U0860607

谨以本辑恭贺魏彌賢先生八十華誕

Dedicaded to Professor Doctor Michael Weiers's 80th Birthday

西域歷史語言研究集刊

第十輯

中國人民大學國學院西域歷史語言研究所　編

沈衛榮　主編

科學出版社
北京

內容簡介

《西域歷史語言研究集刊》是由中國人民大學國學院西域歷史語言研究所主辦的學術刊物，以刊登國內外學者關於中國西北邊疆地區少數民族歷史、語言、考古、地理、宗教等方面的最新研究成果爲主要宗旨，發表具有原創性的學術研究論文、書評和研究綜述等，以期推動國內學界在西域歷史語言研究方面的進步。

本書適合於從事中國西北邊疆地區民族語言、歷史、考古、地理以及宗教研究的國內外學者和相關專業的大專院校師生參考閱讀。

圖書在版編目（CIP）數據

西域歷史語言研究集刊. 第十輯 / 沈衛榮主編；中國人民大學國學院西域歷史語言研究所編. —北京：科學出版社，2018.3

ISBN 978-7-03-056921-9

Ⅰ. ①西… Ⅱ. ①沈…②中… Ⅲ. ①西域–文化史–研究–叢刊 Ⅳ. ①K294. 5-55

中國版本圖書館CIP數據核字（2018）第049713號

責任編輯：郝莎莎 / 責任校對：鄒慧卿

責任印製：肖 興 / 封面設計：陳 敬

科學出版社 出版

北京東黃城根北街16號

郵政編碼：100717

http://www.sciencep.com

中国科学院印刷厂 印刷

科學出版社發行 各地新華書店經銷

*

2018年3月第 一 版 開本：787 × 1092 1/16

2018年3月第一次印刷 印張：37 1/2 插頁：1

字數：865 000

定價：218.00圓

（如有印裝質量問題，我社負責調換）

Historical and Philological Studies of China's Western Regions

No. 10

Institute for Historical and Philological Studies of China's
Western Regions, Renmin University of China

Shen Weirong Editor-in-Chief

Science Press
Beijing

《西域歷史語言研究集刊》編委會

主　　辦　中國人民大學國學院西域歷史語言研究所

主　　編　沈衛榮　　中國人民大學國學院西域歷史語言研究所

編　　委　烏雲畢力格　中國人民大學國學院西域歷史語言研究所

沈衛榮　　中國人民大學國學院西域歷史語言研究所

孟憲實　　中國人民大學國學院

孫家洲　　中國人民大學歷史學院

成崇德　　中國人民大學歷史學院

羅　豐　　寧夏文物考古研究所

榮新江　　北京大學中國古代史研究中心

劉迎勝　　南京大學民族與邊疆研究中心

余太山　　中國社會科學院歷史研究所

達力扎布　中央民族大學歷史系

朱玉麒　　北京大學中國古代史研究中心

吴玉貴　　中國社會科學院歷史研究所

張德芳　　甘肅文物考古研究所

李　肖　　中國人民大學國學院西域歷史語言研究所

松川節　　日本大谷大學文學部

杉山正明　日本京都大學文學部

荒川慎太郎　日本東京外國語大學亞非研究所

Max Deeg　英國卡迪夫（Cardiff）大學宗教系

Kirill Solonin　中國人民大學國學院西域歷史語言研究所

Ruth Dunnell　美國肯揚（Kenyon）學院歷史系

Peter Schwieger　德國波恩大學中亞語言文化研究所

Karénina Kollmar-Paulenz　瑞士伯爾尼大學宗教系

文本批判中發現歷史真相

——慶祝魏彌賢教授80華誕

烏雲畢力格

第二次世界大戰後，在德國成長了一大批優秀的東方學家，在很長一段時間內引領了西方漢學研究領域。波恩大學中亞語言文化研究所自20世紀60年代以後的四十年內一直是德國乃至歐洲蒙古學、藏學、中亞突厥學和滿學研究的領頭羊。作爲波恩大學中亞語言文化學研究所的奠基人，中國蒙古學研究界對海西希（Walther Heissig）教授非常熟悉，一致認爲海西希教授是戰後德國蒙古學的奠基人、領路人和優秀的學者。但是，中國蒙古學界對中亞語言文化學所的其他學者了解不多，對這個曾經的國際中亞學研究的勁旅缺少整體認識。海西希教授毫無疑問是這個團隊的偉大的組織者，但不能忘記他身邊有一批大學問家，他們成就了中亞所。著名的藏學家迪特・舒（Dieter Shuh）、克勞斯・薩迦斯特（Klaus Sagaster）、魯道夫・卡謝夫斯基（Rudolf Kaschewski）、彼得・史衛國（Peter Schwieger）和著名的中亞突厥學家漢斯—萊納・肯培（Hans-Rainer Kämpfe）都是這個研究所的佼佼者。其實在這個團隊裡應該首屈一指的還有一位大學者，他就是筆者的博士生導師彌沙艾勒・瓦雅思（Michael Weiers）先生。

先生漢文名魏彌賢，1937年12月26日出生在德國巴伐利亞州史坦伯格湖岸邊的伯恩裡德村。1958年畢業於慕尼黑古代語言與人文學高中後，先後在德國慕尼黑大學、意大利羅馬大學、那不勒斯大學和德國波恩大學學習，所涉獵學科領域之廣讓人驚歎。比如，先生師從Anton Spitaler, Sabatino Moscati和 Otto Spies等教授修閃米特語言文學；師從Erich Haenisch, Herbert Franke, Helmut Hoffman, Joachim Kissling, Giuseppe Tucci, Luciano Petech, Francesco Gabrieli, Alessio Bombaci, Walther Heissig等教授學習東方學與亞洲研究學，攻讀滿學、蒙古學、漢學、藏學、突厥學、伊斯蘭學和中亞語言文化學等方向；師從 Gustav Mensching教授學習比較宗教研究。他在德國和意大利幾座名校轉校學習，是爲了得到以上提及的當時世界上最優秀的閃米特學和東方學其他分支的名師們的指點。先生除了拉丁語、古希臘語和當代歐洲諸語言外，還掌握了阿拉伯語、波斯語、察哈台語、滿語、蒙古語、藏語和漢語等東方諸語言，是一位博才多學、才華橫溢、具有超強語言天賦的學者。

先生在20世紀60年代在波恩大學攻讀博士學位，主專業爲中亞語言文化學，副專業爲閃米特語言文學研究和比較宗教研究。1965年他撰寫博士學位論文《前古典時期蒙古語的歷史語法研究》，以優異成績畢業，並留校任中亞語言文化系助教。從此以後，他主要從事蒙古學、滿學和中亞突厥學的語言學與史學方向的研究，1971年完成了題爲《阿富汗赫爾塔省莫格勒語（語言資料、語法和詞彙表）》的教授資格論文，次年晉升爲波恩大學中亞語言文化研究所教授，一直到2003年退休。這期間，魏彌賢教授擔任過波恩大學中亞語言文化研究所所長十年（1991—2001），自1991年以來一直被聘爲內蒙古大學榮譽教授。

先生十分重視掌握"遺留性史料"，爲此不辭辛苦地進行大量田野調查，收集資料。在1969—1972年間，先生在阿富汗多地進行過每年若干個月時間的莫格勒語調查。1971年到臺灣各博物館、圖書館和檔案館收集滿文檔案文書資料，在臺灣宜蘭縣收集清中葉的滿漢碑文拓片。他還到過蘇聯時期的烏兹別克斯坦和吉爾吉斯斯坦收集中亞研究的相關資料。1975年，先生在伊朗進行了幾個月的研究工作，研究從13、14世紀流傳下來的蒙古語遺留，收集蒙古時代的硬幣，並做了相關硬幣目錄。他還查訪了伊利汗國統治者們在Tabrīz、Soltāniye和Marāghe等地所居的建築物遺跡。1990年至1994年，先生在中國內蒙古進行了蒙古語方言調查，編寫了調查問卷及其詞彙表，並在中國多個使用蒙古語的地区進行調研。魏彌賢教授特別重視中國第一歷史檔案館所藏滿蒙文檔案資料，親自到該檔案館查閱相關檔案。他還熱心經營學術出版物，和其他學者聯合主編學術刊物《中亞研究》（Zentralasiatische Studien）、《滿學研究叢書》（Aetas Manjurica）和《通古斯西伯利亞研究叢書》（Tunguso Sibirica）等。《中亞研究》是波恩大學中亞語言文化研究所的期刊，由海西希教授創刊和主編，是國際中亞研究領域的頂級刊物之一，1991—2001年先生擔任研究所所長期間主編該刊物。《滿學研究叢書》和《通古斯西伯利亞研究叢書》是由先生主導並聯合德、意、俄同行共同編輯的學術刊物，爲推動歐洲滿學研究發揮了重要作用。

先生知識廣博，東西兼通，在很多領域建樹頗多，但他首先是一位優秀的語言學家和史學家，並且尤其發力於蒙古學和滿學領域的研究。以我的認識，先生的主要研究路徑和特色在於，將歷史學與語言學研究相結合，以史料學批判爲研究的出發點，用語文學研究方法從事歷史的和批判的實證研究。先生爲人和藹可親，平易近人，但在學術問題上桀驁鋒利，富有批判精神，語言犀利甚至刻薄。先生治學態度嚴謹，工作極其勤奮，追求學問孜孜不倦，在學術田野中日夜耕耘，從不知疲倦。先生在語言問題上是一位"民族主義者"，講究典雅漂亮的德文寫作，卻很少用英文發表。他沉浸在閱讀和研究工作中，樂此不疲，但吝惜時光，足不逾戶。因爲這些緣故，先生在學界幾乎成爲了一位"獨行者"，但他學術眼光遠大，視野寬闊，思維敏捷，洞察力尖銳，在同一領域內而言，在學術高度和研究深度上，和先生同一代的學者中很少出其右者。

下面，筆者僅舉兩個方面的例子淺談對先生"歷史批判主義"治學特點的印象。

先生在語言研究方面大致有三大貢獻比較顯著。其一是對古蒙古語語法的研究，其二是對蒙古方言的研究，其三是莫格勒語研究。我們看看他第一個方面的研究的一個例子。要讀先生的成名之作《前古典時期蒙古書面語的歷史語法研究》（*Untersuchungen zu einer historischen Grammatik des präklassischen Schriftmongolisch*，《亞洲研究叢書》第28卷，烏托・哈喇索維茲出版社，1969年），就會清楚地看到貫穿他畢生研究的“歷史批判主義”的實踐。筆者所説的“歷史批判主義”就是德語的Historisch-kritische Metodenlehre，概言之，就是通過對研究資料的歷史考察和真僞正誤的價值判斷，求得達到研究目的的可靠可信的依據，借此盡最大限度地接近研究對象的真相。比如，先生的《前古典時期蒙古書面語的歷史語法研究》這本書，一方面研究並利用13世紀到17世紀初期間的畏吾體蒙古文、八思巴蒙古文、漢字音寫蒙古文、阿拉伯字音寫蒙古文等蒙古語資料，從語音學和形態學\詞法學兩個方面總結了“前古典時期”（即13世紀至17世紀初）蒙古語的語法特點，另一方面爲史學家和文獻學家們提供了可以用來爲那些沒有成書年代或晚近成書的蒙古語文獻較準確地判斷年代的語言學和文獻學依據。這裏不僅可以讀到先生對古蒙古語（他所稱的“前古典時期蒙古語”）語法特點的種種新的見解，而且還可以看到他對語言資料所進行的研究方法與路徑，即歷史的和批判的觀察與分析。在蒙古語研究領域一直存在著一種病態：即無批判狀態。首先，對語言資料缺乏文獻學批判，隨手拿來一本文獻就用，不論它的版本品質、手抄或出版年代。其次，對語言資料缺乏歷史的批判，不考慮文獻的歷史性，用晚近語言資料中的語言現象去“論證”古代蒙古語早期的語言特點，等等。魏彌賢先生其實早在20世紀60年代就已經指出這些現象的危害，並以自己的研究實例給學界提供了歷史批判主義的研究範式。

蒙古史和滿蒙關係史是魏彌賢先生的又一個重要研究領域。他研究《蒙古秘史》和蒙古帝國史，尤其是對以阿拉伯語和波斯語文獻爲支撑的四大汗國史研究領域有很大貢獻。但在這裏筆者特別想提及的是他的17—18世紀蒙滿歷史研究。筆者認爲，先生在這個領域把“歷史批判主義”運用得爐火純青，淋漓盡致。在這裏他特別注意以下幾點：一是史料學批判（Quellenkritik）。先生特別重視史料學理論，強調史料的不同性質和層次，每研究一題，必先評判其史料，擇其可靠者做立足之本。二是史料的“流傳史”（Überlieferungsgeschichte）。先生借鑒《聖經》研究方法，探究某一史料經不同歷史時期在不同編寫因素作用下的從最初到後期的各種流變和傳承，從中發現不同時代不同人群不同目的的歷史書寫的差異，進而復原被改造的歷史的原來面貌。三是文本研究（Textkritik）。先生對文本的性質、內容、內外特徵、語言文字以及其形成的背景和各文本之間的關係等環節予以充分的重視。在他的研究中，文本研究和語文學研究相輔相成，通過對文本的多層次和多視角的考察，揭示其內容，判斷其價值，汲取其合理內涵。先生從1970年代初開始的利用滿文原檔研究滿洲興起史、滿蒙關係史和清代前中期國史編纂史的一系列研究論文（詳見本書《魏彌賢教授論著目録》），充分實踐了他的這些理念。1969年臺灣故宫博物院影印出版了《舊滿洲檔》，這是清宫所藏1607—1636年間的老滿文檔案，是清太祖太宗兩朝《實録》的原料，也是乾隆朝“皇朝史學”的重要資料，史料價值彌足珍貴。先生敏鋭地感覺到它的重大史料學價值，開始對清朝前期歷史和前中期史學史進行研究，取得了重大進展。他的這一研究爲德國乃至整個西方開闢了17—18世紀滿洲史和蒙古史研究的新天地，而且在方法論方面爲整個國際學界樹立了好的榜樣。

關於先生的學術成果和治學思想有很多要寫的，但因爲時間關係只好到此止筆了。筆者今生有機會受到先生的栽培，倍感幸運和榮幸。在慶祝先生80華誕之際，表達我衷心的謝意，並祝願他晚年健康幸福！

2017年秋於北京

目　録

文本批判中發現歷史真相——慶祝魏彌賢教授80華誕……………………烏雲畢力格（i）

魏彌賢教授論著目錄……………………………………………………………………烏雲畢力格（1）
從新疆鄯善縣洋海墓地出土木質火鉢探討火崇拜與拜火教的關係……………………
……………………………………………………………………………李　肖　馬麗萍（23）
再議新疆吐魯番出土"秦王鏡"……………………………………………………劉志佳（35）
新疆出土垂直焊接雙環耳飾的研究………………………………………………林鈴梅（57）
古代青金石的定名與清朝皇室青金石、催生石來源及使用之探討……………張永江（79）
《聖彼德堡梵德大辭典》前言……………………………………………………劉　震（95）
Some Notes on the Sanskrit Fragments of the *Ajātaśatrukaukṛtyavinodana* in the
　Schøyen Collection and Their Extant Parallels……………………Wu Juan（吴　娟）（109）
《善說集》（*Subhāṣitasaṃgraha*）文本概述——以Bendall編校本與新見尼泊爾
　梵文寫本爲中心……………………………………………………………………陸辰葉（147）
從《心經》音譯本及其他文獻看梵文jña的發音……………………………………李建強（157）
故宮藏西夏文《高王觀世音經》考釋………………………………………………孫伯君（165）
西夏文《聖金剛能斷至勝慧彼岸大經顯理燈炬記》初探…………………………李夢溪（183）
清代禁書運動對蒙古語文獻的影響——以《登壇必究》之《北虜譯語》爲例……
………………………………………………………………………………………布日古德（201）
《雲使》在蒙古……………………………………………………………………薩其仁貴（215）
捨身飼虎本生的文本和圖像研究——兼論德國佛教藝術史研究方法………孟　瑜（229）
一個成功的誤解？——西藏博物館所藏《噶瑪巴爲明太祖薦福圖》再考…………
……………………………………………………………………………………姚　霜（241）
A Dream of the Emperor and the Translation of A Buddhist Scripture…………………
…………………………………………………………Hanmo Zhang（張瀚墨）（263）
後藏地區金剛界曼荼羅的傳播路徑之重構——以後弘初期爲中心…………阮　麗（309）
"和尚之教"在西藏——以寧瑪派對摩訶衍及其教法的詮釋、辯護與批判爲例
……………………………………………………………………………………楊　杰（335）
"他空見"詮釋的出發點——論朵波巴·攝囉監燦班藏布之二諦見………石　美（367）
蘇卡悉地研究………………………………………………………………………索朗卓瑪（377）
談白一平—沙加爾上古音体系的幾個問題………………………………………高永安（391）

《上古漢語：構擬新論》音義關係指誤……雷瑭洵（397）
白一平、沙加爾《上古漢語：構擬新論》若干例證商榷——兼談對西方學術評價的反思……向筱路（409）
從上古文獻看白一平—沙加爾上古音構擬……趙團員（421）
曹議金東征甘州回鶻史事證補——浙敦114號《肅州府主致沙州令公書狀》譯釋……任小波（433）
Жаруудын үүсэл гарлын тухай……Боржигдай Оюунбилэг（443）
The Influence of Mongol Law during the Yuan Dynasty……Florence Hodous（457）
馬可·波羅與蒙古法：擴大文明的範圍，縮小野蠻的範圍……Florence Hodous 撰；高 宇 趙佰悅 譯；馬曉林 校（469）
《皇輿全覽圖》東北大地測繪考——以滿文檔案爲中心……承 志（479）
新見三封明廷賜封西番剌麻勅諭及其考釋……沈衛榮（519）
清代後期内モンゴル・ハラチン地域におけるアルバン・タリヤについて……包呼和木其爾（533）
西域察合台文史籍中阿闌豁阿感光而孕故事……特爾巴衣爾（549）
“五族共和”在邊疆的實踐——基於綏遠五族學院的考察……樊志強（557）
民國北京政府時期察哈爾的土地開墾與設治述略……蘇日朦（569）

《西域歷史語言研究集刊》第十輯作者名録……（585）

CONTENTS

Foreword ······ Borjigidai Oyunbilig (i)

Michael Weiers—Bibliography ······ Compiled by Borjigidai Oyunbilig (1)
Zoroastrianism and Fire Worship ······ Li Xiao & Ma Liping (23)
Reconsideration of the "Qin Wang Mirror" unearthed from Turfan, Xinjiang ······ Liu Zhijia (35)
Study of Earrings with Two Vertically Welded Looms Found in Xinjiang ······ Lin Lingmei (57)
Discussion on the Name of Ancient Lapis Lazuli , the Lapis Lazuli and Hasten Parturitian Stone's Source and Usage of the Royal Household in Qing Dynasty ······ Zhang Yongjiang (79)
The Preface of "Großes Petersburger Wörterbuch" ······ Liu Zhen (95)
Some Notes on the Sanskrit Fragments of the *Ajātaśatrukaukṛtyavinodana* in the Schøyen Collection and Their Extant Parallels ······ Wu Juan (109)
An Overview of the *Subhāṣitasaṃgraha*:Based on Bendall's Edition and a New Sanskrit Manuscript from Nepal ······ Lu Chenye (147)
On the Pronunciation of Sanskrit akṣara jña based on the Transcriptional Material of *hṛdaya sūtra* and Others ······ Li Jianqiang (157)
Textural Research on the Tangut Version of *Gaowang Guanshiyin Jing* preserved in the Palace Museum of Beijing ······ Sun Bojun (165)
A Primary Study on a Tangut Commantory of the *Diamond Sutra* ······ Li Mengxi (183)
The Influences of the Book-Banning Movement on Mongolian Documents in Qing Dynasty: A Comparative Study on the Edition of a Sino-Mongol Glossary Known as the Bei-lu Yi-yu ······ Kereidjin D. Bürgüd (201)
Meghadūta in Mongolia ······ Saqirengui (215)
On Texts and Images of the Tigress Story—Using German Research Methodology of Buddhist Arts History ······ Meng Yu (229)
A Successful Misunderstanding? : A Reexamination of the Painting Collection Handscroll "The Fifth Karmapa's Miracles in Nanjing" in Tibet Museum ······ Yao Shuang (241)
A Dream of the Emperor and the Translation of a Buddhist Scripture ······ Hanmo Zhang (263)
Re-mapping the Historical Dissemination of Vajradhātu-maṇḍala Iconography in Central Tibet During the Early Period of the Later Diffusion of Buddhism ······ Ruan Li (309)
Hwa-shang's Teachings in Tibet: In the Case of rNying-ma School's Interpretations,

Defenses and Criticisms of Hwa-shang Mahāyāna and His Teachings ········ Yang Jie（335）
The Starting Point of the Interpretation of gZhan stong View: the Satya-dvaya thought of Dol po pa shes rab rgyan mtshan ········ Shi Mei（367）
A Brief Study of Sukhasiddhi ········ Sonam Drolma（377）
Note on Baxter- Sagart' Reconstruction of old Chinese Phonology ········ Gao Yong'an（391）
The Phonetic-Semantic Relation Errors in *Old Chinese: A New Reconstruction* ········ Lei Tangxun（397）
A Discussion about Several Evidences in *Old Chinese: A New Reconstruction*—Also Rethinking the Western Academic Evaluation ········ Xiang Xiaolu（409）
Critical Remarks on the Reconstruction of Old Chinese by Baxter and Sagart ········ Zhao Tuanyuan（421）
New Evidence on the History of Cao Yijin's Conquest of Ganzhou Uighurs:A Study on Tibetan Manuscript Zhejiang 114 from Dunhuang, the *Official Letter from Suzhou Fuzhu to Shazhou Linggong* ········ Ren Xiaobo（433）
A Study on the Origin of Jarud ········ Borjigidai Oyunbilig（443）
The Influence of Mongol Law during the Yuan Dynasty ········ Florence Hodous（457）
Marco Polo and Mongol Law: Pushing Further the Limits of Barbarity ········ Florence Hodous（469）
Land Surveys in the Northeast for the "*Huangyu quanlan tu*" ········ Cheng zhi（Kicengge）（479）
Three Newly Discovered Ming Edicts to Tibetan Lamas: Text and Interpretation ········ Shen Weirong（519）
Studies on Alba's Farm Land（alban tariy-a）in Kharchin Banner during the Late Qing Period ········ Borjigin Huhmuchir（533）
Research on Alan Goa's Giving Birth thanks to a Ray of Light in the Historical Writings in Chaghatai ········ Torubayar（549）
Harmony among Five Nations in Frontier Region：Based on the Research of Suiyuan Five Nations College ········ Fan Zhiqiang（557）
Studies on the Land Reclamation and Establishment of New Administrative Units in Chakhar during the Peking Government of Republican China ········ Surimeng（569）

List of Contributors ········（585）

魏彌賢教授論著目錄

烏雲畢力格 編

Abkürzungen

Reihen- und Zeitschriftentitel:

AdW	Akademie der Wissenschaften
AF	Asiatische Forschungen
AOH	Acta Orientalia Academiae Scientiarum Hungaricae
BOH	Bibliotheca Orientalis Hungarica
CAJ	Central Asiatic Journal
CMR	Canada-Mongolia Review
JAOS	Journal of the American Oriental Society
OE	Oriens Extremus
OLZ	Orientalistische Literaturzeitung
S.P.A.M.	Stipes Philologia Asia Maiorishttp://www.zentralasienforschung.de/spam
TUNSIB	Tunguso-Sibirica
UAJb	Ural-Altaische Jahrbücher
ZAS	Zentralasiatische Studien
ZDMG	Zeitschrift der Deutschen Morgenländischen Gesellschaft

Sonstige Abkurzüngen

(H) Herausgeber

(R) Rezension

1966

1. *Untersuchungen zu einer historischen Grammatik des präklassischen Mongolisch*, Dissertation, Bonn 1966, 249 Seiten.

2.„Register der geographischen und Personennamen“ aus: *Qad-un ündüsün-ü erdeni-yin tobčiya* „Eine Pekinger Palasthandschrift“, E. HAENISCH (H), *AF* Band 14, Wiesbaden1966, S. 586-596.

1967

3.„Zum Textfragment TM 40 aus der Berliner Turfansammlung", in: *ZDMG* 117:2 (1967), S. 329-352.

4. „Die Entwicklung der mongolischen Schriften", in: *Studium Generale*, Jg. 20, Heft 8 (1967), S. 470-479.

5. „Mongolische Reisebegleitschreiben aus Čaγatai", in: *ZAS* 1 (1967), S. 7-54.

6. Artikel: „Burjatisch" in: *Brockhaus Enzyklopädie*[17], Band 3 (1967).

1968

7. „Mongolische Arbeiten auf dem Gebiet der mongolischen Sprachforschung 1957-1968", in: *ZAS* 2 (1968), S. 307-367.

8. (R) A. RóNA-TAS, *Tibeto-Mongolica. The Tibetan Loanwords of Monguor and the Development of the Archaic Tibetan Dialects*, in: *Oriens* 20 (1968-1969), S. 539-540.

9.-11. Artikel: „Dagurisch", „Dariganga", „Dschu-Uda-Dialekte", in *Brockhaus Enzyklopadie*[17], Bde. 4 und 5 (1968).

1969

12. *Untersuchungen zu einer historischen Grammatik des präklassischen Schriftmongolisch*, = *AF* Band 28, Wiesbaden 1969, 238 Seiten.

13. „Vorläufiger Bericht über sprachwissenschaftliche Aufnahmen bei den Moghol von Afghanistan", in: *ZAS* 3 (1969), S. 417-429.

14. „Die Sprachen von Afghanistan" (von R. FARHADI, Kabul), ins Deutsche übertragen von Michael Weiers, in: *ZAS* 3 (1969), S. 409-416.

15. (R) N. POPPE, *The Twelve Deeds of Buddha. A Mongolian Version of the Lalitavistara*, in: *JAOS* 89.1 (1969), S. 270-273.

1970

16. „Zur Frage des Verhältnisses des Altmongolischen zum Mittelmongolischen", in: *Mongolian Studies* = *BOH* XIV (1970), S. 581-590.

17. *Historische Mandschutexte*, aus dem Nachlaß von E. Haenisch mit Anmerkungen, herausgegeben von Michael Weiers, *AF* Band 29, Wiesbaden 1970, 21 Seiten + 114 Tafeln.

18. „Weiterer Bericht über sprachwissenschaftliche Aufnahmen bei den Moghol von Afghanistan", in: *ZAS* 4 (1970), S. 475-481.

19. „Zu den langen Vokalen in der Moghol-Sprache", in: *ZAS* 4 (1970), S. 467-473.

20.-23. Artikel: „Kalmückisch", „Khalkha-Mongolisch", „Khartschin-Tumut-Dialekte ",

„Khortschin-Mongolisch“, in: *Brockhaus-Enzyklopadie*[17], Bde. 9 und 10 (1970).

1971

24. „Das Moghol-Vokabular von W. R. H. Merk“, in: *ZAS* 5 (1971), S. 157-190.

25.-32. Artikel: „Moghol“, „Mongolische Literatur“, „Mongolische Schriften“, „MongolischeSprachen“, „Mongolistik“, „Monguor“, „Oiratisch“, „Ordossisch“, in: *BrockhausEnzyklopädie17*, Bde. 12 und 13 (1971).

1972

33. „Ein arabisch-mongolischer Wörterspiegel aus der Biblioteca Corsini in Rom“, in: *ZAS* 6 (1972), S. 7-61.

34. „Bericht über Sammeltätigkeit in Taiwan, 1971“, in: *ZAS* 6 (1972), S. 585-601.

35. *Die Sprache der Moghol der Provinz Herat in Afghanistan (Sprachmaterial · Gram matik · Wortliste)*, Materialien zur Sprache und Literatur der Mongolen von Afghanistan I = *Abhdl. d. Rhein.-Westf. AdW* Band 49, Opladen 1972, 190 Seiten.

36. „Bericht über weitere Arbeiten bei den Moghol von Afghanistan“, in: *ZAS* 6 (1972), S. 573-584.

37. Artikel: „Paoan-Mongolisch“, in: *Brockhaus Enzyklopädie*[17], Band 14 (1972).

1973

38. „Das Verhältnis des Ligdan Khan zu seinen Völkerschaften“, in: *Serta Tibeto-Mongolica*, Wiesbaden 1973, S.365-379.

39. „Eine fünfsprachige Wörtersammlung aus dem Gebiet der Moghol von Herat in Afghanistan“, in: *ZAS* 7 (1973), S. 503-523.

40. (H) *Serta Tibeto-Mongolica*, Festschrift für Walther Heissig, Wiesbaden 1973.

41. „Die mo. Sprache des 16. und 17. Jhdts. und die klassische mongolische Schriftsprache“, in: *Akten des 2. Internationalen Mongolistenkongresses*, Band 1, Ulaanbaatar1973, S. 88-90.

42.-44. Artikel: „Santa“, „Schira-Uigur“, „Schriftmongolisch“, in: *Brockhaus Enzyklopädie*[17], Bde. 16 und 17 (1973).

1974

45. „Tibetisch in mandschurischer Schrift“, in: *ZAS* 8 (1974), S. 333-406.

46. „Grundzuge der Sprache der Moghol von Afghanistan“, in: *XVIII. Deutscher Orientalistentag, Vorträge*, Supplement II, Wiesbaden 1974, S. 567-571.

47.-52. Artikel: „Tsakhar-Dialekte“, „Tung-hsiang-Dialekte“, „Üdsümütsin-

Mongolisch“, „Ulan-Tsab-Dialekte“, „Urat-Mongolisch“, „Tungusische Sprachen“, in: *BrockhausEnzyklopädie17*, Band 19 (1974).

1975

53. „Zwei mandschurische und mongolische Schreiben des Sure Han aus dem Jahre 1635“, in: *ZAS* 9 (1975), S. 447-477.

54. „Die Sprache der Hazara und der Mongolen von Afghanistan in lexikostatistischer Sicht“, in: *Afghanistan Journal*, Jg. 2, Heft 3 (1973), S. 98-102.

55. *Schriftliche Quellen in Moġolī. 2.Teil: Bearbeitung der Texte*, Materialien zur Sprache und Literatur der Mongolen von Afghanistan III = *Abhdl. d. Rhein.-Westf. AdW* Band 59, Opladen 1975, 173 Seiten.

56. (R) L. LIGETI, *Trésor des sentences, Subhāṣitaratnanidhi de Sa-Skya Paṇḍita*, in:*OLZ* 1975, Nr. 1, S. 91a/b.

57. (R) L. LIGETI, Titel wie 56., *Indices Verborum*, in: *OLZ* 1975, S. 92-93.

58. (R) L. LIGETI, *Monuments en écriture ’Phags-pa*, in: *OLZ* 1975, S. 93-94.

1976

59. „Ein Schreiben südostmongolischer Stammesfürsten an den Mandschuherrscher Sure Han aus dem Jahre 1636“, in: *Tractata Altaica*, Wiesbaden 1976, S. 755-766.

60. „Zum Nominativ **i* des altaischen Personalpronomens der 3. Person Singular“, in: *ZAS* 10 (1976), S. 431-437.

61. „Beispiele für Sprachmischung in der geschriebenen Moghol-Sprache und deren Bezugauf Forschungsziele in der Altaistik“, in: *Altaica Collecta*, Wiesbaden 1976, S. 361-368.

62. „Hypotaktische Modellsprachen und parataktische Replikasprachen - ein Beitrag zur Linguistik des sprachlichen Kontakts –“, in: *ZAS* 10 (1976), S. 411-429.

63. (R) J. G. HANGIN, *A Concise English-Mongolian Dictionary*, in: *Oriens* 25-26(1976), S. 430.

1977

64. „Prinzipien für Notation und Notierung im Wörterbuch einer Mischsprache“, in: *ZAS* 11 (1977), S. 389-409.

65. *Schriftliche Quellen in Moġoli. 3. Teil: Poesie der Mogholen*, Materialien zur Sprache und Literatur der Mongolen von Afghanistan IV = *Abhdl. d. Rhein.-Westf. AdW* Band 62, Opladen 1977, 202 Seiten.

66. „Typen verbaler Personendifferenzierung im Mongolischen“, in: *CAJ* XXI (1977), S. 295-325.

1978

67. „Münzaufschriften auf Münzen mongolischer Il-Khane aus dem Iran“, in: *CMR* IV:1(1978), S. 41-62.

68. „Bemerkungen zur Phonetik der dagurischen Mundart von Butha“, in: *ZDMG* 128:1(1978), S. 123-160.

69. „Voraussetzungen für Sprachwandel bei Sprachen im Kontakt“, in: *CAJ* XXII (1978), S. 286-319.

70. (H) mit G. DOERFER, *Beiträge zur nordasiatischen Kulturgeschichte = Tungusica* 2(1978), Wiesbaden 1978, 271 Seiten.

1979

71. *Die Verträge zwischen Russland und China 1689-1881*, Bonn 1979, XI+271 Seiten.

72. „Mandschu-mongolische Strafgesetze aus dem Jahre 1631 und deren Stellung in derGesetzgebung der Mongolen“, in: *ZAS* 13 (1979), S. 137-190.

73. „Die Kuang-ning Affäre, Beginn des Zerwürfnisses zwischen den mongolischen Tsakharund den Mandschuren“, in: *ZAS* 13 (1979), S. 73-91.

1980

74. „Fragment einer Anweisung zur Moxibustion oder Akupunktur in mandschurischer Sprache“, in: *Heilen und Schenken*, Wiesbaden 1980, S. 139-144.

75. „Specimina mandschurischer Archivalien aus der K‘ang-hsi Zeit“, in: *ZAS* 8 14/1(1980), S. 7-40.

76. *Linguistische Feldforschung. Ein Leitfaden*, Wiesbaden 1980, 83 Seiten.

77. (R) H. WALRAVENS (Hrsg.), *Berthold Laufer. Kleinere Schriften*, Bde. 1-4, Wiesbaden1976-79, in: *Monumenta Serica* 34 (1979-80), S. 563-565.

1981

78. „Gesetzliche Regelungen für den Außenhandel und f‘ür auswärtige Beziehungen derMongolen unter Kangxi zwischen 1664 und 1680“, in: *ZAS* 15 (1980), S. 27-52.

79. (R) Catalogue du Fonds Mandchou, Paris 1979, in *ZAS* 15 (1981), S. 550/51.

1982

80. „Der russisch-chinesische Vertrag von Burinsk vom Jahre 1727“, in: *Florilegia Manjurica in Memoriam Walter Fuchs = AF* Band 80, Wiesbaden 1982, S. 186-204.

81. „Aus der Poesie der Mogholen“, in: *AOH* XXXVI (1982/83), S. 563-574.

82. (H) Tungusica II: U. JUGEL, *Studien zur Geschichte der Wu-liang-ha im 15. Jh.*, Teil1, Wiesbaden 1982.

83. (H) zusammen mit G. STARY (Venedig), *Florilegia Manjurica in Memoriam WalterFuchs*, = *AF* Band 80, Wiesbaden 1982.

1983

84. (H) zusammen mit D. SCHUH: *Archiv für Zentralasiatische Geschichtsforschung*, Sankt Augustin, Heft 1-6, 1983.

85. (H) *Documenta Barbarorum*, Festschrift für Walther Heissig zum 70. Geburtstag =Veröffentlichungen der Societas Uralo-Altaica, Band 18, Wiesbaden 1983.

86. *Zu mongolischen und mandschurischen Akten und Schriftstücken des 17. bis 20. Jahrhunderts* = Archiv für zentralasiatische Geschichtsforschung, Heft 3, 52 Seiten (71-120), St. Augustin 1983.

87. „Der Mandschu-Khortsin Bund von 1626", in: *Documenta Barbarorum*, S. 412-435, Wiesbaden, 1983.

88. „Walther Heissig und die deutsche Mongolistik nach dem Kriege", in: *Documenta Barbarorum*, S. XI-XV, Wiesbaden 1983.

89. (R) *Studia Sino-Mongolica*. Festschrift für Herbert Franke, hrsg. v. WOLFGANG BAUER = Münchener Ostasiatische Studien, 25, in: *UAJb*, Neue Folge Band 3 (1983), S. 248/49.

90. (R) STARY, Giovanni, *Die chinesischen und mandschurischen Zierschriften*, Hamburg:Buske 1980, in: *UAJb*, Neue Folge Band 3 (1983), S. 275.

1984

91. „Münzaufschriften auf Münzen mongolischer Il-Khane aus dem Iran, Teil zwei", in:*UAJb*, Neue Folge, Band 4 (1984), S. 171-186.

92. (H) zusammen mit W. HEISSIG: *Zentralasiatische Studien* 17 (1984), Wiesbaden, 237 Seiten.

1985

93. „Zum mongolischen Nomen *buši* / *biši* und seiner diasystematischen Differenzierung", in: *ZAS* 18 (1985), S. 68-89.

94. (H) zusammen mit W. HEISSIG: *Zentralasiatische Studien*, 18 (1985), Wiesbaden, 313 Seiten.

95. (H) zusammen mit D. SCHUH: *Archiv für zentralasiatische Geschichtsforschung*, Heft 7-9, St. Augustin, 168 Seiten.

96. (H) *Tungusica* 3: G. DOERFER, *Mongolo-Tungusica*, Wiesbaden, 305 Seiten.

1986

97. (H) *Die Mongolen. Beiträge zu ihrer Geschichte und Kultur*, BWR 86, Darmstadt, 632 Seiten.

98. (H) zusammen mit W. HEISSIG: *Zentralasiatische Studien*, 19 (1986), Wiesbaden, 290 Seiten.

99. „Zur Stellung und Bedeutung des Schriftmongolischen in der ersten Hälfte des 17. Jahrhunderts“, in: *ZAS* 19 (1986), S. 38-67.

100. „Die Mandschu-mongolischen Strafgesetze vom 16. November 1632“, in: *ZAS* 19(1986), S. 88-126.

101. „Vorwort“ zu: *Die Mongolen* (vgl. 97.), S. IX-XX.

102. „Nahöstliche und europäische Quellen“, in: *Die Mongolen* (vgl. 97.), S.18-28.

103. „Zur Herausbildung und Entwicklung mongolischer Sprachen. Ein Überblick“, in:*Die Mongolen* (vgl. 97.), S. 29-69.

104. „Zur anthropogeographischen Betrachtung der mongolischen Geschichte, Gedankenüber eine zukünftige Forschungsrichtung“, in: *Die Mongolen* (vgl. 97.), S. 149-154.

105. „Von Ögödei bis Möngke - das mongolische Grosreich“, in: *Die Mongolen* (vgl. 97.), S. 192-216.

106. „Das Khanat Tschaghatai“ in: *Die Mongolen* (vgl. 97.), S. 290-299.

107. „Die Mongolen in Iran“, in : *Die Mongolen* (vgl. 97.), S. 300-344.

108. „Die Goldene Horde oder Das Khanat Qyptschaq“, in: *Die Mongolen* (vgl. 97.), S.345-378.

109. „Münzaufschriften auf Münzen mongolischer Il-Khane aus dem Iran, Teil drei“, in:*UAJb* N. F. 5 (1985-1986), S. 168-186.

1987

110. (H) mit W. HEISSIG, K. SAGASTER und V. VEIT: Asiatische Forschungen Band 94, *Die Eroberung der Burg von Sum-pa* von R. KASCHEWSKY und P. TSERING, 2 Bde., Wiesbaden, 173 / 206 Seiten.

111. (H) mit M. GIMM und G. STARY: *Aetas Manjurica*, Tomus 1, Wiesbaden, 479 Seiten.

112. „Die Vertragstexte des Mandschu-Khalkha Bundes von 1619/20“, in: *Aetas Manjurica*1 (1987), S. 119-165.

113. „Konkordanz zum Aktenmaterial der *Chiu Man-chou Tang* und *Man-wen Lao-tang*Jahrgänge l620-1630“, in: *Aetas Manjurica* 1, (1987), S. 166 - 479.

114. Neufassung des Artikels „Dagurisch“, in: *Brockhaus Enzyklopädie*[19].

1988

115. Neufassung des Artikels „Galik-Alphabet“, in: *Brockhaus Enzyklopädie*[19].

116. Artikel: „Galdan“, in: *Brockhaus Enzyklopädie*[19].

117. Artikel: „Geser-Khan-Epos“, in: *Brockhaus Enzyklopädie*[19].

118. Artikel: „Heissig, Walther“ in: *Brockhaus Enzyklopädie*[19].

119. „Der erste Schriftwechsel zwischen Khalkha und Mandschuren und seine Überlieferung“, in: *ZAS* 20 (1987 / erschienen 1988), S. 107-139.

120. (H) zusammen mit W. HEISSIG: *Zentralasiatische Studien* 20 (1987 / erschienen 1988), 366 Seiten.

121. Artikel: „Goldene Horde“, in: *Brockhaus Enzyklopädie*[19].

122. (R) HANS-RAINER KÄMPFE, *Das Asaraγči neretü-yin teüke des Byamba erke daičingalias Šamba Jasaγ (Eine mongolische Chronik des 17. Jahrhunderts)* = *AF* 81, Wiesbaden1983, in: *Monumenta Serica* 36 (1984-85) [erschienen 1988], S. 696-98.

123. (R) PAUL RATCHNEVSKY, *Činggis Khan*. Sein Leben und Wirken = Münchener OstasiatischeStudien 32, Wiesbaden 1983, in: *Monumenta Serica* 36 (1984-85) [erschienen1988], S. 681-83.

124. (R) RAINER VON FRANZ: *Die unbearbeiteten Peking-Inschriften der Franke-LauferschenSammlung* = *AF* 86, Wiesbaden 1984, in: *Monumenta Serica* 36 (1984-85), [erschienen 1988], S. 678-81.

125. (R) GIOVANNI STARY: *Emu tanggü orin sakda-i gisun sarkiyan. Erzählungen der 120 Alten. Beiträge zur mandschurischen Kulturgeschichte* = *AF* 83, Wiesbaden 1983, in: *Monumenta Serica* 36 (1984-85) [erschienen 1988], S. 691-92.

126. Kurzbiographie „Kotwicz“, in: *Brockhaus Enzyklopädie*[19].

127. „Bemerkungen zu mongolischen Ortsnamen“, in: *UAJb*, Neue Folge, Band 7, 1987(= 1988), S. 233-240.

1989

128. (H) zusammen mit W. HEISSIG: *Zentralasiatische Studien* 21 (1988 / erschienen 1989), 237 Seiten.

129. „Zum Verhältnis des Ch'ing-Staats zur lamaistischen Kirche in der frühen YungchengZeit“, in: *ZAS* 21 (1988, erschienen 1989). S. 115-131.

130. „Einigung unter Činggis“, in: W. HEISSIG / C.C. MULLER (Hrsg), *Die Mongolen* (Haus der Kunst München, Katalog), Innsbruck 1989, 52-53.

131. „Vorstoß an die Grenze“, in: *op. cit.* 130., 86-88.

132. „Stämme und Verbreitungsgebiete; Sprache, Wesenszuge“, in: *op. cit.* 130., 113-117.

133. „Bemerkungen zu einigen sprachlichen Eigenheiten des Südostmongolischen im 17.Jahrhundert“, in: *Gedanke und Wirkung*, Festschrift zum 90. Geburtstag von Nikolaus Poppe = Asiatische Forschungen, Band 108, Wiesbaden 1989, S. 366-372.

134. „Geschichte der Mongolen“, in: A. EGGEBRECHT (Hg.), *Die Mongolen und ihr Weltreich*, Mainz 1989, S, 45-114 + 52 Abb..

135. „Westliche Boten und Reisende zu den Mongolen im 13. und 14. Jahrhundert“, in:*op. cit.* 134., S. 185-195 + 5 Abb..

1990

136. „Alltag der Mongolen“, in: *Frankfurter Allgemeine*, Nr. 6, 8. Januar 1990, S. 23.

137. Artikel: „Mongolei“, in: *Brockhaus Enzyklopädie*[19].

138. Artikel: „Muslims in the Modern Mongolian People's Republic“ in: *The Encyclopediaof Islam*.

139. Artikel: „Mongolen“, in: *Brockhaus Enzyklopädie*[19].

140. Artikel: „Mongolische Volksrepublik“, in: *Brockhaus Enzyklopädie*[19].

141. Artikel: „Mongolische Literatur“ (Neufassung), in: *op. cit.* 140.

142. Artikel: „Qalqa“, in: *op. cit.* 140.

143. Kurzbiographie: „Nikolaus Poppe“, in: *op. cit.* 140.

144. Kurzbiographie: „G. J. Ramstedt“, in: *op. cit.* 140.

145. Kurzbiographie: „B. Rintschen“, in: *op. cit.* 140.

1991

146. (H) zusammen mit M. GIMM und G. STARY: *Klassische, moderne und bibliographische Studien zur Mandschuforschung* = *Aetas Manjurica* 2 (1991), Wiesbaden 1991, 270 Seiten.

147. „Mandschurische Dokumente zu einer neu eingefuhrten Kanzleipraxis der frühestenYung-Cheng Zeit“, in: *Aetas Manjurica* 2 (1991), S. 254-270.

148. Kurzbiographie: „Sanschejew“, in: *Brockhaus-Enzyklopädie*[19].

149. Kurzbiographie: „Isaak-Jakob Schmidt“, in: *op. cit.* 148.

150. Artikel (Neufassung): „Santa“, in: *op. cit.* 148.

151. Artikel (Neufassung): „Schriftmongolisch“, in: *op. cit.* 148.

152. (H) zusammen mit W. HEISSIG: *Zentralasiatische Studien* 22 (1989-1991), Wiesbaden1991, 317 Seiten.

153. „Mongolenpolitik der Mandschuren und Mandschupolitik der Mongolen zu Beginnder dreißiger Jahre des 17. Jahrhunderts“, in: *ZAS* 22 (1989-1991), S. 256-275.

154. (R) MICHEL HOANG, *Gengis Khan*, Librairie Arthéme Fayard, Paris 1988, in: *ZAS*

22(1989-1991).

155. „Mongolische Lexikographie", in: F.J. HAUSMANN, O. REICHMANN, H. E. WIEGAND, L. ZGUSTA (Hgg.), *Wörterbücher. Ein internationales Handbuch zur Lexikographie(Dictionaries. An International Encyclopedia of Lexicography)*, dritter Teilband (thirdVolume), Berlin · New York, 266., S. 2623-2626.

1992

156. „Wer Mongolen waren und wer heute Mongolen sind", in: *Mongolische Notizen* 1(1992), S. 11-14 (Teil I).

157. Kurzbiographie: „Wladimirzow", in: *Brockhaus-Enzyklopädie*[19].

158. (H) zusammen mit W. HEISSIG: *Zentralasiatische Studien* 23 (1992), Wiesbaden 1992, 215 Seiten.

159. „Das Schriftmoġolī der Mongolen von Afghanistan. Ein Abriß", in: *ZAS* 23 (1992), S.60-66.

160. „Auswirkungen des mongolischen Weltreichs auf das europäische Russland und aufMittelasien", Projektbeschreibung in: *Nord-Sud-Dialog*. Entwicklungsländerforschun gan der Universität Bonn, unter A3, 26/27.

161. „Dialektatlas der mongolischen Sprache der Inneren Mongolei", Projektbeschreibungin: *Nord-Süd-Dialog* (wie 160.), unter A5, 30/31.

162. „Geschichte Innerasiens vom 17.-20. Jahrhundert", Projektbeschreibung in: *Nord-Süd-Dialog* (wie 160.), unter A7, 34-36.

163. (H) zusammen mit M. GIMM und G. STARY: *Historische und bibliographische Studienzur Mandschuforschung = Aetas Manjurica* 3 (1992), Wiesbaden 1992, 479 Seiten.

164. „Nurhacis Verlautbarungen über die Staatsführung aus dem Jahre 1622 und ihre Überlieferung", in: *Aetas Manjurica* 3 (1992), S. 432-478.

1993

165. (H) *Tungusica*, Band 4, Wiesbaden 1992 (=1993).

166. „Wer Mongolen waren und wer heute Mongolen sind", in: *Mongolische Notizen* Nr. 2(1993), S. 27-31 (Teil II).

167. „Argun aller alten Herren, Čingiz aller Könige, und die nächtliche Reise des Propheten.Mongolische Tradition und muslimische Inkulturation in der Dichtung der Mongolenvon Afghanistan" in: *AOH* XLVI : 1 (1992/93), S. 61-79.

1994

168. (H) zusammen mit W. HEISSIG: *Zentralasiatische Studien* 24 (1994), Wiesbaden

1994, 237 Seiten.

169. „Die historische Dimension des Jade-Siegels zur Zeit des Mandschuherrschers Hongtaiji“, in: *ZAS* 24 (1994), 119-145.

170. „In memoriam N. N. Poppe“, in: *ZAS* 24 (1994), 233.

1995

171. (H) zusammen mit H.-R. KÄMPFE: *Tunguso-Sibirica* 1, Wiesbaden 1995, 146 Seiten.

172. (H) zusammen mit W. HEISSIG und G. VERHUFEN: *Zentralasiatische Studien* 25 (1995), Wiesbaden 1995, 196 Seiten.

173. (H) zusammen mit H.-R. KÄMPFE, *Tunguso-Sibirica* 2, Wiesbaden 1995, 365 Seiten +3 Karten.

174. „Bemerkungen zum Gebrauch von *bui* im Schriftmongolischen“, in: *ZAS* 25 (1995), S.164-175.

1996

175. „Zum Mandschu-Kharatsin Bund des Jahres 1628“, in: *ZAS* 26 (1996), S. 84-121.

176. (H) zusammen mit W. HEISSIG und G. VERHUFEN: *Zentralasiatische Studien* 26(1996), Wiesbaden 1996, 247 Seiten.

177. „Materialien zur Vorgeschichte der Qing-Dynastie - Einleitung“, in: G. STARY (Hrsg.), *Materialien zur Vorgeschichte der Qing-Dynastie*, Wiesbaden 1996, S. 1-10.

178. „1635 on-u qaračin-u neyilegülülte“, in: B. Oyunbilig, L. Naranγoo-a (Hrgg.), *Elbegbütügel. Professor Doktor Jayčid Sečen-ü nayan nasun-u oi-du*, Sinhua-Verlag des HulunBuir Aimak, o.O., 1996, 89-104.

1997

179. „Herkunft und Einigung der mongolischen Stämme: Türken und Mongolen“, in: S.Conermann/J. Kusber (Hrsg.), *Die Mongolen in Asien und Europa*, Kieler Werkstucke, Reihe F: Beiträge zur osteuropäischen Geschichte 4, Peter Lang, Frankfurt am Main1997, 27-39.

180. „Temüdschin trennt sich von Dschamukha. Essay zur Geheimen Geschichte der Mongolen“, in: *Mongγol teüke sudulul = Studia Historica Mongolica*, 1997, 22-31.

1998

181. „Centers of Writing in the East“, in: *The Fifth Seal*, Calligraphic Icons, Kathmandu1998, 23-27.

182. (R) R. Kullmann, D. Tserenpil, „Mongolian Grammar“, in: *ZAS* 27, (1997 = 1998), 212-214.

183. (R) Ch. Bawden, „Mongolian-English Dictionary“, in: *ZAS* 27, (1997 = 1998), 210-211.

184. (H) *Zentralasiatische Studien 27* (1997 = 1998), 222 Seiten.

185. (H) Beiträge zur Geschichte, Sprache und Kultur der Mandschuren und Sibe (= AetasManjurica 6, 1998), 335 Seiten.

186. „Die unruhigen Grenzen des Aisin-Staats Ende der 20er und Anfang der 30er Jahre des17. Jahrhunderts“, in: *Aetas Manjurica 6*, 1998, 193-249 + 1 Karte.

187. „Zur Registratur der mandschurischen Holztäfelchen über Ajiges Invasion der Mingim Jahre 1636“, in: *Aetas Manjurica 6* , 1998, 251-313.

188. „Allgemeine Hintergrundliteratur“, in: *Literaturangaben*, http://www.zentralasienforschung.de

189. „Erste hinführende Literatur zu Zentralasien“, in: *Literaturangaben*, http://www.zentralasienforschung.de

190. „Grundlagenliteratur zur Historie“, in: *Literaturangaben*, http://www.zentralasienforschung.de

191. „Literatur zur historisch kritischen Methode und Textwissenschaft“, in: *Literaturangaben*, http://www.zentralasienforschung.de

192. „Literatur zur Lexikologie und Lexikographie“, in: *Literaturangaben*, http://www.zentralasienforschung.de

193. „Literatur zum Problem Gattung - Textsorte“, in: *Literaturangaben*, http://www.zentralasienforschung.de

194. „The scientific approach to writing systems“, in: *Literaturangaben*, http://www..zentralasienforschung.de

195. „Hunnen“, in: *Abrisse zur Geschichte innerasiatischer Völker*, http://www.zentralasienforschung.de

196. „Awaren“, in: *Abrisse zur Geschichte innerasiatischer Völker*, http://www.zentralasienforschung.de

197. „Türken in Westeurasien“, in: *Abrisse zur Geschichte innerasiatischer Völker*, http://www.zentralasienforschung.de

198. „Türken, Protomongolen und Prototibeter im Osten“ in: *Abrisse zur Geschichte innerasiatischerVölker*, http://www.zentralasienforschung.de

199. „Xyon, Kidariten, Hephthaliten“, in: *Abrisse zur Geschichte innerasiatischer Völker*, http://www.zentralasienforschung.de

200. „Xiongnu (ostliche Hunnen)“, in: *Abrisse zur Geschichte innerasiatischer Völker*,

http://www.zentralasienforschung.de
201. „Xianbi“, in: *Abrisse zur Geschichte innerasiatischer Völker*, http://www.zentralasienforschung.de
202. „Tuyuhun“, in: *Abrisse zur Geschichte innerasiatischer Völker*, http://www.zentralasienforschung.de
203. „Prototibetische Qin“, in: *Abrisse zur Geschichte innerasiatischer Völker*, http://www.zentralasienforschung.de
204. „Tabgatsch“, in: *Abrisse zur Geschichte innerasiatischer Völker*, http://www.zentralasienforschung.de
205. „Türkische (hunnische) Xia“, in: *Abrisse zur Geschichte innerasiatischer Völker*, http://www.zentralasienforschung.de
206. „Rouran“, in: *Abrisse zur Geschichte innerasiatischer Völker*, http://www.zentralasienforschung.de
207. „Kök-Türken“, in: *Abrisse zur Geschichte innerasiatischer Völker*, http://www.zentralasienforschung.de
208. „Qarluq“, in: *Abrisse zur Geschichte innerasiatischer Völker*, http://www.zentralasienforschung.de
209. „Tschigil und Tuxs“, in: *Abrisse zur Geschichte innerasiatischer Völker*, http://www.-zentralasienforschung.de
210. „Uiguren“, in: *Abrisse zur Geschichte innerasiatischer Völker*, http://www.zentralasienforschung.de
211. „Kirgisen“, in: *Abrisse zur Geschichte innerasiatischer Völker*, http://www.zentralasienforschung.de
212. „Yagma“, in: *Abrisse zur Geschichte innerasiatischer Völker*, http://www.zentralasienforschung.de
213. „Kimek“, in: *Abrisse zur Geschichte innerasiatischer Völker*, http://www.zentralasienforschung.de
214. „Oguz“, in: *Abrisse zur Geschichte innerasiatischer Völker*, http://www.zentralasienforschung.de
215. „Uigurennachfolger“, in: *Abrisse zur Geschichte innerasiatischer Völker*, http://www.zentralasienforschung.de
216. „Shatuo“, in: *Abrisse zur Geschichte innerasiatischer Völker*, http://www.zentralasienforschung.de
217. „Tanguten“, in: *Abrisse zur Geschichte innerasiatischer Völker*, http://www.zentralasienforschung.de
218. „Das tibetische Reich“, in: *Abrisse zur Geschichte innerasiatischer Völker*,

http://www.zentralasienforschung.de

219. „Bohai“, in: *Abrisse zur Geschichte innerasiatischer Völker*, http://www.zentralasienforschung.de

220. „Datierungsfragen“, in: *Varia*, http://www.zentralasienforschung.de

221. „Zum grammatischen Sprachbau der uigurisch-mongolischen Schriftsprache“, in: *Varia*, http://www.zentralasienforschung.de

222. „Temüdschin der Schwurbrüchige“, in: *Zentralasiatische Studien* 28 (1998), 31-44.

1999

223. „Dihqan Dynastien“, in: *Abrisse zur Geschichte innerasiatischer Völker*, http://www.-zentralasienforschung.de

224. „Die Eingliederung der Kharatsin“, in: *ZAS* 29 (1999), 37-85.

225. „Ein Blockdrucktext betreffend die orthographische Präzisierung der Buchstaben ohnePunkte und Kreise durch Dahai“, in: *ZAS* 29 (1999), 87-96.

226. (R) W. Romanovsky, *Die Kriege des Qing-Kaisers Kangxi gegen den Oiratenfursten Galdan.* Wien: Verlag der Österreichischen Akademie der Wissenschaften 1998, in:*ZAS* 29 (1999), 256-258.

227. (H) zusammen mit H.-R. KÄMPFE: *Tunguso-Sibirica* 6, Wiesbaden: Harrassowitz Verlag1999, 163 Seiten.

228. (H) zusammen mit W. HEISSIG: *Zentralasiatische Studien* 29, Wiesbaden: HarrassowitzVerlag 1999, 258 Seiten.

229. (H) zusammen mit D. SCHUH: *Archiv für zentralasiatische Geschichtsforschung*, VEBVerlag, St. Augustin.

2000

230. „Einleitung zu den Indices des Bodogon-i bithe von 1789“, in: Indices der Personen-, Orts-, Stammes-, Fluß-, Gebäude- und Behördennamen im Daicin gurun-i fukjin doroneihe bodogon-i bithe und im Huang qing kai guo fang lue = Aetas Manjurica 7, Wiesbaden:Harrassowitz Verlag 2000, VII-XII.

231. (H) zusammen mit M. GIMM UND G. STARY: *Aetas Manjurica* 7, Wiesbaden: HarrassowitzVerlag 2000, 252 Seiten.

232. „Zum Textmaterial der Aisin-Zeit und seiner Quellenauffassung“, in *ZAS* 30, Wiesbaden:Harrassowitz 2000, 125-141.

233. (H) zusammen mit W. HEISSIG: *Zentralasiatische Studien* 30, Wiesbaden: HarrassowitzVerlag 2000, 219 Seiten.

234. „Die politische Dimension des Jadesiegels zur Zeit des Mandschuherrschers

Hongtaiji", in: *ZAS* 30, Wiesbaden: Harrassowitz 2000, 103-124.

235. „Randbemerkungen zum Mandschu-Kharatsin Bund des Jahres 1628", in: *Studia Historica Mongolica*, Hohhot: Inner Mongolian University 2000, 173-178.

236. Mit Carsten Näher: „Mandschuristik und Mandschu-Tungusologie an der Universität Bonn", in: *Asien* 76, Hamburg: Deutsche Gesellschaft für Asienkunde 2000, 136-146.

237. „Vom Mythos zur Historie. Aus der Werkstatt der Zentralasienwissenschaft", in: ZGS2, 82-89.

238. (R) Roth Li, Gertraude. *Manchu. A Textbook for reading Dokuments.* Honolulu, Hawaii: University of Hawa'i Press, 2000, in: *ZAS* 30: 202-207.

239. „1628 on-u manǰu - qaračin-u qolboγan-u tuqai nökübüri čoqulta", in: *Arkivs ba mongγol teüke sudulul* 1, Hohhot 2000, 1-10.

240. „Ein unbekannter Übersetzer und sein herrscherlicher Adressat. Zur Kommunikativen Kompetenz in mandschurischen Briefübersetzungen aus dem Mongolischen", in: L.Bieg, E. von Mende, M. Siebert (Hg.), *Ad Seres et Tungusos. Festschrift für MartinGimm.* Opera sinologica 11, Wiesbaden: Harrassowitz Verlag 2000, 441-450.

241. Linksammlung Mandschu-Tungusologie: http://www.zentralasienforschung.de

2001

242. (H) zusammen mit H.-R. KÄMPFE: *Tunguso-Sibirica* 7, Wiesbaden: Harrassowitz Verlag2001, I-XV + 199 Seiten.

243. (H) zusammen mit D. SCHUH: *Archiv für Zentralasiatische Geschichtsforschung* Heft12, Bonn: VGH Wissenschaftsverlag.

244. (H) zusammen mit D. SCHUH: *Archiv für Zentralasiatische Geschichtsforschung* Heft13, Bonn: VGH Wissenschaftsverlag.

245. „Schriftzentren des Ostens", in: Rolf A. Kluenter (Hg.), *Aworldwide.* Königslutter-Rhode, 24-27.

246. Linksammlung Mongolistik: http://www.zentralasienforschung.de

247. Linksammlung Zentralasiatische Turkologie: http://www.zentralasienforschung.de

248. (H) zusammen mit W. HEISSIG: *Zentralasiatische Studien* 31, Wiesbaden: HarrassowitzVerlag 2001, 229 Seiten.

249. „Die drei Amtshofe des Schriftwesens im spaten Aisin-Staat", in: *ZAS* 31, Wiesbaden:Harrassowitz 2001, 65-88.

2002

250. „Einige Bemerkungen zur Geschichte der Entwicklung der mandschurischen Schrift", in: *AOH* 55, 2002, 265-275.

251. *Mongolische Literatur?*, der ursprünglich digitalisierte Beitrag findet sich in Papierformin: *Ultra Paludes Maeoticas 1 = Tunguso Sibirica*, Band 23, Wiesbaden:
Harrassowitz Verlag, 11-22.

252. *Liegnitz und die Mongolen*. Der ursprünglich digitalisierte Beitrag findet sich in überarbeiteter Fassung sowie in Papierform vgl. unten unter Nr. 265.

253. *Bemerkungen zu Titel und Titelhinweis im älteren mongolischsprachigen Schrifttum*, in: *Opera altaistica professori Stanislao Kałużyński octogenario dicata*, in: *Rocznik Orientalistyczny*, Tom LVIII, Zeszyt 1, 242-246.

254. *Die Siegel des Ayuširidara, die politischen Ideologien der Mongolen, und ihre Geschichtsschreibung*.Der ursprünglich digitalisierte Beitrag findet sich in Papierform
in: Michael Weiers, *Erbe aus der Steppe. Beiträge zur Sprache und Geschichte der Mongolen = Tunguso Sibirica*, Band 28, 28-51.

255. (H) zusammen mit H.-R. KÄMPFE: *Tunguso Sibirica* 8, Wiesbaden: Harrassowitz Verlag, 219 Seiten.

256. „Zum Wert mandschusprachiger Quellen für die Erforschung der Geschichte Innerasiens", in: Naeher/Stary/Weiers (Hrsg.), *Proceedings I.C.M.T.S. Volume 1: Trends in Manchu and Tungus Studies*. Wiesbaden: Harrassowitz Verlag, 199-218.

257. (H) zusammen mit H.-R. KÄMPFE: *Tunguso Sibirica* 10, Wiesbaden: HarrassowitzVerlag, 193 Seiten.

2003

258. *Analyseanleitungen*. Der ursprünglich digitalisierte Beitrag findet sich in überarbeiteterund stark erweiterter Fassung in Papierform unter dem Titel *Zum grammatischen Sprachbau der uigurisch-mongolischen Schriftsprache*, in: Michael Weiers, *Erbe ausder Steppe. Beiträge zur Sprache und Geschichte der Mongolen = Tunguso Sibirica*, Band 28, 9-20.

259. (H) zusammen mit H.-R. KÄMPFE: *Tunguso Sibirica* 11, Wiesbaden: Harrassowitz Verlag, 262 Seiten.

260. (H) zusammen mit H.-R. KÄMPFE: *Tunguso Sibirica* 12, Wiesbaden: Harrassowitz Verlag, 178 Seiten.

261. „Moghol", in: *The Mongolic Languages*. Edited by Juha Janhunen. Routledge Language Family Series. London and New York: Routledge, 248-264.

262. *Heutige mongolische Schriftsprachen, Sprachen, und Dialekte (eine Aufzählung)*. Der ursprünglich digitalisierte Beitrag findet sich in Papierform in überarbeiteter, und zueiner Tabelle verkürzte Fassung als Anhang des Beitrags: „Zum grammatischen Sprachbau der uigurisch-mongolischen Schriftsprache", in: Michael Weiers, *Erbe aus der Steppe. Beiträge zur Sprache und Geschichte der Mongolen = Tunguso Sibirica*, Band 28, 19-20.

263. (H) *Zentralasiatische Studien* 32, Bonn: VGH Wissenschaftsverlag GmbH, 181 Seiten.

264. „Abendländer in China vermißt", in: H. LINK und TH. MULLER-BAHLKE (Hg.), *Zeichenund Wunder. Geheimnisse des Schriftenschranks in der Kunst- und Naturalienkammerder Franckeschen Stiftungen. Kulturhistorische und philologische Untersuchungen= Kleine Schriftenreihe der Franckeschen Stiftungen* 4, Halle: Franckesche Stiftungen zu Halle, 229-251.

265. *Liegnitz und die Mongolen* (uberarbeitete Fassung von Nr. 252), in: *Mongγol teüke sudulul*, Tomus 7, Hohhot: Inner Mongolia University Press 2003, 77-91.

2004

266. (H) zusammen mit H.-R. KÄMPFE: *Tunguso Sibirica* 14, Wiesbaden: Harrassowitz Verlag, 146 Seiten.

267. *Geschichte der Mongolen*, Stuttgart: Kohlhammer Urban-Taschenbücher, Band 586, 269 Seiten, ISBN 3-17-017206-9.

268. *Zur Erforschung der Geschichte der Mongolen des 17. Jahrhunderts. Ein Ausblick.* Der ursprünglich digitalisierte Beitrag findet sich in Papierform in: Michael Weiers, *Erbe aus der Steppe. Beitrage zur Sprache und Geschichte der Mongolen = TungusoSibirica*, Band 28, 52-78.

2005

269. *Zur Bearbeitung von Überrest-Dokumenten zur Geschichte des östlichen Innerasiensin der ersten Hälfte des 17. Jahrhunderts.* Der ursprünglich digitalisierte Beitrag findetsich in Papierform in: Michael Weiers, *Erbe aus der Steppe. Beiträge zur Sprache und Geschichte der Mongolen = Tunguso Sibirica*, Band 28, 79-100.

270. (H) zusammen mit H.-R. KÄMPFE: *Tunguso Sibirica* 13, Wiesbaden: Harrassowitz Verlag, 166 Seiten.

271. „Reiche der Reitervölker, Tschingis Khan und das mongolische Weltreich", in: *Vernissage.Die Zeitschrift zur Ausstellung*, Nr. 10/05, Heidelberg: Vernissage-Verlag GmbH& Co. KG, 30-44.

272. „Steppe und Steppenreiche bis Činggis Khan", in: Ausstellungskatalog: *Dschingis Khan und seine Erben. Das Weltreich der Mongolen*, 36-38; ISBN 3-7774-2545-1.

273. „Loyalität und Fürsorge – Činggis Khan, seine Nachkommen und das Weltreich bis1260", in: Ausstellungskatalog: *Dschingis Khan und seine Erben. Das Weltreich der Mongolen*, 92-95; ISBN 3-7774-2545-1.

274. „Sprache und Schrift der Mongolen", in: Ausstellungskatalog: *Dschingis Khan*

undseine Erben. Das Weltreich der Mongolen, 106-107; ISBN 3-7774-2545-1.

275. „Die Goldene Horde in Russland“, in: Ausstellungskatalog: *Dschingis Khan und seine Erben. Das Weltreich der Mongolen*, 222; ISBN 3-7774-2545-1.

276. „Das Khanat Čaγatai“, in: Ausstellungskatalog: *Dschingis Khan und seine Erben. Das Weltreich der Mongolen*, 241-243; ISBN 3-7774-2545-1.

277. „Ein Reich zerfällt“, in: *Damals. Das Magazin für Geschichte und Kultur* Nr.6/2005, Leinfelden-Echterdingen: Konradin Medien GmbH, 38-44.

278. (H) zusammen mit M. GIMM UND G. STARY: *Aetas Manjurica* 10, Wiesbaden: Harrassowitz Verlag 2005, 118 Seiten.

279. (H) zusammen mit M. GIMM UND G. STARY: *Aetas Manjurica* 11, Wiesbaden: Harrassowitz Verlag 2005, 369 Seiten.

280. „Bemerkungen zu Titel und Titelvermerk im älteren mongolischsprachigen Schrifttum“, in: *Opera altaistica professori Stanislao Kałużyński octogenario dicata = Rocznik Orientalistyczny*, T. LVIII, Z. 1, 2005, 242-246.

281. „Zum Synkretismus moderner mongolischer Sprachen“, in: G. Hauska (Hrsg.), *Gene, Sprachen und ihre Evolution*, Schriftenreihe der Universität Regensburg Band 29, Regensburg: Universitatsverlag Regensburg, 197-212; ISBN 3-930480-46-8.

2006

282. (H) zusammen mit H.-R. KÄMPFE: *Tunguso Sibirica* 15, Wiesbaden: HarrassowitzVerlag, 175 Seiten.

283. (H) Alessandra Pozzi, Juha Antero Janhunen and Michael Weiers, *Tumen jalafun jecenakū. Manchu Studies in Honour of Giovanni Stary = Tunguso Sibirica* 20, Wiesbaden:Harrassowitz Verlag, 320 Seiten.

284. „Wie geht es Ihnen? – Mir geht es gut“, in: Alessandra Pozzi, Juha Antero Janhunenand Michael Weiers, *Tumen jalafun jecen akū. Manchu Studies in Honour of GiovanniStary = Tunguso Sibirica* 20, Wiesbaden: Harrassowitz Verlag, 309-317.

285. (H) zusammen mit H.-R. KÄMPFE: *Tunguso Sibirica* 17, Wiesbaden: Harrassowitz Verlag, 154 Seiten.

286. (H) zusammen mit M. GIMM UND G. STARY: *Aetas Manjurica* 12, Wiesbaden: Harrassowitz Verlag, 207 Seiten.

287. *Zweitausend Jahre Krieg und Drangsal und Tschinggis Khans Vermächtnis = Tunguso Sibirica* 21, Wiesbaden: Harrassowitz Verlag, 168 Seiten.

288. *Tschinggis Khans politisches und territoriales Erbe.* Der ursprünglich digitalisierte Beitrag findet sich in Papierform in: Michael Weiers, *Erbe aus der Steppe. Beiträgezur Sprache und Geschichte der Mongolen = Tunguso Sibirica*, Band 28, 101-120.

2007

289. (H) zusammen mit H.-R. KÄMPFE: *Tunguso Sibirica* 22, Wiesbaden: Harrassowitz Verlag, 189 Seiten.

290. „Aufbruch der Reitervolker – Das „Weltreich“ Čingis Chaans“, in: U. B. Barkmann(Hrsg.), *Čingis Chaan und sein Erbe. Das Weltreich der Mongolen.* Materialien der Konferenzen des DAAD und der DFG anlässlich der Ausstellung der Kunst- und Ausstellungshalleder Bundesrepublik Deutschland „Čingis Chaan und seine Erben – Das Weltreich der Mongolen“ Bonn 16. Juni – 25. September 2005, Ulaanbaatar: Centrefor Mongol Studies, National University of Mongolia, 259-265 (Übersetzung insKhalkha-Mongolische *ibid.*, 55-62).

291. (H) zusammen mit H.-R. KÄMPFE: *Tunguso Sibirica* 24, Wiesbaden: Harrassowitz Verlag, 141 Seiten.

292. (H) zusammen mit H.-R. KÄMPFE: *Tunguso Sibirica* 18, Wiesbaden: Harrassowitz Verlag, 162 Seiten.

293. (H) zusammen mit H.-R. KÄMPFE: *Tunguso Sibirica* 19, Wiesbaden: Harrassowitz Verlag, 184 Seiten.

294. (H) zusammen mit H.-R. KÄMPFE: *Tunguso Sibirica* 16, Wiesbaden: Harrassowitz Verlag, 113 Seiten.

2009

295. „Die Mongolen und der Koran“, in: Volker Rybatzki, Alessandra Pozzi, Peter W. Geierand John R. Krueger (Eds.). *The Early Mongols · Language, Culture and History · Studies in Honor of Igor de Rachewiltz on the Occasion of His 80th Birthday*, Bloomington: Indiana University Uralic and Altaic Series 173, 209-217.

296. *Geschichte Chinas. Grundzüge einer politischen Landesgeschichte*, Stuttgart: Verlag W. Kohlhammer, 268 Seiten.

297. *Erbe aus der Steppe. Beitrage zur Sprache und Geschichte der Mongolen = Tunguso Sibirica* 28, Wiesbaden: Harrassowitz Verlag, 181 Seiten.

298. „Zum grammatischen Sprachbau der uigurisch-mongolischen Schriftsprache“, in:*Erbe aus der Steppe* (vgl. Nr. 297.), 10-20.

299. „Randbemerkungen zum Mandschu-Kharatsin Bund des Jahres 1628“, in: *Erbe aus der Steppe* (vgl. Nr. 297.), 21-27.

300. „Die Siegel des Ayuširidara, die politischen Ideologien der Mongolen, und ihre Geschichtsschreibung“, in: *Erbe aus der Steppe* (vgl. Nr. 297.), 28-51.

301. „Zur Erforschung der Geschichte der Mongolen des 17. Jahrhunderts. Ein Ausblick“,

in: *Erbe aus der Steppe* (vgl. Nr. 297.), 52-78.

302. „Zur Bearbeitung von Überrest-Dokumenten zur Geschichte des östlichen Innerasiensin der ersten Halfte des 17. Jahrhunderts“, in: *Erbe aus der Steppe* (vgl. Nr. 297.), 79-100.

303. „Tschinggis Khans politisches und territoriales Erbe“, in: *Erbe aus der Steppe* (vgl. Nr.297.), 101-120.

304. „Achthundert Jahre Herrscher Tschinggis Khan (1206-2006)“, in: *Erbe aus der Steppe*(vgl. Nr. 297.), 121-145.

305. „Zur „Versorgung“ von Mongolen in der Aisin-Zeit“, in: *Erbe aus der Steppe* (vgl. Nr.297.), 146-155.

306. „Die Mongolen kommen – Kampf der Kulturen im Mittleren Osten“, in: *Erbe aus der Steppe* (vgl. Nr. 297.), 156-168.

307. (H) zusammen mit H.-R. KAMPFE: *Tunguso Sibirica* 27, Wiesbaden: Harrassowitz Verlag, 151 Seiten.

308. „Vom Mythos zur Historie. Aus der Werkstatt der Zentralasienwissenschaft“, in: HugoSchmale, Marianne Schuller, Gunter Ortmann (Hrsg.), *Wissen/Nichtwissen*, München:Wilhelm Fink Verlag, 151-162.

309. „Ersuchen an den Herrscher“, in: *Zentralasiatische Studien* 38 (2009), 345-356.

2010

310. (H) zusammen mit H.-R. KÄMPFE: *Tunguso Sibirica* 29, Wiesbaden: Harrassowitz Verlag, 174 Seiten.

311. „Үнэнч зүтгэлийн хариуд ивээл халамж - Чингис хаан, түүнийг залгамжлагчид ба 1260 он хүртэлх Их Монгол улс“ (Loyalität und Fursorge als Antwort auf aufrichtige Bemuhungen – Tschinggis Khan, seine Nachfolger, und das Mongolische Grosreichbis 1260), in: *Quaestiones Mongolorum Disputatae* VI, Tokyo 2010, 6-12.

2011

312. *Zu einem Auftrag zur Globalisierung im 13. Jahrhundert und zu seinen Folgen*. Eineüberabeitete und erweiterte digitale Fassung vgl. unten unter Nr. 318.

313. „Zur Geschichte der Beziehungen zwischen Tibetern und Mongolen“, in: R[uth] Erken(Hg.), *1000 Jahre asiatisch-europäische Begegnung*, Frankfurt am Main: Peter Lang. Internationaler Verlag der Wissenschaften, 175-188.

314. *Zu den Throneingaben aus dem Lifan yuan. Eine Anleitung zu ihrer Untersuchung*. Der ursprünglich digitalisierte Beitrag findet sich erweitert sowie in Papierform vgl.unten Nr. 316.

315. „Going along the frontier. Qing-China's northern territories 1653-1739", in: *Quaestiones Mongolorum Disputatae* VII, Tokyo 2011, 1-10.

2012

316. „Zu den Throneingaben aus dem Lifan yuan. Eine Anleitung zu ihrer Untersuchung", in: *Quaestiones Mongolorum Disputatae* No. 8, Tokyo 2012, 1-24.

317. „Übersetzung im Lichte von Textkategorie, Textsorte, Texttyp und die Sehepunkte derGeschichte" in: Vgl. überarbeitete und erweiterte Papierfassung unten Nr. 328, dort S.40-71.

2013

318. „Zu einem Auftrag zur Globalisierung im 13. Jahrhundert und zu seinen Folgen", Überarbeitung von Nr. 312 sowie erweiterte Paperfassung in: Vgl. unten Nr. 328, dort S. 13-39 sowie: http://www.zentralasienforschung.de/spam/spam042002.pdf .

319. „Von Grammatiken, Grammatikern, Philologen, und Linguisten – ein kurzgefaßter Überblick nebst Literatur", in: Vgl. überarbeitete und erweiterte Papierfassung unten Nr. 328, dort S. 186-193.

320. „Zur Inschrift auf dem Hohen Wegtor in Fatiḥpūr Sīkrī", in: Vgl. überarbeitete und erweiterte Papierfassung unten Nr. 328, dort S. 72-87.

321. *Die Schlacht von Wahlstatt bei Liegnitz und die Mongolen* http://www.zentralasienforschung.de/spam/spam022002.pdf

322. „Zur Symbolik der Leber und ihrer Verbreitung", in: Vgl. uberarbeitete und erweiterte Papierfassung unten Nr. 328, dort S. 120-129.

2014

323. „Bemerkungen zum Gebrauch der uighurisch-mongolischen und mandschurischenSchrift", in: Vgl. uberarbeitete und erweiterte Papierfassung unten Nr. 328, dort S.130-153.

324. „Beispiele für ein rhetorisches Stilmittel in der Geheimen Geschichte der Mongolen", in: Vgl. überarbeitete und erweiterte Papierfassung unten Nr. 328, dort S. 154-162.

325. *Von der Parataxe zur Hypotaxe — Formen und Funktionen*, Teil I http://www.zentralasienforschung.de/spam/spam092006.pdf

326. „Philologische Überlegungen zu Sprache und Text in uighurisch-mongolischer un dmandschurischer Schriftsprache", in: Vgl. uberarbeitete und erweiterte Papierfassungunten Nr. 328, dort S. 88-119.2015

327. „Die Dynastien Yuan und Qing im Blickfeld Politischer Strategie", in: Vgl. überarbeiteteund erweiterte Papierfassung unten Nr. 328, dort S. 163-185.

328. *Beiträge zur Mandschuristik und Mongolistik und ihrem Umfeld* = Michael Weiers(H), *Tunguso Sibirica*, Band 38, Wiesbaden: Harrassowitz Verlag, 2015, 193 Seiten.

329. *Staatlich verordnete Digraphie für die Mongolische Republik*

http://www.zentralasienforschung.de/spam/spam152015.pdf

330. *Mit Feuer in den Augen, mit Glanz im Gesicht*

http://www.zentralasienforschung.de/spam/spam162015.pdf

331. *Der Begriff Horn in der Vision des Qorči aus der Geheimen Geschichte der Mongolen*

http://www.zentralasienforschung.de/spam/spam172015.pdf

332. *Anordnungen Tschinggis Khans für seine Nachtwachen – Notizen für eine historische Textanalyse der Geheimen Geschichte der Mongolen*

http://www.zentralasienforschung.de/spam/spam182015.pdf

2016

333. *Zum Werktitel mongolischer Handschrifttexte*

http://zentralasienforschung.d e/spam/spam192016 . pdf .pdf

334. *Von 'Phags-pa zu Sayang Sečen — ein Spiel mit Ort und Zeit*

http://www.zentralasienforschung.de/spam/spam202016.pdf

335. *Bemerkungen zu einem Stempelsiegel aus Čayatai und seiner Inschrift*

http://www.zentralasienforschung.de/spam/spam212016.pdf

336. *Urkundliche Hinweise auf den politisch-kulturellen Umbruch im östlichen Innerasien des 17. Jahrhunderts*

http://www.zentralasienforschung.de/spam/spam222016.pdf

337. *Eine Notiz zu Neyiči Toyin*

http://www.zentralasienforschung.de/spam/spam232016.pdf

338. „The Lifanyuan: A Review Based on New Sources and Traditional Historiography", in: *Managing Frontiers in Ching China.* Edited by Dittmar Schorkowitz and Chia Ning, Leiden | Boston: Brill (*Brill's Inner Asian Library 35*), S. 70-91.

2017

339. *Bemerkungen zur Terminologie in der uighurisch-mongolischen Schrift*

http:www.zentralasienforschung.de/spam/spam242017.pdf

340. *Zur Funktion der Redefigur figura etymologica in der Geheimen Geschichte der Mongolen*

http:www.zentralasienforschung.de/spam/spam252017.pdf

從新疆鄯善縣洋海墓地出土木質火鉢探討火崇拜與拜火教的關係*

李　肖　馬麗萍

1987年，新疆吐魯番地區鄯善縣洋海墓地和達浪坎墓地被盜，新疆文物考古研究所委派張鐵男研究員會同吐魯番地區文物管理所前往處理，共收繳清理文物130件並發表了簡介①。此後，吐魯番地區文管所又在農民家裡和墓地收回、採集到部分流散文物②。在這次清理中，採集到一件木鉢（編號87CYP：108），由於受當時考古發掘資料所限，並未認識到這件器物的重要性，只是當成了一件很普通的圜底木鉢登記入庫，2010年吐魯番地區博物館時將其鑒定爲館藏三級文物（圖1）。該木鉢用吐魯番盆地北側天山上的雪嶺雲杉（Schrenk Spruce）製成，通長37、寬15、高13厘米（圖2）③。由於當時的器物編號隨意性較大，除了“87”這個代表1987年發掘年份的數字規範外，第一個字母應該是代表鄯善縣的拼音頭一個字母“S”，但這裡寫成了“C”；第二個字母“Y”是代表洋海墓地的拼音首字倒是沒有歧義，按照考古規範第三個字母應該是“墓葬”拼音的首字母“M”，結果卻寫成了“P”，可能是“被盜墓”的首字拼音，

圖1　木鉢（87CYP：108）（周芳攝）

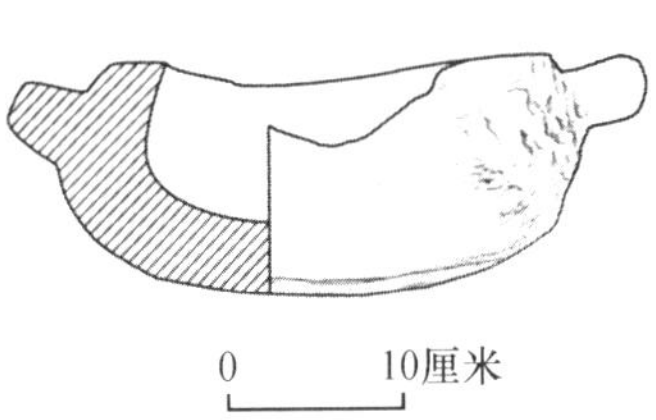

圖2　木鉢線圖（陳新勇、佘秀紅繪）

* 本文系國家社科基金重點項目“新疆地區中西文化交流”（項目編號：12AZD085）階段性成果。

① 新疆文物考古研究所《“鄯善古墓被盜案”中部分文物之介紹》，《新疆文物》1989年第4期，34頁。

② 吐魯番地區文物局《鄯善洋海墓地出土文物》，《新疆文物》1998年第3期，28頁。

③ 吐魯番地區文物局《1987年收繳的洋海墓地被盜出土器物》，《吐魯番學研究》2011年第2期，12頁。

但由於新疆方言“b”“p”音不分，所以才出現這種讓人不容易搞明白的文物編目[④]。木鉢利用樹幹的半個側面整體切削掏挖而成整，加工粗糙，平面爲圓角長方形，在其長軸方向的兩端各有一個凸出部分，爲搬動時的手柄。口沿較爲平滑，但其中的一側由於長期使用而磨損凹陷（圖3）。底部爲圜底，由於長期使用而磨得較爲光滑（圖4）。由於是清理被盜擾的的墓葬，所以這件器物的出土位置、用途、裡面的隨葬品都不得而知，發掘者可能是由於當時能夠對比的材料不多而未做進一步的深入研究。但重新觀察後不難發現鉢內尚殘留有灰燼，內壁和底部有嚴重燒灼的痕跡（圖5、圖6），甚至在損毀口沿的外側也能見到燒灼後的碳化部分（圖7）。

圖3　木鉢（87CYP：108）（周芳攝）

圖4　木鉢（87CYP：108）（周芳攝）

圖5　木鉢（87CYP：108）（周芳攝）

圖6　木鉢（87CYP：108）（周芳攝）

自從在吐魯番洋海墓地發現了距今2500年前的大麻實物後[⑤]，包括新疆在內的，歐亞大陸中西部古代印歐人群普遍吸食大麻的現象又一次引起學術界的關注，但在吐魯番洋海墓地裏未發現、或鑒別出如同俄國阿爾泰—南西伯利亞地區青銅時代墓葬裏出土的

④　此編號的由來是通過請教當時清理這批墓葬的親曆者，現新疆吐魯番學研究院研究員張永兵先生後才得以釋疑。

⑤　Jiang HE, Li X et al., “A new insight into Cannabis sativa(Cannabaceae) utilization from 2500-year-old Yanghai Tombs, Xinjiang, China”, *Journal of Ethnopharmacology*, 2006 Dec 6; 108(3), pp. 414-422.

吸食大麻的工具而成爲一個未解之謎[⑥]。

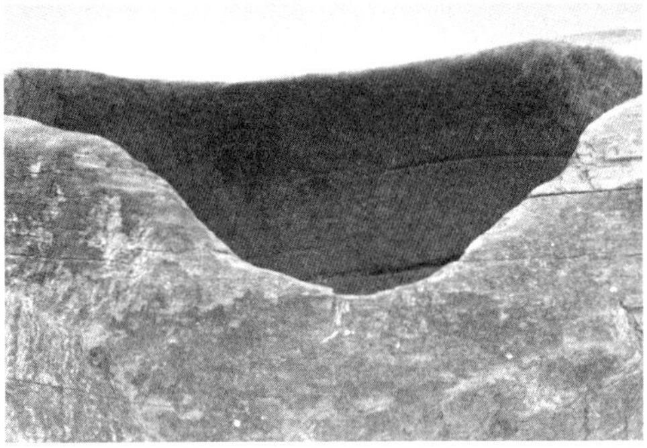

圖7 木鉢（87CYP：108）（周芳攝）

2013年，中國社會科學院考古研究所在新疆塔什庫爾干縣發掘了吉爾贊喀勒墓地（又稱“曲曼墓地”），在M11、M12、M15號墓葬中出土了木鉢狀容器，裏面放有長期爲火燒灼而變黑的十幾粒卵石，作者在介紹墓地的文章中稱其爲木制火壇，是歐亞大陸迄今發現最早最原始的明火入葬火壇（圖8、圖9）。發掘者認爲這是在歐亞大陸範圍内首次發現距今2500年左右的拜火教遺跡；拜火教起源有波斯或中亞說，這一發現支持了中亞起源說，並有可能把中亞起源地定於塔里木盆地周緣或直接定在帕米爾高原[⑦]。

圖8 B區M12墓葬二次葬和木鉢（巫新華攝）

圖9 M2墓葬出土的“火壇”（巫新華攝）

古波斯的瑣羅亞斯德教（Zoroastrian）因爲崇拜聖火而被周邊其他文明稱之爲拜火教。然而，在歐亞大陸諸多民族，無論其居住地域是在東方或是西方，抑或內亞地區，在其歷史發展的早期階段都有過崇拜火的習俗。所以，著名學者林悟殊先生指出：“有火崇拜的宗教，未必就是瑣羅亞斯德教；有火崇拜習俗的民族，未必就是拜火民族。不過，瑣羅亞斯德教特別強調火崇拜，這卻是

⑥ 李肖、呂恩國、張永兵《新疆鄯善洋海墓地發掘報告》，《考古學報》2011年第1期，99頁。
⑦ 巫新華《2013年新疆塔什庫爾干吉爾贊喀勒墓地的考古發掘》，《西域研究》2014年第1期，124頁。

不爭的事實”[⑧]。

古希臘地理學家斯特拉波（Strabo，公元前64/63—公元23），其生活的年代正處於波斯帕提亞王朝（公元前274—公元226）的中葉，他最早記載波斯境內拜火教徒崇拜火廟的習俗，“在卡帕多奇亞地區（Cappadocia）有一種教派，被稱爲‘燃火者’，他們有火廟、圍場。火廟正中有火壇，其上有大量灰燼，祭祀使火保持持久不息”[⑨]。可以看出，拜火教的火壇是建在火廟內的，而不是其他地方，更沒有將儲存火種的火罐當做隨葬品埋入墓裏的任何記載和考古發現。所以，新疆塔什庫爾干縣吉爾贊喀勒墓地（以下簡稱該墓地）發現“拜火教徒”將儲存火種的木質容器放在墓裏隨葬的現象是歷史文獻和考古發掘都未曾記載或證實過的事情。

關於瑣羅亞斯德教徒喪葬習俗的文字記載，最早可追溯到公元前5世紀，當時希臘的著名學者希羅多德（Herodotus）在其名著《歷史》第一卷第一四〇節中寫道：據說波斯人的屍體是只有在被狗或是禽撕裂之後才埋葬的。麻葛僧有這種風俗，那是毫無疑問的，因爲他們公然這樣實行的[⑩]。

拜火教的重要經典《阿維斯陀》中有《梵迪達特》（Vendidad），意思是“驅魔之法”，計有22章，其中第六章記載了拜火教徒如何處理屍體的方法，也即是驅魔之法。阿胡拉瑪玆達要求信徒將屍體放在最高處讓鳥獸啄食，而且要用金屬或石塊、獸角將屍體頭髮、雙足縛住，否則鳥獸會將其拖入水中或植物中間，玷污大地和水。“對於被鳥獸吃剩下的遺骸應該放在容器中，避免與獸類接觸，也可不玷污雨水。如果無法置辦容器，則可任其安放在地上，讓日光來照射”[⑪]。

希羅多德記載波斯拜火教徒用狗或禽處理屍體的時代是公元前5世紀，和新疆塔什庫爾干縣吉爾贊喀勒墓地（又稱“曲曼墓地”）的時代相當，可見這裏的喪葬習俗和伊朗高原的拜火教徒的存在著巨大的差異。在時代稍晚幾個世紀的《魏書》卷120《西域傳·波斯國條下》記載道：“死者多棄屍於山，一月著服。城外有人别居，唯知喪葬之事，號爲不淨人，若入城市，搖鈴自别。”所以，沒有任何記載證明拜火教徒的墓葬如同該墓地這樣把逝者未經處理，也沒有放入專門的容具內就埋葬的；再者，拜火教的教義認爲將死者直接埋入地下是嚴重觸犯戒律的行爲，是必須要處死的重罪。在《小阿維斯陀經》（Khurtak Avistak）就有“玷污死物（Nasa），將死物在火上烘烤，或將它投入諸水中，或將它埋在地下”，都是要判死刑的重罪[⑫]。

根據目前學術界對拜火教的研究，拜火教的創始人瑣羅亞斯德生活在公元前1400

---

⑧ 林悟殊《波斯拜火教與古代中國（Zoroastrianism & Ancient China）》，台北：新文豐出版公司印行，1995年，51頁。

⑨ Strabo, *Geography*, XV 3.15(Loeb Classical Library).

⑩ Herodotus, *History*(Loe Classical Library). 參見徐松岩譯著《歷史》，北京：中信出版社，2013年，第一卷，第140節，71頁。

⑪ 拜火教經典《阿維斯陀》（Avistak）中的一部分，它摘自其他經典的經文，供每日祈禱時念經之用，見龔方震、晏可佳《祆教史》，上海：上海社會科學出版社，1998年，8頁。

⑫ Dhabhar, *Zandi Khurak Avistak*, 1963, pp.132-134.

年—公元前1000年的時代裏[13]，那個時代的拜火教徒其喪葬儀軌雖不如大致在公元以後那樣將遺骸放入納骨器中，但也是要將屍體搬運至一塊平整的坡地或戈壁沙漠，任憑飛禽走獸將屍體吃光，骨殖另行埋葬，免得污染水、火或者其他阿胡拉馬茲達的創造[14]。所以，該墓地如果是拜火教信徒的墓地，就沒有理由不嚴格按照拜火教的儀軌將遺骸按照教規處理，而是和其他印歐人一樣實行土葬。該墓地的遺骨保存完整，二次葬的墓葬所佔比例極低，發掘的41座墓葬中，只有3座是二次葬（即使是二次葬也不能說和拜火教有關），大部分都是完整下葬，此外，將“火壇”埋入墓中則更是玷污聖火的大罪，解釋不通。

這個地處帕米爾山結東麓塔什庫爾干地區的墓地，初步斷定其時代是公元前5世紀左右，所反映出的考古文化尚處在青銅時代—早期鐵器時代，可見其文化發展遠遠滯後於周邊諸文明，甚至落後於塔里木盆地周緣的綠洲文明。在與該墓地相對應的時代裏，西側伊朗高原上已經建立起了波斯阿契美尼德（Achaemenian）王朝（公元前550—前330），拜火教已作爲國教，在帝國境內風靡流行[15]。縱觀世界文明發展史，任何能夠發展成爲宗教的信仰毫無例外地都出現在有著深厚文明積澱的地區，而帕米爾高原由於其嚴苛、貧瘠的自然環境，至今都不是人類宜居之地，所以不具備成爲包括拜火教在內的，任何古代宗教的發源地。從考古材料和文獻記載來看，原始印歐人（Proto-Indo-Europeans）均實施土葬或火葬，但只有拜火教把逝者放入專門的寂沒之塔（dakhma）內讓鷹、犬等動物將軟組織食盡後，把遺骸放入專門的石函（圖10）[16]或陶質的納骨器之中，這是教義的嚴格規定，直至今天在印度的拜火教徒仍然保持著這種傳統的葬俗[17]。

圖10　石函

開鑿于伊朗納格什—魯斯塔姆附近懸崖上

最後，新疆地區雖然發現了不少和拜火教有關的，諸如納骨器等遺物（圖11）[18]，但至今也沒有發現像伊朗雅茲迪遺存的寂沒之塔（圖12）和火壇等遺跡。所以，認爲該墓地是拜火教徒的遺存缺乏依據。

拜火教崇尚光明和給萬物帶來生機的水，大約從公元前5000年起，生活在南俄草原上的

⑬ Mary Boyce, *Zoroastrians,Their Religious and Practices*,London: Routledge & Kegan Paul, 1979, p.78.

⑭ 龔方震、晏可佳《祆教史》，72頁。

⑮ 林悟殊《波斯拜火教與古代中國（Zoroastrianism & Ancient China）》，2頁。

⑯ 〔美〕布朗主編、王淑芳譯《波斯人：帝國的主人》，北京：華夏出版社，2002年，177頁。

⑰ 龔方震、晏可佳《祆教史》，340頁。

⑱ 祁小山、王博《絲綢之路·新疆古代文化》，乌鲁木齐：新疆人民出版社，2008年，125頁。

圖11　鄯善縣吐峪溝出土的納骨器（祁小山攝）

圖12　伊朗亞茲德（Yazd）的寂沒之塔（李肖攝）

原始印歐人將就祭水視爲重大活動；同樣，對光明的載體——火的祭祀也不亞於對水的祭祀，他們每日三次，在晨禱、午禱和晚禱時，將清潔的木材、一些香料和一小塊動物脂肪（早期爲動物腹內的網膜）等三樣祭品投入家裏爐竈的火焰中進行祭祀。公元初年，希臘地理學家斯特拉波（Strabo，公元前64—公元23）曾經目睹波斯人祭火，“加入干燥的沒有枝杈的木柴，把軟化的油脂置於火上”[19]，可見祭火儀式並未放在墓葬中進行。

除了祭祀水、火外，他們還向諸神獻祭，目的是博得諸神的庇佑，求得今生和來世的福祉等等。這其中獻給諸神的植物祭品有某些植物的汁液、石榴、小麥、蔬果，其中，最主要的是一種稱作豪麻（haoma，梵語soma，漢譯“蘇摩”）的植物。據《阿維斯陀》記載，豪麻爲一種綠色植物，種類繁多，多汁多肉，柔韌芳香，遍生於高山幽谷之間，以其釀制的豪麻酒（parahaoma）功效很大，武士飲之可以增加力量和勇氣，祭祀飲之將頓生智慧和靈感。豪麻又是草藥之冠，可以治療疾病，有益健康。伊朗—雅利安人把豪麻在石臼裏搗爛，取其汁與石榴汁、牛乳調和成豪麻酒，具有麻醉/興奮作用飲品。但是，豪麻究竟爲何種植物，祆教經典語焉不詳，目前學術界較爲認可的觀點分爲三種，一是認爲豪麻爲大黄屬植物；再就是認爲是蛤蟆菌（也稱“鵝膏菌”）菌類植物（*Amanita muscaria*），如沃森（R.G.Wassen）在其大作《蘇摩：神聖的仙菌》（1968）中旁征博引，詳加考證，但這種菌類在中亞地區似乎極少分布；1984年，美國加利福尼亞大學的史華慈（M.Schwartz）則考證它爲野芸香[20]。但無論是什麽成分，豪麻都是榨成汁飲用而不是放在火裏熏煙。此外，在新疆阿勒泰山脈裏雖然也有食後能夠

⑲　Strabo,*Geography*, XV 3.15(Loeb Classical Library).

⑳　史華茲、佛拉瑞特《蘇摩和芸香》，加利福尼亞：加利福尼亞大學出版社，1984年，6頁。

至幻的蘑菇——美麗毒蠅鵝膏菌（*Amanita muscariavry* Formosa(Pers.:Fr)Bert），但由於其毒性太強，根本無法控制用量，所以也沒有任何使用的記載（圖13）[21]。所以，到了漢代以後，信仰拜火教的粟特人來到新疆和中國內地，他們在舉行祭祀活動時所飲用的豪麻汁裏面加入的興奮劑肯定不是用上述兩類材料制成。反之，歐亞大陸西部直到包括新疆在內的中亞東部，吸食大麻的傳統卻歷史悠久[22]。

圖13 美麗毒蠅鵝膏菌

希羅多德在《歷史》第四冊中描述道："在葬禮完成之後，斯基泰人會自己清洗一番，他們先塗膏油於頭上，然後再清洗掉，最後他們清洗身體。在這些準備工作完成之後，他們就架設三根桿子，上面鋪蓋一張氈毯，並將這些東西安置牢固，然後在桿子與毛氈之間放一個盆子，再將燒紅灼熱的石頭丟到盆子裏。然後斯基泰人便拿著大麻籽爬行入帳，並且將大麻種子放到燒熱的石頭上，在灼熱的石頭上會冒出強烈的煙氣，這個時候他們開始吸食這些煙氣。斯基泰人喜歡這種蒸氣浴，他們樂在其中並且興奮嚎哭，這是斯基泰人的沐浴。"

在阿爾泰地區巴澤雷克二號墓的墓室內埋有一男和一女，在墓室西南邊發現一捆總共有六支的桿子，在這捆桿子的下方有一個方形的四角銅器，銅器之內裝有碎裂的石頭，這些包有樺樹皮的桿子長122.5厘米，直徑2—3厘米，一條小皮帶在這些桿子最上端下面2厘米處把它們捆綁在一起（圖14）[23]。在墓室西半邊有另外一個銅器，裏面同樣填放了石頭，其上也有以六根桿子所捆綁組

圖14 俄羅斯南西伯利亞巴澤雷克冰室墓中出土的吸食大麻工具

㉑ 王仁主編《新疆阿爾泰山脈野生植物圖譜》，烏魯木齊：新疆科學技術出版社，2011年，66頁。

㉒ Herodotus, *History* (Loe Classical Library), Ⅳ.75.

㉓ M.L.Artamonov, "Frozen tombs of the Scythians", *Scientific American*, 1965, 212(5), p.108.

成的架子，在這些架子上面覆蓋有一張150厘米×170厘米的披肩。這張披肩是用作吸食大麻時所需的小幕帳（圖15）。在六根桿子的其中一根桿子上固定著一個皮囊，皮囊內裝有大麻籽。容器內的石頭之間所殘留下來的大麻籽，有些被燒得焦黑，容器的把手用樺樹皮包裹著（圖16）㉔。對於生活在這一地區的原始印歐人來說，吸食大麻在他們的日常生活與祭祀當中都是很重要的㉕，很多學者認爲，墓中出土的大麻是作爲亡者在另外一個世界裏固定使用所需，也不排除爲葬禮上舉行祭祀儀式所用，但這些解釋不通爲何在同一墓地裏只有極少數墓葬裏隨葬和吸食大麻有關的物品並且與墓葬的規格無關？通過對新疆鄯善縣吐魯番洋海墓地的研究，這一疑問似乎已經找到最接近事實的答案，那就是隨葬上述物品的墓葬，其墓主人生前很可能是專司祭祀的薩滿（圖17）㉖，同類遺物在哈薩克斯坦阿爾泰地區早期鐵器時代的墓葬裏也有出土（圖18）㉗。

圖15　吸食大麻示意圖

張文玲依據*Cat. Bonn*, Barkova L., KalašnikJu. *Zwei Gesichter der Eremitage. Die Skythen und ihr Gold*, 1997, Bonn, S.159之圖繪制

圖16　大麻熏爐

由此可見，無論是鄯善縣洋海墓地還是塔什庫爾干縣吉爾贊喀勒墓地，這類裝滿燒黑石塊的木質容器應該是用來的吸食大麻的工具，而不是拜火教用來貯存聖火火種的火盆。因爲這類出土遺物都與薩滿和祭祀有關，在祭典當中，薩滿通過吸食大麻來達到極度興奮之態，以期和神靈溝通。從古至今，在波斯以及中亞地區常常可以見到通過吸食大麻來得到薩滿式興奮狀態的人們㉘。

㉔ 張文玲《黃金草原：古代歐亞草原文化探微》，上海：上海古籍出版社，2012年，116頁。

㉕ Gisela Wolf und Frank M.Andraschko und Heulen vor Lust, “Der Hanf bei den Skythen”, vom: *Gold der Steppe,Archaeoloie der Ukraine*, Schleswig, 1991, S.157, 159. Hermann Parzinger, Die Skythen (Beck Wissen), Verlag C. H. Beck, München, 2004, S. 52-53.

㉖ 李肖、呂恩國、張永兵《新疆鄯善洋海墓地發掘報告》，99頁。

㉗ Зайнолла Самашев, Берел · Berel, Издательский дом«Таймас», Алматы, 2011, c. 26.

㉘ Gisela Wolf und Frank M.Andraschkound Heulenvor Lust,1991, S.157,159.

簍

圖17 隨葬裝滿大麻葉容器的薩滿墓葬（張永兵攝）

圖18 哈薩克斯坦阿爾泰地區出土的大麻熏爐

新疆地區在青銅時代—早期鐵器時代雖不是拜火教的發祥地，但火崇拜的存在是確鑿無疑的。2001年，俄罗斯著名中亞考古學家馬爾沙克（Boris I.Marshak）先生在北大演講，在會間休息時，筆者專門就新疆及哈薩克斯坦七河流域等地出土的祭火銅盤是否爲拜火教遺物時，老先生的回答是："這些都屬於火崇拜而非拜火教。"正如前文引用林悟殊先生的話："有火崇拜的宗教，未必就是瑣羅亞斯德教；有火崇拜習俗的民族，未必就是拜火民族。不過，瑣羅亞斯德教特別強調火崇拜，這卻是不爭的事實。"在吐魯番的阿拉溝古墓中就出土了祭火的銅盤（圖19）㉙。這些年來新考古材料的湧現更加證實火崇拜的普遍存在。吐魯番勝金店墓地爲戰國末至漢代初期當地居民的墓地。在墓地規模最大、規格最高的M13號墓葬裹出土一盞葦燈（圖20），位於墓室壁東端（圖21）。葦燈緊貼墓壁，下葬前點燃，隨著墓室封閉缺氧而熄滅（圖22）。

圖19　吐魯番阿拉溝古墓出土的銅盤（馮斐攝）

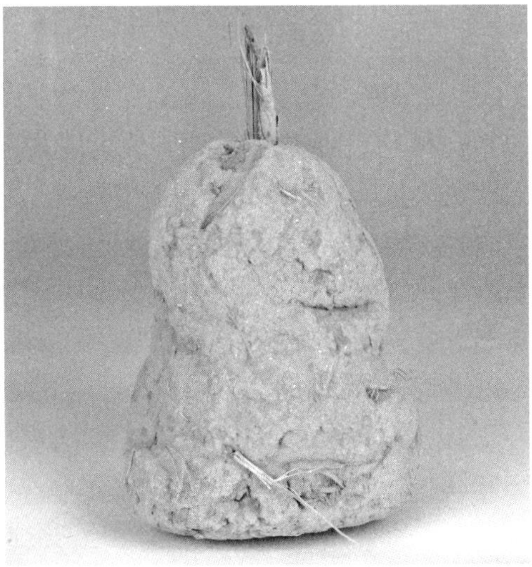

圖20　泥座葦燈（張永兵攝）

生活在歐亞草原地區的原始印歐人普遍存在拜火的習俗，只是部分文化發達地區演化成了宗教——拜火教，而其他地區由於社會生產方式等原因，仍然停留在火崇拜階段，一直到了歷史時期這種古老的習俗才爲宗教習俗所取代。

附記：此文的完成得到了新疆吐魯番學研究院張永兵先生，新疆吐魯番地區博物館周芳女士，中國科學院植物研究所李金峰先生的幫助，在此一並表示誠摯的感謝。

㉙　龔方震、晏可佳《祆教史》，131頁。

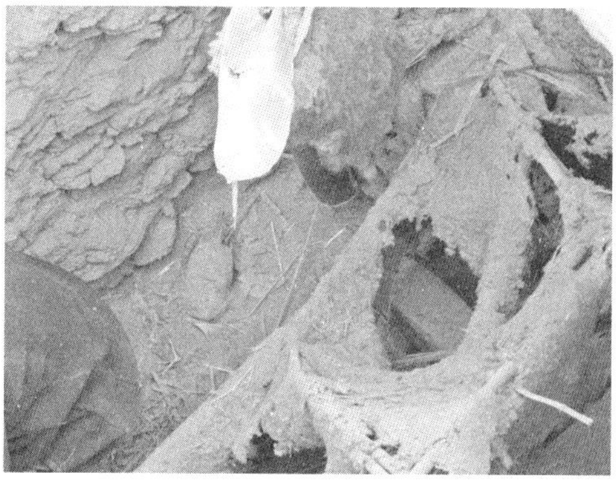

圖21 泥座葦燈出土情況（李肖攝）

圖22 M13墓室泥座葦燈出土位置（李肖攝）

Zoroastrianism and Fire Worship

Li Xiao & Ma Liping

Archaeology has always been important for the study of Zoroastrianism, but there have always been some conceptual issues that need to be clarified, such as the differences between Zoroastrianism and fire worship. In essence, Zoroastrianism is a type of worship that sublimated and separated from more primitive fire worship. From the perspective of ethnicity, whether the later Zoroastrianism or the early fire worship, these were beliefs of the ancient Indo-European people who lived in the southern Russian Steppe to the north of today's Black Sea- Caspian Sea about 10 000 years ago. In the next thousands of years their movement spread to Central Asia, the Iranian plateau, the northwestern Indian subcontinent and the area of southern Siberia – Altai mountains. The worship of fire was brought to the above areas and left many relics and remains relevant to fire worship.

As a branch of the Indo Europeans who were the original residents who lived in the Central Asian steppe regions from about 4000 years ago, the Aryans moved into the Iranian plateau and then became the ancestors of the Iran Aryans. They developed their own culture through contact and exchange with the ancient culture of the Middle East. They were polytheistic, worshipping fire in particular, and the worship of the God of light or Ormuzd Ahura Mazda was placed in a very prominent position and carried out through complicated sacrificial rites. Between 3400 to 3000 years ago Zarathustra, who was born into a noble and priestly family, had accepted the Oracle, reformed the traditional fire worship, and founded Zoroastrianism. He became the founder of the religion.

However, only Iran Aryans sublimated fire worship into a religion. The ancient Indo-European people who lived in other areas, especially the Xinjiang region which is located in Eastern Central Asia, were still in the stage of fire worship, under they came under the influence of Buddhism. With some of the new achievements of Xinjiang archaeological researchers in recent years, we try to analyse these materials and clarify the similarities and differences between fire worship and Zoroastrianism, as well as their origin.

再議新疆吐魯番出土“秦王鏡”*

劉志佳

一、前　　言

2005年，新疆吐魯番文物局對木納爾三號墓地進行發掘，M311被盜墓中出土銅鏡一面，名爲“秦王鏡”[①]。李春長曾在《新疆文物》撰文討論此鏡[②]，但對此鏡的斷代及銘文考證方面仍需作進一步探討。

從20世紀50年代至今，除新疆吐魯番外，河南、陝西、安徽、湖南、四川以及俄羅斯的圖瓦共和國均出土了同類銅鏡[③]，鏡背鐫有“賞得秦王鏡，判不惜千金。非關欲照膽，特是自明心”20字銘文，並多伴有瑞獸紋飾。

此類銅鏡亦常見於古代金石典籍中，國内各大博物館亦有展陳，是各收藏家趨之若鶩的珍品。各家對其稱謂不一，或按銘文内容、或按主題紋飾、或二者兼具，如“自明鐵鑒”“明心鑒”“秦王鏡”“四神鏡”“秦王瑞獸鏡”“秦王四駿鏡”等（附表）。其在隋唐兩代極爲風行，目前，尚無其他任何一款銘文鏡有如此廣泛的傳布。實際上，隋唐銅鏡五言銘較四言駢體銘爲少[④]，而現存的五言銘文鏡卻以“賞得”銘帶鏡存量最多，其内外區演變軌跡清晰，屬最易歸納分類者。

目前學界尚缺乏對此類銅鏡的分類梳理與考訂字句等方面的研究，各出土、館藏及圖錄中對其描述鑒別各異，甚者影響與出土物相關聯的史實的判斷。因此，對此類銅鏡的裝飾布局、演變規律進行分析，深入探討銘文典故，考訂釋義，解決仿鏡鑒別、斷代等問題，實有裨益於學界提高對此類銅鏡裝飾藝術及文化内涵的認識。

---

*　本論文系中國人民大學研究生科學研究基金項目成果之一，項目名稱：中國古代“賞得秦王銘瑞獸銅鏡研究”（項目編號：16XNH034）。

①　李肖、張永兵、張振峰《新疆吐魯番地區木納爾墓地的發掘》，《吐魯番學研究》2006年第2期，1—36頁；《新疆吐魯番地區木納爾墓地的發掘》，《考古》2006年第12期，27—46頁。

②　李春長、徐靜《吐魯番出土的“秦王鏡”》，《新疆文物》2013年第3—4期，112—116頁。

③　〔日〕岡崎敬著，姚義田譯《中亞發現的唐鏡》，《文博》1992年第3期，33頁。

④　梁上椿《岩窟藏鏡》，北京：北京大業印刷局暨育華印刷所，民國31年（1943），8頁。

二、銅鏡分類

根據目前搜集到的資料，按照此類銅鏡的外觀差異及鏡背主題紋飾的繁簡變化，對具有“賞得秦王鏡”銘帶的銅鏡進行歸類。有些銅鏡數量極少，雖與他類銅鏡有相似之處，但自身特徵突出，擬單獨歸類。

A型　銅質，方鏡，圓紐。

Aa型　方鏡，圓紐，圓紐座。雙凸弦將鏡面分爲内外兩區，内方圈無紋，紐外兩條相對的龍首尾相連。外區有“賞得秦王鏡，判不惜千金。非關欲照膽，特是自明心”20字隸楷之間銘文，外區四角有花草紋。素緣（圖1）⑤。此方鏡内區浮雕寫意性雙龍紋，首尾相連。雙龍形體纖長，盤曲卷折，後肢與尾部糾結，繞紐飛舞。

Ab型　方鏡，圓紐，圓紐座。雙凸弦將鏡面分爲内外兩區，内方圈弦紋，“繞紐配置”四獸，瑞獸形態飄逸，繞紐奔馳。外區有“賞得”等20字隸楷之間銘文，外區四角有花草紋。無緣（圖2）⑥。風格與1955年3月西安東郊郭家灘第646號隋墓出土“玉面方窺四獸鏡”一致⑦。

圖1　隋・龍紋方鏡

圖2　隋唐・賞得秦王鏡銘神獸鏡

B型　圓鏡，圓紐。依紋飾、銘文及材質分爲三亚型。

Ba型　銅質，圓鏡，圓紐，花瓣紐座。雙凸弦紋或鋸齒紋將鏡面分爲内外兩區，内區由四V形飾與大方格平行分爲四區。V形飾内有半圓加點狀凸紋，“規矩配置”，

⑤　郭玉海《故宫藏鏡》，北京：紫禁城出版社，1996年，74頁；何林主編《故宫藏鏡》，北京：紫禁城出版社，2008年，78頁；彩版見何林《你應該知道的200件銅鏡》，北京：紫禁城出版社，2007年，92頁。

⑥　日本千石唯司藏，見王綱懷、孫克讓《唐代銅鏡與唐詩》，上海：上海古籍出版社，2007年，32頁。

⑦　陝西省文物管理委員會編《陝西省出土銅鏡》，北京：文物出版社，1959年，90頁。

各分區置一站立或行走跳躍瑞獸，形態似獅似豹，間以折枝花草紋。外區有“賞得”等銘文，楷書。邊緣有三角、弦紋、櫛尺紋等（圖3）[⑧]。

圖3 Ba型銅鏡

1. 隋唐·賞得秦王鏡銘瑞獸鏡 2. 隋唐·賞得秦王鏡銘神獸鏡 3. 初唐·秦王鏡 4. 唐·四神鏡 5. 唐·明心鑒 6. 唐·秦王鏡

圖3分别源自公私收藏、發掘出土及金石典籍著錄。因保存條件不一，材質成分差異，著錄品質有别，造成有些細節如各鏡重量未知，鏡背細部難以辨認。然其關鍵信息尚存，又時代相近，從裝飾圖案及配置、各鏡尺寸來看，可歸納稱爲“同形鏡”[⑨]。此類鏡尺寸大多在16—17厘米之間（見附表）。整體風格與1954年12月西安東郊郭家灘第61號隋大業七年（611）墓出土之“窺莊益態鏡”、1956年11月西安東郊韓森寨東南第153號隋墓出土“昭仁鏡”相似[⑩]。

⑧ 圖3：1見王綱懷、孫克讓《唐代銅鏡與唐詩》，31頁；圖3：2見王綱懷《清華銘文鏡——鏡銘漢字演變簡史》，北京：清華大學出版社，2011年，144頁；圖3：3見新鄉博物館藏，圖版亦見楊秀清、胡秉鈞《介紹幾面館藏銅鏡》，《中原文物》1988年3期，90頁；圖3：4見湖南省博物館編《湖南出土銅鏡圖錄》，北京：文物出版社，1965年，117頁；圖3：5 見（清）王傑等撰《西清續鑒甲編》卷二十，《續修四庫全書》1108冊《子部·譜錄類》，上海：上海古籍出版社，347頁；圖3：6見劉體智藏並輯《小校經閣金石文字》，1935年石印本，卷十六葉百一正。

⑨ “同形鏡”未必同範，也可能是因爲同模，或同了祖範，或相同設計方案。何堂坤《中國古代銅鏡的技術研究》，北京：中國科學技術出版社，1992年，160頁。

⑩ 陝西省文物管理委員會編《陝西省出土銅鏡》，91—92頁。

1994年，咸陽市秦都區公安分局破獲一起倒賣文物案件，繳獲文物內即有一枚“秦王鏡”，型制、年代與圖3：3一致，尺寸有0.3厘米差異，當爲年代久遠損耗所致，亦爲“同形鏡”⑪。

Bb型　銅質，圓鏡，圓紐，紐外有一圈聯珠紋，花瓣紐座。雙凸弦紋或鋸齒紋將鏡面分爲內外兩區，內區無四V飾，僅有大方格，“四方配置”。四瑞獸仍置於大方格四方，站立或行走跳躍，或昂首，或回首，或前行，形態似虎似豹似馬，以寶相花紋隔開。外區爲“賞得”銘文帶，楷書。外圈爲凸弦紋或三角紋。素緣或窄素緣（圖4）⑫。

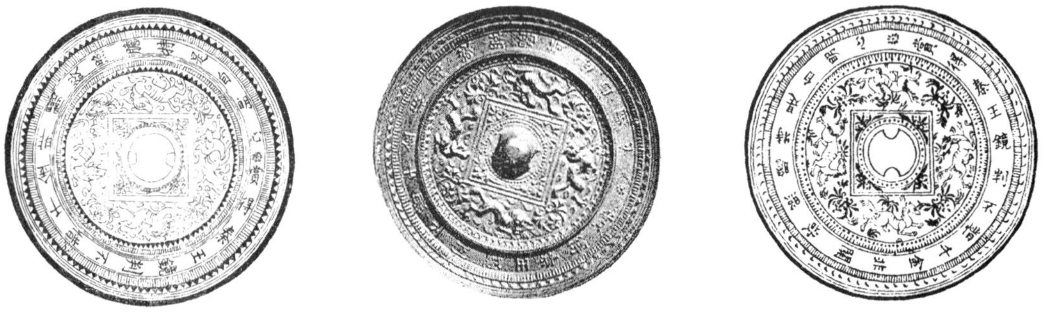

1　　2　　3

圖4　Bb型銅鏡

1. 唐·秦王鏡　2. 唐·秦王鏡　3. 唐·秦鏡

Bb型鏡主要見於金石典籍著錄及考古發掘，其分區及配置一致，惟內區瑞獸及裝飾的花紋有別。圖4：1與圖4：2內區中瑞獸與大方格之間以卷草紋或波紋隔開，而圖4：3內區中的瑞獸與大方格之間則以寶相花紋隔開。圖4：2中瑞獸似虎、似豹，或臥伏仰首，或奔馳側視，或趨步前行，或奔跑回首。形態各異，豐柔矯健，極富動態美。圖4：1中瑞獸形態與圖4：2基本一致，惟尺寸，重量有别（見附表）。此二枚銅鏡既不可能同母模，亦不同範，當是源自相同的設計方案。

圖4：3中的瑞獸與上述二枚銅鏡有別，似馬、似鹿，相對的兩只奔跑回首，另兩只奔馳前行，體態舒展有力。《金石索》並無圖4：3尺寸、重量等具體信息，僅在卷六云：“《博古錄》載有‘唐自明鐵鑒’，較大，其孚飾亦不同，惟其五言四句詩無異。故列於唐，此葉東鄉所得。其中‘闟’字作‘閧’，從門內並，亦別。”⑬可見其尺寸明顯小於‘唐自明鐵鑒’。有關銘文差異，下文將詳作探討。

⑪　銅鏡現藏咸陽市文保中心，圖版分別見趙彩秀、楊新文《四龍紋金鐲與秦王鏡》，《文博》1998年2月，85—86頁；劉曉華、張瑛《稀有的秦王銘帶鏡》，《收藏家》2003年第6期，22頁。

⑫　圖4：1見[清]錢坫《浣花拜石軒鏡銘集錄》，清嘉慶元年（1796）刻本，卷二葉七正；圖4：2 見陝西省文物管理委員會編《陝西省出土銅鏡》，第100頁；圖4：3 見馮雲鵬、馮雲鵷《金石索》卷六，據邃古齋藏本影印《萬有文庫》本，第一集一千種，上海：商務印書館，1929年，121頁。

⑬　馮雲鵬、馮雲鵷《金石索》卷六，122頁。

Bc型　銅質，圓鏡，圓紐，圓紐座。

Ⅰ式：凸弦紋將鏡面分爲內外兩區，“繞紐配置”，瑞獸似狻猊、似獅，繞紐追逐。外區有“賞得”等銘文，邊緣主要爲幾何點線紋、三角紋或弦紋（圖5）[⑭]。

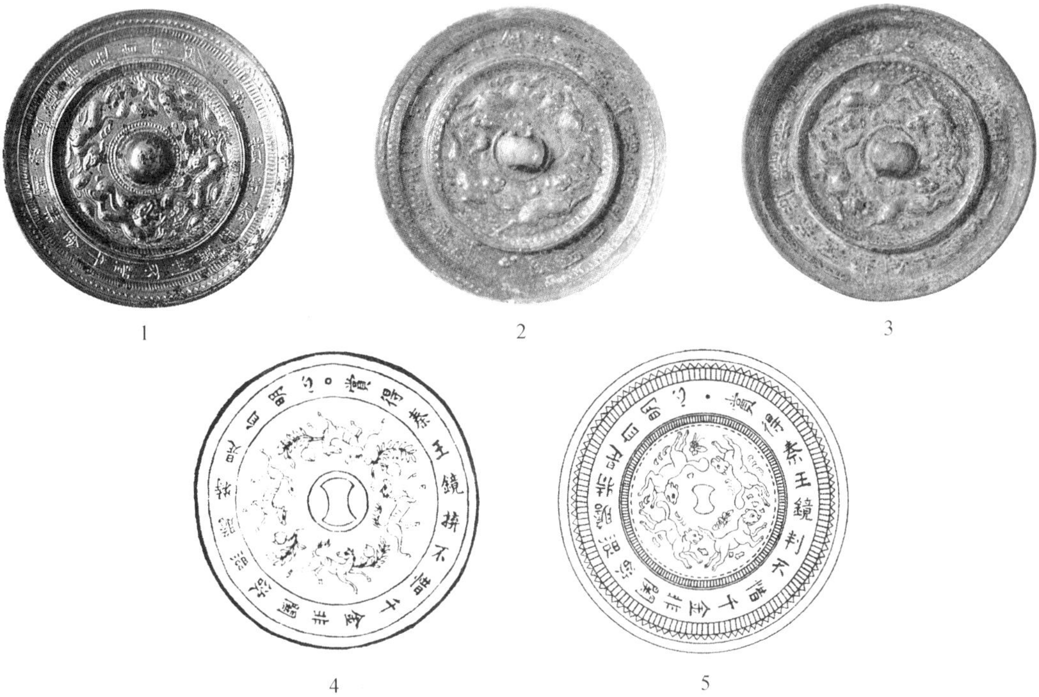

圖5　Bc型Ⅰ式銅鏡

1. 隋唐·賞得秦王鏡銘神獸鏡　2. 隋唐·秦王鏡　3. 唐·賞得秦王銘四瑞獸鏡　4. 唐·秦王鏡二　5. 唐·秦王鏡

此類銅鏡數量最多，普遍見於各公私收藏、考古發掘及金石圖錄中。《小校經閣金石文字》收有5枚此類銅鏡圖錄，其中兩枚外區凸棱無裝飾，另外3枚外區飾有凸弦紋[⑮]；《善齋吉金錄》收錄2枚，較爲清晰。張廷濟《清儀閣所藏古器物文》收錄1

⑭　圖5：1見王綱懷、孫克讓《唐代銅鏡與唐詩》，32頁；圖5：2見吐魯番博物館藏，器物編號M311：1，圖版亦見李肖、張永兵、張振峰《新疆吐魯番地區木納爾墓地的發掘》，27—46頁；圖5：3見蚌埠市博物館《蚌埠市博物館藏銅鏡集萃》，北京：文物出版社，2014年，96頁；圖5：4見馮雲鵬、馮雲鵷《金石索》卷六，第122頁；圖5：5見劉體智輯《善齋吉金錄（鏡丙）》，民國二十三年（1934），卷三“鏡錄”葉七八正；圖6：1四川博物館藏，圖版亦見四川省博物館、重慶市博物館合編《四川省出土銅鏡》，北京：文物出版社，1960年，94頁；圖6：2見安徽文物考古研究所、六安市文物局《六安出土銅鏡》，北京：文物出版社，2008年，242頁；圖6：3藏陝西歷史博物館，圖版亦見陝西歷史博物館編《千秋金鑒——陝西歷史博物館藏銅鏡集成》，西安：陝西出版集團、三秦出版社，2012年，578頁；圖6：4見儀征博物館《儀征館藏銅鏡》，南京：鳳凰出版傳媒集團、江蘇美術出版社，2010年，148頁。

⑮　劉體智藏並輯《小校經閣金石文字》，卷十六葉百二。

枚[16]；梁上椿《岩窟藏鏡》收錄2枚[17]；洛陽博物館、旅順博物館、陝西歷史博物館等亦有收藏[18]。本文僅選取幾類具有代表性的銅鏡加以介紹。

Bc型Ⅰ式鏡背題材多爲四瑞獸加銘帶，惟《金石索》收錄之“秦王鏡二”（圖5，4）鏡背題材爲“瑞獸蒲桃紋”加銘帶。張鐵山先生收藏的“賞得秦王鏡銘神獸鏡”（圖5，1），紐座外有一圈聯珠紋，是其餘各鏡所無。《中國青銅器全集·16銅鏡》圖一〇四隋“賞得秦王神獸鏡”除鏡紐無聯珠紋外，裝飾配置與圖5：1一致，尺寸略微有別[19]。此二鏡四瑞獸形態飄逸，周邊間有云氣紋，生動活潑，雕刻技法圓潤。與其他Bc型Ⅰ式鏡相比，圖5：1尺寸稍大（見附表）。吐魯番博物館所藏“秦王鏡”（圖5，2）與蚌埠博物館藏“賞得秦王銘四瑞獸鏡”（圖5，2）的紋飾、配置基本一致，但銹色、大小均有別。其與洛陽博物館、旅順博物館及《岩窟藏鏡》所收錄的此類銅鏡大小、紋飾幾乎相同，直徑均在9.5厘米左右（見附表），然這些銅鏡並非同範所造。梁上椿在《岩窟藏鏡》就已經提到關於其收錄的二枚銅鏡，“直徑雖相同，但非同範”[20]，尤其是各博物館及《岩窟藏鏡》所收錄的Bc型Ⅰ式鏡重量有明顯差别。因此，這類銅鏡可能是採用了相同的設計方案，或個別銅鏡使用了相同的母模，亦屬於“同形鏡”。

Ⅱ式：仿鏡，凸弦紋或凸棱將鏡面分爲內外兩區，“繞紐配置”，瑞獸呆板不靈動，繞紐追逐，線條較粗。外區有“賞得”等銘文，字體不甚規整。邊緣或有弦紋，或僅爲凸棱，表面粗糙（圖6）。

Bc型Ⅱ式鏡多爲仿唐鏡，主要分兩類：一類是仿隋唐“瑞獸銘帶”鏡，另一類是仿唐“瑞獸葡萄紋銘帶”鏡，數量以後者居多。

在制鏡工藝上，宋以後往往用漢唐銅鏡直接翻模，一枚銅鏡便可翻制多枚，鑄成的銅鏡鏡型相同，尺寸因以類相從。就目前已知的信息，此類帶“賞得”銘文的仿鏡直徑尺寸大概分兩種，一種直徑8.8厘米，另一類直徑在15.4厘米左右（見附表）。除此之外另有借摹本仿照制模，往往僅得其意，未得其法。如帶“賞得”銘文的“瑞獸葡萄紋”銅鏡在鏡背紋飾上與前代有偏差，下文將詳作探討。

C型　銅質，圓鏡，圓紐，圓紐座，僅有銘文，無裝飾，寬素緣，屬非典型“賞得”銘帶鏡。銘文分六輪。第一輪十二格，每格六字；第二輪爲“明齊滿月”等24字銘文帶，無格；第三輪十二格，每格六字；第四輪24格，每格一字，爲“賞得秦王鏡，判不惜千金。非關欲照膽，特是自明心。蒲山謹讃”24字銘文；第五輪二十四格；外輪

[16] 張廷濟《清儀閣所藏古器物文》（第四冊），民國十四年（1925）涵芬樓影印，葉十一。

[17] 梁上椿《岩窟藏鏡》，20頁。

[18] 洛陽博物館《洛陽出土銅鏡》，北京：文物出版社，1988年，74頁；旅順博物館《旅順博物館藏銅鏡》，北京：文物出版社，1997年，100頁；陝西歷史博物館編《千秋金鑒——陝西歷史博物館藏銅鏡集成》，350頁。

[19] 中國青銅器全集編輯委員會編《中國青銅器全集·16銅鏡》，北京：文物出版社，2005年，104頁。

[20] 梁上椿《岩窟藏鏡》，20頁。

圖6　Bc型Ⅱ式銅鏡

1. 宋・秦王鏡　2. 宋・瑞獸葡萄紋鏡　3. 宋・仿唐瑞獸紋鏡　4. 元・仿唐賞得秦王銘瑞獸鏡

二十四格[21]（圖7）。

此鏡計有銘文五百六十九字，當屬銅鏡類銘文最多的一款，“賞得秦王鏡”銘抑或是工匠從當時流行的鏡銘中選取使用。徑一尺五分，鏡面很大。從佈局上看，此鏡的設計採用了12等分圓周法，此種“等分刻度法”便於銘文的雕刻與制坯，再由等分好的坯型拼裝成一個整圓[22]。這點可從銘文第一輪及第三輪的分格排列中獲知。第二輪24字銘文帶雖未分格，但每字向外輻射正位於第四輪至第六輪24格每格格線上。其24格又由12等分圓周獲得。

D型　鐵質，圓形，圓紐，柿蒂紋紐座，紐座外有兩圈三角凸弦紋。《宣和博古圖

㉑　圖7見國家圖書館藏劉體智藏並輯《小校經閣金石文字》，卷十六葉一百七；圖版亦見氏輯《善齋吉金錄（鏡丙）》，卷三“鏡錄”葉八六。

㉒　有關銅鏡的等分圓周法，可參賈亦顯、李婷《銅鏡文化與圖案》，北京：北京工藝美術出版社，2007年，10—11頁；李迪《從古代銅鏡上的花紋探討古代等分圓周方法》，《內蒙古師範學院學報》1977年第1期，66—71頁。

錄》云：“五金皆金，莫不有序。以泉貨言之，則銅上，鐵次之。以方言之則，銅者南方之金，而鐵之位北也。於是凡銅鑒者先焉，鐵者置其後。”[23]有基於此，筆者將鐵質鏡列爲最後一類。

銅鏡分内外兩區，内區分八格，每格以兩道凸弦紋隔開。“青龍、白虎、朱雀、玄武”（四靈）配置在大格内，並分别被小格内的變形寳相花紋隔開。外區有“賞得”等二十字銘文帶，楷書。外圈爲凸三角紋，素緣（圖8）[24]。

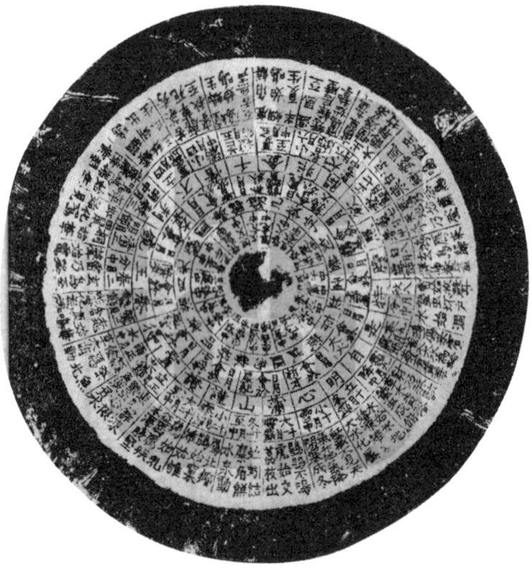

圖7　唐・唐月令鏡

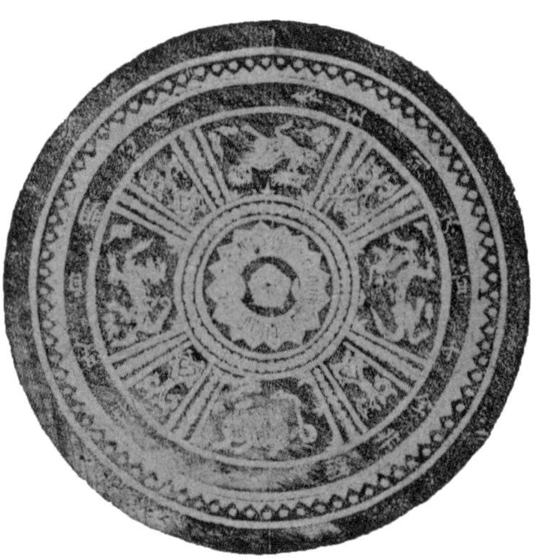

圖8　唐・自明鐵鑒

鐵質鏡極易氧化銹蝕，因此完整的鏡子保存下來的不多，帶有“賞得”等20字銘文的鐵鏡更是難得。惟宋代王黼所編之《宣和博古圖錄》收有此鐵鑒拓片圖影，極爲珍貴。名爲唐自明鐵鑒，“徑七寸一分，重二斤十有四兩”[25]。

陸繼輅《合肥學舍劄記》曾著錄“青綠雙麐鳳鏡一”，鏡銘亦爲“賞得”等銘文。從命名中可以看出，其裝飾題材爲“雙麐鳳”，且鏡銘爲“隸書”[26]，與上述所載之銅（鐵）鏡均不同。但未見圖版，其配置紋樣等資訊亦闕，因而並不單獨列出。

因大部分銅鏡的出土年代不清晰，缺少紀年墓作爲參考，各圖錄及館藏對其斷代亦不甚精確，給此類銅鏡發展脈絡的研究帶來許多混亂與困擾。就類型劃分的結果來看，此類銅鏡的演變軌跡基本符合徐殿魁、孔祥星、徐燦平等人對隋唐銅鏡的分期斷代。但此五言詩體銘銅鏡特點突出，其鏡背紋飾的演化又略有不同。

總體來看，Aa型、Ab型鏡風格迥異，前者風格古樸，有漢魏銅鏡遺風；後者做工

㉓　（宋）王黼《宣和博古圖錄》，泊如齋重修明萬曆1603年本，卷三十葉十七。

㉔　同㉓，葉十正。

㉕　同㉓，葉十六背。

㉖　（清）陸繼輅《合肥學舍劄記》卷十，《續修四庫全書》據華東師大圖書館藏清光緒四年興國州署刻本影印，1157冊，389頁

精良，内區由a型的對龍紋變爲四瑞獸紋，四獸形態飄逸，間雜云氣紋。

值得注意的是，Aa型“龍紋方鏡”不似戰國時期爬蟲類的蟠螭紋，亦不似漢式鏡中一角四足似哺乳類的龍紋。唐代流行的龍紋鏡是單個盤龍，龍紋構圖飽滿，鱗紋清晰，氣勢宏大。出土的唐鏡中典型的雙龍紋鏡尚未見存，宋代雙龍鏡最多㉗，但紋飾粗糙，整體龍紋趨於平和，尺寸較小。而此“龍紋方鏡”雙龍紋靈動飛舞，形體纖長，隱有飛動之勢，頗具隋代龍紋鏡典型特徵㉘。因此，《故宫藏鏡》將其著爲隋代，應當無誤。

Ab型鏡整體風格類似隋“玉面方窺四獸鏡”，但裝飾更爲華美，内外區分界處有一圈聯珠紋，四角又有端莊的寶相花紋，内區四瑞獸又開B型鏡四瑞獸繞鈕奔走之先，四瑞獸瀟灑飄逸。方形瑞獸鏡所見甚少，又缺乏紀年方面的資料印證，僅從瑞獸和四方枚的風格上推測，似更接近於初唐鏡㉙。因此，此鏡時代約爲隋末至唐高宗時期。

B型“賞得”銘文鏡a、b、c亚型之間的演變軌跡比較明顯。Ba型承襲了“四神規矩鏡”的風格㉚，與隋“窺莊益態鏡”“照仁鏡”相似，規矩配置，内區分置四獸。此類型規矩配置加銘文銅鏡時間上限爲隋大業七年（611）㉛。現存的Ba型鏡多缺少墓葬信息，圖3：4銅鏡出土於1957年湖南長沙陳家大山墓1，缺墓葬紀年，從同墓出土的陶器、銅錢等，將其定爲唐墓。陳燦平先生將此類鏡下限定爲初唐㉜，可見Ba型鏡時代約爲隋大業末至唐高宗時期。

Bb型鏡略去V飾，將其置換爲規整的寶相花紋，仍規矩配置，整體風格與Ba型鏡相似。Bb型鏡中圖4：2於1955年西安東郊灞橋第146號唐墓出土，缺墓葬資料。目前尚未見到與Bb型鏡相匹配參考的其他銅鏡材料，此種配置或爲“賞得”銘帶鏡獨有。Bb型鏡當與Ba型鏡時代相當或略晚，大致時代爲武德至高宗時期。

Bc型鏡完全略去規矩紋，四獸繞紐配置。Bc型Ⅰ式鏡内區瑞獸體現出兩種截然不容的形態，一類瑞獸飄逸靈動，另一類瑞獸豐腴柔健，瑞獸間留白較多。前類直徑稍大，後一類直徑稍小。圖5：1銅鏡與《中國青銅器全集·16銅鏡》收錄的“賞得秦王神獸鏡”屬前類，後者於1988年陝西長安南裏王村出土，年代爲隋㉝，但隋代此類四獸紋尚不流行。龍朔元年（661）許夫人墓出土一枚Bc型Ⅰ式型鏡，殘存三分之一，從圖版來看，此瑞獸飄逸瀟灑，屬於前類㉞。與此鏡類似的還有河南三門峽廟底溝M183出土的“環繞四獸銘帶鏡”，銹蝕嚴重，出開元錢，爲盛唐墓。仔細辨認，此鏡亦屬於前類。

㉗ 孔祥星、劉一曼《銅鏡鑒賞與收藏》，長春：吉林科學技術出版社，1994年，218頁。

㉘ 方素萍《淺析龍紋在銅鏡歷史發展中的演化過程》，《大眾文藝》2015年第17期，116頁。

㉙ 徐殿魁《唐鏡分期的考古學探討》，《考古學報》1994年第3期，305頁。

㉚ 洛陽博物館《洛陽出土銅鏡》，72頁。

㉛ 陝西省文物管理委員會《西安郭家灘隋墓清理簡報》，1957年第8期，65頁。

㉜ 陳燦平《隋唐墓葬出土銅鏡研究》，北京大學2011年博士學位論文，11頁。

㉝ 中國青銅器全集編輯委員會編《中國青銅器全集·16銅鏡》，104頁。

㉞ 廣東省博物館、茂名市博物館、電白縣博物館《廣東電白唐代許夫人墓》，《文物》1990年第7期，56—57頁。

因此，Bc型Ⅰ式型鏡前一類時代約爲隋末至玄宗開元時期。

Bc型Ⅰ式型鏡後一類瑞獸紋豐腴柔健，至晚期稍顯瘦長。除吐魯番木納爾墓地M311出土的“秦王鏡”，其他銅鏡均缺乏墓葬信息。且木納爾M311爲被盜墓，此鏡系從被盜墓中清理而出，並無更多出土器物參考，時代被定爲麴氏高昌國至唐西州時期[35]。俄羅斯圖瓦的凱諾塔夫墓出土過一枚秦王鏡，尺寸紋飾均符合後一類，同墓出開元錢、馬具等，爲盛唐墓。旅順博物館與蚌埠博物館所藏此類銅鏡瑞獸稍顯瘦長，形態亦不似前代有神，瑞獸風格類似咸通十年（869）偃師杏園李棁墓出土四獸鏡。因此，Bc型Ⅰ式型式鏡後一階段約爲玄宗開元至懿宗時期。

仿鏡多以Bc型鏡爲主，數量不多。吴文清先生收藏一枚明代仿鏡，鏡背爲傳統瑞獸紋[36]。仿鏡中出現了“瑞獸葡萄紋”主題，瑞獸及銘文均呆板不規整。時代爲宋元明時期。

C型鏡不甚典型，鏡背不分區，鏡背分格，格内皆是銘文。“賞得”銘文僅據一輪，或僅作爲流行語被工匠選入。銘文的重心在於“月令”，但此月令非《唐月令》（《禦刊定禮記月令》）[37]，《唐月令》避睿宗諱改“鶡鴠”爲“鶡鳥”，而此鏡銘文未避睿宗諱，因此，此鏡當鑄於《唐月令》成書之前。聯繫下文“賞得”銘文或爲隋蒲山公李密所作，因此C型鏡時代當在隋末至玄宗前。

D型鏡爲鐵鏡，擬單獨列出。鏡内區配置與隋唐淮南起照銘神獸鏡相似，規矩配置，分八格，格内四靈被寶相花紋隔開[38]。區别是D型鏡的裝飾紋樣不如隋鏡繁複，外區銘文帶外亦無花紋。D型鏡爲鐵鏡，鐵鏡具有明確的時代性，主要集中在隋至初唐，盛唐已不多見，中晚唐更少[39]。内區四靈的裝飾主要流行於初唐，最晚至貞觀後期[40]。因此，D型鏡的時代約爲隋末至貞觀年間。

三、銘文典故分析

“賞得秦王鏡”銘銅鏡始流行於隋唐之際，其五言詩體銘第一句又含“秦王”二字，因而對此五言銘的正確解讀尤爲重要。對“秦王鏡”典故如何解讀不僅關係此類銅鏡的時代劃分，亦影響與此五言銘相關史實的判斷，甚至於影響對此類銅鏡裝飾藝術及文化内涵的認識。

目前學界對“秦王鏡”的認識約分兩類，一類直謂此“秦王”乃李世民，因“秦

㉟ 李肖、張永兵、張振峰《新疆吐魯番地區木納爾墓地的發掘》，27—46頁。

㊱ 吴文清《賞鏡斷代説秦王》，《收藏界》2003年6月，21頁。

㊲ 《新唐書》卷五十七《藝文志》，北京：中華書局，1975年，1434頁。

㊳ 中國青銅器全集編輯委員會編《中國青銅器全集·16銅鏡》，105頁。

㊴ 陳燦平《隋唐墓葬出土銅鏡研究》，35頁。

㊵ 王綱懷《止水集——王綱懷銅鏡研究論集》，上海：上海古籍出版社，2010年，130頁。

王”是李世民在唐高祖年間的封號[41]；另一類謂“秦王”當指秦始皇，此“秦王鏡”典故當源自《西京雜記》。

持第一種觀點者，如《四龍紋金鐲與秦王鏡》、《稀有的秦王銘帶鏡》、《一面罕見的秦王銘帶鏡》等文，認爲此類銅鏡是李世民爲秦王時賞賜身邊功臣之物[42]。魏訓田在《山東陵縣出土〈唐東方合墓誌〉考釋》亦持此説，並用以考證東方合生平事蹟，具有一定的影響力[43]。早在民國年間，莊陔蘭援引《唐書·太宗本紀》，認爲“此鏡當系秦王宮人所鑄。借古事以紓丹誠，非泛詠秦鏡也。鐫馬其上，亦以頌其武功耳”[44]。徐殿魁先生亦認爲太宗以前，鏡背花紋中很少有駿馬賓士的形態，秦王鏡將“秦王”與駿馬熔鑄於一個畫面，此鏡當有頌揚秦王李世民金戈鐵馬、馳騁疆場的含義[45]。

此五言銘句首有“賞得”二字，又隋唐間銅鏡償作爲君臣之間賞賜、敬獻之物，便有認爲此“賞得秦王鏡”意指“秦王”李世民賞賜銅鏡於有功之臣者。李世民爲太宗時曾僎撰《金鏡述》，“貞觀二年正月庚午，著《金鏡述》以示群臣”[46]。《尚書考靈曜》有云：“秦失金鏡，魚目入珠。”宋均注：“金鏡，喻明道也。”[47]觀此述文，皆興亡之道，此“金鏡”當非實物。貞觀十八年，高季輔爲吏部侍郎時，曾被賜鏡，“凡所銓敘，時稱允當。太宗嘗賜金背鏡一面，以表其清鑒焉”[48]。

從工藝上看，包金、貼金或鎏金均能使銅鏡具有金背效果，如兩面唐金殼花鳥鏡[49]，唐金銀平脱葵花鏡[50]、唐銀背鎏金鳥獸菱等[51]，但最爲典型的莫過於2002年西安市東郊馬家溝村東唐太州司馬閻智夫婦墓出土的一枚金背禽獸葡萄菱花鏡，此鏡不像常見的貼金或包金，高浮雕金背殼爲熔模法鑄造而成，分鑄金殼與銅胎後，將金殼背面的高浮雕空腔填平，使用黏結劑將二者粘合在一起[52]。根據墓誌資料，閻智卒於聖曆二年（699），神龍二年（706）與夫人合葬。從出土時間與銅鏡工藝來看，此鏡當最接近太宗賜高季輔的“金背鏡”，而此類金背鏡多無銘文，工藝上又與“賞得”銘帶鏡千差萬別。可見，太宗確曾“賞鏡”，但卻不是“賞得”銘帶鏡。

㊶ （後晉）劉昫等撰《舊唐書》卷一《高祖本紀》，北京：中華書局，1975年，6頁。

㊷ 趙彩秀、楊新文《四龍紋金鐲與秦王鏡》，85—86頁；劉曉華，張瑛：《稀有的秦王銘帶鏡》，22頁；王清波、郝建保《一面罕見的秦王銘帶鏡》，《中國文物報》2001年7月25日第004版。

㊸ 魏訓田《山東陵縣出土唐東方合墓誌考釋》，《文獻》2004年第3期，93—94頁。

㊹ 莊陔蘭纂修《重修莒志》，民國二十五年（1936）本，卷五十一葉五背。

㊺ 徐殿魁先生曾在此觀點下出注“一説’秦王’指秦始皇”，但未作探討。徐殿魁《唐鏡分期的考古學探討》，304頁。

㊻ 吴玉貴撰《唐書輯校》卷三，北京：中華書局，2008年，1224頁。

㊼ （清）趙在翰輯，鐘肇鵬、蕭文郁點校《七緯》（附〈論語讖〉），《齊文化叢書·文獻集成》4，濟南：齊魯書社，1997年，593頁。

㊽ 《舊唐書》卷七十八《高季輔傳》，2703頁。

㊾ 洛陽博物館《洛陽出土銅鏡》，圖版115、116。

㊿ 中國青銅器全集編輯委員會編《中國青銅器全集·16銅鏡》，132頁。

(51) 同㊿，122—127頁。

(52) 楊忙忙、楊軍昌《唐金背禽獸葡萄鏡鈣化鏽的清除及研究》，《考古與文物》2006年第5期，111頁。

《四龍紋金鐲與秦王鏡》與《稀有的秦王銘帶鏡》二文以太宗“三鏡自照”爲例[53]，以佐證鏡銘裏的“秦王”爲李世民說。而宋王楙認爲太宗“三鏡自照”正周武王之意。案武王鏡銘曰：“以鏡自照者見形容，以人自照者知吉凶。非出於此乎。”[54]可見，太宗“三鏡自照”事典於《武王鏡銘》，卻與《武王鏡銘》一樣均無“明心、照膽”等語，因此在內涵上當與“賞得”鏡銘無涉。太宗此說於魏征死後，而隋鏡中早有“賞得秦王鏡”銘，且李世民封秦王始於高祖建唐之時，銘文亦早於其封號。因此，此五言鏡銘中的“秦王”非指秦王李世民。既非李世民，那麼鏡背紋飾爲“功狗”之說則難以成立，而“駿馬”的形象亦與五言詩體銘沒有直接關係。

與《稀有的秦王銘帶鏡》發表同期，吴文清先生撰有《賞鏡斷代說秦王》一文，吴先生反對銘文中“秦王”爲李世民的觀點，認爲此“秦王鏡”典故源自《西京雜記》，王綱懷《唐代銅鏡與唐詩》與胡珊珊《唐鏡銘文文學研究》亦同此說不過各家均未作有力論證[55]。筆者亦認爲此鏡銘典出《西京雜記》，下文擬詳作探討。

《西京雜記》（下文簡稱《雜記》）卷三“咸陽宫異寶”：“高祖初入咸陽宫，周行庫府，金玉珍寶，不可稱言。其尤驚異者，……有方鏡，廣四尺，高五尺九寸，表裏有明，人直來照之，影則倒見。以手捫心而來，則見腸胃五臟，厲然無硋。人有疾病在內，則掩心而照之，則知病之所在。又女子有邪心，則膽張心動。秦始皇常以照宫人，膽張心動者則殺之。”[56]

《雜記》的抄録者爲東晉葛洪，或有言其爲葛氏後人於六朝時集體編纂[57]，而至梁初已流行世間。梁武帝敕殷芸撰《小說》，皆鈔撮故書，其中引《雜記》甚多，“咸陽宫異寶”[58]條即在其中。北周庾信《鏡賦》：“鏡乃照膽照心，難逢難值。”《酉陽雜俎·語資》云：“庾信作詩，用《西京雜記》事。”雖後追改曰：“此吴均語。”[59]可見自梁初已有典出《雜記》者。

然而《雜記》的廣泛流傳當自隋始，《隋書·經籍志》著録《西京雜記》二卷，撰者失載[60]。《隋書·經籍志》著録書目主要利用隋代國家藏書並加工整理而成，且“煬帝

---

[53] 指“夫以銅爲鏡，可以正衣冠；以古爲鏡，可以知興替；以人爲鏡，可以明得失。朕常保此三鏡,以防己過”，見《舊唐書》卷七十一《魏徵列傳》，2561頁。

[54] （宋）王楙撰，王文錦點校《野客叢書》，北京：中華書局，1987年，332頁。

[55] 吴文清《賞鏡斷代說秦王》，20—21頁；王綱懷、孫克讓《唐代銅鏡與唐詩》，31頁；胡珊珊《唐鏡銘文文學研究》，浙江大學2013年碩士學位論文，29頁。

[56] （晉）葛洪撰，周天遊校注《西京雜記》，西安：三秦出版社，2006年，140—141頁。

[57] 關於《西京雜記》的作者，歷來爭議頗多，筆者較認同葛洪說與集體編纂說。可參丁宏武《〈西京雜記〉非葛洪僞託考辨》，《圖書館雜誌》2005年第11期，68—75頁；王守亮《〈西京雜記〉作者問題考述》，《臨沂大學學報》2012年第2期，56—58頁。

[58] （梁）殷芸撰《小說》，附於魯迅先生紀念委員會編《魯迅全集》第八卷《古小說勾陳》，北京：人民文學出版社，1972年，204—205頁。

[59] 《鏡賦》見（北周）庾信《庾子山集》卷一，北京：中華書局，1980年，57頁；“庾信作詩”事見（唐）段成式撰，方南生點校《酉陽雜俎》前集卷一二《語資》，北京：中華書局，1981年，112頁。

[60] 《隋書》卷三十三《經籍二》，北京：中華書局，1973年，966頁。

好學，喜聚逸書，而隋世簡編，最爲博洽”[61]。隋煬帝在位十三年，加之太子時前後二十年，不斷修撰文化典籍，擴建圖閣，《隋大業正御書目》正是在此基礎上成書，《隋書·經籍志》又是以此書爲基礎。可見，隋代《雜記》已進入史官視野。

又如著名的傳奇小說《古鏡記》，其在晉葛洪所記鏡異之事的基礎上踵事增華，集古今鏡異之大成[62]。《古鏡記》作者王度爲隋唐間人，主要生平活躍於隋[63]，與道士及陰陽占卜之士來往比較密切，《中說·天地篇》曾載：“芮城府君（王度）重陰陽。”《古鏡記》敘事起自大業七年五月，至大業十三年七月十五日止，“事雖出隋代，記則實入唐初”，《古鏡記》當爲隋末唐初的作品[64]。從作者生平、成書年代及內容上看，其雖號爲“唐人小說之開山”（汪辟疆），實則反應隋人的精神世界。而《古鏡記》所載之“照見妖魅，洞徹腑臟，驅邪除妖，治病救人”諸事均典出《雜記》“咸陽宮異寶”條，可見，隋人對《雜記》尤其是其中所抄錄的鏡異之事相當熟悉。

至唐，《雜記》流傳更廣，並引起廣泛討論。宋晁載之《續談助·洞冥記跋》引張柬之語曰：“昔葛洪造《漢武內傳》《西京雜記》，……並操觚鑿空，恣情迂誕。”[65]《漢書·匡衡傳》顏師古注稱“今有《西京雜記》，其書淺俗，出於里巷，多有妄記。”[66]《唐書·藝文志》亦有著錄。

與此相呼應，唐代傳奇小說則將鏡異之事進一步發揚，在此僅舉二例。《異聞錄》“李守泰”一則云：“唐天寶三載五月十五日，揚州進水心鏡一面。……斯鏡可以辟邪，鑒萬物。秦始皇之鏡，無以加焉。”[67]《酉陽雜俎》卷十《物異》云：“秦鏡。儛溪古岸石窟有方鏡，徑丈餘，照人五藏，秦皇世號爲照骨寶，在無勞縣鏡山。”[68]可見小說中所謂“秦始皇方鏡”“秦鏡”均與《雜記》“咸陽宮異寶”條中的“方鏡”有某種繼承關係。受《雜記》的廣泛傳播與鏡異小說發展的影響，“秦鏡、秦宮鏡、照心照膽”的典故亦在唐人詩文中屢見不鮮，限於篇幅，在此不逐一列舉[69]。

從館藏及考古實物來看，目前尚未見到含此類鏡銘的漢魏銅鏡。《清稗類鈔》“唐松泉藏鏡條”曾著錄：“又六朝海馬鏡一，徑二寸八分，重四兩四錢。”鏡背爲“賞得”等二十字銘文，惜未附有圖影，缺乏詳細信息，是否確爲六朝銅鏡難以斷定，徐柯

---

61 《舊唐書》卷四十六《經籍上》，1962頁。

62 王光福《晉人葛洪所記鏡異事與唐人鏡異小說之關係》，《中國文言小說研究》2010年3月，149頁。

63 韓理洲先生認爲王度生卒年均存疑，但大致應與魯迅對其生平考證相合，“蓋生於開皇初年，大業七年五月，自禦史罷歸河東……八年，冬，複入長安，兼著作郎，奉詔修國史，九年秋，出於兼芮城令”，卒於武德間。見韓理洲《〈古鏡記〉作者辨》，《中國文學研究》1986年第2期，24—25頁。

64 汪辟疆校錄《唐人小說·古鏡記》，上海：上海古籍出版社，1978年，10頁；關於《古鏡記》成書年代的討論，可參程國賦《〈古鏡記〉研究綜述》，《晉陽學刊》1992年第6期，71—100頁。

65 （宋）晁載之《續談助》，《叢書集成初編》，上海：商務印書館，1937年，16—17頁。

66 《漢書》，北京：中華書局，1962年，3331頁。

67 汪辟疆校錄《唐人小說·古鏡記》，10頁。

68 （唐）段成式撰，方南生點校《酉陽雜俎》前集卷一二《語資》，93頁。

69 王綱懷、孫克讓《唐代銅鏡與唐詩》與胡珊珊《唐鏡銘文文學研究》中舉例尤多。

亦稱“觀詩語，當是陳、隋時物”[70]。可見，六朝時存有此類銘文的銅鏡亦寥寥無幾。而六朝後，鏡銘中含“阿房照膽，仁壽懸宫”“同心照膽，知幽察微”“秦王辟惡，漢帝懷香”“銷兵漢殿，照膽秦宫”“膽照光來”等語的銅鏡驟然湧現，且多爲隋唐之物，如隋照膽（四神）鏡，隋唐盤龍六瑞獸銘帶鏡，隋唐秦王辟惡四靈八卦十二生肖鏡，隋阿房四神十二生肖紋銅鏡，唐同心簇六團花銘帶鏡，隋照心團花鏡，唐鳳凰雙鏡葵花鏡等[71]。此類鏡銘逐漸脱胎於鏡異，雖仍事典於《雜記》，卻引申出忠貞、清明之勵志表述。除“賞得”等二十字銘文内含“秦王鏡”，紀年爲開元十年的“開元十年銘家史鏡”亦含“秦王之鏡，照膽照心”銘文[72]，可確證此“賞得”等銘文中所謂之“秦王鏡”當源自“咸陽宫異寶”中的“方鏡”，此“秦王”當指秦始皇。可以看出，鐫有此類銘文銅鏡的發展與《雜記》、鏡異小說及詩文的流傳是同步行進的。

銅鏡中事典於《雜記》的五言鏡銘僅“賞得秦王鏡”銘一例，唐人詩作雖多有“秦鏡”“秦臺鏡”“秦時鏡”等語，而含“秦王鏡”的詩作僅見此五言鏡銘。此“秦王鏡”典故一入五言銘便賦予了更廣闊的内涵，後世詩作，如“奩展秦王鏡，塵生神女竇”“妾有秦王鏡，瑩瑩照面真”“願以秦王鏡，相將照妾心”“妾有秦王鏡、照人無隱情”等詩句中所謂之“秦王鏡”均自“賞得秦王鏡”銘始[73]。

四、銘文字體分析

工匠刻鑄鏡銘，詞句多從當時流行的鏡銘中選用、拼湊，抄刻時亦多不校正。又漢字筆劃多，在泥模上刻印，往往難以下刀，因此鏡銘中減筆字、異體字極多。簡省偏旁，僅用形聲字的聲符替代是常有之事，甚至有掉字漏句的現象。又因部分銅鏡保存狀況不善，鏡背紋飾及銘文多不清晰，在不參校其他銅鏡的情況下，釋讀銘文頗易出錯。

前文已述及，“賞得秦王鏡”銘在隋唐五言銘文中極爲流行，從各家抄錄及圖版上的“賞得秦王鏡”銘文來看，亦有使用減筆字或異體字的現象。這其中既有工匠刻鑄的原因，亦有後人摘錄時的誤讀。

關於“賞”字，各鏡皆爲賞（有謂“貴、買”者，皆誤讀），陸繼輅《合肥學舍劄

---

⑰ （清）徐柯編撰《清稗類鈔》第九册，北京：中華書局，1986年，4345頁。

⑱ 張孜江《館藏漢唐銅鏡賞析》，《收藏界》2010年6月，117—118頁；孔祥星、劉一曼：《中國青銅圖典》，北京：文物出版社，1992年，516頁；王綱懷《唐鏡與唐詩》，上海：上海人民出版社，2016年，22—23頁；黄啟善《廣西銅鏡》，北京：文物出版社，2004年，150頁、170頁；陳佩芬《上海博物館藏青銅鏡》，上海：上海書畫出版社，1987年，圖版六十八、八十七。

⑲ 王綱懷、孫克讓《唐代銅鏡與唐詩》，40頁。

⑳ 以上詩作分别見自（明）何白《汲古堂集》卷二，明萬曆刻本；（明）李濂《嵩渚文集》卷三十一，明嘉靖刻本；（明）張時徹《芝園集》卷三“樂府”，明嘉靖刻本；（清）劉大櫆《海峰詩集》“古體詩四”，《續修四庫全書》據天津圖書館藏清刻本影印，集部1427册。

記》：“賞蓋償字之省。”[74]《說文解字》：“償，還也。從人賞聲……賞以償之也。”《漢語大字典》：“賞，通償。報償。《韓非子·飾邪》：群臣賣官於上，取賞於下。王先慎集解：賞，讀爲償。《新書·脩政語上》：學黄帝之道而賞之。俞樾平議：賞讀爲償。”可以看出，“賞償”相通時，取報償之意。

又如“王”字抄錄成“玉”。《岩窟藏鏡》收錄兩枚“賞得”銘帶鏡圖版，銘文清晰可辨，但正文中卻錄爲“賞得秦玉鏡”，此處或爲梁上椿誤讀，或有意爲此。《尚書帝命驗》曰：“桀失玉鏡，用其噬獸。”鄭玄注：“玉鏡喻清明之道。”[75]梁上椿或另有理解，因而改王爲玉。

《清稗類鈔》錄“王”爲“皇”，或徐柯所見確爲“秦皇”，或爲徐柯誤讀，但“皇”與“王”字體構造差别甚大，除非徐柯故意如此，當不致有此錯誤，或在徐柯看來，此銘文即是指秦始皇。

再如“判”字，圖5：4、圖6：2、圖6：3、圖6：4均作“拚”。張相《詩詞曲語辭匯釋》云：“判，割捨之辭；亦甘願之辭。自宋以後多用拚字或拼字，而唐人則多用判字。……拚或拼，則宋詞中最習見。晏幾道《鷓鴣天》詞：‘彩袖殷勤捧玉鐘，當年拚卻醉紅顔。’周邦彥《解連環》詞：‘拼今生對花對酒，爲伊淚落。’”[76]圖6：2、圖6：3、圖6：4均爲宋以後鏡，符合張相對判的異體字發展的判斷。惟圖5：4《金石索》斷爲唐鏡，觀此圖版，在Bc型Ⅰ式鏡中實屬另類，整體紋飾比較簡單，内區“易蒲桃爲桃李之桃”[77]，卻與Bc型Ⅱ式鏡的整體風格一致。文獻中有以“桃”“蒲陶”“陶”代指葡萄的記載[78]，然而觀漢唐“海馬（獸）葡萄鏡”實物，極少有以“桃”代“葡萄”圖案者。而唐以後，瑞獸鏡及葡萄鏡的製作工藝均衰落，工匠們在鑄鏡時對以往習見的主題已不甚熟練，往往只求神似，並不求貼近原型，從而有“易蒲桃爲桃李之桃”的情況。因此，從銘文及裝飾風格可以判斷，圖5：4當爲仿唐鏡。《小校經閣金石文字》卷十六著錄有“唐秦王鏡二”“唐秦王鏡三”，鏡背紋飾及銘文均模糊扭曲，細觀銘文，可以辨出“拚”字，且内區四獸紋之間的植物與圖5：4、圖6：2等一致，爲“海馬葡萄鏡”主題。凸棱，無紋飾，素緣[79]。可見，此二鏡亦爲仿唐鏡。四川博物館藏有一枚宋“秦王鏡”，出土於成都羊子山淳熙壬寅年（1182）墓。觀其銘文，無宋代慣用的“拚”字，仍作“判”，且鏡背紋飾及瑞獸配置與仿鏡有較大差别，因此，此鏡當爲宋墓隨葬前代鏡，此鏡當爲唐鏡。

A型鏡中的兩枚方鏡，“惜”作“昔”，僅取聲符，而B類鏡均作“惜”。方鏡中

---

[74] （清）陸繼輅《合肥學舍劄記》卷十，389頁。

[75] （清）趙在翰輯，鐘肇鵬、蕭文郁點校《七緯》（附〈論語讖〉），607頁。

[76] 張相著《詩詞曲語辭匯釋》卷五，北京：中華書局，1977年，640—641頁。

[77] 馮雲鵬、馮雲鵷《金石索》卷六，122頁。

[78] 可參陳習剛《吐魯番文書中葡萄名稱問題辨析——兼論唐代葡萄的名稱》，《農業考古》2004年第1期，154—162頁；楊友誼《明以前中西交流中的葡萄研究》，暨南大學2006年碩士學位論文；陳習剛《再論吐魯番文書中葡萄名稱問題——與劉永連先生商榷》，《古今農業》2010年第2期，57—75頁。

[79] 劉體智藏並輯《小校經閣金石文字》，卷十六葉百一背。

"昔"字似隸似楷，字形與敦煌文書P.2965《佛說生經》："守者連昔饑渴"的"昔"字相似。各鏡的"關"字，有作"關""閞""闗""関"者，似無明顯規律可循。"特"字，錄文有作"持""恃""將"者，爲誤讀。關於銘文字體，兩枚方鏡似隸書。Ba型鏡雖爲楷書，但字體瘦長，有漢隸筆劃。吴文清亦收有一枚銅鏡，型制與Bc型Ⅰ式鏡中圖5：1一致，但字體與Ba型鏡相似[80]。陸繼輅《合肥學舍劄記》卷十著錄的"青綠雙麐鳳鏡"，銘文字體爲隸書。除此之外，其他式鏡皆爲楷書。從字體上看，銘文於隸楷之間，或似隸書者，年代稍早，爲隋或隋唐之交。

五、詩體銘釋義及作者考述

從詩歌的角度來看，此詩銘是一首整齊的五言四句的古詩，其平仄與近體詩的要求不符，所以誕生時代很可能在初唐及以前。但作者顯然又對"一句之中，平仄交替出現"的詩歌語言規律有所注意，因此每一句的第二字和第四字都平仄相對，顯示出高度律化的特徵，因而誕生的時代也不會太早，當在六朝至初唐這一時間段內。從詩的風格來說，它明白如話、直抒胸臆又頗有氣骨，應該是受到了北方文學的影響，而與風格纖弱、注重詞藻修飾的六朝詩歌大有不同。總而言之，該詩自明心志、擲地有聲，無纖弱浮華之弊，有音情頓挫之美，似已具備初唐陳子昂所倡的"骨氣端翔，音情頓挫，光英朗練"之詩歌風貌。

關於此五言詩銘，各金石典籍及圖錄均未言及作者，陳尚君先生認爲此詩作於唐，《全唐詩補編》卷五十六收錄此詩，題爲"唐鏡銘"，亦未提及作者[81]。《隋文紀》卷八亦收錄此詩銘，未言著者，梅鼎祚認爲此詩作於隋[82]。從現存隋鏡即含此鏡銘的情況來看，梅鼎祚的判斷是正確的。

至於作者，C型鏡（圖7：1）第四輪"賞得"鏡銘末鐫刻有"蒲山謹讚"四字，可見，此詩銘當爲"蒲山"所作的讚。隋唐之際並無名爲"蒲山"又具詩才之人[83]，惟隋末領導農民起義的代表人物李密或與此"蒲山"有關，"密字玄邃，一字法主。……開皇中，襲父爵蒲山公"[84]。《北史》卷六十謂李密"才兼文武，志氣雄遠，少襲爵蒲山公"[85]。《新唐書·李密傳》卷八十四："十三年，讓分兵與密，别爲牙帳，號蒲山

---

[80] 吴文清《賞鏡斷代說秦王》，20頁。

[81] 陳尚君輯校《全唐詩補編》卷五十六，北京：中華書局，1992年，1636頁。

[82] （明）梅鼎祚《隋文紀》卷八，《影印文淵閣四庫全書》第1400冊，臺北：臺灣商務印書館，1986年，401頁。

[83] 唐高宗時，有名衛蒲山者，《新唐書》卷四："乙未，殺丘神勣、左豹韜衛將軍衛蒲山。"此衛蒲山乃武將，史載寥寥，斷無此詩情。

[84] 《隋書》卷七十《李密傳》，1624頁。

[85] 《北史》卷六十，北京：中華書局，1974年，2132頁。

公。”[86]《資治通鑒》謂“號蒲山公營”[87]，顧祖禹《讀史方輿紀要》略云：“密襲爵爲蒲山郡公，因爲軍號蒲山，無食土，蓋所食封戶之名。”[88]古人喜以最顯貴的官爵稱人，“密以蒲山公之後，爲天下所矜也。天下之初亂也，人尤重虛名以爲所歸”，因此，李密自號蒲山乃情理之事。

雖李密於大業十三年（617）稱魏公，但爲時不長，且瓦崗寨中依附於李密的骨幹力量爲“蒲山公營”。因此，魏公尊號雖顯，但從習慣上，還是慣用“蒲山公”爲號。李密爲王世充所敗後，投靠李唐，拜光祿卿，封邢國公，而事後李密對此多不以爲然，這點可以從《李密墓誌銘》中可以看出，“公威未振，主自爲謀，蓋當世舊部先附，多出其右，故吏後來，或居其上。懷漁陽之憤憤，恥從吴耿後列；同淮陰之快俠，羞與絳灌爲伍。負其智勇，頗不自安”[89]，就李密一代雄主，必恥於以邢國公自稱。

唐以後，亦有指“蒲山”爲李密者。清孫志祖引唐皇甫枚《三水小牘》“内蛇死而鄭厲入，群鼠奔而蒲山亡”之事，認爲皇甫枚所謂之蒲山即李密，“李密屯營，群鼠銜尾，西北渡洛，經月不絕，見《新唐書》本傳，密父寬封蒲山公，故云蒲山亡爾”[90]，判斷準確。唐袁郊《甘澤謠》“魏先生”條：“及隋末兵興，楊元感戰敗。謀主李密亡命雁門，變姓名以教授。……今方捕蒲山黨，得非長者乎？”[91]清樂鈞作《魏先生》詩，自云“唐袁郊《甘澤謠》，凡九事，雖荒陋而可喜，各系一詩於後”，詩曰：“先生乃先覺，何物蒲山兒。”[92]元張憲《玉笥集》：“代田舍翁詞補魏征諫錄云：‘出仕蒲山公，蒲山愎諫自用，故臣言不用。’”[93]清黄恩彤《鑒評别錄》：“時有李代楊之讖，本屬無稽，乃蒲山先起，唐公繼之。”[94]可見，後世所謂之“蒲山黨”“蒲山兒”“蒲山”皆指李密。

元明清詩作中，多有吟詠李密事蹟者，其中亦常見以“蒲山”指代李密。如元汪克寬《題李密營丘畫驪山老姥賜李密火星劍圖》：“蒲山鋭額千牛客，蒲韉跨犢行無跡。掛角青編一束書，夢對重瞳意相得。”[95]明張以寧《翠屏集》卷一《蔣仲誠墨牛圖二首》：“嗟哉蒲山子，區區讀何書。”明沈德符《清權堂集》卷六《省牛四首》：

---

⑯ 《新唐書》卷八十四《李密傳》，3680頁。

⑰ 《資治通鑒》卷一八三，北京：中華書局，1956年，5711頁。

⑱ （清）顧祖禹撰，賀次君、施和金點校《讀史方輿紀要》卷四，北京：中華書局，2005年，186頁。

⑲ 蘇小華考證出土的《李密墓銘》是在傳世本《李密墓誌銘》基礎上删改寫刻而成，見蘇小華《傳世本〈李密墓誌銘〉與出土〈李密墓銘〉的先後關係辯證》，《古籍整理研究學刊》2009年第4期，43—45頁；傳世本《李密墓誌銘》分别見於《全唐文》卷一百四十一及《文苑英華》卷九四八。

⑳ （清）孫志祖《讀書脞錄》，嘉慶十二年（1807）刻本，卷七葉十八。

㉑ （唐）袁郊撰《甘澤謠》（附錄），北京：中華書局，1985年，1頁。

㉒ （清）樂鈞《青芝山館詩集》卷三，《清代詩文集彙編》編纂委員會編《清代詩文集彙編》481冊，上海：上海古籍出版社，2010年，94—95頁。

㉓ （元）張憲《玉笥集》卷二，《影印文淵閣四庫全書》1217冊，379頁。

㉔ （清）黄恩彤《鑒評别錄》卷三十六，《四庫未收書輯刊·二輯》29冊，北京：北京出版社，1997年，639頁。

㉕ （明）曹學佺《石倉歷代詩選》卷三百六十一，《影印文淵閣四庫全書》1391冊，880頁。

“自從齊相歌時扣，直到蒲山掛漢書。”皆是借用李密“牛角掛書”的典故。《新唐書·李密傳》：“聞包愷在緱山，往從之。以蒲韉乘牛，掛《漢書》一帙角上，行且讀。”[96]

又如王世貞《詠史》其十八：“兵謀歸蒲山，盜道推建德。”[97]清紀邁宜《重過濬縣懷古》：“三策蒲山智略長，英雄亡命起黎陽。”卷九《洛口倉歌》：“錦帆天子揚州去，洛口之倉棄誰聚。蒲山亦是不世人，一呼百萬雄獅聚。”[98]皆頌李密起兵抗隋之事。

李密不僅是隋末農民起義中的領導人物，而且頗具才學。《隋書·李密傳》：“後更折節，下帷耽學，尤好兵書，誦皆在口。師事國子助教包愷，受《史記》《漢書》，勵精忘倦，愷門徒皆出其下。”[99]其師包愷，字和樂，東海人，“從王仲通受《史記》、《漢書》，尤稱精究。大業中爲國子助教。於時《漢書》學者，以蕭包二人爲宗匠。聚徒教授者數千人”[100]。

從包愷治《漢書》尤稱精究，李密師從包愷，愷門徒皆出其下的事實來看，其當不會忽略與《漢書》淵源頗深的《雜記》。因爲班固《漢書》殆是全取劉歆，僅小有異同，而《雜記》二卷又出自劉書，爲班固《漢書》所未取。《西京雜記跋》云：“洪家世有劉子駿《漢書》一百卷，……洪家俱有其書，試以此記考校班固所作，殆是全取劉書，有小異同耳。並固所不取，不過二萬許言。今抄出爲二卷，名曰《西京雜記》，以裨《漢書》之闕。”且劉歆《漢書》存世寥寥，爲“世人稀有，縱複有者，多不備足。”葛洪家又曾遭焚書之厄，“書籍都盡，僅《雜記》兩卷在洪巾箱中，故得猶在”[101]。因此，從李密的知識體系及《雜記》與《漢書》的關係來看，其對《雜記》當有一定瞭解，而其所作之贊（“賞得秦王鏡”銘）事典於《雜記》亦爲情理中事。

李密亦頗具詩才，其逃歸淮陽時曾作五言詩一首：“金風蕩初節，玉露凋晚林。……寄言世上雄，虛生真可愧。”[102]李密作爲關隴貴族出身，詩作能吸收南朝文風，又能剔除纖巧，感情質實，風格慷慨沉鬱，善用事典，對偶工整，與“賞得”詩體銘風格一致。

最後，初步判斷此“賞得秦王鏡，判不惜千金。非關欲照膽，特是自明心”五言四句詩作者爲隋蒲山公李密，此詩當爲隋詩。

因此，詩歌銘文大意當爲：我曾得到了秦王鏡，爲了它不惜拋去千金。不是由於要用它來照我的心膽，只是我明白自己的內心。言下之意是我的內心天地可鑒，無須千金寶鏡來照了。

---

[96] 《新唐書》卷八十四《李密傳》，3677頁。

[97] （明）王世真《弇州山人續稿》卷四《影印文淵閣四庫全書》1282冊，45頁。

[98] （清）紀邁宜《儉重堂詩》卷七，《清代詩文集彙編》243冊，561、595頁。

[99] 《隋書》卷七十《李密傳》，1624頁。

[100] 《隋書》卷七十五《包愷傳》，1716頁。

[101] （晉）葛洪撰，周天遊校注《西京雜記》，275頁。

[102] 《隋書》卷七十《李密傳》，1626—1627頁。

六、結　　語

最後，從類型劃分、斷代及典故分析的結果看，吐魯番木納爾墓地出土的“秦王鏡”當爲唐西州時期，具體時代爲玄宗開元前後。其鏡背銘文事典於《西京雜記》，初步判斷爲隋蒲山公李密所作。關於詩體銘的創作時間、創作背景及與《唐月令鏡》的關係，筆者擬另撰文探討。

附記：本論文撰寫得到中國人民大學李肖教授、新疆師範大學薛天緯教授、首都師範大學秦邦興博士、四川的汪怡夢女士、吐魯番學研究院舍秀紅女士等的大力支持，特此致謝！

Reconsideration of the “Qin Wang Mirror” unearthed from Turfan, Xinjiang

Liu Zhijia

In 2005, a “Qin Wang Mirror” was unearthed from the Munaer cemetery M311. On the back of this mirror there is engraved a 20-character inscription— “Though I receive the Qin Wang mirror as a reward, though no cost was spared in producing it, it is not for checking my loyalty, but only to see my sincere and true heart.” Through an in-depth discussion of this literary quotation found on the mirror, we can figure out the periodization, decorative meaning and special characteristics of this bronze mirror. In the end, we can draw the conclusion that the character inscription was written by Duke Pu Shan Li Mi during the Sui Dynasty.

附　表

型式		出處/單位	圖號	名稱	時代	形制	重量（克）	直徑/邊長（厘米）	分期
A型	a	《故宮藏鏡》	圖1	龍紋方鏡	隋	方	119.6	6.6×6.8	隋末
	b	《唐代銅鏡與唐詩》	圖2	賞得秦王鏡銘神獸鏡	隋唐	方			隋末至高宗時期
B型	a	《唐代銅鏡與唐詩》	圖3，1	賞得秦王鏡銘瑞獸鏡	隋唐	圓	465	16.7	隋大業末至高宗時期
		《清華銘文鏡——鏡銘漢字演變簡史》	圖3，2	賞得秦王鏡銘神獸鏡	隋唐	圓	465	16.7	
		新鄉博物館	圖3，3	秦王鏡	初唐	圓		16.5	
		《四龍紋金鐲與秦王鏡》		秦王鏡	唐初	圓		16.8	
		《湖南出土銅鏡圖錄》	圖3，4	四神鏡	唐	圓		16	
		《西清續鑒甲編》	圖3，5	明心鑒	唐	圓	（十三兩）約484.9	（五寸一分）16.32	
		《朝陽博物館藏銅鏡》		方格四神紋秦王銘文鏡	隋	圓（殘）		17.1	
		《小校經閣金石文字》	圖3，6	秦王鏡	唐	圓			
	b	《涴花拜石軒鏡銘集錄》	圖4，1	唐秦王鏡	唐	圓		（六寸）19.2	武德至高宗時期
		《陝西省出土銅鏡》	圖4，2	秦王鏡	唐	圓		13.8	
		《金石索》	圖4，3	唐秦王鏡一	唐	圓			
	c Ⅰ	《唐代銅鏡與唐詩》	圖5，1	賞得秦王鏡銘神獸鏡	隋唐	圓	510	12.4	隋末至玄宗開元時期
		河南三門峽廟底溝M183		環繞四獸銘帶鏡	盛唐	圓（殘）		12.5	
		《中國青銅器全集・16銅鏡》		賞得秦王神獸鏡	隋	圓		12	
		《山東陵縣出土〈唐東方合墓誌〉考釋》		秦王鏡	唐	圓（殘）		12.5	

续表

型式		出處/單位	圖號	名稱	時代	形制	重量（克）	直徑/邊長（厘米）	分期
B類	c Ⅰ	《岩窟藏鏡》（河南出土）		秦王四獸鏡	隋末唐初	圓	170	9.5	玄宗開元至懿宗時期
		《岩窟藏鏡》（陝西出土）		秦王四獸鏡	隋末唐初	圓	145	9.5	
		吐魯番博物館	圖5，2	秦王镜	隋唐	圓		9.5	
		《洛陽出土銅鏡》		秦王四駿鏡	唐	圓	141	9.4	
		《旅順博物館藏銅鏡》		秦王瑞獸鏡	唐	圓	140	9.5	
		《蚌埠市博物館藏銅鏡集萃》	圖5，3	賞得秦王銘四瑞獸鏡	唐	圓	221	9.1	
		《千秋金鑒——陝西歷史博物館藏銅鏡集成》		賞得秦王鏡瑞獸紋鏡	唐	圓	180	9.9	
		《善齋吉金錄》	圖5，5	唐秦王鏡	唐	圓		（四寸五分）約15	
		《金石索》	圖5，4	唐秦王鏡二	唐?	圓			
	c Ⅱ	《四川省出土銅鏡》	圖6，1	秦王鏡	宋?	圓		8.8	宋元明
		《六安出土銅鏡》	圖6，2	瑞獸葡萄紋鏡	宋	圓		8.8	
		《千秋金鑒——陝西歷史博物館藏銅鏡集成》	圖6，3	瑞獸紋鏡	宋	圓	516	15.3	
		《儀征館藏銅鏡》	圖6，4	仿唐賞得秦王銘瑞獸鏡	元	圓		15.4	
C型		《小校經閣金石文字》	圖7	唐月令鏡	唐	圓		（一尺五分）約35	隋末至玄宗前
D型		《宣和博古圖錄》	圖8	唐自明鐵鑒	唐	圓	（二斤十有四兩）1719.25	（七寸一分）約21.8	隋末至貞觀年間

註：按此類銅鏡甚多，筆者僅就所見並具有代表性銅鏡的進行統計；表内“時代”一欄爲各金石典籍、館藏及報告所劃分的時代。年代後標示問號的，正文内當專做探討，仍留存原定時代。

新疆出土垂直焊接雙環耳飾的研究*

林鈴梅

耳飾作爲一種重要的人體裝飾物，在古代社會是身份和財富的象徵，也能在一定程度上反映人群的族屬。除了審美功能，特殊的耳飾樣式也往往被賦予祭祀的內涵。其樣式及承載的工藝更是能夠反映不同地區不同人群之間的互動與交流。新疆考古調查收集與發掘所得耳飾種類繁多，文化內涵豐富，對於瞭解新疆古代裝飾文化具有重要意義，也爲研究新疆與周鄰地區的文化交流提供了另一套參照系統。其中，垂直焊接雙環耳飾是新疆地區早期鐵器時代廣泛流行的一種耳飾樣式，具有典型意義。

一、新疆發現的垂直焊接雙環耳飾

垂直焊接雙環耳飾指的是一大一小雙環垂直焊接的耳環或耳墜。焊接雙環的耳環可以單獨佩戴，也可以添加墜飾作爲耳墜佩戴，這種類型的耳墜在新疆有較多的發現。值得注意的是，有些耳墜出土時墜部已經脱落或者由於擾亂遺失，這種情況下常常被誤認爲是單獨的耳環，如和靜縣阿爾夏一號墓M3出土有焊接雙環的耳飾，與蜻蜓眼珠一類的料珠同出，表明雙環下原本應垂掛有墜飾。發現垂直焊接雙環耳飾的地區主要有：伊犁河流域、吐魯番—天山中段北麓、哈密—巴里坤、塔里木盆地北緣、阿勒泰地區。

1. 伊犁河流域地區

尼勒克縣一級電站東麥里墓地M40：2（銀）、M41：1（金），墓地年代在公元前8到前3世紀，相當於春秋至戰國時期（圖1，1、2）[①]。尼勒克縣加勒克斯卡茵特墓地M52：1（金）一對，小環爲金絲纏繞三匝。內徑分別是1.5、1.8厘米，外徑分別是2、2.2厘米。墓葬年代大致在公元前5世紀至公元前後，相當於戰國至漢代（圖1，3、

---

* 本文为中國人民大學科學研究基金（中央高校基本科研業務費專項資金資助）項目成果，項目批準號：17XNH027。

① 新疆文物考古研究所《尼勒克縣一級電站墓地考古發掘簡報》，《新疆文物》2012年第2期，36頁，圖一三，35、36。

4）[②]。鞏留縣山口水庫M17：4（金），通高1.6厘米；M35：2（金），雙環下連接一套環，用金絲擰成。墜飾可分爲兩部分，上部飾有三隻中空的山羊，以金箔模壓合扣而成，下焊飾小金珠組成交錯三角紋，下墜黑色炭精。墓地年代在公元前後至公元3、4世紀，相當於漢至魏晉時期（圖1，5、6）[③]。特克斯—牧場墓群出1件葡萄墜金耳環，環徑1.3厘米，下垂8粒空心的葡萄串墜。墓群年代約在公元前3至前2世紀，相當於戰國末至西漢初年（圖1，7）[④]。新源縣阿尤賽溝口墓地M1：8（金），大環直徑1.2厘米，金絲截面直徑0.1厘米。雙環下套一小環，下端穿飾一上部包金的綠松石墜，長1.1厘米。耳環通長3.2厘米。墓地年代約在公元前3至前2世紀，相當於戰國晚期至西漢前期（圖1，8）[⑤]。烏吐蘭漢代墓地出土兩件金耳墜，雙環下垂掛一顆橢圓形紅寶石，紅寶石上端用長條形金片包裹，金片上焊飾由金珠組成的三角紋（圖1，9）[⑥]。

2. 吐魯番—天山中段北麓地區

瑪納斯縣清水河鄉團莊子村M5出土1件雙環耳環，金絲加扭，墓葬年代約在公元前7世紀，相當於春秋晚期（圖1，10）[⑦]。阿拉溝墓地M3：8（金），下端綴一紅色瑪瑙珠。通長4.1、環直徑1.5厘米，墓葬年代約在公元前7至前5世紀，相當於春秋戰國時期（圖1，11）[⑧]。烏魯木齊南山魚兒溝墓地32號墓出1件金耳墜，雙環下連接一穿綠松石的掛墜，墜下面焊接四顆小金珠，通長2.6厘米；38號墓出1件相似形制的金耳墜，環部已缺失，墜部由金絲盤結成圓形，對稱焊接4個小環，兩邊小環各套一穿石珠的墜，下面小環連接一魚尾形綠松石墜。墓葬年代約在公元前5世紀，相當於戰國時期（圖1，12、13）[⑨]。洋海三號墓地M312：1（金），雙環下吊金絲、連接蚌殼片，通長4.1厘米，約在公元前5至前1世紀，相當於戰國到西漢時期（圖1，14）[⑩]。勝金店墓地

---

② 新疆文物考古研究所《尼勒克縣加勒克斯卡茵特墓地發掘簡報》，《新疆文物》2007年第3期，12頁，圖二三，10。

③ 新疆文物考古研究所《2005年度伊犁州鞏留縣山口水庫墓地考古發掘報告》，《新疆文物》2006年第1期，38頁，圖七〇，2、4。

④ 新疆文物局等主編《新疆文物古蹟大觀》，烏魯木齊：新疆美術攝影出版社，1999，373頁，圖1061。

⑤ 新疆文物考古研究所《新源縣阿尤賽溝口墓地、喀拉奧依墓地考古發掘報告》，《新疆文物》2013年第2期，14頁，圖四，8。

⑥ 新疆維吾爾自治區文物考古研究所《2013—2014文物考古年報》，37頁。

⑦ 新疆昌吉回族自治州文物局編《絲綢之路天山廊道——新疆昌吉古代遺址與館藏文物精品》，北京：文物出版社，2014年，196頁，圖183a。

⑧ 新疆文物考古研究所《烏魯木齊市魚兒溝遺址與阿拉溝墓地》，《考古》2014年第4期，32頁，圖二六，13。

⑨ 文昊主編《新疆百科圖志・文物文化卷》（1），烏魯木齊：新疆美術攝影出版社，2014年，512頁。

⑩ 新疆文物考古研究所、吐魯番地區文物局《鄯善縣洋海三號墓地發掘簡報》，《新疆文物》2004年第1期，64頁，圖二五，4。

M13：37（金），雙環下綴穿金絲珊瑚墜，墓地年代約在公元前2至前1世紀，相當於西漢時期（圖1，15）[11]。

3. 哈密—巴里坤地區

伊吾托背梁墓地M5：13（金），通長2.1厘米；M1：1-2，形制相同。M1：1，通長5.6厘米，由大金環、小金環和紅瑪瑙墜三部分組成。大金環下焊接一小金環，下垂掛兩小金環，末端穿飾梯形紅瑪瑙墜。墓地年代上限應晚於公元前5世紀，相當於戰國至西漢時期（圖1，16、21、22）[12]。東黑溝墓地出土了兩對耳墜，其中M011：12、M011：13，形制基本相同，雙環下連接1顆綠串珠。另外一對M011：11（金）與M011：6（金）雖不是雙環結構，但樣式、風格、工藝與前邊一對非常一致。M011：6，總長6.2厘米，按結構可分八部分，從上向下依次是金掛鈎、金螺旋飾、籠狀金飾、環狀金飾（3個小環焊接在大環上）、金掛鈎、綠串珠（2顆）、金螺旋飾、紅瑪瑙串珠。東黑溝墓葬年代約在公元前2至前1世紀，相當於西漢前期（圖1，17—20）[13]。伊吾縣沙梁子墓地M1出土一對金耳墜，雙環下垂掛兩個墜飾，墜飾一端彎成螺旋狀，一端穿一顆紅色圓形瑪瑙，墓葬年代約爲公元前5至前1世紀，相當於戰國至西漢之間（圖1，23、24）[14]。巴里坤縣西溝遺址1號墓出土一件金耳墜，總長4.6厘米，重3.4克。整體由七部分構成：上邊圓環，兩端各焊有四顆金珠；環下連接一錐形飾，表面滿飾金珠；下邊連接一方形金框，內鑲嵌綠松石，金框邊框焊一圈金珠，在兩側裝飾金珠塔；方形金框下接一金圈，金圈邊緣也焊飾金珠，兩側裝飾金珠塔；金圈中穿套螺旋形金絲，盤繞三圈；向下延伸的金絲穿一綠松石串珠；金絲末端墜一紡錘體金飾，金飾上下邊緣位置都焊飾金珠，四面焊飾金珠塔。墓葬年代初步定在在公元前3至前2世紀，相當於中原戰國晚期至西漢早期（圖1，25）[15]。

4. 塔里木盆地北緣地區

察吾呼一號墓地M204：9（金），直徑1.2厘米，墓地年代在公元前10至前7世紀，相當於西周至春秋時期（圖1，26）[16]。庫爾勒上戶鄉古墓葬M1：7（金），絲徑0.15厘米，重1.228克，墓葬年代可能晚於群巴克墓葬，約在公元前7世紀至前3世紀，相當於

---

⑪ 吐魯番學研究所《新疆吐魯番市勝金店墓地發掘簡報》，《考古》2013年第2期，38頁，圖二○。

⑫ 西北大學文化遺產保護與考古學研究中心等《2009年伊吾縣托背梁墓地考古發掘簡報》，《新疆文物》2014年第2期，54頁，圖一七，10—12。

⑬ 新疆文物考古研究所、西北大學文化遺產與考古學研究中心《2006年巴里坤東黑溝遺址發掘》，《新疆文物》2007年第2期，52頁，圖二七，2、3。

⑭ 新疆維吾爾自治區文物考古研究所《2013—2014文物考古年報》，52頁。

⑮ 西北大學絲綢之路文化遺產保護與考古學研究中心、哈密地區文物局、巴里坤文物局《巴里坤縣西溝遺址1號墓考古發掘簡報》，《新疆文物》2016年第1期，87頁，圖一○，1。

⑯ 中國社會科學院考古所新疆隊、新疆巴音郭勒蒙古自治州文管所《新疆和靜縣察吾乎溝口一號墓地》，《考古學報》1988年第1期，92頁，圖一五，3。

春秋至戰國時期，年代下限當在漢代以前（圖1，27）[17]。和靜縣阿爾夏一號墓地M3：6（金），通高2.4厘米，直徑1.5厘米，絲徑0.1厘米；M3：4-1（金），通高2.7厘米，直徑2.1厘米，絲徑0.1厘米，同出的有一蜻蜓眼珠M3：4-2。另外，M4：3（金），雙環下掛金鏈，其下墜有一小海貝。通長5.2厘米，金鏈長2.5厘米，耳環絲徑0.1厘米，海貝直徑1.1厘米。墓葬年代在公元前後，相當於漢代（圖1，28、29、33）[18]。和靜縣巴侖台至伊爾根鐵路沿線發現2件金耳環，墓葬屬於察吾呼文化的範疇（圖1，30、31）[19]。和靜重工業園區古遺址M7：8（金），墓葬年代在公元前後，相當於漢代（圖1，32）[20]。阿合奇縣庫蘭薩日克墓地93AKM8：1（金），耳墜上部纏繞八周細金絲；中部穿兩個筒形金珠和一個石珠，金珠兩端各焊接兩行細金珠，中部焊接三朵橢圓形花瓣；下部懸掛一魚尾飾，總長7.2厘米。墓葬年代約在公元前5至前1世紀，相當於戰國至西漢（圖1，34）[21]。

5. 阿勒泰地區

喀拉蘇墓地M15出土1件，金質，雙環下套接三個首尾相接的小金環，下邊連接一金絲，金絲上穿一金珠花環，底端墜一段螺旋狀飾物，墓葬年代仍未確定（圖1，35）[22]。

出土雙環垂直焊接耳飾的墓葬主要分布於天山山間盆地及南北麓地帶，目前爲止，阿勒泰地區的喀拉蘇墓地也發現了一件此類的耳墜。現有的材料顯示，新疆發現的雙環垂直焊接耳飾可能可以早到公元前7世紀，在公元前7至前5世紀（相當於中原春秋時期）有少量的發現，主要爲耳環樣式。這種耳飾集中流行於公元前5至前1世紀（相當於中原戰國至西漢），這一時期耳墜樣式豐富。在之後的公元前1至公元3、4世紀（相當於漢代至魏晉時期）仍有一些發現，並且製作精美（圖2）。由於涉及的單個墓葬沒有較爲科學、明確的定年，報告提供的整個墓地的年代划定過於寬泛，我們對新疆發現的最早的垂直焊接雙環耳飾的年代仍存疑問。《絲綢之路天山廊道——新疆昌吉古代遺址與館藏文物精品》一書基於瑪納斯縣清水河鄉團莊子村M5出土物與圖瓦阿爾然2號墓同類物的比較，包括圓錐體金耳墜、鶴嘴鋤等，將M5號墓年代定在公元前7世紀，似乎並

---

⑰　巴音郭楞蒙古自治州文物保護管理所《新疆庫爾勒市上戶鄉古墓葬》，《文物》1999年第2期，36頁，圖九，14。

⑱　新疆文物考古研究所《和靜縣阿爾夏一號墓地考古發掘報告》，《新疆文物》2013年第2期，75、77頁，圖一五、一八、二二。

⑲　新疆維吾爾自治區文物考古研究所《2013—2014文物考古年報》，60頁。

⑳　新疆文物考古研究所《2012年和靜縣和靜重工業園區古遺址考古發掘報告》，《新疆文物》2015年第1期，圖版4。

㉑　新疆文物考古研究所《阿合奇縣庫蘭薩日克墓地發掘簡報》，《新疆文物》1995年第2期，27頁，圖十二，3。

㉒　新疆維吾爾自治區文物考古研究所《2013—2014文物考古年報》，41頁。

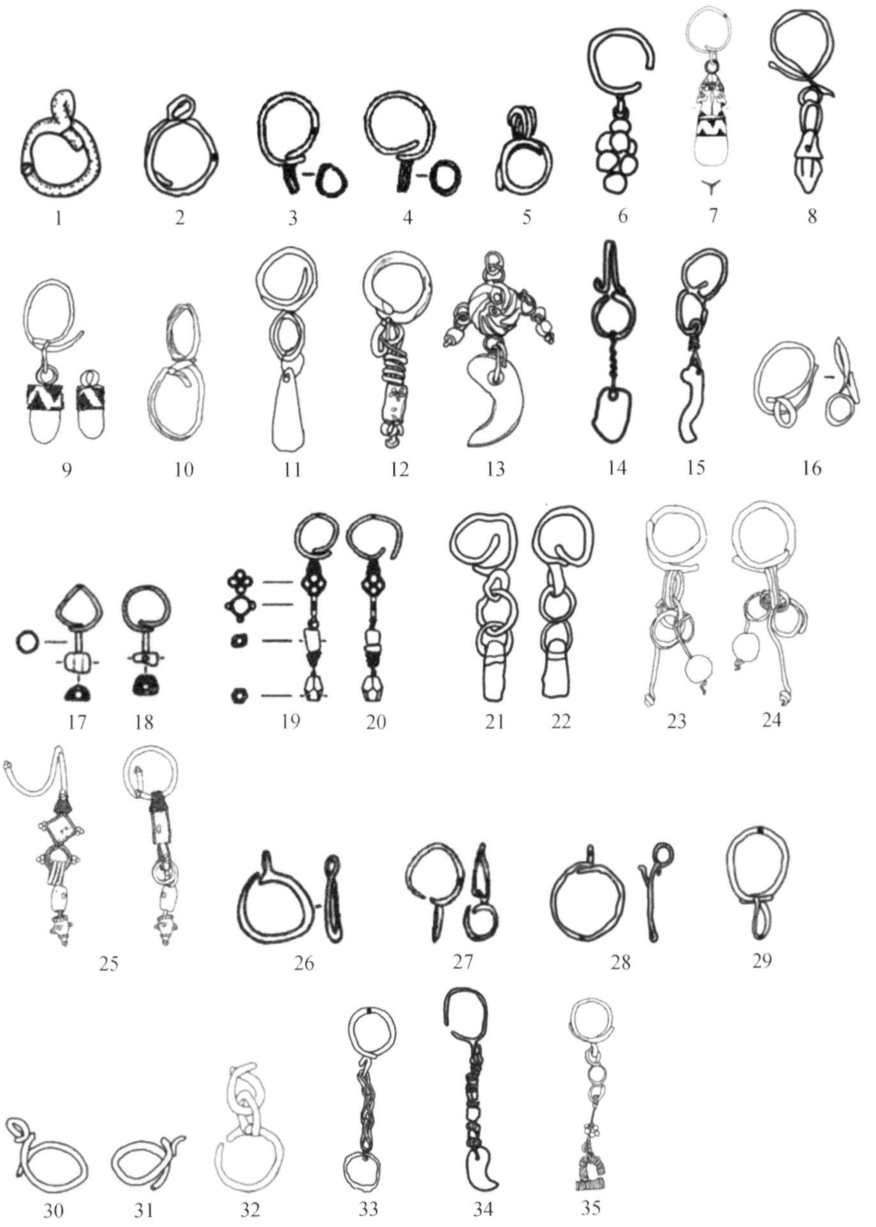

圖1

1、2. 東麥里墓地（M40：2、M41：1） 3、4. 加勒克斯卡茵特墓地（M52：1） 5、6. 鞏留縣山口水庫（M17：4、M35：2） 7. 特克斯一牧場墓群 8. 阿尤賽溝口墓地（M1：8） 9. 烏吐蘭漢代墓地 10. 團莊子村M5 11. 阿拉溝墓地（M3：8） 12、13. 魚兒溝墓地（32、38號墓） 14. 洋海三號墓地（M312：1） 15. 勝金店墓地（M13：37） 16、21、22. 托背梁墓地（M5：13、M1：1-2） 17—20. 東黑溝墓地（M011：12、M011：13、M011：11、M011：6） 23、24. 沙梁子墓地（M1） 25. 西溝遺址1號墓 26. 察吾呼一號墓地（M204：9） 27. 上戶鄉古墓葬（M1：7） 28、29、33. 阿爾夏一號墓地（M3：6、M3：4-1、M4：3） 30、31. 巴侖台至伊爾根鐵路沿線 32. 和靜重工業園區古遺址（M7：8） 34. 庫蘭薩日克墓地（93AKM8：1） 35. 喀拉蘇墓地M15（1. 銀 2—35. 金）

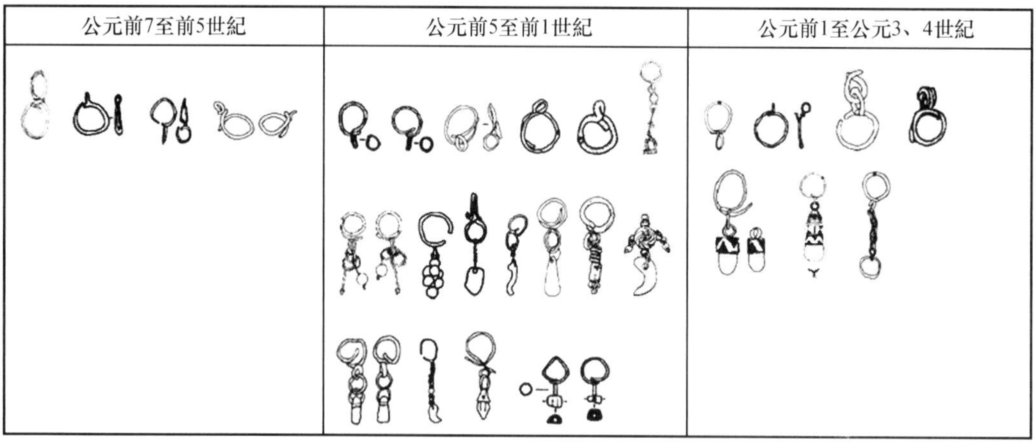

圖2　新疆發現的垂直焊接雙環耳飾的年代分布

未提供相關的測年數據[23]。學者一般認爲，圓錐體耳墜最早出現於圖瓦地區，是阿迪—拜爾（Aldy-Bel）文化（公元前7至前5世紀）的典型器物[24]。但在圖瓦地區公元前7至前5世紀的遺存裏，我們並未發現雙環垂直焊接的耳飾。團莊子村M5雙環焊接耳環與圓錐體耳墜同出的情況十分特殊，無論如何，它反映了新疆出現雙環焊接耳飾的時間較早。

二、新疆周鄰地區發現的雙環垂直焊接耳飾

雙環垂直焊接耳飾是歐亞草原早期鐵器時代傳播廣泛、沿用時間跨度長的一種耳飾樣式。從地域上來看，東邊從薩彥—阿爾泰地區至哈薩克草原，南至中亞西天山山區，西至南烏拉爾地區都有較多發現，新疆東邊的內蒙古草原地區也有個別發現。從時間跨度上來看，這種耳飾在公元前6至前1世紀這一時段流行於新疆周鄰地區[25]。

阿爾泰山區及其邊緣、鄂畢河上游有較多發現，且年代較早，主要發現於巴澤雷克文化、卡緬文化（Каменская Культура）、卡爾干達斯類型（Коргантасские Тип）遺存。巴澤雷克文化遺存包括：位於阿爾泰西伯利亞地區的拜卡（Бике）Ⅲ號墓地1號墓出土了兩件此類耳環，有銀質與金質的，年代約在公元前5至前4世紀（圖3，1、2）[26]。在阿爾泰山西部邊緣的波內爾（Берел）墓葬出土了一件焊有三個小環的金耳

㉓　新疆昌吉回族自治州文物局編《絲綢之路天山廊道——新疆昌吉古代遺址與館藏文物精品》，196頁。

㉔　可參考林鈴梅《新疆出土圓錐體耳墜的研究》，《絲綢之路研究》（第一輯），北京：三聯書店，2017年，166—186頁。

㉕　Ю. Ф. Кирюшин, Н. Ф. Степанова, *Скифская эпоха Горного Алтая. Ч. III: Погребальные комплексы скифского времени Средней Катуни*, Барнаул, Издательство Алтайского Университета, 2004, с. 96.

㉖　Vladimir D. Kubarev, Novosibirsk, "Skythische Kurganeaus den Gräberfeldern Bike I und II am mittleren Katun', Sibirien", *Eurasia Antiqua*, Band7, 2001, S. 142, Abb.10-4、5. Ю. Ф. Кирюшин, Н. Ф. Степанова, *Скифская эпоха Горного Алтая. Ч. III: Погребальные комплексы скифского времени Средней Катуни*, с. 223, рис. 42, 7, 8.

環，同出的有焊綴金珠的墜飾，墓葬年代約在公元前4世紀（圖3，3）[27]。魯金科指出巴澤雷克墓葬的耳環被盜，但在阿拉格爾（Арагол）墓地5號墓中保存了金耳環，是雙環焊接的結構，大環直徑1.6厘米，小環直徑0.75厘米（圖3，4）[28]。阿拉格爾墓地屬於巴澤雷克文化早期遺存，年代在公元前6世紀中葉至前5世紀中葉[29]。他還提到吉謝列夫在烏爾蘇爾（Урсул）河谷的卡拉庫爾（Коракол）村的一座石冢裏也發現了這樣的耳環[30]。杜特傑斯肯（Тыткескень）Ⅵ號墓地M14出土了兩件金耳環，M27出土了兩件金耳環，雙環下的金鏈飾已經脱落，墓葬年代在公元前6世紀中葉至前5世紀中葉（圖3，5—8）[31]。卡爾—克齊（Кор-Кечу）墓葬出土銀耳環，墓葬屬於巴澤雷克文化早期遺存，年代在公元前6世紀下半葉（圖3，9）[32]。

位於鄂畢河上游的卡緬文化遺存包括：卡緬（Камен）Ⅱ號墓地15號墓出土了一件金耳環（圖3，10）[33]，墓葬年代在公元前6世紀下半葉至前5世紀[34]。噶羅錫（Рогозиха）1號墓地6號墓出土一件金耳環，墓葬年代在公元前6世紀下半葉至前5世紀上半葉（圖3，11）[35]。位於阿爾泰山西段山麓的葉魯尼納（Елунино）Ⅱ號墓地1號墓出土了一件金耳墜，墓葬年代在公元前6至前5世紀（圖3，12）[36]。

卡爾干達斯類型遺存確定於哈薩克斯坦中部，在阿勒泰地區也發現了該類遺存，有學者認爲，這一類型的遺存可能與更東邊的人群向西遷徙有關系[37]。卡爾干達斯類型遺存也發現該類耳飾，克爾—克齊（Кер-Кечу）墓地出土一對金耳墜，雙環下帶鏈飾，末端

㉗ Зайнолл Самашев, *Ђерел·Berel*,Алматы, Баспа үйі, 2011, с.136.

㉘ Sergei I. Rudenko, translated and with a preface by M. W. Thompson, *Frozen Tombs of Siberia, the Pazyryk Burials of Iron Age Horsemen*, London, J. M. Dent & Sons Ltd, 1970, p. 106.

㉙ В. Д. Кубарев, П. И. Шульга, *Пазырыкскаякультура (курганыЧуи и Урсула),* Барнаул, Издательство Алтайского государственного университета, 2007, с. 25.

㉚ S. V.Kiselev, “Report on the Altaian Expedition of the State Historical Museum in 1934*”, Soviet Archaeology*, vol. I, 1935.

㉛ Ю. Ф. Кирюшин, Н. Ф. Степанова, А. А. Тишкин, *Скифская Эпоха горного Алтая, Часть II, Погребально-поминальные Комплексы Пазырыкской Культуры*, Барнаул, Издательство Алтайского Университета, 2003, с. 183, рис. 15, 2. В. Д. Кубарев, П. И. Шульга, *Пазырыкскаякультура (курганыЧуи и Урсула)*, с. 275, рис. 80.

㉜ В. Д. Кубарев, П. И. Шульга, *Пазырыкскаякультура (курганыЧуи и Урсула)*, с. 213, рис. 18-7.

㉝ В. А. Могильников, А. В. Куйбышев, “Курганы«Камень II»(Верхнее Приобье) пораскопкам 1976 г.”, *Советская Арехеология,* 1982(2), с. 115, рис. 2-3.

㉞ А. П. Уманский, А. Б. Шамшин, П. И. Шульга, *Могильник скифского времени Рогозиха-1 на левобережье Оби,* Барнаул, Издательство Алтайского Университета, 2005, с. 76.

㉟ А. П. Уманский, А. Б. Шамшин, П. И. Шульга, *Могильникскифскоговремени Рогозиха-1 на левобережье Оби,* рис. 136, с. 15, 5.

㊱ Ю. Ф. Кирюшин, Я. В. Фролов, “Комплекс памятников эпохи раннего железа в районе с. Елунино, Сборник научных трудов”, *Древние Поселения Алтая,* Барнаул, Издательство Алтайского государственного университета, 1998, с. 136, рис. 11-1.

㊲ В. Д. Кубарев, П. И. Шульга, *Пазырыкская культура (курганы Чуи и Урсула)*, с. 17.

穿肉紅玉髓珠，墓葬定在公元前6世紀中葉至公元前5世紀前葉（圖3，13、14）[38]。同屬於該文化類型的西伯爾卡（Сибирка）1號墓地位於阿爾泰西北部，墓地出土了一件8字環金耳環（圖3，15）[39]。墓葬年代在公元前6世紀中葉或稍晚[40]。

此外，位於阿爾泰邊疆區的烏什特—伊舒多夫卡（Усть-Иштовка）1號墓地，M7出土了兩件銅耳環，M15、M12、M10各出土了一件金耳環，樣式有雙環垂直焊接及8字環，墓葬年代定在公元前4世紀末至前3世紀（圖3，16—20）[41]。哈薩克阿爾泰地區也發現了4件耳環、耳墜，用金絲纏繞作墜鏈，下邊穿綴半寶石，有的還綴有金珠裝飾，年代約在公元前2至前1世紀（圖3，21—24）[42]。

圖瓦地區也有一些發現。位於圖瓦中部的烏賓（Урбюн）Ⅲ號墓地3號墓出土一件金耳墜，雙環下墜金鏈，金鏈末端連接金片製成的鈴形飾。墓葬的年代定在公元前5至前4世紀（圖3，25）[43]。艾爾梅雷克墓地(Аймырлык)出土有穿綴綠松石的雙環耳墜，墓葬年代在公元前5至前3世紀（圖3，26—28）[44]。在稍後的蘇魯克—赫姆（Сулуг-Хем）Ⅰ號墓中也能看到這種耳環樣式，墓葬年代在公元前3至前1世紀（圖3，29）[45]。

哈薩克斯坦東部及七河流域也有較多發現。東哈薩克斯坦的齊列克塔5號墓地4號墓出土一件金耳墜，垂直焊接雙環下帶鏈飾，下端綴四瓣葉形飾。墓葬年代定在公元前5至前4世紀（圖4，1）[46]。伊塞克古墓群也出土了2件類似的雙環耳環，年代在公元前4至前3世紀（圖4，2、3）[47]。著名的伊塞克金人墓墓主佩戴了一件造型獨特的穿綴綠松

㊳ П. И. Шульга, *Снаряжение верховой лошади в горном Алтае и верхнем Приобье, Часть II(VI-III вв. до н. э.)*, Новосибирск, РИЦ НГУ, 2015, с. 248, рис. 19, 11.

㊴ П. И. Шульга, *Снаряжение верховой лошади в горном Алтае и верхнем Приобье, Часть II(VI-III вв. до н. э.)*, с. 244, рис. 18, 5.

㊵ В. Д. Кубарев, П. И. Шульга, *Пазырыкская культура (курганы Чуи и Урсула)*, с. 17.

㊶ А. Л. Кунгуров, А. А. Тишкин, "Результаты Исследования памятника эпохи раннего железа Усть-Иштовка 1 на Алтае", Сборник, посвященный памяти антрополога А.Р. Кима, *Археология, антропология и этнография Сибири*, Барнаул, Издательство АГУ, 1996, с. 127, рис. 3, 6-10.

㊷ *The Centaurs of the Great Steppe*, Tasmagambetov I., 2003.（影像資料附圖片）

㊸ Д. Г. Савинов, "Могильник Урбюн-III и некоторые вопросы археологии Тувы скифского времени", *Археология Южной Сибири(ИЛАИ)*. Вып. 11. Кемерово, КемГУ, 1980, с. 113, рис. 6, 3.

㊹ А. М. Мандельштам, "Ранние кочевники скифского периода на территории Тувы", *Степная полоса Азиатской части СССР в скифо-сарматское врем, Серия: Археология СССР,* Москва, Издательство «Наука», 1992, с. 427, табл. 77, 7-9.

㊺ Vladimir Seme'nov, *Suglug-Hem and Khayrakan. The Cemeteries of Skythian Time of Central Tuva Basin*, St. Petersburg Centre for Oriental Studies, 2003, p. 99.

㊻ Телеубаев Э. Т., Үмітқалиев Ұ. Ү., Жуматаев Р. С., "Щілікті жазығындағы тас жәшікті жерлеу ескерткіштері", *Материалы международной научной конференции: Археология Казахстана в Эпоху независимости: итоги, перспективы,* посвященной 20-летию независимости республики Казахстан и 20-летию института археологии им. А. Х. Маргулана, 12-15 декабря 2011 г., г. Алматы, Том II, Алматы, 2011, 109-сурет, 4-сур, А.

㊼ K. Akishev, *Ancient Gold of Kazakhstan*, АΛМА・АТА・ΘНЕР, 1983, p. 132.

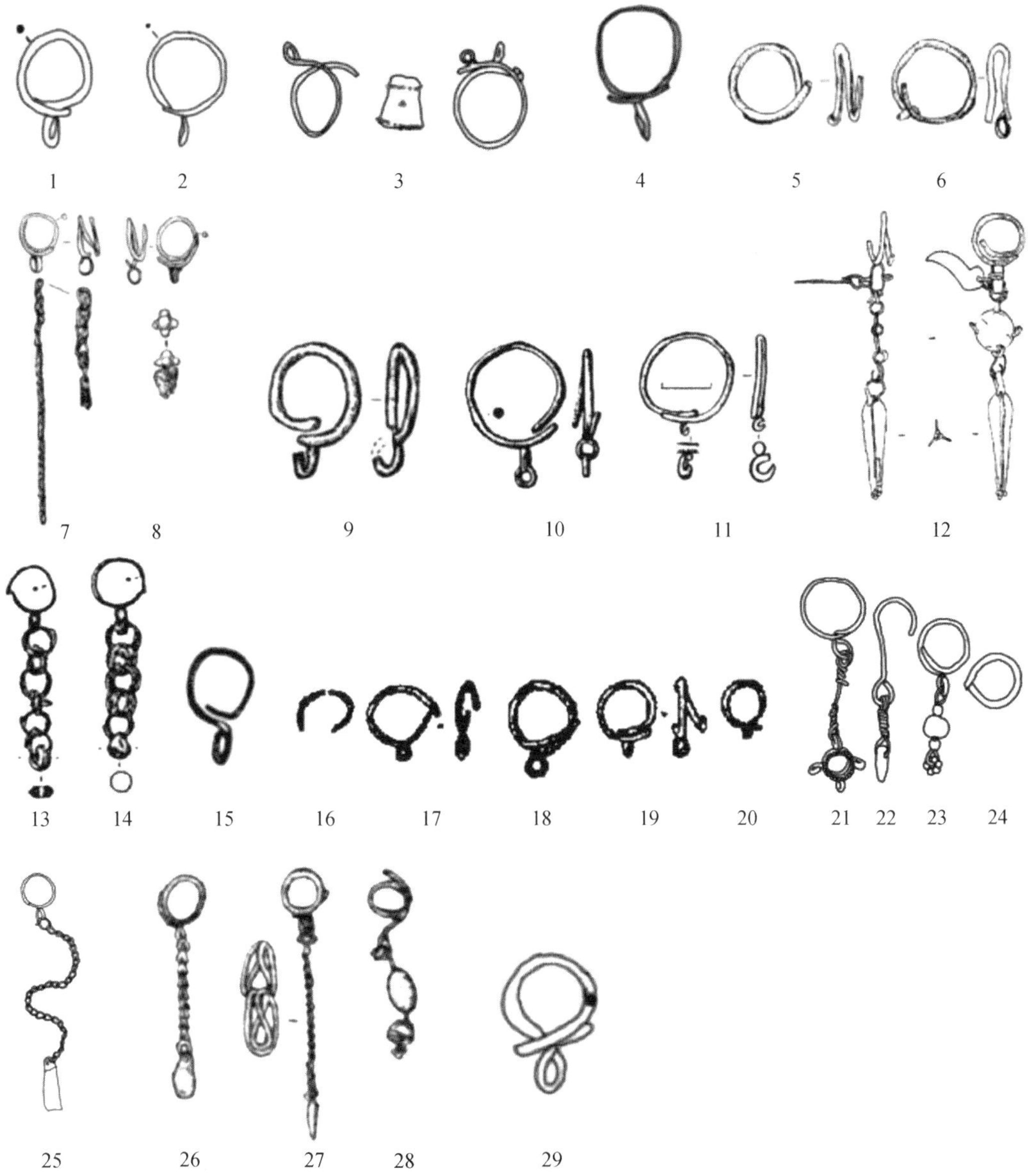

圖3 薩彥—阿爾泰地區發現的垂直焊接雙環耳飾

1、2. 拜卡Ⅲ號墓地1號墓 3. 波內爾墓葬 4. 阿拉格爾墓地5號墓 5—8. 杜特傑斯肯Ⅵ號墓地M14、M27 9. 卡爾—克齊墓地 10. 卡緬Ⅱ號墓地15號墓 11. 噶羅錫1號墓地6號墓 12. 葉魯尼納Ⅱ號墓地1號墓 13、14. 克爾—克齊墓地 15. 西伯爾卡1號墓地 16—20. 烏什特—伊舒多夫卡1號墓地 21—24. 哈薩克阿爾泰地區 25. 烏賓Ⅲ號墓地3號墓 26—28. 艾爾梅雷克墓地 29. 蘇魯克—赫姆Ⅰ號墓（1、9. 銀 16、17. 銅 2—8、10—15、18—29.金）

石的耳墜，墓葬年代定在公元前5至前4世紀（圖4，4）[48]。位於七河流域的薩里布拉克（Сарыбулак）墓出土了一件金耳墜，在雙環下垂一條編織的金鏈，金鏈的尾端原來是否有墜飾則不得而知了。另出一件金耳墜，雙環下用金絲纏繞，原本應穿綴綠松石，末端飾有金珠塔，墓葬年代在公元前4至前1世紀（圖4，5、6）[49]。科克圖馬（Коктума）墓葬出土了7件此類耳飾，以綠松石或紅玉髓作墜，墓葬年代約在公元前4至前1世紀（圖4，7—13）[50]。位於阿拉木圖郊區的尼什尼卡緬（Нижнекаменский）墓地5號墓和4號墓各出土一件雙環焊接的金耳環，К. А. Акишев將墓葬年代定在公元前4至前3世紀（圖4，14、15）[51]。吉斯拉維斯（Кызылауыз）1號墓地11號墓出土銅耳墜，雙環垂直焊接，下帶石墜。墓葬年代定在塞人文化晚期，公元前5至前4世紀（圖4，16）[52]。位於七河流域東部的卡塔托別（Катартобе）墓地2號墓2號墓室墓主頭骨左側出土一件金耳墜，墓葬年代在公元前3至前2世紀（圖4，17）[53]。卡拉沙（Караша）1號墓地56號墓出土一對銀質雙環焊接耳環，墓葬年代在公元1至3世紀（圖4，18）[54]。烏古爾卡拉（Унгуркора）1號墓地28號墓出土一件雙環垂直焊接耳環，К. А. Акишев認爲其年代在烏孫時期（圖4，19）[55]。

往南至中亞西天山地區也有少量發現。位於今吉爾吉斯斯坦境內的科特曼—秋別（Кетмень-Тюбе）墓葬出土了兩件金耳墜，一件墜部爲金箔製成雙鳥形象，一件墜部穿綠松石珠，墓葬年代約在公元前4至前3世紀（圖5，1、2）[56]。位於今吉爾吉斯斯坦天山地區科奇科爾（Кочкор）谷地的庫姆—秋別（Кум-Дёбё）墓地2號墓出土了一件金耳墜，雙環下帶螺旋鏈飾並穿綠松石墜。該墓葬屬於天山地區早期遊牧民的遺存。墓中可能埋葬了一位35—45歲男性。墓葬被盜嚴重，除了金耳飾還發現了一件穿孔骨器（圖5，3）[57]。再往南的阿賴山山區也有個別發現，年代在公元3至4世紀（圖5，4）[58]。

---

[48] K. Akishev, *Ancient Gold of Kazakhstan*, p. 126.

[49] K. Akishev, *Ancient Gold of Kazakhstan*, pp. 136、137.

[50] K. Akishev, *Ancient Gold of Kazakhstan*, pp. 139-141.

[51] А. З. Бейсснов, “Серьги сакской эпохи”, *Вестник Томского государственного университета*, История, 2014, №6(32), c. 125, рис. 7, 1, 2.

[52] А. З. Бейсенов, “Серьги сакской эпохи”, c. 124, рис. 8, 1.

[53] Чотбаев А., Онгар А., “Некрополь катартобе-памятник кочевой элиты восточного жетысу”, *Всадники Великой степи: традиции и новации,* Астана, 2014, c. 73, рис. 12, 4.

[54] А. З. Бейсенов, “Серьги сакской эпохи”, c. 124, рис. 7, 3.

[55] А. З. Бейсенов, “Серьги сакской эпохи”, c. 124, рис. 8, 2.

[56] Parzinger G. *Die frühen Völker Eurasiens vom Neolithikum bis zum Mittelalter*, München, Verlag C.H.Beck, 2006, S. 663.

[57] А. К. Абетеков, “Исследования шамшинского археологического отряда КИАЭ в 1987-1988 гг”. Часть 1. 1987 год, *Материалы и исследования по археологии Кыргызстана,* выпуск 4, Бишкек, «Илим», 2009, c. 23, рис. XXVI-1.

[58] Ю. А. Заднепровский, “Ранние кочевники Кетмень-Тюбе, Ферганы и Алая”, *Степная полоса Азиатской части СССР в скифо-сарматское врем, Серия: Археология СССР,* Москва, Издательство «Наука», 1992, c. 385, табл. 35, 77.

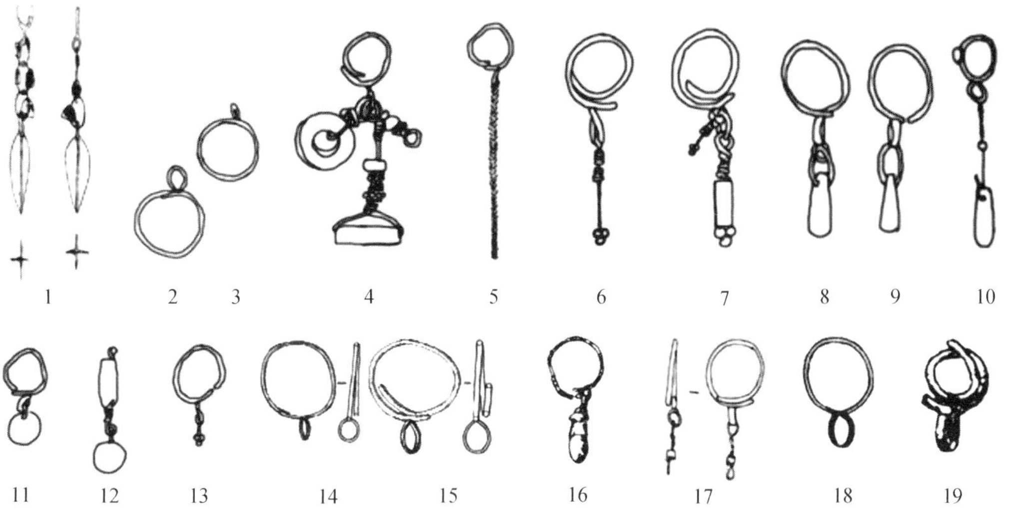

圖4

1. 齊列克塔5號墓地4號墓　2、3. 伊塞克古墓群　4. 伊塞克金人墓　5、6. 薩里布拉克墓葬　7—13. 科克圖馬墓葬　14、15. 尼什尼卡緬墓地5、4號墓　16. 吉斯拉維斯1號墓地11號墓　17. 卡塔托別墓地2號墓2號墓室　18. 卡拉沙1號墓地56號墓　19. 烏古爾卡拉1號墓地28號墓（1—15、17、19. 金　16. 銅　18. 銀）

哈薩克斯坦中部也有少量發現。卡拉乾達地區的納加涅斯克(Nagornensk)墓地出土了兩件金耳墜，帶空心球飾，底端還焊飾金珠，墓葬年代在公元前5至前3世紀（圖5，5、6）[59]。塔沙拉爾（Тасарал）3號墓地2號墓出土一件金耳墜，雙環下垂一鈴形飾，內鑲嵌橢圓形彩色石頭，鈴形飾的邊緣焊飾一圈的金珠（圖5，7）[60]。

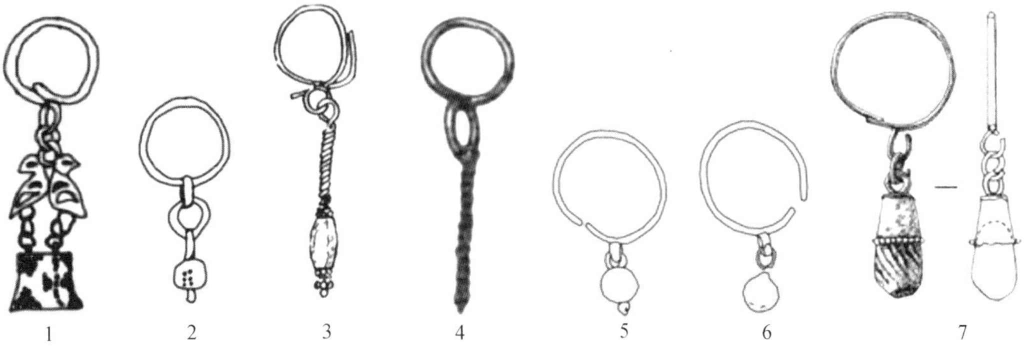

圖5

1、2. 科特曼—秋別墓葬　3. 庫姆—秋別墓地2號墓　4. 阿賴山山區　5、6. 納加涅斯克墓地

7. 塔沙拉爾3號墓地2號墓（1—7. 金）

---

⑲ Grigore Arbore Popescu, Chiara Silvi, Karl Baipakov, *L'UOMO D'ORO, La cultura delle steppe del Kazakhstan dall' età del bronzo alle grandi migrazioni*, Electa, Milano, Elemond Editori Associati, 1998, p. 201, fig. 382, 383.

⑳ А. З. Бейсенов, "Серьги сакской эпохи", с. 124, рис. 6, 1.

南烏拉爾地區有大量的發現。吉雷克—奧巴（Кырык-Оба）Ⅱ號墓地23號墓出土一對金耳墜，圓環下垂直焊接又編織金鏈圍成的金環，下套接多個纏繞多圈的金環，末端焊接一金球，金球表面滿飾僞金珠。墓葬年代在公元前6至前5世紀（圖6，1、2）[61]。菲力波夫卡1號墓地出土了數量較多的此類耳飾，約爲18件，樣式相近，但大多細部造型變化豐富。上環有的由簡單的金絲彎曲而成，有的由表面呈多棱面的粗環彎曲而成。下環有的由一至兩組編織金飾帶彎曲而成，有的由金絲纏繞幾圈而成，有的爲光素無紋的扁環。上下雙環垂直焊接之處往往焊飾細金珠。菲力波夫卡1號墓地的年代定在公元前5至前4世紀（圖6，3—20）[62]。位於奧爾斯克市東郊的新庫瑪克（Новый Кумак）墓地也出土了一件相似的耳飾，上環由包金銅絲環繞兩圈而成，下環爲編織金飾帶彎成的扁環（圖6，21）[63]。吉曲吉諾（Кичигино）墓地3號墓4號墓室出土一對銀耳飾，下環由纏繞多圈的銀絲構成，墓葬的年代在公元前5世紀末至前4世紀（圖6，22、23）[64]。列別傑夫卡墓地多見此類耳飾及其變體，六號墓地23號墓出土一對銀耳環；26號墓出土一對銅耳環，上環穿套一寬扁圓環，圓環表面有突棱（圖6，24—27）[65]。列別傑夫卡Ⅱ號墓地6號墓出土了一對金耳墜及一件墜飾，金耳墜的雙環並未採取垂直焊接，下垂金鏈，其上墜眾多的小金球，金鏈末端墜石榴狀金飾，表面有金珠焊飾的紋樣，底部垂掛豐富的錐形飾，通長20厘米；另一件墜飾由金鏈帶金球墜構成，金球上滿飾金珠，金鏈上垂掛一顆綠松石珠。此外，Ⅱ號墓地9號墓還出土了一件雙環垂直焊接的耳墜，金鏈下帶多瓣葉形飾，末端焊飾若干粒金珠。該墓地年代約在公元前5世紀（圖6，28—31）[66]。阿克秋別地區的別斯—奧巴（Бес-Оба）墓地出土了兩件該類耳飾，其中一件與卡拉乾達地區

---

[61] С. Ю. Гуцалов, “Погребальные памятники кочевой элиты южного Приуралья середины I тыс. до н. э.”, *Археология, этнография и антропология Евразии,* 2(30), 2007, с. 80, рис. 8, 4.

[62] *Золотые олени Евразии,* СПБ, 2001, с. 76, кат. 16; Л. Т. Яблонский, *Отчет о раскопках курганов 2 и 29 могильника Филипповка 1 на территории Илекского района Оренбургской обл. РФ в 2008 году,* 2009, рис. 38, 1, 2; 98, 1, 6, 3, 5; 99, 2; 135.转自Е. В. Лылова, “Об одном типе серег из погребений ранних кочевников Южного Урала”, *Вестник Челябинского государственного университета,* 2009, № 37(175), История, вып. 36, рис. 1,11; 2, 1; 3, 1; 1, 6-10; *2, 7; Сокровища сарматских вождей (Материал раскопок Филипповских курганов),* Под общей научной редакцией Л. Т. Яблонского, Оренбург, Печатный дом«Димур», 2008, кат. 34; 80; 102; 118; А. Х. Пшеничнюк, *Отчет о раскопках Филипповских курганов в Илекском районе Оренбургской области в 1987 году,* Уфа, 1988, рис. 86, 1, 2; 97. 转自Е. В. Лылова, “Об одном типе серег из погребений ранних кочевников Южного Урала”, рис. 2, 3, 4, 5.

[63] Савельева К. Ф., Смирное К. Ф., “Ближневосточные древности на Южном Урале”, *ВДИ*, № 3, 1978, с. 107, рис. 1, б. Из Е. В. Лылова, “Золотые серьги из IV прохоровского кургана”, *Археологические памятники Оренбуржья,* Выпуск VI, Оренбург, Издательство ОГПУ, 2004, с. 73.

[64] А. Д. Таиров, “Исследования курганного могильника Кичигино в 2007 году (предварительные результаты)”, *Ранние кочевники Волго-Уральского региона,* Оренбург, Издательство ОГПУ, 2008, с. 141, рис. 2, 1, 2.

[65] Б. Ф. Железчиков, В. М. Клепиков, И. В. Сергацков, *Древности Лебедевки(VI—II вв. до н. э.)*, Москва, Издательская фирма «Восточная литература» РАН, 2006, с. 104, рис. 53, 11; 57, 7.

[66] С. Ю. Гуцалов, “Погребальные памятники кочевой элиты южного Приуралья середины Iтыс. до н. э.”, *Археология, этнография и антропология Евразии,* 2(30), 2007, с. 76, рис. 3, 2-4; *Unbekanntes Kasachstan Archäologie im Herzen Asiens*, Band II, Bochum, Deutsches Bergbau- Museum Bochum, 2013, S. 762, Tafel. 500.

納加涅斯克墓地出土的耳墜非常接近，雙環下帶空心金球飾，雙環焊接處還焊飾金珠；另外一件金耳墜帶金鏈，下墜空心扁金球。墓葬年代在公元前6至前5世紀（圖6，32、33）[67]。位於南烏拉爾地區的帕哈羅夫卡（Прохоровка）大墓出土了一件雙環垂直焊接的耳飾，上環處垂掛一鏤空金球，金球由金絲編織而成，並間隔點綴一組三顆的細金珠，墓葬年代在公元前5世紀（圖6，34）[68]。

彼得大帝的西伯利亞寶藏中也有雙環垂直焊接耳墜，其中一件環部穿兩件金環，環面焊接金珠；另外一件上環兩端都焊飾了金珠（圖6，35、36）[69]。新疆東邊的內蒙古地區西溝畔2號墓出土了一對金耳墜，雙環下穿金絲繞成的喇叭形飾和石珠。墓葬年代約在公元前3世紀，相當於中原戰國時期（圖6，37、38）[70]。

國外學者對境外各區域發現的垂直焊接雙環耳飾都有較多的研究，形成了較爲一致的觀點。他們指出，焊接雙環耳飾流行於公元前6至前5世紀的阿爾泰地區，與其相關的8字環耳飾年代可能稍晚。根據薩彥—阿爾泰地區的材料，在某些時期，兩種耳飾是共存的，但總的來說，焊接雙環耳飾年代要早於8字環耳飾，它可能爲後者提供了樣式的模板[71]。值得注意的是，新疆地區發現的8字環耳飾也往往與垂直焊接雙環耳飾同出。垂直焊接雙環耳飾在七河流域、哈薩克斯坦東部及西天山山區也有較多發現，年代在塞人文化晚期。在烏孫文化早期的遺存中也有相似的耳飾，年代在公元前3至前2或前1世紀[72]。南烏拉爾地區這一耳飾樣式集中流行於公元前5至前4世紀，此外還發現了此類耳飾的變體，如帕哈羅夫卡（Прохоровка）4號墓出土的耳環，小環通過一截小管與大環相接，使其能夠活動；阿赫列彼納（Охлебино）墓地出土的耳環，小環直接套入大環，而不是焊接。它們的年代可能稍晚，約在公元前4世紀末[73]。

在這些研究基礎上，將新疆地區發現的同類耳飾納入考察，可以對這種耳飾的流傳與使用的時空跨度都會有更全面的認識。

---

⑰ Grigore Arbore Popescu, Chiara Silvi, Karl Baipakov, *L'UOMO D'ORO, La cultura delle steppe del Kazakhstan dall' età del bronzo alle grandi migrazioni*, Electa, Milano,Elemond Editori Associati, p. 147, fig. 182, 183.

⑱ Grigore Arbore Popescu, Chiara Silvi, Karl Baipakov, *L'UOMO D'ORO, La cultura delle steppe del Kazakhstan dall' età del bronzoallegrandimigrazioni*, Electa, Milano,Elemond Editori Associati, p.172.

⑲ С. И. Руденко, *Сибирская коллекция Петра I,* Свод Археологических источников, Д3-9, 1962, табл. XX, 10, 11.

⑳ 伊克昭盟文物工作站、內蒙古文物工作隊《西溝畔匈奴墓》，《文物》1980年第7期，7頁，圖一二。

㉑ П. И. Шульга, *Могильник скифского времени Локоть-4а,* Барнаул, Издательство Алтайского государственного университета, 2003, с. 60; А. З. Бейсенов, “Серьги сакской эпохи”, с. 125, 126.

㉒ А. З. Бейсенов, “Серьги сакской эпохи”, с. 126; Чотбаев А., Онгар А., “Некрополь катартобе-памятник кочевой элиты восточного жетысу”, с. 72.

㉓ Е. В. Лылова, “Золотые серьги из IV прохоровского кургана”, *Археологические памятники Оренбуржья,* Выпуск VI, Оренбург, Издательство ОГПУ, 2004, с. 70-71, рис. 2, 4, 5.

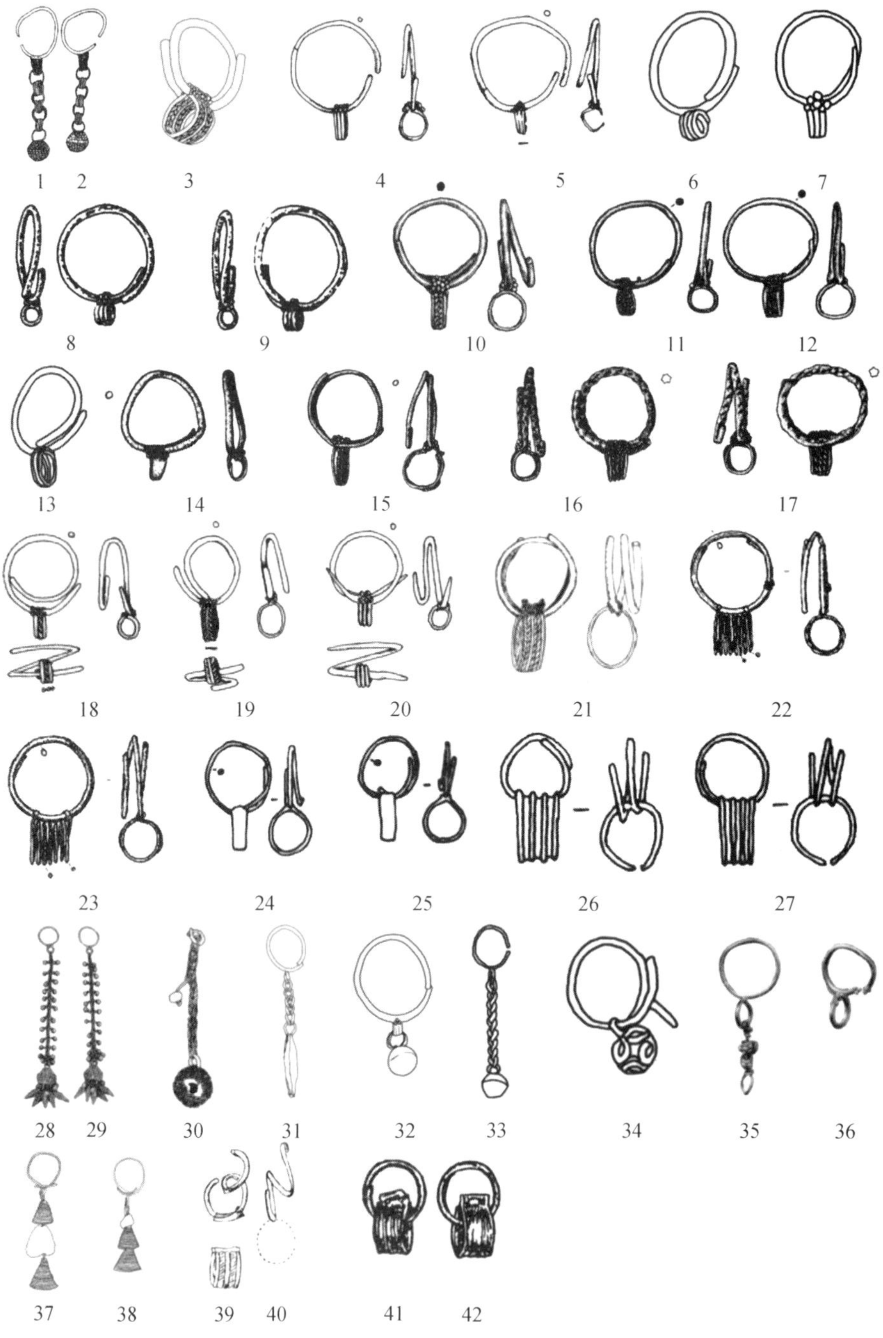

圖6

1、2. 吉雷克—奥巴Ⅱ號墓地23號墓　3—20. 菲力波夫卡1號墓地（3. 1號墓　4、5. 2號墓1號墓室　6. 4號墓5號墓室　7—9. 7號墓　10. 15號墓2號墓室　11、12. 16號墓2號墓室　13. 28號墓1號墓室　14—17. 29號墓2號墓室　18—20. 29號墓5號墓室）　21. 新庫瑪克墓地　22、23. 吉曲吉諾墓地3號墓4號墓室　24—27. 列別傑夫卡六號墓地（24、25. 23號墓　26、27. 26號墓）　28—31. 列別傑夫卡Ⅱ號墓地（28—30. 6號墓　31. 9號墓）　32、33. 別斯—奥巴墓葬　34. 帕哈羅夫卡大墓　35、36. 西伯利亞寶藏　37、38. 西溝畔2號墓　39、40. 帕哈羅夫卡4號墓　41、42. 阿赫列彼納墓地（1—21、28—38. 金　22—25. 銀　26、27. 銅　39—42. 銅包金）

三、新疆出土的垂直焊接雙環耳飾與周鄰地區同類物的比較及其反映的文化互動與交流

（一）新疆與其西邊發現的雙環焊接耳飾的比較研究

薩彥—阿爾泰、中亞七河流域、天山地區西至南烏拉爾地區發現的雙環焊接耳飾都反映出與新疆所見有著千絲萬縷的聯繫。

尼勒克縣一級電站東麥里墓地M40：2（銀）、M41：1（金），尼勒克縣加勒克斯卡茵特墓地M52：1（金），阿拉溝墓地M3：8（金），伊吾托背梁墓地M1：1-2（金），垂直焊接的小環都由多圈金屬絲環繞而成，與哈薩克斯坦西部及南烏拉爾地區發現的同類物非常接近（圖7，1—8）。

位於西天山地區的科特曼—秋別大墓出土的金耳墜，垂直焊接雙環下垂掛一墜飾。墜飾由上下兩部分構成，上部是兩只鳥（鷹）的形象，相對而立，雙雙做回首狀，鳥身原本應該鑲嵌了半寶石，現已遺失。墜飾的下部是用金片製成的略呈圓台狀且中空的飾物，金片在上下沿焊飾一圈金珠，中間間隔裝飾由金珠組成的豎線紋、菱形紋和上下相對的三角紋。這件耳墜與鞏留縣山口水庫出的耳墜，無論是形制，工藝還是風格都極爲相似（圖7，9、10）。從形制上來看，兩者都是由上部的耳環與下部的墜體組成，上部的耳環又由焊接的大小兩環組成，下部墜體的頂部都焊接了一個小圓環，用來與耳環相接；從製作工藝上來看，兩件耳墜主體部分的動物紋樣，其表現方式略有不同，鞏留縣山口水庫的是用金片壓制出山羊的形象，科特曼—秋別大墓出土的這件則是鳥狀的金飾牌，鳥身或許鑲嵌了寶石。但兩者明顯存在的共同之處是它們都使用了金珠裝飾工藝，且金珠構成的圖案也相似；從藝術風格來看，兩件耳墜都帶有明顯的草原風格，羊和鳥（鷹）都是草原民族鍾愛的圖案。值得一提的是，烏吐蘭墓地發現的兩件金耳墜，墜部有金片製作的環形裝飾帶，上邊有金珠組成的上下相錯的三角紋，這與鞏留縣山口水庫墓地以及科特曼—秋別大墓出金耳墜的裝飾風格是一致的（圖7，11）。這也反映出，在公元前4世紀至公元前後，在天山西段流行著一種幾何紋的金珠裝飾紋樣。

阿合奇縣庫蘭薩日克、烏魯木齊市南山魚兒溝及哈巴河縣喀拉蘇墓葬出土的耳飾反映出與阿爾泰、中亞七河流域、天山地區密切的聯繫。阿爾泰山區尤其是鄂畢河上游地區發現了較多八字環耳墜，墜部用金屬絲繞纏，並在墜部穿綴綠松石等串珠。如屬於巴澤雷克早期文化遺存的博拉套（Баротал）1號墓地100號墓出土的銅耳墜，下墜兩顆玻璃珠，墓葬年代在公元前5世紀下半葉（圖7，15）[74]。鄂畢河上游的卡緬文化遺存更是發

---

[74] В. Д. Кубарев, П. И. Шульга, *Пазырыкская культура (курганы Чуи и Урсула)*, с. 215, с. 257, рис. 62, 15; с. 235, рис. 40, 21.

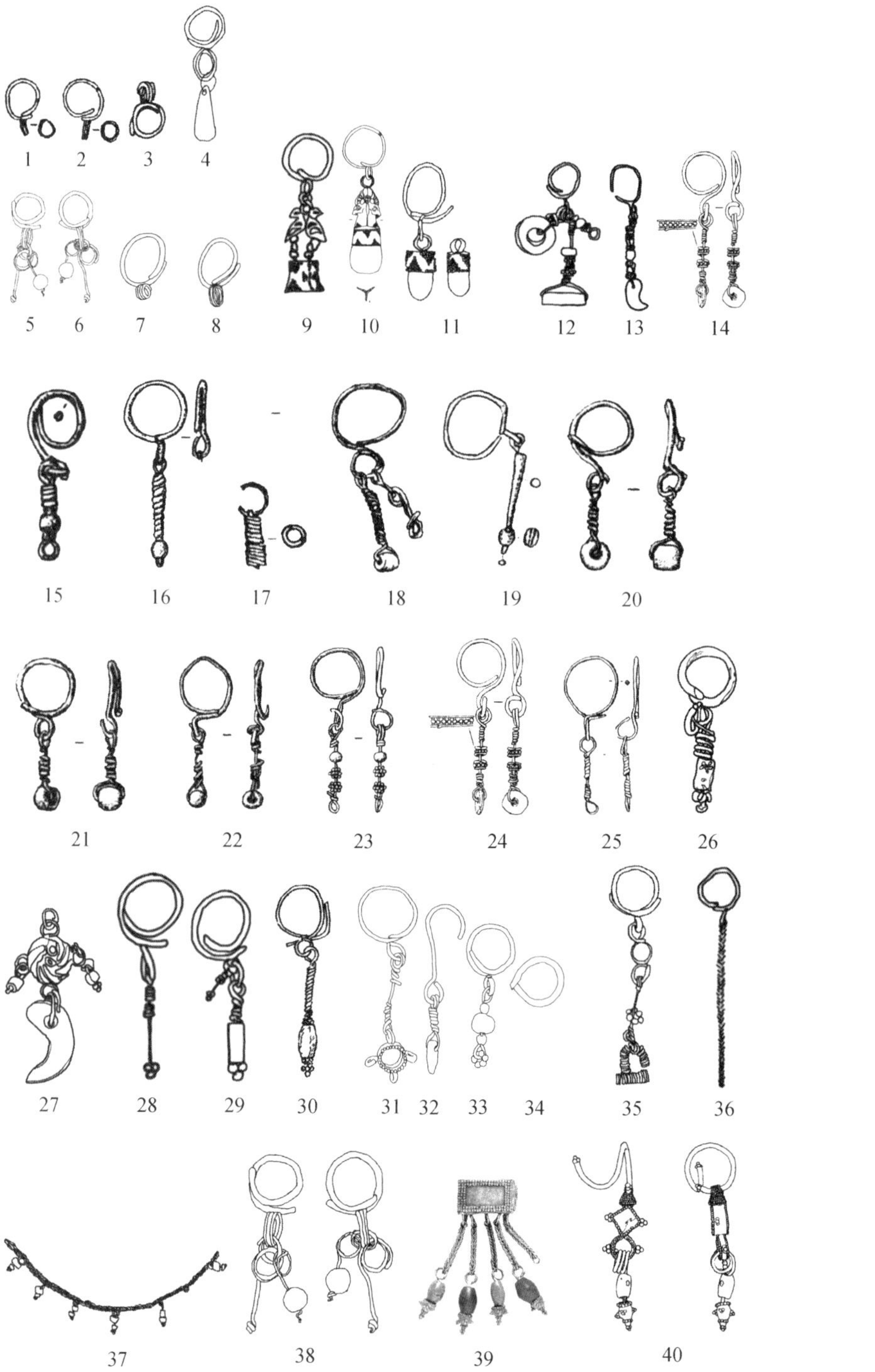

圖7

1、2. 東麥里墓地（M40：2、M41：1） 3. 加勒克斯卡茵特墓地（M52：1） 4. 阿拉溝墓地（M3：8） 5、6. 托背梁墓地（M1：1-2） 7、8. 菲力波夫卡一號墓地4號墓5號墓室、28號墓1號墓室 9. 科特曼—秋别大墓 10. 鞏留縣山口水庫（M35：2） 11. 烏吐蘭墓地 12. 伊塞克金人墓 13. 庫蘭薩日克墓地（93AKM8：1） 14、20—25. 洛卡其4號墓地（14、24. 9號墓1號墓室 20. 1號墓 21. 2號墓1號墓室 22. 4號墓3號墓室 23. 4號墓1號墓室 25. 9號墓3號墓室） 15. 博拉套1號墓地100號墓 16—19. 噶羅錫1號墓地（16. 8號墓 17、18. 19號墓 19. 8號墓） 26、27. 魚兒溝墓地 32. 38號墓 28、36. 薩里布拉克墓葬 29. 科克圖馬墓葬 30. 庫姆—秋别墓地2號墓 31—34. 哈薩克阿爾泰地區 35. 喀拉蘇墓地M15 37. 阿拉溝墓葬 38. 沙梁子墓地M1 39. 精河縣南土墩墓 40. 西溝遺址1號墓（1. 銀 2—14、20、21、23—40. 金 15—19、22. 銅）

現了數量較多的此類耳墜，年代在公元前6世紀下半葉至前5世紀（圖七，16—25）[75]。其中，洛卡其（Локать）4號墓地9號墓出土的金耳墜尤爲矚目，墜部穿有圓環飾，由上下兩層金絲夾金珠焊接而成。另外，著名的伊塞克古墓也出土了一件相似的耳墜，這件形制特殊的金耳墜由“金人武士”佩戴，墜部由三部分組成，每一部分都串聯或垂掛綠松石珠。這兩例耳墜及新疆阿合奇縣庫蘭薩日克墓葬發現的金耳墜驚人地相似，環部都採用金絲纏繞的形式，間隔穿套由大小金珠組成的圓環以及綠松石串飾，體現著濃郁的草原遊牧文化的風格，既精緻又透露著粗獷的格調（圖7，12—14）。伊塞克古墓的這件耳墜，金絲的纏繞大膽粗率，綠松石墜飾質樸厚重，墜部結構枝節叢生，形制複雜多變，透露著一種不對稱的美感。如此風格獨特、製作精緻的耳墜，正正襯托了墓主人極爲尊貴的身份地位。值得注意的是，洛卡其4號墓地還出土了刻畫特殊圖案的銅鏡（撥浪鼓），學者指出，墓葬發現的金珠飾品及銅鏡（撥浪鼓）可能是作爲儀式執行者（巫師）的工具[76]。這啓示我們，這些製作複雜、精美的長條金耳墜可能不是用於日常的佩戴，而是在祭祀場合使用，它的佩戴者可能有著巫師一類的身份。

從目前的材料來看，墜部用金屬絲纏繞並穿石珠的裝飾樣式在阿爾泰山區、鄂畢河上游出現得比較早，在公元前6世紀下半葉至前5世紀。這種裝飾樣式很快在中亞七河流域及西天山地區流行，如七河流域薩里—布拉克墓葬和科克圖馬墓葬出土的金耳墜，年代在公元前4至前1世紀；天山地區庫姆—秋別墓地2號墓出土的金耳墜。烏魯木齊市南山魚兒溝發現的兩件金耳墜，造型、工藝與前邊三例均非常接近，細部表現也驚人一致，墜飾末端都焊飾三或四顆金珠。哈薩克阿爾泰地區發現的金耳墜也具有此類造型，其中一件耳墜穿瑪瑙珠，並在末端穿一圈由六顆金珠焊接而成的花環。新疆哈巴河縣喀拉蘇墓地出土的金耳墜，也懸掛了同樣的金珠花環（圖7，26—35）。

魚兒溝和阿拉溝墓葬出土的包括耳墜在內的飾物尤其值得注意。魚兒溝處在艾維爾溝和阿拉溝交匯處，艾維爾溝是天山山脈中部的一條東西向的狹長溝谷，沿著溝谷向北可以穿越天山至烏魯木齊。阿拉溝是一條東西向的山谷，沿溝西行再往北穿越冰達阪可到達烏魯木齊，向西可到巴音布魯克草原甚至到伊犁河谷，向南可到天山南麓的焉耆盆地[77]。可見，魚兒溝和阿拉溝在天山地帶溝通東西及南北的通道上佔據極爲重要的位置。阿拉溝墓葬出土了一件金鏈。通長25厘米（圖7，37）[78]。金鏈由金絲編織而成，與薩里—布拉克墓出的金耳墜鏈墜的工藝是一致的（圖7，36），年代也相近。項鏈上間隔垂掛6件小墜飾，結構相似，穿一大一小形狀不同的綠松石珠，底端焊飾小金珠塔飾，由4顆小金珠組成，並用纏繞的金絲將墜飾與項鏈連接。這件項鏈與魚兒溝墓地、中亞

---

⑮ А. П. Уманский, А. Б. Шамшин, П. И. Шульга, *Могильник скифского времени Рогозиха-1 на левобережье Оби*, рис. 142, с. 21, 6; рис. 159, с. 38, 4, 6; рис. 174, с. 53, 10. П. И. Шульга, *Могильник скифского времени Локоть-4а*, с. 147, рис. 5, 6, 8; с. 155, рис. 13, 3; с. 158, рис. 16, 4; с. 159, рис. 17, 17; с. 180, рис. 38, 5; с. 186, рис. 44, 12.

⑯ П. И. Шульга, *Могильник скифского времени Локоть-4а*, с. 60.

⑰ 新疆文物考古研究所《烏魯木齊市魚兒溝遺址與阿拉溝墓地》，19頁。

⑱ 祈小山、王博《絲綢之路新疆古代文化》，烏魯木齊：新疆人民出版社，2008年，130頁。

七河流域所出金耳墜的風格也是如此的相似。如果仔細觀察阿拉溝墓地出土的這條金鏈，穿綠松石墜的金絲繞幾圈，與金鏈相扣接。伊吾縣沙梁子墓地出的金耳墜，每件下垂掛兩墜體，雖然穿綴的是瑪瑙珠，但是穿綴的方式與阿拉溝墓地的金鏈是一致的（圖7，38）。精河縣城南土墩墓出土的一件金掛飾，長5、寬2厘米，年代相當於漢代，以同樣的方式穿綴各色半寶石，末端有紡錘體金飾，用金珠細緻裝飾（圖7，39）[79]。巴里坤縣西溝遺址1號墓出土的耳墜，下端懸掛綠松石部件及紡錘體金飾，其結構與精河縣南土墩墓所出幾乎一模一樣（圖7，40）。

阿拉溝墓葬還出土了一批金器[80]，其中虎紋圓金牌、對虎紋金箔帶、獅形金箔的造型與風格也與哈薩克斯坦伊塞克金人冠飾的豹子相近（圖8，1—5）[81]。阿拉溝墓葬出土的方座承獸銅盤在哈薩克草原有較多的發現，年代在公元前4至前2世紀（圖8，6、7）[82]。所有這些都反映了阿拉溝、魚兒溝墓葬與天山西端的草原地帶有著千絲萬縷的聯繫。

圖8

1—3. 阿拉溝墓葬出土金器（1. 獅形金箔　2. 虎紋圓金牌　3. 對虎紋金箔帶）　4、5. 伊塞克金人墓冠飾上的豹紋裝飾　6. 阿拉溝墓葬出方座承獸銅盤　7. 哈薩克草原發現銅盤（祭壇）

此外，和靜縣阿爾夏一號墓地出土的金耳墜（M4：3）所帶鏈飾也值得我們注意（圖9，1）。鏈飾工藝特殊，由單環對折形成U形環，再環環嵌套而成。這種鏈飾在歐亞草原上有較多發現，如鄂畢河上游另外發現的一件金耳墜也帶相似鏈飾，末端垂

[79] 新疆維吾爾自治區文物局編《絲路瑰寶——新疆館藏文物精品圖錄》，烏魯木齊：新疆人民出版社，2011年，294頁。

[80] 新疆社會科學考古研究所《新疆阿拉溝豎穴木槨墓發掘簡報》，《文物》1981年第1期。

[81] Dr. Claudia Chang, *Of Gold and Grass: Nomads of Kazakhstan*,Washington, Access Industries, 2006, p. 117, fig. 50-51.

[82] Dr. Claudia Chang, *Of Gold and Grass: Nomads of Kazakhstan*, p.125，fig. 67.

四瓣葉形飾，墓葬年代在公元前6世紀（圖9，2）[83]。鄂畢河上游鄂畢—普列斯（Обские Плесы）2號墓地出土不少的銅耳墜，墜部即採用此種結構的鏈飾，墓葬年代在年代定在前5至前4世紀（圖9，3）[84]。圖瓦地區雙環焊接耳墜也見此類鏈式，年代在公元前5至前3世紀（圖9，4、5）。南烏拉爾地區的帕哈羅夫卡（Прохоровка）墓地出土一件金耳墜，半月形墜飾下端垂掛五條環環嵌套的金鏈，金鏈末端連接水滴形墜飾，內本有鑲嵌物，墓葬年代在公元前4世紀左右（圖9，6）[85]。近來，哈薩克斯坦中部塔樂迪（Талды）2號墓地4號墓出土一件金耳墜，僅存墜部，由環環嵌套的金鏈帶金球墜組成（圖9，7）[86]。研究者將該墓地的年代定在公元前7至前6世紀左右，並指出，帶有此類編織鏈飾的耳墜在塞人文化早期就已經出現，其後十分迅速地向東西兩邊傳播[87]。內蒙古的阿魯柴登也發現了此類鏈飾，艾瑪·班克女士認爲在內蒙古發現的這種鏈飾可能不是本土製造，而是從更遠的中亞或西亞地區的金屬加工中心輸入[88]。可以看到，中亞地區公元前1千紀後半葉已經熟練掌握這種鏈飾的製作工藝，但由於新疆阿爾夏一號墓地及內蒙古阿魯柴登發現的同類鏈飾數量單一，我們無法判斷其爲本地製作還是從中亞輸入的，但無論如何，它們都反映了與中亞地區微妙的文化聯繫。

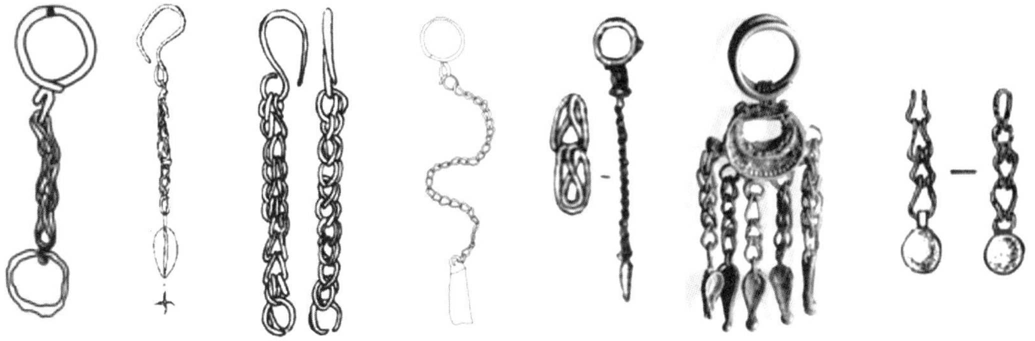

圖9

1. 阿爾夏一號墓地（M4：3） 2. 鄂畢河上游 3. 鄂畢—普列斯2號墓（銅） 4. 烏賓III號墓地3號墓 5. 艾爾梅雷克墓地 6. 帕哈羅夫卡墓地 7. 塔樂迪2號墓地4號墓（1、2、4—7. 金 3. 銅）

---

[83] К. В. Чугунов, “Локально-хронологические особенности культуры Тувы в середине 1 тысячелетия до. н. э.”, *Евразия сквозьвека,* СПб, 2001, табл.1, 28.

[84] С. Д. Ведянин, А. Л. Кунгунов, “Грунтовый могильник староалейской культуры Обские Плесы 2”, *Погребальный обряд древних племен Алтая*, Барнаул, Изд-во Алтайского университета, 1996, рис. 13, 1-9, 18, 19.

[85] *Сокровища сарматских вождей (Материал раскопок Филипповских курганов),* под общей научной редакцией Л. Т. Яблонского, с. 27, рис. 3.

[86] А. З. Бейсенов, “Серьги сакской эпохи”, с. 124, рис. 5, 2.

[87] А. З. Бейсенов, “Серьги сакской эпохи”, с. 123.

[88] Emma C. Bunker, “Gold in the Ancient Chinese World: A Cultural Puzzle”, *Artibus Asiae*, vol. 53, no. 1/2(1993), p. 45.

（二）新疆與其東邊發現的雙環焊接及相關耳飾的比較研究

新疆發現的垂直焊接雙環耳墜與其東邊地區發現的同類物的聯繫也同樣值得關注。東天山地區巴里坤東黑溝墓葬和巴里坤縣西溝遺址1號墓出土的金耳墜在造型、工藝和風格方面與內蒙古阿魯柴登[89]、碾房渠窖藏[90]、西溝畔2號墓，以及河北易縣燕下都辛莊頭M30出土的金耳墜[91]比較接近（圖11，1—7）。尤其東黑溝墓葬和西溝遺址1號墓出土的耳墜上都穿飾一大環四周各焊接一小環或金珠飾，與阿魯柴登出土的一模一樣。西溝遺址1號墓金耳墜上懸掛的螺旋狀墜飾，不僅與中亞地區聯繫緊密，而且與河北易縣燕下都辛莊頭M30出土的金耳墜也很接近。內蒙古阿魯柴登墓葬和碾房渠窖藏發現的耳墜都帶有金葉飾，耳墜上裝飾金葉的例子在阿爾泰地區有不少發現，如尤斯底（Юстыд）、阿卡—阿拉哈（Ак-Алаха）、葉魯尼納墓地出土的耳墜，年代約在公元前6至前3世紀（圖11，8—11）[92]。

值得注意的是，層疊地穿綴綠松石的等料珠，並在墜飾底部焊飾金珠塔的做法在甘肅張家川馬家塬戰國墓地中也能看到（圖10，12）[93]，表明這種裝飾傳統可能以新疆作爲過渡地帶，繼續向東傳播。

總　結

通過垂直焊接雙環耳飾，我們可以看到公元前1千紀下半葉新疆地區，尤其是天山一帶與歐亞草原地區緊密的文化聯繫，這種文化聯繫也向東擴展到甘內蒙古、甘肅地區，並一直延續到之後的歷史時期。天山地帶對於垂直焊接雙環耳飾的傳播起著重要的作用。天山地帶自古以來都是遊牧民族活動的場所，也是古代東西方人群往來的自然通道、文化交流的前沿地帶。天山山間的通道也連通著天山以南的綠洲定居人群與天山以

---

⑧⑨ 田廣金、郭素新《內蒙古阿魯柴登發現的匈奴遺物》，《考古》1980年第4期，圖版拾一，4。

⑨⓪ 伊克昭盟文物工作站《內蒙古東勝市碾房渠發現金銀器窖藏》，《考古》1991年第5期，406頁，圖三，1、2。

⑨① 陳靜《戰國時期燕國金飾件賞析》，《東方收藏》2014年第6期，70頁，圖11。

⑨② В. Д. Кубарев, *Курганы Юстыда*, Новосибирск, Наука, 1991, табл. XXI-12, 13；Н. В. Полосьмак, *Всадники Укока*,Новосибирск, Издательство «ИНФОЛИО-пресс», 2001, с. 163, рис. 109, б；Н. В. Полосьмак, "Исследование второго кургана могильника Пазырыкской культуры Ак- Алаха I", *Археологические Вести*, №.4, 1995, с. 93, рис. 4; Ю. Ф. Кирюшин, Я. В. Фролов, "Комплекс памятников эпохи раннего железа в районе с. Елунино", Сборник научных трудов, *Древние Поселения Алтая*, Барнаул, Издательство Алтайского государственного университета, 1998, с. 136, рис. 11-1.

⑨③ 早期秦文化聯合考古隊等《張家川馬家塬戰國墓地2007—2008年發掘簡報》，《文物》2009年第10期，42頁，圖四七。

圖10

1. 東黑溝墓地（M011：11、M011：6）　2. 西溝遺址1號墓　3. 阿魯柴登墓地　4. 碾房渠窖藏　5. 西溝畔2號墓　6、7. 燕下都辛莊頭M30　8. 尤斯底　9. 阿卡—阿拉哈1號墓地1號墓　10. 阿卡—阿拉哈1號墓地2號墓　11. 葉魯尼納墓地　12. 馬家塬戰國墓地（M14：4-13）（全部金）

北的草原遊牧人群，承擔新疆地區內部文化交流的橋梁作用[94]。

耳飾作爲一種重要的人體裝飾物，對文化特徵有著極強的指示作用。相互之間有著密切聯繫的人群可能使用相似形制風格的耳飾，反映著他們在相似的文化背景中產生的認同感。耳飾也可以通過貿易交換從一地流轉到另一地，於是它成爲不同地區人群貿易往來巨大體系的一個縮影。耳飾作爲一種載體，也傳播著審美價值和工藝。焊接雙環的耳飾樣式帶著濃郁的草原文化的特質，並將穿綴瑪瑙、綠松石和焊飾金珠工藝帶到新疆地區。這些工藝對此後新疆地區及其以東地區的裝飾文化都起著極爲重要的作用。

---

[94] 松田壽男著，陳俊謀譯《古代天山歷史地理學研究》，北京：中央民族學院出版社，1987年，3—5頁。

Study of Earrings with Two Vertically Welded Looms Found in Xinjiang

Lin Lingmei

Earrings with two vertically welded looms were widely spread along the Tianshan area of Xinjiang during the 5th century BC to the 1st century BC. A number of analogues have been found in Sayan-Altai, Semirechye, the Western Tianshan and even the Southern Urals. The east-west and north-south passways in Tianshan played a significant role in the transmission of this type of earring. With Xinjiang as the transit point, earrings with two vertically welded looms spread even further east to Inner Mongolia and Gansu, bringing with them decorations using turquoise and granulation which profoundly influenced the decorative culture of Xinjiang and areas further east in later history.

古代青金石的定名與清朝皇室青金石、催生石來源及使用之探討*

張永江

青金石，古玩收藏界也稱“帝王石”“帝王青”，是一種稀見的天藍色半寶石。地質學上定義爲以含鹼性鋁矽酸鹽礦物爲主的礦石，含有少量的黄鐵礦、方解石等雜質的隱晶質集合體。現代已經作爲一級玉石，與紅寶石、綠松石、珊瑚等並稱。

現代寶石界對青金石的分級，主要依據顏色、純度、大小標準分爲四級：青金石級、青金級、金克浪級和催生石級。其中最低的催生石級定義爲，不含黄鐵礦，含較多白色方解石等雜質礦物，呈藍白混雜或藍星點分佈。這和清代的分類不同。清代青金石、催生石二者並稱，雖關係密切，但屬於兩類寶石。

目前學術界關於青金石的研究，主要集中在以下幾個領域。首先是地質學的寶石鑒定[①]方面，側重研究產地、寶石學特徵、分級和鑒定問題；其次是文物及藝術品鑒賞[②]領域，介紹其質地、工藝和文化價值；其三是史學領域成果，著眼於青金石利用的歷史文化視角[③]，但多屬於一般性的介紹。現在，學術界、收藏界公認，中國青金石的大量利用始於清代，皇室和官方是主要消費者，但只限於零星介紹[④]。青金石在古代中國經歷了怎樣的認知過程？清代爲什麼能夠大量使用青金石？這些青金石的來源和途徑如何？其使用範圍有何規定？都尚未研究。本文通過有關的檔案、文獻記述，試做鉤稽探討。

---

* 本文爲教育部人文社科重點研究基地重大項目“內地化與一體化：清代邊疆民族區域社會發展長期趨勢研究”的階段性成果，項目號：10JJD770019。

① 代表性的如伏修鋒、干福熹、馬波、顧冬紅《青金石產地探源》，《自然科學史研究》2006年第3期；白洪麗《青金石及其鑒藏》，《收藏家》2011年第6期。

② 楊晨《青流雅素，金外之音——談兩件青金石雕山子的藝術價值》，《數位時尚（新視覺藝術）》2013年第2期。

③ 阿布力克木·阿不都熱西提《西域青金石與東西方經濟文化交流》，新疆大學碩士論文，2003年；阿合買提江·艾海提、阿布力克木·阿布都熱西提《青金石古今中外名稱考》，《絲綢之路民族古文字與文化學術討論會會議論文集》，2005年；葉舒憲《蘇美爾青金石神話研究——文明探源的神話學視野》，《中南民族大學學報》2001年第4期。

④ 馮伯群《清代官員的頂子》，《中國檔案報》2001年12月21日；黄德晃《清朝官員的頂戴》，《中國商報》2002年5月23日。

一、清代以前對青金石的認知與青金石定名

青金石作爲寶石在中國使用的歷史，可以早至漢代。但直到今日，人們對它傳入史的認識仍很有限。在中國古代資料中，與青金石有關的美稱有許多，如璆琳、金精、瑾瑜、蘭赤、金螭、青黛、琉璃、瑟瑟等。佛教稱爲吠努離或璧琉璃，來自西方，是佛教七寶之一，也是古代東西方文化交流的見證物。上述名稱常常被研究者作爲青金石的古代稱呼。但實際上，古代對寶石的分類，並沒有現在這樣清晰，上述稱呼是籠統的指碧色（包含藍綠及相近顏色）寶石，包含青金石而非專指青金石。

我們先從學術界的研究和史料上做一番梳理。青金石的信息最早見於《魏書·西域傳》："大月氏國，……自乾陁羅以北五國盡役屬之。世祖時，其國人商販京師，自云能鑄石爲五色瑠璃，於是採礦山中，于京師鑄之。既成，光澤乃美於西方來者。乃詔爲行殿，容百餘人，光色映徹，觀者見之，莫不驚駭，以爲神明所作。自此中國瑠璃遂賤，人不復珍之。"張星烺先生在"五色瑠璃"之下注釋："今代之骨克察河（Kokcha）上流，仍有著名之瑠璃礦（Lapis lazuli）。"[⑤]骨克察河，今譯科克奇河，位於今阿富汗巴達赫尚省，自古以來就是著名的青金石產地。顯然，這裏的"五色瑠璃"，被視爲青金石了。但嚴格講古來瑠璃就是冶煉合成品，是古代玻璃，雖然色澤近似青金石，與取自自然的青金石礦物仍然有别。"璆琳"，對應漢語作"瑠璃"或者"琉璃"。商周時代已經開始煉製，實物亦不鮮見。因此，古代典籍中出現的"璆琳""瑠璃"以及"頗梨"，儘管包含青金石，但多數可以排除在青金石之外。真正與現代青金石含義接近的稱呼應該是"瑟瑟""金精""蘭赤"。這些稱呼的出現，都在南北朝時期之後。瑟瑟，關於其確切含義，學者的看法尚不完全一致。著名東方學家勞費爾認爲，瑟瑟（sit-sit）是薩珊朝波斯的寶石。含義複雜，有時指建築石材（如孔雀石），有時則是裝飾寶石（如翡翠一類）[⑥]。不同時代，瑟瑟所指並不相同。他沒有排除包括青金石的可能。而謝弗則斷定是天青石或青金石[⑦]。語言學者也證明，明代《高昌館雜字》中讀作xixir（sirsir），有譯爲瑪瑙或水晶的。另有一詞Naqewar，漢譯爲"石青"，正確寫法應爲Laqewar，是伊朗語詞Lazhuward的對應詞。因此，瑟瑟包括兩個含義：①指青金石或天青石；②不僅用來指青金石，還可指顏色相近的瑪瑙、綠松石、孔雀石等[⑧]。從史料上看，瑟瑟也見於《魏書·西域傳》："波斯國，……出金、銀、鍮石、珊瑚、琥珀、車渠、馬腦，多大真珠、頗梨、瑠璃、水精、瑟瑟、……等物。"[⑨]"康國，……出馬、駝、驢、……阿薛那香、瑟瑟、麞皮、氍毹、錦、

⑤ 《中西交通史料彙編》第三冊，北京：中華書局，2003年，1337頁。

⑥ 勞費爾《中國伊朗編》，林筠因譯，北京：商務印書館，1964年，345—350頁。

⑦ 謝弗《唐代的外來文明》，吴玉貴譯，北京：中國社會科學出版社，1995年，500頁。

⑧ 阿布力克木、阿布都熱西提《與青金石有關的突厥語寶石名稱考》，《西域研究》2008年第3期，111頁。

⑨ 《魏書》卷102《西域傳》，北京：中華書局，1974年，2270頁。

疊。”[10]既然同一史籍中同時出現了頗梨、瑠璃、瑟瑟的記載，不可能同時與青金石有關。此外，《周書·異域傳下·波斯》記載：“〔波斯國〕又出白象、師子……馬瑙、水晶、瑟瑟。”[11]還有，《新唐書·高仙芝傳》：“仙芝爲人貪，破石，獲瑟瑟十餘斛。”[12]談到唐西域邊將高仙芝攻破中亞地區屬於昭武九姓集團的石國，獲取大量寶石。石國即今中亞塔什干城，“東南有大山，產瑟瑟”。大山，應該是興都庫什山。《冊府元龜》載，同屬昭武九姓的康國（撒瑪律幹）也產瑟瑟，但應該是貿易所得。開元五年，康國王還遣使向唐朝進貢毛錦、青黛[13]。可貴的是，《新唐書》還記載了著名的寶石產地庫克察河流域。當時這一地區歸屬于俱蘭國，緊鄰吐火羅國。“俱蘭，或曰俱羅弩，曰屈浪拿，與吐火羅接。環地三千里，南大雪山，北俱魯河。出金精，琢石取之。”還提到吐火羅國北部有頗黎山，在開元、天寶年間數次向唐朝“紅碧玻璃”[14]。類似記載也見於《冊府元龜》，開元二十九年，吐火羅遣使獻紅頗黎，碧頗黎，生瑪瑙、生金精等物[15]。按張星烺先生注釋，俱蘭，或曰俱羅弩，曰屈浪拿，名見玄奘《西域記》卷十二[16]，其原音爲kuran，在今骨克察河（Kokcha R.）上流，拉其瓦特（Lajwart）地方，以產琉璃馳名[17]。與此記載可以相互印證的還有《馬可波羅遊記》的相關記述，“此州出產巴剌思紅寶石（rabisbalais），此寶石甚美，而價甚貴。……同一境內別有一山，出產瑟瑟（azur，lapis-lazuli），其瑩澤爲世界最。產於礦脈中，與銀礦同”[18]。這裏azur、lapis-lazuli譯爲“瑟瑟”，但一般直接譯爲“青金石”。勞費爾同樣引證了這一段，但中譯本逕自譯爲“青金石”。勞費爾還引用了馬可波羅研究專家亨利·玉爾的注釋：“lajwurd礦（由此字轉寫出l'azur和lazuli）一如紅寶石礦，馳名已久。礦在科克恰河上游之可蘭山谷中揚甘地帶。通俗的語原是Hamah-kan或‘萬礦山’。1838年伍德曾視察這些礦山。”[19]還提到最優等的在布哈拉出售。綜合中西兩種史料。可以確認以下幾點：①現今阿富汗東北部，毗連塔吉克斯坦、烏茲別克斯坦的興都庫什山區自古就是出產包含青金石在內的各種寶石的富礦區；②金精就是青金石，提取方法是在原礦石（生金精）中“琢制”[20]；③唐代的青黛、瑟瑟、琉璃，一定包含青金石在內。所以直到民國時代，馮承鈞、張星烺仍用“琉璃”“瑟瑟”指代青金石。

---

⑩ 《魏書》卷102《西域傳》，北京：中華書局，1974年，2281頁。

⑪ 《周書》卷50《異域傳》下，北京：中華書局，1974年，920頁。

⑫ 《新唐書》卷135《高仙芝傳》，北京：中華書局，1974年，4578頁。

⑬ 《冊府元龜》卷966、971，北京：中華書局，1985年。

⑭ 《新唐書》卷221《西域傳》（下），6252頁。

⑮ 《冊府元龜》卷971。

⑯ 《大唐西域記》卷12，上海：上海人民出版社，1977年。原文爲“屈浪拿國，睹貨邏（即吐火羅）國故地也，……有山岩中，多出金精，琢析其石，然後得之”。

⑰ 《中西交通史料彙編》第三冊，1408—1409頁。

⑱ 馮承鈞譯《馬可波羅遊記》第1卷第46章，《巴達哈傷州》，上海：上海書店出版社，2000年，75頁。

⑲ 勞費爾《中國伊朗編》，林筠因譯，350頁。

⑳ 勞費爾不很肯定，但大體承認“唐時金精似指青金石”。勞費爾《中國伊朗編》，林筠因譯，349頁。

另一方面，史料也提示我們：至遲到元代，人們已經開始意識到青金石與綠松石的區別，從而使用新的稱呼加以區別。著名的例子是出使西亞常德口述，劉鬱整理的《西使記》中的兩處記載。一處記載報達（巴格達）的富庶，稱"所產大珠曰太歲強（彈）、蘭石、瑟瑟、金剛鑽之類"。校注者陳得芝注曰："蘭石，薄乃德（俄國學者）注稱可能是指天青石（lapis lazuli）的波斯語名（lajward）之首音。瑟瑟，薄乃德注稱，並非G.Pauthier（法國漢學家頗節）所言樂器，而是一種寶石。"李時珍《本草綱目》卷八"寶石"條："《山海經》言騩山多玉，淒水出焉，西注於海中。多採石。採石即寶石也，碧者，唐人謂之瑟瑟；紅者，宋人謂之靺鞨。今通呼爲寶石。"另一處說"蘭赤生西南海山石中，有五色，鴨思價最高"。注釋指出："蘭赤、鴨思，均爲寶石的譯名。前者可能復原爲碧琉璃（lapis lazuli）的波斯語名Lajward；後者似可復原爲阿拉伯語的yashm/yashb（碧玉——引者注）。"[21]可見當時漢語中出現了青金石的新名稱"蘭石"或"蘭赤"，是當地波斯語、阿拉伯語稱呼的漢語音譯。因爲常德身臨其地，有條件將其與瑟瑟區分開。不過，這個新名稱只此一見，同樣生活在元代江南的陶宗儀就不知道這一名稱。他專門記述了五種"回回石頭"，包括紅石頭、綠石頭、鴉鶻、貓睛和甸子，沒有提到瑟瑟和蘭石。與青金石有關的應該是鴉鶻。鴉鶻也稱亞姑，有紅、青、黄、白各類。青亞姑名下列又有三種："青亞姑，上等深青色；你蘭，中等淺青色；屋撲你蘭，下等如冰樣，帶石，渾青色。"[22]陶宗儀專門請教過回回商人，"鴉鶻"一名無疑來自阿拉伯語。應該是yagut（寶石）一詞的音譯。在江南，"鴉鶻"更流行，直到明代，談到域外寶石的書籍常常提到"鴉鶻石"，留下了"鴉青""鴉青色"等形容詞。而"蘭石""蘭赤"在內地社會上並未普及。常德眼中的瑟瑟，江南陶宗儀稱爲"甸子"，也稱"靛子"，就是綠松石。

明代資料中仍有瑟瑟，但所指似乎已轉向綠松石。明初所修《元史》記述成宗七年六月"西京道宣慰使法忽魯丁以瑟瑟二千五百余斤鬻於官，爲鈔一萬一千九百餘錠。有旨除御榻所用外，餘未用者宜悉還之"。至大二年八月"詹事院臣啟金州獻瑟瑟洞，請遣使采之，帝曰：'所寶惟賢，瑟瑟何用焉；若此者，後勿複聞'"[23]。數量如此之多的瑟瑟，只能是綠松石。到明後期，沈德符《萬曆野獲編·外國·烏思藏》則明言："其官章飾，最尚瑟瑟；瑟瑟者，緑珠也。"清楚地將瑟瑟定義爲綠色寶珠，即西藏常見的綠松石。同時，在明代的官方文獻中我們第一次明確地看到了"青金石"一詞的出現。《明實錄》中記載："禮部言，比土魯番速壇阿黑麻王並其妻哈屯呵嗒各具番書，遣使貢馬。本部已請賜馬價、表裏。此外又貢磁（硫）黄、青金石，非邊關驗放之數未敢進收。"[24]明代嚴從簡的《殊域周諮錄》也提到哈密部落"其貢有玉、速來蠻石、青

㉑ 陳得芝《［常德］〈西使記〉校注》，《中華文史論叢》2015年第1期，99頁。

㉒ 陶宗儀《南村輟耕錄》卷7《回回石頭》，北京：中華書局，1958年，84頁。

㉓ 《元史》卷21《成宗本紀》，453頁；卷24《仁宗本紀》，北京：中華書局，1974年，537頁。

㉔ 《明孝宗實錄》卷29，弘治二年八月壬子，臺北："中研院"史語所校印本，1962年。

金石、把咱石等”[25]。與“蘭石”“蘭赤”等譯名不同，青金石是漢語標準的名稱，一直使用至今。但青金石這一名詞在明代資料中也很罕見，如前所述，在江南，仍流行元代以來的“鴉鶻石”一類外來語譯名。推測當時只限於極少數直接接觸西域貢使者才得以獲知和使用這一名稱。《明實錄》的記載當然來自嘉峪關的報告，而嚴從簡則長期擔任禮部行人司官員，專事貢使接待工作。前述西域吐魯番王阿黑麻夫婦進貢的青金石，雖然被明朝拒收，但可知明代的青金石仍然來自中亞方向。而且，無論是吐魯番還是哈密，都不出產青金石，這些貢物顯然也是通過貿易等方式從更西方的阿富汗獲得。

有研究者認爲，青金石在中國社會流行，始於明清時期。這一看法並不準確。明代無論文獻還是實物中都少見青金石的信息。上引《明實錄》等記載雖然重要，卻是僅有的記載。原因何在？恐怕與接觸條件有關。即取決於中原與西域的政治交往與物資流動。明前期，在嘉峪關外保留著哈密衛等軍政機構，其重要性在於“西域三十八國入貢經哈密”，“令爲西域之喉襟，以通西番之消息”[26]。明與西域諸國維持著政治聯繫的同時，保有與中亞的寶石產區物資交流通道。這裏應該提及，明朝皇室和上流社會崇尚奢靡，玉石的消費需求很大，主要仰給於中亞方面的朝貢貿易。皇室優先選取上等玉石，通過實物賞賜完成交易。剩餘次等玉石才能出售，獲得銀兩。好玉價值很高，索價萬兩白銀。由於從皇室所獲得物資價值有限，與市場形成巨大反差，貢使遂想方設法行賄主管官員減少貢玉，留下好玉出售獲利；而士大夫也請托這些官員購買玉石。長期尋租的結果，終於釀成嘉靖四年禮部主管貢玉官員陳九川等勾結他人，侵吞天方國貢玉，“竊賣利己”的大案，牽出禮部通事、翰林譯臣、審案官員直至大學士等多人[27]。

由於政治紛爭，嘉靖初年明朝所設的哈密衛最終被葉爾羌汗國吞併，之後明於嘉峪關閉關絕貢，切斷了與西域的聯繫。儘管此後中亞的寶石轉而遠道繞經印度洋，從海路輾轉運到廣州，但畢竟極爲不便。由此青金石的來源斷絕，明代社會不見記載和使用也就不難理解了。

簡而言之，青金石進入中國並被認知，大致經歷了四個階段。①漢代到隋代，一般名之爲“璆琳”“瑠璃”（琉璃）以及“頗梨”，系外來語，混同在古老朦朧的寶石（包括人工製品）群中。②唐宋時代，主要名“瑟瑟”，偶爾稱“金精”。前者爲寶石統稱，外來語；後者爲專稱，漢語專名，但不普及。③元代，多稱呼“鴉鶻”，寶石統稱，外來語。偶爾稱“蘭石”“蘭赤”，屬外來語專稱。④明清時代，“青金石”的漢語專名確立，並沿用至今。偶見“金星石”的用例[28]，應該是唐代“金精”的餘緒。在明代部分時段，部分地區，仍使用“鴉鶻石”的舊稱。

㉕ 余思黎點校本誤斷爲“其貢有玉、速來蠻、石青、金石、把咱石等”，意義遂不可解。見“中外交通史籍叢刊”本《殊域周諮錄》，北京：中華書局，1993年，428頁。

㉖ 《殊域周諮錄》，412、414頁。

㉗ 《殊域周諮錄》，394—400頁。

㉘ 李賢《明一統志》卷89，《于闐》，《景印文淵閣四庫全書》第473冊，臺北：商務印書館，1986年，886頁。

二、清代皇室青金石的來源及使用

古代中國長期不識青金石的真面目，主要原因是其稀有和罕見。考古文物資料顯示，直到清代以前，利用青金石鑲嵌製作的實物都很少，且多爲小件器物，如戒指、石硯鑲嵌物等，未見大件器物。

清初，至少在雍正以前，文獻中關於青金石的信息仍然較少。基本上都是蒙古、西藏地方首領作爲貢禮進獻的青金石念珠。

《清太宗實錄》在元年（1636）記載："察哈爾國公主，具盛筵進上。複獻金茶桶、金盆、金壺、玉數珠、珍珠衫、蟒緞、糚緞、翠緞、倭緞衣服，嵌松子石、青金石鞦轡等物。"[29]所述爲新俘獲的蒙古大汗林丹汗的公主向新主人皇太極呈獻一批財寶，包含有綠松石、青金石嵌飾物件。應該是蒙古汗廷世代相傳的寶物。由此滿洲政權初識青金石，其時，長城以內還是明朝崇禎帝的天下。

崇德八年有歸化城蒙古甲喇章京套布克向清皇后進獻青金石念珠一串[30]。

順治四年，青海顧實汗福晉獻禮順治皇后、蒙古墨爾根濟農獻禮多爾衮青金石念珠各一串[31]。

順治六年西藏商吉德巴獻禮攝政王多爾衮青金石念珠。

順治九年四世班禪呈獻順治皇帝的禮物中包括青金石佛像一尊，青金石念珠一串[32]。

同年（1653）冬，五世達賴喇嘛應清廷之邀自西藏來京晉見順治皇帝，南苑初見時進呈了以珊瑚、琥珀、青金石念珠數串、氆氇、蔗糖、唵叭香數包以及馬匹、羔皮各千件爲主的貢禮[33]。

順治十年返藏途中駐留青海的達賴喇嘛回獻清廷禮物中包括青金石數珠。

順治十一年，顧實汗以受封金冊金印事回謝禮物也有青金石念珠一串。

順治十五年，五世達賴奏請聖安的隨書獻禮有青金石念珠。

康熙三年，五世達賴貢獻清廷的禮單中有青金石念珠一串108顆[34]。

青海西寧的寺院也有貢進青金石念珠的，如順治年間開始"西寧西納演教寺國師，貢舍利、琥珀數珠、珊瑚數珠、青金石數珠、菩提數珠、花毯、西絨毯、氆氇、腰刀、

㉙ 《清太宗實錄》卷32，崇德元年十一月〇甲辰，北京：中華書局，1986年。

㉚ 《清內秘書院蒙古文檔案彙編漢譯》，崇德八年八月二十七日"歸化城土默特部古祿格章京爲首所獻禮物記錄"，北京：社科文獻出版社，2015年。

㉛ 《清內秘書院蒙古文檔案彙編漢譯》，順治五年三月十日收"顧實汗福晉表請皇后安並獻禮物書"；"墨爾根濟農爲問安獻禮事致皇叔父王文"。

㉜ 《清內秘書院蒙古文檔案彙編漢譯》。

㉝ 《五世達賴喇嘛羅桑嘉措傳》下冊，陳慶英等譯，臺北：全佛文化事業有限公司，2003年，488頁。

㉞ 均見於《清內秘書院蒙古文檔案彙編漢譯》。

猞猁猻皮、艾葉豹皮、金錢豹皮、狼皮、狐皮、馬、駝、牛、酥油等物。”[35]其來源尚不清楚。

這些來自西藏的青金石製品，是否西藏出產尚不清楚。但是，存在著經由準噶爾蒙古信衆之手自外界輸入西藏的可能性。例如，乾隆九年、十三年在準噶爾使團赴藏熬茶的檔案中記錄了進獻大昭寺的禮物有青金石鉢兩個，青金石輪兩個，青金石盤子一個[36]。當然，這些都是成品，而非原石。

上述經由蒙古、西藏上層進獻渠道進入清廷的青金石製品作何用途不得而知。無論如何，大規模地制度性使用青金石，的確是從清代開始的。

清初開始，皇室人員冠服較多使用青金石作爲裝飾。包括：

（1）皇帝祭天時佩戴的朝珠、朝帶。尋常時朝珠用珍寶雜飾，“惟祀天以青金石爲飾”。祭祀時龍文金方版朝帶“其飾祀天用青金石”。這是因爲青金石“其色如天”，以其裝飾可以營造“天人合一”的氣氛，增強儀式的莊嚴感。

（2）皇帝儀仗。凡遇皇帝升殿，或祭祀壇、廟，除鑾儀衛儀仗外，設金頂黃糚緞曲柄傘，並備嵌珊瑚、松子石、鋄金玲瓏四方鞍十副，夏季用青金石、珊瑚、松子石、鋄金玲瓏、西牛尾踢胸，冬季用嵌青金石、珊瑚、松子石、鋄金玲瓏、染就青狐尾踢胸[37]。

（3）皇后、貴妃、妃嬪冠服。皇后冬、夏朝冠，均飾以珍珠或東珠，間以金銜青金石結或青金石珠。皇貴妃朝冠大體相同。其餘妃嬪朝冠、皇子、皇孫福晉朝冠也鑲嵌青金石結或青金石珠。區別只在珍珠數量遞減。

（4）親王、郡王甲胄、櫜鞬、佩刀都鑲嵌有青金石[38]。

（5）奉恩將軍冠頂、縣君額駙冠頂，都飾以青金石[39]。

清廷何時實施這一規定，記載並不明晰。有確切時間記載的是，奉恩將軍冠頂用青金石在雍正八年，縣君額駙冠頂用青金石在雍正五年[40]。後來在乾隆五十一年，又補充制定了固倫公主朝冠飾用青金石的規定[41]。

雍正五年（1727）以後，清朝官方文獻如《實錄》《會典》等書中關於青金石的記載驟然出現並增多，主要是制訂了關於青金石使用的規定。是年九月，議定了王公大臣官員等階層的常服頂帶規制。“尋議，諸王及大小臣工平時所戴暖帽涼帽，俱照朝帽頂分別，令其戴用。凡親王、世子、郡王、長子、貝勒、貝子、入八分公，俱用紅寶石

㉟ 《清會典事例》，卷986，《理藩院·甘肅河州等處喇嘛貢物》，北京：中華書局，1991年。

㊱ 《清代軍機處滿文熬茶檔》，《祝藏辦事副都統索拜奏報準噶爾使臣等進獻達賴喇嘛等物件數目折》，檔號：03-1742-1-24；《侍郎玉保等奏報準噶爾人等進獻各寺廟物件佈施銀兩數目折附件》，檔號：03-1742-1-21，上海：上海古籍出版社，2010年。

㊲ 允祿等監修：《大清會典》（雍正朝），卷233，《近代中國史料叢刊三編》789冊，臺北：文海出版社，1995年。

㊳ 《清會典事例》，卷893，《工部·軍器》，北京：中華書局影印本，1991年。

㊴ 《清會典事例》卷326、327，《禮部·冠服》。

㊵ 《清會典事例》卷327，《禮部·冠服》。

㊶ 《清會典事例》卷1188，《內務府·典禮》。

頂。未入八分公、固倫額駙、和碩額駙，民公、侯、伯、鎮國將軍及一品大臣，俱用珊瑚頂。輔國將軍、奉國將軍、多羅額駙、二品、三品大臣，俱用起花珊瑚頂。奉恩將軍、固山額駙、及四品官員，俱用青金石頂。五品、六品官員，俱用水晶石頂。七品以下及進士、舉人、貢生，俱用金頂。生員、監生，俱用銀頂。從之。”[42]這一次規定沒有收錄到《會典事例》中，是否實施不得而知。雍正八年，再次議定二品以下官員帽頂規制，重申“奉恩將軍及四品官，俱用青金石或藍色涅玻璃”[43]。這一記載見於《會典事例》，“四品官上銜青金石或藍色涅玻璃，中飾小藍寶石”[44]。此前，按照順治二年制定的冠服規定，“四品官冠用鏤花金頂，上銜藍寶石，中飾小藍寶石”[45]。按清朝規制，正、從四品官包括京外文武數十種官缺，特别是數量極大的地方道員、知府、佐領、都司，涉及數千人。突然由藍寶石改用青金石，雖然只是一顆頂珠，但總量也會不少，而且並非一次性使用，再加上皇室的使用，都需要有較爲穩定的來源。那麼，清朝的青金石來源在哪裏呢？

除了前述青金石製品作爲貢物或禮品進入清廷外，至少目前我們尚未看到平定準噶爾政權以前清朝獲得青金石原料的記載。這裏還只能推測。考慮到當時青金石產地的唯一性，主要的來源和方向只能是蔥嶺以西，沿古老的絲綢之路經嘉峪關進入内地。這條通道的必經之路——新疆（當時的西域）在準噶爾汗國的控制之下，清朝與準噶爾之間雖然兵戎相向，但真正隔絶交往的時間並不長，不過是1688—1697年的十年時間。其餘多數時間中存在著朝貢和遣使名義下的貿易往來。玉石作爲商品之一，雖不常見，應該有輸入。康熙末年，清朝的西、北兩路大軍扼守巴里坤和科布多，控制了新疆與内地的交易通道。雍正五年開始，清軍採取攻勢，一度進至哈密和額爾齊斯河地區。清朝從這一方向獲得青金石並不令人意外。《會典事例・兵部・郵政》中保存著一條規定“又定，西北兩路將軍大臣回繳朱批摺奏，應由奏事之便匯繳。其每年恭進馬匹玉石果膏等項，交與該處，遇有卡倫侍衛内換班引見人員之便，照料解送”[46]。可見，西、北兩路將軍每年都要向清廷繳送玉石等項物資。此外，也存在著西藏輸入青金石的可能。由於和碩特蒙古顧實汗與五世達賴喇嘛接受了清朝的冊封，所以西藏經由青海、甘肅進入内地的商路是暢通的。康熙末年，義大利人德西迪里曾報導西藏婦女穿用青金石的飾物。約成書於乾隆年間的《西藏記》也記載“洛隆宗南去二日，有浪岩山，產青金石”。洛隆宗即今西藏江達縣。如果這一礦藏在清初已經開採利用的話，輸入内地也不困難。

毫無疑問，清朝真正徹底解決青金石的來源問題，是從平定了準噶爾勢力，控制了新疆，從而掌控了絲綢之路開始的。

目前還沒有找到平準時期清朝從新疆直接獲得青金石的直接證據。但是，當時清朝

[42] 《清世宗實錄》卷61，雍正五年九月丙寅。

[43] 《清世宗實錄》卷87，雍正八年冬十月庚子。

[44] 《清會典事例》卷327，《禮部・冠服》。

[45] 《清會典事例》卷327，《禮部・冠服》。

[46] 《清會典事例》卷699，《兵部・郵政・給驛二》。

內務府儲存和使用青金石的記錄也許可以從側面證實。已經公佈的乾隆時期內務府造辦處的《行取物料清冊》和《收貯物料清冊》以年爲單位，清楚地記載了每一種材料存留和加工、使用情況。青金石屬於“玉作”，其資料如表1所示。

表1

增減數量 年代	舊存	新進
乾隆二十五年	3兩7錢	青金字4個，青金珠15個，青金鑲嵌27塊（重五分），青金小墜1件[47]
乾隆二十六年	青金小花籃1件，青金滿漢字12件，青金字12個，青金鑲嵌57塊（重3兩7錢3分4厘），青金帶面6塊，重1兩5錢，青金珠大小52個，青金塔大小4個，重1錢5分，碎青金6錢5分，青金墜角1件	2兩1錢4分[48]
乾隆二十七年	4錢1分	青金石腰箍4個，青金小花籃1個，青金字24個[49]
乾隆二十八年	青金帶面6塊，青金珠大小44個，青金塔大小4個，青金墜角1件，青金石腰箍4個[50]	未查到
乾隆二十九年	28兩1錢8分8厘[51]	無
乾隆三十年	27兩1錢9分8厘[52]	無

乾隆二十四年清軍底定新疆，其時清宮庫存青金石只有3兩7錢，此後則逐漸增加，五年之後竟然增加到9倍數量。其中關聯，耐人尋味。

乾隆四十三年發生了高樸偷賣官玉萬餘斤的大案。乾隆帝曾說：“自平定回部以來，所產玉石，除文官所餘，招商變價外，其回民違禁私賣，奸商潛蹤私買，載回內地，制器牟利者，並不始於此時。”[53]爲防止此類事件，清朝從新疆大規模運送已開採的玉石到北京。爲此在喀喇沙爾所屬10處軍台，共設置鐵輪車18輛。運送玉石完竣後這些車輛分給直接各站使用[54]。

催生石、青金石雖然不是嚴格意義上的玉石，但作爲有特殊用途的寶石，應該是與玉石一起繳送的。而且，在清宮，青金石的加工也歸屬內務府的“玉作”管理。

青金石記載較少，大概有兩方面原因。一是此物非新疆出產，輸入數量本身就少，另一方面與清朝政策上的寬鬆管理也有關係。青金石雖然稀有，但不是玉石，不在官

㊼ 《清宮內務府造辦處檔案總匯》第26冊，北京：人民出版社，2005年，12、20頁。

㊽ 《清宮內務府造辦處檔案總匯》第27冊，4、92頁。

㊾ 《清宮內務府造辦處檔案總匯》第27冊，97、761、769頁。

㊿ 《清宮內務府造辦處檔案總匯》第28冊，582頁。

(51) 《清宮內務府造辦處檔案總匯》第29冊，303頁。

(52) 《清宮內務府造辦處檔案總匯》第29冊，315頁。

(53) 《清高宗實錄》卷1070，乾隆四十三年十一月丁亥。

(54) 《清會典事例》卷695，《兵部·郵政·驛車》。

方的壟斷和禁令範圍。早期甚至不徵收關稅。這裏通過幾個案例予以說明。一是乾隆四十六年新疆宜禾知州瑚圖里違法案，追查出其家人陸明與迪化州商人張五合夥做生意，經營玉器首飾，以465兩5分白銀在南路買獲青金石72塊，計508斤4兩。被起獲後"隨押送交軍機處查收辦理"[55]。在一起偶發的案件中交易的青金石就達到500餘斤，遠超過清宮的庫存。二是乾隆五十五年查獲商民張子敬私販俄羅斯皮張案，皮張自然沒收，同時查獲的還有催生石、青金石，"並非禁物，亦令入官"。乾隆諭令陝甘總督勒保"令將秀林查獲之此項皮張、催生石、青金石中應送京城者，送往京城；其餘次者，俱在彼變價辦理"[56]。其三，同一年，哈密辦事大臣伊桑阿奏報，查獲民人瑪希金行囊攜帶催生石30餘斤、青金石30斤。乾隆帝明確諭令"白玉石、綠玉石系產自回地瑪納斯山河，特令嚴禁私自開採，而回地產物，並未蓋行禁止。催生石、青金石並非玉石，毋庸禁止"[57]。說明到乾隆後期，中亞輸入的青金石已不稀見，以至於政策上已無須限制。其四，乾隆五十六年，葉爾羌辦事大臣明興奏稱"巴達克山前來貿易攜入之催生石、青金石內，因青金石不收稅銀，奸詐商人爲逃稅謊報者甚多"。請示嚴加核查。對此，乾隆帝明令"葉爾羌僅將貿易之催生石收稅，青金石（不）收稅銀，均系原任大臣辦理錯謬。今明興等既查出，擬定嗣後貿易之青金石，較催生石加收十倍稅銀，尚屬在理。即照伊等所奏辦理可也"[58]。由此可知，此前的三十年，新疆對青金石的輸入貿易是免稅的。而且青金石產地的巴達克山商人直接進入新疆葉爾羌口岸貿易。免稅政策導致徵稅的催生石冒充青金石免稅入境貿易。另外，結合前引史料，青金石貿易額動輒數十斤，輸入量已達到一定的規模。青金石之路重新打開，促進了中國內地青金石加工、消費的繁榮。

清廷在必要的冠服朝珠、頂戴製作之外，佛珠、佛塔、佛像、藏經盒等宗教法物也離不開青金石，娛樂賞玩性質的青金石藝術品加工也出現了。存世的青金石作品中，大部分是乾隆朝製作的。特别是大件作品。見於拍賣記錄和文獻報導的就有：

"清乾隆青金石松泉人物山子"（寬19厘米）

"乾隆青金石御制詩山子"（寬30.3厘米）

"乾隆青金石獸面圖龍耳蓋爐"

"青金石訪友圖山子"（高36.5厘米）

"松間浮雲暢舟山子"（高18.5厘米）

"清青金石嵌珠寶象"

---

[55] 中國第一歷史檔案館藏"軍機處錄副奏摺"，烏魯木齊都統明亮《奏報起獲瑚圖裏家人陸明有寄存青金石事》，檔號：03-1317-013，縮微號：092-2188。

[56] 《乾隆朝滿文寄信檔譯編》，乾隆五十五年十一月初六日《寄諭陝甘總督勒保著將查獲商民私販禁物挑選送京餘者變價》，長沙：嶽麓書社，2011年。

[57] 《乾隆朝滿文寄信檔譯編》，乾隆五十五年三月初一日《寄諭陝甘總督勒保等著民人攜帶之物非回地瑪納斯玉石概勿查禁》。

[58] 《乾隆朝滿文寄信檔譯編》，乾隆五十六年五月二十四日《寄諭葉爾羌辦事侍郎明興等著嗣後攜來貿易之青金石俱照所請收稅》。

“青金石山水人物御題詩文插屏”

特別是北京瀚海拍賣的“清乾隆青金石描金御題詩七巧插屏”，體量巨大，製作精美。上有乾隆御筆：“偶詠《宋人名流集藻畫冊》中李迪《雞雛待飼圖》，惻然有懷于災壤饑民之無救也。因摹其畫，即用題迪畫韻成什，命泐石以示爲民父母之官。”之後是御題五言詩一首：“雙雛如仰望，其母竟何之。未解率場啄，誰憐空腹饑。展圖一絜矩，觸目切深思。災壤民待哺，慎哉群有司。”落款“戊申中秋上澣御筆”[59]。

這幅作品有助於解答這樣一個問題，清廷爲什麽會選定青金石作爲道、府等四品官的頂戴？直接原因恐怕與青金石本身的顏色有關，統治者著眼的不是材質的貴賤而是“其色如天”的顏色寓意。地方道府一級官員作爲“爲民父母之官”，歷來被小民視作“青天大老爺”，青金石帽頂恰似頭頂青天，誠當如包拯一般爲民做主。這也可以解釋，在雍正朝未採用青金石之前，四品官帽頂使用藍寶石或者藍色涅玻璃的理由。

要回答清朝皇室爲何如此重視、珍愛青金石這一外來寶石的問題，就涉及更大範圍的民族文化心理層面。一方面，青金石作爲藏傳佛教的傳統七寶，和藏、蒙民族一樣，滿族出於同樣的宗教情感尊崇和喜愛。更根本的原因，則在於青金石的顏色與滿族的民族文化的心理底色吻合一致。這個心理底色，就是靛藍——天青色。滿族從上到下，無分貴賤，都喜愛和尊崇這一顏色。其形成當然有長久的歷史基礎，也不排除鄰近民族如蒙古文化傳播的影響。

青金石的增加，使清廷不再只是單向地接受來自西藏的禮物，也開始回贈。乾隆四十六年，爲了表彰妥善處理六世班禪意外圓寂於內地事件的西藏堪布額爾德尼諾門汗阿旺粗勒提木，乾隆帝賞賜的禮物中就包括青金石佛頭珊瑚素念珠一掛[60]。

嘉道時期，清廷進一步擴大了青金石的使用範圍。開始將青金石製品賞賜給作戰有功的大臣和將領。如嘉慶六年，賞賜作戰有功的賽沖阿青金石扳指一個。九年，賞前線作戰的賽沖阿、豐紳、馬瑜、田朝貴等將領以青金石扳指[61]。道光二十二年，賞賜大臣青金石紅喜字扳指一個，由內務府領發[62]。

光緒年間，清廷仿照西方國家實行授勳制度，稱爲“寶星之制”。青金石和其它寶石一樣被選爲裝飾材料。寶星分五等，分別授贈不同身份的外籍人士，其中第四等授各國兵弁，“四等，用法藍地銀雙龍中嵌青金石綠龍醬色帶”[63]。

另一方面，內地民間社會也有機會消費青金石，甚至形成了一定的市場。筆記、野史、小說中屢見記載。

例如，清代北方朝野流行的青金石數珠，乾嘉時在嶺南也有製作和銷售，“數珠

---

[59] 參見白洪麗《青金石及其鑒藏》。

[60] 《乾隆朝滿文寄信檔譯編》，乾隆四十六年正月三十日《寄諭駐藏辦事副都統恒瑞著賞賜堪布額爾德尼諾門汗阿旺粗勒提木》，檔號：03-136-1-007。

[61] 《嘉慶帝起居注》，嘉慶六年正月二十日；嘉慶九年八月，桂林：廣西師範大學出版社，2006年。

[62] 《清代軍機處隨手登記檔》，道光二十二年十二月初四日，北京：國家圖書館出版社，2013年。

[63] 邵之棠輯《皇朝經世文統編》卷107，《雜著三》，光緒二十七年刊本。

一百八粒，或用碧霞洗，或用珊瑚及青金石、伽南香之類，價不過三四千金。”[64]

在揚州，傳聞明末已經有周姓富豪創制鑲嵌百寶的工藝，號稱“周制”，“其法以金、銀、寶石、真珠、珊瑚、碧玉、翡翠、瑪瑙、玳瑁、硨磲、青金石、綠松石、螺甸、象牙、蜜蠟、沉香，雕爲山水、人物、樹木、樓臺、花卉、翎毛，嵌於花梨漆板之上，大而屏風、桌椅、窗戶、書架，小而筆筒、茶具、硯匣，五色陸離，真未有之奇玩也。”[65]清中期修建的市肆中有玉寶塔一座，高九尺九寸，仿報恩寺塔式樣製作，分九重，“第一層白玉佛四。八方殿宇牆垣，皆刻玉佛八十有八。其餘八層，內貯金佛四尊。門外以青金石爲扁額”[66]。

清後期，甚至個人也有了消費青金石的能力。安徽歙縣一位許姓徽商，家資數百萬兩，開鋪肆四十餘處，後以子孫豪奢張揚，許翁懼禍而一朝散盡家財。俞樾曾親見此人，“其冠戴青金石，頂綴鶡羽藍翎焉，而意氣猶甚雄爽也”[67]。此翁職歷不詳，也可能通過花錢捐納獲得了佩戴四品官青金石帽頂的資格。

儘管稀見，但市場上已經有了公開的交易。長江流域的水陸碼頭上，“金、銀、珠玉、水晶、瑪瑙、密蠟、翡翠、珊瑚、青金石、碧霞洗、古窯器、新磁，以及朝珠、念珠、手串、齋戒牌、如意盒、香囊，無不鱗集”[68]。

最後，青金石的廣泛使用，也促進了知識界對青金石的正確認知和概念的精確化。至遲在乾隆時期編纂的《五體清文鑒》中，含義分類上已經清楚地將其與磁、琺瑯等人工製品分類在一起。對應的蒙古語作sil，滿語作aikan，維吾爾語音譯作loli/luli。而青金石則和珊瑚、綠松石等自然物放在一起，和漢語的“青金石”相對，滿語、蒙古語均作“nomin”，藏語作“mu-men”，維吾爾語作“lajward”[69]，各有其命名。社會上，青金石也作爲專名固定了下來。表明在漢語世界裏，青金石終於走完了其漫長的認知過程。

三、神秘的催生石

催生石（hasten parturition stone）是青金石的一個品種。當青金石中混雜的白色方解石多於藍色時，呈淺藍或灰藍色，又名雪花催生石。從寶石的角度看，催生石品質不高，也不受重視。清代以前，文獻上鮮見記載。經常爲人們所提及的是明代朱孟震《西南夷風土記》中的一段記載，“土產，孟密東產寶石、產金，南產銀，北產鐵，西產催生文石”。孟密，也寫作猛緬，指今天緬甸北部。據此可知，緬甸是催生石的一個產

---

[64] 趙翼《簷曝雜記》卷4，“廣東珠價”，北京：中華書局，1982年，61頁。

[65] 徐珂《清稗類鈔》，“工藝類·王盧仿周制”，北京：中華書局，1986年，2374頁。

[66] 李鬥《楊州書舫錄》卷4，北京：中華書局，1960年，99—100頁。

[67] 易宗夔《新世說》，陳麗莉、尹波點校，成都：四川大學出版社，1998年，162頁。

[68] 章學誠《湖北通志檢存稿》一，《食貨考》，北京：文物出版社，《章學誠遺書》卷24，影印本，1985年，25頁。

[69] 《五體清文鑒》（第二冊），卷22，“貨財類”，北京：民族出版社，1957年，3109頁。

地。後經雲南永昌、騰越輸入中國内地。這一地區因爲開採技術落後，產量不大。催生石最主要的產地，仍然是阿富汗的巴達赫尚地區，與青金石處於同一礦脈。阿富汗也是世界上催生石的最主要產區。其他地方據説也有出產。民初地質學家章鴻釗《石雅》提到“今俗有名崔生石者，亦青金石之屬，相傳出塔什干”。並引述清代周靄聯《竺國紀遊》，謂“碩板多地方產催生石，似青金石而紋理粗劣，色亦黯”[70]。據此，則清代西藏也有出產，但章氏未做肯定。史料中也沒有看到西藏或蒙古上層向清廷貢進催生石物件的記録。不過，地方誌中有滇藏毗連的中甸地方出產催生石的記載，“中甸距前藏凡四十七站，……所產則藏綢、……催生石，上品曰京青，蓋以輸京局者，青礦隸三寶法王”[71]。如果這一記載無誤，中甸應該是清廷催生石的重要來源。

目前爲止，資料中尚未發現清代以前的催生石加工物件的記述，出土實物中也未見報告。事實上，清代乾隆朝才是催生石真正被開發、利用的時期。

清初文獻中雖不見催生石的蹤跡，鮮爲人知的是，清宮檔案中並不乏催生石的信息，只是不爲外界所知。和青金石一樣，阿富汗的催生石輸入正是伴隨著準噶爾問題的解決實現的。

在西域戰事剛剛結束不久的乾隆二十六年四月，乾隆帝密信給新疆的參贊大臣阿桂“先前，兆惠在伊犁，在噶爾丹策零貯藏玉石之豁吉格爾地方房内，尋得催生石三塊送京。富德于伊犁豁吉格爾巴克地方亦尋得一塊送京。再喇嘛伊西車木比勒告知兆惠，伊犁河對岸察汗烏蘇、維霍爾里克一帶舊房内尚有此石，亦未可料。著寄信阿桂等，於此等地方留心尋找，酌量送京。欽此。”並囑咐“將此寫入加封，入伊奏事夾板内送發”[72]。可知在平准戰爭期間，將軍兆惠、富德等人已經開始爲清廷尋找青金石送往北京。阿桂接旨後即著手尋找，“阿桂等奏，伊犁河兩岸，從前大軍數次經過，並無玉石等物。奴才等詢知情者，相繼掘獲大小玉石十五塊，大小催生石十四塊，大玉盤二個。分別裝入四匣内，交與侍衛鄂鐸送往京城”。接報後當年八月，乾隆帝再諭阿桂“將此等挖掘玉石之事，不必專做一事具奏”。“唯將所得玉石酌量送京，不必專折具奏。”[73]看來，乾隆帝對尋找催生石一事不欲更多人知道，故有保密考慮。從内務府的檔案看，乾隆二十五年造辦處只有催生石存貨4兩4錢5分，但二十六年新進催生石數量達到95斤12兩[74]。一年以後，乾隆帝再次寄信諭令伊犁將軍明瑞、葉爾羌辦事大臣新柱，“從前伊犁曾送催生石，恐回疆亦有此物。著傳諭明瑞、新柱等，留意查找送京。欽此，欽遵。先前在伊犁。豁吉格爾、柏興、察汗烏蘇等地，獲得厄魯特埋藏之青金石送京，唯不知何地出產。著大臣等詢問厄魯特、回子等知情者，究系何處出產催生石，

---

⑩ 章鴻釗《石雅》，《民國叢書》第二編本，上海：上海書店出版社，1989年，79頁。

⑪ 王崧《道光雲南志鈔》，《邊裔志下·西藏載記》，昆明：雲南社會科學院文獻研究所，1995年，290頁。

⑫ 《乾隆朝滿文寄信檔譯編》，乾隆二十六年四月初十日，《寄諭參贊大臣阿桂等將伊犁豁吉格爾等處尋得催生石乘便送京事》，檔號：03-129-1-062。

⑬ 《乾隆朝滿文寄信檔譯編》，乾隆二十六年八月二十日，《寄諭參贊大臣阿桂等將掘獲玉石之處不必專折具奏》，檔號：03-129-2-024。

⑭ 《清宮内務府造辦處檔案總匯》，北京：人民出版社，2007年，第26冊，27頁；第27冊，97頁。

即派人前往採掘。若于厄魯特、回部地方不產此物，即出價購買。唯留意尋覓大塊上好者。一應得獲，即刻乘便送京”。透露了乾隆帝不擇手段，必欲獲得催生石的迫切心情。信末尾卻又說“此物可得可不得，不可當做要事”[75]。這又反映出乾隆帝欲蓋彌彰的矛盾心理，令人莞爾。讀過這幾份檔案，首先浮現的問題就是，乾隆帝爲何急於獲得催生石?

催生石品質不及青金石，更無法媲美於紅寶石、藍寶石，乾隆帝一定有更隱秘的理由。合理的解釋，恐怕與傳說中的催生石具備催產助生神奇功效有關，雖然這不可能得到史料的證實。

漢語“催生石”一名，其來源有兩說。其一是廣爲流傳的孕婦在以傳統方式分娩時此石能起催生作用。或說此名源于古人用此石作產婦催生藥之說。或說古代印第安人曾用其作爲婦女催生之藥，故名。這些都來自民間傳聞，沒有看到醫書和文獻上的證據。但古埃及人認爲青金石有安神，治療神經狂躁功能，則上述傳聞或有一定道理。古代婦女生產，生死攸關，即便皇家也不例外。乾隆帝相信此說，也可以理解。另有一說，認爲催生石中“催生”二字乃藏語方言譯音，並不以催生爲義。根據是周靄聯《竺國紀遊》[76]，實則這是章鴻釗的看法。周氏只是在“催生石”一詞之後“原注謂‘俗語相傳，不知果此二字否？’”[77]表示不確定而已。

乾隆後期，不知是皇帝本人對催生石的熱情已經消退，還是朝廷通過其他途徑獲得了足夠的供應，總之是政策上放鬆了對催生石的管控。乾隆四十六年，吐魯番領隊大臣圖思義循慣例扣押了攜帶催生石的內地商人王增。隨後商請烏什參贊大臣綽克托，希望定例嚴查商民貨物。此舉遭到乾隆帝的申飭，斥其不明事理，“甚是過分”，重申禁止的是“私攜偷帶玉石”，要求將王增立即放行[78]。

在清代，催生石，滿語作cui sheng wehe，應該是漢語的音譯。與青金石nomin是明顯區别的石種。與青金石在清代大範圍的使用不同，催生石則不那麼爲人所知。催生石的采進、加工，和青金石一樣，都歸內務府造辦處玉作管理。

從內務府檔案看，催生石的製品主要有佛頭塔珠（朝珠的一部分）、珠兒、八寶、小蟾、小磬、小刀把等小件物。但結合其他資料看，催生石作品遠不止這些。

一類是賞賜嬪妃的催生石裝飾品。如乾隆三十六年六月初四，來自西域回部的容嬪封妃，乾隆帝賞賜有青金石挑花垂掛、垂簾，金鑲催生石金箍垂掛等多件。

第二類是宗教法物。如乾隆三十五年內務府如意館玉匠七十兒奉旨將一塊重16斤的催生石照章嘉國師的繪本雕刻成一尊呀嗎達嘎（大威德金剛）[79]。紫禁城齋宮西暖閣佛堂

---

[75] 《乾隆朝滿文寄信檔譯編》，乾隆二十七年八月二十六日，《寄諭伊犁等處辦事大臣明瑞等著於回疆留意查找催生石送京》，檔號：03-129-4-052。

[76] 臺北故宮博物院編輯委員會編輯《清代服飾展覽圖録》，臺北故宮博物院編印，1986年，18頁。

[77] 章鴻釗《石雅》，79頁。

[78] 《乾隆朝滿文寄信檔譯編》，乾隆四十六年七月二十六日，《寄諭烏什參贊大臣綽克托等著傳諭圖思義遵照成例查辦過往商民》，檔號：03-136-1-066。

[79] 熊文彬等《藏傳佛教藝術發展史》下冊，上海：上海書畫出版社，2010年，831頁。

供奉有催生石釋迦牟尼佛一尊。乾隆四十四年，六世班禪來到熱河預備覲見乾隆帝。清廷賞賜他“催生石手持金剛白玉救度佛母一堂”，上嵌珍珠寶石，總重108兩5錢⑧⁰。班禪圓寂於北京後，乾隆帝特賜金塔並指示鑲嵌松石、珊瑚、催生石三色，以增華麗⑧¹。嘉慶二十五年，道光帝以催生石小朝珠一盤，賞賜西藏濟嚨呼圖克圖之呼畢勒罕⑧²。

第三類，有重大意義的寶璽、冊頁。乾隆五十七年，清廷指令揚州工匠以催生石雕刻了國子監御寶“表章經學之寶”，重達44兩3錢6分。同時以催生石製作了“御制石刻蔣衡書十三經”冊頁12頁。置於辟雍亭⑧³。

第四類是各類擺件。如故宮甯壽宮花園養和精舍一層陳設有催生石羅漢仙山一座；二層陳設著催生石伏獅羅漢仙山一件。避暑山莊則設置有催生石鼓10件。清末，慈禧的隨葬品中也出現了三件催生石玩器。

值得思考的是，與青金石不同，清代民間鮮有催生石物件。從而使催生石顯得很神秘。這究竟是乾隆帝獨特的審美趣味和偏愛所致，還是另有原因，尚待進一步研究。

17、18世紀清朝經過長期對峙，最終成功地解除準噶爾政權的威脅，實現了大一統。其意義不僅體現在政治統一，版圖擴大，民族融合諸方面。清朝重新打通了隔絕已久的絲綢之路，促進了西域與中原的經濟文化交流，也暢通了中亞與中國的物資流動，進而影響了中國朝野的審美趣味、奢侈品和藝術品創作、宗教藝術，乃至世俗的社會風尚等方方面面。本文探討的青金石、催生石流動不過是一個很小的側面，本文的研究也僅僅是一個初步的嘗試而已，期待未來會有更多更深入的研究出現。

Discussion on the Name of Ancient Lapis Lazuli , the Lapis Lazuli and Hasten Parturitian Stone's Source and Usage of the Royal Household in Qing Dynasty

Zhang Yongjiang

When the Lapis Lazuli entered China , it was recognized after a long time. It Often referred to general terms of foreign words, such as “Beautiful Jade”（璆琳）, “Colored Glaze”（琉璃）, “Po Li”（颇梨）, “SeSe”（瑟瑟）, “Ya Hu”（鸦鹘） and so on in literature, sometimes to be called the “blue stone”（兰石，兰赤）and other designations or the Chinese special name “Aurin”（金精）, “Venus Stone”（金星石）, but not very usually. The Chinese name of “Lapis Stone” has been confirmed during Ming and Qing period and still in use. In

⑧⁰ 第一歷史檔案館、中國藏學研究中心合編《六世班禪朝覲檔案選編》，《英廉等送往熱河備賞班禪各物清單》，北京：中國藏學出版社，1996年。

⑧¹ 王曉晶編著《六世班禪進京史實研究》，北京：民族出版社，2013年，169頁。

⑧² 《清宣宗實錄》卷8，嘉慶二十五年十一月甲子。

⑧³ 《欽定國子監志》卷21，北京：北京古籍出版社，2000年。

Early Qing Dynasty, A little bit Lapis Lazuli has been introduced to the court via the Northwest Mongolian and Tibetan channels. The Lapis Lazuli was systematically used in the bead of official's hat, royal dresses, religious objects and the decoration of artwork during the reign of Emperor Qianlong and Yongzheng, they could access to stable source because the Qing regime opened up and controlled the Western Regions. The same kind of Hasten Parturitian stone caused special attention for the Qianlong emperor at one time, although some works handed down, rare records of the function, so it generates a sense of mystery.

《聖彼德堡梵德大辭典》前言

劉　震

奥托・尼古拉斯・馮・波特林克（Otto Nikolaus von Böhtlingk）1815年6月11日生於聖彼德堡，1904年4月1日卒於萊比錫。他早年在聖彼德堡學過阿拉伯語和梵語，20歲時前往柏林求學於語言學家波普（Franz Bopp），而後到波恩轉投印度學家施萊格爾（A. W. Schlegel）和拉森（Christian Lassen）。1842年，他就職於聖彼德堡科學院，後來成爲院士。在俄國政府的許可之下，1868年，他遷到耶拿（Jena），1885年，又到了萊比錫。

在波恩的時候，年僅24歲的波特林克就完成了兩卷本的《波尼你語法八章書》（*Pāṇini's acht Bücher grammatischer Regeln*, 1839/40），1887年，又以《波尼你語法》（*Pāṇini's Grammatik*）爲題出版了修訂本。此書至今仍然是學習古代印度語法的必修讀物。此外，他還編輯了婆缽提婆（Vopadeva）的語法（1846）和金月（Hemacandra）的詞典（1847）。關於印度的戲劇，他編輯和翻譯了迦梨陀娑（Kālidāsa）的《沙恭達羅》（*Śakuntalā*, 1842）和首陀羅迦的《小泥車》（*Mṛcchakaṭikā*）。詩學方面，他編譯了檀丁的《詩鏡》（*Kāvyādarśa*, 1890）。哲學和吠陀文獻方面，他編譯了《唱贊奥義書》（*Chāndogyopaniṣad*, 1889）和《大林奥義書》（*Bṛhadāraṇyakopaniṣad*, 1889）。有關吠陀的重音，他還寫過一篇重要的文章——"關於梵語的重音"（Über den Accent im Sanskrit, 1843）。在印度的箴言文學方面，他編纂翻譯過三卷本的《印度格言》（*Indische Sprüche*, 1863-1865, ²1870-73），這是他的梵語字典的副產品。在梵語教學方面，他編輯了《梵語文選》（*Sanskrit-Chrestomathie*, 1845, ²1877, ³1909 R. Garbe）。可以說，這位高產的學者爲印度學研究的衆多領域作出了奠基性的貢獻，而且這些成就至今尚未能取代或者超越。

波特林克的語言天賦還表現在：他根據他人在西伯利亞的田野調查記錄，寫出了《關於雅庫德人的語言》（*Über die Sprache der Jakuten*，1851）一書。

當然，他留給後世最最輝煌的成就，毫無疑問是他與羅特共同編纂的七卷本《梵語辭典》（*Sanskrit-Wörterbuch*, 1855-1875）——又被稱作的"聖彼德堡大辭典"（Großes Petersburger Wörterbuch），與以此爲基礎的、波特林克所編的七卷本《縮編梵語辭典》（*Sanskrit-Wörterbuch in kürzerer Fassung*, 1879-1889）——又被稱作"聖彼德堡小辭典"（Kleines Petersburger Wörterbuch）。

魯道夫・馮・羅特（Rudolf von Roth）1821年4月3日生於斯圖加特，1895年6月23

日卒於圖賓根（Tübingen）。1838年起，他在圖賓根學習神學，而後學習東方語言，於1843年博士畢業。接下來，他參訪各大圖書館，在巴黎與布諾夫（Eugène Burnouf）一起研讀寫本，而後前往倫敦和牛津。此次遊歷的成果——《關於吠陀文獻與歷史》（*Zur Litteratur und Geschichte des Weda*, 1846）使之一舉成名。回國之後，他的圖賓根完成了教授資格考試，1848年成爲編外教授，1856年成爲梵語的正式教授（1865—1866院長，1866—1867校長），同時也是大學圖書館館長。

羅特是德國吠陀文獻研究以及吠陀語法、詞源學和注疏作品研究的奠基人。根據他自己抄錄的寫本，羅特編輯了不少文獻，首先是最早的語法學家的作品之一，一部帶有同義詞列表的注釋—語法作品，同時也是一部吠陀研究的重要工具書：《耶色伽的〈詁訓〉及〈詞彙〉》（*Jāska's Nirukta sammt den Nighaṇṭavas*, 1852）。他還與惠特尼（William Dwight Whitney）合作出版了《阿闥婆吠陀本集》（*Atharva Veda Sanhita*, 1856, [2]1924 v. Max Lindenau）。在與波特林克合作編纂《聖彼德堡大辭典》時，羅特負責吠陀文獻和醫藥—自然科學類的詞彙。這些詞彙是他寫本閱讀時所積累的。羅特用文獻學、辭典和語法來研究吠陀文獻，其準則就是基於文獻本身來理解文獻，這與印度本土的注疏家勢必相違。此外，他還從事伊朗的阿維斯陀（Avesta）研究。

1852年，波特林克給羅特寫了第一封信，從此開始了長達二十多年的編纂《聖彼德堡大辭典》的合作。在工作最爲緊張的19世紀五六十年代，幾乎每個禮拜，在聖彼德堡和圖賓根之間均有信件往來。這些信件傳遞著辭典的文稿和樣書，以及雙方在編纂細節上的意見和對學界同仁的評價，見證了他們從距離遙遠的“最尊敬的教授先生”，發展到親密無間、開誠佈公的“親愛的朋友”。其實他們素未謀面，首次會面要直到1866年在圖賓根。辭典的第一卷出版於1855年，最後一卷出版於1875年。結束之後，波特林克馬上就利用新的文獻出處，著手《聖彼德堡小辭典》的編纂工作①。

下面就從《聖彼德堡大辭典》各個分冊的前言中節譯一些段落，可以讓我們瞭解辭典的體例和編輯的艱辛過程，另外還有一些小花絮②。當然，他們得以在有生之年編纂出一部至今仍爲最權威的梵語辭典，其對完整性和完成力之間的平衡掌握，依然值得今世之學人學習。

第一卷前言：

> [III]自從威爾遜（H. H. Wilson）在加爾各答出版了《梵英詞典》，三十多年來，我們的梵語語言和文學研究取得了卓越的進步，因此通過重新修訂詞彙，去嘗試爲不斷擴展和增高的大廈提供堅實的支柱，是恰逢其時的。

① 波特林克寫給羅特的484封信件，於1993年在圖賓根大學圖書館的羅特遺書中被找到，由Agnes Stache-Weiske整理，Heidrun Brückner和Gabriele Zeller編輯，以《1852—1885年間關於聖彼德堡辭典的書信》（*Briefe zum Petersburger Wörterbuch 1852-1885*）爲書名由Wiesbaden的Harrassowitz出版社於2007年出版。

② 原文使用的舊式轉寫系統在此被代之以新式轉寫系統。原文使用的天城體字母在此被代之以拉丁字母轉寫。在翻譯過程中，得到了慕尼克大學印度日爾曼系的博士候選人潘濤先生的大力協助，再此表示感謝——譯者。

接下來他們批評了威爾遜的資料過分依賴印度本土班智達，而未能用現代學術規範來甄別。

我們的辭典由兩部分組成，但不能完全分割：源自印度學者搜集的詞彙和我們自己從梵語文獻中搜集的。如果可能的話，搜集整理所有流傳至我們這個時代的梵語文學作品，那麼印度本土搜集的詞彙語料——反正與該語言的整個詞庫相比，是微不足道的——即便擱置一旁也並無大礙，或許我們真的不必去重複印度學者所提供的材料中無數的錯誤和偏差。不過，對此既缺乏資金也缺乏人力，所以我們的工作中，只能用印度本土材料的內容來補充我們自己所搜集資料的不足，爲此我們不得不對它們的缺陷做出妥協。

印度的工具書與可考的語言用法之間特殊的自相矛盾的例子，在本書中，人們可以發現足夠多；還有更多的情況是，前者只描述了真正用法的一部分。考慮到在某一個我們無法獲取的，或者沒有被關注到的文獻出處中，可能存在另一種語言用法，那麼印度本土辭書犯錯的概率便無法完全被排除，而這恰恰因爲在該錯誤中，還隱藏著對真相不可忽視的暗示。不過，正如人們相信自己親眼所見某部古老《梵書》的話語，而不信其他持異議者——儘管人數衆多——的話語一般，此處在本書中所見的，也應該比注釋家的證據更有說服力。

我們必須標出這些錯誤和偏差，我們要關注，印度辭書中沒有在現實語言運用中出現的殘餘，甚至要關注那些被注疏家對文獻明顯曲解的詞彙，爲的是不將時不時會出現的有用的東西與糟粕一起掃除，我們還沒有富足到可以將它們揚棄的地步。

基於這一觀點，希望我們處理【印度——譯者】語法學家和辭書學家所傳的詞彙的方式方法能得到體現。

[IV]與之相反，我們盡了最大努力，對自己所收集的詞彙進行了更大的擴充，以此爲辭書學奠定唯一牢固的基礎。在前言末尾，用一個目錄單獨羅列了已經出版的和還處於手稿狀態的作品，有些是完整地被我們摘引，有些則是甄選了標誌性的和較爲重要的部分，而有些只是簡略地參考。

特別是我們完整地整理了吠陀文獻中最重要的書籍，以此作爲我們工作的正確開端。這樣，一個全新的領域被開啟，從中收穫了一筆意想不到的財富，流入了梵語詞匯寶庫。所得的收穫並不僅限於梵語詞匯的增長，對於整個語言寶庫的理解來說，其收穫也是相當可觀的。人們只能尾隨語言寶庫紛繁蕪雜的現象，一旦確定其源頭之後，才能從中厘清概念線索。或者，在後期的語言運用中，一個詞語的原本概念變得模糊不清，似乎散於一些看似無關的不同詞義中，就像一枚磨損或者被殘缺的錢幣，這時人們可以回歸到吠陀寶藏中，從而能獲悉完整的、未受磨損的印紋，以及原初的面值。

有些詞根，後來完全消失了，而豐富的構詞類別，除少數派生形式外，滅亡殆盡，但是在這裡【吠陀——譯者】人們可以發現這些詞根和構詞類別仍然充滿活力，通過它們也可以懂得後續的演變形態。因此，通過解讀古代語言，詞源學尤其會得到發展，而語言比較本就應該比迄今所做的更加嚴格地基於詞彙中可考的最古老部分。

如果只從希羅多德和偉大悲劇作家開始，卻根本無視更古老的作品，那麼希臘語辭書編纂將遭受巨大損失，而梵語辭典將會蒙受同樣或者數倍於此的損失，如果捨棄了廣義的吠陀文獻，且古代文獻數量越大，損失就越嚴重。

然而，五十年前科爾布魯克（H. T. Colebrooke）就正確地指出，在很長時間裡，吠陀語言的艱深和困難將會阻礙對此浩如煙海的文獻研究的深度和廣度，不過最近幾十年所作的工作使得這座原始森林多少有徑可循，以至於我們所嘗試的研究沒有變得徒勞無功。這一嘗試可以被稱爲是一次大膽的冒險，因爲真正的注釋工作開始之前，應該要完成一部辭典。在運算的各個因素被確定前，人們卻盼望完成運算並獲得答案。因爲不得不承認，幾乎全部用於注疏準備工作的材料，與其說在困境中給予我們指引，還不如說是誤導了我們。除了本菲（Th. Benfey）關於《娑摩吠陀》的工作，目前爲止還沒有成規模的符合一般學術注疏規範的作品問世，即便如此，我們也不能一味追隨這位前輩。如果朗洛瓦（Langlois）的《梨俱吠陀》譯本能夠名副其實的話，我們的工作可能差不多已經完成一半了。只有在那些初學者想犯錯誤也很難的地方，這部翻譯才有用，但是即便是在這些地方，它也是處處盡力讓文本南轅北轍。”

接下來，他們繼續批判首部《梨俱吠陀》譯本——朗洛瓦的法譯本的低級錯誤。

對於理解吠陀文本來說，既然我們從今人那裡所獲幫助有限，那麼我們就尤其要轉向印度的知識界，他們自己爲了解釋這些文本所做的工作，即那些注疏。事實上，對於吠陀文獻兩個部分——神學和儀式——的任何一個，最好的嚮導莫過於那些在所有細節上都力求精確的注釋。這些詳細的注疏逐字逐句地依照文本，不厭其煩地在各處重複已有的解釋，即便是在只是貌似會有誤解的地方，有時候好像與其說是爲那些在此觀念和印象之下成長起來的祭司學徒而寫的，不如說是爲我們這些外人而寫的。[V]此處【吠陀文本的注疏——譯者】便是屬於這些祭司學徒的領域，那些分支衆多的、意味深長的、多爲吹毛求疵的儀軌象徵都需要去解釋，也需要去闡明所有不計其數的細節，因爲在侍奉神靈時對它們的重視與否，直接決定了是獲得永恆的福祉還是墮落。因爲在《梵書》中飄蕩著同樣的精神，它處於完全正統的婆羅門神學體系的影響下，並充斥于那些婆羅門學派之中，這些婆羅門學派幾百年前曾如此努力地研究和解釋其古代神學文獻中的傑出作品。

不過，如果這些人試圖去解釋古代歌集則是另外一回事了。這些文本既非通過神學冥想而創造的，亦非從某個規定嚴格的、細緻的祈禱儀式中發展而來，根據其絕大部分來看，它們卻是最古老的宗教詩歌作品，作爲日常的祭祀和祈禱，其詩歌藝術同樣與家族或者種姓無甚關係；在它們中間存在著一個神的世界，反映了一種與《梵書》中所教授的體系大相庭徑的信仰；他們使用的語言與《梵書》所用近乎經典梵語的語言間的差距之大，就像薩里詩歌的拉丁語有別于馬庫斯·特倫提烏斯·瓦羅（M. Terentius Varro）的。這裡不僅需要完全不同的詮釋技巧，還需要評判的自由度、更廣闊的視野和歷史觀。然而，所有古代異教民族的祭司知識界都缺乏評判的自由度，且在印度，人們從未獲悉它的任何歷史發展。

同樣的特質使得那些注疏家成爲了理解神學書籍的傑出嚮導，卻不適用於那個古老得多、且完全不同類的領域。——在所謂的經典梵語裡駕輕就熟的語言應用，他們也在吠陀詩歌裡尋找這樣的用法；對他們來說，既然儀式的程式是毋庸置疑的，且自開天闢地以來就存在著，那麼那些印度祭神的始祖們也一定是如此祭祀的：如果對他們來說，神譜和彼時的世界秩序是不可觸碰的和已經啟示的真理，那麼同樣的神譜和秩序肯定在啟示的核心、在與諸神互相信任地生活的、具有遠高於後世的智慧的古代仙人（Ṛshi）的歌曲中，一定能夠重現。

論證這一情況的例子毋庸贅述，同樣地，對於我們從注疏家們並不完美的作品中獲益匪淺的事實，人們也無需期待去愈加彰顯。這一整體情況既不難辨識，也並非别具一格。這一古老民族的聖書在隨後的數百年間完全按照盛行的神學體系，按照或高或低的學術水準，來作解釋，並且普遍如此：這種詮釋以傳統自封，也就是說，自稱古老和權威的，在事實上不一定名副其實。也沒人想到，比如，希伯來語的《舊約》要依據《塔木德》和拉比們，而要根據娑衍那（Sāyaṇa）、摩醯陀羅（Mahīdhara）等人來翻譯，被認爲是一位細緻的吠陀解釋者的義務，亦是一例。我們也不像威爾遜[③]那樣相信，比如，娑衍那比每一位歐洲的解釋者都更好地理解吠陀的文句，我們除了對他亦步亦趨就無事可幹了；而我們相信，一位細緻的歐洲解釋者能夠遠遠比娑衍那更正確。更好地理解吠陀；我們並不認爲下一個任務是去達到幾百年前在印度大行其道的對吠陀的理解水準[④]，而是要尋找詩人自己置於其歌曲和箴言裡的含義。因此，我們認爲，娑衍那和其他注疏家的文字並非解釋者的準繩，而只是一種輔助工具，用於完成這項無法一蹴而就、且無法獨自一人解決的艱難任務。我們非常遺憾，繆勒（Müller）爲人稱道的《梨俱吠陀》注疏編輯本，就這點而言，尚未有更新的進展。

因此我們嘗試走一條語言學所規定的道路：通過比對所有在遣詞造句方式或者內容方面有關聯的出處，讓文本自己交代其含義；這是一條緩慢而艱難的道路，過往的注疏家和譯者都無法指引我們。所以，對我們來說，這是一項兼

③ *ṚIG-VEDA-SANHITÁ. A collection of ancient Hindu hymns of the Rig-Veda, the oldest authority for the religious and social institutions of the Hindus. Translated from the original Sanskrit*. By H. H. Wilson. London 1850. I, p. 25.

④ Wilson，同③，II, p. XXIII。

任注疏家和辭書家的雙重任務。詞源學的處理方式本身是不可能指向正確目標的，因爲那些詞源學家肯定會[Ⅵ]試圖去猜測一個詞的意思，而不去關注他們所處理的出處之外，該詞再次出現的十個或者二十個例子。即便是依照語言法則處理，爲了每次都擊中目標，對於詞語的解釋會陷入過於寬泛的邏輯範疇，並且會產生過於普遍和平實的概念，這些概念或許包含了詞語固定的內涵和明晰的外延，但是卻無法再現其特殊性以及相關的力量和美感。

這就是成就這些注疏家們的工作方法，由此確證無疑：他們沒有同時掌握這些書中的所有詞彙，同樣地，他們也沒有依據固有的傳統解釋來處理每一個單獨的出處。由此，吠陀中不計其數的詞被他們簡單解釋爲"力量""祭祀""食物""智慧"，大量的動詞被解釋爲"行走""運動"，而所有這些詞都不同於彼此地擁有特定的含義和鮮明的內容，但也經常會與那些一般性的概念有些許交集。人們只有爲這些無法理解的詞彙重新找回他們已經逝去的正當解釋時，吠陀才能獲得令人信服的意義、力量和豐富性，從而向我們呈現出上古時代思想世界的一幅截然不同的圖景。

誰能夠認識到這一工作的困難，他將會諒解我們無法否認的衆多錯誤，在工作進程中，這些錯誤首先一覽無餘地彰顯在我們自己面前。辭典的這一部分，既是最新的，也是最先過時的，因爲很多致力於吠陀的出色的協同工作將會迅速促進對於吠陀的理解，並且比起我們這第一次嘗試會更加真實和準確地確定很多內容。數百年來人們致力於理解荷馬的詞彙，可是對他的詞彙釋義還是未能窮盡，但是在語言層面上，荷馬的難度還是不可與吠陀同日而語的。這些遠古時代的紀念碑，唯獨於此處以文字的形式流傳至今，人們怎麼能期待它們和一本現代的出版物一樣可以被輕易譯出！

經過Röer博士先前的不懈努力，他在加爾各答得到了《鷓鴣氏本集》（*Taittirīya-Saṃhitā*）的一個非常好的複本，在辭典付梓期間，我們得以處理全部的吠陀本集（Saṃhitā），並且考慮窮究《梨俱吠陀》和《阿闥婆吠陀》，《勝利本集》（*Vājasaneyi-Saṃhitā*）與《娑摩吠陀》獨有的部分，還要列出複合詞；我們沒有延伸到《鷓鴣氏本集》，因爲根據其主要內容，它不屬於歌集，而是屬於《梵書》類別，考慮到空間限制和並不顯著的成效，對《梵書》的處理並不能達到完全的列舉。

在康涅狄格州紐黑文市的惠特尼（W. D. Whitney）教授給了我們《阿闥婆吠陀》完整和精確的詞彙列表，這是一個很有價值的助力。

現在收入辭典的梵書和經書（Sūtra）文獻，篇幅相當可觀，柏林的韋伯博士（Albrecht Weber）給我們提供了《百道梵書》（*Śatapathabrāhmaṇa*）、迦旃延（Kātyāyana）經豐富的材料，之後又有商羯衍那（Śāṅkhāyana）和波羅奢那（Pāraskara）的，方始成爲可能。若沒有這些幫助，我們可能至少在這部作品開始的時候，就會局限於《愛多列雅梵書》（*Aitareyabrāhmaṇa*）、阿濕伐羅耶那（*Āśvalāyana*）的兩部經，以及喬屍迦（Kauśika）對《阿闥婆吠陀》的注釋。我們認爲自己也有義務，並很樂意公之於衆：從開始到現在，韋伯傾其全力，對這一集衆人之力的工作投入了極大的熱情。

阿達爾貝爾特·庫恩（Adalbert Kuhn）博士開始爲我們的詞典搜集商羯衍那的《家庭經》（*Gṛhyasūtra*）中的詞彙。

奧夫萊西特（Aufrecht）博士在前往牛津之前，提供了吠陀領域中到agra（不含）爲止的詞彙支持。

我們要感謝施坦茨勒（Stenzler）教授，他留下了《摩奴法典》的完整索引，包含了所有詞彙及其所有出處；這位學者還告知我們各種尚未編輯的印度詞典的摘要，這些詞典被《野人和阿周那》（*Kirātārjunīya*）和《童護伏誅》（*Śiśupālavadha*）的注疏家所引用，最後還將波普的《梵語詞匯》的初版交由我們自由使用，此書中波普有時會列出不同作家的生僻詞和詞義。

我們感謝科學院的希夫納爾（Schiefner）多次告知佛教文獻裡的內容，即梵藏詞典《翻譯名義大集》（*Vyutpatti*）。

對我們來說，最弱的是哲學文獻，我們將帶著特別的謝意，接受這方面專家可能提供的幫助。

[Ⅶ]這些可以方便獲得的威爾遜、豪頓（Haughton）、維斯特加特（Westergaard）、波普、拉森、吉爾德邁斯特（Gildemeister）和本菲的詞典、詞根彙編和詞彙表，我們理所當然地使用過，但沒有一個詞彙、沒有一個詞義，是不經過檢視就吸納入我們的辭典的。羅陀犍陀（R ā dh ā k ā nta）的《音如意樹》（*Śabdakalpadruma*）在很多方面爲這位博學的印度人贏得了極大的尊重，這部作品讓我們得以利用大量未曾編輯的印度本土詞典以及這些字典的注疏，而後者的寫本我們都無法獲得。摘引自已編輯和未編輯文本中的詞彙，尤其是豐富的植物名稱的同義詞讓我們獲益匪淺⑤。這部無法購置的珍貴作品，皇家科學院感謝編者慷慨贈予的樣書。

爲了方便讀者使用我們的辭典，特作如下提示。我們從動詞詞根中將母音ṛ、ṝ、ḷ完全剔除，同樣的，詞根中的複合元音也被去除；名詞主題母音ṛ，被ar取代。名動詞（Denominativa）到目前爲止以詞根的形式被引用，而我們則加上了名動詞尾。

我們用最簡單的方式標注重音，不過這種方式在印度不通用。相反，對於吠陀文獻中的例子，我們保留寫本慣用的標注方式。動詞詞根的類別並未給出，因爲從所附的第三人稱單數現在時來看，特別是注意到重音的話，這就不言自明瞭。

我們的工作如此分工，其中一位編輯者（Roth）負責處理吠陀文獻和吠陀

⑤ 我們高興地聽說，這位博學的印度人打算在他作品的第二版裡使用我們的辭典。1855年5月17日，他從加爾各答寫信給我們，……（略）。

工具書，以及善聞（Suśruta）的《生命吠陀》（*Āyurveda*），此外還關注植物名稱，而其他的文獻以及整理全部材料的工作，則由另一位編者來完成。

本辭典的有些缺憾，要歸咎於兩位合作者相隔太過遙遠，從而僅有幾次會面的機會。我們的工作因此變得非常艱難。我們的工作——爲此，十年來的努力還不足夠——有著內外雙重困難，如果説我們還是能夠保持勇氣的話，那麼但願人們從中認識到：我們在自己的領域內是如何勤奮地從事科學工作的。我們希望這份同樣的勤奮——如果我們未能完成已經開始的工作的話——喚醒後繼者，像我們一樣或者比我們更好地完成任務。

第二卷前言（1858年10月14日，聖彼德堡—10月26日，圖賓根）：

我們在此所公佈的這部辭典的第二卷，比第一卷完成得更快，儘管它包含了與之同樣多的頁數。在此期間，材料明顯增多，這一點每位細心的讀者立刻就能發現。不僅是本辭書的編輯者，而且他們的朋友韋伯，從開始就年年擴大所搜集文獻的範圍，並且從字母ga開始，韋伯的一位勤奮的學生，在赫龍洛（Groenlo）的凱爾恩（Kern）博士，借助婆羅訶密醯羅（Varāhamihira）只存於寫本的作品提供了非常有價值的貢獻。

下略。

第三卷前言（1861年7月1日，聖彼德堡—7月13日，圖賓根）：

該辭典的第三卷，根據我們起初的估計，還得包含na，並且完成整部作品的一半，結果還是沒有包含na，因爲我們不願意讓本卷的篇幅超過前兩卷太多。隨著工作的進展，我們確信，對整部作品篇幅的預估，後來總是被證明不準確。因此，至na爲止整部作品的一半將完成這一預設也不再成立。我們未曾想過將一卷結束於一個字母的半當中，這卻是無需辯解的。

對我們來説，非常棘手的是：那些內容和形式上皆值得高度關注的文獻，卻仍有很大的批判和解釋的空間，我們視之爲己任，爲本辭典去處理這些文獻。諸如伐致呵利（Bhatṛhari）和《五卷書》（*Pañcatantra*）中的格言之類，就屬於這類文獻。第一部作品，我們感謝希夫納爾和韋伯，他們羅列了各種異讀，具有極高的價值，有了他們的説明，在大部分情況下，可得一個解讀無礙的文本。對《五卷書》的批判和理解，本菲的作品曾經對於我們意義巨大，不過該作品的韻文部分，構成了本辭典的一個豐富的源泉，根據那些注解——我們中的一個針對本菲的譯文作了發表（註腳略）——仍舊需要某些補充，達到完全的理解——在人們可以收穫稱讚之前。這是吃力不討好的事情，因爲人們每次都試圖將所謂正確的文本在最後一刻展示出來。

這樣一種工作方式的不良後果讓其中一位編者想到，首先借助現有的工具確定伐致呵利的格言文本，服務於自身，而後由此減輕辭典工作的負擔。一部以此方式修訂的文本，希望能在其本身和一個更大的範圍內得到認可，將其他印度思想家和詩人的格言併入這個集子，或許未嘗不可。爲了查找方便，或許應該嚴格按照字母順序排列（根據格言第一個詞彙）；每句格言要給出所有的出處；此外，編者或許有義務，至少告知比較重要的異讀。給出格言的翻譯無疑也是恰如其分的，不過首當其衝的是給出一部盡可能完整的關鍵字索引，通過它的説明，人們根據隻言片語的記憶，也能找出每句格言。

對於我們的朋友惠特尼，在第一卷的前言裡，我們已經感謝了他對吠陀文獻的幫助，而現在我們想對其來自《日成究竟》（*Sūryasiddhānta*）的貢獻致以誠摯的謝意。

因爲我們的同事和朋友希夫納爾的不懈努力，從現在起，佛教文獻得到了更多的關注。新收入的這方面文獻的目錄，可見"第三卷中新增縮略語解釋"⑥。

第四卷前言（1864年11月17—29日）：

一部大型辭典的編纂者會面臨雙重危險：要麼追溯得太深，在細枝末節裡面迷失方向，要麼他在年事已高時方才著手工作，使得他的作品很可能無法完成，而一部未完成的詞典相比其他的未竟之作利用率更低；另外一重危險就是，當他尤其想將工作真正結束時，他通過犧牲精確性和完整性來加快工作進度。我們以威爾遜詞典的第二版爲標準，目前我們工作的五分之三已經完成；這一部分，我們花了大約十二年半。按照同樣的速度，我們可能還需要八年半的時間才能完成剩下的五分之二的工作，依照常人的情況我們應該可以活這麼久。根據對作品的整體設計，我們並未陷入第一重危險中，由此不會被人指責草草地進行了一項無法預見盡頭的作品，而對此作品我們是不可以指望後繼者的。我們也時刻警惕第二重危險，因爲在開始這部作品時，我們已經決定，將一段漫長的歲月全部奉獻給這部辭典，心無旁騖。

這部辭典的缺陷，我們完全清楚，不過當我們意識到，我們傾盡全力工作，且我們的成果爲數百人所利用，並且激勵他們作進一步研究，我們就獲得了在艱難的道路上不屈不撓前行的勇氣和動力。

我們感到非常惋惜，因爲凱爾恩博士移居貝拿勒斯一事使我們損失了他對字母pha的貢獻，但我們也樂觀地期待，後續字母的材料，同樣能夠豐富如前。

我們感謝我們的朋友惠特尼，除了前述貢獻，他還從《美國東方學雜誌》（*Journal of the American Oriental Society*）上所發表梵語銘文中整理了一份較爲重要詞彙的索引。

借此特殊機會，我們要特別感謝我們的朋友A.韋伯的參與，他所收集的材料日益增長，重要而且豐富，有些部分只有他能見到，而在這部辭典中，對於每一個涉及由他告知的出處的見解，他的觀點的表述並非全部見於紙上。

第五卷前言（1868年5月1日，聖彼德堡—5月13日，圖賓根）：

這第五部分，內容和外觀上與之前的四部分看上去大相徑庭，同時包含了

⑥ 指的是波特林克編纂翻譯過三卷本的《印度格言》（*IndischeSprüche*, 1863-65, 2 1870-73）——譯者。

進行調整的條件：在外觀上，如果之前的每兩卷合成一冊，它則以相當的篇幅自成一冊；內容上，儘管修訂和增補部分篇幅不小，但查閱工作並沒有變困難，反而還變簡單了，因爲所有對之前每部分的增補從現在起可以被捨棄了。

在修訂和增補的過程中，爲了不耽誤作品的繼續和按時完成，我們無法對之後獲取的文獻進行系統梳理，也不能對衆多詞條進行徹底的修訂。我們更多地只能收錄我們自己歷年來收集的內容，以及在此期間從所出版的索引和詞典中相對輕鬆地可以摘取的內容，以及那些樂於助人的朋友們，諸如凱爾恩、庫恩、施坦茨勒和韋伯⑦所提供的材料。雖然這部字典並不完美，我們仍然希望它對字典的使用者是有説明的。

首先，我們認爲目前整理吠陀詞條並不合適，奥夫萊西特一部針對吠陀文本的詳盡的字典和繆勒的《梨俱吠陀》譯文都在準備中。人們不要責備我們讓他人先行一步，他們做起來比我們十六年前輕鬆多了，也不要責備我們現在沒有去作修訂，我們希望這兩部作品真的會很快問世，那樣我們至少可以將他們的成果用於我們辭典的一部分之中。將來我們完成編纂之後，時間和條件允許的話，重拾吠陀的難點亦爲時未晚。

第五卷前半本中需要我們提請注意的是，在確定一個詞開頭是寫作ba還va的時候，我們依照了吠陀文獻的優質寫本和孟買的版本。在這方面，這裡提到的版本比加爾各答版更加可靠，因爲馬拉地語（Mahrattisch）至今都明確區分ba和va，而在孟加拉文中這兩個音合二爲一了。對baka、bakula、baṭu、bandi、bandin、bandī、bandhura、bandhula、barbara、balāhaka、bāṣpa和biḍāla這些詞的解釋還需要參考增補。

在此機會，請允許我們解釋一下，我們如何看待一本詞彙手冊和一本詳盡的辭典之間的關係，我們又會如何使兩者相得益彰的。

要編纂一本詞典，追求完整性這一不可達成的目標，編輯者有義務從最遙遠的、他偶然涉入的領域，收集一切新東西；那麼詞彙手冊的編者必須精確地限定其領域，避免哪怕一次越界。

要編纂一本詳盡的辭典，需要毫無保留地將自己的知識儲備傾囊而出；如果詞彙手冊的編者，在所能展示給讀者的那點貧乏的材料之外，就不知道更多的了，那麼他的作品就很糟糕了。

如果一部大辭典的編者在他的長途跋涉中，在某些地方仍忽略了近在咫尺的東西時，人們會原諒他；而對於詞彙手冊的編者，人們有理由要求他完全掌握其狹小的領域，作爲一名受雇的嚮導不可適逢緊急情况時丢下業餘的遊客——其作品的使用者。

在詳盡的辭典裡面，最最精確的出處是不可或缺的；不過將這些例證轉移

⑦ 惠特尼的增補來得太晚，將在這部作品的最後給出。

到詞彙手冊裡面卻並無用處。後者或許應該給出一個詞在哪類文本中被賦予特定的含義的一般性資訊。如果一個詞彙或者詞義早在吠陀中已經出現——即便原則上不太可能，那麼它也應該被注明，因爲沒人可以將如此一張貴族證書等閒視之。爲了我們辭典的使用者的利益，我們卻曾希望過，一本詞彙手冊的編者可以標注他所給出的一切新的東西，還有他改變表達方式的一切舊的東西，通過在這種情況下特別地附上引文，但這可能也會讓這本詞彙手冊原本的目標群體爲此支付更多。吉爾德邁斯特在拉森《梵語文選》（*Anthologia Sanscritica*——譯者）的詞彙表中用星號標出了我們所缺的詞彙和詞義，對此我們表示感謝。

在一部大辭典裡，大膽的詞源學解釋或者語彙比較，相對地無傷大雅，因爲通常只有學者使用它；一本詞彙手冊是在初學者手中，必須提供給他們完全可靠的東西，由此隨著時間的推移，他們習慣於謹慎，並獲得獨立于一切學術權威的、判斷正確或可能的感覺，這對於語言研究者是不可或缺的。

附上梵語詞匯的轉寫是適得其反的，因爲這不僅沒用,且讓本書價格更貴。誰要是讀梵語文本，必須認識梵語字母；而誰要是不識梵語字母，那麼這本辭典不應用於語言比較。在印度日爾曼比較語言學領域裡，當今有那麼多大師，以至于我們並不需要濫竽充數之輩。對比較語言學者來說，一本詞彙手冊根本不能取代一部大辭典，因爲前者對一個詞彙菁蕪不分。

下面的話是針對辭書家、語法家和系統性的反對者的。根據印度語法家的方式，將ṛ、ṝ、ḷ、e、ai和o保存在詞根裡，而卻隨手拋棄了詞根其他的特點，比如詞根起始音ṇa和ṣa——事實上起始音是na和sa——的應用，多少是違背印度語法家的做法，人們比實際情況更少地展現這些特點，但卻完全與歐洲的學術標準相對立，因爲人們除了印度語法家的權威之外無法爲這樣的寫法辯護，不過人們也忘記了，這個不是爲了符合理論的權威，而是追求與實踐一致的權威。首位將詞根以ṝ和o結尾的方式列示出來的印度語法學家聲稱，他確信這樣的詞根實際存在，也就是說可以認爲，他沒有正確理解一個完型的詞與原型的區別，因爲他有時也將此（不過出於純粹實用的目的）稱作pada（完型的詞）。帶著對波尼你一條規則的單純理解，人們沒有認識到波尼你的學術立場。有鑑於此，對我們理解波尼你有所補益的，也不是後期語法家的研究本身，而卻是不帶偏見的文獻學理解。比如，car帶有ā，構成不規則的形式āścarya，當波尼你要描述這種情況的話，他說道：āścaryam anitye，就是說，如果該詞有“異常”的意思的時候，人們構詞爲āścarya，對此唯有迦旃延才會想到去說，他的前輩應該用adbhute（奇跡）代替anitye才對。不過，當一位歐洲學者嘗試調和這兩位元語法家表面上的矛盾時，他設想，āścarya一詞可能在波尼你和迦旃延之間的時期裡經歷了詞義的變化，如此造成一種假像，似乎這位學者在運用數學量去操作，比起運用只能通過文獻學深厚功底才能準確衡量的量，更加得心應手。如果爲了混淆視聽，現在還去熱捧語法家根深蒂固的怪癖，如此產生的奇怪情況不能強求實幹家去面對。

回顧我們作品迄今爲止的命運，我們完全有理由感謝它已經得到的認可和影響力，即便它還有不足。個別人用了我們的辭典，我們爲他減輕了工作負擔，他不僅認爲並無必要去承認這點，還越發熱衷於尋找或創造機會來對我們吹毛求疵，爲了能讓自己的光芒放到燭臺上更加明亮，不過，我們對作品的滿意不應由此而削弱。誰對此感到驕傲，他都可以獲得這份虛榮；我們認爲，在此還留有空間給許多人，莫用同樣的東西來報答我們的作品，而要跨過它，不受打擾地繼續我們的道路，而我們的前路仍然既漫長又艱難。

第七卷前言（1875年8月4日，耶拿和圖賓根）：

持續了將近二十五年的工作之後，我們終於完成了這部辭典。在所有方面，它還仍未圓滿，而人們有時間自己去發現其優缺點：因此我們不必去詳細闡述。

只有一點，我們認爲趁此機會應該提醒大家，當年我們著手工作時，梵語文獻水準和數量與今日不可同日而語；當時我們所缺乏的許多材料，如今人們對它們已並不陌生；當時文獻僅有少量的前期處理可供我們直接使用或在編輯過程中給予我們幫助。

儘管如此，我們仍舊冒險將整個文獻納入視野，只要我們能夠得到的，就會採用。經常通過我們的努力，原本只有殘篇可用的文本漸漸可以獲得全本，如此這部辭典在編纂過程中逐步擴容成一部百科全書。假若我們只是囿於當初存在的文獻，並且在此希望做到圓滿，那麼這種圓滿可能很快就會變成可悲的殘缺。我們拓展至所有方面的文獻，竭盡所能從各方收集可用材料，即便是由殘片綴合而成且要耗費時間和精力；只要能夠服務於編纂，我們不憚於使材料顯得不均衡。即便是我們在相關領域搜集的材料也有可能殘缺不全，我們記下這些，會有助於現在的使用者以及未來的後繼者⑧。

對於吠陀，我們曾徒勞地期待過索引和專門詞典的出現，然而這一切皆落後於我們。自始至終，人們給予了我們作爲先行者的未曾期待的敬意。

我們原本的同仁們自始至終都支持我們，首先是我們的朋友韋伯，他無私地花費自己寶貴的時間和精力，從那些對辭書意義重大的、部分地唯有他可見到和熟悉的《梵書》和《經》的部類中，收集詞彙，爲我們的作品錦上添花。其次，貢獻最大的是凱爾恩、施坦茨勒、惠特尼。如果我們要最後感謝希夫納爾的話，希望我們就如此說道：他提供了梵語詞典罕用的材料，出自他所駕輕

⑧　繆勒（M. Müller）在其《梨俱吠陀》編輯本的第六冊前言（第X頁）你問道："爲什麼在《聖彼德堡辭典》中沒有這些技術術語（原文如此），比如gītin、śiraḥkampin？"在我們的辭典中有很多缺漏，不過這兩個詞卻沒有漏掉。它們就在正文裏（並非在增補裏），帶有正確的釋義，每個包含迄今爲止所知的唯一一個出處。我們能否可以反詰道：有人怎麼可以如此輕率地責難？

就熟的佛教文獻。

正如我們要感謝這些幫助，我們還應該說明一點，我們重視所有同行的評價，它們總體上來說是愛護和認可我們的，激勵著我們，伴隨我們到如今。

而我們作品的贊助者——皇家科學院，賜予我們命運中不可多得的恩惠，來完全執行它的委託，對於我們圓滿完成任務的方式，我們希望它不吝掌聲。

Some Notes on the Sanskrit Fragments of the *Ajātaśatrukaukṛtyavinodana* in the Schøyen Collection and Their Extant Parallels*

Wu Juan

The *Ajātaśatrukaukṛtyavinodana* ("Dispelling of Ajātaśatru's Remorse"; hereafter AjKV) is one of the first Mahāyāna *sūtra*s translated by the Indo-Scythian monk Lokakṣema into Chinese in the late second century CE.① It had not come down to us in any Indian-language version until its discovery in the Schøyen Collection. So far, at least twenty Sanskrit fragments of the AjKV, belonging to a palm-leaf manuscript of a Mahāyāna *sūtra* compendium, have been identified in the Schøyen Collection.② The manuscript was found along with other Buddhist manuscripts in caves near the Bamiyan valley in Afghanistan. It is written in a northwestern Gupta Brāhmī script dating probably from the fourth-fifth centuries CE.③ It has been reasonably suspected that "further pieces of the same manuscript may be preserved" in

---

* An earlier version of this paper was presented in the colloquium "Religions and Religious Texts on the Silk Road" held at the School of History, Archaeology and Religion, Cardiff University, on 6-7 March 2009. I thank the organizer, Professor Max Deeg, and the participants for their valuable remarks. The delay in the publication of this paper was partly due to the failure to materialize an original plan to publish the proceedings of the colloquium. The paper was slightly revised in June 2016 during my postdoctoral fellowship at Leiden University, under the sponsorship of the Robert H. N. Ho Family Foundation administrated by the American Council of Learned Societies. I am grateful to Professor Shen Weirong for including my humble paper in this volume. Any errors that remain are mine alone.

① While the Sanskrit title of this text is often given as *Ajātaśatrukaukṛtyavinodanā*, as Miyazaki (2010: 29; 2012: 25) rightly points out, this title is not attested in any extant Indian-language source. Based on a careful survey of Tibetan transliterations of the title of the AjKV in various Kanjur editions, Chinese translations of the title, and references to the AjKV in other Mahāyāna texts, Miyazaki (2010: 33; 2012: 31) suggests two possible titles under which the AjKV may have circulated in ancient India: **Ajātaśatru-kaukṛtya-(prati)vinodana* and **Ajātaśatru-parivarta/-sūtra*.

② See Harrison and Hartmann 1998, 2000a, 2000b, 2002. These 20 fragments are from 16 folios.

③ See Harrison and Hartmann 1998: 71; Matsuda 1999: 364. According to Sander (2000: 293), the script of this Mahāyāna sūtra manuscript "stands at the end of the development leading to the ornate 'Gilgit/Bamiyan Type I'. A dating into the 5th century is therefore reasonable."

the Schøyen Collection and "may still come to light."④

This paper will begin with a brief introduction to the AjKV as a whole, and will then compare the Sanskrit fragements of one section of the text from the Schøyen Collection with their extant Chinese and Tibetan parallels. The section concerns a matricide who, after confessing his crime to the Buddha and receiving ordination, quickly attains arhatship and enters *parinirvāṇa*. This section, which is interesting in a number of ways, has not been given due attention in previous scholarship. It is hoped that the present study will not only help us better understand the fragmentary Sanskrit version of this section preserved in the Schøyen Collection, but will also help to illuminate some of the problematic aspects of contents and terminologies of the Chinese and Tibetan versions of this part of the text.

The Content and Versions of the AjKV

The AjKV centers around a story in which the Bodhisattva Mañjuśrī, through expounding the "emptiness" (*śūnyatā*) of all phenomena, successfully dispels the "remorse" (*kaukṛtya*) of the Magadhan king Ajātaśatru who has committed patricide, one of the five most serious crimes according to Indian Buddhist ethics, namely, the "crimes of immediate karmic retribution [of descent into hell in the next birth]" (*ānantaryakarma*).⑤ As Paul Harrison and Jens-Uwe Hartmann so aptly put it in this text "the notion of 'emptiness'... is applied unflinchingly to the problems of moral responsibility and personal continuity, in short, to the central Buddhist doctrine of karma, illustrated, as it were, with the 'worst case scenario' represented by the parricide Ajātaśatru."⑥ The text shows that through listening to Mañjuśrī's exposition of emptiness, Ajātaśatru is almost entirely freed from the bad karmic consequence of his patricide. He is said to be reborn in hell only for a short while and to feel no pain there. Most spectacularly, he is predicted to eventually attain Buddhahood and *parinirvāṇa* in the future.⑦ Such an extremely positive stance radically distinguishes the AjKV

---

④ See Harrison and Hartmann 2002: 45. Recently Ye, Li and Kanō (2013: 41-42) have identified two folios from the set of miscellaneous texts in Śāradā palm-leaves from Zha-lu ri-phug (a hermitage near Zha-lu monastery), dating "between ca. the 12th to the 13th centuries" (p.35). These two folios correspond to the portion of the AjKV that extends from the end of Chapter III to the beginning of Chapter XI (the chapter divisions are adopted from Dharmarakṣa's Chinese translation T. 627, and are not found in any other version of the AjKV). According to Ye, Li and Kanō (2013: 42), the Sanskrit text preserved in the two folios "seems a kind of selection of excerpts or summary of the sūtra."

⑤ For a detailed study of the five crimes, see Silk 2007.

⑥ See Harrison and Hartmann 2000a: 169.

⑦ For more discussions on the AjKV's prophecy of Ajātaśatru's future rebirths and final Buddhahood, see Granoff 2012: 204 n. 60; Miyazaki 2013: 3-5; Wu 2012: 214-225; 2014: 158-160; 2016: 129.

from a well-known canonical Buddhist text dealing with the remorse of Ajātaśatru, namely, the *Śrāmaṇyaphalasūtra* ("Scripture on the Fruits of the Ascetic Life"; hereafter ŚPS). In almost all extant versions of the ŚPS (except T. 22) we are told that precisely because of his patricide Ajātaśatru fails to make any substantial spiritual progress during his visit to the Buddha.[8] The AjKV's attribution of future Buddhahood to Ajātaśatru, as Harrison suggests, represents one of the strategies used by the Mahāyāna authors to scripturally legitimize their new goal of Buddhist practice through "scraping the bottom of the historical barrel," that is to say, through recycling those personages whose spiritual attainments were previously unknown or simply precluded in pre-Mahāyāna Buddhist canonical literature.[9]

Besides the salvation of Ajātaśatru, another major theme of the AjKV is the glorification of the Bodhisattva Mañjuśrī. It is interesting to note that in this text Mañjuśrī instead of the Buddha Śākyamuni manages to dispel Ajātaśatru's remorse. Mañjuśrī is featured prominently almost throughout the text.[10] Especially in Chapter III he is not only depicted as being superior over all the great disciples of Śākyamuni, but also as the one who inspired Śākyamuni in one of his past lives to embark on the path to awakening.[11] The ultimate purpose of such construction of the authority of Mañjuśrī is perhaps not to exalt this bodhisattva alone, but to promote the bodhisattva path exemplified by him.[12]

The AjKV is usually regarded as one of the earliest Mahāyāna texts translated into Chinese by Lokakṣema in the late second century CE.[13] His translation survives as T. 626 *Asheshi-wang-jing* 阿闍世王經 ("Sūtra on King Ajātaśatru") in the Taishō canon. Some scholars have expressed misgivings over the traditional ascription of T. 626 to Lokakṣema, based on the observation that T. 626 exhibits a number of terminological and stylistic features uncommon to Lokakṣema's corpus.[14] Those features suggest two possibilities: first, T. 626, as we now have it, may not have come from Lokakṣema's own hands, but from the

⑧ T. 22 is the only version of the ŚPS that speaks of Ajātaśatru's multiple spiritual achievements during his visit to the Buddha, including, *inter alia*, his complete destruction of outflows (**āsrava*), which is equal to the realization of arhatship (cf. 276a13-16). It is hard to say to what extent T. 22 reflects the content of its Indic original, especially given that Ajātaśatru's arhatship is unattested elsewhere. On T. 22, see MacQueen 1988: 224-226; Wu 2012: 98–117.

⑨ See Harrison 2000: 181-183.

⑩ Chapter IV is an exception in which Mañjuśrī makes no appearance. Miyazaki (2008a) suggests that this chapter was probably originally an independent text and later incorporated into the AjKV.

⑪ For an English translation of the Tibetan version of Chapter III of the AjKV, see Harrison 2004.

⑫ Harrison (2000: 172) notes that the exaltation of Mañjuśrī appears not only in the AjKV, but also in a number of other Buddhist texts translated by Lokakṣema, which reflects "the emergence of Mañjuśrī as an important archetypal bodhisattva figure by the middle of the second century CE, be it in one milieu or in many."

⑬ On the ascription of T. 626 to Lokakṣema, see Zürcher 1991: 299; Harrison 1993: 152-156.

⑭ See Nattier 2006: 187 n. 10; 2008: 79, 84-85; Miyazaki 2007a; 2007b.

hands of members of his school; second, if T. 626 was indeed a work of Lokakṣema, it must have undergone some degree of revision after his time. In any event, the status of T. 626 as the oldest Chinese translation of the AjKV is beyond doubt.

Alongside T. 626, two other complete Chinese versions of the AjKV have also survived. One is T. 627 *Wenshuzhili-puchao-sanmei-jing* 文殊支利普超三昧經 ("Sūtra on the Universal and Transcendent Samādhī of Mañjuśrī") translated by Dharmarakṣa in the late third century CE,⑮ and the other T. 628 *Weicengyou-zhengfa-jing* 未曾有正法經 ("Sūtra on the Unprecedented True Dharma") produced by Fatian 法天 in the tenth century. It has been noted that Fatian's version differs from the two older Chinese versions in striking ways.⑯ For instance, all mentions of parricide are missing in his version and even the title is colored with a positive hue, insofar as it can hardly, at first sight, be linked with the remorse of Ajātaśatru. As we will see, Fatian's bowdlerizations are particularly notable in the section of the AjKV to be discussed below, where all references to parricide have been replaced with generalized expressions such as "to commit murder" (*zao-shaye* 造殺業), or simply "to commit a crime" (*zao-zuiye* 造罪業). Fatian probably deliberately made such changes in order to fit the text into a Chinese ethical context, and thus his version is more like "a free adaptation of the text rather than a straight translation of an Indic original."⑰ Besides the three Chinese versions, there is also a full Tibetan translation of the text, revised by the Indian

⑮ The oldest extant Chinese Buddhist catalogue *Chu-sanzang-jiji* 出三藏記集 (T. 2145) compiled by Sengyou僧祐 around 515 CE reports Dharmarakṣa's two translations of the AjKV: (1) 7b25. 普超經四卷 (……舊錄云文殊普超三昧經，太康七年十二月二十七日出), "The *Puchao-jing* in four fascicles (the old catalogue calls it'*wenshu-puchao-sanmei-jing*,' issued on the twenty-seventh day of the twelfth month of ...the seventh year of the Taikang reign [= January 28, 287 CE])"; (2) 9a28. 更出阿闍世王經二卷, "The re-issued [?] *Asheshi-wang-jing* in two fascicles" (the Song 宋, Yuan 元 and Ming 明 editions add: 建武元年四月十六日出, "[It was] issued on the sixteenth day of the fourth month of the first year of the Jianwu reign [= 304 CE]"). Boucher (1996: 193) suggests that according to Sengyou's records Dharmarakṣa may have translated the AjKV twice, separately in 287 CE and 304 CE. However, the second date (304 CE) is problematic, for the Jianwu reign only started from the seventh month of that year (= August 304 CE). Thus the second date may well be a later and unreliable addition, as it has happened to Dharmarakṣa's many other works listed in the *Chu-sanzang-jiji*, particularly in the Song, Yuan and Ming editions (on this problem, see Nattier 2008: 8). We can be sure that the present T. 627 corresponds to the version from 287 CE. This is not only supported by the resemblance of their titles, but also because the version from 304 CE was already lost at Sengyou's time (cf. T. 2145 [lv] 9b27 [*juan* 2]).

⑯ See Harrison 1993: 154-155.

⑰ See Harrison and Hartmann 2000a: 167. Miyazaki (2008b) has looked into what caused Fatian to make such bowdlerizations of the AjKV. According to his investigation, Fatian seems to have made deliberate changes not only in his version of the AjKV, but also in his two other translation works (T. 3 and T. 363), and the causes may be related to the technical incompetence of his translation team, the influence from fellow Chinese monks, and the influence from the royal court that supported and supervised his translation activities.

monk Mañjuśrīgarbha and the Tibetan scholar Ratnarakṣita in the early ninth century.[18]

Before the discovery of the Sanskrit fragments of the AjKV, all our knowledge about this text came from the derivative Chinese and Tibetan versions introduced above, as well as from a few citations also extant only in Chinese or Tibetan.[19] In other words, there was no Indic-language version of this text available to us at all. The discovery of a Sanskrit version of the AjKV in the Schøyen Collection, though in fragmentary form, has at least alleviated the situation to some extent. Recent studies have already demonstrated the benefits of having these Sanskrit fragments. For instance, the Sanskrit version confirms the hypothesis Harrison earlier raised regarding *dharmadhātu* ("realm of *dharma*s"), instead of *dharmakāya* ("body of *dharma*s"), as the Indic original of the term *fashen* 法身 used in T. 626.[20] Moreover, as Tenshō Miyazaki shows, the Sanskrit fragments help to discern a terminological shift from **bodhisattvadharma* (or **bodhisattvabhūmi*), translated as *pusa-fa* 菩薩法 in T. 626, to *mahāyāna*, that occurred in the transmission of the AjKV.[21]

---

⑱ As Harrison and Hartmann (1998: 68 n. 5) have observed, "[n]one of the available editions of the Kanjur gives any hint as to the identity of the original translators." For a detailed introduction to the Tibetan translation and its extant editions, see Miyazaki 2010: 4-5, 249-272. In this paper I use the Derge, sTog Palace and Peking editions of the AjKV (Derge Kanjur 216, *mdo sde*, Tsha 211b2–268b7; sTog Kanjur 223, *mdo sde*, Za 266b7-351a7; Peking Kanjur 882, *mdo-sna-tshogs*, Tsu 220a5-281a5).

⑲ There are five citations from the AjKV in the Tibetan version of the *Sūtrasamuccaya* traditionally ascribed to Nāgārjuna (see Pāsādika 1989: 21, 94, 97, 146, 182). There are also brief references to the AjKV in several eighth-century Sanskrit and Tibetan commentarial works, but no citations are found (see Harrison and Hartmann 1998: 67). The story of Mañjuśrī's salvation of Ajātaśatru as told in the AjKV is alluded to in a number of Mahāyāna texts. For instance, in the Tibetan version of the *Drumakinnararājaparipṛcchā*, the kinnara King Druma says to Ajātaśatru (Harrison 1992b: 253.4-8): *rgyal po chen po khyod kyis gang gi phyir dge ba'i bshes gnyen bcom ldan 'das dang 'jam dpal gzhon nur gyur pa rnyed de / de gnyis las khyod kyis dam pa'i chos thos nas / des mi shes pa'i mun pa dang / gti mug gi ling tog chen pos mtshams med pa'i 'gyod pa byung ba'i sems bsal nas / khyod kyis chos la chos kyi snang ba chen po thob ste /* My translation reads: "O Great king, because you have gained two good friends, the Blessed One and Prince Mañjuśrī. Having heard the true Dharma from these two, your darkness of ignorance, great veil of delusion, and thought of remorse for the *ānantarya* crime has been removed. You have gained the great illumination in the Dharma" (see the Chinese counterparts at T. 624 [xv] 364b12-14 [*juan xia*]; T. 625 [xv] 385b20-23 [*juan* 4]). In the *Tathāgatācintyaguhyanirdeśa* Ajātaśatru says to the Buddha that owing to Mañjuśr ī his remorse has been removed and his mind illuminated (see T. 310 [xi] 76c11-12 [*juan* 14]; T. 312 [xi] 746c2-3 [*juan* 19]). In the **Mahāprajñāpāramitāśāstra* (T. 1509 [xxv] 506b12-14 [*juan* 63]) and the **Daśabhūmikavibhāṣā* (T. 1521 [xxvi] 49a21-22 [*juan* 6]), it is said that because of the Buddha and Mañjuśrī Ajātaśatru's weighty crime of patricide has become diminished.

⑳ See Harrison and Hartmann 2000a: 168 n. 4.

㉑ See Miyazaki 2008b: 34-35. In another paper Miyazaki (2007c: 1104) uses the Sanskrit fragments to determine the language of the source-text of the extant Tibetan version of the AjKV, which has been mistakenly recorded as being translated from Chinese in the *Den-kar-ma,* one of the oldest catalogues of Tibetan Buddhist canonical literature.

The discussion below is an attempt to further explore the fragmentary Sanskrit version of the AjKV found in the Schøyen Collection, through a case study of one section of the text concerning the salvation of a matricide. A careful comparison will be made between the Sanskrit version and its Chinese and Tibetan parallels, so as to identify the differences between these versions in content and terminology. As I will argue, some of the differences (especially substantial ones) may be classified as recensional variations, that is, variations of different Indic recensions of the text, while some other differences may have been brought about by the translators due to their stylistic preferences or idiosyncratic word choices. Thus the differences offer windows into the recensional history of the AjKV and into its translation processes. As mentioned earlier, the paleographical analysis of the Sanskrit fragments of the AjKV show that they were copied during the fourth-fifth centuries, closest to the time when Dharmarakṣa's translation was made. In the discussion that follows I do not intend to date the form of the text represented by the Sanskrit fragments, but will rather consider from a philological perspective its relationships with the Indic originals underlying the Chinese and Tibetan versions.

One Example: The Salvation of a Matricide

The section to be examined belongs to the first half of Chapter XI of the AjKV, if we follow the chapter divisions in Dharmarakṣa's version. It tells how a matricide, after confessing his crime and receiving ordination from the Buddha, quickly attains arhatship and *parinirvāṇa*. This story stands as one of the most fascinating scenes in the narrative framework of the AjKV. It vividly illustrates two main concerns of the text, namely, the annihilation of the law of *karma* and the salvation of one who has committed an *ānantarya* crime, although here instead of Ajātaśatru a matricide becomes the one to be saved. Since matricide represents a type of paradigmatic sinfulness according to Indian Buddhist ethics, the final spiritual liberation of a committer of this crime therefore constitutes a paradigmatic demonstration of the salvific power of the savior who, in the present case, refers to the Buddha.[22] In this story, the teaching the Buddha preaches to the matricide

[22] It is noteworthy that in this story the Buddha, rather than Mañjuśrī, plays the role of redeemer, although Mañjuśrī is said to be the one guiding the matricide into the Buddha's presence. Thus this story appears to be inconsistent with the second half of Chapter XI, which, like most other parts of the text, lays emphasis on Mañjuśrī and his capabilities. The first and second halves of Chapter XI are also inconsistent in terms of their narrative settings (see discussion in Miyazaki 2008b: 42-43).

centers around the notion that "the nature of mind is originally pure."㉓ This notion, as Akira Hirakawa says, "would later develop into *Tathāgatagarbha* doctrine and form an important type of Mahāyāna thought."㉔ The teaching surely deserves examination in its own right. In the present study, my focus will not be on the teaching but on the narrative frame enclosing the teaching. Particular attention will be given to the differences between the presentations of this frame in the extant versions of the text.

The part preceding this section, which forms the beginning of Chapter XI of the AjKV, may be summarized as follows: After preaching to Ajātaśatru, Mañjuśrī leaves the king's palace. On his way back, he sees a matricide sitting under a tree, regretfully weeping. In order to convert him, Mañjuśrī transforms into a man walking with his parents, who are also conjured up by Mañjuśrī. Not far from the matricide, the phantom man (transformation of Mañjuśrī) provokes a quarrel with his parents and kills them. He then approaches the matricide to express his remorse for the parricide and his fear of the immediate retribution of descent into hell. He advises the matricide to go with him to ask the Buddha for help, and the matricide agrees. In front of the matricide, the phantom man confesses his parricide to the Buddha who thereupon expounds the original purity of mind.

The discussion below concerns what happens afterwards. It covers three events:(1) the phantom man's ordination and *parinirvāṇa*; (2) the matricide's confession; (3) the matricide's ordination and *parinirvāṇa*. Four versions will be translated and compared, including the fragmentary Sanskrit version (Skt.), Lokakṣema's translation (Lk.), Dharmarakṣa's translation (Dh.) and the Tibetan translation (Tib.); reference will also be made to Fatian's version when necessary.

(1) The Phantom Man's Ordination and Parinirvāṇa

<Skt.> folio 538v2-4:㉕

atha khalu sa nirmi(taḥ puraṣo bhagavanta)m etad uvāca <|> āścaryam idaṃ

㉓ Lokakṣema's version has 心者本淨 (T. 626 [xv] 403c5 [*juan xia*]); Dharmarakṣa's version has 心者清淨 (T. 627 [xv] 425a6 [*juan xia*]). The Buddha's sermon to the matricide is abbreviated in the Tibetan version (see Harrison and Hartmann 2000a: 198), where no correspondent to the Chinese phrases can be found; the Sanskrit fragment is damaged at the place in question (ibid.: 199, folio 540r1). Earlier in the AjKV the Buddha delivers the same sermon to a phantom man conjured up by Mañjuśrī, which is given in full in the Tibetan. There we find *kye skyes bu sems ni rang bzhin gyis dang ba yin te* "O Man, mind is by nature pure" (Derge 216, *tsha* 258b1-2; sTog 223, 334b7-335a1), which matches 心者本淨 in Lokakṣema's version (T. 626 [xv] 403b2 [*juan xia*]) and 心者清淨 in Dharmarakṣa's version (T. 627 [xv] 424b29 [*juan xia*]). Harrison and Hartmann (2000a: 195, folio 538r2-3) reconstructs the Sanskrit as *cittaṃ* (*hi bhoḥ puruṣa prakṛtiviśuddhaṃ*...).

㉔ Hirakawa 1990: 251.

㉕ The text is quoted from Harrison and Hartmann 2000a: 197.

bhagavan yāvad idaṃ tathāgatena supratividdhā[26] *dharmadhā(tu)ḥ a(*...**v3**...*)* *sarvadharmāḥ* <|> *labhe ahaṃ bhagavato 'ntikāto*[27] *pr(avrajyām...) ehi bhikṣūti*[28] | *atha sa nirmitaḥ pravrajita iti saṃdṛśyate* | *sa avocat* | *prāptābhijño 'smi (***v4**...*bha) gavān āha* <|> *yasyedānīṃ bhikṣoḥ kālaṃ manyase i(...)e* | *svakena ca (t)ejodhātunā kāyo dhyāpitaḥ* | Then the phantom man said to the Blessed One, "It is wonderful, O Blessed One, how the Tāthagata has well penetrated the realm [i.e., totality] of *dharma*s...all *dharma*s...I want to take ordination from [i.e., by] the Blessed One... "Come, O monk!" Then the phantom man appeared as if ordained. He said, "I have attained the supernatural knowledges···" The Blessed One said, "It is now time for a monk to do as you think fit." His body was burned by his own element of fire.

<Lk.> T. 626 [xv] 403b9–15 [*juan xia*]:[29]

其化人則言："善哉，善哉，如怛薩阿竭以法身而自成佛。今知如佛所說，以信不疑，無作者，無受罪者。無生者，無所滅者，如諸法。願樂得爲沙門。"佛言："如子之願。"應時，其化人便如沙門。即白佛："我所犯罪殺父母已脱，而得阿羅漢。今欲般泥洹。"佛言："從意，如所欲。"是化比丘飛去地二十丈。在於虛空，便般泥洹。從身火出，還自燒身。

The phantom man then said, "Excellent! Excellent! One such as the Tathāgata has, with the body of *dharma*s, attained Buddhahood by himself. Now I know that just as the Buddha said, which I believe without doubt,[30] there is no performer of [an action], nor is there anyone experiencing [the result of] a crime. Nothing is born, and nothing perishes, as is the case with all *dharma*s. I want to become a monk." The Buddha said, "As you wish." Immediately, the phantom man appeared as a monk. Then he told the Buddha, "I have been absolved of the crime I had committed by killing my parents, and have attained arhatship. Now I want to undergo *parinirvāṇa*." The Buddha said, "Follow your will. Do as you wish." The phantom monk flew away

---

㉖ The ending *-ā* of *supratividdhā* ("well penetrated") appears to be inconsistent with the masculine singular ending *-uḥ* of *dharmadhā(tu)ḥ*. For the occasional use of *dhātu* as a feminine noun in Buddhist Hybrid Skt., see BHSD, s.v. dhātu.

㉗ As Harrison and Hartmann (2000a: 197 n. 83) point out, the ending of *antikāto* appears to be "a BHS abl. sg." (cf. BHSG, §8.50-51).

㉘ The form *bhikṣūti* (= *bhikṣu iti*) may result from the loss of the initial vowel *i* of *iti* in the sandhi, with the compensatory lengthening of the final vowel *u* of *bhikṣu* (see BHSG, §4.18).

㉙ See a Japanese translation in Sadakata (1989: 152-153).

㉚ The expression今知如佛所說，以信不疑 ("Now I know that just as the Buddha said, which I believe without doubt") has no parallel in Dharmarakṣa's version or in the Tibetan. The Sanskrit fragment has a lacuna here.

from the ground [to the height of] twenty *zhang*. While in mid-air, he underwent *parinirvāṇa*. Fire erupted from his body, and then burned his body.

<Dh.> T. 627 [xv] 424c9-16 [*juan xia*]:

於時化人即而歎曰："得未曾有，天中之天，如來所因成最正覺，了知法界，無有作者，亦無有受。無有生者，無滅度者，無所依猗。願得出家，因佛世尊，得作沙門，受具足戒。"佛言："比丘，善來。"於時化人前作沙門。即白佛言："唯然，世尊，吾獲神通，今欲滅度。"佛之威神使彼化人去地四丈九尺。於虛空中，而取滅度。身中出火，還自燒體。

Then the phantom man immediately exclaimed, "I have learnt something unprecedented, O God among Gods, the way in which the Tathāgata has attained supreme, perfect awakening and has thoroughly comprehended the realm of *dharma*s [in the sense that] there is no performer [of an action] nor is there anyone experencing [the result of an action]. Nothing is born, and nothing ceases, with nothing to depend on.[31] I hope that I can go forth from the household life, and that because of the Buddha, the World-Honored One, I can become a monk and take full ordination."[32] The Buddha said, "O Monk, welcome!" At that moment, the phantom man went forward and became a monk. Then he told the Buddha, "O World-Honored One, [since] I have gained supernatural power, now I want to enter extinction." The divine power of the Buddha caused the phantom man to depart from the ground [to the height of] four *zhang* and nine *chi*. While in mid-air, he entered extinction. Fire erupted from his body, and then burned his body.

<Tib.> Derge 216, *mdo sde*, Tsha 258b6-259a2; sTog 223, *mdo sde*, Za 335a7-b2; Peking 882, *mdo-sna-tshogs*, Tsu 270b2-6:[33]

de nas bcom ldan 'das la |[1)] *skyes bu sprul pa des 'di skad ces gsol to* || *bcom ldan 'das de bzhin gshegs pas chos kyi dbyings yongs su dag pa* | *las ma mchis pa* | *rnam par smin pa ma mchis pa* | *ma skyes pa* | *ma grub pa* | *mngon par rdzogs par sangs rgyas pa ngo mtshar to* || *bcom ldan 'das bdag rab tu 'byung bar 'tshal na* | *bde*[2)]

㉛ The phrase 無所依猗 ("with nothing to depend on") has no parallel in Lokakṣema's version or in the Tibetan. The Sanskrit has a lacuna here.

㉜ Dharmarakṣa mentions both the initial ordination *pravrajyā* ("going forth into the ascetic life"), which he translates as 作沙門 ("to become a monk"), and the full ordination *upasaṃpadā*, which he translates as 受具足戒 ("to take full ordination"). There is no explicit reference to *upasaṃpadā* in any other versions of the text, although the formula beginning with *ehi bhikṣu* ("Come, O monk") is indeed one of the four forms of *upasaṃpadā* (cf. BHSD, s.v. *ehibhikṣukā*).

㉝ The text is also edited and translated in Harrison and Hartmann (2000a: 198).

bar gshegs pa rab tu dbyung[3] *bar gsol | dge slong tshur shog || tshangs par spyad pa spyod cig ces* |[4] *bcom ldan 'das kyis de la de*[5] *skad gsungs pa dang | de'i mod la de rab tu byung bar snang ste | bcom ldan 'das bdag gis mngon par bgyi ba*[6] *thob kyis* |[7] *mya ngan las 'da' bar 'tshal lo zhes de skad kyang smras so* ||[8] *de*[9] *lta ste | dge slong de sangs rgyas kyi mthus steng gi bar snang la shing ta la gang tsam du 'phags nas | bdag gi me'i khams kyis lus bsregs*[10] *pa dang* |

1) DP omit *shad* 2) P: *bda* 3) S: *'byung* 4) P omits *shad* 5) P: *'di* 6) S: *bar* 7) DP omit *shad* 8) P omits double *shad* 9) P: *'di* 10) P: *sregs*

Then the phantom man said to the Blessed One, "O the Blessed One, it is wonderful that the Tathāgata has become fully awakened to [the fact that] the realm of *dharma*s is thoroughly pure, without *karma*, without maturation [of *karma*], unborn and unperfected.[34] O Blessed One, I want to take ordination. O Sugata, please ordain me!"[35] The Blessed One said to him, "Come here, O monk, lead the pure life!" Immediately he appeared as ordained. He said, "O Blessed One, since I have attained completion [?],[36] I want to undergo *parinirvāṇa*." Thus this monk, by the power of the Buddha, rose into the air to the height of a *tāla* tree. His body was burned by his own element of fire.

The passage above concerns a man, though in phantom form, who has committed two *ānantarya* crimes (patricide and matricide) but still receives ordination and finally enters *parinirvāṇa* after attaining arhatship. This scenario appears to run against the conventional rules of monastic ordination, since in all traditions of Indian Buddhist monasticism it is forbidden to ordain one who has committed an *ānantarya* crime, and if a monk is discovered after ordination to have committed such a crime, he is to be, at least in principle, expelled from the Buddhist monastic community.[37] In the AjKV, however, the situation is radically different. The Buddha himself grants ordination to the phantom man with full awareness of the double parricide (killing both parents) the man has committed. Here the ordination of the phantom man, together with his subsequent attainments

---

㉞ This sentence, compared with its counterparts in the two older Chinese versions, gives one more detail, i.e., the nature of *dharma*s as being thoroughly pure (*yongs su dag pa*). This detail only finds a parallel in Fatian's version (T. 628 [xv] 445b6-7 [*juan* 5]: 希有，世尊善說法界自性清淨 "It is wonderful that the World-Honored One well expounded the realm of *dharma*s as being innately pure").

㉟ The sentence "O Sugata, please ordain me" (*bde bar gshegs pa rab tu 'byung bar gsol*) finds a parallel in Fatian's version (T. 628 [xv] 445b7-9 [*juan* 5]). There is no parallel in the two older Chinese versions, and the Sanskrit has a lacuna here.

㊱ On *mngon par bgyi ba thob kyis*, see discussion below.

㊲ For more discussion, see Silk 2007: 276-282.

of arhatship and *parinirvāṇa*, serves to demonstrate the salvific power of the Buddha and of his teaching. It illustrates a revolutionary view of the authors of the AjKV on *karma* and karmic responsibility. This view is articulated through the mouth of the phantom man at the beginning of the passage: there is no performer of an action, or any experiencer of the result of an action.

The table below gives a basic comparison of the Sanskrit, Chinese and Tibetan versions of this passage describing the phantom man's ordination and *parinirvāṇa*. Since my purpose is to show the differences between the four versions, no mention is made of the cases where all four versions agree, or where nothing can be found in (or reconstructed from) the fragmentary Sanskrit manuscript.

Table 1 A Comparison of the Sanskrit, Chinese and Tibetan Versions of the Portion of the AjKV on a Phantom Man's Ordination and Parinirvāna

No.	Skt.	Lk. (T. 626)	Dh. (T. 627)	Tib.
1	*bhagavan* "Blessed One"	—	天中之天[38] "God among Gods"	*bcom ldan 'das* "Blessed One"
2	*supratividdhā* "well understood"	—	了知 "thoroughly know"	—
3	*dharmadhā(tu)ḥ* "realm of *dharmas*"	法身 "body of *dharmas*"	法界 "realm of *dharmas*"	*chos kyi dbyings* "realm of *dharmas*"
4	*sarvadharmāḥ* "all *dharmas*"	諸法 "all *dharmas*"	—	—
5	*bhagavato 'ntikāto* "from [i.e., by] the Blessed One"	—	因佛世尊 "because of the Buddha, the World-Honored One"	—
6	*ehi bhikṣu* "Come, O monk!"	如子之願 "As you wish"	比丘善來 "O monk, welcome!"	*dge slong tshur shog tshangs par spyad pa spyod cig* "Come here, O monk, lead the pure life!"
7	—	我所犯罪殺父母已脫 "I have been absolved of the crime I had committed by killing my parents"	—	—

㊳ Boucher (1996: 210-214) observes that in Dharmarakṣa's corpus the Chinese 天中天 corresponds mostly to *bhagavat* in Sanskrit texts, and only occasionally to *devātideva* or other epithets of the Buddha (e.g., *tathāgata*). This observation also holds true in the present case. In Dharmarakṣa's translation of the AjKV 天中天 and its variant form 天中之天 occur ten times. On four occasions where the Sanskrit is available for comparison, they all correspond to the vocative *bhagavan*.

续表

No.	Skt.	Lk. (T. 626)	Dh. (T. 627)	Tib.
8	*prāptābhijño* "with the supernatural knowledges attained"	得阿羅漢 "attained arhatship"	獲神通 "attained supernatural power"	*mngon par bgyi ba thob* "attained completion [?]"
9	*yasyedānīṃ bhikṣoḥ kālaṃ manyase* "It is now time for a monk to do as you think fit."	從意，如所欲 "Follow your will. Do as you wish."	—	—

Of the nine cases listed above where no agreement is reached among the four versions, Dharmarakṣa's version (T. 627) matches the Sanskrit in seven cases (nos. 1, 2, 3, 5, 6, 7 and 8), with the highest frequency. The Tibetan version matches the Sanskrit in four cases (nos. 1, 3, 6 and 7), plus one more case (no. 8) subject to discussion. Lokakṣema's version (T. 626) matches the Sanskrit in two cases (nos. 4 and 9). More notably, there are four cases (nos. 3, 6, 7 and 8) where the expressions used by Lokakṣema are not attested in any other versions. Let us take a close look at these expressions:

In no. 3 Lokakṣema uses the term *fashen* 法身 (lit. "*dharma*-body") in the sentence 如怛薩阿竭以法身而自成佛 ("One such as the Tathāgata has, with the body of *dharma*s, attained Buddhahood by himself").[39] Harrison suggested that the term *fashen* 法身, though appearing as the standard equivalent of *dharmakāya*, is used throughout T. 626 to denote the "totality of *dharma*s" where the Indic original is supposed to have had *dharmadhātu*.[40] This suggestion is confirmed by the Sanskrit folio (538v2) which does have *dharmadhātu* at the place in question: *yāvad idaṃ tathāgatena supratividdhā*[41] *dharmadhā(tu)ḥ*... ("the extent to which the Tāthagata has well penetrated the realm of *dharma*s..."), with *dharmadhā(tu)* ("realm of *dharma*s") corresponding to *fashen* 法身 in T. 626.[42] Since the counterparts in Dharmarakṣa's translation and in the Tibetan also have standard equivalents of *dharmadhātu* (Chin. *fajie* 法界, "realm of *dharma*s"; Tib. *chos kyi dbyings*), it is most likely that *dharmadhātu* instead of *dharmakāya* was the Indic word underlying *fashen* 法身 in the above sentence from T. 626. In his pioneering study of T. 626, Harrison states that one thing which seems enigmatic is "his [= Lokakṣema's] insistence on employing the Chinese word *shen*, given that this never means 'collection' ".[43] In fact

㊴ On *da-sa-a-jie* 怛薩阿竭, a transliteration of Gāndhārī **tasa-agada* (< Skt. *tathāgata*), see Karashima 2010: 98.

㊵ Harrison 1992a: 64-65, 67.

㊶ On the ending-ā used here, see above n. 26.

㊷ Harrison and Hartmann (2000a: 168 n. 4) show that this suggestion is confirmed by at least two Skt. folios from the Schøyen Collection, i.e. folio 538(v2) under discussion and folio 534 (r2-v2).

㊸ See Harrison 1992a: 67. Square brackets are added by the present author.

that *shen* 身 can sometimes mean "collection" and has been used by Lokakṣema as an equivalent of *skandha* ("aggregate") in his translation of the *Aṣṭasāhasrikā Prajñāpāramitā* (T. 224).[44] The use of *shen* 身 to render *dhātu* is, to some extent, analogous to the use of *shen* 身 to render *skandha*.

What does seem enigmatic to me is the fact that in the present Chinese sentence *fashen* 法身 is not used in the same way as *dharmadhā(tu)* in the Sanskrit, *chos kyi dbyings* in the Tibetan, or *fajie* 法界 in Dharmarakṣa's version, because it appears to refer to a particular attribute with which the Tāthagata is endowed, rather than an object he has intellectually penetrated or become awakened to. This is indicated by the word *yi* 以 ("with, by means of"), an instrumental particle in Classical Chinese, that precedes *fashen* 法身. It is unclear to me why Lokakṣema formulated the Chinese sentence in this way. In any event, his preference for using *fashen* 法身 to render *dharmadhātu* in this and other parts of T. 626, as Harrison suggests, may reflect his intention to preserve the primary meaning ("body") of Skt. *kāya* / Chin. *shen* 身 and his underlying conception of "the *dharma-kāya* as a 'body' of some kind, even if only metaphorically" behind such word choice.[45]

Further, in no. 6 where the Buddha replies to the phantom man's request for ordination, both the Sanskrit (538v3) and Dharmarakṣa's version have "Come, O monk" (Skt. *ehi bhikṣu*; Chin. *biqiu-shanlai* 比丘善來), a standard formula of admission into the monastic community. The Tibetan has *dge slong tshur shog tshangs par spyad pa spyod cig* ("Come here, O monk, lead the pure life"), indicating **ehi bhikṣo cara brahmacaryaṃ*, a variation of the formula. Unlike them all, Lokakṣema uses *ru-zi-zhi-yuan* 如子之願 ("As you wish"). In no. 9 he uses two similar phrases—*congyi* 從意 ("Follow your will") and *ru-suoyu* 如所欲 ("As you wish")—as the Buddha's reply to the phantom man's request for *parinirvāṇa*, which corresponds to *yasyedānīṃ bhikṣoḥ kālaṃ manyase* ("It is now time for a monk to do as you think fit") in the Sanskrit (538v4). Given this correspondence, it is likely that Lokakṣema's Indic original had the formula *yasyedānīṃ (...) kālaṃ manyase* on both occasions, as the Buddha's replies to the phantom man's requests for ordination and for *parinirvāṇa*. The same situation also occurs in the case of the matricide to be discussed later, where Lokakṣema's Indic original also seems to have used *yasyedānīṃ (...) kālaṃ manyase* twice, as the Buddha's replies to the matricide's requests for ordination and for *parinirvāṇa*.

In nos. 7 and 8 about the phantom man's request for *parinirvāṇa*, Lokakṣema's version has the longest sentence among all four versions: 我所犯罪殺父母已脫, 而得阿羅漢, 今欲般泥洹 ("I have been absolved of the crime I had committed by killing my parents, and have attained arhatship. Now I want to enter *parinirvāṇa*").[46] Compared with its counterparts

---

[44] See Karashima 2010: 418-419, s.v. 身 shēn.

[45] Harrison 1992a: 67-68.

[46] T. 626 [xv] 403b13-14 [*juan xia*].

in the other versions, this sentence has two distinctive features: one is the phantom man's statement on being absolved of his double parricide, and the other in his the mention of attainment of arhatship, instead of acquisition of supernatural power.

In no. 7 the phantom man acknowledges his being absolved of his crime immediately after he hearing the Buddha's sermon and receives ordination. Thus his acknowledgement serves as a testimony to the salvific power of the Buddha and of his teaching. It is hard to say whether Lokakṣema's Indic original really had this detail. Given the lack of parallel in all the other versions, it is possible that this detail was an interpretive gloss added by Lokakṣema himself.

The situation is more complex in no. 8, where Lokakṣema's version speaks of the phantom man's attainment of arhatship. The Sanskrit (538v3) has *prāptābhijño 'smi...* ("I have attained the supernatural knowledges..."), which matches 吾獲神通,今欲滅度 ("I have attained supernatural power. Now I want to extent extinction") in Dharmarakṣa's version.[47] The Tibetan (Derge, Tsha 259a1; sTog, Za 335b3; Peking, Tsu 270b5) reads *bcom ldan 'das bdag gis mngon par bgyi ba thob kyis mya ngan las 'da' bar 'tshal lo* ("O Blessed One, since I have attained completion, I want to undergo *parinirvāṇa*"). It puzzles me what the expression *mngon par bgyi ba* (literally "complete action") refers to here. It could denote the phantom man's completion of ordination, given that he makes this request just after receiving ordination, but it could also be a variant of *mngon par shes pa,* the standard Tibetan equivalent of *abhijñā* ("supernatural knowledge").[48] If the second hypothesis is correct, the Tibetan would agree with the Sanskrit and with Dharmarakṣa's version at this point. It is clear that both *abhijñā* in the Sanskrit and the word *shentong* 神通 ("supernatural power") in Dharmarakṣa's version refer to the stereotyped set of six supernatural knowledges (*ṣaḍabhijñā*) attributed to a Buddha or an arhat.[49] By attaining the six supernatural knowledges, the phantom man attains arhatship. This can also be known from the way in which he enters *parinirvāṇa*. He is said to do so through self-cremation in mid-air, as usually performed by Buddhist saints when they pass into *parinirvāṇa*. Thus, although the Sanskrit and Dharmarakṣa's versions —and perhaps also the Tibetan version—mention the phantom man's acquisition of supernatural knowledges (Skt. *abhijñā*; Chin. *shentong* 神通; Tib. *mngon par bgyi ba* [variant of *mngon par shes pa*]), they actually imply his attainment

---

⑰ T. 627 [xv] 424c14 [*juan xia*].

⑱ Tib. *mngon par* represents the Skt. prefix *abhi-*, and *bgyi ba* is usually used to render derivatives of √*kṛ* "to do" (cf. TSD, ii. 657, s.v. *bgyi ba*; iii. 1018, s.v. *mngon par*). Harrison and Hartmann (2000a: 198) translate *bdag gis mngon par bgyi ba thob kyis* as "since I have attained realisation" but it is still unclear to me what the "realisation" exactly refers to here.

⑲ The set of five mundane *abhijñā*s (*pañcābhijñā*) attainable for both Buddhists and non-Buddhists (for instance, Brahmanical sages) makes no sense in the present context.

of arhatship. Lokakṣema's version differs from them all by making this point explicit. Such a difference may have resulted either from Lokakṣema's own interpretation, or from a recensional variation of his Indic original.[50]

In sum, among the four versions of this part of the AjKV depicting the phantom man's ordination and *parinirvāṇa*, Dharmarakṣa's version matches the Sanskrit text in most cases. His Indic original may have been the closest to the Sanskrit text as far as this part is concerned. The Tibetan version matches the Sanskrit in fewer cases and contains some details only attested in Fatian's version, which suggests the closeness between the underlying Indic recensions of the Tibetan and Fatian's versions.[51] Lokakṣema's version has the fewest matches with the Sanskrit and, moreover, it shows three significant differences from the other versions:

i) Lokakṣema uses *fashen* 法身 (lit. "*dharma*-body") in places where the Sanskrit text uses *dharmadhā(tu)* ("*dharma*-realm"). We can be sure that his Indic original also had *dharmadhātu* instead of *dharmakāya*, and that the difference was caused by his preference for employing the word *shen* 身, which most often means "body" but sometimes can also mean "collection," to render *dhātu*.

ii) While the Sanskrit, Tibetan and Dharmarakṣa's versions all use the formula "Come, O monk" (*ehi bhikṣu*) or its variation "Come here, O monk, lead the pure life" (**ehi bhikṣo cara brahmacaryaṃ*) as the Buddha's reply to the phantom man's request for ordination, Lokakṣema's version uses 如子所願 ("As you wish") which seems to have been based on **yasyedānīṃ (...) kālaṃ manyase*.

iii) In Lokakṣema's version the phantom man says that he is absolved of his double parricide. This detail finds no parallel in any other versions. It may well be an interpretive gloss added by Lokakṣema to highlight the salvific power of the Buddha and the efficacy of his teaching.

iv) Lokakṣema's version mentions the phantom man's attainment of arhatship, instead of his mastery of the six supernatural knowledges as in the Sanskrit and in Dharmarakṣa's versions, although the two achievements are equivalent in function.

In comparison with the foregoing versions of the text, Fatian's version has two extra details: one is the phantom man's monastic appearance after ordination,[52] and the other the

---

[50] Fatian's version neither mentions the attainment of arhatship nor the acquisition of supernatural power (cf. T. 628 [xv] 445b11-12 [*juan* 5]).

[51] Harrison and Hartmann (2000a: 167) already noted the closeness between the Indic originals of the two versions, on the basis of their similarity in abbreviating the Buddha's sermon to the matricide.

[52] T. 628 [xv] 455b10-11 [*juan* 5]: 是時化人，於剎那間，鬚髮自落，袈裟被身，成苾芻相 ("At that time the phantom man, in an instant, with his hair and beard automatically falling off, with his body clad in the *kāṣāya* robe, obtained the marks of a monk").

vanishment of the phantom man's cremation remains.[53] Neither detail is found in the two older Chinese versions. As we will see, the Sanskrit version gives the second detail only in reference to the matricide; the Tibetan version gives both details also only referring to the matricide. Unlike them all, Fatian's version has the two details in both cases of the phantom man and the matricide, which may reflect a later development of the AjKV.

(2) The Confession of a Matricide

<Skt.> folio 539r1–3:[54]

ānaṃtaryakārī dvitīyaḥ puruṣaḥ taṃ nirmitaṃ puruṣaṃ parinirvāyaṃtaṃ t(āṃ) c(a) dh(armadeśanāṃ...**r2**...*) mātā jīvitād vyavaropitā* <|> *eṣa ca bhagavatsakāśe pravrajitvā parini(r)v(ṛtaḥ*...**r3**...*ma)yāpi bhagavan mātā jīvitād vyaparopitā* |

The second man who has committed a crime of immediate retribution [saw] the phantom man undergoing *parinirvāṇa* [and heard the exposition of the Dharma]... [thinking, "I] took the life of [my] mother, and that man, having taken ordination in the presence of the Blessed One, underwent *parinirvāṇa*..." ... "O Blessed One, I too took the life of my mother."

<Lk.> T. 626 [xv] 403b16–21 [*juan xia*]:[55]

其殺母者見是人已般泥洹具足，聞怛薩阿竭所語，則自念言："其人所作甚逆，今作沙門而得度脱般泥洹。我罪尚可行。何爲不自歸佛？亦可到是。"便前爲佛作禮，自白："我所作非法，自殺我母。今以身自歸。"

The matricide saw that this man [= the phantom man] had accomplished *parinirvāṇa* and, having heard what the Tathāgata said, he thought, "What this man had done is very heinous, [but even so] he has now become a monk and attained liberation through undergoing *parinirvāṇa*. My crime is less serious. Why don't I take refuge in the Buddha? [Thereby] I can also attain the same result." Then he went forth to pay homage to the Buddha and said, "What I did is unrighteous, [because] I killed my mother. Now I take refuge [in the Buddha]."

<Dh.> T. 627 [xv] 424c16-21 [*juan xia*]:

於時，逆子見彼化人得作沙門，聽受經法。聞佛所説，心自念言："向者彼人自危二親，在世尊前而作沙門，便得滅度。今吾何故不効彼人而作沙門？亦當滅度。"作是念已，往詣佛所。稽首聖足，前白佛言："我亦造逆，自危母命。"

㊾ 445b13-14: 化火自焚，滅盡無餘，同彼虚空 ("He conjured fire to burn himself, and vanished completely without remainder, just like the empty sky").

㊿ The text is quoted from Harrison and Hartmann 2000a: 197.

55 See a Japanese translation in Sadakata (1989: 153-154).

At that time, the treacherous son [= the matricide] saw the phantom man become a monk and heard the teaching. Having heard what the Buddha said, he thought, "Just now this man took the life of both his parents, [but even so] he has become a monk in front of the World-Honored One and then attained liberation. Now, why don't I follow this man to become a monk? [Thereby] I will also attain liberation." After having thought this, he went to where the Buddha was. Having bowed his head at the Blessed One's feet, he went forth and said to the Buddha, "I also committed a crime, [because] I took the life of my mother."

<Tib.> Derge 216, *mdo sde*, Tsha 259a2-4; sTog 223, *mdo sde*, Za 335b4–7; Peking 882, *mdo-sna-tshogs*, Tsu 270b6-7:[56]

skyes bu yang dag pa des chos bstan pa 'di dag thos so || thos nas kyang 'di snyam du gyur te | skyes bu des ni pha dang[1)] *ma gnyi ga'i*[2)] *srog bcad kyang |*[3)] *de yongs su mya ngan las 'das na |*[4)] *bdag gis ni ma 'ba' zhig*[5)] *gi srog bcad du zad pas |*[6)] *ci'i phyir bdag yongs su mya ngan las mi 'da' snyam nas | de de'i tshe bcom ldan 'das kyi drung du song ste | bcom ldan 'das kyi zhabs la mgo bos phyag 'tshal nas |*[7)] *bcom ldan 'das la 'di skad ces gsol to || bcom ldan 'das bdag gis*[8)] *kyang ma'i srog bkum mo ||*

1) S omits *dang* 2) S *ka'i* 3) DP omit *shad* 4) DP omit *shad* 5) P *shig*[57] 6) DP omit *shad* 7) DP omit *shad* 8) P omits *gis*

The real man heard this exposition[58] of the Dharma. Having heard it, he thought, "That man has undergone *parinirvāṇa*, even though he had taken the lives of both his parents. Since I only took the life of my mother, why can't I undergo *parinirvāṇa*?" Immediately he went up to the Blessed One, and bowed his head at the feet of the Blessed One. He said to the Blessed One, "O Blessed One, I too took the life of my mother."

The table below gives an overview of the significant differences between the four versions of this part of the AjKV. As in the preceding Table1 here no mention is made of the cases where the Sanskrit is not available for comparision.

---

[56] The text is also edited and translated in Harrison and Hartmann (2000a: 198).

[57] I adopt the reading'*ba' zhig* ("only") in the Derge and sTog editions, rather than '*ba' shig* in the Peking edition, where *shig* is probably an orthographical variant of *zhig*.

[58] Tib. *chos bstan pa 'di dag*. As Hahn (1974) has amply shown, the particle *dag* does not necessarily indicate plurality, and there are many cases where "noun + *dag*" corresponds to a Sanskrit singular. Here it seems more suitable to translate *chos bstan pa 'di dag* as "this exposition of the Dharma" [i.e., the Buddha's sermon on the original purity of the mind] instead of "these expositions of the Dharma". The Sanskrit (539r1) is damaged at the place in question (Harrison and Hartmann 2000a: 197).

Table 2 A Comparison of the Sanskrit, Chinese and Tibetan Versions of the Portion of the AjKV on the Confession of a Matricide

No.	Skt.	Lk. (T. 626)	Dh. (T. 627)	Tib.
1	*parinirvāyaṃtaṃ* "undergoing *parinirvāṇa*"	般泥洹具足 "to accomplish *parinirvāṇa*"	得作沙門 "to become a monk"[59]	—
2	*dh(armadeśanāṃ)* "exposition of the Dharma"	怛薩阿竭所語 "what the Tathāgata said"	經法 "scriptural Dharma, teaching"	*chos bstan pa* "exposition of the Dharma"
3	...*mātā jīvitād vyavaropitā* "[I] took the life of [my] mother"	—	—	—
4	*eṣa ca bhagavatsakāśe pravrajitvā* "That man, having taken ordination in front of the Blessed One"	今作沙門 "He has now become a monk"	在世尊前而作沙門 "He has become a monk before the World-Honored One"	—
5	—	今以身自歸 "Now I take refuge [in the Buddha]"	—	—

Of the five cases listed above, Dharmarakṣa's version matches the Sanskrit in three cases (nos. 2, 4 and 5). Both Lokakṣema's version and the Tibetan match the Sanskrit in two cases (nos. 1 and 4; nos. 2 and 5). Let us now look at them in detail.

In no. 2 the Tibetan has *chos bstan pa* ("exposition of the Dharma"), the standard equivalent of *dharmadeśanā*. The Sanskrit folio (539r1) is badly damaged at the place in question, insofar as only an akṣara *dh(...)* is legible. The current reconstruction **dh(armadeśanāṃ)* is based on the Tibetan. Lokakṣema uses the phrase 怛薩阿竭所語 ("what the Tathāgata said") to refer to the Buddha's teaching. Dharmarakṣa uses the term *jingfa* 經法 which, as Vetter and Zacchetti have observed, often (though not always) has the same function as *dharma* in early Chinese Buddhist texts, referring either to Buddhist teaching or to states of existence in general.[60] For instance, in Dharmarakṣa's translation of the *Saddharmapuṇḍarīka*, most occurrences of *jingfa* 經法 are found where the Sanskrit parallel has *dharma*, referring to Buddhist teaching.[61] In Dharmarakṣa's translation of the AjKV, *jingfa* 經法 occurs totally eleven times, and in two occurrences (not including the present one) where the Sanskrit is

㊾ Like Dharmarakṣa's version, Fatian's version also mentions the phantom man's ordination instead of his *parinirvāṇa* at this point (cf. T. 628 [xv] 445b15 [*juan* 5]).

㊿ See Vetter and Zacchetti 2004; Karashima 2010: 266-269, s.v. 經法 (jīng fǎ).

(61) See Vetter and Zacchetti 2004: 159-166; Karashima 1998: 226-227, s.v. 經法 (jīng fǎ).

available for comparison, *jingfa* 經法 corresponds to *dharma*.⑫ Given such correspondences, it might also be possible to reconstruct the Sanskrit word as **dh(armaṃ)* referring to the Buddha's teaching.⑬

Nos. 3 and 4 concern the matricide's decision to confess his crime to the Buddha. In the Chinese and Tibetan versions, the matricide reflects that the phantom man, although having killed both his parents, still attains *parinirvāṇa*. The Sanskrit (539r2) reads: *...mātā jīvitād vyavaropitā eṣa ca bhagavatsakāśe pravrajitvā parini(r)v(ṛtaḥ...)*, "...[I] took the life of [my] mother, and that man, having taken ordination before the Blessed One, underwent *parinirvāṇa*..." Here the phrase *mātā jīvitād vyavaropitā* is unexpected, given that the Chinese and Tibetan versions all mention the phantom man's double parricide and thus all suggest something like **tena puruṣeṇa mātāpitarau jīvitād vyavaropitau*.⑭ Although Lokakṣema's version and the Tibetan speak of the matricide's reflection on his own crime, in both versions this detail appears only after the mention of the phantom man's *parinirvāṇa*.⑮ Since the Sanskrit folio is damaged both before *mātā jīvitād vyavaropitā* and after *parini(r)v(ṛtaḥ...)*, for the time being it is hard to draw any conclusion regarding the original structure of the Sanskrit sentence in question.

Interestingly, in Fatian's version the matricide says, "That man [= the phantom man]

---

⑫ The two occurrences are as follows: (1) T. 627 [xv] 425c29-426a1 [*juan xia*]: 彌勒如來緣不動菩薩說此經法 ("The Tathāgata Maitreya will, because of the Bodhisattva Immovable, preach this teaching"). Here *jingfa* 經法 matches *dharmaṃ* in the Sanskrit (Harrison and Hartmann 2000a: 210, folio 544v3: *[...ākhyātāvī]naṃ bodhisatvam ārabhya tathā tathā dharmaṃ de(śa)yati yathā...*, "[The Bodhisattva Maitreya] will preach the Dharma regarding the Bodhisattva Ākhyātāvīna in such a way that..."), and *chos kyi rnam grangs* (**dharmaparyāya*) in the Tibetan (Derge, Tsha 261b6–7; sTog, Za 340a7); (2) 423c11-13 [*juan xia*]: 吾今覺了一切諸法。所覺了法，於諸經法，亦無所得趣於地獄、若生天上、般泥洹者 ("Now I [= Ajātaśatru] have become awakened to all *dharma*s. Among all *dharma*s, there is no *dharma*, into which I have become awakened, going to hell, being reborn in heaven or entering *parinirvāṇa*"). The Sanskrit reads (Harrison and Hartmann 2000a: 188, folio 534r3): *tathā abhisaṃbuddhe maṃjuśri sarvadharmaiḥ tad apy ahaṃ dharmaṃ na samanupaśyāmi (yaḥ...)*, "Mañjuśrī, with all *dharma*s perfectly comprehended [by me] in this way, I do not see any *dharma* [going to hell...]." Harrison and Hartmann (2000a: 188 n. 53) point out that *tathā abhisaṃbuddhe...sarvadharmaiḥ* seems to be "a poorly Sanskritized 'instrumental absolute (perhaps from *abhisaṃbuddhehi sarvadharmehi*)" which functions as the Classical Sanskrit locative absolute *abhisaṃbuddheṣu sarvadharmeṣu*. It is possible that Dharmarakṣa's Indic original had *tathābhisaṃbuddheṣu...sarvadharmeṣu*, and that he translated *sarvadharmeṣu* twice, once as the locative absolute which underlies 吾今覺了一切諸法 ("Now I become awakened into all *dharma*s"), and once as a simple locative which underlies 於諸經法 ("among all *dharma*s"). If this was the case, *zhu-jingfa* 諸經法would match *sarvadharmeṣu* and *jingfa* 經法 would still correspond to *dharma*.

⑬ This means that the latter part of folio 539r1 might be reconstructed as *t(aṃ) c(a) dh(armaṃ...)*.

⑭ The phrase *tena puruṣena/putreṇa mātāpitarau jīvitā vyavaropitau* does appear elsewhere in the Skt. text. It is partially preserved in the Schøyen fragment (536r1-v4) of the AjKV, concerning Mañjuśrī's encounter with the matricide (cf. Harrison and Hartmann 2000a: 192; 2002: 47).

⑮ In T. 626 and the Tibetan, having reflected on the phantom man's double parricide and *parinirvāṇa*, the matricide compares his crime with the phantom man's (T. 626 [xv] 403b19 [*juan xia*]: 我罪尚可行, "My crime is less serious"; Tib. *bdag gis ni ma 'ba' zhig gi srog bcad du zad pas*, "Since I only took the life of my mother"). The comparision is not explicit but implied in Dharmarakṣa's version.

and I both committed a crime. He attained liberation first. Now I had better also request the Buddha to convert and convey me to deliverance."[66] Unlike the other versions of the text, which all suggest the lower severity of the real man's matricide in comparison with the phantom man's double parricide, Fatian's version equates the two crimes. The equation is understandable since throughout his version, in order to avoid explicitly mentioning parricide and matricide, Fatian consistently uses obscure expressions, such as *zaoye* 造業 ("to commit an act"), *zao-shaye* 造殺業 ("to commit an act of murder") and *zao-zuiye* 造罪業 ("to commit a criminal act"), to refer to the crimes committed by the phantom man and by the real man. The obscuration was intended to adapt the text into a Chinese ethical context. Since there is no distinction between the references to matricide and double parricide, Fatian might have found it difficult—and perhaps also unnecessary from his point of view—to differentiate the severity of the two crimes. Seen from this perspective, the equation is both an illustration and a result of the bowdlerization policy adopted by Fatian in translating the AjKV.

Lastly, in no. 5 about the matricide's statement of confession, Lokakṣema's version has 今以身自歸 ("Now I take refuge [in the Buddha]") which may be a gloss added by Lokakṣema himself, given the lack of parallel in the other versions. Fatian's version formulates the matricide's confession as follows: "O World-Honored One, I have committed an act of murder and am afraid of falling into the great hell in the future."[67] Here Fatian again uses *zao-shaye* 造殺業 ("to commit an act of murder") to refer to matricide, but the mention of the man's fear of hell—which is surely a gloss added by Fatian—clearly indicates the *ānantarya* nature of the crime. Futher, in Fatian's version the matricide's confession is followed by his entreaty to the Buddha for help, "May the Buddha show compassion and grant me salvation,"[68] which has no parallel in the other versions. Almost the same phrase also occurs earlier in Fatian's version as the entreaty of the phantom man, where it matches *bcom ldan 'das bdag la skyabs mdzad par gsol* ("I entreat the Blessed One to protect me") in the Tibetan (Derge, Tsha 258a3; sTog, Za 334a5; Peking, Tsu 269b6).[69] Fatian's version is more developed than the Tibetan as far as this detail is concerned, since it mentions the entreaty in both cases of the phantom man and the matricide, while the Tibetan only mentions it in the case of the phantom man.

In sum, in this part of the AjKV concerning the matricide's confession, two remarks

---

[66] T. 628 [xv] 445b16-17 [*juan* 5]: 此人與我同造罪業。彼先解脫，我今亦宜求佛化度.

[67] 445b18-19: 世尊，我造殺業，怖於當來墮大地獄.

[68] 445b19: 願佛慈悲而垂救度.

[69] See 445a18-19. No entreaty is found in the two older Chinese versions, and the Sanskrit is not available for comparison (cf. Harrison and Hartmann 2002: 47-48).

may be made on the Sanskrit text in comparison with the other versions:

i) The Sanskrit (539r1) has the akṣara *dh(...)* where Dharmarakṣa uses *jingfa* 經法 and the Tibetan has *chos bstan pa*. The current reconstruction *dh(armadeśanāṃ)* is based on the Tibetan. In view of the repeated correspondences of *jingfa* 經法 to *dharma* in Dharmarakṣa's translation corpus, we might suggest **dh(armaṃ)* as another candidate for reconstruction.

ii) The Sanskrit text differs from the other versions by placing the matricide's reflection on his own crime before his reflection on the phantom man's *parinirvāṇa*. Since the folio is badly damaged, nothing conclusive can be said about the extact structure of the Sanskrit sentence in question.

Moreover, Fatian's version differs from the foregoing versions in three aspects:

First, he consistently uses obscure expressions to refer to matricide and patricide, in order to make the text more acceptable for Chinese audiences.

Second, instead of differentiating the real man's matricide and the phantom man's double parricide, Fatian equates the two crimes. The equation is explicable, if we take into account his bowdlerization policy in translating the AjKV.

Third, in Fatian's version the matricide's confession is followed by his entreaty to the Buddha, which is a repetition of the earlier entreaty of the phantom man. In this regard, his version is more developed than the Tibetan which only has the entreaty in the case of the phantom man.

(3) The Matricide's Ordination and Parinirvāṇa

In the Sanskrit text and the two older Chinese versions of the AjKV, in response to the matricide's confession, the Buddha repeats verbatim to him the sermon earlier preached to the phantom man. The repetition is abbreviated both in the Tibetan and in Fatian's version, which reflects a significant similarity between the underlying Indic rencessions of the two versions.[70] The Buddha's sermon concerns the original purity of mind. Since the focus of this

[70] On this similarity, see Harrison and Hartmann (2000a: 167). In the Tibetan the Buddha responds to the matricide's confession as follows: Derge, Tsha 259a4–5; sTog, Za 335b7–336a2; Peking, Tsu 270b8–271a2: *de nas bcom ldan 'das kyis skyes bu de la legs so zhes bya ba byin te /* [1] *legs so legs so // skyes bu khyod kyis de bzhin gshegs pa ma bslus* [2] *mod kyi / kye skyes bu khyod sems gang gis ma'i srog bcad* [3] *pa sems kyi rgyud la rtogs shig ces rgya cher bka' stsal te / zhib tu* [4] *sprul pa'i skyes bu ji lta ba de*[5] *bzhin du bya'o //*

1) DP omit *shad* 2) P *slus* 3) P *bcod* 4) P *du* 5) S omits *de*

"Then the Blessed One applauded that man: 'Excellent! Excellent! O Man, although you have not lied to the Tathāgata, O Man, you should examine in your course of thinking (*sems kyi rgyud*, Skt. **citta-saṃtati/-saṃtāna*) with which thought you took the life of your mother,' and so on, as it was told in detail to the phantom man." See also a translation in Harrison and Hartmann (2000a: 198). In Fatian's version, the Buddha's sermon to the phantom man is given in full, but in the case of the matricide, only the first sentence of the sermon is given (cf. T. 628 [xv] 445b19–21 [*juan* 5]).

study is on the frame story of the salvation of the matricide, I will not discuss the doctrinal content of the sermon in any detail. The translation below is made from the passage that appears immediately after the sermon. It shows how the matricide, following in the footsteps of the phantom man, takes ordination and then attains *parinirvāṇa*.

<Skt.> folio 540v1-541r2:[71]

(...) sa atrāṇo duḥkhārdito bhagavaṃtam etad avocat | dahyāmi[72] *bhagavan| trāyasva m(e) suga(ta | ...***v2***) pratiṣṭhāpite tasya śirasi pāṇau bhagavatā* |[73] *atha tasya puruṣasya sarvā duḥkhā (...***v3** *pravraj)i(ṣy)e 'haṃ bhagavan* <|> *pravrajāhi me sugata | tam evaṃ bhagavān āha | ehi bhikṣūti pra(...)* **(v4** *duḥkhaṃ duḥkhasamudayaḥ duḥ)khanirodhaḥ mārgaḥ tasya virajo vigatamalaṃ dharmeṣu dharmacakṣur viśud(dham...)* **(541r1***...) āha* <|> *parinirvāyiṣye bhagavan | parinirvāṇakālasamayo me bhagavan | āha* <|> *y(asyedānīṃ bhikṣoḥ kālaṃ manyase...***r2***...) dahyataḥ*[74] *na chavikā*[75] *na maṣiḥ prajñāyate* <|> *devatāśatasahasrāṇi cāsya pūjā a(...)*

...Without protection, afflicted by pain, he said to the Blessed One, "O Blessed One, I am on fire. O Sugata, please save me! ..." As soon as the Blessed One put his hand on his [= the matricide's] head, then all that man's painful [sensations...][76] "O Blessed One, I shall take ordination...O Sugata, please ordain me." The Blessed One said to him, "Come, O monk! ..." [...suffering, the origin of suffering,] the cessation of suffering, and the path to the cessation of suffering. He gained the dust-

---

⑪ The text is quoted from Harrison and Hartmann 2000a: 200–201.

⑫ The word *dahyāmi* is a Buddhist Hybrid Skt. passive form of √*dah* ("to burn"), with an active ending (cf. BHSG, §37.12–14).

⑬ Here *(...) pratiṣṭhāpite tasya śirasi pāṇau bhagavatā* appears to be a locative absolute construction, given the locative endings of *pāṇau* (locative singular of *pāṇi*, "hand") and *pratiṣṭhāpite* (locative singular of the past passive participle of the causative *pratiṣṭhāpayati*, "place upon"). The Chinese and Tibetan versions all mention the golden color of the Buddha's hand (cf. *jinshou* 金手 ["golden hand"] in T. 626 [xv] 403c14 [*juan xia*]; *jinse-bi* 金色臂 ["golden arm"] in T. 627 [xv] 425a17 [*juan xia*]; *phyag gser gyi kha dog lta bu* ["hand of gold-like color"] at Derge, Tsha 259a6, and Peking, Tsu 271a3; *phyag g.yas pa gser gyi kha dog lta bu* ["right hand of gold-like color"] at sTog, Za 336a4). The Sanskrit folio may have had this detail in the lacuna before *pratiṣṭhāpite*.

⑭ Here *dahyataḥ* is probably the genitive (or ablative) masculine singular form of *dahyat* ("being burned"), an example of Buddhist Hybrid Skt. present passive participle of √*dah* with active ending (see BHSG, §37.15), equivalent to *dahyamāna* in Classical Skt. The corresponding Tibetan reads *bsregs pa de'i tshe* ("when it was burned"), which suggests that the Sanskrit may well have had an absolute genitive construction here.

⑮ Emended to *chāyikā* (cf. Harrison and Hartmann 2000a: 201 n. 97).

⑯ Harrison and Hartmann (2000a: 201 n. 91) rightly point out that the plural form *duḥkhā* at 540v2 may have been followed by *vedanāḥ*.

free, stainless and pure Dharma-eye into *dharma*s... He said, "O Blessed One, I shall undergo *parinirvāṇa*. O Blessed One, it is the time, the occasion, for me to undergo *parinirvāṇa*." [The Buddha] said, "[It is now time for a monk to do as you think fit]..." [When his body] was being burned, no ashes or soot was found, and a hundred thousand gods paid homage to him...

<Lk.> T. 626 [xv] 403c12-21 [*juan xia*]:⑰

其殺母者，應時身諸毛孔一一孔，泥犁之火從其孔出，痛不可言。則自陳說："今自歸怛薩阿竭。惟哀加護，令得安隱。"佛則時以金手著其人頭上。應時火滅，苦痛則除。便前長跪，願欲作沙門。佛言："如所欲。"則時以爲沙門。怛薩阿竭以四諦法而說之。應時得法眼。深入其事，則得阿羅漢。便白佛言："今我欲般泥洹。"佛言："如所欲。"飛在虛空，去地百四十丈。便於是上，其身火出，還自燒身。諸天億百千人悉飛而來供養。

The matricide, immediately with fire of hell coming out of each pore on his body, suffered inexpressible pain. Then he said, "Now I take refuge in the Tathāgata. Please grant protection and set me at peace." The Buddha thereupon put his golden hands above the man's head. Immediately the fire was quenched and his pain ceased. Then he went forth and prostrated, wishing to become a monk." The Buddha said, "As you wish." There and then he became a monk. The Tathāgata preached to him the teaching of the four [noble] truths. Immediately he obtained the Dharma-eye. Having penetrated the matters,⑱ he attained arhatship. Then he said to the Buddha, "Now I want to undergo *parinirvāṇa*." The Buddha said, "As you wish." He flew into the air to [the height of] one hundred and forty *zhang* away from the ground. At that height, fire erupted from his body, and then burned the body. Myriads of deities came flying here to pay homage.

<Dh.> T. 627 [xv] 425a14-25 [*juan xia*]:

於時逆人，地獄之火從毛孔出，毒痛甚劇而無救護。則白佛言："我今被燒。惟天中天，而見救濟。歸命大聖。"於是世尊出金色臂，著實人頂上。火時即滅，無復苦痛。見如來身若干相好，身痛休息，而得安隱。又前白佛："欲作沙門。"佛尋聽之，即爲寂志。於時，世尊爲說四諦。其人聞之，遠塵

⑰ See also a Japanese translation in Sadakata (1989: 155-156).

⑱ The phrase 深入其事 ("to penetrate matters") seems to refer to the matricide's penetration into the Buddha's teaching. The Sanskrit is not available here. The counterpart in Dharmarakṣa's version reads: T. 627 [xv] 425a21 [*juan xia*]: 修行法教 ("[Having] practiced the teaching of the Dharma"). The Tibetan (Derge, Tsha 259b3; sTog, Za 336b4; Peking, Tsu 271a8) reads: *yang* (S: *'ang*) *lam bsgoms nas* ("having further cultivated the path").

離垢，得法眼淨。修行法教，逮得往還，證至得羅漢。又白佛言："欲般泥洹。"世尊告曰："隨意所存。"於時，比丘踊在虛空，去地四丈九尺。身中出火，還自燒體。百千天人於虛空中而來供養。

At that time, the treacherous man [= the matricide], with fire of hell coming out of his pores, suffered extreme pain but did not have any protection. Then he said to the Buddha, "Now I am on fire. May the God among Gods save me! I take refuge in the Great Sage." Then the World-Honored One stretched out his golden arm and put it above the real man's head. The fire was immediately quenched, and he felt no more pain. When he saw the Tathāgata's body [endowed with] a number of excellent physical marks and minor characteristics,[79] the pain in his body ceased and he gained peace. Furthermore, he went forth and said to the Buddha, "I want to become a monk." The Buddha thereupon permitted him. Immediately he became a tranquil-minded one. At that time, the World-Honored One preached to him the four [noble] truths. When the man heard this, free from dusts and stains, he gained the purity of the Dharma-eye. Practicing the teaching of the Dharma, he attained the state of going-and-returning (*sakṛdāgāmin*),[80] and realized the attainment of arhatship. Further, he said to the Buddha, "I want to undergo *parinirvāṇa*." The World-Honored One said, "As you wish."[81] At that time, the monk jumped into the air to [the height of] four *zhang* and nine *chi* away from the ground. Fire erupted from his body, and then burned the body. A hundred thousand celestial beings in the air came to pay homage.

<Tib.> Derge 216, *mdo sde*, Tsha 259a5-b5; sTog 223, *mdo sde*, Za 336a2-b7; Peking 882, *mdo-sna-tshogs*, Tsu 271a2-b2:[82]

de nas de'i tshe skyes bu de'i ba spu'i khung bu thams cad nas sems can dmyal ba'i me byung bar gyur te | de tshig cing mgon med pa dang | bcom ldan 'dasla 'di skad ces gsol to || bcom ldan 'das bdag ni tshig par gyur na |[1] *bde bar gshegs pa mgon mdzad du gsol |*[2] *bcom ldan 'das la skyabs su mchi'o || de nas bcom ldan 'das kyis*[3] *phyag*[4] *gser gyi kha dog lta bu skyes bu*[5] *de'i spyi bor bzhag go || phyag bzhag ma thag tu de nas de'i tshe |*[6] *skyes bu de'i tshor ba de thams cad rgyun chad par*

---

⑲ There is no mention of the Tathāgata's major physical marks (**lakṣaṇa*) or minor characteristics (**anuvyañjana*) in Lokakṣema's version or in the Tibetan. The Sanskrit has a lacuna here.

⑳ Dharmarakṣa mentions not only the man's final attainment of arhatship, but also his intermediate attainment of the state of once-returning. This latter detail is not found in Lokakṣema's version or in the Tibetan, and the Sanskrit is not available here.

㉑ The text has 隨意所存, lit. "stay wherever you wish."

㉒ The text is also edited and translated in Harrison and Hartmann (2000a: 201-202).

gyur to || de lus bag yangs shing bde bar gyur nas |[7] *de bzhin gshegs pa la shin tu gus par gyur te | bcom ldan 'das la 'di skad ces gsol to || bcom ldan 'das bdag ni rab tu 'byung bar 'tshal na |*[8] *bde bar gshegs pas rab tu 'byung*[9] *bar gsol | bcom ldan 'das kyis de la dge slong tshur shog || tshangs par spyad pa spyod cig ces de skad bka' stsal pa dang | de'i tshe de nyid du de mgo bregs | chos gos sbyar ma bgos | skra dang kha spu bregs nas zhag bdun lon pa*[10] *tsam du gyur te | dge slong bsnyen par rdzogs nas lo*[11] *brgya lon pa'i spyod lam du gnas par gyur to || de bzhin gshegs pas tshur shog ces gsungs nas || mgo bregs lus ni chos gos sbyar mar ldan |*[12] *de ma thag tu dbang po rab zhi zhing || sangs rgyas dgongs pa'i cha lugs gnas par gyur |*[13] *de nas bcom ldan 'das kyis dge slong de la 'phags pa'i bden pa bzhi dang ldan pa'i gtam bshad pa dang | des de thos nas chos la rdul med cing dri ma dang bral ba'i chos kyi mig rnam par dag pa'i steng du yang*[14] *lam bsgoms nas |*[15] *dgra bcom par gyur te | des bcom ldan 'das la 'di skad ces gsol to || bcom ldan 'das bdag ni yongs su mya ngan las 'da' bar 'tshal lo || bde bar gshegs pa bdag ni yongs su mya ngan las 'da' ba'i dus dang man*[16] *la bab bo || bcom ldan 'das kyis bka' stsal pa | dge slong khyod da*[17] *de'i dus la bab par shes par gyis shig || des de'i tshe steng gi bar snang la shing ta la bdun tsam na 'dug ste | bdag gi*[18] *me'i khams kyis lus bsregs so || bsregs pa*[19] *de'i tshe sol ba dang thal ba yang*[20] *med par gyur nas |*[21] *lha brgya stong dag kyang de la phyag 'tshal bar gyur to ||*

1)DP omit *shad* 2) D: double *shad* 3) P: *kyi* 4) S adds *g.yas pa* 5) S omits *skyes bu* 6) S omits *shad* 7) D omits *shad* 8) P omits *shad* 9) P: *dbyung* 10) P omits *pa* 11) P: *tshe lo* 12) D: double *shad* 13) D: double *shad* 14) S: *'ang* 15) P omits *shad* 16) P omits *dang man* 17) S omits *da* 18) P omits *gi*; S: *gis* 19) S: *pa'i* 20) S: *'ang* 21) DP omit *shad*

Then, at that moment, from all the pores on that man's body, fire of hell came forth. Being burned without protection, he said to the Blessed One, "O Blessed One, I am on fire. O Sugata, please protect me! I take refuge in the Blessed One." Then the Blessed One put his hand of gold-like color on the top of that man's head. As soon as he put his hand there, all that man's [painful] sensations[83] ceased. Having experienced bodily relief and become at ease, he felt great devotion to the Tathāgata.[84] He said to

---

⑧③ As Harrison and Hartmann (2000a: 201 n. 91) observe, the Tibetan only has *tshor ba* (**vedanā*), with nothing correspondent to *duḥkhā* in the Sanskrit fragment.

⑧④ The sentence *de bzhin gshegs pa la shin tu gus par gyur te* only finds a parallel in Fatian's version: T. 628 [xv] 445b24-25 [*juan* 5]: 此人即時身火得滅，離其苦惱。得大快樂，起淨信心 ("The fire on that man's body was immediately quenched, and he was relieved from pain. Having gained great happiness, he gave rise to a mind of pure faith"). The Sanskrit is not available for comparison.

the Blessed One, "O Blessed One, since I want to take ordination, O Sugata, please ordain me." The Blessed One said to him, "Come here, O monk, lead the pure life!" At the very moment he became head-shaved, clad in a monastic cloak,[85] with hair and beard shaved only for seven days, showing the deportment of a monk fully ordained for one hundred years. As soon as the Tathāgata said, "Come here," with his head shaved and his body clad in a monastic cloak, his senses immediately became tranquil, and he appeared in the attire intended by the Buddha. Then the Blessed One preached to this monk a discourse regarding the four noble truths. Having heard this, his dust-free and stainless Dharma-eye into *dharma*s was purified, in addition to which, having cultivated the path, he became an arhat. He said to the Blessed One, "O Blessed One, I want to undergo *parinirvāṇa*. O Sugata, the time, the occasion for me to undergo *parinirvāṇa* has come." The Blessed One said, "O monk, you should know that the time for it has now come." Then sitting up in the air at the height of seven *tāla* trees,[86] his body was burned by his own element of fire. When it was burnt, no charcoal or ashes were left. A hundred thousand deities also paid homage to him.

In comparison with the earlier account of the phantom man's ordination and *parinirvāṇa*, the above depiction of the matricide is constructed in a different way. It does not start with the matricide's reaction to the Buddha's sermon as in the case of the phantom man, but with his torment by the fire of hell and the Buddha's saving him from torment. This depiction has two implications: first, the fire of hell symbolizes the infernal punishment the matricide is supposed to experience in his next life, as a karmic result of his crime; second, the Buddha's act of quenching the fire and relieving the matricide from the torment symbolizes his power of saving the matricide from the presupposed fate of hell. Thus the quenching of fire is a scene challenging the traditional theory of *karma*. It almost totally annihilates the power of *karma* through an exaltation of the salvific power of the Buddha. The above depiction of the matricide also contains two details not found in the earlier account of the phantom man: 1) the Buddha's exposition of the four noble truths, which causes the matricide to attain the pure Dharma-eye and finally arhatship; 2) two incidents during the matricide's *parinirvāṇa*, including the vanishment of his cremation remains and the homage paid by the gods. Below I list all significant differences between

---

⑧⑤ Regarding *chos gos sbyar ma bgos*, Harrison and Hartmann (2000a: 201 n. 93) state, "*Chos gos* is standard for *cīvara*, but *sbyar ma* is less clear." On *sbyar ma* as an equivalent of *saṃghāṭī*, see TSD, ix. 4132, s.v. *sbyar ma*. Thus *chos gos sbyar ma* may have been based on **cīvaraṃ saṃghāṭiṃ*. On *saṃghāṭī* referring to "some sort of cloak," one of the three garments of a monk, see von Hinüber 2006: 13 (cited in SWTF, s.v. *saṃghāṭī*); Karashima 2012: III. 516 ("*saṃghāṭī*~ 'Obergewand'").

⑧⑥ The detail of seven *tāla* trees is also found in Fatian's version (T. 628 [xv] 445c7-8 [*juan* 5]).

the four versions of this part of the text:

Table 3 A Comparison of the Sanskrit, Chinese and Tibetan Versions of the Portion of the AjKV on a Matricide's Ordination and Parinirvāṇa

No.	Skt.	Lk. (T. 626)	Dh. (T. 627)	Tib.
1	*atrāṇo* "without protection"	—	無救護 "without protection"	*mgon med pa* "without protection"
2	*duḥkhārdito* "afflicted by pain"	痛不可言 "afflicted with inexpressible pain"	毒痛甚劇 "afflicted with extreme pain"	—
3	*dahyāmi bhagavan* "O Blessed One, I am on fire"	—	我今被燒 "Now I am on fire"	*bcom ldan 'das bdag ni tshig par gyur na* "O Blessed One, I am on fire"
4	*pravrajāhi me sugata* "O Sugata, please ordain me"	—	—	*bde bar gshegs pas rab tu dbyung bar gsol* "O Sugata, please ordain me"
5	*ehi bhikṣūti* "Come, O monk!"	如所欲 "As you wish"	佛尋聽之 "The Buddha thereupon permitted him"	*dge slong tshur shog tshangs par spyad pa spyod cig* "Come here, O monk, lead the pure life!"
6	(possibly parallel to T. 626 and T. 627)[87]	則時以爲沙門 "There and then he became a monk"	即爲寂志 "Immediately he became a tranquil-minded one"	*de'i tshe de nyid du de mgo bregs* | ... | *sangs rgyas dgongs pa'i cha lugs gnas par gyur* | "At that very moment he became head-shaved, …, and he appeared in the attire intended by the Buddha"
7	*(duḥkhaṃ duḥkha-samudayaḥ duḥ)kha-nirodhaḥ mārgaḥ* "[suffering, the origin of suffering,] the cessation of suffing, and the path"	四諦法 "Dharma on the four [noble] truths"	四諦 "four [noble] truths"	*'phags pa'i bden pa bzhi dang ldan pa'i gtam bshad pa* "discourse concerning the four noble truths"

⑧⑦ The Skt. folio is damaged here. As Harrison and Hartmann (2000a: 201 n. 94) rightly point out, the insufficient space in the Skt. fragment indicates that the manuscript originally had no such detailed depiction of the monastic appearance of the matricide as that found in the Tibetan.

续表

No.	Skt.	Lk. (T. 626)	Dh. (T. 627)	Tib.
8	*tasya virajo vigatamalam dharmeṣu dharmacakṣur viśud(dham...)* "He gained the dust-free, stainless and pure Dharma-eye into *dharmas*"	得法眼 "[He] gained the Dharma-eye"	遠塵離垢，得法眼淨 "Free from dust and stains, [he] gained the purity of the Dharma-eye"[88]	*chos la rdul med cing dri ma dang bral ba'i chos kyi mig rnam par dag pa* "[His] dust-free and stainless Dharma-eye into *dharmas* was purified"
9	*parinirvāṇakālasamayo me bhagavan* "O Blessed One, it is the time, the occasion for me to undergo *parinirvāṇa*"	—	—	*bde bar gshegs pa bdag ni yongs su mya ngan las 'da' ba'i dus dang man la bab bo* "O Sugata, the time, the occasion for me to undergo *parinirvāṇa* has come"
10	*...dahyataḥ na chavikā na maṣiḥ prajñāyate* "[When the body] was burnt, no ashes or soot was found"	—	—	*bsregs pa de'i tshe sol ba dang thal ba yang med par gyur nas* "When it was burnt, no charcoal or ashes were left"

As shown in this table, Lokakṣema's version T. 626 matches the Sanskrit in three cases (nos. 2, 7 and 8), including one case (no. 8) where the Sanskrit has a partial parallel in T. 626, and another case (no. 7) where the Sanskrit enumerates the four noble truths, while T. 626 only summarizes them. Dharmarakṣa's version matches the Sanskrit in five cases (nos. 1, 2, 3, 7 and 8), including one case (no. 7) where it also summarizes the four noble truths. The most striking is the Tibetan version. On the one hand, it matches the Sanskrit in the most cases (nos. 1, 3, 4, 5, 7, 8, 9 and 10), and in three cases (nos. 4, 9 and 10) the Sanskrit only finds parallels in the Tibetan. On the other hand, the Tibetan also appears to be the most divergent from the Sanskrit, since it contains a detailed depiction of the monastic appearance of the matricide after his ordination, which finds no parallel in the Sanskrit or in the two older Chinese versions. Let us look at some of the differences in detail:

---

⑱ Dharmarakṣa's Indic original was likely written in a Prākrit language in which neutral and masculine endings of *a*-stems could have fallen together in pronunciation. According to Pischel (1900), "Das Geschlecht des Skt. ist im Pkt. nicht immer bewahrt geblieben" (§356), and "Wie die Neutra auf *-as*, sind auch viele Neutra auf *-a* im Pkt. dialektisch zu Masculinen geworden" (§357). As he observes, in Ardhamāgadhī and Māgadhī the nominative singular neuters of the *a*-stem frequently end in *-e* or *-o*, both also the endings of nominative singular masculines of the *a*-stem (i.e., *-e*, *-o* = *-aḥ*; cf. §345). Dharmarakṣa's Indic original possibly had **virajo vigatamalo* or **viraje vigatamale* (or a similar form applicable to both neuter and masculine), which was read as masculine by him (or by his translation assistants). Dharmarakṣa seems to have already made such reading in his translation (T. 585) of the *Viśeṣacintibrahmaparipṛcchā* in 286 CE, where this problematic Chinese phrase first occurs.

In no. 5 about the Buddha's reply to the matricide's request for ordination, the Sanskrit (540v3) has the ordination formula *ehi bhikṣu* ("Come, O monk"), as in the case of the phantom man. Lokakṣema uses the phrase 如所欲 ("As you wish") which, as we have seen, also appears earlier in his version as the Buddha's reply to the phantom man's request for *parinirvāṇa*, where it corresponds to *yasyedānīṃ bhikṣoḥ kālaṃ manyase* in the Sanskrit (538v4).[89] Moreover, he also uses this Chinese phrase as the Buddha's reply to the matricide's request for *parinirvāṇa*, where the Sanskrit (541r1) only has the akṣara *y(...)*, which probably originally initiated *y(asyedānīṃ bhikṣoḥ kālaṃ manyase)*.[90] Lokakṣema's use of the same phrase as the Buddha's replies to the matricide's requests for ordination and for *parinirvāṇa* indicates that his Indic original may have had the formula **yasyedānīṃ (...) kālaṃ manyase* on both occassions. As I argued earlier, in the case of the phantom man, Lokakṣema's Indic original seems to have used this formula as the Buddha's replies to the phantom man's two requests. Thus unlike the Sanskrit text using *yasyedānīṃ (...) kālaṃ manyase* twice, as the Buddha's replies to the phantom man's and the matricide's requests for *parinirvāṇa*, Lokakṣema's Indic original may have used this formula four times, as the Buddha's replies to the phantom man's and the matricide's requests both for ordination and for *parinirvāṇa*. Also in no. 5, Dharmarakṣa uses the phrase 佛尋聽之 ("The Buddha thereupon permitted him"), which might be a loose rendering of the same formula **yasyedānīṃ (...) kālaṃ manyase*. The Tibetan has *dge slong tshur shog tshangs par spyad pa spyod cig* ("Come here, O monk, lead the pure life"), clearly indicating **ehi bhikṣo cara brahmacaryaṃ*.

Immediately following the Buddha's reply, in no. 6 the Tibetan version differs from the Sanskrit and from the two older Chinese versions by including a detailed depiction of the matricide's monastic appearance after his ordination. This depiction comprises two sentences. In the first sentence, the matricide is said to become head-shaved (*mgo bregs*), wearing a monastic cloak (*chos gos sbyar ma*), "with hair and beard shaved only for seven days" (*skra dang kha spu bregs nas zhag bdun lon pa tsam du gyur te*) and showing the "deportment of a monk fully ordained for one hundred years" (*dge slong bsnyen par rdzogs nas lo brgya lon pa'i spyod lam*). The second sentence, which partly overlaps with the first one, says that as soon as the Tathāgata pronounced 'Come here,' with his head shaved and his body clad in a monastic cloak, the matricide's "senses became tranquil" (*dbang po rab zhi zhing*) and he "appeared in the attire intended by the Blessed One" (*sangs rgyas dgongs pa'i cha lugs gnas par gyur*).

In their note on the first sentence of the depiction, Harrison and Hartmann state that

---

⑲ See discussion above p. 123.

⑳ Harrison and Hartmann 2000a: 201 n. 96.

since this sentence only finds a parallel in Fatian's version, it "must therefore reflect a different and possibly later recension of the AjKV"; they suggest, "if we bracket it as a later interpolation then the last sentence of the section no longer seems redundant."[91] Harrison and Hartmann are certainly right in classifying the first sentence as "a later interpolation". In fact, the interpolation probably consists not just of the first sentence alone. Rather, both the first and second sentences as a whole may have been later added into the AjKV. They correspond to a type of formula used in some Buddhist Sanskrit texts. For instance, in the *Jyotiṣkāvadāna* (No. 29) of the *Divyāvadāna* we find the following depiction of Jyotiṣka's monastic appearance after his ordination:[92]

> *bhagavato vācāvasānam eva muṇḍaḥ saṃvṛttaḥ saṃghāṭīprāvṛtaḥ pātrakaravyagrahastaḥ saptāhāvaropitakeśaśmaśrur varṣaśatopasaṃpannasya bhikṣor īryāpathenāvasthitaḥ* | *ehīti coktaḥ sa tathāgatena muṇḍaś ca saṃghāṭīparītadehaḥ sadyaḥ praśāntendriya eva tasthau nopasthito*[93] *buddhamanorathena* |
>
> "As soon as the Blessed One finished the words, he became shaved, clad in a monastic cloak, holding the ring of the almsbowl in his hand,[94] with hair and beard shaved for seven days, standing [there] with the deportment of a monk fully ordained for one hundred years. When the Tathāgata said 'Come here,' he immediately became head-shaved, clad in a monastic cloak. Even his senses became tranquilized. He stood there, dressed according to the Buddha's will."[95]

Basically the same passage, with some variations, can be found, for instance, in

---

[91] Harrison and Hartmann 2000a: 201 n. 94.

[92] Divy 281.23–28. There is no counterpart to this passage in the newly identified Sanskrit fragments of the *Jyotiṣkāvadāna* in the Schøyen Collection, which only cover parts of the story prior to Jyotiṣka's request for ordination (Baums 2002: 287-302 [especially 296, 299]).

[93] On *nopasthita* as a variant of *nepatthita* ("clothed, garbed"), the denominative past passive participle of *nepathya* ("costume, attire"), see BHSD, s.v. *nepatthita*.

[94] On *pātrakara* as a variant reading of *pātrakāṭaka* ("ring on which the almsbowl is fastened"), see BHSD, s.v. *-kāṭaka*.

[95] As Lamotte (1944-1980: II.632-633 n. 4) notes, "L'ordination par « Ehi bhikṣo » est généralement accompagnée d'une prise d'habit miraculeuse, dont le Vinaya pāli ne dit rien, mais qui est décrite en termes stéréotypés dans tous les textes sanskrits: « Le Buddha n'a pas plus tôt prononcé cet appel que le candidat se trouve rasé (*muṇḍa*), revêtu du manteau (*saṃghāṭīprāvṛta*), tenant en main le bol et le vase (*pātrakaravyahasta* [emended to °*vyagrahasta*, added by the present author]), etc.» (cf. Divya, p. 48, 281, 341)." The Sanskrit passage cited here is the full form of what Lamotte cites from the *Divyāvadāna*.

the *Avadānaśataka* and the Mūlasarvāstivāda *Saṃghabhedavastu*.[96] The depiction of the matricide's monastic appearance in the Tibetan version of the AjKV may have been based on a Sanskrit original very similar to the above passage from the *Divyāvadāna*. Such a depiction, as Edgerton puts it, "tells how after ordination by the *ehibhikṣukā* formula, the signs of worldly life were magically replaced in the initiate(s) by monkish insignia."[97]

In Fatian's version we find the following depiction of the matricide's monastic appearance: "There and then this man, with his hair and beard automatically falling off, with his body clad in a *kāṣāya*, obtained the marks of a monk. Just like a monk ordained for one hundred years, all his faculties were well-adjusted and his deportment was in good order, which fulfilled what was wished [by the Buddha]."[98] This depiction may have also been based on an Indic (probably Sanskrit) formula similar to that used in the *Divyāvadāna*. Perhaps aware of the partial overlap between the first and second sentences of the Indic formula, Fatian gives a conflated rendition by mentioning only once the matricide's shaved head and his monastic attire.[99] The first half of Fatian's rendition, "with his hair and beard automatically falling off, with his body clad in a *kāṣāya*, [he] obtained the marks of a monk," also occurs earlier in his version, referring to the phantom man's monastic appearance after ordination, where it finds no parallel in the Tibetan or in any other version of the text.[100]

Nos. 7 and 8 concern the spiritual attainments of the matricide after hearing the Buddha's teaching of the four noble truths. In no. 7, unlike the Chinese and Tibetan versions using the general term *sidi* 四諦 ("four [noble] truths") or *'phags pa'i bden pa*

---

[96] See almost the same passage at SBhV I.206.15-22, where the latter part *ehīti coktaḥ···buddhamanorathena* is in verse. In Avś I. 284.7-11 the latter part is also in verse and, instead of *varṣaśatopasaṃpannasya* ("ordained for one hundred years"), we find *dvādaśavarṣopasaṃpannasya* ("ordained for twenty years"). In Avś I. 347.6-348.1 the order of the two parts of the passage is reversed and *ehīti coktaḥ... buddhamanorathena* remains in verse.

[97] While Edgerton's comment is made regarding a variant form of the depiction in the *Mahāvastu* (cf. BHSD, s.v. *sumbhaka*), it characterizes well the function of this type of formula in general. In terms of wording, the formula used in the *Mahāvastu* (e.g. Mvu III.65.3-6, 92.8-11) is very different from the passage cited above from the Divy. The Sanskrit original of the Tibetan passage in question should have been closer to the formula used in the Divy, than that used in the Mvu.

[98] T. 628 [xv] 445c1-3 [*juan* 5]: 即時，此人鬚髮自落，袈裟被身，成苾芻相。如百臘者，諸根調適，威儀庠序，所願圓滿.

[99] Fatian's use of *jiasha* 袈裟 indicates that the formula on which his rendition was based had *kāṣāya* instead of *saṃghāṭī*. See Yaśomitra's commentary on the *ehi-bhikṣukā* formula mentioned in the *Abhidharmakośa* (AKVy 374.9-11: *ehibhikṣukayeti ehi bhikṣo cara brahmacaryam iti bhagavato vacane ehīti coktas sugatena tāyinā muṇḍaś ca kāṣāyadharo babhūveti*, "The fomular 'Come, O monk' refers to the Blessed One's words " 'Come, O monk, lead the pure life!' When a holy one such as the Sugata said 'Come,' the person became shaved, dressed in a *kāṣāya*").

[100] See above n. 52.

bzhi (**catvāry āryasatyāni*), the Sanskrit (540v4) has *(··· duḥkhaṃduḥkha samudayaḥ duḥ-) khanirodhaḥ mārgaḥ* ("[··· suffering, the origin of suffering,] the cessation of suffering, the path leading to the cessation of suffering"). Harrison and Hartmann rightly point out, "the nominatives here suggest that in the Sanskrit the four noble truths are 'unpacked' after a word like *yad uta*."[101] Strictly speaking, this "unpacked" form is still an abbreviation and belongs to what K. R. Norman calls the "mnemonic" set, a shorthand way of referring to the four noble truths.[102]

In nos. 9 and 10 the Sanskrit (541r1-2) has *parinirvāṇakālasamayo me bhagavan* ("O Blessed One, it is, the time, the occasion for me to undergo *parinirvāṇa*") and *dahyataḥ na chāvikā* [emended to *chayikā*] *na maṣiḥ prajñāyate* ("[When the body] was being burnt, no ashes or soot was found"). Both phrases find parallels in the Tibetan, but not in the two older Chinese versions. These are formulae which also occur elsewhere referring to the *parinirvāṇa* of others.[103] In no. 10 the Sanskrit also has a parallel in Fatian's version,[104] which is similar to the earlier depiction of the phantom man.[105] By mentioning the vanishment of cremation remains of both the phantom man and the matricide, Fatian's version once again appears to be more developed than the Tibetan.

To sum up, in this part of the AjKV describing the matricide's ordination and *parinirvāṇa*, Dharmarakṣa's version has more matches with the Sanskrit than Lokakṣema's version. The Tibetan version has the most matches with the Sanskrit, but meanwhile it gives a detailed depiction of the matricide's monastic appearance after ordination, which finds no parallel in the Sanskrit or in the two older Chinese versions. At least three observations may be made regarding these versions:

i) Lokakṣema's version uses 如所欲 ("As you wish") as the Buddha's replies to the matricide's two requests separately for ordination and for *parinirvāṇa*, which suggests that his Indic original may have had the formula **yasyedānīṃ (...) kālaṃ manyase* on both occasions.

ii) The depiction of the matricide's monastic appearance in the Tibetan version, as well

---

[101] Harrison and Hartmann 2000a: 201 n. 95.

[102] Norman 1982: 379.

[103] See Pāli Ud 92.28-93.4: *ekamantaṃ nisinno kho āyasmā dabbho mallaputto bhagavantaṃ etad avoca parinibbānakālo me dāni sugatā ti ... parinibbutassa sarīrassa jhāyamānassa ḍayhamānassa n'eva chārikā paññāyittha na masi* ("Sitting on one side, the Venerable Dabbha, son of Malla, said to the Blessed One: 'O Sugata, now is the time for me to undergo *parinibbāna* .' ···When the body of the one [= Dabbha Mallaputta] who had attained *parinibbāna* was being cremated and burnt, neither ashes nor soot was found"); also translated in Masefield (1994: 181).

[104] T. 628 [xv] 445c8 [*juan* 5]: 化火焚身，滅盡無餘 ("He conjured fire to burn himself, and vanished completely without remainder").

[105] See 445b13-14 (translated above in n. 53).

as its counterpart in Fatian's version, seems to have been based on a formula similar to that used in the *Divyāvadāna* and in some other Buddhist Sanskrit texts. This depiction reflects a later development of the AjKV.

iii) In narrating the matricide's *parinirvāṇa*, the Sanskrit version uses the stock phrases *parinirvāṇakālasamayo me bhagavan* and *dahyataḥ na chavikā na maṣiḥ prajñāyate*, which find parallels in the Tibetan but not in the two older Chinese versions. Fatian's version uses the two stock phrases in both cases of the phantom man and the matricide, and thus appears to be more elaborated on this detail than any other version of the text.

Conclusion

The present paper has examined one section of the AjKV, through a close comparison of the Sanskrit version preserved in the Schøyen Collection with its Chinese and Tibetan parallels. The section concerns a matricide who, after being ordained by the Buddha, attains arhatship and then enters *parinirvāṇa*. This story constitutes a building block of the larger narrative framework of the salvation of the patricide Ajātaśatru in the AjKV and illustrates "the strong antinomian tendencies of the text".[106] The examination has shown that of all the extant versions of this section Dharmarakṣa's Chinese translation is the closest to the Sanskrit version in overall terms, although there are cases where the Sanskrit is not supported by Dharmarakṣa's version but by one or more of the other versions.

Compared with Dharmarakṣa's version, Lokakṣema's version T. 626 is less close to the Sanskrit in this part of the text. The disagreements between T. 626 and the Sanskrit are not only found where T. 626 lacks counterparts to the Sanskrit, but also where T. 626 contains expressions which find no or different counterparts in the Sanskrit. Among these expressions, *fasheng* 法身 (lit. "*dharma*-body") is an idiosyncratic rendition reflecting Lokakṣema's word-choice preference. The phantom man's statement on being absolved of his crime of parricide and the matricide's announcement of taking refuge may be seen as glosses added by Lokakṣema. Further, his repeated use of the phrase *ru-zi-zhi-yuan* 如子之願 or *ru-suoyuan* 如所欲 ("As you wish"), both indicating **yasyedānīṃ (...) kālaṃ manyase*, as the Buddha's replies to the phantom man's and the matricide's requests for ordination and for *parinirvāṇa*, may reflect a recensional variation of his Indic original.

It has also been observed that the Tibetan version of this section differs from the Sanskrit and the two older Chinese versions by including a detailed depiction of the matricide's monastic appearance. This depiction was probably translated from a formula

---

[106] Boucher 2002: 255.

similar to that found in the *Divyāvadāna* (281.23-28). It only has a parallel in Fatian's version, and may well represent a later development of the text. Besides this depiction, the Tibetan and Fatian's versions also share a number of other details not found in the Sanskrit, Lokakṣema's or Dharmarakṣa's version. Thus there can be little double that the underlying Indic originals of the Tibetan and Fatian's versions were relatively close to each other.

Discussion has also been made on the bowdlerization tendency of Fatian's version. The tendency is not only shown in Fatian's replacement of all references to parricide with general or obscure expressions, but also in his choice to equate the phantom man's double parricide and the real man's matricide, rather than differentiating the serevity of the two crimes as in the other versions.

Taken as a whole, two basic recensional lines may be identified in this section of the AjKV: the first line is represented by the Sanskrit version and by the Indic originals underlying the two older Chinese versions; the second line is represented by the Indic originals underlying the Tibetan and Fatian's versions. The primary differences between the two lines lie in the abridgement of the Buddha's sermon to the matricide, and in the interpolation of a formula depicting the matricide's monastic appearance after ordination. Interestingly, these two differences separately reflect the abbreviation and expansion tendencies of the AjKV over time. The observations above are based on a study of one section of the text. Further research is needed to see whether this is a consistent pattern.

Abbreviations

AjKV *Ajātaśatrukaukṛtyavinodana*

AKVy *Sphuṭārthā Abhidharmakośavyākhyā by Yaśomitra*. Edited by Wogihara Unrai. Tokyo: The Publishing Association of *Abhidharmakośavyākhyā*, 1932-1936.

Avś *Avadānaçataka: A Century of Edifying Tales Belonging to the Hīnayāna*. 2 vols. Edited by Jacob Samuel Speyer. St.-Pétersbourg: Commissionnaires de l' Académie Impériale des Sciences, 1906-1909.

BHSD Franklin Edgeton: *Buddhist Hybrid Sanskrit Grammar and Dictionary*. Vol. II: Dictionary. New Haven: Yale University Press, 1953.

BHSG Franklin Edgeton: *Buddhist Hybrid Sanskrit Grammar and Dictionary*. Vol. I: Grammar. New Haven: Yale University Press, 1953.

D *Bka' 'gyur* (*sde dge par phud*). 103 vols. Tibetan Buddhist Resource Center, TBRC W22084. Delhi: Delhi karmapae chodhey gyalwae sungrab partun khang, 1976-1979.

Divy *The Divyāvadāna: A Collection of Early Buddhist Legends*. Edited by Edward B. Cowell and Robert A. Neil. First Published, Cambridge 1886. Reprint: Amsterdam: Oriental Press NV / Philo Press, 1970.

Mvu *Le Mahāvastu, texte sanscrit publié pour la première fois et accompagné d'introductions et d'un commentaire*. 3 vols. Edited by Émile Senart. First published in Paris, 1882–1897. Reprint: Tokyo: Meicho Fukyūkai, 1977.

P *Bka' 'gyur pe cin par ma*. 109 vols. Woodblock print preserved at National Library of Mongolia, Ulaanbaatar. Digitally published and distributed by Digital Preservation Society, Tokyo. 2010.

S *Bka' 'gyur* (*stog pho brang bris ma*). 109 vols. Tibetan Buddhist Resource Center, TBRC W22083. Leh: Smanrtsis shesrig dpemzod, 1975-80.

SBhV *The Gilgit Manuscript of the Saṅghabhedavastu: Being the 17th and Last Section of the Vinaya of the Mūlasarvāstivādin*. Edited by Raniero Gnoli. 2 vols. Roma: Is. M. E. O., 1977-1978.

ŚPS *Śrāmaṇyaphalasūtra*

SWTF *Sanskrit-Wörterbuch der buddhistischen Texte aus den Turfan-Funden und der kanonischen Literatur der Sarvāstivāda-Schule*, begonnen von E. Waldschmidt, hg. von H. Bechert, K. Röhrborn, J.-U. Hartmann, Bd. I ff., Göttingen 1994 ff.

T. *Taishō shinshū daizōkyō* 大正新脩大蔵経. Edited by Takakusu Junjirō 高楠順次郎 and Watanabe Kaikyoku 渡辺海旭. Tokyo: Taishō issaikyō kankōkai 大正一切経刊行会, 1924-1934.

TSD *Tibetan-Sanskirt Dictionary*. 16 vols. Edited by J. S. Negi et al. Sarnath, Varanasi: Dictionary Unit, Central Institute of Higher Tibetan Studies, 1993-2005.

Ud *Udāna*. Edited by Paul Steinthal. First published in 1885. Reprint: London: The Pali Text Society, 1982.

References

Baums, Stefan. 2002. "*Jyotiṣkāvadāna*." In *Manuscripts in the Schøyen Collection III*: *Buddhist Manuscripts, Volume II*, edited by Jens Braarvig et al, 287-302. Oslo: Hermes Publishing.

Boucher, Daniel. 1996. *Buddhist Translation Procedures in Third-Century China: A Study of Dharmaraksa and His Translation Idiom*. Ph.D diss., University of Pennsylvania.

______. 2002. "Review of Jens Braarvig (ed.), *Buddhist Manuscripts, Volume I*." *Indo-Iranian Journal* 45 (3): 245-259.

Hahn, Michael. 1978. "On the Fuction and Origin of the Particle *Dag*." In *Tibetan Studies Presented at the Seminar of Young Tibetologists, Zürich, June 26-July 1, 1977*, edited by P. Kværne and M. Brauen, 137-147. Zürich: Völkerkunde-museum der Universität Zürich.

Harrison, Paul. 1992a. "Is the Dharma-kāya the Real 'Phantom Body' of the Buddha?" *Journal of the International Association of Buddhist Studies* 15 (1): 44-94.

________. 1992b. *Druma-kinnara-rāja-paripṛcchā-sūtra: A critical edition of the Tibetan text (Recension A) based on eight editions of the Kanjur and the Dunhuang Manuscript Fragment*. Studia philologica Buddhica. Monograph Series 7. Tokyo: The International Institute for Buddhist Studies.

______. 1993. "The Earliest Chinese Translations of Mahāyāna Buddhist Sūtras: Some Notes on the Works of Lokakṣema." *Buddhist Studies Review* 10 (2): 135-177.

_______. 2000. "Mañjuśrī and the Cult of the Celestial Bodhisattvas." *Chung-Hwa Buddhist Journal* 13 (2):

157-193.

______. 2004. "How the Buddha Became a Bodhisattva?" In *Buddhist Scriptures*, edited by Donald S. Lopez, 172-184. London: Penguin Classics.

Harrison, Paul, and Jens-Uwe Hartmann. 1998. "A Sanskrit Fragment of the *Ajātaśatru-kaukṛtya-vinodanā-sūtra*." In *Sūryacandrāya: Essays in Honour of Akira Yuyama On the Occasion of His 65th Birthday*, edited by Paul Harrison and Gregory Schopen, 67-86. Swisttal-Odendorf: Indica et Tibetica Verlag.

______. 2000a. "*Ajātaśatrukaukṛtyavinodanāsūtra*." In *Manuscripts in the Schøyen Collection I. Buddhist Manuscripts, Volume I*, edited by Jens Braarvig et al., 167-216. Oslo: Hermes Publishing.

______. 2000b. "Two additional fragments of the *Ajātaśatrukaukṛtyavinodanāsūtra*." In *Manuscripts in the Schøyen Collection I: Buddhist Manuscripts, Volume I*, edited by Jens Braarvig et al., 301-302. Oslo: Hermes Publishing.

______. 2002. "Another Fragments of the *Ajātaśatrukaukṛtyavinodanāsūtra*." In *Manuscripts in the Schøyen Collection III: Buddhist Manuscripts, Volume II*, edited by Jens Braarvig et al., 45-49. Oslo: Hermes Publishing.

Hirakawa, Akira 平川彰. 1990. *A History of Indian Buddhism from Śākyamuni to Early Mahāyāna*. Translated from the Japanese and edited by Paul Groner. Honolulu: University of Hawai'i Press.

Karashima, Seishi 辛嶋静志. 1998. *A Glossary of Dharmarakṣa's Translation of the Lotus Sūtra*. Bibliotheca Philologica et Philosophica Buddhica I. Tokyo: The International Research Institute for Advanced Buddhology, Soka University.

______. 2010. *A Glossary of Lokakṣema's Translation of the Aṣṭasāhasrikā Prajñāpāramitā*. Bibliotheca Philologica et Philosophica Buddhica XI. Tokyo: The International Research Institute for Advanced Buddhology, Soka University.

Lamotte, Étienne. 1944-1980. *Le Traité de la Grande Vertu de Sagesse*. 5 vols. Reprint: Louvain: Université de Louvain, reprint, 1970-1981.

MacQueen, Graeme. 1988. *A Study of the Śrāmaṇyaphala-sūtra*. Wiesbaden: Otto Harrassowitz.

Masefield, Peter. 1994. The *Udāna*. Oxford: The Pali Text Society.

Matsuda, Kazunobu 松田和信. 1999. "Sukoien-korekushōn no shinzayikyō dankan nitsuite"スコイエン・コレクションの『新歳経』断簡について [Sanskrit Fragments of the **Pravāraṇāsūtra* in the Schøyen Collection]. *Indogaku bukkyōgaku kenkyū* 印度學佛教學研究 48 (1): 366-359.

Miyazaki, Tenshō 宮崎展昌. 2007a. "*Ajaseōkyō* (T626) no kanyakusha ni tsuite"『阿闍世王經』（T626）の 漢訳者につい [The Translator of the *Asheshi-wang-jing*]. *Indotetsugaku Bukkyōgaku Kenkyū*. インド哲学仏教学研究14: 57-71.

______. 2007b. "*Tonshindarashomonnyōraisammaikyō* no kanyakusha ni tsuite"『伅眞陀羅所問如來三昧經』の漢訳者について [The Translator of the *Tunzhentuoluo suowen rulai sanmei jing*]. *Bukkyō bunka kenkyū ronshū*仏教文化研究論集11: 18-39.

______. 2007c. "Discerning the Original Language of the Tibetan Version of Mahāyāna Sūtras: From a Simple

Mistake in the *lDem kar ma* Regarding the *Ajātaśatrukaukṛtyavinodanāsūtra*." *Journal of Indian and Buddhist Studies* 55 (3): 1101-1105.

______. 2008a. "Background to the Compilation of Chapter IV of the *Ajātaśatrukaukṛtyavinodanā-sūtra*: was Chapter IV Originally a Separate Text?" *Journal of Indian and Buddhist Studies* 56 (3): 1110-1113.

______. 2008b. "*Ajaseōkyō* no hensanjijō ni kansuru ichi kōsatsu"『阿闍世王経』の編纂事情に関する一考察—「大乗」「無生法忍」などの術語の用例に関連して— [A study of the compilation of the Ajātaśatrukaukṛtyavinodhāna-sūtra: with reference to examples of the word "mahāyāna" and "anutpattika-dharmakṣānti" and other words]. *Bukkyō bunka kenkyū ronshū*仏教文化研究論集12: 26-49.

______. 2009. "Hōtenyaku *misōu-shōbō-kyō* ni tusite" 法天訳『未曾有正法經』について [A Study of the *Weicengyou-zhengfa-jing* translated by Fatian]. In 第4次韓國佛教學結集大會論集 *The Proceedings of the Fourth Annual Buddhist Studies Conference in Korea*, 113-118. Seoul.

______. 2010. *Ajaseōkyō no kenkyū*『阿闍世王経』の研究 [A Study of the **Ajātaśatrukaukṛtyāvinodanā—sūtra*]. Ph.D diss., University of Tokyo.

______. 2012. *Ajaseōkyō no kenkyū: Sono hensan katei no kaimei wo chūshin toshite* 阿闍世王経の研究—その編纂過程の解明を中心として [A Study of the *Ajātaśatrukaukṛtyavinodana*: Focusing on the Compilation Process]. Bibliotheca Indologica et Buddhologica 15. Tokyo: The Sankibo Press.

Nattier, Jan. 2003. *A Few Good Men: The Bodhisattva Path according to The Inquiry of Ugra* (*Ugraparipṛcchā-sūtra*). Honolulu: University of Hawai'i Press.

______. 2006. "The Names of Amitābha/Amitāyus in Early Chinese Buddhist Translations (1)." *Annual Report of the International Research Institute for Advanced Buddhology at Soka University* 9: 183-199.

______. 2008. *A Guide to the Earliest Chinese Buddhist Translations: Texts from the Eastern Han* 東漢 *and Three Kingdoms* 三國 *Periods*. Tokyo: The International Research Institute for Advanced Buddhology, Soka University.

Norman, K[enneth] R[oy]. 1982. "The Four Noble Truths: A Problem of Pāli Syntax." In *Indological and Buddhist Studies: Volume in Honor of Professor J. W. de Jong on his Sixtieth Birthday*, edited by L. A. Hercus, F. B. J. Kuiper, T. Rajapatirana and E. R. Skrzypczak. Canberra: the ANU Faculty of Asian Studies.

Pāsādika, Bhikkhu. 1989. *Nāgārjuna's Sūtrasamuccaya: A Criticial Edition of the mDo kun las btus pa*. Copenhagen: Akademisk Forlag.

Pischel, Richard. 1900. *Grammatik der Prakrit-Sprachen*. Strassburg: Trübner.

Sadakata, Akira 定方晟. 1989. *Ajase no Satori* 阿闍世のさとり [The Awakening of Ajātaśatru]. Kyoto: Jinbun Shoin.

Sander, Lore. 2000. "A brief palaeographical analysis of the Brāhmī manuscripts in volume I." In *Manuscripts in the Schøyen Collection I. Buddhist Manuscripts, Volume I*, edited by Jens Braarvig et al., 285-300. Oslo: Hermes Publishing.

Silk, A. Jonathan. 2007. "Good and Evil in Indian Buddhism: The Five Sins of Immediate Retribution." *Journal of Indian Philosophy* 35 (3): 253-286.

Vetter, Tillman, and Stefano Zacchetti. 2004. "On *jingfa* 經法 in Early Chinese Buddhist Translations." *Annual Report of the International Research Institute for Advanced Buddhology at Soka University* 7: 159-166.

Wu, Juan. 2012. *From Perdition to Awakening: A Study of Legends of the Salvation of the Patricide Ajātaśatru in Indian Buddhism*. PhD diss., Cardiff University.

______. 2014. "Violence, Virtue and Spiritual Liberation: A Preliminary Survey of Buddhist and Jaina Stories of Future Rebirths of Śreṇika Bimbisāra and Kūṇika Ajātaśatru." *Religions of South Asia* 8 (2): 149-179.

_______. 2016. "The Rootless Faith of Ajātaśatru and Its Explanations in the **Abhidharma-mahāvibhāṣā*." *Indo-Iranian Journal* 58 (2): 101-138.

Ye, Shaoyong, Li Xuezhu, and Kanō Kazuo. 2013. "Further Folios from the Set of Miscellaneous Texts in Śāradā Palm-leaves from Zha lu Ri phug: A Preliminary Report Based on Photographs Preserved in the CTRC, CEL and IsIAO." *China Tibetology* 20 (1): 30-47.

Zürcher, Erik. 1991. "A New Look at the Earliest Chinese Buddhist Texts." In *From Benares to Beijing: Essays on Buddhism and Chinese Religion*, edited by Koichi Shinohara and Gregory Schopen, 277-304. Oakville: Mosaic Press.

《善說集》（*Subhāṣitasaṃgraha*）文本概述*

——以Bendall編校本與新見尼泊爾梵文寫本爲中心

陸辰葉

Subhāṣitasaṃgraha，譯名《善說集》①，又譯《妙言集》②、《善說經集》③、《善巧語集》④（下文簡稱SS），是一部以梵文和部分中古印度俗語（主要是Apabhraṃśa，訛誤語）輯錄的印度晚期佛教文選，匯集了各種顯密經典。作者不詳，未發現存有藏譯與漢譯。英國學者Cecil Bendall根據他在尼泊爾發現的梵文寫本編校出版了該文本⑤。Bendall將SS的內容分爲兩部分，前半部宣說諸位上師先賢之至高無上性與空性相關教理，後半部開示證得大手印成就之實修法門⑥。從文本所主張的最終目的而言，SS可以劃歸大手印文本。實際上，在尼泊爾還存有該文本的另一種梵文寫本，這在Bendall編校本之外又提供了一種解讀文本的可能性。隨著當下佛教晚期尤其是密教研究的升温，該文本的多重研究意義也浮現出來。

---

* 本論文得到國家留學基金資助。

① 該譯名由日本學者高田仁覺首創，後來日本學者大多沿用該譯名，具有一定代表意義。參見高田仁覚《*Subhāṣita-saṃgraha*（善說集）における大乘思想の斷片について》，《印度學佛教學研究》2（2），1954，pp. 184-185。

② 該譯名參見〔荷〕高羅佩著，李零、郭曉惠等譯《中國古代房内考》，上海：上海人民出版社，1990年，460頁。

③ 該譯名參見〔英〕凱思著，宋立道、舒曉偉譯《印度和錫蘭的佛教哲學：從小乘佛教到大乘佛教》，上海：上海古籍出版社，2004年，263頁，註3。可能所指並非該文本，而是標題相同的其他文本。

④ 該譯名參見李學竹《月稱及其〈入中論〉》，《中國藏學》2006年第2期，236頁。

⑤ Cecil Bendall ed.,"Subhāṣita-saṃgraha: An Anthology of Extracts from Buddhist Works complied by an unknown author, to illustrate the Doctrines of scholastic and of mystic (tāntrik) Buddhism", *Le Muséon: Études Philologiques, Historiques et Religieuses*, Nouvelle série IV, 1903, pp. 375-402; Part I: Nouvelle série V, 1904, pp. 5-46; Part II, pp. 245-274: Appendix et Index.

⑥ 參見賴富本宏《*Subhaṣitasaṃgraha*の引用文献をめぐって》，《密教文化》96, 1971, pp. 50-37；《*Subhaṣitasaṃgraha*に関する一考察—その構成と内容を中心として—》，《印度學佛教學研究》19（2），1971，pp. 862-865。

一、Bendall編校本

英國學者Cecil Bendall⑦（1856—1906）是著名東方學家、印度學家。他中學即從George Frederick Nicholl學習梵文。Bendall後來進入劍橋大學就讀，跟隨劍橋首位梵文教授Edward Byles Cowell閱讀梵文，並深受其影響從而決定了他日後的學術道路走向。在取得劍橋大學一等榮譽學士學位之後，Bendall開始在劍橋從事梵文教學工作。他在梵文寫本方面的研究成績突出，兩次探訪尼泊爾與北印度，獲取寫本，編寫了多個寫本目錄。他在印度古文字、碑銘等方面都是專家⑧。

SS的梵文寫本是Bendall在1899年1月第二次訪問尼泊爾時獲得的。當他正準備結束在Mahārāja的圖書館的工作時，圖書館館長Viṣṇuprasāda班智達好心地向Bendall展示了館長個人收藏的幾種稀有寫本，其中就有這部SS的寫本原本。寫本是以一種古孟加拉字體書寫在貝葉上，很可能是15世紀左右書寫的。館長送了該寫本的複本給Bendall，複本是在館長指導下由圖書館工作人員爲Bendall製作的，附有館長簽名。複本中有加爾各答的Vinodavihārl Bhaṭṭācārya班智達做的修訂，但如這位班智達所言，他的修訂不徹底。編輯一個單獨的現代複本有難度，如果抄錄複本者不理解寫本語言，那就會增加難度。這點尤其適用於解讀SS這部使用了難懂的Apabhraṃśa這種俗語的情況。Bendall指出，SS的發現說明使用Apabhraṃśa作爲佛教文獻的一支是存在的，而佛教俗語的使用此前衹有藏文材料曾提到過，SS是第一部確實的文獻證明。爲了彌補寫本材料的不足，Bendall通過SS中引用段落來尋找對應的藏譯本，從而進行編輯校對。由於SS中沒有給出編纂者的姓名及年代等外部證據，Bendall也沒有從印藏書籍中找到該文本的信息，他衹能從其中引文及其作者的年代來判斷SS的年代，其中可能年代最近的是寂護（Śāntideva），也就意味著SS至少是8世紀或之後成書的⑨。

根據Bendall的描述，SS寫本共有103頁。Bendall將SS內容分爲兩部分,且概括了段落大意。第一部分是賢者篇（scholastic），1至38頁；第二部分是秘密篇（mystic），39至103頁。第一部分又分爲兩章。第一章1至16頁，是一系列意圖不明的摘錄，但主要是處理教義時如宜教授的重要性。這一章中提出，愚者必不可能成上師；空性教義中的教導必須是漸次的；當還是一個弟子時，人無自主（svātantrya）；般若波羅蜜多（prajñā-pāramitā）中的教導適用於弟子生涯的多個次第；此波羅蜜多爲各乘（yāna）所共許。第二章16至38頁，主要是佛教本體論，尤以中觀派的論點爲主。這一章中提到

⑦ 中譯名有班達爾、本達爾、本多爾、本道爾、賓達等。

⑧ Cf. W. B. Owen, “Bendall, Cecil (1856-1906)”, rev. R. S. Simpson, in *Oxford Dictionary of National Biography*, ed. H. C. G. Matthew and Brian Harrison ,Oxford: OUP, 2004; online ed., ed. Lawrence Goldman, September 2014, http://www.oxforddnb.com/view/article/30702 (accessed April 16, 2016).

⑨ Cecil Bendall ed., “Subhāṣita-saṃgraha: An Anthology of Extracts from Buddhist Works complied by an unknown author, to illustrate the Doctrines of scholastic and of mystic (tāntrik) Buddhism”, pp. 375-376.

四句偈（catuḥkoṭi），分別引出龍樹（Nāgārjuna）、月稱（Candrakīrti）及種種經典中（nānāsūtre）的論述；也提到對心（citta）與色（rūpa）的思擇導向空性的教義；以及二邊（antadvaya）教義與名言字句的表達⑩。

第二部分同樣分爲兩章。第一章39至82頁，重在討論慧（prajñā）與方便（upāya）。其中涉及如各種續中提到的方便；無法通過這兩項原則之一單獨地達到佛性，而要完全通達二者；密續中關於本性的解釋；密宗瑜伽的本性；瑜伽士不被激情（rāga，passion）所染污，反而能以激情克服激情⑪；瑜伽士必須去除所有善業，惡業更不用說；思擇分別與空性；必須修習空與不空；禮敬金剛（vajra）；得正樂位（satsukhapada），並討論心與菩提心（bodhicitta）；概述如慧、方便與慾（kāma）的密教教義。第二章83至103頁，說各種證得“圓滿”的密教修習。此章下又二分。第一節言及智印（jñāna-mudrā）的修習；隱居中齋戒與禪修；瘋狂律儀（unmattavrata）；行如鬼怪，食殘羹，衣著破爛或著“天衣”（digamabara），禁言禪修；三種證得大手印（mahāmudrā）之方便：平和、中等與內相（adhyātma-nimitta），第二種是在夢中實現的；圓滿必由串習（abhyāsa）證得，而非僅憑知識；各種證得無上瑜伽之修法與方便；人必須宣說法（dharma）而實現其終極願想，但習咒（mantra）的知識也是必須的；這些甚至對罪大惡極之人也行之有效。最後一小節則是來自前密教文獻（pre-tantrik literature）摘錄，與一位悔僧及十惡有關；抑制造惡趨勢的如宜加行，此加行可在上師的指引下通過該文本實行⑫。

根據筆者的調查，Bendall所使用的這份寫本複本現存於英國劍橋大學圖書館。根據劍橋圖書館的描述，該寫本（也被看作是寫本）編號MS Or.679，紙質，僅正面有字，有Bendall的注釋，105頁（69頁重複並末尾另附一頁），梵筴裝，保存完好，以黑色墨水、尼泊爾文字（Nepālākṣarā）書寫。1906年4月27日入藏圖書館⑬。

二、基於Bendall編校本的《善說集》研究述評

Bendall編校本問世之後一段時間，一度無人問津。直到1931年，著名的法國佛教學者Louis de La Vallée Poussin在《關於聖天的〈心清淨論〉》（À propos du

---

⑩ Cecil Bendall ed., “Subhāṣita-saṃgraha: An Anthology of Extracts from Buddhist Works complied by an unknown author, to illustrate the Doctrines of scholastic and of mystic (tāntrik) Buddhism”, p. 378.

⑪ rāga在古代佛經中常被漢譯爲“貪慾”（藏譯’dod chags），如此而言，我們似乎也可以將這裏的“以激情克服激情”（conquers passion by passion）簡單地理解爲常說的“以慾止慾”，但這麼理解與西方學者們普遍沿用的“passion”這一譯語含義不完全一致，或許這點值得思考。

⑫ Cecil Bendall ed., “Subhāṣita-saṃgraha: An Anthology of Extracts from Buddhist Works complied by an unknown author, to illustrate the Doctrines of scholastic and of mystic (tāntrik) Buddhism”, pp. 1-2.

⑬ Cf. http://cudl.lib.cam.ac.uk/view/MS-OR-00679/1(accessed April 20, 2016). 該網頁上將Bendall的姓氏誤作Bendal。

Cittaviśuddhiprakaraṇa d' Āryadeva）一文中，提到SS中有《心清淨論》的片段，從而確認了該論的梵文名⑭。

1961年，荷蘭著名漢學家高羅佩出版了《中國古代房內考》（*Sexual Life in Ancient China*）⑮。該著作成爲他代表作之一。高羅佩是看似第一個對SS中的文字進行援引解讀之人，實則不經推敲。在該著作中，他“引用”了SS的一句話，作爲附錄一“印度和中國的房中秘術”之“佛教金剛乘房中秘術”一節中的論據：

> 這種修煉方法的關鍵性步驟是，第一部首先要從女性配偶獲得刺激以形成精滴。有些書把她說成是由凝心定慮產生的一種形象，與她結合是一種精神結合。但更多的書卻說，她必須是個真正的女人，甚至乾脆說“佛在女性生殖器中”（buddhatvaṁ⑯ yoṣit-yoni-samāśritaṁ）參看本達爾（C. Bendall引《妙言集》[the Subhāṣita-saṁgraha]，載*Muséon*，1903—1904年），並說子宮實際上就是般若（參看*ITB* 102頁以下及*SM* 32頁）⑰。

這裏，“buddhatvaṁyoṣit-yoni-samāśritaṁ”一句被高羅佩譯爲“佛在女性生殖器中”（Buddha-hood abides in the female organ）⑱，從而強調金剛乘的修習實際上是房中術，隨即與印度教性力派的修習混爲一談。這種論證方式至今仍會被不假思索地繼承⑲。可事實是，Bendall編校本中沒有這句原文。究竟這句語出何處？抑或高羅佩自行構擬？單就這點，高羅佩粗疏謬誤便又添一例⑳。回頭來分析這句“引文”的句意：samāśritaṁ是過去分詞的業格形式，詞根爲sam-ā-√śri，意爲“依靠”；yoni除了“女性生殖器”，還有“根源、產地”之意。此句直譯爲佛性依止女性子宮，可引申理解爲佛性與生俱來之意，這就出現了與高羅佩截然不同的見解。

同年，A. Bharati在《密續中的密意語言》（Intentional Language in the Tantras）一文中，在提到菩提心（bodhicitta）最爲激進的密意用法時，在注釋中提及SS中也有意義相近的段落。這種激進的解讀方式說明了密意（sandhā-bhāṣā）包含了一種系統性的歧義，這提醒人們回歸古代先賢在詮釋文本上的分歧：按字面（mukhya）還是用比喻的（gauṇa）方式去解讀。而每個個體詮釋者的決定實際上如印度格言那樣：“選擇

---

⑭ Louis de La Vallée Poussin, “À propos du Cittaviśuddhiprakaraṇa d'Āryadeva”, *Bulletin of the School of Oriental Studies* 6(2), 1931, p. 411.

⑮ Robert H. van Gulik, *Sexual Life in Ancient China: A Preliminary Survey of Chinese Sex and Society from ca. 1500 B.C. till 1644 A. D.*, Leiden: Brill, 1961.

⑯ 中譯本1990版誤作buddhatvain。

⑰ 〔荷〕高羅佩著，李零等譯《中國古代房內考——中國古代的性欲社會》，北京：商務印書館，2007年，328頁。

⑱ Robert H. van Gulik, *Sexual Life in Ancient China: A Preliminary Survey of Chinese Sex and Society from ca. 1500 B.C. till 1644 A. D.*, p. 342.

⑲ 例見李南《論佛教身體曼荼羅》，《南亞研究》2008年第2期，64—74頁。

⑳ 對高羅佩該著作的評論，參見沈衛榮《大師的謬誤與局限——略議〈中國古代房內考〉的問題》，《東方早報》2011年6月5日第5版。

你最想要的”（yathecchasi tathā vṛṇu）[21]。這既表明了其時對密教的一種認知狀況，似乎在一定程度上也可以拿來解釋高羅佩的“引用”意圖。

後來學者們可能逐漸意識到SS中保存了不少經續的段落，於是越來越多的研究會利用其中的段落而將其納入參考文獻[22]。在Ronald M. Davidson的《印度密教：密教運動社會史》（*Indian Esoteric Buddhism: A Social History of the Tantric Movement*）中，論述密教成就者的修習範式的發展時，言及九世紀的《秘密成就》（*Guhyasiddhi*）第六品中的瘋狂律儀（unmattavrata），便以SS中的概括性文字來說明：靜默禪修，行如惡魔，食用剩飯，遊走乞食，拒絕滿足感，衣著腐爛等[23]。

日本學界對SS的研究大多集中在文本本身。日本學者首次注意到了這部文本是在20世紀50年代。高田仁覺在1954年分别發表了《*Subhāṣita-saṃgraha*（善說集）における大乘思想の斷片について》與《善說集に示されたる密教的學道（一）》兩篇文章，可謂日本學界對SS的研究開端。他從SS中找出大乘思想的片段，根據SS的引用順序羅列爲：《華嚴經》與月稱的《入中論》的片段、《般若波羅蜜多經》與Saraha（即大手印第一傳承薩羅訶）之說的片段、龍樹的《中論》、月稱的《中論注》、龍樹的《菩提心注》、寂天的《入菩提行論》、《入楞伽經》、*Ekanaya-nirdeśa-sūtra*、《諸法本無經》等。又對SS中的密教學道的四個問題做了分析：密教學道首要條件之弟子必須有上師（guru），弟子應該如何侍奉上師與阿闍梨（ācārya），如何能遇到密教的上師與阿闍梨，以及密教上師如何指導弟子[24]。此後，瓜生津隆真注意到了SS中有

㉑ A.Bharati, “Intentional Language in the Tantras”, *Journal of the American Oriental Society* 81(3), 1961, p. 270.

㉒ 這類論著有：Alex Wayman, *Calming the Mind and Discerning the Real: Buddhist Meditation and the Middle View. From the Lam rin chen mo of Tsoṅ-kha-pa*, New York: Columbia University Press, 1978; David Seyfort Reugg, *The Literature of the Madhyamaka School of Philosophy in India*, Wiesbaden: Otto Harrassowitz, 1981; Robert A. F. Thurman, *Tsong Khapa's Speech of Gold in the Essence of the True Eloquence: Reason and Enlightenment in the Central Philosophy of Tibet*, Princeton, New Jersey: Princeton University Press, 1984; KodoYotsuya, *The Critique of Svatantra: Reasoning by Chandrakīrti and Tsong-kha-pa. A Study of Philosophical Proof According to Two Prāsaṅgika Madhyamaka Traditions of India and Tibet*, Stuttgart: Franz Steiner Verlag, 1999; Kurtis R. Schaeffer, *Dreaming the Great Brahmin: Tibetan traditions of the Buddhist poet-saint Saraha*, New York: Oxford University Press, 2005; Kevin A. Vose, *Resurrecting Candrakīrti: Disputes in the Tibetan Creation of Prasaṅgika*, Boston: Wisdom Publications, 2009; Shingo Einoo,*Genesis and Development of Tantrism*, Tokyo: Institute of Oriental Culture, University of Tokyo, 2009; Christian K. Wedemeyer, *Making Sense of Tantric Buddhism: History, Semiology, and Transgression in the Indian Traditions*, New York: Columbia University Press, 2013; Vincent Eltschinger, “Is There a Burden-bearer? The Sanskrit Bhārahārasūtra and Its Scholastic Interpretations”, *Journal of the American Oriental Society* 134(3), 2014, pp. 453-479. 等等。

㉓ Ronald M. Davidson, *Indian Esoteric Buddhism: A Social History of the Tantric Movement*. New York: Columbia University, 2002, p. 222.

㉔ 高田仁覚《*Subhāṣita-saṃgraha*（善說集）における大乘思想の斷片について》，《印度學佛教學研究》2（2），1954，pp. 184-185；《善說集に示されたる密教的學道（一）》，《印度學佛教學研究》3（1），1954，pp. 264-267.

《入中論》的第44偈和184偈的梵文，作《月稱造“入中論”の梵文佚文》一文[25]。再到70年代初，賴富本宏在高田仁覺的基礎上，對SS的內容作了更爲細緻的介紹，形成《*Subhaṣitasaṃgraha*に関する一考察——その構成と内容を中心として》一文。他還將Bendall編校本的索引中舉出的SS引用文獻及文獻作者的情況作了日譯對照，並且按照顯密，按經、論、儀軌與註疏進行分類，形成《*Subhaṣitasaṃgraha*の引用文献をめぐって》一文[26]。SS中所有引用過的文獻可以此文爲基礎進行查找。至此，日本學者對SS研究告一段落，研究進度僅僅停留在初步文獻梳理。20世紀90年代的日本學者在論文中利用SS進行研究的例子多了一些。苫米地等流的論文《*Pañcakrama*研究（2）——*Caryāmelāpakapradīpa*における引用文献》中提到*Ekanayanirdeśa*時，會注明參考SS[27]。山口益在《般若思想史》一書的第十章“中觀思想的密教化”中簡介了SS。他認爲，印度密教實際上是由所謂的“中觀思想的密教化”的形態演變而來，SS正是體現這種傾向性的著作，且將SS與歸於聖天名下的《心障清淨論》（*Cittāvaraṇaviśodhana*）[28]並舉[29]。2008年，松森大樹再次將目光投射到了SS上，參考了苫米地等流的相關論文，研究了其中引用聖天的《行合集燈》（*Caryāmelāpakapradīpa*）的部分，以明妃禁戒（vidyāvrata）與智印等至（jñānamudrāsamāpatti）爲要點，就兩部文獻中的修習口訣（bhāvanopadeśa）進行了簡要的比較，作《*Subhāṣitasaṃgraha*に見られる*Caryāmelāpakapradīpa*の引用について》一文[30]。

目前尚未發現以SS爲題的漢文研究成果。今人的相關研究也主要以SS作爲參考文獻。李學竹2006在《月稱及其〈入中論〉》一文中提及《善巧語集》（即SS的另一漢譯名）引用了《入中論》[31]。後又以SS校對月稱（*Candrakīrti*）《入中論》（*Madhyamakāvatāra-kārikā*）[32]。2010年，台灣學者釋見弘法師在其文《二諦之區別與空之三要點——以〈明句論〉第二十四章爲主》中提及SS，因爲SS引用了《入中論》

㉕ 瓜生津隆真《月稱造〈入中論〉の梵文佚文》，《印度學佛教學研究》8（2），1960，pp. 556-557.

㉖ 賴富本宏《*Subhaṣitasaṃgraha*の引用文献をめぐって》，《密教文化》96，1971，pp. 50-37；《*Subhaṣitasaṃgraha*に関する一考察——その構成と内容を中心として》，《印度學佛教學研究》19（2），1971，pp. 862-865.

㉗ 苫米地等流《*Pañcakrama*研究（2）——*Caryāmelāpakapradīpa*における引用文献》，《印度學佛教學研究》41（1），1992，pp. 396-391.

㉘ 這與上文提到聖天的*Cittaviśuddhiprakaraṇa*與之題目類同，它們之間的關聯有待研究。Seyfort Ruegg指出，在SS提到丹珠爾中有歸於聖天名下的*Cittāvaraṇaviśodhana-nāma-prakaraṇa*和歸於Indrabhūti-pāda名下的*Cittaratnaviśodhana*，皆於11世紀翻譯成藏文，但它們之間的關聯不明。參見David Seyfort Ruegg, *The Literature of the Madhyamaka School of Philosophy in India*, Wiesbaden: Otto Harrassowitz, 1981, p. 106.

㉙ 〔日〕山口益編，肖平、楊金萍譯《般若思想史》，上海：上海古籍出版社，2006年，82—83頁。

㉚ 松森大樹《*Subhāṣitasaṃgraha*に見られる*Caryāmelāpakapradīpa*の引用について》，《印度學佛教學研究》56（2），2008，pp. 933-929.

㉛ 李學竹《月稱及其〈入中論〉》，《中國藏學》2006年第2期，227—236頁。

㉜ Li Xuezhu, "*Madhyamakāvatāra-kārikā* Chapter 6", *Journal of Indian Philosophy* 43, 2014, pp. 1-30.

的一句偈頌，但衹言及世俗諦，沒提及勝義諦[33]。

簡而言之，SS的獨特之處就在於其中往往摘錄了常見經論的段落異讀與某些鮮見的密續內容。

三、新見尼泊爾梵文寫本

新見尼泊爾梵文寫本出自尼泊爾-德國梵文寫本保存項目（Nepal-German Manuscript Preservation Project，簡稱NGMPP）[34]，由曾任該項目主任的德裔奧地利學者Klaus-Dieter Mathes提供該寫本微縮膠片的複本。寫本原件現存於尼泊爾加德滿都國家檔案館。複本首尾各有三頁後期整理的文字，包括起止頁（第一頁“START”和末尾頁“END”）、寫本信息（首尾各有一頁，內容一致）和題跋。寫本標題爲*Subhāṣitasaṃgraha*，卷號A 1057/20，編號MS No. 3-652，散裝紙質寫本，顏色棕黃，正文共26頁，一頁大小爲32.1厘米×12.1厘米，用城體（Nagari）書寫，1986年1月8日拍攝成微縮膠片。由於筆者無法觸及寫本本身，寫本更多的原始信息無從知曉。

相較於Bendall所使用的百頁之巨的寫本，該寫本從體量上明顯不全，是一個殘本，它總共26頁，雙面皆有文字，每面八行。從文字上來看，它的第1頁從正面第一行有數個字母，之後有大片空白，直到倒數第三行開始有三行梵文。從倒數第三行即第五行起始段落，可辨認出對應Bendall編校本正文第一部分第9頁底部段落[35]，隨後寫本到26頁正面第五行結束全文。新寫本缺少開頭部分內容，從Bendall編校本的信息來看，大約是劍橋圖書館所藏MS Or.679前7頁的篇幅。新寫本是紙質，使用城體書寫，年代可能比較晚近。新寫本文字書寫較爲清晰，可惜錯誤較多，往往一行會出現十幾處抄寫錯誤。然而，這是目前筆者僅可利用的寫本資料，在文獻價值上來看依舊難能可貴。Bendall編校本並非完美無缺，其中有幾處空缺，恰好可以通過這個寫本得到啟發，從而修正與補足Bendall編校本。新寫本有自己的段落層次，這點對文意的解讀提供了一些新的方向。

鑒於新寫本本身存在不少錯誤，引入藏文材料、通過梵藏對勘的研究方法，對於該寫本而言是較好的處理方式，也能較爲明顯地體現出它的價值。由於SS目前未見藏譯，衹能以SS中標明出處的文本藏譯來對勘研究。筆者目前正以SS作爲梵文支持來編校僅有藏譯本的《入真實論》，因爲在SS中有部分與《入真實論》內容重合的地方，

㉝ 釋見弘《二諦之區別與空之三要點——以〈明句論〉第二十四章爲主》，《法鼓佛學學報》2010年第7期，67—106頁。

㉞ 該項目介紹參見張曦：《尼泊爾梵文寫本整理情況》，《南亞研究》1988年第3期，87頁；Franz-Karl Ehrhard, “The Nepal German Manuscript Preservation Project”, *European Bulletin of Himalayan Research* 2, 1991, pp. 20-24；https://www2.uni-hamburg.de/ngmcp/ngmpp_top_e.html(access April 20 2016).

㉟ 即Cecil Bendall ed., “Subhāṣita-saṃgraha: An Anthology of Extracts from Buddhist Works complied by an unknown author, to illustrate the Doctrines of scholastic and of mystic (tāntrik) Buddhism”, p. 383.

這些文字沒有明確的出處，有可能是SS作者引用了《入真實論》，而這是此前Bendall等研究者未曾發現的一點。反過來說，SS中有些沒有明確標明段落出處的文字能夠通過《入真實論》的藏文來進行校對。筆者主要的依據來自Klaus-Dieter Mathes的研究，他曾撰文提到智稱（Jñānakīrti）《入真實論》（*Tattvāvatāra*, *De kho na nyid la 'jug pa*）。印度阿闍梨俱生金剛（Sahajavajra）爲闡釋其師慈護（Maitrīpa）的《十真如》（*Tattvadaśaka*）所寫的《十真如注》（*Tattvadaśaṭīkā*）中，征引了《入真實論》中的一段關於瑜伽士結合觀修而得大手印的偈頌，出現在教化利根者的開篇[36]。有趣的是，這段偈頌也出現在SS中，卻是處於明確的密教語境之中。因此，《入真實論》與SS可以對校。當新寫本在與Bendall編校本有異讀時，該寫本便能起到了補充及提供新想法的作用。例如，在Bendall編校本第397頁的一句：

yā sā sarvaprapañcānām abhūmir vacasām abhūḥ |
vittiḥ sā citta—— prajñeti parikīrtitā ||

在Bendall所用寫本中，citta後的文字缺失。而在新見寫本中該詞是完整的，見於第7頁反面第一行：cītupārakya，可惜該詞拼寫有誤。通過《入真實論》的藏文：

gang zhig spros pa thams cad kyi |
| gnas dang tshig tu ma gyur pa'i |
| 'jug de thugs kyi rdo rje yis |
| shes rab ces ni yongs su grags |[37]

結合其中thugs kyi rdo rje yis，該處空缺可回譯爲citta<vajreṇa>（以意金剛）。而根據新見寫本的字母推測，則傾向於citta<*vajrasya*>（意金剛的）這樣的寫法。因此有兩種釋讀可能。

四、《善說集》研究問題的幾點思考

概括而言，SS文本的研究意義可有四個方面。

一，在語文學上，因爲該文本引用了多種顯密文獻，有些少見的文獻也保存其中，這便使其很適合用於梵藏經論的校對，起到修補、考訂和解釋其他文本的作用。顯然，這點已經在過往與當下的研究中受到普遍認可。

㊱ Klaus-Dieter Mathes,"Blending the Sūtras with the Tantras: The Influence of Maitrīpa and his Circle on the Formation of Sūtra Mahāmudrā in the Kagyu Schools", in Ronald M. Davidson and Christian K. Wedemeyer eds., *Tibetan Buddhist Literature and Praxis: Studies in its Formative Period, 900-1400: Proceedings from the Tenth Seminar of the International Association of Tibetan Studies*, Leiden, Boston: Brill, 2006, pp. 201-227; *A Direct Path to the Buddha within:Gö Lotsāwa's Mahāmudrā Interpretation of the Ratnagotravibhāga*, Boston: Wisdom Publications, 2008, pp. 35-40.

㊲ 德格版（sDe dge）《丹珠爾》（*bsTan 'gyur*），3709號，rGyud，tsu，43v2。TBRC W23703. 78: 79-153, Delhi: Karmapae Choedhey, Gyalwae Sungrab Partun Khang, 1982-1985. http://tbrc.org/link?RID=O1GS6011/O1GS601137884$W23703.

二，在印度佛教史的研究上，SS提供了佛教晚期在印度的一個側影。Bendall認爲，就當時而言，已經有大量關於印度佛教早期的研究，一些關於中期經院派與哲學的研究，但幾乎沒有關於如密教文獻中所顯示的佛教末期衰落狀況的研究。SS這部文選展示了《集學論》（*Śikṣāmuccaya*）的教義，並將我們帶向該系統在其誕生地上的歷史發展盡頭[38]。當前，未有從《集學論》（即作者歸屬有爭議的《大乘集菩薩學論》）的教義出發來解釋SS的研究，有必要考察Bendall如何得出如此的論斷。

三，在佛教語言上，SS是俗語Apabhraṃśa研究的好例子，尤其是後者。如前所述，Apabhraṃśa也是佛教文獻的寫作語言，主要是密教文獻在使用。就語言系統而言，Apabhraṃśa是俗語（Prakrit）的一種。最狹義的俗語單指Mahārāṣṭrī，最廣義的俗語則包括了中期印度所使用的非梵語意外的所有其他雅利安語言，這裏的俗語就是指後者。Apabhraṃśa是新層俗語的總稱，年代指向7、8—11世紀，細分來說將近三百種，也有三種至二十七種的分法。有些耆那教文獻也使用Apabhraṃśa書寫[39]。關於Apabhraṃśa研究不多，它主要是語言學學者的關注點，佛教學者關注較少。一方面是這類文獻本身有限，相對梵文文獻來說資料較少，該語言也不易掌握；另一方面是目前密教研究很多集中於藏傳佛教，利用藏文文獻的比例較大，較少涉及Apabhraṃśa。而在SS中摘錄的道歌（Doha）使用的是Apabhraṃśa，道歌研究則是密教研究中富有多義性的一項。爲此，Bendall特地在附錄中輯錄出了SS中使用Apabhraṃśa的28頌詩，單做了一篇研究，與梵文和藏文做了比較，英譯了大部分詩句，並且加以分析[40]。這樣的研究還可深入下去。

四，在文類研究上，“善說集”（Subhāṣita-saṃgraha）實際上是一種印度的文類，作品冠以這一題名很大程度上就意味著“無名氏”。關於我們所討論的SS的作者不詳這一點，可能與這一類稱爲“善說集”的文類有關。很多梵文作者的作品遺失了，但他們的詩句卻被保留在很多“善說集”之中[41]。印度文學史上歷來不斷有名爲“善說集”或類似名稱的作品問世，形成了一種以善說（subhāṣita）或妙語（sūkti）來抒情、說理或演講等的文類，重在內容，而非作者，類似於諺語集。佛教“善說集”是用來宣揚佛法的。其他印度宗教也運用這種文類。對這類作品的整理和研究很有限，現存數百部這類“善說集”中，僅有少數被編輯過[42]。當然，我們依然可以選擇追查這部“善說集”的作者究竟是誰，但不可忽略作者隱去姓名而終無結果的可能。

㊳ Cecil Bendall ed., “Subhāṣita-saṃgraha: An Anthology of Extracts from Buddhist Works complied by an unknown author, to illustrate the Doctrines of scholastic and of mystic (tāntrik) Buddhism”, pp. 376-377.

㊴ 參見水野弘元著，許洋主譯《巴利文法》，臺北：華宇出版社，1986年，1—11頁。

㊵ See Cecil Bendall ed., “Subhāṣita-saṃgraha: An Anthology of Extracts from Buddhist Works complied by an unkhown author, to illstrate the Doctrines of scholastic and of mystic (tāntrik) Buddhism”, pp. 245-265.

㊶ Ludwik Sternbach, “Ravigupta and hi gnomic Verses”,*Annals of the Bhandarkar Oriental Research Institute* 48/49, Golden JubileeVolume 1917-1967 (1968), p. 137.

㊷ Ludwik Sternbach,*A History of Indian Literature Vol. IV, 1: Subhāṣita, Gnomic and Didactic Literature*, Wiesbaden: Otto Harrassowitz, 1974, pp. 1-43.

五、余　　論

在過往的研究中，SS除了得到了文獻梳理外，較多的價值是被當做輔助支持性文本來引用，這是由該文本內容旁征博引的特性所決定的。相較而言，該文本精準校對的完整性、具體的成文年代、作者考證、語言內涵、義理分析等研究工作仍然有待展開。在新寫本的發現之後，文本的諸多問題可以藉此機會繼續研究。和很多佛教原典的研究相同，僅僅依靠這兩部寫本與Bendall編校本來說，很難解決所有相關問題，因此，希望更多不同地區和年代的寫本仍然存世並被我們所發現。

An Overview of the *Subhāṣitasaṃgraha*:Based on Bendall's Edition and a New Sanskrit Manuscript from Nepal

Lu Chenye

The *Subhāṣitasaṃgraha* is an anthology of extracts from different kinds of Buddhist sutras and tantras in Sanskrit and partly in Apabhraṃśa, compiled by an unknown author, which reflects the condition of late period Indian Buddhism. Cecil Bendall found the manuscript of this work in Nepal and edited it, publishing his edition in 1903-1904. The anthology is divided into two parts by Bendall: Part I is scholastic and Part II is mystic. Actually, it is a text about Śūnyatā and Mahāmudrā. Now, a new Sanskrit manuscript from Nepal has been discovered by the Nepalese-German Manuscript Preservation Project, providing new clues and ideas to make a more accurate edition and to interpret its meaning. The study of this work will also contribute to developing new approaches to Buddhist philology, Indian Buddhist history, Buddhist linguistics, Indian literature genres and so forth.

從《心經》音譯本及其他文獻看梵文jña的發音*

李建強

一、引　　言

在早期的婆羅迷（Brāhmī）字母中，jña是ja和ña兩個字母的疊加，比如在貴霜（Kushāṇa）時代，這個字母寫作[①]。William Dwight Whitney的*Sanskrti Grammar*談到梵文的j源自g[②]，但沒有論及字母組合jña。Adolf Friedrich Stenzler的Elementarbuch der Sanskrit-Sprache第十七版第7條之Ⅶ在連寫字母jña後有個注，季羨林先生的中文版作：發音作dnya。該書德文版第十八版小注有了改動，段晴先生譯爲：今天一般讀作dnya或gnya。這兩個版本都沒有提到可念成[ʥȵa]。德國海德堡大學南亞所古典印度學部Thomas Lehmann的梵語講義Sanskrit für Anfänger Ein Lehr-und Übungsbuch§1.9.4提到了jña的發音，德文原文如下：Zu beachten ist die Aussprache der Lautkombination jñ. Diese wird je nach Region wie dt.“gnj”, “gj” oder “dnj” ausgesprochen. Beispiel: ajña wird wie dt. “agnja/agja/adnja” gesprochen[③]. 我的同事張麗香老師漢譯如下“應當注意的是複合音素jñ的發音。按照地域的不同，這個音分别讀如德文裏的‘gnj’，‘gj’或‘dnj’。例：ajña讀如德文裏‘agnja /agja/adnja’”[④]。同樣也沒有提到念[ʥȵa]。

聶鴻音先生根據梵文複合字母jña在12、13世紀之交河西地區的音譯，指出其在西夏、蒙元時代並沒有統一的讀法，表現出[kȵa][dzȵa][tȵa]三種念法，這是盛唐密宗佛教傳入河西以後，譯者由於師承各異而產生的不同翻譯習慣所致[⑤]。如果跟Lehmann教

---

* 本文为中国人民大学科学研究基金（中央高校基本科研业务费专项资金资助）项目成果，批准号：15XNL014。

① Ram Sharma, *Brāhmī Script—Development in North-Western India and Central Asia*, Delhi: B. R. Publishing Corporation, 2002, p. 249.

② William Dwight Whitney, *Sanskrit Grammar*, Mineola, New York: Dover Publications, Inc., reprint, 2003. 見該書第42條，15—16頁。

③ 該講義未正式出版，德文版由張麗香老師惠賜。

④ 張麗香《梵文入門教程》，上海：中西書局，2018年（待刊）。

⑤ 聶鴻音《梵文jña的對音》，《語言研究》2008年第4期，14—16頁。

材中的講法兒相比，多出了[dzn̥a]，少了‘gj’。

John Beames談到了jña在印度七種方言中的發音，下面把這段話翻譯並引在這裏：

除了Gujarati、Sindhi、Marathi之外的所有方言區，這個字符規則地念作*gy*，所以ājñā念作āgyā，jñān念作gyān。Bangali和Oriya方言保持着jña這個拼寫，而Hindi和Panjabi方言寫法和讀音一致。Marathi方言念作dny，Gujarati方言念得像jn或dn。⑥

作者列舉的方言材料中，除了Gujarati方言的jn和[ʥn̥]有些近似，其他方言都沒有念[ʥn̥a]。另外，他試圖探討gy這樣的音出現的時代，但所找的材料已經是晚到公元16世紀左右莫臥兒王朝Akbar皇帝時代的文獻，以及比Akbar早兩個半世紀的Chand的文獻，那也到了14世紀左右了。漢語及其他語言轉寫梵語的對音文獻，早於14世紀的反映jña語音線索的文獻比比皆是，這不僅能研究漢語的語音面貌，也能爲印度歷史語言學研究提供些線索。

本文打算利用《心經》及其他對音材料探討梵文jña在不同譯本中所體現的梵語語音面貌。

二、《心經》音譯本關於jña的對音概況

梵文字符jña主要出現在動詞jñā（知道）及其派生的詞中，梵本《心經》中有大量含有jñā這個詞根的詞。目前來看，現存的漢語音譯本中譯經時代最早的是唐代不空譯本，保存在房山石經中；敦煌文獻中S2464、S5648、P2322、S5627、S3178譯經時代不好確定，至晚也是10世紀的文獻；另外，房山石中還保存有辽代慈賢譯本。這些音譯材料是探討梵文字母jña發音的主要材料。

《心經》當中含有jñā的音節有prajñā、saṃjñā、vijñā、jñāna、jñātavya，對音情況如下：

表1　《心經》jñā的對音

	prajñā	saṃjñā-	vijñānam	na vijñānaṃ	na jñānaṃ	prajñā	jñātavyam	prajñā paramitā
S2464	鉢囉(二合)誐攘(二合)	散誐攘	尾誐攘(二合)喃		曩誐攘喃	鉢囉誐攘(二合)	誐攘(二合)哆尾演	鉢囉誐攘(二合)播囉弭哆
S5648	鉢囉(二合)誐攘	散誐攘	尾誐攘(二合)喃	曩尾誐攘(二合)喃	曩誐攘喃	鉢囉誐攘(二合)	誐攘(二合)哆尾演	鉢囉誐攘(二合)播囉弭哆
P2322	鉢囉(二合)誐攘	散誐攘	尾誐攘(二合)喃	曩尾誐攘(二合)喃	曩誐攘喃	鉢囉(二合)誐攘	誐攘(二合)哆尾演	鉢囉(二合)誐攘(二合)播囉弭跢
S5627	鉢囉 穰	散誐攘	尾誐攘喃	曩尾誐攘喃	曩誐攘喃	鉢囉攘	誐攘 哆演	鉢囉攘 播囉弭跢
S3178	鉢囉 穰	散誐攘	尾誐 喃	曩尾誐攘喃				
不空	鉢囉(二合)枳娘(二合)	僧(去)枳娘(二合)	尾枳娘(二合)曩	曩尾枳娘(二合)曩	曩枳娘(二合)曩(引)	鉢囉枳娘(二合)	枳娘(二合)怛尾焰(二合)	鉢囉(二合)枳娘(二合)播囉弭跢
慈賢	鉢囉(二合)倪也(二合)	僧擬惹(二合)	尾倪也(二合)喃	拏尾倪也(二合)捺	拏倪也(二合)喃	鉢囉(二合)倪也(二合)	倪也(二合)馱尾焰(二合)	鉢囉(二合)倪也(二合)播囉弭跢

⑥ John Beames, *Comparative Grammar of the Modern Aryan Languages of India*, Volume 1: On Sounds, London: Cambridge University Press, first published in 1872, digitally printed in 2012, p. 303.

複合字母jñā，不空用“枳孃二合”來對，敦煌寫本用“誐攘二合”對，有時也寫作“誐穰”，攘、穰形近，似乎是抄寫的問題。還有單寫一個“穰”的。慈賢用“倪也二合”“擬惹二合”對。

除了《心經》之外，其他的對音材料中也會偶爾見到jñ-的對音，恐怕不能窮盡性搜集，所以只作爲《心經》對音的補充。

三、梵文jña念gnya的證據

“誐攘二合”能夠體現不空一派的對音特點：次濁聲母能對梵文的不送氣濁塞音。敦煌寫本《心經》中，疑母字誐對ga，儼對gam，蘖對g（蘖嚕二合對grū），彥對gan，泥母字怒對d（怒嚕二合對drū），那對da，你對d（你也對dya），耨對du，明母冒對bo，沒對bud。所以“誐攘二合”之“誐”，記錄的是梵文音[ɡ]。S5627中“攘”也有寫作“穰”的。問題在下一個字“攘”或“穰”上。攘穰，《廣韻》只有日母音，《集韻》中“攘”字除了日母音外，還收有娘母一讀，庚韻尼庚切，用在疊韻聯綿詞“搶攘”（搶，鋤庚切）中，但是庚韻的主要母音很少對長元音ā，恐怕不該取這個音。日母字對梵文的舌面鼻音ñ[ȵ]，雖然是玄奘的對音習慣，不過根據劉廣和先生的研究，不空對音，日母也有的對ñ、ny[7]，所以“誐攘二合”可以還原成梵音ɡnya。“攘穰”也有可能是“孃”的誤字。《慧琳音義》卷十釋《仁王護國般若波羅蜜多經下卷》云：“枳孃二合，上雞以反，孃取上聲，經從禾，誤也。”孃字一般對ṇa[ɳa]，音近替代可對ña[ȵa]，則“誐攘二合”可以描寫梵文音[ɡȵa]。這說明至晚公元10世紀，梵文jña念[ɡȵa]在漢語文獻中就有記錄了。

四、不空“枳孃二合”的對音

萬金川先生檢索CBETA中的用例，發現在不空、慧琳等人的著作中，都出現“枳孃二合”這種形式，他推測，“這個轉寫語形或可視爲是不空翻譯集團的標誌之一”[8]。他引用柯蔚南的觀點[9]，指出在《慧琳音義》中“枳”字章母“之耳反”一讀只出現在“枳園”等專有名詞中，見母一讀，一是用於植物名“枳椇上吉以反，下俱宇反”中，除此之外，“所有其他的用例都只出現在梵文語詞的漢音轉寫裏”。至於“枳孃”對應jña[10]的問題，由於萬金川先生認爲梵語jña只讀[ʥȵa]，“枳”字的對音只好算作“慧琳音譯系統

⑦ 劉廣和《音韻比較研究》，北京：中國廣播電視出版社，2002年，115頁。

⑧ 萬金川《石室〈心經〉音寫抄本校釋初稿之一》，《佛學研究中心學報》2004年第9期，84頁。

⑨ W. South Coblin, “A Compendium of Phonetics in Northwest Chinese”, *Journal of Chinese Linguistics*, Monograph Series Number 7(1994), pp. 1-117, 119-504.

⑩ 柯尉南認爲“枳孃”轉寫-jñyaḥ，萬金川先生作了糾正。

裏的一項例外”[11]。但是《慧琳音義》中“枳孃”之“枳”的注音清清楚楚爲見母：“枳孃二合，枳音雞以反。”且“枳”字在《廣韻》中也有“居紙切”的讀音，與慧琳注音声母相同。所以聶鴻音先生推測，在不空一派的僧人中，jña讀作[kȵa][12]。

我們檢索《大正藏》不空譯咒中“枳”字的梵文對音形式，除了“枳孃”之外，“枳”都對梵文的ki 或k-。如果從對音字表示讀音的單一性方面考慮，“枳孃”之“枳”也應讀見母，那麼jña讀作[kȵa]或近似的音。可是《金剛頂一切如來真實攝大乘現證大教王經》中，不空用“惹拏二合”對𑖕𑖿𑖗𑖯（jñā）[13]，而且出現多次。“惹”是日母字，不會有舌根音的成分，應該是描寫[dʑ]。拏，娘母，一般對ṇ[ɳ]，與ñ[ȵ]音近，“惹拏二合”可還原成[dʑȵa]。按照John Beames的說法[14]，梵文詞語jñā的讀音在有的方言中和形態變化有關，作爲動詞，在Panjabi、Oriya、Gujarati、Marathi、Sindhi方言中變成jāṇa°，在Hindi、Bangali方言中變成jāna°；作爲名詞，在Panjabi、Oriya、Hindi、Bangali方言中都有gyāna這樣的形式。不空所譯的“惹拏”若不加“二合”，對jāṇa正合適。不過，不空的譯音材料中，jña的讀音是否和語法功能相關還需要對每個詞逐一分析，現在還不是下結論的時候，把線索寫在這兒，供大家參考。

五、梵文jña念gya的證據

《心經》慈賢譯本中，jñā的對音，“倪也二合”出現11次，“擬惹二合”出現2次[15]。萬金川先生[16]認爲，“倪也二合”之“倪”，“對譯梵語舌面塞擦音串jñ，而在實際音讀裏，因於語流音變而出現了……舌面塞擦音j的‘減音’現象。”他引用儲泰松先生的觀點，北宋時期，疑母三四等由於介音的影響，使得前面的ŋ的發音部位前移而變成ȵ，所以能夠對梵文的ñ。這種解釋的不足之處在於必須承認存在j[dʑ]的脫落，而且疑母細音已經變成ȵ。可是實際情況是，慈賢譯本《心經》中，疑母字儼對gam，孽對g（孽嚕對grū），巘對gan，誐對ga，儼孽巘都是細音，但都對g，由此可推理，“倪”字也應對應g。可見萬先生的推測不符合慈賢對音事實。“也”，以母，一般對ya，那麼“倪也二合”正好對gya，慈賢用的梵本，jñā讀作[ɡja:]。至於“擬惹二合”，顯然也是記錄梵文jñā。“擬”是疑母，表示音素[ɡ]沒有什麼問題，日母字“惹”之後有“二合”，說明此字僅取聲母之後的部分[ja]，正如“吠鉢哩惹二合娑”對viparyāsa，“哩惹二合”ryā一樣。

---

⑪ 萬金川《石室〈心經〉音寫抄本校釋初稿之一》，85頁。

⑫ 聶鴻音《梵文jña的對音》，14—16頁。

⑬ 《金剛頂一切如來真實攝大乘現證大教王經》在《大正藏》第十八冊874號經，“惹拏二合”出現多次，比如第318頁下欄；梵本在《大正藏》875號經中，比如第324頁中欄20行有𑖕𑖿𑖗𑖯（jñā）。

⑭ John Beames, *Comparative Grammar of the Modern Aryan Languages of India*, Volume 1: On Sounds, p. 303.

⑮ 表1中把重複的句子去掉了，“倪也二合”出現7次，“擬惹二合”出現1次。如果重複的句子也算，則應是文中所列的結果。

⑯ 萬金川《石室〈心經〉音寫抄本校釋初稿之一》，85—86頁。

所以“擬惹二合”所對的jñā讀作[gja:]。另外，宋施護譯《聖觀自在菩薩不空王秘密心陀羅尼經》“倪踰二合引”對jño，“倪也二合”對jñā，倪，疑母，踰也，以母，同樣是梵文jñ讀gy的證據。所以，梵語方言jñā讀作[gja:]的證據至晚在宋辽時期就已經有了。

六、jña讀作[dȵa]的證據

聶鴻音先生曾指出，prajñā中的jñā，失譯西夏文《般若心經》作[illegible]，對音漢字爲“（波囉）得娘”⑰。西夏文[illegible]，李範文先生《夏漢字典》擬音爲[tjɨ]，聶先生猜想，這個音是經過藏文dzñā轉換而來⑱。但結合梵語方音想一想，這可能就是jña讀[dȵa]的證據。在敦煌藏文文獻中能找到旁證。《不空羂索陀羅尼》梵本中有jñopavīta、sarva jñā這樣的詞，P.t.0056藏文本分別作dnyopavīta、sarva dnya。藏人用dny記錄jñ，說明他們聽到的音是[dȵ]。敦煌文獻一般是8—10世紀的，所以梵文方言jña讀[dȵa]至晚在10世紀就已經存在了。

七、jña讀作其他音的證據

全面收集整理梵漢對音中有關jña的材料，一時還不具備條件，這裏只談目前所見到的材料中，jña的語音面貌。

1. jña讀作[ʥȵa]

闍那崛多《不空羂索呪經》“社儒”對jño，“腎若”對jñā。菩提流志譯《不空羂索咒心經》“實乳”對jño、“實若而可切”對jñā。菩提流志譯《不空羂索神變真言經》“腎二合饒去”對jño，“腎二合惹”對jñā。“社實腎”都是禪母，是濁塞擦音，“儒乳若饒惹”都是日母字，有舌面鼻音成分，故所依據的梵本，梵文jñ念[dʑȵ]。

義淨《金光明最勝王經》“僧慎爾耶”對saṃjñeya⑲，“鉢喇底慎若”對prati-jñā⑳，禪母字“慎”加上日母字“爾、若”一起對jñe、jñā㉑，說明他所傳的梵文jñ念[dʑȵ]。

⑰ 聶鴻音《西夏文藏傳〈般若心經〉研究》，《民族語文》2005年第2期，25頁。

⑱ 聶鴻音《梵文jña的對音》，15頁。

⑲ 《大正藏》中所附的梵文作sañciñjaya，顯然是個誤字。段晴新發現了兩片于闐文的《金光明最勝王經》殘片，恰也有對應的這一段咒語，相應的詞是saṃjñeya，見Duan Qing（段晴），“Two New Folios of Khotanese Suvarṇabhāsottamasūtra”, *Annual Report of the International Research Institute for Advanced Buddhology at Soka University for the Academic Year 2006,* vol. 10, Tokyo 2007, pp. 325-336.

⑳ 《大正藏》中所附的梵文作pratiśiñjā, 顯然是prati-jñā之誤。

㉑ 柯蔚南認爲義淨對音禪母字“慎”能對ś和c，他依據是《大正藏》所附的錯誤的詞形，結論顯然是靠不住的。參看W.South Coblin（柯蔚南），*A Survey of YIJING's Transcriptional Corpus*，《語言研究》1991年第1期，68—92頁。

施護譯《佛說智光滅一切業障陀羅尼經》“惹拏(二合)曩”對jñāna，而日母字“惹”加上娘母字“拏”對jñā，與不空譯《金剛頂一切如來真實攝大乘現證大教王經》中的現象一致，前面的討論已經說過，有讀[dʑɳa]的可能。但是施護譯《聖觀自在菩薩不空王秘密心陀羅尼經》中jñ念[gj]，這兩部經主譯都是施護，jña的念法不同，其原因有待深入研究。

2. jña讀作ña[ɳ̥a]

于闐高僧提雲般若等譯《智炬陀羅尼經》“南無 壤奴嗢迦(上)寫(斯舸反)”對namo jñānolkasya，單用日母字“壤”對jñā，中原音日母字是個舌面鼻音，說明此處jñ讀作ñ[ɳ̥]。這個念法還有一條旁證，梵詞saṃjñā在于闐語《贊巴斯特之書》中作saṃñā[22]，jñā就轉成ñā。

施向東先生指出，玄奘是把jñ念成ñ，用日母字對[23]，根據施先生提供的線索，找出相關證據如下：《大般若波羅蜜多經・理趣分》卷578“鉢剌壤波囉弭多曳……奴壤多，邺壤多”，“鉢剌壤”對譯prajñā，“奴壤多，邺壤多”《慧琳音義》作“弩(鼻)枳孃(二合上引)多，闕枳孃(二合引)多(上引)曳(引)”，則“壤”對jñā。《阿毗達磨顯宗論》“爾焰”是對jñeyaṃ，“爾”對jñe。另外補充一個例證，玄奘譯《地藏十輪經咒》出現了“鉢剌惹”，是對prajñā。這都是單獨的日母字對jñ[24]，jñ讀作ñ[ɳ̥]。

jña用日母字對音，在隋唐之前的對音材料中經常出現。比如，法顯《大般泥洹經》、曇無讖《大般涅槃經》都有字母對音和釋義，齶音第五母ña分別譯爲：

顯譯：若者，智也。知法真實，是故說“若”。

讖譯：喏者，是智慧義。知真法性，是故名“喏”。

從二人的釋義來反推，所舉的梵語例詞應該大概是jñāpana，包含jñā這樣的音。爲ña舉例證卻舉了個包含jña的詞，可見他們所傳的音，jña大概念ña。

後漢三國時期的對音材料中，也能發現這類對音現象。不過，人們一般把早期對音中的這類現象解釋爲轉寫巴利語或其他語言。俞敏先生《後漢三國梵漢對音譜》jña對“若”，加了說明“P.ñ=skt. jñ”[25]。劉廣和先生《東晉譯經對音的晉語聲母系統》指出“對音材料裏有pali文音的影響，比如般若，與其說是對梵文的prajñā，不如說對巴利式的pañña”[26]。如果把這類對音也算上，那麼jña讀[ɳa]的證據至晚要推到後漢三國了。

㉒ 段晴《于闐・佛教・古卷》，上海：中西書局，2013年，105頁。

㉓ 施向東《音史尋幽——施向東自選集》，天津：南開大學出版社，2009年，16頁。

㉔ “惹”前面是曷韻字“剌”，應當有個t或d韻尾。若和後一個音節連起來讀就是dña。可是“爾焰”前頭又沒有d韻尾字。

㉕ 俞敏《後漢三國梵漢對音譜》，載於《俞敏語言論文集》，北京：商務印書館，1999年，12頁。

㉖ 劉廣和《音韻比較研究》，150頁。

八、結　　語

根據梵漢對音的證據，梵文jña至晚在10世紀就有[gȵa]和[dȵa]的念法，至晚在宋辽時期，就有[gja]的念法。另外jña還可以讀成[ʥȵa]和[ȵa]，而且，後兩種讀音的證據比前面三種的早。梵文教材不錄後兩種讀音，是沒照顧到漢語對音文獻所反映的梵語歷史面貌。

On the Pronunciation of Sanskrit akṣara jña based on the Transcriptional Material of *hṛdaya sūtra* and Others

Li Jianqiang

In the common text books of Sanskrit, the instructions of akṣara jña are not unanimous. By the proofs of the Sanskrit-Chinese transcription, the akṣara jña were pronounced as [gȵa]、[dȵa] no later than 10 century AD, and as [gja] no later than the Song and Liao Dynasties. Furthermore, the akṣara jña can also be pronounced as [ʥȵa] and [ȵa]. The proofs of last two pronunciations existed earlier than the former three. The common text books of Sanskrit ignored the last two pronunciations probably because of no considering the historical Sanskrit recorded by Chinese characters in transcriptional materials.

故宫藏西夏文《高王觀世音經》考釋

孫伯君

一

北京故宫博物院所藏西夏文刻本《高王觀世音經》是目前存世的有確切紀年的最晚的西夏文物之一，對確定西夏文的使用下限和西夏後裔在明朝的宗教活動以及《高王觀世音經》的傳行情況均具有重要意義。據《中國藏西夏文獻》題錄，西夏文《高王觀世音經》編號B51.002，卷子裝刻本，上下雙欄，紙幅高17厘米，長260厘米，版框高12.5厘米。卷首有版畫，所反映的是序言所述故事。卷尾有發願文，共34行，內容包括刊刻時間，即“大明朝壬子宣德五年（1430）正月十五日”，“發願者緣旦監剉”，以及眾多助緣人的名字。卷首有“肇祥鑒藏”，卷中朱印也有“周肇祥”字樣，卷末有“百鏡庵藏古雕刻記”鈐記，說明此本曾周肇祥所收藏。周肇祥（1880—1945），浙江人，近代著名的書畫家和鑒藏家。著述甚豐，曾著有《琉璃廠雜記》《百鏡庵鏡異錄》《遼金元古德錄》《壽安山志》《婆羅花樹館題記》《遼金元官印考》等①。此前，西夏文《高王觀世音經》只有史金波、白濱、李範文、聶鴻音等學者對卷尾發願文進行過研究和討論，迄今未見全文釋讀。

關於此本的刊刻時間，史金波和白濱在《明代西夏文經卷和石幢初探》一文中曾通過對卷尾發願文的初步翻譯，判斷其刊刻於洪武五年（1372）②；李範文則指出西夏文“[illegible]”實爲明代漢語“宣德”年號的音譯，從而認定其刊刻於宣德五年（1430）③。聶鴻音先生在《明刻本西夏文〈高王觀世音經〉補議》一文中成功地釋讀了“[illegible]”實爲藏語人名Yon tan rgya mtsho（緣旦監剉）的音譯，從而結合《明實錄》“永樂十三年二月庚午”條的記載“命禪師緣旦監剉爲灌頂慈慧妙智大國師，領占端竹爲灌頂慧應弘濟國師，皆賜誥、印”，進一步認定這部經的刊行時間爲宣德五年（1430）④。

黑水城出土文獻中存有幾種漢文本《高王觀世音經》，見藏於俄羅斯科學院東方文

---

① 參考周肇祥撰，趙珩、海波點校《琉璃廠雜記》之“史樹青序”，北京燕山出版社，1995年。

② 史金波、白濱《明代西夏文經卷和石幢初探》，《考古學報》1977年第1期。

③ 李範文《關於明代西夏文經卷的年代和石幢的名稱問題》，《考古》1979年第5期。

④ 聶鴻音《明刻本西夏文〈高王觀世音經〉》補議》，《寧夏社會科學》2003年第2期。

獻研究所。其中俄藏TK117爲經折裝刻本，且清晰完整[⑤]。通過對照翻譯，故宫藏西夏文本與俄藏漢文本非常接近，可以判斷兩種文本有淵源關係。值得注意的是，西夏文本卷首版畫與黑水城漢文本頗有不同，黑城本卷首版畫（見圖1）畫面右側主體是觀音像，國王與王后在左側頂禮，而作爲故事主角的孫敬德和拿著斷刀的行刑武士則只在左側遠處有所勾勒。顯然，版畫所反映内容不只是與序分内容相呼應，更强調的是國王和王后頂禮觀音的場面，極具西夏繪畫風格，尤其是國王和王后的服飾和水月觀音像等與黑水城出土佛畫中的服飾和形象頗爲相似[⑥]。

西夏文本卷首版畫（見圖2）内容分四組，中間有西夏文榜題，分别是“[illegible]”（夢中誦眾經可解）、“[illegible]，[illegible]”（敬德審處，不能損身）、“[illegible]”（千卷經）、“[illegible]，[illegible]”（何有感通，王問敬德），所反映的内容與序言所述故事更爲貼切。從繪畫風格來看，顯示了中原佛畫的典型特徵，尤其是國王和行刑武士，其服飾均具有明代漢族服飾的特點。説明明代西夏後裔所信仰的《高王觀世音經》，已非西夏時期的國王詔敕、舉國誦持，而純粹是一種民間修行。

圖1　黑水城出土漢文本《高王觀世音經》卷首版畫（俄藏TK117）

⑤　俄羅斯科學院東方研究所聖彼德堡分所、中國社會科學院民族研究所、上海古籍出版社編《俄藏黑水城文獻》第三册，1996年，36—38頁。

⑥　歷史博物館編譯小組編輯，許洋主譯《絲路上消失的王國——西夏黑水城的佛教藝術》，臺北：歷史博物館，1996年，180、199頁。

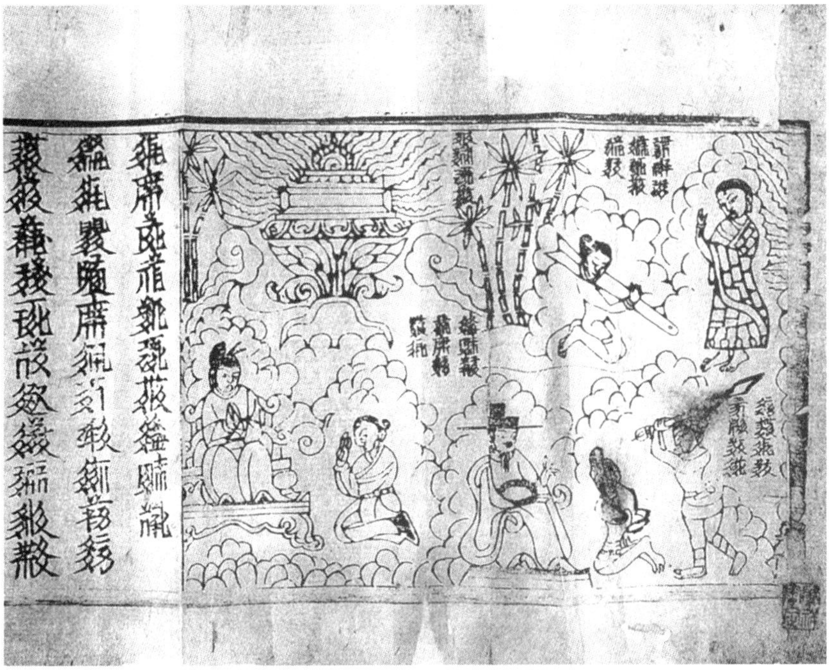

圖2　故宫博物院藏西夏文本《高王觀世音經》卷首版畫

我們知道，《高王觀世音經》是南北朝東魏天平（534—537）年間開始流行的一部經典，其由來是元魏定州募士孫敬德因冤獲罪，臨刑夢沙門開示而誦《觀世音經》千遍得以免刑的感應故事，道宣《大唐内典錄》卷10“歷代眾經應感興敬錄”曰[7]：

昔元魏天平年中，定州募士孫敬德，在防造觀音像。年滿將還，在家禮事。後爲賊所引，不堪拷楚，遂妄承罪。明日將決，其夜禮懺流淚，忽如睡夢，見一沙門教誦《救生觀世音經》。經有諸佛名，令誦千遍得免苦難。敬德如夢所緣，了無參錯，遂誦一百遍。有司執縛向市，且行且誦，臨刑滿千。刀下斫之，折爲三段，皮肉不傷。易刀又斫，凡經三換，刀折如初。監司問之，具陳本末。以狀聞丞相高歡，乃爲表請免死。因此廣行於世，所謂《高王觀世音》也。敬還，設齋迎像，乃見項上有三刀痕。

存世《高王觀世音經》的漢文本版本眾多，最早的是房山石經本，敦煌文獻中有幾個版本，《大正藏》所收爲其中一種，編號2898[8]。在這些文本中，上述孫敬德誦經感應故事均沒有與經文一起刊行。而在俄藏漢文本中，上述故事則作爲序分加在了經文之前，且感應故事也被鋪陳演繹，如把孫敬德籍貫換成了相州，高歡變成了國王，孫敬德的身份演繹成了寶藏宮的看守，臨刑前已誦經100 遍變成了900遍等。還增加了孫敬德與監守的對話、高歡對監獄合死犯人的試驗，以及高歡詔敕誦經等内容。此外，《大

⑦　（唐）道宣《大唐内典錄》，載《大正藏》卷55，第2149號，339頁上欄。

⑧　《高王觀世音經》，載《大正藏》卷85，No. 2898，1425頁中欄—1426頁上欄。

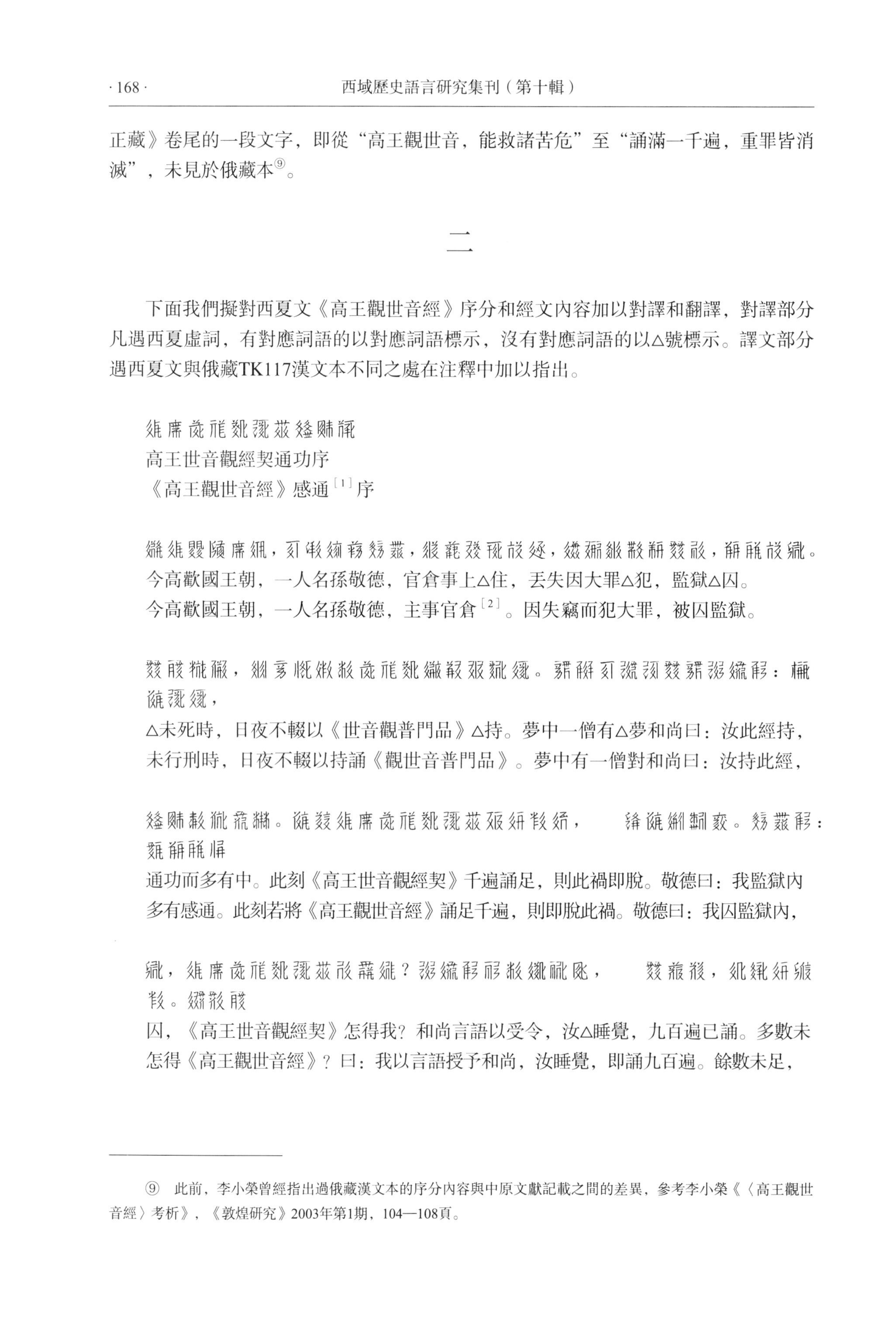

正藏》卷尾的一段文字，即從“高王觀世音，能救諸苦危”至“誦滿一千遍，重罪皆消滅”，未見於俄藏本[9]。

二

下面我們擬對西夏文《高王觀世音經》序分和經文內容加以對譯和翻譯，對譯部分凡遇西夏虛詞，有對應詞語的以對應詞語標示，沒有對應詞語的以△號標示。譯文部分遇西夏文與俄藏TK117漢文本不同之處在注釋中加以指出。

[illegible]
高王世音觀經契通功序
《高王觀世音經》感通[1]序

[illegible]
今高歡國王朝，一人名孫敬德，官倉事上△住，丟失因大罪△犯，監獄△囚。
今高歡國王朝，一人名孫敬德，主事官倉[2]。因失竊而犯大罪，被囚監獄。

[illegible]
△未死時，日夜不輟以《世音觀普門品》△持。夢中一僧有△夢和尚曰：汝此經持，
未行刑時，日夜不輟以持誦《觀世音普門品》。夢中有一僧對和尚曰：汝持此經，

[illegible]
通功而多有中。此刻《高王世音觀經契》千遍誦足，則此禍即脫。敬德曰：我監獄內
多有感通。此刻若將《高王觀世音經》誦足千遍，則即脫此禍。敬德曰：我囚監獄內，

[illegible]
囚，《高王世音觀經契》怎得我？和尚言語以受令，汝△睡覺，九百遍已誦。多數未
怎得《高王觀世音經》？曰：我以言語授予和尚，汝睡覺，即誦九百遍。餘數未足，

---

⑨　此前，李小榮曾經指出過俄藏漢文本的序分內容與中原文獻記載之間的差異，參考李小榮《〈高王觀世音經〉考析》，《敦煌研究》2003年第1期，104—108頁。

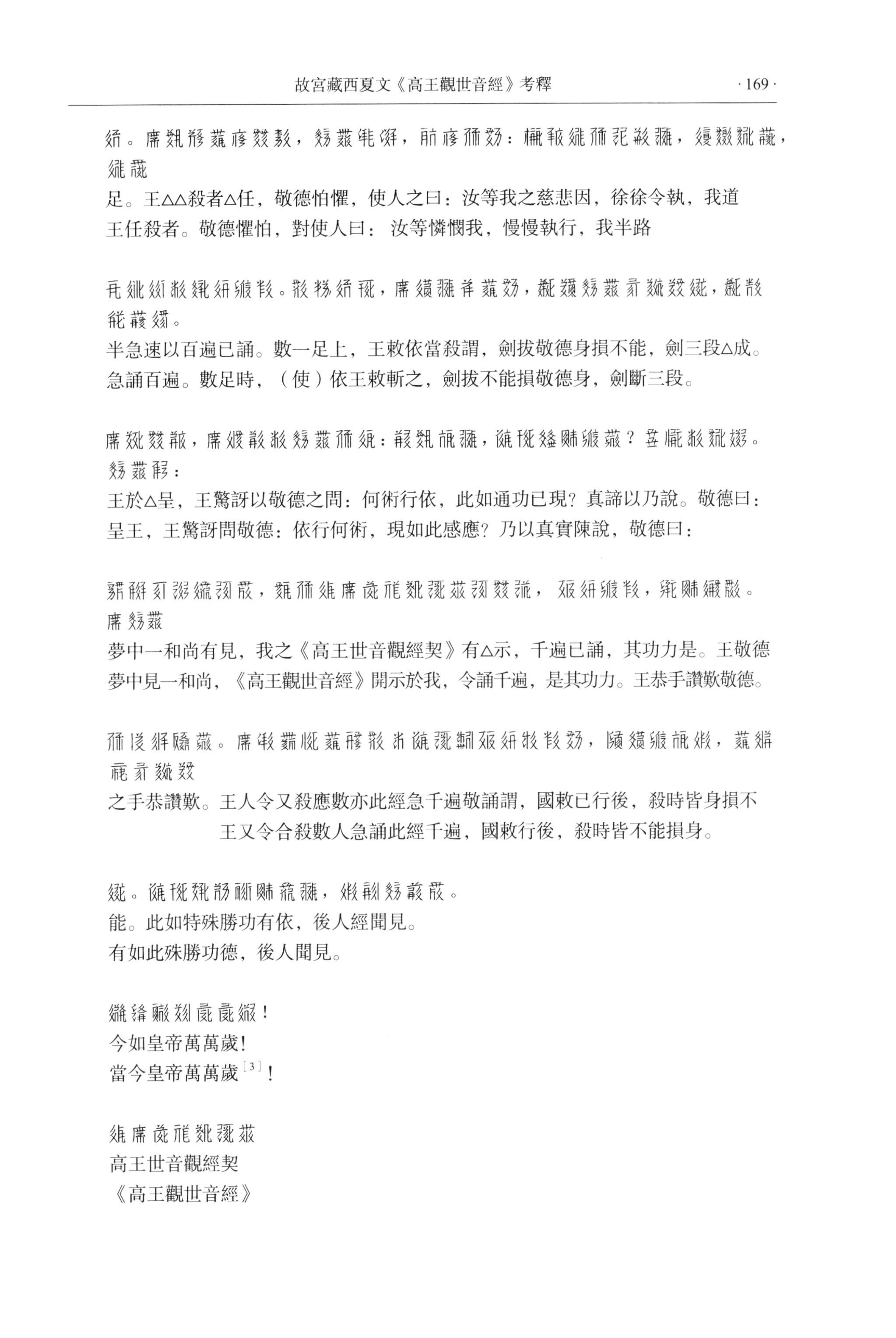

[illegible]
足。王△△殺者△任，敬德怕懼，使人之曰：汝等我之慈悲因，徐徐令執，我道
王任殺者。敬德懼怕，對使人曰：汝等憐憫我，慢慢執行，我半路

[illegible]
半急速以百遍已誦。數一足上，王敕依當殺謂，劍拔敬德身損不能，劍三段△成。
急誦百遍。數足時，（使）依王敕斬之，劍拔不能損敬德身，劍斷三段。

[illegible]
王於△呈，王驚訝以敬德之問：何術行依，此如通功已現？真諦以乃說。敬德曰：
呈王，王驚訝問敬德：依行何術，現如此感應？乃以真實陳說，敬德曰：

[illegible]
夢中一和尚有見，我之《高王世音觀經契》有△示，千遍已誦，其功力是。王敬德
夢中見一和尚，《高王觀世音經》開示於我，令誦千遍，是其功力。王恭手讚歎敬德。

[illegible]
之手恭讚歎。王人令又殺應數亦此經急千遍敬誦謂，國敕已行後，殺時皆身損不
王又令合殺數人急誦此經千遍，國敕行後，殺時皆不能損身。

[illegible]
能。此如特殊勝功有依，後人經聞見。
有如此殊勝功德，後人聞見。

[illegible]
今如皇帝萬萬歲！
當今皇帝萬萬歲[3]！

[illegible]
高王世音觀經契
《高王觀世音經》

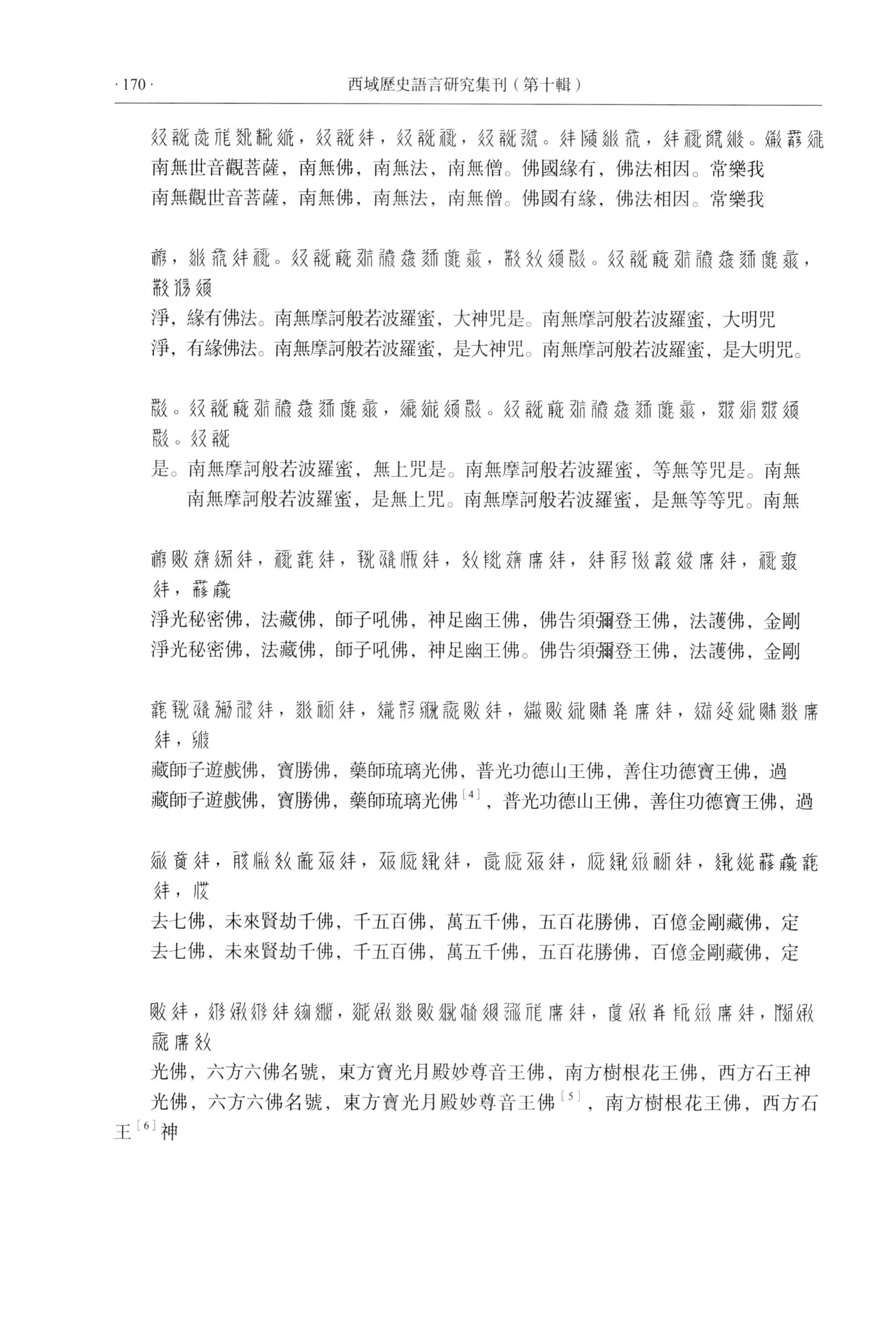

[illegible]
南無世音觀菩薩，南無佛，南無法，南無僧。佛國緣有，佛法相因。常樂我
南無觀世音菩薩，南無佛，南無法，南無僧。佛國有緣，佛法相因。常樂我

[illegible]
淨，緣有佛法。南無摩訶般若波羅蜜，大神咒是。南無摩訶般若波羅蜜，大明咒
淨，有緣佛法。南無摩訶般若波羅蜜，是大神咒。南無摩訶般若波羅蜜，是大明咒。

[illegible]
是。南無摩訶般若波羅蜜，無上咒是。南無摩訶般若波羅蜜，等無等咒是。南無
南無摩訶般若波羅蜜，是無上咒。南無摩訶般若波羅蜜，是無等等咒。南無

[illegible]
淨光秘密佛，法藏佛，師子吼佛，神足幽王佛，佛告須彌登王佛，法護佛，金剛
淨光秘密佛，法藏佛，師子吼佛，神足幽王佛。佛告須彌登王佛，法護佛，金剛

[illegible]
藏師子遊戲佛，寶勝佛，藥師琉璃光佛，普光功德山王佛，善住功德寶王佛，過
藏師子遊戲佛，寶勝佛，藥師琉璃光佛[4]，普光功德山王佛，善住功德寶王佛，過

[illegible]
去七佛，未來賢劫千佛，千五百佛，萬五千佛，五百花勝佛，百億金剛藏佛，定
去七佛，未來賢劫千佛，千五百佛，萬五千佛，五百花勝佛，百億金剛藏佛，定

[illegible]
光佛，六方六佛名號，東方寶光月殿妙尊音王佛，南方樹根花王佛，西方石王神
光佛，六方六佛名號，東方寶光月殿妙尊音王佛[5]，南方樹根花王佛，西方石王[6]神

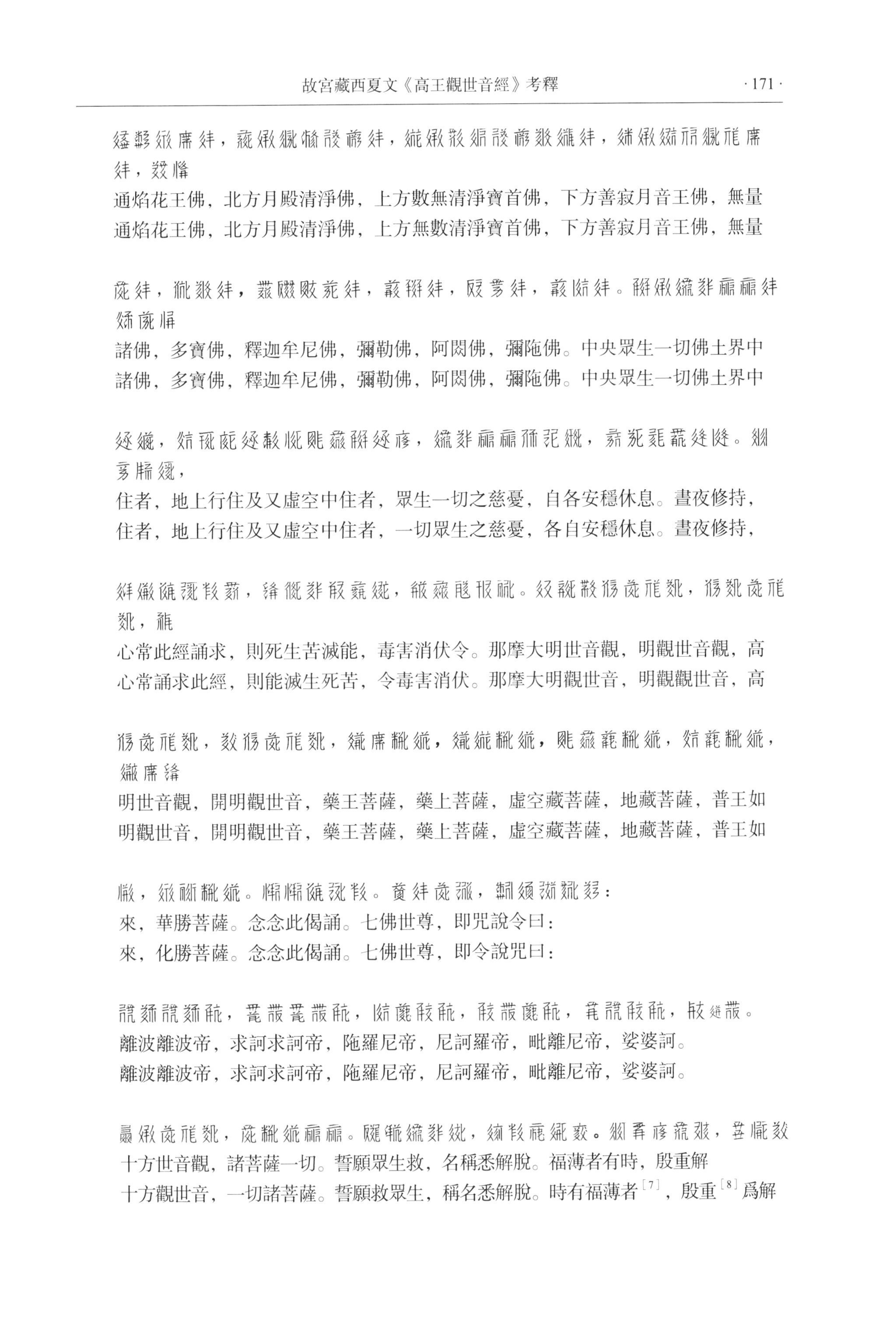

[illegible]

通焰花王佛，北方月殿清淨佛，上方數無清淨寶首佛，下方善寂月音王佛，無量

通焰花王佛，北方月殿清淨佛，上方無數清淨寶首佛，下方善寂月音王佛，無量

[illegible]

諸佛，多寶佛，釋迦牟尼佛，彌勒佛，阿閦佛，彌陁佛。中央眾生一切佛土界中

諸佛，多寶佛，釋迦牟尼佛，彌勒佛，阿閦佛，彌陁佛。中央眾生一切佛土界中

[illegible]

住者，地上行住及又虛空中住者，眾生一切之慈憂，自各安穩休息。晝夜修持，

住者，地上行住及又虛空中住者，一切眾生之慈憂，各自安穩休息。晝夜修持，

[illegible]

心常此經誦求，則死生苦滅能，毒害消伏令。那摩大明世音觀，明觀世音觀，高

心常誦求此經，則能滅生死苦，令毒害消伏。那摩大明觀世音，明觀觀世音，高

[illegible]

明世音觀，開明觀世音，藥王菩薩，藥上菩薩，虛空藏菩薩，地藏菩薩，普王如

明觀世音，開明觀世音，藥王菩薩，藥上菩薩，虛空藏菩薩，地藏菩薩，普王如

[illegible]

來，華勝菩薩。念念此偈誦。七佛世尊，即咒說令曰：

來，化勝菩薩。念念此偈誦。七佛世尊，即令說咒曰：

[illegible]

離波離波帝，求訶求訶帝，陁羅尼帝，尼訶羅帝，毗離尼帝，娑婆訶。

離波離波帝，求訶求訶帝，陁羅尼帝，尼訶羅帝，毗離尼帝，娑婆訶。

[illegible]

十方世音觀，諸菩薩一切。誓願眾生救，名稱悉解脫。福薄者有時，殷重解

十方觀世音，一切諸菩薩。誓願救眾生，稱名悉解脫。時有福薄者[7]，殷重[8]爲解

[illegible]

脫所。但因緣有者，讀誦口不綴。經誦千遍滿，念念心不絕。火焰傷不能，刀杖

脫。但有因緣者，讀誦口不綴。誦經滿千遍，念念心不絕。火焰不能傷，刀杖

[illegible]

立摧折。恚怒歡喜生，死者變活成。此事虛莫言，諸佛妄不說。

立摧折。恚怒生歡喜，死者變成活。莫言此事虛，諸佛不妄說。

[illegible]

高王世音觀經契 竟。

《高王觀世音經》 竟。

注　釋

［1］　俄藏漢文本無"感通"（[illegible]）兩字，且以下序分內容並非與俄藏漢文本逐字對應。

［2］　今高歡國王朝，一人名孫敬德，主事官倉，俄藏漢文本作"昔高歡國王在相州爲郡，有一孫敬德，爲主寶藏宮"。

［3］　當今皇帝萬萬歲，俄藏漢文本與《大正藏》本均無，爲西夏文本所加。

［4］　藥師琉璃光佛，俄藏漢文本與《大正藏》本均作"藥師琉璃光王佛"。

［5］　東方寶光月殿妙尊音王佛，俄藏漢文本作"東方寶光月殿妙音尊王佛"，而《大正藏》本作"東方寶光月妙尊音王佛"。

［6］　石王（[illegible]），俄藏漢文本與《大正藏》本均作"皂王"。

［7］　時有福薄者，俄藏漢文本作"恐有福薄者"。

［8］　[illegible]，義爲"真諦"，這裡與"殷重"對譯。

由西夏文內容可知，此本與俄藏漢文本頗爲一致。首先，夏、漢兩種文本序分內容基本一致，尤其是孫敬德感應故事被鋪陳演繹部分，如西夏文本也稱高歡爲國王，臨刑前已誦經亦作900遍，增加了孫敬德與監守的對話、高歡對監獄合死犯人的試驗，以及高歡詔敕誦經等內容。其次，《大正藏》卷尾的一段文字，即從"高王觀世音，能救諸苦危"至"誦滿一千遍，重罪皆消滅"，亦未見於西夏文本。再次，經文部分俄藏漢文本與《大正藏》本出入之處，西夏文本也有出入。上述特徵均顯示西夏文本與俄藏漢文本之間有淵源關係。

三

西夏文本卷尾還存有一篇發願文，史金波和白濱在《明代西夏文經卷和石幢初探》

一文中曾對發願文有過初步翻譯[10]，後來史金波在《西夏佛教史略》中又做了全文譯釋[11]，但囿於當時條件，譯文還有不盡人意的地方，尤其是對文中出現的年號和人名的翻譯，由於沒有遵從大字、小字並用的拼合原理加以復原，只是照搬《番漢合時掌中珠》的對音字，故未能確切還原真正的年號和歷史人物，使得其中的很多歷史資訊沒有被揭示出來。

李範文曾指出西夏文《高王觀世音經》發願文中所用的音譯方法是仿照漢語的“反切法”而來，並首次把小字作爲前一大字的韻尾加以拼合，認定西夏文“□□□□”實爲明代漢語“宣德”年號的音譯[12]。史金波和白濱在《明代西夏文經卷和石幢再探》一文中雖然堅持把西夏文“□□□□”譯作“須能斗盈”，卻承認《高王觀世音經》中西夏字後所加小字實際表示前一字的韻尾，並指出元代遺存西夏文文獻爲梵語和漢語標音均使用這種方法[13]。聶鴻音在《明刻本西夏文〈高王觀世音經〉補議》一文中則進一步揭示了發願文中人名的拼合實際上遵從了西夏時期爲梵文、藏文和漢字標音的做法，並用大字和小字，小字代表母音和輔音韻尾，例如“□”代表-n，“□”代表-m，等等[14]。

由於西夏語的複元音和輔音韻尾不如藏語、蒙古語和明代北方漢語發達，因此，《高王觀世音經》發願文在翻譯藏族、蒙古族和漢族人名時，爲求準確，遇到複元音和輔音韻尾時，便採用了大字加注小字的拼合形式，小字往往代表的是大字的韻尾。這種注音形式是西夏人創立的。12世紀下半葉，西夏仁宗（1139—1193年在位）曾主持翻譯了大量的西夏文佛經，並爲準確標定陀羅尼中的梵文音節重新確立的一套規則，西田龍雄、聶鴻音、孫伯君等均在相關論著中總結過這套梵漢對音規則[15]。其核心是遇到梵文與西夏文不同的複輔音、長元音和輔音韻尾時，用大字加小字的拼合形式，如：①表示梵語的複輔音時，使用一個大字和一個小字的組合，以替代中原梵漢對音中的“二合”形式，如梵文tra，法國吉美博物館藏西夏文《法華經》校譯本譯作“□□”，唐代密宗經師習慣在音節後面用小字注“二合”，不空譯作“怛囉二合”；②表示梵文長母音時，在音節後加注小字“□”，如梵文nā，西夏文譯作“□□”，與唐代不空等加注“引”字，即nā譯作“娜引”的做法相應；③表示梵文中的收尾輔音-n、-ṃ、-ṇ、-ṭ、-r，分别在音節後加注小字“□”“□”“□”“□”“□”等。

正如學者在前述論文中指出過的，西夏時期創立的這套標音規則在元代得以沿用，

⑩ 史金波、白濱《明代西夏文經卷和石幢初探》。

⑪ 史金波《西夏佛教史略》，銀川：寧夏人民出版社，1988年，327—328頁。

⑫ 李範文《關於明代西夏文經卷的年代和石幢的名稱問題》。

⑬ 史金波、白濱《明代西夏文經卷和石幢再探》，白濱編《西夏史論文集》，銀川：寧夏人民出版社，605頁。

⑭ 聶鴻音《明刻本西夏文《高王觀世音經》補議》。

⑮ 参考西田龍雄《西夏语研究と法華經》（I），《東洋學術研究》第44卷第1号，2004年；聶鴻音《〈仁王經〉的西夏譯本》，《民族研究》2010年第3期；孫伯君《西夏佛經翻譯的用字特點與譯經時代的判定》，《中華文史論叢》86，2007年。

元代刊行的《金光明最勝王經》和居庸關六體石刻中西夏文《佛頂尊勝陀羅尼》、《如來心陀羅尼》的梵夏對音，以及東壁題記中人名、職銜的翻譯均沿襲了這一規則。如：

《金光明最勝王經》卷四有梵文vitohanti，西夏文對音作“bji^{2}ror^{2}xã^{1}nji^{2}tjij^{1}”，其中han，用大字“xã^{1}”加小字“nji^{2}”來注音⑯。

居庸關西壁《如來心陀羅尼》中梵文saṃ，西夏文對音作“sja^{1}ŋə^{1}”⑰。

東壁漢文《造塔功德記》有“大都留守安賽罕資政院使金剛義太府太卿”，相應的西夏文翻譯如下⑱：

thej^{1}tu^{1}lji^{1}·^{u2}śji^{1}·^{u2}ŋa^{2}ŋə^{1}sã^{1}·^{jij1}khia^{1}nji^{2}□tśhji^{2}

大　都　留　守　安　賽　罕　資　政

ŋə^{1}ɣjwã^{1}rjɨr^{2}kji^{1}ŋə^{1}kja^{1}gji^{1}thej^{1}xu^{1}thej^{1}khji^{2}nji^{2}。

院　使　金　剛　義　太　府　太　卿

其中“留”對音作“lji^{1}·^{u2}”、“守”對“śji^{1}·^{u2}”、“安”對“ŋa^{2}ŋə^{1}”、“賽”對“sã^{1}·^{jij1}”、“罕”對“khia^{1}nji^{2}”等，均沿用大字加小字的對音形式。

明代編訂的《華夷譯語》和《蒙古秘史》中用漢字爲蒙古語標音也巧妙地運用了這一方法。我們知道，洪武十五年（1382），翰林院侍講火源潔和編修馬沙亦黑奉命編譯了蒙漢對照詞彙集《華夷譯語》，於二十二年（1389）刊行。該書凡十七門，存840條詞語。卷首劉三吾之序詳言編寫功用，其後有凡例六，特别説明了幾則漢字譯寫蒙古語的拼合體例，即涉及“用漢字譯寫胡語，其中間有有聲無字者”，悉採用大字加小字的形式，曰：

> 用漢字譯寫胡語，其中間有有聲無字者，今特借聲音相近字樣，立例於後。讀者依例求之，則無不諧矣。
>
> 字傍小注中字者，乃喉内音也。如中合、中忽之類。
>
> 字傍小注舌字者，乃舌頭音也，必彈舌讀之。如舌兒、舌裡、舌剌、舌魯、舌侖之類。
>
> 字傍小注丁字者，頂舌音也，以舌尖頂上齶（音鄂）讀之。如丁温、丁兀、丁豁、丁斡之類。
>
> 字下小注勒字者，亦與頂舌同。如冰呼莫勒孫之類。
>
> 字下小注黑字者、惕字、克字者，皆急讀帶過音也，不用讀出。
>
> 字下小注蔔字、必字者，皆急讀合口音也，亦不用讀出。

同樣，漢字音寫本《蒙古秘史》的標音也採用了與《華夷譯語》一致的原則。可以想定，西夏時期創立的這套嚴謹的標定外族語的規則，隨著西夏後裔在元朝的任職而被帶到中原，並啟發了《華夷譯語》和《蒙古秘史》的編寫者，爲後世用本族文字音寫外

⑯ 王靜如《金光明最勝王經卷四夏藏漢合璧考釋》，《西夏研究》第二輯，182頁。

⑰ 村田治郎編著《居庸關》第一卷，京都大學工學部，1957年，184頁。

⑱ 村田治郎編著《居庸關》第一卷，292頁。

族語提供了很好的規範，自然，明代刊行的西夏文《高王觀世音經》也遵循了這套標音規則。

事實上，這種大字加小字的譯寫規則一直到清朝仍有所遵循，清朝編定的《同文韻統》卷一《天竺字母後說》規定[19]：

> 其有本字呼聲應長者，三經內用“引”字爲記。今照十二字頭內有餘音字例，將本字疊書，而下一字微小，合爲一字。其本字下帶別音者，即於本字下將別音字細書，合爲一字。其漢字內有音無字者，照釋典本身切例，將所切二字並書，合爲一字。其一字有二音者，如上音分數多、下音分數少，或下音分數多、上音分數少，則將分數多之字正書，分數少之字細書，合爲一字，照國書合聲切法急讀之，即成一音。

其中的“正書”即指用大字，“細書”即指用小字，具體而言，涉及梵文長母音和複輔音等這類無法用單個漢字標音的情況時，均須用大字加小字的形式加以標注，如：ā譯作“阿^{阿}”；kā譯作“嘎^{阿}”；kri譯作“基^{唎}”，kla譯作“^{嘎}拉”等[20]。

四

由於卷尾發願文對確定西夏後裔在明朝的宗教活動以及《高王觀世音經》的傳行情況均具有重要意義，下面我們把西夏文本卷尾發願文加以重譯，文末所現人名根據對音規則和西夏文相關資料加以構擬。

西夏文：

[illegible]
今聞：如來世出，四生惱病△治；　菩薩重現，　三界愚暗中照。　其中世音觀菩
今聞：如來出世，恤治四生惱病；　菩薩重現，　光照三界愚暗。　觀世音菩

[illegible]
薩者，誓願深廣，大海水與匹；　罔極苦救，須彌山等高。　敬寫則必定神現，　受持
薩者，誓願深廣，與大海水相匹；罔極救苦，與須彌山等高。敬寫則必定神現，受持

[illegible]
者殑沙福有。śiə^{2}ljɨ^{1}źjiw^{1}tśhjij$^{1\text{ŋə}1}$sja^{1}，大法處心重。此經通功多有，聞依實信心生。淨錢
有殑沙之福。蘇勒柔丞思[1]，心重大法。此經多有神功，聽聞心生實信。乃舍淨錢，

[illegible]

[19] 《欽定同文韻統》卷一，文淵閣“四庫全書”本，10頁。

[20] 參考聶鴻音《〈同文韻統〉中的梵字讀音和漢語官話》，《滿語研究》2014年第1期。

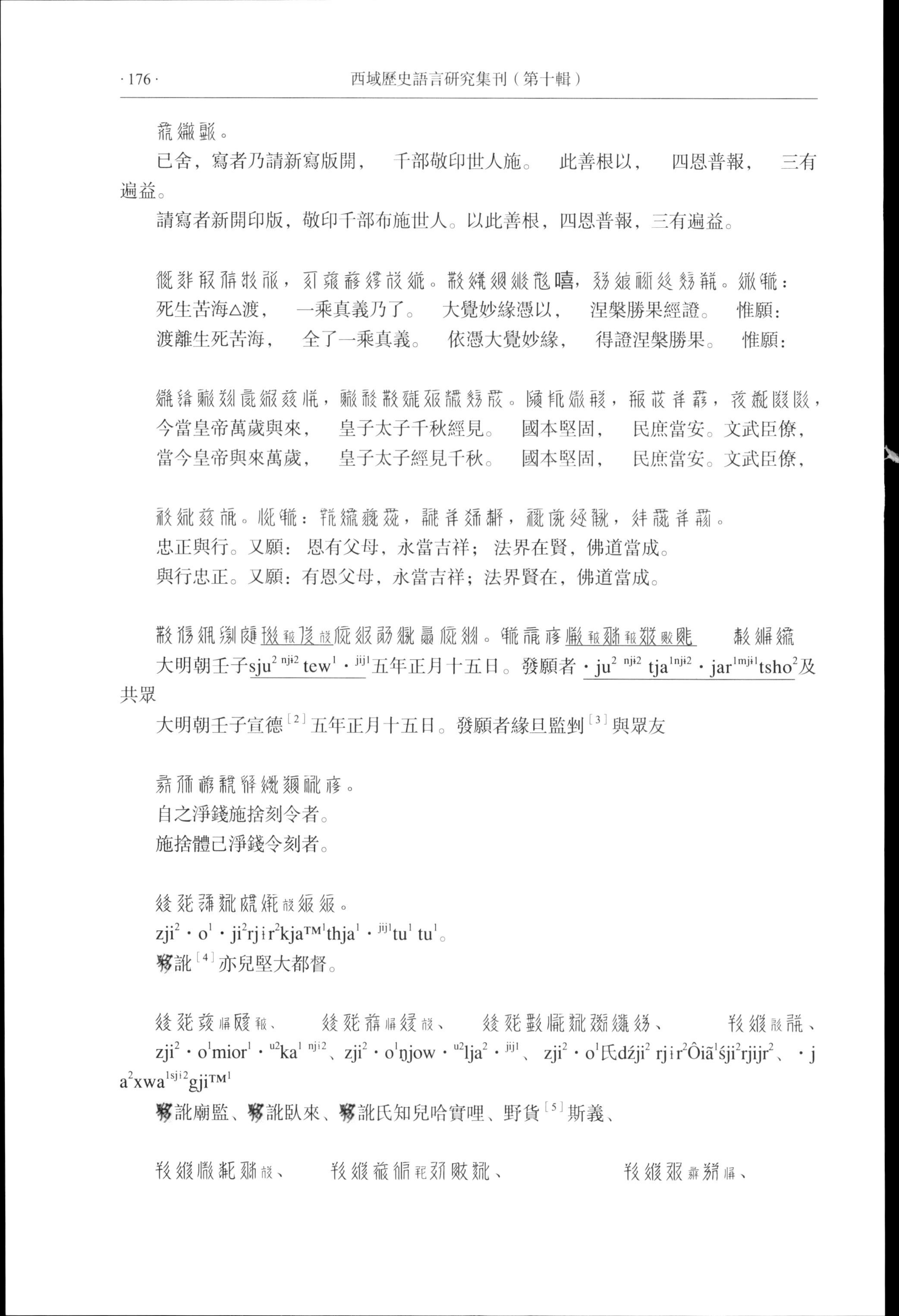

[illegible]。

已舍，寫者乃請新寫版開，　千部敬印世人施。　此善根以，　四恩普報，　三有遍益。

請寫者新開印版，敬印千部布施世人。以此善根，四恩普報，三有遍益。

[illegible]

死生苦海△渡，　一乘真義乃了。　大覺妙緣憑以，　涅槃勝果經證。　惟願：

渡離生死苦海，　全了一乘真義。　依憑大覺妙緣，　得證涅槃勝果。　惟願：

[illegible]

今當皇帝萬歲與來，　皇子太子千秋經見。　國本堅固，　民庶當安。文武臣僚，

當今皇帝與來萬歲，　皇子太子經見千秋。　國本堅固，　民庶當安。文武臣僚，

[illegible]

忠正與行。又願：恩有父母，永當吉祥；法界在賢，佛道當成。

與行忠正。又願：有恩父母，永當吉祥；法界賢在，佛道當成。

[illegible]

大明朝壬子sju^{2} ^{nji2} tew^{1} · ^{jij1}五年正月十五日。發願者 · ju^{2} ^{nji2} tja^{1nji2} · jar^{1mji1}tsho^{2}及共衆

大明朝壬子宣德[2]五年正月十五日。發願者緣旦監剉[3]與衆友

[illegible]。

自之淨錢施捨刻令者。

施捨體已淨錢令刻者。

[illegible]。

zji^{2} · o^{1} · ji^{2}rjɨr^{2}kja^{1}thja^{1} · ^{jij1}tu^{1} tu^{1}。

[illegible]訛[4]亦兒堅大都督。

[illegible]

zji^{2} · o^{1}mior^{1} · ^{u2}ka^{1} ^{nji2}、zji^{2} · o^{1}ŋjow · ^{u2}lja^{2} · ^{jij1}、zji^{2} · o^{1}氏dźji^{2} rjɨr^{2}Ôiã^{1}śji^{2}rjijr^{2}、· ja^{2}xwa^{1sji2}gji^{1}

[illegible]訛廟監、[illegible]訛臥來、[illegible]訛氏知兒哈實哩、野貨[5]斯義、

[illegible]

·ja2xwa1bu1Ôa2tja1·jij1 ·ja2xwa1khja™1 bja1kjiw1thjɨj1mo2 rjɨr2 ·ja2xwa1tjij1ŋə1pã1·u2

野貨不花歹、野貨恰巴克帖木兒、野貨丁保、

[illegible]

phjij1śjo2khia1rar2dźia2 ŋə1、tow1ba2la1、tow1so2no1·jar1、tow1rjir1kə1ta1 bu1Ôa2、lji2mja1ŋə1 kja™1·jij1、

並尚[6]卡剌張、多把拉、多桑那延、多哩疙瘩不花[7]、李[8]忙該、

[illegible]

lji2 bu1da2·jij1、ŋa2nji2khow1to2tśji2、ŋa2nji2na1·ja2nji2thjɨj1mo2rjɨr2、na1·jij1mja1tjɨ1tśhjo2ljɨ1gja2、

李部歹、安郭門智、安那延帖木兒、乃馬得楚裡嘎、

[illegible]

wow1·ji2khja2、wow1tow1kə1ta1ka1nji2、phjij1ŋə1bu1ɣa2thjɨj1mo2rjɨr2、·o1gji1rar1thow1ɣa2tśji2、

王[9]依迦、王杜疙瘩敢、平不花帖木兒、訛義剌達花赤、

[illegible]

·o1gji1rar1dźia2gji1 ·o1gji1rar1thow1la1nji2、·o1gji1rar1bia2bu1kja1等圍繞住住。

訛義剌紮義、訛義剌達蘭、訛義剌八部迦等處處圍繞。

[illegible]

法界內情有一切，現在時短災間斷害事， 讒舌毀壞，及身老時上，最樂淨土

法界內一切有情，現在災害禁斷，讒舌毀壞以及身死時往生與最樂淨土

[illegible]

內往生。

[illegible]

nwə1ŋə1zjinji2tśjow1·u2·ja2nji2lji2ŋə1刻印。

能仁[10]周彥陵刻印。

注　　釋

［1］　西夏文“□śiə^{2}□ljɨ^{1}□źjiw^{1}□tśhjij^{1}□ŋə^{1}□sja^{1}”，可對譯作“蘇勒柔丞思”，待考。

［2］　據李範文考證，西夏文“□□□□”（sju^{2} nji^{2} tew^{1} · jij^{1}）爲明宣宗年號“宣德”（1426—1435）的音譯，宣德五年，即1430年。實際上，按照干支推算，明代宣德五年是庚戌年，宣德七年（1432）才是壬子年。

［3］　據聶鴻音考證，西夏文“□□□□□□□”（· ju^{2} nji^{2}tja^{1}nji^{2} · jar^{1} mji^{1} tshọ^{2}）爲藏文Yon-tan rgya-mtsho的音譯，明代譯作“緣旦監剉”，華言“功德海”，永樂十三年（1415）被敕封爲“灌頂慈慧妙智大國師”。

［4］　“□□”（zjị- · o）爲西夏姓氏，見西夏文《三才雜字》“番姓氏”第42，李範文等譯作“□訛”㉑。

［5］　“□□”（·ja-xwa）爲西夏姓氏，見西夏文《三才雜字》“番姓氏”第175，李範文等根據黑水城出土元代遺存文獻譯作“耶和”㉒。孫伯君曾據黑水城出土漢文《雜字》“番姓名”第10譯作“野貨”㉓。漢字“野”“耶”古代同爲餘母字；漢字“貨”，《廣韻》呼臥切，曉母果攝過韻字，與西夏字𗰜（xwa）音近。

［6］　“□□”（phjij-śjo）爲西夏姓氏，見西夏文《三才雜字》“番姓氏”第115，李範文等曾譯作“平尚”，可以與黑水城出土漢文《雜字》“番姓氏”第49“並尚”勘同㉔。另，保定西夏文經幢中有此姓。漢字“並”，《廣韻》蒲迥切，並母梗攝迥韻字，西夏時期河西方音並母清化讀爲送氣清音，與“平”同音，兩字在河西方音中失落-ŋ韻尾。

［7］　按，西夏文《三才雜字》“人名”第23有“□□□”（kə-ta-djij），李範文譯作“格怛賢”㉕。

［8］　“□”（lji）爲西夏漢姓“李”的音譯，見西夏文《三才雜字》“漢姓氏”第3。西夏皇族曾被唐朝賜姓“李”。

［9］　“□”（wow）爲西夏漢姓“王”的音譯。見西夏文《三才雜字》“漢姓氏”第2。

［10］　能仁（□□□□），當指大能仁寺，是明代藏傳佛教著名的寺院。據記載，大能仁寺，建於元代延祐中，初名能仁寺，明洪熙元年（1425）修，加賜大能仁寺額。該寺與大慈恩寺、大隆善護國寺並稱京師三大寺院。該寺在今北京西城兵馬司胡同北㉖。

㉑ 李範文、中島幹起《電腦處理西夏文雜字研究》，82、118頁。

㉒ 李範文、中島幹起《電腦處理西夏文雜字研究》，83、121頁。

㉓ 孫伯君《西夏番姓譯正》，《民族研究》2009年第5期，83—90頁。

㉔ 孫伯君《西夏番姓譯正》，83—90頁。

㉕ 李範文、中島幹起《電腦處理西夏文雜字研究》，83、123頁。

㉖ 黃顥《在北京的藏族文物》，北京：民族出版社，1993年，15頁。

余　論

明代《高王觀世音經》的刊行當是由大能仁寺的喇嘛組織的。我們知道，明代對西藏實施“多封眾建”政策，使得大批藏族僧人來到內地並得到朝廷供養，歷代諸帝更是紛紛賜給高僧大德各種封號。據考證，住持大能仁寺的喇嘛曾先後受封法王的有西天佛子索南監參（bsod nams rgyal mtshan）和結斡領占（rje bo rin chen），受封佛子的有紮巴藏播（grags pa bzang po），受封灌頂國師的有索南加（bsod nams rgyal）等。北京西郊翠微山明代《法海禪寺記》碑陰就記載了很多受賜法王、西天佛子的著名僧人捐助了該寺的修建，曰[27]：

敕賜法海禪寺助緣法王、尚師、國師、禪師、僧官、剌麻、僧眾、官員人等。

萬行妙明真如上勝清淨般若弘照普應輔國顯教至善大慈法王西天正覺如來自在大圓通佛釋迦也失，妙法清修淨慈普應輔國闡教灌頂弘善西天佛子大國師啞蒙葛，弘通妙戒普惠善應輔國闡教灌頂淨覺西天佛子大國師班丹紮釋，淨修弘智灌頂國師鎖南釋剌，弘善妙智國師舍剌巴，妙勝禪師鎖南藏卜□□□□大師，戒行禪師班卓兒。

僧錄司左善世大旺，右覺義南浦。右善世祖淵。諸山長老道觀、懷閏、恩常、正榮、覺海、妙山，首座福寬、了玄、知藏善秀。

官員人等王琦、梁員（等三百七十六人略）。

開山第一代主持福壽。同開山剌麻領占巴、紮失乳奴、紮失遠丹。

本山僧眾（略）

正統八年歲次癸亥十月望日。建寺功德主太監李福善、董工中貴賀佛信、阮覺保等立石。

其中班丹扎釋即是於正統十二年（1447）主持重刊《聖勝慧到彼岸功德寶集偈》（房山雲居寺本）的著名僧人班丹箚釋巴藏卜（dpal ldan bkra shris dpal bzang po），史載他是波忒國三疊人，世代在甘肅岷州爲官，其傳記見載於正統十二年（1447）編纂的《金剛乘起信莊嚴寶鬘西天佛子源流錄》[28]　。而戒行禪師班卓兒，即班卓兒藏卜（dpal'byor dpal bzang po），也作班卓爾藏卜、班卓巴藏卜，他曾於明正統十年受封爲“清心戒行國師”，是班丹扎釋的侄子，《西天佛子源流錄》的校正者，同時也是把《聖勝慧到彼岸功德寶集偈》付梓刊行的僧人也釋巴的老師[29]。此外，法海寺的“同開山剌麻”領占巴原是甘肅河州普綱寺、永昌寺僧人，其祖端月堅藏曾於洪武六年（1373）赴南京朝覲，洪武二十六年（1393）被任命爲河州衛番僧綱司都綱。領占巴則繼任爲第二任都綱，紮失巴則爲第三任[30]。可見，明代的著名藏傳佛教高僧中不乏來自河西地區的

[27] 張淑霞主編《北京法海寺》，北京市石景山區文物管理所，2001年9月，49—53頁。

[28] 張潤平、蘇航、羅炤編著《西天佛子源流錄——文獻與初步研究》，中國社會科學出版社，2012年。

[29] 羅炤《藏漢合璧〈聖勝慧到彼岸功德寶集偈〉考略》，《世界宗教研究》1983年第4期，4—36頁。

[30] 黃顥《在北京的藏族文物》，31頁。

僧人。而從西夏文《高王觀世音經》的刊佈、發願文的助緣人中出現了很多西夏姓氏，以及《聖勝慧到彼岸功德寶集偈》採用西夏時期鮮卑寶源所譯漢文本爲底本這些跡象看，明代在北京各寺院住持的僧人中一定有西夏後裔。正如元代藏傳佛教在內地的傳播與西夏遺僧有千絲萬縷的聯繫一樣，西夏後裔也是明代藏傳佛教得以興盛的一股不可小覷的力量。

附錄：俄藏黑水城出土漢文本《高王觀世音經》

高王觀世音經序[1]

昔高歡國王在相州爲郡，有一孫敬德，爲主寶藏宮，犯法囚禁在獄中。知慮就死，持誦《觀世音普門品經》，日夜不輟。於睡中夢僧言曰：汝持此經不能免死，持取《高王觀世音經》一千遍，當離刑戮。敬德曰：今在獄中，何時見本？僧曰：口受與汝，睡覺無遺失。志心誦持，得九百遍。文案已成，付都市斬之。敬德怕懼，問使人曰：都市近遠？使曰：何故？敬德曰：昨夜夢一僧，令教受持《高王觀世音經》一千遍，當得免死，今欠一百遍，請求使慢行。隨路急念，持經一千遍，數滿使乃令斬之。敬德身不損，其刀爲三段。將刀呈王，王宣敬德問曰：汝有何術得如此？敬德曰：實無術，獄中怕死，持《觀世音普門品經》，夢見一僧令持《高王觀世音經》一千遍，獲福如是。王謂敬德：汝勝於我，與聖何異？王處分獄中更有合死之人，將此經各令持誦一千遍，斬之，是人悉得如此。王勑下，國人悉令持誦此經，普壽百歲，水陸怨債，讬化梵文，更無輪報矣。

《高王觀世音經》

觀世音菩薩，南無佛，南無法，南無僧。佛國有緣，佛法相因。常樂我淨，有緣佛法。南無摩訶般若波羅蜜，是大神咒。南無摩訶般若波羅蜜，是大明咒。南無摩訶般若波羅蜜，是無上咒。南無摩訶般若波羅蜜，是無等等咒。南無淨光秘密佛，法藏佛，師子吼佛[2]，神足幽王[3]佛。佛告須彌登王佛，法護佛，金剛藏師子遊戲佛，寶勝佛[4]，藥師琉璃光王佛，普光功德山王佛，善住功德寶王佛，過去七佛，未來賢劫千佛，千五百佛，萬五千佛，五百花勝佛，百億金剛藏佛，定光佛，六方六佛名號，東方寶光月殿妙音尊王佛[5]，南方樹根花王佛，西方皂王神通焰花王佛，北方月殿清淨佛，上方無數清淨[6]寶首佛，下方善寂月音王佛，無量諸佛，多寶佛，釋迦牟尼佛，彌勒佛，阿閦佛，彌陁[7]佛。中央一切眾生在佛土界[8]中者，行住於地上，及在虛空中慈憂于一切眾生，各令安穩休息。晝夜修持，心常求誦此經，能滅生死苦，消伏於毒害。那摩大明觀世音，觀明觀世音，高明觀世音，開明觀世音，藥王菩薩，藥上菩薩[9]，虛空藏菩薩，地藏菩薩[10]，普王[11]如來化勝菩薩，念念誦此偈。七佛世尊，即說咒曰：

離波離波帝，求訶求訶帝，陁羅尼帝，尼訶羅帝，毗[12]離尼帝[13]，娑婆訶。

十方觀世音，一切諸菩薩。誓願救眾生，稱名悉解脱。恐有薄福者，殷重爲解脱[14]。但是有因緣，讀誦口不綴。誦經滿千遍，念念心不絕。火焰不能傷，刀兵立摧折。恚怒生歡喜，死者變成活。莫言此是虚，諸佛不妄説。

《佛説高王觀世音經》

説　明

［1］ 此段“高王觀世音經序”，《大正藏》本無。

［2］ 《大正藏》本無“佛”字。

［3］ 幽王，《大正藏》本作“由王”。

［4］ 《大正藏》本“寶勝佛”之後有“神通佛”。

［5］ 月殿妙音尊王佛，《大正藏》本作“月妙尊音王佛”。

［6］ 清淨，《大正藏》本作“精進”。

［7］ 陁，《大正藏》本作“陀”，下同。

［8］ 土界，《大正藏》本作“世界”。

［9］ “藥上菩薩”之後，《大正藏》本有“文殊師利菩薩，普賢菩薩”。

［10］ “地藏菩薩”之後，《大正藏》本有“清涼寶山億萬菩薩”。

［11］ 普王，《大正藏》本作“普光”。

［12］ 毗，《大正藏》本作“毘”。

［13］ “毘離尼帝”之後，《大正藏》本有“摩訶迦帝，真靈虔帝”。

［14］ 此句《大正藏》本作“若有智慧者，殷懃爲解脱”。

Textural Research on the Tangut Version of *Gaowang Guanshiyin Jing* preserved in the Palace Museum of Beijing

Sun Bojun

The Tangut version of *Gaowang Guanshiyin Jing* preserved in the Palace Museum of Beijing is one of the latest Tangut relics found in China with exact date. The present paper interprets the full text and pointed out that the Tangut version originally relates to the Chinese one preserved in Russia by comparison with the two Chinese versions there collected in the *Taishō Tripiṭaka*. The different style frontispieces of the Tangut and Chinese version show that the faith of *Gaowang Guanshiyin Jing* inherited by Tangut descendant in Ming dynasty was a kind of folk practice whereas used to be recited by whole people according to the imperial edict in Xixia.

西夏文《聖金剛能斷至勝慧彼岸大經顯理燈炬記》初探

李夢溪

一、《金剛經》文本群在西夏的流行情況

《金剛經》在西夏極爲流行。在現存刻本、寫本資料中，我們可以看到衆多西夏文[1]、漢文[2]《金剛經》殘片；此外，西夏擁有針對《金剛經》的專門儀軌，並留存了其漢文文本記錄[3]。西夏流行的《金剛經》，經文本身以鳩摩羅什譯本爲主，尚存約七種基於此譯本而作的《金剛經》注釋類文獻[4]，推測翻譯自漢文佛經文本，玆列如下：

（1）《[illegible]》（[illegible]）［《金剛般若波羅蜜多經》（宗密

---

① 克恰諾夫《西夏文佛教典籍目錄》中第34至63號文獻下即所收錄《金剛經》殘片，黑水城出土。Института Востоковедения Поссийской Академинн Наук, Составитель Е. И. Кычанов: Каталог Тангутских Буддийских Памятников, Университет Киото, 1999г, с. 278-288. 中國藏西夏文《金剛經》文獻分别出土于黑水城、綠城，現藏于敦煌、甘肅、内蒙古等地博物館，黑水城出土文獻如：G11・035［D.0669］；G11・036［B128：11］；G11・037［B121：35-1—3］（敦煌），G11・037［13214］（甘肅），G11・009［6735］；G11・009［6736］；G11・009［6737］；G11・009［6739］；G11・009［6742］；G11・009［6743］；G11・009［6744］；G11・009［6748］（武威），《中國藏西夏文獻》（16），甘肅：甘肅人民出版社；敦煌文藝出版社，2005年；綠城出土文獻，如：M1・242-267 [無編號]，塔拉、杜建錄、高國祥主編《中國藏黑水城民族文字文獻》，北京：中華書局；天津：天津古籍出版社，2013年。M11・006; 007; 008; 009（内蒙古），《中國藏西夏文獻》（17）。此外，日本也有少量黑水城出土西夏文《金剛經》文獻，如：39-13b，武宇林、荒川慎太郎《日本藏西夏文文獻》，北京：中華書局，2010年。

② 黑水城出土漢文《金剛經》文獻，如：M1・1429［F13：W51］；M1・1430［83H・F13：W52/0403］；M1・1431［83H・F13：W53/0404］；M1・1432［F19：W9］；M1・1433［F19：W10］；M1・1435［F15：W1］，塔拉、杜建錄、高國祥主編《中國藏黑水城漢文文獻》（8），北京：國家圖書館出版社，2008年。

③ 《〈金剛經〉菩提道場前行儀軌》，M1・1426 [F209: W13-1]; M1・1426 [F209: W13-2]，塔拉、杜建錄、高國祥主編《中國藏黑水城漢文文獻》（8）。

④ 以下所有提及文獻的西夏文标題，西田龍雄和克恰諾夫的目錄收錄一致，笔者對标題進行了重譯。

科判）］[⑤]

（2）《[illegible]》（《金剛般若義解記》）[⑥]

（3）《[illegible]》（《金剛般若略記文》）[⑦]

（4）《[illegible]》（《金剛般若記文》）[⑧]

（5）《[illegible]》（《金剛般若科次經頌義解纂要略記》）[⑨]

（6）《[illegible]》（《金剛經》）[⑩]

（7）《[illegible]》（《金剛經集（纂）》）[⑪]

西夏文《[illegible]》（[illegible]）（《金剛般若波羅蜜多經》（宗密科判））是對漢文《梁朝傅大士頌金剛經》的翻譯，其科判部分相當於漢文《金剛般若經疏論纂要》中宗密的注釋[⑫]。《[illegible]》（《金剛般若科次經頌義解纂要略記》）是對（《金剛般若波羅蜜多經》（宗密科判））的注釋。索羅寧研究認爲：《纂要略記》的序言對鳩摩羅什的生平進行了演繹，如將其

---

⑤ 此文獻即《梁朝傅大士頌金剛經》，題記：[illegible]（姚秦三藏法師鳩摩羅什譯），[illegible]（唐涼大崇福寺沙門宗密科），題目：[illegible]（金剛般若波羅蜜多經）。據荒川《西夏文金剛経の研究》，克恰諾夫《西夏文佛教典籍目錄》中收錄了兩個版本，編號爲：Танг. 386，Инв. No. 7580與Танг. 386，Инв. No. 8131。西田龍雄《西夏譯佛典目錄》沒有收錄。此文本另一版本爲M21. 166［F6：W36］，見《中國藏西夏文研究（17）》。〔日〕荒川慎太郎《西夏文金剛経の研究》，京都：松香堂，2014年，10—12頁。〔日〕西田龍雄《西夏文華嚴經（III）：西夏譯佛典目錄·西夏語漢語對照語匯》，京都：京都大學文學部，1977。

⑥ 克恰諾夫《西夏文佛教典籍目錄》中記錄了兩個版本，Танг. 385，Инв. No. 929和Танг. 385，Инв. No. 886。克恰諾夫《西夏文佛教典籍目錄》，466頁。西田氏編號爲：Leningrad Cat. 385，西田龍雄《西夏譯佛典目錄》，25頁。《大正藏》收錄《金剛般若義記》（No. 2740）。

⑦ 克恰諾夫《西夏文佛教典籍目錄》中記錄了三個版本，Танг. 383，Инв. No. 4129；Танг. 383，Инв. No. 4375和Танг. 383，Инв. No. 4129，見克恰諾夫《西夏文佛教典籍目錄》，579頁。西田氏編號爲：Leningrad Cat. 384，西田龍雄《西夏譯佛典目錄》，25頁。

⑧ 克恰諾夫《西夏文佛教典籍目錄》沒有收錄。西田氏編號爲：Leningrad Cat. 383，西田龍雄《西夏譯佛典目錄》，25頁。

⑨ 克恰諾夫《西夏文佛教典籍目錄》收錄了兩種版本，Танг. 200，Инв. No. 5934，題記：[illegible]（黑山沙門善信集），與Танг. 302，Инв. No. 4895，克恰諾夫《西夏文佛教典籍目錄》，573—574頁。西田氏編號爲：Leningrad Cat. 387，西田龍雄《西夏譯佛典目錄》，25頁。索羅寧《〈金刚般若科次经颂义解纂要略记序〉及西夏汉藏佛教的一面》。對該文獻有所討論，此處依據索羅寧譯名。參見索羅寧《〈金剛般若科次經頌義解纂要略記序〉及西夏漢藏佛教的一面》，《中國藏學》2016年第2期，93—101頁。

⑩ 克恰諾夫《西夏文佛教典籍目錄》中記錄號碼爲：Танг. 381，Инв. No. 4161。荒川慎太郎《西夏文金剛経の研究》提及此文本另一版本，Танг. 381，Инв. No. 6806，13頁，並收於附錄。西田龍雄《西夏譯佛典目錄》沒有收錄。

⑪ 克恰諾夫《西夏文佛教典籍目錄》中記錄號碼爲：Танг. 382，Инв. No. 7107。克恰諾夫《西夏文佛教典籍目錄》，582頁。西田龍雄《西夏譯佛典目錄》沒有收錄。

⑫ 荒川慎太郎《西夏文金剛経の研究》，10—11頁。

等同於“有相”唯識代表人物陳那（Dignāga），或金剛亥母與中有傳承體系的蓮花戒（Kamalaśīla）。這兩方面原因說明該文獻具有漢傳、藏傳佛教的雙重屬性。其題注“黑山沙門善信集”，說明該文獻屬於“西夏本土著作”，西田氏判斷其爲“宗義書”文獻⑬。

《[illegible]》（《金剛經》）與《[illegible]》（《金剛經集（纂）》）爲同本異版，且皆相應于漢文《金剛經纂》⑭。其理由在於：《[illegible]》（《金剛經集（纂）》）結尾句爲：[illegible]（《金剛般若經》一卷終）⑮。

在上述注釋文本的名稱中，“[illegible]”是西夏文對漢文的逐字翻譯，分別對應漢字“金”與“剛”。與此相對，《天勝律令》將西夏僧衆分爲漢與番藏兩類，《金剛經》被列爲一等番藏僧衆的必讀經目。其文曰：“一等番羌所誦經頌：《仁王護國》《文殊真實名》《普賢行願品》《三十五佛》《聖佛母》《守護國吉祥頌》《觀世音普門品》《竭陀般若》《佛頂尊勝總持》《無垢淨光》《金剛般若》與頌全。一等漢之所誦經頌：《仁王護國》《普賢行願品》《三十五佛》《守護國吉祥頌》《佛頂尊勝總持》《聖佛母》《大□□》《觀世音普門品》《孔雀經》《廣大行愿頌》《釋迦讚》。”⑯這在西夏多流行漢地鳩摩羅什譯本《金剛經》的背景下需特別注意。而這一現象亦與本文所研究文獻的性質相呼應，列該文獻於下：

（1）《[illegible]》（《聖金剛能斷至勝慧彼岸大經顯理燈炬記》，即本文所研究文獻）⑰

（2）《[illegible]》（《聖金剛王能斷至勝慧彼岸大乘經》）⑱

在這兩篇文獻中，“[illegible]”對應藏文rdo rje，意爲“石王”，是“金剛”的意譯。《聖金剛能斷至勝慧彼岸大經顯理燈炬記》中有如下段落，亦印證此含義：

[illegible]，[illegible]，[illegible]，[illegible]：[illegible]，[illegible]，[illegible]，[illegible]，[illegible]。

---

⑬ 索羅寧《〈金刚般若科次经颂义解纂要略记序〉及西夏汉藏佛教的一面》，98—99頁。

⑭ 荒川慎太郎《西夏文金剛経の研究》，13—23頁。

⑮ 荒川慎太郎《西夏文金剛経の研究》，附錄三。

⑯ 史金波、聶鴻音、白濱譯註《天盛改舊新定律令》北京：法律出版社，2000年，404—405頁。

⑰ 該寫本由79頁殘片構成，爲注釋的開始部分，每頁中間六列下方缺三到六字不等。由於譯師慧照爲五明現生寺禪師，故疑該文本出自該寺藏經樓。文本題記：[illegible]（法師松波上尊集），[illegible]（沙門慧照番譯），題目：[illegible]（《聖金剛能斷至勝慧彼岸大經》顯理——燈燭記第一）。克恰諾夫《西夏文佛教典籍目錄》、西田龍雄《西夏譯佛典目錄》中無此文本。

⑱ 克恰諾夫《西夏文佛教典籍目錄》中記錄號碼爲：Танг. 81，Инв. No. 2561，克恰諾夫《西夏文佛教典籍目錄》，484頁。西田氏編號爲：Leningrad Cat. 81，西田龍雄《西夏譯佛典目錄》，49頁。

七者，因爲不混雜而是金剛。譬如：如金剛寶不與金剛石沙礫體性相混，此經典大寶亦爾，以三慧修習，則分析三次所轉法輪，（《金剛經》與彼三者）本質不混雜。

這段引文將《金剛經》比作現實中之金剛石，以説明其相比於其他經典文獻的殊勝特性。這種翻譯方式，與西夏文對其他藏傳佛教文獻中出現的術語“金剛”的翻譯方式相類，如“金剛亥母”類文獻中，“金剛亥母”皆被寫作“[illegible]”。

需要特别説明的是，筆者從聖彼得堡的收藏中得到第一篇文獻，但這篇文獻的題名似乎未收錄於西田隆雄與克恰諾夫的目錄中。西田龍雄、克恰諾夫目錄中收錄了第二篇文獻，集者、譯者與筆者所見第一篇文獻相同，且西田氏將第一篇文獻的“[illegible]（乘）”字用括號標出，似乎他在文本中未見此字，而科恰諾夫直接將括號去除，留下“[illegible]”字，可見二人都認爲這兩篇文獻爲同一篇。荒川慎太郎與索羅寧亦沿襲了這一觀點。但是除此以外，這兩篇文章第一篇以“顯理燈炬記”結束，“顯理”放在句末符合藏文的語言習慣，其本義爲“顯明金剛經之理”，“燈炬記”爲文章副標題，而第二篇文獻以“經典”二字結束。可以看出，第一篇文獻爲《金剛經》的闡釋文本，而第二篇言“大乘經”似乎説明該文獻是《金剛經》本身。基於此，確有兩種文獻指同一篇的可能，但亦可能是慧照法師翻譯了兩部松波上尊的著作。

以上爲目前所能確認的所有與《金剛經》直接相關的西夏文注釋類文獻。從中可見西夏以流傳漢傳佛教傳統的西夏文《金剛經》注釋爲主，但仍有代表藏傳佛教特色的文本傳世。而這兩個傳統並非截然對立，如《金剛般若科次經頌義解纂要略記》即體現出融合的傾向。在這一背景下，有必要探求《聖金剛能斷至勝慧彼岸大經顯理燈炬記》中的義理出處，及其以何種方式融入了西夏《金剛經》傳播的漢傳佛教傳統。

二、作者及相關研究文獻

《[illegible]》（《聖金剛能斷至勝慧彼岸大經顯理燈炬記》）題記云：

[illegible]，[illegible]
法師松波上尊集，沙門慧照番譯

以下討論作者和譯者的可能性：

1. [illegible]（松波上尊）

[illegible]二字可能對應藏文Sum pa，是西夏文對原文字的音寫。克恰諾夫目錄出給出了兩個和“松波”相關的名號：[illegible]（松波上尊）、[illegible]（松巴明滿）。

（1）[illegible]（松波上尊）

在荒川氏《西夏文金剛経の研究》附錄三首頁所給出的照片中，《[illegible]》（《金剛般若心真（言）》）緊承上文所述文獻《[illegible]》（《金剛經》）而撰寫，其題記爲：[illegible]（松波法師傳），該文獻亦爲般若類經典文獻。[19]

此外，西夏文阿底峽尊者撰《[illegible]》（《四十種空幢要論》）正文中出現了[illegible]（松波譯師）的字樣，疑與此松波上尊爲一人，屬於藏傳佛教傳統[20]。

（2）[illegible]（松巴明滿）

松巴明滿對應藏文爲Sum pa Sangs rgyas，俄藏黑水城文獻中有其一篇《[illegible]》（《亥母耳傳記文》）[21]，索羅寧認爲此師即上云“松波上尊”，屬於從帕當巴桑傑（Dam pa Sangs rgyas，也即小黑足）到無生（Skye med，āsu）的一支金剛亥母傳承[22]。

雖然學者對上述二師的傳承進行了初步分析，但沒有明確證據證明二者爲同一人。Sum pa可爲氏族或地域名稱，其地位於衛藏東北方向。山口瑞風氏認爲Sum pa位於北至黃河發源地區南岸的色末地區，南至小金川一帶，以松潘爲中心[23]。此地區爲黨項人舊居地，與西夏王朝中心聯繫緊密。或可推測有多位元Sum pa地區上師來至西夏傳法，或西夏人去往Sum pa之地求法。

2. [illegible]（慧照）

慧照是西夏末期非常活躍的論師之一，根據聶鴻音、魏文等學者的研究，其活躍時代大概在公元1194年至公元1227年西夏亡國間：

首先，《[illegible]》（《仁王護國般若波羅蜜多經》）於天慶元年（1194）刊刻，乃羅太后爲紀念仁孝皇帝駕崩週年而舉行法會而作，其題記中慧照被稱爲慧照禪師[24]。這是可見最早有關慧照的記載。其次，名爲李慧明[25]的譯師

⑲ 索羅寧《〈金刚般若科次经颂义解纂要略记序〉及西夏汉藏佛教的一面》，94—95頁。並參見荒川慎太郎《西夏文金剛経の研究》，附錄三。

⑳ 索羅寧《〈金刚般若科次经颂义解纂要略记序〉及西夏汉藏佛教的一面》，94—95頁。

㉑ 克恰諾夫《西夏文佛教典籍目錄》，579頁。

㉒ 〔俄〕Solonin, K., “Dīpaṃkara in Tangut Context, Part 1,” *Acta Orientalia*, 68, No. 4 (2015), p.435.有關此金剛亥母傳承的考證，參見孫鵬浩《有關帕當巴桑傑的西夏漢文密教文獻四篇》，載于沈衛榮主編《文本中的歷史：藏傳佛教在西域何中原的傳播》，北京：中國藏學出版社，2012年，85—97頁。

㉓ 對松巴地理位置的研究，最早有伯希和、圖齊等學者的論文，他們基本認爲松巴地域範疇不確定，但總體位於衛藏東北方向。伯希和認爲松巴也即蘇毗。山口瑞鳳駁斥了他們的觀點，而將松巴定于北部康區的範圍內，並認爲主要由末氏和朗氏兩大家族統治。譚其驤《中國歷史地圖集》與山口氏觀點不謀而合。

㉔ 《[illegible]》（《仁王護國般若波羅蜜多經》），Танг. 104，Инв. No. 683。參考聶鴻音《〈仁王經〉的西夏譯本》，《民族研究》2010年第3期，44—49頁。此處及本節下文有關時間的推斷，參見魏文《〈最勝上樂集本續顯釋記〉譯傳源流考——兼論西夏上樂付法上師》，載于沈衛榮主編《漢藏佛學研究：文本、人物、圖像和歷史》，北京：中國藏學出版社，2013年，301—330頁。

㉕ 聶鴻音、魏文在其研究中將記此人爲慧明（[illegible]），但克恰諾夫目錄中記作慧照（[illegible]）（克恰諾夫《西夏文佛教典籍目錄》，491頁）。

於光定丙子六年（1216）翻譯了《[illegible]——[illegible]》（《至勝慧彼岸要語教學——現證莊嚴論顯頌》，此李慧明題記中云其乃“講經律論辯番羌語比丘”，與本文所見慧照的身份暗合，或可認爲二者即爲一人。[26]此後，在國圖所藏《最勝上樂集本續顯釋記》（A00969）之卷首署名中，有“講經律論寂真國師沙門惠照[27]傳”字樣，而在上述1216年的題記中慧照尚未受封國師，故《最勝上樂集本續顯釋記》所記載的年代只能處於1216—1227年之間。

上述内容説明本文所研究西夏寫本《金剛經顯理燈炬記》曾流行於西夏晚期，至於其藏文原本寫作年代則難以推定。除本文所涉及以外，慧照還翻譯、講傳了大量經論文獻，主要集中於般若類經典和六法等要語（man ngag）文本，如下：

（1）《[illegible]》（《聖金剛王能斷至勝慧彼岸大乘經》）

（2）《[illegible]》（《金剛般若義解記》）[28]

（3）《[illegible]——[illegible]》（《至勝慧彼岸要語教學——現證莊嚴論顯頌》）

（4）《[illegible]》（《入二諦論義解記》）[29]

（5）《[illegible]》（《勝住法事》）[30]

（6）《[illegible]——[illegible]》（《菩提勇識所學——道、果顯釋寶炬》）[31]

（7）《[illegible]——[illegible]》（《長壽定全部次第——受取次第要語》）[32]

（8）《[illegible]》（[illegible]）（《欲樂圓融要語》（捺囉巴Nāropāda传））[33]

㉖ 《[illegible]--[illegible]》（《至勝慧彼岸要語教學——現證莊嚴論顯頌》（據藏文原文調整後之題目）），Танг. 101，Инв. No. 5130。參考聶鴻音《俄藏5130號西夏文佛經題記研究》，《中國藏學》2002年第1期，50—54頁。

㉗ 根據魏文《〈最勝上樂集本續顯釋記〉譯傳源流考——兼論西夏上樂付法上師》一文，慧、惠通，也即慧照。

㉘ 即上文所提第二篇《金剛經》注釋文獻，其中克恰諾夫在第二個版本的寫本（Танг. 385，Инв. No. 886）中見到“慧照”字樣。克恰諾夫《西夏文佛教典籍目錄》，466頁。

㉙ 《[illegible]》（《入二諦論義解記》），Танг. 198，Инв. No. 833，克恰諾夫《西夏文佛教典籍目錄》，568頁。題記中云：[illegible]（即“此典籍所有者爲慧照”，其中[illegible]二字不明）。

㉚ Танг. 97，Инв. No. 810，題記中説明是“慧照番譯”，克恰諾夫《西夏文佛教典籍目錄》，490頁。

㉛ 《[illegible]——[illegible]》（《菩提勇識學——道、果顯釋寶炬》）有多個版本，Танг. 120，Инв. No. 5129題記中説明是“慧照番譯”，克恰諾夫《西夏文佛教典籍目錄》，513頁。

㉜ Танг. 322，Инв. No. 4989，克恰諾夫《西夏文佛教典籍目錄》，557—558頁。

㉝ Танг. 325，Инв. No. 5116，題記中説明是“慧照番譯”，此文獻Танг. 325，Инв. No. 2546版本亦提及“慧照”，克恰諾夫《西夏文佛教典籍目錄》，558—599頁。

（9）《[illegible]》（《六法自體要語》）[34]

（10）《[illegible]》（《念定絕害要語》）[35]

（11）《[illegible]》（《六法圓融道次第》（集））[36]

其中，魏文研究認爲慧照爲捺囉巴再傳弟子[37]，可解釋爲何慧照持有、抄寫或翻譯衆多捺囉巴六法文本。此外，《金剛般若義解記》可能爲慧照譯自漢文的文本，將西夏譯漢文《金剛經》注釋文獻與《顯理燈炬記》聯繫起來。

綜合松波上尊和慧照的情況看，《聖金剛能斷至勝慧彼岸大經顯理燈炬記》並非一個孤立的文本，它處在從藏傳佛教角度注釋般若、中觀經論所形成的文本圈之中。松波上尊所傳、慧照所譯《至勝慧彼岸要語教學——現證莊嚴論顯頌》亦是此類文本。《金剛般若義解記》出現了“慧照”字樣，《入二諦論義解記》爲慧照所持有，此二論雖尚未經定性，或亦與此《金剛經顯理燈炬記》有關。本文所述文獻當以此背景考察。

三、文本科判與序分分析

1. 科判

該文本是《聖金剛能斷至勝慧彼岸大經》的注釋書，並非完本。現存部分前半乃其序分（甲一、甲二）與正文（甲三）的起始章節。基於此三部分內容，筆者做出如下科判：

甲一　緣起

分二：說法者佛，與佛所說法

甲二　序分

乙一　說法者

分三：最初“發大菩提心”；其次，（於）“三無數劫”（中），積累具足（福、智）二者；最後，成就如實現前正覺。

丙一　發菩提心

分三次第：以地獄初發悲心，瓦匠子發不真實菩提心，與調禦象心發真實菩提心等三個邏輯遞進的故事，解說何謂發真正菩提心。

丁一　地獄故事

㉞ 有多個版本，Танг. 371，Инв. No. 4698題記中說明是“屬於慧照正書”之文本，克恰諾夫《西夏文佛教典籍目錄》，562—563頁。

㉟ Танг. 415，Инв. No. 2892，克恰諾夫《西夏文佛教典籍目錄》，563頁。

㊱ Танг. 354，Инв. No. 2734，題記中說明是“慧照番譯”，克恰諾夫《西夏文佛教典籍目錄》，590頁。

㊲ 魏文《11—12世紀上樂教法在西藏和西夏的傳播——以兩篇漢譯密教文書和藏文教法史爲中心》，中國人民大學博士論文，2013，第三章。

因爲當初發起了悲心，而生在人間。

丁二　瓦匠子故事

對於了知諸多知識一再發心，（却）一再失去，未得不退悔之心。

丁三　調象故事

發起不退轉之菩提心。此者，即是“發菩提心”。

丙二　三無數劫積累福智資糧

分三：三個無數劫中各佈施佛的名號與數目

丙三　成就如實現前正覺

如何成就真實佛，圓滿受用身佛，及化身佛

乙二　佛所說法

分四部分，前三次第相續：作者依照佛在世三轉法輪，佛涅槃後阿羅漢集結經典，毗婆沙、龍樹創中道學說、無著世親創唯識學說的三次第等三部分介紹佛所說法與後世傳法，最後言及《般若經》的分類。

丙一 佛在世三次轉法輪

分三：瓦拉那西國隨世俗諦轉四諦法輪；王舍城靈鷲峰隨順勝義轉無實有法輪；廣嚴城轉能、所無二法輪

丙二　佛滅度後集經

爲令正法住世而集結經卷

丙三　釋經之三法輪：毗婆沙、中觀、唯識

分四：五百阿羅漢做《大毗婆沙論》；龍樹造“六部中道根本典”；無著、天親做“成立唯識之本母”注疏；慈氏造“慈氏五論”，開顯後二法輪之義理。

丙四　般若注疏

分二大類：十萬頌等廣本、金剛經等略本

甲三　正文

分二：解釋名稱；釋根本文。

乙一　釋名

分二：文本依例釋經名，分爲依梵文釋與依義釋兩部分。後者集合不同注疏的說法，依照功用含義解釋經名之內涵。

丙一　約梵文解說名稱

丙二　約利益解說名稱

分三：依名字次序解釋：聖、金剛能斷、勝慧。

丁一　聖

丁二　金剛能斷

丁三　勝慧

丙三　約餘注疏解說名稱

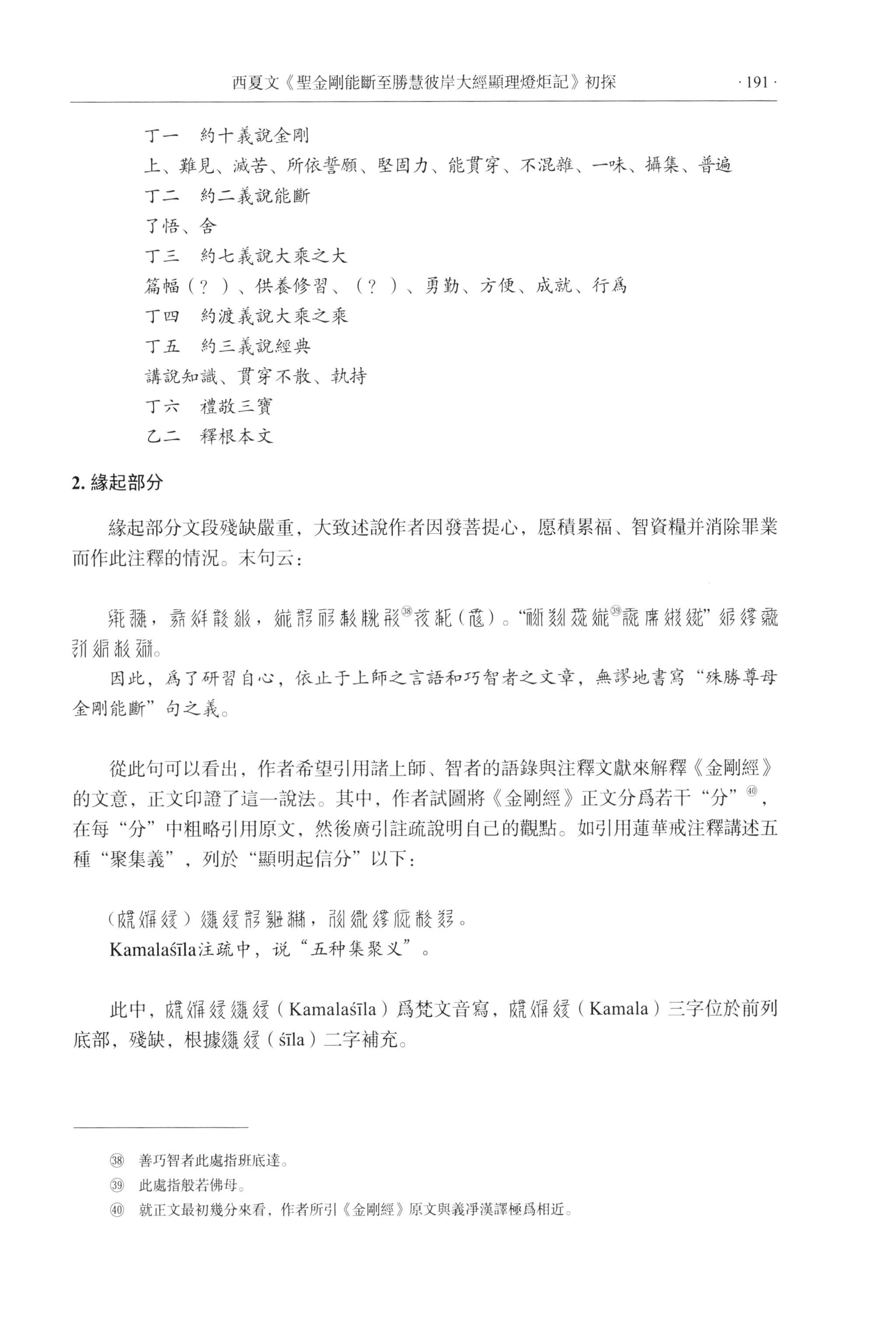

丁一　約十義說金剛

上、難見、滅苦、所依誓願、堅固力、能貫穿、不混雜、一味、攝集、普遍

丁二　約二義說能斷

了悟、舍

丁三　約七義說大乘之大

篇幅（？）、供養修習、（？）、勇勤、方便、成就、行爲

丁四　約渡義說大乘之乘

丁五　約三義說經典

講說知識、貫穿不散、執持

丁六　禮敬三寶

乙二　釋根本文

2. 緣起部分

緣起部分文段殘缺嚴重，大致述說作者因發菩提心，願積累福、智資糧并消除罪業而作此注釋的情況。末句云：

[illegible]，[illegible]，[illegible][38][illegible]（[illegible]）。“[illegible][39][illegible]”[illegible]。

因此，爲了研習自心，依止于上師之言語和巧智者之文章，無謬地書寫“殊勝尊母金剛能斷”句之義。

從此句可以看出，作者希望引用諸上師、智者的語錄與注釋文獻來解釋《金剛經》的文意，正文印證了這一說法。其中，作者試圖將《金剛經》正文分爲若干“分”[40]，在每“分”中粗略引用原文，然後廣引註疏說明自己的觀點。如引用蓮華戒注釋講述五種“聚集義”，列於“顯明起信分”以下：

（[illegible]）[illegible]，[illegible]。

Kamalaśīla注疏中，说“五种集聚义”。

此中，[illegible]（Kamalaśīla）爲梵文音寫，[illegible]（Kamala）三字位於前列底部，殘缺，根據[illegible]（śīla）二字補充。

---

[38] 善巧智者此處指班底達。

[39] 此處指般若佛母。

[40] 就正文最初幾分來看，作者所引《金剛經》原文與義淨漢譯極爲相近。

3. 序分部分（一）：“發菩提心”至“正覺”

緣起以下，說法者與所說法構成了文本的序分。在說法者的部分，我們可以看到世尊從凡夫階段發菩提心及至證覺的過程：此部分又分爲三層，最初“發大菩提心”；其次，（於）“三無數劫”（中），積累具足（福、智）二者；最後，成就如實現前正覺。此三次第在蓮花戒（kamalaśīla）的第一部《修習次第》（Bhāvanākrama）中亦是如此陳列，是印度及藏傳佛教撰論的常見格式。

其中首先松巴上尊討論了何謂“發菩提心”，這在西夏佛教中是十分重要的命題。作者以前後相續的三個故事講述其次第。以序分的兩部分結構而言，第一部分講述的主體是說法者，也即世尊，但在三個故事中主語似乎並不明了。第一段講述世尊本生，也即其在地獄發悲心生人間之事；第二段講述瓦匠子雖發菩提心，卻未能不退轉，此瓦匠子或爲佛陀在人間世之形象；第三段以馴服象獸的故事講述調心的過程，也即發真菩提心。其中特別值得注意的是對何謂“真正”菩提心的探討。文本云：

（1）地獄發悲心而生人間

[illegible][41][illegible][42][illegible]

本师……作为傍生、凡夫时，在地狱中，使其與某……大力救拔者……救拔之時，因为助力弱小，不能救拔。因此，……（力大者）用铁杖击打，（被打者）承受大苦恼。（被打者）言：“吾本师，大……”（本师）说：“你莫要打它，我独自救拔。”（本師）凭借教导……之力，成为救拔之人。（大力者）问（本师）：“你为何慈悲？”用铁杖（擊打），（被打者）將于彼上送命。（本师）因为当初发起了悲心，而生在人间。

（2）瓦匠子發不真實菩提心

[illegible][43][illegible]

一名瓦匠……时，世间一佛诞生，名为“释迦牟尼”，引导庶民……（瓦匠子）见到所有人都祈求去佛那里，供养他、听闻佛法，自己也想去佛那里，没有其他可供财物，捆草做火炬，奉献于佛。说：“我也与你一样成佛。”发菩提心，并以火炬除暗使

㊶ 寫本中此字右半爲爻。

㊷ 此字龔煌城擬音gej，用作族姓，文意不通。或爲“[illegible]”（貪）之誤寫。

㊸ 寫本中此字右上爲卌。

明，因此，那时候，瓦匠子名作“曜辰”。如彼名称，（瓦匠子）对于了知诸多知识一再发心，（却）一再失去，未得不退悔之心。

（3）象獸喻使王發真實菩提心

表1

	《金剛經顯理燈炬記》	漢譯	《根本說一切有部毗奈耶藥事》[44]
調象師獻象，途遇母象，象驚，王受驚	[illegible]	其後，某國……時，（有一禦人）禮敬王所騎乘的舍象。（王）將（象）群中的一頭象獸……授予（彼）人，令（其）調禦。問：“誰是禦象人？”。答：“（是名爲）‘依法’者。”（調禦畢……），於是奉獻于王。王坐於象脊，禦人……，遇到一群象，（象要）過去……聞母象的香氣……，拉不住。王害怕了，問“怎麼辦？”禦人……。禦象者說：“你拿著樹枝！”因而，在樹近旁時，（王）取得……樹枝。	佛告大王：“乃往古昔無量劫時，有王名曰光明。其光明王有一象寶，身色鮮白如優鉢花，七支圓滿，形貌端嚴，人所喜見。時王即勅調象之人：‘令調此象，堪乘之時，將來見我。’其調象人受王勅已，即將調教。既成就已，還詣王所。王即乘象，並調象人，王在後坐，出城遊獵種種禽獸。然而象王聞母象氣，尋香而走。 “爾時調象師作種種法，不能止息而令象回。又白王言：‘其象走困，願王攀取樹枝，放象隨意。’即逢一樹，王及象師攀枝而住，喻如從死而得再生。
王欲懲罰調象師	[illegible]	回到室內（以後），王生氣了，對禦者說：“你（差點讓）我（因爲）象獸……送了命，對於你的身體，數日（內）你當用爪割成各五兩肉而殺了（自己）。”（王將禦者）下入監牢內。王宮的守護神們在王的夢中這樣說：“雖然已經調伏了象的身體，因尚未調伏（其）心，使王（受到）驚嚇。七日之後，象自己來時如何指令（它）？”因此（又對王）說，“你凡是聽到的都照辦，不要派（人）殺此人。禦象人也據此而告。	王告象師曰：‘汝不調此象成就，便即將來與我乘騎。’白王曰：‘我調成就，然爲彼象聞雌象氣，貪欲醉故不受言教。其象雖去，思憶本處，至第七日，必還來到。所以者何？由見母象，共行欲已，思憶象坊。’至第七日，其象還還來。時調象人速詣白王。

㊹ 此處及下述引文，出自義淨所譯《根本說一切有部毘奈耶藥事》卷15，CBETA, T24, no. 1448, p. 69, a25-p. 73, c5。

续表

	《金剛經顯理燈炬記》	漢譯	《根本說一切有部毗奈耶藥事》
王求可調心之人，與禦象人一起拜謁佛陀	[illegible][45][illegible]	王說："你憑什麼說'身體……你（能）調伏？"那人說："調伏心者，不是我的事，那是（佛能做到的）。"王說："那個調伏心的人，也即佛陀，在哪兒呢？"那時，（佛）在……（他們）一起去了那裡。"因爲聽了調順心之法，我也……憑藉調伏（內心），將會成佛。"**說畢，（發起）一心真實菩提……乃至成佛，連續未曾斷絕。**	王曰：'汝教此象，未好成就。'其人白王：'我調象已。'責曰：'云何調伏？'白言：'請王驗試，即知虛實。'……先白王：'我但調伏其身，不能調心。'王曰：'汝頗見有能調心者？'象師白王言：'有！唯佛世尊能調身心。一切有情欲調其心，由不能調，而皆卻退。……言大王者，有大威力，諸鬭戰中最能殊勝，亦不調心；唯佛世尊無有貪欲心得自在。'"**爾時大王聞佛世尊有精進力，廣行惠施，修諸福業，即發無上菩提之願。**
王因發心而作大布施，供養全部四天王與百柔淨	[illegible]	那時，全部四天王和百柔淨……悉皆供養。後來，如此深深讚歎："在今天，……（心）向菩提，即發心，以此，你今於世界中一切之供事……"因此，發起不退轉之菩提心。此者，即是"發菩提心"。	佛告大王："于意云何？彼時名光明王者，豈異人乎？即我身是。我于爾時，初發無上菩提之意。"

發菩提心後，修行者還需經過積累資糧的過程方可成正覺，因此在說法者部分松巴上尊繼續說明積累資糧的方式。但是這部分故事在阿毘達摩文本中十分常見，並非作者著意之處。其文云：

（4）於三無數劫中積累福、智二資糧

在對於三無數劫積累福、智資糧的論述中，該文本與諸阿毘達摩經典的不同之處在於其配合了資糧、加行、見道、修道等四道來敘述積累次第，且將此四道進一步配合十地。《金剛仙論》中亦有此說法，其文云：

> "前第三段中，已明菩萨现见真如，具足四种深利益心，则能永断四住，出分段生死，离五怖畏，生在佛家，住于**初地大乘法**中。然虽**一大僧祇**行满，**证初地无生见道**之解，并观三种二谛平等照万有，犹地行未圆，一切种智未满，观境未周，断惑未尽，大光明未具足。
>
> 必须重修万行，增习见道，备精（=修）众德，**更径二大阿僧祇**，行满或（惑？）尽，方能进趣证于佛果。是故菩萨若能始从二地，终于远行，以不取心，行诸波罗蜜，
>
> 遣功用相尽，乃得证于**八地已上无功用位**，备（=满）修十地，得一切种

[45] 寫本中此字爲[illegible]，疑爲"[illegible]"的簡寫。

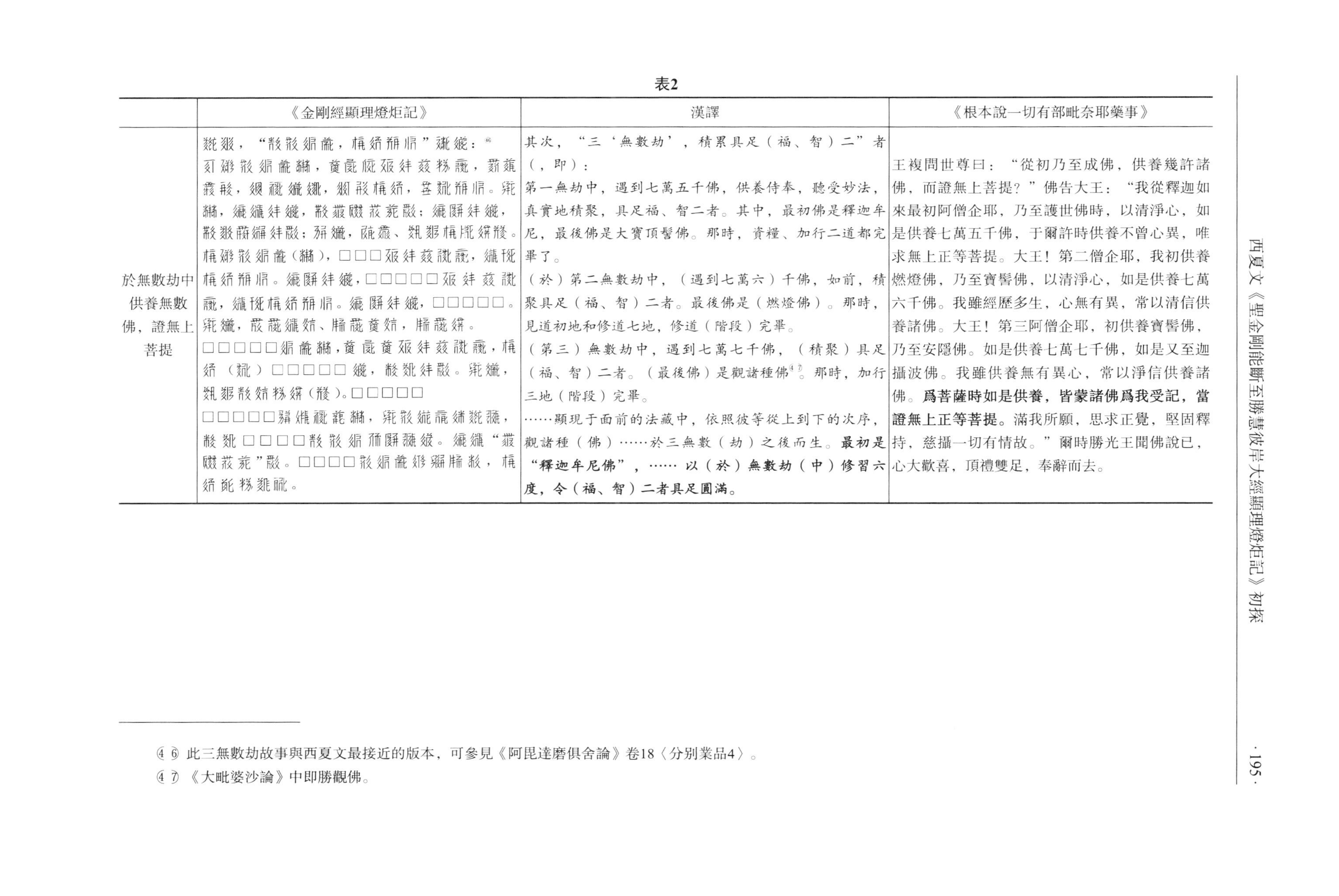

表2

	《金剛經顯理燈炬記》	漢譯	《根本說一切有部毗奈耶藥事》
於無數劫中供養無數佛，證無上菩提	[illegible][46]	其次，“三‘無數劫’，積累具足（福、智）二”者（，即）： 第一無劫中，遇到七萬五千佛，供養侍奉，聽受妙法，真實地積聚，具足福、智二者。其中，最初佛是釋迦牟尼，最後佛是大寶頂髻佛。那時，資糧、加行二道都完畢了。 （於）第二無數劫中，（遇到七萬六）千佛，如前，積聚具足（福、智）二者。最後佛是（燃燈佛）。那時，見道初地和修道七地，修道（階段）完畢。 （第三）無數劫中，遇到七萬七千佛，（積聚）具足（福、智）二者。（最後佛）是觀諸種佛[47]。那時，加行三地（階段）完畢。 ……顯現于面前的法藏中，依照彼等從上到下的次序，觀諸種（佛）……於三無數（劫）之後而生。**最初是“釋迦牟尼佛”，…… 以（於）無數劫（中）修習六度，令（福、智）二者具足圓滿。**	王複問世尊曰：“從初乃至成佛，供養幾許諸佛，而證無上菩提？”佛告大王：“我從釋迦如來最初阿僧企耶，乃至護世佛時，以清淨心，如是供養七萬五千佛，于爾許時供養不曾心異，唯求無上正等菩提。大王！第二僧企耶，我初供養燃燈佛，乃至寶髻佛，以清淨心，如是供養七萬六千佛。我雖經歷多生，心無有異，常以清信供養諸佛。大王！第三阿僧企耶，初供養寶髻佛，乃至安隱佛。如是供養七萬七千佛，如是又至迦攝波佛。我雖供養無有異心，常以淨信供養諸佛。**爲菩薩時如是供養，皆蒙諸佛爲我受記，當證無上正等菩提**。滿我所願，思求正覺，堅固釋持，慈攝一切有情故。”爾時勝光王聞佛說已，心大歡喜，頂禮雙足，奉辭而去。

④⑥ 此三無數劫故事與西夏文最接近的版本，可參見《阿毘達磨俱舍論》卷18〈分別業品4〉。

④⑦ 《大毗婆沙論》中即勝觀佛。

智。……

就此经中始未（+亦）具明三道。何者是前之住分？**局在初地，即是见道；此如实修行分，二地已上，至于七地，即是修道。下断疑分中言，违于不住道者，即是八地至十地无功用道也。**”⑱

此中所云：第一無量劫中菩薩住于初地，證無生見道；第二住於二地以上，至於七地；至於不住道，方入八地以上。本文與此種說法相近，並在其中加入資糧、加行二道，至於初地之前。

調象和三無數劫的故事散見於諸“根本說一切有部律經”、《大毗婆沙論》，以及《俱舍論》。上文舉《根本說一切有部毗奈耶藥事》之例與《金剛經顯理燈炬記》進行對比，因爲二者不僅故事情節大同，邏輯理路亦相近。《藥事》提出三個問題：

（1）於何時初發無上菩提之願?

（2）最初於誰行施得證無上菩提?

（3）從初乃至成佛，供養幾許諸佛，而證無上菩提?

世尊發悲心生人間的部分相當於《藥事》的聖光大王對世尊的提問，也即第一問題。瓦匠子故事對“真實菩提心”的討論在《藥事》並未涉及。后兩個問題分别相應於調象和三無數劫的故事。由此可見，二者都將此成佛過程分爲發心、積資、正覺三部分。此處所用《藥事》爲義淨譯本，從現存文本及此處的相似性看，說一切有部律對西夏佛教產生過影響。藏區流行律經多爲說一切有部律，故此現象亦說明其與藏傳佛教的相關性。

4. 序分部分（二）：三轉法輪

《金剛經顯理燈炬記》序分中所說法部分主要宣說佛法的傳佈的過程，從三轉法輪，至結集經典，最後說毗婆沙、中觀、唯識的佛教流派發展次第。在此部分結尾處，松波上尊將討論集中至般若類經典，並將其分爲長頌與短頌兩類，也即，相對綜合篇幅較長的一類，與強調主題篇幅較短的一類，《金剛經》屬於後者⑲。文本云：

---

⑱ 參見《金剛仙論》卷二，CBETA, T25, no. 1512, p. 807, c4-19。《金剛仙論》，傳爲世親菩薩所造《金剛經》注疏，金剛仙論師釋，菩提流支譯，然吉藏、圓測等師皆云其爲菩提流支所造。此處所見，或可推測其於西夏佛教亦產生過影響。

⑲ Conze首先提出般若經典發展的四階段論：第一階段爲原始佛典的形成期（公元前後百年）；第二階段爲增廣期（公元後一百至三百年），如玄奘《大般若經》；第三階段將長篇中精華部分抽取或分類爲短篇（公元後三百至五百年），《金剛經》屬此；第四階段爲般若經典的密教化（公元後五百至一千二百年），如《心經》的密教詮釋。渡辺章悟氏對此做出詳細地分析。渡辺章悟《金剛般若経の研究》，山喜房佛書林，2009年，24—25頁。

（1）佛在世三次轉法輪

[illegible][50]，[illegible][51][illegible]。“[illegible]，[illegible]；[illegible]、[illegible]、[illegible]，[illegible]。”[illegible]。[illegible]。

瓦拉那西（Varanasi）國附近，轉五……的四諦法輪。謂：“諸蘊處界法實有，無作者、受者與常一之我。”（此即）隨順世俗諦……而說。

[illegible]、[illegible][52][illegible]，[illegible]（[illegible]）[53]□□□[illegible]：“[illegible]”[illegible]，[illegible]（[illegible]）□□[illegible]。

其次，在王舍城靈鷲峰附近，轉四（義）……之無實有法輪：“諸五蘊等法”亦爾，隨順勝義……而說。

[illegible]，[illegible][54][illegible]+{[illegible]}[illegible]，[illegible]□□□□□[illegible]：“[illegible]，[illegible][55][illegible]，[illegible]□□□”，□□[illegible]。

此后，于广严城等宫殿附近，第一次转（诸法）……：“因为遮遣断见，能所无二，诸心……”，随顺于……谛而说。

（2）佛滅度後集經

[illegible]，[illegible]□□□□[illegible]。[illegible]，[illegible]，[illegible]□□□[illegible]，[illegible]。

複次，佛宣說教法之因緣終了，入於滅度……。其後，因爲要令正法流布於長世中，……人們集合佛所說諸種，製作經卷。

（3）釋經之三法輪：毗婆沙、中觀、唯識

[illegible]（[illegible]）□[illegible]，[illegible]，[illegible]《[illegible]（[illegible]）[illegible]》[56]，[illegible][57][illegible]。[illegible]，[illegible]“[illegible]”[illegible]。[illegible]，[illegible]、[illegible]“[illegible]”[illegible]。[illegible]，[illegible][58][illegible]。[illegible][59][illegible]，[illegible]（[illegible]）□[illegible]，“[illegible]”[illegible]。

複次，爲顯明佛所說經典之義，五百阿羅漢聚集，造第一法輪之《分別開顯論》

---

[50] 此處指壇城、道場。

[51] 二字含義不明。

[52] 直譯爲“鳥獸聚”，此處翻譯藏語bya rgod phung po'i ri而來，即靈鷲峰。

[53] 此處及下文括弧中字據文意補，下文“[illegible]（[illegible]）”爲“勝（義）”。

[54] 廣嚴城，梵文：vaiśali，藏文：yangs pa can。佛本於此二轉法輪，說大乘法，但松巴上尊將此地編入第三轉法輪下。

[55] [illegible]，能所之“能”。

[56] 依據意思，構擬爲梵文mahāvibhāṣā，藏文bye brag tu bshad pa，即《大毗婆沙論》。

[57] 此處是否與前“大”字，合併爲“大乘”，待考。

[58] “慈氏世尊”即彌勒。將“慈氏”與“世尊”合起來的這一稱呼，見玄奘所譯五百阿羅漢造《大毗婆沙論》。

[59] 梵文：tuṣita。詞根tuṣ，高興、滿意，故此處西夏文意譯“知足宮”。漢譯：兜率天，彌勒所居。

（《大毗婆沙論》）。其後，龍樹大師造第二法輪之注疏“六部中道根本典”。無著、天親等師作衆多“成立唯識之本母”注疏。繼而，無著師向慈氏世尊祈求修習成就。在知足宫（兜率天宫）内，令後二種法輪之義開顯，作“慈氏五法論”等。

（4）般若注疏

[illegible]，[illegible]□□□□[illegible]，[illegible]、[illegible]□□□□，[illegible]□。□□□□[illegible]，[illegible]“[illegible]”[illegible]，“[illegible]”[illegible][60]□□□□，[illegible]，[illegible]，[illegible]。

複次，憑藉……無著、天親，（即）聖解脱、俗解脱師，以及……（作）多種至勝慧彼岸經之注疏[61]。……（人們）説：“‘勝慧彼岸經’者，即能説‘如實現前了義’……（了）義之能説，（即）希求二部經典，而非隨順。”

□□□□[illegible]：“‘[illegible]’[illegible][62][illegible]　‘[illegible]’[illegible]□□□[illegible]：[illegible]，[illegible]、[illegible]；[illegible]（[illegible]）[63][illegible]。”[illegible]，[illegible]。

云：“是依八種‘如實現前了（義）’所説之（般若波羅蜜多）經與某些‘如實現前了義’兩種：前者是“十萬”、“一億”頌（般若）等六部經典，後者是心經典與“金剛能斷”等。因爲五種道與三地等者，即是“如實現前了義”。

序言部分至此結束。正文中，作者仍依例先釋經名，後進入對根本文的闡釋。釋名又分兩部分：一則按照梵文名稱釋義，二則引用不同注疏釋義。此中涉及衆多名相，於此暫不贅述。

四、結　論

綜上所述，該文獻可能爲譯自藏文的《金剛經》註釋類文獻，翻譯于西夏末期。此文本背後有一批基於漢、藏兩支佛教傳統的般若類經典文獻。雖然這些文獻都譯自梵文，但卻在翻譯中流露出漢、藏兩支傳統自身的特色，因此西夏在轉譯此類般若經典

---

[60] 無法從上下文確定[illegible]是否可翻譯爲“能説”，抑或爲“所説”，後文同。後兩句意義亦不明。

[61] 藏文本有：*'phags pa bcom ldan 'das ma shes rab kyi pha rol tu phyin pa rdo rje gcod pa'i don bdun gyi rgya cher 'grel pa*/（圣佛母般若波罗蜜多能断金刚（经）之七义广释）（北京版无，收德格版3816, sher phyin, ma 178a5-203b7）。汉文本有：（唐）義淨奉制譯，無著造頌，世親釋《能斷金剛般若波羅蜜多經論釋》，大正藏第 25 冊，No. 1513。此处说无著、世亲的多本注疏，不知是否包含此两种。另外，汉文又有无著或世亲单独创作之释论：（北魏）菩提流支譯，世親造，金剛仙論師釋《金剛仙論》，大正藏第 25 冊 No. 1512；（隋）達磨笈多譯，無著造《金剛般若論》，大正藏第25冊，No. 1510a；（隋）達磨笈多譯，無著造《金剛般若波羅蜜經論》，大正藏第25冊，No.1510b

[62] 結合本段上下文及後文所説“十萬”“一億”“金剛能斷”等詞彙推斷。

[63] 據字數及上下文補充。參考Conze對“般若經”的分期，《心經》與《金剛經》屬於同期經典，故大膽猜測。

時，會在一定程度上受到兩隻傳統的影響。

就作者、譯者的情況看，由同一作者Sum pa傳授的《金剛般若心真（言）》可看作此文配套讀本。該注釋文獻之譯者慧照亦是西夏末期名僧，甚至曾出任國師一職，他除關注般若類經典以外，亦傳承了捺囉巴的教法。此二者間有何聯繫，當是進一步考察的有趣點。

就文本內容而言，其中提及五百羅漢造《大毗婆沙論》，該文本僅存漢譯，後於民國時期由法尊法師翻譯爲藏文，顯示出該文本作者對漢傳佛教譯作的熟悉。此外，該文本中的翻譯用語照顧到了西夏人受漢傳佛教影響極大的知識背景，如："大乘（[illegible]）""唯識（[illegible]）"等詞彙，在文本中是以漢文的書寫順序進行書寫的。但是該文本的敘述模式，如以佛在世、佛涅槃、經典後世相傳情形三部分作爲佛所說法的部分，則體現出藏族作者的寫作習慣。在引文中，對蓮華戒"註疏"[64]的引用亦說明作者對藏譯梵文典籍的熟悉。

總之，該文本代表了藏傳顯教文獻在西夏的某種傳播模式，反應出西夏人對漢傳、藏傳佛教所採取的"但爲我所用"的態度。而通過此文獻的體例及其周邊文本瞭解，我們或許亦可推測其用作教學課本的性質。

A Primary Study on a Tangut Commantory of the *Diamond Sutra*

Li Mengxi

As one of the most popular Sutra in Xixia, the *Diamond Sutra* had been spread in this region in various forms. There are not only manuscripts and block-print texts of the Sutra and relative Commentaries, but also special ritual texts based on the Sutra. Most of the extant Tangut texts of the Diamond Sutra are retranslated from the Chinese translation of Kumārajīva, so that it contains the feature of Sino-Buddhism. However, the commentary discussed in this article, which is called *the Lamp illuminating the true meaning of Vajracchedikā Prajñāpāramitā Sūtra*, reflects the Tibetan feature from either the topic and author, or the contents. Therefore, I want to, firstly, discuss who the author and the translator are, and what are the status was before the background of Sino-Buddhism in Xixia; secondly, I will analyse the issues contained in the preface of this text; finally, make a primary identification to the text based on the knowledge above.

---

[64] 蓮華戒對《金剛經》的注釋僅存藏譯，譯名爲：*phags pa shes rab kyi pha rol tu phyin pa rdo rje gcod pa'i rgya cher 'grel pa/*（《金剛般若經廣注》）。蓮華戒（kamalaśīla）作，勝友（jinamitra）、文殊（majuśrī）、智軍（ye shes sde）譯。收於《丹珠爾》，北京版：[P. No.] 5216, sher phyin, ma, 209b4-285b5 (vol.94, p.248-278)；德格版：[D. No.] 3817, sher phyin, ma, 204a1-267a7；那塘版：[N] ma 212a3-291b4；金沙藏：[Kinsha] 3215, ma 279b1 (p.142-1-1)。文中所引是否即此版本注釋待考。

清代禁書運動對蒙古語文獻的影響

——以《登壇必究》之《北虜譯語》爲例

布日古德

在體現中古蒙古語的文獻資料中，用漢字拼寫蒙古語語音的資料，無論是在數量方面還是在種類方面都具有至關重要的學術價值。除了著名的《蒙古秘史》及《華夷譯語》各類版本之外，明代兵書中也收錄了幾部漢語蒙古語對譯辭典，是研究中古蒙古語不可或缺的資料。明代編修的兵書，在清代成爲禁燬書目，相關部分被刪除或修改，而這直接影響到了漢語蒙古語對譯詞典部分。

由於學界對明代兵書所收漢語蒙古語對譯詞典的版本源流及其演變考證不足，一些蒙古語詞彙仍未被正確再構擬，也未得到充分解釋。比較分析版本間存在的差異、追溯其緣由，是再構蒙古語的前提條件。本文將對明代兵書《登壇必究》所收漢語蒙古語對譯詞典《北虜譯語》的版本進行比較分析，並結合清代禁書運動歷史背景，揭示《北虜譯語》不同版本間存在的異同及其緣由，力圖確定最爲可靠且最接近原文的版本。

一、關於《登壇必究》之《北虜譯語》

《登壇必究》是中國明代著名軍事百科全書，成書於1599年。明朝武科進士，廣西總兵，驃騎將軍王鳴鶴編纂。全書共四十卷，七十二類目，近一百萬字。內容包括天文、地理、選將、訓練、賞罰、軍制、敵情、地域攻防等。同時也包含了一些描述周邊民族的歷史、地理、風俗、文化、軍備等方面的內容。

《北虜譯語》也称《譯語》，屬《登壇必究》第二十二卷，是一部漢語與蒙古語的對譯詞典。其中蒙古語部分是用漢字拼寫而成的。這部詞典包括639個詞條，並將其分別收入十七個門類。

1. 天文門　　（42詞條）
2. 地理門　　（70詞條）
3. 時令門　　（40詞條）
4. 人物門　　（82詞條）
5. 珍寶門　　（25詞條）

6. 走獸門　（58詞條）
7. 聲色門　（28詞條）
8. 花木門　（29詞條）
9. 菓木菜門　（31詞條）
10. 飲食門　（47詞條）
11. 衣服門　（53詞條）
12. 飛禽門　（26詞條）
13. 身體門　（38詞條）
14. 馬鞍鞦器械門　（36詞條）
15. 房舍車輛門　（7詞條）
16. 鐵器門　（11詞條）
17. 軍器什物門　（16詞條）

同樣一部對譯詞典也出現在《武備志》中。《武備志》，明茅元儀輯，共二百四十卷，廣采歷代軍事書籍兩千余種纂輯而成。全文二百余萬字，七百三十八幅圖，有明天启元年（1621）刻本。該書第二百二十七卷"北虜考"中收錄了與《登壇必究》之《北虜譯語》如出一轍的漢語蒙古語對譯詞典。但該詞典未註名稱，故有些學者稱該詞典爲《北虜考》[①]。詞典用字方面完全與《登壇必究》之《北虜譯語》相同，在中古蒙古語研究領域中沒有獨立的版本價值，因此本文不做考證。

《登壇必究》版本主要有明萬曆刻本、清復刻本、清刻本等。各版本間存在較大差異。出現這些差異的主要原因是乾隆時期四庫編修背景下的清代禁書政策。

二、清代禁書運動及《登壇必究》

在中國歷史上，各個朝代均有不同程度的文字獄及禁書運動。禁書一詞，最早見於宋人蘇轍《欒城集》之《乞載損待高麗事件札子》一文，謂"不許買禁物禁書及諸毒藥"[②]。王彬對禁書的概念做了如下闡釋："禁書是國家通過行政手段而禁止刊印、流布、閱讀的書籍。（中略）禁書真正作爲具有政治色彩的圖書術語而流傳天下，只是清朝以後的事。"[③]清朝統治階層清楚地認識到，支配知識精英階層就是統治中國的關鍵

① 烏滿都夫《蒙古譯語詞典》，北京：民族出版社，1995年，601頁。

② 蘇轍《欒城集》（卷四十六）《御史中丞論時事札子十三首》。見郭预衡，郭英德主編，新版校評修訂本《唐宋八大家散文總集》"卷10蘇轍"，石家庄：河北人民出版社，2013年，7222頁。

③ 王彬《清代禁書總述》，北京：中國書店出版社，1999年，1頁。

所在。因此，爲鞏固其統治地位，對知識階層的意識形態加強了控制④。

清代文字獄始於順治和康熙年代，乾隆年間發展成爲大規模禁書運動。可以说，禁書運動在乾隆編修四庫全書過程中達到巔峰，成爲一場修書與禁書合二爲一的大規模政治文化運動。這次禁書運動始於乾隆三十九年（1774）。黄裳在其《書林一支——清代的禁書》一文中指出："清代禁書政策的醞釀誕生，實際上怕是始於乾隆三十九年兩廣總督李侍尧查繳屈大均诗文的奏摺。乾隆皇帝從這裏得到啟發，才下决心逐步實施、全面推廣的。"⑤乾隆三十九年八月詔書曾明言"明季末造野史甚多，其間毁譽任意，傳聞異辭，必有詆觸本朝之語，正當及此一番查辦，盡行銷燬，杜遏邪言，以正人心而厚風俗，斷不宜置之不辦"⑥。當時，爲了編修四庫全書，乾隆下令收集整理各地古籍文獻，一方面，對其進行整理抄錄；另一方面，嚴格審查所有典籍文獻中的內容及字句運用特徵。如果發現有違反清政府利益，污衊滿洲與蒙古等北方民族的字句，就將該書徹底銷燬，或者刪除相關部分，甚至進行相應修改。R. Kent Guy在他的*The Emperor's Four Treasures*一書中指出，"編纂四庫全書的陰暗面在於1770年末期至1780年初期，2400部書籍被銷毁，四五百本書籍被刪改"⑦。

乾隆朝禁書運動大約持續了近二十年。孫殿起在其《清代禁書知見錄》自序中指出，"當時對舊籍之追繳燬銷與四庫開館相始終，大都由軍機處、四庫館分別令各省隨處搜繳，先後近二十年"。這期間，各地搜繳過程中，告訐之風應運而起。由於各地漢人官員及文人的舉發，勢利小人挾嫌控告，導致發生了許多文字獄、筆禍事件。文字獄、禁燬書籍的起因大多源於告發與檢舉。然而，對於清代禁書運動的性質，前人過多強調滿人的野蠻與無知，卻忽視了事件起因還在於漢人官員間的權利爭奪。

衆所周知，四庫全書是漢文典籍大型集成，四庫編修過程中產生的禁書政策也是針對漢文典籍的政治措施，蒙古文典籍文獻並不包括在乾隆禁書運動的審查範圍之內。但是，這場禁書運動卻給一些記錄蒙古語的文獻資料帶來了一定程度上的影響。受其影響

---

④ R. Kent Guy, *The Emperor's Four Treasures: Scholars and the State in the Late Ch'ien-lung Era*, Cambridge, Mass.: Harvard University Press, 1987, p. 17. "When the Manchus began to rule China proper in the mid-seven-tenth century, they were confronted with three challenges from intellectuals. The first came from voluntary organizations of literati （wen-she） formed in increasing numbers in the late Ming, partly to influence government policy, but more importantly to influence civil service examiners and thus increase their members' chances in the competition for office. A second challenge to the new regime from the intellectuals was explicit, ethnic anti- Manchuism. Finally, Manchus were confronted with the challenge of having to learn to use effectively the abstract and literary language of Chinese government, including the proper ways of manipulating the classical canon to justify their own rule."

⑤ 《讀書》1987年第3期，92—97頁。

⑥ 王重民輯《辦理四庫全書檔案》，北平：國立北平圖書館排印本，1934年。見乾隆三十九年八月五日諭。另見南炳文、白新良《清史紀事本末》（乾隆朝），上海：上海大学出版社，2006年，1759頁。

⑦ R. Kent Guy, *The Emperor's Four Treasures: Scholars and the State in the Late Ch'ien-lung Era*, p.1. "The darker side of the effort was a campaign of censorship undertaken by the imperial court in the late 1770s and early 1780s.By some courts many as 2400 titles were destroyed in this campaign, and another four or five hundred 'revised' by official fiat."

最深的是收錄漢語蒙古語對譯詞典的明代軍事類百科全書。

明代編纂的军事類書，数量多、內容豐富。如《登壇必究》《武備志》等，都是具有較高歷史文化價值的資料。明代編修的兵書內容主要特點之一在於書中包含了相當一部分描述北方民族歷史、地理、風俗、文化、軍情等方面的重要信息。特别是對蒙古及女真等北方民族的描述篇幅較多、範圍較廣，其中所述軍事戰略方針，主要是針對北方民族。

乾隆四十一年開始，政府部門對明人編修的軍事類圖書進行審查。最詳細的記載見於《大清高宗皇帝實録》自乾隆四十一年五月至乾隆四十三年閏六月，其記載如下：

> 明人所刻類書，其邊塞兵防等門，所有触礙字樣，固不可存，然祇須刪去數卷，或刪去數篇，或改定字句，亦不必因一二卷帙，遂癈全部。他若南宋人書之斥金，明初人書之斥元，其悖於義理者，自當從刪，涉于詆詈者，自当从改，其書均不必燬。使無礙之書，原聽其照舊流行，而應禁之書自不致仍前藏匿，方爲盡善，著四庫館總裁等，妥恊查辦。粘籤呈覧，候朕定奪，並將此通諭中外知之。[⑧]

明代編纂的兵書中描述和闡釋北方民族的部分，使用了較多歧視性、侮辱性字句。這些字句都屬於“違礙字句”。因此，《登壇必究》《武備志》[⑨]等兵書大多成爲禁燬書目。

《登壇必究》是乾隆四十年（1775）由江蘇巡撫薩載奏繳，“載武備事宜”，乾隆四十年三月二十四日奏准[⑩]。另外，乾隆四十二年十一月初二日，浙江巡撫三寶奏繳，“登壇必究八部刊本”[⑪]。乾隆四十三年六月二十九日，江蘇巡撫楊魁重繳“登壇必究二十三部”，“咨解軍機處投收銷燬合併陳明”[⑫]。乾隆四十四年九月初六日閩浙總督三寶再次奏繳“登壇必究三部刊本”[⑬]。

姚覲元《清代禁毁书目・補遺一》中記載了銷燬《登壇必究》的具體事由。記載如下：

> 登壇必究一部三十二册
>
> 查登壇必究係明王鳴鶴撰，皆論次兵家事宜,多係雜湊成書，並無發明，書中有觸礙字句，其二十一至二十四共四卷，原板挖去，均係違礙之處，應請銷燬[⑭]。

從上述奏繳文中可以看出，《登壇必究》之所以成爲禁燬書目的原因在於書中包含

⑧ 《大清高宗純（乾隆）皇帝實録》（二一），台北：華文書局，1963年，15013—15015頁。

⑨ 王彬《清代禁書總述》，北京：中國書店出版社，1999年，454頁。“此書爲安徽巡撫李質穎奏繳，乾隆四十年（1775）十一月二十日奏准禁毁。”

⑩ 參閱雷夢辰《清代各省禁書彙考》，北京：北京圖書館出版社，1989年，152頁。

⑪ 參閱雷夢辰《清代各省禁書彙考》，215—230頁。

⑫ 參閱雷夢辰《清代各省禁書彙考》，159—168頁。

⑬ 參閱雷夢辰《清代各省禁書彙考》，191—203頁。

⑭ 參閱（清）姚覲元《清代禁毁書目補遺一》，北京：商務印書館，1957年，240頁。

了"觸礙字句"，禁燬範圍是"第二十一卷至二十四卷"，禁燬方式爲"原版挖去"，並"銷燬"違礙之處。然而，由於銷燬執行不夠徹底，銷燬方式及手段也有不同。因此各地留存的版本中，第二十一至二十四卷的抽燬程度及範圍存在較大差異。有些版本只在目錄中刪除了這四卷的名稱，原文卻未被抽掉。還有些版本只把違礙字句刪除了，有些版本將觸礙字句刻成墨圍"□□"，有些則對相關字句進行了修改。孫殿起曾指出："四庫館臣以後並議定查辦違礙書目條款，凡宋明人著作中稱遼金元爲敵國者，俱應酌量改正，如有議論偏謬尤甚者，仍行簽出擬銷，卽下至於書中有挖空字面，墨塗字樣，缺行空格，亦指爲意存違悖，語必干犯，都在撤毀之例。卽幸而得存，亦復大加點竄，盡改本來面目。"[15]

漢語蒙古語對譯詞典《北虜譯語》是《登壇必究》第二十二卷的內容。顯而易見，該詞典屬於"違礙之處"，無疑《北虜譯語》是主要禁燬対象之一。

乾隆之後，禁書運動逐漸減弱，禁毀政策開始鬆動，觸礙內容範圍有所縮小。因此道光年間，《登壇必究》得以再版。由于相關"違礙之處"原版已被挖去銷燬，因此再版時有必要對銷燬部分進行重修及補缺。在這一過程中，發生了不同程度的錯改及誤補等現象，導致清刻本與明刻本之間出現了一些名詞術語、內容形式以及用詞用字方面的差異。這些差異主要體現在禁燬部分，即第二十一至二十四卷裏。再版導致漢語蒙古語對譯詞典中的音譯漢字[16]使用方式與明刻本之間有了較大差異，甚至由於過度修改與補充，清刻本裏出現了一些拼寫錯誤問題。

三、《北虜譯語》版本比較

版本學，是研究古籍不同版本特徵和差異、鑒別其真僞優劣的一門學科。研究版本的主要目的之一，是通過版本鑒定，給社會提供最可靠、最全面、質量最好的文獻資料。《登壇必究》版本流傳主要有，明代萬曆二十七年刻本。萬曆之後刊印多次，有明萬曆刻清初印本、清初刻本、清道光活字印本以及一些民間各種抄本。

迄今爲止，我们在中國、日本、美國各大圖書館進行廣泛的調查與搜集，共獲得十五部《登壇必究》文本。通过比較研究《北虜譯語》用字及拼寫特徵發現，這十五部文本屬於六種不同版本。本文以拉丁字母缩略法，分别簡稱這六種版本[17]。具體如下：

HYL　哈佛燕京圖書館藏，明萬曆刻本，編號 T8917/1164。框高21厘米，宽13.5厘米。

---

⑮　孫殿起輯《清代禁書知見錄》，上海：商務印書館，1957年，1頁。

⑯　"音譯漢字"是指拼寫蒙古語語音所使用的漢字。有些學者也稱其爲"漢字注音""漢字音標"等。本文使用"音譯漢字"稱呼拼寫蒙古語語音的漢字符號系統。此概念在本文中，僅限於用漢字記錄蒙古語語音的文獻資料。

⑰　《登壇必究》版本考證需要從封面、牌記、序跋、目錄、版式、字體、紙張、刻工、避諱等諸多內容進行考證鑒定。本文旨在比較漢語蒙古語對譯詞典部分，故版本分類也限於第二十二卷之《北虜譯語》。

PUM　北京大学圖書館藏明萬曆刻本。收《四庫禁燬書叢刊》子部34與35册（北京出版社，1997年）。

ZBJ　中國兵書集成，据明萬曆刻本影印。原書版框高20.7厘米，寬14.2厘米。

HAS　匈牙利科學院圖書館藏版本[18]。

PUQ　北京大学圖書館善本特藏閱覽No.9060.清刻本。原書版框高208毫米，寬308毫米。收《續修四庫全書》子部兵家類960與961册。

IMU　内蒙古大学圖書館藏清刻本。

根據刻印刊行時間，可將這六種版本列入兩類。一類爲明刻本，包括HYL、PUM、ZBJ版本。另一類爲清刻本，包括HAS、PUQ、IMU版本。明刻本之三種版本間版式大致類同，一頁十行，白口單黑魚尾，四周雙邊，版心上鎸書名，中鎸類目名稱及卷次，下鎸頁數字數等。清刻本版式爲一頁九行，白口單魚尾，四周單邊，版心上鎸書名，中鎸卷次及類目名稱，下鎸頁數。

清刻本《登壇必究》之《北虜譯語》，受禁書運動之影響，與明萬曆刻本相比，發生較大變化，尤其是詞典名稱及音譯漢字選用方面有明顯區别。

（一）關於詞典名稱

上述六種對譯詞典版本有兩種不同名稱。一個是《北虜譯語》，另一個是《譯語》。《北虜譯語》這一名稱主要出現在明刻本，而《譯語》這一名稱名称出現在清刻本。究其缘由，还需從清代禁書運動歷史背景解析。

前述，《北虜譯語》屬《登壇必究》第二十二卷，即“違礙之處”，也就是说詞典中包含了一些“觸礙字句”。在清代，什麼樣的字句屬於“觸礙字句”？對此，陳垣在其《舊五代史輯本發覆》中，將清朝避諱字句分爲十个等級。“即忌虜第一，忌戎第二，忌胡第三，忌夷狄第四，忌犬戎第五，忌藩及酋第六，忌伪忌賊第七，忌犯闕第八，忌漢第九，雜忌第十。”[19]

衆所周知，“北虜”或“虜”是中國古代稱北方外族的貶稱。無論是從政治立場，还是血緣關係，清朝統治者都不会認同用“虜”字来稱呼蒙古或北方外族。因此，“北虜”二字成为“觸礙字句”，再版時需加以刪改。結果，清代再版《北虜譯語》時，將“北虜”二字刻意刪除，只留下《譯語》二字作爲詞典名稱。清朝對於“虜”字的避諱，不僅表現在古籍文獻校勘考據方面，就連地名中出現“虜”字，都需刪改。如明永樂初築的寧夏“平虜城”，雍正三年（1725）改爲“平羅縣”。還有寧夏“套虜”改爲“陶樂”等[20]。

---

⑱　Louis Ligeti 在1928—1931年第一次在中國旅行時收集到的版本。

⑲　見陳垣《舊五代史輯本發覆》，北平：輔仁大學，1937年。

⑳　向熹《漢語避諱研究》，北京：商務印書館，2016年，239頁。

在一些研究《登壇必究》之《北虜譯語》的成果中，該詞典被稱爲《譯語》，顯然，這並不是明代刻本中的詞典原名，而是清代刻本中被刪改后的名稱而已。

關於北方族群名稱，詞典中另有兩處違礙字句。即第76詞條與第183詞條的漢語部分。在明刻本裏，這兩個詞條分別爲“北虜”與“女直”。而在清刻本裏，兩個詞條的漢語部分均被挖空墨圍，成爲“□□”的形式。吴哲夫在《清代禁毀書目研究》中指出，不仅“羌胡”“夷狄”“奴戎”“虜蠻”等字句被禁止使用，連“建州”“女真”“女直”等有關滿人的地名，族群名稱也屬於禁忌字句[21]。因此，詞典裏的“北虜”和“女直”二詞，自然是“觸礙字句”，成爲被挖去墨圍的對象。除對譯詞典之外，《登壇必究》其他內容中，也多處出現“北虜”及“女直”等違礙字句。有些清刻本，將“北虜”改爲“北狄”，“女直”改爲“海西”等。這說明，道光年間再版《登壇必究》時，對“狄”字的避諱已經沒有陳垣先生所述那麼嚴格，比乾隆時期鬆弛許多。清代違礙字句在不同時期，界定範圍有所不同，對違礙字句的刪改標準也有區别。“武備志”對譯詞典的版本差異即是較顯著的例子。一些清刻本“武備志”中，唯有“女直”一詞被挖空墨圍，而“北虜”一詞未做同樣處理。從這一點來看，有可能在清代某一段時期，“女直”及“建州”[22]等關於滿人的族群名稱和地名，比“北虜”“夷狄”等更敏感，屬於犯諱更爲嚴重的名稱。

（二）關於音譯漢字之使用情況

在音譯漢字的使用方面，明刻本与清刻本之間最爲顯著的差異在於拼寫蒙古語ča語音的漢字上。有些版本使用“叉”字拼寫蒙古語ča音，而有些版本則用“義”字拼寫。這個拼寫差異共出現在28個詞條中。如表1所示：

表1

詞條序號	漢語	明刻本	清刻本	蒙古語轉寫
11	雪	叉速	義速	času
33	亮了	叉亦把	義亦把	čaiba
35	下雪	叉速我羅難	義速我羅難	času orunam
103	白土廠	叉汪哈兒阿	義汪哈兒阿	čaqan qalγa
104	白塔峪	叉汗速補兒阿	義汗速補兒阿	čaqan suburγa
113	時	叉	義	ča[q]
152	後日	叉只得堵兒	義只得堵兒	čaǰid[ü]dür
232	栢板的	叉兒吉	義兒吉	čargi
294	羝羊	忽叉	忽義	quča

㉑ 吴哲夫《清代禁毀書目研究》，台北：嘉興水泥公司文化基金會，1969年，28—29頁。

㉒ 雷夢辰《清代各省禁書彙考》，84頁，《建州考》謂“書名犯諱”。可見，清代“建州”“女直”等名詞屬於避諱名詞。

续表

詞條序號	漢語	明刻本	清刻本	蒙古語轉寫
307	兒馬	阿叉兒阿	阿義兒阿	ağarγa
318	青白馬	叉哈兒莫林	義哈兒莫林	čaγal morin
320	銀鬃馬	叉必塔兒	義必塔兒	čabidar
324	白馬	叉汗莫林	義汗莫林	čaqan morin
336	粉嘴馬	叉汗忽失文莫林	義汗忽失文莫林	čaqan qusi'un morin
337	豹肚馬	叉哈兒莫林	義哈兒莫林	čaγal/ǰaγal morin
339	騂眼馬	叉兒吉莫林	義兒吉莫林	čalgi morin
349	栢	叉克剌速	義克剌速	ča[q]rasu
383	核桃	叉哈哈	義哈哈	ǰaγa[q]
385	白菓	叉汗者泥四	義汗者泥四	čaqan ǰemis
397	蒜	撒兒叉	撒兒義	sar[im] ča[q]
403	白菜	叉汗奴惡	義汗奴惡	čaqan noγo
435	飽了	叉堵把	義堵把	čadba
454	衣服	忽必叉速	忽必義速	qub<i>času
473	鞋	叉魯	義魯	čaru[q]
504	白	叉漢	義漢	čaqa-n
528	燕兒	哈兒叉	哈兒義	qarča-[i]
529	麻燕	虎克兒哈兒叉	虎克兒哈兒義	hüker qarča-[i]
626	頓項	叉兒吉	義兒吉	čargi/calgi

"叉"和"義"二字，就語音條件來看，顯然，"叉"字的語音成分接近蒙古語ča音，而"義"字的發音與蒙古語的ča相距甚遠，不具備拼寫蒙古語ča音的條件。清刻本用"義"字拼寫出的帶有ča音的詞彙，完全不符合蒙古語原文詞意和語音形式。如表1所示，表示"雪"的蒙古語*času*一詞，明刻本的"叉速"，可構擬爲*času*，符合蒙古語原文語音。而清刻本的"義速"則構擬爲*yisu*，不符合蒙古語原文語音及詞義。以此類推，表1所示28個詞條中，用"義"字拼寫的詞在蒙古語裏不存在，顯然是錯誤的拼寫。清刻本使用"義"字錯誤拼寫蒙古語ča音的原因，在於再版時過度的修改以及參與編修人員不具備蒙古語相關知識所致。

我们收集到的三種明刻本，基本都用"叉"字來拼寫蒙古語ča音。其中PUM與ZBJ兩個版本，則使用"叉"字的俗體字形"义"字來拼寫蒙古語的ča音。此"义"字不同於現代漢語的"义"字。明刻本中出現的"义"字，是"叉"字的俗體字。關於俗體字的概念，《辭源》釋"俗體字是在民間流行的異體字，別於正體而言"[23]。唐顏元孫的

[23] 《辭源》（修訂本），北京：商務印書館，1979年，221頁。

《干祿字書》把漢字分爲俗、通、正三體，並對其概念進行了解釋㉔。凡是區別於正字的異體字，都可以認爲是廣義上的“俗體字”。它可以是簡化字，也可以是繁化字，可以是後起字，也可以是古體字。正與俗的界線是隨著時代而不斷變化的。

關於俗體“乂”字形，張湧泉在《漢語俗字研究》中指出，“乂”字一身而兼三職”㉕。於此同時還列舉實例，對其三職進行了闡釋。“乂”在《清平山堂話本·簡貼和尚》中，代表“叉”字，在同書《快嘴李翠蓮記》中，是“又”字，在《京本通俗小說·馮玉梅團圓》中，是“義”字㉖。除此之外，“乂”作爲“叉”字的俗體字，在敦煌文獻中也頻繁出現㉗。

俗體字同形異字的情況有時會造成辨認或理解上的困難。由於“乂”字“一身兼三職”，因此，《北虜譯語》明刻本中的“乂”字，可以是“叉”字，也可以是“又”字，還可以是“義”字。顯然，清人誤將“乂”看作是“義”字的俗體，生硬地還原其正體字，导致錯誤的蒙古語拼寫。這些錯誤的出现，除漢字俗體字誤讀之外，也與清代文人學術氛圍有直接關係。

清代康雍乾時期，對中國古代典籍進行大規模的訓詁、注疏、校勘、輯佚、辨僞、考訂，在這些過程中，形成了以考證爲特長的“乾嘉考據學派”，使考據成爲清代有別於其他朝代學術思潮的一大特色。考據學派對中國歷史上以儒家經典爲核心的經、史、子、集等各類古籍，從文字、聲韻、校勘入手，一一加以考訂，通過校勘，糾正其訛誤。清代對中國傳統文化的傳承方面呈現出由宋返漢，通經復古的勢頭。強調由文字音訓以明經達道是乾嘉學派的治學理念，也是當時社會文化思潮的顯著特色。在這種復古尊漢的風氣下，俗體字是乾嘉學派文人的禁忌，正統文人對俗體字存有各種偏見。因而，在重刻古籍文本時，清代文人將“粗俗不堪”的俗體字改爲“脫俗儒雅”的正體字，自然合情合理。清人將《登壇必究》明刻本中“叉”字的俗體“乂”字，“復原”爲正體“義”字，不能不说是个時代產物。

除上述“叉”字之外，明刻與清刻本音譯漢字的使用上，另有六處不同。具體如表2：

表2

詞條序號	漢語	明刻本	清刻本	蒙古語轉寫
109	大黑山	哈塔麻得目	塔哈麻得目	qatama dem
130	閏月	揑墨兀兒撒剌	墨兀兒撒剌	neme'ür sara
354	梨树	阿力麻莫多	阿加麻莫多	alima modu
361	粗	伯堵文	伯補文	büdü'ün
582	板腸	穩補速	穩速補	ünbüsü
611	鏵子	安扎速	安扎連	anǰasu

㉔ 顏元孫《干祿字書》，《叢書集成初編》，北京：中華書局，1985年，3—4頁。

㉕ 張湧泉在《漢語俗字研究》，北京：商務印書館，2016年，125頁。

㉖ 張湧泉在《漢語俗字研究》，125頁。

㉗ 參照黃征《敦煌俗字典》，上海：上海教育出版社，2005年，38頁。

表2所示內容可以看出，第109詞條“大黑山*Qatama dem*”一詞，明刻本拼寫爲“哈塔麻得目”，符合蒙古語原文發音，而清刻本所作“塔哈麻得目”，是由於抄錄錯誤導致第一音節與第二音節位置顛倒。第130詞條“閏月*neme'ür sara*”一詞，明刻本拼寫爲“捏墨兀兒撒剌”，而清刻本作“墨兀兒撒剌”，抄錄時遺漏詞首“捏”字。第354“梨树*alima modu*”一詞，明刻本拼寫爲“阿力麻莫多”，而清刻本是“阿加麻莫多”，顯然清刻本將第二音節的“力”字誤寫爲“加”字。第361“粗*büdü'ün*”一詞，明刻本是“伯堵文”，清刻本是“伯補文”，把第二音階的“堵”誤寫爲“補”。第611“鏵子*anǰasu*”一詞，明刻本是“安扎速”，而清刻本是“安扎連”，將“速”字誤抄爲“連”字[28]。

如上所考，清刻本音譯漢字的拼寫錯誤較多，有一些不符合蒙古語語音的詞條，而明刻本音譯漢字的拼寫更接近其原文語音特徵，錯拼誤寫較少。可見，明刻本比清刻本更可靠、更接近原文。

另外需要提到的是，除音譯漢字以外，明刻本與清刻本之間，還存在漢語部分書寫差異。第250詞條，明刻本書寫爲“洙沙”，清刻本則書寫爲“硃砂”。第432詞條，明刻本書寫爲“蜂蜜”，清刻本則書寫爲“烽密”。第577詞條，明刻本書寫爲“膽”，而清刻本則書寫爲“胆”。

明刻本與清刻本《北虜譯語》版本差異，主要在於詞典名稱及蒙古語“ča”音的拼寫方式上。上述分析結果充分說明，這些差異產生的原因與清代禁書運動有直接的關係。考證《北虜譯語》版本源流，比較其異同的目的在於爲再構蒙古語語音提供最可靠的版本。因此，還有必要進一步比較分析明刻本不同版本以及清刻本不同版本之間的差異。

（三）清刻本各版本間差異

根據對該詞典所收詞條的逐一比較，我們發現清刻本三種版本間也存在用字方面的不同。具體如下（表3）：

表3

詞條序號	漢語	PUQ	HAS	IMU	蒙古語轉寫
86	低	孛我你	孛我倫	孛我倫	bo'oni/boɣoni
93	墩臺	墩臺	壞臺	壞臺	qara'ul
455	褀子	禿兒哈	兀哈兒	兀哈兒	tur'a/ uqar
527	鴨	奴谷速	奴塔速	奴塔速	nuɣusu
533	頭	黑乞	奴堵兒	奴堵兒	heki
534	髪	忽速	剌速	剌速	hüsü

---

[28] 第582“板腸，穩補速ünbüsü?”一詞目前無法確定。似與《五體清文鑑》之飯肉類中的一詞“版腸，ümüsü”有關聯。

续表

詞條序號	漢語	PUQ	HAS	IMU	蒙古語轉寫
552	膊子	苦出文	苦印速	苦印速	küǰü'ün
561	脚	苦兒	芳見	芳見	kül
576	心	主兒揹	王兒揹	王兒揹	ǰürken
589	稍繩	敢主阿	敢土阿	敢土阿	γanǰu'a/γanǰuγa
592	皮條	速兒	哈兒	哈兒	sur
593	黏價子	黏價子	黏以子	黏以子	keǰim
595	鞭子	米納	阿納	阿納	mina
625	盔	土剌阿	上剌阿	上剌阿	tula'a

表3所示14個詞條中，12個詞條是蒙古語音譯漢字拼寫方面的差異。第86詞條，“低*boγuni*”，在PUQ中是“孛我你”，而在HAS及“IMU是“孛我倫”。後兩者將末尾音節的“你”誤寫爲“倫”字。第527“鴨*nuγusu*”一詞，PUQ是“奴谷速”，而HAS和IMU中是“奴塔速”，後者將第二音節的“谷”字誤寫爲“塔”字。第533“頭*heki*”一詞，PUQ是“黑乞”，而HAS和IMU都是“奴堵兒”，後者有可能是將其他詞條誤抄所造成。第534“髮*hüsü*”一詞，PUQ爲“忽速”，而HAS和IMU是“剌速”，後者第一音節拼寫錯誤。第552“膊子*küǰü'ün*”一詞，PUQ是“苦出文”，而HAS和IMU都是“苦印速”，顯然後者是拼寫錯誤。第561“脚*kül*”一詞，在PUQ是“苦兒”，而在HAS和IMU都是“芳見”，後者拼寫錯誤。第576“心*ǰürken*”一詞，在PUQ是“主兒揹”，而在HAS和IMU中是“王兒揹”，後者將“主”字誤寫爲“王”字。第589“稍繩*γanǰu'a*”一詞，在PUQ是“敢主阿”，而在HAS和IMU都是“敢土阿”，後者第二音節“主”字被誤寫爲“土”字。第592“皮條*sur*”一詞，在PUQ是“速兒”，而在HAS和IMU都是“哈兒”，後者第一音節被誤寫爲“哈”字。第595“鞭子*mina*”一詞，在PUQ是“米納”，而在HAS和IMU則是“阿納”，顯然後者是拼寫錯誤。第625“盔*tula'a*”一詞，在PUQ是“土剌阿”，而在HAS和IMU都是“上剌阿”，顯然後者將第一音節的“土”字誤寫爲“上”字。

另外，第93與593詞條的漢語部分也有差異。“墩臺”一詞的“墩”字在PUQ中正確，而在HAS和IMU中被誤寫爲“壞”字。第593“黏價子”一詞，在HAS和IMU中誤寫爲“黏以子”[29]。

上述分析說明，PUQ版本的拼寫比較接近明刻本，一定程度上保留了明刻本音譯漢字的使用特徵。而HAS与IMU版本的拼寫方式比較類同，極有可能源於類似的版本。其中，HAS版本的錯拼、誤寫較多，有些個別錯誤是其他版本中不存在的。

㉙ 第455“襖子，禿兒哈 或 兀哈兒tur'a/ uqar”一詞目前無法確定。

（四）明刻本各版本間差異

我们所收集到的三種《北虜譯語》明刻本，在音譯漢字的使用方面大致相同，只有少數幾個詞條的拼寫方式有所不同。如，第288“鹿*buγu*”一詞，在ZBJ版本中爲“僃兀”，而在HYL版本中是“補兀”。第427“甜*amtatai*”一詞，在ZBJ中是“傣塔太”，而在HYL裡則是“俺塔太”。还有第563“拳頭*nudurγa*”一詞，在ZBJ中是“妖堵兒阿”，而HYL中是“奴堵兒阿”。第598詞條的“彎頭*qadar*”一詞，在ZBJ裡是“哈荅完”，而在HYL裡是“哈荅兒”。第75詞條“小壹千*üčüken minγan*”一詞，在HYL中是“五出指民案”，而在PUM 中爲“五山指民案”。這些詞條的拼寫差異完全可以說明，HYL版本的拼寫精確度高于PUM及ZBJ版本。

綜上所述，明刻本與清刻本《北虜譯語》之間，除了六個詞條的誤寫誤抄之差别外，主要版本差異在於詞典名稱及蒙古語“ča”音字的拼寫方式上。以上所分析的結論說明，導致這些差異之根本原因在於清代禁書運動背景下產生的古籍文獻删改現象以及乾嘉學派治學理念所崇尚的“復古風潮”所致。本文結合清代禁書運動歷史背景，通过對《北虜譯語》六種不同版本的比較分析，揭示了各版本間存在的異同之處及產生差異的緣由，從而得出HYL版本是目前最爲可靠、最接近原文版本的結論。因此，我們主張構拟《北虜譯語》蒙古語語音時，應參照HYL版本，即哈佛燕京圖書館藏版本，以此爲根本依據。

The Influences of the Book-Banning Movement on Mongolian Documents in Qing Dynasty: A Comparative Study on the Edition of a Sino-Mongol Glossary Known as the Bei-lu Yi-yu

Kereidjin D. Bürgüd

The Middle Mongolian language is known from written documents that were recorded in many different scripts, including Uighur-Mongol script, Phags-pa script, Chinese script, and Arabic script. Among these, sources written in Chinese script are by far the most important for the phonological reconstruction of Middle Mongolian. These transcriptions are comprised of Chinese terms and their corresponding Mongolian terms, where the phonetic value of Chinese characters is used to denote Mongolian pronunciation. The Mongolian words denoted by the Chinese script represent the sounds of the Mongolian words at the time of compilation.

This is a study of a version of the Sino-Mongol glossary known as the *Bei-lu Yi-yu*北虜譯

語(also known as *Yi-yu*譯語), which is contained in the *Deng-tan Bi-jiu*登壇必究. The *Bei-lu Yi-yu* is a list of words, as well as a Sino-Mongol glossary, which consists of 639 vocabulary words divided into 17 *men* 門 (subject, categories) sections. Each entry consists of a Chinese word followed by its Mongolian translation also written in Chinese script. The present paper compares several editions of the *Bei-lu Yi-yu* and provides a large number of discrepancies between the Ming and Qing editions. Through my exploration of the Chinese characters, I have arrived at the conclusion that the large number of discrepancies mainly comes from the book-banning movement during the Qianlong period, and I conclude that the Harvard-Yenching edition is the most accurate one, and most likely to reflect the original version.

《雲使》在蒙古

薩其仁貴

《雲使》（*Meghadūta*）是古代印度第一部長篇抒情詩，大約創作於公元4—5世紀。其作者迦梨陀娑（Kālidāsa）是古印度“最偉大的古典梵語詩人和戲劇家”。《雲使》代表古典梵語抒情詩歌的最高藝術成就，在印度國內外廣爲流傳。本文在整體介紹《雲使》的基礎上，主要探討《雲使》在蒙古地區的傳播與影響。

一、梵文《雲使》總介

（一）《雲使》的版本以及地位

在印度，《雲使》自問世以來廣泛受到文人評論家的青睞，反復被傳誦、抄錄和作註。據統計，目前《雲使》的手抄本共有40餘種，除了印度，在克什米爾、倫敦、巴黎、柏林和哥本哈根等地收藏。注釋本共50多種，最早的爲10世紀克什米爾學者瓦喇鉢提婆（Vallabhadeva）所注的《難語釋》（*Pañjikā*）。其餘注釋，因其內容和傳承關係已形成了三大體系，即東印度孟加拉體系、西印度耆那教體系和南印度摩利那他體系[①]。《雲使》在漫長的流傳過程中，未免遭到後人的竄改和增添，因而各版本內容不盡相同，詩節總數由110至127不等。耆那教體系詩節總數一般都在120个以上；孟加拉體系爲114—118之間；摩利那他體系爲115个詩節。

到19世紀，西方學者紛紛加入了《雲使》的校勘和翻譯工作。1813年，英國學者H. H. 威爾遜（Wilson）首次把《雲使》翻譯成英文并校勘出版。其后在1817年《雲使》的法文譯本，1847年德文譯本[②]依次出現。德國學者在《雲使》校勘研究方面也做了不少工作，較爲引人注目的有J.吉爾德邁斯特（Gildemeister）1841年的校勘本，A. F.施坦茨勒（Stenzler）1874年的校勘本以及破譯阿育王碑文的德國著名印度學家E.胡爾契（Hultzsch）1911年整理出版的《雲使》最古老的注釋——《難語注》。此外，印度著名版本學家S. K.德博士（Dr. Sushil Kumar De）基於大量資料重新校勘《雲使》，1957

① 摩利那他體系，指以14世紀著名的注釋家摩利那他（Mallinātha）的《更生注》（*Sañjīvinī*）爲代表的註解體系。

② 《雲使》德譯本譯者爲西方宗教學奠基人、著名語言學家麥克斯・穆勒（Max Müller）。

年在新德里出版，學界稱之爲《雲使》精校本。此精校本在校勘過程中比較重視《難語注》，詩節總數也與其相一致，为111个。

迦梨陀娑作品作爲學習古典梵語的典範而在印度的課堂上世代相傳。自10世紀以來迦梨陀娑作品的相關課件已找到約50件[③]，《雲使》是其中一部必不可少的重點教材。同樣在歷代梵語詩學理論著作中，迦梨陀娑的詩句也常被當作典範來運用。《雲使》也曾被多次引用，比如，9世紀的詩學理論家歡增（Ānandavardhana）在其著作《韻光》（*Dhvanyāloka*）中探討“莊嚴”（alaṃkāra）和“味”（rasa）的關係時說：“莊嚴是主者（味）的魅力因素，如同外表的裝飾美化人體。”那麼如何“恰當地使用”呢？他引用了《雲使》的一個詩節：

我在藤蔓裏看出你的腰身，在驚鹿的眼中
看出你的秋波，在明月中我見到你的面容，
孔雀翎中見你長髮，河水漣漪中你秀眉挑動，
唉，好嬌嗔的人呀！還是找不出一處和你相同。

（金克木譯文，《雲使》104節）

並指出“詩人只有這樣運用莊嚴，才能成功地傳達味”[④]。其後在10世紀印度詩學家恭多迦（Kuntaka）的《曲語生命論》（*Vakroktijīvita*）、11世紀的曼摩吒（Mammaṭa）的《詩光》（*Kāvyaprakāśa*）和14世紀毗首那特（Viśvanātha）的《文鏡》（*Sāhityadarpaṇa*）中都引用《雲使》詩句作爲典範。恭多迦還分析《雲使》的個別詩節后動情地寫道：“詩人在這裏展現的這種優美的意義確實是這部名爲《雲使》的作品的生命，令知音喜悅至極。”[⑤]

《雲使》版本眾多、流傳流傳，長期以來不僅被印度文人、理論家們津津樂道，同時也得到了西方學界的一致讚歎，西方學者們對《雲使》研究做出了重大貢獻，德國著名作家歌德先生也曾感慨：“Meghadūta，這雲彩使者，誰不願意把它放進我們的靈魂？”[⑥]《雲使》之所以在東西方文壇上如此顯赫，其原因最終可歸功於它的藝術成就。

（二）《雲使》的內容與藝術成就

《雲使》的主人公是印度神話中的一個小神靈——藥叉[⑦]。這不僅把人間情感表現得淋漓盡致，而且把詩人的想象空間擴展到神界，使詩作的描述背景變得更爲宏偉有氣

③ Daniel H. H. Ingalls, “Kālidāsa And The Attitudes Of The Golden Age”, *Journal of the American Oriental Society*, 1976, Vol. 96, No.1 (Jan-Mar).

④ 黃寶生譯《梵語詩學論著彙編》（上），北京：昆侖出版社，2008年，255—259頁。

⑤ 黃寶生譯《梵語詩學論著彙編》（上），514頁。

⑥ 〔印〕迦梨陀娑著，季羡林譯《沙恭達羅》，北京：人民文學出版社，1954年，譯本序。這裏，歌德先生讀到的應該是《雲使》英譯本和法譯本，因爲到歌德（1749—1832）先生逝世那年《雲使》德文譯本尚未問世。

⑦ 梵文yakṣa，又譯“夜叉”“捷疾鬼”等，能傷人。而在此處，即《雲使》中“藥叉”爲印度神話中的半神或小神靈，是財神俱毗羅的隨從，性情温和而無害。

勢。詩中講的是，居住在北方喜馬拉雅山中的一個藥叉，因疏忽職責受主人財神的懲罰，被貶謫到南方羅摩山靜修林中，承受與妻分離一年的痛苦。在那裏，他因思念愛妻變得如癡如狂，瘦骨如柴。雨季來臨之際，他看到山頂上烏雲密佈，內心更加激動⑧、熱淚盈眶，顧不上雨雲是"有情或無情"便請求它給心愛的妻子捎帶自己安好的訊息。於是他給雨雲指出了一條北行路線，描述了從羅摩山到喜馬拉雅山的名勝古跡、山川河流、城鎮鄉村，從而體現了作者對祖國大好河山的眷戀和熱愛。到了喜馬拉雅山，藥叉又以從遠到近的方式描述藥叉居住的阿羅迦城以及自己的家園，最後引出愛妻，並以18個詩節的篇幅形容愛妻的容貌，想像她在離別日子裏的各種情形。接著對愛妻傾訴衷腸，表述自己的癡情狂愛，並安慰和鼓勵妻子道，團聚的日子即將到來，他們很快會享受愛情的甘甜。最後，藥叉祝福雨雲翱翔天際，永不和閃電夫人相分離。《雲使》構思奇特，想像豐富，詩人别出心裁地選擇"藥叉"和"雨雲"的視角，從而使人間、神界和大自然融爲一體，尤其多次把"雨雲"與"河流"的關係描述爲相思相愛的情人關係，以此渲染整個詩篇濃烈的愛情氛圍，實現了"自然頌"與"愛情贊"的巧妙結合。在愛情方面，雖然在寫分離和思念的痛苦，但整個詩篇洋溢著一種積極樂觀的上進精神，"思念或哀傷的情緒並非占主導地位，而對富貴的展現和激情的抒發才真正使它（指《雲使》——引者）成爲了抒情詩"⑨。

從形式上來講，《雲使》110多詩節，共440多個詩行一律用了同一種格律——"緩進調"（Mandākrāntā）。其特點爲每個詩節有四個音步（詩行），每個音步由長短（重輕）固定的17個音節構成，朗誦時第10個音節後面稍有停頓，即爲"————︶︶︶︶︶— —︶——︶——"⑩。"緩進調"是迦梨陀娑首創，屬於印度詩歌格律中較爲難和少見的，除了《雲使》，在迦梨陀娑的另一篇敘事詩《羅怙世系》中也曾出現。學者指出，"緩進調"因如同雨雲緩緩前行而得名，并根據《雲使》的內容認爲，前四個長音節表示藥叉因思念而惆悵的心情，接著五個短音節表示藥叉焦慮和激動的心情，其後長短音交替表示藥叉思念又焦慮的心情，最後兩個長音節表示藥叉對未來充滿信心而情緒趨於舒緩。可見《雲使》的韻律也很貼切地表達了主人公藥叉的情感波動，從而實現了內容和形式的巧妙結合。

---

⑧ "內心更加激動"的原因是，在印度，雨季裏在外行走極不方便，從而雨季到來之際在外的旅人都會返回家鄉，雨季也成了親人團聚的季節。因此與"每逢佳節倍思親"同理，藥叉看到雨雲（即雨季已經到來）而想到自己無法回家時，內心受到更大的觸動以致托雲送信。

⑨ Sushil Kumar De, *The Meghadūta of Kālidāsa*, 2nd ed., New Delhi: Sahitya Akademi, 1970, p. xxxii.

⑩ 此處"–"表示重音節，"︶"表示輕音節。輕音節，是指含短母音、其後只有單輔音的音節。重音節，一是指含一個長母音、其後跟隨一個或兩個輔音的音節，二是指含一個短母音、其後不只一個輔音相隨的音節。參考〔德〕A.F.施坦茨勒著，季羨林譯，段晴、范慕尤續補《梵文基礎讀本》，北京：北京大學出版社，2009年，7頁。另，以"隨韻"（ṃ/ṁ）和"止聲"（ḥ）結尾的音節也要看作是"重音節"。

二、《雲使》藏譯本與古代蒙古文學

蒙古人最初接觸《雲使》是通過其藏譯本。藏文譯本是《雲使》在印度國外的最早譯本，14世紀初由克什米爾學者、詩人蘇曼室利（Sumanaśrī），藏族譯師祥曲則茂（Byang chub rtse mo）和文法家南卡桑保（Nam mkha` bzang po）在西藏薩迦寺翻譯完成的。從13世紀後期到14世纪前期，這一階段在藏族文學史上具有里程碑意義。此時，印度詩學論著《詩鏡》被介紹到藏地，並在國師八思巴的大力支持下至元十四年（1277）由藏族譯師和印度學者合力完成了《詩鏡》的全部翻譯。這爲藏族文學帶來了新的氣息，《詩鏡》理論極大吸引了藏族高僧和文人的興趣，并影響譯師們開始翻譯印度文學經典，《雲使》正是在這個時候被譯成了藏文。后作爲語言文學理論的典範，入選藏文大藏經《丹珠爾》的“聲明部”，成了《丹珠爾》唯一一部純文學作品。

元代，忽必烈汗及其繼承者們大力支持藏傳佛教及佛經翻譯事業，朝廷中聚集了精通藏語和蒙古語的譯師，他們擔任要職，負責佛教事宜，并翻譯了不少藏文典籍。其中包括藏族高僧大德們的著作，如薩迦班智达貢噶堅贊的《薩迦格言》、國師八思巴的《彰所知論》，以及翻譯成藏文的印度佛教學者們的論著，如《入菩薩行論》（*Bodhicaryāvatāra*）、《聖五護大乘經》（*Pañcarakṣā*）、《金光明經》（*Suvarṇaprabhāsottama*）等。據統計“蒙元時期，蒙古文《甘珠爾》單行本近有二十篇。”[⑪]不僅如此，元代蒙古高僧還用藏、蒙兩種語言並行創作。在他們的創作中，印度文學的正文前後寫序言詩和跋文詩的傳統也已成了慣例。14世紀初的著名譯師、詩人搠思吉斡節兒（chos kyi ’od zer）用蒙古文撰寫了《摩訶迦梨頌》[⑫]，《入菩薩行論注》及其跋文詩的同時還用藏文撰寫了《佛十二行贊》。通過搠思吉斡節兒的詩文，梵語詩學中的“輸洛迦”（śloka）、“拔答迦”（pādaka）等詞彙也融入到了蒙古文學詞彙中[⑬]。可知，蒙古人與藏族人幾乎同時接受了梵文詩學理論，只是在蒙古的流傳沒有那麼廣泛，僅限於精通藏文的蒙古喇嘛文人之中。而《雲使》作爲此時重點介紹到藏文的印度文學作品，自然也會被這些蒙古高僧們所知和欣賞。

而到了16世紀後期，隨著藏傳佛教再度傳入蒙古地區，蒙古佛教文學界掀起了一股

---

⑪ 詳情請見寶力高《蒙古文佛教文獻研究》，北京：人民出版社，2012年，93頁。

⑫ 1902年德國探險隊在新疆吐魯番挖掘出土的文獻中發現了此文共69行殘片。題目爲後人所加，迄今爲止，我們稱它爲《摩訶迦羅頌》（*Mahākāla-yin maγtaγal*），但從其內容看，它實際上是《摩訶迦梨頌》（*Mahākālī -yin maγtaγal*）而非《摩訶迦羅頌》。

⑬ 由梵文的“śloka”和“pādaka”演變而來的蒙古語“silüg”和“badaγ”兩個如今已成爲蒙古文學中的術語，但詞義有所變化。在梵文中“śloka”（關於其來源參見史詩《羅摩衍那》—童年—第二章）指由特定格律形成的詩，其特點爲每個詩節有四個音步，每個音步有8個音節。而在蒙古語中“silüg”泛指“詩歌”。同樣，“pādaka”在梵語中指一個音步，一般一個詩節由4個音步構成，一個音步可以構成一個詩行。而在蒙古語中“badaγ”指一個詩節，而不是一個音步。14世紀初搠思吉斡節兒的用法與其梵文意思相吻合，發生詞義的變化是在後來的使用中造成的。

學習《詩鏡》理論的熱潮，藏語在蒙古佛教文學中的地位日益顯赫，蒙古喇嘛學者們紛紛用藏文撰寫《詩鏡》研究著作，成績斐然。在他們的文學創作中不難看出《雲使》的影響，主要呈現在以下兩個方面。

（一）《雲使》與蒙古喇嘛“書信文學”

在印度文學史上《雲使》曾一度帶來了“信使詩”（saṃdeśakāvya）熱，即《雲使》后出現了一大批模仿《雲使》的詩作，如今能查到的有《風使》《鸚鵡使》《蜜蜂使》《天鵝使》《月使》《杜鵑使》《孔雀使》等。但因爲這些“信使詩”藝術成就無法企及《雲使》而被淹沒在文學長河之中，只有《雲使》長盛不衰，“托雲帶信”的奇特想象也深入人心。黃寶生先生曾指出，在中國古代文學中雖然也有“托雲傳情”的念頭，但總體上覺得雲是漂浮不定而不可信的。如“郁陶思君未敢言，寄聲浮雲往不還”（曹丕《燕歌行》），“浮雲難嗣音，裴徊悵誰與”（任昉《別蕭諮議》）等。那麼，迦梨陀娑的“托雲捎信”的藝術想像，多半是跟印度的熱帶季風氣候有關。印度夏季的氣温高達四、五十度，被稱爲“死亡的季節”。夏季結束便是雨季，當南來的季風吹來帶雨的烏雲，印度人的喜悦心情是不言而喻的[⑭]。因而，迦梨陀娑《雲使》中的“雲”是“烏黑”而“凝重”，它載滿了大量的雨水從印度洋到喜馬拉雅山一路消除人們的煩熱。相比之下，蒙古高原歷來是以“藍天白雲”著稱，也沒有雨季的概念，因而如果沒有外來影響，在蒙古文學中產生《雲使》搬的藝術想像是比較難的。然而在蒙古喇嘛高僧們藏文書信中卻已出現了“新雲使”。18、19世紀著名的蒙古族佛學家阿拉善·阿旺丹德爾（1759—1840）稱自己的信件爲“新雲使”，信件的內容爲“雨水”，信件到達的地方爲“歡樂的園林”，而閱讀信件的聲音如同“雷鳴”般洪亮[⑮]。因而“蒙古喇嘛高僧們在其創作中從迦梨陀的《雲使》中吸取養分”[⑯]是無疑的。在蒙古喇嘛們的信件中，《雲使》的影響還具體體現在：

1.“恩師如雨雲”的比喻

如前所述，《雲使》的產生，與印度的氣候直接相關。在印度，一年分爲春季、夏季、雨季、秋季、露季、冬季六個季節，其中夏季最爲炎熱枯燥，而隨之而來的雨季會驅散炎熱，帶來清涼和濕潤，讓人歡欣鼓舞。因而在《雲使》中给予“雨雲”崇高的人格魅力，稱它爲“焦灼者的救星”而予以信任和希望。因爲“高貴者的成就在於解除受難者的痛苦”。与之类似，在蒙古高僧的信件中歌頌恩師为“以慈悲之清涼陰影，

⑭ 黃寶生《論迦梨陀娑的〈雲使〉》，《梵學論集》，北京：中國社會科學院出版社，2013年。

⑮ G.朝格圖《阿旺丹德爾文集（第四冊）》（蒙古文），呼伦贝尔：內蒙古文化出版社，2014年，1318頁。

⑯ 烏力吉教授曾在1996年出版的書中觀察益西班覺、阿旺丹達等人的書信之後，指出這些“用藏文寫作的蒙古喇嘛作家們從古代印度偉大詩人迦梨陀娑的抒情詩《雲使》吸取養分是較爲肯定的”。詳情請見烏力吉《蒙古族藏文文學研究》，北京：民族出版社，1996年，172—176頁。

拯救萬物灼熱之苦”（阿旺丹德爾《卯年獻給章嘉活佛的奏疏》），或者把自己比作無知的小燕子，把恩師比作爲“雖在高空中遨遊，卻把甘露灑向大地，高尚聰慧的濃雲”（《致瓦剌芒大師的信》），有時候作者把自己的信件比作“報信請安的海鷗鳥”，要求它“快速飛到拯救者雲（比喻收信的尊者）之身旁”。即在蒙古高僧給自己的恩師寫的信件中，往往把恩師比作“拯救萬物灼熱之苦的雨雲”，而這“雨雲”是與迦梨陀娑《雲使》中的“雨雲”聯繫在一起的。在印度神話中把“雲”分爲三類：山的翅膀變來的，梵天的呼吸所生的和從火生的。其中從山的翅膀變來的雲威力最爲強大，帶來的雨水能使世界覆没，是雲中豪傑。《雲使》的雲正屬於此類雲，它不是隨意飄在空中的雲，而是能帶來大量雨水的、驅逐燥熱的雨雲，從這一點上與高僧大德的品質相匹配。

2.“雷聲”“孔雀”等意象

在印度文化中，孔雀是雨雲的親戚，它看到雨雲，尤其是聽到雷聲後便會無比激動而引吭高歌、翩翩起舞。《雲使》中也不止一次描寫到此般情景。在蒙古喇嘛們給良師益友的回信中也反復出現“龍（雷）聲”與“孔雀”的形象，阿旺丹德爾在《辰年給戈壁諾因呼圖克圖的回信》中寫道：“如同孔雀聽到龍聲（雷聲），我的耳朵愉悦於您的言詞。”在《獻給鄂爾多斯吉祥書寺喇嘛之信》中寫道：“聽到龍聲（雷聲）孔雀鳥翩翩起舞一樣，得知您的善事善行，我心非常高興，爲此寫信請安。”除此之外，《雲使》中把“蓮花”與“太陽”比作一對情侣而表達它們之間依存關係，而阿旺丹德爾給老師的信中寫道：“徒兒雖未能前去看望老師，但受恩于老師的厚德而苟活于世，如同蓮花雖未到達太陽之處，太陽仍會照料園中的蓮花一樣。”[17]

信件，對早期蒙古喇嘛而言較爲重要。他們從小出家遊歷各地，常與親人分離，即使在固定地點參與宗教事業，但在其求學路上會有思念和感恩相伴。因而有必要常以書信聯繫表達情意交流心得。想必《雲使》真摯的語言和灼熱的情感在他內心深處產生共鳴，使他們熱愛《雲使》而如斯抒發情感。

（二）《雲使》與蒙古喇嘛“遊記文學”

《雲使》通過雨雲的路程從南到北如數家珍般領略了一番印度北半國的自然風景和人文聖地。從這一層面看，此詩具有遊記文學的特徵。在蒙古喇嘛文人中，也有不少遊記文學或旅途聽聞類的文章。其中，19世紀末一位叫做納木杜拉（Namdul）的布里亞特蒙古喇嘛大師（guru）到俄羅斯莫斯科和聖彼德堡旅遊後撰寫的一部長篇抒情詩（共84個詩節）《空中飛翔》（*Oγtarγui-bar Nisünem*）[18]獨具一格，讓人想起迦梨陀娑的《雲使》中的都市描寫。

據蒙古國學者策·達木丁蘇倫先生分析，此詩原稿爲藏文，后來可能自己翻譯成

---

⑰ G.朝格圖《阿旺丹德爾文集（第四冊）》（蒙古文），1248—1363頁。內容爲本文作者所譯。

⑱ 〔蒙古〕呈·達木丁蘇倫《蒙古古代文學一百篇》（蒙古文），烏蘭巴托，1959年，541—548頁。

了蒙古文。蒙古（譯）文夾雜著大量梵、藏詞彙，不僅讀起來拗口，還使得有些地方不易理解。

此詩描寫的是19世紀末俄羅斯的兩座繁華都市莫斯科和聖彼德堡，其中前11詩節是描寫莫斯科城的，第12—82詩節是描寫聖彼德堡的，最後兩個詩節爲結語，交代了寫作地點和作者。在蒙古古代文學中，以如此規模、如此詳細地描寫城市的作品比較罕見。這首詩雖然是描寫西方都城，但其中充滿了佛教術語和佛教觀念，甚至以佛教宇宙觀去描繪城市結構。在《雲使》中對優禪尼城的繁華富貴如此形容“它好像是天上的居民在享受福報將盡時，把剩餘的福澤換成一角天堂帶來大地”[19]。《空中飛翔》同樣把莫斯科城形容爲“如同天上的一角挪到了地上”。《雲使》中藥叉的故鄉阿羅迦城是福樂的天堂，那裏繁華富饒，男俊女靚，歌舞昇平。《空中飛翔》中的聖彼德堡的情景也與之相同。並且對聖彼德堡城的描寫較爲詳細，幾乎每一巷，每一景幾乎都有所涉及，內容豐富多樣。總之，《空中飛翔》是在蒙古古代文學史上較爲獨特的一首詩。詩中的藝術想像不得不說與《雲使》存在著某種淵源關係。

17、18世紀，“藏文”在蒙古高僧喇嘛們的創作中占主導地位。他們用藏文撰寫的著作，涉及到宗教、哲學、語言、文學等多個領域。《雲使》對蒙古文學的早期影響也是通過藏文實現的。

三、《雲使》四個蒙古文譯本

自18世紀中葉到20世紀60年代，《雲使》共有了四個蒙古文譯本。最早的《雲使》蒙古文譯本是在藏文大藏經《丹珠爾》的蒙譯活動（1742—1749）中產生的，稱蒙古文丹珠爾《雲使》譯本。其餘三個譯本，都是在20世紀中葉分別從《雲使》藏、漢和英文譯本轉譯而成的。除此之外，1956年蒙古國學者策・達木丁蘇倫從藏文丹珠爾轉譯了《雲使》前六個詩節。從版本源流看，從漢文轉譯的譯本來自印度《雲使》摩利那他體系，其餘均來自孟加拉體系文本。下面依次討論《雲使》各譯本以及它們之間的關係。

（一）蒙古文丹珠爾《雲使》譯本

蒙古文丹珠爾《雲使》譯本，是由喀爾喀蒙古政教領袖哲布尊丹巴一世扎納巴咱爾（Jñānavajra，1635—1723）的兩個徒弟洛桑堅贊（Blo bzang rgyal mtshan）和格勒堅贊（Dge legs rgyal mtshan）合譯完成的。按照一般佛經譯本的写作慣例，該《雲使》譯本首先以“頂禮三寶”為開篇語，繼而交代《雲使》的梵、藏和蒙古文名稱，敬禮文殊菩薩，才進入正文內容。與梵、藏文本不同的是，《雲使》蒙古文譯本爲散文體，而非韻文體，因而失去了韻文的一些特徵。又因該譯本產生于集中翻譯蒙古文佛經的活動中，

⑲ 金克木譯《雲使》，人民文學出版社，1956年，21頁。

從而也受到了佛教和佛經翻譯活動的影響。

首先，從翻譯心理上來講，譯者的佛教情感大於文學翻譯。蒙古文丹珠爾《雲使》譯本的譯者爲虔誠的佛教徒，這一點在蒙古文譯本的跋文[20]中記載得比較明確，其中寫道：

> …… 叩首接納聖主之令，心中膜拜佛祖之教，欲爲衆生造福，一心專志譯之。若因無知而錯，請聖賢忍而正之。若是正確無誤，此乃正等正覺之果也。以此造福之力量，企聖上之足下蓮花金剛般堅固，三寶之教如太陽般永遠升起，爲母衆生永得福樂 ……[21]

跋文中，譯者表示以"一心專志"翻譯《雲使》，但這並不是從文學翻譯意義上的"一心專志"而是出於宗教信仰的一種勵志和願望。對佛教信徒而言，佛經翻譯行爲本身就是他們自身的修法形式之一。"歷來認爲，抄寫、供養經典可以得到無限的功德，……虔心收集、翻譯、整理、傳寫、供養、修造佛典與大藏經的人前仆後繼。"[22]從《雲使》的蒙古文譯本看，譯者是想要通過"赤誠之心"而達到"弘揚佛法、造福衆生"，而"如何把它翻譯得更好"這一問題並不是譯者的考慮重點。結果，該譯本更多的是成了一件敬佛之事而很難稱之爲真正意義上的文學翻譯。

其次，從字詞翻譯角度看，《雲使》的翻譯過分依賴和束縛于佛教術語詞典，從而降低了其原本屬性。藏蒙《正字智者之源》[23]（簡稱《智者之源》）是針對大藏經《丹珠爾》蒙古文翻譯活動而編著的藏蒙對照佛教術語詞典。清代，蒙古文佛經翻譯活動處於"鼎盛時期"[24]，主持《丹珠爾》翻譯活動的章嘉呼圖克圖若必多吉（rol pa`i rdo rje，1716-1786）總結以往藏、蒙佛經翻譯活動的經驗，爲了統一和規範翻譯中的名詞術語而組織編寫了這部詞典，並要求譯者們以此爲綱領。其中包含了般若部、中觀部、阿毗達摩部、律藏部、教派部、密咒部、因明部、聲明部、工巧部、醫方部、新舊訓詁學部等類别的藏蒙對照術語。《雲使》雖屬於丹珠爾"聲明部"，但"聲明部"以語言學詞彙爲主，並沒有針對《雲使》翻譯而列出的詞條。這種情況下，譯者還是謹遵《智者之源》，只要《雲使》的詞彙出現在《智者之源》中，就會按照其中的譯法去翻譯，不管它是哪一類詞或適合不適合《雲使》翻譯。比如《雲使》蒙古文譯名爲

---

⑳ 除了藏文譯本的跋文外，蒙古文譯者又加了一篇兩頁之多的蒙古文跋文，表示對佛教的虔誠之心。

㉑ 本文作者譯。蒙古文原文爲：boγda eǰen-iyen kündü ǰarliγ-i orui-bar abču. burqan-u šasin-u ünen ǰirüken-dür-iyen aquluγad. busud olan amitan-a tusa boltuγai kemen sedkiǰü. bučal ügei čing ǰoriγ-iyar orčiγuluγsan egün-e. ülü medeküi-yin erkeber buruγu boluγsan bolbasu. ülemǰi degedü merged-ber(-iyer) küličeǰü ǰasan soyurq-a.. ünen küǰöb boluγsan-u buyan-u qubi ker bükü tegün-i.. üneker tuγuluγsan buddhi qutuγ-un siltaγan bolγan irügemüi. ene metü egüdügsen masi čaγan buyan-u küčün-iyer. eǰen degedüs-ün ülmei-yin lingqu_a vačir metü batutuγad. erdeni-tü šasin naran metü egüride manduǰu. eke boluγsan qamuγ amitan ünide ǰirγaqu boltuγai.

㉒ 方廣錩《蒙古文甘珠爾·丹珠爾目錄》，呼和浩特：遠方出版社，2002年，前言。

㉓ 《正字智者之源》，藏名：dag yig mkhas pa'i'byung gnas zhes bya ba las. 蒙古名：merged γarqu-yin orun neretü toγtaγaγsan taγyiγ. 是蒙古文佛經翻譯史上第一部蒙藏對照佛教術語詞典。

㉔ 蒙古文佛經翻譯活動可分爲萌芽時期（蒙元）、成熟時期（北元）和鼎盛時期（清朝）。

“Egülen-ü ǰarudasun”。蒙古語中“ǰarudasun”意爲“僕人”，經常與“boγul”連用表示“奴僕”。蒙古語中表示“使者”一般用“elčin”一詞，而不用“ǰarudasun”。那麼這裏爲什麼用了“ǰarudasun”？如果查看《智者之源》，在“工巧部”中便會找到藏文的“pho nya”（使者）及其對應詞“ǰarudasun”，即“工巧部”中有個天文學的名詞“dus kyi pho nya”（梵文kālayukta），蒙古文把它譯爲“čaγ-un ǰarudasun”，其中“pho nya”即爲“ǰarudasun”。“sprin gyi pho nya”（雲使）的結構與“dus kyi pho nya”一致，由此推理蒙古文譯者把“sprin gyi pho nya”譯成了“egülen-ü ǰarudasun”。另，在《雲使》蒙古文譯本中“…… eke”（母）一詞出現的頻率也很高，它們是從藏文的“…… ma”翻譯而來。在《雲使》梵文原文中表示女性的詞較多，藏譯本中把它們幾乎都譯成了“…… ma”的形式，接著蒙古文又把它們全部譯成了“…… eke”（母）。在梵文原著里，除了指“大地母親”以外其餘指“女性”的詞並沒有“母”或“母親”的意思，而是指“情人、愛妻、美女”，其中有一部分爲擬人化的河流、花草或城堡。而到了蒙古文譯本中她們卻都成了各種“…… eke”，導致意義說不通。在蒙古語中“eke”表示“母親”，在佛教用語中指“佛母”，如“noγuγan dar-a eke”（綠度母）“čaγan dar-a eke”（白度母）。藏文中，“ma”指“母親”，但在詞尾時，一般表示“女人、女性、陰性”之意。而蒙古文中把它一律譯成“……母”，即譯成了佛教用語，究其原因，這也與《智者之源》有關。在《智者之源》的“般若”、“律藏”、“密咒”和“工巧”部中有藏文“…… ma /mo”與蒙古文“……eke”相對應，此類詞條在“工巧明”部中最多。這些詞大部分爲指“星宿”（天文學）的藻飾詞，來自印度神話中的女性神的名字。本文認爲，《雲使》蒙古文譯本出於遵守蒙古文《丹珠爾》的“名詞術語一致性”原則而把藏文的“…… ma”形式一律譯成了“……eke”。

再次，從翻譯流程角度看，蒙古文丹珠爾《雲使》譯本屬於“過渡性文本”，而非最終文本。“過渡性文本”也叫“半成品”，是指在官方組織的集體佛經翻譯活動中，處於譯經流程的某個中間環節的作品。一般情況下，這些中間環節的作品要繼續經歷譯經流程的全部環節才得以刊行。但也有以“半成品”的形式面世的情況。如唐代漢譯佛經以“半成品”的形式流入到日本的作品較多[25]。

《丹珠爾》的蒙古文翻譯是由官方主持和組織的集體佛經翻譯活動，與藏文佛經翻譯活動一脈相承。蒙古文《丹珠爾》翻譯綱領《智者之源》的翻譯原則主要根據藏文《聲明學要領二卷》制定的。《聲明學要領二卷》是“藏族第一部翻譯理論，標誌著藏族的翻譯理論研究早在一千多年前就已經自成體系，體現了譯經方面的周密分工，設置校對，正義，考證，潤色等環節”[26]。《雲使》蒙古文譯本跋文中記載：“弘揚佛法的哲布尊丹巴格根之徒弟格隆洛桑堅贊、格勒堅贊譯成蒙古文，阿旺松迪寫”，反映了翻譯

㉕ 萬金川《佛典漢譯流程裏“過渡性文本”的語文景觀（第一部）》，《正觀雜誌》第44期，2008年，114頁。

㉖ 拉都《梵藏翻譯方法和翻譯理論形成概述》，《康定民族师範高等專科学校學报》2000年第1期，73頁。

和謄寫兩道工序。然而《雲使》蒙古文譯本最終沒有達到《智者之源》所提出的"語句通順，符合蒙古語的表達方式"的要求。仔細對照《雲使》藏、蒙兩種譯本將會發現，蒙古文譯本只停留對藏文底本的"逐字譯"[27]環節，對藏文只是字對字翻譯，而並沒有從蒙古語的角度進行語序調整和語義潤色。其語序過拘泥于藏文語序，不符合蒙古語的表達方式，甚至句意不通、難以理解，因而降低了該譯本的可讀性，并成爲了以後再譯的客觀原因。

（二）《雲使》20世紀蒙古文譯本

1956年世界和平理事會紀念迦梨陀娑，並把他列入"世界文化名人"之列。這爲各個國家關注和研究迦梨陀娑起到了推動作用。在中國，季羨林和金克木兩位先生分別翻譯迦梨陀娑的《沙恭達羅》和《雲使》來紀念了這位偉人。這一年"蒙古國人民也與世界人民一同紀念迦梨陀娑，並爲增強蒙印兩國政治、文化關係正在努力採取種種措施。"[28]策·達木丁蘇倫先生的《雲使》前六個詩節的譯文正是這個時候翻譯[29]。其後，蒙古國甘丹寺住持大喇嘛額爾敦培勒（Erdenipil）從藏文《丹珠爾》再次翻譯了《雲使》。而此譯本是爲了迎接1959年將在烏蘭巴托舉辦的"首屆國際蒙古學家大會"，目的是要引起國際蒙古學界對《雲使》譯本的關注和研究。據介紹，額爾敦培勒喇嘛1887年出生在今蒙古國紮布汗省，翻譯《雲使》之時他將近70歲高齡。印度學者羅凱什·錢德拉（Lokesh Chandra）在他的論文中提到，1957年5月他在蒙古國見到"在額爾敦培勒的指導下完成《雲使》另一部蒙古文翻譯的譯者Ese-tabkhai"[30]。可知，該譯本是在1956—1957年間完成的，譯者爲師徒二人。但譯本的落款處署名"額爾敦培勒譯"，所以把它稱作"額爾敦培勒譯本"（以下簡稱E譯本）。與此同時，額爾敦培勒還請他的朋友薩嘎拉扎布先生從漢文又一次翻譯了《雲使》。薩嘎拉扎布譯本（以下簡稱S譯本）是從金克木譯本轉譯而成的，因而時間應該在金克木譯本出版的1956年之後，1959年"國際蒙古學家大會"召開前後。E譯本和S譯本均爲散文體，並把每個詩節的序號標在前面，把原來的詩節變成了段落。

還有一部《雲使》蒙古文譯本是由蒙古國著名學者、語言學家、作家賓·仁欽（B. Rinchin）從英文轉譯的。他所依據的是1943年在加爾各答出版的梵孟（孟加拉語）合璧版本中每個詩節後面的英文解釋。即他通過英文解釋理解了意義之後，再把它譯成了蒙古文詩歌。此譯本共有120個詩節，每個詩節由4個詩行組成，用基里爾蒙古文寫成。

㉗ "逐字譯"（word-for-word translation）亦稱"詞對詞翻譯"，即將原文的語句一個詞一個詞地對譯，不考慮詞在語法或詞義方面的差異。見方夢之《中國譯學大辭典》，上海：上海外語教育出版社，2011年，89頁。

㉘ 〔蒙古〕道·策德布《呈·達木丁蘇倫全集》，烏蘭巴托，2004年，229—331頁。

㉙ 該譯文內容少，影響不大，本論文暫不予以討論。

㉚ Lokesh Chandra, "The Mongolian Meghadūta", *Studies in Indo-Asian Art and Culture*, vol.2, New Delhi, 1974, p. 99a.

到目前爲止的所有蒙古文譯本中，賓·仁欽的譯本（以下簡稱R譯本）無論在形式、内容還是在修辭方面，都最爲貼近原文。從蒙古文角度而言，也是相當優美和成功的詩歌翻譯。他的譯本於1962年完成，1963年他把丹珠爾譯本、E譯本、S譯本和自已的譯本（即古今4個譯本）合爲一本在烏蘭巴托出版。1981年，R譯本從基里爾蒙古文轉寫成回鶻體蒙古文，與手抄形式的丹珠爾譯本一起在北京出版。其中，手抄丹珠爾《雲使》譯本充滿了錯誤，無論是對閱讀還是研究，都不可取。另外兩個E譯本和S譯本一直還沒有在中國出版。在蒙古國這兩個譯本的知名度也很小。

E譯本，從内容上看，與蒙古文丹珠爾譯本有較多的重複之處，但也有一些糾正和改動，然而有些改動不僅沒有達到新的高度，反而破壞了傳統表達方式。從文本分析結果看，E譯本除了依據和參考藏、蒙丹珠爾譯本之外並沒有參考《智者之源》等其他文獻。E譯本的主要目的和作用在於正如譯者額爾敦培勒喇嘛提出的那樣“引起國際蒙古學學者們對蒙古文丹珠爾《雲使》譯本的關注，把蒙古文《雲使》納入蒙古文學研究中來”[31]。

S譯本，從内容上看，總體上比較正確和忠實地轉述了金克木譯本的意思。但該譯本的最大問題在於名詞術語翻譯方面採取了從漢文音譯方式，而且同一個詞的前後寫法也不一致。因而譯本中名詞術語較爲混亂，而更重要的是從漢文音譯方式違背了蒙印文學關係上約定俗成的“名從其主”原則。蒙印文學關係中的“名從其主”原則指的是蒙古文中音譯而來的古代印度的名詞，一般都與其原來的梵文名詞相對應。這與早在藏傳佛教傳入蒙古地區之前梵文詞彙通過中亞地區已被吸收到蒙古語詞匯有關。舉個簡單的例子，梵文的“mahākāla”和“skanda”，在蒙古文中仍爲“mahakala”和“skanda”，而從漢文轉譯的《雲使》S譯本中把這兩個詞從漢文音譯成了“mukajiluu”（摩訶迦羅）和“ǰimuluu”（鳩摩羅，skanda的別称），導致本來熟悉的名字變成了陌生而古怪的，有礙於對原文意思的理解。

R譯本，1982年首次被轉寫成回鶻體蒙古文在北京出版之時，編者在前言的介紹中層提到“其中（指《雲使》——引者）的訓諭詞（surγal üges）至今仍被印度人所傳誦”，這一句來自金克木先生《雲使》譯文的前言，但金克木先生說的是“《雲使》的一些名句爲印度人所傳誦”，而在蒙古文“前言”中把“名句”理解成了“訓諭詞”，這可能與蒙古文學歷史上與印藏文學一脈相承的“訓諭詩”比較發達（數量眾多）有關。目前，R譯本是《雲使》知名度最高的一個蒙古文譯本。在形式上，它按照梵文《雲使》四個音步爲一個詩節的格式，並兼顧了蒙古文詩歌押頭韻原則，以第一節爲例具體如下：

Seremǰi aldaγsan nigen yakṣas, kilingtü eǰen-ü bošuγ ǰarliγ-iyar
Sür ǰubqulang-iyan baγuraγulun, üǰesgülengtü amaraγ-ača ǰil-iyer qaγačaγad
Sedkil-dü taγalamǰitu güngǰü-yin ukiyal-du ariγuduγsan mören-ü oyir-a
Següder tegülder γalbawaras modotu rama-yin aγulan-a saγun abai.

---

[31] 〔蒙古〕賓·仁欽等譯《雲使》（基里爾蒙古文），烏蘭巴托，1963年，譯本序，9—10頁。

該譯本語言樸素，行文流暢，至今爲止最能代表《雲使》蒙古文譯本成就而廣爲人知。隨著它在蒙古國首次出版，20世紀60年代在蒙古国也流行了一首歌曲，歌中唱道：

表1

歌詞（基里爾蒙古文）	歌詞大意
Асгарсан бороoны үүл нь ээ хө	灑下細雨的雲啊，
Алсаас ч ирсэн байлгүй дээ хө	是來自遠方的喲，
Амраг хайртай түүний минь	向我心愛的她喲，
Амрыг нь эрээд очоорой доо.	帶到祝福之語吧。
Уулын орой дээрх үүл нь ээ хө	山頂上的雲啊，
Урагшаагаа нүүгээд явчихлаадаа хө	向前方遊走了喲，
Миний хайртай түүнд минь ээ	給我心愛的她喲，
Мэндийг минь хүргээд очоорой доо хө.	送去我的問候吧。

這就是在現代蒙古詩歌中時而會見到的“以雲傳情”意象。天上的白雲促使人們的浪漫想像，成爲了寄託思念的使者。

另一方面，R譯本還吸收和繼承了蒙古文丹珠爾《雲使》譯本的可取之處。上述第一詩節的內容中，“kilingtü eǰen”“bošuγ ǰarliγ”“Sür ǰubqulang-iyan baγuraγulun”“Sedkil-dü taγalamǰitu”“Següder tegülder γalbawaras modotu”等詞組均來自蒙古文丹珠爾《雲使》譯本，這也是R譯本與蒙古文丹珠爾譯本之間重複率最高的一個詩節。其後的詩節中重複率雖然很低，但賓・仁欽先生一直在認真考量丹珠爾譯本中的詞，有價值的盡量傳承到自己的譯本中來。在《雲使》題目的翻譯上，如前所述“egülen ǰarudasu”“egülen elči”二者中賓・仁欽先生採用了丹珠爾譯本的題目“egülen ǰarudasu”，并指出“額爾敦培勒先生在其新譯（指E譯本——引者）中採用‘egülen elči’爲題目是不錯的，關於這一點，我在自己的翻譯中覺得前人的翻譯自有其道理”[32]，因此他保留了“egülen ǰarudasu”這個題目。可知，賓・仁欽先生是比較重視傳統翻譯并在傳統的基礎上再談創新。字詞層面，較爲典型的有“usun bariγči”（持水的，指“雨雲”）、“ünür külgelegči”（乘味者，指“風”）“bütügsed”（成就者，悉檀仙siddha）、“ǰüg-ün ǰaγan”（域龍）、“qormusta-yin nomun”（因陀羅的弓，指“彩虹”）、“ükül ügei er-e em-e”（不死夫妻，指“神仙配偶”）、“γasalang ügei ulaγan modun”（紅色的無憂樹）等等，這些詞組和藻飾詞的譯法不僅在R譯本中得以傳承，而且已成爲了蒙古語詞彙中約定俗成的表達方法。若把它們換成其他詞，會容易導致詞不達意。比如在《雲使》從漢文轉譯的S譯本中把“γasalang ügei ulaγan modun”（紅色的無憂樹）翻譯成了“ulaγan önggetei čenggeltü čečeg”（紅色的喜樂花；漢文：紅色的無憂花），即把“無憂”譯成了“喜樂”。這雖然意思相同，但表達方式脫節了傳統而不易讓人理解。在印度傳說中，“無憂樹”是女人的（左）腳碰觸到才能開花結果。這個意境在《雲使》中出現（請參見金克木譯本第78節，蒙古文R譯本第83節），

[32] 賓・仁欽譯《雲使》（回鶻蒙古文）北京：民族文學出版社，1981年，序，5頁。

并受到了蒙古詩人的深愛，已融入到他們的詩歌中。以蒙古國著名詩人B. Yabuuhulan的詩作《蒙古詩》[33]（Mongγol silüg）爲例：

表2

原文	詩詞大意
Saiqan büsegüi-yin köl	美麗女子的腳
γasalangγui modun-du kürkü-dü	碰觸無憂樹之時
Salaγ-a müčir bükün ni	每個枝節將會
čečegleǰü ǰimislen-e gesen	盛開花朵結果實
Erten-ü mongγol silüg-ün	古代蒙古詩歌
γaiqam-a saiqan sanaγ-a	如此驚人的意境
Ene yabuγ-a nasun-du	在我人生之中
nada-du nige-yi sibeneǰü	對我訴說著什麼
Büür tüürken ulalǰaγsan	燃起了
ongγud-un γal-i mini badaraγaǰu	我朦朧的靈感之光
Büsegüi kümün-i qairalaqu	點亮了
sedkil-i angq-a deberegegsen yum.	我熱愛女人之初心
……	

此詩中，“無憂樹因女人的腳而盛開”已成爲了古代蒙古詩歌的傳統意象。眾所周知，“無憂樹”原產印度，屬於熱帶植物。相傳，佛教創始人釋迦摩尼誕生於此樹下。而這一意象通過佛經傳入蒙古古代文學，再由古代文學傳到現代文學，并在異地他鄉如此“繁茂盛開”。其間，蒙古文丹珠爾《雲使》譯本以及繼承它優點的R譯本起到了關鍵性橋樑作用。因爲在R譯本之前的兩個現代譯本，即E譯本和S譯本中分別把“無憂樹”譯作“γasalang ügei olan modun”（即丹珠爾譯本“γasalang ügei ulaγan modun”的誤抄）和“ulaγan önggetei čenggeltü čečeg”（紅色的喜悅花），而在R譯本中不僅正確承襲蒙古文丹珠爾《雲使》的譯法，而且在譯本序中對其作解釋說明了此樹開花的特殊性。從而被現代蒙古詩歌所吸收，“無憂樹”也成爲了蒙印文學關係中的一棵常青樹。

結　　語

蒙古國著名學者策·達木丁蘇倫（1908—1986）曾說：“要從17、18世紀的蒙古文學當中尋找沒有宗教（指佛教——引者）影響的作品，那就像水中撈幹物一樣。”古代印度古典梵語名詩《雲使》正是在佛教文學盛興的18世紀中葉通過集體佛經翻譯活動由藏文轉譯成了蒙古文。佛經翻譯活動的烙印，一方面使得古代蒙古語《雲使》譯本中保留了蒙古語“經典書面語”[34]的一些詞彙特徵。另一方面，則使它失去了文學性而在閱讀和流傳方面受到了很大限制。但是，此前在14世紀初蒙古人已通過藏文接觸到了《雲

[33] 《B. 亞布呼蘭詩集》（回鶻蒙古文），呼和浩特：內蒙古教育出版社，1990年，614頁。

[34] 17、18世紀蒙古文“譯經語言”，被西方學者稱爲蒙古“經典書面語”（sungγudaγ bičig-ün kele）。

使》。16世紀末起蒙古佛教文學界以藏文閱讀和創作為主，《雲使》的影響也主要體現在蒙古喇嘛文人的藏文創作中。到了20世紀，在“世界文學”的平臺上，經過E譯本和S譯本的探索，到了蒙古國學者賓・仁欽的譯本，才出現了文學意義上的、韻文體的《雲使》蒙古文譯本，推進了《雲使》在現代蒙古文學中的傳播與影響。但R譯本是從英文轉譯而來的，因而對《雲使》梵文原本的閱讀、翻譯以及相關研究留下了餘地。

Meghadūta in Mongolia

Saqirengui

The *Meghadūta* (*Cloud Messenger*) is a long lyrical poem composed by Kālidāsa, the famous ancient Indian poet and dramatist of around the 4th-5th centuries. *Meghadūta* first became known to Mongolians at the beginning of the 14th century through its Tibetan translation. After Tibetan Buddhism was introduced to Mongolia for the second time (in the latter half of the 16th century), the Mongolian Buddhist scholars who were proficient in Tibetan read the Tibetan version of *Meghadūta* and used it in their writings in Tibetan. In the mid-18th century, *Meghadūta* was translated into Mongolian from the Tibetan translation. By the late 20th century, there were three modern Mongolian translations, translated respectively from the Tibetan, from the Chinese and from the English translations of the original work. Following a general introduction about the Sanskrit, this paper mainly discusses how all these Tibetan and Mongolian translations of *Meghadūta* were spread in Mongolia and influenced Mongolian literature.

捨身飼虎本生的文本和圖像研究

——兼論德國佛教藝術史研究方法

孟　瑜

劉震教授在他的《德國佛教藝術史研究方法舉隅：以九色鹿故事爲例》[①]一文中曾對德國佛教藝術史研究的歷史和研究方法進行了詳細的論述。這種研究方法其實是一種窮舉法，即在研究過程中盡可能全面地搜集藝術品與相關文獻，並將二者相結合，通過客觀細緻的比對，發現兩者的異同，從而加深和補充人們對研究對象的認知。這種方法在研究那些流傳甚廣的文獻和藝術作品時顯得尤為重要，下面就以捨身飼虎本生為例進行深入分析。

這一本生的大致情節爲：釋迦牟尼在成佛之前曾歷經多次轉世。在某一次前世中，菩薩無意中看見一隻母虎由於剛剛產下幼子，饑餓難耐，竟想要吃掉自己的幼子充饑。看到此種情形，菩薩心中生大慈悲，於是決定捨棄生命，將自己的身體施捨給了老虎。

這個故事十分著名，先後被十餘種佛教經典所記述，然而這些版本相互間不盡相同。通常情況下，該本生由（佛陀）現在的故事、（佛陀）過去的故事、現在和過去的連接這三個部分組成。“（佛陀）現在的故事”是指，佛陀遊歷到某地後一般會發生一些奇異的現象，而這些現象通常是由於佛陀前世的因緣所致，佛陀便會因此講述過去的故事。“（佛陀）過去的故事”一般是本生的主體敘述，有時會狹義地等同於本生本身。“現在和過去的連接” 通常放在主體敘述之後，在這個部分裡前世的人物會和佛陀當世的人物進行對照，比如，前世捨身的主人公就是現在的佛陀等等。

爲直觀體現該本生各版本間的差異，現將所有版本中主體敘述部分的內容列表如下（表1）：

“（佛陀）過去的故事”即主體敘述部分，一般包含主要角色、主要情節、次要角色和次要情節。

捨身者、母虎以及幼虎毫無疑問是這個本生故事中的主要角色。結合這個版本列表可見，捨身者的身份及名稱並不統一。按照捨身者在捨身時的身份劃分，這些版本大致

---

① 劉震《德國佛教藝術史研究方法舉隅：以九色鹿故事爲例》，《史林》2012年第1期，153—163頁。

表1

出處	捨身者身份及捨身過程	捨身者名稱	幼虎數量	捨身者的陪伴者	死後起塔
Āryaśūra（聖勇）所著*Jātakamālā*（《本生鬘》）中的第1章*Vyāghrījātaka*（《母虎本生》）	婆羅門修行者；從高處投身而下	無；僅被稱爲Bodhisattva（意爲“覺有情”）或Mahātman（意爲“大我”）	不詳	Ajita（意爲“無能勝”）	否
Mahajjātakamālā（《大本生鬘》）中第43章*Brāhmaṇajātakāvadāna*（《婆羅門本生因緣》）②	婆羅門修行者；從高處投身而下	無；被稱爲Mahāsattva（意爲“大有情”）	不詳	Ajita	是
《前世三轉經》（T 178）	婆羅門修行者；以刀刺身	無；僅被稱爲“童子”或“童子道人”	不詳	兩位仙人	否
《銀色女經》（T 179）	婆羅門修行者；以刀刺身	無；僅被稱爲“摩那婆”	不詳	兩位仙人	否
Bodhisattvāvadānakalpalatā（《菩薩因緣如意鬘草》）中第51章*Rukmavatyavadāna*（《金色女因緣》；以下簡稱BAK（I））	婆羅門修行者；以竹片刺頸	Satyavrata（意爲“真誓”）	不詳	兩位仙人	否
Divyāvadāna（《天譬喻經》）中第32章*Rūpāvatyavadāna*（《具色女因緣》）	婆羅門修行者；以竹片刺頸	Brahmaprabha（意爲“梵光”）	2	兩位仙人	否
《六度集經》中第四個故事（T 152，02b08-02b26）	婆羅門修行者；把頭放在老虎口中	無；僅被稱爲“菩薩”	不詳	無	否
《菩薩投身飴餓虎起塔因緣經》（T 172）	一開始是王子，後來出家成爲修行者；從高山上投身而下	栴檀摩提；也被成爲“摩訶薩埵”	7	數百人	是
Jātakastava（《本生贊》）的第五頌	修行者；捨身過程不詳	無	不詳	無	否
《賢愚經》（T 202）中《摩訶薩埵以身施虎品》	王子；以利木刺身	摩訶薩埵	2	兩位兄長：摩訶富那寧、摩訶提婆／大天	是
Bodhisattvāvadānakalpalatā（《菩薩因緣如意鬘草》）中第95章*Vyāghryavadāna*（《母虎因緣》；以下簡稱BAK（Ⅱ））	王子；不詳	Karuṇareṇu（意爲“悲塵”）	2	不詳	否

② *Mahajjātakamālā* 中的*Brāhmaṇajātakāvadāna*是在*Jātakamālā* 中的第1章*Vyāghrījātaka* 的基礎上改寫而來，所以這兩個版本的內容是很接近的。

续表

出處		捨身者身份及捨身過程	捨身者名稱	幼虎數量	捨身者的陪伴者	死後起塔
《金光明經》③	梵文本（Tib. I , Tib. II）	王子；竹片刺頸	Mahāsattva, Mahāsattvavaro, Snying stobs che（*mahākaruṇabala）	5	兩位兄長：Mahāpraṇāda 和 Mahādeva	是
		王子；從高山上投身而下				
	T 663 （及T 664）	王子；尋刀，用竹片刺頸，後從高山上投下	摩訶薩埵	7	摩訶波那羅 / 大波那羅、摩訶提婆 / 大天	是
		王子；從高山上投身而下				
	T 665 （及Tib. III）	王子；尋刀，從高山而下，被神仙捧接， 後竹片刺頸	摩訶薩埵、勇猛	7	摩訶波羅 / 大渠、摩訶提婆 / 大天	是
		王子；從高山投身而下，後竹片刺頸				
《最勝問菩薩十住除垢短結經》（T 309, 970c01-970c10）		身份不詳；從高山上投身而下	無	不詳	慈氏、柔順	無
《分別功德論》（T 1507, 35a27-35b11）		身份不詳；從高山上投身而下並以竹自刺	無	不詳	兩位菩薩	無
于闐文的*Jātakastava*（《本生贊》）的第74和75頌		身份不詳；從高山上投身而下	無	不詳	無	無
一些僅簡略提到捨身飼虎本生的文獻，如《修行本起經》（T 184, 463a19-463a21），《惟日雜難經》（T 760，605b18-605b20，606a27，606b04，606c16-606c17），《佛說菩薩內習六波羅密經》（T 778, 714c19-714c21），《佛本行經》（T 193, 65c06，89c03-89c04），《大智度論》（T 1509, 147a14-147a16，179b26-179c02，669c06-669c07），《入楞伽經》（T 671, 517b06-517b07），《三具足經優波提舍》（T 1534, 361a19-361a21），《佛說月光菩薩經》（T 166, 408a01-408a04），*Rāṣṭrapālaparipṛcchā*（《護國所問經》）的第四個故事		身份不詳；捨身過程不詳	不詳	不詳	無	無

③　《金光明經》（*Suvarṇabhāsottamasūtra*）譯本衆多。主要的譯本有三個中文譯本和三個藏文譯本。中文本分別是：① 北涼曇無讖於西元420 年左右譯出的《金光明經》，在《大正藏》中該譯本編號爲T 663；②隋代僧人寶貴合編前人譯本所著《合部金光明經》，在《大正藏》中該譯本編號爲T664；③唐代義淨譯出的《金光明最勝王經》，在《大正藏》中該本編號爲T66藏文本分別是：①由Mūlāśoka（意爲“根無憂”）和 Jñānakumāra（意爲“智童”）譯出的*'phags pa gser 'od dam pa mdo sde'i dbang po'i rgyal po shes bya ba theg pa chen po'i mdo*（《聖金光明最勝王大乘經》，代稱爲Tib. Ⅰ）；②由 Jinamitra（世友）, Śīlendrabodhi（戒自在菩提）和Ye shes sde（智軍）譯出的*'phags pa gser 'od dam pa mdo sde'i dbang po'i rgyal po shes bya ba theg pa chen po'i mdo*（《聖微妙金光明極勝王大乘經》，代稱爲Tib. Ⅱ）；③由'Gos chos grub（法成）所譯*'phags pa gser 'od dam pa mchog tu rnam par rgyal pa'i mdo sde'i rgyal po theg pa chen po'i mdo*（《聖金光明最上勝王大乘經》，代稱爲Tib. Ⅲ）。

可分爲三類——捨身者爲修行者、王子或身份不詳[②]。

第一類，捨身者在捨身時爲修行者。值得注意的是，在這一類的版本裡，主人公在捨身前大多先經歷了一段非修行者的世俗生活。通常情況下，他先爲一名婆羅門，後出家成爲修行者；只有在T 172中，他由王子身份轉爲修行者。由於*Jātakastava*（《本生贊》）中第五頌的篇幅短小，文中僅提到他修行者的身份。根據上述情況，在第一個大的分類之下需再細分爲以下三個次類：

（1）捨身者先爲婆羅門，繼而在捨身時爲修行者：*Vyāghrījātaka*（*Brāhmaṇajātakāvadāna*）；T 178, T 179, BAK (I) 和*Rūpāvatyavadāna*；T 152；

（2）捨身者先爲王子，繼而在捨身時爲修行者：T 172；

（3）捨身者在捨身時爲修行者：*Jātakastava*的第五頌。

第二類，捨身者在捨身時爲王子：T 202，BAK (II)；《金光明經》。與第一類的版本相比，主人公從出場到捨身的身份未曾發生轉變，均爲王子。

第三類，捨身者在捨身時身份不詳：T 309， T 1507，于闐文的*Jātakastava*以及一些僅簡略提到捨身飼虎本生的文獻。在這類版本中，主人公的身份從未被明確提及，僅以“菩薩”代稱。

從這幾個類別的版本比較來看，第三類中的諸版本內容簡略且與前兩類內容並無太大差異，因此極有可能是從前兩類簡化而來。但就前兩類而言，我們卻無法依據現有的資料進一步推斷哪一個類別的版本產生得更早。在第一類的諸版本中，故事開始于婆羅門或王子的世俗生活，在出家成爲修行者後，他才在山林中遇到老虎，捨身飼虎。而在第二類諸版本中，故事直接開始于王子在山中的漫步，繼而遇虎捨身。無論是哪一種類別，都可以回溯到這樣一個母題：母虎產子，饑餓難耐欲食其子，主人公見狀不忍，捨身飼虎。至於身份的分別，應當是在故事的流傳過程中逐步產生確立的。

捨身者的名字在各版本間也並不完全一致。至於上述名稱中哪個是主人公最本初的名字，哪些是衍生出來的，我們同樣無法確定。

母虎由於產後虛弱想吃掉幼子，這一情節在各個版本中並無二致，此處不再贅言。然而幼虎的數量在各版本間卻不盡相同——從兩隻到七隻不等。本生故事中經常會提到動物，但是一般情況下，這些動物只有爲講述者所熟悉，才會在故事中提及。而從生物學的角度來講，母虎一次生產的幼虎數量很難超過五隻，所以那些幼虎數量超過五隻的版本的編纂者極可能缺乏對老虎的基本認識，因此這些版本不太像是出自早期。

既然是捨身飼虎，那麼主人公的捨身無疑是該本生中最重要的情節，然而他的捨身方式在各版本間差異很大。如表格所示，其捨身方式有兩種：跳崖或用利物刺傷身體。

② 施林洛甫（Dieter Schlingloff）教授將飼虎本生按捨身者的身份分爲兩類：婆羅門修行者和王子。參見D. Schlingloff, *Ajanta – Handbuch der Malereien/ Handbook of Paintings, 1. Erzählende Wandmalereien/ Narrative Wall-Paintings*, Wiesbaden, Harrassowitz, 2000, I, p. 163. 但是這種劃分並不能包含所有的版本，有些版本中捨身者的身份雖是修行者但不一定是婆羅門，有些版本中根本沒有提及捨身者的身份。 因此，筆者在此基礎上再次進行限定，即按捨身者在捨身時的身份劃分類別。

還有一種方式僅在《六度集經》中提到過一次，即捨身者將頭放入老虎口中。但是我們無法得知，爲何同一個本生故事會出現幾種完全不同的死亡方式，也很難確定這些方式的出現孰早孰晚。然而這種明顯的差異至少證明了一個事實——飼虎本生在流傳的過程中衍生出多種版本。

次要角色和次要情節並不一定出現在每個版本中，這與版本內容多寡有關。如果一個版本中包含次要角色和次要情節，那麼在捨身前後主人公的陪伴者以及主人公與陪伴者之間的互動是最重要的次要角色和次要情節，這些內容是爲了反襯主人公異于常人的慈悲和堅毅。另外，值得一提的是，捨身者死後起塔供養這個情節並非見於所有的版本。提到該情節的僅有*Mahajjātakamālā*（《大本生鬘》）中的*Brāhmaṇajātakāvadāna*（《婆羅門本生因緣》）、《菩薩投身飴餓虎起塔因緣經》（T 172）、《賢愚經》（T 202）中的《摩訶薩埵以身施虎品》、《菩薩本生蔓論》中的《投身飼虎緣起》以及《金光明經》，這個因素的加入，極有可能是現實中起塔供養崇拜的信仰在經文中的折射。

通過以上論述，我們可以看出，上述這些版本雖然都是捨身飼虎這個本生故事，但是相互間的主要角色、主要情節、次要角色和次要情節均不完全一致。這些不一致說明，這個本生故事並非從一開始就被完全固定，而是在流傳過程中持續不斷地發展。這些不一致恰恰反映了這個故事的流傳程度之高。另外，根據現存的資料，我們並不能斷定哪個版本是這個本生的源頭。在這個問題上，需要注意的是，判斷一個版本的早晚，不能僅憑其詳略。簡略的版本並不一定是早期的版本，同樣內容豐富的版本也並一定是晚期作品。因此判斷版本早晚必須要從其內容入手。

接下來，我們來看這個本生故事的藝術表現。由於其知名度高，因此圖像表現也十分豐富。迄今所發現的圖像見於印度、斯里蘭卡、東南亞、中亞、中國的新疆、敦煌、中原地區和西藏、日本等地。如同文本的情況一樣，這些地區的圖像表現也存有差異。

與其他地區相比，印度捨身飼虎圖像較少，主要發現于秣菟羅（Mathurā），阿栴陀（Ajaṇṭā），艾荷落（Aihoḷe）和犍陀羅（Gandhāra）等地。

現存最早的圖像出自秣菟羅（Mathurā），位於一根浮雕柱的中部和下部[③]（圖1），其斷代最遲約爲西元150年[④]。中部雕板的保存現狀欠佳，我們只能看到左下方的圓凳上坐著一個修行者，他的右側站著另外一個修行者，在他們的後面可以看到修行茅舍的一角。由於保存狀況的原因，我們並不能很清楚地解釋這兩人之間的關係。一方面，坐著的形象可能爲故事的主人公，那麼站著的人就是他的學生。在這種情況下，這個場景可被解釋爲主人公在教授學生。但同樣有可能的是，主人公是站著的那個人，而坐著的那個人長著長鬍子的老人似爲主人公的老師。那麼這個場景便可以有另一種解釋，即主人公在聆聽老師教誨。與之相比，下部雕板的內容明確許多，即一隻老虎正緊緊咬住主人公的肩膀，背後的修行茅舍清晰可見。通過這個關鍵性場景，我們不僅可以

③ 柱子最上方的浮雕板也許並不屬捨身飼虎本生。參見Vogel, J. Ph.，*The Mathurā school of sculpture, in Archaeological survey of India. Annual report, Calcutta,* 1906-1907，pp. 155-156。

④ 此斷代時間由莫妮卡·茨茵（Monika Zin）教授推斷。

判斷出此浮雕所依據的爲捨身飼虎本生，而且可以進一步限定版本的範圍爲主人公爲修行者的那一類版本。但是我們卻很難再準確推定該浮雕到底是依據哪一個本子，因爲畫面中的主人公已死，那麼最關鍵的細節——主人公的捨身過程——便無法推知。

圖1　秣菟羅（Mathurā）

考古博物館。圖片來自《世界美術大全集》第13卷，插圖90

同樣地，我們也很難推斷另一幅來自犍陀羅（Gandhāra）地區的浮雕的文本依據（圖2）。這件作品可回溯至西元2—3世紀。在現存的一角中，我們可以看到一隻虎正準備撕咬主人公的頭部。主人公著長衫和褲子，頭上似有一個髮髻——這樣的穿著表明他並非一個修行者，而是一位世俗之人。結合上面的表格，若主人公不是修行者，那就只能是一位王子。由於捨身過程沒有被描繪出來，我們只能判斷該圖像依據于主人公爲王子的那一類版本，卻不能準確指出其文本。

如果想準確判斷一個圖像的文本依據，那麼版本中的關鍵細節需要同時齊備。就捨

圖2　犍陀羅（Gandhāra）

政府博物館。圖片來自Quagliotti, A. M.,"A Gandharan relief representing a Jātaka in the Government Museum and Art Gallery, Chandigarh", in *Silk Road art and archaeology* X (2004), pp. 151-165, fig. 1

身飼虎本生而言，捨身者的身份和捨身方式是爲判定版本的標準。例如，在印度阿梹陀（Ajaṇṭā）石窟壁畫中，我們僅憑從高處落下的修行者的下半身以及一側老虎的輪廓，就可以斷定與這幅壁畫最接近的是*Vyāghrījātaka*⑤（圖3），因爲只有在這個版本中講述的是一位婆羅門修行者從高處投身下來，繼而飼虎。至於*Vyāghrījātaka*中其他的內容，如捨身者的學生、幼虎及其數量等，在畫面中不一定都有所體現且表現的方式也不盡相同，例如克孜爾石窟第178窟（圖4）和庫木吐喇石窟第63窟（圖5）的這兩幅圖像都應該是依據*Vyāghrījātaka* 所作，但是畫面的內容卻有所不同。在這兩幅畫面中，都有一個從天而降和一個平躺于地的修行者形象，這表現的是同一個人兩個前後相即的動作——捨身者從高處投身而下，繼而倒地身亡被老虎吞食。在圖4中多繪出了跪在一側禮敬供養的學生以及兩隻幼虎（老虎已被刮去，但是仍可通過其輪廓辨識）。*Vyāghrījātaka*在印度、斯里蘭卡、東南亞、中亞和中國西藏地區十分流行，因而圖像表現也很豐富。但值得注意的是，目前爲止在中國敦煌和中原地區尚未發現該版本的圖像，這大概是由於*Vyāghrījātaka*從未被準確被漢譯⑥，因此這個版本的飼虎本生似不被中國敦煌和中原地區所知曉。

在敦煌莫高窟中，捨身飼虎本生被多次表現。這些畫面情節豐富，充分展現了文本的內容。如在254窟左壁後部中層右端有一幅著名的北魏時期的薩埵太子捨身飼虎圖（圖6），圖中共繪出八個場景：摩訶薩埵王子和他的兩位兄長共游山林，看到母虎欲食初生的幼虎（1）；摩訶薩埵王子捨身——他脫去衣衫，以木刺頸（2），繼而從高山上投身而下（3）；王子倒地身亡，被母虎和她的7只幼虎吞食（4）；兩位兄長回到母虎處，哀悼捨身的王子（5）；兩位兄長討論如何將噩耗告知父母（6）；國王王后聞訊趕來悲慟欲絕（7）；起塔供養，天神禮贊（8）。通過這些情節可以推定，這幅壁畫是依據《金光明經》中的捨身飼虎本生所作。這個版本的知名度頗高，因此圖像表現也很多。除敦煌外，該版本的圖像還見於中亞、中國的西藏和中原地區和、日本等地。總體來講，這些圖像畫面簡單，且與敦煌254窟的這幅壁畫有很大的相似性，因而此處不再贅言。

《賢愚經》（T202）中《摩訶薩埵以身施虎品》也常被用作圖像表現的文本依據。如在莫高窟98窟中便發現一幅五代時期的經變（圖7）。由於保存狀況較差，我們只能識別如下場景：佛陀和阿難陀在城中乞食，路遇一個婦人和她的兩個兒子因盜竊罪即將被處死刑（1）；阿難陀請求國王釋放這三人（2）；阿難陀驚訝於所發生的事情，向佛陀詢問原因（3）；國王一家在山林中漫遊（4）；三位王子繼續前行，路遇餓虎及

⑤ 參見D. Schlingloff, *Ajanta – Handbuch der Malereien/ Handbook of Paintings, 1. Erzählende Wandmalereien/ Narrative Wall-Paintings*, p. 161。

⑥ 北宋時紹德、慧詢等翻譯Āryaśūra（聖勇）所著的*Jātakamālā*（《本生鬘》），定名爲《菩薩本生鬘論》（T 160），十六卷本。但是這個譯本翻譯品質很差，和*Jātakamālā*並無任何聯繫，其中的*Vyāghrījātaka*一篇紹德等人更是以《金光明經》的義淨譯本來頂替。See Brough, J., "The Chinese pseudo-translation of Ārya-śūra's *Jātaka-mālā*", in *Asia major* 1(1964), pp. 27-53, and Meng, Y., Eine Untersuchung zur Vyāghrī-Legende, München, 2017, S. 13-14.

圖3　阿栴陀 (Ajaṇṭā) 石窟

線描圖來自Monika Zin

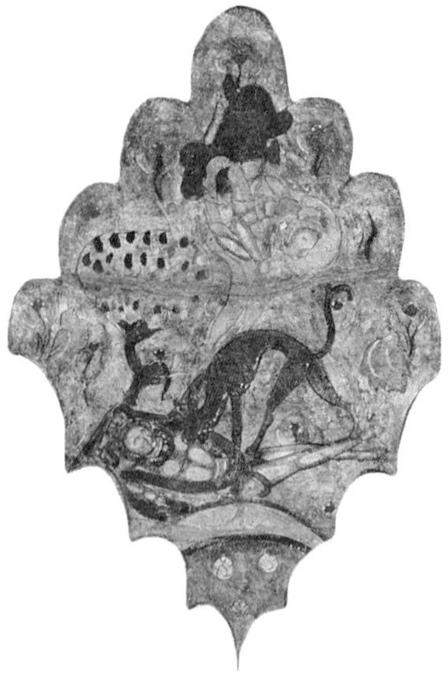

圖4　克孜爾石窟178窟

圖片來自柏林亞洲藝術博物館

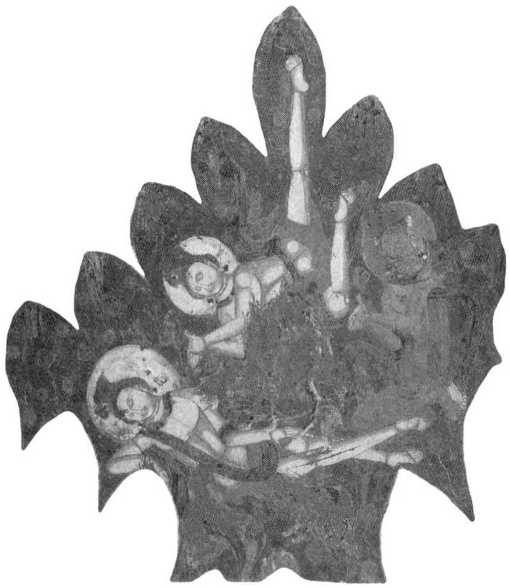

圖5　庫木吐喇石窟63窟

圖片采自《庫木吐喇石窟》圖145

其幼子（5）；三位王子談論老虎（6）；第七個場景並不清晰，似描繪了一個縱身跳下的形象（7）；第八個場景似乎是在描繪老虎啖食王子（8）；起塔供養（9）；阿難陀欣喜於佛陀的講授（10）。這些場景和《賢愚經》中版本基本保持一致。除敦煌外，該版本的圖像還見於中國的西藏和中原地區，此處亦不再煩舉。

我們在分析圖像時，常會碰到這樣一種有趣的情況：即圖像中的絕大部分情節與一

圖6　敦煌莫高窟254窟

圖片采自《敦煌莫高窟（一）》圖36、37；序號由筆者標出

個版本類似，但是其中幾個細節卻更接近另外一個版本。例如上述254窟的那幅壁畫，絕大多數場景都出自《金光明經》中的捨身飼虎本生，但是其中第七個場景卻與《賢愚經》中的描述相似："母扶其頭，父捉其手（T 202, 353a19-353a20）"。這種情形產生的一種可能性爲：曾有多種版本的飼虎本生在某地流行，而畫師在進行創作時，並非完全按照文本內容而是根據自己熟知的版本和圖像模式進行創作。

我們還會遇到另外一種類似的情況，即圖像中的絕大部分情節與某一個版本類似，但是其中幾個細節卻不見於任何已知版本。這種情況存在兩種可能性：一是畫師在進行創作時，在文本內容的基礎上進行了藝術的加工；另一種是在圖像中保留著一個版本，但是這個版本的文字資料尚未被發現。對於這種情況，下面舉例說明：

莫高窟72窟中有一幅五代時期的飼虎本生壁畫（圖8），其絕大多數的場景和題記均接近於《賢愚經》（T202）中《摩訶薩埵以身施虎品》，但是在第六個場景中即"三位王子遇餓虎和其三隻幼虎"中，幼虎的數量不見於任何的版本。這有可能是畫師在文本內容的基礎上進行的藝術發揮，但這也有可能意味著一個尚不爲人所知的文

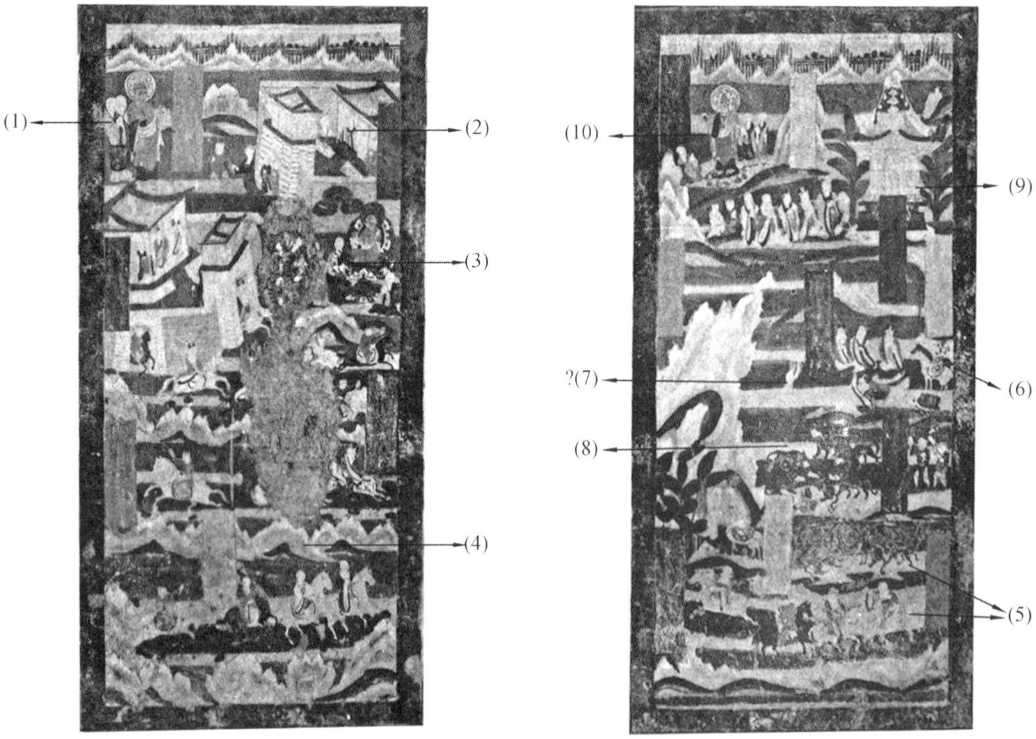

圖7　敦煌莫高窟98窟

圖片采自Pelliot, P., *Les Grottes de Touen-Houang*, 1920, Vol. 3, fig. 36、37；序號由筆者標出

字版本。

又如，在新疆碩爾楚克地區（Šorčuq）有這樣一幅壁畫殘片（圖9），畫面中一位元王子裝扮的人從高空縱身跳下，繼而平躺於地被一隻老虎和兩隻小虎啖食；一位天神立於一側扼腕歎息。從這樣的場景可以推知，在這幅壁畫所依據的文本中，捨身者是一位王子，捨身過程是從高空中跳下，幼虎數量爲兩隻。這些細節卻並不見於迄今所知的版本。當然，這有可能是畫師的自由創造，但是這也爲我們留下一個空白：也許歷史上確有一個這樣的版本符合這些條件。果不其然，在最近的關于一件吐火羅語殘片的研究中[7]，的確發現了這樣一個版本，其内容與畫面中的細節很接近。至此，這件碩爾楚克地區的壁畫殘片終於找到了它可能的文本依據。因此對於上述這種圖像和所知文本並不完全匹配的情況，一定要客觀謹慎對待，不能貿然套用已知的文本，否則也許就失去了發現新文本的可能。

最後值得一提的是，綜觀捨身飼虎的圖像和文本，我們發現並非所有的文本都曾被

⑦　吐火羅殘片338曾被吐火羅語學者西格和西格靈認爲是 *Jātakamālā*（《本生鬘》中的，但是最新研究表明，這張殘片上的內容不僅不是*Vyāghrījātaka*，而且也不與任何一個已知的版本相同，是一個全新的飼虎本生版本。殘片上可識別的內容爲：一位王子從高山上投身而下，捨身給一隻母虎和兩隻小虎。王子捨身後，兩位天神站在一旁禮贊王子。參見Pan, T. /Meng, Y.，*Eine tocharische Vyāghrī-Legende*（待刊）。

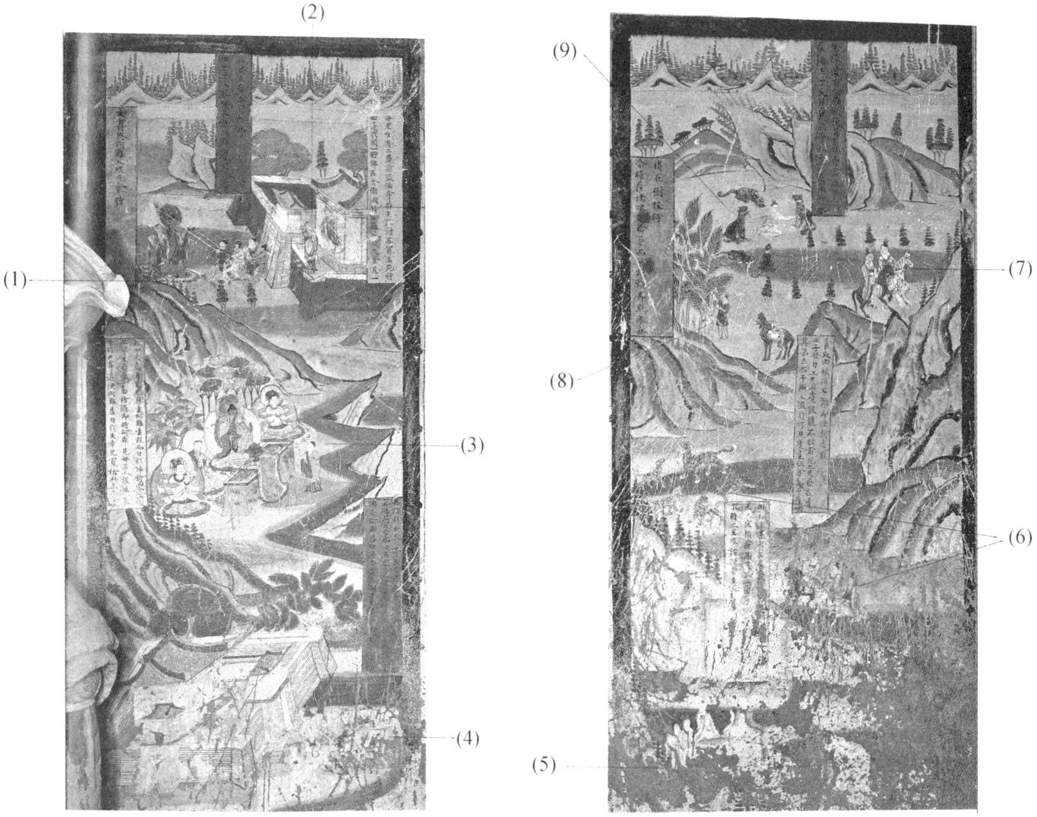

圖8　敦煌莫高窟72窟

圖片采自*Les Fresques de Dunhuang* 1989, Vol. 2, fig. 174；序號由筆者標出

圖9　新疆碩爾楚克（Šorčuq）“寫本窟”

圖片采自Deshpande, O. P. (ed.)，*The cave of one thousand Buddhas – Russian expeditions on the Silk Route, On the occation of 190 years of the Asiatic Museum, exhibition catalogue*, Sankt-Peterburg, Izd-vo Gosudarstvennogo Ėrmitazha, 2008, fig. 117；線描圖采自Schlingloff, 2000, Vol. II, fig. 164, [12]

用作圖像的依據，其原因也許是這些版本流行度較之其他略低。

綜上所述，通過這種窮舉法，仔細比對圖像與文本中的情節，從而可以確定兩者間的對應關係。捨身飼虎是一個古老而又著名的佛教故事，在歷史上所流傳過的文本和圖像一定遠超我們現在所能掌握的資料，因此我們現在得出的這些結論並非不刊之論，對其研究並不能就此打住。如果將來還會有更多的材料被發現，那麼我們需重新客觀審視這個本生故事並對其做出相應的修正 。

On Texts and Images of the Tigress Story —Using German Research Methodology of Buddhist Arts History

Meng Yu

The tigress (*vyāghrī* Sanskrit) story is one of the classic Buddhist Jātaka stories. The variants of this story are attested in Sanskrit, Chinese, Tibetan, etc. and its images can be found in India, Central Asia, East Asia and Southeast Asia. In this paper, the German research methodology of Buddhist Arts History is applied. It features the combination of artistic analysis and philological study. Using this methodology, this paper will bring to light many unknown details of the tigress story.

一個成功的誤解？

——西藏博物館所藏《噶瑪巴爲明太祖薦福圖》再考

姚　霜

對於研究15世紀漢藏交流歷史的學者來説，西藏博物館所藏的歷史宗教長卷《噶瑪巴爲明太祖薦福圖》無疑是一份重要、珍貴的圖像材料。這幅長達五十米的畫卷，通過四十九段繪畫與五體文字的題記，記錄了永樂五年（1407）西藏第五世噶瑪巴德行協巴（De bzhin gshegs ba, 1384—1415）受明成祖（1360—1424）邀請至南京舉行的一系列震撼的宗教活動（圖1）。關於這幅圖的關注，中外學界基本始於20世紀五六十年代。據資料顯示，這幅畫卷原存於噶瑪噶舉的祖庭楚布寺，1960年代由於文物徵集收入西藏文管會，存於羅布林卡，後2000年西藏博物馆成立後遷置於此館，並可謂其鎮館之寶之一。從研究之始出，這幅畫便是研究明初漢藏交流歷史的重要圖像材[1]。但正如台灣學

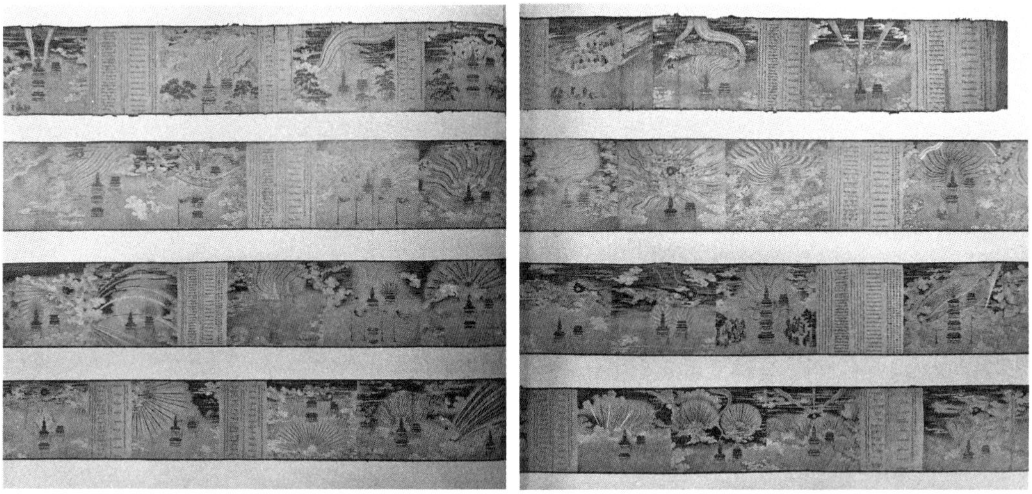

圖1　噶瑪巴爲明太祖薦福圖

畫卷，4768厘米×66厘米，西藏博物館藏（來源：《寶藏：中國西藏歷史文物》北京：朝華出版社，2000年）

① 圍繞這幅畫的歷史背景研究，可謂從韓儒林先生的《明史烏斯藏大寶法王考》（韓儒林《穹廬集》，石家莊：河北教育出版社，2002年），宿白先生《堆龍德慶楚布寺》（宿白《藏傳佛教寺院考古》，北京：文物出版社，1996年）等重要文章，到諸如此類涉及到的人物和其活動的考證，如三寶太監侯顯和大寶法王哈立麻普京行程等等。研究綜述參見駱愛麗《明成祖與大寶法王交流研究——以宗教畫卷〈薦福圖〉爲例》，《新世紀宗教研究》2007年第6卷第1期，45—51頁。

者駱愛麗在總結《薦福圖》研究史時發現，包括五體字的語言考訂，很少有學者關注到了繪畫本身的特質，這些展示的圖像與題記的關係，和題記中的內容與歷史記載的清晰鏈接[②]。本文無疑是需要從繪畫本身出發，試圖在文本、圖像、歷史三者間再次探析這幅存世名畫。

畫卷的製作與版本

首先，關於怎樣解讀這幅畫展現的內容需涉及中國捲軸畫中"讀畫"的問題。張洪興在《重讀中國捲軸畫中的題記》指出，中國繪畫長卷形式上的題跋在11—14世紀大力發展中，並不能單純理解爲書與畫一體的象徵式，或漢字本身的神聖性，由於技術的革新，寫作與繪畫傳統，在裝裱程式的產生與印刷的發明下得到了轉變；讀一幅長卷的方式，正如緩緩攤開一本有前言、腳注和後記的書一樣[③]。從此傳統中國畫卷的製作與觀賞的角度，本畫卷開篇的漢文的題記則如一個書寫規則規範的前言，比如"大明皇帝"與兩個皇字頂格書寫的現象。前言中所述（圖2）：

> 大明皇帝迎請如來大寶法王大善自在佛哈立麻巴，領天下僧眾於靈谷寺修建普度大齋，薦揚皇考太祖高皇帝、皇妣孝慈高皇后，普度天下一切幽靈。自永樂五年二月初五日蕆事之始，有五色卿雲絢爛 [?]紛騰湧凝聚，狀若如意。復有舍利見光塔頂如明月初升，皎潔流動，又見金色光二道[④]。

這一段作爲綱領性的繪畫內容指示，交代了重要的時間、地點、人物與事件的來龍去脈。接下來，如所謂的"連環彩圖"，整卷一共有四十九幅分圖，有的是一幅圖前既有一段題記，有的是一段題記後跟著多幅畫面[⑤]。題記與畫面在此形成了一種互指的關係。然而，當查看一些多幅畫面的連接處，不難發現畫卷存在明顯的分割與拼接的痕跡（圖3）。當對比同類的中國傳統敘述畫（narrative painting）中連貫的畫面時，是否可以猜測這些小單位的繪畫形制在創作後經歷過排列與裝裱？至此，可以觀察到一種書的功能形制在主導著這幅畫卷的製作，而書的功能是否暗示著這幅繪畫的記述功能大於藝術審美目的呢？復次，被鎖定爲"前言"或者"導讀"的題記由五種文字寫成，除了與圖像形成互指外，筆者認爲這樣出現在歌功頌德的石碑牌匾上的多語言文字組合形式更是起了一個彰顯作用。對於這五種文字，基本可以確定爲：漢文、回回文、畏兀兒

---

② 見駱的研究評述與展望於《明成祖與大寶法王交流研究——以宗教畫卷〈薦福圖〉爲例》，49—50頁。

③ Hongxing Zhang, "Re-reading Inscriptions in Chinese Scroll Painting", *Art History*, vol. 28, no. 5, 2005, pp. 606-625.

④ 此段文字句讀將原題記圖像對勘於之前發表文章不同版本記錄所作整理。

⑤ "連環彩圖"一詞出自索文清《明初哈立麻晉京朝覲與"薦福圖"的誕生》,《西藏民族學院學報（哲學社會科學版）》2009年第30卷第1期，19頁。

圖2 噶瑪巴爲明太祖薦福圖（局部）

畫卷，4768厘米×66厘米，西藏博物館藏（來源：《寶藏：中國西藏歷史文物》，北京：朝華出版社，2000年）

圖3 噶瑪巴爲明太祖薦福圖（局部）

畫卷，4768厘米×66厘米，西藏博物館藏（來源：《寶藏：中國西藏歷史文物》，北京：朝華出版社，2000年）

文、藏文、畏兀体蒙古文，這些語言研究已取得豐富的成果⑥。但爲什麼這裡會出現這樣的五體合璧？興許這個答案可以對比放置在此時永樂皇帝的另一個關於藏傳佛教的宏大文化項目中去尋找。在永樂版《大藏經》中，首頁繪圖中可以找到一塊石碑的獨立位置（圖4）。石碑上彰顯皇權的字眼十分醒目，與圖像一道爲接下來的經書文字內容仿佛在開頭做了一種神聖的加持。多體文字合璧常以碑刻形式出現，例如敦煌的五代梵、藏、漢、回鶻的六字真言石刻（圖5），而在元代多文字的六字真言的盛行更是以居庸關的過街塔上的多文字咒語石刻（圖6）爲代表。而根據元代書家盛熙明的記載："今上（妥懽帖木兒）即位之初，聖師大寶葛嚕麻瓦，自西域來京師。解行淵深，福慧具足，明通三世，闡揚一乘。同自在之慈悲，宣六字之神力。上自宮庭王臣，下及士庶，均蒙法施，靈感寔多，不可備錄，將非大士之應化者乎，然江南未之聞也，故略紀其實。若六字咒，師所常誦。唵麻尼巴口能二合口迷吽。"⑦ 由此知，六字真言碑在元代流行開來的源頭之一就是因爲三世噶瑪巴向妥霍帖木兒宣講了"六字之神力"。而從中國藝術史的角度，作爲色目人的盛熙明則作有《法書考》，這本元代關於漢字書學理論傳統的經典不僅在思想上呼應了趙孟頫的推崇二王的復古理念，其中引入了梵文語言語音的比較與從自己的經驗講述不同書體書寫的技巧。所以，與其驚嘆這樣的書體書寫難度

圖4　傳永樂北藏圖版

1440年刻本，白棉紙，36厘米 × 12.5厘米（網絡資料）

⑥　長期以來學界對僅次於漢文後的文字的識別未有定論。台灣學者駱愛麗與其博士生導師劉迎勝最終確認了此字體爲回回文。參見駱愛麗、劉迎勝《噶瑪巴爲明太祖薦福圖回回文初探》，《西北民族研究》2006年第1期，52—63頁。其他文字研究總結見前述注①，駱愛麗《明成祖與大寶法王交流研究——以宗教畫卷〈薦福圖〉爲例》。

⑦　（元）盛熙明《補陀洛迦山傳》；轉引自謝繼勝《居庸關過街塔造像義蘊考——11至14世紀中國佛教藝術圖像配置的重構》，《故宮博物院院刊》2014年第5期，77頁。

圖5　莫高窟六字真言碑

元至正八年（1348）制，敦煌研究院藏

圖6　居庸關雲台

多文字碑刻，元代（網絡圖片）

與難以複製性，像《法書考》類似的由色目人撰寫的工具書的存在至少可以表明在明初要找到一個能夠題寫五字體題記的人並非難事。此外，這幅記載五世噶瑪巴的繪畫採用了這樣的五體合璧的題記，是否是明代宮廷在追溯和延續一個屬於噶瑪噶舉與中央政府交往的傳統？德行協巴如同他的前任一樣得配以有神力的文字。神聖的題記配以分段的圖像記錄，採用多用於經書、繪畫的捲軸式裝幀與經折式的奏折一道成爲了五世噶瑪巴的皇家記錄。

然而，上述畫卷質量的觀察與製作可能性的探討指向了一個不可忽視的問題：畫卷的版本。相較於大量關於畫卷體現的內容的歷史記載的討論，關注到畫卷本身的學者僅有20世紀50年代 H. E. Richardson 在實地調研的基礎上所寫成的《歷史記載的噶瑪派》（*The Karma-pa Sect: A historical Note*）⑧一文。本文將展示蒐集到的關於畫卷本身的文獻記載如下：

1. 藏文文獻《賢者喜宴》⑨

"khyad par tha ma'i nyin nub phyogs nas gser gyi 'od chen po byung bas rgya nag gi rgyal khams thams cad khyab pa bde ba can nas tshe dpag med kyi 'od zer du gzigs pa sogs ngo mtshar mtha'yas pa byung ba rnams nyin so so'i ling tse bkod / bod rgya yu gur sogs yig rigs du ma'i zhal yig dang bcas pa dar yug chen po gcig gi dkyus tsam pa'i ngo mtshar'ja'a sa zhes gsi thang yug dril du ma da lta yod par lta"（漢譯：尤其是最後幾日，從西方升起金色大光，普照漢土諸境，照見了從淨土到無量壽之光輝等等。生起的無盡神奇，記錄展示了每日的分段，帶有漢、藏、畏兀兒等許多文字額題記，如一匹大緞子那麼長的，稱作"（展現）珍奇的詔書"的絲唐，現在見有許多。）

2. 楚布寺藏《歷代噶瑪巴傳》⑩

"nyin re bzhin ngo mtshar mi 'dra ba sna tshogs byung ba rnams gong ma'i bkas ri mor bkod pa dang rgya hor yu gur tu ruska ste yig rigs lnga'i kha byang btab/ de 'dra sgar chen du 'ang yod par gsungs shing rnam thar chen mor yang byung"（漢譯：每日都出現了不同的神奇，在畫上記錄展示了過去的分段，並賦予了漢、蒙、畏兀兒等文字的五種題記。像這樣的"畫卷"，據說噶欽大營還存有，在大傳中也出現過。）

3. 英文文獻《西藏十六世噶瑪巴歷史》（*The History of The Sixteen Karmapas*）⑪

"Emperor Yung Lo decided that the apparently miraculous events which he had witnessed due to his devotion, should be recorded for posterity. He commissioned talented artists to

---

⑧ H. E. Richardson, "The Karma-pa Sect: a Historical Note. Part I", *Journal of the Royal Asiatic Society of Great Britain and Ireland*, nos. 3/4(Oct., 1958), pp. 139-164. Part II: *JRAS*, nos. 1/2(Apr., 1959), pp. 1-18.

⑨ 巴俄・祖拉陳瓦《智者喜宴》，北京：民族出版社，2006年，514頁。

⑩ 此《歷代噶瑪巴傳》（rNam thar chen mo）轉引自H. E. Richardson, "The Karma-pa Sect: a historical note. Part II", p. 16.

⑪ Karma Thinley, Lama Wangchhim, *The History of The Sixteen Karmapas of Tibet*, Boulder: Norbu Publications, 1980, p. 74. 作爲一本當代英文整合著作，作者的敘述顯然運用了多處資料來源。其中，永樂親自的描述很可能混淆了永樂皇帝於五世噶瑪巴離開後與其弟子在靈谷寺再次見到祥瑞之相而作的《御制靈谷寺塔影記》，而五種語言的考訂作者顯然也有自己的判斷。

represent them in painting on large rolls of silk, one of which was kept at Tsurphu. The emperor himself composed a literary account of the miracles, which was transcribed onto the paintings in five languages: Tibetan, Chinese, Mongol, Yugor and Turkic."（漢譯：永樂皇帝決定把這些因爲他的虔誠而親見到的明顯的祥瑞事件爲後世記錄下來。他命天才畫家將之展現畫在巨大的絲卷上，其中一卷保留在楚布寺。皇帝親自爲祥瑞作了文學描述，以五種語言被謄抄在了畫上：藏文、漢文、蒙古文、畏兀兒文和土耳其文。）

4. 漢文文獻《衛藏通志》[12]

> 前藏西北山後大寺噶爾瑪巴瑚圖克圖，系黑教喇嘛，雲南人也，即明時所謂哈立瑪者。藏手卷一軸，長二十餘丈，乃繪永樂初哈立瑪誦經靈谷寺圖。

從這些歷代文獻信息中，可得知在《智者喜宴》的作者巴俄·祖拉陳瓦（Gtsug lag 'phreng ba,1504-1566）時期就確有《薦福圖》的存在，而漢文記載至少可以證實"前藏西北山後大寺"，即楚布寺，在清代仍保存著一幅長卷。但是否就是如今我們看到的這幅呢？不僅如 H. E. Richardson 關注到據楚布寺的《歷代噶瑪巴傳》（*Rnam thar chen mo*）記載說在噶欽大營也有像這樣的，在所示噶瑪巴傳記中都指出了楚布寺藏卷並非唯一。此印證了駱愛麗在總結 H. E. Richardson 與《賢者喜宴》漢譯本時得出的猜測："目前典藏於西藏博物館的《薦福圖》畫卷爲紙質，如果藏文史料記錄與漢文譯文皆未有誤的話，那麼目前見到的這一幅《薦福圖》存世畫卷即非唯一的作品，應該還有絲質質地的畫卷。"[13] 於此，駱的疑惑點很大程度上是來自於對於"gsi thang"這個術語在翻譯中的理解偏差。David Jackson在《西藏繪畫史》（*History of Tibetan Paintings*）中有詳細討論，即"gsi thang"通常指漢地樣式的繪畫，而並不強調其本身材質[14]。所以，結合上述關於其作爲圖書功能性質的討論，情況可能是紙質材質在實用、操作層面上優於慢工細琢的絲帛畫，然後製作完每段記錄後固定在絲卷上，便於攜帶與保存。但是，如文獻顯示，又怎樣看待五世噶瑪巴的傳記中的確有多個版本存在的說法呢？值得注意的是，此段時間作爲西藏繪畫史一個重要發展時期，噶瑪噶舉派扮演了重要的角色。其中，關於16世紀噶瑪噶智畫派的創始人南卡扎西（Nam mkha bkra shis, 生卒年不詳，16世紀中葉至17世紀初），據工珠仁波切（'Jam mgon kong sprul, 1813—1899）在《知識總匯》（*Shes bya kun khyab*）中評述到，南卡扎西在曼拉頓珠（Sman bla don grub, 生卒年不詳，15世紀中葉）後再次引入漢地風格，在暈染和塗色的運用上，其借鑒的是大明的"gsi thang"模板[15]。而格噶喇嘛在他的《西藏藝術的准則》（*Principles of Tibetan Art*）

---

⑫ （清）松筠《西藏志·衛藏通志》，拉薩：西藏人民出版社，1982年，184頁。

⑬ H. E. Richardson, "The Karma-pa Sect: a historical note. Part II", p. 16; 駱愛麗《明成祖與大寶法王交流研究——以宗教畫卷〈薦福圖〉爲例》，50頁。

⑭ David Jackson, *A History of Tibetan Paintings: The great Tibetan painters and their traditions*, Wien: Verlag der Österreichischen Akademie der Wissenschaften, 1996, pp. 132-133.

⑮ David Jackson, *A History of Tibetan Paintings: The great Tibetan painters and their traditions*, p. 173.

一書中明確列出南卡扎西大力模仿的畫本就包括“中國皇帝於1407年獻給五世噶瑪巴德行協巴的 si thang”⑯。因此，從這些資料中看出，《薦福圖》應該在移動的噶欽大營中被噶舉的御用畫師們不斷摹寫。所以，我們在18世紀八邦寺版本的噶舉祖師肖像套畫（圖7）中看到與《薦福圖》近乎一致的靈谷寺瑞祥描繪就不驚奇了。如藏文的記載，

圖7　五世噶瑪巴德行協巴肖像

八邦寺版本，西藏東部，18世紀，100厘米×60厘米，布上礦物著色，Tambaram美術館，紐約

（圖片來源：Himalayan Art Resource）

⑯　David Jackson, *A History of Tibetan Paintings: The great Tibetan painters and their traditions*, p. 173.

“噶欽大營中有這樣的”，所指可能是臨摹的局部，也可能是一整幅仿製品。值得警醒的是，如中國繪畫史屢屢遭遇的鑒定困境，歷史記載中名氣越大，摹本、仿本的存在幾率越高。我們仍需對西藏博物館所藏的這幅畫做進一步的鑒定工作，因爲從該畫目前展現的情況，比如有之前學者指出過的匆促的結尾，畫卷裝裱的質量，並不像其他詔書等皇家記錄有章印、落款等有確切的證據信息表明這是原始本[17]。

再析歷史語境

接下來，對於這本“圖書”的閱讀可以分爲兩部分：一是讀“書”，二是讀“圖”。“書”對於“圖”的指示性在這裡是先決的，因爲當去掉這題記的提示時，幾乎無法在圖像的內部關係指導下讀出任何的敘述性。這種圖像自身即承載著連貫敘述性的畫卷實例在漢地的敘述畫中不勝枚舉，如《韓熙載夜宴圖》（圖8）或明王朝記錄性的《朱瞻基行樂圖》（圖9）。與這些敘述畫不同，《薦福圖》裡的圖像無法單獨存在被識讀。換言之，需先借助“書”，因爲“書”中的信息才是此畫實質的主體。正如之後出有《西天佛子源流錄》這樣記錄西藏上師活動的以文配圖的圖書呈現方式，這樣的記錄實質正是長期以來歷史學家將這幅畫當做重要史料的原因。由於篇幅原因，本文將關注共計二十二篇圖記中的十四篇，即是二月五日至十八日的靈谷寺齋事記錄。後八鋪爲三月的擇日個別實錄，如哈立麻受封“如來大寶法王西天大善自在佛”當日，或哈立麻出發前往五台山等。

圖8 《韓熙載夜宴圖》卷（局部）

五代，顧閎中作（宋摹本），絹本設色，28.7厘米×335.5厘米，故宮博物院藏

⑰ 呼籲對此畫本的質量進行再審核的有駱愛麗文章（駱愛麗《明成祖與大寶法王交流研究——以宗教畫卷〈薦福圖〉爲例》）和羅文華《明大寶法王建普度大齋長卷》，《中國藏學》1995年第1期，89—97頁。

圖9　《朱瞻基行樂圖》卷（局部）

15世紀，絹本設色，36.7厘米 × 690厘米，故宮博物院藏

正如駱愛麗在史料綜述中指出："薦福圖相關史料主要爲藏文史書、漢文梵剎典籍、漢籍史料，三者所強調的重點、記載篇幅與收錄內容互異……"，正是這種"互異"引發了本文對這些敘述的關注。在回歸這幅畫卷上的題記之前，需要確認的是，通過五體書各語言研究表明，漢文後面多語種題記是對漢文的翻譯，到了一些詞彙部分，甚至直接採用漢文音譯模式，而非施加了自己的敘述理念。所以，在此基礎上，本文將漢文文獻作爲理解這些詞彙的大背景書。以下將依次剖析出現在畫卷題記中的重要詞彙：

1. "普度大齋"

這個見於開篇題記的專有名詞指示了明成祖的要求。駱愛麗在文章中就此詞做出了判斷："明成祖爲其父明太祖與皇后所設置了一場'普度大齋法會'，其全名爲'法界聖凡水陸普度大齋勝會'，簡稱水陸會、水陸齋、水陸道場等。"[⑱]關於水陸道場的盛行據說源於梁武帝，這個可以通過佛法威力救度水陸空三界苦難眾生於解脫的法會，最早的存世儀軌見於宋代，並普及全國，尤其成爲了戰爭後朝廷常設的超度法會[⑲]。到了明代亦可從存世的水陸畫（圖9）中一探這種法會的流行。而靈谷寺在五世噶瑪巴到達

⑱　駱愛麗《明成祖與大寶法王交流研究——以宗教畫卷〈薦福圖〉爲例》，2頁。

⑲　關於水陸法會起源的史料："述曰越王出仕之初，登補陀觀大士，聞長身僧之言，許也。日爲師相且囑其諫君上勿用兵，其後張魏公浚果勸孝宗北徵越王，諫之不從及符離兵敗，浚歸見上，上迎謂浚以合，故囑公與諫免生靈塗炭也。史魏公過金山，覽梁武帝水陸儀軌之盛，謂報恩度世之道，在是乃於月波山創殿設十界像，與名僧講究制儀文四卷以四時修供，爲普度大齋，至今百年。"《大正新修大藏經本》佛祖統記，卷四十七，533頁。當代水陸法會研究見聖凱《漢傳佛教水陸法會大觀》，《中國宗教》2003年第9期，56—60頁。

之前曾經就爲宮廷承接著這樣的法事[20]。然而，這樣的普度大齋並非佛教法會的專屬。道教的《靈寶玉鑒》中所描述的普度大齋及其不同的儀軌，也用相似地一連數晝夜、建瑤壇等方式起著相似地開度超升幽魂的作用[21]。而在永樂四年的十一月，在德行協巴抵達南京的前一個月裡，朝天宮也在進行著追薦皇考皇比的普度大齋，同時亦出現了慶雲現、甘露降的情景，記錄在了祭酒兼翰林院侍講胡儼進獻的《孝感醴泉甘露頌》裡[22]。無獨有偶，這樣的群臣進獻也體現在了五世噶瑪巴設法後以內閣首輔胡廣（1269—1418）《聖孝瑞應歌》爲代表的賀表裡[23]。換言之，這種"普度大齋"放置在明王朝的法事傳統裡，可以是多宗教並施的。而根據明《禮部志稿》中"孝之先訓" 的記載"永樂元年五月，禮部尚書李至剛等奏宋制凡忌日於各佛殿誦經設帝後位百官行香今後宜依宋制於天禧等五寺朝天宮令僧道誦經三晝夜……"，結合靈谷寺舉辦薦場的歷史記錄來看，這些法會的目的似乎均指向的是"孝"這個最根本的儒家訴求[24]。

綜上來看，不管是佛教傳統、還是道教傳統，我們看到靈谷寺舉辦普度大齋在這時明王朝的語境下是爲了彰顯孝道的、是爲了安撫爲太平盛世犧牲的亡靈的，這與下達給五世噶瑪巴的聖旨訴說是一致的[25]。而這兩個目的的強調看似與另一個朱棣皇權爲了粉飾自己的合法皇位繼承而在永樂年間出現開啓的系列"瑞應"現象相關，如Patricia Berger在她的文中將五世噶瑪巴的來訪的判定歸於"瑞應"系列，看作爲"朱棣無恥篡

---

⑳ "［洪武二十七年］七月十二日本部官同僧司官華蓋殿欽奉聖旨徵南陣亡病故的官員軍士就靈谷寺做好事普度他恁禮部家用心整理欽此本部儀到靈谷寺修設大齋普度徵南陣亡病故等項……"（明）《金陵梵刹志》萬曆刻天啓印本，卷二，51頁。

㉑ "黃籙普度大齋道場（幾）晝夜伏乞開度某魂超昇所合依律接地建壇。"（明）《靈寶玉鑒》正統道藏本，卷十一，84頁。

㉒ "十一月庚申上修舉金籙齋法於朝天宮神樂觀洞神官追薦皇考皇妣甲子慶雲見朝天宮乙醜甘露降於宮樹丙申慶雲復見既訖事甘露復降孝陵，松柏醴泉由神樂觀上命中使取獻宗廟，分賜廷臣，群臣上表賀聖孝瑞應，上以因祥思懼，不宜怠，忽申傷之，侍臣楊士奇等俱有詩頌。"（明）《國朝典匯》天啓四年徐與參刻本，卷一百十三"禮部"，1469頁。

㉓ "十一月庚午祭酒兼翰林院侍講胡儼獻孝感醴泉甘露頌頌並序欽惟皇上臨御以來聖德廣被治化純利民安物阜世用大康端居穆清孝思罔極重念皇考太祖高皇帝誕膺天命統一環區昭德建中萬世永賴皇妣孝慈高皇后協贊萬幾同勤開創奉神靈之統理萬物之宜共弘大業垂裕後昆緬惟升遐喝勝追慕乃勑禮官徵召天下道流即朝天宮陳金錄普度大齋……聖子神孫萬歲千秋。"《南廱志》民國景明嘉靖二十三年刻增修本，卷二事紀二，36—37頁。

㉔ （明）《禮部志稿》萬曆刻天啓印本，卷二，42頁。

㉕ "大明皇帝致書法尊大乘尚師哈立麻巴：朕承皇考太祖高皇帝、皇妣孝慈高皇后深恩大德，未能上報，夙夜不寧。欲舉薦揚之典，重念奉天靖難之時，將士軍民、徵戰供給，死亡者眾。其時天下將士軍民爲奸惡驅迫，戰鬥供給，死者尤甚眾多。又念普天之下一切幽魂及胎卵濕化、禽獸草木，種種生靈，未得超度。諸如此類，欲與普遍濟拔。今特迎請法尊大乘尚師哈立麻巴，領天下僧眾，以永樂五年二月初五日爲始，於靈谷寺修建普度大齋二七晝夜。以此良因，特伸誠孝。惟願皇考、皇妣超遙佛界，一切幽爽咸脫沈淪，永固皇圖，恩沾萬有。茲特致書，以達朕意。尚師其亮之。"《請於靈谷寺舉辦道場事致哈立麻書》，載於《元以來西藏地方與中央政府關係檔案史料匯編第一冊》，北京：中國藏學研究中心，1993年，97頁。

位的神性正名”[26]。然而，正如明代皇帝的“宗教熱”被諸多學者陸續解密，從洪武時期這樣的從中央到地方藩王的皇家宗教贊助被描述爲“家族傳統”，而從明太祖後鼓勵親王贊助宗教法事活動更是盛行[27]。因此，與其需要解釋此事件爲皇帝的個人宗教信仰與儒家士大夫崇信的仁君的“天助”的調和，不如承認這樣的調和一直存在，因爲明王朝的皇帝一開始就沒有擯棄過佛教、道教，包括在對待藏傳佛教的傳統繼承上[28]。

2.“好事壇場”

既然在明王朝的法事傳統下，通過詔書皇帝的目的如此明確地表達，而德行協巴又作了什麼法與此相應呢？在多處畫面中，靈谷寺建築群的寶塔旁均被標有“如來大寶法王西天大善佛建好事壇場”（圖10）。那具體什麼是“好事壇場”呢？令人驚奇地是，這一具體記錄卻只出現在了藏文文獻裡：

“Zla ba phyi ma'i tshes lnga nas dkyil 'khor phyi nang rnams kyi thig btab pa la drung gis rgyal ba rgya mthso/ rin po ches phur pa/ bka'a bzhi bas gsang 'dus dpon po bas mi tra/ gzhan rnams kyis rdor dbying chos dbyings gsung dbang/ dgyes rdor/ rje btsun ma/ kun rig/ sman bla/ sgrol chog/ thug rje chen po'i gsung sgrub sogs dkyil 'khor bcu gnyis bzhengs”（漢譯：此後月第五日，施內外壇城之線紋，“法王”閣下作“大悲勝海”“紅觀音”，仁波切作“普巴金剛”，噶西瓦作“密集”；首席經師作“米扎百法”，其他人作“金剛界法界語灌頂”“喜金剛”“佛母”“大日如來”“藥師佛”“度母儀軌”“大悲觀音總持修習”等十二壇城。）[29]

如果根據大明皇帝的要求，德行協巴尚可施從二世噶瑪巴噶瑪拔希所傳的、藏傳佛教處理死亡最具代表性的《中陰聞解脫》（*Bar do thos grol*）超度儀軌，而噶舉派的儀軌文本裡，也留下過五世噶瑪巴的一篇《往生西方淨土祈願文》（*bDe ba can du bgrod pa'i smon lam ni*），這些看似更貼近要求的法門卻未被施展或強調，或許它們被用過此場或者而後去五台山爲新逝的仁孝皇后設薦場中也無從得知。而上述的施展的儀軌幾乎涵蓋了當時藏傳佛教無上密法的展示，其殊勝威力可想而知。而根據後大寶法王時代的明朝另一位重要的藏傳佛教高僧大智法王班丹扎釋的記載，“大悲勝海”，又名紅觀音

---

[26] Patricia Berger, “Miracles in Nanjing: An Imperial Record of the Fifth Karmpa's Visit to the Chinese Capital”, *Cultural Intersections on Later Chinese Buddhism*, Hawaii: University of Hawaii Press, 2001, p. 146.

[27] 具體案例分析參見Richard G. Wang, “Ming Princes and Daoist rituals”, *T'oung Pao*, 2nd series, vol. 95, 2009, pp. 51-119。

[28] 最新研究指出“大寶法王”這個名號是依據藏傳佛教噶瑪噶舉傳承名號的藏文漢譯，充分說明宮廷對藏傳佛教傳統本身的瞭解與重視。參見沈衛榮《藏傳佛教在西域和中原的傳播：大乘要道密集》，北京：北京師範大學出版社（即將出版）。

[29] 巴俄·祖拉陳瓦《智者喜宴》，512—513頁；此漢譯借鑒了周潤年版翻譯，在此基礎上亦有修正。周潤年《〈賢者喜宴——噶瑪噶倉〉譯注（六）》，《西藏民族學院學報（哲學社會科學版）》2012年第33卷第1期，62頁。

圖10　寶寧寺水陸畫

明代，山西博物館藏

儀軌，可謂是五世噶瑪巴的特色法門[30]。正是從這一系列金剛乘密法的展示後，皇帝才正式接受了灌頂，於四月聽聞了“六法之導引”，並親自實修。就在這個月德行協巴被賜封了“如來大寶法王西天大善自在佛”。而這一切前後因緣歸結在藏地祖師的敘述中爲：

“phyis rje de bzhin gshegs pa spyan ’dren par bzhed pa’i tse sku gshegs pas de’i sras ta’i ming rgyal po chen pos yab yum gyi thugs dgongs rdzogs dgos par yang dgongs phyad par rgyal po ’di ’jam dpal gyi sku’i bko pa yin yang/ lhag par btsun mo dam po sgrol ma’i sprul pa e dge ba’i bshes gnyin gyi by aba byas pa ste/ rgyal po’i bgyi ba chen pos gyengs/ dam pa’i chos las re zhig gyel bar gyur tse mnal lam du po ta lar spyan ras gzigs mjal du ’gro bar brtsams nas ri la ’dzegs pas ngal te ldog par ’dod tshe utabal sngon po che zhing mtho ba rgyas pa zhig ’dug pa la bzang po’i stabs kyis ngal bsos na slar phyin pa na ri rtse thugs rje chen po dang mjal byin gyi rlab pa’i snang ba byung/ de nas btsun mo dam pa des dam pa’i cho la bkul/ chos kyi rje spyan ’dren pa yang mnyel bsos pas gong mas kyang nga’i dge ba’i bshes gnyen ni btsun mo ’di yin zhes rtag du bngags pa mdzad skad…”（漢譯：此後，又準備迎請法王得銀協巴之時，（太祖皇帝）駕崩，故大明成祖皇帝也考慮需要完成父母之願望。尤其大明成祖皇帝是文殊菩薩之化身；皇后是度母之化身，施以妙善之業。皇帝之偉業“動搖”，使神聖佛法暫時發生亂相之時，據說（皇帝）於夢境中前往普陀拜見觀世音，因爬山之疲憊，正欲離開之時，眼前出現一枝高大而茂盛的青蓮花。（皇帝）趁良機歇息後復返，於山頂上拜見了大悲心佛並得到加持。此後，皇后督促弘揚神聖佛法，迎請法王，並使疲憊的皇帝得到康復，故皇帝曰“朕的妙善者即是此皇后”，對皇后贊不絕口。）[31]

顯而易見，在藏文的敘述中弘揚佛法成爲了大明統治者終極的訴求。明成祖在順帶爲逝去的父親服孝上，得到了大悲心佛的加持，弘揚佛法。法王的到來使皇帝從疲憊中復蘇，而在儀軌修持下，彩虹、大象、獅子、仙鶴、花雨、彩雲上的阿羅漢、諸佛陸續顯現，金光照大地等佛光現象也陸續出現。這樣與漢文敘述中釋道爲一種宗教手段而服務於儒家統治形成了鮮明的對比。正如學者總結過：“雖然，明成祖爲太祖及其皇后舉辦的薦福普度大齋被後人詮釋爲明成祖爲改變篡位者形象而導演的一場成功的政治秀，或者說是明成祖爲導入西藏佛教以強化皇帝的權力而作的宣言式的國家禮儀，但是它無疑亦爲這場秀的主要演員哈立麻尚師提供了一個充分展示番僧之神通和番教之魅力的舞

---

[30] 此信息爲中國人民大學歷史學院安海燕博士於2017年5月10日所作專題講座《大智法王班丹扎釋與明代北京的藏傳佛教——以〈西天佛子源流錄〉爲中心》所示，同名文章即將發表。安指出，班丹扎釋在第五世噶瑪巴處專門受了紅觀音灌頂，傳習其修法儀軌。

[31] 巴俄·祖拉陳瓦《智者喜宴》，514頁；漢譯引自周潤年《〈賢者喜宴——噶瑪噶倉〉譯注（六）》，63頁，有改動。

台。”[32]在這裡，前面的兩種觀點忽略了已經建立好且在中央與地方均盛行的法事傳統，過分強調了番教的神奇帶來的政治效應。

繪畫風格中的漢藏交流

番教的魅力無疑震懾了當時朝廷內外。就目前留下的關於此場景的回顧與後續連鎖奇跡瑞祥的出現，漢文文獻記載可谓從傳統的官史、到高官的文集、還遠至遼東的女僧人和朝鮮使臣。到了明中後期和清朝，類似以此事件爲基礎的民間文學描繪更是層出不窮[33]。此次事件不僅爲漢地豐富的文學文獻提供了內容，神奇的藏傳佛教文化還留下了自己的文化影響足跡：永樂皇帝大量的藏傳佛教造像、定制唐卡中爲漢藏佛教充分交流提供了有力證明。關於這一時期漢藏佛教藝術的交流，學者們之前的研究大量關注著漢風爲西藏藝術帶去的活力。然而，正如 Dora Ching 在研究大明皇家肖像時指出，永樂皇帝的肖像畫的細節中所含藏的藏傳佛教因素說明瞭在藝術製造上皇家層面對藏傳佛教藝術表現的一定的熟悉度[34]。而對於歷史語境的多方位的瞭解可以促使我們更加客觀地賞析這幅畫作的繪畫風格。過去關於此畫藝術表現寥寥的研究中，學者們關注到了此畫具有較高的寫實性，亦有學者提出其政治化宣傳的表現[35]。通過以下畫面細節的討論，本文將進一步論證此畫的寫實性，呼應了畫卷製作中此畫作爲“書”的功能；同時展現奇跡的藝術表現是否如之前學者認爲的具有政治色彩，本文將放置在漢藏藝術交流中評述。

首先，此長卷的繪畫敘述並不複雜：重復的主體建築標明事件發生位置，畫面之間區別在於周圍環境的變幻上。關於這些主體建築，羅在其文中特別對靈谷寺建築的樣式做了分析，對比了民國時期王煥鑣收集了種種古書精華編纂成的南京方志《首都志·附圖》中的“明靈谷寺景”證實了《薦福圖》中所繪的建好事壇場的無梁殿、大法堂和寶公塔均具有寫實性[36]。從此時汉地繪畫史發展來看，金陵作爲明朝的經濟中心，名勝古蹟作爲繁華城市衍生出來的文化消費之一在藝術上促成了“金陵勝景”繪畫題材。縱觀這類題材裡，我們或多或少可以從明中期已降的繪畫作品中看到作爲靈谷寺的標誌之寶公塔的影子（圖11）[37]。此外，至今環繞在南京城郊的松林裡的靈谷寺，以“靈谷深松”爲

㉜ 沈衛榮《“懷柔遠夷”話語中的明代漢藏政治與文化關係》，載於《西藏歷史和佛教的語文學研究》，上海：上海古籍出版社，2010年，589頁。

㉝ 總結見駱愛麗《明成祖與大寶法王交流研究——以宗教畫卷〈薦福圖〉爲例》，43—44頁。

㉞ 參見Dora C. Y. Ching, “Icons of Rulership: Imperial portraiture during the Ming dynasty (1368-1644)”, PhD dissertation, University of Princeton, 2011, pp. 122-130.

㉟ 前者參見駱愛麗《明成祖與大寶法王交流研究——以宗教畫卷〈薦福圖〉爲例》）和羅文華《明大寶法王建普度大齋長卷》，89—97頁；後者參見Patricia Berger, “Miracles in Nanjing: An Imperial Record of the Fifth Karmpa’s Visit to the Chinese Capital”, pp.145-170.

㊱ 羅文華《明大寶法王建普度大齋長卷》，90頁。

㊲ 關於明初城市文化消費見李孝悌編《中國的城市生活》，北京：北京大學出版社，2013年。

圖11　金陵勝景圖（局部）

明，鄒典，紙本設色，29厘米×1272.5厘米，故宮博物院藏

了重要的景色標誌，出現在了天啓版的“金陵四十景”[38]。而在這《薦福圖》畫卷中常有表現的松樹，實並非爲中國山水畫中範式般的環境點綴，或者是表達文人畫意涵松柏的孤傲正氣，其中甚至有單獨一鋪表現虹光大方一片松林（圖12），這些都應屬於紀實性描繪。另一個表現紀實的有趣細節即是在二月十八日，普度大齋最後一日的場景中出

圖12　噶瑪巴爲明太祖薦福圖（局部）

畫卷，4768厘米×66厘米，西藏博物館藏（來源：《寶藏：中國西藏歷史文物》，北京：朝華出版社，2000年）

㊳　天啓版“金陵四十景”總結見呂曉《圖寫興亡——明末清初"金陵勝景圖"研究》，2015年，99藝術網專稿，http://news.99ys.com/news/2015/0723/22_194901_1.shtml；亦可參見明代“金陵勝景圖”的歷史演變研究，呂曉《圖寫興亡：名畫中的金陵勝景》，北京：文化藝術出版社，2012年。

現一個半圓形的池子（圖13）。參照《靈谷寺寺志》："萬工池，一名放生池，在靈谷寺金剛殿之南。明初，靈谷寺建成不久，明太祖朱元璋幸寺，見寺院門前廣後狹，一日役萬工（軍）掘成，岸甃以石，栽蓮數百於內，其土堆爲假山，形如簸箕向裏，俗稱爲駕山，帝駕所臨也。"㊴正如文中所介紹到的形狀特點"簸箕向裡"，四根常用來表示邊界的高旗桿，說明這汪碧池記錄的即靈谷寺門前的萬工池。上述畫面細節的紀實性揭示了畫卷的"詔書"特質，而"珍奇詔書"的神奇處又表現在哪裡呢？

圖13　噶瑪巴爲明太祖薦福圖（局部）
畫卷，4768厘米×66厘米，西藏博物館藏（來源：《寶藏：中國西藏歷史文物》，北京：朝華出版社，2000年）

Berger 在其文中觀察到了這幅記事圖將描繪重點放在了天空的變化，而非人事上。她將這種表現追溯到了北宋時期著名的宋徽宗的《瑞應圖》（圖14），指出這裡政治化瑞應的視覺宣傳㊵。然而，這些祥雲圍繞富麗的建築，加之某些鋪裡出現了仙鶴環繞，這是汉地传统繪畫中表現仙境的慣用手法。即使脫離開宗教繪畫的語境，特別在是山水界畫這一體裁的繪畫中（圖15），或是早已形成裝飾程式的器物上（圖16），我們都可以看出這一傳統絕非具有強烈的政治色彩。這裡對於環境的處理，比如景深的宏觀視角、如意祥雲的勾勒、乘雲而來的仙人們等等漢地樣式成爲藏地繪畫吸收發展的重要導向。這也呼應了前文所提到的關於西藏繪畫史噶瑪噶智畫派發展的歷史記錄。然而，令這幅畫儼然又於即使作爲裝飾，但依然較淡雅清新的漢風繪畫不同的是什麼呢？這裡的強烈視覺差異應來自於這幅畫的豐富的色彩。而這些色彩恰恰是

圖14　瑞鶴圖
宋，趙佶，絹本設色，51厘米×138.2厘米，遼寧博物館藏

㊴　見於《第三章：山水》，《靈谷寺寺志》，2015年整理歷代史料新修，靈谷寺官網網站公佈：http://www.linggusi.net/whiterice/vip_doc/2797644.html

㊵　Patricia Berger, "Miracles in Nanjing: An Imperial Record of the Fifth Karmpa's Visit to the Chinese Capital", p. 150.

圖15　明蟠桃會卷

17世紀作品，仿方椿年（約1225—1264）之作，絹本設色，59.6厘米 × 1007.3厘米，美國華盛頓弗利爾美術館藏

由佔據畫面內容表現主體的、變化萬千的五色毫光（圖17—圖19）。在羅的文章中，他明確的指出了："畫面中常常出現的五色毫光，是西藏唐卡中表現神異景象的慣用手法，而漢地繪畫中極少使用，它顯然是受藏族繪畫藝術影響的結果。"[41]但是羅並未給出他所指的唐卡舉例。本文試圖明確的是，五色毫光的確來自於藏地繪畫的表現，其源

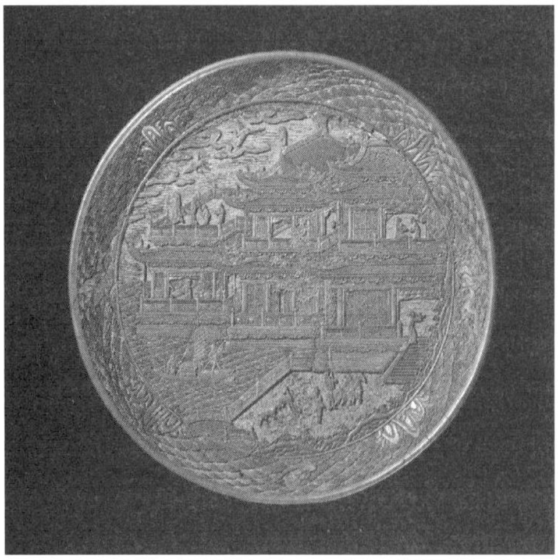

圖16　明代漆盤

平涼王銘作，1489年，中國甘肅，大英博物館藏

圖17　噶瑪巴為明太祖薦福圖（局部）

畫卷，4768厘米 × 66 厘米，西藏博物館藏（來源：《寶藏：中國西藏歷史文物》北京：朝華出版社，2000年）

[41] 羅文華《明大寶法王建普度大齋長卷》，91頁。

圖18　噶瑪巴爲明太祖薦福圖（局部）

圖19　噶瑪巴爲明太祖薦福圖（局部）

頭或應來自於對佛陀背光的表達。而17世紀後出現的神異虹光身的唐卡題材應是漢藏藝術交流的結果，正如這幅畫卷中展現的靈動的流光飛舞。對神異景象的描繪在藏傳佛教繪畫中有一特殊的題材，即佛傳故事中的捨衛城神變。然而，在12—15世紀的佛傳唐卡的表現中並未見對此有用五色毫光來展現這類神通場景的情況。恰恰是在17世紀後的關於這一題材出現的佛陀神變系列畫中，我們看到了相似的光彩表達（圖20）。而無論是在唐卡裡還是在壁畫中，五色毫光用來表現佛陀的背光卻是有靈動的變化。這一點僅從江孜白塔的15世紀的壁畫中（圖21），我們就可以總結出有五色整齊排列的，有波浪線性流動的，有鮮亮的純色的等多種背光的表現形式。作爲佛功德的一種，背光是法性的光輝，彰顯覺者的無所不能。佛光所照之處變得清淨莊嚴。藏地的畫工來自於他們豐富的重彩佛像繪畫經驗，對五色毫光這一繪畫題材的把握無疑更甚於漢地畫工。在《薦福圖》卷裡，五色毫光突破了背光形狀的限制，有橢圓形擬背光的展現，有的是直光，有的是曲光，也有配合以雲層自由穿插的不規則放散狀，有全方位綻放延伸至畫的邊緣，也有彩帶飄逸、寥寥數根就展現了舞動飛天。而這種筆法靈動性，彩虹間著色暈染過渡的自然感，處理空中複雜層次的交疊遠近，恐是漢地繪畫傳統的專長。而像《薦福圖》中表現異彩放光的漢藏藝術交流的成果更是體現在具有里程碑意义的瞿曇寺壁畫多處局部裡[42]。通過回顧上述的歷史圖像材料，因此可推斷《薦福圖》中表現出的繪畫風格很有可能是借鑒了當時西藏繪畫作品的元素，而漢地藝術家進行的發揮。

㊷　壁畫圖片参見金萍《瞿曇寺壁畫藝術研究》，北京：中國藏學出版社，2014年。

圖20　舍衛城神變系列畫

西藏唐卡，德格版版畫，1960年代印，原版制於18世紀中葉，西藏東部，

92.33厘米 × 60.33厘米，紐約魯賓博物館藏

結　　論

本文通過三個方面——繪畫形制與版本、歷史語境、繪畫風格——的討論，試圖將研究重點從研究史中大多歷史宏大敘述的發散移回材料本身的觀察與細節的探究。西藏

圖 21　釋迦牟尼像

15世紀，江孜白塔壁畫，西藏中部，作者攝影照片

博物館所藏《噶瑪巴爲明太祖薦福圖》無論是從繪畫形制的討論、還是藏文文獻的闡述、在功能上可以說是一本“展現珍奇的詔書”；然而，通過對藏、漢、英等歷史文獻的考察，本文明確了此畫卷版本存在的可能性，呼籲《薦福圖》的畫卷的進一步鑒定。其次，在細讀多語言文獻的歷史敘述中，我們看到一個漢、藏兩種文字敘述的、平行的故事：明成祖按照王朝的法事傳統，邀請五世噶瑪巴舉行“普度大齋”，以資孝道與

祈太平；大寶法王爲新皇十分具體地展示了藏傳佛教獨一的密法魅力，折服了皇帝。顯然，這兩個故事的版本分别都是從自己的語境出發，闡述了自己的時代訴求。最後，從這幅精彩的繪畫長卷藝術風格中，我們一窺到此次噶瑪巴的造訪不僅是一個漢藏交流在宗教精神上學習匯貫的實踐，也帶來了物質文化生産的一次互鑒交融。畫卷裡祥雲翻滾、霓虹飛舞，似你中有我，我中有你[43]。

A Successful Misunderstanding? : A Reexamination of the Painting Collection Handscroll "The Fifth Karmapa's Miracles in Nanjing" in Tibet Museum

Yao Shuang

In the Fifth Year of Yongle Reign (1407), Chinese Emperor Ming Chengzu (1360-1424) invited the Fifth Karmapa De bzhin gshes pa, the Tibetan monastic leader of Karma Kagyu School to the contemporary capital Nanjing and this historically significant visit has long been addressed by scholarships. This paper will emphasis on the long painting scroll "the Fifth Karmapa's Miracles in Nanjing" that records the amazing scenes taken place during the Fifth Karmpa's dharma-preaching for the Ming emperor and empress at the imperial temple Linggu Monastery. Through a textual criticism of multilingual historical records-Tibetan, Chinese and English, this paper focuses on the historical narratives of the main body of the painting subjects and endeavor to reconstruct a social and political context of Early Ming dynasty with various façades: What and how did the emperor request? What kinds of religious rituals did the Karmapa conduct? Was there an efficient and full understanding in the Sino-Tibetan court cultural exchanges initiated at the beginning of a post-Mongol new empire? Based on the excellent previous studies on the scroll, the author imports first-hand historical records along with image materials, and embeds them with a philological analysis, leading to a further delineation of parallel narratives for this particular miraculous event as well as a new perspective for reconsidering the scroll's painting style.

㊸ 關於本文標題說明："一個成功的誤解？"一詞來自於不丹宗薩仁波切的主題演講。宗薩解釋到，吉美林巴曾說，"我們思考時是迷惑，我們開口時是矛盾"，所以根本沒有溝通這種事，只有成功的誤解和不成功的誤解。通過本文，可以看到虔誠的皇帝已經被大寶法王的法力所折服，無需思考與討論；而那些明白的或誤解的，就只有留給纂修史書的儒士們評說了。

A Dream of the Emperor and the Translation of a Buddhist Scripture

Hanmo Zhang

Discussion of the origins of Buddhist belief and practice in China elicited from early on a wide array of tentative theories and debates based on related stories and scattered records. Among these theories, the "official"—and perhaps the most widely circulated—version holds that Indic Buddhist belief was introduced into China during the era of the Eastern Han Emperor Ming 漢明帝 (r. 57-75 CE). Details of the legend vary, but the basic elements consist of the emperor's dream, an imperial mission, two (Indian or Rouzhi 月支) monks, and a translated text entitled the *Sishier zhang jing* 四十二章經 (*The Scripture in Forty-Two Sections*), disputably the first Buddhist text translated from a foreign language—Indic, Iranian, or Rouzhi—into Chinese and the one on which the theory rests.

Taking this text as an example, I devote this article to the translation of early Chinese Buddhist texts. How do we understand the texts as well as the legends built up over centuries about their translation? How are we to understand the legends surrounding the original texts? How should we approach issues pertaining to the dating of the translations as well as their authenticity? These questions are the focuses of this article. In the following I will first briefly review the studies on early Chinese translations of Buddhist texts from a methodological perspective, then provide an assessment of the methods encompassed in the studies, and finally, by examining the *Sishi'er zhang jing* that has been wrapped in layers of legend in connection with the similarly legendary stories of An Shigao 安世高 and the translations attributed to him, attempt an alternative understanding of "translatorship," a term I have coined in parallel with "authorship."① The overall

① According to *Webster's Revised Unabridged Dictionary* published 1913 by C. & G. Merriam Co, the word "translatorship" denote "the office or dignity of a translator." This denotation, however, has little to do with the concept of "translatorship" discussed in this article. We shall use it instead as a parallel to the concept of "authorship." Here "translatorship" means a set of attributions of one or more than one translated text from a language other than Chinese. Those translated texts can be even more specifically limited to early Buddhist sutras considered to have been written in Indic or Central Asian languages.

goal of the article is thus to redefine early Chinese Buddhist translations associated with inquiries on the origin and nature of early Chinese Buddhism in terms of their translatorship.

Daoan's Catalogue and the Starting Point

According to the bibliographical information provided by the Southern Dynasties monk Sengyou 僧祐 (445-518 CE), dozens of Indian scriptures had already been translated into Chinese in the Eastern Han dynasty (25-220 CE).② Hundreds more were to come in the ensuing centuries. These early Chinese versions of Indian scriptures are important not only because they reflect the contents of early Buddhism was introduced into early China and how, but also because they preserve primitive versions of early Indian Buddhist texts that have been either lost or so altered over time as to differ substantially from the original versions. Indeed, in the case of a fair number of early Indian scriptures, the transmitted Chinese translations of the Indic texts represent the only medium through which such reconstruction may be attempted.

These texts carry specific philological significance in terms of the Chinese pronunciations of certain Buddhist terms, the vernacular elements of the language used, and the development of a specific literary style heavily influenced by the translation of Buddhist texts. Studies on the Chinese translation of Buddhist texts, albeit largely neglected by early generations of Western Buddhist scholars, have increasingly attracted attention in recent Buddhist studies.③ This trend is observable in the recent publication of papers presented at an international symposium, "Early Chinese Buddhist Translations," held in Vienna in 2007, and in Jan Nattier's *A Guide to the Earliest Chinese Buddhist Translations: Texts from the Eastern Han* 東漢 *and Three Kingdoms* 三國 *Periods* (henceforth referred to as the *Guide*).④

② Shi Sengyou 釋僧祐, *Chu sanzang ji ji* 出三藏記集, ed., Su Jinren 蘇晉人 and Xiao Lianzi 蕭錬子, Beijing: Zhonghua shuju, 1995, pp. 23-233.

③ Deeg, Max, "Introduction to *Early Chinese Buddhist Translations: Contributions to the International Symposium 'Early Chinese Buddhist Translations,' Vienna 18-21 April, 2007*," *Journal of the International Association of Buddhist Studies* 31.1-2 (2008(2010)), pp. 79-82. The philological study of Chinese Buddhist translations in the past hundred years has mainly been carried on by Japanese scholars. In the West only a handful of scholars have conducted research from that perspective; among.them Sylvain Lévi, Paul Pelliot, and Erik Zürcher. Zürcher's works will be discussed in more detail because of their methodological contribution to the study on early Chinese Buddhist translations.

④ Eleven papers presented in that symposium are published in the *Journal of the International Association of Buddhist Studies* 311.2 (2008(2010)) edited by Max Deeg; Nattier, Jan, *A Guide to the Earliest Chinese Buddhist Translations: Texts from the Eastern Han* 東漢 *and Three Kingdoms* 三國 *Periods*, Tokyo: International Institute for Advanced Buddhology, Soka University, 2008.

In these two volumes we can follow not only the revival of Buddhist philology spurred by the discoveries of new textual materials in Afghanistan, Pakistan, Japan, and elsewhere, but also a new enthusiasm for the study of early Chinese translations of Buddhist texts.⑤

Although more attention has been paid to the translations of Buddhist scriptures in comparison with earlier generations of Buddhist scholars, the current trend in Buddhist studies dealing with early Chinese translations has not made any significant methodological breakthrough. Reviewing the arguments made by various scholars in the above-mentioned two volumes, for example, one finds that, however elaborated, the fundamental framework and tools applied rely largely on the oversimplified understanding of translatorship to date, a method heavily influenced by early scholarship in Western Buddhist Studies, such as the works of Erik Zürcher decades ago.⑥ Since the major methods that the Guide adopts derive from such a tradition, a review of how this methodology works in Nattier's monograph is warranted.⑦

The *Guide* deals exclusively with Buddhist texts translated into Chinese during the second and third centuries CE (from the late Eastern Han to the Three Kingdoms). Its main objective is to "make available, in an easily accessible form, the most current information as to which Chinese Buddhist translations can be assigned with confidence to the Han and Three Kingdoms periods." ⑧ To achieve the goal of making her work a handy guide, Nattier compiles three appendices based on the examination of all the

⑤ Harrison, Paul, "Experiencing Core Samples of Chinese Translations of Two Buddhist Sūtras Analysed in the Light of Recent Sanskrit Manuscript Discoveries," In *Early Chinese Buddhist Translations: Contributions to the International Symposium 'Early Chinese Buddhist Translations,' Vienna 18-21 April, 2007* (*Journal of the International Association of Buddhist Studies* 31.1-2 (2008(2010)), pp. 79-504), pp. 205-249; Nattier, *A Guide to the Earliest Chinese Buddhist Translations*, pp. 163-168. Also consult Karashima Seishi 辛嶋靜志, *Fodian yuyan ji chuancheng* 佛典及傳承, Shanghai: Zhongxi shuju, 2016. The word "revival," according to Harrison, may not be accurate to describe the recent increasing scholarly interest in Buddhist philology, for he feels that it should be considered neither dead nor dying given the increasing attention paid to it in recent years.

⑥ Zürcher, Erik, *The Buddhist Conquest of China: The Spread and Adaption of Buddhism in Early Medieval China*, Taipei: Dunhuang shuju youxian gongsi, 1970, pp. 1-80 (especially pp. 10-17, pp. 32-57, and passim); "Late Han Vernacular Elements in the Earliest Buddhist Translations," *Journal of Chinese Language Teachers Association*, 1977.12, pp. 177-203. To his 1977 article, two Chinese scholars add more evidence following Zürcher's argument; see Chen Xiulan 陳秀蘭, "Dui Xu Lihe jiaoshou 'Zuizao de fojing yiwen zhong de Dong Han kouyu chengfen' yiwen de jidian buchong" 對許理和教授《最早的佛經譯文中的東漢口語成分》一文的幾點補充, *Gu Hanyu yanjiu* 1997.2, pp. 55-57; and Zhang Chunxiu 張春秀, "Dui Xu lihe jiaoshou 'Zuizao de fojing yiwen zhong de Dong Han kouyu chengfen' yiwen de zai buchong" 對許理和教授《最早的佛經譯文中的東漢口語成分》一文的再補充, *Hechi xueyuan xuebao*, 28.1 (2008), pp. 55-58. This is another example showing that current discussion on issues regarding early Chinese translation of Buddhist texts still goes on in a discourse created several decades ago.

⑦ Nattier, *Guide*, p. 30.

⑧ Nattier, *Guide*, p. 29.

translations alleged to have been made in those eras. The appendices include an index to translations dated to the Eastern Han and Three Kingdoms periods by their *Taishō* text numbers (Appendix 1), an index of Sanskrit and Pāli titles (Appendix 2), and a list of translations dating from these periods and arranged chronologically with clear attributions to individual translators (Appendix 3). She is at pains to provide a chronology for the "authentic" translations of early Buddhist texts, and all three appendices serve this end. For example, any text, even though ascribed to the periods under discussion in the *Taishō* database, should not be considered genuine in terms of its attribution if it is excluded from Appendix 1; moreover, its Indic origin deserves questioning if this text cannot find a Sanskrit or Pāli match in Appendix 2.[9] The confidence revealed in such argumentation clearly originates from the chronology provided in Appendix 3, a list of translations that are considered to have been authentically produced during the Eastern Han and Three Kingdoms periods.

Notwithstanding the convenience provided by these appendices, questions about how such a chronology is determined need to be asked. For example, how do we judge a translation to be authentic or not? How may it be dated? Why is it ascribed to one instead of another translator? These are among the fundamental questions demanding careful methodological consideration before such a chronology can be undertaken.

The authenticity issue is directly related to the attributions of the Chinese translations, especially regarding how to identify the translator(s) of a specific Buddhist text? Modern Buddhist scholars seem to have no choice but to follow earlier bibliographical works preserved in one form or another to the present day.[10] For the study of early Chinese translations of Buddhist scriptures from this perspective, Daoan's 道安 (312-385 CE) scriptural catalogue, the *Zongli zhongjing mulu* 綜理眾經目錄 (*Catalogue of the Comprehensively Arranged Various Scriptures*) completed in 374 CE, is particularly important. As one of the earliest catalogues of this kind, Daoan's catalogue has usually been considered one of the most reliable sources for the issue of translatorship. Daoan's work, however, is no longer extant. Everything we know about this catalogue relies on another Buddhist bibliographical work, the *Chu sanzang ji ji* 出三藏記集 (*Collection of Notes on Translated Tripitaka*) completed by Sengyou 僧佑 (445-518 CE) around 515 CE. Sengyou compiled the *Chu sanzang ji ji* in consultation with a number of previous bibliographical works and sources available to him, including Daoan's catalogue carefully teased out from the notes in the extant version of the *Chu sanzang ji ji*: Buddhist scholars typically identify such expressions as *gu lu* 古錄 (ancient catalogue), *jiu lu* 舊錄 (previous

⑨ Nattier, *Guide*, p. 29, pp. 169-178.

⑩ Nattier, *Guide*, p. 11.

catalogues), or *An lu* 安錄 (Daoan's catalogue) as from the *Zongli zhongjing mulu*.[11] Such expressions are mainly scattered in Fascicles 2, 3, and 5 of the *Chu sanzang ji ji*, a fifteen-fascicle collection of catalogues, colophons, and biographies of eminent monks.[12] However dispersed they are, it is through the *Chu sanzang ji ji*, the preserver and also the filter, that we are able to catch a glimpse of the major source for the *Guide*.[13]

Sticking to the reconstruction of Daoan's catalogue based on the limited information running through the *Chu sanzang ji ji*, Nattier first determines attributions to a few central translators as the benchmark for other attributions. It seems that she is ready to trust attributions made in Daoan's catalogue as direct links to the actual translation activities, translated scriptures, and translator groups, historicizing them as a result. Once such a cornerstone is established, a few translators are identified, their translatorship is confirmed, and their corresponding literary styles and characteristic vocabularies constructed. Thus a whole set of standards applied to categorize other works, with or without attributions, comes about. The sources—above all the *Zongli zhongjing mulu*, or rather, the *Chu sanzang ji ji*—which provide the essential starting point for the *Guide* are dubbed "external evidence;" whilst the constructed literary style and vocabulary of a specific translated scripture attributed to a specific translator, the "internal evidence."[14] These two kinds of evidence constitute the major strength of Nattier's method. Taking advantage of the convenient word searching tools provided by digitalized Buddhist texts and previous scholarship, Nattier builds links between various translator groups and various literary styles and vocabularies and uses these links to return and check the authenticity of those attributions that enable the construction of the "internal evidence" from what she calls the "starting point."

Since the concept of "starting point" takes on crucial significance, the question deserving our special attention is how credible the information which it provides might be. To this end, it is worth considering what prompted Daoan to catalogue those translated sutras, what sources he relied on when he compiled his catalogue, and how we identify and understand the information from Daoan's catalogue later scatted in Sengyou's compilation. These are among those fundamental questions that need to be addressed to evaluate the above-mentioned approach which is applied not only in Nattier's work but

---

⑪ Other phrases, such as *huo yun* 或云 (some say) and *bie lu* 別錄 (other catalogues) are also frequently seen in Sengyou's commentaries; see Sengyou, *Chu sanzang ji ji*, pp. 23-65 and passim; for a summary of the sources the *Chu sanzang ji ji* relies on, see Sengyou, *Chu sanzang ji ji*, pp. 5-8.

⑫ For a reconstruction of Daoan's catalogue, see Tan Shibao 譚世保, *Han Tang foshi tanzhen* 漢唐佛史探真, Guangzhou: Zhongshan daxue chubanshe, 1991, pp. 67-82.

⑬ Nattier, *Guide*, pp. 163-164, pp. 8-13, and passim.

⑭ Nattier, *Guide*, p. 11.

also widely adopted by scholars of Early Buddhism in general. The following section is designed to fulfill this need. Since the method in question uses the starting point to identify early translators and their translations from the "external evidence," the following section will start by reviewing how related "external evidence" works in defining the starting point.

Scripture Cataloging and Scholar-Monks

The "external evidence" referred to in the Guide comprises two categories: bibliographical materials and biographical materials. Although a number of other catalogues are mentioned in the *Zhongjing mulu* 眾經目錄 (*Catalogue of the Many Scriptures*) attributed to Fajing 法經 dated 594 CE and the *Lidai sanbao ji* 歷代三寶記 (*Records of the Tripitaka of the Past Dynasties*) to Fei Changfang 費長房 dated 597 CE—it is the remaining *Zongli zhongjing mulu* preserved in the *Chu sanzang ji ji* that serves as the most reliable source to identify those early translators and date their translations. Once such a benchmark is established, inconsistent information preserved in other sources must yield to Daoan's authority contained in the *Zongli zhongjing mulu* reconstructed through Sengyou's extant work. A particularly interesting phenomenon is that the number of attributions to early translators of Buddhist scriptures increases in later catalogues as compared to earlier ones. This phenomenon is not explored to elicit meaningful information regarding those attributions in relation to the development of early translatorship. The assumption that the earliest catalogue amounts to be the most reliable source simply dismisses later added attributions as false attributions. The *Lidai sanbao ji* is considered the least reliable source because of its large number of such "false attributions." Similarly, attributions made in Fajing's *Zhongjing mulu* and other catalogues, though not accused as false as those included in the *Lidai sanbao ji*, are also doubted and need additional "careful consideration" when they are not found in Sengyou's catalogue.[15]

Relevant comments made here and there in the *Guide* indicate three reasons as to why the *Zongli zhongjing mulu*, a catalogue that has partially survived, is given so much authority. First, Sengyou's (as well as Daoan's) work "gives the impression of being the product of a careful and critical group of scholars;"[16] and "he (Sengyou) was an exacting scholar who treated his sources with great care," although inconsistencies are by no means

⑮ Nattier, *Guide*, pp. 13-15.

⑯ Nattier, *Guide*, p. 14.

rare in his work.[17] Elsewhere the *Guide* stresses that Daoan was a careful scholar: he not only listed the translated scriptures in his catalogue but "read the texts himself, making his own decisions about the likely authorship of some previously unattributed works."[18] Both Daoan and Sengyou, the "two scholar-monks," "share a well-deserved reputation for high scholarly standards."[19] In short, these comments attempt to convey a simple, direct message: the reliability of the two sources stems from the trustworthiness of their authors, who, portrayed as serious scholars, were primarily concerned with objectivity when compiling their catalogues.

Second, the *Chu Sanzang ji ji* itself is considered an archaic work. To enhance the reliability of the *Chu sanzang ji ji*, the Guide stresses that the *Chu sanzang ji ji* is the oldest extant catalogue of Buddhist scriptures translated into Chinese. As part of the *Zongli zhongjing mulu* has survived to the present day as a result of its inclusion in the *Chu sanzang ji ji*, the *Zongli Zhongjing mulu* must be even earlier; in fact, it is considered the earliest catalogue as such.[20] This notion of valuing the earlier over the later information has to do with the imagination of textual originality: the earlier a text is, the closer it is to its "original form," and, following such reasoning, the greater its validity as testimony for the "original form" of a given text.

Finally, as stated in the *Guide*, the method guiding this project of making a chronology for the early translated Buddhist scriptures needs a starting point with authored and dated translations, and thus gives weight to Daoan's *Zongli zhongjing mulu* preserved in the *Chu sanzang ji ji* fulfills this need.[21] Since Nattier's study is "organized around the names of particular individuals who are said to have played a key role in the initial period of the translation of Buddhist scriptures into Chinese," it requires identifying those individuals based on external evidence. The *Guide* thus hails Daoan's catalogue, disputably the earliest work of this kind preserved in the oldest extant *Chu sangzang ji ji*, as the most suitable source to generate the much needed conversation between translated scriptures and their attributions.

Compared with the bibliographical source (mainly the *Chu sanzang ji ji*), the significance of biographical material—mainly the *Gaoseng zhuan* 高僧傳 for this period—

---

⑰ Nattier, *Guide*, p. 13.

⑱ Nattier, *Guide*, p. 11.

⑲ Nattier, *Guide*, p. 11.

⑳ Nattier, *Guide*, pp. 11-13. Though stating that the date of Daoan's and a few others' catalogues mentioned by Sengyou in the *Chu sanzang ji ji* is still much of an on-going scholarly debate, Nattier does bring up Tan Shibao's theory indicating that neither the *bie lu*, or separated catalogue, nor the *jiu lu*, or previous catalogue, is older than the *Zongli zhongjing mulu*. Tan Shibao, *Han Tang foshi tanzhen*, pp. 33-52.

㉑ Nattier, *Guide*, p. 11.

is downplayed and conflated with the *Chu sanzang ji ji* because of the former's relatively later date. The *Gaoseng zhuan*, compiled by Huijiao 慧皎 (497-554 CE), is said to have been finished around 530 CE, fifteen years later than the completion of Sengyou's catalogue.[22] The opening section of the *Gaoseng zhuan* has long been held essential to the study of the early Chinese translation of Buddhist texts for its inclusion of the biographies of early translator-monks. Nevertheless, because it is dated slightly later than the *Chu sanzang ji ji*, the information that the *Gaoseng zhuan* contains similar to that in the *Chu sanzang ji ji* is considered in the *Guide* to have followed or even replicated Sengyou's work "word by word."[23] The reason that the *Guide* believes that Huijiao "plagiarized" Sengyou's writings has to do with the supposed date of the *Gaoseng zhuan*—fifteen years later than the *Chu Sanzang ji ji*. The method adopted by the *Guide* requires all related sources to be clearly dated and well sorted, so that the earliest and authoritative reference can be determined and the anxiety caused by undated resources eliminated.[24] In fact, although the *Guide* lists the *Gaoseng zhuan* and a few other bibliographical works as "external evidence," the *Gaoseng zhuan* has never been as trusted as the *Chu sanzang ji ji*, if only because it is dated fifteen years later than the latter. The *Guide* has remained fairly consistent in establishing the *Chu sangzang ji ji* (because it contains information on the "earliest" *Zongli zhongjing mulu*) as the single most important source with a few minor adjustments.

Once jump-started by the attributions made in the authoritative *Chu sanzang ji ji* and part of the *Zongli zhongjing mulu* surviving in the former, the ensuing analysis of certain linguistic features of early translations of Buddhist scriptures in conjunction with their attributions becomes possible. A list of "consensus texts," which serve as the core texts to define the translation style and the vocabulary characteristic of the translation style and in the end turn out to be "internal evidence," is based upon both the *Chu sanzang ji ji* and the research of either Ui Hakuju 宇井伯壽 or Erik Zürcher. In other words, the "internal evidence" is a specific database established to pair the translators and the translations according to the analysis of vocabulary, grammar, sentence structure, and literary style of the core texts. Once this sort of database exists, a scholar can employ it to investigate the sub-groups of translations and identify their attributions. This is exactly what the *Guide* has achieved: it provides a chronology of those Buddhist scriptures considered to have

---

㉒ Zürcher, *The Buddhist Conquest of China*, 10.

㉓ Nattier, *Guide*, p. 13, p. 16.

㉔ Nattier, *Guide*, p. 13; Shi Huijiao 釋慧皎, *Gaoseng zhuan* 高僧傳, ed., Tang Yongtong 湯用彤 and Tang Yijie 湯一介, Beijing: Zhonghua shuju, 1992, pp. 1-4.

been translated during the second and third centuries.[25] The chronology, made strictly according to the method widely adopted in the studies of early Buddhism, is expected to join other scholars' works—such as Ui's, Zürcher's, and Sengyou's—as "external evidence" to facilitate further studies on the attributions of early translated Buddhist scriptures.

This chronology results from the attempt to describe the actual circulation of translated Buddhist scriptures among different social groups in early China based on certain linguistic features of the translations that have survived in the Buddhist corpus. Assuming that the translations attributed to early translators have remained basically unchanged throughout their long transmission, scholars of early Buddhism have located vernacular elements in some early translations (especially in those attributed to Lokakṣema (Zhi Loujiachen 支婁迦讖, fl. 168-189 CE)) and try to link them to a possible social, cultural, and geographical environment in which early Chinese Buddhism was fostered.[26] On the basis of this assumption a dichotomy of "vernacular versus literary" is constructed upon limited data. According to the *Guide*, it reveals two distinct audiences to whom the translations were addressed: the literary style reflects the taste of Chinese literati and accordingly the more elegant and classical translations were made by and for the literati; in contrast, the translations containing frequent vernacular expressions and transliteration of terms foreign to Chinese were received by "an audience of immigrants of various nationalities."[27] The *Guide* even speculates that the lack of a style combining vernacular speech with domesticated vocabulary in those early translations attests the absence of "the masses of uneducated, and monolingual, Chinese" among early Buddhist believers.[28] The confidence of making a chronology for early Chinese translations of Buddhist scriptures based on some of their linguistic features is rooted in precisely such an academic trend. It directly supports the belief that some terms and expressions found in early Chinese Buddhist translations—Buddhist names, technical terms, or even pronouns, particles, and the structure of interrogative sentences—can be used to identify the translations as well as the "specific geographical and/or social milieux" with which those translations were associated.[29]

㉕ Nattier, *Guide*, pp. 175-178.

㉖ For example, see Zürcher, "Late Han Vernacular Elements in the Earliest Buddhist Translations," pp. 177-203; Zürcher, "Vernacular Elements in Early Buddhist Texts: An Attempt to Define the Optimal Source Materials," *Sino-Platonic Papers* 71 (1996), pp. 1-31; Zhu Qingzhi 朱慶之, *Fodian yu zhonggu Hanyu cihui yanjiu* 佛典與中古漢語詞彙研究, Taipei: Wenjin chubanshe, 1990, pp. 1-55; Mair, Victor H., "Buddhism and the Rise of the Written Vernacular in East Asia: The Making of National Language," *Journal of Asian Studies* 53.3 (1994), pp. 707-751.

㉗ Nattier, *Guide*, p. 18.

㉘ Nattier, *Guide*, p. 18.

㉙ Nattier, *Guide*, pp. 18-19.

By applying both "external evidence" and "internal evidence" to date and analyze the texts, the *Guide* is able to bring a panoply of sources together and update the scholarship on selected texts. The results, as shown in Appendix 3, suggest that the *Guide* has raised the scholarship to a more "scientific" level. Although the digitized Buddhist corpus and online searching tools are by no means new, the *Guide* has deliberately brought them into the spotlight.[30]

One fundamental question immediately arises, however, when we consider the logic behind this method, whose cornerstone is the starting point, a piece of external evidence with the ultimate authority of guaranteeing a list of earliest translators and the scriptures they translated. Nattier designates Daoan's catalogue that has only partially survived as the starting point because she considers the catalogue an early product and its compiler reliable. But we cannot simply equate a source's antiquity with its objectivity and directly translate Daoan's reputation into the authority of his work. In fact, even if we assume that Daoan's catalogue is the oldest and its parts surviving in the *Chu sanzang ji ji* belong to the original, we still cannot ascertain whether Daoan's attributions of the translations to those individuals reflect the truth. After all, by the time Daoan's catalogue was completed (dated 374 CE), the earliest translation (if the dating is reliable) had been made over two hundred years earlier, and even the latest of the group of translated scriptures regarded as the starting point had been in circulation for around one hundred years (dated 147-280 CE). Lacking secondary sources, written or oral, how could Daoan know exactly who were the translators of the early translated scriptures?

The above-mentioned assumptions become especially suspect when we consider how early Chinese texts were produced and transmitted. Textual and archaeological evidence attests that authors' names do not appear in early Chinese texts.[31] The same convention can be applied to the analysis of early Chinese translations of Buddhist scriptures. According to a passage appearing nearly identically in both Daoan's *Chu sanzang ji ji* biography and his *Gaoseng zhuan* biography, the names of the translators were not in fact recorded in early translated Buddhist scriptures:

自漢暨晋，經來稍多，而傳經之人，名字弗記。後人追尋，莫測年代。安乃總集名目，表其時人，銓品新舊，撰爲經録。衆經有據，實由其功。

From Han to Jin, the number of imported scriptures had gradually increased, but

---

[30] Nattier, *Guide*, p. 30.

[31] Yu Jiaxi 余嘉錫, *Muluxue fawei wai yizhong: Gushu tongli* 目錄學發微 外一種：古書通例, Changsha: Yuelu shushe, 2010; Li Ling 李零, "Chutu faxian yu gushu niandai de zai renshi" 出土發現與古書年代的在認識, *Jiuzhou xuekan* 3.1 (1998), pp. 105-136; Pian Yuqian 駢宇騫 and Duan Shuan 段書安, *Ershi shiji chutu jianbo zongshu* 二十世紀出土簡帛綜述, Beijing: Wenwu chubanshe, 2006.

the names of those who translated the scriptures were not recorded. Later when trying to trace the scriptures, no one could detect their dates. Daoan then collected the lists of translated scriptures, recorded their dates and translators, differentiated the old from the new, and compiled a catalogue for the translated scriptures. That the numerous translated scriptures could be identified was indeed due to his achievement.[32]

As this passage makes clear, in texts from the Han (206 BCE-221 CE) to the Jin (265-420 CE), "the names of those who translated the scriptures were not recorded." It is Daoan who collected and listed the translated scriptures and identified their attributions in his catalogue. Was Daoan the first compiler of this sort of catalogue? Or did he make his own catalogue relying on similar earlier kinds? If his catalogue was the earliest, how could he identify the anonymous translators of those scriptures transmitted over centuries? We do not know the exact answers to these questions. Certain sources suggest the existence of some sort of catalogue prior to the compilation of Daoan's catalogue. For example, in the preface to his catalogue of translations by anonymous translators Sengyou laments that failure to preserve early catalogues directly leads to the absence of translators' names for many translated scriptures:

將是漢、魏時來，歲久録亡；抑亦秦、涼宣梵，成文届止；或晋、宋近出，忽而未詳。譯人之闕，殆由斯歟。尋大法運流，世移六代，撰注群録，獨見安公，以此無源，未足怪也。

Perhaps because the catalogues had long been lost since the times of Han and Wei, or in the Former Qin and Western Liang periods, those who propagated Buddhism stopped at the point when their words were completed [without mentioning the translators], or perhaps because those recent translations appearing in the Jin and the Song eras have been neglected and the details omitted, the translators remain anonymous. One finds in retrospect that since the introduction of Buddhism, six generations have passed. Of the various catalogues that have been compiled and annotated, only Sir An's has survived. For this reason, it is not surprising to find translations without attributions.[33]

The possible loss of earlier catalogues is thus considered one of the reasons leading to the absence of information on the translators of the early translated scriptures. Nevertheless, it seemed an unverifiable assumption even in Sengyou's time because "Of the various catalogues that have been compiled and annotated, only Sir An's has survived." But the message conveyed here is ambivalent: before saying that only Daoan's

---

㉜ Sengyou, *Chu sanzang ji ji*, pp. 561-562.

㉝ Sengyou, *Chu sanzang ji ji*, p. 123.

catalogue survived, Sengyou unambiguously states that there had been various other kinds of catalogues besides Daoan's, although he does not specify whether those catalogues were earlier or later than Daoan's.

The passage may also imply that translating and transmitting early Buddhist scriptures without acknowledging their translators was conventional. Authorship (in this case, translatorship) matters in interpretation rather than in composition (in this case, translation). The Buddha's words were understandably considered more important than the acknowledgment of the translators. When the translated Buddhist scriptures were preached, the priority was doubtless to elucidate the hidden meaning and interpret the Buddha's words. That this convention has remained from the beginning to the late fifth century has led to the large number of orphaned translations and this is attested by long lists of the "anonymous translations of Buddhist scriptures" (*shiyi jing* 失譯經) compiled by both Daoan and Sengyou and preserved in the *Chu sanzang ji ji*.[34] Sengyou lists 450 translated scriptures with attributions, which are far outnumbered by the 1306 translated scriptures without attributions.[35]

These two accounts present a complex picture regarding Daoan's identification of early translators of Buddhist scriptures into Chinese as well as the scriptures they translated. In fact, whether or not Daoan consulted other like catalogues when compiling his own is far from clear. If he did, his catalogue can by no means be considered as the starting point for the discussion of the attributions of early translated scriptures; if he did not, we must address the issue of how he managed to make "reliable" attributions and cannot simply take for granted the credibility of those attributions and ascribe it to his scholarly pursuit of objectivity. In short, the *Guide's* assumption that Daoan's catalogue is the oldest and the most reliable starting point to evaluate other translations and attributions may well be an oversimplification that overlooks the complexity of early Chinese textual production and transmission, the context in which early Buddhist scriptures were translated and circulated. This calls into the question the validity of the whole *Guide* project.

Apocrypha and Foreign Monks

Given the convention revealed in the above *Chu Sanzang ji ji* passage, if translatorship had indeed been by and large neglected in the first one to two centuries of the circulation of early translated Buddhist scriptures, we need to ask why attributions of those translated

---

㉞ Sengyou, *Chu sanzang ji ji*, pp. 91-114, pp. 123-216.

㉟ Sengyou, *Chu sanzang ji ji*, p. 56, p. 211.

scriptures suddenly became so important in the Jin and how catalogues were compiled to find the translators for the early translated scriptures. In his preface to the list of translated scriptures with discernible attributions Sengyou briefly examines the history of the Chinese translation of Buddhist scriptures, mentioning the gradual increase of number of translated texts since the era of Emperor Huan 桓 (r. 146-167 CE) and Emperor Ling 靈 (r. 168-189 CE) of the Eastern Han. He emphasizes Daoan's role in putting those translations into order by compiling a catalogue:

法輪屆心，莫或條叙。爰自安公，始述名録，銓品譯才，標列歲月。妙典可徵，實賴伊人。

"The wheel of dharma" (Buddhist teaching) has reached people's hearts, but no one was able to put the [translated] scriptures in order. It was only from Sir An's time that the names of the translators began to be recorded and transmitted, the talents of the translators were evaluated and appreciated, and the years and months of the translations discerned and listed. That the marvelous canons can be validated indeed relies upon this man.[36]

Although interpretations of this passage may vary, it is safe to infer that Daoan's catalogue was one of the earliest available to Sengyou when he made the above comments. It is also possible that Daoan's catalogue was indeed the earliest, but only in a sixth-century monk's eyes. One can argue that Sengyou must have considered Daoan's catalogue the earliest, otherwise he would not have made the point that it was only from Daoan's time that the attributions of early translated scriptures could be "validated" 可徵, indicating that information regarding the provenance of early Buddhist scriptures had not become available until the completion of Daoan's catalogue. Nevertheless, based on the above passage alone, it is fair to infer that Sengyou considered Daoan's catalogue the most reliable of the earliest catalogues.

Be that as it may, we need to return to the earlier question on how Daoan determined attributions of those translated scriptures with confidence long after those scriptures were translated. Take, for example, the translations attributed to An Shigao. If we believe that An Shigao's biography included in the *Chu sanzang ji ji* contains any truth, most of the translations attributed to him would have been done in the latter half of the second century, approximately two hundred years earlier than the time Daoan's catalogue is dated. In a textual tradition that did not stress the role of the writer or that of the translator, as explicitly pointed out by Sengyou in the above passage, the possible evidence collected by Daoan to identify all those attributions must be scanty, for authorship or translatorship

---

[36] Sengyou, *Chu sanzang ji ji*, p. 22.

had very rarely been substantiated as it was presented later in the history of text making—for instance, to have the name of the author or translator written or printed on a circulated work, as in our present-day printing culture. If Daoan was also seeking a starting point for his project similar to the *Guide*, the evidence, if any, that he could find would hardly be textually verifiable. To fill the evidential void, assumptions about the earliest translators and the dating of their translations should have been made on the demands of Daoan's need when compiling his catalogue.

Is it possible that information on the translatorship of early translated Buddhist scriptures had been orally transmitted through generations of Buddhist believers? Although this assumption is equally unverifiable, it is not unlikely, especially in a religious context in which memory of religious teachings is supposed to last longer. Nevertheless, the *Guide* tends to dismiss this probability. Nattier contends that claiming authorship or translatorship of the texts may have been considered inappropriate both to the author (let alone translator) and to his contemporaries, for the adherents of the Buddha believed that the texts were all *buddhavacana*—the Buddha's words uttered from the Buddha's own mouth.[37] That is to say, memorization of information regarding authorship or translatorship was not encouraged and such information was not expected to be passed down from the very beginning. This accords with Sengyou's claim that no attributions had been included in Buddhist teachings from Han to Jin. On this point, the *Guide* is probably correct, but it exacerbates the dilemma that its putative starting point faces: if Daoan had neither textual records nor orally transmitted memory regarding the translatorship of those early scriptures translated into Chinese one to two centuries before his time, the attributions of those early translated scriptures made in his catalogue could only be considered as his own invention.

Now we must consider the force compelling Daoan to make a catalogue as such. Two factors lead to the need to identify the attributions of the early translated scriptures. One is associated with the fact that a considerable amount of translated scriptures had accumulated by Daoan's time without being properly categorized. Daoan's biography states that the number of the translated scriptures had gradually increased from the Han to the Jin periods.[38] This we can also observe in Daoan's catalogue. Based on what is explicitly mentioned in the *Chu Sanzang ji ji*, in which Daoan's catalogue is partially preserved, the translated scriptures figuring in Daoan's catalogue, including translations labeled as "with attributions," "without attributions," and "forged scriptures," amount to five hundred.[39] Even Daoan himself admitted that "the number of various scriptures is huge" (*zhongjing*

㊲ Nattier, *Guide*, p. 10.

㊳ Sengyou, *Chu sanzang ji ji*, p. 561.

㊴ Tan Shibao, *Han Tang foshi tanzhen*, pp. 67-82.

haoran 眾經浩然).[40] Much as the lengths of different scriptures vary, the quantity of the scriptures as a whole call for some kind of rearrangement.

The other factor deals with the anxiety about the authenticity of the large amount of unprovenanced scriptures. Daoan's biography indicates that by the time Daoan compiled his catalogue, there had been inquiries for the provenance of the translated scriptures in circulation. Buddhist disciples became anxious about when those texts were translated and tried to "trace" 追尋 their origins.[41] In a textual tradition caring less about the authorship of its texts than the texts themselves, the emergence of this kind of anxiety was unusual and seemed to be associated with people's concerns about the authenticity of the texts. Daoan's catalogue reflects the concerns about apocryphal writings that became so influential that the Buddhist apologists felt the urgency to identify and defend the authentic against the apocryphal writings. Daoan's preface to the category of the "dubious scriptures" (*yijing* 疑經) strongly voiced the need to distinguish the authentic teachings from the apocryphal:

> 外國僧法，學皆跪而口受。同師所受，若十、二十轉，以授後學。若有一字異者，共相推校，得便擯之，僧法無縱也。經至晋土，其年未遠，而喜事者以沙糅金，珷玞如也，而無括正，何以別眞僞乎！農者禾草俱在，后稷爲之嘆息；金匱玉石同緘，卞和爲之懷恥。安敢預學次，見涇渭雜流，龍蛇並進，豈不恥之！今列意謂非佛經者如左，以示將來學士，共知鄙倍焉。
>
> According to foreign monastic regulations, monks, when learning Buddhist scriptures, all knelt down and received the scriptures orally. For what they received from their common master, they could teach to later generations only after going it over ten to twenty times. Even if there is a single word different [from what they received from their common master], they would study and collate it together and dismiss [the variant] only after they got it right. Monastic regulations do not tolerate errors. The years when Buddhist scriptures landed in the Jin domain are not far from us, yet those busybodies mix sands with gold: they refine their writings stylistically yet fail to exclude or correct [the wrong]. How could they distinguish the authentic from the apocryphal? If a farmer has grass grow together with crops in field, Hou Ji, God of Millet, would sigh for him; if jade is sealed with stone in the same metal casket, Bian He, knowing jade the best, would feel shameful for it. I, An, dare participate in scripture learning when seeing the Jing and Wei rivers mix together and snakes and dragons move side by side—how could I not feel shameful? Now I list on the left those I do not deem authentic Buddhist scriptures and show them to future

---

[40] Sengyou, *Chu sanzang ji ji*, p. 227.

[41] Sengyou, *Chu sanzang ji ji*, p. 561.

students so that we all know how far astray they have gone.[42]

The list with this preface is credited in the *Chu sanzang ji ji* as "to the Buddhist master An" (*An Fashi zao* 安法師造). If the preface was indeed written by Daoan, we can understand what prompted him to make a catalogue for the translated scriptures: it must be associated with the inquiry about authenticity of translated Buddhist scriptures at the moment Daoan compiled his catalogue. The beginning of the preface represents more of Daoan's own imaginings on how strictly foreign Buddhist monks learned and transmitted Buddhist texts and how seriously they dealt with textual variants. Although they learned and transmitted their doctrines orally, the strictness and seriousness emphasized in their way of learning enabled them to control textual variation and guarantee the reliability of their doctrines. Comparing this scene with what happened soon after Buddhism was introduced into China, Daoan felt the Chinese way of handling Buddhist scriptures disappointing: apocryphal writings crept into Buddhist teaching in no time after the latter landed in China. Condemning the "busybodies" who conflated Buddhist teachings and apocryphal writings, he considered it a shame if a Buddhist student failed to do anything about it.

The reason he compiled the apocrypha list is, thus, clear: in order to protect the true Buddhist teachings, he needed to separate the authentic from the apocryphal. The best way to locate the authentic scripture was to attribute the translated scriptures to eminent Buddhist figures. Once a text was historicized as the result of such attribution, it became immune from the contamination of apocryphal writings and thus established the authority of Buddhist teachings.

Extant Buddhist literature tells us that the efforts of weeding out the apocryphal from the authentic Buddhist writings had been constantly made at least from Daoan's time onward. Daoan lists quite a few "doubtful scriptures" in his catalogue; Sengyou adds more in the *Chu sanzang ji ji* immediately following Daoan's list. He points out that the interpolation of apocryphal writings was a continuing problem from a "corrupt age" (*jiao ji* 澆季):

> 自像運澆季，浮競者多，或憑眞以構僞，或飾虛以亂實。昔安法師摘出僞經二十六部，又指慧達道人以爲深戒。古既有之。今亦宜然矣。祐校閱群經，廣集同異，約以經律，頗見所疑。
>
> Ever since Buddhist teachings were transmitted to a corrupt age, [among those who were interested in Buddhism] those who were superficial and competing with one another have been many. Some created the apocryphal based on the authentic;

---

[42] Sengyou, *Chu sanzang ji ji*, pp. 221-222.

> others confused the substantial by embellishing the fictional. In the past, Master An teased out twenty-six apocrypha; he also pointed out the example of monk Huida as a deep warning [of creating false scriptures]. Once this happened in antiquity, it is natural that it also occurs nowadays. I myself have read and collated a multitude of scriptures and broadly collected similarities and differences among them. Measured by the rules prescribed by the scriptures, many writings are found dubious.[43]

It is hard to pinpoint when this "corrupt age" began, but it must have predated Daoan's (ca. 312-385 CE) time; otherwise he would not have made his list of apocryphal writings resulting from the "corrupt age." If it denotes the chaotic years of the Eastern Han, composing apocrypha may have occurred concomitantly with the introduction of Buddhism to China.

Monk Huida's (if the same Huida referred to by Daoan) biography can be found in the *Gaoseng zhuan*. He is said to have gone to the Buddhist hell when he was thirty-one years old, met the Buddhist master of his previous life, and received the Buddhist teachings from him. He became a monk afterward and had a few prodigies recorded in his biography.[44] Huida's biography contains no information relevant to Buddhist apocryphal writing; it is possible, however, that Daoan alludes to and disputes the manner in which Huida received his Buddhist teachings, a manner resembling Daoist revelation, through which many Daoist writings were produced.[45] This apparently accords with Sengyou's concerns, as we can see in his notes on the list of "miscellaneous scripture." One of the stories told in his notes depicts a prodigy nun, Fani 法尼, who, inspired by the gods, could recite Buddhist scriptures from the age of nine. Sengyou attempted to interview her, but he was prevented from doing so by her family.[46] Following this story Sengyou mentions another prodigy, a Mr. Ding's wife, who suddenly became familiar with a certain Central Asian language and could chant and write Buddhist scriptures in it after an illness toward the end of the Jian'an 建安 era (196-219 CE). In his work, Sengyou casts doubt upon this method of making Buddhist scriptures by categorizing all the scripture attributed to Fani as "dubious scriptures." Nevertheless, relevant to the discussion of translated Buddhist scriptures is the reason given by Sengyou to classify this type of writing as "dubious scripture:"

> 推尋往古，不無此事。但義非金口，又無師譯，取捨兼懷，故附之疑例。

---

(43) Sengyou, *Chu sanzang ji ji*, p. 224.

(44) Huijiao, *Gaoseng zhuan*, pp. 477-479.

(45) Robinet, Isabelle, *Taoism: Growth of a Religion*, trans., Phyllis Brooks, Stanford: Stanford University Press, 1997.

(46) Sengyou, *Chu sanzang ji ji*, pp. 230-231.

In seeking out what happened in the past, we do not lack examples of this kind. Nevertheless, the writings in question were not from the Buddha's golden mouth, nor were they translated by Buddhist masters. To encompass [in my catalogue] both what should be accepted and what should be discarded, I thus attach them as the examples of dubious scriptures.[47]

This passage clearly stipulates the standard through which one distinguishes authentic scriptures from apocryphal writings: an authentic scripture must be either *buddhavacana*, the words of the Buddha, or a translation by Buddhist masters from a foreign language. Since the "golden mouth" does not speak Chinese, authentic Buddhist teachings must be translated from foreign languages. The tension between Buddhist teachings and apocryphal writings, as Sengyou observes from the story of Mr. Ding's wife, started fairly early; it served as a major factor prompting Daoan to compile his catalogue, as he states in the preface preceding the list of apocryphal writings. According to the preface, the purpose of listing apocryphal writings was to warn Buddhist believers of the existence of that type of scripture and eventually eliminate the influence of apocryphal writings. But what occurred from then on indicates a different outcome: the number of the apocryphal writings listed in the catalogues compiled afterward only increased over time. For example, twenty-six "dubious scriptures" are singled out in Daoan's catalogue; Sengyou adds forty-three more to the list following Daoan's; till the *Kaiyuan shijiao lu* 開元釋教錄 compiled in the Tang dynasty (618-907 CE), the listed apocryphal writings number over a thousand, a much longer list than Sengyou's.[48] This phenomenon suggests that the tension between the authentic and apocryphal Buddhist writings had been a continual issue in the culture of Chinese Buddhist scripture making. It also suggests that the tension increased accompanying the prosperity of Buddhism in China. Making catalogues for both the authentic and apocryphal scriptures no doubt reflects the efforts made by the Buddhist apologists to disclose the "dubious scriptures," distinguish the authentic from the "dubious," and eventually aim to eradicate the influence of such "false teachings."

The number of attributions to early translators had also concomitantly increased over time. For example, the *Chu sanzang ji ji* attributes 34 scriptures (40 *juan*) to An Shigao; in Fei Changfang's 費長房 catalogue, the translations attributed to An Shigao rise to 176 volumes (197 *juan*); the *Kaiyuan shijiao lu* revises the number that Fei Changfang proposed by lowering the number of attributions to An Shigao, but it still attributes 95 scriptures (115 *juan*) to him. Similarly, to Lokakṣema 支婁加讖 the *Chu sanzang ji ji* attributes 14 scriptures (27 *juan*), Fei Changfang's catalogue, 21 (63 *juan*), and the *Kaiyuan shijiao lu*,

---

㊼ Sengyou, *Chu sanzang ji ji*, p. 231.

㊽ Sengyou, *Chu sanzang ji ji*, pp. 221-232; *Kaiyuan shi jiao lu, juan* 18, Wenyuange sikuquanshu edition, 1983.

23 (67 *juan*).[49] This also happened to Zhi Qian 支謙 (act. 229-252 CE), a Three Kingdoms period translator, among others.[50]

The increase in the attributions to early translators over time also reflects the tension between the apocryphal writings and the authentic scriptures. Since the "true" Buddhist teachings must be those translated from foreign languages, as emphasized in Sengyou's notes, to secure their authentic status means to find the attributions in one way or another associated with foreign monks or other foreign connections. This phenomenon is especially interesting when we consider how eager Buddhism as a foreign religion tried to connect itself with Chinese culture at the cost of distorting Buddhist teaching by borrowing terms from a foreign tradition to translate and propagate Buddhist teaching and then, after developments during the first one or two centuries, a tendency to differentiate itself from the culture to which Buddhism transplanted itself emerged and continued to grow. This could have happened only after Buddhism had garnered enough power and authority not only to survive but to prosper following its claim that it represented a unique way of thinking different from its Chinese counterpart.

Our understanding of these painstaking efforts seen in those catalogues of Buddhist scriptures to connect early Buddhist scriptures written in Chinese language with Indic and Central Asian origins represented by foreign monks must be embedded in this context. The identification of translators for early Buddhist scriptures would seem in this context a redefinition of Buddhist teaching at a changed stage, and the rethinking of textual authority by compiling catalogues of Buddhist scripture reflects such a redefinition. This is what we see in Daoan's *Zongli zhongjing mulu*, one of the earliest catalogues of Buddhist scriptures, and this is what we continue to see how compiling catalogues for Buddhist scriptures became a weapon to battle against apocryphal writings in order to maintain the authoritative status of the "authentic" scriptures. Viewed from this perspective, the establishment of translatorship of early Buddhist scriptures written in Chinese is a rethinking of textual authority of Buddhist teaching. It is by its nature a later invention and cannot be directly viewed as an effort to keep historical records regarding early translated Buddhist scriptures and their attributions.

The section that follows is a case study dealing with the translatorship of the *Sishi'er*

---

[49] Wang Wenyan 王文顏, *Fodian Hanyi zhi yanjiu* 佛典漢譯之研究, Taipei: Tianhua chuban shiye gufen youxian gongsi, 1984, p. 68. Eric Zürcher also points out such tendency among those who compiled catalogues for Buddhist scriptures, but his approach to this issue is rooted in the age-old *bianwei* 辨偽 (identifying the authentic from forgery) tradition, which prevents him from rethinking the nature of those attributions. See Zürcher, Erik, "A New Look at the Early Chinese Buddhist Texts," in *From Benares to Beijing: Essays on Buddhism and Chinese Religion*, eds., Koichi Shinohara and Gregory Schopen, Oakville: Mosaic Press, 1991, pp. 277-304.

[50] Wang Wenyan, *Fodian Hanyi zhi yanjiu*, pp. 69-70.

zhang jing, or *The Scripture in Forty-two Sections*, arguably the earliest Chinese translation of Buddhist scripture. As vehemently debated topics among such leading scholars as Hu Shi 胡適 (1891-1962 CE) and Chen Yuan 陳垣 (1880-1971 CE) in the first half of 20th century, the authenticity and translatorship of the *Sishi'er zhang jing* are still in dispute today.[51] Most of the discussions, however, are confined in a *bianwei* mode that emphasizes its author or translator so that the texts may be dated and analyzed on the basis of the author's or the translator's biography. The major method of this *bianwei* mode is associated with the misunderstanding of the formation of early Chinese text and authorship. Although I intended the above discussion of the translatorship of early Chinese Buddhist scriptures to provide the context for relocating the discussion on this early Buddhist scripture, it may also shed light on how to approach it.

Dream of the Emperor, Translation of a Scripture

As its title suggests, the *Sishi'er zhang jing* is a scripture consisting of forty-two sections. According to its current form, the Buddha's words are collected piecemeal in each section. The typical opening of a section goes with the phrase "The Buddha says" (*fo yan* 佛言), and the contents follow. Mostly connected to *Xiaosheng* 小乘 (Little Vehicle) scriptures, what is contained in this scripture accords with Eastern Han Daoist thinking in general.[52] Regarding its attribution, the preface says:

後漢西域沙門迦葉摩騰共法蘭譯。昔漢孝明皇帝。夜夢見神人。身體有金色。項有日光。飛在殿前。意中欣然。甚悅之。明日問群臣。此爲何神也。有通人傅毅曰。臣聞天竺。有得道者。號曰佛。輕舉能飛。殆將其神也。於是上悟。即遣使者張騫羽林中郎將秦景博士弟子王遵等十二人。至大月支國。寫取佛經四十二章。在第十四石函中。登起立塔寺。於是道法流布。處處修立佛寺。遠人伏化願爲臣妾者。不可稱數［。］國内清寧。含識之類。蒙恩受賴。

---

[51] Hu Shi 胡適, "Sishier zhang jing kao" 四十二章經考, in *Sishier zhang jing yu Muzi Li huo lun kaobian* (Xiandai fojiao xueshu congkan Vol.11) 四十二章經與牟子理惑論考辨 (現代佛教學術叢刊 11), ed., Zhang Mantao 張曼濤, Beijing: Beijing tushuguan cuhbanshe, 2005, pp. 1-20; Tang Yongtong 湯用彤, "Sishier zhang jing kaozheng" 四十二章經考證, in *Sishier zhang jing yu Muzi Li huo lun kaobian*, pp. 21-34; Wang Weicheng 王維誠, "Sishier zhang jing Daoan jinglu quezai zhi yuanyin" 四十二章經道安經錄闕載之原因, in *Sishier zhang jing yu Muzi Li huo lun kaobian*, pp. 35-42; Liang Qichao 梁啟超, "*Sishier zhang jing bianwei*" 四十二章經辨偽, in *Sishier zhang jing yu Muzi Li huo lun kaobian*, pp. 51-58; Lü Cheng 呂澂, "Sishier zhang jing chaochu niandai" 四十二章經抄出年代, in *Sishier zhang jing yu Muzi Li huo lun kaobian*, pp. 59-68; Tan Shibao, *Han Tang foshi tanzhen*, pp. 272-293.

[52] Tang Yongtong, *Tang Yongtong quanji (Vol. 1): Han Wei liang Jin Nanbeichao fojiao shi* 湯用彤全集 (第一卷): 漢魏兩晉南北朝佛教史, Shijiazhuang: Hebei renmin chubanshe, 2000, pp. 33-34.

于今不絶也。

[The Scripture of Forty-Two Sections was] translated by Western Region monks Jiayemoteng [reconstructed by modern scholars as Kāśyapa Mātaṅga[53]] together with Falan [reconstructed as Dharmaratna] in the Later Han. One night, Emperor Xiaoming of Han dreamed of a god-man with a golden body and sun-shaped light behind his head flying to the front of the Han imperial palace. The emperor was pleased and he greatly liked what he had dreamed. The next day he asked his officials, "What kind of god is this?" Fu Yi, a man of broad knowledge and sound scholarship, answered, "I have heard that in India there is a man who has achieved the Way and is called the Buddha. He is so light that he can rise up and fly. What you dreamed was probably this god." The emperor was thus enlightened, immediately sending a messenger Zhang Qian, the Leader of the Gentlemen of the Palace Guards Qin Jing, and a Student of the Erudite Wang Zun, and so forth, altogether twelve members, to the Larger Rouzhi State. They copied and brought back a Buddhist scripture with Forty-Two sections. It was kept in the fourteenth stone case. Soon a Buddhist pagoda and a temple were erected. After that Buddhist teaching was transmitted and spread, and Buddhist temples were built everywhere. Those who lived far away and wished to humbly cultivate themselves and to be subordinates of the Han were countless. The Han domain remained quiet and peaceful. All that have senses have received favors and blessings from this and this has lasted to the present day.[54]

The preface traces the date of the translation of the *Sishi'er zhang jing* to Emperor Ming (r. 57-75 CE), the second ruler of Eastern Han dynasty (25-220 CE). The emperor dreamed of the Buddha's image one night and then sent a group of imperial envoys to visit India on behalf of the emperor. Whether or not they arrived in India is unknown, but the preface does mention the translation of this scripture undertaken in Larger Rouzhi, better known as the Kushan Empire in northern India. Again, whether the two monks of the Western Region translated the scripture with the help of the Han envoys or by themselves is unclear, but the translation is attributed to them. The envoys returned to the court with the

---

[53] Nattier, *Guide*, p. 35. While supposing that Kāśyapa may be the Indic sounds of Jiaye, we must keep in mind the naming tradition said to be established by Daoan, who adopted 釋, or "Sākya," a part of the Buddha's name, as his "family name" (It was adopted by other monks thereafter). The family names of early foreign monks often indicated their ethnic background. For instance, *zhu* 竺, indicates a monk from India, and *an* 安, a monk from Parthia. Therefore, "Zhu Moteng" 竺摩腾 appearing in the Chu *sanzhang ji ji* and "She Moteng" 攝摩騰 (the reconstructed late Han pronunciations of "攝" and "釋" are both *śap) in the *Gaoseng zhuan*. As we shall see in the following, they are generally considered the names of one person. For a note on the names of Buddhist figures, see Nattier, *Guide*, 27-28.

[54] *Taishō*0784, 17.0722a13-23.

translated *Sishi'er zhang jing*. As a result, the text was included in the imperial collection, and a pagoda and a temple were erected for it, most probably in the Eastern Han capital city Luoyang soon after the imperial envoys brought back the scripture from the west. The preface also claims that Buddhist teachings (rendered as *daofa* 道法, or the Way and the Method) soon spread throughout the Han domain with the Han imperial patronage.

Yet this important scripture relating to the introduction of Buddhism into the Han domain does not figure in Daoan's catalogue. Under the entry of the *Sishi'er zhang jing* on his list of translated scriptures arranged chronologically according to their translators, Sengyou notes:

舊録云，孝明皇帝四十二章。安法師所撰録闕此經。

According to a previous catalogue, [the scripture] is called "Emperor Xiaoming's Forty-Two sections." The catalogue compiled by the Buddhist master Daoan does not include this scripture.[55]

Sengyou's list of the translated scriptures was apparently an enlarged one on the basis of Daoan's. Nevertheless, as shows above, Sengyou believes that the *Sishi'er zhang jing* represents the earliest remaining Buddhist scripture.[56] Songyou also left notes on the translatorship of the scripture. They read as follows:

漢孝明帝夢見金人，詔遣使者張騫、羽林中郎將秦景到西域，始於月支國遇沙門竺摩騰，譯寫此經還洛陽，藏在蘭臺石室第十四間中，其經今傳於世。

Emperor Xiaoming of the Han dreamed of a gold man. He then issued an imperial edict, sending a messenger Zhang Qian and the Leader of the Gentlemen of the Palace Guards Qin Jing to the Western Region. That was the first time they met a monk named Zhu Moteng in the state of Rouzhi. They translated the scripture and then returned to Luoyang. The scripture was stored in the fourteenth room of the stone chamber in the Orchid Pavilion. The scripture has been transmitted to the present day.[57]

Though similar to the story preserved in the preface to the *Sishi'er zhang jing*, the passage differs from the former on several points. First, the "god-man" in the preface becomes a "gold man," possibly a Buddhist statue; second, "the fourteenth stone case" in the preface becomes "the fourteenth room of the stone chamber in the Orchid Pavilion," the Han imperial library and archives; finally, rather than pointing out that Moteng and Falan are the translators as the preface does, Sengyou's notes omit Falan and seem to suggest that the translation resulted from the joint efforts of the foreign monk Moteng and the Han envoys. However, in a note summarizing the Buddhist translations mentioned in

---

55. Sengyou, *Chu sanzang ji ji*, p. 23.
56. Sengyou, *Chu sanzang ji ji*, p. 22.
57. Sengyou, *Chu sanzang ji ji*, p. 23.

Daoan's catalogue, Sengyou leaves out the name of Zhu Moteng, thus seeming to attribute the translation to the two Eastern Han envoys Zhang Qian[58] and Qin Jing:

> 總前出經，自安世高以下，至法立已上，凡十七家，並安公録所載。其張騫、秦景、竺朔佛、維祇難、竺將炎、白延、帛法祖凡七人，是祐校衆録新獲所附入。自衛士度已後，皆祐所新撰。
>
> To summarize the translated scriptures listed afore, their translators, from An Shigao to Fali, seventeen in all, are recorded in the catalogue by Sir An. Others like Zhang Qian, Qin Jing, Zhu Shuofo, Weiqinan, Zhu Jiangyan, Bai Yan, and Bo Fazu, seven in total, are newly discovered and attached to this list based on my own collation of various catalogues. Those listed from Wei Shidu down are all newly compiled by me.[59]

The names of Zhang Qian and Qin Jing clearly shows the inclusion of the *Sishi'er zhang jing* in Sengyou's list, but Zhu Moteng, though mentioned in a previous note following immediately after the title of the *Sishi'er zhang jing*, does not figure here. Also worth noting is the absence of Falan, the other monk mentioned in the preface, from either of Sengyou's notes translated above.

In explaining how these differences came about, Nattier makes the following inference in the Guide. First, she argues that Sengyou attributes the *Sishi'er zhang jing* to Zhang Qian and Qin Jing instead of Zhu Moteng, because the latter's name is not listed in the above summary; nevertheless, Sengyou reiterates that Daoan did not know the attribution to Zhang Qian and Qin Jing; so Nattier suspects that the addition of Zhang Qian and Qin Jing into the list belongs to a later interpolation.[60] This argumentation is not without question. First, Nattier may be right in identifying Zhang Qian and Qin Jing instead of Zhu Moteng as the translators of the scripture, but it only constitutes one of the many possibilities and should not be overstated, especially considering the complex constitution of early translating groups. Even the scarce information regarding early translating teams suggests that at the incipient phase of translation of Buddhist scriptures there should have been more than one person participating in the translation process. Attributions and actual participants were different things entirely: it was common not to attribute a translated scripture to all but only to the leading member(s) of a translating team. Therefore we cannot draw a definite conclusion that Zhu Moteng was not considered by Sengyou as one of the translators, as suggested by Nattier.

Secondly, Nattier may have overinterpreted some of the information included in the source. True, Sengyou clearly states that the *Sishi'er zhang jing* as well as Zhang Qian and

---

⑱ This Zhang Qian is obviously considered an Eastern envoy.

⑲ Sengyou, *Chu sanzang ji ji*, pp. 44-45.

⑳ Nattier, *Guide*, 36-37.

Qin Jing were not recorded in Daoan's catalogue, but this does not imply that Daoan did not know about the story of Zhang Qian and Qin Jing. On the contrary, it is completely possible that, as Wang Weicheng 王維誠 also suggests, Daoan knew the *Sishi'er zhang jing* and the story of Zhang Qian and Qin Jing, but he chose not to include it in his catalogue simply because he doubted its authenticity.[61]

Finally, both Nattier's inference and the reasoning behind it deserve reconsideration. According to Nattier, the passage "suggests that Sengyou's catalogue began with the works of An Shigao, and that the names of the other seven translators (其張騫…凡七人, 'Of these, a total of seven people, Zhang Qian, ...' and so on) should fall between An Shigao and Fali."[62] Following this reasoning, Zhang Qian and Qin Jing as well as the *Sishi'er zhang jing* are placed later than An Shigao. "In fact, however, the text attributed to Zhang Qian and Qin Jing precedes those by An Shigao on Sengyou's list."[63] Therefore, Nattier concludes, "It may well be that this apparent disjunction is the result of a deliberately light revision on Sengyou's part, inserting the new names but leaving the original structure of the passage intact, this encoding a hint that the change had been made under duress."[64]

The opening sentence of the passage cited afore may not mean what Nattier suggests. That sentence simply denotes that, among the translators listed so far, seventeen (from An Shigao to Fali) are mentioned by Daoan, while the other seven names are not listed in Daoan's list but added by Sengyou in an enlarged list compiled by Sengyou himself. Viewed as such, Zhang Qian and Qin Jing should not necessarily fall between An Shigao and Fali in that list at all. Moreover, if we count the translators listed from An Shigao to Fali in the *Chu sanzang ji ji*, we find twenty-two names consisting of both the main translators and their assistants. Five out of the twenty-two translators—Zhu Shuofo, Wei Qinan, Zhu Jiangyan, Bai Yan, and Bo Fazu—plus the other two—Zhang Qian and Qin Jing preceding An Shigao—constitute exactly seven men and they were added by Sengyou when he expanded the list based on Daoan's. The rest, indeed seventeen individuals, are mentioned by Daoan.[65] There is no hint "that the change had been made under duress" suggested by Nattier in this reading.

Nattier moves on to argue that the inclusion of the *Sishi'er zhang jing* in the *Chu sanzang ji ji* may have resulted from a later incursion, for, she contends, the biographies of its

61 Wang Weicheng, "*Sishier zhang jing* Daoan jinglu quezai zhi yuanyin."

62 Nattier, *Guide*, p. 37.

63 Nattier, *Guide*, p. 37.

64 Nattier, *Guide*, p. 37.

65 Sengyou, *Chu sanzang ji ji*, pp. 23-45.

translators would otherwise have been included in the *Chu sanzang ji ji*.[66] While none of the four (Zhang Qian, Qin Jing, Zhu Moteng, and Falan) has a biography in the *Chu sanzang ji ji*, in the *Gaoseng zhuan*, a work alleged to be completed about fifteen years later than the former, both Moteng's and Falan's biographies are included.[67] It seems unlikely that Sengyou did not know of them if he indeed compiled their biographies. Nevertheless, the exclusion of their biographies could have various causes and not necessarily result from an intentional decision on Sengyou's part. Although we cannot take the current version of the *Chu sanzang ji ji* for granted as a work completely out of Sengyou's hands,[68] based on the preface to the list of the translated scriptures under discussion, I would argue that the inclusion of the *Sishi'er zhang jing* as well as the note immediately following it at the beginning of that list does not contradict Sengyou's statement made in the preface:

> 昔劉向校書，已見佛經，故知成帝之前法典久至矣。逮孝明感夢，張騫遠使，西於月支寫經四十二章，韜藏蘭臺，帝王所印。於是妙像麗於城闉，金刹曜乎京洛，慧教發揮，震照區寓矣。竊尋兩漢之季，世構亂離，西京蕩覆，墳典皆散，東都播遷，載籍多亡。子政所覩，其文雖沒，而顯宗所寫，厥篇猶存。東流初法，於斯有徵。祐檢閱三藏，訪覈遺源，古經現在，莫先於四十二章；傳譯所始，靡踰張騫之使。洎章和以降，經出蓋闕。良由梵文雖至，緣運或殊，有譯乃傳，無譯則隱。苟非其人，道不虛行也。逾及桓、靈，經來稍廣。安清、朔佛之儔，支讖、嚴調之屬，翻譯轉梵，萬里一契，離文合義，炳煥相接矣。
>
> In the past when collating the texts, Liu Xiang (77-6 BCE) had seen Buddhist scriptures in the imperial collection. Thus we know that Buddhist canons had arrived long before Emperor Cheng's reign (33-7 BCE). When the time came that Emperor Xiaoming was moved by his dream [of the Buddha], Zhang Qian was sent on a diplomatic trip far westward to Rouzhi to write a scripture with forty-two sections, which was later stored in the Orchid Pavilion with the emperor's seal. From then on, wonderful statues of the Buddha have stood resplendently in the cities, the golden monasteries have shined in the capital city Luoyang, and the teachings of Buddhist wisdom have been initiated and spread, influential and shining everywhere within the domain. I, in private, study the declines of the two Han dynasties, when chaos and separation were created in this world, when the western capital was ruined and the ancient classics scattered. When the eastern capital was fugitively moved,

---

⑥⑥ Nattier, *Guide*, p. 37.

⑥⑦ Zürcher, *The Buddhist Conquest of China*, p. 10.

⑥⑧ For the compilation and transmission of the *Chu sanzang ji ji*, see Sengyou, *Chu sanzang ji ji*, introduction, pp. 1-32.

> most of the texts went lost. The texts that Zizheng (Liu Xiang) had seen were gone. Nevertheless, the pieces written down during the reign of Xianzong (Emperor Ming of Han) still exist. The earliest transmission of Buddhist teachings to the east can find its evidence here. While reading and examining Buddhist scriptures, I seek to check the traces and origin [of the transmission of Buddhism to China]. Among the ancient scriptures that have survived till now, none is earlier than the *Scripture of the Forty-Two Sections*. As for the beginning date of transmitting and translating Buddhist scriptures, it was not earlier than the time of Zhang Qian's diplomatic journey. From the reigns of Emperor Zhang (r. 75-88 CE) and Emperor He (r. 88-105 CE) onwards, there had been a lack of translated scriptures. This is because that even though the Indic scriptures did arrive, chance and fortune moved in a different direction: when translated, they were transmitted; when not, they were hidden. Without the right persons, the Way would not run in vain. To the times of Emperor Huan (r. 147-167 CE) and Emperor Ling (r. 168-189 CE), the range of the scriptures that arrived had gradually widened. Peers like An Qing and Shuofo and fellows like Zhi Chen and Yan Tiao have translated Buddhist scriptures from Indic language into Chinese. These two languages, though used in places ten thousand *li* away from each other, are connected by translation. The meanings conveyed by different languages meet and are brilliantly articulated.[69]

This clearly composed passage narrates the early history of the introduction of Buddhist texts to China. If we consider that the preface was associated with Sengyou, we have no reason to view the entry of the *Sishi'er zhang jing* as a later incursion. The preface unambiguously demonstrates how Sengyou conceived the position of the *Sishi'er zhang jing* in early Chinese translation of Buddhist scriptures: "Among the ancient scriptures that have survived until now, none is earlier than the *Scripture of the Forty-Two Sections*. As for the initial date of transmitting and translating Buddhist scriptures, it was not earlier than the time of Zhang Qian's diplomatic journey." Besides, more than just a simple statement that the *Sishi'er zhang jing* was the currently earliest Buddhist scripture translated from an Indic language, the above passage also points out the lacuna between the introduction of the *Sishi'er zhang jing* and the later thriving of Buddhist translation toward the end of Eastern Han period. It explains that the translation of the *Sishi'er zhang jing* initiated the influence of Buddhist teachings upon early China, at least in metropolitan areas, but the translation of Buddhist scriptures failed to gain popularity immediately following the introduction of one of the earliest scriptures. In short, available information does not

---

⑥⑨ Sengyou, *Chu sanzang ji ji*, p. 22.

suggest that Sengyou ever considered it problematic to situate the *Sishi'er zhang jing* in the early history of Buddhist translation as the earliest Buddhist scripture introduced into China.

The above passage also serves as a response to the accusation of its being anachronistic in using the Western Han envoy Zhang Qian's name to invent a story that happened in the Eastern Han period. Maspéro argues that the lacuna of three hundred years between the two unrelated events reveals a glaring contradiction and that the change of Zhang Qian's name to Cai Yin⑳ 蔡愔 as the Eastern Han envoy to search for Buddhism in the west betrays the belated attempt to smooth such inconsistency. The entire tale of the mission to the West culminating in the translation of the *Sishi'er zhang jing*, according to Maspéro's argument, turns out to be nothing but a poorly woven web of fabrication.㉑ Here Sengyou points out that Zhang Qian's diplomatic journey to the West and the translation of the *Sishi'er zhang jing* were Eastern Han events and had nothing to do with the Western Han envoy of the same name but traveling to the West for different purposes. It seems unlikely that a person as learned as Sengyou would follow such obvious anachronism were this Zhang Qian indeed regarded as the Western Han Zhang Qian. Viewed from this perspective, Maspéro's argumentation oversimplifies the sources. Sengyou as well as his contemporaries, I would contend, could not have been as ignorant as Maspéro considers.

The change of Zhang Qian's name to Cai Yin, nevertheless, indeed occurs in Zhu Moteng's biography included in the *Gaoseng zhuan*:

> 漢永平中，明皇帝夜夢金人飛空而至，乃大集群臣以占所夢。通人傅毅奉答："臣聞西域有神，其名曰'佛'，陛下所夢，將必是乎？"帝以爲然，即遣郎中蔡愔、博士弟子秦景等，使往天竺，尋訪佛法。愔等於彼遇見摩騰，乃要還漢地。騰誓志弘通，不憚疲苦，冒涉流沙，至乎雒邑。明帝甚加賞接，於城西門外立精舍以處之，漢地有沙門之始也。但大法初傳，未有歸信，故蘊其深解，無所宣述，後少時卒於雒陽。有記云：騰譯《四十二章經》一卷，初緘在蘭臺石室第十四間中。騰所住處，今雒陽城西雍門外白馬寺是也。
>
> One night in the Yongping era (58-75 CE) of the Han, Emperor Ming dreamed that a gold man, flying across the sky, arrived. He then gathered all his officials to divine what he had dreamed. Fu Yi, a personage of broad knowledge and sound scholarship, received the imperial order and answered, "I have heard that in the Western Region there is a god named the Buddha. He must be what Your Majesty dreamed." The Emperor thought that what Fu Yi said was correct. He immediately sent the Gentleman of the Interior Cai Yin, Student of the Erudite Qin Jing, and so forth, on

---

⑳ Huijiao, *Gaoseng zhuan*, 1.

㉑ Maspéro, Henri, "Le songe et l'empereur Ming: Étude critique des sources," *Bulletin de l'École Française d'Extrême-Orient* 10.1 (1910), pp. 95-130.

a diplomatic mission to India to search for Buddhist teaching. Cai Yin and others met Moteng in India and invited him to return to the Han domain with them. Moteng made an unshakable resolution to promote and transmit Buddhist teaching [to China], braved fatigue and bitterness, risked traveling through moving sands, and arrived in Luoyi (Luoyang) in the end. Emperor Ming rewarded him and treated him well by erecting a monastery outside the western gate of the capital city for him to reside in. From then on the Han began to have Buddhist monks. However, in the beginning when Buddhist teachings was introduced to the Han, no one else was converted to Buddhism. Therefore, Moteng hid his deep understanding of the Buddhist teachings and did not preach or transmit anything. Shortly thereafter Moteng died in Luoyang. A record says that Moteng translated the *Sishi'er zhang jing*, one *juan*, sealed in the fourteenth room of the stone chamber in the Orchid Pavilion in the beginning. The place where Moteng used to live is now the White Horse Monastery outside the western city gate—the Yong Gate.[72]

According to Maspéro, the theory that holds Zhang Qian to be the main Messenger to the West appeared older, while the change of Zhang Qian to Cai Yin came later in order to cover up the historical error in the older version of the story.[73] Does this change truly reflect later intentional editing efforts to smooth over the differences regarding the translation of the *Sishi'er zhang jing*? Or does it simply result from a different version of this legend with no intention to correct the supposed mistake—if people consider it a mistake at all—appearing in other versions of the same story? Comparing the version of the story in Zhu Moteng's biography with that in the preface of the *Sishi'er zhang jing*, we find that Cai Yin's appearance is not necessarily intended to replace Zhang Qian. Zhang Qian is mentioned in the preface as a Messenger; Qin Jing, the Leader of the Gentlemen of the Palace Guards; and Wang Zun, Student of the Erudite. In Zhu Moteng's biography, however, Cai Yin holds the official tile the Gentleman of the Interior, and Qin Jing, Student of Erudite. One would wonder why a later intentional synthesis as suggested by Maspéro would still have resulted in such inconsistencies if at all. In fact, we do not see a tidy correspondence between the two sets of name and official tile lists supporting Maspéro's inference that Cai Yin's appearance in Moteng's biography is a planned rearrangement to take Zhang Qian's place in this story. More probably, the variations occurring among different versions indicate how some elements of a story as such could be rather flexibly altered in its transmission in early and medieval Chinese culture of text making. It is likely that for a considerably long period after the story about Emperor

[72] Huijiao, *Gaoseng zhuan*, pp. 1-2.

[73] Maspéro, "Le songe et l'empereur Ming," p. 126.

Ming's dream and his sending envoys to the West was created, it did not have a fixed form. People added details in or took some elements out of the narrative based on different oral or/and written traditions. It is possible that later writers or editors might deliberately alter the story to fit specific needs, but this does not explain all the variants appearing in different versions of the same story, nor is this the only way to explain all these changes. Similarly, in the case of the *Sishi'er zhang jing*, we should avoid the tendency of dismissing its authenticity and its possible early date simply through the examination of the inconsistencies among different sources regarding the making of this scripture.

In addition to the above passages, the story of Emperor Ming's dream related to the search for Buddhist teaching from his court appears in a number of other sources. For example, in the *Lihuo lun* 理惑論 (*On Disposing of Error*), a text allegedly composed by a Master Mu (Muzi 牟子) in late Eastern Han, it mentions, as follows,

> 昔孝明皇帝夢見神人，身有日光，飛在殿前，欣然悦之。明日，博問群臣："此爲何神？"有通人傅毅曰："臣聞天竺有得道者，號曰佛，飛行虚空，身有日光，殆將其神也。"於是上寤，遣使者张骞、羽林郎中秦景、博士弟子王遵等十二人，於大月支寫佛經四十二章，藏在蘭臺石室第十四間。時於洛陽城西雍門外起佛寺，於其壁畫千乘萬騎，繞塔三匝，又於南宮清涼臺，及開陽城門上作佛像。
>
> In the past Emperor Xiaoming dreamed that a god-man, with sunlight around his body, flew to the front of the Han imperial palace. The emperor took delight in it. The next day he asked all his officials, "What kind of god is this?" Fu Yi, a man of broad knowledge and sound scholarship, answered, "I have heard that in India there is a man who has achieved the Way and is called the Buddha. Surrounded by sunlight, he flies in empty space. What you dreamed was probably his spirit." The emperor was thus enlightened and sent a Messenger Zhang Qian[74], the Leader of the Gentlemen of the Palace Guards Qin Jing, the Student of the Erudite Wang Zun, and others, twelve in all,[75] to the Larger Rouzhi State to copy a Buddhist scripture with forty-two sections. It was stored in the fourteenth room of the stone chamber in the Orchid Pavilion. At the same time a Buddhist temple was erected outside of the Yong Gate, west of Luoyang city. On the walls of the temple thousands of chariots and tens of thousands horses were drawn, forming three circles around the tower. Moreover, the Buddha's images were made on the Qingliang Terrace at the Southern Palace and

⑭ The Taishō edition renders it as "中郎蔡愔" (the Interior Gentleman Cai Yin) instead. See *Taishō* 2102, 52.5a1-2; *Hong ming ji*, juan 1.

⑮ The *Taishō* edition renders it as "十八" (eighteen) instead. See Taishō 2102, 52.5a3.

the Kaiyang Gate.[76]

This is another source mentioning the *Sishi'er zhang jing*, its translators and the place where it was stored when brought back from the west. It also refers to the construction of a Buddhist temple and the making of Buddhist images on the walls of this temple, a palatial terrace, and a city gate. Unlike some other sources, in the *Hongming ji* 弘明集, upon which the *Taishō* edition of the *Sishi'er zhang jing* is based, this passage omits the Messenger Zhang Qian while adding the Interior Gentleman Cai Yin to the team.[77] Such variation could either be the result of the author's deliberate cover-up of the previous anachronistic use of the historical figure Zhang Qian, or that of a later editorial effort. Keep in mind that different versions of the same story could occur over time during transmission.

Other sources do not refer to the *Sishi'er zhang jing* specifically, but they do touch upon the translation of Buddhist scriptures, construction of Buddhist temple(s), or the introduction of Buddha's images to China, in addition to the emperor's dream, the core of the legend. To clarify how this story was involved in the translatorship of the *Sishi'er zhang jing*, I will first translate related passages and then compare the basic narrative elements of the different versions before reaching a conclusion.

The passage in the *Hou Han ji* 后漢紀, compiled by Yuan Hong 袁宏 (328–376 CE), is considered the earliest historic work in which Emperor Ming's dream is recorded. It does not, however, provide such details as the names of the envoys, meeting with foreign monks, or the translation of any specific Buddhist text. Nevertheless, the introduction of Buddhist texts and the Buddha's images are both mentioned. It reads as follows,

> 初，帝夢見金人長大，項有日月光，以問群臣。或曰："西方有神，其名曰佛，其形長大。［陛下所夢，得無是乎？"於是遣使天竺，而問其道術，］遂於中國而圖其形象焉。有經數千萬［言］，以虛無為宗，苞羅精粗，無所不統，善為宏闊勝大之言，所求在一體之內，而所明在視聽之外，世俗之人，以為虛誕，然歸於玄微深遠，難得而測，故王公大人觀死生報應之際，莫不矍然自失。

> In the beginning the emperor dreamed a golden man, tall and big, with sun-and-moon lights behind his head. He asked his officials about it. One official said, "In the west there is a god called the Buddha. Was not he the one Your Majesty dreamed?" The emperor thus sent his messengers to India to search for his methods and

[76] Muzi, "Lihuo lun" 理惑論, in *Zhongguo fojiao sixiang ziliao xuanbian* (Vol. 1) 中國佛教思想資料選編（一）, ed., Shi Jun 石峻 et al, Beijing: Zhonghua shuju, 1981, p. 10.

[77] *Taishō* 2102, 52.5a1-2.

techniques.][78] Afterwards the image of Buddha was drawn in the Middle Kingdom. The [words of the][79] scriptures amount to dozens of millions. The scriptures hold nihility as their principle teaching, covering both the fine and the coarse, and nothing is not united in its teaching. The author of the scriptures is good at making grand, broad, and magnificent speeches. [According to this teaching,] what one seeks is within one's body and what one tries to illuminate is beyond one's seeing and hearing. Common people consider it vain and absurd. However, its essence can be classified as profound, subtle, deep, and far-reaching and can hardly be measured. Therefore, when kings, dukes, and officials observed the moments of retribution among the living and the dead, none of them does not feel fearful and lost.[80]

The central part of the legend also appears in the *Hou Han shu* 后漢書 by Fan Ye 范曄 (398-445 CE), who with careful wording indicates that the account is legendary in nature. The *Hou Han shu* account starts with the word *shi chuan* 世傳, a term indicating that what follows it has been circulated like a legend:

世傳明帝夢見金人，長大，頂有光明，以問羣臣。或曰："西方有神，名曰佛，其形長丈六尺而黃金色。"帝於是遣使天竺問佛道法，遂於中國圖畫形像焉。楚王英始信其術，中國因此頗有奉其道者。後桓帝好神，數祀浮圖、老子，百姓稍有奉者，後遂轉盛。

It has been said through generations that Emperor Ming dreamed of a gold man, tall, big, and with bright light around his head. He asked his officials about it. Someone said, "In the west there is a god called Buddha. His form is a *zhang* and six *chi* tall and he is golden." The emperor then sent his messengers to India asking about the way and method of Buddhism. Afterwards Buddha's images were drawn in the middle kingdom. Ying, Prince of Chu, began to believe the techniques of Buddhist teaching. Because of this, there had been quite a few who respectfully followed its way in the middle kingdom. Later Emperor Huan was fond of worshiping gods. He made sacrifices to the Buddha and Laozi several times. Gradually there also appeared among the masses those who worshiped the Buddha. Soon after that Buddhist teaching gained great popularity.[81]

The *Hou Han shu* account, however, does not mention the translation of any Buddhist

---

⑱ Zhou Tianyou 周天遊 suggests that these sentences should have been added in the narrative based on the *Zi zhi tongjian* 資治通鑒 and other works. See Yuan Hong 袁宏, *Hou Han ji jiaozhu* 後漢紀校注, collated and annotated by Zhou Tianyou, Tianjin: Tianjin guji chubanshe, 1987, p. 299.

⑲ It is understandable why Zhou Tianyou adds the word "言" here. Otherwise the sentence means that the scriptures introduced to Han China amounted to an unbelievable number of dozens of millions.

⑳ Yuan Hong, *Hou Han ji jiaozhu*, p. 299.

㉑ *Hou Han shu* "Xiyu zhuan," 88:2922.

texts. What the envoys brought back seems to have been mainly the Buddha's drawings or statues. The passage also contains information regarding early believers and how the Buddha was worshiped. If we accept this passage as valid, members of the Han imperial family became among the most influential earliest believers. Moreover, in the early stage of the new religion the Buddha was worshiped in tandem with Laozi, the major god of Daoist belief, which indicates that at least in the reign of Emperor Huan (r. 147-167) Buddhism was not yet an independent religion but intertwined with China's native religions.[82]

By comparison, the *Ming xiang ji* 冥祥記,[83] alleged to have been compiled by Wang Yan 王琰, a Southern Qi 南齊 (479-502 CE) official and Buddhist believer, provides more details about Emperor Ming's dream. The narrative goes as follows,

> 漢明帝夢見神人：形垂二丈，身黄金色，項佩日光。以問群臣。或對曰："西方有神，其號曰佛，形如陛下所夢，得無是乎？"於是發使天竺，寫致經像，表之中夏。自天子王侯，咸敬事之。聞人死精神不滅，莫不懼然自失。初，使者蔡愔，將西域沙門迦葉摩騰等賫優填王畫釋迦佛像；帝重之，如夢所見。乃遣画工图之数本，于南宫清凉台及高阳门显节寿陵上供养。又于白马寺壁，画千乘万骑绕塔三匝之像，如诸传备载。
>
> Emperor Ming of Han dreamed of a god-man, whose form was two *zhang* tall, body was golden, and head was adorned with sunlight. He asked his officials about his dream. Someone answered, "In the west there is a god called the Buddha and his appearance resembles what Your Majesty dreamed of. Was not he the god appearing in your dream?" The emperor thus sent his messengers to India to copy scriptures, bring back the Buddha's images, and show them all over the Han domain. From the Son of Heaven to the princes and marquises, they all respectfully served the Buddha. Learning that people's spirits would not perish after death, none would feel fearful and lost. Some time earlier Messenger Cai Yin had guided the Western Region monks Jiaye Moteng and others to bring back Udayana's image and Śākyamuni's statue. The emperor thought highly of them as they resembled what he had seen in his dream. He then dispatched painters to make several copies of the Buddha's image and provided supplies for them on the Qingliang Terrace of the Southern Palace,

---

[82] The relationship between early Chinese Daoism and Buddhism has recently attracted scholarly attention and is discussed in a number of studies. While some scholars warn that we should not overestimate the influence of Daoism over early Buddhism, there is in fact evidence in favor of the existence of such influence. For examples, see Tang Yongtong, *Han Wei liang Jin Nanbeichao fojiao shi*, pp. 33-46; Zürcher, *The Buddhist Conquest of China*, pp. 33-34.

[83] For an English translation and study of this work, see Campany, Robert, *Signs from the Unseen Realm: Buddhist Miracle Tales from Early Medieval China*, Honolulu: University of Hawai'I Press, 2012.

> Gaoyang Gate, and Xianjie Mausoleum. Images of thousands of chariots and ten thousands of horses surrounding the tower's three circles were drawn on the walls of the White Horse temple, as the various biographies record in detail.[84]

Though the above passage does not specifically mention the *Sishi'er zhang jing*, it does point out that the emperor sent the envoys to India to "copy scriptures" and "bring back the Buddha's images" 寫致經像 (*xie zhi jing xiang*). The Messenger whom the emperor sent to India was Cai Yin, who met and brought some Western Region monks, like Jiaye Moteng, back to the Han court. This passage seems to value the introduction of the Buddha's images above the translation of Buddhist texts, given the detailed depiction of the images.

From as early as the Northern Zhou 北周 dynasty (557-581 CE), some began to throw the historical believability of Emperor Ming's dream into doubt by questioning specific details. In his *Xiao dao lun* 笑道論 (*On Mocking Daoism*), the Buddhist proponent Zhen Luan 甄鸞 (535-566 CE) mocks the statement in the *Hua hu jing* 化胡經 (*Scripture of Cultivating Foreigners*) by denying that Emperor Ming dispatched Zhang Qian to India. He basically holds that the Zhang Qian who "exhausted the origin of the Yellow River" lived during Emperor Wu's reign (r. 141-87 BCE) and could not still be serving in Emperor Ming's (r. 57-75 CE) court more than one hundred years later. The *Hua hu jing* states:

> On the jiazi day in the seventh year of the Yongping era during the Han Emperor Ming's reign, the Jupiter star appeared in the daytime and the west was bright at night. The emperor dreamed of a god-man one *zhang* and six *chi* tall with sunlight around his head. The next morning he asked his officials [about his dream]. Fu Yi said, "This was the sign showing that the foreign prince in the west had achieved the Way." Emperor Ming immediately sent Zhang Qian and others to explore the origin of the Yellow River, crossed thirty-six states, and arrived at Shewei. Since the Buddha had achieved nirvana, the imperials convoys copied scriptures of 605,000 words and returned in the eighteenth year of the Yongping era.[85]
>
> 至漢明永平七年甲子，歲星晝現，西方夜明，帝夢神人，長一丈六尺，項有日光。旦問群臣，傅毅曰：西方胡王太子成道，號佛。明帝即遣張騫等，窮河源，經三十六國，至舍衛，佛已涅槃，寫經六十萬五千言，至永平十八年乃還。

Zhen Luan's inquiry may have represented an influential strain of thought of his time and thereafter. The "Shi Lao zhi" 釋老志 ("Records of the Buddha and Laozi") chapter of the *Weishu* 魏書 compiled by Wei Shou 魏收 (505-572 CE), from the perspective of its

---

⑭ Wang Yan 王琰, *Ming xiang ji* 冥祥記, in *Shuofu zibu* 說郛子部, Shanghai: Shanghai shangwu yinshuguan, 1927.

⑮ *Guang hong ming ji*, juan 9.

attempt to put the elements included the story of Emperor Ming's dream in order, can be read as a response to the accusation of the story's anachronistic nature. It reads as follows,

漢武元狩中，遣霍去病討匈奴，至皋蘭，過居延，斬首大獲。昆邪王殺休屠王，將其衆五萬來降。獲其金人，帝以為大神，列於甘泉宫。金人率長丈餘，不祭祀，但燒香禮拜而已。此則佛道流通之漸也。及開西域，遣張騫使大夏還，傳其旁有身毒國，一名天竺，始聞有浮屠之教。哀帝元壽元年，博士弟子秦景憲受大月氏王使伊存口授浮屠經。中土聞之，未之信了也。後孝明帝夜夢金人，項有日光，飛行殿庭，乃訪羣臣，傅毅始以佛對。帝遣郎中蔡愔、博士弟子秦景等使於天竺，寫浮屠遺範。愔仍與沙門攝摩騰、竺法蘭東還洛陽。中國有沙門及跪拜之法，自此始也。愔又得佛經四十二章及釋迦立像。明帝令畫工圖佛像，置清涼臺及顯節陵上，經緘於蘭臺石室。愔之還也，以白馬負經而至，漢因立白馬寺於洛城雍門西。摩騰、法蘭咸卒於此寺。

During the Yuanshou era of his reign, Emperor Wu of Han dispatched Huo Qubing to attack the Xiongnu. The Han army reached Gaolan, passed Juyan, killed many, and achieved a great victory. The king of Hunye assassinated the king of Xiutu and led 50,000 people to surrender to the Han army. The gold man of the king of Xiutu was captured. Emperor Wu considered him great god and placed him in the Ganquan Palace. The gold man was more than a *zhang* tall. No sacrifice was presented to him. The emperor worshiped him merely by burning incense. That was the initial phase in which the Way of the Buddha began to circulate in Han China. `When the communication with the Western Region was established, Emperor Wu dispatched Zhang Qian as an envoy to Daxia. Zhang returned to spread the words that among Daxia's neighboring states there was one called Shendu, also known as Tianzhu [India]. Only then did people begin to hear of the Buddha's teachings. In the first year of the Yuanshou era in Emperor Ai's reign, Qin Jing, an Erudite Student, received a wide range of Buddhist scriptures orally taught by Yicun, messenger of the king of Darouzhi. People of the Middle Kingdom heard of the Buddha's words, but few believed or understood those words. Later, Emperor Xiaoming dreamed one night that a gold man with sunlight behind his head had flown to the Han imperial court. The emperor asked his officials about this. Fu Yi then answered his question by mentioning the Buddha. The emperor dispatched the Gentleman of the Interior Cai Yin, Student of the Erudite Qin Jing, and others on a diplomatic journey to India to copy the teachings left by the Buddha. Yin then returned eastward to Luoyang with two monks, She Moteng and Zhu Falan. From then on, the Middle Kingdom began to have monks and kneeling worship. Moreover, Yin obtained a Buddhist scripture with forty-two sections as well as a statue of the standing Buddha. Emperor Ming ordered the painters to draw the Buddha's images and put them on the Qingliang Terrace and Xianjie Mausoleum, and to seal the scripture in the stone chamber of the Orchid Pavilion. When Yin returned from the west, he arrived with a white horse carrying the scripture on its back. The Han imperial court thus erected the White Horse Buddhist Temple to the west of the Yong Gate of Luoyang city. Moteng and Falan both died in that temple.[86]

The arrangement of the basic elements of the story regarding the introduction of Buddhism into China presented here seems determined to make itself look more plausible than other versions of the story. It not only eliminates the anachronistic charge of putting the early Western Han official Zhang Qian in the court of an Eastern Han emperor; it also carefully situates all the other elements—for instance, the gold man and the translation of Buddhist scripture—in a historical context to eliminate all the possible inconsistencies. To be sure, whether or not all the events mentioned in this narrative actually occurred is hard to prove, but the different organization of those narrative elements in this version does try to convey the information based on which the translatorship of the *Sishi'er zhang jing* is supposed to be better understood.

To give an overview of how the basic elements are arranged in different versions of the same story, I have arranged them in the table below:

Two points regarding this table need to be made. First, the list of sources containing the story of Emperor Ming's dream in connection with the introduction of Buddhism to Han China is less than exhaustive. However, considering that the main concern of this chapter deals with the translatorship of early Buddhist scriptures in Chinese, the number of the sources is sufficient to present a general picture on how the story involved in the formation of the translatorship of the *Sishi'er zhang jing*.[87]

The second point is that the arrangement of the sources in the table does not follow a chronological order. I tend to believe that there is no meaningful, objective chronological order displaying how the narrative developed in an evolutionary sense; or even if there is such order, it is beyond identification. One common way to date a passage is to assume that its date is identical with that of the text containing the passage, while the text is dated according the author's biographical information. This is the method usually followed

⑯ *Weishu* "Shi Lao zhi," 114:3025-3026.

⑰ For a longer list of the source materials, see Maspéro, "Le songe et l'ambassade de l'empereur Ming," pp. 95-130; Kamata Shigeo 鎌田茂雄, *Zhongguo fojiao tongshi* 中國佛教通史 (Vol. 1), trans., Guan Shiqian 關世謙, Gaoxiong: Foguang chubanshe, 1985, p. 102.

Table1

Sources	1 Buddha in dream	2 Han Envoys	3 Foreign monks	4 Buddhist scripture	5 Buddhist image	6 Buddhist temple
A 后漢書	世傳明帝夢見金人，長大，頂有光明，以問羣臣。	遣使天竺問佛道法。			遂於中國圖畫形像焉。	
B 后漢紀	初，帝夢見金人長大，項有日月光，以問群臣。			有經數千萬［言］。	遂於中國而圖其形象焉。	
C 笑道論	至漢明永平七年甲子，歲星晝現，西方夜明，帝夢神人，長一丈六尺，項有日光。旦問群臣。	明帝即遣張騫等，窮河源，經三十六國，至舍衛。		寫經六十萬五千言，至永平十八年乃還。		
D 理惑論	昔孝明皇帝夢見神人，身有日光，飛在殿前，欣然悦之。明日，博問群臣。	遣使者張騫/中郎蔡愔、羽林郎中秦景、博士弟子王遵等十二/十八人。		於大月支寫佛經四十二章，藏在蘭臺石室第十四間。	於其壁畫千乘萬騎，繞塔三匝，又於南宮清涼臺，及開陽城門上作佛像。	於洛陽城西雍門外起佛寺。
E 四十二章經序	昔漢孝明皇帝。夜夢見神人。身體有金色。項有日光。飛在殿前。意中欣然。甚悦之。明日問群臣。	即遣使者張騫羽林中郎將秦景博士弟子王遵等十二人。	後漢西域沙門迦葉摩騰共法蘭譯。	至大月支國。寫取佛經四十二章。在第十四石函中。		登起立塔寺。於是道法流布。處處修立佛寺。
F 冥祥記	漢明帝夢見神人：形垂二丈，身黃金色，項佩日光。以問群臣。	於是發使天竺，寫致經像，表之中夏。…初，使者蔡愔。	西域沙門迦葉摩騰等。	寫致經像，表之中夏。	西域沙門迦葉摩騰等赍優填王畫釋迦佛像；帝重之，如夢所見。乃遣画工图之数本，于南宫清凉台及高阳门显节寿陵上供养。又于白马寺壁，画千乘万骑绕塔三匝之像，如诸传备载。	
G 出三藏記集	漢孝明帝夢見金人。	詔遣使者張騫、羽林中郎將秦景到西域。	始於月支國遇沙門竺摩騰。	譯寫此經（四十二章經）還洛陽，藏在蘭臺石室第十四間中，其經今傳於世。		

续表

Sources	1 Buddha in dream	2 Han Envoys	3 Foreign monks	4 Buddhist scripture	5 Buddhist image	6 Buddhist temple
H 高僧傳	漢永平中，明皇帝夜夢金人飛空而至，乃大集群臣以占所夢。	即遣郎中蔡愔、博士弟子秦景等，使往天竺，尋訪佛法。	愔等於彼遇見摩騰，乃要還漢地。	有記云：騰譯《四十二章經》一卷，初緘在蘭臺石室第十四間中。		騰所住處，今雒陽城西雍門外白馬寺是也。
I 魏書	後孝明帝夜夢金人，項有日光，飛行殿庭，乃訪羣臣	帝遣郎中蔡愔、博士弟子秦景等使於天竺，寫浮屠遺範。	愔仍與沙門攝摩騰、竺法蘭東還洛陽。	愔又得佛經四十二章及釋迦立像…經緘於蘭臺石室。	明帝令畫工圖佛像，置清涼臺及顯節陵上。	以白馬負經而至，漢因立白馬寺於洛城雍門西。

by scholars who study the legend of Emperor Ming's dream.[88] However, it is insufficient to disentangle issues regarding the dates and authenticity of the passages pertaining to the authorship or translatorship of the *Sishi'er zhang jing*. For example, even though in later eras people's awareness of the authorship of a work increased, many attributions, especially of the early translated Buddhist scriptures under discussion, were not based on historical records but were deeply embedded in a religious context prompting the apologists to attribute Buddhist scriptures retrospectively to early foreign monks and establish thereby their textual authority and canonical status. The fact that attributions to early translators increased over time, as we observe in a number of catalogues of translated Buddhist scriptures, puts in mind the more fundamental, power-related factors behind such phenomenon.

We must also be cautious about determining which version of the story is more "original" than another when similar passages appear in more than one source. Even if we sometimes agree on the dates of certain works, we should bear in mind that the contents of each work are not homogeneous, which often results in—in the case of the *Sishi'er zhang jing*, for instance— inconsistencies between the date of the source material and that of the story. Indeed, in most cases it is difficult, if not totally impossible, to determine which version of a story presented in a string of similar passages is more "original" than another. Take, for example, the passages recorded in the *Hou Han shu* (A) and the *Hou Han ji* (B). Since similarities between the wordings of A1 and B1 and between A5 and B5 are obvious, some—Maspéro, for instance[89]—would jump to the conclusion that the version in A is a variation of that in B because Fan Ye (398-445 CE) (the author of A) lived later than Yuan Hong (328-376) (the author of B). The major weakness of this theory is that it ignores the possible existence of a third source based on which both Fan and Yuan respectively compiled their works. Even if we assume that it was Yuan Hong himself who wrote down the story in B, he was probably not the one who invented it. Moreover, since both A and B have been passed down to us after many generations of editing that is difficult to trace, we simply cannot exclude the possibility that the similarities between the two works are later editorial interpolation or alteration. Finally, if we agree that more sophisticated versions of a legend generally postdate less sophisticated ones, we may infer that the passage in A

---

[88] Maspéro, "Le songe et l'ambassade de l'empereur Ming," pp. 95-130; Liang Qichao, "*Sishier zhang jing* bianwei," pp. 51-58; Tang Yongtong, *Han Wei liang Jin Nanbeichao fojiao shi*, pp. 23-34; also see Tang Yongtong, "*Sishier zhang jing* kaozheng," pp. 21-34; Lü Cheng 呂澂, *Zhongguo foxue yuanliu lüejiang*中國佛學源流略講, Beijing: Zhonghua shuju, 1979, pp. 19-31; Ren Jiyu 任繼愈, *Zhongguo Fojiao shi* (vol. 1) 中國佛教史（第一卷）, Beijing: Zhongguo shehui kexue chubanshe, 1981, pp. 94-104; Kamata Shigeo, *Zhongguo fojiao tongshi* (Vol. 1), pp. 103-116; Tan Shibao, *Han Tang foshi tanzhen*, pp. 272-293.

[89] Maspéro, "Le songe et l'ambassade de l'empereur Ming," pp. 95-130.

is earlier than that in B because B emphasizes the introduction of scriptures while A does not.

Another questionable point originally made by Maspéro but inherited by the *Guide* is that the version in the *Chu sanzang ji ji* (G) is no more than an abbreviation of the preface to the *Sishi'er zhang jing* (E).[90] To be sure, compared with the E version, the G version is rather short. Their differences, however, are still discernible. Besides the distinctions regarding the Buddha's figure in Emperor Ming's dream (between G1 and E1) and the place where the *Sishi'er zhang jing* was stored (between G4 and E4), the biggest difference between the two is how the foreign monk(s) took a part in the story's structure. While the two monks to whom the translation of E is attributed do not appear in the narrative of the story, only one of them is mentioned in G, and he plays a role in the story initiated by the emperor's dream (between G2, G3 and E2, E3, respectively). The danger of the point made by Maspéro essentially results from an oversimplified method for dealing with the transmission of early and early medieval Chinese texts as well as the formation of their authorship or translatorship. In fact, even a preliminary browse through the passages from G, E, D, F, and H reveals the complex textual entanglement among them. Whereas the core of the story remains basically unchanged in all these versions, no two versions are even nearly the same. Based on the above observation, I maintain that rather than searching for information to help date the source materials, we ought to view all the above versions as parts of an informative lore suggestive of the formation and translatorship of the *Sishi'er zhang jing*.

The story of Emperor Ming's dream, as the table shows, includes a number of narrative building blocks, the number of which varies according to the varying analytical strategies. Even though the core of the story (Column 1), the emperor's dream, for the most part remains unchanged in its various versions, the situation of the rest of the building blocks (Columns 2, 3, 4, 5, 6) is more intricate. Questions on which building blocks are included, in what form, and how linked directly to our view on the relationship between the translatorship and the development of the lore of the *Sishi'er zhang jing*. The following is a classification of the listed versions highlighting their different narrative foci:

Type I: no Buddhist scripture mentioned (A);
Type II: at least one Buddhist scripture mentioned (B, C, D, E, F, G, H, I);
Type III: passages in Type II mentioning the *Sishi'er zhang jing* (D, E, G, H, I);
Type IV: passages in Type III indicating only Chinese envoys as translators (D, I);

⑽ Nattier, *Guide*, p. 36.

Type V: passages in Type III indicating that the translation of the *Sishi'er zhang jing* was a joint project by both Chinese envoys and foreign monks (G);

Type VI: passages in Type III indicating only foreign monk(s) as translator (E, H).

The above classification gives us reason to assume that the story of the emperor's dream was not specifically conceived to fit the reconstruction of the *Sishi'er zhang jing*'s translatorship. The Type I version shows that Buddhist scriptures do not always provide the legend's focus. Even when scriptures do become the focus, they are not all exclusively related to the *Sishi'er zhang jing*, as we see in Type II. And as we see in Type III some of the versions tie the legend specifically with the translatorship of the *Sishi'er zhang jing*. The five versions listed in Type III change their focus to highlight different individuals as the text's translators. Some of the versions (D and I) indicate that the Chinese envoys were the translators, while others (E and H) consider the foreign monks as the translators. One of Sengyou's notes preserved in the *Chu sanzang ji ji* (G) seems to suggest that the translation of the *Sishi'er zhang jing* was a joint project carried out by both the emperor's envoys and Zhu Moteng, a foreign monk, but according to another note in the same work, Zhu Moteng was not considered a translator. In the preface to the *Sishi'er zhang jing* and Moteng's and Falan's biographies we learn that the translation of the text is attributed to two foreign monks.[91]

The attribution of a translated scripture to one or more than one Buddhist monks is important for the scripture, for it was a crucial step towards establishing its authenticity and authority. Like many other translated scriptures, the *Sishi'er zhang jing* was an anonymous translation before the story of the Han emperor's dream played a role in the process of forming of this scripture's translatorship. Although available evidence makes the initiation of the process difficult to detect, we now have confidence to speculate that efforts to distinguish the *Sishi'er zhang jing* from the apocryphal writings constituted a motivating factor. Attributing it to one or more than one foreign monk or the Han officials connected to foreign monks reflects the intention to establish its authenticity and canonical status. This accords with one of Sengyou's notes recorded in the *Chu sanzang ji ji*: the authenticity of a Buddhist scripture depends on its translatorship—if a piece of Buddhist writing cannot be linked to "the Buddha's golden mouth"[92] or "translated by Buddhist masters,"[93] it would be considered a "dubious scripture."[94]

---

⑨① For the attribution of the *Sishi'er zhang jing* and other texts to Zhu Falan, see Huijiao, *Gaoseng zhuan*, p. 3.

⑨② Sengyou, *Chu sanzang ji ji*, p. 231.

⑨③ Sengyou, *Chu sanzang ji ji*, p. 231.

⑨④ Sengyou, *Chu sanzang ji ji*, p. 231.

Conclusion

Current evidence would indicate that the translatorship of the *Sishi'er zhang jing* had not taken shape by Daoan's time in a manner capable of securing its authenticity even if the *Sishi'er zhang jing* had been available then. And even if the text had in fact taken shape, Daoan was not convinced by its attribution. For the reason that Sengyou has well articulated, it is understandable that attributions of early translated scriptures to Chinese translators did not contain enough authority as foreign monks. After all, Buddhism is a foreign religion and the original Buddhist teachings had to be written in foreign languages. Listing the earliest translation of Buddhist scriptures as having been made by Chinese translators is somewhat awkward, which is why in more developed versions foreign monks become a part of the narrative, a phenomenon evident in Sengyou's note indicating the translation of the *Sishi'er zhang jing* as the result of joint efforts by both Chinese envoys and foreign monks.

We can also infer that the text of the emperor's dream must have been deeply embedded in the formation of the *Sishi'er zhang jing*'s translatorship by Sengyou's time. Even though from the early phase of the development of Buddhism in China (the sixth century, for instance, as we see in Zhen Luan's *Xiao dao lun*), part of the legend had been mocked for their absurdity, Sengyou, widely admired as a learned scholar-monk, accepted it as authentic in dealing with the translatorship of this text. One of the details under vehement attack is that Zhang Qian, an envoy sent by Emperor Ming to the west, appears anachronistically in this story. This has been pointed out by Zhen Luan in the sixth century, by Maspéro in an article published 1910, by Nattier very recently in the *Guide*, and by many others on different occasions.[95] But as we have mentioned before, Sengyou may not have been so ignorant about Han history, and the role Zhang Qian plays in the story seems not absurd to him at all. One way of explaining such seeming inconstancy is that, as Nattier proposes, the entry recorded in the *Chu sangzang ji ji* belongs to a later interpolation. Another way to explain it is simply that Sengyou believed that the story was true, or at least he would not challenge a saying representing the common wisdom of the time.

The use of Zhang Qian in the legend is, no doubt, evocative of the bygone contact between the Han Empire and the west, but its readers, especially those as learned as Sengyou, cannot be too ignorant to overlook the glaring anachronism related to the historical figure Zhang Qian. This may be a reason for some other versions of the story

---

[95] *Guang hong ming ji*, juan 9; Maspéro, "Le songe et l'empereur Ming," pp. 95-130; Nattier, *Guide*, pp. 35-37.

to employ Cai Yin to replace or avoid Zhang Qian's name appearing in the story (as we see in D, F, H, I), even though we need to keep in mind that textual variations may have been more complex than expected. Most probably, in Sengyou's mind Zhang Qian was a useful—because influential—name to evoke people's memory of the past when some of the earliest contacts between China and the west occurred, yet he would certainly know enough, if asked, how to resolve so obvious an anachronism by replying that the Zhang Qian involved in the story was not the Zhang Qian serving in Emperor Wu's court. In fact, the only account that intentionally responds to the accusation of the story's being detectably anachronistic is the "Shi Lao zhi" chapter of the *Weishu,* an account that makes painstaking efforts to render all the elements included in the legend read meaningfully and appear reliable.[96] For example, it separates Zhang Qian from Emperor Ming's dream, deliberately restoring the historical event of Zhang Qian's diplomatic journey to the Daxia as the beginning of the Han people's acknowledgment of India and Buddhism. This account even goes further in laying out a precursor for the translation of the *Sishi'er zhang jing* and, therefore, eliminating the doubt that the Han envoys could have the translation by themselves because they did not know foreign languages.[97]

The above discussion enables us to infer confidently that the translatorship of the *Sishi'er zhang jing* was a later attribution in the legend of the Eastern Han Emperor Ming's dream and his dispatch of envoys to the west in search of Buddhism. The different versions of attribution may have resulted from the practical need to distinguish true Buddhist teachings from apocryphal writings. Some of the versions thus reflected their responses to the critiques on the story tied to the attribution. Even though the *Sishi'er zhang jing* itself may have been available before Daoan, the decision to attribute it to either the Han envoys or the foreign monks came later. Nevertheless, the connection between the translation of the scripture and the emperor's dream together with his sending the envoys to the west must have been well established by Sengyou's time.

Moreover, the above conclusion is not limited to the case of the *Sishi'er zhang jing*; it may extend to other early translated Buddhist scriptures. Take, for example, the attributions to An Shigao, who has long been considered the first translator in the history of Chinese Buddhist translation.[98] Scholars usually accept these attributions mainly based on Daoan's catalogue.[99] When consulting An Shigao's biography for the information of his life, on the basis of which the translations are dated, attributed, and analyzed, we must give

---

[96] *Weishu* "Shi Lao zhi," 114:3025-3026.

[97] *Weishu* "Shi Lao zhi," 114:3025-3026.

[98] Nattier, *Guide*, p. 38.

[99] Zürcher, "A New look at the Early Chinese Buddhist Texts," pp. 277-304.

it a second though before accepting the attributions as records of historical facts that had really taken place and can be analyzed according to An Shigao's biography. A careful reading of the scattered information about An Shigao's life, mainly found in a few postfaces to Buddhist scriptures and his biography preserved in the *Chu sanzang ji ji*,[100] reveals that even the supposedly earliest biography is mostly a later construction consisting of stereotyped narratives and materials from various legendary sources.[101] In these sources An Shigao is portrayed as a Bodhisattva (菩薩) or a man with magical power and secret knowledge from a royal family in a certain Parthian state. One source claims that An Shigao translated "several million of words" (數百萬言) and "as a result Buddhist teachings spread throughout the Han domain" 于是漢邦敷宣佛法,[102] while another maintains that he understood the languages of birds and animals, knew how to interpret omens of heaven and earth, and possessed transcendent knowledge about diagnosing and curing people's diseases.[103] Furthermore, the narration often begins with "有…者" (Once there was …), "昔…" (In the past), or other similar phrases conveying the implication that the ensuing words are more hearsay or story-telling than a statement of historical fact. Indeed, that concrete dates or places are usually avoided in such accounts indicates that they are legendary in nature. Finally, the hagiographic stories included in his biography further suggest that it resembles a potpourri of various legendary narratives using a foreign monk of uncertain provenance as its center. Much as Nattier defends the idea that the material woven into these stories might actually have occurred in terms of her "principle of embarrassment"—an approach to hagiographical writings—little historical information can be gleaned from such vague narration.[104] The defense of the historical accuracy of An Shigao's biography is by no means convincing.[105]

I would also argue that even the attributions of the prefaces or colophons need to be treated with caution. It is necessary to inquire into such questions as when they were written and in what situation, where they were attached and by whom, how they were collected and for what reason. More often than not, early Chinese colophons or postfaces written by compilers or editors as the result of their arrangements of the texts, tend to postdate the text to which they were attached, but they were rarely circulated independently. Whether or not the colophons preserved in the *Chu sanzang ji ji* have

---

[100] Sengyou, *Chu sanzang ji ji*, p. 244, p. 245, p. 248, p. 369, pp. 508-510.

[101] Zürcher, *The Buddhist Conquest of China*, pp. 32-34.

[102] Sengyou, *Chu sanzang ji ji*, p. 369.

[103] Sengyou, *Chu sanzang ji ji*, p. 242, p. 508.

[104] Nattier, *Guide*, p. 39.

[105] Nattier, *Guide*, pp. 38-41.

similar origins is unknown. Nor is there any evidence showing who, why, and how the colophons were collected. If they were indeed written by later editors who faced the same problem as Daoan did when compiling his catalogue, they probably cannot be used as primary sources, especially for the purpose of dating and attributing early Chinese texts.

Finally, I would briefly bring up the issue regarding the material form of the texts, an issue that, while not intensively discussed in this article, is crucial to the study of early Chinese translated Buddhist scriptures.[106] As D. F. McKenzie points out, the material form of a text is a determinate factor in both defining meaning and providing a way of reading the text.[107] Consequently, the change of a text's material form will bring about a change in the circulation of the text, the way it generates meaning, and the way it is received. From this perspective, the study of early Chinese translation of Buddhist text should first of all explore its form, be it on palm tree leaves, birch barks, or oral delivery, when imported into China. Scholars tend to believe that early Buddhist monks and Buddhist teachings traveled to China along with adventurous early foreign merchants.[108] In a recent study Erik Zürcher proposes that the transmission of Buddhism to China did not move gradually from India, Central Asia, the Serindia regions and thence to the Han domain; rather, Buddhism entered the Han urban areas through a distant path starting from India and its adjacent regions.[109] Should this postulation be valid, we may infer that the earliest Buddhist texts, if indeed delivered to China in written form, may have been on palm tree leaves or birch barks and possibly used mainly to serve foreign merchant communities. The translation of early Buddhist teachings appeared only when there was a need on the part of the later generations of foreign merchants increasingly attuned to Han culture and Chinese language and thus beginning to forget their original language, or the activity of translating Buddhist scriptures occurred to fulfill the need of Han native residents who were interested in or even converted by Buddhism. No matter how the Buddhist scriptures before being translated looked like, either in their written forms or being memorized by heart, once translation was attempted, the translated scriptures were arranged according to the Han Chinese textual tradition, namely written down on bamboo strips (evidentially,

---

[106] For a more detailed study on early Chinese texts from this perspective, consult Zhang Hanmo, *Authorship and Text-making in Early China*, Berlin and Boston: Walter De Gruyter GmbH, forthcoming.

[107] Mckenzie, D. F., *Bibliography and the Sociology of Texts*, Cambridge: Cambridge University Press, 1999.

[108] For example, Ji Xianlin 季羡林, "Shangren yu fojiao" 商人與佛教, in *Ji Xianlin xueshu lunzhu zixuanji* 季羡林學術論著自選集, Beijing: Beijing shifan xueyuan chubanshe, 1991, pp. 416-538; Nattier, *Guide*, p. 18.

[109] Zürcher, "Han Buddhism and the Western Region," in *Thought and Law in Qin and Han China: Studies Dedicated to Anthony Hulsewé on the Occasion of His Eightieth Birthday*, eds., William L. Idema and Erik Zürcher, Leiden: Brill, 1990, pp. 158-182; for its Chinese version, see Zürcher, "Handai fojiao yu xiyu" 漢代佛教與西域, trans., Wu Xuling 吴虚領, *Guoji Hanxue* 2(1998), pp. 291-310.

paper was invented as early as in the second century BCE, but was used widely as writing material from the end of the fourth and the beginning of the fifth century CE[110]), following Chinese editing and circulating conventions, and claiming authority not only through the Buddha's name but also appealing to elegant Chinese literary forms. Consequently, we find that, unlike later Buddhist scriptures, early translations tended to be much shorter; and as in other early Chinese texts translators' names were not usually affixed to the translated texts. Finally, we clearly see a tendency to retranslate or reorganize earlier scriptures and translate new materials in more elegant ways.[111]

Thus the study of early Chinese Buddhist translations must take into account the material forms of the scriptures before being translated, the convention of early text making, and the context of their social and religious functions. The translatorship of early Chinese Buddhist scriptures should also be understood in this context. In the initial phase of the spread of Buddhist belief in China, a translator's name was not important to the scriptures he translated. The translators' names were not attached to the translated scriptures; it was present only when such a need as discriminating the orthodox Buddha's words from apocryphal writings arose, and could be constructed only in a retrospective, sometimes a legendary, sense, especially where early translations are concerned. Accordingly, caution must be taken when translatorship, a special from of authorship, is applied as a historical source to date a text or establish its authenticity and authority.

(I dedicate this article to the memory of Professor Michael Henry Heim, late of UCLA, and an unforgettable mentor to many; and I dedicate this article to him not only in thanks for his dedicating time in the last few days of his life to read it through, but also with respect to his having inspired me to be a better human being. Any errors that remain are, of course, my own.)

---

[110] See Tsien, Tsuen-Hsuin, *Paper and Printing: Science and Civilization in China, Chemistry and Chemical Technology* V (Part 1), Cambridge: Cambridge University Press, 1985.

[111] Durt, Hubert, "Early Chinese Buddhist Translations—Questions from the Early Translations in Anthologies of the Sixth Century," in *Early Chinese Buddhist Translations: Contributions to the International Symposium 'Early Chinese Buddhist Translations,' Vienna 18-21 April, 2007* (*Journal of the International Association of Buddhist Studies* 31.1-2 (2008(2010)), pp. 79-504), pp. 119-140; Silk, Jonathan A., "The *Jifayue sheku tuoluoni jing*—Translation, Non-translation, Both or Neither?", in *Early Chinese Buddhist Translations: Contributions to the International Symposium 'Early Chinese Buddhist Translations,' Vienna 18-21 April, 2007* (*Journal of the International Association of Buddhist Studies* 31.1-2 (2008(2010)), pp. 79-504), pp. 369-420.

後藏地區金剛界曼荼羅的傳播路徑之重構

——以後弘初期爲中心

阮　麗

一、問題的提出

後弘初期，後藏地區遺存的金剛界曼荼羅圖像甚少，最初僅知有圖齊教授早年記錄的江浦寺（rKyang phu）[①]。然而，隨著近年西藏考古的推進，在乃甲切木石窟（gNas mjal che mo）、恰姆（Chag mo）石窟相繼發現了此時期以金剛界曼荼羅扎題材的塑像，頗受藏學界的關注。此外，筆者2014年在西藏考察時發現的拉孜縣木絜山石窟（Mu kra'i brag phug），亦可能是一幅簡略形式的金剛界曼荼羅。

乃甲切木石窟、恰姆石窟相距不遠，位於日喀則地區南崗巴縣和定結縣。詳細調查報告已有何強先生對乃甲切木石窟[②]，西藏自治區文物保護研究所、中國藏學研究中心西藏文化博物館對恰姆石窟[③]的公佈。相關主要研究成果還有艾米·海勒（Amy Heller）博士[④]、霍巍教授[⑤]、筆者[⑥]、謝繼勝教授[⑦]及其學生王瑞雷博士[⑧]等，學者們就石窟開鑿年代、圖像的風格特徵、文本依據及其傳播路線等方面展開了綜合性的考證。

---

① 〔意〕圖齊（Tucci, Giaseppe）著，魏正中、薩爾吉編譯《梵天佛地》第四卷第一冊，67—85頁，上海：上海古籍出版社，2009年（原版爲*Indo-tibetica*,1932—1941年，以下略）。

② 何強《西藏崗巴縣乃甲切木石窟》，載於四川大學博物館、西藏自治區文物管理委員會編《南方民族考古》第四輯，1992年，179—186頁。

③ 西藏自治區文物保護研究所、中國藏學研究中心西藏文化博物館，夏格旺堆、熊文彬、何偉、邊頓、洛桑次仁、曲扎《西藏日喀則定結縣恰姆石窟初步調查與研究》，《中國文物報》2012年3月2日第8版。西藏自治區文物保護研究所、中國藏學研究中心西藏文化博物館《西藏定結縣恰姆石窟》，《考古》2012年第7期，68—82頁。

④ Amy Heller, "The caves of gNas mjal che mo", in D. Klimberg-Salter and E. Allinger, eds., *The Inner Asian International Style, 12-14th Centuries*, Wien: Austrian Academy of Sciences, 1998. pp. 135-150.

⑤ 霍巍《關於衛藏地區幾處佛教石窟遺址的調查與研究》，《西藏研究》2002年第3期，52—60頁。

⑥ 阮麗《敦煌石窟曼荼羅圖像研究》，中央美術學院博士論文，2012年5月，73—83、23—26頁。

⑦ 謝繼勝《羌姆石窟——終於找到了藏區腹地佛教造像樣式來源的關鍵證據》，《中國國家地理》2012年第8期，36—71頁。

⑧ 王瑞雷《從乃甲切木石窟看慶喜藏金剛界壇城在後藏的傳播》，《敦煌研究》2014年第5期，10—19頁。

然而筆者認爲，在以往的研究中，關於傳播路徑仍有兩個問題需要進一步探討[⑨]。一是，以圖齊教授爲代表，傳統認爲後弘初期的金剛界曼荼羅現存實例基本都是依據仁欽桑布譯慶喜藏（Ānandagarbha）釋《真性作明》（*Tantratattvālokakarī*）所繪。圖齊教授在《梵天佛地》一書中，將塔波寺和白居寺金剛界殿金剛界曼荼羅皆以慶喜藏此本作爲文獻依據，但是卻未將二圖像與文本核實[⑩]。此後，受到圖齊教授的影響，西方學者喬伯（Roger Goepper）在研究阿奇寺時[⑪]，盧恰尼茲（Luczanits）博士在研究塔波寺時[⑫]亦同樣判定是根據此本。艾米海勒博士再次引用圖齊、喬伯和盧恰尼茲觀點並同時指出，不僅是塔波寺，阿奇寺（Alchi）、那科寺（Nako）、東噶石窟（Dunkar）、乃甲切木石窟，雖然圖像之間略有不同，但可能均與慶喜藏釋相關[⑬]。另外，日本學者田中公明博士對白居寺（dPal' khor chos sde gling）金剛界殿、托林寺（mTho lding）和扎不讓（Tsa pa rang）[⑭]，森雅秀教授對白居寺吉祥多門塔（bKra shis sgo mang mchod rten）第五層壁畫[⑮]進行比對後，均認爲所依文本是慶喜藏釋《真性作明》。如此，慶喜藏釋《真性作明》就成了西藏金剛界曼荼羅最爲普遍的文本，並且是由譯者仁欽桑布傳入西藏。筆者、王瑞雷博士亦先後跟隨了這一觀點[⑯]。不過筆者很快意識到，《真性作明》對曼荼羅每尊的持物，甚至包括兩手的姿勢、位置都有嚴格的規定，若將其按照文本描述重新核實，在上述石窟中，僅有白居寺金剛界殿[⑰]及吉祥多門塔第五層、托林寺和扎不讓與《真性作明》[⑱]基本一致，其他實例皆與此本有明顯差異，尤其是阿奇寺，就連《真性作明》最基本特徵的四波羅蜜菩薩爲三昧耶形都不相符。由此推測，慶喜藏釋《真性作明》以外，後弘初期西藏或許傳入了極其豐富的金剛界曼荼羅文本及圖像。

另一是，謝繼勝教授從恰姆石窟與塔波寺具有相同的金剛界33尊系統、懸塑技術，

---

⑨ 本文主要觀點於2015年10月第六屆西藏考古與藝術國際學術討論會（杭州）口頭發表，會議中宣講內容全文提交會議組（未發表）。

⑩ 〔意〕圖齊（Giaseppe Tucci）著，魏正中、薩爾吉編譯《梵天佛地》第三卷第一冊，26—28頁。

⑪ Roger Geopper, *Alchi: Ladakh's hidden Buddhist sanctuary: the Sumtsek,* London, Serindia Publications, 1996.

⑫ Christian Luczanits, "The Clay Sculptures", in Deborah E. Klimburg-Salter (ed.), *Tabo- a Lamp for the Kingdom, Early Indo-Tibetan Buddhist Art in the Western Himālaya,* Milan, Skira Editore, 1997, pp. 189-205.

⑬ Amy Heller, "The caves of gNas mjal che mo".

⑭ 田中公明《ペンコルチューデ寺院の金剛界立体曼荼羅》，《東京大学文学部文化交流研究施設研究紀要》通号8，1988年，pp. 81-101。《西チベット、トリン寺とツアパラン遺跡の金剛界諸尊壁画について》，《密教図像》11，1992年，pp. 11-22（L）。

⑮ 森雅秀《ペンコルチューデ仏塔第5層の〈金剛頂経〉所説のマンダラ》，《チベット仏教図像研究国立民族学博物館研究報告》別冊第18号，1997年，pp. 269-318。

⑯ 阮麗《敦煌石窟曼荼羅圖像研究》，論文將乃甲切木石窟判定爲慶喜藏另一文本《一切金剛出現》；王瑞雷《從乃甲切木石窟看慶喜藏金剛界壇城在後藏的傳播》一文認爲，後葬地區金剛界曼荼羅皆爲慶喜藏《真性作明》本。

⑰ 田中公明博士將圖齊教授最初考察的白居寺金剛界殿圖像與文本逐一對比。

⑱ 本文所指《真性作明》，僅以37尊尊容爲中心，其餘內容暫不做探討。

以及供養人的髮辮與東噶皮央石窟吐蕃裝束女性相似的幾點特徵，新近提出“我們以往研究西藏石窟，都是單獨地考察喀什米爾、藏區西部與衛藏中部零星湧現的石窟，沒有把藏西的石窟與屬於衛藏的石窟聯繫起來考察，沒有考察石窟與寺院造像體系的內在聯繫——因爲沒有一個年代確鑿並保留了原始風貌的石窟作爲參照系。恰姆石窟的出現啟動了于闐、敦煌樣式經由藏西挺進至衛藏地區的證據鏈”，其傳播路徑是“由喀什米爾或敦煌經於闐進入札達、普蘭等藏西石窟，延伸至衛藏定結、崗巴的恰姆與乃甲切木石窟，沿著亞東山口東向轉到康馬艾旺寺”[19]。筆者認爲這一看法還值得商榷。

鑒於此，本文在前賢研究成果的基礎上，將對下列問題提出質疑：

（1）乃甲切木石窟、恰姆石窟、木紮山石窟的文本依據是否爲慶喜藏釋《真性作明》？

（2）慶喜藏釋《真性作明》究竟是怎樣的傳播路徑？

（3）其傳播路徑是否與藏西、敦煌有關？

二、西藏金剛界曼荼羅的文獻及圖像差異

1. 文本

金剛界曼荼羅是依據《真實攝經》（漢譯本稱《初會金剛頂經》）所繪，《真實攝經》由金剛界品、降三世品、遍調伏品、一切義成就品四大品，及教理分、流通分六部分的龐大經軌群構成，其中四大品又包含大、三昧耶、法、羯磨、四印、一印曼荼羅六章。各章均由大曼荼羅開始，大曼荼羅是其他五種曼荼羅的根本，共計有28種曼荼羅。我們通常所說的金剛界曼荼羅是指狹義上的《真實攝經》第一品的第一個曼荼羅，即其根本曼荼羅，又稱爲金剛界大曼荼羅或金剛界三十七尊曼荼羅，它由五佛、四波羅蜜菩薩、十六大菩薩、八供養菩薩和四攝菩薩的37尊構成。此外，有時還繪入賢劫十六尊或賢劫千佛，尊像數達53尊或1037尊，賢劫尊常見於壁畫或唐卡中，而塑像作品極爲少見。

《真實攝經》是瑜伽部根本怛特羅，現存經軌的藏譯本主要有：

11世紀中葉喀什米爾大譯師信相鎧（Śraddhākara-varman）入西藏時與仁欽桑布（Rin chen bzang po，958—1055）共同譯出藏文本《一切如來攝真實集成大乘經》（簡稱《真實攝經》，*De bzhin gshegs pa thams cad de kho na nyid bsdus pa zhes bya ba theg pa chen po'i mdo*，德格No. 479，北京No.112），此本收錄於德格版密教部na帙（1-142a），相當於一部儀軌集成，共分爲九品，與梵文本《一切如來真實攝經》（*Sarvatathāgatatattvasaṃgraha nāma mahāyānasūtra*）[20]及漢譯本宋大中祥符八年施護

⑲　謝繼勝《羌姆石窟——終於找到了藏區腹地佛教造像樣式來源的關鍵證據》。

⑳　梵文貝葉經《一切如來真實攝經》原本是圖齊1932年在尼泊爾發現，現藏於尼泊爾國立古文書館，圖齊並將寫本全部抄寫帶回國（稱爲Devanāgarī本）。

譯《佛說一切如來真實攝大乘現證三昧大教王經》[21]內容基本一致。

《西藏大藏經》還收入了對《真實攝經》的藏文注疏，格魯派創始人宗喀巴（1357—1419）在《真言道次第》中稱《真實攝經》的“三大論書”是：①佛密（Buddhaguhya）釋《怛特羅義入》（*Tantrāthāvatāra*，*rGyud kyi don la 'jug pa*，德格No. 2501，北京No. 3324），是經典內容大意的注疏，略晚於漢譯本或屬同一時期。蓮花金剛（Padmavajra）又對此書進行了複注，即《怛特羅義入注釋》（*Tantrāthāvatāra-vyākhyāna*，*rGyud kyi don la 'jug pa'i 'grel bshad*，德格No.2502，北京No.3325）。② 釋友（Śākyamitora）釋《俱差羅莊嚴真實攝疏》（*Kosalālaṃkāra-tattvasaṃgrahaṭīkā*，*De kho na nyid bsdus pa'i rgya cher bshad pa ko sa la'i rgyan*，德格No.2503，北京No.3326）略早於佛密本。③ 慶喜藏（Ānandagarbha）釋《真性作明》（*Tantratattvālokakarī, De bzhin gshegs pa thams cad kyi de kho na nyid bsdus pa theg pa chen po mngon par rtogs pa zhes bya ba'i rgyud kyi bshad pa de kho na nyid snang bar byed pa*，德格No. 2510，北京No.3333），是三大論書中最龐大的一部注疏，內容與釋友本相似，對經典逐句有詳盡的解釋。佛密、釋友、慶喜藏三人都是印度活躍於8—9世紀瑜伽部密教的三大學匠，由此推測《真實攝經》完本的成立時間下限應是8世紀末[22]。

慶喜藏還著有一部關於金剛界曼荼羅的儀軌書《一切金剛出現》（*Vajradhātuma-hāmaṇḍalopāyikā-Sarvavajrodaya, rDo rje dbyings kyi dkyil 'khor chen po'i cho ga rdo rje thams cad 'byung ba*，德格No. 2516，北京No. 3339），是以《真實攝經》的金剛界大曼荼羅品爲中心製作的儀軌。

無畏生護（Abhāyakaragupta，11世紀後半—12世紀初）編撰的曼荼羅觀想集成《究竟瑜伽鬘》（*Niṣpannyogāvalī*）以及與其相對應的曼荼羅儀軌書《金剛鬘》（Vajrāvalī）中第十九章是金剛界曼荼羅，《究竟瑜伽鬘》對諸尊尊容進行了具體描述。

《真實攝經》注疏還有14世紀布頓（Bu ston，1290—1364）著《入瑜伽怛特羅海之舟》（*rNal 'byor rgyud kyi rgya mtshor 'jug pa'i gru gjins*，德格No. 5104），書中也提到了佛密、釋友和慶喜藏三人。

與《真實攝經》相關的還有一短篇文獻，即慕底達克沙（Muḍitakoṣa）譯《金剛界大曼荼羅一切諸尊建立》（*Vajradhatumahamandala savadevavyavasthana, rDo rje dbyins kyi dkyil 'khor chen po'i lha rnams kyi rnam par gzhag pa*，德格No.2504，北京No.3327），內容與《一切金剛出現》相近。

19世紀俄寺僧蔣揚洛特旺波（Jamyang loter wang po）編纂的曼荼羅集成《續部總集》（rGyud sde bsdus）第四卷包含有慶喜藏傳承的金剛界曼荼羅，雖然此文獻成立較

㉑ 大正藏，第18冊，No. 0882。

㉒ 松長有慶《密教経典成立史論》，法藏館，1980年，p. 195。慶喜藏被看作是波羅朝瑪赫波羅（Mahipala）一世時代的人，關於瑪赫波羅（Mahipala）一世原認爲在位時間是847—899年，但據印度學者最近的研究也有說法是988—1038年在位。參見松長惠史《インドネシアの密教》，法藏館，1999年，p. 218。

晚，但是對於研究俄寺傳承具有極高的參考價值。《西藏俄寺曼荼羅集》是依據這部文獻而製作㉓。

此外，還有尼泊爾密教僧庫拉達塔（Kuladatta，11世紀中？）的梵文寫本儀軌集成《所作集細疏》（Kriyāsaṃgrahapañjikā），其中包含有金剛界曼荼羅的儀軌，寫本遺存數量較多，年代最早的推測爲1216年㉔。依此文獻製作的“金剛界念誦次第”在加德滿都河谷一帶十分流行。

2. 圖像

上述西藏諸文獻中，與曼荼羅圖像相關的文獻僅有慶喜藏釋《真性作明》及其他的儀軌書《一切金剛出現》、與無畏生護的《究竟瑜伽鬘》㉕。其中《真性作明》對諸尊尊容的描述最爲詳細，《續部總集》個尊與《真性作明》一致。《俱差羅莊嚴真實攝疏》描述了五佛的形象，五佛不持持物，與其他諸本相異。

三本文獻共通的特徵是，五佛均呈菩薩形，鳥獸座，並持代表性持物。區別主要是，慶喜藏兩本的大日如來是四面二臂，四波羅蜜菩薩是三昧耶形；而《究竟瑜珈鬘》是四面八臂或一面二臂，四波羅蜜菩薩是人形，並且左手結期克印，並持羂索。此類圖像在西藏實例極少，也就是說《究竟瑜珈鬘》在西藏並不流行。《真性作明》最顯著的特徵是，十六親近菩薩中有金剛光、金剛幢等五身菩薩以及四攝菩薩中金剛鈴菩薩的左手都是撫在蓮座上。金剛鈴菩薩左手扶座還說明四攝菩薩是坐姿，而不是我們通常見到的展左腿的明王形。《一切金剛出現》雖然與《真性作明》持物一致，但是由於其中沒有詳細敘述兩手的姿勢，所以這兩本是否爲相同的粉本尚不明確。然而，兩本的金剛業菩薩都是在胸前持羯磨杵，金剛牙菩薩都是藥叉的忿怒形等特徵，對於辨識圖像是否爲慶喜藏本有一定的幫助。

四波羅蜜菩薩的尊形在西藏以三昧耶形最爲常見，或許正因爲如此，很容易誤把四波羅蜜菩薩爲三昧耶形的慶喜藏本看作是西藏金剛界曼荼羅的主要依據。另外，還有幾例金剛界曼荼羅塑像不見四波羅蜜菩薩，僅存33尊，如塔波寺、白居寺金剛界殿、江浦寺。但是，文獻中金剛界曼荼羅都作37尊，即所謂的三十七菩提分法，並沒有所謂的33尊系統。換言之，不論四波羅蜜菩薩是三昧耶形還是人形，都當算作37尊曼荼羅中的4尊。因此，金剛界曼荼羅塑像中常常不見有四波羅蜜菩薩可能是由於這四身大多表現爲三昧耶形，三昧耶形如持物般大小，很容易遺失的緣故吧。我們在唐卡作品中一般就不會見到缺少四波羅蜜菩薩的金剛界曼荼羅。圖齊教授也曾這樣解釋，“塔波寺曼荼羅天衆數目與慶喜藏、宗喀巴或薩迦派論書所述之間的差異是少了四天衆，但我認爲這不是傳規的不同……天衆本該有或塑或雕的明確標識，而這些在今天的塔波寺裡已蕩然無

㉓ ギャッツオ・ソナム著、立川武蔵編《西蔵曼荼羅集成》，講談社，1983年，No. 22。

㉔ 乾仁志《Kriyāsaṃgraha所説の金剛界曼陀羅》，《印度學仏教學研究》通號87，1995年，pp. 149-153（L）。

㉕ 由於《續部總集》文獻略晚，而且與《真性作明》圖像完全一致，未列入。

存，即使在持有標識的手等塑像最脆弱的部分也不見此類的跡象”[26]。雕塑作品遺存年代久遠，這種情況是極有可能發生的。

尼泊爾庫拉達塔的《所作集細疏》雖然描述了諸尊的標誌性持物，但亦沒有具體描述二手的姿勢。圖像特徵是四波羅蜜菩薩是三昧耶形，四攝菩薩明確記爲忿怒尊。持物與其他本不同的是金剛語菩薩持海螺。獨特之處還有在《所作集細疏》排除魔障的禮儀一節中記有，四攝菩薩的金剛鉤展右，金剛索展左，金剛鎖呈氏宿姿（vaiśākapada，叉開兩腿站立），金剛鈴呈曼荼羅步（maṇḍalapaśa）的姿勢。類似的圖像可見有塔波寺、爪哇島出土銅像的金剛界曼荼羅，四攝菩薩是一身展左、一身展右，二身蹲坐勢。[27]另外，賢劫十六菩薩在《所作集細疏》中是各自持不同持物，而慶喜藏釋《真性作明》是與各自方位的四轉輪王菩薩持物相同，即東方四身持金剛杵和金剛鈴，南方四身持摩尼寶，西方四身持蓮花，北方四身持羯磨杵。《一切金剛出現》僅錄入賢劫千佛的尊名。由於《所作集細疏》與《一切金剛出現》較爲接近，以及金剛語菩薩持海螺在西藏極少見，所以此本尚無法判斷是否爲西藏流行的粉本。

三、乃甲切姆與恰姆石窟的曼荼羅與相關圖像問題的討論

1. 乃甲切木石窟

乃甲切木石窟位於崗巴縣城以西約30千米的昌龍鄉乃村，與錫金毗鄰，海拔5000米。據藏文史書記載，8世紀中葉蓮花生大師應贊普赤松德贊之迎請入藏，在返回印度時途徑崗巴，並在此傳授過密法。崗巴縣境內的多吉曲登尼瑪寺（意爲金剛太陽塔寺）相傳是在赤松德贊的授意下創建，至今在西藏及錫金、尼泊爾的佛教信徒中仍很有影響[28]。

乃甲切木石窟現存5個洞窟，距地面10余米，洞口皆面向南方，自西向東順序排列。金剛界曼荼羅塑於第4號窟內，窟室平面呈圓角方形，進深3.2、橫寬3.7、高3.2米，窟頂壁畫已殘毀不清，四壁從窟底1.5米以上部分均爲賦彩的石胎泥塑浮雕造像，但彩繪經後代補繪。塑像是完整的金剛界37尊曼荼羅，五佛皆一面二臂，菩薩形，左肩斜披絡腋，高髮髻，結跏趺坐於須彌座上，並帶有鳥獸座，臂釧、項飾、腰飾均爲雙重連珠樣式。艾米·海勒認爲其身體比例具有印度—尼泊爾風格，而尊像面部特徵的寬臉、眉毛交匯於鼻樑正中眉心處、眼修長，更接近印度紐瓦爾民族或尼泊爾的特徵[29]。

北壁正中爲主尊大日如來及四波羅蜜菩薩（圖1），大日如來雙手交至胸前，手部殘毀，似結智拳印，結跏趺坐於“工”字形須彌座上，座內有二獅子。最引人矚目的

㉖〔意〕圖齊（Tucci, Giaseppe）著，魏正中、薩爾吉編譯《梵天佛地》第三卷第一冊，44—45頁。

㉗ 乾仁志《Kriyāsaṃgraha所説の金剛界曼陀羅》，《印度學仏教學研究》通號87，1995年，pp. 149-153（L）。

㉘ 霍巍《關於衛藏地區幾處佛教石窟遺址的調查與研究》。

㉙ Amy Heller, “The caves of gNas mjal che mo”.

是，大日如來兩側三昧耶形四波羅蜜菩薩中的羯磨杵内還露出一女尊的頭部，這是三昧耶四波羅蜜菩薩與女尊身形的一種混合圖像，在現存實例中僅此一例。

圖1　乃甲切木石窟大日如來

夏格旺堆提供

四佛配置於東西兩壁，周圍各有四親近菩薩，由左下方沿順時針方向排列。門口處南壁上方的立像是八供養菩薩及四攝菩薩。十六親近菩薩的持物雖然大多殘毀，但以二手的位置、姿勢並結合經典不難推測出各尊的尊格及其圖像特徵。乃甲切木石窟與慶喜藏二本、《究竟瑜伽鬘》及《所作集細疏》三本文獻對比如下：

（1）與《究竟瑜伽鬘》的不同有，四波羅蜜菩薩是三昧耶形，而不是結期克印的菩薩形。金剛薩埵翻轉右手持金剛杵的姿勢與文本的右手豎中指施天杖印並置五股金剛杵，金剛語菩薩持舌與文本的持海螺，金剛牙菩薩的菩薩形與文本的忿怒形等。

（2）與慶喜藏二本的不同在於，主尊大日如來爲一面二臂與慶喜藏二本的四面二臂相異。十六親近菩薩不見有《真性作明》中左手扶於座上的姿勢。金剛薩埵握持金剛杵的右手向外翻轉與慶喜藏二本右手豎中指施天杖印並置五股金剛杵，金剛愛菩薩弓箭持於胸前與慶喜藏本的張弓射箭，金剛利菩薩持劍於胸前與慶喜藏本揮劍的姿勢皆有別。另外，金剛業菩薩（圖2的左下方）二手上舉至頭頂，與慶喜藏二本右手在胸前持羯磨杵，左手於腰間持金剛鈴（或搖鈴）相異。金剛業菩薩二手舉至頭頂現存有兩種圖像，一種在《究竟瑜伽鬘》提到的二手舉過頭頂並持羯磨杵。另一種唐密系中傳9世紀文秘所作《秘藏記》是二手舉至頭頂合掌，現圖成身會等圖像中亦見類似形象。但乃甲切木石窟的金剛業菩薩屬於哪種持物無法辨識。

圖2　乃甲切木石窟西壁北側

夏格旺堆提供

（3）與《所作集細疏》的主要區別是，大日如來是一面二臂與文本的四面二臂；金剛語菩薩持舌與文本的持海螺相異。然而，四攝菩薩二身明王形，展左及展右勢，另二身是肌肉凸顯的力士形（一身殘毀），立姿。四攝菩薩與《所作集細疏》略有相似之處，但力士形的表現僅見於乃甲切木石窟。

顯然，乃甲切木石窟與四文本的諸多差異證明，乃甲切木石窟皆不是出自包括慶喜藏二本在內的上述文獻。

2. 恰姆石窟

恰姆石窟位於日喀則地區定結縣瓊孜鄉（Khyung rtse）恰姆村南3千米，2008年由日喀則地區文物普查隊發現，2012年發佈了詳細的調查報告。考古報告中對泥塑木樁碳十四測定的結果是1020—1160年（即11—12世紀），報告又結合其他西藏早期作品將年代斷於11世紀，同時恰姆石窟群可分爲三區，約105個洞窟，推測爲金剛界曼荼羅塑像的分佈於一區1號窟。該窟坐西朝東，單室，平面呈馬蹄狀。泥塑和壁畫分佈於西、北、南三壁，東壁辟門。窟內塑像現皆無，僅存32組（還有1組殘毀）泥塑的頭光、身光和高浮雕五鳥獸座。南壁和北壁泥塑身光底部還有不少題記框，其中兩個框內題有文字"金剛因"（rDo rje 'khra lo）及"金剛薩埵"（rDo rje semes pa），但考古報告認爲可能是後代補寫。各尊的配置是正壁西壁（圖3）9個背光外，北壁和南壁分别有13個背光。再加上南北兩壁最東端和東壁南北兩端因窟壁坍塌而被毀的2尊佛像，1號窟內原有泥塑應爲37尊，數量和配置與金剛界曼荼羅37尊完全吻合[30]。

圖3　恰姆石窟主壁（西壁）

夏格旺堆提供

恰姆石窟不是33尊，據考古報告，窟內現存有塑像背光、木樁等37尊的痕跡和鳥獸座，筆者在仔細核對後發現也是37尊。謝老師可能沒有注意到入口處門上方坍塌的地方還有四組三角形的木樁洞，這裡是四攝菩薩的位置。

謝繼勝教授僅數有33尊[31]，可是，如果以33個背光按照曼荼羅配置排列的話，發現無

[30] 西藏自治區文物保護研究所、中國藏學研究中心西藏文化博物館《西藏定結縣恰姆石窟》。

[31] 謝繼勝《羌姆石窟——終於找到了藏區腹地佛教造像樣式來源的關鍵證據》。

法合理安置於其中，再次核對後才注意到，入口上方的坍塌處還發現了四組“∴”形木樁痕跡（圖4），這應該是四攝菩薩的尊位。因此該窟窟內佈局是，西壁是9尊，南北壁各12尊（其中1身殘毀）的33尊，再加上東壁門上方的4尊，共計37尊。而且，從中央主尊兩側四波羅蜜菩薩位置的背光前，還殘存有腿部木胎的痕跡看，應該是人形而不是三昧耶形。因此，可以肯定地説，恰姆石窟與塔波寺沒有文本的傳播關係，同時也不是慶喜藏本。

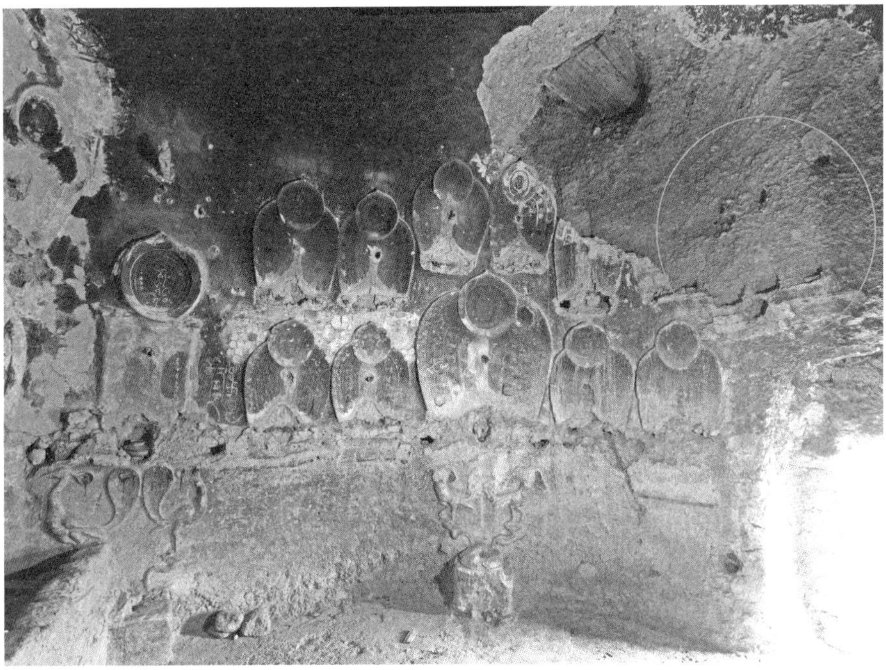

圖4　恰姆石窟北壁

夏格旺堆提供

然而，37尊的數量、佈局、鳥獸座並不是金剛界曼荼羅所特有的特徵，同樣的配置還出現在《金剛頂經》系瑜伽部具密派（gSang ldan）攝族文殊曼荼羅、攝族毗盧遮那曼荼羅，惡趣清淨曼荼羅中的一切智毗盧遮那37尊曼荼羅等。例如，拉達克地區阿奇寺壁畫（13世紀早期）的攝族文殊曼荼羅（圖5）、攝族毗盧遮那曼荼羅（圖6）。具密派攝族曼荼羅被認爲是金剛界系曼荼羅的一種，攝族文殊曼荼羅出自《文殊師利真實名經》（Nāmasaṃgīti），結構是中央主尊爲四面八臂本初佛文殊，第二重八葉蓮瓣形狀內的四方是金剛界四佛，四隅是四波羅蜜菩薩。第三重十六葉蓮瓣內配十六大菩薩。其外側內院配內四供養菩薩，外院配賢劫十六尊、外四供菩薩和四攝菩薩，共計53尊。攝族毗盧遮那曼荼羅亦與攝族文殊曼荼羅完全的結構一樣。可見，具密派攝族曼荼羅、一切智毗盧遮那曼荼羅雖然與金剛界曼荼羅形狀不同，但是，在恰姆石窟的雕塑作品中是無法區別出來的。因此，在窟內不存一身塑像的情況下，確認其內容是金剛界曼荼羅尚缺乏足夠的證據。

圖5　阿奇寺三層堂3層北壁 具密派攝族文殊曼荼羅

撮影：森一司；監修：田中公明『ラダック・ザンスカールの仏教壁画』，渡辺出版，2011年，pp.186

圖6　阿奇寺大日堂後壁右 具密派攝族毗盧遮那曼荼羅

撮影：森一司；監修：田中公明『ラダック・ザンスカールの仏教壁画』，渡辺出版，2011年，pp.183

3. 木紮山石窟

木紮山石窟位於定結縣以北約180千米的拉孜鎮拉孜村西，東連薩迦縣、西南接定日縣，西靠昂仁縣，北鄰謝通門縣，自古以來就是交通要道。木扎山形似一巨石，石窟海拔是3950米，東側山下是拉孜曲德寺。據《拉孜曲德寺簡志》載，該石窟開鑿於819年左右的前弘後期，11世紀後弘初期比丘嘎耶達熱（Gayadhara）曾在此洞窟內修煉過。從造像特徵看，可能是11—12世紀之作。

洞窟面闊2.65、高3.2、進深3.5米。窟內正壁是主尊大日如來及四菩薩（圖7），兩側各設有二細長形拱形龕，龕內塑像不存。大日如來像高1.53米，菩薩形，一面二臂、雙手結智拳印，結跏趺坐於蓮花座上，座下有二獅子。兩側有四身菩薩，高0.53米，四菩薩的一手分別持四佛的象徵性持物，即金剛杵、如意寶、蓮花、羯磨杵，當地人稱之爲五佛[32]。但是，四菩薩中的二身結跏趺坐，二身卻是呈輪王坐坐姿，而通常輪王坐是不作爲如來的坐姿，所以這四菩薩當不是金剛界四佛。四菩薩的尊格有兩種可能，一是四波羅蜜菩薩，一是四轉輪王菩薩。若是四波羅蜜菩薩，兩側壁就可能是四佛，窟內則是

圖7　木紮山石窟大日如來

羅文華攝

㉜　這裡順便值得一提的是，僅具備金剛界五佛並不能稱其就是金剛界曼荼羅，例如在莫高窟第465窟窟頂、榆林窟第3、4窟曼荼羅或經變畫上方、西夏黑水城出土佛畫上方等，這些都不是金剛界曼荼羅，正如圖齊說過"每個怛特羅儀軌皆需觀想五佛，這是每個儀式的前行。一想及此，五佛的出現就很容易解釋了"（同注圖齊Tucci, Giaseppe著，魏正中、薩爾吉編譯《梵天佛地》第三卷第二冊，28頁）。因此，謝繼勝教授在《羌姆石窟—終於找到了藏區腹地佛教造像樣式來源的關鍵證據》一文中將昌珠寺殘存五方佛塑像以及恰姆石窟東南方楚坦尼瑪拉雪山與周邊地區"五寶庫大雪山"都看做是金剛界曼荼羅壇場的看法筆者認爲似乎不夠妥當。

由金剛界五佛及四波羅蜜菩薩構成的金剛界九尊曼荼羅。若是四轉輪王菩薩，窟內可能是金剛界曼荼羅另一種的四印曼荼羅，這樣兩側壁則是四攝菩薩。然而無論是其中哪一種情況，從大日如來一面二臂的圖像上判斷，其文本肯定不是慶喜藏二本。

四、從江浦寺看慶喜藏釋《真性作明》在後藏地區的出現及其傳播

上述後弘初期的金剛界曼荼羅塑像（包括恰姆石窟、木紮山石窟）均不是慶喜藏本，那麼慶喜藏本到底是什麼時候出現的呢？筆者發現，最早且最爲接近於慶喜藏釋《真性作明》的圖像是江浦寺。但是，還有一點令人質疑的是，江浦寺的年代是否會早到目前學術界普遍接受的圖齊、維塔利觀點的11—12世紀？本節將探討這座後藏地區早期的重要寺廟中金剛界曼荼羅塑像的時代及其圖像特徵。

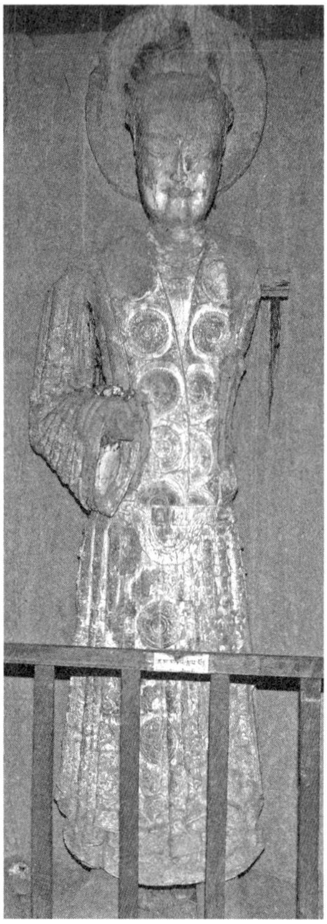

圖8　艾旺寺無量壽佛殿菩薩

羅文華攝

江浦寺位於錫金江孜商道亞東大道左側，日喀則地區康馬縣南部的薩瑪達鄉，是著名的薩瑪達（sa ma mda'）寺院之一。在斷代上圖齊顯得猶疑不定，他在最初看到江浦寺塑像時寫道："薩瑪達的這座寺院建於11世紀曲吉洛卓（Chos kyi blo gros，10世紀後半至11世紀前半，仁欽桑布的弟子）時代，如今所見應爲薩迦袞噶洛卓堅贊任座主時所進行的擴建和修復，最早的遺存只有一些銅像、前殿和底層佛殿的壁畫。但祖拉康二樓和院子四周回廊四間佛殿的塑像年代並不那麼久遠，它們丟棄了初期的神聖樸實，修飾更繁富，華麗寬大的裙褶垂曳，與其他佛陀神像的貼身袈裟形成對比。"[33]可是，如果將他這些塑像斷在薩迦派掌權時期（13—14世紀），就會與同屬薩瑪達寺院的艾旺寺（e-vam）年代相矛盾，所以圖齊最終還是將這批寺院定於後弘初期的11—12世紀[34]。其後，維塔利又找到了一些關於薩瑪達寺院的新史料，據這些史料他將江浦寺、艾旺寺列爲薩瑪達類型中最早的一批，年代可能比1037年的孜乃薩寺（rTsis gNas gsar）嘉丕殿還早，約在1030年左右或更早[35]。

然而，筆者在對金剛界曼荼羅諸尊尊像比定時卻發

㉝ 〔意〕圖齊（Tucci, Giaseppe）著，魏正中、薩爾吉編譯《梵天佛地》第四卷第一冊，85頁。

㉞ Tucci, *Transhimalaya*, trans. James Hogarth, Geneva, Nagel Publishers, 1973, pp. 91-94.

㉟ Robeter Vitali, *Early Temples of the Central Tibet*, London:Serindia Publications,1990.pp95.

現，史料大多年代與實際塑像的風格難以匹配，江浦寺塑像明顯晚於艾旺寺。比較一下艾旺寺無量壽佛殿的菩薩像（圖8）與江浦寺金剛界曼荼羅塑像便一目了然：

艾旺寺衣著厚重、團花顯得粗略，身體比例上，頭部較大，體態僵硬，缺乏變化，形象更加古樸。而江浦寺薄衣貼體，團花刻畫非常細膩，身上的裝飾也極其精緻繁縟，身體比例均勻，肌肉感突出，腰部已經明顯拉長，表現出較晚的時代特徵。孜乃薩寺（圖9）與江浦寺（圖10）比較同樣，孜乃薩寺團花刻畫明顯粗略。

圖9　孜乃薩寺無量光佛

Von Schroeder, Ulrich, *Buddhist Sculptures in Tibet II*, Hong Kong: Visual Dharma, 2001.pp.841,fig.XIII-11

圖10　江浦寺“普明殿”大日如來

Von Schroeder, Ulrich, *Buddhist Sculptures in Tibet II*, Hong Kong: Visual Dharma, 2001.pp.845,fig.fig.XIII-17

艾旺寺與雪朗寺（Zho nang）中，雪朗寺如來像（圖11）很明顯袈裟輕薄，袖口與腿部衣紋細緻，線條流暢，而艾旺寺（圖12）的袖口、衣褶就表現得很厚重。雪朗寺如來像與江浦寺的表現手法十分相似，應時代接近。

此外，艾旺寺菩薩頭戴三葉冠，江浦寺眷屬菩薩中頭冠既有三葉冠，又出現有數量較多的五葉冠（圖13），冠葉雕刻極爲精緻。目前學界一般成熟的五葉冠最早是以14世紀的夏魯寺壁畫作爲時代參照物。而且，江浦寺甚至與15世紀白居寺菩薩像（圖14）都可以找到很多相似之處，如冠葉、項飾的吊墜、耳璫、面容等。可見，白居寺金剛界殿塑像不論在佈局、懸塑的技法形式，還是尊像特徵上都明顯受到了江浦寺的影響，二者看上去絕不會相距有四個世紀那麼遙遠。

因此，筆者認爲以上薩瑪達類型寺院的塑像不能籠統地歸入一個時期，大致可分爲

圖11　雪朗寺如來像

Von Schroeder, Ulrich, *Buddhist Sculptures in Tibet II*, Hong Kong: Visual Dharma, 2001.pp.851,fig.fig.XIII-32

圖12　艾旺寺如來像

羅文華攝

圖13　江浦寺金剛王菩薩

〔意〕圖齊（Tucci, Giaseppe）著，魏正中、薩爾吉編譯《梵天佛地》第四卷第三冊圖版28局部，上海：上海古籍出版社，2009年，29頁兩個階段，第一個階段是11世紀後弘初期江浦寺、艾旺寺的修建時期，包括圖齊所說的江浦寺中的“一些銅像、前殿和底層佛殿壁畫”及降魔殿懸塑，艾旺寺、孜乃薩寺塑像均屬於這一時期，但不排除艾旺寺、孜乃薩寺亦有部分可能曾在後期重修。第二個階段是13世紀大規模重修時期，包括江浦寺“普明殿”、度母殿及雪朗寺等，其下限是布頓到夏魯寺之前的14世紀初。圖齊此前提出的薩瑪達寺院在11—13世紀一直持續的說法仍值得重視。

江浦寺有兩處金剛界曼荼羅，祖拉康第一間殿內的銅鎏金佛塔及二層右側“普明殿”（Kun rig lha khang）內的塑像。由於兩處作品皆已無存，幾乎沒有學者對曼荼羅尊像做過具體的研究。其實，祖拉康第一間殿內的銅鎏金佛塔眷屬尊照片中雖然可確認的圖像很少，但幸運的是，仍然可以找到其圖像的主要特徵。“普明殿”從圖齊在這個殿內拍攝的照片中可以找到27尊，尊像特徵基本上都可以辨識出來。

圖14　白居寺金剛薩埵菩薩

羅文華攝

第一間佛殿稱作南殿（gTsang khang lho），殿內有一座極其精美的銅鎏金佛塔（圖15），裡面裝有某位上師的舍利。塔有十三層相輪，塔基浮雕金剛界曼荼羅。圖齊認爲此塔可能不是一件尼泊爾藝術品，而是一件由尼泊爾傳至藏地的晚期波羅時代（12世紀）的孟加拉藝術品[36]。

金剛界曼荼羅的結構是，最上層四面的中央是大日如來，環繞大日如來的四佛有一尊缺失。大日如來兩側有三昧耶形金剛杵、摩尼寶、蓮花、羯磨杵，當是四波羅蜜菩薩。第二層四方的中央設四拱門，拱門內是四佛，四佛僅留存有不空成就如來的照片，不空成就手指筆直，似不曾持物，但在台座正中刻有標識性持物羯磨杵及金翅鳥。從局部照片中還可見，四佛兩側各二菩薩是十六親近菩薩，呈輪王坐姿，由上至下排列。第三層兩側是位於四隅的外四供養菩薩和寶瓶，中部的中央是明王形四攝菩薩及賢劫十六菩薩。賢劫十六菩薩遊戲坐，各方的四尊尊形完全相同。由此可見，塔是由金剛界37尊中缺少外四供養菩薩的33尊及賢劫16尊，共計49尊構成，外四供養菩薩的位置被四花瓶所替代。

㊱ 〔意〕圖齊（Tucci, Giaseppe）著，魏正中、薩爾吉編譯《梵天佛地》第四卷第一冊，71—72頁。

圖齊照片中可以找到右手上舉的是金剛寶菩薩，持蓮花的金剛法菩薩，和右手揮劍、左手持般若經的金剛利菩薩。更具有說明性的是，金剛寶菩薩下方的金剛光菩薩（圖16）和金剛利菩薩對面的金剛語（圖17）二身左臂直立於身側，與《真性作明》的圖像一致。但是，仍然其他眷屬中仍發現有四攝菩薩是明王形與《真性作明》相異[37]。

圖15　江浦寺南殿銅鎏金佛塔

〔意〕圖齊（Tucci, Giaseppe）著，魏正中、薩爾吉編譯《梵天佛地》第四卷第三冊圖版18，上海：上海古籍出版社，2009年，18頁

圖16　銅鎏金佛塔局部一

〔意〕圖齊（Tucci, Giaseppe）著，魏正中、薩爾吉編譯《梵天佛地》第四卷第三冊圖版16，上海：上海古籍出版社，2009年，16頁

二層右側佛殿當地俗稱“普明殿”，但主尊並不是普明大日如來，而是四面二臂結智拳印的金剛界大日如來（上述圖10）。筆者從圖齊的照片並結合筆錄復原出殿內的結構（圖18，但佛殿朝向不明）。“主尊比例最大，位於中央，沿著牆壁於盛開蓮座上入定的是構成該部族的三十六天衆。”[38]四佛配置於周圍三面，四佛左右懸塑十六親近菩薩，靠近門口處兩側是四攝菩薩及八供養菩薩，圖齊共載有曼荼羅中27尊照片[39]，缺少四波羅蜜菩薩、十六親近菩薩的四身及四攝菩薩的二身。

㊲　但是圖片中不見有金剛牙菩薩，因此，不能判斷金剛牙菩薩是否與後述普明殿形象是否一致。

㊳　〔意〕圖齊（Tucci, Giaseppe）著，魏正中、薩爾吉編譯《梵天佛地》第四卷第一冊，75頁。

㊴　〔意〕圖齊（Tucci, Giaseppe）著，魏正中、薩爾吉編譯《梵天佛地》第三卷圖版，25—31頁。

圖17　銅鎏金佛塔局部二

〔意〕圖齊（Tucci, Giaseppe）著，魏正中、薩爾吉編譯《梵天佛地》第四卷第三冊圖版14，

上海：上海古籍出版社，2009年，146頁

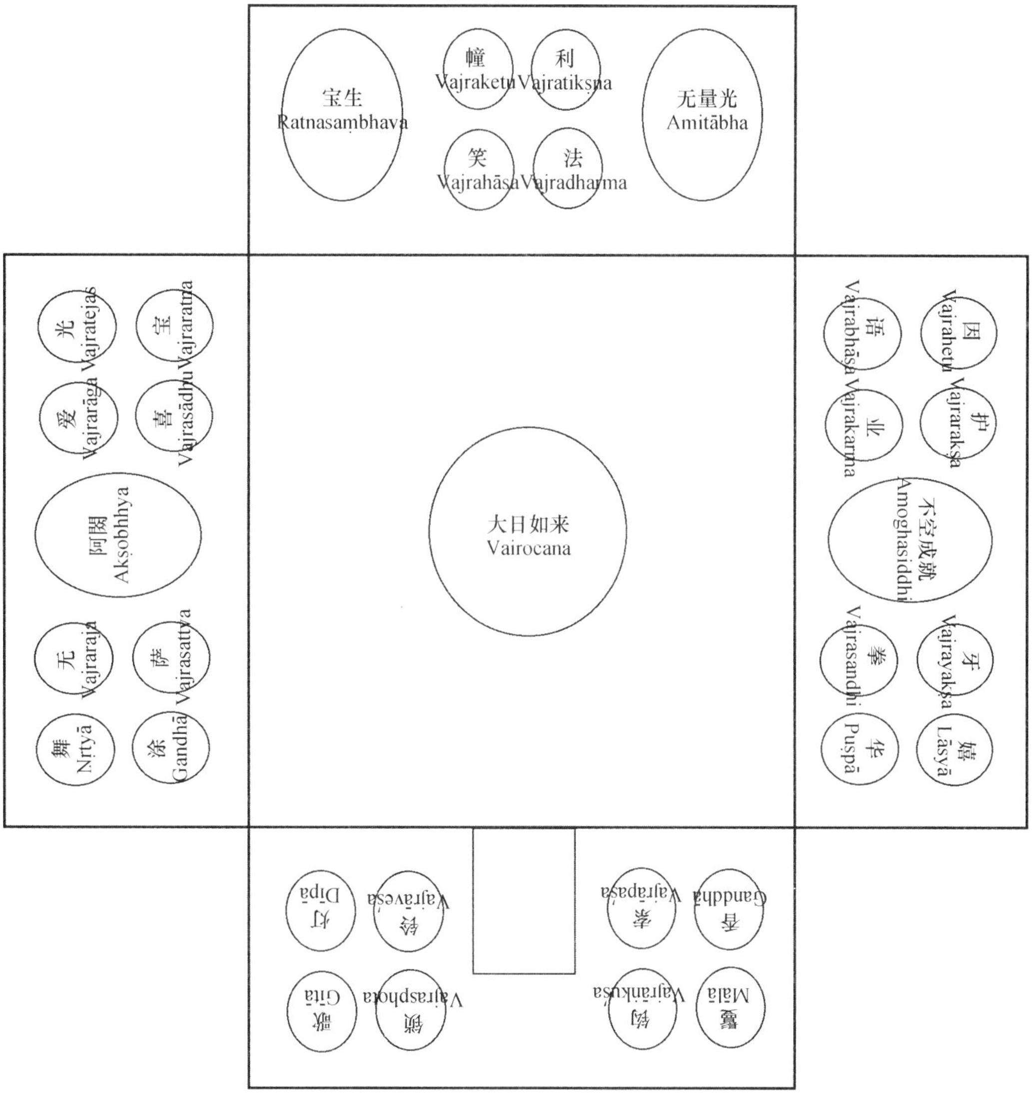

圖18　金剛界曼荼羅復原平面圖（筆者繪）

五佛中有四佛的上身右肩均斜挎圓形團花裝飾帶，下裙亦對應同樣的團花圖案。唯有無量光佛斜挎裝飾瓔珞，瓔珞極其精美華麗。五佛底層皆有木柱支撐，具鳥獸座。阿閦、寶生、不空成就施印的手指略帶彎曲，說明原當持有標識物，但持物皆缺失。照片中不見四波羅蜜菩薩，是三昧耶形的可能性較大，或已缺失，或在大日如來的台座上。

眷屬尊持物大多缺失，將二手的姿勢、印契與文本對照其實並不難辨識每尊的尊格，十六大菩薩是以左下→左上→右上→右下順時針方向排列，八供養菩薩位於十六大菩薩的外側，以橫向排列，四攝菩薩無疑是守護在門的兩側。諸尊圖像特徵釋讀如下：

圖中（圖19）寶生如來的左側有四菩薩，靠近寶生如來兩身的下方右手舉至頭頂，持物缺失，左手於腰間，當是金剛寶菩薩。其上方的菩薩右手當胸，持物漫漶，右手扶於座，當是金剛光菩薩。其左側兩身菩薩的上方左手當胸，右手伸出體側似握金剛鈴，從手的印契和尊像的方位推測，當是阿閦如來四親近菩薩中作搭弓射箭姿勢的金剛愛菩薩，因此右手持物的金剛鈴或許是遺落後被誤放在此處的。其下方二手胸前結金剛拳作善哉勢，無疑是阿閦如來四親近菩薩中的金剛喜菩薩。

圖中（圖20）無量光如來的左側有四菩薩，靠近無量壽如來兩身的上方當是金剛因菩薩，右手中指豎立，持物缺失，左手扶於座上。下方菩薩金剛語菩薩右手持舌，左手扶於座上。再右側兩身的下方右手於胸前，立中指，持物缺失，從手的印契及方位看當是不空成就如來四親近菩薩中的金剛業菩薩。其上方二手抬至兩肩前，大指與頭指相撚姿勢，是不空成就如來四親近中的金剛護菩薩，持物甲胄缺失。

圖中（圖21）有二菩薩、四女尊。其中左側上方二手舉至臉頰兩側的菩薩，是不空成就如來四親近中的金剛牙菩薩。下方二手於胸前，右手壓左手的菩薩亦不難看出是不空成就如來四親近菩薩中的金剛拳菩薩。其左側上方二手於腰間的女尊是內四供養菩薩中的金剛嬉菩薩，下方右手於胸前，左手於腰間的是外四供養菩薩中持香爐的金剛香菩薩。正面二身亦是女尊，上方爲持花鬘的金剛鬘菩薩，下方是持蓮花的金剛華菩薩。

圖中（圖22）有二菩薩、四女尊及二明王。右側下方菩薩右手於胸前作托物姿勢，持物缺失，左手不明，當是阿閦如來四親近菩薩中的金剛薩埵菩薩。其上方菩薩右手於胸前持金剛杵，右手似於腰間，從右手的印契及方位看當是阿閦如來四親近菩薩中持鉤的金剛王菩薩，因此筆者懷疑右手的金剛杵可能是下方的金剛薩埵持物遺落後被誤放到了此處。再左側的上方女尊左手舉於頭上，右手於腰間的是內四供養菩薩的金剛舞菩薩，下方女尊二手於胸前，左手作托物姿勢，當是外四供養菩薩的金剛塗菩薩。朝向正面的二女尊中上方一身右手在下，左手在上的是正在彈琵琶的金剛歌菩薩。下方右手在右肩前方，左手於腰間的是金剛燈菩薩。二明王是四攝菩薩，展右，持物缺失，按照八大供養菩薩的配置順序的規律，上方當是金剛鎖菩薩，下方是金剛鈴菩薩。

塑像中十六大菩薩的金剛光、因、語三身菩薩皆左臂垂直於身後，並扶在蓮座上，毫無疑問是出自慶喜藏釋《真性作明》。此外，金剛愛菩薩張弓射箭，金剛業菩薩右手置於胸前的位置，亦完全遵循了《真性作明》的描述。僅稍有出入的是，金剛牙菩薩爲菩薩形，而不是《真性作明》的忿怒形。四攝菩薩明王形，展左，區別於《真性作明》

圖19 “普明殿”寶生如來及眷屬

〔意〕圖齊（Tucci, Giaseppe）著，魏正中、薩爾吉編譯《梵天佛地》第四卷第三冊圖版26，上海：上海古籍出版社，2009年，27頁

圖20 “普明殿”無量光如來及眷屬

Von Schroeder, Ulrich, *Buddhist Sculptures in Tibet II*, Hong Kong: Visual Dharma, 2001.pp.847,fig.fig.XIII-20

圖21 曼荼羅眷屬一

Von Schroeder, Ulrich, *Buddhist Sculptures in Tibet II*, Hong Kong: Visual Dharma, 2001.pp.847,fig.fig.XIII-22

圖22 曼荼羅眷屬二

Von Schroeder, Ulrich, *Buddhist Sculptures in Tibet II*, Hong Kong: Visual Dharma, 2001.pp.847,fig.fig.XIII-23

四攝菩薩中的金剛鈴菩薩左手扶於座的姿勢。可見，塑像與鎏金塔圖像當是一致的。

江浦寺隨後不久，更加忠實於《真性作明》原本的圖像先後出現在夏魯寺、薩迦寺（Sa skya筆者推測）、俄寺（Ngor）、白居寺金剛界殿及吉祥多門塔第五層等，金剛牙菩薩是忿怒形，四攝菩薩亦是菩薩形，與《真性作明》完全吻合。也就是說，這一成熟的圖像出現的年代均不早於14世紀，從這些實例中，可以聯想到的人物顯然唯有布頓大師。

江浦寺是當時研習佛法的重要中心，尤其對密法傳歸及其教義在後藏地區的傳播作出了重要貢獻[40]，與金剛界曼荼羅的傳播亦有著密切關係。桑噶（Zangs dkar）譯師帕巴協饒（'Phags pa shes rab，出生於阿里普蘭）、尼泊爾大悲班智達及印度班智達熏奴奔巴（gZhon nu bum pa）也曾滯留於江浦寺翻譯佛經。桑噶譯師比曲洛晚半個多世紀，專攻《金剛頂怛特羅》及《真性作明》，《真性作明》上品由仁欽桑布譯出，下品就是由大悲班智達及桑噶譯師譯成。但是，需要指出的是，江浦寺的金剛界曼荼羅塑像是《真實攝經》四大品中第一品所說的第一個曼荼羅，即四大品的根本曼荼羅。因此，我們所見到的江浦寺塑像在仁欽桑布翻譯的上品最初的部分就已經全部出現，而桑噶譯師譯出《真性作明》下品的內容與江浦寺塑像並沒有直接關聯。

13世紀初，著名弘法者迦濕彌羅班欽釋迦室利（Śākyaśrī）入藏傳教時，最早的駐錫地也是江浦寺，江浦寺是釋迦室利寫作的地方，在此地他著出《菩薩道次第略攝》（*rGyal sras lam rim bsdus*），江若地區因而名揚雪域，江浦寺與艾旺寺亦皆因釋迦室利在藏史上顯赫。布頓大師是釋迦室利的隔代轉世，他的老師一切智帕臥雲丹嘉措的住寺是江喀地方的貝鄔瑪寺（sPe'u dmar），布頓大師年輕時代就是在貝鄔瑪寺聽受了全部瑜伽修習法、時輪續兩種傳規的注釋和口訣、袞邦巴所傳卓派時輪等所有精深法門[41]。他對《真實攝經》的各注疏、儀軌亦極其精通，還著有《真實攝經》注疏《入瑜伽怛特羅海之舟》。

布頓大師將《真性作明》首先繪製於夏魯寺（1333—1335年）的西無量宮。遺憾的是，夏魯寺此曼荼羅現已被櫃子遮擋，無法確認到圖像。然而，夏魯寺使用《真性作明》本有幾個證據，一是慶喜藏的《真性作明》在《真實攝經》28種金剛界曼荼羅基礎上發展成44種，這44種金剛界曼荼羅最早繪製於夏魯寺後，又沿用在白居寺吉祥多門塔第五層[42]。其二，第五層壁畫下方還有銘文記載是出自於布頓大師的《夏魯寺之無量宮殿東南西北方配置的曼荼羅等之目錄》（*Sha lu'i gtsug lag khang gi gshal yas khang nub ma, byang ma, lho ma rnams na bshugs pa'i dkyil 'khor sogs kyi dkar chag*，德格No. 5171，簡稱《夏魯寺目錄》）。在《夏魯寺目錄》西無量宮的金剛界曼荼羅最初部分既指出，"金剛界曼荼羅有阿闍梨佛密、釋友、慶喜藏、無畏生護的四種不同配置，在此

㊵ 〔意〕圖齊（Tucci, Giaseppe）著，魏正中、薩爾吉編譯《梵天佛地》第四卷第一冊，72—75頁。

㊶ 張亞莎《艾旺寺雕塑研究及其藝術風格分析》，《中國西藏》2002年第3期，87—106頁。

㊷ 森雅秀《ペンコルチューデ仏塔第5層の〈金剛頂経〉所説のマンダラ》。據森雅秀教授的研究，五層壁畫中至少確認有金剛界曼荼羅44種中的40種以上。

處主要是依據慶喜藏的觀點”[43]。證明夏魯寺的金剛界曼荼羅與白居寺吉祥多門塔五層壁畫應該是一致的。

白居寺三層大殿內金剛界殿塑像和吉祥多門塔第五層金剛界（大）曼荼羅已被確認是出自慶喜藏釋《真性作明》。金剛界殿僅缺少四波羅蜜菩薩[44]，但值得一提的是，在第五層壁畫中就繪有金剛界殿中所不見的三昧耶形四波羅蜜菩薩，說明金剛界殿很可能當初塑有三昧耶形四波羅蜜菩薩。

薩迦派傳承同樣採用布頓大師傳播的慶喜藏本的理由是，據薩迦派傳承的《續部總集》記載，金剛界曼荼羅爲慶喜藏傳承。根據《續部總集》繪製的俄寺曼荼羅集中亦可以看到，除缺少五佛的鳥獸座以外，與《真性作明》的描述完全一致（圖23）。俄寺是由薩迦派第21代住持俄爾欽貢噶桑波1429年創建，該寺以弘傳薩迦南寺密法爲主，是晚期薩迦派在後藏傳播的重要場所。又據記載薩迦寺曾繪有大量的曼荼羅，薩迦寺法王索南堅贊也跟隨布頓大師學法，都暗示著我們薩迦寺繪有布頓大師選用《真性作明》本的可能性極大。

由此可見，以《真性作明》爲文本依據的金剛界曼荼羅是在布頓大師以後才作爲定

圖23　俄寺金剛界曼荼羅

《西藏曼荼羅集成》，講談社，1983年，No.22

㊸　川崎一洋《シャル寺の曼荼羅壁画について(III) プトゥンの金剛界曼荼羅理解》，《密教図像》通号21，2002年，pp. 37-47。

㊹　田中公明先生在白居寺金剛界殿塑像與慶喜藏釋《真性作明》比對的表格中，金剛索菩薩尊形在白居寺的圖像與《真性作明》所描述的形象並不一致，但經筆者核對，金剛索菩薩不是田中先生表格中記載右手扶座姿勢，實際與《真性作明》圖像完全一致。

本在後藏地區廣泛流傳開的。從這一流傳路徑可以看出，江浦寺年代斷於13世紀當更爲妥當。

另外，江浦寺釋迦殿和艾旺寺降魔殿出現了11世紀左右降魔變的懸塑，這種題材的懸塑在藏西並不流行，因此筆者認爲懸塑技術是由藏西地區傳入的觀點還需謹慎。

五、結　論

通過本文的考證，筆者認爲後弘初期後藏地區金剛界曼荼羅的傳播路徑大致是：

（1）後弘初期，瑜伽部根本怛特羅《真實攝經》及其注疏先後傳入西藏，與此同時，藏西與後藏地區金剛界曼荼羅題材的造像、壁畫隨之盛行起來。但這一時期尚未發現依據慶喜藏釋《真性作明》所造的實例，後藏地區的乃甲切木石窟、恰姆石窟、木扎山石窟皆不是此本，並且粉本各不相同。

（2）江浦寺金剛界曼荼羅的年代應略晚於圖齊、維塔利判定的11—12世紀，推測是13世紀在江浦寺大規模重修時期塑造，其下限是布頓大師到夏魯寺之前的14世紀初。因此，最早且最爲接近於慶喜藏釋疏《真性作明》的實例是13—14世紀初的江浦寺，但仍略有區別。隨後，更加忠實於《真性作明》原本的圖像當先後出現在夏魯寺、薩迦寺、俄寺、白居寺金剛界殿及吉祥多門塔第五層等，是14世紀以後由布頓大師廣泛傳播開來，並成爲14—15世紀後藏地區普遍流行的的主要文本。

（3）後藏地區的金剛界曼荼羅與藏西和敦煌沒有發現傳播關係。

與藏西地區的區別是，在西藏西部現存仁欽桑布遺跡中，包括塔波寺、東噶石窟、阿奇寺、拉隆寺、松達寺等早期寺院在內，卻未發現一處與《真性作明》相一致的作品，僅在15—16世紀重修的托林寺和扎不讓壁畫中確認出此文本的圖像，但圖像區別於江浦寺，四攝菩薩爲菩薩形，很可能是由後藏地區傳入的布頓大師傳播的《真性作明》本，此外，托林寺和扎不讓還融入了不見於衛藏地區的其他粉本的圖像。

與敦煌同樣有很多明顯差異，後藏地區的五佛大多爲四面二臂（亦有一面二臂），具鳥獸座、菩薩形，印契、持物、身色都與《真實攝經》所說的一致。四波羅蜜菩薩大多爲三昧耶形（或有人形）。而榆林窟、東千佛洞五佛皆爲一面二臂肉身色的如來形，並且不具鳥獸座、不持持物，印契的圖像、四方色都具有敦煌獨特的風格特徵，五佛印契中寶生與不空成就手彎曲向外，並向上或向下翻轉，與唐密系五佛相近。菩薩形的四波羅蜜菩薩在後藏地區亦尚未發現過類似的圖像或文獻。

江浦寺與敦煌除了文本間存在根本性的不同以外，造像風格、懸塑形式等方面都截然不同。江浦寺嚴格地遵循文本而製作，塑像的技術水準遠勝於榆林窟、東千佛洞。而榆林窟、東千佛洞曼荼羅諸尊的配置方位等出現有很多錯誤，反映出畫工對金剛界曼荼羅並不熟悉[45]。二者之間難以找到其中的關聯。

㊺ 阮麗《敦煌石窟曼荼羅圖像研究》，61—74頁。

總之，後弘初期後藏地區的金剛界曼荼羅都不是慶喜藏本，並且粉本各不相同，說明當時可能傳入了豐富的金剛界曼荼羅圖像粉本或文獻，而且存在著不同傳承和階段性差異，可能是由印度、尼泊爾直接流入。而慶喜藏釋《真性作明》是到了14—15世紀才成爲後藏地區普遍流行的主要文本。

附記：文中承故宫博物院研究院羅文華研究員提供考察時拍攝的木紮山石窟、艾旺寺圖片，以及西藏自治區文物保護研究所夏格旺堆先生提供的乃甲切木石窟、恰姆石窟圖片，謹致謝忱。

附表　《一切金剛出現》《真性作明》《究竟瑜伽鬘》中尊像比較表

	《一切金剛出現》（Sarvavajrodaya）		《真性作明》（Tattvālokakarī）		《究竟瑜伽鬘》（Niṣpannyogāvalī）	
尊名	右手	左手	右手	左手	右手	左手
毗盧遮那	覺勝印中五鈷杵四面二臂		覺勝印中五鈷杵四面二臂		覺勝印中五鈷杵（四面八臂或一面二臂）	
阿閦	觸地印持五鈷杵		觸地印持五鈷杵		觸地印持五鈷杵	
寶生	與願印持金剛寶		與願印持金剛寶		與願印持金剛寶	
無量光	禪定印持蓮華輪		禪定印持金剛蓮華		禪定印持金剛蓮華	
不空成就	施無畏印持羯磨金剛杵		施無畏印持羯磨金剛杵		施無畏印持羯磨金剛杵	
金剛波羅蜜	五鈷金剛杵（三昧耶）		五鈷金剛杵（三昧耶）		五鈷金剛杵	期剋印並持羂索
寶波羅蜜	五鈷杵前持如意寶珠（三昧耶）		五鈷杵前持如意寶珠（三昧耶）		五鈷杵前持如意寶珠	期剋印
法波羅蜜	十六葉蓮瓣上五鈷杵（三昧耶）		十六葉蓮瓣上五鈷杵（三昧耶）		帶五鈷杵的蓮華	蓮華
羯磨波羅蜜	十二鈷羯磨杵（三昧耶）		十二鈷羯磨杵（三昧耶）		十二鈷羯磨杵	期剋印
金剛薩埵	擲金剛杵	傲慢相持鈴	中指天杖印齊於胸前持金剛杵	傲慢相持鈴	右手中指立金剛杵於胸前	傲慢相持鈴
金剛王	持金剛鉤		持金剛鉤		持金剛鉤　羂索	
金剛愛	持金剛弓箭		射金剛弓箭		持金剛弓箭	
金剛喜	二手作金剛拳善哉姿勢		二手作金剛拳善哉姿勢		二手作金剛拳善哉姿勢	
金剛寶	額上置寶珠	搖鈴	額上置寶珠	持鈴	額上置寶珠	持鈴
金剛光	持金剛日輪		持金剛日輪	扶座上	二手胸前持金剛日輪	
金剛幢	持如意寶幢		持如意寶幢	扶座上	二手持如意寶幢	
金剛笑	金剛笑的喜悦		持金剛齒鬘	扶座上	右手持帶一排牙的金剛杵，左手金剛齒列欲放口中	
金剛法	胸前開蓮華	持蓮華莖	胸前開蓮華	持金剛蓮華	胸前開蓮華	持蓮華莖

续表

<table>
<tr><td></td><td colspan="2">《一切金剛出現》
（Sarvavajrodaya）</td><td colspan="2">《真性作明》
（Tattvālokakarī）</td><td colspan="2">《究竟瑜伽鬘》
（Niṣpannyogāvalī）</td></tr>
<tr><td>尊名</td><td>右手</td><td>左手</td><td>右手</td><td>左手</td><td>右手</td><td>左手</td></tr>
<tr><td>金剛利</td><td>揮劍</td><td>胸前持般若經</td><td>揮劍</td><td>般若經</td><td>揚劍</td><td>胸前持般若經</td></tr>
<tr><td>金剛因</td><td colspan="2">右手中指轉八輻輪</td><td>右手中指尖
轉八輻輪</td><td>扶座上</td><td colspan="2">右手中指轉左掌上的八輻輪，
結轉法輪印</td></tr>
<tr><td>金剛語</td><td colspan="2">以金剛舌語姿</td><td>金剛舌</td><td>扶座上</td><td>握獨鈷杵前端</td><td>持海螺</td></tr>
<tr><td rowspan="2">金剛業</td><td rowspan="2">胸前持羯磨杵</td><td rowspan="2">羯磨杵的鈴</td><td rowspan="2">中指立羯磨杵
於胸前</td><td rowspan="2">持羯磨鈴
傲慢相</td><td>胸前持羯磨杵</td><td>羯磨杵的鈴</td></tr>
<tr><td colspan="2">或二手持羯磨杵於頭頂</td></tr>
<tr><td>金剛護</td><td colspan="2">金剛甲冑</td><td colspan="2">二手持金剛甲冑</td><td colspan="2">二手持金剛甲冑</td></tr>
<tr><td>金剛牙
（夜叉）</td><td colspan="2">金剛牙放自身口中，威赫勢</td><td colspan="2">臉兩側口中的獠牙（鼓腹）</td><td colspan="2">兩手小指持金剛牙於口前忿
怒相</td></tr>
<tr><td>金剛拳</td><td colspan="2">金剛拳中壓五鈷杵</td><td colspan="2">二手三昧耶拳中置金剛杵</td><td colspan="2">二手金剛拳中壓五鈷杵</td></tr>
<tr><td>金剛嬉</td><td colspan="2">金剛慢勢二手持金剛杵</td><td colspan="2">二手慢印持五鈷杵</td><td colspan="2">持金剛杵，做金剛慢勢</td></tr>
<tr><td>金剛鬘</td><td colspan="2">持寶珠鬘</td><td colspan="2">持寶珠鬘</td><td colspan="2">持寶鬘</td></tr>
<tr><td>金剛歌</td><td colspan="2">彈琵琶</td><td colspan="2">彈琵琶</td><td colspan="2">彈琵琶</td></tr>
<tr><td>金剛舞</td><td colspan="2">二手握三鈷杵作舞</td><td colspan="2">二手握三鈷杵作舞</td><td colspan="2">二手握三鈷杵作舞</td></tr>
<tr><td>金剛香</td><td colspan="2">持香爐</td><td colspan="2">持香爐</td><td colspan="2">未詳述</td></tr>
<tr><td>金剛華</td><td colspan="2">持華籠</td><td>散華</td><td>持金剛華器</td><td colspan="2">未詳述</td></tr>
<tr><td>金剛燈</td><td colspan="2">持燭臺</td><td colspan="2">持燈燭</td><td colspan="2">未詳述</td></tr>
<tr><td>金剛塗</td><td colspan="2">持香器</td><td>塗香雲</td><td>持法螺</td><td colspan="2">未詳述</td></tr>
<tr><td>金剛鉤</td><td colspan="2">持鉤</td><td colspan="2">持金剛鉤</td><td colspan="2">與前述曼荼羅同，持標識型持物</td></tr>
<tr><td>金剛索</td><td colspan="2">持金剛索</td><td colspan="2">持金剛索</td><td colspan="2">與前述曼荼羅同，持標識型持物</td></tr>
<tr><td>金剛鎖</td><td colspan="2">持金剛鎖</td><td colspan="2">持金剛鎖</td><td colspan="2">與前述曼荼羅同，持標識型持物</td></tr>
<tr><td>金剛鈴</td><td colspan="2">持金剛鈴</td><td>持金剛鈴</td><td>扶座上</td><td colspan="2">與前述曼荼羅同，持標識型持物</td></tr>
</table>

註：松長恵史《インドネシアの密教》，法藏館，1999年，pp. 222-223，並在此基础上校對後略做修改。

Re-mapping the Historical Dissemination of Vajradhātu-maṇḍala Iconography in Central Tibet During the Early Period of the Later Diffusion of Buddhism

Ruan Li

In the study of Tibetan Buddhist iconographies, there have remained different scholarly views on the historical dissemination of the iconography of the vajradhātu-maṇḍala i in Central Tibet during the early periodof the Later Diffusion of Buddhism (*phyi dar*).

Previous scholars, represented by the Italian Tibetologist Giuseppe Tucci (1894-1984), generally attributed the textual source of the Tibetan vajradhātu-maṇḍala to the early eleventh-century translation by Rin chen bzang po (958-1055) of the *Tantratattvālokakarī* by the Indian master nandagarbha (c. 8th-9th century). However, with the examination of recent archaeological discoveries of cave temples such as gNas mjal che mo, Chag mo and mu kra'i brag phug grottoes, my research has found a different iconographical attribution than the previous studies of nandagarbha versions namely, these images are of various origins, with texts and paintings that could come from diverse traditions imported into Central Tibet in the early *phyi dar* period.

My paper aims to re-delineate a historical map of the dissemination of vajradhātu-maṇḍala iconographies, by which the iconographical tradition of Tibetan Buddhism parallels their great literary history. In general, the earliest iconographical representations most possibly related to nandagarbha's *Tantratattvālokakarī* are found in mural paintings of the rKyang phu Monastery. Later, iconographies attributed to the *Tantratattvālokakarī* s started to appear in mural paintings of major monastic institutions, such as Sha lu Monastery, Ngor Monastery, dPal 'khor chose sde Monastery and its affiliated Great Stupa of bKra shis sgo mang mchod rten (murals on the fifth floor) and so on, but all these images seem to owe their textual origins to the contemporary translation by Master Bu ston (1290-1364), which prevailed from the fourteen century and became the primary textual basis during the fourteenth to fifteenth centuries in Central Tibet.

“和尚之教”在西藏

——以寧瑪派對摩訶衍及其教法的詮釋、辯護與批判爲例

楊 杰

一

衆所周知，“吐蕃僧諍”（或云“桑耶僧諍”，792—794）這一歷史事件連同參與這場辯論的漢土和尚摩訶衍（8世紀後期）及其教法在藏土歷來備受矚目，隨著現代藏學的發展，諸多學者也對其中相關的歷史叙事和教法義理給予了高度的關注和深入的研究，富于啓發性的著作層出不窮[①]。通過對藏文文獻的廣泛檢視，我們發現對摩訶衍及其教法的討論遍布各宗各派歷代上師的著作，乃至在現當代的藏文文獻中，仍能頻頻見到相關的論述，可以說，摩訶衍及其教法幾乎成了一個熱度持續不退的“熱點話題”，它滲透到了教法源流（chos ’byung）、辯論文書（rtsod yig）以及宗義建立（grub mtha’i rnam bzhag）等各種體裁的文獻，而它在這些文獻中所呈現出的面貌又因作者的傳承歸屬、宗義立場以及相關的歷史因素而變得紛繁多樣。針對這一話題，學術界的研究大致可分爲兩個方向，一是通過梳理和比較包括敦煌文本在内的古藏文文獻以及相關的漢文史料，力求還原“吐蕃僧諍”的歷史原貌以及摩訶衍、蓮花戒（Kamalaśīla）二者的傳承與教法的本來面目，二是通過分析各派歷代上師著作中的相關討論，揭示出後世對摩訶衍及其教法的理解、詮釋，以及對摩訶衍形象的再創造。直至目前，學界在以上兩方面的持續努力已然表明，藏土語境下的摩訶衍及其教法在很大程度上是一個由西藏人創造出來的傳統[②]，隨着時間的推移，摩訶衍這一形象逐漸脱離其歷史原型，繼而演變成一個單純的“文化符號”，最終在出于各種目的的辯護或妖魔化的貶斥中，成爲五花八門的義理辯諍和教法開示的工具與載體。平心而論，解讀與比較後世對摩訶衍及其教法的闡釋與相關的歷史追溯與重構工作一樣，應當得到同等的重視，因爲前者對我

---

① 自從20世紀30年代E. Obermiller將《布頓佛教史》譯爲英文以來，全世界幾乎所有著名藏學家乃至漢學家都或多或少地涉及過有關吐蕃僧諍的研究，有相關專著出版者包括Marcelle Lalou, Paul Demiéville, Giuseppe Tucci, Rolf Stein, L. Gómez, Samten Gyaltsen Karmay以及上山大峻、山口瑞鳳、今枝由郎、沖本克己、木村隆德、小畠宏允、原田覺、饒宗頤等，發表過相關論文者亦不勝枚舉，于此不一一列述。

② 參沈衛榮《西藏文文獻中的和尚摩訶衍及其教法——一個創造出來的傳統》，《新史學》十六卷一期，2005年3月，1—50頁。

們深入理解西藏人創造摩訶衍教法傳統的動機、藏傳佛教各派以摩訶衍教法爲支點所作的交流與互動以及由此彰顯出的各派之間見修之細微差异，無疑有着顯著的意義[③]。然而，學界在這方面傾注的力度還明顯不足，現有的研究大多局限于某一派别某一上師的孤立論述，而未能以歷史的縱軸爲脉絡，展現對摩訶衍教法的闡釋在歷代上師之間形成的傳承與遞變，亦未能在派别之間作出横向比較，展示出各派在摩訶衍教法的闡釋上形成的差异和相互影響。本文將以寧瑪派（rNying ma pa）爲例，在回顧總結相關背景的基礎上，著重以努佛智（gNubs chen Sangs rgyas ye shes, 8—9世紀）、龍青巴（Klong chen rab ’byams pa, 1308-1364）、無畏洲（’Jigs med gling pa, 1730-1768）以及不敗尊者（Mi pham rgya mtsho, 1846-1912）等著名寧瑪派上師的相關論述爲考察對象，分析各自的理論來源、寫作動機，由此全面展示歷史上寧瑪派對摩訶衍教法的詮釋以及其間的演變軌迹，并通過比較寧瑪派内部以及寧瑪派與他派在詮釋上的异同，深入分析這些詮釋所受到的派内與派外在歷史與宗教上的影響因素。

二

西藏歷史和宗教傳統中對吐蕃僧諍的描述早已爲學界所熟知，其過程大體如下：漢土和尚摩訶衍來到吐蕃教授禪宗的頓悟法門，主張行者不需精勤于六度，以不思、不觀、不作意爲修道，頓證無分别智，直趣佛果。其教法雖然在吐蕃廣受歡迎，却與寂護（Śāntarakṣita）所傳的瑜伽行中觀（Yogācāra-Madhyamaka）之漸門修習相悖，這一系修習主張行者踐行六度，于道上以如理思擇之觀察慧（so sor rtogs pa’i shes rab）依次第作觀修，最終契證無分别智（rnam par mi rtog pa’i ye shes）。兩派在見地上針鋒相對的差异逐漸上升至使用暴力在内的嚴重衝突。在兩相爭執不下的情况下，赤松德贊不得不迎請寂護的弟子蓮花戒入藏，令其與摩訶衍各陳自宗，相互辯駁，以决正理。最後，這場辯論以摩訶衍的失敗告終，而他本人也被逐出吐蕃，蓮花戒所倡之瑜伽行中觀漸門修習則被吐蕃贊普詔立爲佛法之正宗[④]。

以上這種對吐蕃僧諍的表述顯然已經滲透到了整個藏傳佛教圈，隨着時間的推移，這種表述模式在代代相傳的過程中被不斷重復、强化，如前所言，摩訶衍本人最終僵化爲一個充滿負面色彩的文化符號，其所代表的教法也成爲异端的代名詞，藏土鮮有人對這種固定的表述提出質疑、對摩訶衍教法的真相作出追問。然而，當今學界則對這一

③ 此即如D. Seyfort Ruegg所言：“藏學家應當不只是關心試圖重構所謂的‘桑耶僧諍’中實際發生了些什麼，而且也應當關心西藏之史學與教法傳統認爲什麼東西是這一事件及其主題的重要性，也就是說，也要關心這一事件對于西藏文明的意義。”見D. Seyfort Ruegg, “On the Tibetan Historiography and Doxography of the ‘Great Debate of bSam yas’”, in *Tibetan Studies: Proceedings of the 5th Seminar of the International Association for Tibetan Studies*, Narita 1989, Vol. 1, *Buddhist Philosophy and Literature*, ed. Ihara Shōren and Yamaguchi Zuihō (Naritasan Shinshoji, 1992), p. 244.

④ 參沈衛榮上揭文，13頁。

被廣泛接受的表述傳統是否反映了歷史的真實表示高度懷疑，學者們甚至懷疑吐蕃僧諍這一事件是否真正發生過，抑或這場所謂的僧諍是否原本只是一系列的討論和書面交流[⑤]。依據包括敦煌文本在内的藏、漢文文獻對吐蕃僧諍的重構表明，真實的故事與後世的表述之間存在較大差异，而且後世的表述也從未形成完全統一的論調。首先，值得注意的是，我們在據説是蓮花戒于僧諍後所造的《修習次第論》（*Bhāvanākrama, bsGom rim*）[⑥]中，并未發現對這場辯論和摩訶衍有任何提及[⑦]。其次，對于後世的表述所依據的藍本《巴協》（*dBa' bzhed*，或*sBa bzhed*、*rBa bzhed*），有三個版本爲學界所熟知[⑧]，Matthew Kapstein據其對現存最早版本的《巴協》的研究以及與《巴協》英譯者之一巴桑旺堆的私人交流，指出其中對摩訶衍所主之頓門派的記述與同載此事的漢文文獻《頓悟大乘正理决》所言[⑨]甚爲一致[⑩]，《巴協》早期的作者（或作者群）對8世紀漢傳佛教在藏土的活動抱以認可與贊許的態度[⑪]。要言之，通過檢視早期的藏文文獻，我們可以看出，有關吐蕃僧諍的歷史叙事確曾歷經演變，其對應的叙事文本經歷過不斷的修改與增删[⑫]，而這些改動主要發生在"黑暗期"之後新譯密咒時期。最終，基于《巴協》而逐漸定型的叙事，將摩訶衍及其教法徹底推向否定乃至妖魔化的深淵，而這一叙事本身則成爲整個藏民族共同的"文化記憶"（cultural memory），繼而對後世

⑤ Sam van Schaik, *Tibet: A History*, New Haven and London, Yale University Press, 2011, p. 39.

⑥ 《修習次第論》共分三篇，有關三篇的相關文本校訂與翻譯分别見：*sGom pa'i rim pa dang po* (Bhāvanākrama [I]), S. Yoshimura (ed.), *Tibetan Buddhistology*, Kyoto, 1953; G. Tucci, *Minor Buddhist Texts II, Serie Orientale Roma IX. 2*, Rome, 1958, pp. 229-282; *sGom pa'i rim pa bar ma* (Bhāvanākrama [II]), S. Yoshimura上揭書；*sGom pa'i rim pa tha ma* (Bhāvanākrama [III]), S. Yoshimura上揭書。E. Lamotte對其所做的部分翻譯見與P. Demiéville,*Le concile de Lhasa: Une controverse sur le quitétisme entre Bouddhistes de L'inde er de la Chine au VIIIe siéle de L' ére chrétienne*, Pairs, Impreimerie, National de Paris, 1952, Appendix II, pp. 336-353.

⑦ 值得注意的是，我們的確在《修習次第論》中找到了與《巴協》中蓮花戒、巴·桑希（'Ba' Sang shi）和巴·吉祥音（dBa' dPal dbyangs）對摩訶衍的批評高度一致的段落，我們有理由懷疑這場僧諍是否真實發生過，也有理由推測《巴協》的作者可能是基于《修習次第論》而加以演繹。參Flemming Faber, "The Council of Tibet According to the sBa bzhed", *Acta Orientalia*, 47, 1986, pp. 48-49；G. W. Houston, *Sources for a History of the bSam yas Debate*, Sankt Augustin, VGH Wissenschaftsverlag, 1980, p. 62.

⑧ 《巴協》有各種不同的版本，既有廣、中、略三版（rgyas bsdus 'bring），又有正本（khungs ma）、淨本（gtsang ma）和雜本（lhad ma）等，現存的三個版本實際上都非最原始的古本，其中最早的一種已是11世紀的産物，其後一種則出于12世紀，最晚的一種更是晚至14世紀。顯然巴塞囊（dBa' gSal sang）并非其唯一作者，該書或應成書于10世紀中葉，而後歷經後人的種種增删與修訂。

⑨ 其文云："至戌年正月十五日，大宣詔命曰：'摩訶衍所開禪義，究暢經文，一無差錯。從今以後，任道俗依法修習。'"引自上山大峻《敦煌佛教の研究》，京都：法藏館，1990年，541頁。

⑩ 值得注意的是，儘管《巴協》的確提到漢傳佛教的書籍被普遍召回，但却只是封藏于桑耶寺，而且還特别强調這些書籍并未被銷毁。見巴色朗《巴協》（*sBa bzhed*），北京：民族出版社，1980年，75頁。

⑪ Matthew Kapstein, *The Tibetan Assimilation of Buddhism: Conversion, Contestation and Memory,* New York, Oxford University Press, 2000, p. 214, n. 11.

⑫ 在前注提到的民族出版社出版之《巴協》中還有一大段關與"萬應白蓮"（dkar po chig thub）的論述，其中曾借摩訶衍之口對萬應白蓮加以定義，如果没有證據表明摩訶衍教法與萬應白蓮的關係在八世紀時就已確立的話，這一處即有可能是後世的增補。參巴桑旺堆《〈韋協〉譯注》，《中國藏學》2011年第2期，197頁，注9。

的藏土論師産生了深遠的影響。

究竟是什麽樣的因素促成了有關吐蕃僧諍叙事的轉變？創造否定和妖魔化摩訶衍的傳統之形成動力從何而來？我們不妨回顧一下相關的歷史背景。10世紀末、11世紀初，積極倡導佛教復興的吐蕃宗室子弟天喇嘛智光（lHa bla ma Ye shes 'od, 959-1024）發起了對藏土密教圈的肅清與淨化，其動機在于他對舊譯密咒時代所傳教法、所譯經典真實性、可靠性的懷疑，從而積極致力于從印度重新尋求佛法之正宗，由此開啓了新譯密咒時代⑬。在新譯密咒時代的初期，藏土總體上都處在“印度至上”的話語模式下，現有教法中被認爲是製造“雜染”與“不純”的非印度元素遭到全面清算，此中即包括西藏本土的元素和漢傳佛教滲入的元素。在這種清算和新譯密咒著力于構建自我身份的語境下，隨之而來的歷史叙事開始逐漸將漢傳佛教對藏土的影響一一擦除，從而確立真實佛法的唯一來源爲聖域（'Phags yul）印度而非漢土，同時通過創造和固化摩訶衍在辯論中慘敗的叙事傳統，力圖將其代表的漢傳教法永久性地貼上异端邪說的標簽，乃至在後世的辯論中，爲了達到貶斥論敵的目的，往往會將論敵的觀點與摩訶衍挂鈎⑭。

縱觀整個藏傳佛教體系，被辯駁者通過與“和尚教”挂鈎捆綁而遭到頻繁抨擊的教法無疑是噶舉派（bKa' brgyud pa）的大手印（Mahāmudrā）和寧瑪派的大圓滿（rDzogs chen）。儘管12—13世紀的薩迦班智達慶喜幢（Sa skya paṇḍtia Kun dga' rgyal mtshan, 1182-1251）非如Roger Jackson所説的那樣是唯一和最早將摩訶衍的教法説爲“萬應白蓮”并將大手印法和大圓滿法與之相提并論的上師，但在將後兩種教法與早已被醜化的摩訶衍建立聯繫的傳統上，薩班無疑是一個具有决定意義的人物，鑒于他在話語上的權威地位，他所造的《能仁密意極明論》（*Thub pa'i dgongs pa rab gsal*）和《三律儀判别》（*sDom gsum rab dbye*）⑮中有關摩訶衍教法的評述的確將其與大手印、大圓滿的關係推向了高度明朗化的層面，這些評述也被後世論師頻頻徵引。薩班的出發點本身是要批評當時盛行的有關不作意（yid la mi byed pa）的觀修，他將批評對象與早已作古且被醜化的摩訶衍扯上關係，多少有點借古諷今的意味。然而，這種做法并非毫無根據，因爲大手印和大圓滿的教法中的確充斥着衆多以不作意、無念等爲修道的教授，而無分别、不作意這些名相也確實是這些文本中的高頻詞彙，乍一看，它們與摩訶衍的教法是有某些相似性。雖然整個大乘佛教都共許最終的佛果是要圓證離諸作意的無分别智，但在無分别、不作意只能作爲佛果境界還是也可以作爲修道的問題上，大乘佛教内部有不同意見，薩班等新譯密咒上師反對入手即以無分别爲道的頓門修習，因

---

⑬ 有關智光所發布的文告（bka' shog）及相關歷史背景的研究，見Samten Karmay, *The Arrow and the Spindle: Studies in History, Myths, Rituals and Beliefs in Tibet*, Kathmandu, Mandala Book Point, 1998, pp. 3-16.

⑭ Donald Lopez, "Polemical Literature (dGag lan)", in José Ignacio Cabezón ed., *Tibetan Literature: Studies in Genre*, ed. Ithaca, Snow Lion Publications, 1996, p. 219.

⑮ 該論英譯及研究見Jared Douglas Rhoton, *A Clear Differentiation of the Three Codes: Essential Distinctions among the Individual Liberation, Great Vehicle, and Tantric Systems*, Albany, State University of New York Press, 2002. 另參李夢妍《薩思迦班智達所作〈三律儀分别〉與西藏的“三律儀”文獻》，收沈衛榮主編《文本中的歷史：藏傳佛教在西域和中原的傳播》，北京：中國藏學出版社，2012年，301—316頁。

此我們不難理解他們何以會在批評這種修習的同時，爲批評對象貼上此前已被异端化的摩訶衍的標簽。此外，在《遍作王續》（*Kun byed rgyal po*）等早期大圓滿文獻中也有大量篇幅對于道上的淨障積資、六度的修習等一切勤作作了種種否定，這同樣不免讓人聯想起《巴協》中記載的摩訶衍教法。

鑒于大圓滿法與摩訶衍教法表面上的諸多相似，混淆二者的現象古已有之，從努佛智的《禪定目炬》（*bSam gtan mig sgron*）可知這種現象在前弘期就已存在，而新譯密咒的諸多上師又因上述相似性而對大圓滿法多有誤讀和抨擊，寧瑪派内部不可能沒有任何反應，首先它不可能察覺不到自身教法與摩訶衍教法的模糊關係，其次它也不可能對相應的抨擊所帶來的話語壓制默不作聲。實際上，寧瑪派在判定摩訶衍教法、厘清其與大圓滿法的异同上付出過長期的努力，接下來筆者將按時間先後順序，逐次梳理寧瑪派歷史上判定、詮釋摩訶衍教法的上師所造的相關論著，同時結合薩班等影響藏土主流觀點的人物的有關論述，以反映寧瑪派内長期被學界忽視的細緻討論、這些討論理路的延續、遞變、多元以及影響這些討論的潛在因素。

三

（一）努佛智（8—9世紀）

在寧瑪派的早期上師中，唯一且最早詳細評述過摩訶衍之頓門教法，且將之與大圓滿法進行比較者，無疑當爲努佛智，他所造的判教類論書《禪定目炬》（亦作《瑜伽目之禪定》（*rNal 'byor mig gi bsam gtan*））依據修習層次的高低將證悟無分別智的法門分爲四大類，由下往上即印度瑜伽行中觀所主之漸門派（rim gyis pa / tsen min）、漢土禪門所主之頓門派（cig car ba / ston mun）、藏土無上密咒乘之大瑜伽（rNal 'byor chen po / Mahāyoga）和大圓滿（rDzogs pa chen po / Atiyoga）。關于努佛智的出生年，不同的材料有不同的說法[16]，但大致上應屬于公元8—9世紀的人，而根據Samten Karmay的考證，《禪定目炬》或當成書于10世紀[17]。無論如何，這部論書保留了大量不見于後弘期的藏文禪宗材料，鑒于後弘期論師在無法接觸到早期藏文禪宗材料的情况下，依據《巴協》等零星材料的對漢土禪法作出片面且充滿臆斷歪曲的想像，我們要想了解新譯密咒興起之前，藏土對摩訶衍禪法的認識，《禪定目炬》無疑是一份彌足珍貴的材料。

---

⑯ 有关努佛智生平的考證見Dylan Esler, "On the Life of gNubs-chen Sangs-rgyas ye-shes", in *Revue d'Etudes Tibétaines*, no. 29, Avril 2014, pp. 5-27; Jacob Dalton, "Preliminary Remarks on a Newly Discovered Biography of Nubchen Sangyé Yeshé", in Benjamin Bogin and Andrew Quintman eds., *Himalayan Passages: Tibetan and Neware Studies in Honor of Hubert Decleer*, Boston, Wisdom Publications, 2014, pp. 145-162.

⑰ Samten Karmay, *The Great Perfection: A Philosophical and Meditative Teaching of Tibetan Buddhism*, Leiden, E. J. Brill, 2007, p. 34.

對于《禪定目炬》中有關頓門派修習討論，學界已有專文對其加以詳論[18]，兹就相關要點加以歸納與補充。總體而言，努氏依見（lta ba）、修（sgom pa）、行（spyod pa）、果（'bras bu）四科對四大法門加以判别和比較，與後期的傳統截然相反的是，他不僅不以摩訶衍所傳頓門爲异端，還將其置于漸門之上，僅置于大瑜伽法門之下。努氏認爲，這四種法門對無分别智的理解有層次上的差别，故將其差别喻爲梯級，逐級向上[19]。在第二章比較頓漸二門時，一開始就指出漸悟者爲蓮花戒之主張（'dod gzhung），乃不了義之經（drang ba don gyi mdo sde）、未究竟圓滿之論書（yongs su ma rdzogs pa'i gzhung），而頓入者爲菩提達摩傳至摩訶衍之宗，乃究竟圓滿之經論[20]。至于頓門派何以較漸門派爲勝，努氏從方便（thabs）、入軌（'jug lugs）、行持（spyod pa）等方面列舉了前者的十大殊勝處（khyad par bcu 'phags），綜觀這些比較，不難發現漸門修習的特點乃有所作、有所爲、有所緣，作意于對治分别、積集福德資糧、以身語之行作利他，而頓門修習的特點爲無所作、無所爲、無所緣，不作意與對治分别而令分别自生自息，依等持而同時圓積二資糧，以等持作利他。于第五章依見、修、行、果專説"頓門派之傳規"（ston mun cig car 'jug pa'i lugs）時，與後世在根本不參考禪宗文獻的情况下，將頓門學説簡化爲毫無細節可言的不思不觀、全離作意的做法不同，努氏詳細解説了頓門派完備的修證次第，他先依菩提達摩《二入四行論》解説行者依教、理二門而作"理入"，復説行者于無所緣境界中看心（sems la lta）從而成辦安心，繼而修止觀雙運，令無生本覺、法爾光明現前，由此證得菩提。在行持方面，努氏仍依《二入四行論》説行者于出定後得位以四行的行持來于日常生活中保任、圓融座上之覺受，并持此覺受境界，不違世俗、不舍善業而作利他行，故而于無貪無求之本覺境界中，無需著意而能任運成就佛事業，這與後世被宗喀巴等人猛烈抨擊的廢止方便善行而墮入虛無、斷滅的摩訶衍教法形成鮮明對比。在果方面，努氏强調行者于神通、光明、佛像等一切希有境界均不生貪執，于一切黑白業皆無所緣，這實際上就是平等性的現證。

在談到頓門派與大圓滿的差别時，努氏指出[21]：

---

⑱ 參沈衛榮上揭文，16—25頁。關與漸門派的章節見于《禪定目炬》65—118葉，關于頓門派的章節見于118—186葉。針對這兩章的解釋研究分别見：宮崎泉《〈禪定燈明論〉漸門派章について》，《日本西藏學會會報》，48，東京，2002年10月，43—50頁；乙川文英《〈禪定燈明論〉研究（2）——第五章（頓門派章）の構成》，《印度學佛教學研究》，43：2，東京，1995年，214—216頁。

⑲ de dag gi khyad par skad(skas) kyi gdang bu bzhin te / dper na skad gdang la mtho dman yod par dang 'dra ste //《禪定目炬》，Leh, S. W. Tashigangpa, 1974, 60—61葉。

⑳ 據Karmay所言，頓入之究竟圓滿即"究竟圓滿之了義經"（nges pa'i don gyi mdo sde yongs su rdzogs pa），與前述漸門派之"不了義、未究竟圓滿之論書"相對應，參Karmay上揭書，92頁。

㉑ ston mun ni rdzogs chen dang skad mthun / bya ba med bsgrub pa med par ston yang / gzhi mi 'byung ba yongs su grub pa la dgongs nas / don dam pa'i bden pa ma skyes stong pa'i gzhi la smra ste / de la ni brtags na da dung bden pa re mos pa dang / stong pa'i ngang la 'dris par byed pa dang / rtsol ba yod de / bden pa gnyis med pa la spyod kyang ma myong ste //《禪定目炬》，490葉。

頓門雖與大圓滿名言類似，同倡無所作、無所修，然彼以無生之基爲圓成（yongs grub），遂將勝義諦說爲無生空性之基。于彼若加觀察，則彼仍希求真實，于空性境界中作串習與勤作，雖能運用二諦無別（之說），却未能親證。

這就是說頓門派雖與大圓滿有諸多相似的名相，然其無所作仍未究竟，仍于空性有勤作，雖能在見地上體認二諦無别，却未能真實現證。對于這種比較，努氏說道[22]："于（寫作）《禪定目炬》之際，因頓門與大圓滿相似，（有人）將其誤解，故作詳細安立。"

由此可知，努佛智所處的時代，已有人將頓門派與大圓滿混淆，因此努氏撰寫《禪定目炬》的其中一個目的就是廓清二者的界限，而他所作的比較非常全面而細緻，就其評述來看，頓門派的教法并非入手即以單純而片面的無分别、無作意爲修道正行，而是有環環相扣的見地抉擇、止觀修習及行持的配合。他在解說頓門派時的引文不僅包括禪宗初祖菩提達摩所傳的《二入四行論》，于今保留在敦煌文獻中的藏文禪宗文書，還包括《般若波羅蜜多經》《大寶積經》《維摩詰經》等多種經典，這不僅爲頓門派教法提供了共通大乘的經教依據，而且也讓作者的論述能以禪宗自身文本爲本，避免了帶有高度傾向性的想象和臆斷，由此可見作者是在廣泛而詳細地研究了他當時能接觸到的藏譯禪宗文本後才作的總結。與後世對摩訶衍教法的否定式評價不同，努氏對其評述相當正面而客觀，這至少可以說明在努氏的時代，後世關于"吐蕃僧諍"的表述傳統尚未形成，否則努氏便有故作驚人語之嫌。然而不但努氏所引的大部分材料于後弘期再未曾見，努氏本論的判教框架和理論幾乎被後世的寧瑪派傳統完全忽視和遺忘[23]，更不用說對新譯密咒群體產生較大的影響。

（二）娘日光（Nyang ral Nyi ma'od zer, 1124—1192）（或其弟子）

在努佛智之後，涉及吐蕃僧諍的一部重要史書便是據說爲寧瑪派著名伏藏師娘日光所撰寫的《教法源流・華藏蜜粹》（*Chos 'byung me tog snying po sbrang rtsi'i bcud*，以下簡稱《華藏蜜粹》），Daniel Hirshberg認爲該書由娘氏的第一代弟子所寫，通過對現存寫本的仔細比對研究，他發現該書前後經過了大量的修改，而這些修改都涉及教義和歷史[24]。在有關吐蕃僧諍的部分，我們看到辯論的整個過程與《巴協》大致

㉒ rnal 'byor mig gi bsam gtan gyi skabs 'dir / ston mun dang / rdzogs chen cha 'dra bas gol du dogs pa'i phyir rgyas par bkod do //《禪定目炬》，186葉。

㉓ 也有極個别的特例，如17世紀噶陀壽自在寶（Kaḥ thog Tshe dbang nor bu）曾在其著述中引用過《禪定目炬》的相關論點，詳見下文的討論。

㉔ Daniel A. Hirshberg, "Discerning the Words of a Master: Textual Criticism and Scholarship in the Digital Age" (Indiana University, Bloomington, Indiana, September 4, 2012), http://www.indiana.edu/~iaunrc/newsevents/past_events/discerning-words-master-textual-criticism-and-scholarship-digital-age.

相近，雖然也以摩訶衍的失敗告終，但值得高度注意的是，贊普在辯論結束後作的評判[25]：

> 于修道傳規中，有和尚之頓入法，此乃根器極利且具修習者之道，而對（中根）以下行人而言，則可令其誣蔑十法行、心識昏沉、不積資糧、阻礙他人修心，且致正法衰微，故當禁止。

這段話的後半部分與晚出版本的《巴協》相同，但在前面却多出了重要的前提，此中首先肯定了摩訶衍所傳頓門教法爲佛法修道傳規之一種，其次指出其乃根器極利者之修道，只是不能作爲中下根人的修道而已，以其能致後者生出上述過患，考慮到廣大吐蕃臣民根器多非利根，所以加以禁止。這種以頓門派爲利根行人修道的說法對後世寧瑪派的影響頗爲深遠，在龍青巴、無畏洲以及噶陀・格澤班智達等人的論述中，仍可見到，關于這一點，後文將會詳述。

與《巴協》類似，《華藏蜜粹》的成書也應非一人之功，而在其撰寫和多次修改的過程中，所運用的材料也來源不一[26]，正如Sam van Schaik所言，西藏史家在書寫歷史時會依賴于多種來源的材料，但却鮮有對其材料出處的說明[27]，這也給我們對其中叙事來源的確定帶來困難。儘管如此，從客觀上而言，《華藏蜜粹》對摩訶衍教法性質的肯定，與《巴協》現存最早的版本中所說相呼應，其作者可能參考了這一版本甚或更早的已佚失的版本，同時就時代而言，他（們）也可能接觸到了12世紀較晚的版本。

（三）薩迦班智達（1182—1251）

如前文所言，較娘日光略晚的大學者薩迦班智達在吐蕃僧諍傳統的發展過程中是一位標志性的人物，他的相關論述也對後世造成了巨大的影響[28]。他在《能仁密意極明

㉕ lam sbyong lugs la ha shang gi chos cig car du ’jug mchis pa de / dbang po yang rab sbyangs pa can gyi lam yin la / dbang po ['bring] man chad chos spyod bcu la skyon bkal / sems ni bying / tshogs ni ma bsags / gzhan gyi blo sbyong ’phro bcad pas chos kyang nub par gyur pas / ’phro chod la khyed rang yang sgoms shig //娘・尼瑪韋色《娘氏宗教源流》，拉薩：西藏藏文古籍出版社，2011年，376頁。

㉖ Hirshberg指出，娘氏的弟子在撰寫該書時，運用了娘氏本人有關赤松德贊與蓮花生事迹的傳記，此中涉及的材料可能包含口傳、文本及回憶的片段。

㉗ Sam van Schaik and Lewis Doney, “The Prayer, the Priest and the Tsenpo: An Early Buddhist Narrative from Dunhuang”, in *Journal of the International Association of Buddhist Studies*, Vol. 30, 2009, p. 176.

㉘ 有關薩班對吐蕃僧諍相關論述的研究，可參見Roger Jackson, “Sa skya Pandita’s Account of the bSam yas Debate: History as Polemic”, *The Journal of the International Association of Buddhist Studies*, 5 (1982), pp. 89-99.該文指出薩班將摩訶衍的教法與“萬應白蓮”挂鈎的做法視爲年代的錯置，由此引起了同行的反駁，David Jackson先後以專文和專著詳加駁斥，見David Jackson, “Sa-skya Pandita the‘Polemicist’: Ancient Debates and Modern Interpretations”, *Journal of the International Association of Buddhist Studies*, 13:2, 1990, pp.17-116; David Jackson, *Enlightenment by a Single Means*, Wien, Verlag der Österreichischen Akademie der Wissenschaften, 1994. 另見Leonard van der Kuijp, “ On the Sources for Sa-skya Pandita’s Notes on the bSam-yas Debate”, *Journal of the International Association of Buddhist Studies*, 9, 1986, pp. 147-153.

論》中提到了吐蕃僧諍，並將摩訶衍說爲失敗者，在其《三律儀判別》中，他批評了有關"無作意"的修法，尤其是當時噶舉派的"萬應白蓮"，其中指出：當時有人自稱修習大手印，唯求壓制分別念，以這種所謂的無分別爲大手印，而不知生圓二次第引生之智方爲大手印，這些愚人所修的大手印大多淪爲旁生（dud 'gro）之因，即便不如此，也會令行人往生無色界（gzugs med khams），或墮落爲聲聞之寂滅，這類觀修乃"今日之大手印"（da lta'i phyag rgya chen po）和"漢傳之大圓滿"（rgya nag lugs kyi rdzogs chen），只是將"上升"（mas 'dzegs）和"下降"（yas 'bab）易名爲頓門、漸門而已[29]，本質上和漢傳頓門法無差別，而寂護對這種現象早有授記，授記說漢土比丘將于藏土弘揚"萬應白蓮"頓門道，他與蓮花戒辯論失敗後，其修法雖遭王令禁止，但後來有人僅依據其所傳文字，而將"萬應白蓮"之原名隱去，喬裝改扮爲大手印，當今之大手印大多爲此漢傳法[30]。薩班進一步指出，他所承認的大手印是由灌頂所生智（dbang las byung ba'i ye shes）、二次第之禪定所生之自然智（rim pa gnyis kyi ting 'dzin las 'byung ba'i rang byung ye shes）。事實上，薩班對吐蕃僧諍事件及摩訶衍教法的描述不是照抄《巴協》，就是轉引《華藏蜜粹》，[31]作爲新譯密咒杰出代表人物的他精通梵文，視印度材料與傳統爲佛法的唯一權威來源，對印度以外的來源或許已有先入爲主的偏見，再加上他也很有可能在先前已然形成的吐蕃僧諍傳統中，選擇性地接受了所有有關摩訶衍的負面評論，從而將充當反面教材的摩訶衍作爲論辯工具來抨擊他所認爲的錯誤修習，儘管他的重點不是專論摩訶衍，但從客觀上却無疑加深了摩訶衍的負面色彩，强化了摩訶衍與"萬應白蓮"的聯繫，推動了將摩訶衍作爲抨擊工具的傳統的形成與發展。

㉙ da lta'i phyag rgya chen po dang / rgya nag lugs kyi rdzogs chen la / yas 'bab dang ni mas 'dzes gnyis / rim gyis pa dang cig char ba / ming 'dogs bsgyur ba ma gtogs pa / don la khyad par dbye ba med //薩迦班智達《三律儀論說自注》，拉薩：西藏藏文古籍出版社，2012年，65頁。

㉚ phyi nas rgyal khrims nub pa dang / rgya nag mkhan po'i gzhung lugs kyi / yi ge tsam la brten nas kyang / de yi ming 'dogs gsang nas ni / phyag rgya chen por ming bsgyur nas / da lta'i phyag rgya chen po ni / phal cher rgya nag chos kugs yin //薩迦班智達《三律儀論說自注》，65—66頁。

㉛ Leonard van der Kuijp通過仔細比對兩個版本的《華藏蜜粹》及薩班之《能仁密意極明論》，有力地證明了薩班的論述的確是對前者的轉引，至少不能排除二者有徵引一個更早的共通材料的可能性，因此，將摩訶衍教法與"萬應白蓮"建立聯繫的傳統應在薩班之前已然形成，甚至早至後弘期之前。參見Leonard van der Kuijp, "On the Sources for Sa-skya Pandita's Notes on the bSam-yas Debate," pp.147-151。另可參見Faber, "The Council of Tibet According to the sBa bzhed", pp. 53-54；David Jackson, *Enlightenment by a Single Means*, pp. 169-175.

值得注意的是，薩班在此中并沒有直接批評寧瑪派的大圓滿[32]，但却將被認爲是摩訶衍所傳的“萬應白蓮”說爲“漢傳之大圓滿”，這無疑也暗示了大圓滿法與摩訶衍教法的相似性，尤其是在無分別、無作意的觀修方面。《三律儀判別》問世後對後世産生了巨大而長遠的影響，在數量相當可觀的注疏中，注家們往往大作發揮，認爲薩班對無分別、無作意修習的批評同樣針對寧瑪派的大圓滿，那些抨擊寧瑪派大圓滿法的論師也常持之以爲據。這種普遍存在的現象當然引起了寧瑪派上師的高度重視，在無畏洲、格澤班智達等上師的著作中，我們可以見到，爲了抗衡與抵消上述現象的影響，在無分別、無作意修習的問題上，展開了詳盡的討論來廓清摩訶衍教法與大圓滿教法關係，後文也將進一步詳述這一點。

（四）龍青巴（1308—1364）

在摩訶衍教法日趨异端化、負面化的大環境下，藏土不少上師選擇在默許主流批判的前提下，與摩訶衍教法劃清界限，從而維護自身教法的正當性，令其免受抨擊。然而，也有上師敢于積極地肯定摩訶衍的教法，并將之置于自宗教義體系中極高的地位，通過指出摩訶衍教法并無過失，從而證明與之相合的自宗教法無可指責，14世紀的著名寧瑪派上師龍青巴便是其中的一位典型代表。龍青巴一生著述頗豐，其主旨在于以大圓滿法爲軸心、以大圓滿見爲究竟抉擇見，對佛法一切顯密道次第的見、修、行、果作了全面的判定和詮釋，并著重對大圓滿法中的諸多概念加以準確界定，澄清相關的誤解，以清晰的綱目對大圓滿法的各個層面作出有序而系統化的闡釋。龍青巴著作中有關摩訶衍教法的討論僅有一處，然其態度已然非常鮮明，這一討論見于其著名的《七寶藏》（*mDzod bdun*）中之《實相寶藏論》（*gNas lugs rin po che'i mdzod*）及其釋論[33]，該論以“無有”（med pa）、“平等”（phyal ba）、“任運”（lhun grub）、“唯一”

㉜ 同樣，就薩班此處對大手印的批評而言，往往也被後世一些論師解讀爲對所有大手印教法的評破，他們却忽略了薩班的上下文語境，斷章取義而加以發揮。薩班其實并非不接受大手印法，《三律儀判別》有言：我（所許）之大手印，乃由灌頂所生智，以及二次第禪定，所引生之自然智。（nged kyi phyag rgya chen po ni / dbang las byung ba'i ye shes dang / rim pa gnyis kyi ting 'dzin las / 'byung ba'i rang byung ye shes yin //《三律儀論說自注》，頁64）。在19世紀不分派運動的背景下，工珠·功德海（Kong sprul Yon tan rgya mtsho, 1813-1899）于其《見地抉擇餘論》（*lTa ba gtan la 'bebs pa las 'phros pa'i gtam skabs lnga pa lung dang rig pa'i me tog rab tu dgod pa*）中認爲：如是實相大手印，一切經續皆明說，且合大圓滿心部，至尊薩迦五祖師，皆許細品中觀宗，以及大手印見地，爲諸權宜之所需，于《三律儀判別》中，遮破達波大印等，然于《無我母贊釋》，實則承許（大手印）。（de lta'i gnas lugs phyag chen da'ang / mdo rgyud kun tu gsal bar gsungs / rdzogs chen sems sde'i grub mthar mthun / sa skya'i rje btsn gong ma lngas / grub mtha' phra ba'i dbu ma dang / lta ba phyag rgya chen po bzhed / 'on kyang gnas skabs dgos dbang gis / dwags brgyud phyag chen la sogs pa / sdom gsum rab dbyer bkag mdzad kyang / rang bzhed bdag med bstod 'grel lags // *rGya chen bka' mdzod*, Paro, Ngodrup, 1975-1976, Vol. 9, ff. 64-65.）

㉝ 本論英譯見Richard Barron (trans.), *The Precious Treasury of the Way of Abiding and The Exposition of the Quintessential Meaning of the Three Categories*, Junction City, Padma Publishing, 1998. 漢譯見隆欽燃絳巴尊者造論，劉立千翻譯，《實相寶藏論詳釋》，北京：民族出版社，2007年。

（gcig pu）四金剛處（rdo rje'i gnas bzhi）詮說諸法實相，于解說"無有"時，龍青巴以抉擇諸法無自性之定解慧决定無有（chos thams cad rang bzhin med par gtan la 'bebs byed nges shes kyi blo dang bcas pa med par la bzla ba），此中强調了諸法自性超越善惡因果，這很容易讓人想起《巴協》中摩訶衍關于黑白善惡的著名表述[34]：

一切皆由心之分别生，由愛憎造諸善不善業，遂嘗受善趣或惡趣之果，流轉于輪回。一無所思，無所作意，由此得從輪回中究竟解脱。如是即無所思。行布施等十法行乃爲無善緣、劣慧鈍根之士夫開示，對于往昔已經修心之利根者而言，善與惡皆成障蔽，猶如白雲黑雲，俱障虚空。

摩訶衍這一段話常被後世視爲否定善惡因果、妨礙行者積集資糧、令行者于惡業上放任身心的"斷見"（chad lta），而龍青巴對此則指出[35]：

自然本覺勝義如大日　善惡白黑二種雲所障
貪執取捨精勤電所燒　苦樂迷亂顯現大雨降
輪回種子六趣葉包裹　嗚呼悲慘六趣誠可憫
于彼究竟義之决定藏　金帶繩帶同能作系縛
法與非法同能系縛心　黑白雲聚同能作障蔽
善惡二者皆能障本覺　是故通達此義瑜伽士
應重超越善惡與因果

其釋論云[36]：

---

[34] 依拙譯，藏文：thams cad sems kyi rnam par rtog pas bskyed pa / dga' mi dga'i dbang gis / las dge mi dges mtho ris dang ngan song gis 'bras bu myong zhing 'khor ba na 'khor te gang zhig ci la'ang mi sems ci yang yid la mi byed pa de 'khor ba las yongs su thar bar 'gyur ro / de lta bas na / ci yang mi bsam mo / sbyin pa la sogs pa'i chos spyod bcu spyod pa ni skye bo dge ba'i 'phro med pa blo zhan pa dbang po rtul ba rnams la bstan pa yin / sngon blo sbyangs pa dbang po rnon pa dag la / sprin dkar nag gang gis nyi ma sgrib pa ltar dge sdig gnyis kas sgrib pas⋯//德吉編，《〈巴協〉彙編》，北京：民族出版社，2013年，50—51頁。另可參見韋・賽囊著，巴擦・巴桑旺堆譯，《〈韋協〉譯注》，拉薩：西藏人民出版社，2012年，22頁。

[35] rang byung rig pa don dam nyi ma la / dge sdig dkar nag gnyis ka'i sprin gyis bsgribs / blang dor 'bad rtsol zhen pa'i glog gis gdungs / bde sdug 'khrul snang char gyis rgyun babs pas / 'khor ba'i sa bon 'gro drug lo 'dab rgyas / kye ma nyam thag 'gro drug snying re rje / mthar thug don gyi nges pa'i snying po la / gser sgrog thag sgrog 'ching bar mnyam pa ltar / chos dang chos min sems kyi 'ching bar mnyam / dkar nag sprin tshogs sgrib par mnyam pa ltar / dge sdig gnyis ka rig pa'i sgrib par mnyam / de bas 'di nyid rtogs pas rnal 'byor ba / dge sdig rgyu 'bras kun las 'das pa gces //百慈藏文古籍研究室《隆欽繞降智麥威賽文集》，北京：中國藏學出版社，2009年，第14册，413、415頁。

[36] dbyar gyi dus na char sprin glog dang char du bcas pas nyi ma'i dkyil 'khor bsgribs pa ltar / las dge ba dang mi dge ba 'dus byas pa'i sprin blang dor 'bad rtsol gyi glog dang bcas pa bde sdug tha dad kyi char du 'bab pas / so so rang byung gi ye shes chos sku don gyi nyi ma mthong ba la bsgribs te / gtan du 'khor ba na 'khyams pa snying rje'i gnas su de kho na nyid rtogs pa'i rnal 'byor pas mthong ste /⋯slob dpon chen po ha shang gis gsungs pas de dus blo dman pa'i blor ma shong yang don la de bzhin du gnas so / theg pa 'og ma la gsang ba blor mi shong bas skur pa btab dus kho las des ngan song du ltung ba'i phyir ro /⋯rig pa'i don la zang ka chos sku rjen par sangs te / gang gis ma gos cis kyang mi mtshon pa thams cad las 'das pa nyi ma'i snying po lta bu la / chos su 'dzin pa dang zhen pa dang bya rtsol thams cad sgrib pa dang 'ching ba mnyam pas kyad med de / sprin dkar pos kyang bsgribs / nag pos kyang bsgribs dang / gser gyi sgrog gis kyang 'ching / thag pa'i sgrog gis kyang 'ching ba bzhin te //百慈藏文古籍研究室《隆欽繞降智麥威賽文集》，413—415頁。

猶如夏時，雨雲雷電具足，遂障蔽日輪，集聚善不善業之雲連同取捨精勤之雷電降下苦樂不同之雨，由是障蔽別別自然智法身勝義之大日，長久漂泊于輪回中，證悟真實之瑜伽士則能見此爲可悲之處……大阿闍黎和尚所言爲當時劣慧之心所不容，然而真實中原本如此。諸下乘者，心不能容秘密，遂興誹謗，彼由此惡業而墮惡趣……

于本覺境中，通透之法身赤裸覺醒，不受任何染污，亦無可表示，超越一切，猶如日光藏。于法所起之一切執著、貪愛及勤作皆同爲障蔽與系縛，無有差別。此如白雲是障，黑雲亦是障，金帶能縛，繩帶亦能縛。

由上可見，龍青巴于根本頌中直接借用了摩訶衍的黑雲白雲之喻，以說明對于本覺而言，善惡二業皆成障蔽，皆爲束縛心性之戲論，儘管二者能令行者往生善趣或惡趣，但終究不能脱離輪回六趣。龍青巴認爲，摩訶衍所言合乎諸法實相，只是當時的人智慧淺薄，無法接受無上秘密教法，因爲下乘行人難以容忍究竟了義。對于龍青巴的觀點，我們應結合其造論語境和依據加以考慮，論中所說實以諸多早期大圓滿密續爲據，依于其中的見地來抉擇諸法實相，其中頻頻徵引的就有著名的大圓滿古續《遍作王續》（屬于心部（sems sde））[37]，該續以“十自性”（rang bzhin bcu）[38]將九乘次第（theg pa rim pa dgu）中阿底瑜伽以下八乘的種種勤作和落于善惡取捨等相對法的修習加以概括幷一一評破，龍青巴據此指出究竟現證諸法實相的阿底瑜伽必須超越善惡取捨，[39]但這幷不意味著龍青巴將這種超越泛化至九乘次第的每一乘，亦即在不顧道次第的情況下對善惡、取捨、因果等作出一刀切的武斷否定。若依龍青巴的思路，我們可以看出，摩訶衍所受攻擊的一個重要原因即在于，批評者將其所揭示的果位（'bras bu）所證之離戲論實相倒置于遵循如理取捨與精勤的具戲論道位（lam）現相上，由此得出其以斷見破壞道上修習的結論，因此，龍青巴的潛臺詞意在提醒行人不能忽略摩訶衍的觀點所立足的層面，同樣，也不能將圓證實相的阿底瑜伽大圓滿孤立地抽離其所屬的九乘次第體系，忽視整個體系由下至上漸離戲論的完整階梯，以至指責《遍作王續》等大圓滿續典的主張破壞了作爲其基礎的下八乘之觀修。

㊲ 該續爲心部三主續之一，有關大圓滿三部各自所依之主要續典，參見Tulku Thondup, *The Practice of Dzogchen*, Ithaca, Snow Lion Publications, 1989, pp. 32-35.

㊳ 《遍作王續》第九品以十自性概括了阿底瑜伽相比于下八乘而具有的十大特徵，概括如下：①無見（lta med）；②無守護（bsrung med）之律儀；③無尋求（btsal med）之事業；④無障（bsgribs med）之本智；⑤無淨治（sbyangs med）之淨得；⑥無所行（bgrod med）之行道；⑦無所執（gzung med）之能執；⑧無二（gnyis med）之相屬；⑨真實（bden pa）之決定；⑩無言詮（brjod med）之能詮（rjod byed）。見*bKa' ma rgyas pa*, Kalimpong: Dupjung Lama, 1982-1987, Vol. 17, ff.43-44。另參見E.K. Neumaier-Dargyay, *The Sovereign All-Creating Mind the Motherly Buddha*, Albany: State University of New York Press, 1992, pp. 36-38; David Germano, “Architecture and Absence in the Secret Tantric History of the Great Perfection (*rdzogs chen*)”, in *Journal of the International Association of Buddhist Studies*, 1994, Vol. 17, pp. 207-208.

㊴ 龍青巴對“十自性”的解釋見其《菩提心遍作王法義導引 · 寶舟》（*Byang chub kyi sems kun byed rgyal po'i don khrid rin chen gru bo*），收《隆欽繞降智麥威賽文集》，第22册，480—508頁。

（五）宗喀巴（Tsong kha pa, 1357—1419）

在龍青巴之後，要考察寧瑪派對摩訶衍教法的觀點，我們無法回避的便是格魯派創始人宗喀巴的相關論述，因爲宗喀巴是繼薩班之後，在摩訶衍問題上對整個藏土産生巨大影響的上師，在其《菩提道次第廣論》（*Lam rim chen mo*）中，可見到對摩訶衍所作的反復破斥。

> 然由支那和尚堪布解了空性未達扼要，以是因緣，謗方便分，遮止一切作意思惟，損減教法，爲蓮華戒大阿闍黎善破滅已，抉擇勝者所有密意，爲恩極重……[40]
>
> 又說一切分別是相執故，障礙成佛，弃舍一切觀察之修，此爲最下邪妄分别，乃是支那和尚堪布之規。破除此執，于止觀時，兹當廣說。又此邪執障礙敬重諸大教典，以彼諸教所有義理，現見多須以觀察慧而思擇故……[41]
>
> 支那堪布等，于如此道顛倒分别，有作是云："凡是分别，况惡分别，即善分别亦能系縛生死，其所得果不出生死。金索繩索皆是系縛，黑白二雲俱障虛空，黑白狗咬皆生痛苦，是故唯有無分别住是成佛道。其施、戒等，爲未能修如是了義愚夫而說。若已獲得如是了義，更修彼行，如王爲農，得象求迹。"和尚于此引八十種《贊嘆無分别經》根據成立。此說一切方便之品，皆非真實成佛之道，毁謗世俗，破佛教之心藏，破觀察慧思擇無我真實義故，故亦遠離勝義道理，任何勝進終唯攝于奢摩他品，于此住心執爲勝道，是倒見中最下品者[42]。

由上可見，宗喀巴對摩訶衍的批評理路與《巴協》中蓮花戒的批評和赤松德贊的裁决如出一轍，特别是在善惡黑白問題上，與龍青巴的觀點截然相反，他認爲摩訶衍的教法謗拔方便分，輕慢道次第，破壞布施、持戒等六度修習，且唯重寂止（zhi gnas），而不能以觀察慧作勝觀（lhag mthong）及止觀雙運（zhi gnas zung 'jug）。宗喀巴對摩訶衍的嚴厲破斥與他本人的佛學主張密不可分，衆所周知，宗喀巴往往被後世塑造爲宗教改革家的形象，他强調佛教經典的漸次修學，由顯入密，且極重戒律，而傳統表述中的摩訶衍教法無疑與其在《菩提道次第廣論中》鋪設的修證道路大相徑庭，依《廣論》所言，行人當由皈依發心入道，思惟四諦、十二緣起，繼而入大乘修學六度、四攝法、止觀，最終入金剛乘，整個過程都離不開思擇、對善惡的取捨等等一切如理作意行，故而對于宗喀巴而言，摩訶衍的主張勢必有礙于這一漸修體系。隨着《廣論》的流傳，宗喀巴的論述也基本奠定了格魯派對摩訶衍的批判基調。

從15世紀中葉至17世紀中葉，格魯派對辯論日趨重視，同時其注疏傳統則趨于式

㊵ 依法尊法師譯《宗喀巴大師集》，北京：民族出版社，2003年，卷1，32—33頁。

㊶ 同㊵，76頁。

㊷ 同㊵，253—254頁。

微[43]，重視辯經的經院式教學模式在16—17世紀時得到大力的推廣，而貫徹這種模式的頂級寺院便是在藏土居于核心地位的拉薩三大寺，以辯經取代注疏的趨勢也使得格魯派與宗見與己有异的他派筆戰頻仍，隨着五世達賴喇嘛以後格魯派在政治上的勢力日益增盛，其話語霸權的地位也得到進一步的鞏固，在這樣的大背景下，他派學者在討論相關話題時，便不得不考慮格魯派的看法，有關摩訶衍的爭議自然也不例外。

（六）噶陀·壽自在寶（Kaḥ thog Tshe dbang nor bu, 1698—1755）

繼龍青巴之後，我們在18—19世紀的寧瑪派文本中看到了有關大圓滿與摩訶衍禪法的更多、更爲集中的討論，這些討論并未告訴我們歷史上大圓滿與摩訶衍禪法原初的真實關係，但却細緻地呈現了寧瑪派上師針對人們所認爲的二者關係所作的辯答與回應。

首當一提的是18世紀噶陀寺著名學者壽自在寶[44]所著的《和尚教法史·能淨意垢之善流》[45]（下稱《善流》），這部以藏土上師身份評述漢土教法源流的專論已經受到學界的關注，在格魯派占據宗教話語霸權而導致"反和尚"之風盛行的背景下，《善流》對摩訶衍教法的積極肯定顯得格外引人注目。作者記述了始于菩提達摩、包含摩訶衍在內的漢土禪法傳承，其中直接或間接運用了包括《禪定目炬》在內的諸多早期的材料。壽自在寶非常明確地點出，其闡述頓門派有兩大目的，一是鑒于摩訶衍教法與大圓滿有相似之處，爲避免混淆、誤解故需說明，二是承許摩訶衍教法爲正道（yang dag pa'i lam）[46]，這無疑與《禪定目炬》中所說之造論動機相合。壽自在寶依循《禪定目炬》的模式，判別頓門派居于漸門派之上、大瑜伽與大圓滿之下，并且指出頓門派所依爲顯乘經教，尤以三轉法輪爲重。通過徵引漢譯《大般涅盤經》，作者指出并非所有行人都必須歷經長劫漸修而證覺，若能通達善巧方便，即可頓證，由此成立頓門修習的合理性。

---

[43] George Dreyfus, "Where Do Commentarial Schools Come From? Reflections on the History of Tibetan Scholasticism", in *Journal of the International Association of Buddhist Studies* 28, No. 2, 2005, p. 293.

[44] 該師出生于康區，早年于噶陀寺學習，其後造訪衛藏地區并值遇當時包括覺囊派在內之各派著名上師，最終成爲寧瑪派內弘揚他空見與時輪教法的重要上師之一，下文所涉及的格澤班智達即爲其轉世。參見Hugh Richardson, "A Tibetan Antiquarian in the 18th Century", *Bulletin of Tibetology* Ⅳ, No 3, pp. 5-8; Gene Smith, *Among Tibetan Tetxs*, Boston, Wisdom Publications, 2001, pp. 20-21.

[45] 全名爲《略說漢土和尚教法史及其論敵之宗見·能淨意垢之善流》（*rGya nag hwa shang gi byung tshul grub tha'i phyogs snga bcas sa bon tsam smos pa yid kyi dri ma dag byed dge ba'i chu rgyun*），見噶妥·仁增次旺諾布《噶妥·仁增次旺諾布文集》，北京：中國藏學出版社，2006年，卷2，379—389頁。關于該論中涉及摩訶衍教法的部分的研究，見張淩暉《漢僧的歷史——一則十八世紀寧瑪派的辯教案例》，《文本中的歷史：藏傳佛教在西域和中原的傳播》，607—626頁。

[46] dgos pa ni rdzogs chen dang cha 'dra bas mi nor ba'i tshad du yin par gsung ba dang / hwa shang gi chos de yang yang dag pa'i lam du bzhed pa'o //《噶妥·仁增次旺諾布文集》，384頁。

而後，作者著重指出頓門派在次第上低于密咒乘㊼：

最初，唯歷經資糧道及加行道而得初地，此時大部分（行人）趣入密咒道，雖有因外相示現之緣故而于八地之前不入（密咒道）者，然而自八地起，彼等亦將不假外緣、憑藉自力而得了知并趣入密咒自性。因此，雖有開示云"顯乘道者需入密咒道"，然而自八地以上，將自然了知并趣入（密咒）道，且無中斷之機會。此外，最初之入門顯密皆可，然最終需入密咒（道）。因此，得正圓覺果時，無顯佛密佛之差別，如是考慮而宣說，故無過失。

由此可見，壽自在寶認爲就證果而言，無論是由顯還是密入道，都無關緊要。行者可依顯乘道漸次歷經十地，但是到八地時，將自然進入密咒道。從初地開始就入密咒道的利益就是可以讓行者證果更加迅速，然而壽自在寶爲了將摩訶衍的頓門法納入標準的顯乘道模式，明顯忽視了其本身的諸多不共特徵，摩訶衍所主并非依次歷經十地，而是直趨十地㊽。

針對當時的情形，壽自在寶提到㊾：

即使在當今，漢土禪師和尚亦唯授宗門，于此藏土，亦有説"不分在家出家，一律接受心導引"者，主張入手即專注于甚深內義，此（趨勢）大體上已趨衰微，然其與（漢土宗門）僅屬部分相似。

壽自在寶似乎是在指涉當時有些大圓滿與大手印上師輕視漸門道，而這一風氣已然沒落，他的重點是在于强調這些藏土上師所傳的教法與漢土禪師所主之頓門道只有少分相似，後者廢聞思（thos bsam）而以禪定（bsam gtan）爲修道的全部，漸門道則圓具此三分㊿。爲了證明大圓滿也含攝漸門道，他引用了口訣部（man ngag sde）"十七續"的《日月和合續》（*Nyi zla kha sbyor*），指出其中有開示依次作七種行持（spyod pa bdun）(51)。

㊼ thog mar tshogs sbyor gyi lam mdo lam 'ba' zhig pas bsgrod nas sa dang po thob pa'i skabs su sngags lam la 'jug par shas che zhing gal te tshul ston gyi dbang gi sa brgyad pa'i bar du mi 'jug pa dag yod srid kyang sa brgyad pa nas gzhan rkyen la ltos pa ma yin par sngags kyi ngang tshul rang stobs kyi shes bzhin du 'jug tu yod pa yin pas des na mdo lam du sngags la 'jug dgos so zhes ma bstan kyang sa brgyad pa yan chad nas ngang gi shes pa'i dbang gi la ma tshang ba dang chad pa'i go skabs med la / gzhan yang thog ma'i 'jug sgo mdo sngags gang yin kyang rung mthar sngags la gzhol dgos pas yang dag par rdzogs pa'i sangs rgyas kyi 'bras bu thob tshe mdo sngags tha dad kyi sangs rgyas dbye ru med pa'i phyir de ltar dgongs te gsungs pas skyon med pa'o //《噶妥·仁增次旺諾布文集》，385頁。

㊽ 見《〈巴協〉彙編》，51頁。另見巴桑旺堆上揭書，22頁。

㊾ da lta yang rgya nag tu bstan 'dzin mkhan hwa shang tsung men rnams tshul de kho na yin 'dug la / bod 'dir yang yang btsun pa dang khyim pa ris su med par sems khri nod do zhes thog ma nas zab mo nang don la gzhol bar 'dod pa phal cher 'di rnams kyang de dang cha mthun pa las gzhan tu ma dmigs so //《噶妥·仁增次旺諾布文集》，385頁。

㊿ de yang cig car 'jug pa ni thos bsam gyi bya ba gzhan gtso bor mi byed pa rnam pa kun tu bsam gtan don bsgom lhu ru blangs pa ste //《噶妥·仁增次旺諾布文集》，385頁。

(51) thos bsam sgom gsum la rim gyis 'jug par bzhed de / rdzogs chen nyi zla kha sbyor gyi rgyud las spyod pa bdun rim can du gsung ba dang gnad gcig go //《噶妥·仁增次旺諾布文集》，385頁。

最後，壽自在寶認爲頓漸之分源于漢土，實不見于印度，而當佛法從印度和漢土傳入藏土時，方可分頓漸[52]：

因此，當知追隨昔日印度堪布寂護之智自在（Jñānanendra）大師等依止三慧（shes rab gsum），是爲漸門派，追隨漢土堪布摩訶衍者唯精進于禪定，是爲頓門派。

在壽自在寶看來，在印藏佛教的語境中使用頓、漸的名相是錯誤的，頓門道唯見于漢土，而不見于主流的印藏佛教傳統。因此，從總體上看，壽自在寶與努佛智相似，他并不拒斥頓門道，而是將其地位加以合理的判攝，雖然他在經教中找到了頓證可能性的依據，但他并不認爲判教意義上的頓漸區分傳統源自印度。

（七）無畏洲（’Jigs med gling pa, 1730—1768）

從噶陀·壽自在寶開始，我們可以看到寧瑪派上師既未刻意與摩訶衍劃清界限，也未簡單地肯定摩訶衍，他們在摩訶衍教法問題上的回應愈加精細，從宏觀的教相簡別深入到立足于實修細節的具體問題，他們試圖尋求一個平衡點來解决頓漸二門之間的張力。無畏洲便是此中的典型代表[53]，作爲寧瑪派的著名上師，他不但編纂了寧瑪派的密續合集，還撰寫了包括《功德藏》（*Yon tan mdzod*）在内的論著來對佛教的修道做全面的闡釋，但最終令他蜚聲整個藏土的無疑還是他所發掘的密意藏（dgongs gter）[54]——《龍青寧提》（*Klong chen snying thig*）[55]，據記載，這部伏藏是他三次在定中面見龍青巴後從心間流露的法要，其中包含一些密續和大量成就法，以及由無畏洲本人寫作的有關大圓滿的導引文與釋論，在這些伏藏根本文和無畏洲的導引中，我們見到了有關摩訶衍禪法的重要討論。在其中一篇名爲《遍智言教》（*Kun mkhyen zhal lung*）[56]的釋論

---

[52] des na sngon rgya gar mkhan po zhi ba ’tsho yi rjes su ’brang ba bandhe chen po ye shes dbang po la sogs pas shes rab gsum bsgrags mar mdzad pa la brten rim gyis pa dang rgya nag mkhan po ma hā ya na’i rjes ’brang rnams kyi bsam gtan kho na la gzhol bas cig char bar grags pa shes par bya’o //《噶妥·仁增次旺諾布文集》，386頁。

[53] 對無畏洲生平背景及其自傳的研究，見Janet Gyatso, *Apparitions of the Self: The Secret Autobiographies of a Tibetan Visionary*, Princeton, Princeton University Press, 1998.

[54] 關與伏藏的定義及分類的討論，見Andreas Doctor, *Tibetan Treasure Literature: Revelation, Tradition, and Accomplishment in Visionary Buddhism*, Ithaca, Snow Lion Publications, 2005, pp. 17-30.

[55] 有關《龍青寧提》中大圓滿的頓、漸修習的詳細討論，見Sam van Schaik, *Approaching the Great Perfection: Simultaneous and Gradual Approaches to Dzogchen Practice in Jigme Lingpa's Longchen Nyingthig*, Boston, Wisdom Publications, 2004. 該書對《龍青寧提》的源流、内容作了全面的介紹，通過翻譯其中的十篇有關大圓滿的論述，集中討論了無畏洲對大圓滿教法中頓、漸教法的闡釋與抉擇。

[56] 全名爲《持明空行歡喜密語·粉碎伺察宗義之錘·發顯心要、攤開掌心之口訣·密主極喜勇父之即興歌·遍智言教甘露滴》（*Rig ’dzin mkha’ ’gro dgyes pa’i gsang gtam / yid dpyod grub mtha’ ’jig pa’i tho lum / snying phyung lag mthil bkram pa’i man ngag / gsang bdag dga’ rab dpa’ ’o’i thol glu / kun mkhyen zhal lung bdud rtsi’i thigs pa*），收于Ngodrup and Sherab Drimed, *Rin chen gter mdzod chen mo*, Buthan: Paro, 1978, Vol. 108, ff. 529-555。英譯見Sam van Schaik上揭書，208—224頁。

中，無畏洲針對將大圓滿等同于摩訶衍所傳無分别修習的批評作出了明確的回應，其回應乃立足于大圓滿口訣部對心（sems）與本覺（rig pa）的辨别[57]，他指出[58]：

就區分有對境之心與無對境之通透本覺而言，和尚不得要領，故而于不辨心與本覺之無記（lung ma bstan）心識狀態中，令一切憶念、思惟、覺受停息，遂偏墮于愚痴之一邊，猶如昏厥或沉睡。于大圓滿中，依于無對境之智，不落于對有對境之心所作之伺察，而于如無垢水晶球之本覺憶念境界中，令諸遍計得以隱沒，無增無減，無有變遷，住于邊際解脱之廣大界密意中。故二者并無相似之處。

依汝等所許，和尚具此謬見，遂將其安立爲一無所思而如卵蛋之敵論。然而和尚實了知《華嚴經》等衆多經典，蓮花戒于論辯中以杖繞首，藉此表徵而問輪回之因，（和尚）抖披風之雙襟，以示（其因）乃能所二取[59]，彼實乃根器極利之補特伽羅，無可争議。若無所念、無所作即生舍離觀察慧之過失，則《般若經》亦有此過失。因此，于真實中，和尚之見地究竟如何，唯圓滿佛陀能知，他人則不能。

由上可見，無畏洲非常謹慎，他顯然是在回應批評的同時，對批評者預設的摩訶衍教法提出了質疑，他認爲，就吐蕃僧諍過程的相關記載所展現的一些迹象來看，摩訶衍應屬根器極利之人，其教法亦與《般若經》無違，歷史上真實的摩訶衍教法究竟是何面貌，唯佛能知。在承認史實難考的前提下，無畏洲只能依循批評者基于《巴協》的叙事所定義的摩訶衍教法，指出其過失在于不能辨别心與本覺，唯求暫時壓制分别，從而落

---

[57] 大圓滿口訣部依“十七續”展開四重辨别，分别爲辨别心與本覺、辨别意與般若、辨别識與智、辨别阿賴耶與法身，詳細解説見摧魔洲（bDud ’joms gling pa, 1835-1904）所造《無修佛道》（*Ma bsgom sangs rgyas*），收《化身大伏藏師摧魔洲甚深伏藏秘密法匯》（*sPrul pa'i gter chen bdud ’joms gling pa'i zab gter gsang ba'i chos sde*）, Timphu, Lama Kuenzang Wangdue, 2004, Vol. 16, ff. 97-364. 英譯見Richard Barron, *Buddhahood Without Meditation: A Visionary Account Known as Refining One's Perception (Nang-jang)*, Junction City, Padma Publishing, 2006. 漢譯與研究見談錫永導論、許錫恩譯，《無修佛道：現證自性大圓滿本來面目教授》，北京：華夏出版社，2010年。

[58] ha shang la yul sems rtog dang yul med rig pa zang ka mar phyed pa’i gnad med pas / sems rig skabs ma phyed pa’i shes pa lung ma bstan gyi ngang du dran bsam tshor ba thams cad ’gags nas brgyal ba’am / gnyid ’thug lta bu’i gti mug phyogs gcig tu lhung ngo snyam dang / rdzogs pa chen po yul sems rtog la yul med ye shes kyis rtog dpyod ma shor bar rang rig gi dran pa shel gong g.ya’ dag ba lta bu’i ngang du kun rtog bag la zha nas rang ngo la bri gang dang ’pho ’gyur med pa mtha’ grol klong yangs chen po’i dgongs pa la bzhugs pa gnyis mtshungs pa’i yul med la //收《化身大伏藏師摧魔洲甚深伏藏秘密法匯》（*sPrul pa'i gter chen bdud ’joms gling pa'i zab gter gsang ba'i chos sde*）, ff. 536-537.

[59] 這一細節所涉爲摩訶衍與蓮花戒在辯論前的首次會面，相關記載可見于《西藏王統記》（*rGyal rabs gsal ba'i me long*），參見Per Sørensen, *Tibetan Buddhist Historiography: The Mirror Illuminating the Royal Genealogies*, Wiesbaden: Harrassowitz, 1994, p. 401; Tucci, *Minor Buddhist Texts* (part I & II), Kyoto, Rinsen Book Company 1978, p. 365. 不過，在《西藏王統記》中，摩訶衍是將披風擲于地上（sa la brdabs），而非抖動（sprugs）雙襟。無畏洲所述與《巴協》所載更爲相合，《巴協》對應段落爲：hwa shang gis cha tshur kha na ber gyi thu ba nas bzung nas sprugs /，見巴色朗《巴協》，北京：民族出版社，1982年，67頁。

于昏昧無記之愚痴境界，而大圓滿則令行者住于明淨無垢之本覺境界，一切遍計分別無需刻意壓制，即能于通透光明之廣大界中自然解脱。因此，摩訶衍之無分別教授與大圓滿實具天壤之别，對于這種差别，無畏洲另有一篇名爲《大圓滿三要辨别》（*rDzogs pa chen po'i gnad gsum shan 'byed*）[60]的偈頌從三方面詳加陳述，其中包括辨别阿賴耶與法身、辨别心與本覺、辨别寂止與勝觀，由此鄭重强調大圓滿絕不落于摩訶衍教法所住之昏昧無記、具諸所緣、迷糊黯淡之阿賴耶、心識以及單純之寂止邊。

儘管無畏洲迫于大圓滿所受的批評而指出了批評者心中定義的摩訶衍教法所犯過失，從而令大圓滿與之劃清界限，然而如前所説，就無畏洲本人的觀點來看，摩訶衍屬于利根行人，無畏洲對他的態度和對寧瑪派的印度前賢甚爲相近，在其所著之《白蓮花》（*Padma dkar po*）[61]中有云[62]：

> 復次，殊勝利根化機如極喜金剛（dGa' rab rdo rje）、自生蓮花生（Padmasambhava）與因陀羅菩提（Indrabhūti）等壇城主，僅于共通化機面前示現入道之相，故而彼等已自然得聞解脱，然而漸門之補特伽羅却不能如是觸證，故于此際仍追求解脱。

作爲龍青巴精神繼承人的無畏洲，他的這段話也明顯呼應了前者在《勝乘藏》（*Theg mchog mdzod*）中所言[63]：

> 達至彼本性之大瑜伽士直言因果善惡皆無有，例如蓮花生、無垢友及帝洛巴等，我等雖能如是了知，却未能由串習而成現證，故將不畏懼本性和警惕微細因果結合而宣説。

由此可見，無畏洲與龍青巴一致，皆視蓮花生等印度上師乃頓證實相之利根行人，其所證實相超越善惡因果，摩訶衍的特徵無疑與此相符，因此無畏洲實際上已將摩訶衍的地位視爲與諸位印度大成就者無异，然而他的最終目的并非局限于爲摩訶衍作積極的辯護，因爲在承認摩訶衍所傳頓門道亦爲正道後，如何處理頓漸二門的緊張關係便成爲無法回避的問題，而這一緊張關係恰好就内嵌在《龍青寧提》的各類文本中。整個《龍

---

[60] 收《無畏洲全集》（*'Jigs med gling pa'i bka' 'bum*），成都：阿宗曲嘎印經處，1999年，卷12，101—104葉。英譯見Sam van Schaik上揭書，162—165頁。

[61] 全名爲《金剛乘成熟解脱道次第所出口訣之所依·白蓮花》（*rDo rje theg pa smin grol lam gyi rim pa las 'phros pa'i man ngag gi rgyab brten padma dkar po*），*Rin chen gter mdzod chen mo*, Vol. 108, ff. 471—527. 英譯見Sam van Schaik上揭書，173—207頁。

[62] de yang dbang po rnon mchog gi gdul bya dga' rab rdo rje dang / rang byung padma indra bhū ti sogs pa ni dkyil 'khor gyi bdag po nyid thun mong gdul bya'i snang ngor lam la 'jug pa'i tshul bstan pa tsam yin phyir rang byung thos grol du gyur kyang / gang zag rim gyis pa la ni / de lta'i reg pa mi 'gro ste / de'i phyir skabs 'dir yang grol ba don du gnyer ba zhig yin phyin chad //《金剛乘成熟解脱道次第所出口訣之所依·白蓮花》（*rDo rje theg pa smin grol lam gyi rim pa las 'phros pa'i man ngag gi rgyab brten padma dkar po*），*Rin chen gter mdzod chen mo*, f. 486.

[63] gshis der phebs pa'i rnal 'byor pa chen po rnams la rgyu 'bras dge sdig med pa thod drang du bshad de padma dang / bi ma la dang / te lo pa la sogs pa bzhin no / rang cag rnams la blos de ltar rtogs kyang goms pas thog du ma 'phebs pas / gshis la mi skrag cing las 'bras cha phra ba la 'dzem pa dang sbyar nas bshad do // *Theg mchog mdzod kyi glegs bam phyi ma*, in *mDzod bdun*, Gangtok, Sherab Gyaltsen and Khyentse Labrang, 1983, Vol. 6, ff. 1595-1596.

青寧提》的主體部分是大瑜伽部的修習儀軌，而少部分則屬于大圓滿。這些大圓滿文本大致可以分爲伏藏文本和由無畏洲本人寫作的非伏藏文本，與頓門有關的論述即見于大部分伏藏文本和少部分非伏藏文本，而與漸門有關的論述則主要見于非伏藏文本。在前一類文本中，頻頻强調本覺周遍一切有情，有情本具覺性，經由上師之直指教授，行者可頓證本覺，例如在《無上智》（*Ye shes bla ma*）[64]中，作者即指出[65]：

> 于今，藉上師之教誡，可于剎那間證覺，對本性不作整治，無有渙散、無所觀修而安住于（本性），此即明說爲本初佛普賢王如來之心要。

而在《口訣大圓滿後續》（*Man ngag rdzogs pa chen po'i rgyud phyi ma*）中，又有云[66]：

> 精勤于心識造作之法、八乘言說之宗義、由分別假立之空性，由此掌握之體悟無法觸及實相。

此即如早期的心部本續《遍作王續》一樣，立足于阿底瑜伽大圓滿，對九乘次第中下八乘具有作意、未離言說之見地加以批評。此外，無畏洲還圍繞觀修，指出薩迦、噶舉以及寧瑪自宗的種種觀修都是依二次第漸證，亦即首先抉擇一切顯現皆爲心，繼而决定心本身亦爲空，然而大圓滿中則無此二次第，唯有一次第，亦即行者現證俱生本覺，一旦現證，即無需其他觀修方便[67]。與此相應，無畏洲更對五道十地的漸修模式加以否定，强調唯有一地，即包含直證本覺之唯一方便的大圓滿。

然而，似乎與此矛盾的是，《龍青寧提》的其他文本却大倡漸門修習，無畏洲將大瑜伽和大圓滿的具體操作都納入漸修框架，他在《白蓮花》中即詳述了金剛乘標準的漸修模式，例如先尋找具格上師，而後受灌頂、修前行、修生圓二次第等。在《無上智》

---

[64] 本論英譯見Lama Chönam and Sangye Khandro (trans.), *Yeshes Lama*, Ithaca, Snow Lion Publications, 2008。漢譯見智悲光尊者著，劉立千譯《大圓勝慧本覺心要修證次第》，北京：民族出版社，2000年。

[65] da ni bla ma'i gdams ngag gis rig pa skad cig ma'i 'tshang rig pa tsam nas yin lugs kyi thog tu bzo mi 'chos shing / 'di las gang du'ang ma yengs / gang du'ang mi sgom par 'jog pa ni / gdod ma'i sangs rgyas kun tu bzang po'i dgongs pa'i mthil lhag ger bstan pa yin te // Ngagwang Sogpa (ed.), *rDogs pa chen po klong chen snying thig gi gdod ma'i mgon po'i lam gyi rim pa'i khrid yig ye shes bla ma*, in *Klong chen snying thig*, New Delhi, A 'dzom chos sgar par khang, 1973, Vol. 3, f. 325.

[66] ci phyir blo yis byas pa'i chos / theg brgyad tshig gi grub mtha' dang / rtogs pas brtags pa'i stong pa nyid / rtsol bas gcun pa'i shes nyams la / gnas lugs yin du mi re bar // Ngagwang Sogpa (ed.), *rDogs pa chen po klong chen snying thig gi gdod ma'i mgon po'i lam gyi rim pa'i khrid yig ye shes bla ma*, f. 103.

[67] snang ba sems su ngo sprad pas sems la byan tshud / sems nyid stong par ngo sprad pas stong pa bde bas rgyas gdab / stong pa rig par ngo sprad pas rig pa nyid dbyings dang gnyis su med pa de kho na chos sku'o zhes pa ltar / snang ba sems kyis bzos par ngo sprad pas bden 'dzin rang rgyud pa ldog / de ltar bzo byed kyi sems stong bar ngo sprad pas phyi yul don du zhen pa spong / stong pa rig par ngo sprad pas chos nyid chad ltar mi gol ba'i gnad tsam la kha drangs te khrid pa'o / de ni snying thig gi dgongs pa'i phyogs la nye ba ma yin par da gdod go ste / … gzhan du sems don dam du med / kun rdzob tu yod par btags nas lta sgom dmigs gtad can lam du byed cing de bzhin du zung 'jug gi chos skad kyang yod pa gnyis gcig la gcig 'brel gyi zung 'jug 'chos pa dang / 'dir rdzogs pa chen po gdod nas rig stong mnyam rdzogs chen por slar zung du 'jug rgyu med pa tha dad ris med chen po'i khyad 'dug pa'i phyir ro // *Klong chen snying thig*, Vol. 3, ff. 322-323. 英譯見Lama Chönam and Sangye Khandro上揭書，47—49頁。

中，又先後分述了大圓滿修行的立斷（khred chod）、頓超（thod rgal）二次第，在《大圓滿洞見實相》（*rDzogs pa chen gnas lugs cer mthong*）[68]及《白蓮花》中甚至還將大手印之"專一"（rtse gcig）、"離戲"（spros bral）、"一味"（ro gcig）、"無修"（sgom med）四瑜伽（rnal sbyor bzhi）次第配合頓超之"現見法性"（chos nyid mngon sum）、"證量增長"（nyams snang gong 'phel）、"明體進詣"（rig pa tshad phebs）、"窮盡法性"（chos nyid zad pa）四顯現（snang ba bzhi）修習[69]。

無畏洲顯然意識到了《龍青寧提》中頓漸二門表面上的緊張對立，爲了圓融地處理這一問題，他首先將行者的根器區分爲上、中、下三種，儘管他認爲利根者可頓證悟入大圓滿，然而絕大多數行者却難以如此成辦，因此他只能教授基于四瑜伽次第的漸修法[70]。既然頓證者只能是根器極利者，亦即蓮花生、無垢友、因陀羅菩提、摩訶衍（鑒于無畏洲個人認爲摩訶衍也屬極利根器），那麽屬于中下根器的普通人只能依漸門悟入。由此可見，頓門道對于漸修之普通人而言在實修上不具有可操作性，那麽頓門道對于後者是否毫無意義呢？事實上并非如此，在無畏洲的著作中，頓門所扮演的角色實爲漸門的抉擇見（lta ba），與頓門有關的闡述强調輪涅無二、超越善惡因果的實相，由此在見地上導引行者離二者的相對邊。這樣的闡述散見于《龍青寧提》中的伏藏類大圓滿文本，也見于指導漸修的非伏藏文本，如《無上智》與《白蓮花》等，頓門式的闡述在漸修類文本中顯然并不是以修道指南的角色出現，而是作爲究竟見的開示，行者不可以取其字面意義而在入手實修時就否定因果等等，而應當依照漸門道的施設與建立，區分輪回與涅盤，依道次第逐步累積證悟，以臻究竟圓證。因此，從總體上來看，《龍青寧提》巧妙地在頓漸二極之間建立了平衡的橋梁，無畏洲一方面藉其中屬于伏藏類的密續等文本闡釋了體現頓門特色的見地，用以抉擇諸法實相，揭示本覺之俱生與周遍，另一方面又通過劃分行者根器的方式承認頓證的可能性，同時將普通人與頓證模式隔離開來，從而指出漸門修習的必要性與合理性。

回過頭來，如果我們對噶陀·壽自在寶與無畏洲這兩位同屬于18世紀的上師對摩訶衍教法的論述加以比較的話，可以發現二者的理路具有明顯的差异，無畏洲承龍青巴的觀點，視摩訶衍爲一獨立的人物而非一宗派之代表，其證悟相當于無垢友、帝洛巴等大

---

[68] 英譯見Sam van Schaik上揭書，235—238頁。

[69] 無畏洲以"專一"等噶舉派大手印的法名言（chos skad）來概括《龍青寧提》的修證次第，以二者都屬與瑜伽行中觀之系統故。無畏洲甚至指出，一般都認爲此四瑜伽次第源自岡波巴（sGam po pa bSod nams rin chen, 1079-1153），其實不確。此四瑜伽實出自《勝樂本續》，阿底峡教授俱生合和（lhan cig skyes sbyor）之四瑜伽時，也以《勝樂》爲本，而該續不應偏屬與某一派。無畏洲又引伏藏師般若光（Phreng po gter ston Shes rab 'od zer, 1518-1584）之伏藏《解脱滴密意自解脱》（*Grol thig dgongs pa rang grol*）之説，將世間瑜伽（'jig rten gyi rnal 'byor）、見道瑜伽（mthong lam gyi rnal 'byor）、修道瑜伽（sgom lam gyi rnal 'byor）、無學道瑜伽（mi slob pa'i lam gyi rnal 'byor）等四瑜伽次第配合大乘瑜伽行的五道，前一屬加行道，後三分屬見道、修道和無學道，"專一"等四瑜伽亦配合此四道。參*Rin chen gter mdzod chen mo*, Vol. 108, ff. 492-495. 另見Sam van Schaik上揭書，186—187頁。

[70] 見Sam van Schaik上揭書，187頁。

圓滿或大手印之成就者[71]，且爲當世所罕見。壽自在寶的做法更近于努佛智，他是將摩訶衍視爲漢土頓門派禪法的代表，并在肯定其教法屬于正道的前提下，在教法系統中給予其相應的定位，亦即高于漸門派，低于金剛乘。就出發點而言，無畏洲是基于修行實踐來評定摩訶衍，而壽自在寶則是基于判教目的而加以考量，但是二者無疑都是在意識到自宗大圓滿在過去飽受批評的情況下對摩訶衍教法做出了正面評價，他們也很清楚這樣的評價極有可能招來更多的批評，這的確需要一定的勇氣，他們對摩訶衍教法的評價處處彰顯著寧瑪派自宗的不共見解以及背後隱含的宗派身份强調。這一現象實際上與17—18世紀寧瑪派的發展有關，當時藏土的寧瑪派寺院數量急劇增加，而伏藏主洲（gTer bdag gling pa, 1646—1714）和法吉祥譯師（Lo chen Dharmaśrī, 1654—1717）等人也對寧瑪派文本進行了大規模的整理與彙編；另一方面，寧瑪派又受到了準噶爾部等諸多力量的迫害，不少著名上師遭到殺害[72]，這種迫害一直延續到壽自在寶與無畏洲的時代，前者甚至寫信給七世達賴請求停止對寧瑪派的迫害[73]。寧瑪派自身建設的迅猛發展爲其帶來的與日俱增的自信和自我身份意識，及其所受到的頻繁迫害，共同構成了包括上述兩位上師在內的18世紀寧瑪派行人文本書寫的歷史大環境，這種環境使他們不得不認真考慮如何在對摩訶衍教法等重大問題的討論上最大限度地突顯自宗的不共特性。

（八）噶陀·格澤班智達（1761—1829）

格澤班智達不變壽自在勝成（dGe rtse Paṇḍita 'Gyur med tshe dbang mchog grub，以下簡稱格澤班）是噶陀寺第一世格澤活佛[74]，他的聞名主要源于他編纂的德格版《寧瑪十萬續》，除此之外，學界對其著作的研究一直相對匱乏，迄今爲止只有幾部對其“他

---

[71] 將摩訶衍等頓門派行者的證悟等同于大圓滿行者的證悟的做法也可見于伏藏師鄔金洲（O rgyan gling pa, 1329—1367）的《大臣遺教》（*Blon po bka' thang*），其翻譯收錄于G. Tucci, *Minor Buddhist Texts II*。

[72] 有關這一段歷史，參見Luciano Petech, *China and Tibet in the Early Eighteenth Century*, Leiden, E. J. Brill, 1950.

[73] Kaḥ thog Tshe dbang nor bu, *Gong sa bdun pa skal bzang rgya mtsho'i zhabs su zhu yig phul ba ngang pa'i bu mo'i glu dbyangs*, in *Selected writings of Kaḥ-thog Rig-'dzin Tshe-dbaṅ-nor-bu*, Darjeeling, Kargyud Sungrab Nyamso Khang, 1973, Vol. 1, ff. 717-723.

[74] 關于歷代格澤班智達的生平，見江陽吉澤《噶妥寺志》（*Kaḥ thog pa'i lo rgyus mdor bsdus*），成都：四川民族出版社，1996年。另參Michael Jann Ronis, *Celibacy, Revelations, and Reincarnated Lamas: Contestation and Synthesis in the Growth of Monasticism at Katok Monastery from the 17th through 19th Centuries*, PhD dissertation at University of Virginia, UMI, 2009. 有關將格澤班智達確定爲噶陀寺第一任寺主的討論，見Helmut Eimer and Pema Tsering, "A List of Abbots of Kaḥ-thog Monastery According to Handwritten Notes by the Late Katok Ontul", *Journal of the Tibet Society* 1, 1984, pp. 11-14.

空”（gzhan stong）及密教論述所作的翻譯與研究[75]。格澤班曾爲薩班的《三律儀判別》寫過一部注疏，名爲《斷除由〈三律儀判別論〉引發之對舊譯（寧瑪派）之諍論·無爲庫》（*sDom gsum gyi rab tu dbye ba'i bstan bcos chen pos snga 'gyur phyogs la rtsod pa spong ba 'dus ma byas kyi gan mdzod*），其中也通過爲摩訶衍教法的辯護而爲他宗基于薩班《三律儀判別》對寧瑪所作的批評做出回應。

針對密乘律儀部分關于大手印、大圓滿與摩訶衍關係的批評（第三品，頌167—175），格澤班的闡釋顯得與衆不同。主流闡釋普遍認爲薩班在批評摩訶衍時也在針對藏土的大手印與大圓滿，然而格澤班却認爲[76]：

> （薩班之）用意在于成立大車之追隨者——漸門派爲正（法），名爲頓門派者乃了義，此雖無誤，然其乃利根者之道，故而遮止一切鈍根者入彼（道），因此，（薩班）所言無疑具有密意。

格澤班認爲，摩訶衍教法本身無錯，錯在批評者對它的理解[77]：

> 然而，後世僅識ka、kha之愚者將和尚教法說爲錯誤，且誤將其來源視爲外道與野蠻不化之人。

爲了消除這種誤解，格澤班分兩步成立摩訶衍的教法爲正法，首先指出它源于印度且傳承未斷，其次證明其教法本身無誤且無過失[78]。格澤班指出，從印度傳入漢土的佛教可分爲三大傳規，一爲戒律，二爲密咒乘，三爲波羅蜜多乘。其中密咒乘傳規包含事續、行續、瑜伽續，而不包含無上瑜伽續。波羅蜜多乘也分三支，一爲廣大行傳承（rgya chen spyod pa'i brgyud pa），亦即源于彌勒與世親、由玄奘譯介的瑜伽行派，二爲甚深見傳承（zab mo lta ba'i brgyud pa），亦即由文殊、龍樹、清辨、月稱等祖師傳下的中觀派[79]。三爲修傳勝義傳承（sgrub rgyud don gyi brgyud pa），亦即宗門、

---

[75] 見Tomoko Makidono, Kaḥ thog Dge rtse Mahāpaṇḍita's Doxographical Position: The Great Madhyamaka of Other-Emptiness (gzhan stong dbu ma chen po)", *Indian International Journal of Buddhist Studies*, vol. 12, 2011, pp. 77-119; Tomoko Makidono, "The Turning of the Wheel of Mantrayāna Teachings in the Rnying ma rgyud 'bum dkar chag lha'i rnga bo che by Kaḥ thog Dge rtse Mahāpaṇḍita 'Gyur med tshe dbang mchog grub", *Indian International Journal of Buddhist Studies*, vol. 13, 2012, pp. 149-186; Gyatrul Rinpoche, *The Generation Stage in Buddhist Tantra*, Ithaca, Snow Lion Publications, 2005.

[76] dgongs gzhi rim gyis pa'i lugs shing rta chen po'i rjes 'brangs tshad mar sgrub pa'i gsung yin la / cig car par grags pa nges don du 'khrul ba med kyang dbang rnon gyi lam yin pa'i phyir dbang po rno rtul thams cas der 'jug pa dgag pa'i phyir dgongs pa can gyi gsung du nges so //甘孜州藏傳伏藏文化協會《格澤班智達文集》，成都：四川民族出版社，2014年，第6卷，144—145頁。

[77] 'on kyang phyis su byis pa ka kha shes pa yan chad kyis hwa shang gi chos log ces mu stegs dang kla klo tsam du nor ba'i khungs byed pa zhig 'dug ste //甘孜州藏傳伏藏文化協會《格澤班智達文集》，145頁。

[78] thog mar rgya nag mkhan po'i chos de nor ba yang dag pa yin min la dpad dgos pas / chos de'i khungs bshad pa dang / de nyid skyon med par bstan pa'o //甘孜州藏傳伏藏文化協會《格澤班智達文集》，145頁。

[79] de la rgya chen spyod pa'i brgyud pa ni / rgyal tshab ma pham pa dang / thogs med sku mched /dharmārkṣita / slob dpon dga' bo / 'dul bzang ste /… zab mo lta ba'i brgyud pa ni / 'jam dbyangs / klu sgrub / zla grags / legs ldan 'byed / prajñārasmi …//甘孜州藏傳伏藏文化協會《格澤班智達文集》，146頁。

佛語傳承、實修加持傳承（nyams len byin brlabs brgyud pa）、覺空大手印（rig stong phyag rgya chen po），在藏土即名爲"心要勝義教法"（snying po don dyi bstan pa）或"心要勝義傳承"（snying po don gyi brgyud）[80]。格澤班將始于菩提達摩、包含摩訶衍在内的漢土禪宗歸入第三種傳規，并描述了達摩爲慧可等漢土弟子傳法的過程，有意思的是，格澤班指出其所傳之禪法即爲大手印[81]，通過這一描述，格澤班展示了大手印以具有象徵意義的一切行爲舉止（brda）來教授的方式并不適用于所有人，只適用于利根行人。

在談到吐蕃僧諍事件時，格澤班與無畏洲一樣，也提到了摩訶衍抖雙襟以答蓮花戒的細節，由此指出"二位阿闍梨皆住于聖者位，無可爭議"[82]。在辯論的具體問題上，格澤班就蓮花戒對摩訶衍教法中不作意、不積二資糧的批評，指出摩訶衍所提倡的不作意、不積二資糧實際上是爲了修習"無所緣"（dmigs med），對格澤班而言，在究竟證悟的境界中絕不容許有絲毫執著，在勝義層面，即便是布施等六度的修習都不應有任何所緣境[83]，人們的誤解就是將摩訶衍對無所緣修習的强調視爲對二資糧的徹底否定。至于摩訶衍所說的不作意，格澤班認爲其意趣在于令行者不執著于空性[84]：

> 以意識思惟"諸法皆空性"，遂執著于彼（空性）而修習者，不離執空之心，且具五蘊之相續，故無觸證本初法性之機會。

---

⑧⓪ sgrub rgyud don gyi brgyud pa 'dir tsung min zhes bya ste / bka'i brgyud par bsgyur du rung ba / nyams len byin rlabs brgyud pa dang / rig stong phyag rgya chen por yang bod cog pa snying po don gyi bstan par grags te //甘孜州藏傳伏藏文化協會《格澤班智達文集》，147頁。

⑧① "考慮到爲彼等開示之方式有落入油滑理論之危險，（其教授）即非如ka、kha字母之學習，遂藉表示以發問、令（弟子）作答之方式傳授大手印口訣，其義即契入（弟子）心中，思所成慧得以增勝，由是趣入觀修，此非單純之釋續理論，返觀于内後，則唯與觀修相合，此故事即與阿底峽所言相符：'非由聞知由修知。'不僅如此，一切大乘觀修所出之言說皆不逾越彼實相，以世尊處處宣說'此法超越言說與文字，非名言與推理境界'故。" de dag la chos ston tshul ni / dred po go yul du shor ba'i nyen 'byung bar dgongs te ka kha slob pa ltar gang yang mi slob ste / brda bstan pas dris pa la lan ldon pa'i tshul du phyag rgya chen po'i man ngag byin nas don la bsam du bcug / bsam byung gi shes rab brtas pa na bsgom du bcug pa sogs bshad rgyud kyi go yul tsam min par kha nang du log nas sgom pa'i don kho na la skyor bar mdzad pa'i lo rgyus'di ni / jo bo chen po'i zhal nas / thos pas mi shes bsgoms pas shes / zhes gsungs pa dang ma 'das te / bcom ldan 'das kyis / chos 'di ni tshig dang yi ge shin tu 'das pa / sgra dang rtog ge'i yul ma yin pa / dpe dang gtan tshigs kyis gtan la mi 'phebs pa / zhes rnam pa kun tu bstan pa'i phyir to //甘孜州藏傳伏藏文化協會《格澤班智達文集》，149頁。

⑧② de'i tshe bsam yas su slob dpon hwa shang dang zhal 'dzom pa na ka ma la shī las phyag shing slad du lan gsum bskor ba'i brdas khams gsum du 'khor ba'i rgyu dris pa / hwa shang chen pos ber gyi thu ba gnyis nas phyag gis bzung ste sprugs pa'i brdas gzung 'dzin gnyis yin par lan btab skad / 'di la dpyad na slob dpon gnyis ka 'phags pa'i sar bzhugs pa rtsod pa med de //甘孜州藏傳伏藏文化協會《格澤班智達文集》，152頁。

⑧③ 例如，三大悲（snying rje gsum）中就有緣有情大悲（sems can la dmigs pa'i snying rje）、緣法大悲（chos la dmigs pa'i snying rje）、無緣大悲（dmigs pa med pa'i snying rje），而無緣大悲乃究竟勝義之大悲。

⑧④ yid kyi rnam par rig pas chos thams cad stong pa nyid do snyam nas de la 'dzin pa dang bcas sgom par byed pa ni stong 'dzin gyi blo dang ma bral zhing phung po lnga'i rgyun dang ldan pas gnyug ma'i chos nyid la reg pa'i skabs med //甘孜州藏傳伏藏文化協會《格澤班智達文集》，157頁。

在此基礎上，格澤班針對宗喀巴等人批評摩訶衍唯重安住修（'jog sgom）而不作觀察修（dpyad sgom）的問題，指出在根本定（mnyam bzhag）中不應作意于觀察修，那些倡言在聖者根本定中也需要作分别觀察修的人實際上已偏離佛教傳統[85]。通過徵引薩羅哈（Saraha）的說法，他點出薩羅哈的見地實同于摩訶衍關于不作意的教法[86]，而推理尋思者（rtog ge pa）對大手印與大圓滿的誤解源于他們自身對分别（rnam rtog）的執著。最後，與無畏洲類似的是，格澤班也從史料可靠性的角度對批評者眼中的摩訶衍教法提出了質疑，他寫道[87]：

> 一般而言，雖然（爾等）都是在說"此乃和尚禪師之主張"後，就于言說上對其加以衆多增益，然而應該以所有人共許之（和尚）宗見爲本，由闡明其過失之方式加以駁斥。按《巴協》所安立之說法，彼（和尚之教法）于前弘期已被封藏，後世之人將《巴協》等所述視爲（和尚）之主張，從而將其作爲敵論而加以復述，此無非草率之舉，既然未曾親見所破之宗究竟如何，《巴協》等所述即唯成無有旁證之一偏之詞。其次，又以《巴協》爲據而說：
>
> 于彼漢土堪布宗　僅僅依其文字相
>
> 將其本名隱藏後　易爲大手印之名
>
> 此等說法亦難免妨害《巴協》本身，因爲其中已說一切漢土堪布之宗皆已封藏不現，若問"彼宗（于後弘期）從何而來？最初出自何人之手？"（爾等）實無話可說。——此乃遍知白蓮花尊者所言。況且當時之反駁者蓮花戒阿闍梨無疑爲中觀自續師，（自續）是否爲中觀之究竟尚不確定……

---

⑧⑤ chos nyid ji lta ba mngon sum tu mjal bar byed pa ni sgom byung rtog bral gyi shes rab nyid yin pas man ngag rig pa rnams kyis mnyam bzhag la dpyad sgom mi mdzad pa ni man ngag gi gnad gsang bla na med pa mkhyen pa yin la / kha cig 'phags pa'i mnyam bzhag la'ang rtog dpyod dgos par smra ba ni sangs rgyas pa'i lugs las gzhan du gyur pa ste nang pa'i grub mtha' smra ba tshad ldan thams cad kyis rnam rtog dngos gzhir dgos pa'i mnyam bzhag ma bshad pa'i phyir //甘孜州藏傳伏藏文化協會《格澤班智達文集》，158頁。

⑧⑥ sa ra has / 'di ltar dus gsum rnam pa thams cad du / yid la byar med ma bcos gnyug ma'i ngang / de nyid skyong la sgom zhes tha snyad gdags / zhes pa 'dis ni bsam gtan mkhan po'i dgongs pa la shin tu 'jug cing tshad mar byed pa'i phyir ro //甘孜州藏傳伏藏文化協會《格澤班智達文集》，159頁。

⑧⑦ spyir yang hwa shang bsam gtan mkhan po'i 'dod pa yin zer nas sgro btags mang po tshig gi lam du 'dren par byed mod kyang / de'i gzhung lugs thams cad kyi mthun snang du grub pa zhig gzhir bzhag nas skyon rig pa'i sgo nas rgol par 'os pa la / de ni bstan pa snga dar gyi skabs nas gter du sbas pa'i gtam rba bzhed du bkod pa ltar na phyis kyi smra ba po rnams yis rba bzhed sogs su de'i bzhed pa yin rgyu ba 'ga' zhig phyogs sngar bkod pa la bskyar zlos mdzad pa rnams ni gya tshom tsam las ma 'das te dgag bya'i gzhung gang yin pa dgnos su ma mthong phyin rba bzhed sogs su bkod pa de ni dpang po med pa'i thal mo ya gcig kho nar gyur pas so / de yang rba bzhed la khungs byed bzhin du / rgya nag mkhan po'i gzhung lugs kyi / yi ge tsam la brten nas kyang / de yi ming 'dogs gsang nas ni / phyag rgya chen por ming bsgyur nas / zhes pa la sogs gsungs pa 'dis ni rba bzhed nyid la'ang gnod pa bzlog dka' ste der rgya nag mkhan po'i gzhung lugs thams cad gter du sbas nas med zin par bshad na gzhung lugs de gang du byung / thog mar su'i lag tu byung zhes dris nas smra bcad dgos pa'i phyir ro / zhes thams cad mkhyen pa padma dkar pos gsungs so / skabs de nyid kyi rgol ba po ka shī dpon slob ni dbu ma rang rgyud par nges pa'i phyir / dbu ma'i mthar thug pa yang der ma nges shing //…甘孜州藏傳伏藏文化協會《格澤班智達文集》，159—160頁。

以上格澤班的質疑與反駁可以說在上引無畏洲夾注的基礎上又作了進一步的深化和拓展，他立足于史料的運用直指批評者在歷史根據上的缺陷，點明了他們對摩訶衍教法的印象通通來自《巴協》，在沒有其他文獻作爲旁證的情况下，《巴協》的說法只能是一家之言，故而不足爲信，同時，既然《巴協》說摩訶衍教法在前弘期已經遭禁而中斷，那麼後弘期的人又是如何將早已失傳的摩訶衍教法改頭換面而造出大手印呢？按當今的史學觀點來看，格澤班的質疑顯然很有說服力。

（九）不敗尊者（1846—1912）

時至19世紀，在與絨宋法賢、龍青巴齊名的寧瑪派大學者不敗尊者著作中，摩訶衍的教法仍然是熱議的對象，尊者一生中與格魯派有頗多激烈論爭，在諸多宗義與實修問題上與格魯派筆戰頻仍，他在摩訶衍教法問題上的闡述在這一背景下也同樣具有極强的針對性。在不敗尊者之前以及他同時代的格魯派上師著作中，可以看到格魯派在遮遣（dgag pa）、勝義諦以及空性觀等多方面認爲寧瑪派是在擁護摩訶衍，從而加以大力批判。他們聲稱，寧瑪派對諸法的遮遣、將勝義諦說爲非有非無或者二俱、二俱非以及對執空的批評都是在復述摩訶衍的斷見。鑒于前文所述各大寧瑪派上師沒有對摩訶衍加以直接而徹底的否定，這一點也就不足爲奇。

到不敗尊者這裏時，情况發生了變化，他本人對摩訶衍的觀點既不同于格魯派，也不同于其寧瑪派前輩，因爲他并未如格魯派一般將摩訶衍斥爲斷見者，也未如寧瑪派前輩一般在大乘佛教傳統中賦予摩訶衍較高甚至與部分寧瑪古德齊平的地位。對于摩訶衍在聞思修三者中獨重修而輕聞思、在修道上不重觀察與思擇的態度，尊者表示不贊同，他在駁斥摩訶衍時，語氣也往往十分謹慎。爲了說明他不同意完全肯定或完全否定摩訶衍，他在爲辯答格魯派上師洛桑繞賽（Blo bzang rab gsal, 1840—1910?）所寫的《略答他宗辯難・理路極明・能顯真實》（*gZhan gyis rtsod pa'i lan mdor bsdus pa rigs lam rab gsal de nyid snang byed*，下稱《能顯真實》）中說道[88]：

---

[88] de'i phyir sngon gyi rgya nag dge slong gis ci yang yid la mi byed pa'i rgyab brten du mdo sde brgyad bcu khungs su byas zhes grags pa'i gtam rgyun tsam las / mdo sde'i lung drangs pa dang / de'i don ji ltar gtan la phab pa'i yig cha gang yang deng sang mi snang bas/ de dang gzhan 'dra mi 'dra yang ji ltar shes nus te / 'dra gzhi ma nges pa'i phyir ro // gal te des rnam par mi rtog pa'i ye shes mdo dang bstan bcos chen po rnams nas ji skad gsungs pa ltar gtan la phab yod na / sbyin sogs thabs kyi cha bkag pa 'ba' zhig tu bstan pa skad du deng sang bshad pa'i rna thos gtam rgyun 'di yang mi bden par nges te/ thabs tshul rigs pa de thams cad rnam par mi rtog pa'i ye shes bskyed pa'i sgo dang / rnam par mi rtog pa'i ye shes kyis zin pas sbyin sogs thabs kyi cha dang ldan pa'i rnam kun mchog ldan gyi stong nyid rgyal ba sras dang bcas pas bgrod gcig lam ji bzhin gtan la phab yod na de la de 'dra'i lugs ngan pa 'dzin pa'i smra ba 'byung mi rigs la / kamalaś ī la sogs kyis dgag par yang mi rigs te / rgyal ba'i lam yang dag pa 'gog pa'i nang pa'i mkhas pa su yang mi srid do / gal te mdo sde khungs su drangs kyang mdo sde'i don ji bzhin ma shes par log par bshad na des rgyab brten du drangs pa tsam gyis lung de dag la da lta gtad so cha ba thams cad de'i lugs su ga la 'gyur te / des rang blo'i dri mas sangs rgyas kyi bka'i don bslad kyang / sangs rgyas kyi bka' ni bka' ma yin par mi 'gyur bas ... //局・迷旁《慧寶》（*sPyod 'jug sher 'grel ketaka*），成都：四川民族出版社，2010年，288—289頁。

> 據說昔日漢土比丘爲支撑其不作意（教法）而以八十部經爲據，然此僅爲傳說而已，今時已不見任何一部徵引此等經教并抉擇其法義之文書。因此，如何能知他宗與之相似與否？[89]若（摩訶衍）如實依經論所言而抉擇無分别智，則今時唯言其遮破布施等方便分之道聽途說必不屬實。若彼如實抉擇一切方便法與理皆爲生起無分别智之門徑，且抉擇具足無分别智所攝布施等方便分之具遍善空性（rnam kun mchog ldan gyi stong nyid）——亦即佛與菩薩所行之唯一道，則不應惡語指責其爲如是（斷見）之傳規。即使是蓮花戒等人也不應將其辯破，因任何佛教學者皆不可能破遣佛之正道。若（摩訶衍）確曾引諸經教以爲據，却未如實了知經義而作邪説，焉能僅憑彼曾引用此等經教以支撑（其説），遂將一切于此等經教中求諸依據者説爲（依循摩訶衍）之傳規？此純屬以自心之污垢染污佛語之義，而佛語亦將不成佛語……

由此可見，在沒有充分的歷史證據證明摩訶衍教法真相的情况下，不敗尊者并不願意對摩訶衍教法武斷地下定論，其次他認爲，引述的經教和摩訶衍重叠并不意味著就是在依循摩訶衍的教法，而且既然是經教，當然可以引用，否則只能説明經教本身有誤。事實上，格魯派在摩訶衍問題上對寧瑪派的抨擊主要集中于對空性的抉擇與觀修，在格魯派看來，但凡教授“一無所執”者，都屬于摩訶衍的傳統。不敗尊者認爲，這種觀點無非暴露出他們自身無視離戲論勝義、與甚深實相相悖的過失，尊者區分出兩種無所執，其一是屬于勝義，由究竟觀察生起决定，從而離諸執著；其二屬于世俗，亦即格魯派眼中的摩訶衍所主張的無所執。如果不做上述區分，則會誤將佛的不作意與摩訶衍的不作意混爲一談，而後者實爲執著于征相（mngon rtags su 'dzin pa）。尊者于其《决定寶燈》（*Nges shes rin po che'i sgron me*）第三品討論聖者于根本定（mnyam bzhag）中是否需執境相時，簡明扼要地對這兩種無所執作出了定義[90]：

> 護持見地正行時　有説一切皆不執
> 一無所執之義理　分爲善證與邪證
> 一爲離四邊戲論　聖者見其無所住
> 故諸境執自然消　如望光明虚空際
> 二爲無念和尚宗　無觀察但置心空
> 既無勝觀諸明相　如深海石住平庸
> 譬如同説無所有　中觀實見其爲無

[89] 言下之意即：汝宗如何得知我宗與摩訶衍教法相似？

[90] lta ba'i dngos gzhi skyong ba'i dus / kha cig cir yang mi 'dzin zer / cir yang mi 'dzin zhes pa'i don / legs par rtogs dang log rtogs gnyis / dang po mtha' bzhi'i spros bral te / 'phags pa'i ye shes kyi mdun na / gang yang gnas na med mthong bas / 'dzin stangs ngang gis zhig pa ste / stong gsal mkha' la lta dang mtshungs / gnyis pa dran med ha shang lugs / ma dpyad tse ner bzhag pa yis / lhag mthong gsal ba'i cha med par / mtsho gting rdo bzhin tha mal gnas / dper na ci yang med ces pa / dbu mas med par mthong ba dang / gzugs med med par mos pa ltar / tshig tsam mtshung pa 'di dag kyang / don la mi mtshungs gnam sa bzhin //《不敗尊者全集》（*Mi pham bka' 'bum*），成都：雪域經典古籍搶救協會，2007年，卷17，512—513葉。

彼則唯信無形色　語同義理殊天地

此中即說明，第一種無所執實爲依中觀之如理觀察而現見、决定無所有，第二種只是信受無形色便自認爲證空。尊者在《中觀莊嚴論釋·文殊上師歡喜教言》（*dBu ma rgyan gyi rnam bshad 'jam dbyangs bla ma dgyes pa'i zhal lung*）[91]中，將兩種無所執比作都在聲稱自己沒有偷竊的賊人與無罪者，儘管二者都以同樣的方式否認偷竊，但在內容上却迥异，其中一方所說爲真，另一方爲說謊。和尚的無所執是不見任何所執境、繼而無如理之觀察、無所决定，由此引生的無所執實際上只是作意于無念來强行壓制心識活動，這種作意于無所執的狀態實際上連有邊都未能離，更不用說離四邊[92]。對如理觀察的强調實際上是貫穿不敗尊者著作的一個重點，他認爲由觀察思擇而生决定是顯、密（包括大圓滿在內）一切修道的關鍵，在《决定寶燈》中，他指出，即便是大圓滿的本淨立斷修習都離不開中觀應成見[93]：

欲通本來清淨義　則需窮盡應成見
從離戲論方面言　二者說爲無差別

不敗尊者認爲，摩訶衍的無所執并未超越“想”（'du shes）的範疇，以其具相執（mtshan mar 'dzin pa），故而仍落于作意與分別，這種表面上的無分別修習實際上最多只能算寂止。由于缺失勝觀境界中的明分（gsal cha），這種修習易落入昏昧而一無所知的境界，鑒于這種歧路（gol sa）對大圓滿修習能造成重大妨礙，故而尊者另造有專論《具證長老直指心性教授·除暗明燈》（*rTogs ldan rgan po rnams kyi lugs sems ngo mdzub tshugs kyi gdams pa mun sel sgron me*）[94]加以鄭重說明，其中指出，同樣名爲無分別，明空雙運的澄明通透境界與一無所知的無記狀態實具天壤之別，前者爲本覺，後者則爲無明，由此，尊者也同無畏洲一樣，將此中的要點歸結爲大圓滿口訣部對本覺與無明、阿賴耶與法身、識與智等等的辨別[95]。格魯派認爲，摩訶衍的這種修習落于斷見，以其否定了有、無、是、非等，同時也否定了相應的觀修，尊者則持相反意

---

[91] 英譯見Padmakara Translation Group, *The Adornment of the Middle Way: Shantarakshita's Madhyamakalankara with Commentary by Jamgon Mipham*, Boston & London: Shambhala Publications, 2005。

[92] ha shang la sogs pa ni dngos zhen thams cad khegs nas dmigs gtad kyi mtshan ma ci yang ma mthong nas yid la mi byed pa min gyi / sems la 'gyu 'phro thams cad bkag pa tsam la mtha' thams cad sel ba lta ci / yod mtha' yang sel ba'i rgyu mtshan med la / rnam par mi rtog pa ni de lta bu ma yin te /…de ltar mnyam bzhag gi spyod yul du gyur pa'i gnas lugs mthar thug gi dbang du na / mtha' bzhi'i dmigs gtad med cing sgra rtog gi yul min pas khas kyang mi len pa yin gyi / dmigs gtad yod bzhin du khas mi len pa ni g.yo sgyu'i lta ba yin te / de gnyis khas mi len pa tsam 'dra yang / don la bden rdzun gyi khyad yod de / rkun po yin pa zhig gis brkus par khas ma blangs pa ltar yin no // 局·迷旁，《中觀莊嚴論詳解》，成都：四川民族出版社，2009年，88—90頁。

[93] ka dag gdar sha chod pa la / thal 'gyur lta ba mthar phyin dgos / spros bral tsam gyi cha nas ni / de gnyis khyad par med do gsung //《不敗尊者全集》（*Mi pham bka' 'bum*），卷17，518葉。

[94] 見《不敗尊者全集》，卷32，363—368葉。

[95] 有關該論的翻譯與討論見楊杰《寧瑪派說阿賴耶》，收沈衛榮主編《大喜樂與大圓滿：慶祝談錫永先生八十華誕漢藏佛學研究論集》，北京：中國藏學出版社，2014年，43—44、49—51頁。

見，他認爲，如果真如格魯派所言，那麼摩訶衍反倒遠離了諸戲論邊，如果確實如此，摩訶衍理應已證無分别智，且已洞見實相。針對這一問題，尊者于《能顯真實》中補充道[96]：

如今，但凡有（主張）心一無所執者，即説之爲和尚宗，且爲斷見，此外，將和尚對“一無所執”想之執著視爲未超越執著，故而未達無分别智之一分，遂將其説爲斷見，此實無意義。斷見者，無疑乃謗拔因果等義之見地，如何能將一無所執視爲斷見？因此，説和尚宗爲斷見者，非從見地方面説，而是依據彼除無所執外，主張不需布施等一切道相，從而安立爲斷見。然而，當今説無所執爲斷見者本身不能辨識斷見，又如何能了知（某宗）是否屬于斷見？

實際上，對不敗尊者本人而言，要批評他所認爲的錯見，完全無需使用摩訶衍這一符號。但對格魯派而言，摩訶衍却是具有十足斷見意味的符號，他們常常借助這一符號來抨擊寧瑪派的見修。鑒于不敗尊者所處的19世紀正是不分派運動（ris med）興盛之時，各大宗派與格魯派交鋒不斷，從未退去熱度的摩訶衍此時更是在宗見交流過程中高頻出現，因此，作爲對格魯派的回應，不敗尊者不得不圍繞這一符號來給出他自己的詮釋與判斷，并借此爲自宗作辯護。與無畏洲等前輩相似，他通過指出主流印象中的摩訶衍教法與大圓滿在諸多關鍵問題上名同實异，實質差别甚大，從而澄清、維護大圓滿，而不是像格魯等余宗上師一樣，將摩訶衍教法與大圓滿劃等號，從而加以批判。尊者顯然熟知龍青巴和無畏洲等人對摩訶衍所持的積極態度，因此他理應意識到了他個人的闡釋與前輩的相异之處，然而到尊者的時代，作爲教法符號的摩訶衍早已與作爲歷史人物的摩訶衍相剥離，從無畏洲對論敵所描述的摩訶衍與真實的摩訶衍所作的區分，可知而這種剥離在無畏洲時代已經被意識到。正如Karma Phuntsho所言，我們很難確定不敗尊者是否相信他所討論的摩訶衍與真實的摩訶衍一致，[97]因爲他對摩訶衍教法的描述與評定實質上是作爲輔助性的工具來服務于他對自身學説體系的構建以及對論敵的回應，他筆下的摩訶衍使得他在抨擊摩訶衍相關錯誤的同時，又對其所主張的離四邊境界保留出肯定的餘地，這種既异于寧瑪自宗前輩又异于余宗的處理方式同時讓自宗與余宗行人都不得不重新思考摩訶衍教法與大圓滿各自的特徵與彼此間的差异，而這也不失爲一種謹慎而微妙的策略，因爲這能够在摩訶衍教法問題上，讓寧瑪派在一定程度上與格魯派的主流觀點靠攏，從而部分地消解自宗由力挺摩訶衍而與格魯派形成的針鋒相對的緊張關

---

[96] deng sang ni blos cir yang ma bzung phan chod ha shang gi lugs yin par byas nas de la chad lta'o zhes zer yang / ha shang gis cir yang 'dzin par mi bya'o snyam du 'dzin pa de 'dzin pa las ma 'das pas rnam par mi rtog pa'i ye shes kyi phyogs su ma phyin kyang chad lta zhes brjod pa don med de / chad lta ni rgyu 'bras sogs yod pa'i don la skur 'debs kyi 'dzin stangs can du nges la / cir yang ma bzung ba la ci zhig chad par lta / de'i phyir ha shang gi lugs de la chad lta zhes brjod pa ni / lta ba'i thad nas brjod pa ma yin te / ci yang mi 'dzin pa de las gzhan sbyin sogs lam gyi rnam pa kun mi dgos par 'dod pa de'i cha nas chad ltar btags pa yin kyang deng sang 'dzin med la chad ltar brjod pa de dag gis ni chad lta kho rang yang ngos zin mi snang na / chad lta yin min ga la shes //《慧寶》，345頁。

[97] Karma Phuntsho, *Mipham's Dialectics and the Debates on Emptiness*, London and New York, RoutledgeCurzon, 2005, p. 198.

係，在此基礎上來細緻剖析大圓滿與摩訶衍教法的异同，以令論敵更容易接受其對大圓滿的澄清與維護。

四

上文的梳理已爲我們大致呈現了摩訶衍及其教法的形象在寧瑪派傳統的歷史軸綫上所經歷的形成與演變過程[98]，從中我們可以看出，對摩訶衍教法的種種評述實際上都是時代的産物，這些評述或褒或貶，但都無一例外地被打上了當時的歷史與宗教背景的烙印，仔細審視這些特定的背景有助于我們理解相關叙事傳統形成的原因，以及對摩訶衍教法的種種態度背後的影響因素。在努佛智的時代，藏土上師尚能接觸到豐富的藏譯禪宗文獻，而關于吐蕃僧諍的叙事傳統也未形成，努佛智本人無需與論敵辯諍，所以在他的判教作品《禪定目炬》中能够給予摩訶衍的頓門教法足够細緻的解讀和相當正面的評價。在努佛智之後，我們見到了歷經修改的《巴協》，不同版本的《巴協》中吐蕃僧諍叙事的流變見證了摩訶衍教法的負面化過程，最終《巴協》完成了吐蕃僧諍叙事傳統的

---

⑱ 對摩訶衍教法加以論述的寧瑪派上師實不限與上文所列，與近現代，仍有不少著名寧瑪派上師在相關著作中以專章討論摩訶衍的教法，限于篇幅，此處不再詳細列舉論述，其中具有代表性者即敦珠仁波切（bDud ’joms ’Jigs bral ye shes rdo rje, 1904—1987）和義成活佛（sPrul sku Don grub, 1939—），前者的討論見與其所著《寧瑪派教法史》（全名《依舊譯派——雪域一切佛法來源而開顯：金剛乘寶貴教法史·帝釋天遍勝大戰鼓雷音》（*Gangs ljongs rgyal bstan yongs rdzogs kyi phyi mo snga ’gyur rdo rje theg pa'i bstan pa rin po che ji ltar byung ba'i tshul dag cing gsal bar brjod pa lha dbang g.yul las rgyal ba'i rnga bo che'i sgra dbyangs*），收*bDud ’joms ’jigs bral ye shes rdo rje'i gsung ’bum dam chos rin chen nor bu'i bang mdzod*, Kalimpong, Dupjung Lama, 1979-1985, Vol. 1, ff. 1-845）第七品“大圓滿見”部分，其中指出：“大圓滿本性，乃一離所作之宗輪；當對不住于因緣和合界中之本智，爲其究竟了義作直指教授時，解說云：毋須有待于黑白因果上精進之有爲法。有等藏人詫而斥之，認爲此即隨順摩訶衍’斷行’之說。”（依許錫恩譯《勝利天鼓雷音·金剛乘教法史》，台北：全佛文化，2017年，606頁。）敦珠仁波切并未質疑論敵對摩訶衍教法的定性，而是遙承龍青巴之觀點，認爲大圓滿所證乃諸法實相，其基道果皆不落于分別、取捨與希疑，故而安住于三解脫門，在此基礎上，敦珠仁波切廣引顯經密續證明大圓滿所示超越黑白因果之實相不違經教。敦珠仁波切此書藏文原著撰寫于1962年，其時《禪定目炬》尚未出版面世（其出版日期爲1974年），書中未見引用《禪定目炬》。而義成活佛與其*Buddha Mind: An Anthology of Longchen Rabjam's Writings on Dzogpa Chenpo*（Ithaca, Snow Lion Publications, 1989，後來于2002年再版時更名爲*The Practice of Dzogchen*）一書中專論大圓滿與和尚摩訶衍時，則認真參考了《禪定目炬》提供了相關信息，高度强調了該論的重要性，并據之而對《巴協》《賢者喜宴》《布頓教法史》等傳統史書中的記載表示懷疑，其中提到：“閱畢所引（《禪定目炬》）上文後，當能管窺摩訶衍之見地一二，及其是否與禪宗或大圓滿相似。若和尚摩訶衍之教授住于無所思維，此即非大乘或大圓滿之經典所教授。若彼謂與體證法性究竟義後，應無念而住，因任何念頭皆能障蔽行者住與證境故，如此則與大圓滿教授無忤。然而此法只與體證此等成就之行人應機，而非對吾等只具凡夫心識、生活、見地及情緒之人而說。大乘確有說頓悟者，尤以密乘與大圓滿爲著。然此乃對心成熟、根器已利、善業已積之人而說，蓋其于今生或宿世，已曾修學故也。”（依許錫恩譯《九乘次第論集》，臺北：全佛文化，2008年，183頁）義成活佛此說與無畏洲的觀點明顯有一脉相承的意味。舉上來二例，可一窺寧瑪派近人對摩訶衍教法及其與大圓滿關係所持的態度，也可知寧瑪派對摩訶衍問題的關注度直至近現代依然不减。

構建，并奠定了對摩訶衍教法的批判基調。這一過程時值新譯密咒的興起，由新譯密咒上師倡導的“印度至上”話語模式對藏傳佛教中非印度元素的排斥與清算對上述叙事産生了直接的影響，代表漢土佛法的摩訶衍在這一語境下被貼上异端的標簽。由于後弘期的上師無法接觸到前弘期的藏譯禪宗文本，他們對摩訶衍教法的印象幾乎都來源于《巴協》，《娘氏教法源流》等教法史中對吐蕃僧諍的記載以及薩班等上師的相關論述實際上都是照搬《巴協》。不過，《娘氏教法源流》與其他同類作品的不同之處在于首先肯定了摩訶衍教法的正當性，而後才指出它由于不適用于作爲鈍根的普羅大衆而遭禁，這也爲後世寧瑪派上師基于根器的劃分而回護摩訶衍教法打下了伏筆。在薩班的時代，强調不作意、離分别的大手印、大圓滿修習盛行于藏土，由于這些修習在薩班眼中與正統的密咒乘修習有種種相悖，而與傳統所載的摩訶衍禪法有頗多相似之處，故而薩班視之爲受摩訶衍禪法影響的錯誤修習，由是加以猛烈批判，這種批判對後世造成了深遠的影響，其後的寧瑪派上師開始針對這種强有力的宗教話語，在澄清大圓滿與摩訶衍禪法的异同、維護大圓滿教法的地位方面付出了長期而艱巨的努力。同樣具有强大話語權的宗喀巴對摩訶衍也持全面否定的態度，他本人對僧團建設和戒律極爲重視，不重六度修學以及積集資糧等道上方便的摩訶衍教法自然與之相悖，故而淪爲宗喀巴筆下的斷見而遭到批評。寧瑪派在摩訶衍教法問題上對新譯密咒上師作出回應時，其總體態度傾向于積極肯定，而非簡單粗暴地將摩訶衍推向自身的對立面以便與之劃清界限。具體而言，龍青巴認爲摩訶衍教法在超越善惡因果方面與大圓滿法高度一致，二者在揭示究竟實相方面均無過失；壽自在寶主要承繼《禪定目炬》的理路成立摩訶衍教法爲正道并賦予其合理的判教地位；到無畏洲的時代，格魯派的主導地位日趨穩固，因此無畏洲及其後的寧瑪派上師無法回避格魯派在摩訶衍教法問題上對寧瑪派所作的抨擊，他們的回應顯示出極强的針對性。從無畏洲開始，到後來的格澤班智達與不敗尊者，我們看到了寧瑪派對吐蕃僧諍叙事傳統日益明朗化的質疑，其意旨即在于從教理上廓清大圓滿與摩訶衍教法的同時，從歷史的角度動搖以《巴協》所載爲唯一依據而將大圓滿等同于摩訶衍教法的合理性。不敗尊者與上述上師相比甚爲不同，他對摩訶衍的部分肯定承繼了寧瑪前輩的觀點，對摩訶衍的駁斥則在一定程度上循從了格魯派的理路。在以格魯派爲代表的經院式教學盛行、格魯派宗見占據主導地位的時代背景下，不敗尊者受其上師之托，力圖强化寧瑪派自身的寺院教育，爲寧瑪派學人提供顯密經教釋讀的注疏範本，并且系統而旗幟鮮明地構建起寧瑪派自宗的見地系統，以便與格魯派的宗教霸權相抗衡，在此過程中，他時刻面臨格魯派針鋒相對的挑戰，因此其著作針對的受衆往往同時包括自宗和格魯派學人，在此前提下，他力求在摩訶衍問題上尋求寧瑪派與格魯派之間的平衡點，亦即在批判的同時保留肯定的餘地，以使其所定義的摩訶衍形象能同時爲寧瑪與格魯二宗認可，從而令二宗行人都能重新審視大圓滿與摩訶衍教法的關係，并接受他本人的分析與評判。

如上所言，在不同的時代背景下，不同的上師所討論的摩訶衍承載的宗教内涵各各相异，整個藏土其實并不存在一個統一的摩訶衍形象，在辯護與批判的交叠聲中，歷史上真實的摩訶衍及其教法早已變得模糊黯淡，甚至面目全非。每一位上師在討論摩訶衍時，都是在《巴協》叙事傳統的基礎上根據其本人的需要而給予不同程度的重新定義，摩訶衍最終成爲教法辯諍的工具，那些批判摩訶衍的人無非只是在借用甚至改造這一工具來批判他們所認爲的錯誤修習，以宗教指導爲首要目標的他們無意于肩負歷史學家的責任而去追問摩訶衍其人其法究竟如何。然而從無畏洲開始，寧瑪派上師愈發意識到論敵所認爲的摩訶衍教法和歷史上真實的摩訶衍教法之間的區隔，在沒有充分的史料可資稽考的情况下，他們無法還原摩訶衍教法的真相，不過對他們而言，真相已然不重要，重要的是如何澄清論敵定義的摩訶衍教法與自宗教法的關係并闡明二者的不同，從而回護自宗。簡而言之，藏土上師對摩訶衍無論是批判還是辯護，其根本目的無非屬于破遣他宗、回護自宗的範疇，而不是針對摩訶衍本身，儘管每個教派都在討論摩訶衍，實際上却沒有哪家的說法能有助于我們了解歷史上真實的摩訶衍及其教法，但從另一方面而言，梳理與比較各宗對摩訶衍的討論并非沒有意義，因爲這些討論本身就是藏傳佛教史上每一個時代的縮影，它們見證了藏傳佛教各宗派交流互動的生動歷史，其間激蕩出的細緻精微的思辨火花爲我們提供了深度了解各宗派見修細節以及各時期政教背景的窗口，就本文選擇的寧瑪派的相關討論而言，我們清楚地看到了寧瑪派上師對以摩訶衍教法爲代表的漢傳佛法的解讀與詮釋，以及他們在摩訶衍問題上爲回應新譯密咒上師而付出的長久努力，這些的回應也爲我們正確而深刻地理解大圓滿中諸多重要的名相、理念及具體修習提供了極大的幫助。

Hwa-shang’s Teachings in Tibet: In the Case of rNying-ma School’s Interpretations, Defenses and Criticisms of Hwa-shang Mahāyāna and His Teachings

Yang Jie

Through the use of both Tibetan and Chinese historical materials, scholars have made significant contributions to the reconstruction of the great debate of bSam-yas which had always been one of the hottest topics of Tibetan studies. In spite of the fact that the historical narrative related to this debate has been strongly proved to be essentially a tradition invented by Tibetans, the attention paid to later Tibetans’ understandings and interpretations of Hwashang Mahāyāna’s teachings was still far from enough. Taking the rNying ma school as an example, this article comprehensively demonstrated the development of its interpretation of Hwashang’s teachings with an examination of related works of some important masters from this school. Based upon the comparison of the interpretations within rNying ma school itself and other schools, the author analyzed the historical and religious factors influencing those interpretations.

“他空見”詮釋的出發點

——論朵波巴・攝囉監燦班藏布之二諦見

石　美

二諦（bden gnyis, satya-dvaya）思想是佛教，尤其是大乘學說中關於認識真理的一個重要理論，二諦分爲世俗諦（kun rdzob bden pa，saṃvṛti-satya）和勝義諦（don dam bden pa，paramārtha-satya，又稱第一義諦），通常指兩種真實或實在的道理。隨著印度佛教分別於漢藏兩地傳入，其中的二諦思想也在兩地得以重視和發展。如在藏傳佛教發展過程中，諸多學人都對二諦思想有所論及，但不同派別的宗義體系，卻對二諦見有不同認識。這種不同雖然早在印度佛教的不同派別中就已存在，但更多的確是部分西藏學人根據自己的學說體系和宗義需要對二諦思想進行的不同詮說。

朵波巴・攝囉監燦班藏布（Dol po pa Shes rab rgyal mtshan dpal bzang po，1292—1361，以下簡稱朵波巴）爲藏傳佛教覺囊派的重要人物，爲覺囊派他空見思想的實際開創者，其於《山法了義海》（*Ri chos nges don rgya mtsho*）中所闡釋之“他空見”，開覺囊派他空教法之先河，引起自14世紀起直至今日藏傳佛教内部“他空”與“自空”的諸多論爭。其“他空見”詮釋的基礎，則是建立在他獨特的二諦理論基礎上，爲闡明自己的二諦觀點，他撰寫《二諦顯明日光》（*bDen gnyis gsal ba'i nyi ma*）[①]一文，系統論述了自己的二諦見，本文即主要圍繞該文，就朵波巴二諦見的相關問題進行探討。

一、四部宗二諦見概說

在瞭解朵波巴二諦思想之前，我們首先就傳統意義上所劃分的四部宗的二諦思想進行簡要論說。

關於二諦思想的起源問題，其於大乘佛教興起之前的小乘佛教及部派佛教中就早有涉及。如《大毗婆沙論》（*Abhidharma Mahāvibhāṣā Śāstra*）第七十七有云：“尊者世友作如是說，能顯名是世俗，所顯法是勝義。復作是說，隨順世間所說名是世俗，隨順賢聖所說名是勝義。大德說曰，宣說有情瓶衣等事，不虛妄心所起言說是世俗諦。宣說緣性緣起等理，不虛妄心所起言說是勝義諦。尊者達羅達多說曰，名自性是世俗，此是

---

① 收錄於《壤塘版袞欽朵波巴全集》第六函，壤塘印經院，697—728頁。

苦集諦少分。義自性是勝義，此是苦集諦少分。”②

儘管在早期佛教中與二諦理論比較接近的一些名詞和概念已經出現，但其義理與大乘佛教所討論的二諦理論有明顯不同，即使在後來所逐步形成的說一切有部（Sarvāstivāda）、經量部（Sautrāntika）、唯識宗（Vijñānavāda）、中觀宗（Madhyamaka）的宗派義理中，其相應的二諦思想的內涵也各不相同。

說一切有部，又稱毗婆沙部（Vaibhāṣika），該宗之二諦觀如《阿毗達磨俱舍論·分別顯聖品》第六之一（*Abhidharmakośa*）所云：“諦有二種，一世俗諦，二勝義諦。其相云何。頌曰：彼覺破便無，慧析余亦爾，如瓶水世俗，異此名勝義。”③說一切有部許一切法三世實有，其二諦見亦承彼實有宗見而立，認爲經不起思維理智分析的爲世俗諦，如瓶，經分析後“瓶”的概念即受破壞，其存在即僅爲世俗諦上的有，經得起思維理智分析的爲勝義諦，如無分方的極微、無刹那的心識、無爲的虛空等，無論如何分析，其概念亦不受破壞，其存在即爲勝義諦上的有。世俗諦定義下的有雖真實的存在，但並非實體有，可稱爲“假有”（prajñapi），而勝義諦定義下的有則爲實體有。

經量部，又分隨教行經部宗（Lung gi rjes ’brang gi mdo sde pa）及隨理行經部宗（Rigs pa’i rjes ’brang gi mdo sde pa）④。二諦理論於經部宗而言，不僅是一種認識理論，而且是一種將外境加以分別的方式⑤。經部宗認爲心能了別者即外境，而外境無非世俗和勝義，共相和自相。在二諦的定義上，經部宗與毗婆沙宗完全相反，經部宗認爲依賴名言概念施設才能夠成立的事情，是世俗諦，如無爲法等。不需要依賴名言概念即存在的事情，是勝義諦，如瓶等。其許共相爲世俗諦，因彼共相由名言概念提煉而來，一落名言，即有分別，則非勝義。許自相爲勝義諦，因有自相，即無需設施的名言概念即能成立，爲勝義真實。

唯識宗許三界唯心，唯識無境，許一切法依遍計（parikalpita）、依他（paratantra）、圓成（pariniṣpanna）三自性而安立。儘管其二諦理論並沒有像在中觀宗中那麼重要，但唯識宗亦依照自己的學說框架成立了自己的二諦學說。簡要言之，唯識宗認爲我們有兩種思擇觀察方式，一爲名言，一爲勝義，如對瓶進行思維觀察即是名言，對瓶的空性的觀察即是勝義，因而，他們認爲觀察思擇名言建立之境爲世俗諦，觀察思擇勝義建立之境即爲勝義諦。此外，其將三自性與二諦相攝，認爲依他起爲世俗諦中的真實，遍計執於世俗諦中亦非真實，在勝義諦的層面，唯圓成實爲真實。

依格魯派宗義，中觀宗又可分爲中觀自續派（Svātantrika）與中觀應成派（Prāsaṅ-

② 玄奘譯，大正藏［毗曇部］NO1545。關於二諦理論來源的相關介紹可參考姚衛群《印度幾部重要佛典中的“二諦”觀念》，《佛學研究》2012年第1期，98—105頁。

③ 玄奘譯，大正藏，［毗曇部］NO1558。

④ 關於兩類經部宗的特徵、異同等相關知識可參閱日慧法師著《佛教四大部派宗義講釋》（上），北京：宗教文化出版社，2004年。亦可參閱廖本聖《蔣央協巴〈宗義理論〉藏本譯注毗婆沙宗與經部宗》，《正觀》第六十期，2012年；陳法菱《論述［隨理行經部宗］的宗義主張》，《大專學生佛學論文集》，2012年，台北。

⑤ 關於經量部對於外境的六種分類方式，可參閱敦珠法王等著，談錫永、沈衛榮、邵頌雄、許錫恩譯著《寧瑪派四部宗義釋》，北京：中國藏學出版社，2012年，68—69頁。

gika），該系統承襲龍樹《中論》之緣起中道思想，內部建立了一系列龐大的二諦認識理論，如世俗諦又可分正世俗、倒世俗，勝義諦又分名言勝義、離異門勝義諦等。但概括說來，兩派之二諦理論皆認爲，名言概念皆屬世俗諦，於勝義諦中，無微塵法有自性。兩派之不同之處在於，自續派認爲一切法雖無自性，但在世俗諦的名言範圍內，承認諸法以自相而存在，而應成派則認爲即使在名言範圍內，亦不許諸法有相，僅存"妙有"之功用。

以上是對於傳統意義上所謂四部宗的二諦思想的簡要概述，目的在於在我們分析朵波巴二諦思想之前，能夠對以上幾種較爲普遍的二諦思想有一個總體的認識，若要詳加闡述，則非只言片語可以明析，因爲這一部分並非本文主要研究對象，所以不再贅述。

二、朵波巴的二諦見

作爲14世紀時期西藏著名的佛教人物，朵波巴重新思考整理了整個佛學義理框架，並創造性的提出了"他空"思想，而其詮釋他空見地的出發點便是其獨樹一幟的二諦理論。

《二諦顯明日光》乃朵波巴爲專門闡述其二諦思想而作，全文分四個部分展開論述，本文即主要依據最體現其二諦觀點的第一、二部分概括總結其主要見地。

1. 了知二諦分別之功德以及不了知之過失

朵波巴引用智藏（Jñānagarbha，Ye shes snying po，8世纪人）之《二諦分別論頌》（*bDen pa gnyis rnam par 'byed pa'i tshig le'ur byas pa*）⑥中的一頌："能了二諦義，於法不昏昧，彼從積資糧，圓滿得解脫"⑦，以此來說明二諦對於通達佛法的重要性以及正確了知二諦能夠獲得的功德。相反，若不能就二諦有正確的認知，則定生過失，其引用龍樹《中論》（*rTsa shes*）中的一頌說明未了二諦之過失，"若人不能知，分別於二諦。則於甚深法，不知真實義"⑧。

2. 抉擇二諦之自性

朵波巴分四點加以論述二諦之自性，分別爲：性相（mtshan nyid）⑨、名相

---

⑥ 關於智藏《二諦分別論》目前尚沒有漢譯本，英譯本及相關研究可參考Malcolm David Eckel, *Jñānagarbha on the Two Truths*, New York: State University of New York, 1987 (First Indian Edition: Delhi, 1992)。

⑦ 《壤塘版袞欽朵波巴全集》第六函，696頁：*bden gnyis rnam dbye shes pa dag/thub pa'i bka' la mi rmongs te/de dag ma lus tshogs bsags nas/phun tshogs pha rol 'gro ba nyid/*。

⑧ 此處依《中論》鳩摩羅什譯本翻譯，大正藏，［中觀部］No.1564。

⑨ 可理解爲事物之性質，如能托屋梁是柱的性相。

（mtshon bya）[10]、異門（rnam grangs）[11]、事相（mtshan gzhi）[12]。其中，尤其詳細的論述了性相分。

性相分上，朵波巴首先給出了二諦定義。他明確指出："識之境，本質而言真實自性爲空，即世俗諦之性相；聖智之境，本質而言真實自性不空，即爲勝義諦之性相"[13]。並再次引用並闡釋智藏《二諦分別論》裡的一頌，認爲識境的顯現爲世俗，智境的顯現爲勝義。世俗非真實爲自空，是識上之顯現而非智上之顯現。勝義真實非自空而爲他空，是智上之顯現而絕非識上之顯現。其又引寂護《中觀莊嚴論注》（*dBu ma mdo sde rgyan rtsa 'grel*）、月稱《入中論》（*dBu ma 'jug pa*）等論著來說明勝義諦實相清淨、無二、無戲論。其亦將三自性理論引入自己的二諦見，認爲遍計依他自性非有，圓成則自性非無。

在對二諦作出清晰定義後，朵波巴認爲要通達此二諦之真實義，則要斷除五種關於二諦的錯誤認識。

第一要斷除勝義自空見。朵波巴在論述上採用了佛教論典中經常使用的一問一答的形式。若問："如勝義非自空，那麼《入楞伽經》中所云：世俗中一切皆有，勝義中非有故，於同一事物，有無不成相違，因而說一切所知爲有是世俗上的有，說無則是勝義上的無，這難道不對嗎？"[14]於此疑問，朵波巴認爲此處經典實爲針對世俗所攝諸法之開示，因其安立一事物，事物即有爲，有爲即世俗。之後，他又引用多種經論如龍樹之《中論》、《法界贊》（*Chos dbyings bstod pa*）、《菩提心釋》（*Byang chub sems 'grel*）、《修習次第》（*sGom rim*），彌勒之《辨中邊論本頌》（*dBus mthar*）、《經莊嚴論》（*mDo sde rgyan*）、《寶性論》（*rGyud bla ma*，又稱《無上續論》）以及《大空經》（*sTong ba nyid chen po'i mdo*）、《大涅槃經》（*Myang 'das chen po*）等來論證勝義不空。如《菩提心釋》云：善念與惡念，斷續之性相，諸佛說空相，除此不許空[15]。《大涅槃經》亦云："涅槃爲不空之空，除彼之外爲空之空。"[16]如是，朵波巴廣引經論，論證煩惱世俗爲自空，法界勝義爲他空。

---

⑩ 名言三法所行之對境，如云所知、實事和瓶皆是名相。

⑪ 品類、差別、門類、異名，指事物的不同名稱。

⑫ 性相所表名相事例，如云金瓶，即是瓶之事相。

⑬ 《壤塘版袞欽朵波巴全集》第六函，697頁：*rnam shes kyi yul gang zhig/gshis la rang gi ngo bo bden pas stong pa ni/kun rdzob bden pa'i mtshan nyid dang/'phags pa'i ye shes dam pa'i yul gang zhig/gshis la rang gi ngo bo bden pas mi stong pa ni/don dam bden pa'i mtshan nyid de/*。

⑭ 《壤塘版袞欽朵波巴全集》第六函，699頁：*gal te don dam rang gis mi stong na/lang gshegs su/kun rdzob tu ni thams cad yod/dam pa'i don du yod ma yin/de phyir dngos po gcig nyid la/yod dang med pa ji ltar 'gal/zhes shes bya thams cad yod par bshad tshul kun rdzob tu yod pa dang/med par bshad tshul don dam du med par gsungs so zhe na ma yin te/*。

⑮ 《壤塘版袞欽朵波巴全集》第六函，700頁：*dge dang mi dge'i rnam rtog ni/rgyun chad pa yi mtshan nyid can/sangs rgyas rnams kyis stong nyid gsung/gzhan ni stong par mi bzhed do/*。该引文出自龙树《菩提心释》第五十颂。

⑯ 《壤塘版袞欽朵波巴全集》第六函，701頁：*myang ngan las 'das pa ni mi stong pa'i stong pa nyid do/de las gzhan ni stong pa'i stong pa nyid do/*。

第二要斷除勝義無對境之見。朵波巴引《寶性論》云："佛性佛菩提，佛法及佛業，諸出世淨人，所不能思議，此諸佛境界。"⑰又引《辨中邊論》云："略說空異門，謂真如實際，無相勝義性，法界應當知。由無變無倒，相滅聖智境，及諸聖法因，異門義如次。"⑱意在說明勝義諦爲聖者聖智之行境，而非無有對境。他指出，心識（blo）、覺（rig pa）、心（sems）、識（shes pa）等皆於二諦中以兩種方式而存在，世俗之心等爲識，勝義之心等爲智，因此勝義雖非世俗心之對境，但卻是勝義心之對境。之後，其引《法界贊》云："此如深深地下水，未經沾染純然淨，故煩惱中本覺智，離諸假障而圓滿"⑲，以此來闡發勝義智境本來清淨，但爲客塵遮障之理。

第三要斷除世俗爲智境之見。在這一點上，朵波巴又從五個角度進行了駁斥，即從導師佛語，慈氏之教理，無著兄弟之教理，龍樹父子之教理，寂天之教理五個方面，分別引述相應之經典展開破斥。

於導師佛語而言，《華嚴經》（*Phal chen*）云："如是正觀法，悉皆如虛空"⑳。《般若攝論》（*sDud pa*）云："色及受等不可見，想無所見心不見，識及心意不可見，此名見法如來說，有情言說見虛空，虛空豈見觀此義"㉑。《瑜伽師地論·菩薩地真實義品》（*Byang sar don gyi sde tshan gyi mdo*）云："世間諸世俗，牟尼皆不著，無著孰能取，見聞而不愛。"㉒以上所引經文大致是說，佛爲究竟之勝觀，於此勝觀上並沒有世俗三界之顯現，而對於世俗之一切，佛智無有絲毫執與取。通過上述論說，朵波巴認爲佛陀密意在於開示世俗三界並非勝義智境。

於慈氏之教理而言，朵波巴援引《辯法法性論》（*Chos nyid rnam 'byed*）、《經

---

⑰ 《壤塘版袞欽朵波巴全集》第六函，701頁：*sang rgyas khams dang sang rgyas byang chub dang/sang rgyas chos dang sang rgyas 'phrin las te/dag pa'i sems can gyis kyang bsam bya min/'di ni 'dren pa rnams kyi spyod yul yin/*。此處漢譯依《寶性論》勒那摩提譯本翻譯（大正藏，No1611）。

⑱ 《壤塘版袞欽朵波巴全集》第六函，701—702頁：*stong ba nyid ni mdor bsdus na/de bzhin nyid dang yang dag mtha'/mtshan ma med dang don dam dang/chos kyi dbyings ni rnam grangs so/gzhan min phyin ci log ma yin /de 'gags 'phags pa'i spyod yul dang/'phags pa'i chos kyi rgyu yi phyir/rnam grangs don ni go rim bzhin/*。

⑲ 《壤塘版袞欽朵波巴全集》第六函，703頁：*sa yi dkyil na yod pa'i chu/dri ma med par gnas pa ltar/nyon mongs nang na ye shes kyang/de bzhin dri ma med par gnas/*。該處漢譯依《法界贊》談錫永譯本。《四重緣起深般若》附錄法界贊譯文，談錫永著，北京：華夏出版社，2010年。

⑳ 《壤塘版袞欽朵波巴全集》第六函，704頁：*lhag mthong gis ni mthong gyur na/thams cad mthong ba med pa yin/*。此處漢譯依《大方廣華嚴經》佛陀跋陀羅漢譯本（大正藏，No.0278）。

㉑ 《壤塘版袞欽朵波巴全集》第六函，704—705頁：*gzugs rnams mi mthong tshor ba dag kyang mi mthong zhing/'du shes mthong ba med la sems pa mi mthong zhing/gang la rnam par shes dang sems yid mthong med pa/'di ni chos mthong yin zhes de bzhin gshegs pas bstan/nam mkh' mthong zhes sems can tshig tu rab brjod kyang/nam mkh' ji ltar mthong ste don 'di brtag par gyis/*。此經又稱《佛說佛母寶德藏般若波羅蜜經》（寶賢譯，大正藏，No0229），此處寶賢譯本的相應漢譯文爲：色無相以受無相，乃至想行亦復然，識亦如是五法同，是法無相佛佛說，其虛空見眾生相，虛空無相不可得。

㉒ 《壤塘版袞欽朵波巴全集》第六函，705頁：*byang sar don gyi sde tshan gyi mdo drangs par/'jig rten dag na kun rdzob gang ci'ang rung /de kun thub pa'i zhal gyis mi bzhes te/gzigs dang gsan la bzhed pa mi mnga' bas/de ni zhal gyis mi bzhed gang gis 'dzin/*。此處譯文依玄奘漢譯本翻譯（大正藏，No.1579）。

莊嚴論》、《辨中邊論本頌》、《現觀莊嚴論》（*mNgon rtogs rgyan*）的相關偈頌，尤其對《辯法法性論》的內容進行了大量的引用，以此證明智境唯有勝義而無世俗。如《辯法法性論》云："彼現法性隱，彼沒法性現"[23]，如是，若佛爲世俗，則不現勝義法性。《經莊嚴論》云："依於名與義，顯現名與義，非正分別因，遍計之法相，顯現三三相，所取能取相，非真分別念，依他起法相"[24]，朵波巴解釋此經曰，第一個顯現三相是顯現處、境、身[25]，此爲所取之性相。第二個顯現三相是染污意、五根識、意[26]的顯現，此爲能取之性相。因此，若世俗爲智境，則智境落於遍計執及依他起。《現觀莊嚴論》云："由佛以現智，不見諸法故。"[27]其依以上慈氏諸論，明析世俗非智境，智境無世俗。

於無著兄弟教理而言，朵波巴不僅引用了無著《攝大乘論》（*Theg bsdus*）、《阿毗達磨集論》（*Kun btus*）、世親《辨中邊論》等，還引用馬鳴《般若十萬頌註疏——摧伏損害》（*'bum Tik*）、陳那《八千頌攝義論》（*brGyd stong don bsdu*）、月官《文殊贊》（*'Jam dbyangs la bstod pa*，全稱《薄伽梵聖文殊師利具有加持贊》）等來論證智境上無有世俗顯現。如《攝大乘論》云："無分別智行，諸義皆不現，當知無有義，由此亦無識"[28]。《八千頌攝義論》云："因何無明所變現，彼非實有唯顯現，能將非有顯現者，彼即說之爲無明"[29]，如是認爲世俗因無明而現，非智境之現。

於龍樹父子教理而言，朵波巴認爲若遍知爲世俗有法[30]，則遍知可見迷亂，未遠離分別，未斷除習氣，成不淨之昏昧顯現。龍樹《六十正理論》（*Rigs pa drug cu pa*）云："如是無明緣，佛爲世間說，世間謂分別，有何不應理"。又引聖天《中觀破迷論》（*dBu ma 'khrul 'joms*）論之，認爲凡夫迷亂地以"有"爲無和無常，以"無"爲有和常恆，待智慧眼開，如同於無明習氣之睡眠中醒來，現起善逝無垢智，爾時一切分別迷

㉓ 《壤塘版袞欽朵波巴全集》第六函，705頁：*chos nyid rnam 'byed du/de snang chos nyid mi snang zhing/de mi snang bas chos yid snang/*。此處譯文依法尊法師漢譯文翻譯，另亦有談錫永譯、韓鏡清譯，具體內容可參閱談錫永、邵頌雄釋著《辯法法性論及釋論兩種》，北京：中國藏學出版社，2013年。

㉔ 《壤塘版袞欽朵波巴全集》第六函，705—706頁：*ming dang don du snang ba dang/don dang ming du snang ba dang/yang dag min rtog mtshan nyid ni/kun btags pa yi mtshan nyid do/rnam gsum rnam gsum snang ba can/gzung dang 'dzin pa'i mtshan nyid de/yang dag ma yin kun rtog ni/gzhan gyi dbang gi mtshan nyid do/*。

㉕ 處，指顯現器世界；境，指色聲香味觸法六境；身，指眼耳鼻舌身意六根，此爲所取法方面。

㉖ 染污意，緣阿賴耶爲我，五根識爲能取，意爲分別，此爲能取法方面。

㉗ 《壤塘版袞欽朵波巴全集》第六函，706頁：*mngon rtogs rgyan du/ci phyir zhe na sangs rgyas kyi/mkhyen nas chos rnams ma gzigs phyir/*。

㉘ 《壤塘版袞欽朵波巴全集》第六函，706頁：*'phags pa thogs med kyi theg bsdus su/ye shes rgyu ba rtog med la/don rnams thams cad mi snang phyir/don med khong du chud par bya/de med pas na rnam rig med/*。此處譯文依《攝大乘論本》玄奘譯本翻譯（大正藏，No1594）。

㉙ 《壤塘版袞欽朵波巴全集》第六函，707頁：*gang phyir ma rig pas sprul pa/de ni med pa kho na snang/med pa ston par nus pas na/de ni ma rig ces brjod do/*。

㉚ 藏文典籍裡的有法（chos can）一般有兩種意思，一是一切法得以成立的基體，二是一切法。另外雙方在辯論時，承載著爭論的那個載體亦可稱爲chos can。此處爲第二個義項，指世俗一切法。

亂皆不現。月稱《三皈依七十頌》（*Skyabs gsum bdun cu pa*）[31]云："無明睡眠之顛倒，於眾生言皆顯現，彼之虛妄如夢境，無明睡眠相續斷，清淨之智定生起，凡醒覺者即佛陀，如說眾生眠中醒，翳眼所見發和月，無翳眼中無所現，如已覺識亦無現"[32]，因而，一切世俗法，於眾生言皆顯現，於諸佛言皆不現。

於寂天之教理而言，《入菩薩行論》（*Byang chub sems dpa'i spyod 'jug*）云："誰制燒鐵地，眾火從何出，佛說彼一切，皆由惡心造"[33]，因此若遍知爲世俗有法，則遍知即成惡心。

綜合上述五個方面，朵波巴認爲若佛爲世俗有法，則佛即世間，則佛非究竟涅槃，所以定要斷除世俗爲智境之見。

第四要斷除智上不現即不能知的見地，此即是說要斷除那種認爲智境上既然無有世俗，則智於世俗無法了知之見。朵波巴認爲於佛智境，一切法不現，而法性遍一切法，依佛智力，依現證法性之力，故可間接了知一切法。如《寶性論》云："究竟所知智，照見眾有情，具遍知法性，故能盡所有"[34]。

第五要斷除認爲二諦自性相異之見。朵波巴認爲，二者自性非一非異。若二者自性爲一，則凡夫既能見世俗即可見勝義，若見勝義，即成解脫；若二者自性爲一，如果於世俗上有漏增長，則勝義上亦有有漏增長，則勝義成煩惱之所緣；若二者自性爲一，則勝義無分別，世俗亦成無分別。同樣，若二者爲異亦不應理，若二者爲異，則既見勝義亦不能遮止世俗之實執，勝義亦非世俗所現之法性，亦非世俗成立之基體。因此正如法性與法，二者非一非異。

通過以上需斷除的五種見地的分析，朵波巴總結道："世俗於世俗上真實，於勝義上無有，勝義於勝義上真實，於世俗上無有"[35]。若世俗於世俗上非真實，則與世俗"諦"相違，若勝義於勝義上非真實，則與勝義"諦"相違。

此外，朵波巴還批評了那些認爲"勝義諦於勝義中無有"或"勝義諦僅是世俗中的真實"等見地。指出要把那些損害業因果及二諦，認爲世俗中無有的見地遠遠地拋掉。

名相分上，朵波巴分析了二諦之詞義。世俗諦梵文寫作"saṃvṛti-satya"，"saṃ"

㉛ 藏文全稱爲：*gsum la skyabs su 'gro ba bdun cu pa*，可參見《中華大藏經丹珠爾（對勘本）》第65卷，北京：中國藏學出版社，1994—2008年，685頁。

㉜ 《壤塘版袞欽朵波巴全集》第六函，709頁：*ma rig gnyid kyis log pa yi/'gro la gang gang snang de ni/brdzun te rmi lam bzhin du 'dod/ma rig gnyid ni rgyun chad cing/yang dag ye shes nges 'byung bas/gang zhig rnam sad de sangs rgyas/skyes bu gnyid sad ji bzhin no/zhes rab rib can gyi mig la snang ba'i skra shad dang/zla gnyis sogs mig skyon med la mi snang ba dang/rmi lam gyi snang ba rnams gnyid sad shes pa la mi snang ba ltar/*。

㉝ 《壤塘版袞欽朵波巴全集》第六函，709頁：*lcags bsregs sa gzhi su yis byas/me tshogs 'di dag ci las byung/de 'dra de dag thams cad kyang/sdig sems yin par thub pas gsungs/*。

㉞ 《壤塘版袞欽朵波巴全集》第六函，710頁：*shes bya mthar thug rtogs pa'i blos/thams cad mkhyen pa'i chos nyid ni/sems can thams cad la yod par/mthong phyir ji snyed yod pa nyid/*。

㉟ 《壤塘版袞欽朵波巴全集》第六函，713頁：*kun rdzob ni kun rdzob tu bden par yod kyi/don dam par med pa dang/don dam pa ni don dam par yod kyi/kun rdzob tu med pa dang/*。

爲“真實”義，“vṛti”爲“遮止、障蔽”義，能所二取之顯現遮蔽了勝義空性真如即世俗。但其於世俗上仍爲真實，“satya”即爲“真實、諦實”之意，故稱“世俗諦”。勝義諦梵文寫作“paramārtha-satya”，“prama”爲“極、最勝”義，“artha”爲“趣入不虚妄勝義法性”義，聖智境上爲真實，故稱“勝義諦”。

異門分上，朵波巴指出，唯施設（btags tsam）、名言（tha snyad）、迷亂（’khrul pa）、幻術（sgyu ma）等皆世俗之異名。空性（stong pa nyid）、究竟真實（yang dag mtha’）、無相（mtshan ma med）、法界（chos kyi dbyings）、勝義菩提心（don dam byang chub sems）、最勝菩提心（byang chub sems mchog）以及《般若經》中所說的真如（de bzhin nyid）、法無謬性（chos skyon med pa nyid）、不可思議界（bsam gyi mi khyab pa’i dbyings）等皆爲勝義之異名。

事相分上，朵波巴認爲世俗以緣起爲基，勝義則超越緣起。世俗可分非迷亂顯現之正世俗和迷亂顯現之倒世俗。世俗所攝爲遍計，自相所攝爲依他。勝義可分爲異門勝義（rnam grangs pa’i don dam，即隨順勝義）、非異門勝義（rnam grangs ma yin pa’i don dam，即真實勝義）。又可分爲義勝義（don dam pa）、得勝義（thob pa don dam）、正行勝義（sgrub pa don dam pa）三種。《辨中邊論》云：“義得勝義爲涅槃，此非異門之勝義。正行勝義爲道諦，此即異門之勝義”[36]。

三、朵波巴二諦見對其“他空見”詮釋學說的意義

之所以要討論朵波巴之二諦見，不僅僅是因爲它是其佛學思想的重要組成部分，還因爲此二諦見更是朵波巴他空見學說詮釋的基石和出發點，對其整個他空見思想的建構都有重要意義。

正如唐納德·羅佩茲在文章中指出的那樣：“亞洲佛教思想中各主要宗派的一個共同信念是佛陀並沒有向所有人教授同樣的東西，而是爲了滿足聽眾的具體需要而權宜地改變他的教義。”[37]這樣就使各種不同的教義解釋學說具備了一定的合理性。佛教傳入藏地後，他們就因此可以對印度傳來的各種佛教學說加以系統化。朵波巴即是一位在這一方面具有代表性的人物，他似乎已經意識到，在他那個時代所流行的學說體系也並不是印度佛教直接而來，亦是在藏地前人於佛教不斷詮釋的基礎上發展而來。因此，他亦可以在自己直接觀修的啓示下，詮釋自己的學說見地或宗義體系。

13世紀之前，西藏中觀通行之分類大抵分瑜伽行中觀（Yogācāra Madhyamaka）與經部行中觀（Sautrāntika Madhyamaka），13世紀之後，以中觀應成派（Prāsaṅgika Madhyamaka）、中觀自續派（Svātantrika Madhyamaka）爲主的中觀體系劃分逐步發展

㊱ 《壤塘版袞欽朵波巴全集》第六函，720—721頁：*don dam pa de nyid dang/thob pa don dam pa mya ngan las pa gnyis/rnam grangs min pa’i don dam dang/sgrub pa don dam pa lam gyi bden pa ni rnam grangs kyi don dam mo/*。

㊲ 唐納德·羅佩茲編，周廣榮，常蕾，李建欣譯《佛教解釋學》，上海：上海古籍出版社，2009年，5頁。

起來，並隨著格魯派的壯大逐漸得以確定。而處於14世紀的朵波巴，卻對整個佛學體系進行了重新的思考及詮釋，他將中觀創造性的分爲無相中觀和有相中觀，認爲應成和自續兩派皆屬無相中觀，有相中觀即爲他空中觀，此才是最高見地。

那麼如何詮釋這樣一種學說呢，除藏地學者經常會使用的"四依法"[38]及"三轉法輪"的詮釋方法外，二諦思想始終貫穿其詮釋學體系。

朵波巴將自空、他空框架與世俗諦、勝義諦框架巧妙結合，即認爲世俗諦依識，爲自空，勝義諦依智，爲他空[39]。兩個領域各有分明，這樣，二諦於他就不再僅僅是一個認識方法，更是一種對境。而類似二諦見地，於經論之中亦非毫無端倪，如《顯揚聖教論》即云："世俗諦者，謂名句文身，及依彼義一切言說，及依言說所解了義，又曾得世間心及心法，及彼所行境義。勝義諦者，謂聖智及彼所行境義，及彼相應心心法等"[40]，這裡亦將世俗諦對應言說之行境，勝義諦對應聖智之行境。正是有了這樣一種二諦框架的前提，朵波巴才可以在勝義諦的領域內開許他空見地，而在世俗諦領域內確定自空，因此他並不否認自空見，僅認爲其不如他空見究竟。

另外，朵波巴亦將二諦理論與三自性理論結合，使其成爲一種理解他空的方法。他認爲遍計執是相無自性，是假名有，於世俗中亦無。依他起是生無自性，於世俗中爲有。圓成實即空掉遍計執與依他起，爲勝義無自性，於勝義中有，是遍計執與依他起之基，非爲自空，而爲他空。

因而，正是借助這樣二諦理念，他才能更好的解釋其於實修中現證而來的他空見，所以，可以說其二諦思想對朵波巴所發展出的教法體系具有重要意義，是其他空闡釋學說的出發點和有力工具，值得我們瞭解和研究。

The Starting Point of the Interpretation of gZhan stong View: the Satya-dvaya thought of Dol po pa shes rab rgyan mtshan

Shi Mei

The thought of Satya-dvaya is an important theory of the Buddhism. In terms of its meaning and concept, the Sarvāstivāda、Sautrāntika、Vijñānavāda and Madhyamaka have distinct opinions. Dol po pa shes rab rgyan mtshan who proposed the view of gZhan stong also own his special perspective about the Satya-dvaya. He wrote the work named *bDen gnyis gsal ba'i nyi ma.* In this article, I will analyse the view that Saṃvṛti-satya is the object of Vijñāna and Paramārtha-satya is the object of jñāna, which is raised from this article, and consider this point is significant for Dol po pa's view of gZhan stong.

㊳ 即依法不依人，依義不依語，依了義經不依不了義經，依智不依識。

㊴ 關於他空中觀之二諦見的相關研究可參閱Klaus-Dieter Mathes, "Vordergründige und höcheste Wahrheit im gŻan stong-Madhyamaka", *Annäherung an das Fremde*，第26期，萊比錫：德國東方研究1995年會議。

㊵ 無著造，玄奘譯《顯揚聖教論》卷二，大正藏，No1602。

蘇卡悉地研究

索朗卓瑪

引　　言

*Among Tibetan Texts: History & Literature Of The Himalayan Plateau*者，爲金・史密（E. Gene Smith）於1961—1973年間所撰，由柯帝士・謝弗（Kurtis R. Schaeffer）所編之，玆業乃完，並於2001年得以初版面世。《在藏文文獻之間——喜瑪拉雅高原的歷史與文獻》，顧名思義，是一部有關介紹藏族歷史及其文學的書。此文獻之內容可謂繁複，長凡近乎四百頁，共分六大部分，下分則有十七章。該書有一不容忽視之特點，便是從一種特殊的角度出發，對藏傳佛教各個宗派的興衰流變，以及相關的事項作了扼要的闡述，然敘及要害之處，可謂精心結撰，筆墨不惜。雖然該書作者已有言在先，講明此等文章並非爲一個純粹的學術之作，個中數篇文章皆因他緣而生，即爲方便西方從事藏學的研究機構和學者而做的一番事業。儘管如是，于筆者而言，文中所引的不少歷史人物抑或文獻，悉屬於被束之高閣、無人問津之類，書中所敘及的藏傳佛教香巴噶舉派（Shangs pa bka' brgyud pa）之空行母蘇卡悉地（Sukhasiddhi）便屬於此等情況。故覺其有研究介紹之必要，遂就蘇卡悉地之傳記，於玆略加探討蘇卡悉地以及有關空行母之種種問題，以供深入探討者的參考。而該書中的其餘內容，則擬另題介紹，此處從略。

一、蘇卡悉地是誰？

蘇卡悉地爲一位空行母，系藏傳佛教香巴噶舉派。稍治藏學之人，便知道該派是由賢者穹波乃覺（Mkhas grub khyung po rnal 'byor）大師所傳出的。其之所以被稱爲“香巴噶舉”，皆因爲該派的祖庭香（Shangs）雄雄寺[①]（Gzhong gzhong dgon）所創建的地方在後藏一個名曰“香”（Shangs）的地區（即今天的日喀則南木林縣（Rnam gling rdzong）地區），而且當時在後藏地區，香地區勢力可謂突出，遂以香巴噶舉之名著稱[②]。

穹波乃覺所创建的香巴噶舉派不同于其他任何藏傳佛教派系，其獨特之處在於該派法門源傳自兩位空行母即尼古瑪（Ni gu ma）和蘇卡悉地。其中智慧空行母尼古瑪（Ye shes kyi mkha' 'gro ma ni gu ma）爲香巴噶舉這一派的祖師，如果不算金剛持（Rdo rje 'chang）的話[③]。但她們二者都爲穹波乃覺之不共上師[④]，而且她們都有各自的甚深六法（Zab lam chos drug），是香巴噶舉派甚深密法的根源。

蘇卡悉地所處時代爲宋代，她作爲香巴噶舉派這樣一位舉足輕重的人物，去今如彼其遠，其歷史真相到底若何？到底何謂蘇卡悉地？其來歷何如？其是否生來就是一位空行母？歷來學者們各執一詞的空行母這一名相到底所指何事？其中有沒有隱沒的不曾有人注意到的事蹟？諸如此類問題，雖可在諸藏文文獻中知其一二，但都記載得太過簡略，不能予人以清晰的印象。特別是目前學術界現有的有關蘇卡悉地的研究也多囿於對這些藏文史籍的簡單處理，對帶有歷史成分的傳記資料他們則不甚注意，這大概可能是因爲他們覺著傳記是一種粗制史料。的確，用史學眼光看待人物傳記，其缺點可能甚

---

① 對於雄雄寺的藏文寫法，不同的藏文文獻資料有著不同的記載，目前看來常見的有三種寫法：“Zhong zhong dgon”“Zhang zhang dgon”和“gZhong gzhong dgon”。第一種寫法常見於長條書藏文文獻中，以“Brug lugs chos mdzod chen mo”爲代表。筆者認爲第二種寫法之所以會普遍流行，可能是受到了土觀的影響，因爲見於其作品《宗派源流》中的雄雄寺的藏文寫法便是如此，見其書110頁。但據筆者考證，雄雄寺的正確的藏文寫法應該爲第三種即“Gzhong gzhong dgon”。雄雄寺的全名爲“Gzhong gzhong rdo rje gdan”即雄雄寺金剛座。對於這點佐以文字記載如下：“gzhong gzhong dgon/mtshan rgyas par/gzhong gzhong rdo rje gdan zhes zhu/da lta' i rnam gling rdzong nas spyi le 5tsam gzhong gzhong zhes par song na gzhong gzhong grongagi byang ngos rgyab rir dgon de chags yod/dgon de ni thog mar mkhas grub khyung po rnal' byor gyis phyag btab gnang mdzad/”，載于曲佩（Chos'phel）的《雪域藏地寺廟指南——日喀則寺廟志》（*Gangs can bod kyi gnas yig lam yig gsar ma las gzhis rtses khul gyi gnas yig*），北京：民族出版社，2008年，198頁。同樣在公認的極富學術權威性的《東噶藏學大辭典》（*Dung dkar tshig mdzod chen mo*）上也是用了“Gzhong gzhong dgon”這種寫法，北京：中國藏學出版社，2002年，434—435頁。

② 有關這點，在其他藏文歷史文獻中也有類似的記載，比如于恰白・次旦平措（Chab spel Tshe brtan phun tshogs）的《西藏通史——松石寶串》（*Bod kyi lo rgyus rags rim gyu yi phreng ba*）中記載說：“……於藏曆第二繞迥鐵牛年（1211）至沃如香地方，建造了香雄雄寺，遂以香巴噶舉之名著稱”，拉薩：西藏社會科學院、中國西藏雜誌社、西藏古籍出版社聯合出版，1996年，283頁。

③ 關於這點請見拙作《尼古瑪六法略述》，沈衛榮主編《西域歷史語言研究集刊》第八輯，北京：科學出版社，2015年，411—420頁。

④ 這點在土觀・羅桑卻吉尼瑪（Thu'u bkwan bLo bzang chos kyi nyi ma）所著的《土觀宗派源流》（*Thu'u bkwan grub mtha'*）一書中有如是記載：“他（窮波乃覺）的家屬窮波。幼年時曾學苯教，後知其非，改學“大圓滿法”亦未愜意。乃往尼泊爾依巴蘇莫諦論師（善慧）學梵文，旋赴佛法來源地的天竺，往返竺、尼、藏三地約五十年，親近竺尼大善知識與大成就者約一百五十人。通達顯密經綸及一切要門。他的共同上師有大金剛座主、彌勒巴、趨多瑜伽、羅睺羅等四人；不共的上師有尼古智慧空行母、樂成空行母六人爲主。”該處所指的樂成空行母便爲蘇卡悉地，北京：民族出版社，2000年，61頁。

多，因爲其偏於個人的歷史，但凡所記，皆是記載他小時候如何，壯年如何，生平行事，首尾畢見，看似毫無益處，但這種人物傳記，絕非一個人的起居注這麼簡單，其所有的歷史性質不容質疑。故下來筆者便從《蘇卡悉地傳記》出發[⑤]，一一搜輯與蘇卡悉地相關的史料，但凡與其產生聯繫的，不論直接的或間接的，筆者都將他們全數搜集齊於茲，然後予以深入分析，兼及談論有關空行母的種種問題。其中跟蘇卡悉地有密切關係的，則做專精的功夫並予以詳細之探討；而對與其有關係但事蹟不多的，則略加考證，判斷真僞，如是以來不但可以更好地鉤沉出蘇卡悉地之真實的歷史面貌，而且還可獲得好多有助於研究空行母的好材料，方便考察清楚空行母這一概念之來源去脈。蘇卡悉地的傳記，是筆者在《在藏文文獻之間——喜瑪拉雅高原的歷史與文献》一書中所談及的一本名爲《香巴金鬘》（*Shangs pa gser' phreng*）的藏文文獻中所發現的。其相當於一種“傳記集”，因其收錄了香巴噶舉派三十幾位大德高僧的傳記故事。其中有關蘇卡悉地的傳記部分，題目爲《智慧空行母蘇卡悉地或別名曰樂成之歷史》（*Ye shes kyi mkha' 'gro ma su kha sidhi zhes pa 'am mtshan gzhan bde ba'i dngos grub kyi lo rgyus*）。由於該傳記只有寥寥不到十頁的內容，遂下來先對其作相關介紹，進而再做相關的分析與探討。

二、蘇卡悉地的故事

傳記譯文：梵語名：蘇卡悉地（Sukhasiddhi）、藏文名曰樂悉地（Bde ba'i dngos grub）之歷史。頂禮具德金剛空行母（Dpal ldan rdo rje mkha' 'gro ma）！於印度迦濕弥罗（Rgya gar kha che），有城三百八十萬，其中西部有一城名爲迦濕弥罗城。城中住有一戶八口之家，包括一對夫婦及其六個子女（三男三女），生活极为贫苦，家中僅有一缸糧食，卻未敢享用，封其口而藏之。（隨後）三個兒子往南謀生，三個女兒則往北，其父往西。而後，有一極爲窮困之人向其母乞食。母親打開糧缸，取出糧食布施給他。其夫覓食一無所獲，飢餓難忍，便打算先吃家中所存之一缸糧食后繼續覓食，於是返回其家。三子三女同樣一無所獲，所以也返回家中。他們不約而同，同時抵家，對母親說道：“母親，取出糧食給我們吧。我們大家都已經飢餓不堪。”其母答道：“我以爲你們會尋到食物才回來，有一極爲窮困之人向我乞食，我已將糧食全部布施給他，現已一無所剩。”說罷，其丈夫與孩子們同聲說道：“此前你也做過類似的事，我們已經不悅。而今你不但自己不去覓食，還把我們積攢食物弄沒了，你走吧！”於是將其趕出

⑤ 此傳記名爲《智慧空行母蘇卡悉地/樂成之歷史》（*Ye shes kyi mkha' 'gro ma su kha sidhi zhes pa'am mtshan gzhan bde ba'i dngos grub kyi lo rgyus*），Leh: Sonam w. Tashigang, 1970, 6 ff.(pp. 49-55)。另外，學者Nicole Riggs對香巴噶舉派中的二十幾位著名人物的生平故事做了一個簡單的翻譯，並輯錄成書了，參見Nicole Riggs, *Like an Illusion, Lives of the Shangpa Kagyu Masters*, Eugene: Dharma Cloud Press, 2001.

家門。而後，這位老婦便從迦濕彌羅來到了西方的烏仗那（Nub phyogs o rgyan）[⑥]。烏仗那的男都是勇父（dpa' bo），女子全都是勇母（dpa' mo）。據說，只要來到這個地方，人的覺性便會自然得以澄淨明晰。她遇到了收割的人們，於是得到了一些糧食，她把糧食背到一個城市并釀成酒來賣。當時，阿闍梨密哩斡巴（Birwa pa，又名阿瓦都帝巴A wa dhu ti pa）與手印母阿瓦都帝瑪（A wa dhu ti ma）在烏仗那的密林中作秘密行，這位瑜伽母常去給他買酒。她到了那位賣酒老婦處賣酒，發現其酒比別人的都要醇香。有一天，老婦問她："你是给谁买酒？"瑜伽母回答道："那邊的林中有一位卓越的瑜伽士，我是給他買的。"老婦說道："既然如此，就不收你酒錢了"。並將酒重新挑選了一遍。對此，密哩斡巴問道："你是如何弄到這個免費的酒的？"瑜伽母回答说："這位賣酒的是一位具信者，與之前的那些人不同。她知道我這酒是給我在林中修行的卓越上師時，對您生起了敬信，於是把酒交給了我。"於是，密哩斡巴對那位瑜伽母說道："我要讓這位老婦脫離三界輪迴（khams gsum 'khor ba）。於是該瑜伽母來到那位老婦女面前，問道："您願意過去嗎？"老婦非常欣悅，並帶著酒和豬肉去拜謁上師。之後，密哩斡巴對其做了四灌頂，并授予了生起、圓滿（bskyed rdzogs）次第等秘密成就法，以及懷愛事業（dbang gi 'phrin las），該老婦立即轉爲一智慧空行母（ye shes kyi mkha' 'gro ma）。她被家人逐出家門時，年滿五十九歲。後來在烏仗那賣酒時，正值六十歲。從密哩斡巴處獲得灌頂時，已六十一歲。然而她在一夜之間，由獲得成就之力令六十一歲之異熟身得以清淨，從而轉爲虹身（'ja' lus），現少女相，身色潔白，頭髮散披於身後，仿佛年方十六，儀容佳妙，令人觀之不厭，于虛空中安住七日后，轉爲名曰"蘇卡悉地"之具神變空行母，而後又轉爲出有壞（bcom ldan 'das）無我母（bdag med ma），並成爲密哩斡巴之明妃（gsang yum）。如今，她仍然在世，依舊于六時中以智慧眼觀照三界有情，並對具有清淨境相者說法，并對實修秘密成就法以及向其祈請

---

⑥ "o rgyan"，等同於 "u rgyan"，可音譯爲"鄔堅"或"鄔金"，其意爲飛行。古印度因陀羅菩提王國名。今之阿富汗。亦譯烏仗那、烏丈耶那、歐提耶奈（OTi ya na ste 'phur 'gro zhes pa zur chag pa dang sngar rgya gar nub phyogs kyi rgyal po indra bhu ti byon pa'i yul/），張怡蓀主編：《藏漢大辭典》（*Bod rgya tshig mdzod chen mo*），北京：民族出版社，1984年，3138頁。《蘇卡悉地的傳記》中記載說："烏仗那"這個地方的男的均爲"勇父"（空行男），女的均爲"勇母"（空行女），爲何會如此？對於這點，在金剛乘世界裏有一種說法："傳說烏仗那是一個美麗而又富饒的地方，其統治者爲因陀羅菩提王（Indrabhāti）。因陀羅菩提王想在佛陀面前求一種可以令他寶座、王國、財富抑或家庭永固的佛法。遂佛陀就秘密地對他進行了內密灌頂。其所有的屬民，甚至該地的蟲類都無一例外地修行此法並證得成就，爾後消逝與虹身。這使得烏仗那這個地方變得荒無人煙，後來它就被一個富有慈悲心的蛇神（nāga）施法變成了一湖水。這些蛇神也開始修密宗教法，其兒子們都變成了"勇父"（dākas）、女兒們則都成了"空行母"（*Dākinī*）。由此以來，烏仗那這個地方便成爲了有名的"空行之地"（mkha' ' gro gling）。" Judith Simmer-Brown，*Dākinī 's Warm Breath—The Feminine principle In Tibetan Buddhism*，Boston：Shambhala Publications，2001，p. 267。筆者認爲，Judith Simmer-Brown書中所言及的這個傳說，其傳說之原型應爲《遺教赤銅洲》（*Bka' thang zangs gling m*a）中"因陀羅菩提王爲父以及（花生slob dpon padma 'byung gnas）坐寶座"（rgyal po indrabodhi yab mdzad pa dang rgyal sa bzung ba）之故事，可見於娘惹·尼瑪俄色（Nyang ral Nyi ma 'od zer）：《遺教赤銅洲》（*Bka' thang zangs gling m*a），成都：四川民族出版社，1989年，3—11頁。

者給予加持，并授之以殊勝（mchog）與共通（thun mong）之悉地（dngos grub）。此便爲智慧空行母（蘇卡悉地）之傳記，僅聞其名亦能生起敬信！[⑦]

⑦ 傳記原文：ye shes kyi mkha' 'gro ma su kha sidhi zhes pa 'am mtshan gzhan bde ba'i dngos grub kyi lo rgyus）：gya gar skad du/ su kha siddhi/bod skad du/bde ba'i dngos grub kyi lo rgyus zhes bya ba/ dpal ldan rdo rje mkha' 'gro ma la phyag 'tshal lo/de la rgya gar kha che na/grong khyer 'bum tsho sum cu so brgyad yod pa las/'di nub phyogs kha che'i grong khyer zhes bya ba yin no/de yang grong khyer de na bza' mi gnyis la bu gsum mo gsum dang brgyad yod pas shin tu dbul zhing phongs par gyur pa ste/rgyags 'bras bum pa gang las med pas/de za ma nus pa kha bcad de sbas nas bzhag go/de nas bu gsum po lho phyogs su bza' tshol du song /bu mo gsum po byang du song /pha nub phyogs su song /de nas mal dus gcig na shin tu phongs pa gcig bza' ba slong du byung bas/'bras kyi bum pa kha phyes nas gtsos nas byin no/der pha yis bza' ba ma rnyed bkres pas nyen nas/da ni khyim gyi 'bras bum pa gang bo zos la de nas btsal dgos snyam nas log pa dang /bu gsum gyis kyang ma rnyed par log bu mo gsum gyis kyang de bzhin du log go der khong gsum gros byas pa bzhin du dus gcig tu log nas/ da ni mas 'bras kha phyes nas byin cig bkres shing nyen nas thams cad nyam thag par gyur to/zer ba dang /ma yis smras pa/khyed rnams kyis bza' ba rnyed nas 'ong snyam ste shin tu phongs shing nyam thag pa gcig bza' slong du byung nas/de la 'bras byin nas med byas pas/khyo dang bu mo rnams mgrin gcig bsdebs nas ma la smras pa/khyod kyis de sngar yang 'di ka bzhin du byas pas nged rnams skyid du ma ster/da yang khyod kyis bza' tshol brta mi yong steng nged kyis bsags pa rnams kyang med par byas pas 'di thon cig byas nas khyim nas bton par gyur to/de nas rgan mo de kha che'i yul nas nub phyogs o rgyan du phyin pa dang /o rgyan kyi mi rnams ni/pho skyes thams cad dpa' bo/mo skyes thams cad dpa' mo sha stag tu 'dug la/der phyin pa tsam gyis rig pa rang bzhin gyis dwangs bar 'dug skad/dus der 'bras btsa' ba dang 'dzom nas 'bras bsgrubs pas khal cig rnyed/ de grong khyer gcig tu khyer nas chang tshong ma byas so/de'i dus na o rgyan gyi nags khrod du slob dpon birWa pa zhes kyang bya/a wa ng+hu ti pa zhes kyang bya ba de/phyag rgya a wa nghu ti ma dang gnyis 'grogs nas gsang spyod mdzad kyin yod pa las/rnar 'byor ma des dus rtag tu chang nyo phyin no/de nas ma rgan mo chang tshong ma de la skabs su chang nyos pas chang gzhan las zhim pa sha stag gtsongs so/der rgan mos/rnal 'byor ma khyod chang nyo nas su la khyer byas pas/rnal 'byor mas smras pa/ya ki nags khrod na rnal 'byor pa bzang po gcig bzhugs pas de la 'dren pa yin byas pa dang /rgan mos smras pa/'o na khyod kyis chang rin mi 'dod zer 'bras chang nying sing byas kyi na bskur ro/der birWa pa'i zhal nas/rnal 'byor ma chang rin mi dgos pa'i chang sha stag 'ong pa ji ltar byas pa yin gsung pa dang /de snga'i chang tshong ma dang mi 'dra ba'i dad pa gcig 'dug ste/nga yi bla ma bzang bo gcig nags khrod na yod pa yin te/de la khyer ba yin byas pas/chang tshong ma dad pa skyes nas bskur yin byas pas birWa pa'i zhal nas/rnal 'byor ma/da ci nas kyang rgan mo de ngas khams gsum 'khor de ngas khams gsum 'khor ba nas 'don dgos gsungs pas rnal 'byor ma des rgan mo la khyed 'deng ngam byas pa dang /rgan mo de shin tu mos te/'bras chang bum pa gang dang phag sha bcas khyer nas mjal du phyin no/de nas birWa pas dus de nyid dugs sbub lte ba sbrul 'khor gyi dbang bzhi rdzogs su bskur/bskyed rdzogs gsang sgrub dang bcas pa/dbang gi phrin las bcas gsungs pas dus de nyid du ye shes kyi mkha' 'gro mar gyur to/de yang bu khyo rnams kyis kha che'i yul nas bton pa'i dus su lnga bcu nga dgu lon/o rgyan du phyin nas chang tshong ma byas nas lo drug cu tham pa/birWa pa dang mjal nas dbang zhus pa'i dus su drug cu rtsa gcig lon no/der nub gcig la grub pa thob pa'i stobs kyis drug cu rtsa gcig lon pa'i rnam smin gyi lus de rang dag la song nas 'ja' lus su gyur te/gzhon nu lang tsho dar la babs pa sku mdog shin tu dkar ba/dbu skra sil bus sku rgyab non pa/ bcu drug lon pa'i tshod ltar mdzes shing ltabs chog mi shes pa shing rta la bdun srid tsam gyi nam mkha' la bzhugs pa rdzu 'phrul dang ldan pa'i mkha' 'gro ma su kha siddhi zhes bya bar gyur to/de lang mkha' 'gro ma de bcom ldan 'das bdag med ma dngos su gyur te birWapa'i gsang yum mdzad do/da lta yang 'das grangs mi mnga' bar khams gsum gyi sems can la ye shes kyi gzigs pa dus drug tu 'jug go/des kyang khyad par snang ba dag pa rnams la chos gsungs/gsang sgrub nyams su len pa rnams dang gsol ba 'debs pa rnams la dngos su byin gyis rlob cing /mchog thun mong gi dngos grub ster bar byed do/de ltar ye shes kyi mkha' 'gro ma de'i rnam thar dang /mtshan thos pa tsam gyis shin tu mos par gyur to/, Leh: Sonam W. Tashigang, 1970, 6 ff. (pp. 49-55)。

由此可見，'Bde ba'i dngos grub'是蘇卡悉地空行母之藏文名，意爲“樂成”，故我們也可以稱其爲“樂成空行母”，而蘇卡悉地這一稱號則爲其梵文名字即“Sukhasiddhi”的一種音寫形式。對於蘇卡悉地之出生地，其傳記中也有所敘述，即蘇卡悉地她出生於印度迦湿弥罗。該傳記看似短小而簡單，個中實則充斥著各種密宗學問與知識。正如上文所見，該傳記中出現了很多諸如勇父、空行母以及智慧空行母和無我[⑧]等這類密宗名相。此外，還出現了一些密宗所特有的問題和現象，比如傳記中的蘇卡悉地爲何特以一種“酒商女”[⑨]的形象示人這一問題。悉數這些問題，在下來的腳注中做有相關的解釋和分析，其中有關勇父和空行母部分則擬於下文中予以大篇幅討論與分析。

（一）勇父

何謂勇父？“勇父”，藏文作“dpa' bo”，其意思爲“英雄”，而“勇父”是其在密宗世界中的一個稱法。“勇父”在藏密世界中所扮演的角色可謂重大，他屬於藏密密法修持之中“三根本”（rtsa ba gsum）[⑩]裏面的空行部分。對於“三根本”，《了義炬・大手印四加行簡要合集和正行教學次第》（*Phyag chen sngon 'gro bzhi sbyor dang*

---

⑧ “無我”，藏文作“bdag med pa”，與我見相反，四諦十六行相之一（bdag tu lta ba'i mi mthun pa'i phyogs kyis bdag med pabden bzhi' i rnam pa bcu drug gi nang gses shig），見於東噶・洛桑赤列：《東噶藏學大辭典》（*Dung dkar tshig mdzod chen mo*），北京：中國藏學出版社，2002年，1358頁。對於這點，還可見於談錫永《密宗名相》：“無我，看似是在否定自我，實則並不是自我否定，只是自我認識。認識到“自我”非有實體，可是其功能作用卻宛然實有。如果是以“不常不斷”的態度來認識“自我”，才可以稱爲無我”，北京：華夏出版社，2008年，149頁。關於無我的修持，亦可見於《丹珠爾》對勘版（Bstan 'gyur dpe bsdur ma）卷39，北京：中國藏學出版社，1994—2008年，981—1001頁。

⑨ 人所共知，酒肉是顯乘教法所不許的，爲何密宗裏面卻不視此等爲大忌，甚至有拿酒供佛之現象，如蘇卡悉地傳記之中就有類似的問題。她不但以一個“酒商女”的身份示人，而且還不斷供酒給毗瓦巴。這是爲何？因爲“《結合經》雲：魚肉諸食品，酒爲左所需，能醉品亦可……酒能令歡喜”，見於宗喀巴（Tsong kha pa）著，法尊譯：《密宗道次第廣論》（Sngags rim chen mo），西寧：青海人民出版社，2012年，223頁。宗喀巴於茲所言的酒能令歡喜，是否就是那種由拙火（gtum mo）所產生的四種歡喜快樂，進而出現樂空不二的禪定感受？這點有待深入研究。此外，亦見由羅伯特・薩耶（Robert Sailley）所著，耿昇所譯之《印度—西藏的佛教密宗》一書中所雲的：“據藏族史學家多羅那他認爲《寶石藏》，羅睺羅跋陀可能是接受大手印啟示的第一人，而大手印正是無上“受”和大樂。這應該是由於一名金剛瑜伽行者（Vajrayagini，女神瑜伽行者，yogini），她採用了一“女酒商”的外形。“女酒商”是一種具有雙重意義的稱號：她可以使人飲酒飲得酩酊大醉，也就是一種神秘的醉意。”〔法〕羅伯特・薩耶著，耿昇譯《印度—西藏的佛教密宗》，北京：中國藏學出版社，1999年，78頁。由此可見，於密宗人士而言，酒相當於一種甘露，而且因爲飲酒所產生的神秘效力，故不排除其與空樂大手印間產生關係的可能性。

⑩ 見於東噶・洛桑赤列《東噶藏學大辭典》（*Dung dkar tshig mdzod chen mo*），北京：中國藏學出版社，2002年，1671頁。

dngos gzhi'i khrid rim mdor bsdus nges don sgron me zhes bya ba bzhugs so）[11]中有云：三根本分别爲：加持的根本（byin rlabs kyi rtsa ba）—上師（bla ma）、成就的根本（dngos grub kyi rtsa ba）—本尊（yi dam）和事業的根本（phrin las kyi rtsa ba）—空行護法（mkha' 'gro chos skyong）。他們相對於佛（sangs rgyas）、法（chos）、僧（dge 'dun）“三寶”（dkon mchog gsum）而存在於密宗世界之中。盡管藏傳佛教在修持方面，一度主張顯、密同時共進修持，但二者始終有相對的區别。可以説，一個是於顯乘而言的“三寶”，一個則是於密乘而言的“三根本”。所謂“根本”，即行者要依止的對象。學密法可依多位上師，但根本上師則只有一位，這位上師在傳承系統中的最親上師，則是觀修時的根本上師，例如無垢友尊者、蓮花生大士。修不同的密法亦有各個不同的本尊，但根本本尊亦只有一位。根本本尊既定，則根本空行便亦決定，如毗盧遮那佛爲根本本尊，則根本空行必是佛眼佛母[12]。

勇父作爲密法系統“三根本”中的空行護法部分，其不僅爲一種護法神明，還用來指密宗修行者在行樂空雙運時的修行伴侣。故可以説，勇父他亦是對女性修持者之伴侣的一種稱號。蘇卡悉地傳記中所出現的勇父便屬於第二種情況，即爲一種女性密宗修持者的伴侣，其在密法中所扮演的角色與僧伽在顯宗教法中所充當的角色可以説是一樣的，是爲了支持和指引密宗修持者，使其迅速俱足福慧資糧，證得菩提，圓滿獲得世間法出世間法。“勇父”在梵語中則稱爲“ḍāka”，其跟表示空行母的“dākini”相對應，後者若何，下來有詳論之。

（二）空行母

1. 空行母釋義

對於蘇卡悉地，我們從其傳記故事中了解到，她並非生來就是一個空行母，她是後天在大師毗瓦巴的加持下成爲一位智慧空行母的。那麼到底何謂空行母？她是一個普通的女性還是一個女性神明？抑或是一個原始意象？智慧空行母又是所指何事？是否所有的空行母都可稱其爲智慧空行母？西方學者筆下的空行母形象若何？他們對空行母身份定位的獨到見解是否真正貼近藏傳佛教之意旨？還是他們的一個“想像物”？這些問題

---

⑪ 藏文原文作：dkon mchog gsum zhes pa sangs rgyas chos dang dge ' dun gsum yin/sngags lugs la de' i steng du rtsa ba gsum bsnan dgos te/byin rlabs kyi r+ca ba bla ma/dngos grub kyi rtsa ba yi dam/phrin las kyi rtsa ba mkha' 'gro chos skyong rnams yin/，可見於蔣貢康楚（'jam mgon kong sprul）所著的《文集宝藏》（*Rgya chen bka' mdzod*）中有關《了义炬》（*Phyag chen sngon 'gro bzhi sbyor dang dngos gzhi'i khrid rim mdor bsdus nges don sgron me zhes bya ba bzhugs so*）部分，Paro：Ngodup Publication, 1975-1976, p. 4。

⑫ 談錫永：《密宗名相》，北京：華夏出版社，2008年，13頁。有關這點，亦可見於蔣貢康楚（'jam mgon kong sprul）：《了义炬・大手印四加行簡要合集和正行教學次第》（*Phyag chen sngon 'gro bzhi sbyor dang dngos gzhi'i khrid rim mdor bsdus nges don sgron me zhes bya ba bzhugs so*），Paro：Ngodup Publication，1975-1976，pp. 34-38.

在下文中均有所論。

我們都知道，密宗研究一直受到西方學界廣泛的關注和注意，而空行母作爲密宗世界之中一個不可或缺的元素，近年来亦成了国际学界研究的焦點之一，尤其是西方女性學者，對空行母尤爲關注，研究態勢可謂日趋繁荣。学者们先後对空行母之源流的追溯、身份定位的分析及其與西方世界之間的交通之跡等等问題方面，都有相当激烈的争论與探討。雖然很多問題迄今都還未能形成一個定論，但每一學者所加以研究的有關空行母的問題本身却为我们理解該議題提供了一個极大的帮助。相較之下，在國内空行母這一議題卻相對邊緣化了，未能得到應有的關注。

空行母一詞，藏文作“mkha’ ’gro ma”，亦可音寫作“Khandroma”；其梵文則作“Dākinī”。一般意義上來講，“mkha’”意爲“虛空”或“天空”；“’gro”則意指“行走”；“ma”爲陰性詞詞尾。所以“mkha’ ’gro ma”[13]三個字完整的意思爲“虛空中行走的女性”。空行母這一議題看似非常平常而又簡單，實則不然。正如美國學者Janice D. Willis在其“空行母：對其本質與意義的相關論述”一文中所說：毋庸置疑，空行母是密宗宗教裹面最爲重要的、最強有力的（potent）以及最爲活躍的一個象徵、觀點和符號。而正是因爲她的那種活力和力量以及她那無所不包的象徵性，所以想去界定它抑或對它進行一種單一性質的定義幾乎都是不可能的[14]。所以，（西方學者）對於空行母之意義，始終沒有形成一個定論抑或說達到一種共識，那些力圖进一步界定和描述空行母之本質及其作用方面的的各种尝试亦可謂失當[15]。由此可見，西方學者在如何準確地看待和解釋空行母方面可謂各執一詞，互爲牴牾，頗存紛歧異趣。早期學者如L. Austine Waddell[16]、Evans Wentz[17]傾向於把空行母定義爲一種“復仇女神”（furies）抑

---

⑬ 對於這點，西方學界有幾種不同的聲音：首先，學者Herbert V. Guenther認爲，“mkha’”意指一種“空性”（藏文作stong pa nyid；梵文作Śūnyatā），而“’gro”則表明一種“證悟”（to understand），因此在他看來，空行母表示的是“證悟空性的女性”，不僅如此，“dākinī”的陽性對等詞“dāka”亦表示是證悟空行的人，見於Herbert V. Guenther, *Treasures on the Tibetan Middle Way*, California: Shambahla Publications, 1976, p. 103. 對於這點，我們可以在後來的學者Judith Simmer- Brown所撰之*Dākinī 's Warm Breath: The Feminine principle In Tibetan Buddhism*一書中看到對其做的詳盡的解釋: Judith Simmer- Brown, *Dākinī 's Warm Breath: The Feminine principle In Tibetan Buddhism,* Boston：Shambhala Publications, 2001, p. 51.

⑭ Janice D. Willis，“Dākinī: Some Comments on its Nature and Meaning”，in *The Tibet Journal*，Vol.1，12，No. 4(1987)，pp. 56-71.

⑮ Janice D. Willis, “ Dākinī: Some Comments on its Nature and Meaning”, pp. 56-71.

⑯ A. Waddell, *Tibetan Buddhism*, New York: Dover Publications, 1972, p. 366（Willis, 69）. A. Waddell還認爲空行母等同於瑜伽女修行者（Yogini），因爲他覺得“furies”和“yogini”都在意指一種“具有神力的女神”，認爲她們是被一種自然和超自然之力所賜予的。

⑰ W. Y. Evans-Wentz, *Tibetan Yoga and Secret Doctrines*, London: Oxford University Press, 1935 (Willis, 69).

或“女巫”（witch）；而和其差不多同時代的Sarat Chandra Das[18]和較後的Robert Paul[19]則將空行母釋義成“仙女”（fairy）抑或“精靈”（sprite）。然而，於密宗手（tantric adept）而言，空行母扮演的則是一種類似“信使”（messenger）或者“女先知”（prphetesses）、“女護法”（protectress）以及“鼓勵者”（inspirer）的角色；但有的時候，他們也被視爲“明妃”（rig ma）抑或一種“神秘伴侶”（mystic consort）[20]。後來，晚期學者David Snellgrove通過一種宏觀視角，著眼於整個的佛教之發展歷史，梳理了前人們對於空行母的各家看法，亦廓清了一些有關空行母的謬論，還提出了自己的一些看法：他認爲，密宗文本裏常以瑜伽士之伴侶而出現的女性人物，她們是空行母。瑜伽士去參觀朝聖之地，她們都會緊隨跟來。她們之所以被人視爲“女巫”，是因爲她們的出現與一種性式儀軌相關，而且還因爲她們的活動充斥著一種陰森恐怖和較爲猥褻的怪調，這就使得人們給其冠以一個“女巫”的稱號。但是當她們進入藏地神話世界之後（也就是密宗入藏），她們一改往日形象，不再是昔日印度佛教密宗之中的那種駭人形象既吃人肉又飲人血，而是以一種較爲柔和的形象示人，盡管在外形上還保有一點兇猛之相。她們入藏密系統後，身份便變得不同往日，於藏密她們代表的是一種個人智慧的象徵，是神秘教法的賜予者和神聖供品的提供者。因此,David Snellgrove他覺得把空行母看作是一種“女巫”或者“仙女”的見解顯得有些欠妥[21]。由此可見，空行母經歷了一種從早先印度密宗中嗜血駭人之形象到成爲藏傳佛教密宗中代表智慧的一種護法形象。而這正是佛教密宗之印度和西藏的分界問題。我們知道，印度大乘佛教開始出現密教化是在公元第7世紀左右，當時波羅王朝的勃興和超行寺的建立，就是後期大乘佛學的性質開始出現密教化的標誌，發展到後來則是完全融合於密教之中，而這一切皆是因爲當時大乘佛學之繁瑣理論不爲群眾所接受，故爲了爭取群眾，便採取了印度教的方法，而密教的性質同印度教相接近，這便是印度佛教密宗產生的主要原因（《印度佛學源流略講》[22]）。印度佛學密宗一直發展到13世紀初伊斯蘭教入侵印度滅佛爲止。當時超行寺的毀滅，便是印度佛教終止發展的一個象徵。後來，密宗通過蓮花生大士之力傳入西藏，形成了具有藏地特色的藏傳密宗，相應地空行母的身份定位也隨之發生了變化。故研究需從印度佛教密宗中的空行母（密宗入藏前）和藏傳佛教中的空行母（密宗入藏後）這兩種角度來進行研究，不然任何一種忽略歷史的看法都沒法解釋和認識空行母的來龍去脈。

從前文可知，空行母一詞具有非常多元且甚深的象徵含義所闡述的內容，但若要

---

⑱ Sarat Chandra Das, Rai Bahadur, *A Tibetan-English Dictionary with Sanskrit Synonyms*, Delhi: Motilal Bonarsidass, 1970, p. 180.

⑲ Robert Paul, *The Tibetan Symbolic World : Psychoanalytic Exploration*, Chicago：The University of Chicago Press，1982，p. 132.

⑳ Janice D. Willis, “Dākinī: Some Comments on its Nature and Meaning”, p. 56.

㉑ Snellgrove, *Buddhist Himalaya*, Oxford: Bruno Cassirer, 1957, p. 175（Willis, 69）.

㉒ 呂澂《印度佛學源流略講》，上海：上海人民出版社，2005年，200—217頁。

從類型上判別的話，其主要分爲兩種類型：即“世間空行母”（‘jig rten pa’i mkha’ ’gro ma）和“智慧空行母”（Ye shes kyi mkha’ ’gro ma）。所謂“世間空行母”，是指不住清淨刹土，而出現在凡間人世的空行母，如卓瓦桑姆等（Dag pa’i zhing du bzhugs pa min par ’jig rten gyi tshul bzung ba’i mkha’ ’gro ma ’gro ba bzang mo lta bu）[23]抑或叫“世俗空行母”，是指一種獲得神通變化的凡人瑜伽母（Rdzu ‘phrul thob pa’i so so skye bo’i rnal ’byor ma）[24]；而“智慧空行母則指一種出世間空行母或指那種證得三乘（Theg pa gsum）之見（mthong）、修（sgom）、無學（mi slob）此三聖道而現女人身者即爲“佛母”或“聖母”（‘phags ma），亦可叫金剛瑜伽母（‘jig rten las ’das pa’i mkha’ ’gro ma’am/’phags ma’am rdo rje rnal ‘byor ma）[25]。“世間空行母”和“智慧空行母”，二者區别若何，於此略述一二：其一，從二者發展演變的歷史來看[26]，前者更接近於早前印度傳統中的空行母形象，也就是説其是印度前佛教時期（pre-buddhist）[27]的一個文化遺物，對於這點學者Martin Kalff在其所撰的“上樂金剛傳承中的空行母”（Dākinī in the Cakrasamvara Tradition）一文中作有詳細的闡釋，他認爲印度前佛教時期的空行母如同邪魔（Demons）一般，是一個不良女性（harmful female）；其二，盡管很多時候於密宗語境中，智慧空性母在所依靠的出現之方式上，跟世間空行母並無大異，但其有一個世間空行母所不具備之特點，即她有三只眼睛，第三只眼睛垂直立於其額頭中間[28]。除此之外，更多關於空行母之其他問題，可通讀《蓮花遺教》（*Padma bka’ thang*）[29]一書，其中對於密宗入藏前後的相關事宜皆有敘及，盡管其中有些内容有待深入研究。

2. 西方學者的空行母研究範式

學者Keith Dowman曾在其*Sky Dancer*：*The Secret Life and Songs of the Lady Yeshe Tsogyel*這一書中提到：空行母這個詞把一個珍貴的新概念引進了西方世界。這概念的價值正是在於它缺乏精確的定義；它涵蓋了一系列的涵義——女性的原則、一個精神上

㉓ 可見於張怡蓀主編《藏漢大辭典》（*bod rgya tshig mdzod chen mo*），北京：民族出版社，1984年，895頁。

㉔ 張怡蓀主編《藏漢大辭典》（*bod rgya tshig mdzod chen mo*），895頁。

㉕ 張怡蓀主編《藏漢大辭典》（*bod rgya tshig mdzod chen mo*），2594頁。

㉖ 對於世間空行母和智慧空行母之歷史演變以及二者區别若何問題，可見於Judith Simmer-Brown所撰之*Dākinī 's Warm Breath: The Feminine principle In Tibetan Buddhism*一書中對此所做的詳盡的討論，Judith Simmer-Brown, *Dākinī 's Warm Breath: The Feminine principle In Tibetan Buddhism,* pp. 53-65.

㉗ Martin Kalff, “Dākinī in the Cakrasamvara Tradition”, *Tibetan Studies*, Zurich: Völkerkundemuseum der Universität Zurich, 1978, pp.149-162（Willis, 69）.

㉘ See Judith Simmer-Brown, *Dākinī 's Warm Breath: The Feminine principle In Tibetan Buddhism*, p. 64.

㉙ 《蓮花遺教》（*Padma bka'thang*），青海：塔爾寺出版，2001年。

融合的時機、上師的明妃、女性性伴侶——這些加總起來成爲一個迷和矛盾[30]。嚴格意義上來講，空行母對於西方世界而言，始終是一個“他者”的存在，而且是一個神秘的“他者”形象，因此西方學者在解讀空行母時難免會以一種“他者化”的視角來建構其相關理論抑或文化意識形態。對此，學者Judith Simmer-Brown在其所撰寫的*Dakini's Warm Breath: The Feminine principle In Tibetan Buddhism*[31]一文中，概述了西方學界對於空行母這一議題所產生的較爲流行的幾種研究範式：其一爲榮格心理學中的靈魂論，認爲其是一種与无意识（unconcious）密切相关的女性之原型（archetype），嵌於男人的靈魂（psyche）之中。這種範式是西方最早應用於空行母研究的一個學術路徑，其反映了榮格對早期西方學者所產生的深遠的學術影響，比如揚名於國內外藏學界的學者Giuseppe Tucci便是其中一個典型的例子，他將榮格觀點應用於解釋[32]曼荼罗；第二種研究範式爲女性主義論，這種主張近年來尤爲流行，尤其深受西方女性學者們的厚待，引起了她們廣泛的關注。

持榮格靈魂論的學者們認爲，空行母是異性的一個幻想（fantasy of opposites）。Judith在其書中提到，榮格與西藏密宗之間的交通之跡始於W.Y.Evans-Wentz 學者讓他爲前者所編的有關西藏密宗文本一書即*The Tibetan Book of the Great Liberation: or the Method of Realizing Nirvana through Knowing the Mind*[33]之中的幾篇文章發表心理學式的評論。對於《西藏解脱書：或通過意識瞭悟涅槃之方便》一書，學者Donald S. Lopez在其著作*Prisoners of Shangri-la: Tibetan Buddhism and the West*[34]中有大篇幅的闡述。榮格初次接觸藏傳密宗的經歷，爲其後來的學術無疑產生了一定的影響[35]。但他本人對於靈魂與空行母之間的關係從未發表過任何一種直接的言論。更爲諷刺的是，Judith認爲榮格本人甚至可能不會提倡從靈魂原理去解讀空行母，因爲他可能覺得“東方視野”（eastern view）偏於保守，所以一切把空行母箍於靈魂原理之下去分析和解讀空行母的行爲都顯得不妥；此外他亦不覺得西方複雜靈魂之外向性，需要的是一個無形的個人實體（personal entity），一個處於不同與我們世界的個體。由此可見，榮格本人其實

---

[30] Keith Dowman, *Sky Dancer: The Secret Life and Songs of the Lady Yeshe Tsogyel*, New York: Snow Lion Publications, 1996, p. 273. 其原文爲：“The word Dākinī, or Khandroma, has introduced a valuable new concept to the western world. The value of the concept is in its very lace of precise definition; it embraces a range of meaning—the female principle, a moment of spiritual integration, the Guru's Consort, a female sexual partner—that adds up to an enigma and paradox”。該句被學者June Campbell引述於其*Traveller in Space: Gender, Identity and Tibetan Buddhism*這一書中，並對其進行了一定的抨擊，相關中文譯作見呂艾論，臺灣：正智出版社，2012年，219頁。

[31] See Judith Simmer-Brown, *Dākinī 's Warm Breath: The Feminine principle In Tibetan Buddhism*, pp. 12-17.

[32] Judith Simmer-Brown, *Dākinī 's Warm Breath: The Feminine principle In Tibetan Buddhism*, p.12.

[33] W.Y. Evans-Wentz, Donald S. Lopez, C. G. Jung, The Tibetan Book of the Great Liberation: *or the Method of Realizing Nirvana through Knowing the Mind,* London: Oxford University Press, 2000.

[34] Donald S. Lopez, *Prisoners of Shangri-la: Tibetan Buddhism and the West*, Chicago: University of Chicago Press, 1998, pp. 47-50. 而對於該書，沈衛榮教授發表了一篇具有深刻見解的文章，見《美国藏学主流的学术传承和学术批评》一文，文章來源《東方早報》，2016年4月10日。

[35] See Simmer-Brown, *Dākinī 's Warm Breath: The Feminine principle In Tibetan Buddhism,* p. 12.

更傾向於將空行母視作一種“靈魂數據”[36]（psychic data），而非一種“集體無意識”（collective unconscious）。換言之，就是榮格把靈魂視作爲一種個人主體性（personal subjectivity）抑或一種內在生活（inner life），一種與公開形象（public persona）截然相反的東西，或者應說靈魂不是外在形象能夠表達或顯現出來的一種東西，因爲它是無形的、是直覺的，它還与更深层次的精神力量相联系，以一種符號或以象徵的形式呈現於意识之中，並對每一个决定，行为和观点產生影響[37]。由此看來，“空行母是異性的一個幻想”這一說是後來學者從榮格靈魂原理之中衍生出來的一個學說。因爲在他們看來，空行母就像靈魂一樣，代表的是一種外在所缺乏的東西。這種研究範式尤其側重於異性論、雙性共生（contrasexuality）以及性別意象的終極性和心理層面的解讀。總之，於筆者而言，這種透過靈魂之棱鏡來解讀空行母的範式頗爲新穎，無論好壞，其都爲我們瞭解問題本身提供了一個极大的幫助。

至於女性主義研究範式，其徹底顛覆了空行母原有的傳統形象即女性護法或佛母。西方學者所具有的這種女性主義研究視角，跟其所處的環境是有一定的關係的。我們都知道，20世紀60年至70年代，女性主義的第二次浪潮席卷了西方世界，此運動大概一直持續到了80年代。該運動的發生，對西方社會產生了極大的影響，其中性別研究的興起便是其中之一，80年代以降，西方世界就便出現了很多各種不同的女性主義派别。而近年以來，這種情況尤甚，女性主義的觸角也開始從政治學、社會學的領域延伸到了宗教世界，空行母這一議題亦毫無例外地成爲了女權主義者們熱衷研究與討論的對象。

迄今，西方學界用兩性視角去檢視空行母問題方面，湧現出了不少作品，於此略舉一二，比如首當其衝的Judith Simmer-Brown的*Dakini's Warm Breath: The Feminine principle In Tibetan Buddhism*；Michaela Haas所著的*Dakini Power: Twelve Extraordinary Women Shaping the Transmission of Tibetan Buddhism in the West*[38]；還有Rita M. Gross所寫的*Buddhism after Patriarchy: A Feminist History, Analysis, and Reconstruction of Buddhism*[39]；學者Ann Carolyn Klein所著之*Meeting the Great Bliss Queen: Buddhists, Feminists, and the Art of the Self*[40]；Tsultrim Allione的*Women of Wisdom*[41]；以及Keith Dowman的*Sky Dancer*：*The Secret Life and Songs of the Lady Yeshe Tsogyel*[42]和June Campbell的*Traveller in Space:*

㊱ Simmer-Brown, *Dākinī's Warm Breath: The Feminine principle In Tibetan Buddhism,* p. 12.

㊲ Simmer-Brown, *Dākinī's Warm Breath: The Feminine principle In Tibetan Buddhism,* p. 13.

㊳ Michaela Haas, *Dākinī Power: Twelve Extraordinary Women Shaping the Transmission of Tibetan Buddhism in the West,* New York: Snow Lion Publications, 2013.

㊴ Rita M. Gross, *Buddhism after Patriarchy: A Feminist History, Analysis, and Reconstruction of Buddhism,* New York: State University of New York Press, 1993.

㊵ Ann Carolyn Klein, *Meeting the Great Bliss Queen: Buddhists, Feminists, and the Art of the Self,* New York: Snow Lion Publications, 2008.

㊶ Tsultrim Allione, *Women of Wisdom,* New York: Snow Lion Publications, 2000.

㊷ Keith Dowman, *Sky Dancer: The Secret Life and Songs of the Lady Yeshe Tsogyel.*

Gender, Identity and Tibetan Buddhism[43]等這一系列的作品。這些作品以不同的看法對藏傳密宗中的空行母問題各抒己見，無論是對金剛乘中空行母之性別問題還是其身份定位問題，都有所敘及。雖然有些作品並非針對與藏傳密宗而作，但其中不乏與空行母這一議題相通之處，故提及於茲以供大家討論。

如前所述，"空行母"藏文作"mkha''gro ma"，其名中自帶有一種表示陰性的"ma"字，也許正是因爲這點，使得個別學者對其產生了謬見。比如學者Simmer-Brown在其書中所說的那樣，傳統意義上，空行母會被視爲一種可貴的象徵、符號，或者爲一種內在精神之旅的秘密。而這一正面形象卻被西方女權主義者們加以利用把其改造成了一種"女性中心主義者的聖騎士"（gynocentric crusader）或"厭女者的受害人"（misogynized victim）。顯然，美國佛教的這種性別戰爭扭曲了其真正的教義。此外，Simmer-Brown[44]還認爲如果這種異性對立論或政治上的性別之爭滲透到宗教世界的現象一旦成爲美國佛教發展的一個趨勢的話，那麼這無疑會對佛教教義的完整傳播會構成巨大的威脅。因此，作者呼籲西方學者，尤其是西方女權主義學者，停止用政治學、社會學或女性主義來審視空行母這一宗教議題，而應把其置入其所在的領域，也就是說對待空行母應該用宗教的視角去分析之。對此，筆者深表認同。

總而言之，筆者于該文中，通過搜羅相關文獻並對其進行梳羅抉別之後，對有關空行母蘇卡悉地及其相關問題，略述了一番。如此以來，對在藏文史籍中沒有載或有記載而太過簡略的，甚至在旁的書籍中也記載很少的有關空行母蘇卡悉地方面具有填補空白的作用，可以彌補不少缺憾。其中，西方學者的空行母研究範式作爲一個大的議題，有待日後更爲深入更爲詳盡的探討，而此處所述僅供探討者的參考。

A Brief Study of Sukhasiddhi

Sonam Drolma

Sukhasiddhi was an Indian teacher of Vajrayana Buddhism and master of meditation. She was also one of root teachers of the Tibetan yogi Khyungpo Nenjor, who founded the Shangpa Kagyu school of Tibetan Buddhism. Her six dharmas is one of the main religious teachings of Shangspa Kagyu. Although it still forms the very core of the Shangpa Kagyu lineage currently, it enjoys very little attention and understanding from the academia for a dearth of related documents. So I will explore here who is Sukhasiddhi in order to get a clear perspective of its important role in the Shangpa Kagyu lineage. And I will also give a brief discussion on the methodology employed by western scholars currently on the topic of Dākinī.

[43] June Campbell, *Traveller in Space: Gender, Identity and Tibetan Buddhism.*

[44] See Simmer-Brown, *Dākinī 's Warm Breath: The Feminine principle In Tibetan Buddhism, pp.* 5-6.

談白一平—沙加爾上古音体系的幾個問題

高永安

最近讀William H. Baxter（白一平）and Laurent Sagart（沙加爾）的新著*Old Chinese: A New Reconstruction*（《上古漢語的新構擬》）①，感覺兩位先生徵引博贍、論證宏闊，博學多聞！兩位先生都是從事漢語歷史研究多年，對漢語的上古音構擬花費了很多心血，成績卓著！兩位先生的構擬試圖擺脱“有一分證據説一分話”的實證方法，讓人耳目一新。而兩位先生把其最新著作的主要構擬成果放到網絡上②，供大家免費下載使用，其公益之心，令人感動！但是儘管如此，我在閱讀過程中有些疑惑之處，還是願意提出來，就教于兩位先生和大方之家！

一

作者引證非常豐富，從古代典籍到現代理論，從《詩經》押韻到漢字諧聲，從甲骨文到六國文字，從中古語音系統到古今方言，能夠駕馭這麼浩繁的文獻，真是需要功力！但是，其中一些對前人結論的徵引，竊以爲缺乏審慎的選擇。例如奧德里古爾的漢語聲調來源說。

奧德里古爾（André G. Haudricourt）《越南語聲調的起源》認爲越南語的聲調是受漢語影響產生的③。而6世紀前後，越南語有六個聲調，清濁搭配，可以歸結爲三類：平聲（清）與弦聲（濁）爲一類，問聲（清）與跌聲（濁）爲一類，鋭聲（清）與重聲（濁）爲一類。三類聲調的韻，在韻尾上都有表現：第一類（平、弦）爲舒聲，具有鼻音、元音韻尾或者無韻尾；第二類（問、跌）具有喉塞音韻尾，即-ʔ；第三類（鋭、重）具有清擦音韻尾，即-s。

越南語：	平聲（弦聲）-n	中古漢語：平聲
	問聲（跌聲）-ʔ	上聲

① William H. Baxter and Laurent Sagart, *Old Chinese: A New Reconstruction,* New York: Oxford University Press, 2014.

② 網址是：http://ocbaxtersagart.lsait.lsa.umich.edu/.

③ 奧德里古爾(André G. Haudricourt)《越南語聲調的起源》，見馮蒸《冯蒸音韵论集》，北京：学苑出版社，2006年，68—82頁。

銳聲（重聲）-s　　　　去聲

既然漢語的平聲韻尾跟越南語的平聲（弦聲）一致，上聲和去聲豈不是也跟越南語的問聲（跌聲）、銳聲（重聲）一致嗎？這個研究似乎很巧妙，但是卻經不起推敲。根據王力的《漢越語研究》，漢越語聲調跟漢語聲調的對應並不整齊，問聲對漢語上聲，銳聲對漢語去聲字的對應並不占絕對數量④。薛才德研究認爲，藏語的-s不支持漢語聲調具有-s韻尾的假說⑤。其後反對這一學說的論文大量出現，基本上否定了這個說法。但是白一沙二位先生還採用這個說法作爲其構擬上古漢語韻尾（這兩個韻尾預示著未來的聲調產生）的依據，不能不說是一大缺憾。

目前構擬上古漢語聲調的方案有很多，但是最成功的方案還是王力的平、上、長入、短入說。王力的方案是從清人段玉裁的“上聲備於三百篇，去聲備于魏晉”，以及黄侃“上古有平入二聲”的先聲來的。而這個理論主要來自對先秦韻文的押韻狀況。但是王力的方案經常被問到一個問題：如果中古的平上去入四聲來自上古平上入三聲，那麼是怎樣的發展關係呢？例如，部分去聲從長入而來，但是去聲裏的陽聲韻字是哪裏來的？答案當然是從平上聲來的⑥。這個問題白一沙兩位的回答看似近理。比如：

表1　白一沙的後來發展爲聲調的韻尾示意表

	甲類	乙類	中古聲調
A	巴*pˤra	方*paŋ	平
B	把*pˤraʔ	丙*praŋʔ	上
C	霸*pˤrak-s	傍*[b]ˤaŋ-s	去
D	白*bˤrak		入

表1中，A、B、C、D分別對應于中古音的四個聲調：平上去入。在甲類中，除去後來發展爲聲調的韻尾-ʔ和-s，A、B兩行韻母相同，可以一起押韻；C、D兩行韻母相同，可以一起押韻。但是，C行与D行一起押韻比較多的是所謂的祭部字，他們在中古音裏發展爲去聲；但是在上古音裏，他們經常跟入聲有關涉，所以，他們被構擬爲“*pˤrak-s”是可以的。但是C行裏还有另一类，比如“事忌意禦助”都來自古上聲，“畏”來自古平聲，這些字並不像第一类字那樣經常跟入聲押韻，卻可以偶爾跟平上聲一起押韻。對於這些字來說，在上表中就是A、B、C爲一類，而D自成一類。那麼我們怎麼解釋一些韻的字要實現類似“ak-s”與“a/ aʔ/”押韻而與“ak”相遠呢？但在王力的系統裏就沒有這樣的問題。因爲王力的上聲、去聲都不是用韻尾來表示的，那麼平上去的押韻就可以實現了。如：

---

④　又參見丁邦新《丁邦新語言學論文集》，北京：商務印書館，1998年，83—105頁。

⑤　參見薛才德《漢語藏語同源字研究》，上海：上海大學出版社，2001年。

⑥　王力說：“魏晉時代產生去聲。陰聲韻的去聲字，多由長入字轉來（去聲產生後不再存在長入聲），少數由平上聲轉來；陽聲韻的去聲字由平上聲轉來。”王力《漢語語音史》，北京：中國社會科學出版社，1985年，162頁。

表2 王力的上古聲調示意表

	甲類	乙類	中古聲調
A	巴*peaa	方*pɨaaŋ	平
B	把*pea	丙*pɨaŋ	上
C	霸*peaak	傍*baŋ	去
D	白*beak		入

表2中A、B兩類押韻的障礙是，長短元音是否可以押韻。這個問題可以參考一個旁證材料。高永安《漢藏語系一些少數民族語言詩歌押韻情況簡析》[⑦]調查了現在具有長短元音對立的語言的詩歌押韻實例，發現對立的長短元音之間押韻的情況，雖然不能說是常例，但是數量很大。也就是說，在王力的系統裏，平聲和上聲偶有押韻是沒問題的。第二個問題是，如果說去聲是长入聲脱落塞音韻尾而來的，那麼陽聲韻裏的平上聲變爲去聲的條件是什麼？這個問題可以根據當時（即去聲產生的漢魏時期）的用字狀況推測。當時去聲剛從入聲中獨立出來，成爲一個新的獨立聲調，所以它具有很強的標記性。這個標記大概跟四聲别義的時尚結合起來了，就產生了大量的去聲。在四聲别義的實踐中，語義、語法等不管是什麼關係，最終變爲去聲的居多[⑧]。這可能就是當時去聲大量出現的原因。這裏面可能有個疑問，難道一個聲調產生可以不需要語音條件嗎？其實真不需要。一個聲調的產生未必都是爲了補償音段音位，比如語義、語法、語用，都可能影響聲調。駐馬店方言的入聲分派，受到連讀變調的影響，就是一個例子。駐馬店話屬於中原官話，其清入聲應該都歸陰平。但還是有一些入聲字今歸了陽平。據考察，原來這些歸在陽平的古入聲字，在使用中常常放在雙音詞的詞首部位，而這個位置，正好有陽平的變調。如黑豆、鐵路、雞蛋，前字都是陽平，但單獨讀的時候就是陰平。其中，“雞”是平聲字，不會改變聲調；而“黑、鐵”都是入聲字，他們如果是處在入聲消失的時候，新的聲調還沒有固定，就容易改變原來的聲調類别。上述“鐵”就改變了，單獨用於形容一個人有力氣，就用“鐵”陽平。去聲的產生大概有似於此。這種語言的使用情況影響聲調歸屬的實例應該不少，如果按照白—沙的思路，這些都應該構擬爲韻尾的區别，那就距離事實太遠了。

二

白—沙的系統裏，前置音節的構擬也很值得商榷。白—沙參考了侗台語（或叫卡岱

⑦ 高永安《漢藏語系一些少數民族：語言詩歌押韻情況簡析》，《語言學論叢》第34輯，北京：商務印書館，2006年，38—49頁。

⑧ 孫玉文把四聲别義叫做變調構詞，認爲是一種詞彙派生的手段。孫玉文《漢語變調構詞研究》（增訂本），北京：商務印書館，2007年，371頁。“四聲别義主要是平、上、入聲字，變爲去聲，其意義主要是由其他詞性變爲意義有關聯的動詞。”高永安《聲調》，北京：商務印書館，2014年，189頁。

語Kra-Dai）的冠音，認爲上古漢語也應該有一套冠音，或叫前綴音。這個前綴音可以是一個輔音音素，也可以是一個小的、内部結構相對簡單的音節。這個思路沒有處理好語言的層次，從幾個方面來說都是行不通的。

所謂層次，有同源的，就是不同時代的疊加。例如，爸和父就是同源的層次，兩個詞都是父親的意思，只是一個是古代用的，一個是今天用的。兩個詞有歷史關係，但是還不能說“父”上古音就讀如“爸”。因爲那時古代的語音系統裏的音，按照今天的構擬，它應該有一個介音。“爸”在“父”的古音構擬上可以有參考價值。所謂異源層次，就是有不同來源的層次。例如，宣城方言裏古日母字有[z][ȵ]兩個音。如果按照一般的構擬，就爲它早期構擬一個[zȵ]，以解釋这兩個音的來源。但是，宣城話的這兩個音應該是有不同的來源。鼻音的來源是本地的自源讀音，擦音的來源應該是外來的影響。怎麼知道呢？可以比較周圍的方言，對宣城話影響最大的是江淮官話，而江淮官話中的日母讀音就是擦音。而宣城所屬的吴語，其日母則一般是鼻音。這個比較只是一個線索，在詞彙中的表現才是根據：古日母字在宣城話裏分讀擦音和鼻音的時候，在詞彙裏往往有書面和口語的差别。例如，“人民”的“人”就是擦音，“媒人”的“人”則是鼻音。媒人是生活用詞彙，不需要上台面，所以就用本土讀音；要上台面的，要在官場說的詞彙，其讀音則很容易受到強勢方言的影響。所以，就宣城話本身來看，如果要爲這個方言日母字構擬出早期的形式,就要摒棄外來的擦音一讀,僅僅構擬出鼻音即可。

儘管有很多學者論述到漢藏語系其他語言有前冠音，比如謝蓓蒂、張琨[⑨]、陳其光[⑩]認爲古苗瑤語有前冠音，戴慶廈[⑪]認爲古藏緬語有前冠音、王太春[⑫]認爲古侗台語有前冠音。但是，是不是漢藏語系的其他三大語族都有前冠音，漢語就一定有前冠音呢？這些資料只能說提供了一個概率，並不能證明上古漢語一定有前冠音。羅傑瑞認爲，閩語有一種弱化聲母，根據泰語前加成分能够促使聲母弱化，推測原始閩語也有一套帶前加成分的聲母[⑬]。後來有人竟然發現了漢語方言也有前冠音（鼻冠音）聲母[⑭]。但是這種前冠音的來源卻值得商榷，因爲那其實很有可能是早期的層次，因爲這些帶前加成分的語言或方言都集中在一個毗鄰的地域空間，也有可能是异源层次[⑮]。

---

⑨ 謝蓓蒂、張琨《苗瑤語藏緬語漢語的鼻冠塞音聲母》，《史語所集刊》第47本第8分，臺北，1977年，467—561頁。

⑩ 陳其光《古苗瑤語鼻冠閉塞音聲母在現代方言中的反映形式的類型》，《民族語文》1984年第5期，11—22頁。

⑪ 戴慶廈《彝緬語鼻冠聲母的來源及發展——兼論彝緬語語音演變的“整化”作用》，《民族語文》1992年第1期，42—48、51頁。

⑫ 王太春《仡佬語鼻冠音聲母研究》，中央民族大學2008年硕士学位论文，4—8頁。

⑬ Norman, Jerry（羅傑瑞）, “The Initials of Proto-Min”, *Joural of Chinese Linguistics*, 1974, 2(1), pp. 27-36.

⑭ 胡方《論廈門話[-mb -ŋg -nd]聲母的聲學特性及其他》，《方言》2005年第1期，9—17頁。

⑮ 參見王福堂《閩北方言弱化聲母和“第九調”之我見》，《中國語文》1994年第6期，430—433頁；王福堂《原始閩語中的清弱化聲母和相關的“第九調”》，《中國語文》2004年第2期，135—144、191—192頁；王福堂《漢語方言語音的演變和層次》（修訂版），北京：語文出版社，2005年，121—149頁。

其次，我們且不說三大語族的語音特徵未必能推論出漢語早期必須具有前冠音。就前冠音這個具體問題看，三大語族的前冠音（不論是音素還是音節）可能是地區性的。因爲所謂前冠音是一個語音問題,地域相連的不同語言或方言可能相互借用相同的語音特徵或要素。比如，安徽寧國在太平天國時期人口損失很大，後來有很多湖北人移民于此形成湖北話方言島。但是，如今他们的方言具有的陽聲韻鼻化並進一步脱落的特徵，跟移民來源地湖北話不同，而跟移民目的地相同。也就是說，湖北移民接受了當地的語音特徵，但是仍保留著原來方言的主體。如果我們要根據這個移民方言島來構擬它的早期形式，要不要構擬出陽聲韻鼻化的特徵呢？那顯然就選錯了道路。那麼，三大語族的前冠音是不是由於地區毗鄰才具備的呢？

況且，白一沙採用的是他們認定爲三個語族中的早期漢語借詞，且不說時代上的參差會帶來錯位，這些借詞的來源方言是哪種方言也可能會影響到借詞的形式,比如越南的漢越語,其來源方言就有長安話說、平話說、粵語說。而借詞的語音形式可能是這些方言才具有的，而這些形式又可能是該方言的底層。举一个白一沙用例：

（49）瓦*C.ŋʷˤra[j]ʔ> *ngwaeX* > w ǎ “屋頂”

比較：瓦，原始閩語：*ŋh-，梅縣客家話：/ŋa 3/，越南語：ngói [ŋɔi B1]，聲調是高調域。

這裏的*C.表示一個不確定的前冠音，他们構擬的目的是爲了解釋閩方言、客家話和越南語早期借詞中的陽域聲調（upper-register tones）。如果這些毗鄰地區的陽調都有共同的來源，而屬於一個歷時層次，那麼這個構擬就把問題複雜化了。例如，孟慶惠⑯、劉福鑄⑰先後報導漢語徽方言、閩方言和畲語都有成套邊擦音聲母（tɬ、tʰɬ、ɬ），但是在漢語古音構擬時，還沒有人採用這套聲母作爲其聲母系統的一員，爲什麼？因爲大家基本同意這是古百越語的底層。前冠音会不会也是這樣？

三

爲什麼“白一沙”會努力把所有的上古漢語語音特徵，和古方言特徵、相關語言及其借詞的特徵，都展現在他們的系統中呢？最直接的原因還是，儘管他們本來計劃要構擬出一個特定時代的上古漢語，但是還是太想構擬出一個漢語的祖語，並且用它來解釋所有漢語語音演變。白一沙的構擬目標是什麼時期呢？該書對這一點有明確的說明，其時間跨度是從商代晚期（公元前1250）到秦統一中國（公元前221）。並且意識到，這個時期漢語的在時間和地域上都產生了很多變體⑱。順便說一句，如果漢語真的是一源分化的，這個目標就沒有錯,如果漢語是多源融合的,或者有分化又有融合的,那麼這個目

⑯ 孟慶惠《黃山話的tɬ、tʰɬ、ɬ及其探源》，《中國語文》1981年第1期，46—49頁。

⑰ 劉福鑄《莆仙方言邊擦音[ɬ]聲母探源》，《莆田學院學報》2007年第3期，93—98頁。

⑱ William H. Baxter and Laurent Sagart, *Old Chinese: A New Reconstruction,* 見1.1。

標就稍微有點兒錯位。這裏白一沙大概是假設漢語是一源的。這個問題先放在一邊，在這一千年左右的時間内，這個語言既然在時間和地域上都有差别，那麼這個差别有多大？是一個基本同質的語言，還是前後有很大差别？或者甚至是到了互相不能通話的地步？

从地域差别来看，春秋戰國時期的楚語、齊語、吴語都已經特徵明顯，相互之間差距很大，甚至於需要專門學習才能掌握。这都是有歷史記載的。從時間差别來看，商代的語言可能還不是漢語，而是漢語祖先華夏語與藏緬語沒有分家時的共同語。所以，武王伐紂時，武王的講話羌戎軍隊不用翻譯就能明白[19]。但是至遲到魯襄公十四年，姜戎氏就抱怨與華夏人"言語不達"，說明華夏語已經與藏緬語分家了[20]。這麼說，如果把甲骨文跟六國文字放在一起，來探討他們的共同語，可能是不合適的。

另一個問題是，我們現在正在使用的語言真的只是從商代晚期開始的嗎？漢語更早的歷史真的是子虛烏有的嗎？如果我們能找到我們語言的更早的證據，那麼今天我們構擬的這個用來解釋所有漢語方言的共同語，是不是還不夠格呢?有研究表明，我們使用的這種語言與親屬語言的祖語在五六千年之前已經存在了，而這種祖語就是今天我們說的漢藏語系諸語言的祖先。這個說法聽起來仿佛神話，但它有大量的史籍呈現的古今口傳歷史、考古文化的支持，又經過語言比較的驗證（即三重證據法），所以是可信的。那個時代就是五帝時代，那個時代的語言有個名字叫華夷語系[21]。

接下來的問題是，從五帝時期（大約仰韶文化晚期，公元前3000）到秦統一（公元前221），這就不是一千多年，而是三千多年了。不管五帝時代的語言狀況是怎樣的，儘管今天我們無法確切知道，但是，那種語言是從那時候就存在的，而且一直延續到今天。而它在稍晚的夏代是怎樣的？商代又是怎樣的？都是可以探討的問題。但是可以肯定，夏商時代的語言，由於它不是最早的源頭，所以也不必試圖構擬爲最早的共同語言祖先。那麼，我們還能夠指望構擬一個以春秋戰國時期的語言特徵爲主體的共同語，來解釋後來所有語言的演變嗎？

Note on Baxter- Sagart' Reconstruction of old Chinese Phonology

Gao Yong'an

William H. Baxter (白一平) and Laurent Sagart' (沙加爾) new reconstruction of Chinese, *Old Chinese: A New Reconstruction*, have made some progress. However, some fundamental theorles in this book, such as André G. Haudricourt' tone theory, and the reconstruction of pre-initial sounds, are not strong enough.

---

⑲ 俞敏《俞敏語言學論文集》，北京：商務印書館，1999年，204頁。

⑳ 何九盈《重建華夷語系的理論和證據》，北京：商務印書館，2015年，52頁。

㉑ 參見何九盈《重建華夷語系的理論和證據》。

《上古漢語：構擬新論》音義關係指誤*

雷瑭洵

白一平（William H.Baxter）與沙加爾（Laurent Sagart）兩位教授的論著*Old Chinese: A new reconstruction*①（《上古漢語：構擬新論》）在古代文獻的處理上有不少失當之處，其中音義關係處理爲其中一大宗。《新論》在此基礎上構擬出一套上古漢語的形態系統，同樣難以成立。

語言是一種符號系統，包含形式和意義兩個方面，二者不可分立。語言的符號性決定了語言研究必須以正確的音義結合爲基礎。音義關係的研究涉及語言單位同一性的判定、注音的準確性、釋義的準確性，以及進一步判定單位與單位之間是否有滋生關係等十分基礎的問題。《新論》對音義關係的不當認識和不當處理，從根基上動搖了其構擬的可信程度。

上古漢語的音義關係的性質，決定了上古漢語不是形態語言。《新論》對音義關係的認識不當，因此爲上古漢語構擬出一套形態系統。爲上古漢語構擬形態的做法，前人已經提出有力的批評，請參看郭錫良②、耿振生③、孫玉文④等學者的著述，本文不做贅述。

姑且拋開這一套形態系統不論，《新論》對文獻材料中音義關係的處理也存在大量失當之处，主要有下述幾種情況：①將別義的異讀處理爲不別義的異讀；②語音和語義的配合不當；③滋生方向有誤；④誤判同源詞；⑤對音義關係的年代認識不當。

下文在既往研究的基礎上，結合古代注音釋義等材料，試舉例說明。

---

* 本文的寫作受到北京大學中文系上古音小組討論的啟發，在孫玉文教授的指導下完成。在寫作過程中參考了上古音小組共同翻譯的《上古漢語：構擬新論》書稿，並得到邵永海、李建強、萬群、趙團員、劉翔宇、程悅、劉敏旗等老師和學友的幫助，本文還得到“北京大學翁洪武科研原創基金項目”資助，謹致謝忱。文中若有謬誤，概由筆者負責。

① William H.Baxter and Laurent Sagart, *Old Chinese: A New Reconstruction*, New York: Oxford University Press, 2014.下文簡稱《新論》。

② 郭錫良《歷史音韻學研究中的幾個問題——駁梅祖麟在香港語言學會年會上的講話》,《古漢語研究》2002年第3期，2—9頁；郭錫良《音韻問題答梅祖麟》，《古漢語研究》2003年第3期，2—17頁。

③ 耿振生《論諧聲原則——兼評潘悟云教授的“形態相關”說》，《語言科學》2003年第5期，10—28頁。

④ 孫玉文《兩漢至明清漢語的音變構詞例證》，《語言科學》2006年第5期，13—21頁；孫玉文《上古漢語詞綴構擬析評》，收入陳燕、耿振生主編《繼往開來的語言學發展之路》，北京：語文出版社，2008年，232—257頁；孫玉文《上古漢語音變構詞中的特指構詞》，《民俗典籍文字研究》第七輯，2010年，北京：商務印書館，107—125頁；孫玉文《上古音叢論》，北京：北京大學出版社，2015年。

一、將别義的異讀處理爲不别義的異讀

漢字的異讀，有的區别意義，有的不區别意義。結合文獻材料，辨析異讀是否别義，是研究音義關係的基礎工作。而《新論》在分辨異讀是否别義這項工作上存在失誤，將許多别義異讀處理爲不别義異讀的情況，如“呼 call out, shout”（pp. 341-342）[5]、“借 loan, borrow”（p. 346）、“削 scrape, pare”（p. 368）、“炙 roast, broil”（p. 376）等。下文以“借”爲例進行分析。

借

《新論》（364頁）在詞表中對“借”的注音和釋義如下[6]：

借$_1$ jiè *tsjaeH*< *[ts]Ak-s ‘loan, borrow’: 226; see also jiè<*tsjek*

借$_2$ jiè *tsjek*< *[ts]Ak ‘loan, borrow’: 226; see also jiè<*tsjaeH*

按：“借”的兩條讀音，分别對應《廣韻》“子夜切”（去聲，“借$_1$”）與“資昔切”（入聲，“借$_2$”）[7]。“借”的兩讀，《新論》用“loan, borrow”釋義，將兩讀處理爲不區别意義的異讀，這一處理與語言事實不合。

事實上，讀去聲的“借$_1$”與讀入聲的“借$_2$”别義，古人早已指出：

（1）《左傳·莊公十八年》：“王命諸侯，名位不同，禮亦異數，不以禮假人。”杜預注：“侯而與公同賜，是借人禮。”音義：“是借，子夜反。”正義：“假、借同義，取者假爲上聲，借爲入聲；與者假、借皆爲去聲。”

孔穎達已經明確地指出，“借”的去入兩讀是“借出”與“借入”的差别。賈昌朝《群經音辨》也明確收錄了“借”的兩讀的意義差别：

（2）《群經音辨·辨彼此異音》：“取於人曰借，子亦切；與之曰借，子夜切。”

“借”的兩讀别義，在經師的音注材料中也有明確反映：

（3）《史記·周本紀》：“秦**借道**兩周之間，將以伐韓。周恐**借之**畏於韓，**不借**畏於秦。”正義：“上‘借’音精夕反，下音子夜反。”

“秦借道兩周之間”，“借道”指“秦國從其他國家借入道路，掌握道路的控制權”，是“借入”；而“周恐借之畏於韓”，“借之”指“周國將道路借給秦國”，是“借出”：根據《史記正義》的注音，“借入”與“借出”分别讀入聲與去聲，這與孔穎達的處理一致。

---

⑤　例字在《新論》中至少出現兩次。除第四節列舉同源詞之誤時列出正文頁碼，本文列舉時僅列出例詞在詞表中的頁碼，在正文中的頁碼可以通過詞表索引查到。

⑥　原文所無數字序號1、2，爲了方便行文，筆者在引文的字頭下加標數字序號。下同。

⑦　這是上古長入與短入的差異在中古的反映，《新論》則處理爲有無-s尾的差異。本文暫不擬討論詞綴的構擬問題。這兩種處理意見都是將讀音分爲兩類，因此不影響對音義配合的討論。下同。

（4）《漢書·文帝紀》："群臣袁盎等諫說雖切，常假借納用焉。"蘇林注："假音休假，借音以物借人之借。"

"某音某某（之某）"，這種將上下文語境標明的注音方式往往意味着被釋字有兩讀别義的情況，如：

（5）《漢書·郊祀志》："始秦得水德，及漢受之，推終始傳，則漢當土德。"顔師古引鄭氏注："音亭傳。"自注："音張戀反。"

"傳"異讀别義，故而在例（5）中，經師在注音時須注明其語境"亭傳"，從而起到注音兼釋義的作用。因此，例（4）中蘇林將"借"的讀音注爲"'借'音'以物借人'之'借'"，正說明了"借"的異讀别義。

"借"的異讀别義，今人周祖謨[⑧]、Downer[⑨]、周法高[⑩]、孫玉文[⑪]均著錄。Downer直接將去入兩讀的讀音差異譯爲"to lend"和"to borrow"的差别[⑫]。由此可見，"借"的兩讀别義，前人早已分辨得很清楚。《新論》將兩讀處理成不别義的異讀，顯然是不合適的。

《新論》的處理與高本漢（Bernhard Karlgren）《漢文典》（*Grammata Serica Recensa*，1957）[⑬]的意見相同。高本漢也誤認爲"借"的兩讀不别義，將"loan, borrow"歸併在一個義項中。但是，在前人說法存在分歧的情況下，《新論》卻不加甄别和論證，而徑取一家之說。即使沒有見到前人的成果，通過對具體的材料分析，求真辨僞，仍然能得出"借"字去入兩讀的詞義分别，不至於誤認爲兩讀不别義。

在《新論》中，類似"借"這類前人早已得出明晰的科學結論而未加採納，以致出現知識性錯誤的地方並不少見。作爲立志建立上古漢語形態的一部著作，卻不能在既往研究的基礎上，合理地辨析一個漢字的異讀是否别義，不僅顯得粗疏，也背離了自己的研究目標。

二、語音和語義的配合不當

音義配合是音義關係研究的核心工作之一。對於别義的異讀，應該明確語音和語義

⑧ 周祖謨《四聲别義釋例》，《輔仁學志》13卷1、2合期，1945年，75—112頁。後收入《問學集》，北京：中華書局，1966年，81—119頁。

⑨ G. B. Downer, "Derivation by Tone-Change in Classical Chinese", *Bulletin of the School of Oriental and African Studies*, 1959 (22), pp. 258-290.

⑩ 周法高《中國古代語法·構詞編》，臺北：臺灣"中研院"歷史語言研究所，1962年。

⑪ 孫玉文《"假""借""丐"變調構詞三則考辨》，《湖北大學學報》（哲學社會科學版）2000年第5期；孫玉文《漢語變調構詞考辨》，北京：商務印書館，2015年。

⑫ G. B. Downer, "Derivation by Tone-Change in Classical Chinese", pp. 281, 282.

⑬ Bernhard Karlgren, *Grammata Serica Recensa*, Stockholm: The Museum of Far Eastern Antiquities, 1957, p. 210. 下文如不說明，所說《漢文典》均指1957年版的修訂本。中譯文可參〔瑞典〕高本漢《漢文典》，潘悟云等譯，上海：上海辭書出版社，1997年。

的配合關係，做到音義匹配。《新論》的注音和釋義，存在大量配合不當的情況，如華（p. 342）、亢（p. 338）、鉛（p. 371）、治（p. 376）、祝（p. 249, p. 377）、濯（p. 378）等。下文以“祝”“鉛”爲例進行分析。

祝

請看《新論》（249頁）對“祝”音義關係的處理：

$祝_1$ *[t]uk>*tsyuwk*>zhù ‘pray, recite’

$祝_2$ *[t]uk-s >*tsyuwH*>zhòu ‘to curse’

按：上述“祝”的兩條讀音，分别對應《廣韻》“之六切”（入聲，“$祝_1$”）與“職救切”（去聲，“$祝_2$”）。《新論》處理爲“祈禱”與“詛咒”的差别，這一處理與語言事實不合。根據孫玉文《漢語變調構詞考辨》對“祝”的研究，“$祝_1$”爲“主贊詞之人”，“祈禱”與“詛咒”義均爲“$祝_2$”[14]。

“$祝_1$”義爲“主贊詞之人”，古人早已指出：

（1）《説文·示部》：“祝，祭主贊詞者。从示，从人、口。一曰：从兑省。《易》曰：兑爲口，爲巫。”大徐音：“之六切。”

大徐本的注音指明“主贊詞之人”之義當讀入聲。賈昌朝也明確指出“$祝_1$”表示“祭主贊詞者也”：

（2）《群經音辨·辨字音清濁》：“祝，祭主贊詞者也，之六切；謂贊詞曰祝，之又切，《禮》有六祝。”

《經典釋文》的注音也與之相合，試舉兩例：

（3）《儀禮·聘禮》：“**僕爲祝**，祝曰：‘孝孫某，孝子某，薦嘉禮于皇祖某甫，皇考某子。’”音義：“祝祝，上之六反，下之又反。”

（4）《莊子·逍遥遊》：“庖人雖不治庖，**尸祝**不越樽俎而代之矣。”音義：“尸祝，之六反。傳鬼神辭曰祝。”

例（3）中，“僕爲祝”之“祝”，指祭祀活動中的祝禱之人，名詞；“祝曰”之“祝”，當爲動詞，即“祝禱”。而《釋文》特意指明了兩處“祝”的讀音不同，作爲名詞的“祝”注了入聲。又例（3）中，“尸”與“祝”均是祭祀活動中的兩個重要的參與者，“尸祝”連用，而且《釋文》解釋“祝”的作用爲“傳鬼神辭”，同時注入聲。兩條例證，均反映入聲的“$祝_2$”，義爲“主贊詞之人”。

而“祝禱”之義，根據經師音注，應該讀去聲，爲“$祝_2$”，本小節例（3）中“祝禱”之“祝”，《釋文》注去聲，即此明證。試再舉一例：

（5）《詩·魯頌·閟宫》：“魯侯燕喜，令妻壽母。”鄭箋：“則善其妻，壽其母，謂爲之**祝慶**也。”音義：“祝慶，之又反。下同。”正義：“燕於内寢，則善其妻，壽其母，謂爲之祝慶，使妻善而母壽也。”

---

⑭ 孫玉文《漢語變調構詞考辨》（上册），北京：商務印書館，2015年，228—230頁。

“祝慶”連用，且《正義》中明言“使妻善而母壽也”，是一種中性的祝禱的行爲，《釋文》注去聲，可證“祝禱”之義音去聲，當爲“祝$_2$”。

總之，《新論》將“祝禱”之義列在“祝$_1$”之下，是不合適的。“祝$_2$”音項下當列“主贊詞之人”之義，不應列“祝禱”之義；而“祝$_1$”下同時有“祝禱”與“詛咒”之義，不能僅列一義。

《新論》的處理與《漢文典》的處理基本相同。在《漢文典》（267頁）中，“祝”的入聲裏列了“prayer, recite; pray; pray-master”等義，去聲則列“to curse”一義。“pray-master”在入聲是對的，“prayer, recite; pray”歸入入聲則不當。《新論》捨棄了高氏正確的意見，而因襲了高氏錯誤的處理，犯了失考之誤。

高本漢《漢文典》是20世紀30年代至50年代的產物，其中多有錯訛，早已爲學界所批評。因此使用該書去研究上古音構擬，不能照抄其結論，必須審慎對待並加以檢驗，這是學界共識。高書出版至今已70多年，當時漢語音義關係研究還不深入，高氏出現音義配合失當的錯誤，可以理解；近二三十年來，漢語音義關係研究已有很大進展，《新論》沒有吸收新的成果，出現常識性錯誤，是非常遺憾的。

鈶

《新論》（56頁）解釋“鈶”的音義如下：

鈶 *sə.ləʔ>*ziX*>yí ‘handle of plow or sickle’ (< ‘instrument of holding’)

按：“鈶”又作“枱”。

（1）《説文·木部》：“枱，耒端也。从木台聲。**鈶，或从金，台聲**。𣟴，籒文从辝。”大徐音“弋之切”。段玉裁注：**“許意上曰耒，下曰枱。”**又云：“以其木也，故從木；以其屬于金也，故亦從金。”

（2）《玉篇·木部》：“枱，弋之切，耒端木也，**亦作鈶**。𣟴，籒文。”

（3）《集韻》盈之切：“枱鈶𣟴耜，《説文》‘耒耑也’，**或作鈶𣟴耜**。”

又：

（4）《集韻》象齒切：“枱𣟴，耒耑，或作𣟴，**通作鈶**。”

根據故訓，“鈶”有“耒端”義。段注講得清清楚楚，“下曰枱”。《王力古漢語字典》釋爲“古農具，耒端用于起土的部分”。此義有弋之切（餘母之韻開口三等平聲）、象齒切（邪母止韻開口三等上聲）兩讀，不别義。

“鈶”與“耜”是同源字：

（5）《玉篇·金部》：“鈶，辝理切，**亦作耜**。”

（6）《玉篇·木部》：“耜，詳以切，耒端木。”

（7）戴侗《六書故·木部》“梩”字注：“（梩），又作枱，耒端也，或作鈶，从金。”

（8）《説文·木部》“枱”段玉裁注：“枱，今经典之耜。耒下曰‘耕曲木也'，此云'耒耑也'，與京房'耜，耒下耓也'、'耒，耜上句上（当作'木'）也'相合。"

《廣韻》"耜"作"詳里切"，與"象齒切"同音。且"耜""鈶"兩字上古同爲之部，讀音相近，語義相通，又有故訓爲證，應爲同源字。"鈶"又有"詳茲切"（邪母之韻開口三等平聲）一讀：

（9）《集韻》詳茲切："柌枱鈶檕，《博雅》'柄也'，或作枱鈶。"

（10）《廣雅·釋器》："柌，柄也。"

（11）《玉篇·木部》："柌，似咨切，鐮柄也。"

例（9）—（11）則反映"鈶"讀"詳茲切"時義爲"鐮柄"，與"柌"同。

综上，古注中反映出"鈶"的兩讀區别意義。"鐮柄"義時應爲"詳茲切"，根據《新論》中古音轉寫規則，其中古音應注爲"*zi*"；"耒端"義爲"象齒切"或"弋之切"，應注爲"*ziX*"或"*yi*"。

再來看《新論》的處理。"鈶"的讀音注爲"*ziX*"，釋義爲"犁或鐮刀的柄"，這一處理至少有兩點不當：

第一，釋義有誤。"耒端"不是"柄"，而是指"耒下端"。

第二，音義配合不當。"鐮柄"義時讀"詳茲切"，當注爲"*zi*"。

這一處理也與《漢文典》相同。《漢文典》（257頁）將"鈶"釋爲"handle of a plough or a sickle"。《新論》沒有注明出處，也沒有在此基礎上深入研究，沿襲了高氏之誤。

《新論》認爲"鈶"是由"以"通過前綴"s_2-"派生，經過"instrument of holding"義演變而來。現在"鈶"（*sə.ləʔ>*ziX*）的"柄"之義已經無從落實，這一同源判定也就不成立了。這種情況屬於下文第四節"同源詞判定不當"的情況，此處不做過多論述。

三、滋生方向有誤

確定詞義滋生過程中的原始詞和滋生詞，判斷詞義的滋生方向是音義關係研究的一項重要工作。《新論》對詞義滋生方向的判斷存在失誤，下文以"喪"爲例進行分析。

喪

《新論》（143頁）認爲表"死亡，葬禮"之義的"$喪_1$"加-s尾派生出表"失去"義的"$喪_2$"，茲錄如下：

$喪_1$ *s-mˤaŋ>*sang* >sāng 'mourning, burial'

$喪_2$ *s-mˤaŋ-s >*sangH*>sàng 'lose; destroy'

按："$喪_1$"和"$喪_2$"的滋生方向有誤。"$喪_2$"滋生出"$喪_1$"，是一種委婉的表達，古人早已言明。

（1）《白虎通·崩薨》："喪者，何謂也？喪者，亡也。人死謂之喪何？言其喪亡，不可復得見也。不直言死，稱喪者何？爲孝子之心不忍言也。"

（2）賈公彦《儀禮·喪服》篇題《疏》引鄭玄《三禮目錄》："不忍言死而言喪。喪者，棄亡之辭。若全存居於彼焉，已亡之耳。"

因爲不忍直言死，所以用"失去"進行委婉地表達，進而滋生出"死"的意思，這也是非常自然的一條滋生方向。

"喪"與"亡"的平行演變也證明了這一點，"亡"也有"失去"義：

（3）《易·旅》："射雉一矢亡。"正義："射之而復亡失其矢。"

通過"失去"委婉表達"死亡"，從而滋生出"死"的意思。《説文·亡部》"亡"字條段玉裁注："亦謂死爲亡。孝子不忍死其親，但疑親之出亡耳。"

因此，《新論》將"喪$_2$"（s-mˤaŋ-s）構擬成"喪$_1$"（s-mˤaŋ）加-s尾，實質是認同"喪$_1$"出現在前，並且滋生出"喪$_2$"，這與語言事實相違背。《新論》如果不同意前人的分析，就應論證，"喪"是由"死亡"義引申出"喪失"義。

必須指出，《新論》在沒有提供過硬證據的前提下，提出一種與學界公認看法相左的處理意見，並作爲構擬的基礎。這種做法忽視了已有研究成果，難以吸收前人研究中合理的意見，因此造成了許多不應該出現的錯誤。

四、同源詞判定不當

同源詞的判定與音義關係研究密切相關。《新論》所判定的同源詞，有許多難以成立。如"晶—淨"（p. 55）、"兜—頭"（p. 55）、"亡—喪"（p. 56）、"以—鈶"（p. 56）、"臭—朽"（p. 57）、"見—瞯"（p. 58）等等。下文以"見—瞯""兜—頭"爲例進行分析。

見—瞯

《新論》（55頁）認爲"見"和"瞯"是同源詞，注音釋義如下：

見 *[k] ˤen-s >*kenH*>jiàn 'see (v.)'

瞯 *m-[k] ˤ<r>en>*hean*>xián 'spy on, watch'

按："瞯"的音義處理不恰，"瞯"與"見"不具有同源關係。

（1）《説文·目部》："瞯，戴目也。从目閒聲。江淮之間謂眄曰瞯。"段玉裁注："戴目者，上視如戴然。"大徐音："戶閒切。"

可知匣母平聲音有兩義："眼珠多白色"、"斜視"。故訓可證：

（2）《爾雅·釋畜》："一目白，瞯。"

（3）《廣韻》戶閒切："瞯，人目多白。"

（4）《方言》："瞯，眄也……吴揚江淮之間或曰瞯，或曰䀨。"郭璞注："音閑。"

（5）《玉篇·目部》："瞯，胡間切，眄也。"

又有見母去聲一讀：

（6）《集韻》居莧切："覵瞯，視也，或从目。"

（7）《孟子·離婁下》："王使人瞯夫子。"朱熹注："瞯，古莧反……瞯，竊視也。"

"瞯"與"覵"同：

（8）《廣韻》古莧切："覵，視也。"

（9）《玉篇》："覵，古莧切，視也。"

（10）《廣雅·釋詁》："覵，視。"曹憲《博雅音》："覵，古莧。"王念孫疏證："覵之言閒也。卷三云：閒，覗也……瞯與覵同。"

綜上，"窺伺"義之"瞯"當注見母去聲一讀爲宜。

"瞯"當與"閒"同源，王念孫早已指明。"閒"有"偵候、刺探"一義。如：

（11）《左傳·僖公三十年》："狄閒晉之有鄭虞也，夏，狄侵齊。"音義："狄閒，閒厠之閒。"

（12）《國語·魯語下》："齊人閒晉之禍，伐取朝歌。"韋昭注："閒，候也。"

（13）《韓非子·外儲説右上》："內閒主之情以告外。"

"閒"的本義是"縫隙"：

（14）《說文·門部》："閒，隙也。从門，从月。"大徐本注："徐鍇曰："夫門夜閉，閉而見月光，是有閒隙也。"

由"縫隙"引申出"偵候"之義，進而寫作"覵""瞯"等。"瞯"的語源十分清楚，與"見"無涉。《新論》認爲"見"與"瞯"同源，既沒有加以論證，也沒有駁倒古人對"閒""瞯"同源的看法，不能令人信服。與之相關的詞頭*-m的構擬也就無從落實。

兜—頭

《新論》（55頁）認爲"兜"派生出"頭"：

Prefix *m2- occurs in names of human body parts:

兜 *tˤo>*tuw*>dōu 'helmet, hood'

頭 *[m-t]ˤo>*duw*>tóu 'head'

按："兜鍪"是一個侯部疊韻的聯綿詞，又可寫作"兜鉾""兜鞪""兜牟"等，音轉爲"鞮鍪"，"兜"只有表音的作用。

（1）《說文·兜部》："兜，兜鍪，首鎧也。"《冃部》："冑，兜鍪也。"

（2）《廣雅·釋器》："兜鍪謂之胄。"王念孫疏證："《說文》：胄，兜鍪也。兜鍪，首鎧也。《急就篇》作'兜鉾'。《後漢書·禰衡傳》：'更著岑牟單絞之服。'李賢注云：岑牟，鼓角士胄也。鍪、鍪、鉾、牟並通。《韓策》云'甲盾鞮鍪'，卽兜鍪之轉也。"

（3）《急就篇》："弓弩箭矢鎧兜鉾。"顔師古注："兜鉾，首甲也，古謂之胄。"

（4）《漢書·韓延壽傳》："被甲鞮鍪居馬上。"顔師古注："鞮鍪卽兜鍪也。"

可見"兜鍪"不可分訓，將"兜"單獨釋爲"頭盔"的處理是不當的。根據故訓，"兜鍪"和"胄"同源。

《新論》對"兜"的釋義與高本漢1940年版的《漢文典》⑮處理相同，這一版本的《漢文典》（158頁）"兜"下列"helmet, head-covering"（头盔）和"（put a hood over head:）deceive"（（頭巾遮住頭〉）欺騙）兩個義項，"頭盔"義不確，上文已論。"欺騙"之義，其例證如下：

（5）《國語·晉語六》："在列者獻詩，使勿兜。"韋昭注："兜，惑也。"

例（5）中"兜"爲"兆"之誤，清儒已經指出：

（6）王引之《經義述聞》"使勿兜"條："引之謹案：兜當爲兆。《說文》：'兆，廱蔽也。從人，象左右皆蔽形，讀若瞽。''勿兆'謂'勿廱蔽'也。《說文》之訓，殆出賈侍中《國語》注乎？韋注訓爲惑，則其字益當作'兆'。蓋'兆'之爲言，猶蠱也。蠱，惑也。《爾雅》曰：'蠱，疑也。'疑，亦惑也。昭元年《左傳》曰'女惑男謂之蠱'，是也。'兆'與'兜'形相似，後人多見'兜'少見'兆'，故'兆'譌爲'兜'矣。"

（7）《說文·兆部》："兆，廱蔽也。"段玉裁注："此字經傳罕見，音與'蠱'同，亦蠱惑之意也。《晉語》曰：'在列者獻詩，使勿兜。'疑'兜'或當爲'兆'。韋曰：'兜，惑也。'"

《說文》中，"兆"作""，"兜"作""，形近易訛。《國語》這條例證不能作爲"兜"有"欺騙"義項的例證，其源頭爲"頭巾遮住頭"的說法就難以成立了。高本漢在修訂《漢文典》可能注意到這一項失誤，1957年修訂本《漢文典》（50頁）刪除了1940年第一版（158頁）中"兜"的釋義。《新論》沒有注意到高氏的變化，仍然沿用高本漢1940年第一版之誤⑯。

⑮ Bernhard Karlgren, *Grammata Serica*, Stockholm: The Museum of Far Eastern Antiquities, 1940, p. 158. 中譯本，59頁。

⑯ 高本漢《漢文典》（修訂本）中只收錄了"兜"的字形，沒有注音和釋義。《漢文典》（修訂本）的中譯本（59頁）沒有採納高氏的修訂意見，仍列出"兜"的釋義。《新論》的參考文獻中也沒有列*Grammata Serica Recensa*一書。

“兜鍪”出現在漢代。《说文·冃部》“冑”字條段玉裁注：“古謂之冑，漢謂之兜鍪，今謂之盔。”已經不在《新論》所定義的上古漢語的範圍之內[17]。

再看“頭”。王力收錄“頭”與“首”這一對同源字，兩字“定審鄰紐，侯幽旁轉”[18]：

（8）《說文·頁部》：“頭，首也。”《百部》：“百，頭也，象形。”

（9）《廣雅·釋親》：“首謂之頭。”

“頭”的用例在先秦已有，出現在“兜鍪”之前。如：

（10）《禮記·曲禮上》：“頭有創則沐。”

《新論》將“頭”和“兜”處理成同源詞，而沒有加以論證；根據上文的論證，這一同源關係的處理不能成立；進而認爲“兜”加*m-詞頭派生出“頭”，更是認爲滋生詞在原始詞之前出現。總之，這一滋生關係的判定是不能成立的。

五、對音義關係的年代認識不當

字的音義結合可以發生變化。同一個字，在不同年代的音義關係可以不同。因此，音義關係的研究還必須辨明某一種音義配合的出現的時代。《新論》將一部分先秦以後才有的詞義和音義配合歸入上古，如“椅”（p. 371）、“正”（p. 376）等等。下文以“正”爲例進行分析。

正

《新論》（168頁）用“正”與越南語進行語音對應：

正 * C.teŋ>*tsyeng*>zhēng ‘first (month)’ *giêng*[ziʌŋ A1] ‘the first month’

按：在“一年的第一個月”的“正月”[19]中，“正”讀平聲是秦代以後的事情，古人已經指出，孫玉文進一步分析了“正”的音義[20]。茲引述故訓材料如下：

（1）《史記·秦始皇本紀》：“秦始皇帝者……以秦昭王四十八年正月生於邯鄲。及生，名爲政，姓趙氏。”

《集解》：“徐廣曰：‘一作“正”。’宋忠云：‘以正月旦生，故名正。’”

《索隱》：“《系本》作‘政’，又生於趙，故曰趙政。”

《正義》：“正音政，‘周正建子’之‘正’也。始皇以正月旦生於趙，

⑰ 《新論》所說的上古漢語，指先秦漢語。參見該書第1頁。

⑱ 王力《同源字典》，北京：商務印書館，1982年，190頁。

⑲ 正月有“正陽之月”義（《小雅·正月》），音去聲，此處不涉。毛傳中已有論述，具體分析詳見孫玉文《〈漢語歷史音韻學·上古篇〉指誤》，《古漢語研究》2002第4期，13—24頁；張猛《關於〈小雅·正月〉中“正月”的訓詁問題》，《古漢語研究》2004年第1期，17—19頁。

⑳ 孫玉文《〈漢語歷史音韻學·上古篇〉指誤》，13—24頁。

因爲政，後以始皇諱，故音征。”

秦始皇因爲在正月出生，故名“政”。又因爲避諱，將“一年第一個月”的“正月”中“正”改讀音“征”，平聲[21]。因此，這一平聲讀法是在秦代才出現的。不在《新論》所討論的先秦音的範圍之內。此音能與漢越語中的借詞對上，正説明借貸關係至早發生在秦代以後。並不能作爲論證《新論》所界定的上古音的證據。造成這種失誤的原因，正是因爲忽視了音義關係的年代性。

六、結　　語

音義關係的研究在語言研究中佔據非常基礎的地位。缺乏對音義關係的關注，甚至連語言中的基本單位都難以準確地確定。上文分别從不同的角度舉例説明《新論》對音義關係的失當處理。這種不符合語言事實的音義關係處理，造成了與該書基本目標的背離。

《新論》（3—4頁）批評了傳統的研究集中在古音構擬，不夠重視形態與句法語義特征的重建，並嘗試重建上古漢語的形態系統：

The focus has been on phonetic reconstruction, with relatively littleattention to morphology or to the syntactic and semantic properties of thereconstructed forms.

We also believe that the reconstruction of Old Chinese phonology has progressed tothe point that it is productive to use the techniques of internal reconstruction to reconstructthe morphology of Old Chinese.

《新論》的批評是不能成立的，高本漢[22]、Downer[23]、周法高[24]等學者均作了構擬上古漢語形態的嘗試，而孫玉文[25]等一系列研究從構詞的角度分析上古漢語的音變，不能説既往的研究不重視詞彙的重建。

丁邦新[26]曾經對Sagart的《上古漢語詞根》[27]提出一點意見：“周法高在四十年前出

㉑ 針對這一説法，近代雖有不同意見，但均不足以駁倒張守節《正義》之説。

㉒ Bernhard Karlgren, *Word families in Chinese*, Stockholm:The Museum of Far Eastern Antiquities, 1933. 參見[瑞典]高本漢《漢語詞類》，張世禄譯，上海：商務印書館，1937年。

㉓ G. B. Downer, “Derivation by Tone-Change in Classical Chinese”, *Bulletin of the School of Oriental and African Studies*, 1959 (22), pp. 258-290.

㉔ 周法高《中國古代語法·構詞編》，“中研院”歷史語言研究所專刊之三十九，1962年。下同。按丁邦新原文引爲“構詞篇”。

㉕ 孫玉文《漢語變調構詞研究》，北京：北京大學出版社，2000年。又：增訂本，北京：商務印書館，2007年；孫玉文《上古漢語詞綴構擬析評》，232—257頁；孫玉文《漢語變調構詞考辨》，北京：商務印書館，2015年。

㉖ 丁邦新《上古漢語的構詞問題——評Laurent Sagart: *The Root of Old Chinese*》，《語言學論叢》第二十六輯，北京：商務印書館，2002年，1—11頁。

㉗ Laurent Sagart, *The Roots of Old Chinese*, Amsterdam/Philadelphia: John Benjamins Publishing Company, 1999.可參見〔法〕沙加爾《上古漢語詞根》，龔群虎譯，上海：上海教育出版社，2004年。

版的《中國古代語法·構詞篇》是他出名的著作，專論上古漢語的構詞法。Sagart完全不加引用，書目中也未見，令我很驚訝：這本書是第一本系統地討論古漢語構詞問題的書，舉出許多詞頭、詞尾，也有插詞‘之’。有些說法確鑿無疑，不知Sagart何以不引用？”

如今十年過去了，在Sagart作爲第二作者的《新論》中依然沒有見到引用周法高的《構詞編》，甚至在參考文獻的列表中也沒有出現，更不必說近些年相關領域的研究進展了。這一點同樣讓我們驚訝，不知《新論》何以不引用？是前人不夠重視形態或詞彙的重建，抑或是《新論》不重視前人的研究呢？

無論如何，重建上古漢語的形態系統，首先要建立在能夠正確地處理音義關係、研究清楚這種形態系統的性質的基礎之上。而《新論》恰恰在音義關係的處理上存在很多問題，因此這一套形態系統也是建立在沙灘之上，其準確性是十分可疑的。例如不能正確地區分異讀是否別義、不能正確地進行音義配合、不能正確地判定同源詞和滋生方向，等等。究其原因，表面上是盲從一家之說，忽視前人有分歧的討論；其實質是沒有從材料着手，缺乏對上古漢語音義關係深入的研究。這樣的構擬難以經得起材料的檢驗，不能取信於人。

更深層的原因，恐怕是他們試圖建立的上古漢語的形態系統，不符合漢語的實際情況，故而得不到漢語材料的支撐。上古音構擬確實應該考慮和語義變化相關的音變，但是這類音變現象應該屬於構詞範疇，很難抽象到語法形態。目前，音變構詞研究取得一定的規模[28]，在這個基礎上進行上古音構擬的深入探索，或許能取得新的突破。

The Phonetic-Semantic Relation Errors in *Old Chinese: A New Reconstruction*

Lei Tangxun

This article reviews the Phonetic-Semantic Relation errors in *Old Chinese: A New Reconstruction* by Prof. Baxter and Prof. Sagart. These errors can be separated into following five situations: 1) Confusing variant pronunciations that distinguish different meanings sources with those that do not, 2) Wrong matchings between pronunciations and meanings, 3) Reversed direction of derivation, 4) Wrong assertions of cognate words, 5) Incorrect age of Phonetic-Semantic Relation. The inappropriate analyses and treatments of original data result in the unreliability of reconstruction in this book.

㉘ 比如，孫玉文《漢語變調構詞考辨》，北京：商務印書館，2015年；張忠堂《漢語變聲構詞研究》，北京：中國書籍出版社，2012年；趙團員《上古漢語變韻構詞研究》，北京大學博士學位論文，2016年。

白一平、沙加爾《上古漢語：構擬新論》若干例證商榷*

——兼談對西方學術評價的反思

向筱路

引　言

白一平（WilliamH.Baxter）和沙加爾（Laurent Sagart）的新著《上古漢語：構擬新論》（*Old Chinese: A New Reconstruction*）（以下簡稱《新論》）在2014年由紐約的牛津大學出版社出版，據該書前言所述，這本書在他們以往的研究基礎上，利用了新的材料、採用了新的方法對上古漢語音韻、形態和詞彙提出了一個更加科學的構擬方案①。這本書也獲得了美國2015年布龍菲爾德圖書獎（Leonard Bloomfield Book Award），有人評價它"不僅是現代學術的驚艷之作，而且是一部將會對漢語史、中國古代歷史和文化研究產生更廣泛而持久影響的著作"（this is not only an impressive piece of modern scholarship; it is also a book that will have lasting impact on the study of Chinese linguistic history and of ancient Chinese history and culture more broadly）②，由此可見，美國主流語言學界對這本書是高度讚賞和認可的。但是我們仔細閱讀這本被譽爲"驚艷之作"的書，發現其中存在諸多可議之處，難以讓人滿意，上面所引的這段評價也沒有得到大家的公認。下面舉出幾個例子作具體分析，指出《新論》存在的問題，同時也對西方學術評價發表一些個人看法，不當之處，敬祈方家教正。

---

* 本文的思路是在2015年9月開始的北京大學中文系上古音小組討論會上逐漸形成的，具體寫作得到了孫玉文、李建強二位先生的悉心指導，趙團員、汪春濤等學兄也提出了寶貴意見，寫作過程參考了上古音小組共同翻譯的《上古漢語：構擬新論》書稿，本文也得到中国人民大学科学研究基金项目（15XNL014）的支持，在此一併表示感謝。文中錯誤概由筆者自己負責。

① William H.Baxter and Laurent Sagart, *Old Chinese: A New Reconstruction,* New York: Oxford University Press, 2014, p. 1.

② 參見：http://www.linguisticsociety.org/news/2015/11/17/old-chinese-new-reconstruction-wins-bloomfield-book-award.

若干例證舉隅

（一）

《新論》認爲“工”和“公”在中古是同音字，以往的學者認爲在上古它們也是同音，但是在先秦文獻中，“工”和“公”沒有出現混用的例子，這説明它們在先秦不同音，因此“工”構擬成*kˤoŋ，“公”構擬成*C.qˤoŋ，這樣也能解釋以“公”爲主諧字的諧聲字都有小舌音聲母③。

按：《新論》中的這個論斷是基於作者的一個方法論前提，即語音構擬不僅要解釋已經出現的現象，也要解釋爲什麽有些現象不能出現。例如在談到上古漢語韻文材料的時候，他們説：“一個合理的上古音構擬的要求之一就是要能解釋在《詩經》里哪些字能互相押韻，並且同樣重要的是要能解釋哪些字不能互相押韻。”④從擬音是否客觀反映韻部遠近的角度看，這個看法大體是正確的，而且我國學者很早就在他們的研究中體現了這個觀點。例如段玉裁分古韻爲十七部，他雖然沒法用國際音標爲每個韻部構擬音值，但是卻按照心目中音值的遠近來排列韻部，他把古韻十七部分爲六大類：之部是第一類；宵幽侯魚音近，是第二類；蒸侵談音近，是第三類；東陽耕音近，是第四類；真文元音近，是第五類；脂支歌音近，是第六類。拿我們今天的古音構擬成果來看，段玉裁的這種安排也是比較合理的，它能夠解釋古書中的合韻、音轉等現象，也就是哪些韻部相近，但同時也能解釋韻部相遠的現象，例如先秦魚部和宵部相差甚遠，往往不能一起押韻，段玉裁雖然將它們同列第二類，但分居首尾，説明段玉裁認爲它們讀音仍然有較大區別⑤。段玉裁對先秦韻部的這種安排是根據對材料的精細考察、分析而得出的，所以具有科學性。

然而反觀《新論》，其中很多推理都值得進一步推敲，不能接受材料的檢驗。例如書中認爲“五”和“午”是兩個常見的聲符，但是在先秦它們沒有出現相通的情況，直到《説文》時代才有交替的例子，這説明它們先秦不是同音字，因此《新論》把“五”的聲母構擬爲*C.ŋˤ-，把“午”的聲母構擬爲*m.qʰˤ-⑥。最近何大安先生在給《新論》所作的書評中詳細地批駁了這個看法，指出至晚在西周晚期就有“五”和“午”相通的例子。何先生認爲《新論》這個推理的問題主要有兩點：一是我們依據的往往是不全面的材料（incomprehensive materials），因此有些語言現象沒有反映出來，但沒反映（not attested）並不一定代表不存在（not existed）；二是《新論》往往只依靠一些工具書，而沒有親自去查閲原始材料。針對這種情況，何先生還特別引用了趙元任先生給王力先

③ WilliamH.Baxter and Laurent Sagart, *Old Chinese: A New Reconstruction,*p. 28, 66.

④ WilliamH.Baxter and Laurent Sagart, *Old Chinese: A New Reconstruction,*p. 21.

⑤ 參考林燾主編《中國語音學史》，北京：語文出版社，2010年，248—249頁。

⑥ WilliamH.Baxter and Laurent Sagart, *Old Chinese: A New Reconstruction*, pp.128-131.

生《中國古文法》的評語“言有易，言無難”[⑦]，發人深省。

此處《新論》對“工”“公”的處理同樣存在問題。我們也查閱了一些《通假字典》類的工具書，發現在《新論》設定的上古音範圍內（即公元前221年秦統一中國之前），目前確實沒有找到“公”“工”混寫的情況。這可能有兩種情況，一是確實先秦“公”和“工”不相通；二是目前保存的先秦文獻較少，“公”、“工”先秦就有相通的情況，只不過文獻沒有記錄下來（not attested），至少沒有被收入到這些工具書當中。這都有待對材料進一步發掘才能得出確鑿的結論。

但至晚在漢代，“公”“工”相通的例子就已經比較普遍了，這也同漢代流傳下來的文獻更多有關係。《史記·封禪書》：“受此書申公。”《孝武本紀》“申公”作“申功”，“功”从“工”得聲。《詩·大雅·靈台》：“蒙瞍奏公。”《楚辭·九章》“矇瞍謂之不章”王逸注引《詩》作“蒙瞍奏工”，《呂氏春秋·侍君覽·達鬱》“矇箴師誦”高誘注引《詩》作“矇叟奏功”。

也許有人會爲《新論》辯護，認爲先秦沒有出現“公”“工”相通的例子，而漢代有這種情況，這可能是因爲到了漢代兩字讀音才變得相同。我們認爲這個看法不能成立。首先，目前我們沒有找到先秦“公”和“工”聲母讀音不同的內證材料，研究上古音，必須充分利用一切反映上古語音面貌的內證材料，尋求科學合理的解釋，就筆者目力所及，目前所有直接的內證材料都沒有顯示出“公”“工”讀音有別，那麼有些人認爲它們先秦不同音便沒有充足的理由。第二，王力先生《漢語語音史》在談到漢代音系時說：“關於漢代的聲母，我們沒有足夠的材料可供考證，這裡缺而不論。可以假定，漢代聲母和先秦聲母一樣，或者說變化不大。”[⑧]這是在仔細研究材料后得出的實事求是的結論，如果沒有堅強的理由，我們不能輕易拋棄。上面我們引了漢代“公”和“工”相通的例子，說明那時它們讀音就相同或相近，書面語要滯後於口語，那麼很可能先秦口語中它們讀音就是一樣的。第三，文字相通的成因是複雜的，《新論》把這個問題想得太簡單，也暴露出作者在基礎知識和邏輯推理上的漏洞。如果兩個字有通假的情況，並不能就此認爲它們的讀音一定相同，有可能是由於字形相似造成的誤寫，因爲詞義的引申而新造一個分化字，分化字和本字也可能會出現相通的現象；相反，即使兩個字讀音相同，它們也不一定會相通。其實我們只要看看郭錫良先生的《漢字古音手冊》（增訂本）就會發現，中古和上古都同音但在上古卻不相通的字有很多，例如“畢篳蓽韠趩蹕滭斁滭熚彃樿縪罼必珌”中古都是幫母質韻字，上古同屬幫母質部，但是先秦文獻中“畢篳蓽韠趩蹕滭斁滭熚彃樿縪罼”等字不與“必珌”相通，它們分屬兩個諧聲系列；又如“暄萱諼吅喧諠讙颵”中古都是曉母元韻字，上古同屬曉母元部，但先秦文獻中“吅”和其他字不相通，它們分屬不同的諧聲系列。這樣的例子還有很多，《新論》爲什麼不按照處理“公”“工”那樣的辦法來爲它們構擬不同的上古音呢（在《新

⑦ Ho Dah-an, Such Errors Could Have Been Avoided—Review of Old Chinese: A New Reconstruction, *The Journal of Chinese Linguistics*, Vol.44, No.1(2016), pp.198-210.

⑧ 王力《漢語語音史》，北京：中華書局，2014年，81頁。

論》里，"叩諠喧"的上古音都是*q^{wh}ar）？這難道不是自相矛盾嗎？究其原因，還是在於他們這樣做的目的。《新論》之所以非要認爲"公"和"工"上古讀音不同，是要以此作爲所謂"小舌音假設"（uvular hypothesis）的證據，在《新論》的上古音系統里，共有四套小舌音聲母，這個構擬在白一平和沙加爾之前的文章中有論述，他們認爲當一個特定的韻類中有兩個對立的諧聲系列、並且它們在中古有同樣的舌根音聲母時，通常情況是其中一個系列在上古是小舌音，也就是"舌根音+ʔ-、x-、h-"的形式，另一類則是普通的舌根音，他們舉出了主元音是-o-的四個例子："冓：句""侯：后""工：公""角：㱿"，每個配對中的前一個是舌根音聲母，後一個是小舌音聲母⑨。關於這個假設，我們可以再討論，但至少"工：公"這個例子是不能成立的，那也就是說所謂的小舌音假設是存在漏洞的。

就這個例子來看，《新論》爲了給自己的一個理論找證據，首先設立一個方法論前提，再去主觀地找材料，只取對自己有利的例子，並且對材料也沒有做正確的分析。這種做法帶有明顯的先入爲主的觀念，用材料來遷就理論，是難以得出正確的結論的。

（二）

《新論》認爲"魯"的上古音是*r.$ŋ^{ʕ}$aʔ，"魚"的上古音是*[r.ŋ]a，這樣構擬可以解釋：①"魯"中古讀來母，來母的上古讀音是*r；②"魯"以"魚"爲聲符，"魚"中古是疑母字⑩。

按：《說文·魚部》："魯，鈍詞也，从白，鮺省聲，《論語》曰'參也魯'。"段玉裁駁正，認爲"鮺省聲"爲淺人所改，今正爲"魚聲"。或許《新論》就是依據段注認爲"魚"是"魯"的聲符。

但是現代學者多認爲"魯"不是形聲字，而是會意字，字形也並非从"白"，而是"口"的訛誤，例如于省吾先生說："按甲骨文魯字作𩵋，从魚从口，口爲器形，本象魚在器皿之中，說文偽爲从白。"⑪儘管于先生對會意的具體說解後人有不同意見，但大家基本上都同意"魯"是會意字。可見前輩學者對"魯"的字形分析有不同的看法，那麼爲什麼《新論》只取一種"少數派"的意見呢？

我們認爲，《新論》之所以認爲"魯"是以"魚"爲聲符，是要爲前冠音*r的構擬找證據。《新論》認爲上古漢語存在前冠音（preinitial），前冠音必須是輔音，《新論》相信目前有證據支持的前冠音有*p、*t、*k、*r、*m、*N（*n、*ŋ），他們說"支持*r作爲前冠輔音的證據非常有限"，這有限的例子就是"魯：魚"，也就是說，在他

---

⑨ Laurent Sagart, "Reconstructing Old Chinese uvulars in the Baxter-Sagart system (ver. 0.97)",40th International Conference on Sino-Tibetan Languages and Linguistics, Sep 2007, Harbin,China.

⑩ WilliamH.Baxter and Laurent Sagart, *Old Chinese: A New Reconstruction*, p. 52.

⑪ 于省吾《甲骨文字釋林·釋魯》，北京：中華書局，1979年，52頁。

們自己的體系中，如果這個例子不成立，那構擬出的前冠音*r根本就站不住脚。從科學研究的角度看，這種只憑極個別例子就歸納出一種理論的做法是非常危險的。

（三）

《新論》認爲帶前冠音*N-的詞可以和不帶*N-的詞構成及物-不及物的配對，在中古表現爲曉母和疑母的對立。舉出的一個例子是“嚇”$*q^{hʕ}$<r>ak，“使害怕”（to frighten）：“愕” $*N\text{-}q^{hʕ}ak$，“害怕的”（scared）[⑫]。

按：關於“嚇”的詞義，王力、孫玉文等先生有詳細的考證，“嚇”在上古漢語中沒有“害怕，使害怕”的意思，這個意思口語中大約產生在六朝時期[⑬]。

此外，“愕”在上古也沒有“害怕”的意思，而只有“吃驚”的意思，“愕”可能和“遻”（后也寫作“遌”）是同源詞，《說文・辵部》：“遻，相遇驚也。”《廣雅・釋詁》：“愕，驚也。”《戰國策・燕策三》：“秦王還柱而走，群臣驚愕。”宋玉《高唐賦》：“卒愕異物，不知所出。”

《新論》認爲“愕”有“害怕”的意思，可能是看到《爾雅・釋詁》里有“驚，懼也”這樣的訓釋，由此推出“愕”也有“懼”的意思。我們猜想，他們的邏輯是：古訓中有“A，B也”，又有“B，C也”，由此則“A，C也”。但是這種邏輯推理必須符合“同一律”，也就是說在正確思維的同一過程中，同一概念的內涵必須保持同一，違反這一要求的邏輯錯誤，稱爲“混淆”或“偷换概念”。具體到這裡，至少存在三種違反“同一律”的情況。第一，B是一個多義詞，古訓中用B的甲義來解釋A，而C解釋的是B的乙義，可以記作“A，$B_{甲}$也”“$B_{乙}$，C也”，那麼A怎麼可能和C同義呢？第二，古訓中的訓解大多是近義詞爲訓，我們知道，一種語言中的同義詞（等義詞）數量是很少的，這是語言交際的必然要求，因此經師往往找不到完全等義的詞來作訓，只能選擇近義詞，我們可以記成A≈B，B≈C，那麼A和C充其量只能看做是近義詞關係。第三，古人給詞作訓解，是爲了讀懂文獻，所以往往隨文釋義，訓釋的詞義通常只是語境義，我們只有把語境義進一步概括分析，才能得到詞的準確詞義。也就是說，如果B只是解釋A的語境義，即使B和C是同義詞，C和A也不可能是完全同義的。

王力先生曾專門談到在訓詁中要避免出現偷换概念的毛病，他說“何況《爾雅》《廣雅》這一類的書只把故訓羅列在一起，並非定義式的解釋，我們在利用這些書的時候，一不小心，就會偷换概念”，“古代學者（包括清人在內）由於時代的局限性，常常陷於偷换概念而不自覺；現在我們如果再重蹈這覆轍，那就不應該了”[⑭]，前輩學者的這些告誡必須引起我們的重視。

---

⑫ WilliamH.Baxter and Laurent Sagart, *Old Chinese: A New Reconstruction*, p. 121.

⑬ 孫玉文《〈漢語歷史音韻學・上古篇〉指誤》，《古漢語研究》2002年第4期，22頁；又收入《上古音叢論》，北京：北京大學出版社，2015年，81—82頁。

⑭ 王力《訓詁學上的一些問題》，載《談談學習古代漢語》，濟南：山東教育出版社，1984年，58—59頁。

其實王力先生主編的《古代漢語》和郭錫良先生主編的《古代漢語》都已經對“畏、懼、恐、怕、驚”這幾個詞的詞義做了清楚的辨析，“驚”是突然受到刺激而精神緊張，例如《呂氏春秋·察今》：“溺死者千有餘人，軍驚而壞都舍。”賈誼《論積貯疏》：“安有爲天下阽危者若是而上不驚者！”這兩個“驚”是強調精神緊張，是驚駭，而不是害怕。雖然古書中有時候也有“驚恐”連用的情況，但那是既驚又恐，不能說“驚”就是“恐”[15]。另外古注也清楚地告訴我們“驚”是“驚駭”的意思，宋玉《招魂》：“宮廷震驚，發激楚些。”王逸注：“震，動也。驚，駭也。”但是人們在感到吃驚的時候，尤其是面對一些可怕異常的情況時會伴隨有害怕的情緒，此乃人之常情，這時“驚”和“懼”的意思就比較接近，所以古訓中會出現“驚，懼也”的訓釋，但這只是用近義詞解釋“驚”的語境義，並不能由此就認爲“懼”是“驚”的一個固定詞義。

由此可見，《新論》對“嚇”“愕”詞義的分析都是錯誤的，在判定同源詞的問題上主觀性太強，“嚇”在先秦根本沒有“使害怕”的意思，“愕”也沒有“害怕的”這個含義。之所以發生這個錯誤，恐怕在於沒有親自爬梳材料，也沒有對前人的既有研究成果加以吸收。《新論》想舉這對例子來構擬所謂的*N-前綴看來是不成功的。

（四）

《新論》認爲“鼻”記錄了兩個詞，“鼻子”和“用鼻子聞氣味”，這個分別在閩語里還有保留，因此把記錄“鼻子”義的“鼻”的上古音構擬爲*m-bi[t]-s，而記錄“用鼻子聞氣味”義的“鼻”構擬成*Cə-bi[t]-s，記錄這兩個意思的“鼻”中古都讀*bjijH*[16]。

按：“鼻”在上古沒有“用鼻子聞氣味”這個意思，《漢語大詞典》“鼻”下列有“用鼻子聞”這個義項，給出的書證是明清時代的，明劉基《郁離子·牧豭》：“鼻糞壤而食腥穢。”清李漁《閑情偶寄·種植下·草本》：“此皆言其可目者也，可鼻則有荷葉之清香，荷花之異馥。”這些例證都比較晚，完全不在《新論》所說的上古音範圍內，而且我們懷疑“用鼻子聞氣味”這個意思可能不是“鼻”的固定義項，而是在語境中臨時活用造成的，例如上舉第二例“可鼻”與“可目”對舉，《漢語大字典》、《王力古漢語字典》都沒有爲“鼻”列“用鼻子聞氣味”這個義項。

的確，在現代閩方言中，有些地方“鼻”有兩個意思，並且讀音有別，例如石陂話“鼻頭”表示鼻子，“鼻”讀[p‘i]，而表示“聞；親嘴”義時讀[bi][17]，但是既然“用鼻子聞氣味”這個意思在上古根本沒有出現，我們又怎麼能把現代漢語方言中的這種讀音區別機械地推到上古去呢？我們在利用歷史比較法的時候也不能忽視歷史文獻的作用。

---

⑮ 郭錫良等編著《古代漢語》（修訂本），北京：商務印書館，2014年，898—899頁。

⑯ WilliamH.Baxter and Laurent Sagart, *Old Chinese: A New Reconstruction*, p. 132, 188.

⑰ 秋谷裕幸《福建石陂方言音系》，《方言》2004年第1期，79頁。

此外，雖然《切韻》系韻書中“鼻”只有去聲讀法，但從現代漢語方言和其他歷史文獻來看，“鼻”在古代應該還有入聲一讀，前人早已論證過這個問題⑱，我們要注意吸收前輩學者的研究成果。

（五）

《新論》認爲“尼”上古有兩個讀音，一是*nˤərʔ，演變爲中古的*nejX*，意思是“停止”（可能是不及物動詞）；一是*nˤərʔ-s，演變爲中古的*nejH*，意思是“停止、阻止”（可能是及物動詞）⑲。

按：“尼”有“停止”的意思，《孟子·梁惠王下》：“行或使之，止或尼之。”趙岐注：“尼，止也。”爲什麼“尼”會有“停止”的意思呢？于省吾先生有詳細的論證，他說：“尼字的構形既然象人坐于另一人的背上，故《爾雅·釋詁》訓‘尼’爲止爲定；人坐于另一人的背上，則上下二人相接近，故典籍多訓尼爲近……由于尼字之訓止訓近，故从尼之字多含有停留之義。《論語·子張》的‘致遠恐泥’，鄭玄謂‘泥謂陷滯不通’。《爾雅·釋邱》謂‘水潦所止，泥邱’。《易·姤》初六的‘繫于金柅’，馬融注謂‘柅者在車之下，所以止輪不動也’。甲骨文有秜字，《說文》謂‘秜，稻今年落來年自生謂之秜’。按自生之秜，無須人之勞動培植，故也與止義相因。”⑳

既然“尼”有“停止”的意思，那是不是像《新論》中所說，有及物和不及物的區别，並且各自有不同的讀法呢？我們考察文獻，發現恐怕並非如此。

《經典釋文》爲“尼”注音共4次，其中1次是爲“仲尼”注音，讀女持反。其他3次分别是《爾雅·釋詁》：“尼，止也。”《釋文》：“尼，施女乙反，謝羊而反。”這一條黄焯先生有校語：“吴云：‘……施乾讀如字，而謝嶠所見本疑並作𡰥，與夷同音，合音羊脂反，其作羊而反者，當時脂、之已不能明辨，作音諸家每多錯互耳。’”㉑如此則羊而反並非爲“尼”注音。又《爾雅·釋詁》：“即，尼也。”嘉慶本十三經注疏附《釋文》：“尼，女乙切。”通志堂本《釋文》：“尼，本亦作昵，同女乙反，謝羊而反，顧奴啟反，下同。”陸德明說的“下同”指的是下一條“尼，定也”。《爾雅·釋訓》：“宴宴、粲粲，尼居息也。”嘉慶本十三經注疏附《釋文》：“尼，女乙切。”通志堂本《釋文》：“尼，女乙反，謝羊而反，又奴啟反。”根據通志堂本《經典釋文》，顧野王爲“尼”注有奴啟反的讀法，《篆隸萬象名義》爲“尼”注兩個讀音，奴啟、女飢二反，《宋本玉篇·尸部》：“尼，奴啟、女飢二切，安也，

⑱ 參見李榮《陸法言的〈切韻〉》，載《音韻存稿》，北京：商務印書館，1982年，39頁；王恩保《吴淑〈事類賦〉用韻研究》，《古漢語研究》1997年第3期，17頁。

⑲ WilliamH.Baxter and Laurent Sagart, *Old Chinese: A New Reconstruction*, p. 147.

⑳ 于省吾《甲骨文字釋林·釋尼》，北京：中華書局，1979年，304—305頁。

㉑ 黄焯《經典釋文彙校》，北京：中華書局，2006年，844頁。

止也，和也，息也。”通過這些材料我們可以發現，陸德明認爲“尼”表示“停止”義和“接近”義時讀娘母質韻音（女乙切）是“會理合時”的，宋代孫奭《孟子音義》爲前引“尼之”注音也是女乙切，但同時可能其他經師或者在其他方言區中有别的讀法。

“尼”《廣韻》只收一個讀音，脂韻：“尼，和也，女夷切。”《集韻》收四個讀音，脂韻女夷切：“《說文》‘從後近之’，徐鍇曰‘昵也’。”（從趙振鐸《集韻校本》改）脂韻延知切：“《說文》‘平也，東方之人也’，或作‘𡰥’‘尼’，古書作‘夸’。”薺韻乃禮切：“《爾雅》‘定也’。”質韻尼質切：“《爾雅》‘止也’，一曰‘近也’。”《集韻》所收的四個讀音都可以找到它們的來源。

根據《新論》所使用的注音符號，*nejX*表示中古是泥母薺韻音，應該對應《集韻》中的乃禮切，顧野王注的奴啟反；*nejH*表示中古是泥母霽韻音，可是我們目前沒找到古人給“尼”注霽韻讀法的材料。我們推測，或許《新論》把“泥”的音義强加到“尼”上來，“泥”中古有去聲霽韻的讀法，《廣韻》注音奴計切，讀這個音時有“陷滯不通”的意思，但是這個意思並不是由“尼”的“停止”義滋生來的，而是由“泥”讀平聲時表示的“含水的半固體狀的土”這個意思引申出來的，關於“泥”的變調構詞，孫玉文先生有詳細的論述[22]，此處不贅。因此，《新論》認爲“尼”有泥母霽韻讀法，它的意思是及物用法（可能）的“停止”，這是毫無根據的。

（六）

《新論》認爲“袂”（衣袖）中古有兩個讀音：第一個是*kwet*，按照《新論》中的系統，應該是見母屑韻；第二個是*mjiejH*，按照《新論》中的系統，應該是明母祭韻。《新論》進一步認爲這兩個讀音分别有它們的上古來源，爲它們構擬了不同的上古音，並且認爲現代漢語普通話的mèi是來自中古的*mjiejH*，而不是*kwet*[23]。

按：“袂”《廣韻》只收一個讀音，祭韻：“袂，袖也，彌獘切。”《集韻》收有三個讀音，祭韻儒稅切：“袂，衣袖，《莊子》‘被髮褕袂’，李軌讀。”祭韻倪祭切：“襒袂，《方言》‘複襦謂之筩襒’，或作袂。”祭韻彌獘切：“袂，《說文》‘袖也’。”都沒有注“袂”有見母讀法。《經典釋文》爲“袂”注音共17次，其中15次注明母祭韻音（彌世反、面世反、武世反、緜世反、滅制反），1次兼注又音“李音芮”，這和《集韻》的儒稅切是一致的，可能有的經師或方言讀這個音。另外《儀禮·少牢饋食禮》：“實于左袂，掛于季指。”釋文：“袂，音決。”這可能就是《新論》認爲“袂”中古有見母屑韻音的依據，《廣韻》“決”注音古穴切。但很多學者對《釋文》“袂，音決”表示疑議，黄焯《經典釋文彙校》：“宋本‘袂’作‘抉’。阮云、段玉裁云：‘袂不當有決音，《儀禮》嘉靖本、鍾人傑本皆作抉。’今案《五經文字》、《九經字樣》俱無‘抉’字，《宋人重修玉篇》始載之，未知是古字否。至錢大

㉒ 孫玉文《漢語變調構詞考辨》，北京：商務印書館，2015年，945—951頁。

㉓ WilliamH.Baxter and Laurent Sagart, *Old Chinese: A New Reconstruction*, p. 152.

昕謂‘袂當作秧，陸所見本已譌’，此又當别論也。”[24]由此則“音決”不是爲“袂”注音。

隋唐以後“袂”應該已經是一個常用詞了，人們已經熟知它的讀法，《史記》三家注、《漢書》顔師古注、《後漢書》李賢注、《文選》李善注都不爲“袂”注音，如果“袂”中古真有見母屑韻讀法，應該會在這些材料中記錄下來，畢竟它不是一個常見的讀音。由此可見，“袂”中古存在見母屑韻音的可能性很小，《新論》據此構擬出一個上古讀音是不可靠的。而且，據《集韻》，“袂”還有疑母、日母讀法，爲什麼《新論》不按照歷史比較法也爲它們構擬出不同的上古讀音呢？我想，這與《新論》引證這個例子的目的有關，《新論》是將這個例子放在“帶前冠音*p、*t、*k的聲首”（onsets with preinitial *p、*t、*k）來說的，核心觀點是說如果某個字的上古讀音是*k.m-，那它到中古的演變路徑就會是下面兩種中的一種：*k.m- > *km- > $^{*}k^{w}$- >*kw-*，或*k.m- >*m-*。“袂”在現代漢語普通話中讀mèi是屬於第二種，如果不爲“袂”的上古讀音找到一個*k聲母的話，就不能把它放到這個演變中去了，而剛好《經典釋文》中“袂”注有“音決”。這顯然是強材料以就我，先假定一個演變機制，再去挑選一些看似合適的材料來論證。

（七）

《新論》認爲“乞”是“气”的聲符，同時“气”（吸進去的東西，空氣、氣息、水蒸汽等）的詞根是“吸”（吸入）。因此把“气”最初的上古音構擬成*C.q^{h}əp-s，“吸”的上古音構擬成*q^{h}(r)əp[25]。

按：“气”不是形聲字，而是象形字。《說文·气部》：“气，雲气也，象形，凡气之屬皆从气。”許慎就認爲“气”是象形字。甲金文中，“气”通常寫作三，後來爲了和“三”區别，寫成，字形進一步變易，寫成气[26]，正是象雲气升騰之形，段玉裁說“气本雲气，引伸爲凡气之偁”，甚確。那麼“气”怎麼可能是形聲字、以“乞”爲聲旁呢？事實上，“气”可以借用來表示“乞求”之義，後來寫作“乞”，段玉裁明確說：“借爲气假於人之气，又省作乞。”于省吾先生也指出，甲骨文中的“气”可以訓气求（乞求），並舉了幾條卜辭爲證，可從。總而言之，將“气”看成是形聲字，這是一個知識性的錯誤。

另外，“气”的“吸進去的氣體、氣息”義是由自己的“气體（總稱）”義發展而來，而不是由“吸”的“吸收”義發展而來。上文已經說過，“气”可以作爲氣體的總稱，例如《莊子·齊物論》：“夫大塊噫氣，其名爲風。”（表示氣體的“气”後來寫作“氣”，這裡不詳細討論。）由此發展出“吸進去的气體、氣息”的意思是很自然的

---

[24] 黄焯《經典釋文彙校》，北京：中華書局，2006年，349頁。

[25] William H.Baxter and Laurent Sagart, *Old Chinese: A New Reconstruction*, pp. 169-170.

[26] 參考于省吾《甲骨文字釋林·釋气》，北京：中華書局，1979年，81頁。

詞義引申，可以看作特指構詞，《玉篇・气部》：“氣，息也。”而“吸”的本義就是向內吸氣，《說文・口部》：“吸，內息也。从口，及聲。”它和“气”的“吸進去的氣體”義沒有引申關係。

《新論》之所以非要胡亂地斬斷詞義引申脈絡，認爲“气”和“吸”在詞義上有引申關係，完全是爲了他們的上古音構擬服務。他們認爲上古的*C.q^h-會演變爲中古的溪母，爲了給這一理論找證據，他們便想辦法把“乞”“氣”“气”“吸”串聯起來，但其實並非如此。這也是歪曲材料以就我的錯誤做法。

余　論

上文僅對《新論》中的7個例子進行了辨析，便暴露出該書存在的諸多問題，例如對文字通假的實質認識比較淺顯，研究詞義關係時偷換概念，將不同時代的讀音和意義強扭在一個共時平面，對字形的分析有失準確，沒有吸取前輩時賢的研究成果，隨意選擇利用材料以遷就自己的理論等等。歸根結底，在於《新論》作者沒有踏踏實實地深入到漢語文獻內部，沒有仔細地爬梳材料，因此得出的一些看似很巧妙新穎的結論往往得不到材料的支持，有些更是無異於空中樓閣。作爲西方學者，對中國的語言史感興趣、並願意去探索，應該得到我們的讚賞和鼓勵，在具體研究過程中提出一些吸引眼球的觀點，也可以理解。但是就這本著作本身的質量而論，學術界一些人對它大加推崇，就與科學精神相違背，也不利於良好學風的創建。

據美國語言學會網站上的介紹，布龍菲爾德圖書獎是認可那些對我們理解語言和語言學作出突出貢獻、具有持久價值的著作的一項獎勵（this award recognizes a volume that makes an outstanding contribution of enduring value to our understanding of language and linguistics），獲此獎勵的著作須達到四項要求：創新性（novelty），實證意義（empirical import），觀念上的重要性（conceptual significance）和表述的清晰性（clarity）。一些在學術界頗有影響的著作都曾獲得過這個獎勵，例如拉波夫（William Labov）的《語言演變原理：內部因素》（*Principles of Linguistic Change: Internal Factors*）獲得1996年布龍菲爾德圖書獎，而1998年的榮譽則頒給了哈里斯（Alice C. Harris）和坎貝爾（Lyle Campbell）合著的《歷史句法學的跨語言視角》（*Historical Syntax in Cross-Linguistic Perspective*），這兩部著作應該是達到了上面提到的四項標準，並經受住了時間的考驗，近二十年過去了，它們仍爲學術界所重視。相比之下，《新論》實在是相形見絀得多，它被授予布龍菲爾德獎，實在讓人驚詫。由此也反映出西方的漢學研究尤其是漢語音韻學、音義關係方面的研究水平與國內的研究存在較大差距，以至于不能正確地對相關研究成果作出客觀公允的評價，同時評審們在評價《新論》時恐怕並沒有嚴格貫徹布龍菲爾德圖書獎的四項標準。這兩點是密切相關的。

那麼，我們應該怎樣進行正確的學術評價呢？下面結合《新論》簡單談談自己的看法。

首先，既然是進行科學研究，那是否具有科學性應該成爲評價中最重要的標準。所謂科學性，簡單來說，就是要在科學思想的指導下對客觀材料進行如實可靠的分析和研究，進行合理的推論，這就是布龍菲爾德獎要求的實證意義。拋棄客觀材料、主觀臆測都不符合科學性的要求。上文我們提到，《新論》在探討具體詞的詞義時，有偷換概念的錯誤，有不顧詞義產生的時代性的錯誤，在論證“公”和“工”的使用情況和讀音關係時，有主觀猜測的錯誤，自己訂立的原則不能貫徹到底等等。這些都與科學精神相悖，所得出的結論也不能接受材料的檢驗，與實證意義的要求大相徑庭。

其次，對一項研究進行評價，需要與其他同類的研究進行比較，看是否在前人基礎上做出了新的貢獻，這實際上就是布龍菲爾德圖書獎的另一項標準——創新性。但所謂創新，必須在已有的研究上進行，批判地繼承已有的研究成果和研究方法，並在行文中出註說明，這不僅是學術進步的必由之路，也是學術規範的具體要求。這一點，王力先生《中國語言學的繼承和發展》一文有精闢的闡述，此處不贅[27]。其實上面提到的《新論》中的一些失誤是完全可以避免的，例如“驚”的詞義問題、“魯”和“气”的字形結構問題，前人都已經對它們進行了研究，並且言之有據，作者本人或者是沒注意到，或者是注意到了而不予採納，但都沒有進行說明，這既不符合學術規範，也不利於自己的研究。如果沒有實證作爲基礎，所謂的創新往往也是站不住腳的。

最後，《新論》把漢語上古音系統和形態問題結合起來作爲研究，在一些學者看來，是一種新的研究思路，在研究觀念上做出了重大貢獻。關於上古漢語是否存在西方語言中的形態、是否具有各種詞綴，國內外的學者分歧很大，相關的討論也有很多。學術乃天下之公器，對學術研究的評價只能基於學術本身，不能受自己先入爲主想法的束縛。受印歐語系的語言影響，一些西方學者也傾向於認爲上古漢語也存在形態，但是《新論》在面對這個問題時，對相關爭論和研究動態隻字不提[28]，這缺乏科學研究最基本的客觀性，而對現有構詞研究成果的評價，也有失公允。我們很難想象，這樣一種無視現有研究成果和觀點分歧的做法能夠稱得上具有觀念上的重要性。

江永在《古韻標準・例言》里說得好：“余謂凡著述有三難，淹博難，識斷難，精審難。”這三點雖難，但卻是我們要努力達到的目標。分而言之，在具體實踐中，只要肯花時間、勤於動手，藉助方便快捷的網絡資源和電子檢索工具，是能夠較爲充分地佔有材料、達到淹博的程度。但是識斷和精審則需要研究者個人付出極大的努力，也更考驗他們的水平，尤其是現在新理論、新方法層出不窮，面對的語言事實也複雜多樣，如何選擇合適的理論框架、從中吸取有用的思路和方法，如何細緻科學地分析材料、總

㉗ 參看王力《中國語言學的繼承和發展》，載《王力文集》第16卷，1990年，濟南：山東教育出版社，48—63頁。

㉘ 例如丁邦新、孫玉文等先生曾對爲上古漢語構擬詞綴的做法進行過正面批評，詳參丁邦新《上古漢語的構詞問題——評Laurent Sagar: The Roots of the Old Chinese》，《語言學論叢》第26輯，北京：商務印書館，2002年，1—11頁；孫玉文《上古漢語詞綴構擬析評》（上、下），《江漢大學學報》2007年第3期，39—46頁，《江漢大學學報》2007年第4期，58—75頁，又收入《上古音叢論》，27—57頁。

結規律、得出結論，都是研究者不得不面對的問題。關於如何做到這一點，《中國語言學》的發刊詞里的一段言簡意賅的話給我們指出了方法，即“以中國語言學的優良傳統爲根，取世界語言學的精華而融通之，堅定地走自主創新之路，爲繁榮中國語言學而奮鬥”。我想只有具備這樣素質的學者才能真正爲中國語言學的傳承與發展做出貢獻，也只有符合這樣要求的著作才能真正獲得人們的認可和讚譽。

A Discussion about Several Evidences in *Old Chinese: A New Reconstruction*—Also Rethinking the Western Academic Evaluation

Xiang Xiaolu

Old Chinese: A New Reconstruction by Prof. William H.Baxter and Prof. Laurent Sagart was thought highly of in American mainstream linguistic field, and even received Leonard Bloomfield Book Award in 2015. However, after examining this book carefully, we found that there are many problems, and it failed to satisfy the readers. In this article, we chose 7 evidences to analyze specifically in terms of the analysis on materials, logical reasoning, etc., and further rethought the western academic evaluation.

從上古文獻看白一平—沙加爾上古音構擬*

趙團員

白一平（Baxter）、沙加爾（Sagart）《上古漢語：構擬新論》①用“上古漢語”這個術語來指稱“在公元前221年秦朝統一中國以前的種種漢語變體”。他們看起來非常強調上古漢語文獻的重要性：“雖然我們不能確定，但看起來我們掌握的最早的漢語文獻——包括卜辭、青銅銘文和最早的漢語經典文獻——都沒有從這個共同祖語那兒偏離太遠。”②但我們在通讀全書後發現，白—沙構擬在解釋上古文獻方面有很大的問題。我們從三方面來討論其文獻方面的問題，一是白—沙構擬與同源詞研究；二是白—沙構擬的預測性問題；三是*-r韻尾構擬的問題。

一、白—沙構擬與同源詞研究

白—沙構擬的一個詞是由詞根和詞綴組成的，“当兩个詞有同样的詞根而有不同的詞缀时，可以看作属于同样的语族”③。他們也承認上古漢語中存在相互關聯的語根（related roots）。他們說：“兩個構擬出來的獨立的詞根具有相似的意義和相近但不相同的讀音，這種情況並不罕見。”④這些語音的不同包括咽化（pharyngealization）與非咽化聲母⑤的區别，送氣與不送氣的區别，*-ʔ與*-k⑥的區别。無論是屬於同樣的語族，還是相互關聯的詞根，都可以看作同源詞。白—沙構擬的前綴很豐富，而中綴只有一個<r>。前綴影響聲母的演變，中綴同時影響聲母和韻母的演變。但僅僅靠中綴及“相互關聯的語根”，不能解釋所有韻母不同的同源詞。

---

* 本文爲遼寧省社科聯2016年青年項目L16CYY008、大連理工大學科研基金（中央高校基本科研業務費專項資金）資助項目DUT16RC（3）083的階段性成果。寫作過程中，北大中文系上古音小組孫玉文、李建强等先生提出寶貴意見，在此表示感謝。

① William H. Baxter and Laurent Sagart, *Old Chinese: A New Reconstruction*, New York: Oxford University Press, 2014.本文引用主要根據北大中文系上古音小組的中文翻譯，個别語句有調整，同時標示原文頁碼。下文書名簡稱《新論》，這種構擬稱爲白—沙構擬。

② 《新論》，2頁。

③ 《新論》，59頁。

④ 《新論》，60頁。

⑤ 即王力上古音系統中一、二、四等與三等。

⑥ 即王力上古音系統中的上聲與入聲。

（一）白—沙構擬與“旁轉”現象的矛盾

從白—沙的設定來看，不存在詞根主元音不同的同源詞。例如他們在討論“飢”的押韻問題時，提到：“一般字典中（飢）歸入脂部明顯是個錯誤，‘飢’（飢餓）顯然與‘饑’（饑荒）相關，而‘饑’字每個人都歸入了微部。”[⑦]白—沙用“飢”“饑”語義的相關，證明二者同部[⑧]。该例可進一步證明他們認爲同源詞詞根的主元音要相同。但這與上古漢語中存在“旁轉”[⑨]的事實矛盾。王力先生《同源字典》有“旁轉”一類，即上古主元音不同的同源詞，如“飢”“饑”在《同源字典》中是一對脂微旁轉的同源詞，分別構擬作ki əi，kiei[⑩]。

但是不少類似的配對詞，在白—沙的構擬中看不出同源的痕跡。下面舉二個例子說明。王力《同源字典》證明“dzio聚：dziu遒（侯幽旁轉）”爲一對同源詞[⑪]，白—沙分別構擬爲“*m-tsʰoʔ”“*tsu”[⑫]。主元音不同，“聚”有前綴，“遒”沒有。王力：“həm含：ham函（侵談旁轉）”[⑬]，白—沙分別構擬爲“*Cə-m-kˤ[ə][⑭]m”“*[g]ˤ[o]m”，除主元音不同外，聲母也不同，而且“含”有前綴*m-，以及鬆散結合的前冠音（loosely attatched preinitials）*Cə，而“函”沒有，兩者完全沒有同源的跡象。這兩對同源詞先秦都有用例，白—沙構擬不能體現二者的同源關係，這與上古文獻反映的事實不符。

（二）白—沙構擬與變等構詞的矛盾

白—沙構擬的介音-r-，“它或者是詞根的一部分，或者是佔據相同位置的中綴*<r>[⑮]”[⑯]。這個-r-既與中古的捲舌音有關[⑰]，又對韻母的發展有影響[⑱]。-r-同時承擔語音和中綴功能，常常會產生矛盾。白—沙構擬“爲中古漢語的三種音節構擬元音前的

⑦ 《新論》，285頁。

⑧ 根據王力先生的系統，“饑”與“飢”分別是微部和脂部，主元音不同。本文暫不涉及這個具體問題，主要討論“旁轉”是否存在的問題。

⑨ 《新論》，234—235頁，也提到“耕元旁轉”的問題，僅僅是語音問題，而不是同源詞的問題。

⑩ 王力《同源字典》，北京：商務印書館，1982年，393頁。

⑪ 王力《同源字典》，197頁。

⑫ 白—沙的擬音，我們採取的是白—沙2015年10月13在網上更新的擬音，網址：http://ocbaxtersagart.lsait.lsa.umich.edu/。

⑬ 王力《同源字典》，605頁。

⑭ 白—沙構擬中[ ]號表示不確定。

⑮ 白—沙構擬中<>號表示中綴。

⑯ 《新論》，51頁。

⑰ 參看《新論》，80—81頁。

⑱ 參看《新論》，其中稱爲前元音（prevocalic），213—219頁。

*-r-：①中古具有捲舌𪘲音聲母(*tsr-, tsrh-, dzr-, sr-, zr-*)或捲舌塞音聲母(*tr-, trh-, dr-, nr-*)的音節；②二等音節；③特定的三等音節（包括很多重紐三等音節）”[19]。通過等的變化構造新詞的現象可稱爲變等構詞。變等構詞與中綴*<r>有密切的關係。根據白—沙構擬的設定，在涉及變等構詞時，以上三類音節從理論上只能是滋生詞，而不是原始詞。這些都是從其語音構擬及中綴設定推出來的結論，但很難得到上古材料的支持。

以一等韻和二等韻之間的變等構詞爲例，白—沙構擬中一等韻上古沒有-r-介音，二等韻有-r-介音。那麼涉及一二等之間的變等構詞，似乎只能一等韻爲原始詞，二等韻爲滋生詞。Baxter& Sagart已經如此處理[20]。因爲如果一等爲滋生詞，則一等有*<r>中綴，與語音設定矛盾。

而上古漢語中存在原始詞爲二等，滋生詞爲一等的變韻構詞。孫玉文在《漢語一二等韻之間語音轉換的變韻構詞舉例》中，以充分的文獻證據證明存在原始詞爲二等韻、滋生詞爲一等韻的例子，此文中他例舉了三個例子：“行*$_{c}$ɣe ɑ ŋ：行*$_{c}$ɣ ɑ ŋ；獲*ɣo ǎ k：穫*ɣu ǎ k；横*$_{c}$ɣo ɑ ŋ：璜*$_{c}$ɣu ɑ ŋ。”他同時指出：“因爲有人給上古二等韻構擬了一個-r-介音，於是根據這種類型（一等韻增生介音構造新詞）的原始詞沒有-r-介音，滋生詞有-r-介音，就把這個-r-處理爲所謂中綴。這種做法非常不科學。”[21]這是很有道理的。

白—沙系統中二等和四等之間的區别也是靠介音，即二等有介音-r-，四等無介音-r-，特定的三等音節可以有介音-r-。那麼涉及到三四等之間的變等構詞，似乎四等不能作滋生詞。但實際上古漢語中存在三等滋生四等的例子。如“資：齎”這一對詞。資，原始詞，錢財，財物，即夷切。《左傳·定公五年》：“夏，歸粟于蔡，以周亟，矜無資。”（2139-2[22]）滋生詞，特指出行所持的財物，一般寫作“齎”，祖稽切。《禮記·奔喪》：“若所爲位，家遠，則成服而往。”鄭玄注：“謂所當奔者，外喪也。外喪緩而道遠，成服乃行，容待齎也。”（1655-2）陸德明《經典釋文》：“待齎，子西反，資糧也，一音咨。”（14-11-2）[23]“一音”表明“咨”音爲陸德明所不取。根據郭錫良《漢字古音手冊》（修訂版），上古讀音分别爲*$_{c}$ts ĭ ei：*$_{c}$tsiei，是三、四等的區别。按照白—沙構擬，“資”上古音爲*[ts]ij，“齎”未見擬音，白—沙“齊”和“躋”分别構擬爲*[ts]ˁəj，*[dz]ˁəj，我們根據同諧聲必同部的原則，推斷白沙“齎”很可能構擬爲*[ts]ˁəj[24]，兩者主元音很可能就不同，讀音上看不出同源關係。

---

⑲ 《新論》，213頁。

⑳ William H. Baxter and Laurent Sagart, *Word formation in Old Chinese.New approches to Chinese word formation:morphology,phonology and the lexicon in Mordern and Ancient Chinese*, ed.Jerome L.Packard,Berlin:Mouton de Gruyter, 1998, pp. 62-64.

㉑ 孙玉文《漢語一二等韻之間語音轉換的變韻構詞舉例》，《中華字典研究》第二輯下，北京：中国社会科学出版社，2010年，668—680頁。

㉒ （清）阮元校勘《十三經注疏》（嘉慶刊本），北京：中華書局，1980年。數字代表第2139頁第2欄。下同。

㉓ （唐）陸德明《經典釋文》，北京：中華書局，1983年。

㉔ 白—沙構擬中懠的上古音爲*[dz]ˁ[i]j，所以不排除他把“齎”主元音構擬爲i的可能。

如果白—沙想表現二者的滋生關係，則應該擬爲*[ts]<r>ij，但這既與四等不能帶-r-介音的設定矛盾，也與他們把大多數齊聲字聲母構擬爲əj的做法矛盾。

值得注意的是，我們上文所舉的“旁轉”諸例，主元音不同，白—沙所謂“相互關聯的語根”不包括這一類型。對於一二四等到三等變化的變等構詞，白—沙構擬有兩種可能的處理，一種是處理爲相互關聯的詞根，一種是爲三等構擬<r>中綴。從三等到一二四等變化的變等構詞，三等到二等很可能處理爲中綴的有無，而三等到一等、四等則似乎只能處理爲“相互關聯的詞根”，因爲處理爲中綴的有無則與語音的設定矛盾。同樣是變等構詞，爲什麼會有不同的處理方案？白—沙的答案是：“上古漢語中這樣的語音交替並不能產，我們把它們處理爲上古漢語的祖語中曾經能產的形態交替的殘留。”㉕我們認爲，是否能產還是得從上古漢語內部材料中去總結，而不是僅僅依靠某種語音構擬來推測。上古二等到一等，三等到四等的變等構詞例子很多㉖，很難認爲是殘留。

（三）中綴例證中的問題

《新論》3.3.2.6爲中綴<r>例舉了9對例子，其中只有例（123）配對詞之間只有<r>有無的區別，其他8例配對詞之間都還有其他方面的語音對立。如（117）配對詞讀音既有中綴的區別，也有後綴及最小音節（minor syllable）有無的區別㉗。既然存在多種語音對立，怎麼確定語義區別用中綴表示的，而不是由於前綴或後綴，作者並沒有充分的證明，從邏輯上來看是有很大漏洞的。同時，例（117）字與詞的對應關係也不妥當。其配對詞語音的對應不成立，從而詞綴的構擬不能成立。該例涉及“洗”與“洒”“灑”三個字形：

洗 *[s]ˁərʔ>*sejX* > xǐ ‘wash’

洒～灑 *Cə.s<r>ərʔ-s >*srjeH*>*sreaH*> sǎ ‘sprinkle’㉘

srjeH反映的是《廣韻》“所寄切”，中古支韻字（舉平以該上去，下同）在上古一般歸爲支部或歌部，未見歸入文部或微部的。就白-沙構擬而言，聲符“麗”*[r]ˁe-s，以及從“麗”的得聲的字，如“纚”*sreʔ、“曬”*sre-s都是支部字。白-沙“洒～灑”的上古擬音實際反映的是“洒”（汛）的讀音，而不是“灑”的讀音。上古“洒”與“汛”表示的爲同一個詞，後來讀同“灑”，是訓讀的結果。

段玉裁已經指出“洒”“汛”在表示“灑水”時同詞。《說文解字·水部》：“汛，灑也。”段玉裁注：“然謂‘洒’即‘汛’之假借，則于古音尤合。蓋‘洒’從

㉕ 《新論》，61頁。

㉖ 據我們統計，僅在《同源字典》中，三等到四等變化的配對詞就有11對，而四等到三等變化的配對詞則只有3對。

㉗ 其他諸例語音對立，可參看《新論》，57—58頁。

㉘ 《新論》，57頁。

西聲，‘西’古音如‘詵’也。”[29]段玉裁首先从古音证明，然後用音注材料證明。《漢書·東方朔傳》：“一日卒有不勝洒掃之職。”顔師古注：“洒音信，又音山豉反。”[30]“洒音信”，與“汛”讀音相同，段玉裁指出這是“《漢書音義》舊說”，可從。此外，《原本玉篇殘卷》水部有“洒”字：“洒……《聲類》亦汛字也，汛，灑也。”[31]《聲類》明確指出“‘洒’亦‘汛’字”。《集韻》稕韻：“汛洒，思晉切。《說文》：灑也。或作洒。”[32]可進一步證明上古時期“洒”“汛”音義皆同[33]。而“洒”在先秦文献中占主导的形式，“灑”到战国晚期才出现，到漢代逐渐占优势，所以後来“洒”（汛）訓讀爲“灑”。兩者在表“灑水”義時語義相同，是同義詞，而不是同一個詞的不同分化形式。

“洗”在上古爲“洗足”義。《說文》：“洗，洒足也。”徐鉉引《唐韻》注音：“穌典切”。段玉裁注：“《內則》曰：‘面垢，燂潘請靧。足垢，燂湯請洗。’此洒面曰靧，洒足曰洗之證也。洗讀如跣足之跣。自後人以洗代洒滌字，讀先禮切。”[34]《漢書·高祖本紀》：“沛公方踞床，使兩女子洗。”顔師古注：“洗，洗足也。洗，音先典反。”[35]表示“洗滌”義，上古常寫作“洒”而不是“洗”，僅寫作“洗”也是不妥當的。

由此可見，這兩組字与詞音義對應都有問題。更重要的是，“洒”上古音應該對應中古的“思晉切”，爲心母三等真部字[36]。按照白—沙構擬，上古不能有介音-r-，所以這個例子很難成立。

二、白—沙構擬的預測性問題

無論在諧聲還是在通假中，白-沙強調“在大多數情況下，每個聲符代表一種音節類型，該音節類型的音首發音位置、主元音和韻尾都是確定的。”[37]這可以看作白—構擬的諧聲、通假原則。但是我們看到他們的構擬常常違背這個原則。同時，白一平在 *A Handbook of Old Chinese Phonolog*（《上古音手冊》）中把元部分成三個主元音*-an, *-en,*-on，這樣《詩經》等韻文中的元部就新增了一些不和諧的押韻，他試圖用文獻傳

㉙ （清）段玉裁《說文解字注》卷二一，上海：上海古籍出版社，1988年，565頁。

㉚ （漢）班固《漢書》卷六五，北京：中華書局，1987年，2854頁。

㉛ （梁）顧野王《原本玉篇殘卷》，北京：中華書局，2004年，375頁。此爲黎昌庶本。

㉜ 趙振鐸校《集韻校本》，上海：上海辭書出版社，2114頁。

㉝ 詳細考證可參見趙團員《“洒、汛、灑”音義考》，《中國典籍與文化》2016年第3期。

㉞ （清）段玉裁《說文解字注》卷二一，564頁。

㉟ （漢）班固《漢書》卷一上，18頁。

㊱ Baxter, William H. and Laurent Sagart, *Word formation in Old Chinese.New approches to Chinese word formation:morphology,phonology and the lexicon in Mordern and Ancient Chinese*, p. 63.〔法〕沙加爾《上古漢語詞根》，龔群虎譯，上海：上海教育出版社，2004年，124—125頁。這兩處都討論了這個例子，存在類似的錯誤。

㊲ 《新論》，65頁。

抄導致的變化以及先秦到兩漢的音變兩種因素來解釋不和諧的押韻[38]。《新論》中繼承了這種思路，并引入出土文獻的資料，用《詩》和《老子》的例子試圖證明他們的上古音系具有預測性。他們聲稱："和傳統的韻部分析及以其爲基礎的各種構擬相比，我們的構擬是更好的文獻研究工具。"[39]但他們所舉的例子是不能成立的，所謂預測性並不存在。

（一）"四矢□兮"例

首先討論《詩》中的例子。《齊風·猗嗟》"四矢□兮"，毛詩作"反"，韓詩作"變"[40]。白一平之前認爲，該字所處韻段其他韻腳字"孌、婉、選、貫、亂"主元音都是*on，"反"的主元音是*an，"變"的主元音是"on"，"變"能反映《詩》文本更古老的面貌。[41]《新論》則進一步提出，上博簡《孔子詩論》[42]引用此句，寫作"𢆶"，他們根據李家浩《釋"弁"》[43]的考證認爲該字讀爲"弁"，然後，他們說"弁"經常作"變"的通假字，因此上博簡的用字證明白一平之前的預測是正確的[44]。

我們認爲，他的預測并沒有得到證明。首先，即便承認該字只能通假"變"，也不能證明先秦只有這一個版本，不能證明毛詩的版本"反"在先秦沒有出現。另外，我們全面考察上博簡中與"弁"字形有關的諸例後發現，認爲該字可以和"反"通假。在上博簡六中，《用曰》："民道绅多，而亦不可沽。"。"绅"的聲符與《孔子詩論》中的字形相同，整理者注釋："'绅多'，讀爲'繁多'或'煩多'皆可。"[45]"繁""煩"白一沙構擬爲*[b]ar，*[b]a[n]，主元音都是[a]，而"弁"的讀音爲*C.[b]ro[n]-s，绅韻部也應該是on，這樣"绅"與"繁""煩"主元音不同，而且比這兩個字多個前綴。白一沙構擬不能解釋上文通假現象。而且"绅"既然可以通"繁"或"煩"，而"繁""煩"與"反"讀音無論是根據王力體系還是根據白一沙構擬，讀音都是相近的，這樣就很難排除"弁"通"反"的可能。

白一沙體系不能解釋"绅"和"繁""煩"的通假，傳統的元部說則能解釋清楚，他們聲母相同，韻部相同，自然可以通假。至於爲什麼"弁"經常作"變"的通假字，而不常作"反"的通假字，也可以從傳統元部的角度來解釋。以郭錫良《漢字古音手

㊳ William H. Baxter, *A Handbook of Old Chinese Phonology*, Berlin:Mouton de Gruyter, 1992, pp. 355-361，pp. 370-389.

㊴ 《新論》，208頁。

㊵ 《經典釋文》，67頁。

㊶ William H. Baxter, A Handbook of Old Chinese Phonology, pp. 364-366.

㊷ 馬承源主編《上海博物館藏戰國楚竹書》（一），上海：上海古籍出版社，2001年，图版34頁，释文151—152頁。

㊸ 李家浩《釋"弁"》，《古文字研究》，第一輯，1979年，391—395頁。

㊹ 《新論》，208—209頁。

㊺ 馬承源主編《上海博物館藏戰國楚竹書》（六），上海：上海古籍出版社，2007年，圖版127頁，釋文305頁。

冊》（增訂本）的構擬爲例，弁*bǐan，變pǐan，繁*bǐwan，反*pǐwan。“弁”“變”韻母和聲調都相同，只有聲母有清濁的區别；而“弁”與“繁”“反”則聲調與開合口都不同，相對而言，“弁”“變”讀音更接近，所以通假較多。但是由此確定“變”爲更原始的面貌，證據并不充分。而且上文已經證明“弁”通“反”的可能性是確確實實存在的，白—沙所聲稱的預測性很難成立。

（二）“萬物無以生將恐滅”例

其次討論《老子》的例子。王弼本第38章“萬物無以生將恐滅”這句話在馬王堆帛書甲、乙本《老子》中未出現。而白沙構擬“滅”與“裂”“發”“歇”“竭”“蹶”主元音不同。他們認爲這能體現其構擬的優越性，因爲他們的構擬能預測“萬物無以生將恐滅”不能出現，也能解釋後來這句話出現的原因，因爲漢代以後“滅”的主元音變得和其他韻腳字一致了[46]。白—沙的論證有兩個方面的問題，首先，同上一例一樣存在邏輯問題。“萬物無以生將恐滅”這句話在馬王堆帛書中未出現，这與“滅”能不能與“裂”“發”“歇”“竭”“蹶”押韻是兩回事。即使先秦所有《老子》文本中都沒有這句話[47]，也不能證明 “滅”不能與“裂”“發”“歇”“竭”“蹶”押韻。此外，我們有連綿詞的材料證明先秦“滅”能與“裂”押韻。《莊子·則陽》：“君爲政焉勿鹵莽，治民焉勿滅裂。”[48]《釋文》“鹵，音魯。莽，莫古反，又如字。滅裂，猶短草也。李云：謂不熟也。郭云：鹵莽滅裂，輕脫末略，不盡其分也。司馬云：鹵莽，猶麤粗也。謂淺耕稀種也。滅裂，斷其草也。”（28-12-8）“魯莽”“滅裂”都是疊韻連綿詞，兩者聲母别是l-m-，m-l-，恐怕也是作者有意的運用技巧。這則例子能證明“滅”“裂”先秦同韻部，主元音相同。孫玉文指出，大多數上古疊韻連綿詞的等是相同的[49]。“滅裂”上古都是開口三等，也是這一規律的體現。白沙構擬“滅裂”擬音爲*[m]et *[r]at，也不能體現連綿詞的疊韻關係，由此可進一步看出白—沙構擬的缺陷。

三、*-r韻尾構擬中的問題

白—沙韻尾*-r的构擬承自斯塔羅思京[50]，用來解釋元部、真部、文部及歌部、脂

㊻ 《新論》，210—211頁。

㊼ 馬王堆帛書《老子》沒有這句話，並不一定意味着先秦所有《老子》文本中肯定没有这句话。

㊽ 郭庆藩《莊子集釋》，北京：中華書局，2012年，889—890頁。

㊾ 孫玉文《先秦連綿詞的語音研究》，原載劉麗文、趙雪主編《古代語言現象探索》，北京：北京廣播學院出版社，2003年，34—81頁。又收入論文集《上古音叢論》，北京：北京大學出版社，2015年，192—234頁。

㊿ 〔俄〕斯塔羅思京《古漢語音系的構擬》，張興亞譯，北京：北京大學出版社，2012年，166—168、202—208頁。白—沙與斯塔羅思京一個很大的不同是，白—沙的-r尾字有二等字，比如下文的“山”字，而斯塔羅思京明確排除掉二等字，這樣兩者-r尾字的範圍明顯不同，而且兩者論據并不完全相同。這一點白—沙沒有指明，而經何大安指出，參看Ho, Dah-an, “Such errors could have been avoided: Review of Old Chinese: A New Reconstruction”, *Journal of Chinese Linguistics*, 1(44), 2016, pp.175-230。

部、微部的一些字中古同時有陰聲和陽聲[51]讀法的現象。但是通過《詩》韻他們系聯了一些與陰聲韻未有任何交涉的字。如5.5.1.2 所引韻段197.8（即《小雅·小弁》）：“山，泉，垣。”首先，該韻段白一平之前韻腳字爲：“山，泉，言，垣”[52]，與此不同。其實從顧炎武開始，諸家“言”字皆入韻，並無疑義。作者此處“言”不入韻，大概是因爲看到“言”*-r尾的證據比較弱，而採取的處理，這種處理理由並不充分。此外，“泉”字作者未提供任何與陰聲韻交涉的證據，“山”作者提供了一條與陰聲韻有交涉的證據，即《釋名》的聲訓“山，崖也”[53]，何大安已經指出此條引用爲版本的錯誤，當爲“山，產也”。所以實際上並沒有證據[54]。而《說文》從山得聲有五個字：“仚，訕，邖，疝，汕”，都與陰聲韻未有交涉。這一類的例子不少。作者認爲：“*-r在現代漢語方言中推通常的表現是[n]，但是在先秦階段，我們已經有證據有一些方言中的*-r已經變成了[j]。”[55]可見白-沙構擬中的*-r尾字在文獻中表現是不一致的，不少字和陰聲韻沒什麼瓜葛，文獻依據很薄弱。

此外，他們通過與*ar，* ər的的類比，構擬了*-ir，但是只有一個例子“牝”[56]。而這個例子恰好是有問題的。根據前人研究，“牝”在先秦兩漢都只有陰聲韻的讀法，陽聲韻讀法是後起的。

“牝”字是陽聲讀法後起的典型例子。顧炎武《唐韻正》從押韻和音義的角度，證明先秦兩漢“牝”只有陰聲一讀，這是可以信從的[57]。顧炎武列舉了8個韻段[58]。《老子》叶“死，牝（是謂玄牝）[59]”（《列子》同）；《大戴禮·易本命》叶“死，牝（溪谷爲牝）”（《孔子家語》《淮南子》同）；《淮南子·兵略訓》叶“死，牝（左牡而右牝）”；《文子·守弱》叶“牝（爲天下牝），死”；《自然》叶“牝（非雄非牝），死”；《太玄經·居·次八》叶“幾，牝（雙其牝），旨”；《飾·次五》叶“水，牝（實以天牝）”；晉郭璞《山海經·豪彘贊》叶“彘，矢，牝（自爲牧牝）”[60]。這8例“牝”都是指雌性動物，或者其比喻義。經過我們進一步調查，先秦兩漢的韻文中“牝”字確無與陽聲字押韻者。

顧氏還以《說文》爲證，“牝”從匕得聲，“匕”與陽聲韻未有交涉。我們還可以

---

[51] 本文的陰聲韻和陽聲韻以王力先生的中古音和上古音系統作爲參照。

[52] William H. Baxter, A Handbook of Old Chinese Phonology, p. 672.

[53] 《新論》，148頁。

[54] Ho, Dah-an, “Such errors could have been avoided: Review of Old Chinese: A New Reconstruction”.

[55] 《新論》，252頁。

[56] 《新論》，292頁。

[57] （清）顧炎武《音學五書》，北京：中華書局，1982年第1版，2005年第2次印刷，334頁。

[58] 重複不計。

[59] “牝”字所在語句，據顧炎武所引版本，這有助於判斷韻腳字的義項。另外，《廣韻》之韻、脂韻、支韻，顧炎武上古音爲一個韻部，根據王力先生的上古三十部我們重新確定了韻腳字。

[60] 雖然有5例“牝”“死”押韻，但具體語句不同，應該能反映實際讀音。

從同諧聲的其他字來看，從匕得聲者《說文》有3個字[61]，除“牝”外，其他“疕、吡”中古都是脂韻（舉平以該上去，下同），與陽聲韻沒有交涉。

但至晚到隋唐時期，“牝”的陽聲韻讀法已佔據主流地位。《釋文》爲“牝”注音24例，首音都是毗（頻）忍切，爲陽聲韻。一些音注中保留了陰聲韻讀法。其中記錄注音者名稱的，注者都是徐邈。但徐邈本身也有陽聲韻的讀法。《易・坤》：“坤，下坤上坤，元亨，利牝馬之貞。”（17-3）《釋文》：“利牝，頻忍反，徐邈扶忍反，又扶死反。”（2-2-8）徐邈把“扶忍反”放在“扶死反”之前，說明徐邈讀音中陽聲韻也佔優勢。《老子》六章“谷神不死，是謂玄牝。”[62]《釋文》：“玄牝，頻忍反，舊云扶比反，簡文扶緊反。”（25-2-1）此處陰聲韻前標“舊云”，可見當時此音不常用。

“牝”的陽聲韻讀法產生的上限不容易確定。《周禮・冬官・車人》：“牝服二柯有参分柯之二。”（934-2）《釋文》：“牝服，步忍反，又扶死反，李扶緬反。”（9-31-6）李軌音“扶緬反”，可見“牝”的陽聲韻讀法產生時，很可能仙韻重紐四等字還沒有從真部中獨立出來，只有這樣才能解釋仙韻和真韻兩種不同讀音的分化。根據據丁邦新的研究，魏晉時期，仙、先韻字已經從真部中獨立出去[63]。由此推斷，最早在魏晉之前的東漢，可能已經有陽聲韻的讀法。但是該讀法最初通行範圍很小，在押韻材料中沒有直接體現。“牝”最早押陽聲韻的韻段見東晉殷仲文《南州桓公九井作》：“准，盡，緊，牝（哀壑叩虚牝），隕，菌，軫，引，泯，哂。”[64]徐邈與之時代相近，而比他們時代稍早的郭璞依然押陰聲韻[65]。由此可見，“牝”陽聲韻讀法很可能是後起的。

“牝”爲何會發生這樣的語音演變，顧炎武認爲是因爲回避禁忌字：“後人以其通俗不雅而改爲毗忍，失其本音。猶‘卵’本力管反，後人轉而音羸。‘鳥’本丁了反，後人轉而音嫋。此避俗之曲音，非考文之正說也。當削去併入旨韻。”[66]李榮結合其他文獻以及現代方言，進一步證明了這種說法的合理性[67]。此外，《廣韻》：“牝，扶履切，又毗忍切。一。”《廣韻》中“牝”陰聲韻無同音字，上古“牝”也沒有同音字，這可能也是語音不穩定的一個原因。

白—沙構擬中“匕”構擬爲*pijʔ，與“牝”*[b]irʔ韻尾不同，不能解釋“牝”字的諧聲。他們討論了《老子》中押韻的例子，認爲：“如果我們對韻尾*-r的構擬是對的，並且如果我們知道《老子》這一段是在何時何地創作地，這可能給我們一些關於上

---

[61] 《說文》“尼”“脂”也從匕得聲。由於聲母相差較大，不可從。但是他們也沒有與陽聲韻交涉的例子。

[62] （魏）王弼注《老子道德經注校釋》，樓宇烈校釋，北京：中華書局，2008年，16頁。

[63] 丁邦新《魏晉音韻研究》，臺灣：中央研究院歷史語言研究所專刊之六十五，1975年，154—163頁。

[64] 此段韻腳字見《六臣注文選》，北京：中華書局，2012年，405頁。

[65] 見上文顧炎武《音學五書》所引。

[66] （清）顧炎武《音學五書》，334頁。

[67] 李榮《禁忌字舉例》，《方言》1994年第3期，161—169頁。又收入《方言存稿》，北京：商務印書館，2012年，184—192頁。

古漢語方言中哪些區域*-r變爲*-j的額外線索。”[68]他們認爲這反映了方言現象。但是先秦兩漢所有“牝”入韻的韻段都是陰聲韻，是不是意味着-r韻尾在漢代大多數方言中都變成*-j呢？如果是這樣，爲什麼到隋唐時期，“牝”的陽聲韻讀法反而變成主流呢？如果採用白-沙的擬音，很難解釋文獻中“牝”字的語音的表现。

此外，顧炎武也提到“卵”的兩個讀音，見於《廣韻》，盧管切：“卵，《説文》曰：凡物無乳者卵生。一。”郎果切：“卵，又力管切。”從讀音上看也是陰陽對轉，而且“盧管切”也是只有一個字。現代一些方言中“卵”同時保留了陰聲和陽聲讀法。武漢“卵”有/^{c}nan/、/^{c}no/兩讀，分别對應中古兩讀。/^{c}nan/在“卵子”這個結構中表示睪丸；/$_{c}$no/表示陰囊，也可以表示用於粗話，表示完蛋，或什麼也沒有[69]。南昌“卵”也有對應中古異讀的陰陽兩讀，/^{c}lon/表示男子生殖器，用來罵人。而/^{c}lo/在“卵雞（子）”這個結構中，表示“男性兒童的生殖器”[70]。南昌和武漢音義配合不一致，但都有一個讀音表示罵人。可見顧炎武迴避禁忌字的看法可從。只不過與“牝”不同，從古到今，文獻中“卵”的陽聲讀法都很常見，而陰聲讀法則很少見。據《辭源》，表示“睪丸”，最早的例子見《靈樞經》[71]，當是從“蛋”義引申而來。可見因迴避禁忌產生的陰聲韻讀法當在此之後。白一沙認爲中古兩讀都是從“卵”的上古音*k.rˤorʔ發展而來，陰聲讀法和陽聲讀法是不同方言的演變，也是不合理的。

四、結　論

白一沙構擬對上古文獻的解釋力有限，對於同等性質的材料，他們往往處理不一致。對涉及“旁轉”的同源詞，有的處理爲同韻部，有的則構擬的詞根主元音不同，按照他們的原則只能不同源。這實際上無端排除了一批證據充分的同源詞。對變等構詞，有的處理爲中綴，有的則處理爲“相互關聯的詞根”。他们認識到僅靠詞根加詞綴的方式解決不了詞彙派生問題，這是一個進步。不過他們實際上並沒有嚴格的標準來區分所謂中綴和“相互關聯的詞根”，兩者的認定缺乏堅實的文獻基礎。尤其是中綴<r>的例證，根據我們上文的分析，沒有一例是可靠的。這樣中綴構擬是不能成立的。相反，我們以王力先生的上古音系統爲基礎[72]，主張上古漢語是通過變調、變聲、變韻或聲、韻、調兩種以上的變化來構造新詞，比白一沙氏的理論更適應漢語材料。這與上古漢語單音

[68] 《新論》，292頁。

[69] 李榮主編《現代漢語方言大詞典》之《武漢方言詞典》，南京：江蘇教育出版社，1995年，245、101頁。原書用調值，據音系介紹改爲調類。

[70] 《現代漢語方言大詞典》之《南昌方言詞典》，158—159、64頁。

[71] 《靈樞經》作爲醫書，成書過程很複雜，但該條反映的“卵”的詞義大概不晚於漢朝。

[72] 容許有一些調整。

節的格局有關，單音節格局下只能通過內部曲折的方式構造新詞。[73]加綴法可能適應西方的一些語言，但用在漢語上古材料上，是削足適履。

另外，白—沙常常違反自己設定的“每個聲符代表一種音節類型”的原則，而缺少充分的論證。他們往往把不能解釋的部分歸結爲歷時的變化或方音變化，但是所謂歷時的而變化或方音變化，作者並未提供足夠的有效證據，所以這樣的處理看起來更像是遁詞。他們有時引入出土文獻的證據，似乎增加了關於歷時變化的說服力。我們通過研究《詩》及《老子》的相關例子，發現他們只從對自己有利的角度片面地分析材料，這兩處證據實際并不成立。出土文獻和對應的傳世文獻如何結合，是一個複雜的問題。出土文獻與傳世文獻字形不同，代表的詞可能是相同的，也可能是不同的。如果詞相同，或語音相近，爲通假關係；或者是異體字；或者其中一個有字形的訛誤。如果確定是不同的詞，那麽至少有三種可能，或者傳世文獻代表的是更原始的面貌，或者出土文獻代表的是更原始的面貌，或者傳世文獻和出土文獻是不同的傳本系統，沒有明顯的時代先後關係。實際情況究竟是哪一種，我們需要充分的證明，而不是簡單地選取對自己學說有利的一種可能，來作爲自己學說的證明。這樣即使說有一點證明作用，也是很有限的。

白—沙對傳統韻部的再分部，有很強的主觀性，文獻根據不足。新的分部，一方面要重視歸字的可靠性，一方面也要重視聲韻配合的系統性。他們在這兩方面都有很大的問題。他們僅僅從其內部體系的類比，就構擬出一個類別*-ir。但這個類別他們唯一的例字“牝”也是不成立的，那麽整個類別也不能成立。即使這個例子不存在材料上的問題，爲一個例子設立一個類別，勢必會在聲韻配合體系中留下大量的空格。可見作者的構擬並沒有考慮聲韻配合的系統性，而只是主觀上追求更多的分佈，這種輕易增加語音類別的做法，是存在很大問題的。如果其他的再分部也存在類似的問題，那麽他們的再分部總體上恐怕就很可疑了。

Critical Remarks on the Reconstruction of Old Chinese by Baxter and Sagart

Zhao Tuanyuan

This article discusses three problems in the book *Old Chinese: a new reconstruction* by Baxter and Sagart: ①The phenomenon of pangzhuan and the word derivation through division change can not be fully reflected by the reconstruction with a consistent pattern;②The predictability that they claim has not been confirmed by the early texts;③The reconstruction of coda *-r is questionable.

---

[73] 關於這個問題的探討，可參考王力《漢語詞彙史》，北京：中華書局，2013年，68頁；郭錫良《漢語史論集》（增補本），北京：商務印書館，2005年，145頁。

曹議金東征甘州回鶻史事證補

——浙敦114號《肅州府主致沙州令公書狀》譯釋

任小波

一、引　　言

2000年，浙江教育出版社影印出版《浙藏敦煌文獻》，刊佈了一批以佛典殘頁爲主的藏文寫本。其中，一件墨書秀麗、鈐有朱印的世俗文書頗爲引人注目，此即浙敦114號（浙博89號）藏文寫本。此本首尾、右部俱殘，粘於浙敦113號（浙博88號）漢文寫本紙背，原係著名學者張宗祥（1882—1965）舊藏。就其款式和内容判斷，此本應是吐蕃統治結束以後的一件河西官府文書的正本殘頁，筆者擬題《肅州府主致沙州令公書狀》。《浙藏敦煌文獻》將其斷爲“五代寫本”，擬題則作“河西歷史故事”①。2004年，武内紹人先生發表《吐蕃統治結束直至西夏時期（9—12世紀）藏文在西域行用的社會語言學影響》，簡要提及此本年代當在10世紀末葉（980年代），推定其係曹氏歸義軍壓服了肅州的反抗以後，肅州漢人向歸義軍節度使“令公”的效忠誓辭（a pledge of allegiance）②，然而並未進行文本譯釋和深入研究。

浙敦114號卷首、卷末騎縫之處，分別鈐有署作“肅□之□”“□州□印”的同一枚陽文朱印。浙敦113號騎縫之處的朱印，亦與浙敦114號從同。經過綴合識別，均係“肅州之印”。官府文書上的騎縫朱印，功能在於接續紙張、防止造僞。浙敦113號寫有“同光年”三字，且與印文疊合，表明作爲公文用紙，此紙應接裱於同光年間。同卷題跋“此爲後唐時人書”，即是出自張宗祥手筆。浙敦114號、113號所存印文吻合，表明此本首尾部分雖被揭取，但仍保有原始裝裱狀態。值得注意的是，PT 1190.v號書狀末尾年款上的“肅州之印”，PT 1189號書狀正面下部末尾、背面騎縫之處的“肅州之印”③，亦與浙敦114號、113號相同。PT 1190.v號漢文書狀，尾題“乾符□年正月貳拾

---

① 毛昭晰等主編《浙藏敦煌文獻》，杭州：浙江教育出版社，2000年，圖版207頁，叙録21頁。

② Tsuguhito Takeuchi, “Sociolinguistic Implications of the Use of Tibetan in East Turkestan from the End of Tibetan Domination through the Tangut Period (9th-12th c.)”, in D. Durkin-Meisterernst, S.-C. Raschmann et al. eds., *Turfan Revisited: The First Century of Research into the Arts and Cultures of the Silk Road*, Berlin: Dietrich Reimer Verlag, 2004, pp. 341-343.

③ 森安孝夫《河西帰義軍節度使の朱印とその編年》，《内陸アジア言語の研究》第15號，2000年，118頁。

壹日”，可知年代當在乾符某年（874—879）；PT 1189.r號藏文書狀，據考年代當在乾德五年（967）前後[4]。準此判斷，張氏以及曹氏歸義軍時期，無論對於肅州的實際控制程度和統屬關係如何，肅州官府襲用着同一枚“肅州之印”。

二、浙敦114號藏文録文及漢文譯文

根據《浙藏敦煌文獻》所收浙敦114號藏文寫本彩色、黑白兩種圖版，兹將此本的拉丁轉寫和筆者的漢文譯文迻録如下：

[---] {1} dgongs te gdan gshegs // kam cur pho nya brdzangs // go[-] [---] {2} gin dang / blon po dang / ru ru’i to dog las stsogs pa / zhu ba g[s]o[l] [---] {3} ’tshal zhing / sdums la mchis / tha tshigs gsar du brnan [---] {4} bde ba la bkod nas / yar gshegs // yar gshegs pa’i gti [---] {5} pa ngan pa ma bor nas // sug cur shod ma yang byas / dbang po la [---] {6} glo ba ’phreng nas // leng kong du ma zhus / gros ma bstun ste [---] {7} g.yabs pa dang // pho nya bzungs nas // leng kong gyi thugs [rg]y[al] [---] {8} yang ma legs te nos // rje leng [kong] yang / btsan mag mang po [---] {9} byon // sgo mnan nas / so sor gum chad du gyur nas // [---] {10} ’bangs kyang / sems grangs te / glo ba chung / ’jigs pa ’[-] [---]

{11} $ // slad kyis // rje leng kong yang / byang cub gyi sems rgya b[skyed] [---] {12} ’bangs kyi tshis su / tha tshigs gsar du gso bar gnang // tha [tshigs] [---] {13} du gsos tshun cad // sug cu dbang po dang / ’bangs byin dang / lung ’bangs kyang // he [-] [---] {14} las stsogs pas / kyang // rje leng kong la / snying log par bsam [---] {15} btsal re // ’bangs chang kyu / rje khud par myi bgyi re // yar te [---] {16} te / lha klu gnyen po // mched sum brgya’ drug cu // byang phyo[gs bdag] {17} po byi sha ra ma ne // sha cu’i kyim an shan shin las stsogs pa [---] {18} gzur gsol cig // gos na smos pa las mna’ [---] {19} bya dgur myi legs / bsam dgur ma grub // lo phyugs ma [b]ye[d] [---] {20} sar mtshon sna dgu lus la phog // langs na / mdung dang ral [gri] [---] {21} shog // yul shor nas // ma bzhi g.yas / bu bzhi g.yon du [---]

釋詞：{3} tha tshigs > tha tshig. {7} bzungs > bzung. {8} btsan mag > btsan dmag. {10} grangs > grang. {13} byin > byings. {15} chang kyu > chang khyu. {17} kyim > khyim. {18} gos > bsgos. {21} shor > gshor.

④ 赤木崇敏《帰義軍時代チベット文手紙文書 P.T.1189 訳註稿》，荒川正晴編《東トルキスタン出土〈胡漢文書〉の総合調査》，大阪：平成15—17年度科学研究費補助金研究成果報告書，2006年，83—84頁。

……思慮……並且前往。遣使甘州，祈請……[狄]銀及其臣僚、茹茹都督等，達成和斷，新立咒誓，入於安樂。此後，前往上部。據前往上部者所説，未棄惡劣……其於肅州，亦未通報。對於府主，憂慮……故而，未向令公呈請。商議不諧，調集……扣留使者。於是，令公之憤，亦受不佳……人主令公，遣去衆多勁旅，制服門戍，各各處死。[官]民痛心失望，……苦難。

因此，人主令公，發菩提心，爲求利益百姓，新增咒誓。新增咒誓有云：此後，肅州府主以及一切百姓，龍家、……等，對於人主令公，決不心生邪念。百姓民衆，決不自立爲王。沙州家安善振等，趨前……祈請神龍眷屬、三百六十兄弟、北方之主毗沙門證盟，規誡曉諭。[若違]誓辭，諸事不佳，衆願難遂，農牧無功。所居之處，各色兵器，擊刺其身。一經起身，……戟劍。劃定轄境之後，母族在右，子嗣在左，……

三、曹議金東征甘州回鶻以及遣使後唐

浙敦114號所記史事，當與曹議金（914—935年在位）任歸義軍節度使期間東征甘州回鶻之役有關。根據相關敦煌文書，歸義軍與甘州回鶻之間，相隔不過一年兩次交兵。李軍先生考證，戰事分作甘州（張掖）之戰、肅州（酒泉）之戰兩次戰役⑤。第一次是由於甘州回鶻阻塞歸義軍通貢中原之路，歸義軍主動征討，雙方戰於甘州。根據P 3270號《兒郎偉》，甘州回鶻“數年閉塞東路”，“今遇明王利化，再開河隴道衢。太保神威發憤，遂便點緝兵衣。略點精兵十萬，各各盡擐鐵衣”。此處“明王利化”，係指同光二年（924）五月後唐莊宗授予曹議金歸義軍節度使之事。第二次是由於甘州回鶻兵侵肅州龍家，侵逼歸義軍東境，歸義軍出兵自衛，雙方戰於玉門、肅州。然而，對於戰事的進程和細節，相關論著之中仍有不少歧義。

P 4011號《兒郎偉》頗能貫通戰事全貌，參照原卷圖版以及諸家録文，玆將此本全文釐定如下：

驅儺之法，送故迎新。且要掃除舊事，建立芳春。便獲青陽之節，八方啓（稽）顙來臻。

自從太保利化，千門喜賀殷勤。甘州數年作賊，直擬欺負侵凌。去載阿郎發憤，點集兵鉀（甲）軍人。親領精兵十萬，圍繞張掖狼煙。未及張弓拔劍，他自放火燒然（燃）。一齊披髪歸伏，獻納金銀城川。遂便安邦定國，永世欽伏於前。

不經一歲未盡，他急逆亂無邊。准擬再覓寸境，便共龍家相煎。又動太保心竟（境），跛（叵）耐欺負仁賢。緝練精兵十萬，如同鐵石心肝。黨（當）便充（衝）山進路，活捉獫狁狼煙。未至酒泉小郡，他自魂膽不殘。便獻飛龍

⑤ 李軍《晚唐五代肅州相關事實考述》，《敦煌學輯刊》2005年第3期，96—97頁。

白馬，兼及綾錦數般。王子再拐無數，散髮納境相傳。

因兹太保息怒，善神護我川原。河西一道清泰，天子尉（慰）曲西邊。六蕃總來歸首，一似舜日堯年。大都渴仰三寶，惡賊不打歸降。萬性（姓）齊唱快活，家家富樂安眠。比至三月初首，天使只（旨）降宣傳。便拜三臺使相，世代共賊無緣。萬性（姓）感賀太保，直得千年萬年。

榮新江先生指出，歸義軍趁甘州回鶻内亂、汗位交替之際發動戰爭，戰事當發生於同光二年（甲申，924）末、同光三年（乙酉，925）初，且在同光三年六月以前⑥。同光二年十一月，甘州回鶻可汗仁美之弟狄銀居功奪權、嗣立爲汗，給予曹議金東征可趁之機。尤其根據S 5139.v號《涼州節院使押衙劉少晏狀》所謂“回鶻三五年來自亂”，“曹太保阿郎政直（整治），開以河西老道”，以及尾署“乙酉年六月□日”，戰事應在同光三年六月以前可成定讞。

同光二年末，或即該年十一月狄銀繼任甘州回鶻可汗以後⑦，曹議金親征甘州。同光三年初，亦即該年六月以前，歸義軍與甘州回鶻鏖戰於玉門，進而挺進肅州。根據P 2058.v號《兒郎偉》，甘州回鶻“三五年間作賊，令公親自權兵”，亦與浙敦114號吻合。曹議金東征之役勝利前後，甘州回鶻可汗狄銀亡故，阿咄欲嗣立。根據《新五代史·回鶻傳》，“阿咄欲，不知其爲狄銀親疏，亦不知其立卒”⑧。然據P 4011號“王子再拐無數，散髮納境相傳”，這位“王子”或指狄銀之子阿咄欲。此後，曹議金又將其與甘州回鶻公主李氏所生之女嫁予阿咄欲，改變了此前“可汗是父，天子是子”的甘、沙關係格局。歸義軍兩度擊敗甘州回鶻，打通經由張掖緑洲入貢中原的河西通道，然而終究未能長期控制甘、肅二州。

基於敦煌文書中的紀年史料，榮新江先生揭出曹議金同光二年前後稱司空，同光三年始稱太保，天成三年（928）至長興二年（931）稱令公，長興二年始稱大王⑨。P 4011號記述曹議金東征之役，通篇將其稱作太保，適與如上論斷吻合。鋼和泰（A. von Staël-Holstein）藏卷《于闐使臣上沙州太保書狀》（出自敦煌，925—927），則以藏文The po或The bo對譯曹議金的漢文銜稱“太保”⑩。長興二年正月，後唐以曹議金兼中書令。然於此前，曹議金已在境内冒稱令公、自封使相。根據P 2675.bis.v號《曹議金狀》，曹議金稱“太保兼令公”。此件文書，或即後唐以曹議金兼中書令以後，曹議金上呈某位“相公”的答謝書狀底稿。P 4011號通篇稱曹議金爲太保，然其結尾又稱“比至三月初首，天使只（旨）降宣傳”，“便拜三臺使相”，或係此後傳抄添綴之辭。浙敦114號五次出現“令公”（Leng kong）銜稱，顯然是指曹議金。尤其第7—8行所謂

⑥ 榮新江《歸義軍征甘州回鶻史事表微》，《敦煌研究》1991年第2期，8—10頁；《歸義軍史研究：唐宋時代敦煌歷史考索》，上海：上海古籍出版社，2015年，312—313、324—325頁。

⑦ 馮培紅《敦煌的歸義軍時代》，蘭州：甘肅教育出版社，2010年，327頁。

⑧ 《新五代史》卷七四《四夷附録·回鶻傳》，北京：中華書局，1974年，916頁。

⑨ 榮新江《歸義軍史研究：唐宋時代敦煌歷史考索》，103、107頁。

⑩ G. Uray, “L’Emploi du Tibétain dans les Chancelleries des États du Kan-sou et de Khotan Postérieurs à la Domination Tibétaine”, *Journal Asiatique*, Vol. 269, Nos. 1-2, 1981, pp. 81-82.

“令公之憤”（leng kong gyi thugs [rg]y[al]），“衆多勁旅”（btsan mag mang po）等句，正與P 4011號所谓“去載阿郎發憤”，“親領精兵十萬”，以及“又動太保心竟（境）”，“緝練精兵十萬”相符，均指曹議金東征之役。準此研判，浙敦114號約書寫於天成三年至長興二年之間。

同光年間，歸義軍先後兩次遣使後唐：第一次於同光二年四月抵達洛陽，五月獲授歸義軍節度使；第二次於同光四年（926）正月、二月分作兩批抵達洛陽。此後天成年間，歸義軍是否遣使於史無徵。榮新江先生推斷，P 4011號應係天成二年（927）末曹議金太保、令公銜稱並用，或其將從太保改稱令公時的産物[11]。曹議金稱令公的有紀年的最早書證，見於P 2814號《都頭知懸泉鎮遏使安進通狀》，題作天成三年二月。曹議金冒稱令公以後，或曾還有遣使之舉。浙敦113號上的“州般”二字，當即“沙州入朝般次”之意。同卷内題九字：

中書門下平章事崔□。

根據《新五代史·唐明宗本紀》，天成二年正月“太常卿崔協爲中書侍郎、同中書門下平章事”，卒於四年（929）二月[12]。又據洛陽所出《崔協墓誌》，天成二年正月“制授中書侍郎、平章事”，三年三月“又進門下侍郎、平章事”，卒於四年二月[13]。所謂“崔□”，極有可能便是崔協。天成三年五月，後唐爲“沙州節度使曹義（議）金加爵邑”[14]。如上題字寫於沙州，時間當在天成三年前後，似與後唐加賜“爵邑”相關。

浙敦113號寫本，内有思婦詞、宮詞、《定西番》、願文、王播《題木蘭院二首之一》、雜寫等項[15]。《定西番》所謂“夜久更蘭（闌）欲暮深，聖澤遠聞天下静”，應與歸義軍政治、軍事相關。願文則作：

次（此）則我皇帝之德業也。沙州，最陲西苗裔也。四鄰，並是戎狄也。……次則伏惟我當座都僧統和尚：才明（名）絶代，動必應機。五百挺生，千賢間生。故富通……

雖爲殘抄，然亦可知其係天成三年以後沙州富通和尚所撰。如上“都僧統和尚”，聯繫浙敦114號“令公”以及浙敦113號“崔協”的年代背景，或指河西都僧統陰海晏（926—933年在位），其時正值曹議金任歸義軍節度使的後半期。

---

⑪ 榮新江《歸義軍征甘州回鶻史事表微》，7頁；《歸義軍史研究：唐宋時代敦煌歷史考索》，322頁。

⑫ 《新五代史》卷六《唐明宗本紀》，57、60頁。

⑬ 仇鹿鳴《新見五代崔協夫婦墓誌小考》，杜文玉主編《唐史論叢》第14輯，西安：陝西師範大學出版社，2012年，234頁。

⑭ 《舊五代史》卷三九《唐書·明宗紀》，北京：中華書局，1976年，538頁。

⑮ 黄征、張崇依《浙藏敦煌文獻校録整理》下册，上海：上海古籍出版社，2012年，485—487頁；並參上册《前言》，4頁。

四、多民族、多语言環境下的政治生態

浙敦114號涉及曹議金東征甘州回鶻之役，以及此後肅州官民向曹議金所立的誓辭。兹將相關信息彙釋如下：①第1—2行[---] gin，應指甘州回鶻可汗“狄銀”。此詞源自突厥文Tägin，原指突厥可汗子弟，漢文史籍通常記作“特勤”[16]。這一稱謂，後爲回鶻等族襲用。②第2行Ru ru'i to dog，可以譯作“茹茹都督”。其中Ru ru即是柔然，漢文史籍通常記作“茹茹”“蠕蠕”。至於To dog，當係漢文“都督”之譯音。根據行文，此詞表明茹茹依屬於甘州回鶻。③第6、7、8、11、14行Leng kong，當係漢文“令公”之譯音，均指歸義軍節度使曹議金。④第13行Sug cu dbang po，譯言“肅州府主”。此處dbang po，正是唐宋之際河西漢文官府文書之中“府主”之對稱[17]。⑤第13行Lung 'bangs，譯言“龍家”。根據行文，此詞表明龍家活躍於肅州一帶。⑥第17行Sha cu'i kyim An shan shin，實爲沙州遣往肅州的主盟官員。其中Sha cu'i kyim（< Sha cu'i khyim），譯言“沙州家”。至於An Shan shin，可以譯作“安善振”。根據敦煌漢藏寫本中的“五姓”資料，An正是漢文“安”姓之對音[18]，此人或許具有粟特背景。

浙敦114號第4行yar（上部），當即PT 1189.r號《肅州府主致河西節度書狀》（967）第12—13行所謂yar sha cab phyogs（上部Sha cab方向）。此處Sha cab（< Sha chab，chab係chu之敬語），當即漢文“沙河”之對稱。或因同卷每以Sha cu對譯“沙州”，古藏文中cu ~ chu又常通用，故而選用Sha cab以示區分。根據《大慈恩寺三藏法師傳》，玄奘經行“莫賀延磧，長八百餘里，古曰沙河”[19]。莫賀延磧爲一沙漠地帶，位於歸義軍轄境迤西迤北。根據P 2970號《陰善雄邈真讚》（931年以後），陰善雄曾以歸義軍常樂縣令身份參與東征之役，“達怛犯塞，拔拒交鋒。統領軍兵，臨機變策”，表明甘州回鶻亦曾糾合北境的達怛等部爲其外援。故而“上部”當指玉門、肅州迤北，似爲回鶻所引達怛或茹茹部族的軍帳所在。

浙敦114號中的Lung 'bangs，係指活躍於歸義軍東境的肅州龍家。唐宋之際河西龍家部族，出自西晉以來焉耆龍氏王國。PT 1287號《吐蕃贊普傳記》第381行Lung gi rgyal po，即是出征河隴的吐蕃軍將對於“龍氏國王”的稱謂。PT 1089號《吐蕃職官表狀》（821）第40行涼州軍鎮（mKhar tsan khrom）下的Lung dor，曾有學者推論Lung與吐蕃轄下的龍氏部族有關，然而對於Dor的釋讀並未形成令人信服的結論。840年以

---

⑯ 戴密微（P. Demiéville）《吐蕃僧諍記》（*Le Concile de Lhasa*），耿昇譯，拉薩：西藏人民出版社，2001年，271—272頁。

⑰ G. Uray, “The Title dBaṅ-po in Early Tibetan Records”, in P. Daffinà ed., *Indo-Sino-Tibetan: Studi in Onore di Luciano Petech,* Rome: Bardi Editore, 1990, pp. 419-433.

⑱ 高田時雄《五姓を説く敦煌資料》，《国立民族学博物館研究報告》別冊14號“漢族と隣接諸族”，1991年，261頁。

⑲ 慧立、彦悰《大慈恩寺三藏法師傳》卷一，《大正新修大藏經》第50卷，2053號，224.b.5-6行。

後回鶻西遷，龐特勤率部佔據焉耆，或許正是值此背景，龍氏王族率部流落河西[20]。龍家之名突現於9世紀下半葉的敦煌漢文、胡語文書，適與上述歷史過程相符。PT 1263號《藏漢詞彙》第8行，即以Lung rje對譯龍家首領“龍王”。根據S 367號《沙州伊州地志》（885），“龍部落本焉耆人，今甘、肅、伊州各有首領，其人輕鋭，健鬥戰”，亦與浙敦114號所述甘州（Kam cu）、肅州（Sug cu）地望吻合。

大中三年（849），歸義軍收復吐蕃佔領下的肅州。中和四年（884），甘州龍家等部迫於回鶻的軍事壓力，併入歸義軍轄下的肅州。根據S 389號《肅州防戍都狀》（884），“甘州共回鶻和斷”，“龍家共回鶻和定”。此係歸義軍節度使張淮深（867—890年在位）時期，肅州防戍都基於肅州周邊形勢所上的書狀。此後，歸義軍由於防戍力量有限，逐漸喪失了對肅州的控制，漢人、龍家等部建立肅州政權。張氏後期以及曹氏時期，歸義軍僅保有肅州西境。曹氏後期，肅州日益投附於甘州回鶻，最終成爲甘州回鶻屬郡。根據《新五代史·回鶻傳》，甘州回鶻“又有別族號龍家”[21]，可謂反映了如上歷史過程的結果。張廣達先生指出，唐宋之際河西“各部首領和各地首腦，需要時時通過‘和定’（又稱‘和斷’）來調整彼此的利害關係和結束衝突”[22]。浙敦114號第3行sdums，譯言“調解”“議和”，正可對稱“和斷”等詞。

東征之役勝利以後，曹議金除了遣使後唐、獲取封賜之外，另一舉措便是鞏固肅州防戍、確保東境安定。浙敦114號所記肅州官民向曹議金宣誓效忠，雙方達成和斷，即爲上述舉措的重要內容。肅州對於甘、沙交涉的特殊地位，亦於此役期间再次得以凸顯。暫時掌控肅州局勢以後，曹議金進而謀求與甘州回鶻關係的长久穩定。根據P 2992.v號長興二年《曹議金致甘州順化可汗書狀》：

> 自去年兄大王當便親到甘州，所有社稷久遠之事，共弟天子面對商儀（議）。平穩已訖，兄大王當便發遣一伴般次入京。

長興元年（930）夏秋曹議金親赴甘州，會晤甘州回鶻可汗仁裕（又作“仁喻”）[23]，商議“所有社稷久遠之事”，此後雙方遣使後唐。次年，後唐“以沙州節度使曹義（議）金兼中書令”[24]。準此可知，此时沙、甘關係已是兄弟之國，雙方希望同保河西安定、貢道暢通。歸義軍與肅州之間的盟誓，應在曹議金東行以前。

浙敦114號第13行Byi sha ra ma ne（< Vaiśramaṇa），當指北方天王“毗沙門”（rNam thos sras）。對於此詞，PT 960號《于闐教法史》第16、31行又作Be sha ra ma

---

⑳ 榮新江《龍家考》，陳高華、余太山主編《中亞學刊》第4輯，北京：北京大學出版社，1995年，148—150、155—156頁。

㉑ 《新五代史》卷七四《四夷附録·回鶻傳》，916頁。

㉒ 張廣達《唐末五代宋初西北地區的般次和使次》，《張廣達文集：文書、典籍與西域史地》，桂林：廣西師範大學出版社，2008年，188—190頁。

㉓ 哈密頓（J. R. Hamilton）《五代回鶻史料》（*Les Ouïghours à l'Épouque des Cinq Dynasties d'Après les Documents Chinois*），耿昇、穆根來譯，烏魯木齊：新疆人民出版社，1982年，122頁，注釋1—2；榮新江《歸義軍史研究：唐宋時代敦煌歷史考索》，328—329頁。

㉔ 《舊五代史》卷四二《唐書·明宗紀》，575頁。

ne、Bɨ sha ra ma nɨ。毗沙門天王即多聞天王，係佛教所謂護持世間的四大天王之一，因居北方故稱“北方之主”（Byang phyogs bdag po）。約於6世紀初葉，于闐多聞天王信仰傳入敦煌，受到河西官民的敬奉。中唐以後及至歸義軍時期，多聞天王信仰在敦煌臻於鼎盛。曹氏歸義軍時期，多聞天王信仰與轉輪聖王（Cakravartirāja）觀念相表裏，形成鮮明的政治文化意涵。根據PT 1189.r號，曹元忠（944—974年在位）任歸義軍節度使時期，由於西州回鶻離亂、逃人越境東奔，河西地區劫盜頻發，達怛（Da tar）、仲雲（Ju ngul）、回鶻（Hor，甘州回鶻右翼）等部，於肅州大雲寺（De'i yun zi）內“約以多聞天王證盟”（gnam mtho mtha' tshigs bgos, > rnam thos tha tshig bsgos）[25]。PT 1189.r號第12行mtha' tshigs，亦即浙敦114號第3、12行tha tshigs（咒誓）之别體。正是基於這種護國祐方的政治文化願望，河西官民不僅廣爲崇奉多聞天王，甚至以其作爲重大盟誓的知鑒。P 4011號所謂“善神護我川原”，此處“善神”（*lha dge ba）或即多聞天王。

五、結　　語

浙敦114號所記史事，兹可結合上文所論概述如下：歸義軍節度使曹議金遣使甘州，希望甘州回鶻可汗狄銀君臣、茹茹都督達成和斷，不再侵逼歸義軍東境。此後，肅州府主派員前往上部（甘州回鶻所引之達怛或茹茹軍帳），獲知甘州回鶻不願罷兵。對於如上軍情，甘州回鶻並未事先告知肅州，故而肅州府主未能及時通報沙州。此時，肅州似乎已被甘州回鶻佔領。由於雙方商議不諧，甘州回鶻扣留沙州使者。於是，曹議金憤而出兵玉門、肅州，討擊甘州回鶻。經過激烈戰鬥，甘州回鶻潰敗，肅州亦遭浩劫。東征之役勝利以後，曹議金爲保歸義軍東境安定，遂與肅州府主實現諒解。肅州官民、龍家部族依照先例設立咒誓，皆向曹議金承諾永遠效忠、決不叛離。沙州官員安善振受命前去主盟，並以護國祐方之神北方多聞天王證盟。根據P 4011號，甘州回鶻“准擬再覓寸境，便共龍家相煎”，恰與這一背景和史事吻合。

綜合上文考證，浙敦114號的書寫年代，當在天成三年左右曹議金冒稱令公以後，長興元年夏秋曹議金親赴甘州以前，亦即928—930年之間。武内紹人先生將其斷爲980年代，顯然失之過晚。肅州官民向曹議金宣誓效忠，並非所謂肅州的某次反抗被歸義軍壓服的結果，而是居於甘、沙兩强夾縫下的肅州審度時勢所作出的選擇。參與盟誓的肅州官民，亦非僅是漢人，還有龍家等部。根據浙敦114號，曹議金東征之役的目標，不僅在於打通與涼、靈二州以及中原的政治聯繫，更是在於有效安撫或統合臨邊各部，持續享有絲路上的中轉貿易權益。歸義軍與周邊的回鶻、達怛、茹茹、龍家等部族或政權的交往，造就了唐宋之際河西一帶交融共生的多民族、多語言環境。如若這種交往涉及

---

[25] 任小波《唐宋之際河西地區的部族關係與護國信仰——敦煌PT 1189.r號〈肅州府主致河西節度書狀〉譯釋》，沈衛榮主編《西域歷史語言研究集刊》第7輯，北京：科學出版社，2014年，111—113頁。

三個以上操不同語言的部族，藏語作爲官方通用語言的功能便會凸顯出來。此即吐蕃統治結束以後，藏語得以長期而持續地行用於河西地區的社會語言學機制。這一機制生成的基石，正是盛極一時的吐蕃帝國對於河西乃至西域諸族的軍事征服、政治統合和文化影響。

New Evidence on the History of Cao Yijin's Conquest of Ganzhou Uighurs:A Study on Tibetan Manuscript Zhejiang 114 from Dunhuang, the *Official Letter from Suzhou Fuzhu to Shazhou Linggong*

Ren Xiaobo

This article provides an interpretation of Tibetan manuscript Zhejiang 114 from Dunhung, the *Official Letter from Suzhou Fuzhu* 肅州府主 *to Shazhou Linggong* 沙州令公 written in 928-930 AD. The historical events mentioned in this manuscript must be in the period of Cao Yijin 曹議金 (rg. 914-935 AD), the Linggong (Tib.: Leng kong) of Return-to-allegiance Army 歸義軍. Based on this manuscript and related documents, we have been able to discover some new evidence on the history of Cao Yijin's conquest of Ganzhou Uighurs (Tib.: Hor) 甘州回鶻 in 924-925 AD. According to this manuscript, a pledge of allegiance to Cao Yijin was taken by the Fuzhu (Tib.: dBang po), Chinese inhabitants and Long tribal group (Tib.: Lung 'bangs) 龍家 of Suzhou after the conquest, and meanwhile an oath-taking ceremony was held in front of the image of Vaiśramaṇa (Tib.: rNam thos sras) 毗沙門, who was regarded as a great divine power to preserve peace in the Hexi Corridor region of northwestern China.

Жаруудын үүсэл гарлын тухай

Боржигдай Оюунбилэг

Японы эрдэмтэн Х.Оката Монголын зургаан түмний үүсэл гарлын тухай өгүүлэхдээ Халх түмнийг Юань улсын үеийн Жалайр тэргүүтэй зүүн гарын таван аймгаас бүрэлдсэн гэж үзсэн тул Т.Морикава нар хүлээн зөвшөөрч, улмаар хүн бүр тэгж үздэг болжээ. Халхын бүрэлдэхүүн болсон Жаруудыг таван аймгаас гаралтай гэж үздэг. Халх түмний үүсэл зүүн таван аймагтай нягт холбоотой боловч, түүний бүх отог тэндээс гаралтай хэмээн үзэж болохгүй. Гэвч, би мөн урьд энэ үзлийн нөлөөнд автсан хүмүүсийг даган өгүүлсэн зүйл бий. Иймээс зохиогч тус өгүүлэлдээ Жарууд аймгийн үүсэл гарлын учрыг нэлээд нарийн судалж үзэв. Мэргэд тольдмуй.

Нэг

Жарууд гэдэг нэр Монгол сурвалжид 1662 онд зохиогдсон Саган Сэцэний《Эрдэнийн товч》-ийн Даян хааны үйл хэргийг тэмдэглэсэн хэсэгт анх удаа “Жарууд” гэсэн нэрээр тэмдэглэгдсэн юм. Түүнд өгүүлсэн нь: Даян хаан хөвгүүдээсээ Улсбайхыг Ордос, Түмэд, Юншээбү баруун гурван түмний төрийг засуулахаар илгээтэл, баруун гурван түмний Уйгуудын Ибрай тайш, Ордосын Лэгүш ахлах нар урваж, Улсбайхыг хороожээ. Даян хаан тэр урвалгааныг дарахаар Цахар, Халх, Урианхан зэрэг зүүн гурван түмэн ба Хорчин түмний цэргийг дайчилж баруун гурванд цэрэг мордуулж, Далан тэргүүнд ихэд байлдав. Байлдаан эхлэх үед Даян хаан зарлиг болж өгүүлсэн нь: “Ордос бол эзний найман цагаан гэрийг хадгалсан их заяат улс билээ. Түүн лүгээ Урианхан мөн эзний алтан хөмрөгийг сахисан бас их заяат улс. Хоорчин (Хорчин) Абагтай тусалтугай.” Арван хоёр түмэнтэй арван хоёр отог Халх, Түн их Юншээбүтэй найман отог Цахар тус тус байлд хэмээв. Тэгэхэд, Хорчины Борхай баатар тайж, Урианхайн баатар Баяхай, “таван отог Халхын Баасан тавнан” гэх зэрэг баатрууд эрэлхэглэн дайрчээ[1]. Энэ байлдаанд Даян хааны цэрэг баруун түмнийг дараад,

---

[1] Саган Сэцэн:《Хаадын Үндэсний Эрдэнийн Товч》, Их Хүрээний гар бичмэл, 66г.

зургаан түмнийг нэг жолоонд оруулж авчээ. Далан тэргүүний байлдаан хааны үйлст шийдвэрлэх үйлдэл гаргасан болохоор, тэр дайны ялалтын дараа, Даян хаан түүнд хүчээ өгсөн гавьяат сайд нараа өв тэгш шагнасан аж. Тэдний дотроос анхааруулттай нь “Жаруудын Баасан дархан тавнанд Мандухай хатны ганц охин Төрөлт гүнжийг өгчээ”② гэсэн явдал юм. Энд манай гол сэдэв болсон Жарууд маань “Жаругууд” бичлэгтэй анх удаа гарч буй юм.

Далан тэргүүний байлдааны тухай анх тэмдэглэсэн Монгол сурвалж бичиг бол гол нь XVII зууны эхээр зохиогдсон, зохиогч нь тодорхойгүй 《Хаадын үндэсний хураангуй Алтан товч》（《бага Алтан товч》）юм. Цахарын Борбугын Баян-Өрмэгэр гэх хүн Даян хааны тугийг нууж, оронд нь Урианхайн тугийг босготол, баруун түмний цэргүүд хууртаж, Урианхайн зүг дайрчээ. Тэр дайсныг Хорчины Ортухай ван ба түүний хөвгүүн нь Борхай, Урианхайн Баяхай баатар, Хорчины тавны сайн Чэгч баатар, “таван отог Халхын ноёд ургийн Баасан тавнан тавуулаа хошуу удирдан” тосч байлджээ. Ялсны дараа, Даян хаан “Баасан тавнанд Сайн Мандухай хатнаас төрсөн ганц охиноо өгөв”③. 1677 онд Халхын Шамба тайжийн бичсэн 《Асрагч нэртийн түүх》-д: “Таван отог халхын Баасан”, “Баасанд Мандухай хатнаас төрсөн ганц охиноо өгөв”④ гэдэг. Жарууд Гүүш Дармаагийн 1739 онд бичсэн 《Алтан хүрдэн мянган хэгээст》-д тэмдэглэсэн Далан тэргүүний байлдааны өмнөх хойтох байдлын тэмдэглэл өмнөх бичгүүдээс их ялгаагүй. Харин Баасан тавнанг дурдахдаа “Урианхайн Баасан тавнанд Сайн Мандухай хатнаас төрсөн Гэгээн гүнжийг өгөв” гэсэн ба бас нэг газар “Мандухай сэцэн хатны ганц охин Гэгээн гүнжийг Урианхайн Жим (Зэлмийн эндүү бичлэг)-ийн үр Баасан баатарт өгөөд тавнан болгожээ”⑤ хэмээсэн байна. Хянаваас, Жарууд гүүшийн сүүлийн үг нь 1725 онд зохиогдсон Үзэмчин тайж Гомбожавын “Гангийн урсгал”-аас эх үүсвэртэй ажээ. Гомбожав тэмдэглэсэн нь “Сайн Даян хааны ганц усан (охины эндүү хуулбар) хан (гэгээний буруу бичлэг) гүнжийг Урианхан Зэлмэ (уул зүүлт: Чингис хааны есөн өрлөгийн нэгэн буй)-ийн үрд өгөөд тавнан

② Мөн тэнд, 66r.

③ Quan Rong тулган харьцуулж тайлбарласан: 《Богд Чингис хаан судар》, Үндэстэний хэвлэлийн хороо, 2013 он, гэрэл зураг эх, 513-514-р тал. Zhu Feng, Jia Jing Yan: 《Монголын хураангуй Алтан Товч》 *ийн хятад орчуулга,* ӨМАХХ, 1985 он(дагалдуулал монгол эх),pp:197-198хуудас. Лувсанданзангийн 《Алтан товч》-ын тэмдэглэл 《бага Алтан товч》-той ихээхэн адил (《Эртний хаадын үндэслэсэн төр ёсны зохиолыг товчлон хураасан Алтан товч хэмээх оршив》, Улаабаатар, 1990 он, 165b, 166b).

④ Оюунбилэг: 《Асрагч нэртийн түүхийн судалгаа》, Төвийн Үндэсний Их Сургуулийн хэвлэлийн хороо, 2009 он,(монгол гэрэл зураг эх), 39b-40a, 286-287-р тал.

⑤ Дармаа зохиож, Чойжи харгуулж тайлбарласан: 《Алтан хүрдэн мянган хигээст》, ӨМАХХ, 1987 он, 128-р тал.

болгосноос үржсэн нь, Харчины ноёд тавнан овогт мөн хэмээн зарим олонх дор өгүүлжээ”⑥ гэжээ. Рашпунцагийн Болор эрх-д мөн “Гэгээн гүнжийг Урианхайн Басууд тавнан дор өгүүлэв”⑦ гэжээ.

Монгол бичигт гарсан Баасан (Багасууд) тавнангийн тухай мэдээнүүдийг хураангуйлбал дараах мэт дүгнэлтэд хүрнэ.

“Баасан бол Урианхайн баатар.

Баасан бол Урианхан Зэлмийн үр.

Баасан бол Жарууд отгийн хүн.

Баасан бол таван отог Халхын ноёд ургийн хүн.”

Баасан бол Даян хаан, Мандухай сэцэн хатны дундаас төрсөн ганц охин Төрөлт Гэгээн гүнжийг авсан тавнан. Эдгээр мэдээг нарийн шинжлэн үзвэл, Урианхан=Жарууд=Таван отог Халх гэсэн дүн гарна. Энэ ямар учиртай вэ?

Энэхүү асуудлыг авч ярилцахаас өмнө, урьдаар “уламжлал сурвалжис”-д хамаарагдах сурвалж бичгүүдийн хэрэг явдлыг тэмдэглэх нэгэн онцлогийг цухас дурдах хэрэгтэй. Тэр нь юу вэ гэвэл, хэрэг явдлыг тэмдэглэхдээ сүүлчийн зохиогчид түүхэн хэргийн сүүлчийн үр дүнг үндэслэж, эсвэл бүр түүхэн бичгээ бичсэн тухайн цагийн байдал ба ойлголтоор эрт хуучин цагт болж өнгөрсөн түүхэн үйл явдлыг нэхэн тэмдэглэх нь их. Жишээлбэл, Далан тэргүүний дайны үеийн Баасанг “Баасан тавнан” гэж тэмдэглэсэн нь энэ хүн дайны дараа тавнан болсноос болжээ. Уг нь тэр үеийн Баасанг “Баасан баатар” гэж нэрлэх ёстой. Үүнтэй адилаар, Баасанг “Таван отог халх”-ын хүн гэсэн нь мөн хожмын түүхэнд суурилж бичсэн хэрэг. Учир нь Жарууд (Жаругууд), Баарин, Үжээд, Баяд, Хонгирад таван отог буй болж “Таван отог халх” нэр зүүсэн нь Далан тэргүүний дайнаас наад зах нь хагас зуун жилийн дараах явдал юм. Эдгээр нь бүр Саган сэцэн, Жарууд гүүш зэрэг түүхчид өөрийн цаг үеийн түүхэн нөхцөлд үндэслэж бичсэний үр дүн юм. Тэгэхээр, “Урианхан=Таван отог халх” гэдэг дүгнэлт буруу юм. Үүнийг харин “Урианхан=Таван отог халхын Жарууд” гэж үзвэл зөв болно. Баасан тавнанг “Урианхайн Зэлмийн үр” гэсэн ба “Таван отог халхын ноёд ургийн хүн“ гэсэн нь үүний давхар гэрч. “Таван отог халхын ноёд ургийн хүн” бол хэрэг дээрээ “(Таван отог халхын доторх) Жаруудын ноёд ургийн хүн” гэсэн үг. Энэ нь мөн Жарууд нь Алтан урагтны өмч иргэн болохоос өмнө Баасан тавнангийн эзэмшил иргэд байсан гэсэн хэрэг юм. Үүнийг цаашид хянан үзвэл, Урианхайн Зэлмийн үрс ба Жарууд (Жаругууд)-ын ноёд нь нэг л ургийн угсаа, өөрөөр хэлбэл Жарууд бол Урианхан отог аж.

⑥ Гомбожав зохиож, Чойжи харгуулж тайлбарласан: 《Гангийн Урсгал》, ӨМАХХ, 1980 он, 132-р тал.

⑦ Рашпунцаг зохиож, Хөх-Өндөр харгуулж тулгасан: 《Болор эрх》, ӨМАХХ, 1985 он, 848-р тал.

Хоёр

Сая өгүүлсэн зүйлийг сурвалж бичгийн мэдээнд үндэслэж бичсэн юм. Бид сурвалжийг ярихдаа “үлдмэл” ба “уламжлал” гэж хуваадаг. Урьд өгүүлсэн Монголын он дараалсан түүхэн бичгүүд бол “уламжлалт сурвалж”-д тооцогдоно. Зохиогчид нь хүмүүст түүхэн мэдлэгийг уламжлахын төлөө урьдын хүмүүсийн бичиг баримт, аман уламжлал ба өөрийн үзэж сонссон зүйлсдээ үндэслэж, түүхэн хэргийг тоочин өгүүлжээ. Түүний дотор эндүү ташаа зүйлс олон байлгүй яахав. Түүхчид түүнийг нарийн нягтлахгүйгээр гарын аяар авч хэрэглэж болохгүй. Гэвч алсдаа, түүхийг тэмдэглэн үлдээх гэсэн тусгай зорилгогогүй, харин өөр зорилготой бий болж, санаандгүй түүхэн баримт болдог зүйлийг “үлдмэл сурвалж” гэнэ. Үлдмэл сурвалжид Цогцот үлдмэл⑧, бичгийн үлдмэл⑨, хийсвэр үлдмэл гэж гурван төрөл зүйл байдаг. Түүний дотор хийсвэр үлдмэл гэдэг нь зан заншил, ёс суртахуун, нэр овог зэрэг гарт баригдахгүй, нүдэнд үзэгдэхгүй юмс боловч эртний мэдээ зангийг зорилгогүйгээр, найдвартай уламжилж ирсэн “материалууд”-ыг заана. Жарууд бол Урианхан аймгаас үүсэлтэй гэдгийг гэрчлэх чухал “хийсвэр үлдмэл” олдож байна. Тэр юу гэвэл, Жаруудын язгуур эртнээс уламжилж ирсэн бөөгийн шашны “цахилгаан тэнгэрийн тахилга” юм. Энэхүү тахилгын тухай бөөгийн судлалд мэргэшсэн Жарууд эрдэмтэн Нямаа ийнхүү мэдээлсэн байна: Цахилгаан тэнгэрийн тахилгыг бөөгийн доторх “удмын бөө” хийж гүйцэтгэдэг. Удмын бөө гэдэг нь бөөгийн сахиус нэгэн овгийн дотор үе улиран оршин суудгийг хэлнэ. Удмын бөөгийн дотор үе алгасахгүй эцэг хөвгүүн залгаж суусан нь улам их хүндтэй, иймэрхүү бөө нь бөөгийн бүх ажиллагааг гүйцэтгэхээс гадна “ихэндээ тэнгэр тахих ажлыг хийдэг. Тэнгэрийг буруушаан донгодох онц эрхтэй. Цахилгаан тэнгэрийг тэд тахидаг. Цахилгаан тэнгэрийн тахилга ихэнхдээ зуны зургаа, долоон сарын хур бороо их, аянга догшин үед тохиолддог. Хэзээ хаана тэнгэр буусан бол мөн тэр өдөр, мөн тэр газар нь бөө залж тахилга хийдэг ёстой. Ийм тахилгаар бөө залах хүн бөөгийн үүдэнд хөтөлгөө морьтой очиж морио үг дуугүй гадна нь уяж өгөөд шон дээр нь хадаг өлгөөд гэрт нь орохгүй буцаж явна. Энэ байдлыг үзмэгц бөө учрыг мэдэж тэр дороо тахилгад хэрэглэх тараг⑩, хоёр модон аяга, жад (хутга) авч саяын хүргэж ирсэн морийг унаад өлгөсөн хадгийг нь ташуурын ишээр өлгөн авч өвөртлөөд ирсэн

⑧ тухайлбал, археологийн олдвор гэх мэт.

⑨ жишээлбэл үнэмлэх бичиг, данс хар зэрэг.

⑩ ээдсэн сүү ба түүхий сүүний холимог.

хүний араас ширүүн давхиулж одно. Бөө тэнгэр буусан газар давхиулж хүрвэл мориноосоо их л уур хилэнтэй ширүүн бууж, "ерэн есөн тэнгэрийн аль тэнгэр нь буусан юм?!" гэж бахирч хашгирдаг ба:

"Бороо хур оруулахаараа оруул даа
Буухгүй газар бууж
Бүгд олныг үймүүлдэг нь юу юм бэ?"

гэж тэнгэрийг зэмлэнэ. Бөө нь тэнгэр буухыг тэнгэр таалж байна гэж ч хэлдэг. Тэнгэрийг буруушаан зэмлэж дуусаад, эргээд аваачсан савтай тарагнаасаа хоёр модон аяга хийж аваад: "За, таалахын чинь даваагаар тараг өргье!" гээд хоёр аягатай таргаа хойно хойноос нь "хай! хай!" гэж эгц дээшээ шиддэг. Энэ нь тэнгэрт өгч буй ухаантай. Тэгэхэд нь өнөөх хоёр аяга ёроолоороо бууж ирээд бөөгийн өмнө унахад доторх тараг нь асгардаггүй гэнэ. Үүнээс үзвэл, тэр бөө зохих боловсрол хүртсэн байна... Тахилга хийж байгаа үед ойр орчмын хүмүүс арвин цугларч хувь хувиараа цөм цагаан улаан идээний дээж өргөж, тэнгэрт залбиран мөргөнө. Тэнгэрийн галд алдсан хүн, малын гэрийн эзэн хонины шүүс гаргаж тахил тавьдаг бөгөөд тахилга дуусаад шүүс хонийг бөө аваачина. Хамгийн сүүлд бөө хоёр аягатай таргаа дөрвөн зүг найман зовхист цацаад, тахилгыг төгсгөдөг. "Иймэрхүү тахилга Жарууд, Баарин, Хорчин, Ордост байдаг. Ордосчууд тэднийг "Хувантан" гэдэг. Баарины удмын бөө нар цахилгаан тэнгэрийн тахилгад тэнгэр нарыг буруушаан зэмлэхээр барахгүй заримдаа хараах удаа ч гардаг гэнэ[11]. Би Жаруудад хийсэн өөрийнхөө судалгааг үндэслэвэл, Нямаа гуайн хэлдэг "удмын бөө"-г Жаруудад мөн адил "Дуудаачин" гэдэг байна. Жарууд хошууны Улаанхад сумын Сайбур гацаанд нэгэн Дуудаачин айл байсан. Үр хүүхэд нь одоо хошуундаа амьдрах нь амьдарч, Хөх хотод байх нь байна. Тэд өвөг дээдсээ Дуудаачин явсныг маш тодорхой дурсан ярьж буй бөгөөд дээр үеийнх нь бичиж үлдээсэн зүйлийг ч бага сага хадгалж буй юм. Энэ айл Урианхайтай овогтой, үе үеэрээ Дуудаачин явсан ажээ. Тэдний өвөг дээдэс урьд Мод сумын Наран гацаанд байсан гэнэ. Тэдний дээдсийн онгон нь Баярт хошуу сумын өмнө биеийн Боролжин сүмийн баруунтай байдаг. Хожим тэд Улаанхадын Хороогийн айл руу нүүж, тэнд гаднаа хошууны хүмүүс олшрохоор дахин нүүж, Хөндлөн голын хойд хөвөөний Сайбур гацаанд иржээ. Миний сурвалжилсан айлын хүмүүсийн хэлснээр, нагац эмээ, элэнц эмээ нь бүр Дархан хошууны Боржгин овогт улс бөгөөд тэднийг бага байхад "Танайх бол хуучин Жарууд улс, Дуудаачин аймаг, өвөө ааваас чинь дээш

⑪ Нямаа: 《Бөө мөргөлийн тухай хэдэн асуудал》, Боржигдай Оюунбилэг, Л. Нарангоо нарын найруулсан: 《Элбэг бүтээл-профессор доктор Загчид Сэцэний наян насны ойд》, ӨМСХХ, 1996 он, 271-275-р тал.

үе улиран Дуудаачин явсан. Танайхан хэл ам хатуутай улс, бусад айл аймгийн хүмүүс танайхантай үг ам зөрөхөөсөө айж жийрхдэг юм. Тэнгэр дуугарч аянга буусан тохиолдолд Дуудаачин морьтой давхиулж тэнгэрийг загнан зэмлэж хараан донгоддог. Энэ нь тэдний онц эрх. Тэнгэр буусан газар очиж донгодон зэмлэж ёслол хийсэн хойно сайхан бороо ордог" гэж ярьж өгч байв. Тэдний хэлснээр, 1975 оны зун Хуулин гол хавийн отор нүүдэлд энэ айлын хасаг тэргэн дээр аянга дайрч (тэнгэр буусан гэж хэлж буй). Тэргэн доор борооноос хоргодож байсан гэрийн хүмүүсийг нь хол шидэж, нэг эрэгтэй хүүхэд амиа алджээ. Тэгэхэд энэ явдал гарсны шалтгаан бол соёлын хувьсгалын эцсээр энэ айлынхан Дуудаачины цээрээ алдсанаас болсон гэж нагац нар нь хэлсэн гэдэг. Тэдний хэлснээр Дуудаачин аймгийнхан "Дэлүү идвэл дэлбэрч үхнэ, Олгой идвэл огшуулж үхнэ" гэж малын дэлүү олгой идэхгүй хатуу цээртэй байж. Мэдээжээр, өнөөдрийн Жарууд хошууны Улаанхад сумын ихэнх хэсэг нь Хорчин зүүн гарын дунд хошууны нутаг, 1947 оноос хойш Жарууд хошуунд хуваагдан орж, өнөөдрийн Улаанхад сумыг бүрдүүлжээ. Гэвч, Улаанхадын хүмүүс бүгд өөр хошуунаас ирсэн биш. Энэ Дуудаачин айл шиг Жарууд суугуул улс бас нэлээд бий. Баярт хошуу балгасны Баримт гацаанд Дуудаачин аймгийн хүмүүс амьдарч байна. Тэд нар Дундад иргэн улсын үеийн Жаруудын цуутай Шишү мээрэнгийн хойчис гэж хэлдэг. Тэд өөрсдийгөө Дуудаачин аймаг, Даян овогтой гэж байна. Миний бодлоор, энэ Даян овог нь яг Дуудаачиныг Хятадаар Хуан Тиэн 喚天 гэж орчуулж, түүнийгээ Тиэн 天 хэмээн товчлон, улмаар Хятад овгийг дагуулан нөгөө Хятад овгийн Тиэнийг田 авсан бололтой. Энэ нь орчин үеийн Монголчуудын Хятад овог авах заншилтай нийцэж байна.

Дахин судар бичгийн тэмдэглэлдээ буцаж очъё. XIV зууны эхээр Перст зохиогдсон Рашид-Ад Диний "Судрын чуулган" бол Монголын түүх зан заншлыг дэлгэрэнгүй бөгөөд итгүүштэй тэмдэглэснээрээ цуутай сурвалж бичиг юм. Тус номын нэгдүгээр ботид Монгол аймгуудын олдвор буй. Түүний Монгол Урианхан хэмээх хэсэгт ийн тэмдэглэжээ: "Урианхайчууд өөрсдийгөө Эргүнэ Хунгийн долоон зуухыг ноцооход оролцсон гэж хэлдэг.[⑫] Тэд нарт ийм нэгэн заншил бий: Аянга цахилгаан маш сүрхий гарах үед тэд тэнгэрийг харааж, үүлийг харааж, аянга цахилгааныг харааж, тэдгээрийн зүг бархирч хашгирдаг. Малыг аянга ниргэж алсан тохиолдолд тэд түүнээс зайлж махыг нь иддэггүй. Ингэвэл сая аянга дуугарахаа болино гэж итгэдэг. Бусад монголчууд бол тэднээс алсдаа, аянга дуугарах үед гэрээсээ гардаггүй, айж суудаг", "тэдний бас хэлэхээр, зүйл зүйлийн

⑫ энэ нь Монголчууд Эргүнэ Хунгийн асга хадыг долоон зуухаар хайлуулан шатааж, тэндээс гараад Монголын өндөрлөгт ирснийг дурдсан үлгэрийг хэлж буй-Эшлэгч.

шалтгаанаас болж, чөтгөр шуламс тэдэнтэй ирж хэлэлцдэг. Тэр нутагт иймэрхүү дэмий балай үг яриа зөндөө байдаг⑬ бөгөөд тоолоод барахгүй бөө байдаг. Түүний дотор хамгийн алс хол хязгаар газар суудаг хүмүүстэй хил залгасан газар багтана. Тэр газрыг Барга буюу Баргуужин Дөхөм гэнэ. Тэнд бөө маш олон"⑭ гэжээ. Тодорхойлууштай нь, энд хэлж буй "чөтгөр шуламс" гэгч нь мусульманчуудын үг, Монголчуудын бөөгийн тэнгэр сахиусыг заажээ. Мөн, энд гарсан Баргуужин Дөхөмийн Урианхайчууд гэдэг ч буруу. Урианхайчууд Бурхан Халдунд байснаас биш Баргуужин Дөхөмд байгаагүй⑮. Тийнхүү бөө олонтой гэсэн газар нь Бурхан Халдуны Урианхайн газрыг хэлсэн нь мэдээж юм.

Энэхүү тэмдэглэлээс үзвэл, тэнгэрийг харааж зэмлэдэг онц эрх бүхий бөө нар уг нь Урианхан нарын бөө байсан юм байна. Тэр нь Урианхан нарын бусад Монголчуудаас ялгарах онцгой заншил байж. Тэнгэрийг донгодож хараах эрх бүхий эдгээр бөөг Урианхайчууд угаасаа "Дуудаачин" гэдэг байсан бололтой. Урьд өгүүлсэн Жарууд хошууны Улаанхад сумын удмын бөө Дуудаачид нь Урианхайтай овогтой, тэгэхээр Урианхан язгууртай нь ямар ч мадаггүй. Дашрамд хэлэхэд, Баарин, Ордос, Хорчинд ч "Дуудаачин" байсан нь мөн л Урианхан түмэнтэй хамаатай. Урианхан түмэн XVI зуунд бусад таван түмэнд талагдсан түүхийг анхаарах хэрэгтэй. үүний тухай дараа бас өгүүлнэ. XVI зуунд, Жарууд, Баарин хоёр бүр Их Халх түмэнд багтаж байсан. Халх түмэн бол Урианхан түмнийг устгахад хошуучилсан түмэн. Ордос түмэн ч Урианхайг сөнөөх аян дайнд идэвхтэй оролцож байсан. Тэд Урианхайг сөнөөсний дараа Урианхайгаас олон иргэн хуваан авчээ. Хорчин түмэн нь Урианхайг сөнөөх аян дайнд оролцоогүй боловч, XVII зууны 20-ид онд өвөр таван Халх Манж нарт эвдэгдэх үед Жарууд, Баарин хоёр отог 1627-1628 онд нэг үе Хорчинд орж түшсэн бөгөөд хожим нь Хорчинтой эвдрэлцээд, сая Манжид дагаар орж, Баарин, Жарууд засаг хошууд болов. Энэ үйл явцад Хорчинд нэлээд олон Жарууд, Баарин отгийн ард иргэд хоцрон үлджээ. Тэдний дунд Дуудаачин бөө нар байсан л байлгүй. Тийнхүү Хорчинд Урианхайтай овогт Дуудаачид байсан нь яг энэ үеийн түүхээс улбаатай. Ийм учраас, Баарин, Ордос, Хорчинд бас Дуудаачид байсан нь бүр Урианхайгаас уламжилж очсон хэрэг. Хорчинд Дуудаачин бөөг "Хуан Тиэн" гэж хэлдэг нь

---

⑬ Мэдээжээр, чөтгөр шуламс тэдэнтэй үргэлж хэлэлцдэг.

⑭ Рашид-Ад Дин: 《Судрын чуулган》, Үй Дажэн нарын хятадчилав, нэгдүгээр боть, нэгдүгээр хувиар дэвтэр, Шан Уу хэвлэлийн хороо, 255-256-р тал.

⑮ Жагаачидайн Буяндэлгэр: 《Урианхайн тухай》, Боржигдай Оюунбилэг, Л. Нарангоо нарын найруулсан: 《Элбэг бүтээл-профессор доктор Загчид Сэцэний наян насны ойд》, ӨМСХХ, 1996 он, эндээс лавлана уу.

"Дуудаачин"-г Хятад хэлэнд орчуулж дуудсан төдий. Уг Хятад үг нь Хуан Тиэн 喚天 байсан байлгүй, тэр нь яг тэнгэр дуудна гэсэн үг.

Үүнээс гадна, мөн Жарууд хошууны Баярт хошуу сумын Баримт айлд бас Үү овогтой хүмүүс байдаг. Тэд өөрсдийгөө "Урианхад (urya-qad) гэдэг"⑯. Мөн Гэрэлчулуу сумын Хатан айл гацаанд ч Ү овогт улс бий. Тэд нар өөрийнхөө Монгол овгийг "Тавлах" гэж хэлдэг бөгөөд Ү овог нь 5 五 гэсэн тоог орчуулсан Хятад үг. Түүнээс Хятад овгийн Ү 吴 болсон гэж үзэж байна. Миний бодлоор, эхний Ү овог нь Урианхадын Хятад авианы эхний үсгээс гаралтай нь мэдээж. Гэхдээ Урианхад гэдэг нь Урианхадын гажсан дуудлага болох нь ч магадтай. Харин хоёрдугаар Ү овог нь тавлах гэсэн Монгол овгийг Хятадчилсантай хамаатай гэсэн нь шинэхэн тайлбар ажээ. Үүнийг хараад бид Монголчууд "Тавнан" гэсэн үгэнд хийсэн гүжир тайлбар санаанд орно. Ар Халхын түүхч Галдан туслагчийн 1841 онд бичсэн 《Эрдэнийн эрхи》 гэдэг он дараалсан бичигт, урьд Бөртэ үжинг Модон хотыг эзлэгч Мухар Бор хэмээгч булаан аваачсанд, Урианхайн Зэлмэ аргаар булаан авч, буцаж ирэх замдаа Үжин лүгээ "амгаланг үүсгэж" давхар болсонд, Чингис хаан өршөөж, "тэр хөвгүүн минийх бус боловч миний их хатнаас төрсөн хөвгүүн тул энгийн хүнээс өөр болгож, онц хишиг хүртээж, мөн миний их хатнаас төрсөн хөвгүүн Зүчи, Цагаадай, Өгэдэй, Тулуй дөрвийн дараа тавдугаар ноён хэмээн нэрийдэж яв хэмээн айлдсанаас хойш түүний үрийг цөм тавдугаар ноён хэмээсэн нь сунхуй дор Тавнан (Табунун) хэмээн алдаршсан тэр буй"⑰ гэжээ. Энэ нь тавнанг буруу ойлгож, гажуу тайлбарласан хэрэг юм. Түүхэн үнэнтэй ямар ч холбоогүй. "Тавлах" гэдэг нь үүнтэй адилаар "Тавнан" гэдэг үгийг авиа сэлгэж тавлах гэж хазайлгаснаас болсон биз. Ү овог нь тавлахын тавыг орчуулсан биш, харин тавнан⑱-гийн тавыг орчуулсан байна. Урианхад аймгийн тэргүүн нь адагтаа Басуд тавнангийн үеэс хаадын хүргэд болж, тавнан гэгдэх болсон юм. Энэхүү Ү овогтон нь мөн Урианхадын ноёд язгууртны хойчис болж таарна. Эдгээрийг хамран өгүүлбэл, Жаруудад Урианхан аймагтай хамаатай Урианхад, Дуудаачин, Тавнан зэрэг овог аймаг маш олон байх ажээ. Эдгээр нь "хийсвэр үлдмэл сурвалж"-ийн хувиар Жарууд бол Урианхан гаралтай гэдгийг баттай гэрчилж байна.

---

⑯ Үү овгийн Урианхадын Хятад авианы эхний үсэг гэж үздэг.

⑰ Ц.Насанбалжир харгуулж хэвлэлд бэлтгэсэн: 《Эрдэнийн эрхи》, Улаанбаатар, 57v-58r.

⑱ Уг утга нь таван он, XVI зуунаас хойш Алтан ургийн язгууртнуудын хүргэнийг таван ун гэдэг болжээ.

Гурав

Жарууд аймаг Урианхайгаас үүсэлтэй, энэ ч тодорхой. Гэвч, асуудал энд хүрээд шийдвэрлэгдэхгүй. Мэдээж, Урианхан бол Монголын эртний аймаг. 《Монголын Нууц Товчоон》-д өгүүлснээр, Урианхан нар Бодончарын үеэс Боржгины эзэмшлийн иргэн болсон. Тэдний дотор "Жарчууд аданхан урианхан" гэж байжээ[19]. Чингис хааны үе гэхэд, Тэмүжин эцгээсээ өнчин хоцроод гачигдалтай байсан үед, "Бурхан Халдунаас Урианхадай хүн Жарчидай өвгөн хөөргөө өргөж Зэлмэ нэрт хөвгүүнээ удирдаж ирж өгүүлрүүн: Ононы Дэлүүн болдог бүхүй дор, Тэмүжинг төрөхүй дор Булган нэхий өглөө би. Энэ хөвгүүнээ Зэлмийг өглөө хө би. Өчүүхэн хэмээн авч одлоо. Эдүгээ Зэлмээр эмээлээ тохуул, үүдээ нээлгэ хэмээж өгөв"[20]. Энэхүү Жарчидай өвгөн бол Зэлмэ, Сүбээдэй, Цуурхан нарын эцэг. Түүний хөвгүүд Тэмүжинд туслан улс байгуулж, дэлхий дахиныг байлдан дагуулж их гавьяа байгуулаад хожим нь тэд Урианхайн ноёд болжээ. Их Монгол улс ба Юань улсыг өнгөрөөж Даян хааны үед ирэхэд Урианхан нь хоёр хуваагдан, нэг бүлэг нь тэр цагт их алдаршсан зургаан түмний нэг болж, Урианхан түмэн гэж нэршин, нөгөө нь зургаан түмнээс ангид орших Үлгэ түмэнд багтан Дуюун Ойн Урианхан болжээ. Тэгвэл Жарууд нь чухам хоёр Урианхайн аль бүлэгт нь багтаж байсан бэ? Хэзээ яаж Таван отог Халхад оров?

Урианхан түмнийг доктор Ж.Буяндэлгэр нэлээд сайн судалжээ. Түүний судалгааг үзвэл, Урианхан түмэн нь Хэнтийн нурууны Бурхан Халдуны Урианхайгаас үүсвэртэй. Аль эрт Чингис хааны аравдугаар үеийн элэнц Бодончарын үед Урианхан нь Боржгин ноёдын үүдний боол болсон байв. Чингис хаан Их Монгол улсыг байгуулах үед, Урианхайн Зэлмэ, Сүбэдэй, Урианхайтай ах дүүс их хүч өгсөн бөгөөд хожим Их Монгол улс гадагш өргөтгөх дайн хийхэд Урианхан цэрэг тэдний удирдлагаар Ази, Европын олон улс аймгийг байлдан дагуулжээ. Энэхүү гавьяанаас болж, үүдний боол гаралтай Урианхайн урьдын байр суурь хувирч, Их Монгол улс Юань улсын гавьят сайд, их ноёд болсон юм. Чингис хаан улс байгуулсан хойно, Зэлмийг Мянган өргөмжилж, зүүн гарын түмний дэд ноён болгож, түүний дүү Сүбэдэй, Цуурхан нарыг бас Мянган өргөмжилжээ. Эдгээр ноёдын харьяат Урианхан нар Чингисийн үеэс Бурхан Халдунд амьдарч, Чингис хаанаас хойш түүний алтан хүүр их хоригийг сахих

⑲《Монголын Нууц Товчоон》, 38-р бадаг.

⑳《Монголын Нууц Товчоон》, 97-р бадаг.

үүрэгтэй болов. Эд нар XV-XVI зууны үед Урианхан түмэн болж бүрэлдээд хуучин нутаг Бурхан Халдундаа байжээ[21].

Үлгэ түмний Урианхан буюу Дуюун ойн Урианхан бол Юань улсын Ян Ёоу (延佑) гуравдугаар он буюу 1316 онд байгуулагдсан Дуюун өндрийн Урианхан мянганаас ирэлтэй. Тэдний ноёрхогчид нь Урианхан Зэлмийн үр сад. Мин улсын эхэн үед, Чингис хааны отгон дүү Отчигины үр Ляо Ун Азашир Мин улс дагаснаа, Мин улс түүний эзэмшил нутагт Онгилгууд, Үжээд, Урианхан гурван ой байгуулж, Ляо Унгаар мэдүүлсэн байв. Түүний доторх Урианхайчууд бол Дуюуны Урианхан мянганаас хөгжиж ирсэн улс, тэдний ноёрхогчид Урианхан Зэлмийн үр ач нар, энэхүү гурван ойг Мин улсын түүхэнд “Урианхан хийгээд гурван ой” (兀良哈三衛) гэж, Дуюун Урианхайчуудыг “Урианхан Ой” (兀良哈衛), “Дуюун Ой” (朵顔衛) гэхчилэн нэрийдэж байв. “Ой (衛)” гэдэг нь Мин улсын хил дагуу цэргийн байгууламж, Монголчууд бол харин тэднийг зүгээр л Урианхайчууд гэдэг. Энэ бүлэг Урианхайчууд Дуюун уул, Суул гол дагуу байж байгаад, хожим Хянган давааны өмнө рүү нүүгээд, Отчигин ноёны хойчсын ноёрхол дахь “Үлгэ түмэн” (Хянган давааны Үлгэ буюу Энгэрийн түмэн) болж бүрэлджээ. Үлгэ түмэн нь Отчигин ноёны хойчсын ноёрхолд байж байгаад аль нэгэн үед Урианхайн эзэмшилд орсон байв. XVI зууны түүхчид дөчөөд оноос эхлээд, Их хаан Дайрүсүн Цахар түмнээ авч Хэрлэн голын хавь газраас Хянган даваа даван өмнөш нүүж, Урианхан Ойн хойд хэсгийг эзлэн авахад, хааны хамт Халх түмний зүүн гар Хурхачи баатрын удирдлагаар, Хорчины баруун гар Хүй Мөнх Тасхарын удирдлагаар тус тус Хянган давааны Үлгэд бууж Үжээд Онглигууд хоёр ойг бүр мөсөн эзэмдэж авчээ. Энэ үед, баруун түмний тэргүүн Түмэдийн Алтан хаан тэсэж ядан зүүнш цэрэглэж, Урианхан ойн өмнө хэсгийг байлдан дагуулж, тэднийг Харчины ноёдод хуваан өмчлүүлжээ. Эдгээр цэрэг дайны ажиллагааны үр дүнд, Урианхан ойн Урианхайчууд Цахар, Харчин хоёр аймгийн Алтан урагтны эзэмшилд орж, тэдний тэргүүнүүд нь Цахар, Харчины тайж нарын тавнан болж, Харчинд “Тайж тавнангууд” хэмээх ноёрхогч давхрага бий болжээ. Эдгээр тавнан бол хожмын Чин гүрний үеийн Зостын чуулганы Харчин гурван хошуу ба Түмэд зүүн хошууны засаг тавнан нарын дээдэс юм. Энэ тухай би “Харчин түмний судлал” гэдэг зохиолдоо нэлээд дэлгэрэнгүй өгүүлсэн[22] учраас энд нуршихаа болъё.

Гэвч Үзэмчин тайж Гомбожав Гангийн урсгал-даа Урианхан Зэлмийн үр Баасан тавнангаас үржсэн нь “Харчины ноёд Тавнан овогт мөн хэмээн заримууд

㉑ Жагаачидайн Буяндэлгэр: *Урианхайн тухай,* Боржигидай Оюунбилэг, Л. Нарангоо нарын найруулсан: *Элбэг бүтээл-профессор доктор Загчид Сэцэний наян насны ойд,* ӨМСХХ, 1996 он.

㉒ 烏雲畢力格《喀喇沁萬戶研究》，呼和浩特：内蒙古人民出版社，2005年，45—51頁。

олонх дор өгүүлжээ” гэж дам хэллэгийг тэмдэглэсэнээс болж, хүмүүс Жарууд ноёдыг Харчин Түмэдийн Урианхан ноёдтой нэг гэр гэж үзээд, Жаруудыг Үлгэ түмний Урианхайгаас гаралтай гэж үзэх болсон юм. Гэвч энэ бол эндүүрэл. Энэ эндүүрэл наад зах нь Гомбожавын үед нэгэнт буй болоод, Жарууд гүүш түүнийг итгэн тэмдэглэсэнээс энэ хэллэг улам дэлгэрчээ. Энэ хэллэг эндүүрэл гэдэг нь эргэлзээгүй юм. Хамгийн түрүүнд, Далан тэргүүний дайн болсон 1509 онд, Халх түмэн одоогийн Монгол улсын зүүн өмнө бие ба манай Хөлөнбуйр нутгаар урсаж буй Халх гол дагуу байсан бөгөөд баруун зүүн гарт хуваагдсан их түмэн байжээ. Тэр үед өвөр таван Халх гэж байгаагүй, түүнээс хагас зууны дараа өвөр таван Халх буй болсон юм. Иймээс, Далан тэргүүний дайнд орсон Халх Баасан баатар гэгч Их Халх түмний ноёрхогчдын нэг нь болж таарна. Энэ хүнийг Жаруудын ноён удам гэснээс үзвэл, Жарууд нь Их Халх түмний нэг отог байсан бөгөөд Баасан нь энэ Жарууд отгийн ноён байжээ. Саган сэцэн, Жарууд гүүш нар амьдарч байсан үеийнхээ байдал, мэдлэгт дулдуйдаж, 1509 оны үеийн Жаруудын Баасанг “Өвөр таван Халхын Баасан тавнан” гэж тэмдэглэсэн нь буруу[23]. Хоёрт, Далан тэргүүний дайнд орж их гавьяа байгуулсан Урианхайчууд бол Бурхан Халдуны Урианхан түмний цэрэг, харин Үлгэ түмний Урианхан отог (Мин улсын хэлдэг Урианхан ой) биш. “Эрдэнийн товч”-д тэмдэглэсэнээр, Даян хаан хөвгүүнээ алагдсаныг сонсоод, “Эзэн тэнгэрт зарга заан сацал сацаж мөргөөд, зүүн гурван түмэн, Абга Хоорчин (Хорчин) хийгээдийг аван морилвой”. Тэгээд байлдаанд орохдоо “Ордос эзний найман цагаан гэрийг хадгалсан их заяат улс бөлгөө. Түүнлүгээ Урианхан мөн эзний алтан хөмрөгийг сахисан бас их заяат улс. Хорчин Абгатай тусалтугай”[24]. “Эзний алтан хөмрөг” гэгч нь эзэн Чингисийн алтан хүүрийг бумбалсан авсыг хэлжээ. Үүнээс бид Баасан тавнан бол эзний их хоригийг сахисан Бурхан Халдуны Урианхайн хүн гэж жиших боломж огт алга. Учир нь, эдгээр Урианхан нар Цахар, Харчины тайж нарт хуваагдсан бөгөөд Манж нар эзлэн авах хүртэл Цахар, Харчин хоёр нь Таван Халхад ялагдаж харьяатаа хураалгасан явдалгүй болохоор, тэд дахин Жаруудын тайж нарын албат болж хувирах ёсгүй юм. (Мин улсын Гү Интай гэгч хүн, Урианхан ойн тэргүүн Хуа Дангийн удаах хөвгүүн Барсун их хаантай ураг болоцож Мин улсын дайсан болж байна гэж тэмдэглэсэн зүйл бий.[25] Үүнээс үзвэл, зарим эрдэмтэд Баасан тавнанг энэхүү 把兒孫 гэгчтэй адилтган үзэж, улмаар Жаруудыг Урианхан ойн иргэд

㉓ дашрамд хэлэхэд, би уг нь Ломигийн хэллэгийг дагаж Баасанг Басууд гэж уншсан нь илэрхий буруу болжээ. Энд онцлон залруулъя.

㉔ Саган Сэцэн:《Хаадын Үндэсний Эрдэнийн Товч》, Их Хүрээний гар бичмэл, 66г.

㉕ 谷應泰《明史紀事本末》：“花當次子把兒孫驍勇敢深入，結婚小王子，為中國患滋深矣。”

хэмээн үзсэн нь итгэмээр биш). Үүнээс бид Жаруud бол “Эзний алтан хөмрөгийг сахисан” Урианхан түмний нэгэн отог байсан гэдгийг улам гэрчилж болно.

Тэгвэл Бурхан Халдуны Жарууд нар хэзээ Халх түмэнд багтах болсон бэ? Энэ асуултад хариулахад хялбар. Даян хаан нас барсны дараа, түүний ач Бодь-Алаг хаан Цахар, Халх, Баруун гурван зэрэг таван түмнийг дайчилж, Урианханд хэдэн удаа цэрэглэжээ. Түмэдийн Алтан хааны намтрыг үзвэл, 1524 онд Урианхан түмний төрийн ноён Гэрболд чинсан хоёулаа Халх түмний Бэсүд, Хүрээ хоёр отгийг талсанд, бусад Түмэдийн холбоот цэрэг Урианханд цэрэглэжээ. Түүнээс хойш мөн 1531, 1532, 1538, 1541, 1544 онд дараалан тавантаа аялж, эцэстээ Урианхан түмнийг мөхөөн, түүнийг хуваасан ажээ[26]. Энэ мэт, Урианхан түмэн бусад таван түмэнд хуваагдан оржээ. Урианхан түмний Жарууд отог Халх түмэнд хуваагдан орсон нь яг энэ үеийн явдал байх ёстой.

Дөрөв

Ингээд үзвэл, Жарууд нь Урианхан түмний нэг отог байжээ. Урианхайг таван түмэн хувааж авах үед, 1544 оны орчим Жарууд отог Халх түмэнд хуваагдан, Халх түмний зүүн гарт ороод, Даян хааны хөвгүүн Алчиболдын өмч болсон байна. Үүнээс удалгүй, Халх түмний зүүн гар нь Алчиболдын ганц хөвгүүн Хурхачи Хасар ноёныг даган Дайрүсүн Гүдэн хааныг дагаж Хянган давааны Үлгэд нүүж иржээ. Тэд Үлгэ түмний зарим отог иргэдийг эзлэн авч эрхшээлдээ оруулан улам хүчирхэгжин томров. Хожим Хурхачи ноён нас барах үед, Үлгийн Халхын иргэдээ таван хөвгүүндээ хуваан өмчлүүлсэнд, Үлгийн Халх нь таван Халх болон бүрэлджээ. Энэ бол сая “Өвөр таван Халх”-ын үүсэл юм. Их Халх түмний баруун гарын тэргүүн Гэрсэнз хунтайжийг “Жалайр хунтайж”, зүүн гарын тэргүүн Хурхачи Хасар ноёныг “Жарууд Хурхачи ноён” гэдэг. Энэ нь баруун гарын хамгийн том отог бол Жалайр, зүүн гарын хамаг том отог нь Жарууд байсныг харуулж байна. Мэдээжээр, Жалайр бол Чингис хааны хамгийн их гавьяат түшмэл Гуо ван Мухулайн үр садын аймаг, Юань улсын үеийн зүүн гарын таван аймаг (左翼五投下)-ын ахлах аймаг. Тэр нь хожмын Халх түмний баруун гарын Долоон Халхын ахлах отог болж, Гэрсэнзийн ууган хөвгүүний өмч болжээ. Жарууд нь Чингис хааны дэргэд Мухулайн дараах зүүн гарын хоёр дахь их ноён Зэлмийн аймаг, хэдийгээр Бодь-Алаг хааны үед таван түмэнд талагдсан боловч, Урианхайн

㉖《Эрдэнэ тунамал нэрт судар оршивой》, ӨМНШУХ-ны номын санийн хадгаламж, хулсан үзгийн хуулмал.

ноён аймгийн харьяа болсон Жарууд нь Халх зүүн гарын хамгийн том отог болжээ. Тиймээс, Хурхачи ноён таван хөвгүүндээ өмч хуваахад Жарууд отгийг ууган хөвгүүн Убаш Үйзэндээ өгсөн байна. Ийнхүү Жарууд нь өвөр таван отгийн ахлах отог болжээ. Жаруудын нутаг усыг товч өгүүлбээс, Жарууд нь Урианхайн бүрэлдэхүүн болсны хувьд Бодончарын үеэс хойш XVI зуун хүртэл Хэнтийн нурууны Бурхан Халдунаар төв болсон нутагт үе улиран амьдарч, хожим Хэнтийн нуруунаас Онон мөрний дунд урсгал хүртэл тэлж өргөжжээ[27]. XVI зууны дунд үеэр Халх түмэнд ороод Халх гол дагуу хэсэг хугацаанд байж, удалгүй Хянган давааны өмнө ирж, зүүн Ляохө голын хойгуур, зүүн тийш Хайшийн Зүрчидтэй, зүүн хойгуур Хорчинтой, баруун өмнүүр Хонгириад отогтой тус тус зах нийлж байжээ[28]. XVII зууны эхэн үед гэнэт хүчирхэгжсэн Зүрчиний Айшин гүрэн Монгол аймгуудыг эзэгнэж эхлээд, Монголын Лигдэн хутаг хаантай сөргөлдөв. Лигдэн хаан ба Зүрчин нар өвөр таван Халхыг ширүүн булаалдаж байв. 1626 онд, Баарин, Жарууд хоёр аймаг Айшин гүрний цохилтод өртөж, улмаар Лигдэн хааны довтолгоонд өртөн, арга буюу Нуун Хорчинд очиж түшжээ. Гэвч, тэд Нуун Хорчины дарлал гадуурхалыг амсаж, Хорчинд шахагдаад 1628 онд Хорчиноос салж Зүрчиний Айшин гүрэнд дагаар оров. Тэд Айшин гүрний байлдаанд гавьяа байгуулсан тул, 1636 онд Дай Чин гүрнийг байгуулах үед, Найман хошуунд орсон Жарууд нараас бусдыг нь хоёр хошуу болгон зохион байгуулж, тэдний албат иргэддээ үе улиран ноёлох эрх үлдээж, Шар мөрнөөс хойш Хуулин гол хүрэх газраар нутаг зааж суулгав. Тэр нь өвөр дөчин есөн хошууны Жарууд зүүн, баруун хоёр гарын хошуу болжээ.

Хураангуйлбал, Жарууд бол Урианхан гаралтай, Хэнтийн нуруу Онон гол хооронд нутагтай Урианхан түмэнд харьяалагдах аймаг байгаад XVI зууны 40-өөд онд Халх түмний эрхшээлд оржээ. XVI зууны сүүлийн хагаст Хурхачи Хасар ноёны ахмад хөвгүүний өмч болж, өвөр таван Халхын ахлах отог болов. Чин гүрний үед цөөхөн Жарууд нар Найман хошуунд орсноос гадна бусад ихэнх Жарууд нар нь хоёр засаг хошуунд хуваагдан амьдарчээ.

A Study on the Origin of Jarud

Borjigidai Oyunbilig

This paper combines the study of texts with anthropological fieldwork to investigate

---

㉗ Жагаачидайн Буяндэлгэр, мөн тэнд, 47-р хуудас.

㉘ Дарьжав: 《Мин улсын үеийн говийн өмнөх Монголын түүхийн судалгаа》, ӨМСХХ, 1998 он, 134-136-р тал.

the origin of the Mongolian Jarud tribe, and finds that they originated from the ancient Uriyangqai, living between the Khentii Mountains and the Onon River during the Mongol-Yuan period. The Uriyangqai Tümen, which formed after the collapse of the Yuan, was carved up by the other five Tümens in the 1540s. The Uriyangqai Tümen's Jarud otoγ merged into the Left Hand of Khalkha Tümen and moved to the south of the Hinggan mountains, becoming one part of the Inner Five Khalkha. In the early years of the Qing, the Jarud were divided into two jasaγ banners, left and right.

The Influence of Mongol Law during the Yuan Dynasty

Florence Hodous

1. Introduction

The legal history of the Yuan dynasty contains an interesting paradox, which has not yet been explained satisfactorily. This was a time when a foreign people, considered by some Chinese to be barbarians, invaded and ruled China for over a century, in the process changing and influencing China. Although many Chinese legal procedures and practices continued unchanged, there was a limited Mongol influence as well, despite the fact that Mongol customs often flew in the face of Chinese and Confucian morality.

The paradox is seen when comparing the Yuan dynasty with the other khanates that made up the Mongol empire, after the break-up of the United Empire in 1260-64. Although Mongol influence in China on the law was limited, it was greater than in all the other khanates, a phenomenon which requires explanation. This paper will attempt to give an explanation, and will suggest that not only the bureaucratization of Chinese society, but also a particularly Chinese view of the Emperor as the source and arbiter of law, played a significant role.

2. The influence of Mongol law

The influence of Mongol law can be seen in small but significant aspects of the punishments system in China, which largely was inherited from the preceding Jin and Song dynasties. In China, punishments were traditionally grouped into a 'five punishments' system, where they were graded from the most severe to the least severe, though each had many sub-gradations.

The lowest two gradations were beatings (beating with the heavy stick and beating with the light stick), with a possible number of strokes that were always multiples of ten, up to 110. Under the Yuan dynasty however, unlike during any preceding or following dynasty, the stroke numbers were changed to numbers ending in seven, up to 107.① This highly unusual arrangement was a result of the Mongol preference for the number seven to be connected with punishments, as seen in the *Secret History of the Mongols.*②

Secondly, 'military exile' was adopted as a punishment in China and integrated into the 'five punishments'. This punishment was also typical of the Mongols, who as a nomadic people did not have prisons, so it served as a useful intermediate penalty. During the Yuan dynasty, it was a step above forced labor and a step below the death penalty, so that it came to be used in the case of commuted death penalties.③

Finally, the death penalty itself also underwent changes under Mongol rule. Though traditionally there were two gradations, beheading and strangulation (which was considered less severe), according to the research of Zhou Sicheng, only beheading was routinely used under the Yuan dynasty. This was likely because the Mongols also thought that strangulation was less severe, but reserved this particular penalty for their own nobles (mostly members of Chinggis Khan's family).④

Another, less successful instance of Mongol influence is the levirate, the practice whereby a younger brother would marry the wife of his older brother if he died. Qubilai Qa'an for five years tried to impose such a practice in China, and was opposed by many officials and local magistrates some, but not all of whom, refused to follow his decree.⑤ If we compare this situation with the other khanates, we have no record of the levirate being imposed in the Chaghatai Khanate; it was also not influential in the Ilkhanate; but in the Golden Horde there is a single recorded instance of this practice being imposed, when the wife and younger brother of the deceased Andrew of Chernigov visited Batu Khan, and were forced into such a union.⑥

3. The uniqueness of the Yuan dynasty

Part of the reason for Mongol influence on the law during the Yuan dynasty was the Mongol custom to resolve disputes through discussion and negotiation.⑦ The other part, however, was due to particular characteristics of the Yuan dynasty which made this

① Xu Yuchun, Yuandai fading xing kaobian, pp. 112-120.

② *Secret History of the Mongols,* § 278; see also § 227.

③ Wu Bo, "Chujun zhidu," p. 81.

④ Zhou Sicheng, "Yuandai xingfa zhong de suowei 'qiao' xing yu 'you zhan wu jiao' zhi shuo bianzheng," Beijing shifan daxue xuebao 2015 (2): 154-159.

⑤ Birge, *Women, property, and Confucian reaction,* pp. 238-244.

⑥ Carpini/Dawson, pp. 10-11; Jackson, "The Mongols and the faith of the conquered," p. 60.

⑦ Hodous, *"The quriltai as a legal institution"*, pp. 87-102.

khanate's people more susceptible to Mongol influence. The Chinese themselves were also willing to discuss with the Mongols about which laws should be applied.

The amount of legislation discussed and created under the Yuan is itself unique. Only the Chinese attempted to create, and involve the Qa'ans in creating, a law code and compilations of edicts. As a result, teams of Mongols and Chinese were repeatedly tasked with working together to develop legislation acceptable for all groups. Although most of the legislation developed in this way was not actually promulgated, the process still helped to increase knowledge of each other's legal practices and cherished principles.

This was very different from the Ilkhanate, where most of the inhabitants were Muslim. They believed that the ultimate source of the law is in religion. Therefore, although some local people, especially those who had become close to the Mongols, were judged using Mongol legal procedure, the majority of locals were judged by the religious judges, the qadis (قاضي). And although some of these turned to the Ilkhans to get or secure their positions, they did not turn to the Ilkhans for advice on which laws to apply; thus, their situation was very different from the Yuan dynasty.

The Yuan empire was unique in terms of the dependence of local officials on the Qa'ans. A variety of local officials at the district, prefecture and route levels dealt with legal cases, often in conference. The crucial point is that they were able and willing to communicate regularly with the central government. While legislation sometimes took some years to filter down,[8] communication was more frequent and effective than in any of the other khanates.

4. Confucianism as a powerful motive for cooperation

From the beginnings of imperial Chinese history, the emperors made laws for the people and tried to claim that they alone had the right to do so. This was connected with the claim that the emperors were the 'Sons of Heaven,' having the most direct and most authoritative connection with Heaven. The emperors alone knew the will of Heaven and communicated it to the people. They intended to leave no space for other claims, whether religious or otherwise, to be able to make valid laws.[9]

By the time of the Song and Jin dynasties which preceded the Yuan, Chinese literati viewed the emperor's laws as essential to the ordering of society. In particular, a legal code organized on the model of the Tang code was seen as an absolutely indispensable

---

⑧ Birge, *Women, property, and Confucian reaction,* pp. 240, 245.

⑨ Gu, *The boundaries of meaning and the formation of law,* pp. 79, 162-4; Langlois, "Law, Statecraft, and The Spring and Autumn Annals," pp. 89-152, pp. 103, 108.

tool of rule and necessary for the legitimation of each subsequent dynasty.⑩ While in practice edicts could modify or even reverse rulings in the law codes,⑪ the fact of having a law code with a fixed text had enormous symbolic importance, supposedly lending clarity to the legal system and stability to society.⑫

It is also of immense importance for the case of the Yuan dynasty that while many officials were committed to remaking society according to traditional Chinese principles, at the same time they believed that the law should not remain static. On the contrary, change was expected, especially on the change of dynasties, and during dynasties as well, because the law was meant to be suitable for the times and the particular situations and challenges being lived.⑬

These convictions were the motivation for many Chinese scholars, including Confucians, to serve the Mongols and urge them to produce laws for the empire. While they were interested in Chinese culture being protected, they were convinced that any laws needed to come from the legitimate ruler, and that some changes might be needed to adapt the laws for the current times. This is why they approached the Qa'ans and asked them to issue laws. This would only be the case, however, if they considered the Mongols to be the legitimate rulers of China.

The opinions of southern Song loyalists, scholar-officials who refused to serve the new dynasty due to their attachment to the Confucian idea of loyalty, have long colored the historiography.⑭ However, in fact the Mongols were accepted relatively quickly as legitimate, particularly in northern China, thereby enabling many who were educated in the Chinese tradition to work for and with the Mongols. Many of the inhabitants, officials and scholars of the former Jin empire were favorably disposed towards the Mongols; the Khitans in particular, who could look back with nostalgia to the Khitan Liao empire and many of whom resented Jin rule, welcomed the Mongols.⑮

Many Confucian scholars stressed the value of serving the government; some actively

---

⑩ Langlois, "Law, Statecraft, and The Spring and Autumn Annals," p. 94; Langlois, "Political thought in Chin-hua under Mongol rule," pp. 165-8; Franke,"Jurchen Customary Law and Chinese Law of the Chin Dynasty," pp. 216, 224-6; Franke, "The legal system of the Chin dynasty," pp. 390-2.

⑪ McKnight, "From statute to precedent: an introduction to Sung law and its transformation," pp. 117-123.

⑫ Langlois, "Law, Statecraft, and The Spring and Autumn Annals," p. 98.

⑬ Hu Zhiyu, Zazhu, p. 166; Langlois, "Political thought in Chin-hua under Mongol rule," pp. 181-4.

⑭ Aubin, "The rebirth of Chinese rule in times of trouble: North China in the early thirteenth century," pp. 121, 126, 129.

⑮ Rachewiltz, "Personnel and Personalities in North China," pp. 96-7.

Rachewiltz, "Personnel and Personalities in North China," pp. 96-7.

Aubin, "The rebirth of Chinese rule in times of trouble," p. 142.

encouraged their students to serve the Mongols.⑯ They saw a law code and appropriate laws as essential for the empire. The close connection between Confucianism and the desire to obey laws made by the Emperor is shown by the Mumin zhonggao 牧民忠告 "Frank Advice for Magistrates," written by Zhang Yanghao 張養浩 (1270-1329). Although the work is suffused with Confucian principles, he still states: "Now the law is [the law of] the Son of Heaven. If the people should violate it, they violate the law of the Son of Heaven."⑰

Thus, rather than being a discouragement from working together with the Mongols, Confucianism was on the contrary a strong motivating factor for working together with them, including in regards to legal matters. While Confucian ideals may have prevented a minority of former officials from serving the Yuan, many others had as their aim to 'civilize' or sinicize the Mongols.⑱ In particular, some were motivated to work for and with the Mongols precisely because they wanted to persuade the Qa'ans to issue new laws.

5. Chinese officials' requests for a law code

Requests for the Mongols to issue laws were frequent in the Yuan dynasty. In China there was the tradition that each dynasty should have its own legal code or lü, which was considered essential for preventing disorder. But in 1272, Qubilai declared the Taihelü, the legal code of the Jin dynasty, which had until then still been in use, as no longer valid. From then on, some scholars looked to earlier codes or even the Spring and Autumn Annals to provide a legal basis, while urging the Qa'ans to produce a new laws and a code.⑲

One of the earliest attempts to get the Mongol rulers' cooperation in lawmaking is seen in the Yuan Shi biography of Guo Baoyu郭寶玉, a former Jin commander who submitted to the Mongols in 1211. For him, a new dynasty meant that new laws were required: "When a dynasty is just being established it is appropriate to issue new regulations."⑳

Guo Baoyu was only the first of a long list of Chinese who petitioned the Mongols to produce laws for the empire. Wang Yun王惲 (1227-1304) came from an important legal family that had served the Jin dynasty for many years, while his father spent much

---

⑯ Langlois, "Political thought in Chin-Hua under Mongol rule," p. 163.

⑰ Zhang Yanghao, *Mumin zhonggao,* p. 297, translation taken from Langlois "Law, Statecraft, and The Spring and Autumn Annals," p. 103.

⑱ Jay, *A change in dynasties,* pp. 249, 255-6.

⑲ Langlois, "Statecraft, and the Spring and Autumn Annals," pp. 92-3.

⑳ Yuan Shi, ch. 149, p. 3521, translation taken from Buell, Tribe, 'qan' and 'ulus', pp. 112-113.

time in studying the Confucian classics. In 1268, he proposed that a new code should be adopted.[21] Since this proposal was made before the Jin code had been officially abrogated by Qubilai, his motivation in calling for a new code was not simply the absence of a code but the conviction that a new dynasty should have a new code appropriate for the times. He even recommended using elements from the zhasa, which was believed to the law code of the Mongols.[22]

Hao Jing郝經, from a family of distinguished Confucian sholars, became an advisor to Qubilai Khan. In his memorandums, he urged Qubilai to establish a complete system of laws, "a civil government based on impartial and universal laws."[23] In 1262, Qubilai ordered his senior official Shi Tianze 史天澤 and his advisor and Confucian scholar Yao Shu姚樞 to prepare a Chinese code (which was never promulgated).[24] The delay prompted Wei Qu魏初 to also memorialize about a code and in 1271, he drew attention to the need to update the laws in each dynasty:

"As to li (rites), yüeh (music), hsing (punishment), and cheng (government) they are transitional and are to be modified or expanded according to circumstances nor can they be fixed by a [permanent] code [···]. If [we] expunge [from the T'ai-ho lu] items esteemed by Chin customs as well as laws established by Chin decrees, and then add decrees and rules issued since the beginning of [our] dynasty as well as the established precedents, then a text can be completed and it will become the Chih-yuan Hsin-lü [Chih-Yuan New Statutes].."[25]

Around 1274, Zhao Liangbi 趙良弼 made a similar request to Qubilai that it would be advisable to establish unified laws so as to suppress evil bureaucrats.[26] In 1283, Cui Yu 崔彧, a minister in the Board of Punishments, urged the establishment of unified laws.[27] The efforts of another official, He Rongzu何榮祖, who had started his career as a clerk and had held various positions in the government, were blocked by powerful minister Sengge until his downfall. Subsequently, however, He Rongzu何榮祖 was appointed Senior Chief Councillor of the Central Secretariat, and was able to work with the Mongols on the *Zhiyuan xinge*至元新格 which was promulgated in 1291, and also on a second compilation called Dade lüling 大元律令.

Another official, Zheng Jiefu鄭介夫, held that the Dade lüling needed revision. He

---

㉑ Wang Yun, Qiujian xiansheng daquan wenji, 90:3b.

㉒ Ch'en, Chinese legal tradition, pp. 8-9.

㉓ Lynn, "Hao Ching," p. 354.

㉔ Yuan Shi, ch. 5, p. 82; ch. 158, p. 3714.

㉕ Ch'en, Chinese legal tradition, pp. 14-5.

㉖ Yuan Shi, ch. 159, p. 3746.

㉗ Yuan Shi, ch. 173, p. 4040.

submitted a memorial to the throne saying that one needs to look at both ancient Chinese laws as well as more recent laws including decisions of the current dynasty. Both the Chinese and the Mongol elements should be harmonized into a single document.[28] After Wuzong succeeded to the throne in 1307, the Central Secretariat submitted a memorial in December 1307 or January 1308:

"Statutes and ordinances are urgent matters for governing the state and are to be modified or expanded in accordance with circumstances. [···] Shih-tsu [Qubilai] once again issued an edict ordering that the *T-ai-ho lü* of the Chin be not applied and that elder ministers, who thoroughly understand the laws, consult [laws of] the ancient and present times so as to establish new [legal] institutions. So far it has not been carried out. We, your subjects, think that statutes and ordinances are serious matters and should not be lightly discussed. [We therefore] request that the t'iao-ko put into practice since the succession of Shih-tsu [Qubilai] to the throne be examined and unified [into one code] so that [it] may be observed and put into practice."[29]

Permission was granted for this request to be implemented and it resulted in the compilation of the Dade dianzhang大德典章, of which some fragments are extant.[30]

A further request was made in 1309 by ministers of the Secretariat for State Affairs. This request was accepted but remained without effect since Emperor Wuzong died in 1311 before action could be taken:

"In our country the lands are vast and the people are many, beyond that of former dynasties. The statutes (*ko*) and precedents (*li*) of previous reigns are inconsistent. Officials who enforce the laws issue light and heavy punishments as they like. We request that the more than 9,000 statutes (*ling*) implemented from the reign of T'ai-tsu [Chinggis Khan, i. e. 1206 on] be edited to eliminate the superfluous and render them consistent, and be made into fixed regulations (*ting-chih*)."[31]

Renzong, who took action on the request first approved by Wuzong, was urged on by Xie Rang謝讓 (1246-1311), a minister of the Board of Punishments: "From ancient times to the present day, those who had the country have all had statutes to support their rulings. How could a conscientious holy dynasty like ours have no laws to follow and thus let bureaucrats indulge themselves and people suffer evilness?"[32] The result was a text completed in 1316 with decrees (*zhaozhi*), statutes (*tiaoge*) and precedents (*duanli*), with

---

㉘ Chen, Chinese legal tradition, pp. 19-20.

㉙ Yuan Shi, ch. 22, p. 492, translation taken from Ch'en, Chinese legal tradition, pp. 21-22.

㉚ Ch'en, Chinese legal tradition, p. 22.

㉛ Yuan Shi, ch. 23, p. 516, translation by Birge in: Women, property, and Confucian reaction, p. 212.

㉜ Yuan Shi, ch. 176, p. 4111, translation by Ch'en, Chinese legal tradition, p. 24.

documents covering the years 1234 to 1316. It was expanded and promulgated in 1321 as Dayuan tongzhi大元通制.

From these requests, several of which suggest the use of Mongol laws as well as those that had been promulgated since the Yuan dynasty had been in power, show the officials' belief in the importance of having a new code, which trumped any desire of keeping Chinese laws 'pure' or free from Mongol influence. They considered having up-to-date laws, even if they contained Mongol influences, to be preferable to having outdated 'Chinese' laws. This is what on the Chinese side enabled the discussion and negotiation about the laws that were to be enforced in China.

6. The attitude of local officials

The Chinese officials' requests for the Qa'ans to produce laws would however have been ineffective if the laws had not been respected at the local level. The link between the local level and the central government was in fact crucial. Under the Yuan dynasty, the central government had the same role in the eyes of local officials which it had had during previous dynasties: firstly to make and circulate appropriate legislation, and secondly to act as 'court of appeal' for any difficult cases which could not be decided locally.

That local officials under Mongol rule expected the government to fulfill both these roles is shown both by the contents and by the very existence of a legal compilation known as Yuan Dian Zhang. This was a compilation which was commercially produced in southern China of central government rulings and precedents, organized by topic and date.[33] As a commercial publication, it shows that there was demand for this type of manual, which would have come mainly from those officials dealing with legal matters at various levels of the government. It shows a deep level of interest in and engagement with the laws made by the Yuan rulers, unlike anything that happened in the Ilkhanate or elsewhere in the Mongol Empire.

More evidence that cases were indeed being forwarded up to the central government and were receiving answers come from documents excavated in Qara-khoto, the 'black city' (known in Chinese as 'Hei cheng' 黑城). These documents are one more piece of evidence showing that at least some cases did in fact go up to the central government for review. Because the collection contains some documents from the Qara-Khoto region and some produced in Dadu, one can see how communication regarding such legal matters was very quick. From the Emperor at Dadu, documents could reach Qara-khoto in less

---

㉝ Birge, Women, property, and Confucian reaction, p. 213.

than 20 days.[34]

This is not to suggest that the system of sending cases up for review was entirely free of problems or faultlessly efficient. It is quite possible for example that corrupt officials could have kept some cases from being forwarded up for review; however this may be, the fact that a significant number nevertheless reached the central government shows that there was not only theoretical but also practical reliance on the central government at the local level, which was one of the ways in which Mongol influence could reach the local level and have concrete effects. This means that edicts of the Qa'ans were usually heeded, unlike in the Ilkhanate where firstly less legislation was produced, and secondly, that which was produced was not necessarily respected at the local level.[35]

In terms of the levirate, it is this deference to the Emperor's authority which made Qubilai's attempt to impose it even possible. In none of the other khanates did the Mongols try to impose the levirate, but in China they could because the local officials actively sought out and mostly followed decrees issued by the Qa'an. As for the influence on beatings, military exile, and the death penalty, such changes would not have influenced the local level if officials had not been attentive to the Qa'an.

7. Conclusion

The uniqueness of Yuan history with regards to legal matters lies not so much in the extensive bureaucracy but in the willingness of that bureaucracy to look to the Mongol rulers as the legitimate source of law. This has not so far been recognized as a major factor underlying the extent of Mongol influence in law in China. Both Confucianism and legalism saw the emperor as the legitimate source of law and therefore indirectly led to Mongol influence. Local officials, just like many of the Chinese scholars and officials in the central government, looked to the Yuan emperors as the source of law. This was not only a theoretical opinion, rather they relied on the emperor's edicts in practice to perform their jobs day to day.

The effects of this can be seen in the changes in punishments which affected not only Mongols, but also Chinese, including 'ordinary' Chinese at the local level. They can be explained through the willingness of not only the Mongols but also the Chinese to work together in creating and implementing appropriate laws. Only the flexibility of the Yuan dynasty rulers and elite together with the enthusiasm of the Chinese advisors and officials

---

㉞ Chen Zhiying "'Yuan Huangqing yuannian (gong yuan 1312) shi'eryue Yijinai lu xingfang wenshu' chutan," p. 44.

㉟ Farquhar, The government of China, p. 169.

could have led to this influence of Mongol law within China.

Bibliography

Aubin, Françoise, "The Rebirth of Chinese Rule in Times of Trouble: North China in the Early Thirteenth Century," in: *Foundations and Limits of State Power in China,* ed. by S. R. Schram, London: School of Oriental and African Studies, 1987.

Birge, B, *Women, property, and Confucian reaction in Sung and Yüan China (960-1368),* Cambridge: Cambridge University Press, 2002.

Buell, Paul D, *Tribe, 'qan' and 'ulus' in early Mongol China: some prolegomena to Yüan history,* Ph.D. thesis, University of Washington, 1977.

Carpini, John of Plano, *History of the Mongols, trans.* by Christopher Dawson, in: The Mongol Mission, New York: Sheed and Ward, 1955.

Chen Zhiying陈志英, "'Yuan Huangqing yuannian (gong yuan 1312) shi'eryue Yijinai lu xingfang wenshu' chutan '元皇庆元年(公元1312 年) 十二月亦集乃路刑房文书' 初探, *Neimenggu shihui kexue*内蒙古社会科学, 25/5 (2004), pp. 41-44.

Ch'en, Paul Heng-Chao, *Chinese legal tradition under the Mongols: the Code of 1291 as reconstructed,* Princeton, NJ: Princeton University Press, 1979.

Farquhar, David M., *The government of China under Mongolian rule: a reference guide,* Stuttgart: Franz Steiner, 1990.

Franke, H., "Jurchen Customary Law and Chinese Law of the Chin Dynasty," in: *State and Law in East Asia,* ed. by D. Eikemeir and H. Franke, Wiesbaden: Harrassowitz, 1981, pp. 215-33, reprinted in *Studies on the Jurchens and the Chin Dynasty,* ed. by Herbert Franke and Hok-lam Chan, Aldershot, Hampshire; Brookfield, VT: Variorum, 1997.

Franke, H., "The legal system of the Chin dynasty," in: *Collected Studies on Sung Dynasty Dedicated to Professor James T. C. Liu in Celebration of his Seventieth Birthday,* ed. by Tsuyoshi Kinugawa, Tokyo: Dohosha, 1989, pp. 387-409, reprinted in *Studies on the Jurchens and the Chin Dynasty,* ed. by Herbert Franke and Hok-lam Chan, Aldershot, Hampshire; Brookfield, VT: Variorum, 1997.

Gu, Sharron, *The Boundaries of Meaning And the Formation of Law: Legal Concepts And Reasoning in the English, Arabic, And Chinese Traditions,* Montreal; Ithaca: McGill-Queen's University Press, 2006.

Hodous, Florence, "The quriltai as a legal institution in the Mongol empire," *Central Asiatic Journal,* Vol. 56 (2012/2013), pp. 87-102.

Hu Zhiyu胡祇遹, Zazhu 雜著 [*Zishan daquanji* 紫山大全集, ch. 21] in : *Lixue zhinan*吏學指南, ed. by Huang Shijian 黄時鑑, Hangzhou 杭州: Zhejiang guji chubanshe 浙江古籍出版社, 1988.

Jackson, P, "The Mongols and the Faith of the Conquered," in: *Mongols, Turks, and Others: Eurasian Nomads and the Sedentary World,* ed. by Reuven Amitai and Michal Biran, Leiden; Boston: Brill, 2005, pp. 245-290.

Jay, Jennifer, *A change in dynasties: loyalism in thirteenth-century China,* Washington: Centre for East Asian Studies, 1991.

Langlois, John D, "Political Thought in Chin-hua under Mongol Rule," in: *China under Mongol Rule,* ed. by John D. Langlois, Princeton; Guildford: Princeton University Press, 1981, pp. 137-185.

Langlois, J. D, "Law, Statecraft, and the Spring and Autumn Annals in *Yüan Political Thought," in: Yüan thought: Chinese thought and religion under the Mongols,* ed. by Hoklam Chan and Wm. Theodore de Bary, New York: Columbia University Press, 1982, pp. 89-152.

Lynn, Richard J, "Hao Ching," in: *In the service of the Khan: eminent personalities of the early Mongol-Yüan period (1200-1300),* ed. by Igor de Rachewiltz et al., Wiesbaden: Harrassowitz, 1993, pp. 348-370.

McKnight, B. E, "From Statute to Precedent: An Introduction to Sung Law and its Transformation," in: McKnight, B. E. (ed.), *Law and the State in Traditional East Asia: six studies on the sources of East Asian law,* Honolulu: University of Hawaii Press, 1987, pp. 111-131.

Rachewiltz, Igor de, "Personnel and Personalities in North China in the Early Mongol Period," Journal of the Economic and Social History of the Orient, 9/1-2 (1966), pp. 88-144.

Secret History of the Mongols, a Mongolian epic chronicle of the thirteenth century, trans. and commentary by Igor de Rachewiltz, Leiden; Boston: Brill, 2004.

Wang Yun王惲, *Qiujian xiansheng daquan wenji* 秋澗先生大全文集, reproduced in: Sibu congkan 四部叢刊, Shanghai上海: Shangwu yinshuguan商務印書館, 1919.

Wu Bo武波, "Yuandai xingfa tixi zhong de chujun zhidu tanxi 元代刑法体系中的出军制度探析," *Shanxi Shida Xuebao*山西师大学报 33/2 (2006), pp. 79-84.

Xu Yuchun徐昱春, *Yuandai fadingxing kaobian* 元代法定刑考辨, PhD Thesis, Xinan Zhengfa daxue西南政法大学, 2009.

Zhou Sicheng 周思成, "Yuandai xingfa zhong de suowei 'qiao' xing yu 'you zhan wu jiao' zhi shuo bianzheng 元代刑法中的所谓"敲"刑与"有斩无绞"之说辨正," *Beijing shifan daxue xuebao 北京师范大学学报* 2015 (2): 154-159.

馬可·波羅與蒙古法：擴大文明的範圍，縮小野蠻的範圍

Florence Hodous　撰；
高　宇　趙佰悅　譯；馬曉林　校

前　言

本文擬考察馬可·波羅對於蒙古人法律的認識。蒙古人是當時世界上最偉大帝國的締造者。在研究蒙古法時，《馬可·波羅行紀》並不是經常被引用的文本之一。這位威尼斯人不同於一些歷史學家和政府官員，如服務於蒙古人的志費尼和伊利汗國宰相拉施特，或者是曾公開斥責蒙古人的馬穆魯克王朝史學家馬克里齊，馬可·波羅對蒙古法的談論相對較少。不過，《馬可·波羅行紀》揭示了歐洲人是如何理解蒙古法，以及蒙古法本身爲何。

回到關於馬可·波羅是否到過中國的爭論中，如果批評他在《馬可·波羅行紀》中沒有提到的所有事物，如遺漏了長城、筷子、漢字等重要文化標誌[①]，那麼這個相當奇怪的遺漏列表中也可以加上成吉思汗的大札撒。雖然很多史料談及了這個由成吉思汗或其繼任者之一發布的法典，但都沒有再現大札撒的內容，也沒有給予合理解釋[②]。儘管馬可·波羅沒提到"大札撒"一詞，但是他對蒙古人的法律提供了一些非常準確的認識，這一事實將支持他確實去過中國的推論。

除此之外，馬可·波羅對蒙古法的總體評價也支持他確實去過中國這一觀點。他那

---

① Hans Ulrich Vogel, *Marco Polo Was in China: New Evidence from Currencies, Salts and Revenues*, Leiden: Brill, 2012, p. 43.

② 关于大札撒，参Florence Hodous, *Toluid Dynamics of Asia: Flexibility, Legality and Identity within Toluid Institutions,* PhD Thesis, SOAS, University of London, 2013, pp. 34-56; Chogt, *Chingisu Kan no hō*, Tokyo: Yamakawa Shuppansha, 2010, pp. 48-49; David Morgan, "The' Great Yasa of Chinggis Khan' revisited", in *Mongols, Turks, and Others*, eds. Reuven Amitai and Michal Biran, Leiden: BRILL, 2005, pp. 291-308; Denise Aigle, "Le Grand Jasaq de Gengis-Khan, l' Empire, la culture mongole et la Sharî' a", *Journal of the Economic and Social History of the Orient*, 47/1 (2004), pp. 39-44; David Morgan, "The' Great Yāsā of Chingiz Khān' and Mongol law in the Īlkhānate", *Bulletin of the School of Oriental and African Studies,* 49 (1986), pp. 163-76; David Ayalon, "The Great Yasa of Chingiz Khan: a Reexamination, part A," *Studia Islamica,* 33 (1971), 101-7, 114-6.

個時代的歐洲人並非都知道蒙古人有法律和法律制度，而且他對蒙古人和其他更偏遠的“野蠻民族”的描述也是有明顯差異的。蒙古人被描述爲擁有法律制度；但地處偏遠地區的野蠻人則沒有任何法律或習慣法。因此本文認爲，《馬可・波羅行紀》反映了一個去過中國的人的視角，他瞭解蒙古人，並且不把他們視作野蠻人。

大札撒在哪裏？

如上所述，《馬可・波羅行紀》中並沒有出現“大札撒”一詞。不過，它好像被間接提到了。因此，馬可・波羅認爲，蒙古人的行爲受到他們自己法律的約束。例如，馬可・波羅記錄了阿魯渾指責即將被廢黜的伊利汗阿合馬・帖古迭兒一事，如下：

> 此外，你們很清楚他是如何不遵守我們的法律的，他喪失了信仰，並且成爲一個［很邪惡］的撒拉遜人，還崇拜摩訶末，［侮辱了我們法律］③。

在這裏，馬可・波羅似乎間接提到了衆所周知的大札撒與伊斯蘭教法之間的對立，馬穆魯克王朝的作家一般將其上升爲與伊利汗國、蒙古帝國之間意識形態的鬥爭。根據這個觀點，蒙古人的確有自己的一套可以與伊斯蘭教法相匹敵的法律④。因此，阿合馬・帖古迭兒被指控放棄了蒙古法而支持伊斯蘭教法。另一段與此類似：

> 但我告訴你，如今他們淡化了很多，［並且已經放棄了一些習慣法］，那些留居契丹的人......在生活方式、行爲舉止和風俗習慣上遵從［這些地區］的偶像教，［很大程度上］放棄了他們自己的法律。並且，這些留居黎凡特地區的人［十分］遵從撒拉遜人的行爲方式，［並信奉伊斯蘭教和伊斯蘭教法］⑤。

在這些段落中，馬可・波羅承認蒙古人有他們自己的法律。法律有時候會與宗教混爲一談。他就是不僅熟悉與“宗教”緊密聯繫的伊斯蘭教法，而且非常重視基督教義中的法律部分⑥。事實上，這種宗教與法律的混合，可能是歐洲人或穆斯林認爲蒙古人有“大札撒”的一個原因，而且認爲“大札撒”是對社會生活各個方面有限制的整體性的法律⑦。這樣，我們就可以看到“大札撒”的觀念是如何出現的，以及它如何在蒙古人

③ Marco Polo, *The Description of the World*, trans. by A. C. Moule and P. Pelliot, London: Routledge, 1938, 2 vols, p. 460. 穆勒和伯希和譯本中文字和短語的斜體部分內容不見於法國國家圖書館所藏的法文版，而見於其他抄本。另參馮承鈞譯《馬可・波羅行紀》，上海：上海古籍出版社，2014年，124頁。

④ Denise Aigle, “Le Grand Jasaq de Gengis-Khan, l’ Empire, la culture mongole et la Sharî’ a”, p. 33, pp. 36-37.

⑤ Marco Polo, *The Description of the World*, pp. 174-175. 另參馮承鈞譯《馬可・波羅行紀》, 423頁。

⑥ 馬可・波羅經常談到的是基督法，而不是“宗教信仰”。Marco Polo, *The Description of the World*, p. 78, p. 156, see also p. 350.

⑦ 在承認蒙古人有這樣的框架時，相比較對於野蠻人的刻板印象，他對於蒙古人的觀點更近似於歐洲人對穆斯林的觀點，將其視作某種異端，但在某些方面與基督教相似。W. R. Jones, “The Image of the Barbarian in Medieval Europe”, *Comparative Studies in Society and History,* 13/4 (Oct. 1971), p. 392.

與其他文化的交流中取得如此重要的地位。

然而，這段話的重要性就是在於馬可・波羅承認蒙古人有管理他們生活的法律。當談到“基督法”時，他所指的不僅僅是“基督教義”的另一種說法，而是指法律框架，這也是他身份認同的一部分。蒙古人和歐洲人是不一樣的，因爲他們有不一樣的法律。但不管怎樣，他們是有法律的。

作爲文明標誌的法律

蒙古人有他們自己的法律和法律制度，馬可・波羅對此有明確的認識。這與當時歐洲人對待“野蠻民族”的看法相悖。此種看法也反映在《馬可・波羅行紀》中，但指的是其他人，而不是蒙古人。這很重要，因爲法律像宗教一樣，是歐洲人區分文明民族與野蠻民族的標誌之一。因此，相較於其他野蠻民族，馬可・波羅將蒙古人視爲文明民族。

例如馬修・帕里斯（Mathew Paris），不過他對蒙古人的研究不是來源於第一手資料，但早於馬可・波羅半個世紀，他筆下的蒙古人既不知道摩西律法，也不知道任何其他法律[8]。兩個世紀後，葡萄牙國王杜阿爾特一世（Duarte I）在給教皇尤金四世（Eugenius Ⅳ）的信中表達了類似的看法。他在描述加那利群島的居民時寫道：“他們沒有共同的宗教信仰，也不受法律的約束，缺乏正常的社會交往，像動物一樣生活在這個國家。”[9]

《馬可・波羅行紀》中確實有符合上述模式的描述，即沒有法律的人們像動物一樣生活著。但是，他指的並非蒙古人。其中一種人在“黑暗之州”，馬可・波羅似乎描述的是生活在北極圈裏的人：

> 離王國極北的地方是一個被叫做“黑暗［之谷］”的地區……那裏的人們沒有［使其臣服的國王和任何］統治者，［他們沒有文化並且行爲粗野］（引者按：剌木學本作：他們沒有習慣法[10]），［並且］像動物一樣生活著[11]。

這樣的描述與上面杜阿爾特信中所說的內容類似。他們沒有自己的國王，也沒有任何能規範他們生活的習慣法，這顯示出他們的社會和民衆生活尚未開化。總之，他們像野獸一樣生活著。這可能反映了一個事實，這些人住得太偏遠，以致於馬可・波羅在遠

---

⑧ Matthew Paris, *Chronica Majora*, vol. 4, ed. H. R. Luard, London: Longman, 1872-1883, p. 78.

⑨ Peter Hulme, “Tales of Distinction: European Ethnography and the Caribbean”, in: *Implicit understandings: observing, reporting, and reflecting on the encounters between Europeans and other peoples in the early modern era*, edited by Stuart B. Schwartz, Cambridge, New York: Cambridge University Press, 1994, p. 187.

⑩ Giovanni Battista Ramusio, *Dei Viaggi di Messer Marco Polo, gentiluomo veneziano*, critical digital edition by Samuela Simion and Eugenio Burgio, Ca’ Foscari University of Venice: 2015, book 3, chapter 45: http://virgo.unive.it/ecf-workflow/books/Ramusio/commenti/R_III_45-main.html

⑪ Marco Polo, *The Description of the World*, p. 473. 另參見馮承鈞譯《馬可・波羅行紀》，434頁。

行中遇到的民族都把他們視爲野蠻人。

有類似的章節談到了其他民族。例如，關於唐兀人，馬可·波羅寫道："［此外］，他們娶表姐妹爲妻子，［除了生母外，］他們［也被允許］娶自己父親的妻子，［以及兄弟或其他所有關係的妻子］。［並且］他們不認爲我們有的［非常］多的罪惡是［致命的］罪惡，因爲他們就［以這樣的方式］生活著，像［沒有法律約束的］動物一樣。"⑫更有趣的一點是，雖然馬可·波羅也記載了蒙古人的收繼婚，但他沒有做出相同的判斷，即他們沒有法律或他們活得像野獸。可見，他的看法是清楚的：蒙古人不是野蠻人，只是和歐洲人在法律上有一些不一樣的地方。

對蒙古法的準確認識

《馬可·波羅行紀》除了描述作爲管理生活方式的法律的擁有者蒙古人外，還體現了馬可·波羅在游歷期間對現行法律的一些具體且準確的認識。例如，他記載了對盜竊行爲的懲處，如下：

> 如一人偷盜了［十五頭牛］或一匹馬或其他東西，爲此他理應失去生命，被斬爲兩段［處死］。那麼，確實，如果他能賠付，並賠償所偷物品九倍［的價值］，他可逃脱［死罪，他們也不會用刀處決他。］⑬

在蒙古征服中頻頻施加的懲處措施，把人處以腰斬，儘管這與蒙古的歷史或文化沒有密切的聯繫，但九倍賠償出現在整個內亞歷史中。因爲偷盜牲畜，特别是馬，對牧民意味著嚴重的侵犯。這些牲畜而非任何不動產，代表著包括蒙古人在內的很多內亞民族的財富。九倍賠償條目出現在其他法典中，《俺答汗法典》、1640年《蒙古—衛拉特法典》，以及《喀爾喀法典》（1709—1770年間的一系列法規）⑭。

另外，馬可·波羅的敘述也反映了蒙古人執行不流血的死刑方法，這次以故事的形式而非描述的方式呈現。他描述了乃顏被處死的過程，乃顏是成吉思汗異母弟的後代⑮，事情發生在1287年，如下：

> 當大汗得知乃顏被擒時，［他因此感到非常高興和快樂，］並下令［立即］將其處死。［大汗全然不見乃顏，免得因爲感其爲同族而產生憐惜之情。］於是乃顏按照我要告訴你們的這樣一種方式被處死了。乃顏被［緊緊

---

⑫ Marco Polo, *The Description of the World*, p. 160. 另參見馮承鈞譯：《馬可·波羅行紀》，104、120頁。

⑬ Marco Polo, *The Description of the World*, p. 175. 另參見馮承鈞譯：《馬可·波羅行紀》，124頁。

⑭ As observed by Hans Ulrich Vogel, *Marco Polo Was in China: New Evidence from Currencies, Salts and Revenues*, p. 56; Françoise Aubin, "Some Characteristics of Penal Legislation among the Mongols (13th–21st Centuries)", in: *Central Asian Law: an Historical Overview. A Festschrift for the Ninetieth Birthday of Herbert Franke*, ed. by Wallace Johnson and Irina F. Popova, Topeka, Kansas: Society for Asian Legal History, 2004, p. 141.

⑮ 姚大力《關於元朝"東諸侯"的幾個考釋》，載於《蒙元制度與政治文化》，北京：北京大學出版社，2011年，434頁。

地］捆住，［束縛］在一塊氈子裏，並被殘酷地拖拽、［拋扔］至死。［然後他們將他置留其中，乃顏以此種方式結束了生命。］大汗以此種方式處死乃顏的原因是，［韃靼人說，］他不希望皇室宗系的血液灑在地上，［或向天哀嘆］，或見之於太陽和天空，［也不希望任何動物觸碰乃顏的肢體。］[16]

許多其他材料證實了，有像乃顏一樣的人，以不流血的形式被處死，這符合蒙古族薩滿教信仰。即保留血液以便返回大自然是人與自然世界（特別是動物）生命力交換的一部分，這是薩滿教世界觀的核心，是蒙古人只給予強大和高貴敵人的"特權"。然而，不管是其他遊歷者還是蒙古官員，如志費尼和哈姆杜拉・穆斯塔菲（Hamd Allah Mustawfi），都沒有意識到這種行爲更深層的內涵。所以即使馬可・波羅沒有給出確切的原因，也並沒有顯得他對此太過無知[17]。

此外，關於蒙古法律的實施，《馬可・波羅行紀》提到了另一個有趣的現象，在描述蒙古狩獵時，馬可・波羅說：

一個叫作"孛闌奚赤"的男爵，［用我們的話說］意爲保管無主之物的人。我告訴你，如果一個人［偶然］拾得一匹馬，或一把劍，或一只鳥或是其他［丟失的、無主的］東西，並且他無法找到物件主人，［然後此物就會立刻被］交送至男爵，然後［小心翼翼地］看管、保存［直到物主出現］。找到［任何可能丟失的東西］的人，［一定要立即交還給它的主人。］［另一方面，如果撿拾者沒有這樣做，］如果他沒有及時將物品上交給男爵，他會被當做小偷抓起來（法語本：它是由男爵施行的）。此男爵駐紮在營地的最高處，立著［高聳的］旗幟，所以丟失東西［或是發現東西的］人都能立即［清楚地］看到他［在哪裏］[18]。

《馬可・波羅行紀》宮廷法語本（FB）明確地提到了懲處這些小偷是孛闌奚赤本人。這與帝國建立以前的蒙古現實相符，因爲那時的蒙古人除了薩滿巫師、鐵匠和吟遊詩人外，沒有任何專業人員[19]。法律職責沒有從其他職責中分離出來，所以每個當權者需要做出決定並強制執行[20]。

到忽必烈時期，這種情況隨著札魯忽赤（斷事官機構）的制度化發展發生了改變。雖然成吉思汗首先授予此稱號，但大約在1280年忽必烈設置了大宗正府[21]，並任命諸員

⑯ Marco Polo, *The Description of the World*, pp. 199-200. 另參見馮承鈞譯《馬可・波羅行紀》，150頁。

⑰ Hodous, Florence, "Faith and the Law: Religious Beliefs and the Death Penalty in the Ilkhanate," in: *The Mongols' Middle East*, ed. Bruno de Nicola, Leiden: BRILL, 2016, pp. 114-115.

⑱ Marco Polo, *The Description of the World*, pp. 230-231; Marco Polo, *Le Livre de Marco Polo*, ed. M. G. Pauthier, Paris: Firmin Didot, 1865, p. 307. 另參見馮承鈞譯《馬可・波羅行紀》，188—189頁。

⑲ Thomas T. Allsen, *Commodity and exchange in the Mongol Empire: a cultural history of Islamic textiles*, New York: Cambridge University Press, 1997, p. 30.

⑳ Florence Hodous, *Toluid Dynamics of Asia: Flexibility, Legality and Identity within Toluid Institutions,* pp. 80-85.

㉑ 劉曉《元代大宗正府考述》，《內蒙古大學學報（哲學社會科學版）》1996年第2期，7頁。

札魯忽赤，主要處理涉及蒙古人的案件。儘管如此，很有可能孛闌奚赤至少在狩獵方面繼續持有以往的權力，或者馬可·波羅的敘述反映了札魯忽赤在早期蒙古狩獵中並不起作用[22]。孛闌奚赤懲處違抗他們的人，這反映了蒙古法的實施情況，並且證明了馬可·波羅記敘的準確性。

對元朝法律的準確認識

馬可·波羅除了對蒙古法的實踐有深刻的認識外，他的敘述也準確地反映了受蒙古影響的元朝法律制度。這是任何其他西方旅行者都沒有提及的。例如，關於笞杖他寫道：

> 他們以我現在要向你描述的方式維護公平［和判決］……的確，當一個人偷了一件［不犯死罪的］小東西，他們判處他以笞杖。］［政府用棍棒至少］打其七下，［如果他偷了兩件東西］，［被打］十七下，或者［如果三件東西］，［打］二十七下，或三十七、四十七下，並以此種方式［有時］增至一百零七下。［每偷盜一件東西］，總是增加十下，根據他所盜物品和犯罪程度治罪，他們中的許多人因笞杖而死[23]。

此種敘述符合元朝的事實，因爲它是歷代王朝中唯一一個以“七”爲笞杖尾數的王朝。甚至是最大量刑，即一百零七，這完全準確，並且反映了元朝法律的實施情況[24]。此前歷代王朝刑量以“十”爲單位，如十、二十和三十，直到一百一十。但忽必烈汗改變了這種情況，換以“七”結尾[25]。

對數字“七”的重視反映了蒙古人的偏好，事實上，在《蒙古秘史》中這個數字已經與懲罰有關了。其中，笞打包含三下、七下或三十七下：

> 若輪番護衛士中有人誤班（未到），則誤班者應受杖責三下的教訓；第二次誤班，應受杖責七下的教訓。若該人身體無病，又未向該班長官（怯薛長）請假，而第三次誤班，應受杖責三十七下的教訓；這是該人已不願爲朕效力，當流放遠方[26]。

拉施特也注意到了蒙古刑罰的這一特征。雖然以數字“七”爲尾數的處罰並未在伊利汗國法律中正式出現，但是伊利汗施行此刑罰，臣子也偶爾施行。例如，在1303年，

---

[22] 關於孛闌奚赤，見Miya，Noriko（宮紀子），“ Notes on “bulārghūchī”, *Journal of Oriental Studies*, 2011, pp. 693-740.

[23] Marco Polo, *The Description of the World*, p. 175. 另參見馮承鈞譯《馬可·波羅行紀》，124頁。

[24] 徐昱春《元代法定刑考辯》，西南政法大學博士學位論文，2009年，44頁。

[25] （元）葉子奇《草木子》，北京：中華書局，1959年，64頁；徐昱春《元代法定刑考辯》，35頁。

[26] *Secret History of the Mongols, a Mongolian epic chronicle of the thirteenth century,* trans. and commentary by Igor de Rachewiltz, Leiden, Boston: Brill, 2004, p. 278, see also p. 227. 漢譯文據余大鈞譯註《蒙古秘史》，石家莊：河北人民出版社，2001年，377頁。

當合贊汗得知蒙古軍在敘利亞失利的消息時，他非常生氣，並且召開了一次忽里勒台大會來審判這些異密。他下令笞打他們八十七、七十七或三十七下㉗。

儘管，中國以外的蒙古汗也施行以“七”爲尾數的刑罰，但只有在中國成爲了一個一般性的法規，甚至影響到了當地的居民。正因如此，馬可・波羅對笞打數目，以及從七到一百零七明確範圍的詳盡認識，都強有力地證明他曾到過中國，因爲在其他地方很難獲得這些認識。

馬可・波羅對蒙古法的贊成態度

馬可・波羅不僅對蒙古法和元朝法律的實施有認識準確，而且對這些法律的態度也是中立的，或者說是積極的。這與他在蒙古帝國遊歷多年的經歷相符。雖然帝國之外的作家，如馬修・帕里斯或是馬穆魯克王朝的史學家經常對蒙古法持消極評價，但在帝國工作和生活的史學家，如志費尼和拉施特，對其有積極的評價。例如，當這些穆斯林作家提到蒙古的習俗和法律時，他們試圖說，這些習俗和法律與伊斯蘭教法不沖突，而且彰顯了大汗的強大和公正。

馬可・波羅的積極看法可見於他對忽必烈反穆斯林法的記錄，如下：

> 忽必烈注意到邪惡的撒拉遜教派無論所犯何罪均可被合法化，並且他們可以殺不遵循他們法律的任何人。因此，被詛咒的阿合馬和他的兒子們並不認爲自己作惡多端（引者按：阿合馬是忽必烈時期的一位權臣，其腐敗案暴露於他在1282年被殺之後）。忽必烈非常鄙視且痛惡它，他召撒拉遜人前來，禁止他們做其律法所允許的許多事情。他對撒拉遜人下令，他們娶妻時必須遵循韃靼人的法律，以及食肉時，他們不能像以前那洋割斷動物的咽喉，必須破腹㉘。

這段敘述清楚地表明馬可・波羅是如何贊同這條特定的法律的，以及忽必烈對穆斯林行爲的限制（事實上，這只是暫時的）。它反映出許多歐洲人渴望有一個強大的領導人來幫助他們對抗穆斯林㉙。

當然這條描述很準確，儘管這可能被認爲是馬可・波羅反對穆斯林態度的產物，但

㉗ Rashīd al-Dīn, *Jāmi' al-Tavārīkh*, ed. by M. Roushān and M. Mūsavī, Tehran: Nashr-i Alburz, 1994, 4 vols, p. 1315; Rashīd al-Dīn, *Rashiduddin Fazlullah's Jami'u't-tawarikh: Compendium of Chronicles*, trans. by Wheeler M. Thackston, Cambridge, MA: Department of Near Eastern Languages and Civilizations, Harvard University, 1998-1999, 3 vols, p. 658.

㉘ Marco Polo, *The Description of the World*, p. 216. 另參見馮承鈞譯《馬可・波羅行紀》，124頁。

㉙ 關於歐洲出現的長老約翰傳說的演變，參見Denise Aigle, *The Mongol Empire between Myth and Reality: Studies in Anthropological History*, pp. 41-65.

事實上，拉施特也記錄了同一事[30]，而且《元典章》中也保留了忽必烈的法令[31]。所以，馬可・波羅敘述的準確性再次得到證實。

結　論

正如馬可・波羅沒有提到“文明”的其他方面一樣，大札撒的遺漏是可以被解釋的。事實上，大札撒可能遠不如中世紀史學家所暗示的那麼重要。由於意識形態上的原因，它的重要性被誇大了，如馬穆魯克王朝的史學家想把它與伊斯蘭教法做對比，志費尼想要表明蒙古人有與伊斯蘭教法不沖突的法律。馬可・波羅雖然沒有提到“大札撒”一詞，但他的記述可能比其他歷史學家更接近真實的蒙古法。

如上所示，馬可・波羅關於蒙古法的記述基本上是準確的。從他對草原民族慣例的認識，如支付被盜牲畜九倍價值的賠償、執行不流血的死刑方式，以及元朝法律制度的一些細節，可以看出，與其他歷史學家相比，雖然他關於蒙古法記載的相對較少，但顯示出了他廣博的知識。特別是他對笞杖規則，以及忽必烈反穆斯林法令的敘述，表現了他對元朝法律具體實施方面的熟悉程度。

還需說明的是，與對亞洲一些民族法律的態度相反，馬可・波羅對蒙古法的態度是積極的，這傾向於證實他確實去過中國。馬可・波羅與當時歐洲人以及帝國以外的穆斯林對蒙古人的普遍態度不同，他傳達的大概不是外界對於蒙古法的看法，而是內部觀察。他清晰地論述了蒙古人不是野蠻人，更偏遠地區的民族才是，以此啟發了歐洲對蒙古人的認識，擴大了文明的範圍，縮小了野蠻的範圍。

Marco Polo and Mongol Law: Pushing Further the Limits of Barbarity

Florence Hodous

Although the work of Marco Polo is not the most detailed on Mongol law, it is nevertheless important for understanding European perceptions of the Mongols. Marco Polo is clear that the Mongols have their own laws, an important claim since the law was, in the eyes of many Europeans as well as East Asians, a major marker of civilization. Those who had laws or a legal code belonged to the category of civilized while other

---

[30] Rashīd al-Dīn, *Jāmi' al-Tavārīkh*, p. 921; Rashīd al-Dīn, *Rashiduddin Fazlullah's Jami'u't-tawarikh: Compendium of Chronicles*, p. 451.

[31] P. Ratchnevsky, “Rašīd ad-Dīn über die Mohammedanerverfolgungen in China unter Qubilai,” *Central Asiatic Journal,* 14 (1970), pp. 163-168; 陳高華、張帆、劉曉、黨寶海點校《元典章》，天津：天津古籍出版社，2011年，1893頁，“禁回回抹殺羊、做速納”（57/11a）。

peoples, those without law, were barbarians.

In addition, unlike many other authors, especially those writing from outside the Mongol Empire, Marco Polo seems to have a neutral or positive view of the laws of the Mongols. The information he provides is accurate, comparable with that found in the Persian historian Wassaf or the Secret History. This would tend to confirm that Marco Polo was indeed in China. More than that however, it is his attitude, the contrast between Mongols, who had laws, and other, further peoples, who did not, which reflects the view of a person who is familiar with them. Barbarity, on the other hand, is pushed further away, and applies only to peoples who are even further away and whom Marco Polo probably never met.

《皇輿全覽圖》東北大地測繪考

——以滿文檔案爲中心

承　志

引　言

（前略）其次要提出的問題就是這些教士在確定地點的時候曾否有過中國的助手。但是對於這一點他們仍然是緘默，一如他們對於那二百三十一枚小地圖所包含的經他們所採用的材料一樣。但對於一件事我們要持公正態度的就是中國人自己也是一樣的，在他們一方面也沒有聲明任何一個歐洲的教士爲地圖的合作者，雖然大部分的功績畢竟是要屬於這些教士的（後略）[①]。

福克司在《康熙時代耶穌會士所繪之中國地圖》一文中如此評論《皇輿全覽圖》缺乏相關資料。難道是真的緘默無語嗎？當我第一次閱讀到本文介紹的滿文檔案的時候，突然想起福克司談到參與繪製《皇輿全覽圖》的中外人士都沒有留下詳細資料的問題。耶穌會士與清廷合作進行的如此大規模的測繪活動，在發現滿文檔案之前，除了杜赫德《中華帝國全誌》[②]之外，我們確實看不到其他新的相關資料。但是事過七十六年，我們發現，滿文檔案其實是打破這一緘默的最好的材料。本文介紹的滿文檔案記載了清廷組織主持測繪隊伍中有耶穌會士三人包括在內的十八人的姓名（兩名畫匠不具姓名），還有與此相關的東北各地旗民積極協助調查的具體內容，這些在漢籍資料中鮮為少見，通過這些有利於了解東北各地旗人協助《皇輿全覽圖》測繪調查的具體活動，將會給我們提供更加豐富的歷史圖畫。

衆所周知，有關《皇輿全覽圖》的研究，迄今爲止主要以耶穌會士的書信報告以及記載他們傳教活動的編纂資料爲中心進行研究。在論述其繪製過程時，以往的研究主要側重於強調耶穌會士的功績，特別是通過他們利用科學知識測繪大地的方法等問題爲主

---

① 参看福克司（Walter Fuchs）《康熙時代耶穌會教士所繪之中國地圖》（Der Jesuiten-Atlas von China aus der K'anghsi Zeit，1941年），《中德學志》第三卷（顧華譯中文），433—441頁。

② Jean-Baptiste Du Halde, *Description géographique, historique, chronologique, politique, et physique de l'empire de la Chine et de la Tartarie chinoise, enrichie des cartes générales et particulieres de ces pays, de la carte générale et des cartes particulieres du Thibet, & de la Corée; & ornée d'un grand nombre de figures & de vignettes gravées en tailledouce, 1735.*本文簡稱《中華帝國全誌》。

展開討論這項大地測繪工程在中國地理、地圖史上的重要意義[③]。大多數論作會提及李約瑟評價的“不僅是亞洲當時所有地圖中最好的一種，而且比當時的所有歐洲地圖都好、更精確[④]”這一鼓舞人心的話語，這給我們的歷史地理工作者帶來了莫大的寬慰。但是，我們細究起來就會發現，對於《皇輿全覽圖》我們所知道的，其實可以說是微乎其微。我們在耶穌會士的資料中看到的主要是他們本身參與測繪活動的具體記載，但是，盡管測繪地點是在大清國統治下的中國各地進行，在耶穌會士的書信報告中，我們全然看不到主持這項測繪工程的清廷方面的負責人和參與協助人員的任何情況。先行研究基本上以杜赫德的《中華帝國全誌》的相關耶穌會士報告資料。我們在下面綜述先行研究就會發現這一點。事實上，許多相關研究都在重述杜赫德編(1735)的與耶穌會士測繪相關的內容和零散的一些漢文檔案資料。這一點值得我們思考。最近，滿文、蒙古文、漢文等檔案史料的進一步公布出版，使得我們逐漸看到清廷測繪隊伍的具體人員構成，還有各地協助測繪隊伍的具體活動。

康熙四十七年（1708），康熙帝爲繪製《皇輿全覽圖》，向東北派出包括三名傳教士在內的測繪隊伍，他們帶領向導、畫匠等人，越過山海關，沿著海邊到鳳凰城，然後

---

③ 有關《皇輿全覽圖》的研究，可謂不勝枚舉，這裏就不一一枚舉。主要研究可參看如下論著（按年代順序）：W. Fuchs, *Der Jesuiten-Atlas der Kanghsi-Zeit: seine Entstehungsgeschichte nebst Namensindices für die Karten der Mandjurei, Mongolei, Ostturkestan und Tibet*: mit Wiedergabe der Jesuiten-Karten in Originalgrösse, 1943. Fu-Jen-Universität, Peking. 三上正利《康熙時代におけるゼスイット派の測図事業》《史淵》（51）,1952年，25—50頁，船越昭生《鎖国日本にきた「康熙図」—わが国近代地理学の前駆》《東方学報》（38）,1967年，1—132頁。船越昭生《在華イエズス会士の地図作成とその影響について（明代史の諸問題（特集））《東洋史研究》27（4）,1969年，144—163頁。船越昭生《在華イエズス会士作成地図と鎖国時代の地図：『坤輿萬國全図』『康熙図』の評価・従来の研究をめぐって》《人文地理》24（2），1972年，187—207頁。太田美香《「皇輿全覧図」についての新史料--『宮中档康熙朝奏摺』収録の地図関係奏摺》《史観》（113），1985年，56—69頁，澤美香《檔案史料から見た「皇輿全覧図」とヨーロッパ技術》《史觀》121，1989年，53—64頁，船越昭生《「康熙図」と日本地図史--研究の回顧と展望》《奈良女子大学文学部研究年報》（35），1991年，1—20頁，早坂信子《「康熙銅版皇輿全覧図稿本」考察》《叡智の杜》（2），2005年，8—14頁，和《「康熙銅版皇輿全覧図稿本」考察》（その2）《叡智の杜》（3），2006年，14—20頁。中文論文參看馮寶琳《康熙〈皇輿全覽圖〉的測繪考略》《故宮博物院院刊》1985年第1期，23—35頁。以及李孝聰《馬國賢與銅版康熙〈皇輿全覽圖〉的印製－兼論早期中文地圖在歐洲的傳布與影響》，《東吴歷史學報》1998年第4期，139—154頁；李孝聰《記康熙《皇輿全覽圖》的測繪及其版本》《故宮學術季刊》第30卷第1期，2012年等。最近，利用東西方文獻進行詳細研究的論作參看Mario Cams（康言），The Early Qing Geographical Surveys (1708-1716) as a Case of Collaboration between the Jesuits and the Kangxi Court, *Sini-Wearern Cultural Relations Journal* 34, 2012，pp. 1-20. 和The China Maps of Jean-Baptiste Bourguignon d'Anville: Origins and Supporting Networks, Imago Mundi: The International Jounal for the History of Cartography, 66:1, 2013，pp. 51-69。

④ 全文應該是：（上略）与此同時，清王朝當時曾定了一个很精密的編圖計劃，這個計劃導致了《皇輿全覽圖》的問世，福克斯〔Fuchs（2，3）〕曾翻印過這部地圖集，並細緻地研究過它。這個計劃可能是耶穌會傳教士張誠（Jean Franciois Gerbilion）首先提出的，他勸說康熙皇帝下令組織一次全國普查。這項普查工作從1707年一直進行到1717年，最後所繪成的圖不但是亞洲當時所有地圖中最好的一幅，而且比當時的所有歐洲地圖都更好、更精確（〔英〕李約瑟《中國科學技術史》翻譯小組譯《中國科學技術史》第五卷，地學，第一分冊，北京：科學出版社，1976年，235頁）。

通過長白山西轉到盛京更換乘騎，其後東行到興京，過英額門，經寧古塔，到琿春、隋分河（即綏芬河）、烏蘇里江等地，然後順流進入黑龍江下游地區，完成了第一次測繪調查工作。兩年後，又派出以滿洲旗人爲代表的測繪調查隊，他們抵達第一次調查隊未能到達的黑龍江下游河口、薩哈林等地，第二次進行了東北大地的測繪調查活動。細究這兩次參與測繪活動的參加人員，我們就會發現，先行研究過於注重評價傳教士參與此次測繪活動的重要性，而忽略了清廷派來的主持參與測繪活動的滿洲旗人的具體活動。爲此，我們有必要通過滿文等多種語言資料，重新探討《皇輿全覽圖》大地測量的具體活動。本文旨在主要介紹這些滿文檔案，按例附錄滿文原文等具體內容爲宜，但考慮到篇幅有限，本文僅介紹其中的一部分，以供學界參考。

爲便於行文，除特殊需要之外，所有地名的滿文轉寫均略而不記。康熙時期漢文地名均按《皇輿全覽圖》（漢文，木版）和《康熙起居注》爲據，其他不一一註明。滿文羅馬字轉寫採用了學界通用的穆林德夫轉寫法⑤。

一、《皇輿全覽圖》研究小史

首先，我們簡單地按照年代順序回顧一下有關《皇輿全覽圖》的一些主要研究。

內藤湖南早期在《雷孝思（Pere Régis）等清國地圖製作考》（1911年6月30日）一文中，曾將杜赫德《中華帝國全志》（法文版）序言部分譯成日文，利用雷孝思等耶穌會士的相關資料，研究了清韓邊界。與此同時，他還利用《正教奉褒》一書⑥，指出康熙四十七年（1708）到康熙五十六年（1717）各省地圖繪製工作結束後，白進等人匯成總圖一幅，並將各省分圖，進呈御覽後，得到康熙帝嘉賞的事情⑦。可以說首開研究中國歷史地理利用《皇輿全覽圖》研究之先河。

清末，日本京都帝國大學文科大學派小川琢治、狩野直喜、內藤湖南三位教授和富岡、濱田兩位講師，赴北京學部調查敦煌發掘的古書及內閣傳存古書。當時他們閱覽過不少古地圖。1911年，內閣古書尚未著手整理，他們看到的是未經整理的內閣大庫的內部情形。具體閱覽了如下各種地圖：

> 明代雁門關寧武關垣圖、明代東路邊垣圖說、明代甘肅鎮戰守圖略……大清一統志稿本、清漢字甘肅圖、浙江五府分圖⑧。

此外他們，還看到過明代的直隸全圖，大小有20尺的巨幅輿圖、明代西域地圖。這個時候他們也曾閱覽過和康熙時期耶穌會士繪製的輿圖，也就是《皇輿全覽圖》。通過

---

⑤ P. G. von Möllendorff, *A Manchu grammar, with analysed texts*, Shanghai, 1892.

⑥ 海門黃伯祿編《正教奉褒》，光緒甲午上海慈母堂重印。

⑦ JACAR（アジア歴史資料センター）Ref.B03041212800，間島ノ版図ニ関シ清韓両国紛議一件／附属書（內藤虎次郎嘱託及調查報告）。

⑧ 內藤虎次郎《〈清國派遣教授學術視察報告〉（與狩野・小川・濱田・富岡諸氏合作）內藤湖南全集》第十二卷，1970年，188—211頁。原文載《大阪朝日新聞》，明治44年（1911）2月5日。

圖上書寫的數字，內藤湖南推定爲耶穌會士親自謄寫的地圖。他們將興安嶺、喀爾喀、哈密地方三幅輿圖拍照複寫後，帶回了日本。內藤湖南在他的文章中，提及了一幅東北亞輿圖：

> 清代滿文東北亞地圖，恐爲康熙時期寫本，今次將其原件全部精細模寫而來。這是耶穌傳會士繪製中國地圖以前的地圖。可能是康熙帝等與俄羅斯相戰時，利用過這些地圖。地形繪製非常粗略，山川名稱極爲至當，甚有參考價值⑨。

從這些記載看出內藤湖南等人曾經看過《皇輿全覽圖》繪製以前的一幅東北亞地圖。

此外，談到《皇輿全覽圖》我們不能不提到翁文灝的研究，他的論文對後來研究《皇輿全覽圖》的學者影響至深。翁文灝在《清初測繪地圖考》⑩中指出：

> 中國地圖之重要根據，首推清初聘用西洋天主教士之測量。以後雖經西洋游歷家多次續測，究皆沿循路線，或局於一隅，不及清初之有整個的計劃與普遍的實測。清末及民國初年，中央及各省測量局皆測有詳圖頗多，然皆注意局部地形，而未作全國之大地測量。故迄今亦尚未經始或未完成，而中國全圖乃已告竣，實爲中國地理之大業；雖出異國專家之努力，亦足見中國計劃規模之遠大焉⑪。

從中可以知道，翁文灝高度評價“清初之有整個的計劃與普遍的實測”這一宏大工程。他主要利用了四種西文著作：①蘇西海《印度中國數學天文地理歷史及物理觀察》；②杜赫德著《中國地理歷史政治及地文全志》（*Description geographique historique, chronologique, politique, et physique de l'Empire de la Chine et de la Tartarie chinoise*，1635，1636）（即本文所稱《中華帝國全誌》）；③馬俠《中國通史》（*Histoire generale de la Chine* par Pere de Mailia, 1783）第十二冊；④格羅藉《中國志》（*De la Chine ou description de cet Empire par Abbe Grosier*, 1818）。除此之外，還參考了康維爾（D'anville）以及衣斯爾（Isle）的相關資料。這篇文章爲中文研究者，提供了有關繪製《皇輿全覽圖》方面最基本的知識。由此也可見民國時期，翁文灝高度評價康熙時期測繪事業帶來的重要貢獻⑫。

其後，王庸《中國地理學史》一書中，專設“清初測繪地圖及其影響”一節探討康熙朝測繪全國大地問題，依據翁文灝文章，對康熙朝測繪全國大地，從五個方面進行

---

⑨ 同註⑧，204頁。

⑩ 《地學雜誌》第三期，1929年，405—438頁。該論文後復印以翁文灝著《清初測繪地圖考》，復印民國十九年（1930）九月地學雜志第十八卷第三期，1—34頁。研究者多引用後者，注1930，該本應爲復印本，發表年代應爲1929年。其後，葛劍雄根據英譯本，將杜赫德序言部分譯出，以《測繪中國地圖紀事》（〔法〕J. B. 杜赫德）爲題發表在《歷史地理》（第二輯，上海：上海人民出版社，1982年，206—212頁）。

⑪ 同註⑩，405頁。

⑫ 民國時期地圖學史的綜合評價，參看汪前進《民國時期地圖學史研究的重要成就》，《中國地圖學史研究文獻集成》（民國時期），西安：西安地圖出版社，2007年，序言。

了總結，即：①康熙間測繪地圖之次序與範圍，②測量之方法，③經緯度之根據與觀察，④西藏地圖之測量，⑤新疆地圖之測量等。通過王庸在北平圖書館輿圖部工作和故宮文獻館整理輿圖的經驗，他總結中國地圖的幾點特征如下：

竊謂中國古來地圖，自裴秀以迄明末，即有計里開方之法與傳統之通俗繪法相重疊。及清初測繪地圖，經緯圖法輸入，而地圖繪法乃成三重之局。且由上述諸節，知裴秀以後中國古來地圖之傳統繪法，並未消沉，直至清代猶然。至今北平圖書館及故宮博物院文獻館所藏舊輿圖（均由目錄印行）多有康熙乾隆以後者，而其圖繪不僅無經緯度之法，且並畫方之法而無之。故吾人若於中國地圖史上，將裴秀、賈耽、朱思本、利瑪竇以及清初測繪諸教士等所製之圖，一筆勾銷，則中國地圖之繪法，殆可謂二千餘年如一日也。至於清初測繪地圖之所以不能普及者，一方固由於國人對於科學測繪不甚瞭然，一方亦因內府輿圖之秘藏，僅有少數官吏得見之故。及同治間胡林翼之大清一統輿圖出而後始漸普及，且其時西方學術，亦多輸入，漸爲國人所了解而接受也[13]。

指出中國傳統輿圖繪法，直到清末依然沒有消沉，康熙、乾隆以後繪製的地圖中也有許多沒有經緯度，甚至連傳統的畫方之法也銷聲匿跡的問題。王庸指出康熙、乾隆朝科學測繪地圖與中國古代以來的傳統計里畫方的地圖，當時都已鮮爲少見。

高木菊三郎在他的《中國地圖概觀》一文中，追溯康熙朝測繪全國地圖緣起時，指出首先是康熙二十一年（1682）測繪奉天、吉林等東北地區爲發端，康熙三十五年（1696）南懷仁、白進、安多等人，扈從康熙帝親征噶爾丹，實測沿途各地並繪製東部蒙古，康熙四十七年（1708）以後，開始測繪全國（後略）[14]。他將測繪追溯到康熙二十一年，這從目前掌握的滿文檔案來看，是有一定道理的。有關詳情我們在下文具體討論。

當然，我們不能忘記福克司（W. Fuchs）留下的里程碑式的研究[15]。他早期致力於研究各種中國地圖。福克司整理了早期滿日文化協會、北京人文科學研究所、京城帝國大學附屬圖書館的各種資料，發現耶穌會士地圖有木版圖二十八幅和三十二幅兩種，這表示不同時期繪製而成。最後指出木版圖二十八幅繪製於康熙五十六年（1717），木版圖三十二幅繪製於康熙六十年（1721）。並且指出兩者不同之處在於《黃河河源圖》對揚子江上游、西藏、東土耳其斯坦（即準噶爾）方面地圖的修正，還增加了新的地圖。把哈密圖編入圖三十二幅圖之中，他在論文最後復製出版了包括三十二幅圖在內的如下地圖。

1）盛京全圖 2）烏蘇里江圖 3）黑龍江口圖 4）黑龍江中圖 5）黑龍江源

---

⑬ 王庸《中國地理學史》，北京：商務印書館，1938年，111—126頁。

⑭ 高木菊三郎《支那地圖概観》《地学雜誌》52（12），1940年，577—588頁。

⑮ W. Fuchs, *Der Jesuiten-Atlas der Kanghsi-Zeit: seine Entstehungsgeschichte nebst Namensindices für die Karten der Mandjurei, Mongolei*, Ostturkestan und Tibet: mit Wiedergabe der Jesuiten-Karten in Originalgrösse, Fu-Jen-Universität, 1943, Peking.對福克司論著的評論，參看Bernard, H., “Note complémentaire sur l’Atlas de K’ang-hi”, *Monumenta Serica*, Vol. 11, 1946, pp. 191-200.

圖 6）色楞厄河圖 7）熱河圖 8）河套圖 9）河源圖 10）哈密噶斯圖 11）雜旺阿爾布灘圖 12）金沙瀾滄等江源圖 13）拉藏圖 14）牙魯藏布江圖 15）岡底斯阿林圖 16）河源圖 17）鴉礲（原舊圖無圖名） 18）揚子江湄公河圖（原舊圖無圖名） 19）哈密圖 20）朝鮮圖 21）直隸全圖 22）山東全圖 23）山西全圖 24）陝西全圖 25）河南全圖 26）江南全圖 27）浙江全圖 28）江西全圖 29）湖光全圖 30） 福建全圖 31）廣東全圖 32）廣西全圖 33）貴州全圖 34）四川全圖 35）雲南全圖 36）西藏圖

福克司把包括康熙五十八年（1719）的銅版圖在内的地圖，分木版、銅版各自分類整理成表格列示如下（表1）：

表1　耶穌會士繪製地圖發展階段（福克司）⑯

號碼	圖幅	圖稿完成年代	印刷	年代	地圖形式	地圖內容	地名文字種類	備考（圖號碼爲福克司複製圖號碼
一⑰	28	1717	木版	1711	分圖	地形記載方	漢文	
一a	?	1717	銅版	1711	排圖	式相同	滿漢	馬國賢（Ripa, M）
二⑱	32	1718後期	圖稿	1719	分圖	地形記載方	漢文	
二a	41	1718後期	銅版	1721	排圖	式相同	滿漢	
三	32	1721	木版	1726	分圖	同一、二	漢文	《古今圖書集成》
四	226（231）	1717	木版		分圖		漢文	（1726）職方典所載地圖

從此我們大體知道三十二幅圖有木版區域圖和四十一幅銅版連接圖兩種，前者由同一縮尺圖頁構成，地名均標註漢文。後者上下左右均可拼接可能，塞外地名用滿文標註，內地用漢文。學界一直所稱的《皇輿全覽圖》就是指的這兩種圖的總稱。後來馮寶琳介紹了北京故宮圖書館所藏題名爲《皇輿全覽圖》的木版巨幅地圖兩種（210×226厘米，212×340厘米），馮寶琳推定前者刊刻於康熙五十六年（1717），後者於康熙六十年（1721）刊刻⑲。從此《皇輿全覽圖》又有了一些新的發現，但也有許多問題，特别

⑯ 同註⑮，p. 60. 表格漢譯文，參考了船越昭生《鎖国日本にきた「康熙図」の地理学史的研究》，法政大學出版局，1986年，22頁日文表格。

⑰ 一中的圖1—7增補地名的16—18取代圖9—15.

⑱ 二中圖9，12—14圖中地名增補。

⑲ 馮寶琳《康熙《皇輿全覽圖》的測繪考略》，《故宮博物院院刊》1985年第1期，23—31、35頁。馮寶琳具體詳細介紹如下：

a.《皇輿全覽圖》（圖幅上額墨筆楷書“皇輿全覽圖”，圖背後黄簽題“皇輿遍覽全圖”，又一别名）木刻墨印設色不註比例，註有經緯線，用梯形投影法，經緯線皆成直線。高210厘米，寬226厘米，一幅，故宮圖書館藏。

b.《皇輿全覽圖》（圖幅上額墨筆楷書“皇輿全覽圖”）木刻墨印設色不註比例，有經緯線，用梯形投影法，高212厘米，寬340厘米，一幅，故宮圖書館藏。

有關中國地圖史中，清代的《皇輿全覽圖》的研究，參看海野一隆《東洋地圖學史》，《東洋地理學史研究・大陸篇》，大阪：清文堂，2004年，314—316頁。

是目前具體解讀地圖地名内容的地圖學、地理學方面的專業研究論文畢竟還是少見。

福克司的先行研究，是我們後人研究《皇輿全覽圖》的必讀之作，無論是研究内容還是滿漢地名索引，至今仍有重要的參考價值。以福克司的研究成果作爲基礎，三上正利在《康熙時期耶穌教派測繪事業》一文中，對康熙帝下令繪製全國地圖事業的整個過程進行了介紹⑳。此外，對台灣以及琉球等地測繪過程，方豪有比較詳細的探討㉑。方豪在《中西交通史》（上）中，亦專門對《皇輿全覽圖》如此評價：

> 康熙時之測繪全國地圖，對世界地理學亦有一重要貢獻，即當時雷孝思與杜德美已發現經度長度上下不同，證明地球實爲扁圓形。時牛頓主扁圓說，與喀西尼（Cassini）之長圓說，分壘對峙，在歐洲尚無定論，在中國則由實測已獲得證實扁圓形之不誤矣。十七世紀時，歐洲各國之全國性測量，或尚未開始，或未完成，而中國有此大業，亦中西學術合作之大紀念也㉒。

方豪著意評價康熙時期測繪全國地圖，耶穌會士證明出地球爲扁圓形的問題，提出此偉大事業爲中西學術合作之大紀念㉓。此外，王庸亦指出：

> 當十七八世紀間，歐洲各國的大地測量，或未經始，或尚未完成，而中國卻在十八世紀初期聘用西洋天主教士把中國全圖測繪完成了。雖然這一工作，是由於外國專家們的努力，但這樣偉大的事業總是由中國人主持而規劃的，教士們在整個工作中的地位，不過是傭僱的技師罷了。這是世界學術和文化上一件史無前例的事績。中國從此以後，不但接受了西方地球和經緯度等地理上的新知識，而且把西方的測繪技術，應用到中國地圖上，這比利瑪竇地圖的影響深遠而切實得多了㉔。

1958年這樣一個不平常的年份，王庸强調指出這樣的偉大事業總是由中國人主持規劃，耶穌會士在整個工作中的地位，不過是傭僱的技師罷了的說法，我們考慮到王庸寫這本書正處於較爲特别的歷史時期，如此斷言，也不足爲奇，但現在看來還是值得耐人尋味。以上研究除了内藤湖南之外，基本上都沒有直接涉及東北大地測繪的問題。

藤田元春在介紹《滿蒙合璧清内府一統輿地秘圖》和《乾隆十三排銅版中國圖》的一文中，對《皇輿全覽圖》也進行了一番介紹。通過他的介紹我們可以發現，京都大學的狩野直喜（研究中國哲學、文學）、小川琢治（地質、地理學者）在中國曾閲覽過這

---

⑳　三上正利《康熙時代におけるゼスイット派の測図事業》，《史淵》(51)，1952年，25—50頁。

㉑　方豪《康熙五十三年測繪台灣地圖考》，《文獻專刊》第一卷一期，1949年，28—53頁。方豪《康熙五十八年清廷派員測繪琉球地圖之研究》，《文史哲學報》一期，1950年，157—197頁。

㉒　方豪《中西交通史》（上），長沙：岳麓書社，1987年（初版1953—54年，1—5冊，中華文化出版事業委員会），第三節《康熙時西教士測繪之全國地圖》和第四節《皇輿全覽圖之測繪方法與貢獻》專門簡要介紹了康熙時期的測繪工作。868頁。

㉓　方豪有關論及康熙年間測繪方面的論文，參看方豪《方豪六十自定稿》上、下冊，臺北：臺灣學生書局，1969年。

㉔　參看王庸《中國地圖史綱》，北京：生活·讀書·新知三聯書店，1958年（第十章“第一次中國地圖的測繪”），89頁。

幅銅版地圖。民國十三年（1924）9月，藤田元春到北京旅游，受小川教授囑托探尋這幅地圖，但去北京的圖書館、歷史博物館都未能發現這幅地圖。後來他委托松浦嘉三郎（1896—1945，内藤湖南弟子）[25]，讓他慢慢探尋。最終他們離開北京，藤田也都未能查到地圖的任何消息。從中也可以看出，民國時期，日本學者熱心搜求《皇輿全覽圖》的一個側影[26]。

其實，《皇輿全覽圖》對以後的朝鮮、日本的輿圖製作以及近代地理史的發展起到了不可低估的作用[27]。有關這一點船越昭生曾指出以下問題，他認爲西學東傳的過程中，世界知識、地理知識的傳入，從根本上突破了傳統中華與朝貢世界。在表現全球世界方面，又把中國完整無缺地描繪出來，支撐其基礎的兩根重要支柱，是利瑪竇的“世界地圖”和繪製“康熙圖”（即《皇輿全覽圖》）的兩次地圖繪製事業[28]。船越如此評價是有道理的，他的研究成果《鎖國日本傳來的“康熙圖”的地理學史研究》也證明了這一點。從世界史的眼光來看，可以説《皇輿全覽圖》在法國的出版發行，從根本上不僅改變了滿洲人統治下的中國在歐洲人心目中的形象。也成爲歐洲地理學高度信賴的亞洲東方地圖的重要依據。在國内，測繪的地圖成果也成爲清宫造辦處輿圖房不斷重新繪製、複製地圖的最好的範本（底稿）[29]。也成為中國地圖繪製基本參考資料，特别是杜赫德《中華帝國全誌》（1735年）與康維爾的《中國新地圖》的相繼出版，在歐洲也掀起了一股“中國地圖熱”[30]。

針對法國傳教士在中國的科學活動，藪内清也曾指出，康熙皇帝舉行的全國測繪大地事業，可以説是清朝科學史上最偉大的事業。當時法國自然科學中，大地測量學最爲發達，可以説當時是該領域的最領先的國家，所以大地測量學甚至被稱爲“法國的科學”。有研究指出，測繪全國也是法國路易十四進行佈置的一個計劃。所以，以這些為背景前來中國的法國耶穌會士，參加具體的大地測量工作，成功測繪全國各地，將近用了十年的歲月，康熙五十八年（1719）完成《皇輿全覽圖》的繪製工作。並將其原圖送

㉕ 東亞同文書院畢業後，松浦到北京《順天時報》當記者，後到京都大學跟隨内藤湖南學習，擔任東方文化學院京都研究所初創時期的研究員。編著有《中國法制史論叢》（桑原隲蔵著，松浦嘉三郎等編），東京：弘文堂書店，1935年。曾寫過研究報告《漢書百官公卿表研究》（1934年）提交審查。1929年5月2日開始在東方文化學院京都研究所工作，1934年從研究所辭職，1935年開始在滿洲國大同學院擔任教職。

㉖ 藤田元春《東洋史研究》第十七卷第三號，1958年，497頁。

㉗ 相關研究參看船越昭生《北方図の歴史》，東京：講談社，1976年。船越昭生《鎖国日本にきた「康熙図」の地理学史的研究》，《鎖國日本傳來的“康熙圖”的地理學史研究》，東京：法政大学出版局，1986年。

㉘ 船越昭生《在華イエズス會士の地圖作成とその影響について》，《東洋史研究》27(4)，1969年，158頁。

㉙ 有關内務府造辦處輿圖房相關地圖繪製與複製相關資料，參看中國第一歷史檔案館、香港中文大學文物館合編《清宫内務府造辦處檔案總匯》（55冊），北京：人民出版社，2005年。

㉚ 榮振華著，耿昇譯《在華耶穌會士列傳及書目補編》上、下冊，北京：中華書局，1995年，827頁。在華耶穌會士繪製地圖及其影響參看船越昭生《在華イエズス會士の地圖作成とその影響について》，《東洋史研究》27（4），1969年，506—525頁。最近的研究參看Isabelle Landry-Deron, *La Preuve par la Chine : la « Description » de J.-B. Du Halde, jésuite, 1735*. Paris : EHESS, 2002. 中譯文參看許明龍譯，藍莉著《請中國作證——杜赫德的〈中華帝國全誌〉》，北京：商務印書館，2015年。

到巴黎的耶穌會士杜赫德（Du Halde）之手，除給路易十四閱覽之外，杜赫德把原圖交給地理學家康維爾（d'Anville）印製，後來被收入康維爾的地圖冊中，還收入杜赫德的《中華帝國全誌》第一卷，杜赫德的書於雍正十三年（1735）出版後，開始廣爲中外學界所知[31]。目前，在中國有關《皇輿全覽圖》研究，基本以這本書的英譯本爲主，還沒有法文本的漢譯文版。

2015年，藍莉（Isabelle Landry-Deron）著《請中國作證——杜赫德的〈中華帝國全志〉》（許明龍譯，商務印書館，2015年）的漢譯文在中國出版，使得我們能夠領略到原著前三卷風貌和具體内容，可惜的是作者沒有對涉及滿洲、蒙古、朝鮮、西藏的第四卷進行深入分析。書後的附錄對於理解《皇輿全覽圖》在歐洲的傳播有著很重要的意義。

地理學家陳正祥也指出傳教士熱衷於編印世界地圖來幫助傳教的問題：

> 這批傳教士所繪製的地圖，皆係利用經緯度測繪法，是中國從來所不曾有過的。因爲經緯度測繪法的使用，必須先行觀測各地的經緯度；而能到各地去觀測經緯度，正好附帶去進行傳教活動（後略）[32]。

後來，相繼出版的盧良志編《中國地圖學史》[33]，金應春、丘富科編著的《中國地圖史話》[34]基本上都沿襲翁文灝、王庸的觀點。

在利用清代檔案方面，較早利用《宮中檔康熙朝奏摺》的相關資料，分析康熙朝繪製輿圖進行狀況的論文有太田美香（澤美香）[35]的系列論文。太田美香（1985b）對西藏圖繪製過程進行了考析，值得參考。此外，秦國經也利用中國第一歷史檔案館《宮中檔硃批奏折》，論述了耶穌會士測繪輿圖活動與貢獻[36]。最近，比利時魯汶大學的Mario Cams（康言）也利用《康熙朝漢文硃批奏摺彙編》、《康熙朝滿文硃批奏摺全譯》、《明清史料》丁編、《清中前期西洋天主教在華活動檔案史料》等資料，對江蘇、浙江、江西、四川、雲南、貴州方面的輿圖繪製内容進行了研究[37]。不過Mario Cams忽略

㉛ 藪内清・吉田光邦編《明清時代の科学技術史》，京都：京都大学人文科学研究所，1970年（再版本參看藪内清、吉田光邦編《明清時代の科学技術史》，京都：朋友書店、1997年，1—26頁）。耶穌會士的科學研究問題，參看山田慶兒《耶蘇会士の科学研究》，藪内清、吉田光邦《明清時代の科学技術史》，京都：朋友書店，1997年再刊（初刊1970年），135—146頁。

㉜ 陳正祥《中國地圖學史》，北京：商務印書館，1979年，39—40頁。陳正祥在該書中專門有一節"清初的測繪事業和皇輿全圖"探討清初測繪地圖事業，參看同書，38—45頁。

㉝ 盧良志編《中國地圖學史》，北京：測繪出版社，1984年，177—185頁。

㉞ 金應春、丘富科編著《中國地圖史話》，北京：科學出版社，1984年，130—132頁。

㉟ 太田美香《「皇輿全覧図」について－チベット図作成をめぐって－》，《早稲田大学文学研究科紀要》別冊113冊，1985年，56—69頁，太田美香《「皇輿全覧図」についての新史料—『宮中档康熙朝奏摺』収録の地図関係奏摺》，《史観》（113），1985年，56—69頁，澤美香《檔案史料から見た「皇輿全覧図」とヨーロッパ技術》，《史觀》（121），1989年，53—64頁。

㊱ 秦國經《18世紀西洋人在測繪清朝輿圖中的活動與貢獻》，《清史研究》1997年第1期，37—44頁。

㊲ Mario Cams（康言），"The Early Qing Geographical Surveys（1708–16）as a Case of Collaboration between the Jesuits and the Kangxi Court". Sino-Western Cultural Relations Journal, 34, 2012，pp. 1-20.

了太田美香（澤美香）以及秦國經等先行研究早已利用這批檔案研究《皇輿全覽圖》的進行過研究的問題。Mario Cams最近指出，康維爾經複雜的程序繪製的《皇輿全覽圖》相關地圖，不僅與耶穌會士有關，而且還和俄羅斯彼得堡有密切關聯。他對《皇輿全覽圖》在西方的傳播的幾篇論文，值得參考[38]。

此外，海野一隆也曾指出，真正採用西洋地圖學的人物是滿洲族出身的清朝皇帝。康熙帝的英明果斷開始了西洋式全國地圖的繪製事業，這是在耶穌會士指導下進行的，1718年繪製的《皇輿全覽圖》就是其成果，該圖以北京爲本初子午線，用梯形圖法繪製而成[39]。

余定國在講述清代地圖測繪之際，認爲“朝廷中央受到外國地圖學方法的一些影響，而地方上反對外國的影響則一直持續到十九世紀末葉”[40]，覺得出現兩極現象，這個問題還值得商榷，余定國覺得“滿洲人是否有他們自己的地圖學傳統，我們不知道”，以爲滿洲人入關前和入關後都依賴漢人的地理信息。這是過於片面的論斷，滿洲人入關前繪製的幾幅老滿文地圖，足以證明他們征服明朝之前有他們自己的繪圖傳統，入關後繪製的大量的滿文輿圖，也證明他們依賴的不僅僅是漢人的地理信息[41]。當然，如何界定滿洲人的傳統輿圖也是一個需要思考的問題，但是，滿洲人使用滿文繪製地圖，而不使用漢文，這本身就象征了他們有自己繪製地圖的傳統。

葛劍雄也談到了“康熙時期的經緯度測量和地圖測繪”問題，東北方面指出“1709年（康熙四十八年）5月8日，雷孝思、杜德美和日耳曼神甫費隱（Xavier-Ehrenbert Fridelli）自北京啟程去東北各地測量。儘管這次測繪的地區大多人煙稀少，但由於康熙已下令各地作準備，夫役、馬匹、糧草和物資的供應相當充分。這次測量的地區是北緯40度至45度，繪成的地圖還包括圖們江對岸的朝鮮北部”[42]。當然，此次前往東北各地測量，不只是這三位耶穌會士，還有主持這次測繪隊伍的官方人員，這些問題正好在滿文檔案里有進一步的記載。我們在下面進行詳細論述。

礪波護利用個人收藏的康維爾《陝西省圖》，對中國分省地圖的沿革進行了論述，並梳理羅洪先的《廣輿圖》和清代《皇輿全覽圖》的研究史，又將在歐洲刊行的兩種中國地圖冊，即17世紀的《布朗地圖冊》與18世紀《康維爾地圖冊》進行比較，對《陝西

㊳ Mario Cams , “The China Maps of Jean-Baptiste Bourguignon d’Anville: Origins and Supporting Networks”, *Imago Mundi*: The International Journal for the History of Cartography, 66:1, 2014，pp. 51-69.

㊴ 海野一隆《地図の文化史—世界と日本》，東京：八坂書房，1996年，77頁。

㊵ Cordell D. K. Yee, “Cartography in China”, *The History of Cartography, Volume 2, Book 2, Cartography in the Traditional East and Southeast Asian Societies*, Edited by J. B. Harley and David Woodward(Chicago: The University of Chicago Press, 1994，pp. 35-202, 228-231)，中譯文參看姜道章譯，余定國《中國地理學史》，北京：北京大學出版社，2006年，210—220頁。

㊶ 入關前滿文地圖，參看承志《ダイチン・グルンとその時代—帝国の形成と八旗社会》，名古屋大學出版會，2009年，56頁。康熙朝繪製的相關輿圖研究，參看同書，154—280頁。

㊷ 葛劍雄《中國古代的地圖測繪》，北京：商務印書館，1998年，131頁。

省圖》進行了深入探討[43]。

汪前進、劉若芳《清廷三大實測全圖集》的編輯出版，爲研究者利用《皇輿全覽圖》提供了極大的方便[44]。汪前進在該書的序言中，對《皇輿全覽圖》從五個方面進行了論述，即①起因、②中國政府的主持、③測繪過程、④爲修曆而開展的觀測活動、⑤測繪成果等[45]。

最近，白鴻葉、李孝聰著合著的《康熙朝〈皇輿全覽圖〉》，是一本專門探討《皇輿全覽圖》的著作，其中，第七章第二節專門探討了有關東北測繪部分，以杜赫德測繪中國地圖紀事爲依據，敘述了測量長城口外至盛京地區圖、烏蘇里江、黑龍江地區圖，但基本沒有利用新的檔案資料[46]。

此外，近年來海外收藏中國輿圖資料集的出版物日趨增多，我們已具備了重新探討《皇輿全覽圖》的史料基礎，特别是具體解析每一幅地圖的記載語言、地名特征、版式、自然環境等描述地圖研究最基本的要素，而不是重複前人的成果[47]。

當然，以上主要先行研究沒有詳細探討東北大地的測繪問題。本文在這裏不能將所有的先行研究全部一一介紹，相關的詳細研究，留待今後繼續撰文進行討論。總之，至今爲止有關《皇輿全覽圖》的研究，基本以譯介杜赫德《中華帝國全誌》中的與測繪有關的傳教士書信報告爲主進行展開的，最近開始利用個别零散的康熙朝漢文硃批奏摺，僅停留在繪製年代、地區名稱以及參加人員等方面，也沒有對相關參加人員的歷史背景進行深入探討，特别是對測繪隊伍中的欽天監以及五官正、養心殿筆帖式等曾經專門在八旗官學學習算學專業知識，精通天文曆算等問題，基本沒有人深入進行探討。以下，筆者僅就利用滿文檔案等資料，專門對東北測繪的有關問題進行探討。不當之處，敬請指正。

二、康熙時代繪製的東北輿圖

康熙年間，測繪東北大地大致可以分爲兩個時期。第一，是自入關前至康熙四十八

㊸ 礪波護《中国の分省地図—陝西省図を中心に》，藤井讓治、杉山正明、金田章裕編《大地の肖像—絵図・地図が語る世界》，京都：京都大学学術出版会，2007年，425—447頁。

㊹ 汪前進、劉若芳《清廷三大實測全圖集》，北京：外文出版社，2007年。

㊺ 參看汪前進、劉若芳《清廷三大實測全圖集》，1—3頁。

㊻ 白鴻葉、李孝聰《康熙朝〈皇輿全覽圖〉》，北京：國家圖書館出版社，2014年。該書最後部分也對國外的有關研究按年代順序，進行了一些介紹。

㊼ 美國國會圖書館的地圖資料，參看李孝聰《歐洲收藏部分中文古地圖敘錄》（中、英文對照），北京：北京國際文化出版公司，1996年；同氏《美國國會圖書館藏中文古地圖敘錄》（中、英文對照），北京：文物出版社，2004年。此外還有華林甫《英國國家檔案館藏近代中文輿圖》，上海：上海社會科學院出版社，2009年；林天人編著《皇輿搜覽——美國國會圖書館所藏明清輿圖》，臺北："中央"研究院數位文化中心，2013年；烏雲畢力格等編著《蒙古遊牧圖：日本天理圖書館所藏手繪蒙古遊牧圖及研究》，北京：北京大学出版社，2014年等。

年之前陸續繪製的各類滿漢文輿圖，這些地圖有地方分省小圖，也有全區地圖。東北地區的地圖，有北部一直到西伯利亞以及遠達北冰洋的大范圍的橫跨歐亞的地圖。這些地圖都有一個共同的特點，基本上沒有標注經緯線。也就是說不是我們通常所說的科學測繪地圖，絕大部分地圖用滿文繪製而成，基本反映了當時旗人繪製的獨特的地理觀念和世界觀，與漢文傳統輿圖略有不同。其繪製目的也是多種多樣，反映了編纂各類地方志或通志、《大清一統志》之際，重新調查地理情形的具體情況，是中國古代輿圖的重要組成部分。第二，是《皇輿全覽圖》系列地圖，有木版、銅版、稿本，語言上有滿文、漢文、法文（也包括依照法文繪製的英文、俄文等相關地圖）等。這一系列地圖均標註經緯度（個別除外），康熙朝以後，對其版式歷代都有增訂補充，反復重印複製。致使我們偶爾看到繪寫同一內容的地圖，有大小不同的幾套輿圖。康熙朝《皇輿全覽圖》也有類似的問題，我們目前能夠看得到的墨印、著色、彩繪等地圖，不一定都是在康熙朝印製。這是考量《皇輿全覽圖》需要注意的一個問題。

康熙十一年（1672）正月十六日曾測量京城各門及四周里數，於康熙十五年（1676）正月二十四日，九門提督費揚古奏報具體測量的京城周邊里數[48]。這一時期，康熙帝在遠征之際，也開始攜帶天文測量儀器，隨時隨地開始進行天文觀測和測繪工作。

康熙十六年（1677）四月，滿洲正黃旗覺羅武默訥與一等侍衛塞呼禮等人奉命往差長白山，調查形勢及所在地方。他們五月啟程，從盛京至吉林烏喇地方。六月初二日自厄合納音到達長白山，十三日開始登山，二十八日率領調查隊下山回到納音地方，七月初二日至吉林烏喇，繼續調查所有寧古塔及惠寧等處，八月二十一日回到北京[49]。據推測當時也繪製了《長白山圖》進呈給康熙皇帝[50]。

從吉林到黑龍江地區，康熙二十三年（1684）開始派人從烏喇到愛渾之間設立驛站，開始丈量各地之間的距離等[51]。從此開始開始測繪黑龍江、吉林、盛京三處，具體是爲了設置驛站而開始測繪。從康熙三十年（1691）到三十四年（1695）爲止，兩次以當時鎮守黑龍江等處地方將軍駐守的墨爾根城爲中心，首先是康熙三十年（1691）一月十九日用不到一個月的時間，以墨爾根爲基點，調查了黑龍江地區。主要爲編纂《大清一統志》，以各地建制沿革、四至地名、路程遠近、邊界、地勢、戶口、貢賦、習俗、

---

⑱ 《宮中檔康熙朝奏摺》第八輯（滿文諭摺第一輯），臺北故宮博物院，1977年，9—14頁。漢譯文參看中國第一歷史檔案館編譯《康熙朝滿文硃批奏摺全譯》，北京：中國社會科學出版社，1996年，3頁。

⑲ 《八旗通志初集》卷185，吴默納傳（滿文，39a—44a），4405—4406頁。此外，相關內容參看《大清聖祖實錄》卷69，康熙十六年九月丙子。

⑳ 康熙五十年穆克登查邊與《皇輿全覽圖》的關係，參看馬孟龍《穆克登查邊與〈皇輿全覽圖〉編繪——兼對穆克登“審視碑”初立位置的考辨》，《中国邊疆史地研究》2009年，第3期。

㉑ 《康熙起居注》第二冊，康熙二十三年二月十四日庚戌。

遣往設立烏喇至愛渾一路驛站郎中保奇、能得、額爾賽等奏請諭旨。上諭曰：此乃創立驛站之始，關擊緊要，爾等會同彼處將軍、副都統詢明熟識地方之人，詳加確議安設。凡住驛人役及馬匹生畜需用之物，並所食糧米，今年耕種不及，須要算至明年，加意料理。倘過于儉嗇，食用或至匱乏。必須從長計議，使其久遠可行，毋得狃于目前之見，草率了事。諭畢出。

山河、古城、關津、橋渡、關隘、驛站、衙門、職官、地方特產 、名人、寺廟等項爲主，進行了詳細調查㊷。其調查順序通過兵部來文傳令，黑龍江將軍給各地都統、協領、索倫總管，各地將調查報告送到黑龍江將軍處，最後由黑龍江將軍匯總寄給兵部。調查內容最初開始就用滿漢兩種語言記錄成檔冊。康熙三十四年將調查結果匯總後，寄給兵部。康熙三十八年（1699）開始黑龍江將軍駐守地從墨爾根遷移到齊齊哈爾後，康熙四十八年（1709）爲編纂《大清一統志》，再次開始調查，這次是以齊齊哈爾爲基點進行調查，康熙四十九年（1710）九月提交了調查報告㊸。這一時期正好和北京組織測繪隊伍前來東北進行科學測繪工作同步進行。

康熙二十五年（1686）二月朝鮮民韓得完等二十八人，違禁越江採挖人參，擅放鳥槍，傷害欽差畫地圖人員（《皇朝文獻通考》作繪畫輿圖官役），遣護軍統領佟寶前往朝鮮，會同國王審擬韓得完等二十八人，俱擬立斬㊹。韓得完等人因殺害欽差繪畫輿圖人員，被處以死刑㊺。這個事件也說明清廷派人到中朝邊界繪製輿圖，而這些人員恰好遇到偷採人參的朝鮮人，情急之中繪圖人員中槍遇害。

康熙十四年（1675），俄羅斯派使者斯帕法里帶著《西伯利亞地圖》（1673年繪製）前往中國北京，這幅地圖落入清廷官員手中，被譯成漢文。在摹繪之際，又將俄文《西伯利亞地圖》用中國傳統的山水畫方式，融入了中國風格吸收進來，使得我們初看該圖發覺不了是俄羅斯的《西伯利亞地圖》。康熙時代利用地圖進行文化交流的事實，有時超乎我們的想象㊻。

康熙二十一年（1682），南懷仁扈從康熙帝東巡，開始繪製有經緯度的地圖，範圍從北京到烏喇爲止，以東巡路程爲主的地圖（中國國內目前還未能確認到該幅地圖）。

這張地圖就是依照傳入歐洲的南懷仁地圖繪製的一張世界地圖的一部分。該圖分別繪入不同的世界地圖之中，《亞西亞洲圖》（L'Asie）的一部分，原法文地圖出版後，又贈送到清廷，清宮將其又譯成漢文。這幅圖估計與下面提及的德里格進呈的《西洋地里圖》五幅圖中的一幅地圖有關。漢文將圖名譯爲：

亞細亞洲圖、圖內分四洲之總分緊要之處按拂郎濟亞國天文文學宮所定經緯諸度於拂郎濟亞國五太子講地理者佛爾立法。

㊷ 參看承志《大清國及其時代——帝國形成與八旗社會（ダイチン・グルンとその時代—帝国の形成と八旗社会）》，名古屋：名古屋大學出版会，2009年，197—244頁。

㊸ 同註㊷，225—241頁。

㊹ 《康熙起居注》上册，康熙二十五年二月初二日，1427頁。

禮部題朝鮮國王李焞將本國人民不行嚴飭，致韓得完等三十一人違禁渡江，偷採人參，將遣往畫地圖人員用鳥鎗打傷，應罰銀二萬兩。上曰：李焞將本國人民不行嚴禁，情狀可惡，難從寬免，著依議。

此外，亦可參看《皇朝文獻通考》卷294，四夷考，朝鮮。

㊺ 《康熙起居注》上册，康熙二十五年閏四月十一日，1475頁。

又刑部題，朝鮮國韓得完等將遣畫輿圖官員人等以鳥鎗打死，俱擬斬立決。上月：正法人犯甚多，內有可原情者否？明珠等奏曰：案內韓得完等六人乃執凶器傷人者，金太成等二十二人未曾動手。上曰：韓得完等六名著處斬立決，金太成等二十二人俱著從寬免死，減等發落。

㊻ 具體研究論文參看，承志《マンジュ語地図とシベリア古地図との出会い》，《国語国文》（木田章義教授退職記念特輯（第2））84（5），2015年，473—437頁。

註明了圖名及其來源。此外，圖上還註明了如下內容：

此中國東北及東南面之諸地□□耶穌會士南懷仁□□往此地之南路程。康熙壬戌年，南懷仁奉旨自京都啟程，隨駕往吉林烏喇地。癸亥年，又奉旨自京師啟程隨駕往西大達。自第一路程皆往東北，此路皆往北。

這些文字說明南懷仁奉旨自京城到吉林、烏喇等地。此外圖上還有寧古塔的相關說明：

寧古塔爲大城，古者爲東大達爾國都城，在虎爾哈河北岸。耶穌會士南□□自此城□約四十里□至黑龍江入海之口北口在□□。（□表示文這模糊，無法識讀這處）

通過這些內容可以知道，這裏利用了南懷仁的注釋翻譯的內容，東大達爾國，也就是東韃靼國。滿洲人未曾有過自稱"東韃靼國"的時期。我們通過這一點，明顯就可以知道這是翻譯的內容。這些內容原圖版，文字較小，無法辨識。但可以看出來，當時翻譯補充這些漢文簽條的人員，知道這幅地圖出自南懷仁之手。南懷仁繪製的地圖傳播到西方，編入西方世界地圖之後，又輾轉送到大清國製圖者手上，使我們看到東西方地理知識以及地圖的互動交流的一段歷史，是我們了解當時知識傳播的一個重要的線索之一。

17世紀後期，歷任荷蘭阿姆斯特丹市長、東印度公司社長、駐英國大使尼古拉斯·維特森（Nicolas Witsen, 1641—1717）編纂的《北東韃靼》（*Noord en Oost Tartarye*）中有一幅畫有經緯度和經緯線的《大韃靼新地圖》（Carte nouvelle de la Grande Tartarie）中的一部分，該圖上標有P. Verbiest（南懷仁）的名字，說明這一部分參照了南懷仁繪製的地圖。我們解讀地名之後，就會發現這是一幅中國東北的地圖，有緯線和緯度，沒有經線和經度的記載。圖中具體記載了如下地名（括弧內地名爲筆者翻譯推定）：

PROVINCE DE PEKIKI（北京地區）、PEKIM（北京）、Ville Capitale de la Chine/Située a 40. Degre de /Latitude Septent?（中國首都，緯度40度）、PARTIE DE LA CHINE（中國）、Kam-Hay(山海關？)、PROVINCE DE LEAO-TUM（遼東地區）、Xin-yam/ Leao-tum（沈陽/ 遼東）[Ville Capitale de la province Située a 42. Degr? de Lat? Sept]（首府，緯度42度）TARTARES ORIENTAUX（東韃靼）、Seao Lysto（？）、Torent de Chacay angha（札凱）、Kianghuchen（嘉祐禪）、Feyteri（斐得里）、Torent de Ciam［Ciam小河（哈達河）］、Quaranny Pyra（庫魯河）、Ypatam（一把單）、Ylmen（衣兒門）、Krin（吉林）、Ula（烏喇）、Sum-Hola（松花江）[a 44. Degre Latutude]（緯度44）、Nincrita autresois le Siege［de lEmpire des Tartares］（寧古塔）、Helum R.（黑龍江）、Chacay angha（札凱□）、Torent de Feyteri（斐得里）、Sape Corou（對壕）、Eltem eme Ambaga（阿爾灘訥門）、Suay en ni Pyra［刷煙河（黃河）］、Seuten（搜登、蘇登）

該圖自北向南記載了50、45、40等不同緯度，畫有緯線。南懷仁（1623—1688）在中國繪製的原圖目前下落不明，我們從尼古拉斯·維特森的地圖可以知道，南懷仁繪製後寄給歐洲的地圖，給歐洲地理學界帶去了東方新的地理知識。康熙二十一年（1682）、二十二年南懷仁扈從康熙帝東巡，一邊沿途打獵，扈從捕獵老虎。一邊又進行天文曆算工作，測繪他們自己親自走過的地區，這一時期開始就已開始利用天文觀測的方式測繪東北大地。值得注意的是，這些測繪活動主要以康熙皇帝東巡路程爲中心，沒有針對東北全區進行測繪調查（圖1）。

圖1 中國皇帝（康熙帝）大圍獵圖（Groote jagt vande Keyser van China）[57]

繼承南懷仁繪製東北地圖工作的耶穌會士，有比利時傳教士安多（Antoine Thomas，1644—1709）。安多，康熙二十一年（1682）七月抵達澳門，二十四年（1685）十一月到通州，隨即入京，深得南懷仁關照，一同共事三年。安多曾教授康熙帝幾何學、算術以及儀器用法[58]。其後，南懷仁推薦任欽天監監副。在閔明我出外之際，曾代理擔任欽天監監正。康熙三十五年（1696），安多隨同康熙帝巡幸塞外。四十一年（1702）測量地球一度之長度，約時凡一月，皇三子親視測量。四十四年（1705）與白

---

[57] 南懷仁報告中的插圖，參看Le Comte, Louis, *Beschryvinge Van het machtige Keyserryk China* : Brief van Pater Ferdinand Verbiest Jesuit,1698，p. 384。

[58] 安多在宫廷傳播數學的相關研究，參看韓琦、詹嘉玲《康熙時代西方數學在宫廷的傳播——以安多和〈算法纂要總綱〉的編纂爲例》，《自然科學史研究》22（2），2004年，145—156頁。此外，我們通過康熙時代重要的宫廷數學家陳厚耀的曆算活動，也可以看出康熙四十七年，扈從康熙帝北上的數學家有陳厚耀等人，他一路陪同探討算法、測量法、測量儀器、測日景、圓周率等內容，康熙帝還親自教陳厚耀西洋定位法、開方法、虛擬法等。參看韓琦《蒙養齋數學家陳厚耀的曆算活動——基於〈陳氏家乘〉的新研究》，《自然科學史研究》第33卷，2014年，298—306頁。

進、雷孝思、巴多明等人測繪北京附近兩河氾濫地區，越七十日完成。並將京師以及行宮雕刻成形附於圖上。見於圖者凡城鎮一千七百，村莊無數。傳教士書信中也說這次與皇帝塞外巡幸，給所到之處耆老，傳佈宗教。是行與其說是繪圖，不如說是傳教，說明他們的這次活動除了繪製地圖之外，大力推行傳教活動，並對傳教活動也大爲滿意[59]。可以說安多跟隨康熙帝東巡的其間進行過測繪活動。

康熙三十七年（1698）據安多報告，康熙三十六年（1697），康熙帝抵達寧夏(Nim Hoa)，他繪製了從那里到前往韃靼（西部）遠征的地圖，同年十二月，將繪製好的地圖交給康熙帝後，皇帝格外高興。以此爲契機，爲繪製同樣的地圖，這一年春天，先到東韃靼（遼東）以及到國境地區測繪地圖，答應給予很多旅費，安多欣然答應了康熙皇帝的要求[60]。說明康熙帝特別滿意安多繪製的地圖，並表示繼續支持繪製遼東地區以及從朝鮮到大清國之間邊境地區的地圖。其實，此時安多非常希望能夠到朝鮮傳教。

此外，安多還積極從駐京俄羅斯人手中搜集地圖，有關這一點滿文檔案有記載。康熙四十一年(1702)，赫世亨奏爲安多等人赴俄羅斯館探取地圖未獲事，康熙皇帝斷言“安多死心吧，彼俄羅斯人小氣，決不會告訴安多，安多也絕不能得到”，但安多沒有洩氣，積極與耶穌會士閔明我共商討索取地圖之策，商定如何宴請俄羅斯人，乘機探聽俄羅斯情形，安多數次到俄羅斯館請客吃飯，最終都未能實現索取地圖的願望，最後什麼都沒能探聽到[61]。說明這一時期，清廷有意多方收集俄羅斯信息，耶穌會士不僅熱心傳教事業，還扮演了中俄兩國之間互通訊息的中介者，他們的這些活動直接報告給康熙皇帝，由皇帝具體下令指示下一步活動[62]。

康熙四十八年（1709）六月二十二日晨，安多病故。二十四日，李國屏奏報安多病故的消息後，康熙帝看完奏摺後，內心極度悲痛，硃批：安多自西洋到來後，誠信效力於天文曆法之事，茲聞已故，朕心殊覺惻然。照徐日升例，著李國屏、王道化送去[63]。可見康熙帝惻然悲痛，痛惜失去這樣一位精通天文曆法的人材。

安多在北京期間，曾經繪製過地圖。目前他繪製的地圖藏在意大利羅馬。據A. Florovsky在1951年的《地圖》（Imago mundi）雜誌上介紹當時居住在北京的比利時人耶穌會士安多（Antoine Thomas，1644—1709）繪製了兩幅地圖，一張題名《韃靼地

---

[59] 費賴之著，馮承鈞譯《在華耶穌會士列傳及書目》，上、下冊，北京：中華書局，1995年，403—412頁。

[60] J.G.ルイズデメディナ《遥かなる高麗－16世紀韓国開教と日本イエスス会－》，東京：近藤出版社，1988年，332頁。

[61] 中國第一歷史檔案館、中國海外漢學研究中心合編，安雙成編譯《清初西洋傳教士滿文檔案譯本》，鄭州：大象出版社，2015年，赫世亨奏爲安多等人赴俄羅斯館索取地圖未獲事朱批奏摺（康熙四十一年），282頁。

[62] 耶穌會士與康熙皇帝的關係，參看安雙成《康熙皇帝與西洋傳教士》，《歷史檔案》1994年第1期，91—93頁。

[63] 參看中國第一歷史檔案館編譯《康熙朝滿文硃批奏摺全譯》，北京：中國社會科學出版社，1996年，631頁。

圖》（Tartaria Imago），是一幅東北亞地圖，另一張是《東北亞地圖》，繪製範圍西到莫斯科，南到印度北部以及北印度支那包括在內的亞洲。特別是後者尤其重要，圖上繪有莫斯科、西伯利亞、蒙兀兒連接的路線，圖示從里海到太平洋莫斯科公國的邊界線以及中國的邊界線[64]。該圖註有經緯度，但沒有經緯線。並且，圖上明確記載了1690年安多在北京繪製而成的事實。就在安多繪製這幅地圖的前一年，即1689年，中俄兩國簽訂了尼布楚條約，該圖也反映了中俄簽訂條約後的國界情況。

安多逝去之後，在康熙皇帝身邊活躍的是法國耶穌會士爲中心的科學家。特別是張誠與白晉在北京期間，康熙皇帝專門爲他們請老師，教習滿文。爲了解他們在學習滿文方面的進展，康熙皇帝甚至查考他們，並親自閱覽他們用滿文寫的文章。耶穌會士認爲滿文要比漢語好學得多[65]。康熙四十二年（1703），耶穌會士洪若翰神父致拉雪茲神父的信中，對張誠的狀況如此寫道：

> 我們也差點失去張誠神父，我們的傳教事業在初創時期及其需要他。皇帝派他與安多神父前往韃靼，以便繪製一張精確的地圖。由于他懂滿文，能夠與當地人提問，並與他們交談，所以，他可以從當地人那里得到許多有關那些不屬中國管轄的省份的知識。他在接近克魯倫河的發源地時病倒了，此地離北京有三百多法里。他的病伴隨著使人不舒服的惡心與不停的嘔吐，使他元氣大傷，以至認爲自己快死了。于是，他在給我們寫下其最後的感想後，即準備後事。由于色楞格河附近有一個莫斯科人的居住地，且該居住地距張誠神父等人所在的地方僅有三十法里，有人提出把張誠神父送往那里（後略）[66]。

說明這是指康熙二十八年（1689）首次前往色楞格河與俄羅斯談判的事情，這一年就曾有計劃繪製精確的韃靼地圖，即滿洲人生活的東北地圖。說明法國耶穌會士在康熙身邊的活動，也促使康熙帝下令進行全國測繪活動。

山田慶児介紹，白進受路易十四之命返回法國，于康熙三十七年（1698）帶領十名耶穌會士，再次奉命來到中國。其中有巴多明（Dominique Parrenin）、雷孝思（Jean-Baptiste Regis）等人在內。巴多明後來上奏測量全國，康熙皇帝于康熙四十七年（1708）下令全國範圍内展開天文觀測和大地測量工作。直接參與這一巨大工程的是以白進、雷孝思爲中心的，還有後來的杜德美（Pierre Jartoux）等耶穌會士。康熙五十五

---

⑭ 吉田金一《郎談の「吉林九河図」とネルチンスク条約》62（1·2），1980年，34—35頁。吉田金一《ネルチンスク条約で定めた清とロシアの国境について》，《東洋史研究》42（1），1983年，65頁。

⑮ ［法］杜赫德編，鄭德弟等譯《耶穌會士中國書簡集——中國回憶錄》Ⅰ，郑州：大象出版社，2001年，3 耶穌會傳教師洪若翰神父致國王懺悔師、本會可敬的拉雪茲神父的信（1703年2月15日于舟山，浙江省境内的中國港口，距寧波有18法里），277頁。有關康熙時期耶穌會士學習滿文的問題，參看莊吉發《互動與對話：從康熙年間的滿文史料探討中西文化交流》（台北故宮博物院與北京故宮博物院合作舉辦“兩岸故宮第三屆學術研討會——十七、十八世紀（1662—1722）中西文化交流”2011.11.16，網址：http://www.npm.gov.tw/exh100/academic/download/1/paper/Paper10.pdf）。

⑯ 同註⑮，耶穌會傳教師洪若翰神父致國王懺悔師、本會可敬的拉雪茲神父的信（1703年2月15日于舟山，浙江省境内的中國港口，距寧波有18法里），297頁。

年（1716）實際測繪結束，在杜德美的指導下，康熙五十八年（1719）完成總圖，這就是我們所説的《皇輿全覽圖》。這不僅是耶穌會士在科學研究上取得的巨大成果，也是法國大地測量學的輝煌成果[67]。

我們從《天下輿圖總摺》中選出康熙三十年（1691）到五十三年（1714）間繪製的大清國東北地區地圖來看（參看表2《天下輿圖總摺》所見東北及高麗地圖），這一時期可以説是大量繪製地圖的歷史時期。無論從其繪製年代到地圖名稱、繪製經過等内容來看，每一幅地圖都反映了康熙朝不同時期繪製地圖的歷史，這也從另一方面可以了解到康熙帝積極接受西方天文曆法、醫學、解剖學等各種科學知識，積極開展科學研究，展開文化活動的一個象征[68]。

從表格中的地圖來源來看，我們發現交來輿圖的人員，不僅有康熙帝的近侍大臣浪潭（即郎談）、監造艾保、懋勤殿太監蘇佩升等人，還有西洋人德里格呈進的《西洋地里圖》（伍卷）等西洋地圖資料。此外，有奉旨、傳旨、口外、熱河帶來，甚至還有康熙帝原先在宫中呈覽過的輿圖。譬如在宫中呈覽過的《高麗圖》（一張），還有在暢春園呈覽過的《高麗圖》（一張）。這些都説明康熙帝熱衷于收集閲覽各類地圖資料的事實。

康熙五十年（1711）四月二日，意大利傳教士德里格（亦作德立格、德禮格、德里格）進呈《西洋地里圖》（五張）（參看表2）。他于康熙四十九年（1710）十二月抵達北京，翌年二月覲見康熙帝，四月就給康熙皇帝進獻西洋地圖五張，説明耶穌會士早已了解到康熙皇帝是一位“地圖迷”。

德里格精通音樂、繪畫，曾在宫中擔任樂師，負責爲皇子講授音樂，與衆皇子朝夕相處，深受康熙帝信任。曾參加編纂《律吕正義》一書，其中，首次介紹了歐洲的樂理知識、五線譜等西方音樂知識，也曾經在宫内召開過音樂會。

表2　《天下輿圖總摺》所見東北及高麗地圖

年代	圖名	備考
康熙三十一年2月25日	烏拉寧古塔口外大小圖，伍張	郎潭交來
康熙四十七年1月12日	長白山圖，二張	奉旨交來
康熙四十七年1月12日	烏拉圖，二張	奉旨交來
康熙四十七年1月12日	寧古塔圖，一張	奉旨交來
康熙四十七年1月12日	諾音圖，一張	奉旨交來
康熙四十七年2月15日	口外烏拉長白山等處紙圖，一張	監造艾保交來
康熙四十七年2月15日	口外波爾呵里俄莫圖小紙稿，一張	監造艾保交來
康熙四十八年2月2日	量地球圖稿，一張	奉旨交來
康熙四十八年3月28日	長城圖，一張	奉旨交來

[67] 參看藪内清、吉田光邦《明清時代の科学技術史》，京都：朋友書店、1997年再刊（初刊1970年），143—144頁。山田慶兒將完成總圖的年代記爲1717年，有誤，應爲1718年。

[68] 清朝輿圖繪製與管理參看秦國經、劉若芳《清朝輿圖的繪製與管理》，《中國古代地圖集》，北京：文物出版社，1997年，71—78頁。

续表

年代	圖名	備考
康熙四十八年3月26日	口外小紙圖（自東直門至口外木蘭地方）	
康熙四十八年9月24日	山海關至寧古塔紙圖，一張	口外帶來
康熙四十八年9月24日	熱河至喜峰口紙圖，一張	口外帶來
康熙四十八年11月1日	烏拉關東等處紙圖，三張	奉旨交來
康熙四十八年11月1日	烏拉長白山等處紙圖，一張	奉旨交來
康熙四十八年11月4日	盛京等處圖，一張	本房〔即輿圖房〕傳旨交來
康熙四十八年11月4日	盛京圖，二張	本房〔即輿圖房〕傳旨交來
康熙四十八年11月4日	烏拉種地圖，一張	本房〔即輿圖房〕傳旨交來
康熙四十九年10月29日	口外圖，二張（一張自古北口至所岳爾集期期喀拉圖回至喜峰口。一張自期期喀拉至莫爾根薩哈亮烏拉、烏魯蘇木丹）	奉旨交來
康熙五十年2月24日	松花江黑龍江烏蘇里江三江歸一處到東海圖，二張	奉旨交來
康熙五十年2月24日	熱河盛京長白山烏拉寧古塔等處圖，一張	奉旨交來
康熙五十年2月24日	諾尼烏拉河源圖，一張	奉旨交來
康熙五十年2月24日	古北口至熱河小圖，二張	奉旨交來
康熙五十年4月2日	西洋地里圖，伍卷	西洋人德里格進
康熙五十年4月11日	長白山等處手卷圖，伍軸	奉旨交來
康熙五十年4月11日	西洋坤輿大圓圖，一張	懋勤殿太監蘇佩升交來
康熙五十年9月27日	敦敦至海小圖，一張	奉旨交來
康熙五十年12月27日	口外圖，三張 內（自獨石口至布于魯枯崙圖一張，自科魯崙、吐拉、鄂爾渾色厄圖一張，自推必拉衣懇敖蘭巴汗敖蘭諾名戈必嘉峪關等處圖一張）	奉旨交來
康熙五十年3月14日	烏魯蘇木丹圖，一張	奉旨交來
康熙五十一年1月12日	高麗圖，一張	宮內呈覽過交出
康熙五十一年7月23日	長白山高麗圖，二張	奉旨交來
康熙五十二年9月22日	高麗圖，三張	熱河帶來
康熙五十二年11月11日	高麗圖，一張	暢春園呈覽過
康熙五十三年4月7日	高麗圖，一張	奉旨交來

從表2中列出的地圖名稱以及呈交年代可以看出，康熙三十一年（1692）到康熙五十三年（1714）之間，陸續繪製了東北地區以及包括蒙古、朝鮮在内的各種紙本地圖，其數量驚人。

康熙三十一年二月二十五日浪潭交來五張《烏拉寧古塔口外大小圖》，這些地圖與臺北故宮博物院藏《烏喇等處地方圖》《口外九大人圖》《吉林九河圖》等都有密切關聯。說明大清國在簽訂尼布楚條約之後，爲了編修《大清一統志》積極調查東北各地歷史地理等資料，在當地官員的實際踏查之後，都有詳細的滿文檔案奏報中央，而這些資料基本上沒有全部編入各種編纂資料中，使我們至今難以窺探當時的社會歷史以及地理探查地圖測繪等具體過程。

2010年以來，筆者通過協助調查臺北故宫博物院的滿文輿圖，發現不少康熙時期繪製的滿文輿圖。其中《烏喇等處地方圖》《口外九大人圖》《吉林九河圖》《黑龍江流域圖》等滿文輿圖，可以說都是這一時期滿洲人繪製的中國輿圖的珍貴資料[69]。

此外，康熙四十七年（1708）一月十二日，奉旨交來兩張《長白山圖》，有關這幅輿圖，今西春秋（1935）曾經介紹過，推定該圖於康熙四十九年（1710）至五十年（1711）初[70]繪製。

以下，我們通過中外史料分析一下東北大地的測繪問題，特別是利用滿文檔案，析出測繪隊伍構成人員，並逐一分析這些人員的身份履歷，以此來具體探討清廷主持全國測繪工程的具體問題。

三、《皇輿全覽圖》東北大地測繪隊伍

有資料記載，測繪全國的計劃是由巴多明神甫提出，據《在華耶穌會士列傳及書目》記載：

> 巴多明神甫曾進言康熙皇帝，測繪中國全圖，帝納其言，乃于1708年7月4日命具有學識技能之歐洲傳教師任其事。帝命滿、漢官員隨諸教師前赴各省，隨時供給所需。唯此種官吏之任務，與其謂助理，勿寧謂爲監督。據宋君榮神甫說，彼等似奉朝命勿使諸神甫來往自由。巴多明神甫寵眷隨隆，測地不能逼近俄國邊境，亦不能進至東海沿岸。杜德美神甫奏請測量經過北京之全國子午線，帝嚴爲拒絕。諸神甫將其所繪地圖寄回法國時，明確要求，若無新的指示，不得刊行[71]。

從此來看巴多明曾進言測繪中國全圖，另外，巴多明傳亦記載：

> 中國全國之測繪，雖出諸傳教師手，要應特別歸功于多明。康熙皇帝曾誤以奉天省會沈陽與北京同一緯度，亦位置于三十九度五十六分。多明對帝明言其

---

[69] 筆者對此發表了相關研究論文，參看承志《滿文〈烏喇等處地方圖〉考》，《故宫学術季刊》第26卷第4期，2009年，1—74頁；承志《尼布楚條約界碑圖的幻影——滿文〈黑龍江流域圖〉研究》，《故宫學術季刊》第29卷第1期（秋季号），2011年，147—236頁；承志（2017）《滿文地圖與西伯利亞地圖的邂逅相遇》（待刊）。

[70] 今西春秋《内藤湖南編「增補滿洲写真帖」》，《東洋史研究》（1）1，“批評・介紹”一欄，1935年，55頁。

[71] 〔法〕費賴之著、馮承鈞譯《在華耶穌會士列傳及書目》（上册），北京：中華書局，1995年，538—539頁。

誤，帝命之赴沈陽詳細測驗繪圖進呈。復命以後，帝因疑國內諸省方位或亦有同一之誤，擬繪一總圖，乃命多明選擇能繪圖之傳教師若干人往各省測繪。多明不但主持其事，而且親自測繪，除上述遼東地圖外，1718年曾奉帝命赴煽動登州測驗此城方位，已而從海道赴旅順，又從旅順至沈陽，所過之地皆爲測量⑫。

巴多明體貌魁偉，深受康熙帝器重。康熙帝特派良師給他教授滿漢文字，很快就精通漢文，其滿語流利程度，與其操母語無異⑬。

康熙四十七年（1708）八月初四日，赫世亨（hesihen）奏報白晉（白進）前往測量沿邊地區，不幸中途落馬受傷，已返回京城的消息。康熙帝看完滿文奏摺硃批如下：

白晋原先即不愿去。若白晋气色如故，或許撒謊而回。若回家後痊愈，伊爲傳教之人也，而如此不顧臉面可安心乎？理当痊愈之日，即以自力追去，則彼之大罪，尚有可憐憫之處。爲此我（朕）不明白諸西洋人爲何謝恩？爾如此含混轉奏，理應即行革職，並拿解慎刑司議罪。爾張口即講道統，不知此事載于何書？⑭（參看圖2）

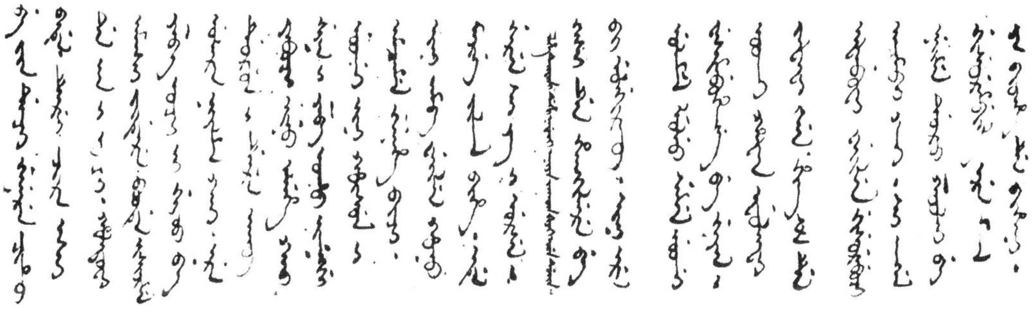

圖2　康熙帝對白進墜馬返京一事寫的滿文硃批（據《康熙朝滿文硃批奏折》膠片）

從硃批內容來看，白進當初有些不願主動參與測繪隊伍的跡象。有關康熙四十七年（1708）开始测绘北京周边地区的資料，據《正教奉褒》記載：

康熙四十七年，上諭傳教西士分赴蒙古各部、中國各省，遍覽山水城郭，

---

⑫　〔法〕費賴之著、馮承鈞譯《在華耶穌會士列傳及書目》（上冊），巴多明，516—517頁。原註引自科拉普羅特《關於亞洲之記錄》卷一，319頁。

⑬　同註⑫，538—539、510頁。

⑭　滿文原文參看《康熙朝滿文硃批奏摺》（膠片2），康熙四十七年八月初四日。漢譯文參看安双成編譯，中国第一歷史檔案館、中国海外漢學研究中心合編《清初西洋傳教士滿文檔案譯本》，郑州：大象出版社，2015年，326頁。筆者比對滿文原文，對原漢譯文做了些微的更改。滿文康熙帝硃批原文如下：be jin daci genere cihakū/ bade, terei cira esi/ da an i oci, holtofi/ amasi jidere boode isinjime/ yebe oci i giyoo be/ ulara niyalma kai, ere/ durun i dere akū/ yabuci inu elehe kao/ giyan i yebe oho inenggi/ utgai[uthai] ini h ū sun i/ amcame genehe bici,/ ini amba weile hono/ amjige jilaka bihe, ede/ geren si yang ni urse i/ kesi de hengkilere be/ bi ulhirakū, sini ere/ ulame lulu seme utgai[uthai]/ wesimbuhengge be giyan i/ uthai hafan efulefi/ jafafi šen hing sy de/ afabufi weile gisurebuci/ acambi kai, si angga/ neime doro kooli be/ gisurembihe ere makan/ ya bithe de biheni,/（筆者按：[ ]內滿文爲後來正字，康熙帝硃批多有[-ha][-ga]不分之處，譬如把cooha（兵）亦多作cooga）。

用西學量法，繪畫地圖，並諭部臣選派干員，隨往照料，並咨各省督撫將軍，札行各地方官，供應一切要需。四月十六日，白進、費隱〔日耳曼人〕、雷孝思、杜德美〔法蘭西國人〕奉派往蒙古等處繪圖。康熙四十七年十月二十九日，費隱、雷孝思、杜德美奉派往直隸繪圖[75]。

康熙四十九年（1710）六月二十六日，費隱、雷孝思、杜德美奉派往黑龍江一帶繪圖[76]。康熙五十六年（1717），各省地圖繪畢，白進等匯成總圖一幅，並將各省分圖進呈御覽，上甚嘉賞[77]。以上內容基本上是以耶穌會士相關資料為根據。

我們來看一下一份滿文奏摺，其中就記載了測繪隊伍以及康熙帝規定具體測繪路線的內容。康熙四十八年（1709）四月十三日卜魁驛站丁齊蘭竇帶來一份文書。其中傳來了康熙皇帝派人前往測繪東北大地的具體計劃：

兵部咨行鎮守黑龍江等處地方將軍等，嚮導護軍參領德克精格（dekjingge）等咨送文書內稱：康熙四十八年三月二十三日，我等會面，奏請訓旨，聖旨：爾等出山海關，沿著海邊測繪前去，到鳳凰城。自鳳凰城不能通達白山，尋求興京前去，至盛京換馬矣。爾等在盛京換乘馬匹，自興京出英額邊門（ingge jase），沿舊道前往過拉法驛站、寧古塔、自寧古塔下到琿春、隋分（即綏芬）、烏蘇里、郭拉（gola），尋吉林河、恒滾河前去。爾等無法抵達之處，爾等問詢名勝之地、大山，繪入圖畫之中。爾等行走之際，若無驛站之處，當即乘騎文武官員馬匹，愛護兵丁馬匹乘騎，不但乘騎彼等馬匹，而且盛京等處文武官員馬匹亦帶去乘騎。彼處衆人盡是富者也。爾等食物亦從彼等之處支取。爾等測量行走之際，從該將軍處，派出循吏勁兵及熟知路途之衆帶去。從盛京等地，派出手快善獵布特哈之衆，讓他們拿上鳥槍、圍網[78]帶去。額真之恩惠，爾等不歡快打獵取得行糧，何故空手而去。我等滿洲等皆前往采挖人參，途中遇見，想必幫助爾等飲食。自恒滾是否有往返到海之人，若有人行走，想必有各種貿易。將此處爾等問詢。爾等前去行走之際，朕之此等指示，若可抵達，隨即前往。若不能抵達，爾等不得以降旨爲由，任意往行。若行糧米等短缺如何行走，拼死奮斗不在此處，朕將爾等送往戰場，前去捐軀奮發之處，可謂有理。但是白白的到不能到達之處，若由此無影無蹤，豈有此理。朕全無詰責爾等之處，朕處理任何事情，均甚公正。又，烏蘇里江等處蚊子蠓虻繁盛之季，若無法行走，爾等返回寧古塔，等候慢走。入秋之后再去。爾等返回寧古塔駐扎之際，自山海關到寧古塔之間，爾等測繪之處繪寫給我奏聞送來。若爾等乘騎馬匹瘦弱疲倦，前來寧古塔換乘再去。等語。謹遵送來。欽派送來之護軍參領德克精格、陶蓄齊、監察御史吴達禮、員外郎舍楞、五官正成

---

[75] 《正教奉褒》，參看韓琦，吴旻校註《熙朝崇正集 熙朝定案》，北京：中華書局，2006年，366頁。

[76] 同註[75]，367頁。

[77] 同註[75]，371頁。

[78] 筆者按，捕捉鳥獸用。

德、西洋人袁費隱（即費隱）、雷孝思、杜德美、養心殿筆帖式布爾賽、嚮導前鋒那蘇泰、明清、畫匠二，又增派郎中關東、藍翎赫木葉、筆帖式噶布喇、塔喇齊、噶布喇。爾等出山海關，沿著海邊到鳳凰城，出邊門前往恒滾河等地。查得，咨文盛京兵部、奉天將軍，牛莊、海州、蓋州、錦州等地軍人備齊馬匹，彼等抵達後，隨即如數送給。因關係聖旨事宜，不得遲延耽誤。又，亦咨文寧古塔、黑龍江將軍等。我等該管理之處備齊馬匹。等語。爲此咨文。三月二十六日（5月5日）[79]。

這是一份兵部寄給黑龍江將軍的滿文咨文。兵部引用了康熙四十八年（1709）三月二十三日，嚮導護軍參領德克精格等人覲見康熙皇帝，奏請訓諭。由康熙皇帝下旨，具體制定的測繪路線是：出山海關沿海邊到鳳凰城，然後折東北到興京，再到盛京換乘馬匹後，再到興京，出英額邊門，到拉法驛站、寧古塔、琿春—隋分（即綏芬）、烏蘇里、郭拉，尋吉林河，恒滾河前往。其間不能到達的名勝地區以及高山等地，均要尋訪當地人員，將其繪入地圖中。若路上遇到沒有驛站的地方，吩咐利用當地文武官員以及盛京等處文武官員的馬匹，並吩咐須要愛護乘騎。並調侃盛京地區全是富人，途中食物亦可以從他們那裏支取。具體測繪工作，由當地將軍派出得力人馬以及熟悉路程的嚮導人員，一同展開工作。隨同測量隊伍的還有從盛京等地派出的善於打獵的布特哈漁獵人員，他們帶上鳥槍、圍網，一路行獵，將獵物作爲糧餉。此外，沿途有滿洲人前往採挖人參人員，他們也會途中協助提供飲食。這說明北京方面派來的測繪隊伍，沒有帶領糧餉部隊，這樣使得他們迅速進行測繪工作。

康熙帝還吩咐如果烏蘇里江等處蚊子蠕虻繁殖時節，無法行走時，可以返回寧古塔，等到入秋後，再行前往。返回寧古塔後，把山海關到寧古塔之間測繪的地圖，繕寫後再給康熙帝寄去。說明當時測繪人員繪製山海關到寧古塔的地圖後，要求寄給康熙帝自己，也就是說繪製的地圖首先寄給北京，讓康熙帝閱覽山海關到寧古塔的地圖。

從滿文咨文的後半部可以看出，測繪隊伍分兩批派出，第一批人馬有欽差護軍參領德克精格、陶蕃齊、監察御史吴達理、員外郎舍楞、五官正成德、西洋人袁費隱、雷孝思、杜德美、養心殿筆帖式布爾賽、嚮導前鋒那蘇泰、明清、畫匠二人，共十三人。第二批人馬是增派人員，有郎中關東、藍翎赫木葉、筆帖式噶布喇、塔喇齊、噶布喇等五人，總共是十八人的測繪隊伍。總之，這些人的乘騎馬匹以及路上生活用的食物，均下令由盛京兵部、奉天將軍、牛莊、海州、蓋州、錦州以及寧古塔將軍、黑龍江將軍準備好供應馬匹提供測繪隊伍乘騎，還有他們生活用的食糧等。這樣就拉開了測繪東北大地的序幕。測繪計劃的具體內容均由康熙皇帝親自指授，吩咐沿途各地盡力從各方面援助測繪隊伍，爲他們提供衣食住行。我們把滿文文書中的測繪隊伍人員名單整理如下。

---

⑲ 《自康熙四十八年吏、兵部、理藩院、盛京兵部來文抄檔》（《黑龍江檔》16-5）四月十三日卜魁驛站丁齊蘭賓咨送文書。

表3　康熙四十八年（1709）測繪隊伍職銜及其名單

	職　銜	人　名	備　考
1	嚮導護軍參領	德克精格	
2	護軍參領	陶番齊	
3	監察御史	吴達禮	
4	員外郎	舍楞	
5	五官正	成德	
6	西洋人	袁費隱（即費隱）	
7	西洋人	雷孝思	
8	西洋人	杜德美	
9	養心殿筆帖式	布爾賽	
10	嚮導前鋒	那蘇泰	
11	嚮導前鋒	明清	
12	畫匠	無名人氏	1人
13	畫匠	無名人氏	1人
14	郎中	關東	增派人員
15	藍翎	赫木葉（黑木葉）	同上
16	筆帖式	噶布喇	同上
17	筆帖式	塔喇齊	同上
18	筆帖式	噶布喇	同上

這次測繪調查人員除了北京派來的十八名專職人員之外，包括當地協助人員共達五十人。有資料記載當時每天宰殺一頭牛，而一頭牛那時要充當五十個人的食物[80]。我們把滿文檔案中出現的測繪隊伍成員，具體分析參加人員的職銜以及履歷等。以下，按以表3順序論述。

1. 嚮導護軍參領德克精格（dekjingge）

滿洲正白旗人，《康熙朝起居注》漢文本作<u>繪畫輿圖護軍參領德克精格</u>。護軍參領一職，屬正三品。據《八旗通志初集》卷205，勳臣傳五，德克精格傳載：

> <u>德克精格</u>，滿洲正白旗人，初任前鋒參領。康熙三十五年，從撫遠大將軍費揚古征厄魯特噶爾丹。由西路進兵，至昭莫多地方，奮勇擊敗賊衆。凱還敘功，授拖沙喇哈番[81]。

⑧⓪　杜赫德編，鄭德弟譯《耶穌會士中國書簡集》Ⅱ，郑州：大象出版社，2001年，耶穌會傳教士杜德美神父致印度河中國傳教區總巡閱使的信（1711年4月12日于北京），53頁。

⑧①　鄂爾泰等修，李洵、趙德貴主點《八旗通志》，長春：東北師範大學出版社，1985年，卷205，勳臣傳五，正白旗滿洲世職官下，4762—4763頁。

但是，康熙五十年（1720）九月因家人關保等人騷擾驛遞等因，被處以枷號一個月，鞭八十。家主德克精格照例革職[82]。説明測繪隊伍除了正式欽派繪畫輿圖人員以外，這些護軍參領都曾攜帶家人，也就是包衣，即私人從僕，使其依仗欽派人員威勢，膽大妄爲騷擾驛站，終致違法，連同家主一同被革職。可見其騷擾程度非同一般。當然，這一事件是在測繪東北大地完成之後，康熙五十年發現非法行為，由刑部進行處理革職。他的事跡其後在南方各地測繪隊伍中我們再也見不到了。

2. 陶蕃齊（toofahaci）

護軍參領陶蕃齊的身世，據《八旗滿洲氏族通譜》卷66、附載滿洲旗分内之蒙古姓氏、各地方博爾濟吉特氏，寨桑札爾固齊（jaisang jargūci）記載：

> 正藍旗人，世居瑚倫博宜爾地方，天聰時同兄弟率部屬来歸，授三等男，編佐領使統之，卒，其子札住襲職，兩遇恩詔，加至一等男，任佐領。卒，其子陶蕃齊（toofanci）襲職，任佐領，卒，其親兄之子瑪尼襲職時，削去恩詔所加之職，承襲三等男，任散騎郎，卒，其子遵珠克現襲職。又寨桑札爾固齊第四弟之子多爾濟，以来歸功授騎都尉，兩遇恩詔，加至三等輕車都尉，卒，其孫丹巴襲職，從征厄魯特噶爾丹於昭莫多地方，奮勇破賊有功，授爲二等輕車都尉，卒，其子劉保襲職時，削去恩詔所加之職，承襲騎都尉兼一雲騎尉，緣事革退，其親弟達色襲職，卒，削去伊父丹巴軍功所得之雲騎尉，其族叔三韋馱，現襲騎都尉。又寨桑扎爾固齊之孫，甘珠爾原任佐領。

瑚倫博宜爾地方，即呼倫貝爾地方。陶蕃齊爲編入滿洲旗分内的博爾濟特氏蒙古人，滿洲正蓝旗人，祖父寨桑札爾固齊，從名字來看，應該是一位蒙古世家顯貴。陶蕃齊，在漢籍史料中，又作陶番齊，據《皇朝文獻通考》卷252记載：

> 三等阿思哈尼哈番介桑貫爾呼奇爾，滿洲正藍旗人。自蒙古歸順封。貫柱、介桑貫爾呼奇爾子，順治六年二月襲，八年二月遇恩詔晉二等。九年正月遇恩詔晉一等。陶番齊，貫柱子，康熙十八年二月襲。馬尼，陶番齊兄子，康熙五十七年十二月降襲三等阿思哈尼哈番〔乾隆元年改爲三等男〕[83]。

介桑貫爾呼奇，即《八旗滿洲氏族通譜》中記載的寨桑札爾固齊，貫柱即札柱（亦作查柱），也就是陶蕃齊父親。通過這些記載，可以說陶蕃齊是一位編入滿洲旗分的蒙古人，曾任佐領，即牛彔章京。陶蕃齊家族世代管理佐領。據《欽定八旗通志》卷14，旗分志十四，八旗佐領十四，正藍旗滿洲佐領記載：

> 第二參領第十七佐領，係天聰三年以庫羅倫布爾地方来歸人丁編立。初以庫色布管理，庫色布故，以寨桑札爾固齊之子查柱管理，查柱從征卒於軍，以其子甘珠珥管理，甘珠珥緣事革退，以其弟阿思哈尼哈番陶藩齊管理，陶藩齊故，以儀素特管理，儀素特故，以宗住普管理，宗住普故，以宗扎普管理，宗

[82] 《清代起居注冊》康熙朝，19，康熙五十年九月二十日丙午。

[83] 《皇朝文獻通考》卷252，封建考七，異姓封爵三，滿洲。

扎普故，以吉爾敏管理，吉爾敏故，以國敏管理。

這充分説明陶蕃齊出身顯貴，歷代管理佐領的蒙古出身的滿洲正藍旗旗人後裔。陶蕃齊，在康熙五十二（1713）年閏五月十日，巡撫江寧等處地方張伯行奏文中也能看到“護軍參領臣陶蕃齊”之名，説明測繪東北之後，與耶穌會士一同繪製江南、河南輿圖，這一年準備前往浙江、福建等地繪畫輿圖[84]。

3. 監察御史吴達禮（udari）

監察御史一職，可以對違法犯罪官員進行監督管理，官職品等爲從五等。監察御史吴達禮，據《福建通志》載：台灣監察御史吴達禮，正紅旗人，康熙六十一年（1722）任台灣監察御史。其他事跡不詳。

4. 員外郎舍楞（šereng）

舍楞，事跡不詳，待考。

5. 五官正成德（cengde）

成德，曾于康熙五十一年（1712）任欽天監監副，乾隆三年（1738）到九年（1744）任太僕寺少卿，期間也任過總管八旗官學生算法以及管理國子監算學等要職[85]。説明對天文日曆算以及算學都有很高的造詣。康熙四十八年（1709）時成德擔任欽天監五官正，屬欽天監時憲科，春夏中秋冬五官正，滿洲、蒙古各二人，從六品[86]。五官正基本都由精通算學人員擔任。著名的數學家明安圖，就曾擔任過欽天監五官正一職。

有關成德相關資料絕少，所屬旗籍也不甚明白。據《清史稿》卷45，時憲志，推步因革記載：

> 五十一年五月，駕幸避暑山莊，徵梅文鼎之孫梅瑴成詣行在。先是命蘇州府教授陳厚耀，欽天監五官正何君錫之子何國柱、國宗，官學生明安圖，原任欽天監監副成德，皆扈從侍直，上親臨提命，許其問難如師弟子。及徵瑴成至，奏對稱旨，遂與厚耀等同直內廷。

説明成德曾在欽天監工作過，且任監副等重要職位。另外，有關成德，在《御制曆象考成》上編，曆理總論，雍正二年（1724）五月十七日奉旨開載纂修編校諸臣職名，考測記載：會考府郎中臣成德。此成德即康熙四十八年赴盛京測繪隊伍中的成德。會考府，爲雍正元年設立，專門爲革除奏銷錢糧不給部費則屢次駁回，勒索地方官的積弊而設，也就是專司察核錢糧的專門機構。成德後來在這裏擔任要職。

---

[84] 中国第一歷史檔案館編《康熙朝漢文硃批奏摺彙編》第四冊，北京：檔案出版社，1984—1985年，康熙五十二年閏五月十日，巡撫江寧等處地方張伯行奏，爲遵旨恭進輿圖事，856—859頁。

[85] 參看臺北國立故宮博物院“清代檔案人名權威資料查詢”數據庫（http://npmhost.npm.gov.tw/ttscgi/ttsweb?@30:813378885:3:1:49@@853118898）。

[86] 參看《大清會典》卷3，卷86，欽天監以及《欽定日下舊聞考》卷71。

從成德在國子監算學任職的經歷來看，説明他是一位精通算學的專門人才。按照規定，國子監算學生，滿洲十二名，蒙古、漢軍各六名，漢人十二名，計三十六名。再加上欽天監附肄業生二十四明，共六十名在內。凡是滿洲、蒙古、漢軍算學生俱于八旗官學生中考取，漢人算學生無論舉人、貢生、生員、童生，由監會同算學考取。欽天監肄業生由該衙門奏撥算學肄業[87]。康熙五十二年（1713），設立算學館于暢春園之蒙養齋，簡大臣官員精於數學者，司其事[88]。可以説成德是八旗官學生中考取欽天監算學的學生出仕。

6. 西洋人袁費隱（Xavier-Ehrenbert Fridelli，1673—1743，滿文作yuwan fei yen）

即費隱，漢文亦作費殷。日耳曼人，是康熙時期測繪大地的主要人物之一。康熙五十四年（1715）十一月初二日的漢文檔案內稱費隱爲“西洋曆法費隱”[89]。據康熙五十四年漢文檔案記載：

> 雲南巡撫奴才甘國壁謹奏，爲欽奉上諭事。案照康熙五十二年五月初十日前撫臣吴存禮準兵部咨內開奉旨派出西洋人費隱等繪畫雲南輿圖，畫完即將圖交該省巡撫本身派出的當家人，敬謹齎送。欽此。又於康熙五十四年三月十四日署撫臣郭 準兵部咨奉旨派出雷孝思、常保到滇同畫輿圖（下略）[90]。

費隱於康熙五十三年（1714）奉命與滿洲人監視武英殿布爾賽、滿洲人護軍參領英柱、滿洲人監副雙德共五人，到雲南。西洋人除費隱之外，還有單爻占[91]。

7. 西洋人雷孝思（Jean-Baptiste Régis，1663—1738，滿文作leo hiyoo sy）

法國耶穌會士，漢名雷孝思，1698年前來中國，熟知天文、數學等科學知識。參與繪製1708—1716年實地測繪的《皇輿全覽圖》繪製工作。據《在華耶穌會士列傳及書目》（上册）記載：

> 雷孝思神甫，字永維。1663年出生于普羅凡斯州之伊斯特雷城。1679年入里昂教区之阿維尼翁城修院。1698年抵中国，因其精通曆算天文，即被召至京師，曾將其偉大測地成績留示吾人。唯其傳教事業與在教生活，惜皆未得其詳焉。

説明雷孝思精通天文曆算，他于康熙三十七年（1698）抵達中國後，很快就被帶到北京。此外，有關測繪東北的年代，據記載：

> 孝思与白晋、杜德美二神甫开始測繪長城一帶地圖。越二月，白晋患病，僅由孝思、德美二人从事測繪，1709年1月10日事畢還京。所繪地圖广十五尺

---

[87] 《欽定國子監志》卷37，生徒三，算學。

[88] 同註[87]。

[89] 參看中國第一歷史檔案館編《康熙朝漢文硃批奏摺彙編》第六册，1984年，605—606頁。

[90] 同註[89]，康熙五十四年六月二十四日，310—313頁。

[91] 參看《雲南通志》卷18下之二。康熙五十四年，測繪雲南人員有乃哥（滿洲人，理藩院官）和覺羅殷泰（滿洲人，康熙五十四年同奉旨至滇，以八表儀器測日影高下，雲南北極高二十四度強）二人。

餘，帝甚嘉許，欲于全国各省悉加測繪。同年5月8日孝思又偕杜德美、費隱二神甫測繪東三省地圖。又在是年十二月十日至1710年7月29日間測繪直隶地圖，終在1710年7月22日至同年十二月十四日間測繪黑龍江外地圖[92]。

康熙四十八年（1709）五月八日，雷孝思與杜德美、費隱進入東北開始測繪地圖。當時對雷孝思等測繪所採用的方法，杜赫德《中華帝國誌》序文中如此記載：

孝思曾云欲成績之良，凡事皆未懈惰疏忽，在各省中曾親自往來各地；檢閱各地之地圖方志；面詢所過諸地之官吏紳耆；而對于所適用尺度之適用從未中斷，俾能與將來之三角測量相和。所采用者蓋爲三角測量法，緣地面廣大城市衆多，如用他法須時過久也。此法尚有他益，蓋其不僅能測定城市之經度，而且可以測定其緯度。夫然後以子午線與兩極星糾正以前之錯誤。尚用別一方法務期求其準確，即復還業已確定之點重在測量之。無論在塞外抑在中國內部，從未忘測驗羅盤磁針之偏差。此類慎重方法以及其他方法皆曾適用，務期使測驗之成績上承帝心而負其保教之至意。吾人所用之唯一尺度即數年前皇帝決定之尺度，別言之中國工部尺是也。安多神父即據此尺以量度數，而定每度爲華里二百里，每華里合一百八十丈，每丈合十尺（中略）則吾人之一大里（lieues）合中國里爲十里[93]。

清代漢文硃批奏摺，亦記載西洋人爲“欽差繪畫輿圖大人西洋曆法雷孝思、西洋曆法費隱”等人 的名字[94]。康熙五十五年（1715）貴州巡撫劉蔭樞的漢文奏摺，經康熙帝閱覽後，發現摺内有“大人”二字，指出“知道了。並無差大臣去。摺內稱[95]大人不合。大人是誰？察明再奏”。劉蔭樞道出“在外各省凡遇欽差不論官品大小，俱稱謂大人，習以爲常”[96]。這也道出了當時各省官員，一般把欽差大臣稱之爲“大人”的一段事實。而這恰恰是康熙帝不喜歡的稱呼。如此君臣間的往復文書，細究起來，饒有趣味。當然，當時的耶穌會士自始至終的主要任務是傳教，他們自己也寫信報告“諸傳教師乘此于所過之處聯絡紳耆，傳布宗教。是行也與其謂爲繪圖，無寧謂之傳教”。[97]可以說這些都道出了耶穌會士他們自己的心聲。

8. 西洋人杜德美（Pierre Jartoux, 1668—1720, 滿文作du da mei）

法國耶穌會士，字嘉平，生于埃夫勒。十九歲入會，其性頗近數學。洪若翰神父信札云：杜德美神甫對分析科學、代數學、機械學、時機學科最爲熟練”。故康熙皇帝頗器其

---

[92] 《在華耶穌會士列傳及書目》二三六 雷孝思，539頁。

[93] 轉引自〔法〕費賴之著，馮承鈞譯《在華耶穌會士列傳及書目》，二三六 雷孝思，540—541頁。

[94] 參看中國第一歷史檔案館編《康熙朝漢文硃批奏摺彙編》第六冊，貴州巡撫督察員右副都御史加三級臣劉蔭樞謹奏，康熙五十四年十一月初二日，605—606頁。

[95] 康熙硃批漢文稱作程。

[96] 《康熙朝漢文硃批奏摺彙編》第六冊，貴州巡撫督察院右副都御史加三級臣劉蔭樞謹奏，康熙五十五年二月初一日，606頁。

[97] 〔法〕費賴之著，馮承鈞譯《在華耶穌會士列傳及書目》一六三 安多，407頁。

材。居京數年，康熙四十七年（1708）與雷孝思、白晉神甫等同奉命測繪中國地圖⑱。杜德美精于解析學、代數、力學與鐘表方面的理論⑲。

杜赫德在他的《中華帝國全誌》序言中，記述了耶穌會士前往東北進行測繪地圖的故事：

1709年5月8日，雷孝思神甫、杜德美神甫和遵旨同行的日耳曼神甫費隱（P. Fridelli），自北京啟程去東韃靼測量，該地是目前統治中國的滿洲人的發祥地。這裏荒蕪多年，對這項須歷時數月的工作缺乏必要的伕役、馬匹和糧秣供應，因此任務頗爲艱巨。但皇上聖明遠慮，早已明詔治理該人煙稀少地區各城鎮的滿人官員。由于他們嚴格遵奉聖旨，所以測量未收到任何延宕。在給地區測繪時，神甫們確定了遼東省（或稱關東省）各主要地點的位置。該省南部以長城爲界，而長城已于上年測定，可作爲依據。時年制成的地圖包括滿洲人的發祥地遼東省，與該省相隔圖門江的朝鮮北界、稱爲魚皮韃子的韃靼人的領地和額真韃子的居住地區，這些地區一直延伸到韃靼地區最大的河流——韃靼人稱之爲薩哈連烏拉、漢人稱之爲黑龍江——的入海口。總之，從45度至40度緯度之間所有漢人稱之爲藏韃子的蒙古王公的領地都已包括在內。神甫們是在40度處折回的。此事深得皇上贊許，那些雖生在北京但眷顧祖宗廬墓的滿人也是如此，因爲花片刻時間從地圖上看到的內容遠比他們向很多旅行者打聽來的爲多⑩。

此外，杜德美曾寫過計算日出入昏刻不同之表，“杜德美曾進過日出入昏刻不同之表，朕比時且叫他那（那，原文如此，應作拿）回去，今有用處，杜德美將進過的表，察明着速報上帶來”⑪。說明曾看完後又叫他拿回去，想用的時候，傳令讓他從速送來。可見康熙帝對此圖表相當重視。

康熙五十年（1711），杜德美寄給印度河中國傳教區總巡閱使的信中記載前往東北地區測繪地圖，途中有機會看到人參，康熙四十八年（1709）七月抵達距離高麗王國很近的一個村子的事情⑫。正如兵部寄給黑龍江將軍的咨文中所引用的康熙皇帝說的一樣，途中遇到採挖人參的滿洲人，想必他們會幫助接濟食物，果然杜德美一行測繪隊伍途中遇到了採挖人參的滿洲人，他們按照所屬旗分安排了具體的採挖地點，然後每百人爲一隊，在指定的地段一字形排開，每十人與另外十人之間保持一定的距離，然後仔細尋找人參的情形⑬。杜赫德對人參進行了詳細的植物學描述，還記錄了當時滿洲人稱人參爲

---

⑱ 同註⑰，594—595頁。

⑲ 〔法〕杜赫德編，鄭德弟等譯《耶穌會士中國書簡集——中國回憶錄》Ⅰ，大象出版社，2001年，24 耶穌會傳教士洪若翰神父致國王懺悔師、本會可敬的拉雪茲神父的信〔1704年1月15日于倫敦〕，309頁。

⑩ 參看〔法〕J. B. 杜赫德、葛劍雄譯《測繪中國地圖紀事》，《歷史地理》第2輯，206—212頁。

⑪ 中國第一歷史檔案館編《清中前期西洋天主教在華活動檔案史料》第一冊，原硃批無年月日，55頁。

⑫ 杜赫德編，鄭德弟譯《耶穌會士中國書簡集》II，大象出版社，2001年，耶穌會傳教士杜德美神父致印度河中國傳教區總巡閱使的信（1711年4月12日于北京），50頁。

⑬ 同註⑫，52頁。

orhoda，即“植物之首”。這和滿文咨文中引用的康熙帝推測可能會遇見採挖人參的滿洲人的記載内容可以互證。

9. 養心殿筆帖式布爾賽（bursai）

滿洲人，是滿洲正藍旗名臣滿丕之子，姓伊爾根覺羅。曾任監視武英殿[104]。布爾賽與西洋人接觸較多，他曾於康熙四十五年（1706）十二月攜西洋人白進、沙國安及其賞物初八日晚到北京[105]。康熙四十五年左右，布爾賽曾任理藩院郎中[106]。另外，據康熙五十四年（1715）九月二十五日記載：

> 又覆請兵部覆原任郎中布爾賽等互爭佐領控告。又閒散宗室佛格等控告滿丕、和理、布爾賽等，原倚仗索額圖欺侮我等，將吏、户、兵三部檔案毁匿，將内閣檔案之字塗註一案。查無圈點檔案所寫係卓科塔，並無朱胡達之名。布爾賽等稱，朱胡達爲伊曾祖，取供時又稱係伊伯曾祖，不合。應將布爾賽等各罰俸一年。佛格等所稱滿丕、和理等，原倚仗索額圖欺侮伊等之處，當時即應控告，乃當時不曾控告，今歲月已久，證據俱無，應無庸議一疏[107]。

上引資料中的原任郎中布爾賽，也就是養心殿筆帖式布爾賽因互爭佐領控告。閒散宗室佛格控告滿丕以及其子布爾賽等人，原先倚仗索額圖氣勢，受到欺壓打擊，又把吏、戶、兵三部檔案銷毁，並將内閣檔案塗改。後來布爾賽等人被各自罰俸一年。滿丕控告滿丕和布爾賽等人，説明滿丕家族與索額圖關係密切。佛格因當時就應該控告，事過多年才上奏控告，以“當時不曾控告，今歲月已久，證據俱無，應無庸議”來退回了佛格的控告[108]。從此也可以看出，康熙五十四年後，基本從滿文和漢文史料中找不到具體記載，也許滿丕以及布爾賽一家曾卷入索額圖事件。

據《雲南通志》記載，康熙五十三年（1714）布爾賽（滿洲人，監視武英殿）、英柱（滿洲人，護軍參領）、郎烏里（滿洲人，郎中）、雙德（滿洲人，監副）等人奉旨偕西洋人費隱、單駁占等人到雲南進行繪圖丈量之際負責嚮導。康熙五十四年由乃哥（滿洲人，理藩院官）、覺羅殷泰（滿洲人）奉旨赴雲南帶上八表儀器測日影高下，進行測繪活動。此後，布爾賽事跡從各種資料中銷聲匿跡，從此我們無從查到他的其他資料。有關布爾賽的相關事跡，有待今後查考。

---

[104] 《雲南通志》卷18，下之二。

[105] 參看中國第一歷史檔案館編譯《康熙朝滿文硃批奏摺全譯》，北京：中國社會科學出版社，1996年，476頁。該書漢譯文將白進作伯金、博津等，應作白進或白晉。

[106] 《康熙起居注》第2冊，康熙四十五年二月二十日，1944頁。

[107] 《康熙起居注》第3冊，康熙五十四年九月二十五日，2198頁。

[108] 同註[107]，2199頁。

上又曰：宗室佛格呈稱，布爾賽之父滿丕，倚仗索額圖行事。雖滿丕當日諂奉索額圖如奴僕，然所行是實。然其時雖不諂奉索額圖？不獨滿丕也。此事原不明白，今所議甚糊塗。將此事并和理奏摺，俱交蘇努，著伊持去，會同該部詳審具奏。

10. 嚮導前鋒那蘇泰（nastai）

事跡具體不詳，待考。

11. 嚮導前鋒明清（mingcing）

具體事跡不詳，待考。

12、13. 畫匠（nirure faksi）

兩位畫匠，滿文檔案未具姓名，由北京派來，係專門繪畫地圖人員。首次通過滿文檔案得知測繪隊伍，有專門的畫匠隨行，應該是精通天文曆法以及算術等知識的專業繪畫人員。滿文檔案中亦作hūwajan（畫匠）。

14. 郎中關東（guwandung）

具體事跡不詳，待考。

15. 藍翎赫木葉（黑木葉）（hemuyen）

正黄旗人，祖上世居寧古塔地方。據《欽定八旗滿洲氏族通譜》卷52，墨爾迪勒氏，佛克楚傳記載：

> 正黄旗人，世居寧古塔地方。來歸年分無考。其曾孫尼酬肯，原任驍騎校，元孫赫穆音（hemuyen），原任頭等侍衛。發丑，現任護軍統領兼佐領。

元孫赫穆音，即測繪隊伍後來增補的黑木葉。從此也可以看出，黑木葉曾擔任過護軍統領和佐領等要職。墨爾迪勒爲滿洲一姓，其氏族散處黑龍江鄂奇村等地方。據康熙五十年（1711）九月二十日記載：

> 又覆請刑部等衙門所題，以差往丈量路程繪畫輿圖護軍參領德克精格等家人關保等騷擾驛遞緣由，應將關保等枷號一個月，鞭八十。德克精格等照例革職。繪畫輿圖西洋人費殷應當議處，今現差往鄂爾多斯等處繪畫輿圖，俟到來日另結一疏。上曰：黑木葉丈量路程繪畫輿圖，頗有勞績，黑木葉從寬免革職，着罰俸三年。西洋人費殷亦從寬免治罪，餘依議[109]。

康熙五十年九月涉嫌德克精格家人關保等人騷擾驛遞之罪，刑部奏題黑木葉因丈量路程繪畫輿圖，頗有勞績，從寬免革職，被罰俸三年。這一年德克精格及其家人關保、西洋人費殷、黑木葉等人都受到調查問罪。除了黑木葉因丈量路程繪畫輿圖有功勞，寬免革職，罰俸三年，費殷被寬免治罪，這和他參與測繪事業多有勞績有直接的關係。

---

[109] 《清代起居注冊》康熙朝·19，康熙五十年九月二十日，10936—10937頁。

16. 筆帖式噶布喇（gabula）

具體事跡不詳，待考。

17. 筆帖式塔喇齊（taraci）

具體事跡不詳，待考。

18. 筆帖式噶布喇（gabula）

具體事跡不詳，待考。

通過以上分析可以知道，京城派來的測繪隊伍，分兩批前來。第一批共有十三人，後來又增派了五位，共由十八人組成。有關這份滿文文書，松浦茂（2011）等將部分內容譯成日文介紹過，認爲十幾位滿洲人參加調查隊伍，與耶穌會士同行，不僅監視他們的行動，還一同協助調查[110]。但是，如此大規模的測繪調查，其主持所有具體工作的還是以滿洲旗人爲主，而且，主要成員均爲康熙皇帝的心腹大臣，他們基本都有天文曆算等知識，自始至終領導了這項巨大測繪工程，這是無可置疑的。先行研究按照耶穌會士書信報道等資料爲據，有關中文資料記載較爲少見，滿文等非漢文資料更是沒有得到挖掘和整理。所以，我們現在看到的《皇輿全覽圖》研究，基本都依據耶穌會士記載的資料，且他們的書信報告中全然不見任何清廷主持人員的蹤影，這些也恰好從另一方面反映了耶穌會士書信報告所獨有的單方面觀點。

我們從上引滿文文書就可以知道，這次大規模測繪活動的最高負責人，就是康熙皇帝。主持工作的也都是康熙帝的心腹大臣，三位耶穌會士的參與，也使得這次大規模調查成爲中外科學技術人員聯手考察的一次絕好機會。

兵部咨文黑龍江將軍沿途關照測量隊伍之後，康熙四十八年（1709）五月初一日，工部咨行黑龍江將軍，具體記載如下：

> 工部咨行镇守黑龙江等处地方将军，为公务事。嚮导巴雅喇参领德克精格等咨文內稱，謹遵上諭，今年丈量路程，繪畫地圖前往之際，出山海關，沿海直到鳳凰城、盛京、寧古塔，英額邊門、恒滚等地前去測量，將此事宜，爾等部院依去年之例，行文所屬地方官員，備齊丈量路程所需設備等物，以及搬運大儀器之四人。等語。是故，將此咨行直隸巡撫，傳令所屬地方官員施行。又，咨札付奉天府通永之道吏，備齊丈量路程所需繩夫等事。若遲延耽擱，指名處罰所屬地方官員，爲此咨文。三月二十六日，將此一事交付副都統宗室勒色里依情，交付事務之都統哈岱，薩海，佐領八十一等。筆帖式岳太蕾書寫[111]。

[110] 參看松浦茂《一七〇九年イエズス会士レジスの沿海地方調查》，《史林》84-3，2001年，77—108頁，後收入《清朝のアムール政策と少数民族》，京都：京都大學出版會，2006年，41—82頁。滿文奏摺日譯文參看同書，56頁。

[111] 《自康熙四十八年正月始工部、盛京工部、奉天、寧古塔將軍、伯都納、黑龍江副都統、墨爾根協領、驛站官咨文抄檔》五月初一日，卜魁驛站丁齊蘭寶送來文書（《黑龍江檔》16-20）。

按照康熙帝指定的路線，測繪隊伍如期到來，希望能夠備齊丈量路程所需設備，還要準備好四位搬運測繪用的大儀器的夫役。將這個內容首先咨文直隸巡撫，傳令各地官員施行。並寄信奉天府，傳令各地備齊繩夫，以協助測量。

康熙四十八年（1709）五月十日，寧古塔副都統咨文琿春噶珊達領催伊珠瑚

副都統咨文琿春噶珊達達巴庫、巴克西蘭、明珠等。欽派大臣丈量綏芬、琿春等地。彼等順便路過爾等之處，選出備齊官員一人、嚮導、熟悉土地善丁，手快之人二十，肉肥體壯馬匹四十頭。若有使用之處儘管使用。若不使用不必派去。又，謹將爾等之處稗子米二倉石，鈴鐺麥米一倉石備齊。豬十頭，依情將烤魚多多備放，大臣等抵達之後，若需要使用即可送去，若不需要不必送去，烤魚務必送去。爲此咨行[112]。

如此我們就知道寧古塔副都統咨文琿春村長等人，吩咐欽派大臣測繪綏芬、琿春等地，除了備齊官員以及嚮導、熟悉土地的善丁，擅長打獵等二十人。可謂準備周全，可以說對測繪隊伍給與無微不至的關照。同時，寧古塔副都統也咨文三姓姓長等人，傳諭欽差繪畫輿圖人員到來之前，做好一切準備工作。我們來看一下康熙四十八年五月十日，正白旗哈爾胡牛彔披甲咨送文書的內容：

副都統咨文三姓姓長堪岱、扎哈拉、蒙克依、額布齊，噶山達瑚阿瑟、春吉喀，尼西蘭、卡爾覺、博倫托、布德勞、法喀拉等人。上諭：派遣大臣到亨滾等地測量。彼等抵達後隨即利用水路前去測繪。爲這些前去大臣等人，選出備齊爾等三姓嚮導八人，派出刀船八艘，不得耽擱。又，採挖人參之漢人等，不得派出與代替爾等噶山各家偷挖人參。爾等之人亦應無數次嚴格巡查。爾等務必到各家各姓之噶山之家，全部曉諭傳令。若將違反此傳令，一併嚴懲姓長、噶山達等。爲此咨行[113]。

三姓姓長需要備齊嚮導八人，測繪隊伍因利用水路前去測繪，所以又要備齊刀船八艘。說明測繪輿圖不僅利用陸路進行調查，還通過水路移動進行測繪工作。其後，寧古塔副都統咨文給琿春噶珊達等人，據同年五月二十八日咨行正黃旗察里布牛彔領催阿蘭泰的文書記載：

副都統咨行琿春噶珊達達巴庫、巴庫西納、莽珠等人，前來測繪土地大臣等不久即可前來。抵達後隨即前往琿春。先前咨文給爾等之處文書內稱,選出備齊與大臣等人一同前往之嚮導、熟知地方之善丁，手快之人二十，肥壯馬四十匹。若有使用之處儘管使用，若不使用不必派出。又，原先咨文，謹將爾等之處稗子米二倉石，鈴鐺麥米一倉石備齊。豬十頭，依情將烤魚多多備放，大臣等抵達之後，若需要使用即可送去，若不需要不必送去，烤魚務必送去。

---

[112] 《康熙四十八年行文档》（《寧古塔》1-11），康熙四十八年五月十日咨文琿春村領催伊珠瑚。

[113] 《康熙四十八年行文档》（《寧古塔》1-11），康熙四十八年五月十日正白旗哈爾胡牛彔披甲（該處押印，文字不清）咨送文書。

派出之嚮導、馬匹、所有食物，立刻準備，不得耽擱。爲此咨行[114]。

到了六月初二日，寄給鑲黄旗雍克牛彔披甲阿爾塔文書，記載了寧古塔副都統咨文姓長（又作哈喇達）等人，要求增派經驗豐富的嚮導十二人，並且吩咐攜帶充分的糧米，若有不足，命令各噶山内湊齊辦理。具體内容如下：

副都統咨文姓長扎哈，額布奇噶山之姓長華塞、春吉喀、尼西拉薩、博倫特、布德婁、徹齊克等人。派人預備選出與前來測量土地之大臣等一同前往之嚮導八人，曾派出刀船八艘。現在增派人材壯健有經驗的嚮導十二人，共達二十人。此等派出嚮導等多預備攜帶糧米。若嚮導等不得糧米，各噶山之内各自湊齊辦理。爲此咨行[115]。

同年六月十日，咨文鑲白旗雍克牛彔領催噶喇庫的文書，又記載了準備刀船以及夫役的内容：

副都統咨文姓長扎哈喇，額布奇，努葉勒姓噶珊達等。先前曾派人令爾等三姓預備派出嚮導二十人，刀船八艘。大臣等前來之後，言稱派出的刀船少，是故從我等此地增派刀船。現在爾等刀船，各刀船派出船夫七人。此次派出之際，努葉勒姓拿出刀船三艘，葛依克勒姓出刀船三艘。瑚西哈里姓出刀船二艘。以前派出二十人之外，另外增派三十六人，每人各攜帶兩個月糧米，不得耽擱。此處刀船盡速出發前去。派人之際，各噶山由扎哈喇親自前去指派，刀船八艘須要修理堅固。爲此咨文[116]。

六月十二日咨行正白旗阿蘭泰牛彔領催之文記載：

副都統咨行水路送刀船之領催碩薩等。爾等逆流而上之水路險惡平安之處抵達之後，選擇停船熟悉之人，逐一逆流而上，不得妄爲犯錯。又抵達呼拉噶河口之後，努葉勒姓三艘刀船，葛依克勒姓三艘刀船，胡什喀里姓二艘刀船，各船均帶去夫役七人。抵達烏蘇里江後，將爾等帶去糧米，交給居住在周圍的阿克頓姓長、噶珊達等，嚴諭留給他們。爾等於一月末前去。抵達雞林烏喇、百都訥二地前往採挖人参之協領等扎營處所之後，替換彼等鐵樁子十五，上等刀船帶去。將此等緣由亦咨文告知協領等。爾等不可耽誤限期之日。擇選前去採挖人参之雞林烏喇、百都訥二地之人帶去的鐵樁子、上等刀船帶去。等於。自寧古塔送去之刀船，抵達爾等之處更換鐵樁子十五、刀船派去。不得耽誤。又，收到的文書内，聖旨：我等滿洲等均去採挖人参，途中遇到，想必給爾等協助食物。等於。爲此咨行[117]。

---

[114] 《康熙四十八年行文档》（《寧古塔》1-11），康熙四十八年五月二十八日咨行正黄旗察里布牛彔領催阿蘭泰文書。

[115] 《康熙四十八年行文档》（《寧古塔》1-11），康熙四十八年六月初二日咨行鑲黄旗雍克牛彔披甲阿爾塔文書。

[116] 《康熙四十八年行文档》（《寧古塔》1-11），康熙四十八年六月十日咨行鑲白旗雍克牛彔領催噶喇庫文書。

[117] 《康熙四十八年行文档》（《寧古塔》1-11），康熙四十八年六月十二日咨行正白旗阿蘭泰牛彔領催之文。

六月十三日同一内容由寧古塔副都統寄給通過水路前往烏蘇里採挖人參的協領色爾特依、覺羅色巴圖等人，要求備好刀船等，嚴令不得耽誤[118]。六月二十日寄給琿春村之賽努的文書中，記載了副都統寄給琿春噶珊達等人協助盡速派出嚮導的事情：

副都統咨行琿春噶珊達達巴庫、巴克西那、莽珠等人。前來丈量土地之大臣等一同前往之熟悉地理之嚮導盡速派出，爲此曾派出巴庫西納。問詢爾等派遣制嚮導薩音柱等人，答稱：自琿春向隋分方向去的路程不太清楚。事關聖旨不得疏忽，派去薩音柱等年輕人大爲不妥，應備齊七、八位年老熟悉地理情形之西蘭、楊古喇、特克新等有經驗之人派去爲宜，大臣等二十日從這裏出發，二十六、七日抵達琿春。此等換派嚮導、馬匹、食物等所有物品，立刻備齊。一刻都不得耽誤，爲此咨行[119]。

各地協助調查計劃，可以說是前所未有的。按杜赫德的《中華帝國全誌》第四卷記載的雷孝思報告，卷末還有各天體觀測地點的表格。我們利用這些資料來說明一下，測繪調查隊伍的具體路線。

康熙四十八年（1709）三月二十九日（陽曆五月八日），從北京出發。他們遵照康熙皇帝設計好的路程，出山海關，沿著渤海沿岸經新店子、牛莊到金州，然後經過正白村到鳳凰城，從鳳凰城路過長白山西側，向西北方面進入盛京。雷孝思他們到盛京五部後，前往郊區的福陵和昭陵觀光。走出盛京後，經得孤村到興京城，謁拜安放清帝祖先的永陵。測繪隊伍從興京返回，再從舊路向英額邊門走去，出了英額門到胖色城，拉法站，六月上旬到達寧古塔[120]。

有關耶穌會士參與繪製的東北地區木版地圖，我們通過福克司的研究來具體看一下。按照木版《皇輿全覽圖》的圖名來看，當時木版地圖名稱以及繪製年代、繪製人員具體如下：

表4 《皇輿全覽圖》東北地區圖

圖號	圖名	繪製年代	繪製者
1—3	盛京全圖、烏蘇里江圖、黑龍江圖	1709.5.8—1709.11	雷孝思（1663—1738）、費隱（1673—1743）、杜德美（1668—1720）
4	黑龍江中圖	1710.7.22—1710.12.14	雷孝思、費隱、杜德美
5	黑龍江源圖	1711.4—1712.1	費隱、杜德美

滿文銅版圖和法國銅版圖無論從圖形上，還是從地名標記上來看，都非常接近。而木版圖從圖形上就與滿文、法文圖版圖大爲不同。木版圖是1943年，福克司在北京輔仁大學任教時，據康熙六十年（1721）木刻版地圖重印[121]。

---

[118] 《康熙四十八年行文档》（《寧古塔》1-11），康熙四十八年六月十三日正黄旗雲騎尉等級章京馬蘭泰咨文。

[119] 《康熙四十八年行文档》（《寧古塔》1-11），康熙四十八年六月二十日寄給琿春村之賽努文書。

[120] 參看松浦茂《一七〇九年イエズス会士レジスの沿海地方調查》，《史林》84-3,2001年，77—108頁，後收入同氏《清朝のアムール政策と少数民族》(東洋史研究叢刊)，41—82頁。

[121] 美國國會圖書館冊藏圖，參看李孝聰編著《美國國會圖書館藏中文古地圖敘錄》，北京：文物出版社，2004年，12—13頁。

據杜赫德《中華帝國全誌》第四卷記載，當時耶穌會士記載的測繪地點具體是，關東（即遼東）共8處，東韃靼共36處，其他東北地區共測繪44處，詳細地點參看表5[122]。

表5

QUAN TONG（关东）	Latitudes（緯度）			Longitudes（經度）			
	deg	min	fec	deg	min	fec	Orient（東）
SIN TIEN TSE（新店子）	41	16	30	5	13	20	東
Nieou tchuang（牛莊）	41	0	25	6	13	20	東
King tcheou（金州）	39	0	0	5	27	50	東
Koulouchannien Cajan（？？噶山）	40	5	30	7	27	50	東
Fong hoang tching（鳳凰城）	40	30	30	7	45	30	東
Ynden hotun（興京城）	41	44	15	8	35	20	東
Tegou Cajan（？？噶山）	41	56	20	7	49	40	東
Moucden hotun ou Chin Yang（盛京或沈陽）	41	50	30	7	11	50	東
TARTARIE ORIENTALE（東韃靼）	Latitudes（緯度）			Longitudes（經度）			
PANSE HOTUN（胖色城）	41	29	0	9	6	40	東
Kirin oula hotun（雞林烏喇城）1	43	46	48	10	24	30	東
TARTARIE ORIENTALE（東韃靼）	Latitudes（緯度）			Longitudes（經度）			
Tondon kiamon（推屯驛）	43	46	48	11	26	0	東
Ningouta hotun（寧古塔城）	44	24	15	13	16	0	東
Source de Houtchi bira	43	31	0	13	15	0	東
Hongta hotun	42	54	1	13	36	0	東
Tchoulghei hotun（朱爾根城）	43	20	10	15	8	20	東
Tchoulghei hotun de Souifong pira（朱爾根城 隋分河）	44	1	12	15	36	30	東
Tapcou hinca bord Midi	44	33	0	16	34	0	東
Tchuolghei hotun de Ousouri pira（烏蘇里江朱爾根城）	44	47	10	18	0	0	東
Niman Cajan（泥滿噶山）	46	55	20	17	44	15	東
Hai tchou Cajan（海州噶山）	47	59	0	18	45	0	東
Houle Cajan（呼勒噶山）	48	50	0	19	3	20	東
Tondon Cajan（鼇鼇噶山）3	49	24	20	19	58	40	東
Edou Cajan（衣禿噶山）	48	9	36	15	37	0	東
Tchesi Cajan（？噶山）	47	49	11	16	11	20	東
Aomili Cajan（?噶山）	47	23	0	15	27	30	東
Mohoro Cajan（木乎勒噶山）	47	18	45	14	40	40	東
Yndamou Cajan（因打母噶山）	46	53	20	14	12	50	東
Nouchon Cajan(奴褚渾噶山)	45	47	45	9	52	0	東
Petouncz hotun（白頭子城）	45	15	40	8	32	20	東
Poroto Cajan（波羅圖噶山）	43	48	0	5	50	0	東

[122] 後來這些經緯度內容又編入*De la Chine, ou Description générale de cet empire*，3e édition， Par M. l'abbé Grosier, Edition 3, Tome 1，1818-1820, pp. 263-264。

续表

Hara paychang（哈喇拜商）	42	18	0	4	3	0	東
Kogin po kiamon	41	4	15	2	46	40	東
Soulai po	41	50	30	1	25	0	東
Sira y jousai po	41	15	36	1	58	20	東
Parin（巴林）	43	35	0	2	15	0	東
Tchacca hotun（塔哈城）	43	59	0	1	26	40	東
Poroto kiamon（博勒多驛）	44	16	48	0	30	0	東
Poro hotun（博勒城）	44	1	30	2	57	30	東
Tchol hotun（戳兒城）	46	39	36	6	36	20	東
Tchiskar（乞啟哈里（齊齊哈爾））	47	24	0	7	27	40	東
Kamnica kiamon（喀母泥喀驛站）	48	41	30	8	27	20	東
Merghen hotun（墨爾根城）	49	12	0	8	33	50	東
Saghalien hotun（黑龍江城）	50	0	55	10	59	0	東
Ouloussou moudan（烏魯蘇穆丹）	51	21	36	10	23	0	東

註：據杜赫德《中華帝國全誌》（1735）卷3，485—486頁，（ ）內地名由筆者對譯。

結　語

通過以上論述，我們大致理清了東北大地測繪隊伍的組編情況和具體參加人員。從測繪隊伍構成人員的簡歷來看，這些人曾在八旗官學就讀，他們大部分是經過嚴格選拔考試後，擁有在內廷行走，侍奉皇帝的經驗。其中，有些人員在算學館擔任過要職，還有人在欽天監擔任五官生的工作，他們精通天文曆算，這些都表明了清廷方面主持測繪工作的人員都是經過嚴格挑選的。另外從欽派嚮導護軍參領德克精格家人騷擾當地人的事件來看，這些測繪隊伍的主要成員，基本上都隨隊帶去家僕隨從，沿途惹是生非，騷擾當地民眾，帶來不少麻煩。從此也可以知道測繪隊伍規模遠比文書中看到的正式人員要多出許多。到了當地之後，有些地區派出多達五十人協助調查，如此大規模的測繪調查，可以說清代歷史上非常罕見。

《皇輿全覽圖》傳入法國之前，南懷仁繪製的東北地圖，以不同方式繪入各類歐洲世界地圖之中，其編入方式較爲特別，僅僅作爲一個參照，並未繪入歐亞大陸的一部分，而是另外作爲參照附圖，配置在世界地圖的右上方。雍正三年（1725）之前，《皇輿全覽圖》傳入法國，南懷仁的地圖很快就被《皇輿全覽圖》取而代之。另外，康熙朝繪製《皇輿全覽圖》的東北亞部分地名，我們通過法文版地圖可以了解到，最初測繪東北大地的成果，由耶穌會士依照滿文、蒙古文的地圖的地名標記，將其以法文音寫的方式，編入法文世界地圖之中。從此東北各地地名以滿語、蒙古語音寫的形式，傳入西方地圖學界，這本身就很有歷史意義。並且在法國繪製的世界地圖上特別註明了滿文、蒙古文與法文對應的表示地理特征的詞彙。具體如下（括弧內文字爲筆者漢譯）：

EXPLICATION（說明、注釋）
Dans langue des Tartares Oriontaux ou Mantcheoux（東韃靼語或滿洲語）
Oula--Fleube ou Grande Riviere（大河）
Pira—Riviere（河）
Omo--Lac ou Etang（湖泊或池塘）

Sekim--Source de Riviere（河源）
Hotun--etpar abreviatin H. Ville.（城）
Cajan--Village.（小城）
Paitchan Lieu serme ou qui aune Enceinte（巡查）
Hiyamen-Parte sur une Route Srequentee.（驛站）
Dansla Langue des Tartares Occidentanx ou Mongols.（東韃靼語或蒙古語）
Mouren-Riviere（河流）
Nor--Lac ou Etang（湖泊或池塘）
Poulac-Fontaine ou siorce（泉水）
Alin—Montagne（山）
Hata-Roche（峰）
Tabahan-Montagne elevee ou passage de Montag（山崗）

康熙二十五年（1696）十月，俄羅斯西伯利亞省向西伯利亞各地下令繪製西伯利亞地圖，其內容要求各地繪製尺幅爲215厘米×140厘米的地區地圖。當時，西伯利亞行政中心托波利斯克繪製了215厘米×280厘米的西伯利亞全圖。各圖中規定記述所有俄羅斯人村莊、當地原住民以及河流名稱、地名、村落及其相互間距離、所需時間等[123]。我們目前看到的列麥佐夫（Ремезов）家族繪製的西伯利亞地圖冊，就是收到這個通知后繪製而成的。目前，列麥佐夫家族留下的西伯利亞地圖集有：①地圖資料集（*Хорографическая Чертёжная книга*），②西伯利亞地圖集（*Чертёжная книга Сибири*），③官用地圖集（*Служебная чертежная книга*）三種。均由全圖和地區圖組成，有目錄、序文、凡例。序文中關於地圖繪製過程的概要以及利用的資料的說明，基本上包含了地圖集所應有的要素[124]。其中，②是俄羅斯帝國第一部俄羅斯地圖集。

1687年，列麥佐夫家族繪製的《西伯利亞全圖》，以西伯利亞及其南部爲中心，地圖上南下北，東爲太平洋沿岸，西達烏拉爾山脈，北爲北極沿海，南到中國北部、青海、重要，東南還能看到日本的一部分。這幅地圖與以往的西伯利亞相關系列地圖相

---

[123] 參看巴格羅夫（Bagrow），Semyon Remezov-a Siberian cartographer，Imago mundi, Vol. 11, 1954，pp. 111-125。

[124] 船越昭生《北方図の歴史》，東京：講談社，1976年，66—76頁。

比，勒拿河到黑龍江之間的東北亞部分明顯越來越趨向詳細分明[125]。但是，該地圖沒有採用地圖投影法，基本上以收集當時未知地區的地理信息爲主要目的。俄羅斯帝國初期繪製的這類西伯利亞地圖集沒有標註經緯度，這與康熙時期開始編纂各地通志以及下令編纂《大清一統志》而繪製的地圖無論在時間上還是在方法上都有相近之處，今後有必要對中俄兩國同時並進的測繪大地事業進一步深入探討。

致謝：本文是在2015年“中央”研究院明清研究國際學術研討會（2015年12月10—11日）參會論文（《皇輿全覽圖》東北大地測繪考——以滿文檔案爲中心）的基礎上增補寫成，感謝主辦單位提供與各位同行交流的機會。本研究受日本學術振興會資助，是研究課題大清帝國國境形成史研究（基盤研究（C），課題番号：26370843）相關研究的一部分，特此致謝。

Land Surveys in the Northeast for the“*Huangyu quanlan tu*”

Cheng zhi（Kicengge）

During the 47th year of the Kangxi reign (1708), the Kangxi emperor for the first time sent out three missionaries as part of a team of surveyors also including an escort, a carpenter, and others, in order to draw part of a map known as the “*Huangyu quanlan tu*”. They traveled through the Great Wall’s Shanhai Pass, along the seashore to the city of Fenghuang, and later west of the Changbai Mountains back to the city of Mukden. After that, they continued eastward, passing Ningguta, Hunchun, the Suifen River, and the Usury River, and on towards the lower reaches of the Amur River. Two years later, the emperor again sent out a team, this time mainly consisting of Manchus. They reached areas that were not visited during the first expedition, such as the mouth of the Amur River and the island of Sakhalin, where they undertook surveying activities. When we look carefully at the people who conducted the surveying activities on both expeditions, we see that the literature has hitherto focused solely on the role of the missionaries, while neglecting the Manchu expedition leaders and representatives of the Bureau of Astronomy. In this presentation, I use Manchu and other language materials to revisit the surveying activities related to the Kangxi-era “Huangyu quanlan tu” and undertaken in the Northeast.

---

[125] 三上正利《一六八七年のシベリア地図》，小牧実繁先生古稀記念會編《人文地理学上の諸問題》天明堂，1968年，425—437頁。有關西伯利亞地圖研究，參看Гольденберг Л. А., *Семён Ульянович Ремезов: Сибирский картограф и географ. 1642 — после 1720 s*. 1965，Наука。 最近的西伯利亞古地圖研究，參看米家志乃布《20世紀前半のシベリア・ロシア極東における植民都市と地図作製》，《法政大学文学部紀要》62，2011年，57—71頁，米家志乃布《ベーリングの第一次カムチャツカ探検とシベリア図》，《法政大学文学部紀要》64，2012年，51—66頁，米家志乃布《レーメゾフの『公務の地図帳』とシベリア地域像》，《法政大学文学部紀要》66,2013年，41—61頁。

新見三封明廷賜封西番剌麻勑諭及其考釋

沈衛榮

一

有明一代，朝廷曾賜予數量眾多的西番高僧以法王、教王、西天佛子、灌頂國師、國師、禪師和剌麻等封號，並視其等級高下頒發以不同類型的詔誥和勑諭，同時還給以相應的圖書（印）、賞賜等。這些封號、詔誥和圖書曾經數量巨大，是紀錄明朝中央與西番地方之間密切交往的第一手資料，也是今天我們研究明朝中央政府與西藏地方之間政教關係史和西藏地方政治、宗教歷史的重要歷史文獻。遺憾的是，能夠保留至今的這類明廷賜封西番剌麻的詔誥和勑諭並不很多，20世紀50年代國家文物部門於西藏進行文物普查期間，曾有不少明代的詔誥被陸續發現、研究和發表，可惜其中的絕大部分只有錄文發表而沒有見到完整的影印圖版[①]。20世紀90年代由西藏自治區檔案館編集、出版的《西藏歷史檔案薈萃》中收錄了此類詔誥八封，這是今藏於西藏自治區檔案館等地之同類詔誥中已爲人所知的部分，而藏於該館內迄今尚未被整理、發表的此類文書相信還爲數不少[②]。此外，於21世紀初出版的題爲《寶藏》的畫冊中，我們又見到了兩封明廷賜封西番僧人的勑諭的完整圖版[③]。還有，於2006年出版的《中國國家博物館館藏文物

---

① 王毅《西藏文物見聞記》（一、二、三、四），《文物》，1959—1961年；西藏文管會《明朝皇帝賜給西藏楚布（普）寺噶瑪活佛的兩件詔書》，《文物》1981年第11期；這兩件詔書分別是：一，洪武八年正月哈爾麻剌麻詔書；二，永樂十一年二月初十日致如來大寶法王書。文竹《西藏地方明封八王有關文物》，《文物》1985年第9期；宋伯胤《明代中央政權致西藏地方詔敕》，中央民族學院藏族研究所編《藏學研究文集——獻給自治區成立二十週年》，北京：民族出版社，1985年；宿白《拉薩布達拉宮主要殿堂和庫藏的明代部分文書》，《藏傳佛教寺院考古》，北京：文物出版社，1996年，208—221頁。

② 西藏自治區檔案館編《西藏歷史檔案薈萃》，北京：文物出版社，1995年，22—33頁。這八封詔誥均漢藏雙語，分別是：一，洪武六年二月賜搠思公失監（Chos kun skyabs）聖旨；二，永樂五年正月十八日致尚師哈立麻書；三，永樂十一年二月初九日賜鎖巴頭目剌昝肖（So pa mgo dpon lHa tsang skyabs）勑諭；四，永樂十二年一月十一日賜高日斡鎖南觀（bKa' bzhi pa bSod nams mgon）勑諭；五，宣德二年三月二十二日賜慧慈禪師葛里麻（Karma pa）勑諭；六，正統十年六月初四日賜尚師哈立麻巴勑諭；七，成化五年四月十一日賜南葛劄失堅參叭藏卜（Nam mkha' bkra shis rgyal mtshan dpal bzang po）勑諭；八，成化二十二年七月十三日賜烏思藏如來大寶法王葛哩麻巴等勑諭。

③ 它們是：一，成化帝封南葛劄失堅參叭藏卜爲輔教王勑諭；二，弘治皇帝允准鎖南堅參巴藏卜承襲淨修圓妙國師封誥。參見《寶藏——中國西藏歷史文物》，第三冊，北京：朝華出版社，2000年，152—173頁。

研究叢書——明清檔案卷（明代）》部分中，我們又見到了國家博物館館藏的明代皇帝頒賜給西番僧人的勑諭和制誥三封[④]。

儘管保存至今的這類由明朝廷賜給西番剌麻的詔誥、勑諭的數量已經不多了，但於當時其數量無疑曾經是十分巨大的。這類詔書的漢文本有一些見於《明實錄》中的直接紀錄，也有一些見於其他各類漢文文獻中的抄錄。例如，在《明太祖文集》中我們曾見到過一件“賜西番國師詔”，而這位“西番國師”據稱是元朝八思巴帝師之後人恭格嘉燦伊實藏布（Kun dga' rgyal mtshan ye shes dpal bzang po）[⑤]。而在時代相應的藏文文獻中，我們見到了更多的這類詔誥、勑諭之藏文版的抄錄文。僅於一部題爲《如願吉祥太陽》（*'Dod pa'i re skong dpal ster nyi ma*）的明封大慈法王釋迦也失（Byams chen chos rje Śākya ye shes）的藏文傳紀中，我們就見到了永樂和宣德二朝先後頒賜給大慈法王的十五封詔書的全錄文。而這部傳紀據稱是根據作者所見的一幅描繪大慈法王替其上師宗喀巴大師出使明廷而於朝廷內外活動的長卷畫傳編寫而成的，所以其中包括的這十五封詔令應當都是從這部長卷中直錄的，而與其中四封相應的漢文版的文本則見於明代釋鎮澄所編《清涼山志》中的“釋迦也失傳”中[⑥]。這即可從一個側面反映出明朝賜封西番剌麻詔諭之頻繁程度是如此之高，明朝皇帝與西番剌麻之間的政教關係是如此之深。

與此類似，在明代漢譯的明封淨覺慈濟大國師、西天佛子、大智法王班丹扎釋的的傳紀《西天佛子源流錄》中，我們也見到了宣德和正統皇帝先後賜封給他的三封詔書的完整錄文，而這三封詔書均不見於《明實錄》之中[⑦]。顯而易見，凡曾入明廷朝覲的番僧、剌麻，特別是曾經獲得過明廷賞賜的法王、國師、禪師、剌麻等稱號者，當無一例外地得到過明朝廷頒賜的封誥和勑諭、圖書等。於此值得一提的是，范德康（Leonard van der Kuijp）教授曾於20世紀90年代初於北京民族宮圖書館中查得明封大乘法王昆澤思巴上師於其入明永樂宮廷朝覲及其前後致永樂皇帝及其皇子等人函共一十七封，足可見其與明皇室書信往還的密切程度，其中多次提到永樂皇帝賜封給他詔書，而他於蛇年（1413）五月八日自明宮城內寫成的一封賜予薩思迦寺僧衆們的法旨中，還全文照錄了

---

④ 中國國家博物館編《中國國家博物館館藏文物研究叢書——明清檔案卷明代》，上海：上海古籍出版社，2006年。其中所錄明朝廷頒賜給西番僧人之勑諭有三封，它們是：一，正統十三年五月十七日頒賜給番僧劄失竹之勑諭，漢藏文合璧；二，正德十年六月二十六日皇帝勑諭陝西岷州衛大崇教寺下院牙兒薩族崇隆寺番僧短竹班丹，漢藏文合璧；三，萬曆四十四年九月二十三日給番僧班着爾領真襲國師之職制誥，漢藏文合璧。

⑤ 《明太祖文集》卷八。實際上，這份詔書的錄文也見於《明實錄》之太祖實錄卷九一，洪武七年七月己卯條中，其中所錄詔書之文字更加準確。

⑥ 關於大慈法王的這部傳紀以及其中所錄的這十五封詔書的錄文和初步研究，參見拉巴平措《大慈法王釋迦也失》，北京：中國藏學出版社，2012年。

⑦ 參見張潤平、蘇航、羅炤編著《西天佛子源流錄——文獻與初步研究》，北京：中國社會科學出版社，2012年，173—181頁。其中的第三件是明英宗加封班丹扎釋爲“西天佛子”時此給他的一封詔誥，其錄文也見於《岷州誌》卷十七，有些文字略有不同。參見陳楠《大智法王考》，氏著《藏史叢考》，北京：民族出版社，1998年，223—246頁。

永樂皇帝頒賜給他的一封詔書⑧。

晚近，還曾有一封爲已故旅德藏胞Namgyel Ronge先生收藏的明嘉靖三十四年（1555）六月二十九日賜予靈藏贊善王灌頂淨修廣慧國師的誥命，多年前曾被德國波恩大學Peter Schwieger教授揭載於世⑨。Schwieger教授還在西藏自治區檔案館中發現了一封嘉靖四十一年（1562）五月二十日賜給怕木主巴灌頂大國師闡化王剳思巴剳失堅參(Grags pa bkra shis rgyal mtshan)的詔令⑩。

二

近日筆者有幸從收藏家手中見到了晚近於民間收集到的明廷賜封西番剌麻勑諭三封，它們分別是：

一，宣德二年（1427）三月二十二日皇帝頒給西寧地面大小官員軍民諸色人等之勑諭，以西寧地面紅崖子溝寺，賜寺名曰華嚴，頒勑護持。

二，永樂十六年（1418）正月二十四日皇帝頒給剌麻恭禪之勑諭。

三，正德三年（1508）七月十六日皇帝剌麻頒給完卜領真列思巴之勑諭。

這三封勑諭均保存完好、齊整，漢藏雙語，與“永樂十六年正月二十四日皇帝勑諭剌麻恭禪”一同賜封的還有“慈悲廣濟圖書”（象牙印）一枚，也保存完好，具有極其寶貴的文物價值。從明代西藏歷史和漢藏關係史的角度來看，第一封給紅崖子溝寺（西寧塔爾寺屬寺）的勑諭，表明明朝廷繼承了元朝頒敕護持西番佛教寺院的傳統，明朝中央政府於西藏地方或具有與元朝政府一樣的權威震攝力量。第二、三封勑諭則表明“剌麻”作爲次於“國師”“禪師”的第三級西番宗教領袖名號，它也必須得到明中央政府的勑諭和承認，其職位可以世襲，憑此可以享受三年一次進京入貢並獲賞賜的特權。這個制度從明初一直延續至明末，是明代中央政府與西番地方政教關係中的一個重要內容。

---

⑧ 范德康教授當年於民族宮圖書館查找到的這十七封信函，以及大乘法王的一份傳紀至今未見出版，也未見有人有對此進行研究的成果問世。本世紀初，筆者曾蒙范教授邀請前往哈佛大學印度梵文研究係作了爲期半年的合作研究，對這些信件做過初步的翻譯，但此後一直未能做進一步的深入研究，殊爲遺憾。自今而後，筆者或將揭載其中的幾封信件，並對它們做一些力所能及的研究。

⑨ 參見Peter Schwieger, A Document of Chinese Diplomatic Relations with East Tibet during the Ming Dynasty, *Tibetstudien: Festschrift fuer Dieter Schuh zum 65. Geburtstag*, herausgegeben von Petra Maurer und Peter Schwieger, Bier'sche Verlagsanstalt, 2007, pp. 209-226.

⑩ Peter Schwieger, Significance of Ming Titles Conferred upon the Phag mo gru Rulers: A Reevaluation of Chinese-Tibetan Relations during the Ming Dynasty, *The Tibet Journal*, Special Issue: *The Earth Ox Papers. Proceedings of the International Seminar on Tibetan and Himalayan Studies*, Held at the Library of Tibetan Works and Archives, September 2009 on the Occasion of the Thank you India' Year, ed. By R. Vitali, Autumn & Winter 2009/ Spring & Summer, 2010, vol. XXXIV, no. 3 & 4/ vol. XXXV, n. 1 &2, Dharamsala, 2010, pp. 312-328.

三、宣德皇帝賜西寧紅崖子溝寺勑諭

皇帝勑諭西寧地面大小官員軍民諸色人等
朕惟
佛氏之興，其來已遠。西土之人，久事崇信。其教以空寂爲宗，以普度爲心，化導善類，覺悟群迷，功德之著，無間幽顯。有能尊崇其教，以導引夫一方之人，去其昏迷，嚮慕善道，強不至凌弱，大不至虐小，息爭鬬之風，無侵奪之患，上下各安其分，長幼各遂其生，同歸於仁壽之中，同安於泰和之世，上足以陰翊皇度，下足以勸善化俗，功德所及，豈不遠哉！今以西寧地面紅崖子溝寺，賜寺名曰華嚴，頒勑護持。所在官員軍民人等，務要各起信心，尊崇其教，聽從本寺剌麻班丹失加等及僧人自在修行，並不許侮慢欺淩。其常住一應寺宇、田地、山場、園林、財產、孳畜之類，諸人不許侵占騷擾，庶俾佛法興隆，法門弘振，而一方之人亦得以安生樂業，進脩善道。若有不遵朕命、不敬三寶、故意生事侮慢欺凌翊沮其教者，論之以法。故諭

宣德二年三月二十二日
zon de'i gnyis pa'i lo zla ba gsum pa'i nyi shu gnyis gi nyin

// rgyal po lung gis

zi nying phyogs kyi sa cha na yod pa'i mi dpon che chung/ dmag mi sde gzhan yang mi sna tshogs rnams la bzlo ba/ nged kyi bsam pa la/ sangs rgyas kyi bstan pa dar ba ni/ yin rung du [yung rin du] (yun rang[11] du) song zhing/nub phyogs na yod pa'i mi rnams kyis yun ring na de la dad cing/ de'i bstan pa ni/ stong ba dang zhi ba la gtsor byas zhing/ sems nyid kun la 'dren pa byed pa dang/ 'dul bya dge ba'i lam la bkod/ ma rig pa 'thoms pa rnams la gsal bar mdzad pa/ yon tan gyi sgron me ni/ nyin mtshan kun tu rgyun 'chad med pa/ gal te sangs rgyas kyi

⑪ rang应为ring。

bstan pa la cher gus byas na/ de'i rtogs(rtog)[⑫] pa las brten nas phyogs gcig gis[⑬] skye bo rnams la dge ba'i lam ston cing/ de dag gis 'khrul pa sel ba/ dge ba'i lam la bkod/ nyom[⑭] che ba rnams kyis nyams chung ba rnams la 'ang brnyas pa med pa dang/ che ba rnams kyis chung ba rnams la 'ang gnod pa med pa dang/ 'thab rtsod kyi bzer bu rab tu zhi zhing/ 'phrog pa dang chom rkun med de/ mthon dman bar gsum rang tshad zin la/ rgan gzhon so sor bde ba dang thams cad mi'i longs spyod myong ba'i ngang nas/ 'jig rten gyi longs spyod la spyod cing/ gong du/ // nged kyi rgyal khams la mi mngon pa'i grogs ldan dang/ 'og tu 'dul bya rnams la dge ba'i lam la bkod cing/ de'i yon tan ni shin tu rgya che ba yin no// da lta zi nying sa cha na yod pa'i hung [ya'i] tsi lung ba'i sde la de'i ming ni hwa yem zhes bya ba gnang bas/ phyogs de na yod pa'i mi dpon dmag mi de la dwog(sogs pa) thams cad so sor dad pa'i sems bskyed nas/ de'i bstan pa la bkur bsti byed pa dang/ sde de'i bla ma dpal ldan skyabs mgo byas dge 'dun rnams la ston(nyon) pa kho rang gar bde rang dbang bsgrub pa byed du chug dbang che brnyas chos snyad brko rdung rdung ma byed pa dang/ 'di lha khang la gtogs pa'i khang gzhi/ sa zhing/ nags ri/ rtswa kha/ char rkyen dngos po dud 'gro sems can la sogs pa la/ mi gang gis kyang gnod 'tsher dang bdag bzung ma byed/ de ltar na/ sangs rgyas kyi bstan pa dar/ chos kyi sgo mo rgya cher 'gyur ba dang/ de phyogs su mi rnams rang rang so sor zhing chu so nam bde skyid la longs spyod pa dang/ dge ba'i lam la brtson 'grus bsgrub par gyis/ gal te// nged kyi lung 'di bzhin du mi nyan cing/ dkon mchog la sa[⑮] mi dad pa yin pas/ de'i don gyis bya ba ngan pa bskyed cing/ de la brnyas chos dang rdung rdung byed pa yin pa dang// sangs rgyas kyi bstan pa la gnod pa byed par yin na/ cis kyang nyes pa gcod pas thar du mi 'jug/

lung yin

zon de'i gnyis pa'i lo zla ba gsum pa'i nyi shu gnyis gi nyin

於迄今已公佈的有數的幾份明代詔誥來看，這份宣德皇帝頒敕護持西寧地面紅崖子溝寺的勑諭是獨有的，其內容對於研究明代中央政府與西藏地方關係史有其特殊的意義。事實上，明代歷朝頒敕護持西番諸佛教寺院是尋常之事，與此敕諭內容相同的文本亦多見於《明實錄》的記載中。例如，永樂八年（1410）“九月庚辰，命番僧綽思吉領禪巴藏卜（Chos kyi rin chen dpal bzang po）爲灌頂弘慈妙濟國師，掌巴監藏 (Byang pa rgyal mtshan)爲淨慈妙智國師，掌巴哈羅思巴 (Byang pa grags pa)爲善濟慧應國師，皆賜誥印圖書，仍給護勑，俾自在修行。其寺田土、山場、園林、財產、孳畜之類，禁諸人毋侵擾，違者罪之。”[⑯]顯然，此處之用辭與前引明宣德皇帝賜西寧地面紅崖子溝

⑫ rtog应为rtogs。

⑬ gis为gi的误写？

⑭ nyom应为nyams。

⑮ 衍字？

⑯ 《明實錄》太宗實錄，卷七十二，永樂八年九月庚辰條。

寺敕諭中的用辭基本一致，可見朝廷頒敕諭護持西番諸佛教寺院實際上是明初開始一直延續的慣例。

這樣的習慣至少一直延續到明朝的中期，例如明英宗正統七年（1442）八月：

辛亥，敕諭河州西寧等處官員軍民人等曰：朕惟佛氏之道，以空寂爲宗，以普度爲用。西土之人，久事崇信。今以黑城子廠房地，賜大慈法王釋迦也失，蓋造佛寺，賜名弘化，頒敕護持。本寺田地、山場園林、財產孳畜之類，所在官軍人等，不許侵占、騷擾、侮慢。若非本寺原有田地、山場等項，亦不許因而侵占、擾害。軍民敢有不遵法者，必論之以重罪。"⑰

不僅如此，由朝廷頒敕護持西番佛教寺院不受他人侮慢侵凌，這本是元朝留下的慣例，我們在元代留下的與西番相關的詔誥，包括帝師法旨、皇后懿旨、諸王令旨中，都見到了大量內容與此類似的文書，可知護持佛教寺院這本是元朝治理西番的一項重要舉措，而明代取代元朝之後，其對西番的治理於這一點上基本上照搬了其前朝的作法。甚至，前引這份"宣德皇帝賜西寧紅崖子溝寺敕諭"其格式也與元代留下的眾多賜給西番佛教寺院的詔令基本一致。例如，元懷寧王海山頒敕給沙魯寺的一封令旨的行文如下：

長生天氣力裏

大合罕福蔭裏

懷寧王海山令旨

向各城的達魯花赤們和長官們，向軍官們，軍人們，往來行走的使臣們宣諭的令旨：

成吉思汗、窩闊台汗、薛禪合罕的聖旨裏都說過："和尚們、也里可溫們、先生們不要承擔任何差發，他們要祈禱上天，「爲我們」祝壽。"如今也這樣，"依照合罕的聖旨，不要承擔任何差發，不要做違背釋迦牟尼教法的事，要祈禱上天，「爲我們」祝壽"。在藏地方的舅舅朵兒只汪術和葛剌思巴監藏所在的沙魯寺裏的僧人們，要向觀世音菩薩常川供奉燈油。"這樣說著，「我」頒給了讓他們執持的令旨。在他們的寺院和房舍裏，使臣們不得下榻，不得索取鋪馬和祇應。不得在他們的莊園（谿卡）裏飼養馬匹和牛，不得徵收地稅、商稅。對他們的土地、園林、碾磨、人口、畜牧，無論什麼東西，任何人不得奪取，不得使用非法的暴力。

再者，他們不要以爲持有令旨而做非法的事，如果做，他們難道不懼怕嗎？我的令旨。蛇兒年秋末月（九月）三十日寫於只剌木禿⑱。

由於以前我們沒有見到過諸如上引元朝懷寧王海山敕諭護持沙魯寺之寺院財產、並給以免除地稅、商稅等種種特權之令旨一樣的明代文書，而且明代詔誥的格式中也缺少"被詔諭者"（publication）和"受制裁"條款（sanction）兩個部分，所以，Schwieger

---

⑰　《明實錄》英宗實錄，卷九十五。

⑱　陳得芝《讀伯希和譯注八思巴字懷寧王海山令旨》，同氏《蒙元史研究叢稿》，北京：人民出版社，2005年，252—265頁；《西藏歷史檔案薈萃》，13—15頁。

先生便認爲明代頒賜給西番僧人和寺院的詔誥中缺失了標明實際權威的因素。顯然，在我們見到這份“宣德皇帝賜西寧紅崖子溝寺勑諭”之後，Schwieger先生的這個説法也就難以成立了⑲。

對於西寧紅崖溝寺我們所知不多，僅見《甘青藏傳佛教寺院》一書中載於今青海省湟中縣有“紅崖溝寺”（Hong ne rgu zi，或稱Brag dmar lung ba'i dgon pa），“位於縣治魯沙爾鎮東南3千米的紅崖溝村。1958年有經堂、僧舍22間，寺僧1人。現有佛堂3間，僧舍4間，寺僧仍1人”⑳。此或當即是我們上引這份勑諭中所提到的獲明朝廷賜名“華嚴”的“紅涯子溝寺”。還有傳紅崖溝寺位於湟中縣魯沙爾鎮所屬紅崖溝村，距塔爾寺僅三公里，乃塔爾寺屬寺。顯然，紅崖溝寺於後代之重要性與其於明代時的地位相比早已經不可同日而語了。

四、永樂皇帝賜剌麻恭禪勑諭

皇帝勑諭剌麻恭禪

朕惟佛氏之道，廣大慈悲，充周
普遍。上足以陰翊皇度，下足以
拔濟有情。功德之弘，被于幽顯。
惟尔恭禪，宿性明通，自然了悟，
爰造毘盧之境，超登般若之迹（道），
妙演真乘，以化善類。眷尔精勤，
良用嘉獎。今特賜以慈悲廣濟
圖書，尔尚嚴潔毘尼，丕闡宗旨，開
導迷惑，賛我皇猷。故諭

⑲ Schwieger, Significance of Ming Titles Conferred upon the Phag mo gru Rulers, pp. 313-314. 事實上，明朝廷對元朝勑諭地方護持番僧所建佛寺的慣例非常熟悉，且多有效法。1970年代，曾於廣東省韶關市曲江縣南華寺發現了元仁宗普顔篤皇帝的兩道聖旨和元朝帝師公哥羅古羅思監藏班藏卜（Kun dga' blo gros rgyal mtshan dpal bzang po）的一道法旨，而這道法旨曾於大明天順八年（1464）五月十五日由大隆善寺淨覺慈濟大國師鎖南領占巴藏卜（bSod nams rin chen dpal bzang po）翻譯成漢文，其云：“皇帝聖旨、帝師公哥羅竹堅參巴藏卜法旨：勑諭文武官員僧俗軍民使臣人等，廣州府南華禪寺、廣州府南華戒院住坐弘園慈濟大師第長老，敬順天道，照依比先聖旨，本寺所有差役人夫吃食等項，盡皆蠲免，亦不許往來諸色人等住坐，攪擾此寺。原有佃戶、財物、河水、水磨、資『孳』畜等項，不許故意生事侵占、攪擾，着他自在修行。因此賜與護勑，敢有違者，奏知朝廷治罪不饒。本寺僧眾倚勑勢力，不許違法。大都大寺內蛇兒年正月三十日。”引自韓小東《大明國師“鎖南領占“考》，《中華論壇》2014年6月16日發布。這位譯者“大隆善寺淨覺慈濟大國師鎖南領占巴藏卜”當是明初著名西番高僧、西天佛子、大智法王班丹扎釋的後人，而後者亦曾模仿元代帝師向於其故鄉甘肅岷州建造的大崇教寺發佈了至少兩通法旨，參見李志明、洲塔《新發現的兩件班丹扎釋法旨及相關史實考述》，《中國藏學》2016年第3期，21—30頁。

⑳ 蒲文成主編《甘青藏傳佛教寺院》，西寧：青海人民出版社，1990年，144頁。

永樂十六年正月二十四日

yung lo bcu drug pa'i lo zla ba cig pa'i nyi shu bzhi gi nyin

//rgyal po'i lung gis

bla ma bsgom chen/ nged kyi bsam pa la/ sangs rgyas kyi lam ni/ byams dang snying rje shin tu che zhing ma kyab pa med pa/ gong du/ nged kyi rgyal khams kyi grogs ldan dang/ 'og tu 'dul bya rnam (rnams) la phan pa mdzad pa/ de'i yon tan rgya chen po ni/ nyin mtshan kun tu rgyun chad ('chad) med pa'o/ khyod bsgom chen/ snga mo nas sems rnam par dag cing rang bzhin du rtogs pa/ rnam dag gyi sa la zhugs pa dang/ pha rol tu phyin pa'i lam la grol ba/ theg pa chen po'i don zab mo bshad te/ skye bo rnams 'dul la/ de'i brtson 'grus legs por yod pa'i don la/ nged sems rab tu spro bas/ da lta nan gyis khyod la tshi ba'i gwong tsi ces yi ge yod pa'i thu'u zhu byin pas/ da phyin chad/ khyod tshul khrims rnam dag lhag par bsrung ba dang/ sangs rgyas kyi bstan pa dar bar byed pa dang ma rig pa 'thoms pa rnams gsal ba'i lam la bkod pa dang/ nged kyi grogs ldan 'ang gyis shig/ lung yin

yung lo bcu drug pa'i lo zla ba cig pa'i nyi shu bzhi gi nyin

五、正德皇帝勑諭剌麻完卜領真列思巴

皇帝勑諭剌麻完卜領真列思巴

朕惟佛氏之教，其體清淨圓明，
其用慈悲利濟，所以陰翊皇度，
化導群迷。凡其徒能闡揚其教
者，國家必褒獎之。尔完卜領真
列思巴，乃已故剌麻恭禪之姪
孫，夙脩善行，恪守清規。今特命
尔襲剌麻之職，尔尚堅持戒律，
益懋進修，丕闡宗風，用廣慈化。
欽哉！故諭

正德三年七月十六日

rgyal po'i lung gis

bla ma dbon po rin chen legs pa la bzlo ba/ nged kyi bsam pa la/ sangs rgyas kyi bstan pa ni/ de'i gzhi pa'i rnam par dag par sgo nas gsal zhing ljogs (sjogs)[21] pa de'i 'khol ba'i byams pa dang snying rjes gzhan la phan par mdzad pas/ rgyal srid la mi mngon par grogs ldan dang/ ma rig pas 'thibs pa rnams la sad par mdzad cing/ gang zhig de'i bstan pa la dar rgyas byed mkhan byung yod na gong gis de la nges par bstod par mdzad pa yin dbon po rin chen legs pa khyod/ 'das pa'i bla ma dgon chen yang tsha bos gzhon nu nas dge sbyor legs par bsgrubs cing/ tshul khrims tshul bzhin tu brtan par bsrung zhing/ da lta lung gis khyod kyi bla ma las ka chab tu bcug pa yin da phyin chad khyod kyis kyang khyad par du tshul khrims legs par bsrung zhing dge sbyor la rab tu bsgrubs cing/ ches cher sangs rgyas kyi bstan pa rgya chen po dar ba dang byams dang snying rjes la brten nas gdul bya rgya chen po brtul bar gyis lung 'di bzhin du gus par gyis shig lung yin

永樂十六年（1418）“賜剌麻恭禪勑諭”和正德三年（1508）“勑諭剌麻完卜領真列思巴”這兩件事及其兩封勑諭均不見於《明實錄》的記載中，這或說明受勑諭者於明代中央政府與西藏政教關係中的重要性或尚不足以吸引明朝宮廷史臣的注意。《明實錄》中實錄了很多類似的勑諭，與見於上錄這兩封勑諭中類似的說辭常見於明代勑諭西番剌麻之詔書、誥命中。例如，明英宗正統十年（1445）六月辛亥勑諭靈藏灌頂國師贊善王班丹堅剉(dPal ldan rgyal mtshan)的誥命中即有如下與見於此誥命中基本一致的表達：“爾尚益堅乃心，益懋乃行，廣宣佛教，化導群迷。俾爾一方之人，咸起爲善之心，永享太平之福。庶克振爾宗風，亦不負朝廷寵命。爾惟，欽哉！”[22]

《明實錄》中記載了大量受封爲法王、教王、西天佛子、大國師、國師以及剌麻、禪師等頭銜的西番僧人，這類僧人數目巨大，然而這些記載恐怕依然還遠不是明朝廷賜封西番各地僧人，並與之交往的全部內容。據新近發現的明封西天佛子、大智法王班丹扎釋的傳紀——《西天佛子源流錄》記載，班丹札釋僅於宣德年間就曾三次受封，第一次是宣德元年正月初八日受封爲“淨覺慈濟大國師”，第二次是同年八月十七日加封爲“弘通妙戒普慧善應輔國闡教灌頂淨覺慈濟大國師”，第三次是宣德乙卯正月加封“西天佛子”，而且每次都獲賜相應的誥命[23]。然而於《明實錄》中，我們衹見到了大明宣宗章皇帝實錄卷十二，洪熙元年十二月戊寅條下“命僧祿司右禪教班丹扎失爲淨覺慈濟大國師”一條記載[24]。可見，即使像班丹扎釋這樣對於明代漢藏關係史的展開具有重大意義的人物，《明實錄》中對他事蹟的記載也是極其有限的。所以，上引這兩封勑諭中的主人剌麻恭禪和剌麻完卜領真列思巴均未見於《明實錄》的記載也是可以理解的。

事實上，國師、禪師、剌麻等職銜並不在明代正常的官僚體制之內，而他們即使作

㉑ sjogs应为rdzogs。

㉒ 《明實錄》英宗實錄，卷一百二十六。

㉓ 張潤平、蘇航、羅炤編著《西天佛子源流錄——文獻與初步研究》，北京：中國社會科學出版社，2012年，173，174，180頁。

㉔ 《明實錄》宣宗實錄，卷十二。

爲朝廷特殊封賞的僧官，其職銜也不高，其中灌頂國師有“賜二品鍍金銀印”者，大國師“皆秩四品，給誥命、金銀印，”國師則“賜五品銀印及誥命”，禪師則“皆秩六品，給勑命、銀印”[25]。而剌麻則似不入品秩，“俱賜勑諭、象牙圖書”[26]。前引永樂十六年正月二十四日皇帝勑諭剌麻恭禪時，賜封“慈悲廣濟圖書”象牙印一枚，即與此體制同[27]。

對於明朝廷於西藏地方封賞、設立國師、禪師、剌麻等僧官的目的，《明實録》太祖實録洪武二十六年（1393）三月丙寅條下有云：

立西寧僧綱司，以僧三剌爲都綱，河州衛漢僧綱司，以故元國師爲失剌監藏（Shes rab rgyal mtshan）爲都綱，河州衛番僧綱司，以僧端月監藏（Don yod rgyal mtshan）爲都綱。蓋西番崇尚浮屠，故立之俾主其教，以綏來遠人。復賜以符曰：自古帝王致治，無間遠邇，設官以理庶務。稽諸典禮，復有僧官以掌其教者，非徒爲僧榮也，欲其率修善道，陰助王化。非真誠寡欲、澹泊自守者，奚足以任斯職？今設僧綱司，授爾等以官，給爾等符契，其體朕之心，廣佛功德，化人爲善。欽哉[28]！

及至明中期的嘉靖二十八年（1549）五月壬辰，復有詔：

以烏思藏等處番僧領占堅參（Rin chen rgyal mtshan）等三十八名，各襲國師、禪師、都綱、剌麻職事，駁回查勘喃哈堅參（Nam mkha’ rgyal mtshan）等三十一名。禮部因奏今歲入貢番僧中多去年已賞今次復來，或同一師僧而襲職異名，或同一職銜而住坐異地，請以後新襲職誥勑，俱開住坐地方及某師某名，不得混冒。又諸番節年襲職守侯誥勑日久，輒令帶原齎誥勑回番，待後入貢之年，赴京補給，以故諸番得假借冒頂，夤緣行私，及今不處，則舊誥舊敕，終無銷繳之期。非但夷情怠玩，抑且國禮未尊，請以後番僧襲職，令將原齎誥敕納還內府，不得如故齎回。其新給誥敕速與關領，庶絕弊端。又各處番僧襲職進貢，本部立文簿一扇，各僧齎到舊給誥敕，所載師僧職名、頒給年月，及今襲替僧徒名字、住坐地方，分別已未領有新誥敕逐一登記備行布政司照式置造。如係應貢年分，即以前冊查對。如係年代久遠，果有老病，方得起送承襲。如已襲未領誥敕，許起送一二人，其餘無得濫放報可[29]。

最後還值得一提的是，於朵思麻、朵甘思地區之西番寺院或多與薩思迦派有較深的聯繫，其寺院領袖的職位傳承多採用薩思迦寺院通行的“叔姪相繼”制度，故西番寺院之國師、剌麻地位的傳襲也多以叔姪相繼。或者，國師、剌麻的姪兒當於西番諸寺

㉕ 《明實録》宣宗實録，卷十四、卷十五。

㉖ 《明實録》宣宗實録，卷十五。

㉗ 《明實録》英宗實録，卷一百三，正統八年四月庚子條有云：“剌麻綽失吉監粲（Chos kyi rgyal mtshan）於陝西廣善寺修行，賜勑諭並圖書，其文曰廣慈宣化。”由此可見明廷賜西番剌麻以“勑諭並圖書”是通常的習慣。

㉘ 《明實録》太祖實録，卷二百二十六。

㉙ 《明實録》世宗實録，卷三百四十八。

院或地方行政管理中曾扮演一個比較重要的角色。於《明實錄》中在番僧名字前常常出現“完卜”，或者“温卜”的稱號，這無疑當即藏文親屬稱謂“dbon po”，今謂“姪兒”之音譯。從“完卜”和“温卜”於《明實錄》中出現的上下語境來看，它實際上指的是與剌麻、國師一様、但地位低於他們的一個職銜或者封號，而不是專指其字面本意“姪兒”。享有“完卜”稱號者可以是某個寺院的“完卜”㉚，也可能是某個“簇”（部落）的“完卜”，故極有可能“完卜”的實際意義是指某一寺院或者地區（部落）的行政管理者㉛。雖然享有“完卜”稱號者常常是承襲國師、剌麻位者之姪兒，例如，《明實錄》中有載成化八年（1472）正月乙卯，“命陝西西寧普法寺妙善通慧國師鎖南巴（bSod nams pa）姪完卜鎖南爾堅剉（*dbon po* bSod nams rgyal mtshan），慧慈弘應國師沙加星吉（Śākya seng ge）姪桑爾加堅參（Sangs rgyas rgyal mtshan），演教寺妙智廣慧剌麻阿節兒（'od zer）姪完卜端約藏卜（*dbon po* Don yod bzang po），各襲其叔原職”。成化八年二月庚辰，“命西寧衛地方寶經寺番僧桑加巴（Sangs rgyas pa）姪完卜桑尔加端竹（*dbon po* Sangs rgyas don grub），廣教寺迦隆鎖南巴（bSod nams pa）姪完卜領真劄失（*dbon po* Rin chen bkra shis），吉祥寺鑽竹領占（Byang chub rin chen）姪完卜繼瓦堅昝（*dbon po* rGyal ba rgyal mtshan），祝洪寺裸古普卜藏姪完卜羅竹堅剉（dbon po Blo gros rgyal mtshan）各襲禪師、剌麻職”。但同様顯而易見的是，在《明實錄》中出現的類似的詔諭中出現的“完卜”這個稱號，哪怕常常與“姪”連稱，但它的意義無疑並非特指“姪兒”。如前引正德皇帝勑諭剌麻完卜領真列思巴中稱“尔完卜領真列思巴，乃已故剌麻恭禪之姪孫”，“完卜領真列思巴”與“剌麻恭禪”二者的生活年代相差近百年，是故前者不可能是後者的直接的姪兒，而只能是同族的“姪孫”。從這個角度看，“完卜”這個稱號的實際意義，或依然與其在吐蕃時期的藏文文獻中一様，指的只是同一部族的男性後裔，或者直系男性子姪擔任行政管理之職責者，而不是特指“姪兒”㉜。這一點我們或還可以引《明實錄》中出現過的“子完卜”這様的說法作爲佐證，明英宗睿皇帝實錄正統十四年九月戊寅朔（一日）條下載：“令故列思麻萬戶府萬戶剌麻堅藏子完卜綽思吉堅粲襲爲指揮僉事；朵甘思宣慰使汪東藏卜子

㉚ 《明實錄》宣宗實錄，卷一百七，宣德八年十二月十九日，“賜湖廣麻寮千戶所故土官舍人向宣烏思藏必力工瓦完卜管著兒監藏等鈔綵幣表裏有差”。從這裏的上下語境來看，“完卜管著兒監藏”當是烏思藏著名的必力工瓦寺的管家之類的行政管理者。

㉛ 《明實錄》宣宗裏實錄，卷一百十五，宣德九年十二月“乙巳，陝西西寧衛國師綽思星吉遣剌麻鎖南星吉、巴哇簇頭目完卜捨剌竹等來朝貢馬”。

㉜ 關於*dbon po*於吐蕃時代藏文文獻及其吐蕃歷史中的意義，參見Helga Uebach, Notes on the Tibetan Kinship Term DBON, *Tibetan Studies, in Honour of Hugh Richardson*, edited by Michael Aris and Suu Kyi Aung San, Oxford,1979, pp. 301-309; Brandon Dotson, “The ' Nephew-Uncle' Relationship in the International Diplomacy of the Tibetan Empire (7th – 9th Centuries,” Contemporary Visions in Tibetan Studies: Proceedings of the First International Seminar of Young Tibetologists, edited by Brandon Dotson, Kalsang Norbu Gurung, Georgios Halkias, and Tim Myatt, Chicago: Serindia Publications, 2009, pp. 223-238。

完卜綽思吉剳巴襲爲指揮僉事。”[33]這説明至少“萬戶府萬戶”或者“宣慰使”的兒子也是可以世襲擔任“完卜”這一職事的。至於“完卜”究竟是指一個何等樣的職事，他於西番宗教和世俗管理體制內具有怎樣的地位，我們還需要尋找新的資料對它做進一步的研究。

Three Newly Discovered Ming Edicts to Tibetan Lamas: Text and Interpretation

Shen Weirong

This article reveals three Ming edicts to Tibetan lamas of mDo smad which are recently discovered by private collector. They are: 1) Edict to Hong yazi gou si monastery in Xining issued on the 22th day of the third month of the second year of the Xuande reign; 2) Edict to the Bla ma bsgom chen issued on the 24th day of the first month of the 16th year of the Yongle reign; 3) Edict to Bla ma dbon po Rin chen legs pa on the 16th day of the 7th month of the 3rd year of the Zhengde reign. Short annotations and interpretation are given in addition to the texts of the edicts in both Chinese and Tibetan. Furthermore, it provides a lists of all Ming edicts to Tibetan lamas so far known to the author.

[33] 《明實錄》英宗實錄，卷一百八十二。

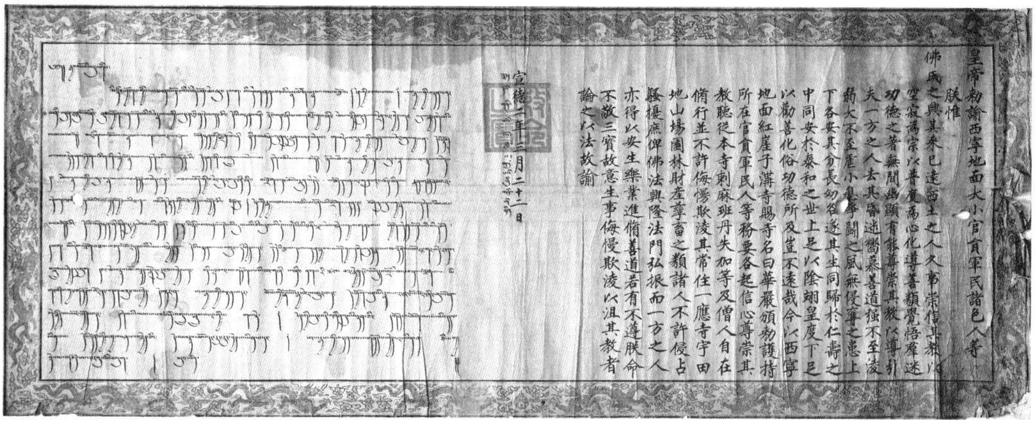

皇帝勅諭西寧地面大小官員軍民諸色人等
朕惟
佛氏之興其來已遠西土之人久事崇信其教以
空寂爲宗以普度爲心化導善類覺悟羣迷
功德之著無間幽顯有能尊崇其教以導引
夫一方之人去其昏迷嚮慕善道強不至凌
弱大不至壓小息爭鬪之風無侵奪之患上
下各安其分長幼各遂其生同歸於仁壽之
中同安於泰和之世上足以陰翊皇度下足
以勸善化俗功德所及豈不遠哉今以西寧
地面紅崖子溝寺賜寺名曰華嚴頒勅護持
所在官員軍民人等務要各起信心尊崇其
教聽從本寺剌麻班丹失加等及僧人自在
脩行並不許侮慢欺淩其常住一應寺宇田
地山場園林財產孳畜之類諸人不許侵占
騷擾庶俾佛法興隆法門弘振而一方之人
亦得以安生樂業進脩善道若有不遵朕命
不敬三寶故意生事侮慢欺淩以沮其教者
論之以法故諭

宣德二年三月二十二日

附圖1

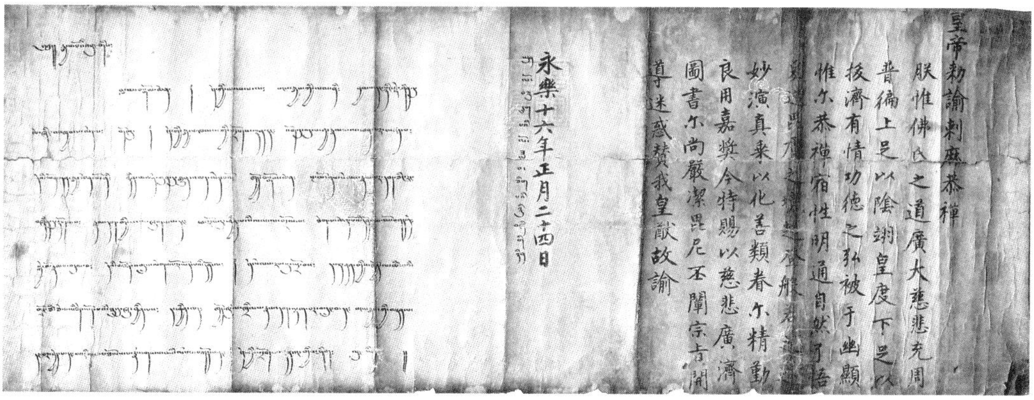

皇帝勅諭剌麻恭禪
朕惟佛氏之道廣大慈悲充周
普徧上足以陰翊皇度下足以
拯濟有情功德之弘被于幽顯
惟尒恭禪宿性明通自然了悟
[illegible]
妙演真乘以化善類眷尒精勤
良用嘉獎今特賜以慈悲廣濟
圖書尒尚嚴潔毘尼丕闡宗旨開
導迷惑贊我皇猷故諭

永樂十六年正月二十四日

附圖2

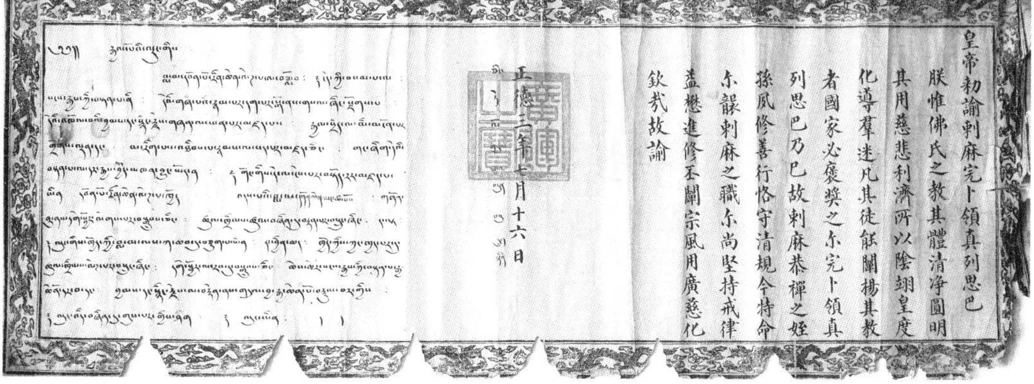

皇帝勅諭剌麻完卜領真列思巴
朕惟佛氏之教其體清淨圓明
其用慈悲利濟所以陰翊皇度
化導羣迷凡其徒能闡揚其教
者國家必褒奬之尒完卜領真
列思巴乃巴故剌麻恭禪之姪
孫夙修善行恪守清規今特命
尒襲剌麻之職尒尚堅持戒律
益懋進修丕闡宗風用廣慈化
欽哉故諭

正德三年七月十六日

附圖3

清代後期内モンゴル・ハラチン地域におけるアルバン・タリヤについて

包呼和木其爾

はじめに

清代後期内モンゴル・ハラチン地域の農耕地は当時のモンゴル旗社会の用途別に則して区分されていた。そのうち佐領箭丁の農耕地は清代モンゴル社会のアルバ問題との関わりで特に重要なので、本稿ではこれについて詳しく論じることとしたい。

アルバとは、義務や公務のことである。清代モンゴル社会のアルバについて、Sh. ナツァグドルジはアルバ供出者や供出形態に基づいて三つに分けている。すなわち、全ての旗や佐領に均分されるアルバ、佐領箭丁だけではなく、ザサグや貴族タイジらも全員供出するアルバ、アルバ負担者が他人を雇用して出させるアルバなどであり、供出されたアルバはその行き先によって滿州皇帝へのアルバ、所属ノヤンへのタタリ・シュース、ホタグト・活仏へのアルバなどに分類されていたとする①。また、Ts. ナサンバルジルはアルバを清朝国家へのアルバと地方行政のアルバの二種類に大別して、さらにそれを幾つかの項目に分けて論じている②。一方二木博史は、清代モンゴル社会における平民が負担する貢租・賦役に注目しながら、旗内の支配隷属関係の変化、特に佐領箭丁と王公貴族の随丁の身分的分化に伴う貢租・賦役負担の変化を指摘している③。

これらの研究から、アルバは清代のモンゴル社会において、旗民が清朝や旗に対して有していた義務であり、主に義務負担者である箭丁（アルバト）や随丁、さらには貴族にも課されていたことが分かる。これをさらに踏み込んで、岡洋樹はハルハ・モンゴルでは駅站・卡倫・牧廠に関わるアルバ、行政費用、宗教信仰に関わる費

---

① Sh. ナツァグドルジ『Сум, хамжлага, шавь ард』Улаанбаатар，1972，59頁。

② Ts. ナサンバルジル1964『Ар монголоос манж чин улсад залгуулж байсан алба 1691-1911 он』Улаанбаатар，1964.

③ 二木博史「清代ハルハ・モンゴルの平民・奴隷の諸義務（Alba）について：18—19世紀前半のトゥシェートゥ・ハン・アイマク、セチェン・ハン・アイマクの事例を中心に」『アジア・アフリカ言語文化研究所通信』，1984，45頁。

用などのアルバがあり、オトグ・バグを単位に配分されていたことを明らかにし、アルバの量は各オトグから佐領に供出する箭丁の数に応じて配分されたのではないかと推測した[④]。これに対して中村篤志は、箭丁の所属単位である佐領はオトグ・バグとは別の特定のアルバを負担していたことを指摘している[⑤]。このように、清代モンゴル社会のアルバ問題についての研究が深められるに従って、アルバ賦課の単位やアルバの種類にはハルハ・モンゴルだけでも地域差が見られることが明らかになっている。

しかし、如何なるアルバでも、それを果たすための財源が必要である。遊牧地帯では家畜が、農耕地帯では農耕地がその財源となった。アルバの負担において、旗当局がどのようなアルバを、如何なる集団に配分するかと言う点で地方差が見られるとしても、実際アルバを供出・遂行する側としては、課されたアルバを果たす財源をどのように確保するのかが課題となる。しかし、旗民がもつ財源がアルバ遂行においてどのように分配・管理・利用されていたのかについては未解明であり、具体的な事例で検討する必要がある。そこで、本稿では内モンゴル・ハラチン地域を事例にアルバン・タリヤが如何に分配・管理・利用されていたのかを明らかにする。

本稿では内モンゴル公文書館所蔵の清代内モンゴル・ハラチン三旗の档案史料から主に農耕地分配の記録、農耕地紛争の訴訟文書、地租紛争の訴訟文書などを用いる。これらの史料からアルバン・タリヤ（アルバ遂行のための財源としての農耕地）を含む旗民の農耕地構成、分配・利用の実態が知られる。また本稿を通じて、モンゴル人社会の農耕地の利用形態を背景とする蒙漢混住地域の社会経済的特徴をも窺うことができる。

第一節　箭丁の農耕地構成

『錦熱蒙地調査報告書』によれば、乾隆十三、十四年以降、箭丁の生活保護を目的として旗の外倉より箭丁に農耕地が支給され、ハラチン中旗では旗民に男女問わず20畝を分給し、左旗では、旗民の十八歳以上の男性に40畝を分給したとされる[⑥]。またハラチンには、旗民が自ら占有した土地や、戦功などの功績に対してザサグから支給された「差役地」、「恩賞地」などがあり、総じて「福分地」と呼ばれていたようである[⑦]。ここから、箭丁が耕作する農耕地には、旗から一律に分配された土地、自ら占有した土地、賞与された土地の種別が存在したことが分かる。ところが『錦熱蒙

④　岡洋樹『清代モンゴル盟旗制度の研究』，東方書店，東京，2007，147—156頁。

⑤　中村篤志「清朝治下モンゴル社会におけるソムをめぐって：ハルハ・トシェートハン部左翼後旗を事例として」『東洋学報：東洋文庫和文紀要』2012，93（3），366—342頁。

⑥　滿洲国土籍整理局『錦熱蒙地調査報告書』（下），1937，1608頁。

⑦　広川佐保『蒙地奉上——滿洲国の土地政策』，汲古書院，2005，140—141頁。

地調査報告書』には、箭丁の農耕地は、三年ごとの戸口調査のたびに家族数の増減に応じて再分配されていたとも記されている⑧。しかし、農耕地を再分配する理由や、再分配されるのが上記の三種類の土地のどれに当たるかについては不明である。そこで以下この問題を解明するために、乾隆60（1795）年に起きたハラチン左旗のジュチン・タボン・ゲル（五家子）村の農耕地をめぐる紛争の事例を取り上げ、これらの農耕地がそれぞれどのように認識され、なぜ再分配されていたのかを明らかにすることから始めたい⑨。

この紛争は、乾隆60（1795）年、ハラチン左旗ジュチン・タボン・ゲル（五家子）村の滋生丁たちが、旗の官員による農耕地分配の不公平を訴えたものである。

同村の住民は、箭丁旧戸43名、箭丁からの滋生丁17名、ダルハチョード旧戸24名、ダルハチョードからの滋生丁16名から成っていた。滋生丁とは、親から独立して自ら一戸分のアルバを果たすようになった成年男子を指す。またダルハチョードとは、特定のアルバが課され、それ以外のアルバから解放された者を指す。彼らは、北京駐在の前ザサグ・ダンバドルジ（在職：1783—1791）、現任ザサグ・ラドナガルディ（在職：1791—1813）、タブナン・グンサンノルブ、タブナン・テグスジャルガランに分属していた。

同旗では、元来旧箭丁、ダルハチョード67戸が持つ農耕地をアルバン・タリヤ、ジンセン・タリヤ、ゴヨルガン・タリヤの項目ごとに統計し、その内のアルバン・タリヤとジンセン・タリヤを合わせて、滋生丁33戸を含む全100戸に、官員なら2分⑩ずつ（ジンセン・タリヤ含む）、平民ならアルバン・タリヤとして1分ずつ与えて、ゴヨルガン・タリヤを現状のままにする方針であった。しかし、村人がゴヨルガン・タリヤであると主張する農耕地であっても、村の役人が確認できない場合は、アルバン・タリヤとして登録した上で均分することにした。そこで、旗印務処から梅林アラハ、扎蘭ツェレブドルジ、アヨルボニヤが派遣され、村に住む官員梅林アラハ、扎蘭ツェレブドルジ、アヨルボニヤ、同村の章京サンバ、アラブダン、アルタンゲレル、書記ユムチュムとともに作業に当たった。

ところが一部のゴヨルガン・タリヤを取り上げられて不満を覚えていたバトルら19人の村人が、派遣された官員に箭丁ボタジャブ、セベグジャブ、トラジャブ、エルデブ、ハルチルハイ、オルトナスト、バヤチホ等が贈賄し、統計冊のゴヨルガン・タリヤの項目に自らの農耕地を載せたとして訴えたのである。

---

⑧　『錦熱蒙地調査報告書』（下），1608頁。

⑨　史料は二つ目録に分かれている。目録503-2-1683「乾隆60年以降、ジュチン・タボン・ゲルの旧戸と滋生丁が農耕地を争った件について」に当事者たちが旗衙門に呈した訴訟文書と供述25通が収録され、目録503-2-1710「タボン・ゲルの滋生丁、ダルハチョード、箭丁の名簿六分」に同村の人口・農耕地の調査記録及び村人たちの証言など22通の文書が収録された。

⑩　ここで、一分農耕地の面積が示されてないが、『錦熱蒙地調査報告書』の記載によればハラチン左旗の場合一分が40畝であったとする。

バトルら原告の訴文の概略は以下の通りである[11]。

（1）旗衙門から派遣された官員は自分が主従関係を持つタブナンの属民に地味の良い土地を与えて一戸の口数に按じて未成年にも一口分の地を与えた。

（2）自分とは主従関係を持たない他のタブナンの属民には、地味の悪い地を与えて、①成年してアルバ供出している子供がいるのに無視し、家族と合わせて一口分の地しか与えなかった（下線は筆者による。以下同様）。

（3）他所のタブナンの属民が官員に賄賂を渡した場合、一戸の口数を按じて未成年にも一口分の地を与えた。

（4）官員が贈賄を受けて、②アルバン・タリヤをゴヨルガン・タリヤとして数人に与えて、逆に賄賂を渡さなかった人のゴヨルガン・タリヤをアルバン・タリヤとして取り上げ、アルバを出す、生計を立てる両方の地を奪った。

（5）官員への見返りとして同村の官員等は勝手に皆のアルバン・タリヤから三人の衙門官員にそれぞれ1頃の地を献上した。

（6）分配後に残った公共用地を寺院に売り渡し、得た金銭を官員等が分かち合った。

（7）旗衙門官員が農耕地分配の時宿泊した諸費用を村の全員で分担したのに、ボタジャブ、セベグジャブ等の家に泊まったと言う理由でアルバン・タリヤから二人に30畝ずつゴヨルガン・タリヤを与えた。

これに対して、訴えられた梅林アラハは[12]、次のように証言している。

（1）村の役員がゴヨルガン・タリヤと認定した農耕地を除いて、残りの農耕地を109分に均等に分けて、③アルバト戸に1分ずつ、官員にジンセン・タリヤとして2分ずつ与えたのは本当であり、同じノヨンの属民を優遇して、他所のノヨンの属民を差別したことはない。

（2）賄賂を受けて未成年にまでアルバン・タリヤを与えたと言うのは誣告である。

また筆帖式ユムチュムは[13]、

村人バイジホは自分のゴヨルガン・タリヤが档冊に記載されなかったという噂を聞いて、自分に確かめるよう頼んだ。確かめた結果、ゴヨルガン・タリヤとして档冊に載っていたため、その旨を伝えた。④その見返りとしてバイジホが渡した銀3両と銭24仟を受け取ったが、他の官員等には黙っていた。

と述べた。

---

⑪ 503-2-1683-7ハラチンのザサグ・ラドナガルディの旗の箭丁バトル、バイホ、シャグダルジャブ、ビンバル、オチルト、マラジャブ、サインチョクト、ソノンピル、ハルジャ、オイト、ナヤンタイ、バイジホ、テグス、ウルジト、トデブ、ハバル、バヤンサン、ボヤンホトグ、サンピル等がザサグ衙門に呈した文書。

⑫ 503-2-1683-9梅林アラハが呈した文書。

⑬ 503-2-1683-14奴才ユムチュムが跪いて事実を報告する。

また贈賄を訴えられた箭丁エルデブは、次のように証言している[⑭]。

（1）弟のドゥーレンが分家して19年になり、昨年から北京でアルバに従事している。そのため、農耕地均分の時報告して彼の分を取った。

（2）長男の⑤エイェートは25歳で、北京で8年間アルバを務めている。次男のバヤリグは19歳になった。そのため、報告して彼らの分（アルバン・タリヤ）を取った。

（3）私は残りの3人の息子と一緒に、従前の一分を取った。⑤現在私たちは3戸分のアルバを出しており、ドゥーレンは分家したため私と関係ない。賄賂を渡して4戸分の地を取ったと言うのは誣告である。

ボタジャブの証言は以下の通りである[⑮]。

（1）旗衙門の使者梅林アラハに賄賂を渡したことを私は知らない。

（2）ツェレブドルジに銭324什を貸したのは本当であるが、私たちは同じノヨンの属民で、以前から互いに金銭のやり取りがあった。今回もお金を貸しただけで、賄賂ではない。

（3）扎蘭アヨルボニヤに銀100両を渡したことはある。それは彼の娘が結婚することになって婚資を出せないため、民人から取る地租を担保にして、仲介人のゴンチョグとウリジホトグの紹介で私から借金したのである。

（4）私は賄賂の見返りとして30畝の地を得たことはない。村の公共費用のため私から高粱7石、大豆3斗を、1斗あたり銭1700什で購入し、その替わりに農耕地30畝を与えようとしたが、私が拒否して現金で返すよう求めた。

以上の証言に対して、ザサグ衙門は以下のような処理を下した[⑯]。

（1）筆帖式ユムチュムは梅林アラハの名を借りて、本来ゴヨルガン・タリヤではない農耕地をバイジホにゴヨルガン・タリヤとして与え、賄賂を取ったため、衙門やタホラシ（村）での筆帖式の職を解き、タホラシの駅站のアルバに発遣せよ。大型（牛・馬・駱駝）家畜5頭を罰とし、50回鞭打ちして戒める外、賄賂として得た金銭を没収して、入官せよ。

（2）バイジホがゴヨルガン・タリヤとして得た農耕地を取り上げて、鞭打ち80回の罰を課する。

（3）バイジホとユムチュムを仲介して銭5什を報酬として得た披甲ジャンバルジャブを50回鞭打ち、得た金銭を入官せよ。

文中の下線部①から成年に達してアルバを供出している息子がいる場合、農耕地の支給を要求できたことが分かる。そして次の下線部②から、アルバン・タリヤとゴ

---

⑭ 503-2-1683-10箭丁エルデブの供述文。

⑮ 503-2-1683-8箭丁ボタジャブの供述文。

⑯ 503-2-1683-15筆帖式ユムチュムが梅林、扎蘭等に随行して五家子の農耕地再分配を行う時、梅林アラハの名を借りて賄賂受けたことを処理したザサグ衙門官員の文。

ヨルガン・タリヤがそれぞれアルバを出す農耕地と生計を立てる農耕地と看做されていたことが分かる。これに反論した梅林アラハの供述の下線部③から、同じく官員に与えられるアルバン・タリヤはジンセン・タリヤと呼ばれ、箭丁のアルバン・タリヤより1分多く給与されており、全員に平等に分配したことが分かる。しかし旗印務処は、下線部④から分かるように、今回の紛争の引き金は筆帖式ユムチュムが賄賂を受けたことによるもので、農耕地の調査に参加した他の官員は贈収賄に関わっていなかったと判断し、筆帖式ユムチュムと彼に賄賂を渡したバイジホ、そして仲介人になったジャンバルジャブを処罰し、当初の方針通り土地の分配を行ったのである。

また、一家族の口数を按じて全員にアルバン・タリヤを与えたとする原告の主張に対して、下線部⑤から、一家族中の口数ではなく、単独でアルバを負担している箭丁の数に応じてアルバン・タリヤが分配されていたことが分かる。

この事例から見ると、ジュチン・タボン・ゲル村の旗民の農耕地はアルバン・タリヤとゴヨルガン・タリヤで構成されていた。その内アルバン・タリヤは専らアルバを負担するために使われる農耕地であり、ゴヨルガン・タリヤは生計を立てるための農耕地として認識されていた。またジンセン・タリヤはアルバン・タリヤの一種であり、官員としてアルバを果たすために支給される農耕地であったのである。漢語の地目に対応させるなら、アルバン・タリヤとジンセン・タリヤは「差役地」、ゴヨルガン・タリヤは「福分地」にそれぞれあたると考えられる。『錦熱蒙地調査報告書』に再分配が行われていたとされるのはアルバン・タリヤとジンセン・タリヤを含む「差役地」に限られていた。外藩モンゴルでは比丁作業が三年に一回行われるため、その時に新しく登録された佐領箭丁にアルバン・タリヤを与える必要から、農耕地の再分配が行われていたと考えられる。では、農耕地の再分配はどのように行われていたのか、節を改めて検討する。

第二節　アルバン・タリヤの分配

乾隆44年（1779）、ハラチン左旗のホジル河のヒヤギン・ブレグ（kiy-a-yin bülüg）、アルバン・ゲル（arban ger）、バダルホギン・アイル（badarqu-yin ayil）三村落の箭丁たちは村内に滋生丁が増えたので農耕地の面積が不均等になったと訴えた[⑰]。そして旗衙門から官員が派遣され、農耕地の再分配を行った[⑱]。

旗衙門の使者が現地に着き、まず分配の対象となる農耕地の総面積を調べた。そ

---

⑰　公文書ではこの3の村落を合わせてヒヤギン・ゴルバン・ブレグという。ホジル地域ではその他にダルハドたちが住む5の村落があり、合わせてダルハド・イン・タボン・ブレグという。

⑱　503-2-2421ヒヤギン・ブレグ、アルバン・ゲル、バダルヒン・アイル三村落の農耕地を均分した档案。

の結果、ザサグ⑲が三村落の章京4人に与えた土地はそれぞれの8頃、領主ノヤンがこの4人に与えた土地はそれぞれの20頃、寺院の香火地として残した土地15頃余を除いて、分配されることになった農耕地はノタギン・タリヤ（nutuγ-un tariy-a）⑳とフデギン・タリヤ（ködege-yin tariy-a）㉑[ヘーリン・タリヤと言う場合もある]を合わせて、総面積は330頃95畝になった。

次に、農耕地を立地、地力などに応じて1、2、3等シャバー㉒に分けて、それぞれ均等に分けた。これを更に、三村落の箭丁149戸に均分すると、戸毎に1等シャバー（ノタギン・タリヤ）60畝、2等シャバー（ノタグに近いフデギン・タリヤ）60畝、3等シャバー（フデギン・タリヤ）95畝ずつの割り当てとなったのである。

分配された土地の地名から見ると、1等シャバーは大体三村落の周辺の農耕地を指し、2等シャバーは村落を少し離れたところ、3等シャバーは村落を遠く離れた川沿いや峡谷の農耕地を指していた。

1、2等シャバーは60畝ずつ四至が明示された農耕地を箭丁に分配し、自種地（tariqu sibaγ-a）と呼ばれていた。ところが、3等シャバーの場合、複数の請負人㉓の名下にある農耕地の総面積を95畝単位で数えて、箭丁複数人に分配している。具体的分配の例は次のようである㉔。

γurbaduγar sibaγ-a-yi ködege-yin γoul ǰabai-ača erüke büri-dü yeren tabuγad mü-ber sibaγalaǰu öggügsen anu,šira γoul-du bou yüng čiuwan-u arban king bögedγucin nigen mü qoyar fün, siüi ǰeng-yin dolun （doluγan） king ǰiran tabun mü, wang züng-yin naiman mü naiman fün, neyite arban naiman king böged tabun mü, egündür, gegerči, dalinsang, nemükür, bayartu, dardung, čangqai, urtu, nančung, bayiqu, nomuǰab, nartu, qada, budaǰab, sarqan, tegülder, odčirsan, čüse, sayinčaqun, baγ-a bayansang tan arban yisün erüke

3等シャバーは野外の川沿い、峡谷から戸毎に95畝ずつ与えたのは、シャラ・ゴル（河）にバウ・ユン・チュアンの10頃31畝2分、シュイ・ジェン

---

⑲ 6代目のザサグ・ホトリンガ（在職：1742—1779）のこと。ホトリンガ以外にも領主ノヨンが現れるが、名前が明示されていない。

⑳ モンゴル語のnutuγは故郷を意味しており、後ろに農耕地を意味するtariy-aが続き、ここでは村の周辺の農耕地を指す。

㉑ モンゴル語のködegeは野原を意味しており、農耕地と合わせてここでは村を離れた場所の農耕地を指す。

㉒ シャバー（sibaγ-a）は元々モンゴル語で籤の意味を現わす言葉である。ここではアルバン・タリヤの単位として使われている。遊牧地帯ではアルバンの家畜をボタ（buda）で数える。但し、シャバーやボタの分量は各旗の決まりによって異なる場合がある。ここでは1、2等地60畝は1シャバー、3等地は95畝1シャバーになっている。

㉓ 主に漢人商人や農民であり、何らかの機会にモンゴル旗の土地を請け負って、更にそれを小作農に耕作させ、自らの小作料との差額を利潤としていた人々で、ハラチンでは攬頭と呼ばれることが多い。

㉔ 前掲ハラチン左旗档案503-2-2421。

の7頃65畝、更にワン・ゾンの8畝8分、あわせて18頃5畝であり、これに当たったのは、ゲゲルチ、ダランサン、ネムグル、バヤルト、ダルドン、チャンハイ、オルト、ナンチョン、バイホ、ノムジャブ、ナルト、ガーダ、ボタジャブ、サルハン、テグルデル、オッドツレン、チューセ、サインチャホン、バガ・バヤンサン等19戸。

ここで分配対象となった農耕地18頃余は3人の耕作者の名下にあった。18頃におよぶ広さの土地をわずか3家族の労働力で経営することはほとんど不可能であり、小作農による小作に出されていたものと考えられる。また、ここでは分配される農耕地の面積だけがあげられており、具体的場所が明示されたわけではない。つまり、3等シャバーの場合、95畝の農耕地よりも、95畝の農耕地から徴収できる地租額を分配したことになる。これは『錦熱蒙地調査報告書』に現れる吃租地㉕に該当するものであり、ハラチン地域ではzüse quriyaqu sibaγ-aと呼ばれていた。

第三節　箭丁による農耕地の利用

前述したように、箭丁の農耕地はアルバン・タリヤとゴヨルガン・タリヤから成っており、アルバン・タリヤには自種地と吃租地の二種類があった。では、農耕地は実際にはどのように利用されていたのだろうか。本節では、箭丁の土地利用状況を調査した旗衙門の記録を用いてこの問題を明らかにする。

ここでは嘉慶元年（1796）、扎蘭セブデンが命令に従ってボーロッド・ブレグ村に赴き、箭丁が民人に農耕地と地租を担保にした状況を調査・報告した史料（所蔵番号503-1-421）を用いる㉖。調査対象となったのはボーロッド・ブレグ村の箭丁111戸である。報告書には箭丁の名前が記され、その下に①アルバン・タリヤとゴヨルガン・タリヤの分量、②担保にした割合、③担保先、④担保とした期間、⑤担保で借りた金額等が記されている。

報告書の内容に基づいて、箭丁111戸の土地利用状況を次の6つの類型に分けることができる。

A. 自種地と吃租地、ゴヨルガン・タリヤを全部担保にしている者43戸。

B. 自種地を担保にし、吃租地とゴヨルガン・タリヤの地租でアルバを供出し、生計を立てている者30戸。

C. アルバン・タリヤを持たない者1戸。

㉕　『錦熱蒙地調査報告書』（下），1608頁。「又例外トシテ左旗ニテハ吃租地十一十二、三畝ヲ普通地一畝ニ換算シテ配給シタトモ言フ。」

㉖　503-1-421命令に従い、扎蘭セブデンがボーロッド・ブレグの箭丁たちが民人に担保にした農耕地、地租を調べた档案。

D.アルバン・タリヤとゴヨルガン・タリヤの一部を担保に出し、一部を残した者15戸。

E.農耕地の利用状況を隠して報告しない者16戸。

F.農耕地を全く担保にしていない者5戸。

また、档案の最後の部分の章京トブダン1戸のアルバン・タリヤについての情報が欠損しており、その利用状況は確認できない。報告書の最後に、以上の111戸が担保にしている地畝の総数を農耕地58頃60畝余、地租738石余と記されている。ここでは、この6項目からそれぞれ一例を挙げて原文を示すと以下の通りである。

A.の例

quyaγ namkai-yin alban-u ǰurγan šabaγ-a, tariqu tariy-a γurban šabaγ-a, züse abqu γurban šabaγ-a, abqu züse arban dan böged dörben deü, γuyulγ-a-u züse qorin qoyar dan nige deü, egünče qorin ǰurγan dan nige deü züse, döcin mü-ü nige sibaγ-a-tai ǰurγan ǰaγun ǰiran mingγ-a ǰoγus-bar arban ǰil-iyer san ǰüi qau-dur dangnaǰu öggüged dörben ǰil ideǰüküi. basa ǰurγan dan züse, γučin mü-ü nige sibaγ-a-tai ǰang liü irgen-dü qorin ǰil-iyer, nige mingγan dörben ǰaγun mingγ-a ǰoγus-u orun-du dangnaǰu öggüged γurban ǰil ideǰüküi. üledegsen öri nige ǰaγun yeren mingγ-a, basa döčin mü-ü qaγas-yi mön ǰang liü irgen-dü nige ǰaγun mingγ-a-bar dingšeü-ber ögǰüküi, nige qaγas-i irgen tiyan γuwang fü-dür yeren mingγ-a ǰoγus-bar dingšeü-ber ögǰüküi oγtu tariqu tariy-a, abqu züse ügei kememü.

披甲ナムカイのアルバン・タリヤ6分あり、自種地3分、吃租地3分ある。取れる地租は10石4斗であり、ゴヨルガン・タリヤの地租は22石1斗である。この内、26石1斗地租、40畝の1分地を660仟銭で10年の期間を設けて、三居号に担保にし、4年間吃租した。また、6石地租、30畝の1分地を民人張六に、1400仟銭（の借金）の代わりに20年間担保とし、3年間吃租した。残った借金は190仟銭残っている。また、40畝の1分地の半分をこの民人張六に、100仟銭の項首で与え、半分を民人田広福に、90仟銭の項首で与えた。耕作する土地や徴収する地租は全くないと言った。

この例から見ると、ナムカイのアルバン・タリヤは6分、つまり6ヶ所にある。その内、3ヶ所は自ら耕作できる土地であり、3ヶ所からは地租を取れるのである。また、ゴヨルガン・タリヤの量が示されていないが、そこから徴収する地租の量は吃租地の2倍以上ある。担保先として、三居号、張六、田広福等の名が現れる。担保とした状況を見ると、三居号に、26石1斗地租と40畝の土地を10年間担保として、660仟銭を借りている。地租と農耕地の面積から見るとアルバン・タリヤとゴヨルガン・タリヤを区別なく担保にしたことが分かる。張六から借りた1400仟銭には、地租6石と土地30畝を20年間担保とした。それでもなお190仟銭の借金が残るため、残りの農耕地を半分ずつ分けて、張六に半分を100仟銭で、田氏に半分を90仟銭で一定期間使用させることにした。この担保とした期間は「受け戻しができない期間である」（アラムス2013：98）。つまり、三居号に担保として置いた分を10年間、張六の分を20年間受け戻すことができないと言うことである。また、借金がなお190銭残ったため、農耕地一分を半分ずつ二人の民人に「頂首」で与えたとしている。寺田浩明によれば「頂首」とは最初、佃戸が地租を滞納することを防止するために導入した「押金」であるが、後にこの「押金」の金額が地価の半分以上となるまで高騰した。そこで、佃戸が事実上は地価の半分を支払ったことになり、佃戸が撤田しない限り田主が農耕地を受け戻すことができなくなったのである[27]。つまり、「頂首」として与えたこの一分の農耕地は、少量の地租が発生するものの、受け戻すことができなくなっていたことを意味する。

B. の例

quyaγ elbeü-yin šabaγ-a ǰurγ-a, tariy-a γurba, züsen-üšabaγ-a γurba, egünü züse arban dan, γuyulγan-u züse arban dan, egünče nige šabaγ-a-u nige dan tabun deü, nige šabaγ-a γučin mü tariy-a-yi nige ǰaγun qorin mingγ-a -bar tabun ǰil-iyer irgen wang buu čin-dü dangnaǰu qoyar ǰil tariǰuqui, yači qorin mingγ-a, nige šabaγ-a-u tabun dan züse-yi öber-iyen idemüi. nige šabaγ-a γučin mü tariy-a-yi nigen ǰaγun γučin mingγ-a-bar tabun ǰil-iyer irgen siüi maü güng-dü dangnaǰu γurban ǰil bolba yači döčin dörben mingγ-a, nige šabaγ-a-u züse γurban dan tabun deü-yi öber-iyen idemüi, basa γuyulγan-u arban dan züse-yi öber-iyen idemüi, tariqu tariy-a ügei kememü.

披甲エルブ一の農耕地6分の内、自種地3分、吃租地3分ある。取れる地租は10石であり、ゴヨルガン（・タリヤ）の地租10石である。この内、1分1石5斗、1分30畝の農耕地を120仟銭で5年の期間民人王宝琴に担保とし、2年耕作した。押契は20仟銭である。（吃租地）1分5石の地租を自ら徴収している。1分30畝の農耕地を130仟銭で5年間民人徐茂公に担保とし、3年経った。押契は44仟銭である。（吃租地）1分の地租3石5斗を自ら徴収している。また、ゴヨルガン（・タリヤ）の地租10石を自ら徴収している。耕作する土地はないと言った。

この例を見ると、アルバン・タリヤの自種地全部、吃租地一部を質入れして、残りの吃租地とゴヨルガン・タリヤからの地租を自ら徴収している。残りの29戸も同様な状況である。

C. の例

quyaγ duγar-un teǰiyebüri-yin γučin mü tariy-a-yi irgen yang tüng ǰeü-dü tabun ǰil-iyer γučin qoyar mingγ-a ǰoγus-bar dangnaǰu öggüged qoyar ǰil ideǰüküi, arban

---

㉗ 寺田浩明「「崇明県志」に見える「承価」「過投」「頂首」について：田面田底慣行形成過程の一研究」『東洋文化研究所紀要』1985，（98），39-178頁.

qoyar mingɣan ǰoɣus-un öri-tei kememü.

披甲ドガルは扶養[28]のため与えられた30畝の農耕地を民人楊同周に5年間32仟銭で担保にし、2年経った。12仟銭の借金があると言った。

ドガルがアルバン・タリヤを持っていなかった理由は説明されていないが、滋生丁だからである可能性が高い。ドガルは32仟銭で民人に土地を貸し与え、30畝の土地を5年間担保に出して、2年間経った後未返済の借金が12仟銭残り、それを原則として残り3年間の契約期間が満了するまでに返済しなければならないのである。

D.の例

quyaɣ gendünǰab-un šabaɣ-a tabu. tariqu šabaɣ-a ɣurba, züse abqu šabaɣ-a qoyar, egünü züse qoyar dan naiman deü, tariqu qorin mü tariy-a-yi li šan ǰüirgen-dür nayan mingɣan ǰoɣus-bar tabun ǰil-iyer dangnaǰü ɣurban ǰil bolba, öri arban tabun mingɣ-a bui, üledegsen-i öbertegen idemüi kememü.

披甲ゲンドンジャブに農耕地5分あり、自種地3分、吃租地2分である。その地租は2石8斗である。自種地の20畝を民人李善柱に、80仟銭で5年間担保とし、3年経った。借金15仟銭ある。残りを自分で使用するという。

本例では、ゲンドンジャブは80仟銭の代わりに20畝の土地を5年間担保とし、3年経って未返済の借金が15仟銭残っている。それを2年後の契約期間満了までに返済しなければならない。残りの農耕地や地租を自ら使用している。

E.の例

qoyaɣ dasiɣ tariy-a zü sen-ütoɣ-a-ban medegülügsen ügei.

披甲ダシグは農耕地や地租の数を報告しなかった。

アルバトたちが農耕地や地租の数を隠して報告しない理由は不明であり、この中にはアルバに従事するために家を離れていた者も含まれていたと思われる。

F.の例

qoyaɣ nimadorǰi-yin šabaɣ-a ǰurɣ-a, čöm öber-iyen tariǰu, idemüi kememü.

披甲ニャムドルジの農耕地は6分ある。全て自ら耕作し、或いは地租を徴収していると言った。

本例のニャムドルジは担保にした土地がなく、アルバン・タリヤとゴヨルガン・タリヤを全て自分で使用収益している。

担保にした農耕地や地租の割合はまちまちであるが、担保とされた農耕地総数の53頃60畝及び地租738石を111戸に割り当てて見ると戸ごとに農耕地48畝余り、地租6石6斗余りとなる。そして、戸数の割合で見ると、ボーロッド・ブレグ村の箭丁111戸の内の43戸は全ての土地、地租を農民に貸し出すか、借金の担保にしている。30戸は自種地を農民に担保として借金し、地租のみで生計を立てている。この73戸は農耕地

㉘ 正式にアルバン・タリヤが分配されていないがアルバを供出しているため、生計が困難な箭丁を養う目的で与える土地。

を全く自分で耕作していないことが確認できる者であり、一村落中66パーセント近くの者は確実に農耕地を農民へ貸し出し、農民が払う地租の収入でアルバを遂行し、生計を立てていた。換言すれば、ボーロッド・ブレグ村の農耕地を耕種している農民が支払う地租は、箭丁のアルバ供出と生計維持の両面で用いられ、アルバ遂行の安定を確保するための不可欠な財源となっていた。

しかし、このような農耕地の利用方法からある問題が発生する。自種地やゴヨルガン・タリヤなど村落周辺にあり、四至が明示された農耕地は、個人的に貸し出すことで管理が可能であるが、村落から遠く、四至が特定されずにまとめて吃租地としていた場合、地租徴収や農耕地の管理がどのようになされていたのかと言う問題である。そのため、次節では吃租地の管理を検討する。

第四節　吃租地の管理と攬頭

吃租地（züse quriyaqu šibaγ-a）[29]とは、個々の箭丁に分配される時すでに耕作者が存在し、行政機関の統一管理のもとに開墾されていたことが窺える土地である。清代後期、旗あるいは佐領との直接交渉で土地を借りて開墾する民人はモンゴル高原南部各地域に広く存在していた。彼らは地商、戸總、二地主、攬頭などと呼ばれ、ハラチン地域では主に攬頭（lanteü）と呼ばれていた。攬頭は借りた土地をさらに小作農に貸し出すことで利益を得ていた。つまり、攬頭は吃租地の実際の経営者なのである。従来の研究は、攬頭の土地経営の性格を地主的土地経営としたり、資本主義農業経営の初期形態であると評価したりしてきた[30]。しかし、こうした議論は攬頭と佃戸の関係をめぐって形成される農業経営形態を論じたものであり、この小世界を包んでいたモンゴル社会との関係がほとんど捉えられていない。攬頭とモンゴル旗の関係は簡単に契約の甲乙双方ではなく、契約後に攬頭は別の小作農を招いて租金を徴収し、吃租地を経営し続けるため、吃租地をめぐる攬頭とモンゴル社会との関係が注目される。

道光12年（1832）、ハラチン左旗のシュジュ営子（sedeng-ün bülüg）のモンゴル人は吃租地の地租を滞納したとして烧鍋杖子の漢人攬頭を訴えた[31]。被告の攬頭李全は次のように弁解している。

öčüken minu gerteki yüng ǰeng qaγan-u on-du süǰü ingzi-yin mongγul

---

㉙　漢語の吃租地と言う用語はモンゴル語のzüse quriyaqu sibaγ -aを現わしており、あらゆる地租徴収が行われている農耕地ではなく、アルバン・タリヤに限って使われていた。

㉚　鉄山博「清代内蒙古の地商経済」『東洋史研究』1994，53（3）、413—442頁；王玉海『発展与変革—清代内蒙古東部由牧向農的転型—』，内蒙古大学出版社，呼和浩特，2000。

㉛　503-2-3392建昌県から、ヌヘン·ゴルの漢人農民li čiüwan、ren zi ou、ren bou tai等が、シュジュ営子のwang wen šeng, wang süng sin等を、攬頭を辞めさせ、地租を増やしたと訴えた案件の巻。

tümensang nar-un tariy-a-yi lanteü bolǰu lüng feng geü-yin atar γaǰar-i türiyesülen abču qaγalǰu tariγad arban dörben čing tabin mü bolbasuraγsan tariy-a bolǰu, ǰil büri ögkü süse qoyar ǰaγun arban lang, γaqai ǰurγ-a, köl-ün ǰoγus qorin dolun mingγ-a, oγtu süse dutaγu ügei, törü gereltü-yin tabuduγar on-du ger-e bičig dakin qaγulba. ene ǰilün qoyar sarada, tümensang nar terigülen ǰalan tung an, qubitu, nurbu tan nigen ǰaγun ilegüü kümün tariy-a-yi kemǰiyeleǰü bačimdaγulun namayi lanteü-ben tülkitügei kemekü böged, baγ-a tariyačin-ud-un süse-yi ösgeǰü teden-ü bey-e-dür tusiyatuγai. sanaqula ünen kü süse ösgeǰü lanteü-yi buliyan abumui.

小民の先祖は雍正年間にショジョ営子のモンゴル人トメンサン等の農耕地の攬頭になり、龍鳳溝の荒地を借りて開墾し、14頃50畝が熟地になった。毎年納める租子210両、豚6頭、使者の出費27仟銭であり、全く租子を滞納したことがない。道光5年（1825）に契約書を更新した。今年の二月、トメンサン等をはじめ扎蘭トンアン、ホビト、ノルボ等百余人が農耕地を丈量し、迫って私に攬頭を辞めさせせようとした上、小作農の地租を増やし、彼ら自身に納めさせようとした。思うに、実は地租を増やして攬頭を奪うのである.

この供述から見ると李氏の先祖は雍正年間ハラチン左旗に移住し、訴訟がおきる道光12年（1832）まで100年余り居住していた。移住後シュジュ営子村のモンゴル人の農耕地を開拓し、代々攬頭としてモンゴル人に地租を供出してきたとしている。しかし、道光12年2月、同村のモンゴル人官員等を百人余が李攬頭をやめさせ、小作農から地租を直接徴収しようとしたのである。これについてシュジュ営子のモンゴル人たちは次のように述べている。

bülüg-un dumdaki nüken-i γoul-un aman-u šouγu ǰangzi-yin alban tariyan-u türiyesün-i uγ-tur čüi teü nar ečiǰü quriyan ačaraγad, erüke-yin toγ-a-bar tügegeǰü öggüdeg bile. ene kedün ǰil čüi teü nar tariyači irgečüd-i dutaγulba kemeged oγtu qaγučin yosuγar türiyesü-yi büridken tügegeǰü ögküügei, šouγu ǰangzi-du alban tariya-u ner-e bayiqu bolbaču, tariy-a ba tariyači irgečüd-i oγtu taniqu ügei tula, bayičaγaǰu olqu ügei. erüke ama olan bolǰu amiduraqui-du üneker berke bolǰuqui, γuyuqu anu tüsimel γarγaǰu tariy-a-yi kemǰiyelen erükebüri-du tegsilen qubiyaǰu olγubasu türiyesü-yi öber öber-iyen quriyan abču alban bariqu ami teǰigekü-dü sayi tusa bolumui.

ブレク中のヌヘン・ゴルの焼鍋杖子にある村のアルバン・タリヤの地租を、元々催頭等が行って徴収し、戸数に按じて分配していた。ここ数年、催頭等は農民が滞納したことを理由に地租を全く昔通りに全額分配しなくなった。焼鍋杖子にアルバン・タリヤの名があるが、農耕地や小作農を全く知らないので、調べることができない。戸口が増えて生活が本当に苦しくなった。請うらくは、官員を派遣して農耕地を丈量し、戸ごとに均分してくれるなら、地租を各人が徴収し、始めて公務遂行や生計の役に立つ。

シュジュ営子村のモンゴル人のアルバン・タリヤは焼鍋杖子にあり、村の催頭と呼ばれる者たちは毎年焼鍋杖子から地租を徴収し、シュジュ営子のモンゴル人の戸数に按じて分配していたのである。ところが、一旦農民が地租を滞納すると実際の農耕地と小作農を知らないため調べる方法がなかったのである。そこで、シュジュ営子のモンゴル人は攬頭を介入させずに、地租を直接小作農から徴収しようとしたのである。この案件を調査するために派遣された旗官員は次のように報告している。

> uɣ-tur tus bülüg-eče ǰalan kibčangɣa, tümensang, ǰanggi sayinbelgetü nar čüiteü bolǰu quriyaqu tariyači irgen ren zi ou, li čiüwan nar-un ner-e-yin dourača abqu amun-u türiyesü ču bui, mönggün-ü türiyesü ču bui.

> 元々同村から扎蘭ヒブチャンガ、トメンサン、章京サインベルゲト等が催頭となり、攬頭任子奥、李全の名下から取る糧租もあり、銭租もある。

このように催頭とは、実は扎蘭、章京など旗官員を指しており、彼らは直接攬頭から吃租地の地租を徴収していた。無論この場合小作農から地租を集めるのは攬頭であり、攬頭の利益はこの過程で発生するのである。上の引用文で名前が現れる任子奥は、シュジュ営子村のハラ・ホショーと言うところにある吃租地を管理していた攬頭である。任子奥と李全は共に吃租地の地租を横領した疑いで攬頭を辞めさせられたのである。

攬頭は農耕地を開拓して水利灌漑システムを導入し、さらにその上に商業作物を植えるなどにした。先行研究では、これが資本主義的経営の特徴もつものとして注目されたのである。しかし、経済的面から見て資本主義的特徴が見いだせたとしても、その農耕地がモンゴル人のアルバ遂行に特化した吃租地であることには変わりない以上、攬頭はそうした吃租地の管理者として、モンゴル社会の要請に掣肘されたのである。

おわりに

もとより、外藩モンゴルの諸ザサグ旗は清朝国家や旗内の貴族タイジ・タブナンに対するアルバの遂行を自らの義務としており、ハラチン地域のザサグ旗も例外ではなかった。アルバの種類や配分する単位は地域によって異なっており、オトグにアルバを賦課することもあれば[32]、佐領（ソム）が自ら特定のアルバを果たす場合もある[33]。重要なのは、そうしたアルバ遂行の財源を如何に確保するかということであろ

㉜ 岡洋樹『清代モンゴル盟旗制度の研究』、東方書店、東京，2007.

㉝ 中村篤志「清朝治下モンゴル社会におけるソムをめぐって：ハルハ・トシェートハン部左翼後旗を事例として」『東洋学報：東洋文庫和文紀要』，2012，93（3），366—342頁。

う。本稿は、ハラチンの農耕社会においてアルバ遂行を目的に設定されていたアルバン・タリヤを取り上げ、これをめぐる土地の利用・管理の実態を考察した。明らかになった知見を次のようにまとめることができよう。

まず、アルバン・タリヤは文字通りアルバ供出のために使用される農耕地である。またその内一部は、官職を持つ者に対してジンセン・タリヤとして箭丁より1分多く支給されていた。また、ゴヨルガン・タリヤは旗民が生計を立てるために用いられる農耕地であり、アルバン・タリヤと混同しない限り、行政機関は関与せず、使用者の意思で処分できるのが原則であった。

アルバン・タリヤの分配には二種類の方法があった。一つは、四至が明示された耕種可能な農耕地を戸ごとに与えるものであり、本稿の事例ではノタギン・タリヤと呼ばれていた。もう一つは、すでに耕種者が存在する農耕地を、四至を特定することなく複数名の箭丁に与えるのであり、本稿の事例ではフデギン・タリヤと呼ばれていた。それぞれ漢語の自種地と吃租地に該当する。

そして、箭丁は農耕地を小作に出す際に、必ずしもアルバン・タリヤとゴヨルガン・タリヤを区別して使用したわけではなく、多くの場合両方を同じ民人に担保にして借金していた。本稿で事例とした村落の場合、村人の7割弱が自ら耕作せずに、地租収入のみでアルバ・生計の両方を賄っていた。

一方旗民個々に配分された土地が特定できない吃租地における地租の徴収や土地の管理の様態を見ると、ハラチン地域では吃租地の地租徴収や管理を担っていたのは、旗や佐領との契約を通じて大土地経営権を得た攬頭であった。催頭と呼ばれる旗の官員と現地で実際に地租を徴収していた攬頭の協力で吃租地が運営されていた。その意味で、攬頭はモンゴル社会のアルバ遂行体制の末端に位置する存在であった。

攬頭が漢人農民を小作農とする過程で、攬頭・佃戸関係に則した社会関係が形成されたことは言うまでもないが、彼らの関係を支えていた土地は、モンゴル旗民にとっての吃租地である限り、この新たに結ばれる社会関係はアルバをめぐるモンゴル旗民の社会関係に包括・掣肘され、それに従属しなければならなかったのである。

Studies on Alba's Farm Land (alban tariy-a) in Kharchin Banner during the Late Qing Period

Borjigin Huhmuchir

As is generally known, the cultivation of farm land in southern part of Inner Mongolia has progressed rapidly during the late half of Qing. The vast and extensive farm lands which lay over the whole area and a large number of Han-Chinese immigrants in the area distinguished from those central and northern parts of Mongolia. How the nature of the traditional society in this area changed and what kind of new society it was formed as a result of the social transformation process requires a close investigation.

The historical view about the land cultivation process in Inner Mongolia has considered as a unilateral one driven by Han-Chinese farmers and unrelated to Mongolians. In this article I would like to emphasize that the cultivation of farm land by Han-Chinese farmers did depends on the necessity of the Mongolians society and had a profound impact on the formation of the regional society in the area.

In conclusion, this article helps us to understand that the vertical connection of Mongolian society tied together by alba relied on the horizontal economic connection between Mongolians and Han-Chinese as shown by the issue of farm land.

西域察合台文史籍中阿闌豁阿感光而孕故事

特爾巴衣爾

阿闌豁阿係朶奔篾兒干之妻。朶奔蔑兒干是成吉思汗先祖孛兒帖赤那第十二代孫，成吉思汗第十一世祖。传说阿闌豁阿在沒有丈夫的情況下感光而孕生下了蒙古黄金家族孛兒只斤氏鼻祖孛端察兒。這一傳說故事在蒙、漢、波斯文史籍中广泛流传。蒙古祖先傳說故事很多，但都不如阿闌豁阿感生故事般流傳如此廣泛。該故事由最初的口傳故事轉變成文本，進入蒙古文歷史書寫，再傳入漢文和波斯文文獻。当然蒙古本土史家們對此津津樂道，幾乎爲後世所有蒙古文史籍所轉載①。而饒有興味的是后世中亚和西域史家们也在不停地转述着該故事。甚至到20世紀初，新疆維吾爾史學家毛拉·穆薩·莎依然米在他著名察合台文史籍《伊米德史》中花費大量筆墨來討論阿闌豁阿無夫而孕之事。總之，在蒙古祖先傳說故事中阿闌豁阿感生故事影響最大，在穆斯林史學界尤其如此。故有必要将其在伊斯蘭史學書寫體系中的流轉情況進行考察。

蒙古人编造阿闌豁阿感光而生的神話，而由此確定了黄金家族的神聖性。該故事劃分了蒙古人核心部落“尼倫”和旁系部落“迭兒列勤”系統。

阿闌豁阿感生故事最早出自《蒙古秘史》，后經《金冊》②逡入波斯文史料《史集》，又經《聖武親征錄》③逡入《元史》。

該故事在《蒙古秘史》中原型如下：

（转写中的序号依次表示卷、节、行数）

01：18：01 urida Dobun mergen-ece töreksen Belgünütei Bügünütei qoyar köbegüd 01：18：02 inu eke-yin-yen Alanqoa-yin ečine ügüleldürün10：18：03 ene eke bidan-u aqa degü üye qaya kümün ügei ere üge-ber 01：18：03 bögetele ede gurban köbegüd törülbi.ger dotora qaqča01：18：04Ma’qaliγ Bayaγudai gümün büyü.ede γurban köbegüd tegün-ü-ei büi-ǰe.gemen01：18：05eke-yin-yen

---

① 除了《阿勒坦汗傳》《十善福白史》等少數史料外，其他蒙古文編年史都收入了阿闌豁阿感生故事。

② 《金冊》之名見於《史集》，蒙古語名稱Altan debter。亦鄰真先生認爲，所謂的《金冊》就是《聖武親征錄》的蒙古文譯本。

③ 現存《聖武親征錄》內容從成吉思汗父親烈祖神元皇帝開始記載，無阿闌豁阿故事。但作爲《元史》第一卷的史料，不難想象，早期的《親征錄》可能包含阿闌豁阿的故事。但後來《親征錄》被收入《說郛》時開頭部分可能被刪除了。

ečine keleldüküy-i eke anu Alanqo'a uqa-ǰu……01：20：01tende Alanqo'a eke inu ügülebi.ta Belgünütei Bügünütei01：20：02qoyar köbegüd minu nama-yi ede γurban köbegüd törülbi.01：20：03kenü yaγun-u köbegüt büyü kemem sereldün keledümüi01：20：04serekü i ber tan-u ǰöb01：21：01sönit büri čegügen šira kümün ger-ün erüge dotoqa-yin gege-yer01：21：02oro-ǰu gebeli minu bili ǰu gege-yen inu gebeli-tür minu01：21：03singgegü bülege.qarurun naran sara-yin kili-yer sira no qai metü01：21：04sičabal ǰaǰu γarqu bülge.deleme yekin ügület ta.01：21：05tegü-ber uqaγasu temd ek inu tenggiri-yin köbegüd büyüǰe.qara terigütü 01：21：06kümün-tür qanilqan yekin ügület ta.qa mua-un qad bolubasu01：21：07qaračus tende uqatǰü.kelebe.④

朶奔蔑兒干在時生的別勒古訥台、不古訥台兩箇兒子背處共說："俺這母親無房親兄弟，又無夫，生了這三箇兒子，家內獨有馬阿里黑伯牙兀歹家，人莫不是他生的麼道。"說間母親知覺了。

……

因那般他母亲阿闌豁阿說："別勒古訥台、不古訥台您兩箇兒子疑惑我這三箇兒子是誰生的。您疑惑的也是。您不知道每夜有黃白色人自天窗門額明處入來，將我肚皮摩挲。他的光明透入肚裏去時即随日月的光恰似黄狗般看来顯是天的兒子，不可比做凡人，久後他每做帝王呵。那時纔知道也者。"⑤

《史集》根據一些貴人的回憶和宮廷珍藏《金冊》所講述內容與《蒙古秘史》基本相同：

據說，—講述者［應對此］負責—阿闌豁阿在丈夫死後過了一段時期，有一天，在家裏睡覺。一線亮光從帳廬的天窗射進來，進入她的肚子裏。由於那種情況，使她驚恐、害怕，沒有對任何人講起這件事。過了一些日子，她知道自己已經懷孕了。當分娩的時日臨近時，她的兄弟們和丈夫的族人們聚在一起說道："一個沒有了丈夫的婦人私下隱瞞丈夫，直到懷孕，這怎麼行呢？"阿闌豁阿回答道："我沒有了丈夫卻有了孩子，不管怎麼樣，你們猜測得對，你們的懷疑表面上看來也對。但是毫無疑問，有些懷疑真是罪過。我怎麼能作出應受責備的可恥的事呢？的確，我每夜都夢見一個紅發藍眼的人慢慢地向我走近來，然後又悄悄地轉了回去。我看得很真！你們對我的任何懷疑都是不對的。我所生的這些兒子，都屬於特殊種類。他們長大了要成爲萬民的君主和汗，到那時，你們和其他合剌出部落才會明瞭我這是怎麼回事。"

阿闌豁阿說罷了這些話，他們根據各種跡象認爲她的貞操不成問題後，便不再向她找茬兒，不再打攪她了。他們知道她的話都是真的，她說的都是實話⑥。

---

④ 《元朝秘史》四部叢刊本，卷1；同時參考了亦鄰真《〈蒙古秘史〉回鶻體蒙古文復原本》，內蒙古大學出版社，1987年。

⑤ 同④，總譯部分。

⑥ 《史集》德黑蘭校本，223—224頁；漢譯本，12—13頁。

18世紀成書于西域地區的察合台文史書*Čingiz-nāma*[⑦]對阿蘭豁阿無夫而孕之事摘抄《史集》，但跟《史集》記載又有些不同：

> 喬比納汗將阿蘭豁阿嫁給了堂兄弟朵（兒）奔伯顏（dorbun bayan）。朵（兒）奔伯顏生了兩個女兒，朵（兒）奔伯顏早逝，阿蘭豁阿當了汗，以貞潔著稱。
>
> 有一天晚上，從天窗照進一束光，這束光照進了阿蘭豁阿嘴裏，兴奋当中她懷孕了。這束光每天晚上從白氈房的天窗照進來再照出去。阿蘭豁阿便開始受到各部首領們的質疑，她統領召開了庫魯台大會，各部（首領）都到了。大家吃喝完畢，各部大人們便羞辱阿蘭豁阿說："哎！阿蘭豁阿，我們一直以爲你是個貞潔乾淨的人，你卻毫不猶豫的做惡事，這段時間你沒有丈夫是怎麼懷孕的？"阿蘭豁阿對他們說："你們猜疑的對，但我從小就乾淨純潔，如今怎麼會讓這種惡事發生在我身上呢？你們可以在我身邊住上幾夜，真主會讓你們明白我的情況。"她從每個部中留兩三位頭面人物住在了家裏。結果，他們發現，從氈房的天窗照進一束光，照到阿蘭豁阿身邊又照了出去。阿蘭豁阿對部落頭人說："這道光第一次照進來的時候，照進了我肚子裏，因這道光我有了身孕。"各部頭人都打消了疑慮，向阿蘭豁阿譴責自己的過錯後而散去[⑧]。

*Čingiz-nāma*與《史集》里故事原型有所差別。《史集》說光照進阿蘭豁阿肚子（شکم），而*Čingiz-nāma*說照進嘴裏（اغزی），此说出自沙拉夫丁·牙孜迪的《勝利者之書》。爲了進一步證明阿蘭豁阿所言真實性，說"留幾個頭面人物在身邊過夜，使他們親眼看到這道光，使其心服口服爲止"云云。這一改編也來自《勝利者之書》：

> （阿蘭豁阿）說：如果你們感到不安，你們可以住到我帳篷裏直到這個秘密被解開讓大家明白事實爲止。大人們等了好幾天，這個事實被證實，直到從帳篷天窗里照進一束光，又照了出去[⑨]。

可以看出，*Čingiz-nāma*作者充分參考了帖木儿朝史籍《胜利者之书》，同时又參考了米尔宏达的《洁净园》、晃迭迷儿的《传记之友》。阿蘭豁阿的故事從《蒙古秘史》到《史集》再到中亚和西域伊斯蘭史書有一種逐漸被放大的過程。《蒙古秘史》將該故事說成家庭內部的事，即阿蘭豁阿與其兩個兒子之間發生的誤會。《史集》將故事擴大成了族人間的事。*Čingiz-nāma*中說各部落首領懷疑她，將故事進一步擴大成了國家大事。描述該故事的文字數量和增飾程度也是越往後越多。帖木儿朝儿部史書雖然互相傳抄，描述雷同，但後期史家對前輩描述絲毫未刪減，反而修飾詞隨著時代推移越來越多，故事的流傳呈現越來越豐富的發展規律。該故事敘述集大成者要數西域伊斯蘭史

---

⑦ 亦名《喀什噶爾史》，成書年代大概在17世紀末18世紀初。作者不詳，但筆者認爲其作者當爲毛拉·米爾薩里·喀什噶爾。該書首先簡單梳理了從亞當、夏娃到成吉思汗及其後裔的歷史，然後重點記述了葉爾羌汗國歷史。

⑧ 《喀什噶爾史》6б—7a 、*čingiz-nāma*，7—8頁。

⑨ 沙拉夫丁·牙孜迪《勝利者之書》，塔什干Fann出版社1972年影印本，63頁，10行。

學後期代表毛拉・穆沙・莎依然米，他將該故事放大到了最大限度，同時也進行了徹底否定。說：

這麼一來，這種情況下，以虛假的和不合法的故事是不存在的。相信這個故事和將它作爲信仰的人是卑賤的惡魔。

……由以上諸證據可知，阿闌豁阿說由白氈房天窗照進一束光由此懷孕而生下孛端察兒之事純粹是不存在的⑩。

《伊米德史》的評論性記述特點在阿闌豁阿故事的敘述中展現的淋漓盡致。《伊米德史》中國社科院藏本從第17頁開始到第22頁，以多達75行的篇幅來討論阿闌豁阿感光而生之事，頗費心思地做了一篇宗教論文否定該故事的真實性。

以往穆斯林學者對阿闌豁阿的故事或深信不疑或作爲一敘述模式迻錄於其著作中。但《伊米德史》作者毛拉・穆薩・莎依然米對該故事進行了質疑和嚴肅批評。他首先從宗教層面進行質疑，認爲聖母只能有一個，那就是麥爾彥，無父而生只能發生在先知爾薩身上，而無父無母而生只能發生在人类的祖先阿丹身上。说：

跟男人沒有接觸的女人生孩子實在是很荒謬的事，也是不可能的事。除了麥爾彥［願真主垂愛她！］其他女人身上不會發生這種事。聖人爾薩（'ys）⑪在沒有父親的情況下由麥爾彥所生。這種奇跡只有在聖人爾薩身上才能發生，除他之外是不容許的。有些伊瑪目記載說，聖母麥爾彥是先知，如果她不是先知，至高無上的真主不會在書（古兰经）中提到她的名字。聖人阿丹⑫以天意在沒有父母的情況下被真主創造出來了。聖人爾薩［願世界與他同在！］在沒有父親的情況下有母親所生。除了他倆之外，其他人在沒父母的情況下出生是不可能的事⑬。

可看出作者是個非常正派的遜尼派穆斯林，反對神秘主義，要求正本清源，也可能在一定程度上受原教旨主義影響。又說：

“真正的造物主安拉一貫以其著作之天威，用神的啟示將天下秩序引入唯一正確的道路。力圖改變安拉所執行的完美秩序和不管在何時何地發生一起有異于安拉習性的怪事是不可能的。難道真主之語需要革新嗎？真主之語有變化嗎？”⑭

作者借此反對一些伊斯蘭教神秘主義者認爲靈魂不死之說，堅持伊斯蘭教所講求的唯一性原則。

蒙古人的宗教相信人的靈魂從一個人的軀體轉移到另一個人的軀體。秦（中國）一部分人和所有印度人都信奉這種學說。有些什葉派和穆塔蘇菲派也

⑩ 《伊米德史》社科院本，21頁；隆德本，8頁右。

⑪ 爾薩在很多時候被譯成耶穌，但爲了使之避免與《聖經》混淆而採用爾薩之譯法。除此還有譯作“伊薩”“牙薩”者。

⑫ 有些地方譯作“亞當”，但避免與《聖經》混淆，筆者譯作“阿丹”。

⑬ 《伊米德史》社科院本，20頁；隆德本，8頁右。

⑭ 《伊米德史》社科院本，20頁；隆德本，8頁右。

傾向於這種學說。實際上，這種學說只是異教徒的東西而已[15]。

作者从宗教層面徹底否定該故事后，緊接著還試圖用自然科學知識解釋這一現象，認爲，即便真有這種現象也只能是自然現象而已，與神靈無關。

安拉知道，據我們嚴謹勘察，太陽和月亮靠近黃道，使兩星距離有六個單位時將會發生這種（從站房天窗照進白光的）現象[16]。

作者從多個層面否定該故事真實性后，進一步質疑阿闌豁阿作爲蒙兀兒人的身份；說：

阿闌豁阿的國家在喀喇沙爾，曾在卡爾梅克（qalmaq）人當中，在荒漠裏當自己國家的首領。他們不知道真實崇高的造物者，不知道仁慈的先知，而且他們都沒皈依過伊斯蘭教，連（真主和先知）的名字都沒聽說過。這些部落的人們敬拜日月和鬼神，全體都誤入歧途，進入了禁區[17]。

他開始觀察到蒙兀兒人與阿闌豁阿時期的蒙古人有本質上的不同，認爲那時候的蒙古人與衛拉特人同種，而跟自己族人蒙兀兒人已經沒太大關係。但需要指出的是，西域史家們對文本做得這一系列處理並非完全是有意的。這一切與作者所生活時代背景、作者知識背景等息息相關。尤其是对阿阑豁阿身份的否定，很大程度上出于其知识背景。

毛拉·穆薩·莎依然米生活在19世紀末20世紀初，開始接觸西方新型思想，包括伊斯蘭教新型思想，富有反思精神。全書主要基調都是反思性的，反思南疆動亂及其後果，反思自己的經歷。作者從新的思想高度來整理傳統文化遺產，重新考察蒙兀兒斯坦歷史進程，對以往的歷史敘述帶有一種批判的眼光。作者一心解構傳統歷史敘述，努力將蒙兀兒人的歷史從蒙古史敘述桎梏中脫離出來。

《伊米德史》花大量筆墨討論阿闌豁阿的故事，並非要凸顯其地位，而是爲了準備捨棄和淘汰該故事。這一做法和其文中的表述也從側面反映了阿闌豁阿故事在西域伊斯蘭史學界有著重大影響力，致使史家們都無法直接繞過或直接捨棄該故事。莎依然米有一種顛覆傳統，創造獨立敘事框架的訴求，他也可能受泛伊斯蘭主義和泛突厥主義思潮影響，作者似乎發出訴求，要將作爲異教徒的蒙古人歷史從突厥穆斯林歷史篇章中剔除出去。

毛拉·穆薩·莎依然米在另一歷史著作《安寧史》中雖然也講到了阿闌豁阿感光而生的故事，但沒有《伊米德史》般長篇評論。而且《安寧史》未質疑故事的真實性，甚至承認阿闌豁阿是聖母麥爾彥的化身。但時隔幾年，作者思想發生巨大變化後撰寫的《伊米德史》，對阿闌豁阿故事的認識發生了如此大的轉變。通過兩書不同記載可以看出，毛拉·穆薩·莎依然米準備從一個傳統封建知識份子轉型成爲新型知識份子的一個側面。

陳崗龍先生說："不管是薩滿教的史詩的說法，還是伊斯蘭教史學家的記載，或是

---

⑮ 《伊米德史》社科院本，20頁；隆德本，8頁右。

⑯ 《伊米德史》社科院本，19頁；隆德本，7頁左。

⑰ 《伊米德史》社科院本，20頁；隆德本，7頁左，8頁右。

蒙古人自己的記錄，包括後來受藏傳佛教思想影響的記錄，阿闌豁阿感光受孕神話一直是一個固定不變的不變項。”[18]與此同時，還有可變項，那就是關於蒙古族源“孛兒帖赤那和豁埃—馬闌勒”的故事。該可變項可由後世史家隨意改編。西域伊斯蘭史家將此可變項直接捨棄不錄，其原因在於伊斯蘭史家爲論證蒙古人的產生授意于伊斯蘭教真主安拉，爲此精心選取一些歷史故事作爲論據。而孛兒帖赤那和豁埃—馬闌勒的故事無助於表達這一思想。對阿闌豁阿故事成爲不變項現象，陳崗龍先生認爲：“從光束中出現的人使阿闌豁阿受孕和阿闌豁阿的身份，是固定不變的不變項。”[19]身份的固定不變指的是其世俗身份。阿闌豁阿在任何宗教語境中其世俗身份固定不變，後世史家未刻意去神話她。在西域伊斯蘭史書中，其身份雖與《史集》和《蒙古秘史》不同，但其世俗身份始終沒變，而且還保持了“從光中出現+藍色眼睛的模式。”[20]如*Čingiz-nāma*“成吉思汗紀”裏講道：

> 阿闌豁阿說過這樣的話：“光從帳篷的天窗照進來，照到我身邊，我看到在光中有一黃色皮膚藍色眼睛的小伙子，又返回出去了。”……也速該把阿禿兒長相和身段與這人一樣，有黃色膚色和藍色眼睛，體態優美[21]。

《史集》說阿闌豁阿爲豁羅剌思部人。《蒙古秘史》說阿闌豁阿父親豁里剌兒台蔑儿干從位於巴児忽真脫古木的豁里禿馬部處遷到不而罕山。而西域伊斯兰史家都把阿闌豁阿說成是乞顔部人。西域史家都參考過《史集》，對阿闌豁阿身世不可能不清楚，但作者硬把她說成是黄金家族的人。西域史家做這一調整目的是爲調和文獻記載矛盾。因爲文獻記載尼倫蒙古孛児只斤鼻祖孛端察兒沒有父親，而母親又是豁羅剌思部人。如此一來，孛端察兒跟乞顔部就脫節了，与其蒙古乞顔部黄金家族身份產生矛盾。爲調和這一矛盾，才篡改阿闌豁阿身份，使成吉思汗母系出自乞顔部，父系是由真主安排而降落的天子。如此安排的另一緣由是爲防止成吉思汗祖上血統來路不明，尤其怕別人質疑其蒙古乞顔部身份，同時更怕別人認爲孛端察兒有其他部落血統。最终所要达到的结果是，以孛端察儿为首的黄金家族，即使其父係來路不明，但至少可保證其母系出自乞顔部。《胜利者之书》等帖木兒朝史書中將阿闌豁說成是余勒都思汗之女，都是從額爾古納—坤出來的乞顔部人。西域史家爲何將余勒都思汗改成伊勒汗，原因不得而知。

該故事也很容易導致大家對成吉思汗祖上身份的質疑。爲了保證黄金家族來自乞顔部神聖血統，不得已將蒙古尼倫部母系設計成乞顔部的人。如同帖木兒大帝父系雖然不是黄金家族，但仗著其母系血統以黄金家族的身份自居。帖木兒朝史家們也許受此啟發才將阿闌豁阿身份篡改成乞顔部人。

感生故事在許多民族和地區都有。目前發現最早感生故事產生於公元前兩千多年的兩河流域。古代最著名、流傳最廣的感生故事是聖母瑪利亞無夫生下耶穌。感生故事在

---

⑱ 陳崗龍《〈烏古斯汗傳〉與蒙古族感光受孕神話》，《長江大學學報》（社科版），2016年第2期，5頁。

⑲ 陳崗龍《〈烏古斯汗傳〉與蒙古族感光受孕神話》，6頁。

⑳ 陳崗龍《〈烏古斯汗傳〉與蒙古族感光受孕神話》，5頁。

㉑ 《喀什噶爾史》9a、*čingiz-nāma*，11頁。

中國少數民族當中也非常多，且形式多樣，有感動植物者、感自然天象者、感神者等多種，阿蘭豁阿感光故事屬於感自然天象。感光而孕現象在感生故事中也比較普遍。如扶餘國祖先由天光而生，高句麗始祖感光而生等。韩儒林先生说："此种感生之说，大抵起于夫余、鲜卑，经畏兀儿及蒙古人承受，将塞北自古相传之苍狼旧说，与之揉合，遂构成因子相同、传说各异之故事。"[22]突厥史诗《乌古思汗傳》中也有"光"因素。阿蘭豁阿感生故事中的"光"可能跟突厥感生故事和高句麗、鮮卑感光故事有關。阿蘭豁阿感生故事原型中有光、有蒼色的狗，可能是蒼狼的化身，還有神人。呈現集天命、圖騰和人爲一體的複合型結構，表現了多族群多文化的交融交錯。但阿蘭豁阿感光而孕故事有濃厚的原始宗教特色，穆斯林學者很難直接接受。故事傳入伊斯蘭史書時，刪除狼狗因子，而保留了光中出現的 "金黃色人"因子。因爲狼在伊斯蘭教意識中沒有神聖性，波斯也不存在狼崇拜文化，而突厥人傳統狼崇拜文化經伊斯蘭教洗禮，已蕩然無存。

感生故事内容一般是女性无性而生育，被生子女父方来自某一神圣物，或为天，或为图腾，或为神人，阿阑豁阿感生故事原型同时包含着这三种类型。感生故事往往跟某一政權或某一族群的起源有關，目的是爲神話統治者身份。如，中国商祖吞玄鸟卵、周祖履巨人迹等，几乎每个朝代创立者身上都有一定程度的感生故事。神話的编造必須讓听众相信，否則就沒有意義。不同地區和不同時期，人們的思想意識有所不同。所以感生故事在流傳過程中必然會不斷發生變化，伊斯蘭史家們一直不斷的努力改造故事之原因在此。許多蒙古傳說故事因無法爲當地學者所接受而被捨棄，而唯獨阿蘭豁阿故事一直在流傳，而且滚雪球式地越加丰富多彩，一直持續到20世紀，可見其生命力之頑強。

Research on Alan Goa's Giving Birth thanks to a Ray of Light in the Historical Writings in Chaghatai

Torubayar

The Islamic tradition in writing Mongolian history was formed during the time of the Il-Khanate, and it became one of the most important traditions for events in Central Asia and the Western Region from then onwards and spread widely. The spread and change of this series of documents reflected the understanding that subsequent historians had of Mongolian history, and at the same time, it also reflected the influence Mongolian history had on the Western Region and other places. This is not only an important issue in the field of Mongolian history, but also in Central Asian history. The story of Alan Goa's giving birth after becoming pregnant through a ray of light is a famous ancient legend of the Mongols. This legend spread widely in Central Asia and had a great influence. But

[22] 韓儒林《穹廬集》，上海：上海人民出版社，1982年，283頁。

scholars of the Western Regions such as Molla Musa Sayrami denied and questioned this story. This reflected how historians of the Western Regions inherited the traditions of Mongolian history studies and their consciousness of Mongol-centrism.

“五族共和”在邊疆的實踐

——基於綏遠五族學院的考察

樊志強

辛亥革命後，南北議和代表經過反復磋商，就“五族共和”问题達成共識。1912年經孫中山倡導，“五族共和”成爲國家民族統一理論，從而在一定程度上具有法律條文的效力[①]。袁世凱及其後的北洋歷屆政府亦奉行不悖。儘管因時代拘囿，“五族共和”在族群涵蓋範圍等問題上，飽受時人詬病，但其在建立和統合多民族國家層面上發揮了一定的歷史作用。

國民教育是構建國族共同體的重要措施，“我們深信五族教育之機會均等是五族合作、五族共和的基礎”[②]。因此在“五族共和”的民族國家理論下，“中華民族既合五大民族而成，自應施以同等教育”[③]，以興辦民族教育整合族群成爲政府和文化教育界關注的重要問題。中華民國臨時政府在南京時，蔡元培主持的教育部，設立了蒙藏教育司，專門負責蒙藏回疆民族教育事務。民國政府遷至北京後，直至1927年，民族教育事務由新設立的管理蒙藏事務機構兼理[④]。北洋政府亦先後頒佈了多項發展民族教育的法規，如1922年教育部頒佈的《學校系統改革案》附有《興辦蒙藏教育辦法案》，提出“今爲對外保存國權計，惟有速興蒙藏教育，取來開化之民而授以正當之知識，庶使知

---

① 孫中山在1912年《中華民國臨時大總統宣言書》中之“國家之本，在於人民。合漢、滿、蒙、回、藏諸地爲一國，即合漢、滿、蒙、回、藏諸族爲一人”，是國內外學界廣泛引用作爲其主張“五族共和”的例證。多數學者認爲“五族共和”系由孫氏首倡，但馮建勇（《近代中國民族國家構建之歷程》，《社會科學》2014年第2期，151—162頁）、沈潔（《革命之後：“五族共和的另一種敘事”》，《讀書》2012年第7期，94—103頁）認爲“五族共和”實則出自康有爲、梁啟超等清末立憲派，在辛亥革命時，經張謇明確提出。另外，日本學者片岡一中（《辛亥革命時期の五族共和論をめぐって》，田中正美先生退官紀念論文集刊行會編《中國近代史諸問題》國書刊行會，1984年，279—306頁）、村田雄二郎（《孫中山與辛亥革命時期的“五族共和”論》，《廣東社會科學》2004年第5期，121—128頁）等人認爲“五族共和”一詞源自1907年楊度所撰之《金鐵主義》。烏雲畢力格、孔令偉《論“五色四藩”的來源及其內涵》（《民族研究》2016年第2期，85—97頁）一文考述了“五色四藩”觀念的產生和流傳，文章結尾提到古代蒙古的“五色”象徵對“五族共和”產生了影響。

② 陶行知《年會感言》，《新教育》1925年第11卷第2期，上海：上海教育共進出版社，148頁。

③ 《教育部關於中華民國大同會創設蒙回藏師範學校請撥開費批》，見《中華民國史檔案資料彙編》（第二輯），南京：江蘇古籍出版社，1991年，479頁。

④ 參見田正平、張建中《近代邊疆教育行政管理機構的創立與演變——以中央政府一級爲中心的考察》，《社會科學戰線》2008年第3期，217頁。

五族一家之利，堅其團結之力，絕其外向之心”[⑤]，以鞏固統一的多民族國家。

當時文教界人士也認識到了開展邊疆民族教育的迫切性，“五族如缺其一，則民國爲不全；政教如有參差，則共和國爲不固。舉世咸知五族爲中華國民而不能辨其爲何族，則五族各宜自認爲中華國民而忘其爲何族。政治所安撫者，中華國民也，非一族人也；教育所造就者，中華國民也，亦非一族人也”[⑥]。陶行知以當時“中華民國”的蒙古文譯文“dumdadu irgen ulus”之謬誤爲例，來說明“五族”對中華民國的誤解，及開展民族教育的迫切性，認爲“我們想要建設一個真正的五族共和，最要緊的方法有兩種：一、是建築四通八達的道路；二、是實行四通八達的教育”[⑦]，並提出“各省區蒙藏，應逐漸設立大學，至少一所，吸收碩學通才，以爲產生文化、整理文化及主張正誼之中心”[⑧]。

雖有政府之計劃及文教界之倡議，但因政局迭蕩、戰爭頻仍，民族教育發展緩慢。以內蒙古地區爲例，“查內蒙各旗近年雖有設立學校者，惟爲數極少，有名無實。中學尤絕少，如察哈爾全區僅有區立中學一處”[⑨]，基礎教育尚且如此，遑論高等教育。在1925年於太原召開的中華教育改進社第四屆年會上，巴圖、伊德欽等十位內蒙古代表在提案中言及：“故自民國以來，年年國防，歲歲籌邊，卒因情形疏隔不收效果。欲破除此種障礙，固非由教育入手不可。……民國三年以來，劃內蒙各旗、特别區統治，然教育設施，仍是有名無實”[⑩]，不僅反映了當時民族教育在蒙地的推行、發展狀況，作爲蒙古族代表，更表達了作爲邊疆教育的受衆對現狀的態度[⑪]。

在滯塞的民國邊疆民族教育中，1925年馮玉祥移節西北，創立的綏遠五族學院，是邊疆地區開辦民族高等教育的有益嘗試。五族學院雖存續時間短暫，但其是在民國“五族共和”思想下在邊疆地區辦學的實踐，且是綏遠地區民族高校的開創之舉。對於“綏遠五族學院”，學界已有不同程度的關注，其中杜曉榮、白燎原在《綏遠五族學院》一文對其創辦、發展進行了基本的梳理，並充分肯定了其在內蒙古高等教育史上的地位[⑫]。其餘有關內蒙古及蒙古民族的通史類著作中，僅作爲一般敘述，予以簡略介紹。本文擬在前人研究的基礎上，搜求相關文書檔案、回憶錄以及當時見諸報端的各項材料

⑤ 《興辦蒙藏教育辦法案》，《中華民國史檔案資料彙編》（第三輯·教育），南京：江蘇古籍出版社，1991年，98—99頁。

⑥ 宮廷璋《促進蒙古教育芻議》，《西北彙刊》1926年第2卷第4期，1頁。

⑦ 陶行知《五族共和與教育者之責任》，《申報·教育與人生週刊》1924年第22期，3月17日。

⑧ 陶行知《中國教育政策之商榷》，《中華教育界》1925年第15卷第4期，6—7頁。

⑨ 《蒙古教育之計劃》，《新教育》1925年第11卷第2期，255頁。

⑩ 《蒙古教育之計劃》，253—254頁。提案者分别爲：巴圖、伊德欽、吴恩和、巴雅爾、王德呢嘛、李鳳崗、林琴、博彥格勒爾、烏勒吉、金永昌。

⑪ 另外，郭道甫稱“從前北京設有蒙藏學校及在黑龍江省設蒙旗學校之舉，但其結果不獨未見何等效力，並其目的亦系完全錯誤”，並提出“吾人此後苟欲徹底提高蒙古民族之程度，使其與其他民族亦有一律平等之資格，應當注重蒙古教育，尤當徹底研究其方針及其辦法”，亦代表了當時內蒙古精英對該地區教育的看法。參見郭道甫《蒙古教育之方針及其辦法》，《新教育評論》1926年第1卷第7期，13—17頁。

⑫ 杜曉榮、白燎原《綏遠五族學院》，《呼和浩特文史資料》第9輯，呼和浩特，1994年，206—210頁。

進一步就其創辦過程、日常管理、課程設計、招生工作、學生去向以及時人對五族共和的理解等問題予以探討。

一、五族學院的籌建

1923年5月11日，北洋政府委任馮玉祥爲西北邊防督辦，負責内外蒙古、新疆一切軍政事務。任命甫一公佈，即招致新疆省議會⑬、新舊土爾扈特盟⑭幾方通電反對，且内蒙境内之熱、察、綏三特别區亦各由勢力强勁的地方集團控制。因此，直至1925年，馮玉祥才離開北京的政治漩渦，移駐張家口，正式出任西北邊防督辦，並由其部下李鳴鐘出任綏遠都統、張之江出任察哈爾都統。

其中綏遠特别行政區是在清代綏遠城將軍轄區的基礎上設於1914年7月，轄八縣、土默特旗及烏蘭察布、伊克昭兩盟十三旗⑮，其地“北控庫倫，西通寧夏，南環秦晉，東綰幽燕，外而長城瀚海，内而青山黄河，形勢雄要，物產豐饒，洵爲西北之重心”⑯。李鳴鐘主政綏遠僅一年有餘，但在興建地方工業、整頓財政、開辦教育、修建公路、剿匪安民等方面，均有顯著建樹⑰。尤其是沙明遠⑱主持下的綏遠教育工作快速、全面地展開，甚至有學者將這一時段稱爲“綏遠教育事業發展的又一黄金期”⑲。

馮玉祥被任命爲西北邊防督辦後，在北京未履職時，就開始關注蒙古問題，廣泛接觸蒙古人士。1923年5月15日，在旃檀寺會見了孫浚黄、金永福二人，二日後又與清末民初活躍於京城的那彦圖會晤，均談及治理蒙古的問題，且研讀《籌蒙芻議》等書籍⑳。馮玉祥移駐張家口後，“首先注意者，爲蒙回子弟之教育，意在提高西北文化，使五族子弟之智識，乃以平等俱進”，意識到了教育對治理西北多民族地區的重要性，

---

⑬ 《新疆省議會通告電北京院部反對西北邊防督辦公署組織條例涉及新疆請劃於西北邊防督辦範圍外函》（九月十八日）《参议院公报》，1923 年第三期第11册，155—158页。

⑭ 《新吐爾扈特盟長親王納木加旺登等聲明反對馮玉祥派兵出關赴新請將新疆地方劃在西北邊防督辦官制之外電》（九月十八日）《参议院公报》，1923 年第三期第11册，211—215页；《舊土爾扈特北部落盟長札薩克親王鄂羅勒莫扎布等仍請將西北邊防督辦事例條例牽涉新疆一層完全取消劃除電》（十一月十二日）《參議院公報》，1923年第三期第13册，99—106頁。

⑮ 民國初年因循清代在蒙古地區的盟旗舊制，綏遠都統對烏伊兩盟的控制力十分有限，詳參Justin Tighe, *Constructing suiyuan: the politics of northwestern territory and development in early twentieth-century china*, Leiden, Brill, 2005, p. 55.

⑯ 澄園《發刊詞》，《綏遠教育季刊》創刊號，1925年2月，1頁。

⑰ 劉映元、張靜文《國民軍進駐綏遠時期——紀念“五原誓師”六十周年》，《史料憶述》第1輯，呼和浩特：内蒙古自治區文史研究館，1986年，2頁。

⑱ 沙明遠（1879—1950年），回族，山東臨清人，歷任陝西、綏遠、甘肅教育廳長，曾爲馮玉祥及西北軍講學，在西北軍中頗有威望。

⑲ 牛敬忠《綏遠地區教育近代化初論》，《内蒙古大學學報》1998年第5期，10頁。

⑳ 馮玉祥著，中國第二歷史檔案館編《馮玉祥日記》（第一冊），南京：江蘇古籍出版社，1992年，1923年5月15日，353—354頁；5月17日，359頁；7月17日，414頁。

並於1924年責成沙明遠籌建五族學院。接受了籌建五族學院的任務後，沙明遠在北京與教育家王鴻一及回族武術名家馬子貞“商議建設及組織種種事項”，擬定了創辦學院的草綱[21]。

據當時報載，“教育廳長沙明遠到任後，甚有意於教育之革新，每早六時即起，各僚屬均于六時到辦公廳，下午六時乃得休息”[22]，在辦理包括籌建五族學院等各項教育工作的同時，教育廳創辦了《綏遠教育季刊》，其中闡釋了創辦五族學院的宗旨：一，團結五族精神；二，發揚東方文化；三，開發西北實業[23]。

在具體籌建中，沙明遠以“教育設施，因地而異同”，首先派員赴包頭、薩拉齊、五原各縣局調查蒙古、回族教育、產業等情況，及宣傳五族學院建立的意義。同時，沙明遠到綏遠次日便拜訪前清歸化城副都統文哲琿，開展聯絡地方上層人士的工作。沙明遠對待地方蒙回兩族上層人士“近則親往訪談，遠則托人迎迓”，如烏拉特之嵩德甫、歸綏回教俱進會會長白志先、包頭回教俱進會會長韓勝海、包頭回教俱進會副會長兼清真學校學董王恩同以及土默特旗的武爾功額、榮祥等人[24]。嵩德甫於二月十五日從包頭到綏遠，對創建五族學院表示出極大的熱忱，“故關於學院建設及招生事宜，尤多所建議”；回族方面，包頭韓勝海、王恩同於二月十七日到綏遠，“報告該地情形及教育狀況”[25]。

在開展調查、聯絡工作的同時，沙明遠從北京邀請“研究教育者”到綏遠進一步完善大綱，“不數日將大綱草就，又經數次修改，始將草案繕出”。在大綱中所體現的“尊師”“實用”“宗教自由”三種精神中，尤其值得注意的是對宗教兼容並包的態度，“故各宗教之建築，儀式仍其舊，且于院內建立各教教堂”[26]，最終在成案通則第六條計劃“凡一切宗教之設備，如福音堂、大雄殿、大成殿、清真寺均設一所，俾各學校有所觀摩，培養其堅固之信仰力”[27]，此舉雖過於理想化，但在一定程度上也符合西北多民族雜居的族群格局與各族學生同校的客觀現實，體現了創辦者尊重各民族風俗習慣、宗教信仰的理念。

另一方面，因主導籌備五族學院的馮、沙諸人，具有極爲濃厚的舊時代氣息，當時論者在肯定沙明遠爲教育工作夙興夜寐之餘，稱“惟各科長多系舊學人員，對於新式教育，頗欠研究。因之對於各學校，亦未能以新教育加以改革，不免爲白圭之玷”[28]。在籌備五族學院時，論及近代學校及當時的高等教育，認爲“近來國內大學林立，徒形式

㉑ 鐘爾強《五族學院事項》，《綏遠教育季刊》1925年創刊號，22—23頁。

㉒ 《綏遠教育之最近狀況》，《中華教育界》1925年第15卷第3期，9頁。

㉓ 劉慶荷《五族學院創設之緣起》，《綏遠教育季刊》1925年創刊號，56—58頁。

㉔ 鐘爾強《五族學院事項》，23—25頁。

㉕ 鐘爾強《五族學院事項》，24頁。

㉖ 鐘爾強《五族學院事項》，25頁。

㉗ 《綏遠教育廳稟督辦呈都統籌備五族學院辦理就緒情形案》，《綏遠月刊》1925年第1卷第1期，教育6頁。

㉘ 《綏遠教育之最近狀況》，9頁。

上觀之，似可追蹤歐美。實則大半空懸大學名號，巧立新奇主義，趨青年于放縱之途，貽社會以詬病之資。且師道墮落，學潮暴烈，將數千年之道德，幾掃地無餘，教育之破產，恐難免矣"，在鄙薄近代大學的同時，卻表達了對傳統書院的思慕，"昔宋明書院之制，規程嚴明，且含有自學輔導主義。故所造人才，率皆品學兼優，應世裕如"，所以"今五族學院即參合古書院之制，培植一般青年，發揚東方文化，闡明孔孟之禮教"㉙，並將此作爲五族學院的創辦主旨之一。貌似以揚棄的態度對待中國傳統文化與舶來之現代教育模式，但五族學院的創辦者似乎仍有保守之嫌。如，《五族學院暫行簡章》第九條"本院以灑掃應對進退爲修身大綱，如故意違抗，由正教用鞭撲督則之，以副嚴格教育之規定"㉚，可謂追求五族共和、弘揚宗教自由進步理念中的"白圭之玷"。

關於校址的選擇，"正式院址擬在歸化新舊城之間建築，中秋節前可望就緒"㉛，建成前借地試辦，招講讀、武術兩部。最後，借用綏遠會館作爲主校址，另外以土默特倉廒爲開辦武術部之場所，兼具體育場的功能。在經費預算方面，核定開辦經費2800餘元，日常費用每月預算爲1900餘元。籌備初期，從財政廳借撥，其後從吸煙卷戶捐稅中抽撥㉜。

在上述辦學大綱、校址、經費等問題落實後，延聘教師和招收學生亦是開辦學校的核心事務。因起初辦學目標甚高，"五族學院爲西北文化中心，且擬逐漸擴充，務使淩駕中原"，故而"但非有各經學大師來此主講，不足以振生氣"，沙明遠充分利用其個人關係網絡，計劃在山東和北京聘請教師㉝，將梅光羲、王鴻一、梁漱溟、賈恩紱等人列入網羅範圍。雖因種種原因上述諸氏並未蒞臨執教，但從這份計劃名單中也可窺知五族學院辦學上較爲保守的一面。後因時間、經費等問題，決定"目前開辦者惟有中學及小學程度之學生，教員不難選聘"㉞，決定先行辦學，暑假再赴各地聘請治傳統學問的知名人士。

在針對民族教育與文化研究方面，擬定延請"札薩克喇嘛十余位，研究黃教，實行保護無量寺、延壽寺、崇福寺等，以內之存經樓及藏經塔，以爲研究上之特別儲備"，另外計劃"購買大號鉛印機器兩架，專請有爾林（即學問）之阿衡，翻譯哥蘭經三十卷，並印清真經典百餘種，恢復亞賴伯之文明"㉟。如此做法，雖與現代學校之研究旨趣、方法相去甚遠，但從保存民族文化、團結各族人士層面來講應有其積極意義。至於

㉙ 劉慶荷《五族學院創設之緣起》，57—58頁。

㉚ 《綏遠教育廳稟督辦呈都統籌備五族學院辦理就緒情形案》，教育16頁。

㉛ 鐘爾強《五族學院事項》，25—26頁。

㉜ 《綏遠教育廳稟督辦呈都統籌備五族學院辦理就緒情形案》，教育5頁；《五族學院概況》，《綏遠教育季刊》1925年第2期，記載35頁。

㉝ 鐘爾強《五族學院事項》，26頁。

㉞ 鐘爾強《五族學院事項》，26頁。

㉟ 鐘爾強《五族學院事項》，26頁。關於延請喇嘛研究黃教，可能是馮玉祥直接授意，1923年5月15日，馮氏與孫浚黃、金永福二人會晤時，孫、金二人對馮玉祥提及："蒙古現在中日俄之範圍下，而其喇嘛教之真精神在世界上有專門研究之必要。"參見《馮玉祥日記》（第一冊），353—354頁。

招生範圍，限定在察綏兩區，雖“五族”兼收，但尤其注重蒙、回兩族。

在籌備期間，沙明遠應馮玉祥之召，於1925年2月8日赴張家口彙報諸項事宜[36]，馮玉祥飭令加緊籌備。經過不足三個月的籌備，于3月22日舉行開院典禮，綏遠五族學院正式成立，雖因條件所限，多項計劃未能如期開展，如大綱中之大學教育暫不開辦，僅試辦類似中、小學程度之班級。但鑒於當時綏遠地區，政局動蕩、教育發展滯後的局面，嘗試創辦民族教育應該予以肯定。李鳴鐘在開學典禮上講到，“不但是五族學院開學的日子，並可以說是我們中華民族五族共和的紀念日子”[37]。下面進一步對五族學院的管理、教學、課程設計及招生授課情況等問題進行梳理，以期深入瞭解其實際運作和歷史影響。

二、設員與管理

新成立的五族學院隸屬綏遠教育廳，廳長沙明遠兼任院長，教務主任由畢業于北京師範大學的鐘爾強代理[38]。在制度設計上以董事會掌全院一切事務，具體設總董一員，副董若干，並聘“各族深負時望之紳耆、鄉老、喇嘛爲名譽共事”[39]。在董事會與院長之下，分設總務、教務、訓育三處，其中教務處分師範、武術、小學、女子、中學、大學六部；訓育處分指導、考核、齋務三股；總務處分註冊、文牘、圖書、庶事、儀器管理五課[40]。對於日常行政工作的處理，採用“合議制度”，並詳細規定了各級、各部門會議的召集人、參會範圍等問題。

在經費管理上，“本院董事會推任基金一人，保管基金。承總董之命令審核本院預算、決算各案”，具體財務流程“凡關於經、常費，除由院長照章具領外，其餘臨時用各款，均由總董命令發佈之”[41]。五族學院每年的經費預算爲23 856元，具體開支專案爲：①學生膳費書籍費、圖書費在內需14 400元；②教職員薪俸（用人工資在內）需7128元；③辦公費用、教學用具及郵電費需1200元；④燃料、房租等雜費1128元[42]。李鳴鐘令悉數由捲煙吸戶捐局撥給，財政來源單一。據《綏遠月刊》所載資料現將1925年

㊱　據馮玉祥日記載，“二月十日，下午二點，沙廳長來，報告在綏遠辦五族學院及通俗講演事”，參見《馮玉祥日記》（第二冊），16頁。

㊲　《五族學院開學李都統訓詞》，《綏遠月刊》1925年第1卷第1期，297—301頁。

㊳　沙星五《我的伯父沙月坡》，《臨清文史》第3輯，臨清：中國人民政治協商會議山東省臨清市委員會文史資料研究委員會1988年，132頁；另外參見許魁元《呼和浩特的舊學府》，《呼和浩特史料》第一集，呼和浩特：中共呼和浩特市委黨史資料徵集辦公室、呼和浩特市地方誌編修辦公室，1983年，294—297頁。

㊴　《綏遠教育廳稟督辦呈都統籌備五族學院辦理就緒情形案》，《綏遠月刊》1925年第1卷第一期，教育6頁。

㊵　《五族學院概況》，記載22頁。

㊶　《五族學院組織大綱草案》，《綏遠月刊》1925年第1卷第1期，教育6頁。

㊷　《五族學院概況》，記載35—36頁。

2—5月綏遠捲煙吸戶捐局撥付五族學院的經費羅列如下（表1）[43]：

表1

月份	數額	來源機構
2	728元8毛2厘	綏遠捲煙吸戶捐局
3	71元1角9分8厘	綏遠捲煙吸戶捐局
4	2668元6角9分6厘	綏遠捲煙吸戶捐局
	2575元9角8分	包頭分局
5	1369元4角9分1厘	綏遠捲煙吸戶捐局
合計	7414.185元	

五族學院月需經費約1988元，現以1925年2—5月爲例，捲煙吸戶捐局平均每月到款約1854元。可見五族學院的經費入不敷出，且據上表可知，捲煙吸戶捐局每月撥款數額差異較大，經費來源並不穩定。當時綏遠財政狀況在李鳴鐘的整頓下有所改觀，但教育經費並不充裕。

五族學院在學生管理方面，"衣食起居均用軍式管理"[44]。在操行方面，要求教職員隨時隨地監督學生，每週匯總研究違規記錄，待期末分甲乙丙丁四等統一考核，且通報家長，其中丙等警告，丁等勒令退學。對優異者亦有相應的獎勵規章，"操行、學業俱列甲等者，特由院長繕給褒狀，以資獎勵"，即爲諸項考核爲甲等的學生頒發獎狀。在綜合方面，規定懲戒學生的方法有五等：①警告；②禁假；③記過；④降級；⑤退學，其中記大過三次，勒令退學。此外，在起居、飲食等方面亦有詳細而嚴格的規章。其中在宿舍分配上，爲體現學校之多族共處特點，"就原有房屋分配宿舍，五族合居爲唯一之配置"，其目的爲"調和種族觀念"。可見，籌建者針對"五族共和"之辦學主旨，在制度設計上頗爲用心[45]。

三、招生與教學

上文述及沙明遠上任後，首先聯絡綏遠蒙、回各族聲望顯著人士，以期獲得地方上層對創辦五族學院的支持。此外，沙明遠派員赴包頭、五原等地調查蒙古、回族的人口及教育狀況。諸項工作開展地頗爲順利，在宣傳五族學院辦學主旨方面起到了積極的作用。但沙明遠及其僚屬的活動範圍幾乎未及烏伊兩盟十三旗的地域。於是，都統署在將創辦五族學院一事照會烏伊兩盟各旗外，又委任麟慶、張汝恢、銀海等人爲勸學大員。

㊸ 據《綏遠月刊》1925第1卷第2期，財政17—18頁；《綏遠月刊》1925年第1卷第3期，財政26—27頁；《綏遠月刊》1925年第1卷第4期，財政13—16頁；《綏遠月刊》1925年第1卷第5期，財政13—14頁。

㊹ 《五族學院組織大綱》，《綏遠月刊》1925年第1期第1號，教育12頁。

㊺ 《五族學院概況》，記載23—30頁。

同時制定了招收第一期學生的計劃，擬招收學生300名，烏伊兩盟十三旗，每旗10名，共130名，土默特20名，蒙古族學生共150名；在各縣局招收回籍學生100名；其餘50個名額由五族學院自行招考，學生免除一切費用[46]。最終在3月26日舉行的分級考試中，有190名學生參加，其中薩拉齊縣選送回籍學生15名、清水河縣選送21名[47]，達拉特旗選送12名[48]，包頭私立清真學堂選送吴懋功、吴佑龍、白子軒等回籍學生20余人[49]。至於蒙古族學生，"蒙古子弟來學者，大抵屬已開化之土默特及半開化之達拉特旗"[50]，烏蘭察布盟盟長"不許將蒙族子弟送到綏遠入學"[51]。

因此，在1925年4月25日於綏遠五族學院召開的烏伊兩盟十三旗王公代表會議上，教育廳鑒於前期在各旗招收學生之窘境，"提議五族學院，業已成立，各旗應多送子弟入學肄業，開通智識案"[52]。吴國棟在1926年刊發的《綏遠遊記》中记载，"教育廳長沙明遠，鑒於歸綏缺乏高等教育，蒙人飽受魚肉，敢怒而不敢言，驟勸其子弟入學，多觀望不前。沙廳長爲特别提倡蒙人教育起見，招集五族聯歡會，蒙古王公多列席。沙詳説五族共和之真諦，某王公大爲感動，當即剪髮易服，誠心内向，派遣子弟入學。數月以來，成效大著。下學期蒙人子弟增至七十餘人，未始非官廳提倡之效也，同人寄寓於此，荷承諸先生竭誠歡迎與詳細賜教，尤爲感謝。"[53]雖照吴國棟所述，烏伊兩盟王公會議可能在擴大招生上起到了一定的作用。但據《西北彙刊》1925年11月所發《西北教育一年來發達之概況》統計，五族學院共有200餘人，蒙古族學生占27%[54]，説明在招收蒙旗學生方面未有根本性改變。

另一方面，爲解決生源不足問題，五族學院在開學三個月後，决定調整辦理蒙古教育的計劃，"本院對於蒙古教育計劃，由'來學'變爲'往教'，最近先由本院所養辦理蒙古教育師資，學成後前往各盟旗就近教育其子弟……現將暑前各縣保送學生百九十人，除一部成績太劣者斥退外，其餘改編爲師範部會，令其專門研究辦理蒙古教育之方法，而符以公費作育師資之通例"[55]。

籌辦期間，沙明遠曾派員至綏遠轄區調查，認爲"各地職業大抵不外農墾畜牧，經濟狀况亦甚平常，河套水利亦可借用"，在瞭解了當時綏遠的社會經濟狀況下，决定

---

[46] 《呈都統爲呈報招生辦法及廣告請鑒核轉令選送文》，《綏遠教育季刊》1925年創刊號，88—89頁。

[47] 《綏遠都統署訓令政字第三百八十七號》、《綏遠都統署訓令政字第三百八十八號》，《綏遠月刊》1925年第1卷第2期，教育2—4頁。

[48] 《1925年烏伊兩盟十三旗王公代表會議錄》，《内蒙古檔案史料》，1993年第1期，43頁。

[49] 政協包頭市東河區委員會文史資料研究委員會、包頭民族宗教志編修辦公室編《包頭回族史料》（内部資料），1987年10月，40頁。

[50] 《五族學院概況》，記載36頁。

[51] 《1925年烏伊兩盟十三旗王公代表會議錄》，《内蒙古檔案史料》，1993年第1期，43頁。關於當時蒙古王公對新式教育的態度，參見《内蒙古通史》第6卷上册，北京：人民出版社，2012年，370頁。

[52] 吴怡庭《綏遠蒙旗會議之議案》，《西北月刊》1925年第25期，22—25頁。

[53] 吴國棟《綏遠遊記》，《農學》1926年第3卷第1期，179—208頁。

[54] 《西北教育一年來發達之概況》，《西北彙刊》1925年第1卷第11期，19—22頁。

[55] 《五族學院概況》，記載36—37頁。

“將來學院正式開幕後，首先設農墾水利、畜牧、制革三科，以適應當地之需要”[56]。因此，在編制學院大綱時，能夠因地制宜，注重結合當地的生產結構和種群分佈狀況，依照學科性質和程度高低初步分爲六部：講讀部、實習部、師範部、女工部、武術部、研究部[57]。1925年3月開學時，先設立講讀和武術二部，期間陸續增設數科，截止本年11月份，“有學生七班，既師範專休科一班；職工科一班；蒙回小學一班；師範預科和第一級、第二級各一班；初級中學一年級一班[58]。在課程編制過程中，同樣結合西北人文、自然環境，在大綱的基礎上對課程進行了調整，“各班加入農業及作工爲主要必修科目”，其中農業每週授課2小時，實習8小時；作工每週4小時，“以製造實用物品及器具爲目的”。此外，“中校課程中添加蒙語爲選修科目”[59]。

五族學院在學生考試設計上，無年考、期考，而是每月考核一次，一年十次。試卷爲百分制，85分以上爲甲等；70分以上爲乙等；60分以上爲丙等；不及60爲丁等，即不及格。十次月考其中若有四次不及格者留級，六次不及格者勒令退學。另外，根據學生專業，“如有一門主要學程不及格者，酌令留級”[60]。

在注重科學文化課程的基礎上，五族學院“對體育異常注意，一切設施莫不精益求精，使學生養成健全之體格，以備將來服務國家也”[61]，Justin Tighe在論及綏遠五族學院時，注意到了該校對體育項目的重視，認爲體育是現代學校教育的重要內容[62]。具體項目設置見表2：

表2　運動項目表

球類	田徑賽		體操		武術	
網球	田賽	徑賽	柔軟體操		團體教練	單人教練
足球	跳遠	半英里接力	軍式體操		拳術	各種兵器
籃球	鐵餅	百米高檻	器械體操	鞦韆	劍術	
隊球	跳高	二百米競走		天橋	棍術	
乒乓球	鐵球	百米競走		木馬		
	標槍	四百米競走		杠子		
	撐杆跳高	百二十米低檻				
		一英里接力				

[56] 鐘爾強《五族學院事項》，23頁。

[57] 《綏遠教育廳稟督辦呈都統籌備五族學院辦理就緒情形案》，教育6頁。

[58] 《西北教育一年來發達之概況》，19—22頁。

[59] 《五族學院概況》，記載23頁。

[60] 《五族學院概況》，記載25頁。

[61] 《五族學院概況》，記載26頁。

[62] Justin Tighe, *Constructing suiyuan: the politics of northwestern territory and development in early twentieth-century China*, p. 178.

在體育鍛煉的時間方面，亦有明確規定，即每日上午練習二十分鐘柔軟體操，“每日午後四句鐘，各隊分班練習”[63]。

課外組織有學生自治會，內設總務、宣傳、編制、教育、衛生五個部門。另外有演說會、雄辯會、新劇團、美術研究社等各類組織，其目的除豐富學生課餘生活外，還擔負著一定的社會責任，如學生自治會計劃在暑假期間“開辦露天學校三處，擬於七月二十日開學教授平民千字課”[64]。

四、對“五族學院”功用的評估

五族學院的設計者，以民國初期五族共和思想爲指導，“所謂五族學院者即融和五族而爲一大民族之最高學府也。招收五族之優秀青年，任其自由信仰宗教，發展各教真正之精神，灌輸五族一家之思想，陶冶合力對外之智慧”[65]，將其規劃爲從大學自小學，涵蓋諸多學科，包容各種思想、蓄納不同宗教的教育機構，並將其定位爲“西北文化中心”。事實上，無論是設計者的經驗和能力，還是當時綏遠，甚至西北的社會經濟狀況都不足以支撑如此理想的教育機構。且從籌備到開學典禮，不足四月，因此諸多設想最終停留在辦學大綱上。即使旨在發展“蒙、回”教育，勉強開辦的幾個部門，也因對烏伊兩盟十三旗教育狀況瞭解不足，而導致諸多問題。因此在以五族學院之名存在的兩年時間裏，其政治象徵意義層面的價值高於其作爲教育機構本身的作用。

綏遠特別行政區爲多族群聚居區域，一方面民國以來中央政府繼續推進清末開始的邊疆—內地一體化進程[66]，而另一方面其轄治之烏伊兩盟十三旗基本上沿襲清朝舊制。制度方面的抵牾和頻繁的政治更迭，導致民國初期綏遠特別區成爲匪患嚴重、鴉片泛濫，社會秩序極爲紊亂的地區。馮玉祥移節西北，創立五族學院，證明其認識到了綏遠、甚至西北多族群並存的現實，通過開辦教育來啟發民智，最終實現開發西北的目的。因此五族學院的建立，至少是一種通過教育手段解決西北問題的嘗試，且其存在象徵了當時“五族共和”的建國綱領，以及能夠團結、凝聚西北各族。當時黃炎培來校做了題爲“正德利用厚生”的演講[67]，農林專家吴國棟亦在其遊記中熱情地對五族學院予以介紹[68]。

另外，五族學院還肩負另外一項實際功能，即作爲處理民族事務的場所。1925年4月26日，由綏遠都統李鳴鐘召集的烏伊兩盟十三旗王公代表會議，在五族學院召開。

---

[63] 《五族學院概況》，記載29頁。

[64] 《五族學院概況》，記載34—35頁。

[65] 劉慶荷《五族學院創設之緣起》，57頁。

[66] 蘇德畢力格《晚清政府對新疆、蒙古和西藏政策研究》，呼和浩特：內蒙古人民出版社，2005年，150—160頁。

[67] 黃炎培著，中國社會科學院近代史研究所整理《黃炎培日記》第2卷，北京：華文出版社，2008年，240頁。

[68] 吴國棟《綏遠遊記》，《農學》1926年第3卷第1期，179—208頁。

之所以選擇“五族學院”作爲蒙旗王公會議的會址，具有向各旗蒙古王公表達“五族共和”政治綱領的初衷。Justin Tighe甚至認爲召開於“五族學院”的“烏伊兩盟十三旗王公代表會議”是綏遠當局處理蒙古事務的准政府機構的組織⑲。

如上文所述，五族學院在行政催產下，倉促成立，問題很多，且其存續時間短暫。但20世紀20年代初期，隨著中國共產黨的成立以及國民黨的改組，革命形勢風起雲湧，在馮玉祥及綏遠都統李鳴鐘的支持下，國共兩黨得以在綏遠地區公開活動⑳。1925年2月，李大釗在張家口與馮玉祥會晤後，派宣俠父、陶新佘等人到馮玉祥部開展活動㉑，同時令歸化城土默特籍共產黨員吉雅泰回綏遠開展工作㉒，“在國共合作統一戰線形成後，國民軍駐綏期間，綏遠地區的革命運動也高漲起來”㉓。當時就讀於五族學院的許多學生正是在這裡接受了革命思想，如楊植霖提到：“馮玉祥國民軍到綏遠後，做了不少於國于民有益的事。開辦設在歸綏的‘五族學院’，就是他們辦的有益於民的大好事之一。正是在這個學院裏，我不僅學到了文化，而且還走上了中國共產黨領導和指引的革命道路。”㉔其中吉雅泰以及五族學院教務長楊紹萱對其影響頗大。回族青年白禎于1925年考入五族學院，“入校後，受學院進步思想的薰陶，和參加綏遠特區工委組織的‘五卅’慘案遊行活動的影響”㉕，未完成學業便考入黃埔軍校。此外，五族學院的部分學生，通過這一平臺，考入更高等級學府繼續求學。如回族青年吴佑龍，從包頭清真高級學堂考入五族學院，其後轉入綏遠省立第一中學，畢業後考取了天津北洋工學院土木工程系㉖。從這一層面來講，五族學院在其存在的短暫時間裏，爲當時在此求學的邊疆各族貧困學生創造了接觸各種政治主張和瞭解國內社會狀況的機會，爲他們打開一扇瞭望外部世界的窗戶。

1926年，國民軍在與直、奉、晉等方聯軍的戰爭中失利西撤，馮玉祥下野赴蘇聯考察，晉系將領商震代理綏遠都統。隨著綏遠政局的跌宕，五族學院，“迨至十六年六月，改名爲中山學院。十六年十一月，因奉軍據綏，反對中山名稱，改爲綏遠公學”㉗。

---

⑲ Justin Tighe, *Constructing suiyuan: the politics of northwestern territory and development in early twentieth-century China*, p. 83.

⑳ 關於當時綏遠及蒙古地區的革命形勢，參見C. P. Atwood, *Young Mongols And Vigilantes in Inner Mongolia's Interregnum Decades,1911-1931*, vol 1, Leiden: Brill, 2002, pp. 278-285。

㉑ 左寶《李大釗與馮玉祥的交往》，《黨史博采》1995年第1期，7—8頁。

㉒ 楊植霖《青山足跡——楊植霖回憶錄》，呼和浩特：內蒙古人民出版社，1995年，12頁。

㉓ 劉映元、張靜文《國民軍進駐綏遠時期——紀念“五原誓師”六十周年》，《內蒙古文史叢書·史料憶述》第1辑，呼和浩特：內蒙古自治區文史研究館，1986年，12頁。

㉔ 楊植霖《青山足跡——楊植霖回憶錄》，11頁。

㉕ 白恩榮《憶黃埔軍校畢業的父親白禎》，《呼和浩特回族史料》第六輯，呼和浩特：政協呼和浩特回民區委員會《呼和浩特回族史料》編輯委員會，2004年，120頁。

㉖ 趙俊《吴佑龍先生一生是追求光明的一生》，《包頭文史資料選編——紀念綏遠“九一九”起義四十年專輯》第11輯，包頭：中國人民政治協商會議包頭市委員會文史資料研究委員會，1989年，135頁。

㉗ 《綏遠通志稿》第六冊，呼和浩特：內蒙古人民出版社，2007年，84—85頁。

1928年6月，閻錫山再次控制綏遠，五族學院最終更名爲中山學院。隨着名稱的變更，馮玉祥、沙明遠等創辦者賦予五族學院的民族教育特性亦逐漸褪祛。

Harmony among Five Nations in Frontier Region：Based on the Research of Suiyuan Five Nations College

Fan Zhiqiang

This article is based upon gazetteers, memorials and government documents of Suiyuan in the 1920s, especially the *Suiyuan Educational Quarterly* and the *Suiyuan Monthly*. These two magazines were sponsored by the local government and published government documents regularly. The author investigates the practice of *Harmony among Five Nations* in the frontier region, through a survey of the establishment of the Suiyuan Five Nations College.

民國北京政府時期察哈爾的土地開墾與設治述略

蘇日嫇

大規模開墾蒙地是民國政府對蒙政策的主要內容之一。在政權建立初期，袁世凱政府十分了解以“放墾蒙地”爲主的清末對蒙“新政”所導致的民族矛盾激化。爲了安撫王公上層，緩和民族矛盾，袁世凱北京政府曾宣布蒙旗“既有閑荒亦暫不放墾”和準許“各旗未放荒地留歸各旗自行開墾”等法令[①]，並未冒然推行放墾。然而隨著袁世凱在全國的統治地位基本鞏固，大部分蒙古王公“决心擁戴共和”之後，袁世凱改變了起初的蒙古地區“暫不放墾”政策，轉而大興蒙墾，積極推進移民墾殖與設治。而新設立的三個特别區，若將其行政區及所屬人口、墾地規模，以及日常行政等各項經費，與內地同一行政級别的省縣保持相當程度，也只有靠遷移內地漢民，放墾蒙地才能維持或實現。因此，放墾蒙地政策的全面啟動，注定成爲民國政府對蒙政策的重要內容。

1915年2月，奉大總統的命令，由財政部會同農商部、蒙藏院，擬訂出“墾辟蒙荒獎勵辦法”七條。9月獲準公布《墾辟蒙荒獎勵條例》。是年11月又頒布《禁止私放蒙荒通則》。前者鼓勵開墾蒙地，數量愈多，獎勵等級愈高。後者則規定，蒙旗未經經管地方長官和中央批準不得自行放墾，若有私放情形，對當事机构相關負責人給予相應的處罰[②]。蒙藏院又制定了《邊荒條例》，明文規定放墾遊牧地，其所得由地方官員和蒙旗分潤。此類通則、辦法、條例的實質爲賦予地方軍閥權力來控制蒙旗土地[③]。

一、察哈爾放墾前的預備工作

1912年11月，察哈爾都統何宗蓮爲籌辦清丈地畝，補墾余荒一案呈請大總統。但該案並未立即得到大總統的批準，其理由爲：“籌辦墾務，自係切要之，清丈地畝一

① 汪炳明《是“放墾蒙地”還是“移民實邊”》，載於《成吉思汗的遺產》，呼和浩特：內蒙古人民出版社，2009年，194頁。

② 烏力吉陶格套《民初科左中旗墾務糾紛與蒙地放墾條例的出台》，*Studies in Inner Asian History and Culture*，No. Mar 2017, p.34，p.45.

③ 色音《蒙古遊牧社會的變遷》，呼和浩特：內蒙古人民出版社，1998年，18—19頁。

事，牽涉頗多，辦理稍一不慎，地方易生枝節，現值邊陲多事，宜稍示懷柔，原議既稱領地各戶蒙民居多，果而推行清丈，誠恐易起驚疑，致滋紛擾，該都統所請設局清丈地畝案，現時機，應暫從緩議。”[④]此時的袁世凱對蒙墾采取的是比較保守的態度，認爲目前並非適合開展蒙墾，應顧忌察哈爾諸旗群總管之意願，從緩實行開墾蒙地。但是，察哈爾都統何宗蓮則提出：

查該部以時機而論，暫從緩議，不爲無見。然局外隱揣，不如當局者詳知底蘊，其間領地各户雖多蒙民，而蒙民素來謹願但求清丈，諒無紛擾，再，清丈補墾，必須雙方進行，於事乃能有濟。蓋原領各民户內竟有原領一頃，私墾至數頃者，有徒領押荒條據，至今未換部照，希圖不納國賦者；甚有一頃不領，私墾盗賣者，其中流弊比比皆是。究其弊端，率由從前包攬大段，欺隱公家，魚肉貧民，一班地痞土棍之所爲。今聞清丈，若輩生畏，難免不設計阻撓，而善良地户知私墾終難久遠，現已紛紛呈請情願清丈。而籌辦墾務不從清丈入手，余荒、夾荒將來終爲彼等欺隱蠶食，則私墾盗賣之弊源終難清。竊維清丈手續雖繁，若辦理得法，似不至枝節旁生。至察境原放之荒，均系內地民户承領，並無蒙民墾種，清丈一事，與蒙民並無幹涉。即有蒙民尚求清丈而不得，決不至有驚疑紛擾之事，其中領地之户雖有教民，若與各教堂主教等宣迎妥洽，自無他項梗阻。此次清丈補墾，與察防用款及八旗生計關系匪淺。現值經濟困難一籌莫展，與其借款仰人鼻息，何若就地籌款，……爲開辟察境利源，籌辦旗民生計起見，擬先篆刻關防，設局籌辦，一俟蒙事稍平，即著手辦理，以便節節進行，逐漸推廣，庶因果兼收，不負國家註重墾務，隱寓實邊之至意[⑤]。

何宗蓮認爲，察哈爾境内原先放墾之荒地，均由內地漢人承領，並無蒙古人墾種清丈之事，與蒙古人無關。既是有蒙古人要求清丈的荒地而未如願，也不至於引起紛擾。而設局籌辦墾務，首先，要清理原先承領蒙地之民戶即漢人中存在的問題。由官府出面清理墾務，消除從前“地痞土棍”包攬大段土地，“欺隱公家，魚肉貧民”之弊端，以保證民戶如實交納國賦。其次，爲加強察哈爾防務，就地籌款，以減輕國家的負擔；再次，蒙古地方一旦穩定下來，即逐漸推廣墾務，以期取得移民實邊之效果。當然，何宗蓮最終目的是爲了建立地方財政，而地方財政則主要靠稅收，因此他對蒙墾持積極態度，想方設法計劃清丈土地，補墾余荒。

推行墾務的另一個關鍵問題，是統一察哈爾政區與墾務管理權問題。察哈爾與綏遠的各廳在清代分屬直、晉二省，而各廳之間界限歷來並不分明。清末察哈爾、綏遠等地的開墾，均由督辦蒙旗墾務大臣辦理，該職屬特設職掌，不以地方爲界。貽谷在察哈爾放墾的目的不是爲了建立地方財政，而是爲了通過放墾收取押荒銀，繳納給清政府。

---

④ “署理察哈爾都統何宗蓮呈大總統報明籌辦察哈爾清丈補墾情形請鑒核飭部立案文並批”，《政府公報》，第260號，1913年1月26日。

⑤ 同註④。

因此也沒有必要十分詳細地劃分墾政與地方民政的界限。設立察綏特別區之前，察哈爾右翼豐鎮、涼城、興和、陶林等四縣墾務屬綏遠城將軍管理。察哈爾、綏遠特別區建立後，察哈爾右翼豐鎮、涼城、興和、陶林四縣劃歸了察哈爾。因此，綏遠都統、督辦墾務大臣潘矩楹因“政區與墾務並無連帶關係”爲由，呈請內務部將察右四縣墾務仍暫由綏遠都統督辦，等清理墾務之後再移交察哈爾[⑥]。

對潘氏的此項要求，內務部經核定之後，呈文大總統：“……查察哈爾右翼四旗豐鎮、涼城、興和、陶林四縣之地自改劃察綏區域以來，該處民事蒙務均歸察哈爾都統管理，所有該地一切事項自願完全移歸察屬，俾一事權，清理墾荒，純系民、旗地畝之事，一切查丈手續，解決爭端，民蒙糾葛均與行政息息相關，若與行政區域分離仍歸綏遠督辦，將來處理一切事件權限不清，必致治絲而芬，自願由察哈爾都統一並管理以昭劃一。”[⑦]從內務部的這一呈文可以看出內務部對潘氏的要求持有否定意見，認爲行政與民事需要統一管理，才能防止權限不清的問題。

其呈文中接著又說道：“墾務與政區並無連帶關係等語徵之，已往事實，自屬實在情形。蓋當日察綏兩處地方，尚未明劃區域，而督辦蒙旗大臣辦理蒙旗墾務，又屬特設職掌，原不以地方爲界限，現在改出區域，既經分別劃清，設置道縣，而蒙旗事宜，亦應由該地方管理。今昔情勢殊異，辦法自宜變通。”[⑧]此段內容也說明民國官員對時局的認識，他們認爲清朝不要求劃分地方界線，但是如今卻不同。

接著又提到：“右翼四旗墾戶，積欠荒價，蒂欠檔冊均在綏遠，其辦理余荒夾荒，各員均係老於墾務之人，未便易生手等語，事屬接替問題，自可安爲籌計，此項卷檔冊籍，既爲清理墾務之根據，應與辦事機關隨之轉移，將來分別點交自無應有所隔閡，其辦事舊員，果係熟習各該地方情形，頗資得力者，即墾務改由察屬辦理，亦必酌量留用。此等事實，雖於察綏兩處，有互相連涉之關，但使接洽安協，尚無事實困難之可言。”[⑨]從這裏可以看出，察哈爾右翼之前開墾的檔冊都在綏遠，辦理墾務的均爲有經驗的官員，所以就算察哈爾接管右翼墾務以後，也應當考慮資歷，留用一部分官員。

又稱：“該地積欠押荒，綏遠已擬作歸還股本抵款一節，查從前撥借公司股本，據稱係爲墾務開渠之用，與他種經費不同，且係指定用途未便聽其無著，自應由察綏會同查明切實數目，將來在清理墾務收入項下，設法提還，以清積欠。”[⑩]上述內容表明，在此之前開墾過程中有收取押荒銀一事，所以察綏兩方應該協同並把實際積欠金額清理，將來在墾務收入中予以償還。

內務部認爲：“總之，察屬右翼四縣之地，爲民蒙交錯雜處之區，而清理該地墾

⑥ “署理察哈爾都統何宗蓮呈大總統報明籌辦察哈爾清丈補墾情形請鑒核飭部立案文並批”，《政府公報》，第260號，1913年1月26日。

⑦ 同註⑥。

⑧ 同註⑥。

⑨ 同註⑥。

⑩ 同註⑥。

荒，又屬民蒙互有糾葛之事，該處民事蒙務，因現行區域之上劃分，既已統屬察哈爾都統管理該地墾務事項，與其俟清理以後再歸察屬致涉紛歧，若按照區域實行劃分清理，各有專責，所有議察哈爾右翼四旗豐、涼、興、陶四縣清理墾務緣由，是否有當理合具呈謹乞。”⑪

由上述文字看，民國初年察哈爾的墾務，不僅僅是清理地畝、開浚利源的問題，更關係到察哈爾與綏遠兩個特別政區劃分轄區問題，而其背後隱藏的是綏遠都統與察哈爾都統的利益角逐。即便當時察哈爾右翼四縣已劃歸察哈爾特別區域，綏遠都統仍力爭維護其舊有的利益，要求察右四縣墾務仍由其暫爲代理。但有鑒於墾務涉及地方民事，不宜將墾務與政區分離，將察哈爾右翼四縣墾務移交綏遠，因此北京政府內務部提議將該四縣墾務改由察哈爾都統一並管理。至此，察哈爾全區諸縣的墾政民政一並歸察哈爾都統管理，察哈爾墾政與政區建設歸於一統，爲此後察哈爾移墾設治的有力推進奠定了初步的基礎。

二、察哈爾全區墾務總局的成立

民國初年，因時局動蕩，內蒙古東西墾務處於停滯狀態。隨著局勢的穩定，民國政府開始著手制定專門法律法規和相應的措施，逐步推進蒙墾。察哈爾地處漠南蒙古中部，其都統所在地張家口是進入中原的咽喉要地，也是京師的門戶。因此，察哈爾的防務和墾政，爲歷代中央政府所重視。民國北京政府爲有效推進察哈爾墾政，專門設立了負責察哈爾特別區全境墾務工作的機構——察哈爾全區墾務總局（簡稱察墾總局）。察墾總局事務由興和道尹監管，各縣酌設分局，以知事爲坐辦委員，與分局局長會同辦理。因清代以來的長期開墾，察哈爾所放地畝多爲各旗群間的“夾荒”或 “余荒”，地段零落，因此，每次放墾時，常發生糾葛，而其他大段荒地多爲王公牧地，交涉更加不易⑫。

1915年4月，民國政府批準財政部呈請，委派龍驤⑬出任察哈爾全區墾務總局總辦一職，在其領導之下，推進清丈及開墾等一系列工作。5月，張家口設立察哈爾墾務總局。次年12月，察哈爾都統向大總統提出將察哈爾墾務總辦一職改爲實官的呈請。其理由有以下兩方面：

（1）察哈爾幅員遼闊，各盟各旗、各廟、各台站之生荒，均係蒙地；換言之，察哈爾尚未開墾的牧地，均屬於各盟旗，根據慣例必須由官府與盟旗接洽、商定後，方能

---

⑪ 同註⑥。

⑫ “留任署察哈爾都統何宗蓮呈察屬墾務擬請援案由道尹等兼任辦理以免面紛更請示文並批令”，《政府公報》，第1079號，1915年5月10日。

⑬ 龍驤：湖北孝感人，1887年出生，畢業於湖北師範學堂，1915年升任察哈爾實業廳廳長兼墾務局總辦。此後，龍驤曾被委派辦理外蒙軍機等重要事宜。1920年，擔任農商部參事，後又任國務院財政部顧問、總統府顧問等要職。

放墾。而盟旗的盟長、寺廟的活佛，以及王公等官階高、職位尤崇。因此，非明令簡任墾務總辦一職，不足與蒙古盟旗交涉。

（2）察哈爾墾務總局統轄包括錫林郭勒盟在內的全區，兼管清丈熟地、開放生荒、設治、屯墾各事宜。其“職掌之重，事務之繁”，不可與內地普通墾務局同日而語。

據此，民國大總統以“察哈爾地區地處蒙疆，寒荒待開，墾務爲綏邊殖民要政，由將全區墾務總辦一職改爲實官，明令簡任以重職守。”由此察哈爾全區墾務總辦便成爲由中央明令簡任的實官，以利於與蒙旗交涉,加快土地開墾的進程。

察哈爾全區墾務總局“掌理全區一切墾務事宜”，並以都統公署爲監督機關，都統爲督辦。但墾務總局的關防則由財政部發文授予。總局建成後，將舊有各墾務總分局所酌量裁並，其應存者一律改爲分局，歸總局直接管轄。墾務總局設總辦、會辦、科長、科員等，除總辦由內務部呈請大總統派委外，以道尹，財政分廳廳長爲會辦。其余科長、科員由總辦商同會辦，秉承督辦，酌定額數，報部核準。墾務總局往來公文程式，對於督辦用詳，對於道尹、財政分廳用咨，對於各縣及各縣墾務局用飭。墾務總局遇有重要事件除呈督辦外，得直接請示財政部。墾務總局經費以裁並原有各機關經費酌量支配報部核定。《綏遠察哈爾各墾務總局辦事權限大綱》自呈準之日施行，其余辦事細則由總辦商同會辦秉承督辦另定之[⑭]。由此可見，墾務總局是直屬民國政府財政部，兼受察哈爾都統監督的特殊的中央政府派出機構。墾務局總辦的官階與道尹、財政分廳相等，對於縣和縣分局以及各旗、群，則是上級官員。

察哈爾全區墾務總局編制爲，督辦一員，由察哈爾都統兼任；總辦一員，由大總統簡任；會辦二員，以興和道尹和特別區財政廳廳長分別兼任，駐局坐辦一員，由察哈爾都統會同主管各部委派[⑮]。總局內分第一科、第二科以及第三科等，分管察哈爾境內的土地開墾沿革調查、審查直轄分局、管理本局所入款項等各項工作[⑯]。

在察哈爾全區墾務總局之下分別設多倫、沽源（原獨石口縣）、陶林、涼城、豐鎮、興和、張北七縣墾務局，分管各縣墾政。此外，還組建了十個屯墾隊，駐各地分管屯墾。察哈爾全區墾務總局編制十分完備,其總辦直接由大總統簡任，各科各司分工詳細明確，足以反映出民國政府對察哈爾移民開墾工作的重視程度。

清代以來察哈爾的開墾分爲官墾和私墾兩大部分，所謂“官墾”，指由官府出面清丈並通過合法程序進行的土地放墾，所謂“私墾”，指蒙漢之間私自授受而放墾，或漢人私占盜墾。如上所述，自清末以來，在察哈爾“私墾盜賣泛濫，流弊叢生”。因此，民國初期察哈爾墾地的清丈整理，無論對中央政府還是對地方政府都顯得十分緊迫。

1915年10月，民國政府頒布《察哈爾縣知事墾務局局長清查余荒夾荒考成條例》，該《條例》共十三條，其主要內容有清查地畝員司之考成由全區墾務總辦會辦考核稟呈

⑭ 察哈爾全區墾務總局編《察哈爾全區墾政輯覽·行政組織上》，沈雲龍主編《近代中國史料叢刊》第三編，臺北：文海出版社，1988年，166頁。

⑮ 同註⑭。

⑯ 同註⑭。

全區墾務督辦執行，先報部備查。具體考成分以下幾個內容：

針對各縣知事兼墾務坐辦及墾務局局長：辦理清丈事件依限完竣者、清丈事竣無控案者、遴用繩丈員書人等能始終慎事者、清丈事件依限完竣、另委抽查毫無作弊者、繩丈人員清丈地畝不誤限期者、辦結人民照界糾葛十起以上者，繪造地圖詳確無訛者，均予以記功或加俸加薪之獎勵。收解荒價達於考成數目以上者，得遵照額外增加獎勵條例之規定，獎勞績年金及各級雙、單金鶴章。辦理延緩不及考成數目者、因清丈發生控案委員查明實係擾民者、任用私人經長官查出舞弊者、委員書繩舞弊不能覺察者，土豪地棍藉端聚眾抵抗不能迅事消弭者、受委員書繩串通辦事不公，經人民訴告委查屬實者，罰俸、罰薪之成數及月數，由全區墾務總辦、會辦臨時酌度辦理，稟承全區墾務督辦執行之；記過次數，得與記功次數相抵消，均予以記過或罰俸罰薪之處分。辦理清丈，疊起風潮，或因循敷衍，不及考成數目五成者，縣知事撤任，墾務局局長撤委，撤任撤委後，倘有賄分贓情，查實褫革官職，依法治罪。

針對科員以及繩丈員：清丈地畝不能依限竣事者、清丈地畝經人民抵抗至二次以上者、繪造圖冊未能詳確者、辦理人民照界糾葛結案後復起爭端者，罰薪之成數及月數，由全區墾務總辦會辦臨時酌度定之，記過次數得與記功次數相抵消，均予以記過或罰俸罰薪之處分。

察哈爾開放旗群台站，大段荒地，設置墾務行局兼設治局局長，所有關於墾務之考成均依上述條例之規定執行[17]。後又頒布《修正察哈爾清查余荒夾荒考成條例》，對原有的條例進行了補充和修訂[18]。

通過獎懲手段考核負責執行清丈、開墾等墾務工作的墾務局局長以及縣知等，以保障墾政的效率和進度。用賞罰分明的考成制度考核大到縣知事、墾務局坐辦、墾務局局長，小到科員、繩丈員等墾務工作人員，一方面勉勵勤於墾務的人員，一方面則嚴懲怠慢墾務者。這一套考核制度無疑從客觀上帶動了墾務工作人員的積極性，爲其後續開墾察哈爾蒙地提供了有效的人力保障。

三、察哈爾開墾章程及開墾概況

民國政府以“察屬地處邊陲，拱衛畿疆，所有理財設治，移民實邊，一切要政無不根基於墾務”爲由，強調禁止旗群牧廠的私墾盜墾，而鼓勵通過合法途徑開墾蒙地，爲此頒布了一系列章程和辦法。除了所有蒙旗通行的《墾辟蒙荒獎勵條例》和《禁止私放蒙荒通則》兩部關於蒙地開墾的重要法令外，民國政府以及地方政府還專門針對察哈爾制定了《察哈爾地區領地承墾章程》以及與之相配套的《察哈爾屯墾章程》《兩翼牧場試辦清丈章程》《繳價領照註冊之辦法》《察哈爾區域推廣兩翼八旗墾務辦法》《察哈

---

⑰　察哈爾全區墾務總局編《察哈爾全區墾政輯覽》，《行政组织下》，163頁。

⑱　《修正察哈爾清查余荒夾荒考成條例》，《政府公報》，第1287號，1915年12月7日。

爾清丈章程》等一系列章程和辦法。

察哈爾幅員遼闊，旗、群、台、王公牧廠幾近占全區十分之八九，察哈爾墾務總局總辦龍驤以及會辦單晉龢、嚴汝誠等一再呈請北京政府在察哈爾旗群大力推行墾務，妥籌蒙、民生計，借以增開縣邑。其所持理由有六端：

> 一，察哈爾特别區域一盟（錫林郭勒盟）八旗（察哈爾左右翼八旗），除舊開七縣暨新開辟一設治局僅占全區面積十分之一二，其余則深閉固拒，久未啟扃，非破除成例，盡開榛莽，無由積縣以成省，此以籌設行省論。
>
> 二，八旗蒙餉爲數甚巨，改革以來久經停撥，各旗官兵勢成坐困，欲籌蒙旗生計，莫如查取户口，按户授田，責令就地耕耘，俾可自存自立，蓋國家撫恤蒙旗，宜使自食其力，以謀永久生理，無取歲撥巨款等，於豢養以致兩困，矧近年欠發蒙餉，積至數十萬元之多，所謂豢養之資，且空懸無著乎，此以蒙旗生計論。
>
> 三，世界列強競行墾殖政策，多由國庫撥款，以經營期事。今吾國財力內外同一艱窘，國庫既無款接濟本區，更無力經營。唯有收集內地資本，借以開拓邊地，如果能將八旗荒地一律開放，則內地資本實業各家，投資墾殖愈增多，此以吸收內地資本論。
>
> 四，清制旗群台站圈地最多，大都自爲風氣，官府絕不過問，如能破例，準令蒙民就地自墾自食，由遊牧而入於耕種，此外另招漢人投資墾辟，俾令雜居，從而統一語言，齊其風俗，則漢蒙可期同化，地方官吏亦可施行行政之權，此以溝通蒙漢論。
>
> 五，全區荒地墾成，則賦額方有增益，其他各項稅捐亦必有人有土方可就地征收。若今之一盟八旗，荒蕪未開，有地等諸石田，籌款安有善策，此以增開利源論。
>
> 六，邊防要政以設險屯軍爲前驅，以移民墾殖爲後盾。今八旗禁例不除，內地富商大賈雖欲投資，亦不可得户口，何由增殖荒地，何由發榮，此以整頓邊防論。而八旗墾務極應推廣者也。⑲

從察墾總辦所述內容可得知，從他們的角度看，墾務有以下益處：①通過開墾設治達到設省一級地方行政組織規模。較之晚清，民國政府的蒙墾政策已不再顧及蒙古地方的特殊性和固有自主地位，也不再區分內屬旗與扎薩克旗的區别了。因此，主張破除前清時期禁止隨意開墾蒙旗牧地的成例，“盡開榛莽”，在察哈爾八旗和錫林郭勒盟一律推進墾殖，從而積縣成省。②八旗官兵的餉銀問題可以就地解決。③可以吸收內地資本，增加財政收入，借以開拓邊地。④通過大規模的移民，同化蒙漢，達到地方統一管理的目的。⑤開放八旗及錫林郭勒盟荒地，開辟利源，從而增加新的稅務，即耕地課稅。⑥極應破除察哈爾八旗土地以往不得隨意開墾的“禁例”，通過增加移民人口，以期達到加強邊防的目的。

---

⑲ 察哈爾全區墾務總局編《察哈爾全區墾政輯覽》，《開放盟旗群台》第二册，9—10頁。

其目的，較之晚清時期的開墾有了質的變化，察哈爾墾務機構將察哈爾的開墾並非看做察哈爾一隅的墾政問題，而是把它和國家的國防戰略和邊疆政策緊密地聯繫起來，強調其重要性，因而對於蒙旗固有的權利和地位基本不予考慮了。

另外察墾總局又制定了察哈爾特別區所轄蒙旗的開墾步驟。察哈爾全區開墾，首先是自察哈爾八旗的開墾入手，漸次推進到錫林郭勒全盟。具體步驟分調查期、籌備期、結束期三步。

第一步，先委派墾務官員派駐各旗，協同總管調查各旗實在户口，並將未開荒（荒地）、廠（牧廠）造冊繪圖，據實報告。這些人員皆委派候補知事或墾務局局長等出任，以重責成，此爲調查期。

第二步，調查結束後，即破除禁墾察哈爾牧地的清代成例，計戶授田；除上年放墾時已劃給隨缺地畝各戶，其余蒙民一律免價，按丁授田五十畝。此外，未開墾的荒、廠悉數放墾，招戶承領；在放墾之旗設立招墾設治局，以原派調查專員爲局長，本旗總管兼充坐辦。放墾面積較小者，聯合不同旗份合爲一區，設立招墾設治局；如地勢不便聯合或荒、廠無多者，可歸並於就近縣治管轄，不另設專局，此爲籌備時期。

第三步，荒、廠放墾完畢，地租征收確有把握後，招墾設治局即改成縣，新設縣的縣知事，從各該局局長、坐辦內擇優尤呈請補任，以酬其功，此爲結束期。

從上述察哈爾全區放墾具體步驟看，民國北京政府厲行移墾設治，推進蒙地漢化的施政目標十分顯著。該計劃呈國務院並分咨內務、財政、農商三部以及蒙藏院查核備案後，即令該總辦擬定辦事細則，遴選合格人員按既定步驟實施⑳。

自從察哈爾全區墾政計劃實施後，察哈爾旗、群、台地開墾規模迅速擴大。到1916年五月爲止， 在察哈爾左右翼八旗及牧群、軍台地界內已註冊的墾牧公司以及墾戶多達二百六十余㉑。

民國政府有關禁止“私墾”，獎勵“官墾”的蒙地放墾法令、法規的實施，對於內地資本家、實業家等投資察哈爾開墾產生了很大的吸引力。期間，察墾總局清查正鑲紅二旗、正鑲白二旗、正鑲黃二旗、正鑲藍二旗等各旗，各王公馬廠、五至十二台㉒以及商都設治區域，各縣官荒蒙荒時，丈出可放之地數萬頃以上。察墾總局呈請大總統，要求變通察哈爾兩翼八旗及錫林郭勒盟舊制，極力推行墾政，借以“積戶成鄉，積鄉成縣，積縣成省”以“鞏固邊疆”。

1915年民國政府頒布了《察哈爾全區墾務總局開放官荒蒙荒情形及領地承墾章程》。承領土地的具體辦法如下：①丈放各旗、群、台廠荒地，其中大段荒地要登報招墾外，還要編列地畝數號、坐落等，將此公布後，聽憑民戶自行承領。②專設墾戶招待室及招待員，與前來承領某號荒段的民戶接洽，或民戶可自行與各縣墾務局及設治局聯

⑳　《察哈爾全區墾政輯覽》，《開放盟旗群台》第二冊，台北：文海出版社，11—12頁。

㉑　《察哈爾墾牧公司及墾戶一覽表》（截至民國六年5月爲止），《察哈爾全區墾政輯覽》，《招墾第三》，4—15頁。

㉒　五至十二台站依次分別爲：奎蘇圖台、扎噶蘇台、明愛、察察爾圖、沁岱、烏蘭哈達、賁巴圖、錫喇哈達。

系。③察區放荒事宜命令禁止賒欠及墾務工作人員與地商勾結，作弊屯留土地。④總局放墾定章、丈地委員，不得爲招墾委員，丈地委員既無所施其巧技，故所丈地畝之廣窄，以及所分等則之高下，均歸核實，絕無蒙蔽取巧等弊。⑤總局及各縣墾務局、行局以及設治局，概無收納現款；凡民戶願領荒地若幹，即核計需欵總數幾何，由該民戶自行送交興業銀行、中國銀行、交通銀行或殖邊銀行，掣取收據，到局驗證，一面過賬，一面填發部照，註明四至，交由該民戶收執。⑥民戶執有察墾總局填發部照，即可馳赴荒地，察懇總局及各墾務局、行局以及設治局等，於荒地所在另派有專員接待，遵章按照撥地。⑦所放地畝分爲上、中、下等，以黑土二尺厚者爲上，一尺厚者爲中，黃土沙城爲下。清丈時，由繩丈委員認真勘察繪圖，注明表內，總局據實注冊編號存記。⑧上地每畝收銀七錢，中地每畝收銀五錢，下地每畝收銀三錢。外加收註冊費、丈費等。⑨領墾荒地以本國人爲限，各民戶領照時，需取具保證書不得抵押或轉賣於外國人。

察墾總局對墾戶的優待及給予的便利條件主要有以下幾方面：①凡從事墾牧，領墾大段荒地者，可赴口外實地調查，察墾總局提供乘墾簡章及有關口外墾牧收支方面的預算書；②凡海內著名實業專家預領大段荒地，親往口外實地調查時，察墾總局要求沿途各墾務局、行局、設治局妥爲接洽；③察區放荒，招墾與設治並行，凡遇開放大段荒地時，同時稟承都統呈準中央政府添設縣治，分駐軍警，保衛地方，俾各墾戶安居樂業。④察區開放新荒，遵照定章以三百六十弓爲一畝，百畝爲一頃，所有沙石城灘、芨芨草灘概行剔除，暫免收價，但此項沙城草灘，在爲補足地價以前，不準向其他人抵押或專賣，至墾成之日，仍應補交地價。⑤放墾新荒自領照之日起，無論上、中、下等則三年之內，均準免升科。⑥領墾荒地，照章須繳清地價，發給部照方準營業，以免賒欠而杜流弊。但有海內著名實業專家承領遠邊大段荒地至四十頃以上，又有確實保證人爲之保證者並準量予變通。⑦凡民戶承墾荒地，遵章繳納荒價，發給部照之後，即可永遠管業。⑧由於近來口外風氣日開，燕晉農民相率出口以工謀生者極眾，戶口繁殖，且今寒帶回溫，各墾牧公司領墾荒段，招佃固易，招工亦極踴躍工價尤廉。⑨察墾總局爲接濟農民，推廣墾殖起見，設立興業銀行以資接濟而便周轉[23]。

在察哈爾土地承領章程及清丈章程等一系列法規的指引下，察哈爾旗、群、台界內的荒地，大多被移居此地的內地農民所承領。

1915年6月，經沽源縣墾務局查明正白旗頭佐之南與牛群連界之五哈爾策魯以內遊牧空閑荒地，由墾務總局出面，命正白旗總管報荒。同月，墾務總局命鑲黃旗查明該旗十一枝箭等處是否有空閑地；命牛羊群總管卓特巴扎布將所屬界內閑荒報局招墾；命和親王府總管將黑山子私開之地遵章報放。同年8月，墾務總局飭令開放魁璋馬廠並開放正白旗牛羊群以及頭台等地。這樣在墾務總局的命令下，察哈爾旗、群、台站的牧地陸續上報墾務總局招墾[24]。以“清丈—劃界—報荒—招墾”爲固定程式的察哈爾墾務迅速推進開來，領墾者遍布察哈爾南北全境，放墾面積日趨擴大。

㉓ 《察哈爾全區墾政輯覽》，《招墾第三》，20—23頁。

㉔ 《察哈爾全區墾政輯覽》，《開放盟旗群台第二》。

根據相關數據，民國北京政府以及察哈爾地方政府在察哈爾推行的開墾政策基本上達到了預期效果。《察哈爾墾牧公司及墾戶一覽表》所列1915—1917年間察哈爾境內被墾牧公司以及墾戶所實際開墾畝數大致情況如下：

表1　羊群暨馬群界內實墾畝數

坐落地點	實墾畝數	坐落地點	實墾畝數
羊群布檔圖土城子	25 800	馬群十一蘇木	4308
羊群察汗諾爾等處	60 787	馬群五菊花八顏花	12 050
羊群花祝秀霍牙爾托洛蓋	36 505	六台羊群等處	18 744
馬群土城子七台西山坡	4133	羊群阿木烏蘇	2000
總計畝數	164 327		

表2　左翼察哈爾界內實墾畝數

坐落地點	實墾畝數	坐落地點	實墾畝數
正白旗大梁底、大小黃羊灘等處	60 000	正藍旗一把樹，正藍旗腦包等處	10 000
正藍旗小城灘等處	50 000	正蓝旗蘆草胡同二道沟等处	5000
正白旗頭枝箭	14 813	達木諾爾	2000
正白旗饅頭山台吐溝等處	20 000	一素溝	10 000
總計畝數	171 813		

表3　右翼察哈爾界內實墾畝數

坐落地點	實墾畝數	坐落地點	實墾畝數
正紅旗二蘇木	9798	鑲藍旗十蘇木	5328
正紅旗四蘇木	5200	正紅旗三蘇木	4864
鑲紅旗十二蘇木	4250	正黃旗牛群霍塔鄂博	3117
正紅旗多與坡八蘇木	3096	正紅旗四七蘇木	3094
正紅旗十二蘇木	12 906	鑲藍旗十一、十二蘇木	11 390
正紅旗火石山	2480	鑲紅旗吉慶莊	2593
正紅旗十五蘇木	2460	鑲紅旗頭蘇木	2300
鑲紅旗四蘇木	2066	鑲紅旗五蘇木	2053
鑲紅旗八蘇木	2150	總計畝數	79 145

表4　群、台站、王公牧廠界內實墾畝數

坐落地點	實墾畝數	坐落地點	實墾畝數
太仆寺	16 923	和親王府馬廠	6000
太仆寺大勝溝	15 796	六台	4333
太仆寺龍虎台	5772	德公府牌雙井子大孤山	2011

续表

坐落地點	實墾畝數	坐落地點	實墾畝數
八台花臥钵英兒等處	8208	德公府牌孤山子沙嶺諾爾等處	2555
德公府牌馬蓮灘大狐山	2154	德公府牌鏵子爐二道溝	2871
博羅柴濟台站	5101	太仆寺閎爐胡同	2800
德公府牌小河子等處	2750	德公府牌西乾溝	2058
德公府牌七裏河豫親王二道窪	2002	豫親王府德公府頭道腦包	2401
德公府牌渝樹溝水泉溝等處	2283	七台及七台十一蘇木	6865
總計畝數	92 888		

表5 察哈爾旗群境内各縣實墾地畝數

坐落地點	實墾畝數	坐落地點	實墾畝數
沽源縣本牌灘烏克河廟	2904	沽源縣水泉溝本牌灘	2880
沽源縣阿古廟井兒溝大西窪	2650	沽源牛角溝庫倫諾楊皮房村	2480
沽源小井溝西案口大紅山大東灘	2470	陶林縣	1631
涼城莫蓋圖等處	5700	豐鎮西界馬廠梁南	6000
沽源黑山嘴本牌灘	4180	涼城永義村東勝莊	4275
沽源西胡同牌王大人廟	2100	沽源十號梁太平溝	2000
沽源本牌灘小官廠子梳妝樓	4040	沽源三道營	2000
總計畝數	4 5310		

註：上列數據均引自《察哈爾墾政輯覽·招墾·察哈爾墾牧公司及墾戶一覽表》。

從上列數據可知，當時推行的蒙地放墾遍及察哈爾八旗、牧廠、台站、前清王公馬廠以及諸縣等察哈爾旗群全境，大批的墾牧公司以及個人墾戶開墾了數量相當可觀的地畝。而且民戶承領荒地之後，就可以“永遠管業”，也就是獲得了土地所有權，於是大片官荒、馬廠以及公共遊牧地轉變爲漢族農民的私有地。民國政府的鼓勵，相對低廉的地價，尤其永遠管業的私有地的獲得，吸引大量內地農民來到察哈爾開墾定居，使該地區農業人口數量迅速增長。

四、察哈爾境内招墾設治局的設立

察哈爾全區墾務總局開始推行墾政後，在察哈爾特別區所轄多倫、沽源、陶林、涼城、豐鎮、興和、張北等七縣均分設墾務局，以監督管理當地墾務。民國政府在“積戶爲鄉，積鄉爲縣，積縣爲省”的基本方針下，開墾與設治雙管齊下，在察哈爾境內設立了若干墾務行局、設治局。設治局制度萌芽於清光緒末年，擬設新縣時，先有設治委員前往劃界，招徠移民墾殖，加強治安，待確有成效後，再正式設立縣治。北京政府時期，設治局名稱正式出現，成爲與縣並列但地位略爲低的地方行政機構[25]。設治局用蒙古語譯爲“siyan-u beledkel tobčiy-a”，其意爲“縣治籌備局”。設治局的成立是察哈爾旗群政區變遷過程中的重要一環，同時也是民國政府拓殖邊疆最有效的舉措之一。

（一）商都招墾設治局的設立

北京政府時期察哈爾境內第一所設治局建在商都牧群，該牧群亦稱大馬群、槼馬廠等。商都官牧場設於清朝乾隆年間，初稱商都牧廠，爲察哈爾正黃旗與鑲黃旗轄境，其地方歸察哈爾都統節制，光緒年間開始陸續放墾此地，大批漢人隨之湧入，逐漸由昔日的遊牧地轉變爲農耕區域。

至1915年9月爲止，大馬群暨羊群界内放墾大段荒地，以三百六十弓[26]，合地一畝計算約地萬數千頃，若以二百四十弓，合地一畝計算已在兩萬余頃以上。經由墾務局派員勘丈、編號、列表布告招墾。招墾之初，有立本墾牧公司及墾戶、千頃墾牧有限公司、寶豐墾牧有限公司，興業墾牧公司等諸多墾牧公司等資本雄厚的公司，以及個别民戶前來領墾大段荒地[27]。但該區域内荒地，距離縣治大都甚遠，或盜賊出沒，或界址毗連遊牧地帶，蒙漢時起紛爭，故農民自行領墾小段者實不多，這使得招墾受到很大影響。因此，墾務局官員主張及早選擇適中地點設立墾務行局兼設治局，一則推廣墾殖，開地利，一則代理訴訟，保護居民。遂陸續有諸多墾牧公司以及墾戶紛紛前來，踴躍承領。

1915年9月，察哈爾都統何宗蓮呈請大總統，擬在大馬群、羊群[28]設立墾務局。具體管轄區域還包括張北縣所管之四台，興和縣所轄之五、六、七台，陶林縣所轄之八台。當時上述各地方荒地尚未盡墾。私墾盜占，訴案糾紛，均因縣治太遠，清理較難，造成國課損失很大。何宗蓮認爲，應將上述地方一並劃入新放墾之大馬群羊群界内大段荒地，另設爲一區。其境域東至馬群，西至蘇尼特，南至三台、北至九台，東西約計一百六十余里，南北約計二百三十余里，統歸新設墾務行局兼設治局局長負責就近招放新荒，清理余荒；並暫行代理所轄境内一切訴訟事宜，會同該管統領節制調遣轄境所駐巡防馬隊。目前放墾的荒地占商都牧群的較多，因此擬請定名爲商都招墾局，擇定七台乾井梁地方爲設治局地點。舉薦前奉天候補同知、現察哈爾張北墾務局局長吴恩溥試署商都招墾設治局局長。試辦一二年後，荒地墾成，地租收入較多時，即請改爲商都縣[29]。

㉕ 傅林祥、郑寶恒著，周振鶴主編《中國行政區劃通史 · 中華民國卷》，上海：復旦大學出版社，2007年，101頁。

㉖ 弓：舊時丈量土地的計量單位,一弓爲五尺、三百六十弓爲一畝。

㉗ 察哈爾全區墾務總局編印《察哈爾全區墾政輯覽》，《察哈爾墾牧公司及墾戶一覽表》，《招墾第三》，3—13頁。

㉘ 大馬群、羊群爲商都牧群及周邊地區牧場的泛稱。

㉙ “留任察哈爾都統兼墾務督辦何宗蓮呈擬於現放大馬群、羊群地方設立墾務行局兼設治局推廣墾殖保護商民以資治而與地方請示文”，《政府公報》，1915年9月4日，第1198號。

1916年1月，經司法、内務、財政及農商等四部會核察哈爾都統所呈後認爲："察哈爾商都地方設立墾務行局兼設治局之事，合理可行，似可照準，以廣墾殖，亦爲設縣治過度之制，宜並將商都墾務行局兼設治局改稱爲商都招墾設治局。"[30]隨之，北京政府將大馬群及羊群之放墾地段以及張北、興和、陶林等三縣之五至八台等地劃歸商都招墾設治局，以七八台之間乾井梁之十蘇木[31]白石山爲設治局所在地，由此拉開了商都設縣的序幕。

1916年3月5日，由察哈爾都統任命吴恩溥爲商都設治局首任局長。9月1日吴恩溥調離，郭成鈞補任商都設治局局長[32]。自1916年6月開始，墾務總局便派員勘定商都設治局邊界，同時命張北、興和、陶林三縣迅速將五至八台墾務交由商都招墾設治局辦理[33]。

《商都招墾設治局辦事大綱十一條》規定了設治局局長權限以及設治局内部編制。文件中首先明文規定該局以"推廣墾殖，保護商民，籌備縣治"爲宗旨。設治局局長按照《縣知事兼理司法事務暫行條例》以及《縣知事審理訴訟暫行章程》代理所轄境内一切訴訟事宜，且對境内所駐巡防軍隊有會同該管統領，節制、調遣之權。招墾設治局局長遇有民政、財政、司法墾務各項要務，應秉承興和道尹、特别區財政廳廳長、審判處處長、墾務總辦分别核示辦理，遇有重大事件亦得呈察哈爾都統示遵。局内設置承審員、科長、科員等辦理應辦事務；雇傭錄事專司繕寫，但須守定部核概算冊，所定名額不得超過。設治局的常年經費由察哈爾墾務總局執撥[34]。同時察墾總局又頒布了《商都招墾設治局招墾科辦事大綱》，共九條内容，規範了該局招墾工作的進行[35]。

自設立商都招墾設治局以來，内地民人及墾牧公司紛紛購置地畝，大興墾荒，到1918年爲止，商都招墾設治局已具備縣治規模，同年11月1日，大總統命察哈爾都統將商都招墾設治局改爲縣缺，改局長爲知事，任命郭成鈞爲商都縣知事[36]。商都招墾設治局作爲察哈爾境内設立的第一個招墾設治局，爲察哈爾墾政的推廣積累了很多經驗，後續設立的諸多招墾設治局紛紛效仿其建制，其對察哈爾旗群界内伸展開來。

（二）寶昌招墾設治局的設立

寶昌招墾設治局是繼商都招墾設治局後在察哈爾設立的墾務管理機構。管轄地域主要位於太仆寺左翼牧群境内。各牧群占地遼闊，水草豐美，土質肥沃。自清中葉以來，

㉚　"司法、内務、財政、農商等四部奏爲會核察哈爾馬羊群地方擬設墾務行局兼設治局"，《政府公報》，第12號，1916年1月17日。

㉛　爲正黄旗第十蘇木。

㉜　《商都縣誌》，《内蒙古自治區地方誌叢書》，海拉尔：内蒙古文化出版社，2007年，30頁。

㉝　察哈爾全區墾務總局編印《察哈爾全區墾政輯覽》，《設治第四》，28頁。

㉞　察哈爾全區墾務總局編印《察哈爾全區墾政輯覽》，《設治第四》，21—26頁。

㉟　同註㉞。

㊱　"内務總長等呈會核察哈爾商都招墾設治局改爲縣缺並任命該局長爲知事擬請照準由"，《政府公報》，大總統第1846號令，1918年11月2日。

隨著傳統畜牧業的衰落，太仆寺左右兩翼各牧群牧地不斷被附近民戶占據，或被盜賣私墾。因此，爲清丈兩翼牧群熟地生荒，民國初年即於墾務總局之下設立了兩翼清丈行局。

1916年11月3日，兩翼牧場清丈行局以“赴經太仆寺境哈辣根台察勘，土地肥沃，有一萬頃，且天氣和暖，以之開墾設治，可籌得二百萬元，較於商都有過之無不及。另於荒廢之地設縣治，於邊塞之區固衛邊隅，開通風之氣，爲國家計萬世之利……”爲由呈請察哈爾墾務總局在太仆寺牧廠設治[37]。

1917年5月6日，由墾務總局派員劃清兩翼牧群界址，察哈爾都統命該地凡已墾熟地及余荒夾荒，不便放牧者，均可清丈放墾；其整段草荒，未被占墾者，留備牧畜。同年，察哈爾都統田中玉[38]向大總統呈請擬於兩翼牧群設立太仆寺招墾設治局，稱：“經數月清丈勘察，查得熟地以三百六十弓折合一畝計算，不下七八千頃；以二百四十弓折合一畝計算，已達萬余頃以上。牧場以北正白一旗，除已墾熟地已劃歸沽源縣外，其未墾生荒以三百六十弓爲一畝計算，亦約有一萬余頃。這一區域位於多倫、張北之間，東接沽源，西趨興和，南靠商都招墾設治局。商都招墾設治局自成立以來，余荒日開，戶口日增，成效顯著。因此，仿照兩翼牧群已墾熟地及正白旗未墾生荒，亟應作爲一區，另設招墾設治局。所有辦事權限，概照商都縣章程辦理。擬一面清丈余荒，開放生荒，推廣墾殖；一面代理訴訟，經征錢糧，籌設縣治。兩翼牧場在清朝原歸太仆寺管轄，日後荒地墾成，地租增益，即改爲太仆縣。同時舉薦前署多倫縣知事現充該處（多倫）墾務局局長林茂亭署理太仆寺招墾設治局局長……”[39]

不過，財政部、陸軍部、農商部及內務部等考慮到兩翼牧群自來系陸軍部軍用馬廠之緣故，提出軍用牧場與放墾區域要劃清界限，禁止越墾。所有放墾所得收入以十分之九批解陸軍部辦理牧政，十分之一撥充放墾及設治經費。此外，對田中玉所請定名爲太仆寺招墾設治局之案，提出異議。因爲兩翼牧群名爲太仆寺左右翼牧群，若以此命名之，將造成墾政與牧政名稱相混。所以要求咨明內務部重新核定名稱，以昭慎重[40]。太仆寺原爲清朝的官用御馬廠，民國建立後，改作陸軍部軍馬場。民國政府在此已投入大量經費，用以改良軍馬品種。因此，對於在此設立招墾設治局，較之前設立商都招墾設治局稍顯謹慎。

1917年5月6日，爲擇定新招墾設治局的名稱，墾務總局令兩翼牧廠清丈行局局長，左翼總管等，將太仆寺牧廠境內寶昌州碑文拓片一份火速送到墾務總局。據太仆寺左翼牧廠總管面稱，太仆寺牧廠界內有唐致和年間寶昌州碑文。但經考證後，得知唐代無致和年號，惟元泰定帝時改元爲致和。因此，總局就此碑是否元泰定帝所立，要求該總管

㊲　察哈爾全區墾務總局編《察哈爾全區墾政輯覽》，《設治第四》，第110頁。

㊳　田中玉（1869—1935），直隸撫寧人，北洋武備學堂學員出身，曾任北洋第一鎮炮隊第一標統帶等要職。1916年任察哈爾都統。

㊴　“大總統會核察哈爾都統請立招墾設治局一案”，《政府公報》，1917年4月2日。

㊵　察哈爾全區墾務總局編《察哈爾全區墾政輯覽》，《設治第四》，171頁。

會同該行局局長查明[41]。後經田中玉一番考證得知，太仆寺牧場境內石碑係元朝元致和元年太歲戊辰六月所立，而建碑者多係當時興和路寶昌州職官。最後，察哈爾墾務總局確定在兩翼牧廠擬設之新設治局定名曰寶昌招墾設治局。

1917年6月8日，察哈爾都統咨內務、財政、陸軍、農商等部稱："……擬即沿襲元代寶昌州舊名定名爲寶昌招墾設治局，將來招墾事竣，設治告成，即徑稱爲寶昌縣，用符名實而垂久遠。"後轉呈財政、陸軍、農商三部備案。此爲寶昌名稱之由來。同年8月，內務部咨察哈爾都統將太仆招墾設治局改成寶昌招墾設治局，太仆寺左翼牧廠與該招墾設治局並存於一地[42]。

察哈爾墾務總局以"自在寶昌設治以來，邊荒逐漸開辟，戶口日增，各屬生荒墾熟已過半數，現在升科地畝均逾六千余頃，額征糧賦正税均達一萬七千余元，與各三等縣缺收入相當，地方行政亦粗具規模，農商群集訴訟漸繁，非設治不足以治理"爲由呈請北京政府擬將寶昌設治局改爲縣治。1925年7月，內務、財政、農商等三部轉呈大總統："……寶昌自民國六年設治以來成績已昭著，自應及時改爲縣治作爲三等縣缺，寶昌設治局定名曰寶昌縣，寶昌招墾設治局局長胡傳璐任命爲寶昌縣縣知事。"[43]

綜上所述，北京政府時期蒙地設治主要以頒布開放蒙荒章程—鼓勵民戶領墾—設立招墾設治局—改設縣治的模式進行，甚至開墾與設治同時進行。這兩個設治局的成立對民國北京政府在察哈爾其他旗群的放墾設治發揮了開路先鋒之作用。

（三）集寧、康保等招墾設治局的設立

集寧在清朝屬蒙古察哈爾正紅、正黃二旗之遊牧地。1921年豐鎮墾務局全局移至集寧，取名爲"平地泉招墾設治局"，此爲集寧設治之始，設治時劃豐鎮之地居多，其次爲興和縣和涼城縣之地。該局局長楊葆初在查干哈達下平曠地會集鄉紳以及土豪進行土地丈量，修建城壕，在五里外，修築土城墻。隨著墾殖的推進，該區域民戶人口迅速增長，形成了楊家灣等諸多村落，民戶約數萬戶。由於其境內有元代的集寧路遺址，因此改平地泉設治局爲集寧設治局[44]。

1922年，由張北、商都兩縣析置康保招墾設治局。此地原爲察哈爾左翼鑲黃旗遊牧地。1925年，康保設治局改爲康保縣。"康保"一名來源於位於境內的一處淖爾，其蒙古語爲"康巴淖爾"，康保爲康巴之諧音，縣名由此而得[45]。

---

[41] 察哈爾全區墾務總局編《察哈爾全區墾政輯覽》，《設治第四》，182頁。

[42] 察哈爾全區墾務總局編《察哈爾全區墾政輯覽》，《設治第四》，182—183頁。

[43] "內務、財政、農商部等呈臨時執政會核察哈爾寶昌、康保兩設治局改爲縣治擬請照準文"，《政府公報》，第3328號，1925年7月8日。

[44] 楊葆初《集寧縣誌》，《中國方志叢書·塞北地方》第一三號，臺北：成文出版社，1968年，25—26頁。

[45] 河北省地名辦公室編《河北省地名志·張家口分冊》，石家莊：河北省地名委員會辦公室，1985年，46頁。

結　　語

清朝覆亡，中華民國成立後，將察哈爾等蒙地改隸於特别區域之下，可謂繼承晚清的籌邊思想，在蒙地與内地的“一體化”方面邁出重要一步，且成效頗大。緊接著爲了穩固邊疆局勢以及建立地方財政，中央及地方政府在察哈爾進行了“有計劃、有組織、有目的”的開墾設治政策。這一時期的開墾，在墾務機構、開墾清丈章程以及開墾力度等各方面均超過了晚清時期，致使察哈爾旗群政區發生了變化，其直接結果爲在察哈爾左右翼八旗以及四牧群界内出現了商都、寶昌、集寧、康保等設治局。隨著移民人口的增長及墾地面積的擴大，這些設治局具備了縣治的規模，不久後被改爲縣治（集寧、康保於國民政府時期改爲縣治），察哈爾十二旗群全域感到墾殖之壓力，這樣凡設縣的地方以漢人爲主體居民的農耕區域不斷擴大，而蒙旗原有的地域則大大縮小，不識農耕的蒙古人不斷北退至干旱地帶。

Studies on the Land Reclamation and Establishment of New Administrative Units in Chakhar during the Peking Government of Republican China

Surimeng

During the New Policies which were practiced in the late Qing to the early Republican China, there were large numbers of Han-Chinese immigrants settled and reclaimed the pasturelands in Chakhar. The central government inherited the policies of reclaiming the pastureland from Qing, in a purposeful, organized, planned manner. Most previous research has concentrated on the land reclamation in the late Qing period, while a few scholars have elaborated on the establishment of new administrative units like Hsien (縣), She ZhiJu (設治局) which is the bureau of preparatory Hsien to manage the Han-Chinese who penetrated into frontier regions. Therefore, in this article, I based on *Government gazette of Republic of China* and *Compilation of Land Reclamation Archives in Chakhar*, focuses on the central government's policies of land reclamation and history processes of change of administrative divisions in Chakhar banners and pastures.

《西域歷史語言研究集刊》第十輯作者名錄

（按作者姓氏拼音排列）

包呼和木其爾	內蒙古大學蒙古歷史學系講師
布日古德	中國社會科學院民族學與人類學研究所副研究員
承　志	日本追手門學院大學教授
樊志强	中國人民大學歷史學院博士生
高永安	中國人民大學文學院副教授
雷瑭洵	北京大學中文系博士生
李　肖	中國人民大學國學院教授
李建強	中國人民大學國學院副教授
李夢溪	中國人民大學國學院博士生
林铃梅	中國人民大學國學院博士生
劉　震	復旦大學文史研究院研究員
劉志佳	中國人民大學國學院博士生
陸辰葉	復旦大學文史研究院博士后
馬麗萍	吐魯番市文物局、吐魯番學研究院文博館員
孟　瑜	清華大學人文學院博士后
任小波	復旦大學歷史地理研究中心副教授
阮　麗	中央美術學院佛教藝術博士、獨立學者
薩其仁贵	中國人民大學國學院博士后
沈衛榮	清華大學人文學院教授
石　美	中國人民大學國學院博士生
蘇日朦	中國人民大學國學院博士生
孫伯君	中國社會科學院民族學與人類學研究所研究員
索朗卓玛	中國人民大學歷史學院博士生
特爾巴衣爾	中國人民大學國學院講師
吴　娟	清華大學人文學院副教授
烏雲畢力格	中國人民大學國學院教授
向筱路	北京大學中文系碩士生
楊　傑	中國人民大學國學院博士後

姚　霜	清華大學人文學院博士生
张瀚墨	中國人民大學國學院副教授
張永江	中國人民大學歷史學院教授
趙團員	大連理工大學人文學院中文系講師
Florence Hodous	中國人民大學國學院博士後